IMMIGRATION AND NATIONALITY LAWS OF THE UNITED STATES

SELECTED STATUTES, REGULATIONS AND FORMS

As Amended to May 15, 2014

Selected by

T. Alexander Aleinikoff
United Nations Deputy High Commissioner for Refugees

David A. Martin
Warner-Booker Distinguished Professor of International Law and Joel B. Piassick Research Professor
University of Virginia

Hiroshi Motomura
Susan Westerberg Prager Professor of Law
University of California, Los Angeles, School of Law

Maryellen Fullerton
Professor of Law
Brooklyn Law School

WEST ACADEMIC PUBLISHING

Mat #41458998

444 Cedar Street, Suite 700
St. Paul, MN 55101
1-877-888-1330

Printed in the United States of America

ISBN: 978-0-314-28820-2

TABLE OF CONTENTS

Page

V. STATE AND LOCAL PROVISIONS

VI. TREATIES AND RELATED MATERIALS

VII. THE CONSTITUTION OF THE UNITED STATES [p. 961]

VIII. SELECTED IMMIGRATION FORMS

BASIC DOCUMENTS

PETITIONS AND APPLICATIONS

VISA APPLICATIONS

EMPLOYMENT

ADMINISTRATIVE REMOVAL AND REINSTATEMENT OF PRIOR ORDER

Page

EXPEDITED REMOVAL

IMMIGRATION COURT

TABLE
IMMIGRATION AND NATIONALITY ACT SECTION CLASSIFICATION TO U.S.C.A.

Date	Pub.L	Ch.	Sec.	66 Stat. Page	U.S.C.A. Title	U.S.C.A. Section
1952–June 27	414	477	101	166	8	1101
			102	173	8	1102
			103	173	8	1103
			104	174	8	1104
			105	175	8	1105
			106	—	8	1105a
			201	175	8	1151
			202	176	8	1152
			203	178	8	1153
			204	179	8	1154
			205	180	8	1155
			206	181	8	1156
			207	—	8	1157
			208	—	8	1158
			209	—	8	1159
			210	—	8	1160
			211	181	8	1181
			212	181	8	1182
			213	188	8	1183
			213A	—	8	1183a
			214	189	8	1184
			215	190	8	1185
			216	—	8	1186a
			216A	—	8	1186b
			217	—	8	1187
			218	—	8	1188
			219	—	8	1189
			221	191	8	1201
			222	193	8	1202
			223	194	8	1203
			224	195	8	1204
			231	195	8	1221
			232	196	8	1222
			233	—	8	1223
			234	198	8	1224
			235	198	8	1225
			235A	—	8	1225a
			236	200	8	1226
			236A	—	8	1226a
			237	201	8	1227
			238	202	8	1228
			239	203	8	1229

TABLE

Date	Pub.L	Ch.	Sec.	66 Stat. Page	U.S.C.A. Title	Section
1952–June 27	414	477	240	204	8	1229a
			240A	—	8	1229b
			240B	—	8	1229c
			240C	—	8	1230
			241	204	8	1231
			242	208	8	1252
			243	212	8	1253
			244	—	8	1254
			245	217	8	1255
			245A	—	8	1255a
			246	217	8	1256
			248	218	8	1258
			249	219	8	1259
			250	219	8	1260
			251	219	8	1281
			252	220	8	1282
			253	221	8	1283
			254	221	8	1284
			255	222	8	1285
			256	223	8	1286
			257	223	8	1287
			258	—	8	1288
			261	223	8	1301
			262	224	8	1302
			263	224	8	1303
			264	224	8	1304
			265	225	8	1305
			266	225	8	1306
			271	226	8	1321
			272	226	8	1322
			273	227	8	1323
			274	228	8	1324
			274A	—	8	1324a
			274B	—	8	1324b
			274C	—	8	1324c
			274D	—	8	1324d
			275	229	8	1325
			276	229	8	1326
			277	229	8	1327
			278	230	8	1328
			279	230	8	1329
			280	230	8	1330
			281	230	8	1351
			282	231	8	1352
			283	231	8	1353
			284	232	8	1354
			285	232	8	1355

TABLE

Date	Pub.L	Ch.	Sec.	66 Stat. Page	U.S.C.A. Title	U.S.C.A. Section
1952–June 27	414	477	286	232	8	1356
			287	233	8	1357
			288	234	8	1358
			289	234	8	1359
			290	234	8	1360
			291	234	8	1361
			292	235	8	1362
			293	—	8	1363
			294	—	8	1363a
			301	235	8	1401
			302	236	8	1402
			303	236	8	1403
			304	237	8	1404
			305	237	8	1405
			306	237	8	1406
			307	237	8	1407
			308	238	8	1408
			309	238	8	1409
			310	239	8	1421
			311	239	8	1422
			312	239	8	1423
			314	241	8	1425
			315	242	8	1426
			316	242	8	1427
			317	243	8	1428
			318	244	8	1429
			319	244	8	1430
			320	245	8	1431
			322	246	8	1433
			324	246	8	1435
			325	248	8	1436
			326	248	8	1437
			327	248	8	1438
			328	249	8	1439
			329	250	8	1440
			329A	—	8	1440-1
			330	251	8	1441
			331	252	8	1442
			332	252	8	1443
			333	253	8	1444
			334	254	8	1445
			335	255	8	1446
			336	257	8	1447
			337	258	8	1448
			338	259	8	1449
			339	259	8	1450
			340	260	8	1451

TABLE

Date	Pub.L	Ch.	Sec.	66 Stat. Page	U.S.C.A. Title	U.S.C.A. Section
1952–June 27	414	477	341	263	8	1452
			342	263	8	1453
			343	263	8	1454
			344	264	8	1455
			346	266	8	1457
			347	266	8	1458
			349	267	8	1481
			351	269	8	1483
			356	272	8	1488
			357	272	8	1489
			358	272	8	1501
			359	273	8	1502
			360	273	8	1503
			361	—	8	1504
			404	274	8	1101nt
			405	274	8	1101nt
			406	275	8	1101nt
			411	—	8	1521
			412	—	8	1522
			413	—	8	1523
			414	—	8	1524
			501	—	8	1531
			502	—	8	1532
			503	—	8	1533
			504	—	8	1534
			505	—	8	1535
			506	—	8	1536
			507	—	8	1537

IMMIGRATION AND NATIONALITY LAWS OF THE UNITED STATES

SELECTED STATUTES, REGULATIONS AND FORMS

I. IMMIGRATION AND NATIONALITY ACT [INA § ___]

TITLE I—GENERAL PROVISIONS

TITLE II—IMMIGRATION

Chapter I—Selection System

TITLE III—NATIONALITY AND NATURALIZATION

Chapter I—Nationality at Birth and Collective Naturalization

Chapter II—Nationality Through Naturalization

TITLE I

GENERAL PROVISIONS

§ 101. Definitions [8 U.S.C.A. § 1101]

(a) As used in this Act—

(1) The term "administrator" means the official designated by the Secretary of State pursuant to section 104(b) of this Act [8 U.S.C.A. § 1104(b)].

(2) The term "advocates" includes, but is not limited to, advises, recommends, furthers by overt act, and admits belief in.

(3) The term "alien" means any person not a citizen or national of the United States.

(4) The term "application for admission" has reference to the application for admission into the United States and not to the application for the issuance of an immigrant or nonimmigrant visa.

(5) The term "Attorney General" means the Attorney General of the United States.

(6) The term "border crossing identification card" means a document of identity bearing that designation issued to an alien who is lawfully admitted for permanent residence, or to an alien who is a resident in foreign contiguous territory, by a consular officer or an immigration officer for the purpose of crossing over the borders between the United States and foreign contiguous territory in accordance with such conditions for its issuance and use as may be prescribed by regulations. Such regulations shall provide that **(A)** each such document include a biometric identifier (such as the fingerprint or handprint of the alien) that is machine readable and **(B)** an alien presenting a border crossing identification card is not permitted to cross over the border into the United States unless the biometric identifier contained on the card matches the appropriate biometric characteristic of the alien.

(7) The term "clerk of court" means a clerk of a naturalization court.

(8) The terms "Commissioner" and "Deputy Commissioner" mean the Commissioner of Immigration and Naturalization and a Deputy Commissioner of Immigration and Naturalization, respectively.

(9) The term "consular officer" means any consular, diplomatic, or other officer or employee of the United States designated under regulations prescribed under authority contained in this chapter, for the purpose of issuing immigrant or nonimmigrant visas or, when used in title III [8 U.S.C.A. § 1401 et seq.], for the purpose of adjudicating nationality.

(10) The term "crewman" means a person serving in any capacity on board a vessel or aircraft.

(11) The term "diplomatic visa" means a nonimmigrant visa bearing that title and issued to a nonimmigrant in accordance with such regulations as the Secretary of State may prescribe.

(12) The term "doctrine" includes, but is not limited to, policies, practices, purposes, aims, or procedures.

(13)(A) The terms "admission" and "admitted" mean, with respect to an alien, the lawful entry of the alien into the United States after inspection and authorization by an immigration officer.

(B) An alien who is paroled under section 212(d)(5) [8 U.S.C.A. § 1182(d)(5)] or permitted to land temporarily as an alien crewman shall not be considered to have been admitted.

(C) An alien lawfully admitted for permanent residence in the United States shall not be regarded as seeking an admission into the United States for purposes of the immigration laws unless the alien—

(i) has abandoned or relinquished that status,

(ii) has been absent from the United States for a continuous period in excess of 180 days,

(iii) has engaged in illegal activity after having departed the United States,

(iv) has departed from the United States while under legal process seeking removal of the alien from the United States, including removal proceedings under this Act and extradition proceedings,

(v) has committed an offense identified in section 212(a)(2) [8 U.S.C.A. § 1182(a)(2)], unless since such offense the alien has been granted relief under section 212(h) [8 U.S.C.A. § 1182(h)] or 240A(a) [8 U.S.C.A. § 1229b(a)], or

(vi) is attempting to enter at a time or place other than as designated by immigration officers or has not been admitted to the United States after inspection and authorization by an immigration officer.

(14) The term "foreign state" includes outlying possessions of a foreign state, but self-governing dominions or territories under mandate or trusteeship shall be regarded as separate foreign states.

(15) The term "immigrant" means every alien except an alien who is within one of the following classes of nonimmigrant aliens—

(A)(i) an ambassador, public minister, or career diplomatic or consular officer who has been accredited by a foreign government recognized de jure by the United States and who is accepted by the President or by the Secretary of State, and the members of the alien's immediate family;

(ii) upon a basis of reciprocity, other officials and employees who have been accredited by a foreign government recognized de jure by the United States, who are accepted by the Secretary of State, and the members of their immediate families; and

(iii) upon a basis of reciprocity, attendants, servants, personal employees, and members of their immediate families, of the officials and employees who have a nonimmigrant status under (i) and (ii) above;

(B) an alien (other than one coming for the purpose of study or of performing skilled or unskilled labor or as a representative of foreign press, radio, film, or other foreign information media coming to engage in such vocation) having a residence in a foreign country which he has no intention of abandoning and who is visiting the United States temporarily for business or temporarily for pleasure;

(C) an alien in immediate and continuous transit through the United States, or an alien who qualifies as a person entitled to pass in transit to and from the United Nations Headquarters District and foreign countries, under the provisions of paragraphs (3), (4), and (5) of section 11 of the Headquarters Agreement with the United Nations (61 Stat. 758);

(D)(i) an alien crewman serving in good faith as such in a capacity required for normal operation and service on board a vessel, as defined in section 258(a) [8 U.S.C.A. § 1288(a)] (other than a fishing vessel having its home port or an operating base in the United States), or aircraft, who intends to land temporarily and solely in pursuit of his calling as a crewman and to depart from the United States with the vessel or aircraft on which he arrived or some other vessel or aircraft;

(ii) an alien crewman serving in good faith as such in any capacity required for normal operations and service aboard a fishing vessel having its home port or an operating base in the United States who intends to land temporarily in Guam or the Commonwealth of the Northern Mariana Islands and solely in pursuit of his calling as a crewman and to depart from Guam or the Commonwealth of the Northern Mariana Islands with the vessel on which he arrived;

(E) an alien entitled to enter the United States under and in pursuance of the provisions of a treaty of commerce and navigation between the United States and the foreign state of which he is a national, and the spouse and children of any such alien if accompanying or following to join him; **(i)** solely to carry on substantial trade, including trade in services or trade in technology, principally between the United States and the foreign state of which he is a national; **(ii)** solely to develop and direct the operations of an enterprise in which he has invested, or of an enterprise in which he is actively in the process of investing, a substantial amount of capital; or **(iii)** solely to perform services in a specialty occupation in the United States if the alien is a national of the Commonwealth of Australia and with respect to whom the Secretary of Labor determines and certifies to the Secretary of Homeland Security and the Secretary of State that the intending employer has filed with the Secretary of Labor an attestation under section 212(t)(1) [8 U.S.C.A. § 1182(t)(1)];

(F)(i) an alien having a residence in a foreign country which he has no intention of abandoning, who is a bona fide student qualified to pursue a full course of study and who seeks to enter the United States temporarily and solely for the purpose of pursuing such a course of study consistent with section 214(*l*) [8 U.S.C.A. § 1184(*l*)] at an established college, university, seminary, conservatory, academic high school, elementary school, or other academic institution or in an accredited language training program in the United States, particularly designated by him and approved by the Attorney General after consultation with the Secretary of Education, which institution or place of study shall have agreed to report to the Attorney General the termination of attendance of each nonimmigrant student, and if any such institution of learning or place of study fails to make reports promptly the approval shall be withdrawn, **(ii)** the alien spouse and minor children of any alien described in clause (i) if accompanying or following to join such an alien, and **(iii)** an alien who is a national of Canada or Mexico, who maintains actual residence and place of abode in the country of nationality, who is described in clause (i) except that the alien's qualifications for and actual course of study may be full or part-time, and who commutes to the United States institution or place of study from Canada or Mexico;

(G)(i) a designated principal resident representative of a foreign government recognized de jure by the United States, which foreign government is a member of an international organization entitled to enjoy privileges, exemptions, and immunities as an international organization under the International Organizations Immunities Act (59 Stat. 669), accredited resident members of the staff of such representatives, and members of his or their immediate family;

(ii) other accredited representatives of such a foreign government to such international organizations, and the members of their immediate families;

(iii) an alien able to qualify under (i) or (ii) above except for the fact that the government of which such alien is an accredited representative is not recognized de jure by the United States, or that the government of which he is an accredited representative is not a member of such international organization; and the members of his immediate family;

(iv) officers, or employees of such international organizations, and the members of their immediate families;

(v) attendants, servants, and personal employees of any such representative, officer, or employee, and the members of the immediate families of such attendants, servants, and personal employees;

(H) an alien

(i)(a) Repealed. Pub.L. 106–95, § 2(c), Nov. 12, 1999, 113 Stat. 1316.

(b) subject to section 212(j)(2) [8 U.S.C.A. § 1182(j)(2)], who is coming temporarily to the United States to perform services (other than services described in subclause (a) during the period in which such subclause applies and other than services described in subclause (ii)(a) or in subparagraph (O) or (P)) in a specialty occupation described in section 214(i)(1) [8 U.S.C.A. § 1184(i)(1)] or as a fashion model, who meets the requirements for the occupation specified in section 214(i)(2) [8 U.S.C.A. § 1184(i)(2)] or, in the case of a fashion model, is of distinguished merit and ability, and with respect to whom the Secretary of Labor determines and certifies to the Attorney General that the intending employer has filed with the Secretary an application under section 212(n)(1) [8 U.S.C.A. § 1182(n)(1)], or **(b1)** who is entitled to enter the United States under and in pursuance of the provisions of an agreement listed in section 214(g)(8)(A) [8 U.S.C.A. § 1184(g)(8)(A)], who is engaged in a specialty occupation described in section 214(i)(3) [8 U.S.C.A. § 1184(i)(3)], and with respect to whom the Secretary of Labor determines and certifies to the Secretary of Homeland Security and the Secretary of State that the intending employer has filed with the Secretary of Labor an attestation under section 212(t)(1) [8 U.S.C.A. § 1182(t)(1)], or

(c) who is coming temporarily to the United States to perform services as a registered nurse, who meets the qualifications described in section 212(m)(1) [8 U.S.C.A. § 1182(m)(1)], and with respect to whom the Secretary of Labor determines and certifies to the Attorney General that an unexpired attestation is on file and in effect under section 212(m)(2) [8 U.S.C.A. § 1182(m)(2)] for the facility (as defined in section 212(m)(6) [8 U.S.C.A. § 1182(m)(6)]) for which the alien will perform the services; or

(ii)(a) having a residence in a foreign country which he has no intention of abandoning who is coming temporarily to the United States to perform agricultural labor or services, as defined by the Secretary of Labor in regulations and including agricultural labor defined in section 3121(g) of the Internal Revenue Code of 1986, agriculture as defined in section 3(f) of the Fair Labor Standards Act of 1938 (29 U.S.C. § 203(f)), and the pressing of apples for cider on a farm, of a temporary or seasonal nature, or **(b)** having a residence in a foreign country which he has no intention of abandoning who is coming temporarily to the United States to perform other temporary service or labor if unemployed persons capable of performing such service or labor cannot be found in this country, but this clause shall not apply to graduates of medical schools coming to the United States to perform services as members of the medical profession; or

(iii) having a residence in a foreign country which he has no intention of abandoning who is coming temporarily to the United States as a trainee, other than to receive graduate medical education or training, in a training program that is not designed primarily to provide productive employment; and the alien spouse and minor children of any such alien specified in this paragraph if accompanying him or following to join him;

(I) upon a basis of reciprocity, an alien who is a bona fide representative of foreign press, radio, film, or other foreign information media, who seeks to enter the United States solely to engage in such vocation, and the spouse and children of such a representative, if accompanying or following to join him;

(J) an alien having a residence in a foreign country which he has no intention of abandoning who is a bona fide student, scholar, trainee, teacher, professor, research assistant, specialist, or leader in a field of specialized knowledge or skill, or other person of similar description, who is coming temporarily to the United States as a participant in a program designated by the Director of the United States Information Agency, for the purpose of teaching, instructing or lecturing, studying, observing, conducting research, consulting, demonstrating special skills, or receiving training and who, if he is coming to the United States to participate in a program under which he will receive graduate medical education or training, also meets the requirements of section 212(j) [8 U.S.C.A. § 1182(j)], and the alien spouse and minor children of any such alien if accompanying him or following to join him;

(K) subject to subsections (d) and (p) of section 214 [8 U.S.C.A. § 1184], an alien who—

(i) is the fiancée or fiancé of a citizen of the United States (other than a citizen described in section 204(a)(1)(A)(viii)(I) [8 U.S.C.A. § 1154(a)(1)(A)(viii)(I)]) and who seeks to enter the United States solely to conclude a valid marriage with the petitioner within ninety days after admission;

(ii) has concluded a valid marriage with a citizen of the United States (other than a citizen described in section 204(a)(1)(A)(viii)(I) [8 U.S.C.A. § 1154(a)(1)(A)(viii)(I)]) who is the petitioner, is the beneficiary of a petition to accord a status under section 201(b)(2)(A)(i) [8 U.S.C.A. § 1151(b)(2)(A)(i)] that was filed under section 204 [8 U.S.C.A. § 1154] by the petitioner, and seeks to enter the United States to await the approval of such petition and the availability to the alien of an immigrant visa; or

(iii) is the minor child of an alien described in clause (i) or (ii) and is accompanying, or following to join, the alien;

(L) subject to section 214(c)(2) [8 U.S.C.A. § 1184(c)(2)], an alien who, within 3 years preceding the time of his application for admission into the United States, has been employed continuously for one year by a firm or corporation or other legal entity or an affiliate or subsidiary thereof and who seeks to enter the United States temporarily in order to continue to render his services to the same employer or a subsidiary or affiliate thereof in a capacity that is managerial, executive, or involves specialized knowledge, and the alien spouse and minor children of any such alien if accompanying him or following to join him;

(M)(i) an alien having a residence in a foreign country which he has no intention of abandoning who seeks to enter the United States temporarily and solely for the purpose of pursuing a full course of study at an established vocational or other recognized nonacademic institution (other than in a language training program) in the United States particularly designated by him and approved by the Attorney General, after consultation with the Secretary of Education, which institution shall have agreed to report to the Attorney General the termination of attendance of each nonimmigrant nonacademic student and if any such institution fails to make reports promptly the approval shall be withdrawn, and **(ii)** the alien spouse and minor children of any alien described in clause (i) if accompanying or following to join such an alien, and **(iii)** an alien who is a national of Canada or Mexico, who maintains actual residence and place of abode in the country of nationality, who is described in clause (i) except that the alien's course of study may be full or part–time, and who commutes to the United States institution or place of study from Canada or Mexico;

(N)(i) the parent of an alien accorded the status of special immigrant under paragraph (27)(I)(i) (or under analogous authority under paragraph (27)(L)), but only if and while the alien is a child, or

(ii) a child of such parent or of an alien accorded the status of a special immigrant under clause (ii), (iii), or (iv) of paragraph (27)(I) (or under analogous authority under paragraph (27)(L));

(O) an alien who—

(i) has extraordinary ability in the sciences, arts, education, business, or athletics which has been demonstrated by sustained national or international acclaim or, with regard to motion picture and television productions a demonstrated record of extraordinary achievement, and whose achievements have been recognized in the field through extensive documentation, and seeks to enter the United States to continue work in the area of extraordinary ability; or

(ii)(I) seeks to enter the United States temporarily and solely for the purpose of accompanying and assisting in the artistic or athletic performance by an alien who is admitted under clause (i) for a specific event or events,

(II) is an integral part of such actual performance,

(III)(a) has critical skills and experience with such alien which are not of a general nature and which cannot be performed by other individuals, or **(b)** in the case of a motion picture or television production, has skills and experience with such alien which are not of a general nature and which are critical either based on a pre-existing longstanding working relationship or, with respect to the specific production, because significant production (including pre- and post-production work) will take place both inside and outside the United States and the continuing participation of the alien is essential to the successful completion of the production, and

(IV) has a foreign residence which the alien has no intention of abandoning; or

(iii) is the alien spouse or child of an alien described in clause (i) or (ii) and is accompanying, or following to join, the alien;

(P) an alien having a foreign residence which the alien has no intention of abandoning who—

(i)(a) is described in section 214(c)(4)(A) [8 U.S.C.A. § 1184(c)(4)(A)] (relating to athletes), or, **(b)** is described in section 214(c)(4)(B) [8 U.S.C.A. § 1184(c)(4)(B)] (relating to entertainment groups);

(ii)(I) performs as an artist or entertainer, individually or as part of a group, or is an integral part of the performance of such a group, and

(II) seeks to enter the United States temporarily and solely for the purpose of performing as such an artist or entertainer or with such a group under a reciprocal exchange program which is between an organization or organizations in the United States and an organization or organizations in one or more foreign states and which provides for the temporary exchange of artists and entertainers, or groups of artists and entertainers;

(iii)(I) performs as an artist or entertainer, individually or as part of a group, or is an integral part of the performance of such a group, and

(II) seeks to enter the United States temporarily and solely to perform, teach, or coach as such an artist or entertainer or with such a group under a commercial or noncommercial program that is culturally unique; or

(iv) is the spouse or child of an alien described in clause (i), (ii), or (iii) and is accompanying, or following to join, the alien;

(Q) an alien having a residence in a foreign country which he has no intention of abandoning who is coming temporarily (for a period not to exceed 15 months) to the United States as a participant in an international cultural exchange program approved by the Secretary of Homeland Security for the purpose of providing practical training, employment, and the sharing of the history, culture, and traditions of the country of the alien's nationality and who will be employed under the same wages and working conditions as domestic workers;

(R) an alien, and the spouse and children of the alien if accompanying or following to join the alien, who—

(i) for the 2 years immediately preceding the time of application for admission, has been a member of a religious denomination having a bona fide nonprofit, religious organization in the United States; and

(ii) seeks to enter the United States for a period not to exceed 5 years to perform the work described in subclause (I), (II), or (III) of paragraph (27)(C)(ii);

(S) subject to section 214(k) [8 U.S.C.A. § 1184(k)], an alien—

(i) who the Attorney General determines—

(I) is in possession of critical reliable information concerning a criminal organization or enterprise;

(II) is willing to supply or has supplied such information to Federal or State law enforcement authorities or a Federal or State court; and

(III) whose presence in the United States the Attorney General determines is essential to the success of an authorized criminal investigation or the successful prosecution of an individual involved in the criminal organization or enterprise; or

(ii) who the Secretary of State and the Attorney General jointly determine—

(I) is in possession of critical reliable information concerning a terrorist organization, enterprise, or operation;

(II) is willing to supply or has supplied such information to Federal law enforcement authorities or a Federal court;

(III) will be or has been placed in danger as a result of providing such information; and

(IV) is eligible to receive a reward under section 2708(a) of Title 22,

and, if the Attorney General (or with respect to clause (ii), the Secretary of State and the Attorney General jointly) considers it to be appropriate, the spouse, married and unmarried sons and daughters, and parents of an alien described in clause (i) or (ii) if accompanying, or following to join, the alien;

(T)(i) subject to section 214(*o*) [8 U.S.C.A. § 1184(*o*)], an alien who the Secretary of Homeland Security, or in the case of subclause (III)(aa) the Secretary of Homeland Security, in consultation with the Attorney General, determines—

(I) is or has been a victim of a severe form of trafficking in persons, as defined in section 7102 of Title 22;

(II) is physically present in the United States, American Samoa, or the Commonwealth of the Northern Mariana Islands, or at a port of entry thereto, on account of such trafficking, including physical presence on account of the alien having been allowed entry into the United States for participation in investigative or judicial processes associated with an act or a perpetrator of trafficking;

(III)(aa) has complied with any reasonable request for assistance in the Federal, State, or local investigation or prosecution of acts of trafficking or the investigation of crime where acts of trafficking are at least one central reason for the commission of that crime;

(bb) in consultation with the Attorney General, as appropriate, is unable to cooperate with a request described in item (aa) due to physical or psychological trauma; or

(cc) has not attained 18 years of age; and

(IV) the alien would suffer extreme hardship involving unusual and severe harm upon removal; and

(ii) if accompanying, or following to join, the alien described in clause (i)—

(I) in the case of an alien described in clause (i) who is under 21 years of age, the spouse, children, unmarried siblings under 18 years of age on the date on which such alien applied for status under such clause, and parents of such alien;

(II) in the case of an alien described in clause (i) who is 21 years of age or older, the spouse and children of such alien; or

(III) any parent or unmarried sibling under 18 years of age, or any adult or minor children of a derivative beneficiary of the alien, as of an alien described in subclause (I) or (II) who the Secretary of Homeland Security, in consultation with the law enforcement officer investigating a severe form of trafficking, determines faces a present danger of retaliation as a result of the alien's escape from the severe form of trafficking or cooperation with law enforcement.

(iii) Repealed. Pub.L. 110–457, Title II, § 201(a)(3), Dec. 23, 2008, 122 Stat. 5053.

(U)(i) subject to section 214(p) [8 U.S.C.A § 1184(p)], an alien who files a petition for status under this subparagraph, if the Secretary of Homeland Security determines that—

(I) the alien has suffered substantial physical or mental abuse as a result of having been a victim of criminal activity described in clause (iii);

(II) the alien (or in the case of an alien child under the age of 16, the parent, guardian, or next friend of the alien) possesses information concerning criminal activity described in clause (iii);

(III) the alien (or in the case of an alien child under the age of 16, the parent, guardian, or next friend of the alien) has been helpful, is being helpful, or is likely to be helpful to a Federal, State, or local law enforcement official, to a Federal, State, or local prosecutor, to a Federal or State judge, to the Service, or to other Federal, State, or local authorities investigating or prosecuting criminal activity described in clause (iii); and

(IV) the criminal activity described in clause (iii) violated the laws of the United States or occurred in the United States (including in Indian country and military installations) or the territories and possessions of the United States;

(ii) if accompanying, or following to join, the alien described in clause (i)—

(I) in the case of an alien described in clause (i) who is under 21 years of age, the spouse, children, unmarried siblings under 18 years of age on the date on which such alien applied for status under such clause, and parents of such alien; or

(II) in the case of an alien described in clause (i) who is 21 years of age or older, the spouse and children of such alien; and

(iii) the criminal activity referred to in this clause is that involving one or more of the following or any similar activity in violation of Federal, State, or local criminal law: rape; torture; trafficking; incest; domestic violence; sexual assault; abusive sexual contact; prostitution; sexual exploitation; stalking; female genital mutilation; being held hostage; peonage; involuntary servitude; slave trade; kidnapping; abduction; unlawful criminal restraint; false imprisonment; blackmail; extortion; manslaughter; murder; felonious assault; witness tampering; obstruction of justice; perjury; fraud in foreign labor contracting (as defined in section 1351 of Title 18); or attempt, conspiracy, or solicitation to commit any of the above mentioned crimes; or

(V) subject to section 214(q) [8 U.S.C.A. § 1184(q)], an alien who is the beneficiary (including a child of the principal alien, if eligible to receive a visa under section 203(d) [8 U.S.C.A. § 1153(d)]) of a petition to accord a status under section 203(a)(2)(A) [8 U.S.C.A. § 1153(a)(2)(A)] that was filed with the Attorney General under section 204 [8 U.S.C.A. § 1154] on or before the date of the enactment of the Legal Immigration Family Equity Act [December 21, 2000], if—

(i) such petition has been pending for 3 years or more; or

(ii) such petition has been approved, 3 years or more have elapsed since such filing date, and—

(I) an immigrant visa is not immediately available to the alien because of a waiting list of applicants for visas under section 203(a)(2)(A) [8 U.S.C.A. § 1153(a)(2)(A)]; or

(II) the alien's application for an immigrant visa, or the alien's application for adjustment of status under section 245 [8 U.S.C.A. § 1255], pursuant to the approval of such petition, remains pending.

(16) The term "immigrant visa" means an immigrant visa required by this Act and properly issued by a consular officer at his office outside of the United States to an eligible immigrant under the provisions of this Act.

(17) The term "immigration laws" includes this Act and all laws, conventions, and treaties of the United States relating to the immigration, exclusion, deportation, expulsion, or removal of aliens.

(18) The term "immigration officer" means any employee or class of employees of the Service or of the United States designated by the Attorney General, individually or by regulation, to perform the functions of an immigration officer specified by this Act or any section thereof.

(19) The term "ineligible to citizenship," when used in reference to any individual, means, notwithstanding the provisions of any treaty relating to military service, an individual who is, or was at any time, permanently debarred from becoming a citizen of the United States under section 3(a) of the Selective Training and Service Act of 1940, as amended (54 Stat. 885; 55 Stat. 844), or under section 454(a) of Appendix to Title 50, or under any section of this title, or any other Act, or under any law amendatory of, supplementary to, or in substitution for, any of such sections or Acts.

(20) The term "lawfully admitted for permanent residence" means the status of having been lawfully accorded the privilege of residing permanently in the United States as an immigrant in accordance with the immigration laws, such status not having changed.

(21) The term "national" means a person owing permanent allegiance to a state.

(22) The term "national of the United States" means **(A)** a citizen of the United States, or **(B)** a person who, though not a citizen of the United States, owes permanent allegiance to the United States.

(23) The term "naturalization" means the conferring of nationality of a state upon a person after birth, by any means whatsoever.

(24) Repealed. Pub.L. 102–232, Title III, § 305(m)(1), Dec. 12, 1991, 105 Stat. 1750.

(25) The term "noncombatant service" shall not include service in which the individual is not subject to military discipline, court martial, or does not wear the uniform of any branch of the armed forces.

(26) The term "nonimmigrant visa" means a visa properly issued to an alien as an eligible nonimmigrant by a competent officer as provided in this Act.

(27) The term "special immigrant" means—

(A) an immigrant, lawfully admitted for permanent residence, who is returning from a temporary visit abroad;

(B) an immigrant who was a citizen of the United States and may, under section 324(a) [8 U.S.C.A. § 1435(a)] or 327 [8 U.S.C.A. § 1438], apply for reacquisition of citizenship;

(C) an immigrant and the immigrant's spouse and children if accompanying or following to join the immigrant, who—

(i) for at least 2 years immediately preceding the time of application for admission, has been a member of a religious denomination having a bona fide nonprofit, religious organization in the United States;

(ii) seeks to enter the United States—

(I) solely for the purpose of carrying on the vocation of a minister of that religious denomination,

(II) before September 30, 2015, in order to work for the organization at the request of the organization in a professional capacity in a religious vocation or occupation, or

(III) before September 30, 2015, in order to work for the organization (or for a bona fide organization which is affiliated with the religious denomination and is exempt from taxation as an organization described in section 501(c)(3) of Title 26) at the request of the organization in a religious vocation or occupation; and

(iii) has been carrying on such vocation, professional work, or other work continuously for at least the 2–year period described in clause (i);

(D) an immigrant who is an employee, or an honorably retired former employee, of the United States Government abroad, or of the American Institute in Taiwan, and who has performed faithful service for a total of fifteen years, or more, and his accompanying spouse and children: Provided, That the principal officer of a Foreign Service establishment (or, in the case of the American Institute in Taiwan, the Director thereof), in his discretion, shall have recommended the granting of special immigrant status to such alien in exceptional circumstances and the Secretary of State approves such recommendation and finds that it is in the national interest to grant such status;

(E) an immigrant, and his accompanying spouse and children, who is or has been an employee of the Panama Canal Company or Canal Zone Government before the date on which the Panama Canal Treaty of 1977 (as described in section 3602(a)(1) of Title 22) enters into force [October 1, 1979], who was resident in the Canal Zone on the effective date of the exchange of instruments of ratification of such Treaty [April 1, 1979], and who has performed faithful service as such an employee for one year or more;

(F) an immigrant, and his accompanying spouse and children, who is a Panamanian national and (i) who, before the date on which such Panama Canal Treaty of 1977 enters into force [October 1, 1979], has been honorably retired from United States Government employment in the Canal Zone with a total of 15 years or more of faithful service, or (ii) who, on the date on which such Treaty enters into force, has been employed by the United States Government in the Canal Zone with a total of 15 years or more of faithful service and who subsequently is honorably retired from such employment or continues to be employed by the United States Government in an area of the former Canal Zone;

(G) an immigrant, and his accompanying spouse and children, who was an employee of the Panama Canal Company or Canal Zone Government on the effective date of the exchange of instruments of ratification of such Panama Canal Treaty of 1977 [April 1, 1979], who has performed faithful service for five years or more as such an employee, and whose personal safety, or the personal safety of whose spouse or children, as a direct result of such Treaty, is reasonably placed in danger because of the special nature of any of that employment;

(H) an immigrant, and his accompanying spouse and children, who—

(i) has graduated from a medical school or has qualified to practice medicine in a foreign state,

(ii) was fully and permanently licensed to practice medicine in a State on January 9, 1978, and was practicing medicine in a State on that date,

(iii) entered the United States as a nonimmigrant under subsection (a)(15)(H) or (a)(15)(J) before January 10, 1978, and

(iv) has been continuously present in the United States in the practice or study of medicine since the date of such entry;

(I)(i) an immigrant who is the unmarried son or daughter of an officer or employee, or of a former officer or employee, of an international organization described in paragraph (15)(G)(i), and who **(I)** while maintaining the status of a nonimmigrant under paragraph (15)(G)(iv) or paragraph (15)(N), has resided and been physically present in the United States for periods totaling at least one-half of the seven years before the date of application for a visa or for adjustment of status to a status under this subparagraph and for a period or periods aggregating at least seven years between the ages of five and 21 years, and **(II)** applies for a visa or adjustment of status under this subparagraph no later than his twenty-fifth birthday or six months after October 24, 1988, whichever is later;

(ii) an immigrant who is the surviving spouse of a deceased officer or employee of such an international organization, and who **(I)** while maintaining the status of a nonimmigrant under paragraph (15)(G)(iv) or paragraph (15)(N), has resided and been physically present in the United States for periods totaling at least one-half of the seven years before the date of application for a visa or for adjustment of status to a status under this subparagraph and for a period or periods aggregating at least 15 years before the date of the death of such officer or employee, and **(II)** files a petition for status under this subparagraph no later than six months after the date of such death or six months after October 24, 1988, whichever is later;

(iii) an immigrant who is a retired officer or employee of such an international organization, and who **(I)** while maintaining the status of a nonimmigrant under paragraph (15)(G)(iv), has resided and been physically present in the United States for periods totaling at least one-half of the seven years before the date of application for a visa or for adjustment of status to a status under this subparagraph and for a period or periods aggregating at least 15 years before the date of the officer or employee's retirement from any such international organization, and **(II)** files a petition for status under this subparagraph no later than six months after the date of such retirement or six months after October 25, 1994, whichever is later; or

(iv) an immigrant who is the spouse of a retired officer or employee accorded the status of special immigrant under clause (iii), accompanying or following to join such retired officer or employee as a member of his immediate family;

(J) an immigrant who is present in the United States—

(i) who has been declared dependent on a juvenile court located in the United States or whom such a court has legally committed to, or placed under the custody of, an agency or department of a State, or an individual or entity appointed by a State or juvenile court located in the United States, and whose reunification with 1 or both of the immigrant's parents is not viable due to abuse, neglect, abandonment, or a similar basis found under State law;

(ii) for whom it has been determined in administrative or judicial proceedings that it would not be in the alien's best interest to be returned to the alien's or parent's previous country of nationality or country of last habitual residence; and

(iii) in whose case the Secretary of Homeland Security consents to the grant of special immigrant juvenile status, except that—

(I) no juvenile court has jurisdiction to determine the custody status or placement of an alien in the custody of the Secretary of Health and Human Services unless the Secretary of Health and Human Services specifically consents to such jurisdiction; and

(II) no natural parent or prior adoptive parent of any alien provided special immigrant status under this subparagraph shall thereafter, by virtue of such parentage, be accorded any right, privilege, or status under this chapter; or

(K) an immigrant who has served honorably on active duty in the Armed Forces of the United States after October 15, 1978, and after original lawful enlistment outside the United States (under a treaty or agreement in effect on October 1, 1991) for a period or periods aggregating—

(i) 12 years and who, if separated from such service, was never separated except under honorable conditions, or

(ii) 6 years, in the case of an immigrant who is on active duty at the time of seeking special immigrant status under this subparagraph and who has reenlisted to incur a total active duty service obligation of at least 12 years,

and the spouse or child of any such immigrant if accompanying or following to join the immigrant, but only if the executive department under which the immigrant serves or served recommends the granting of special immigrant status to the immigrant;

(L) an immigrant who would be described in clause (i), (ii), (iii), or (iv) of subparagraph (I) if any reference in such a clause—

(i) to an international organization described in paragraph (15)(G)(i) were treated as a reference to the North Atlantic Treaty Organization (NATO);

(ii) to a nonimmigrant under paragraph (15)(G)(iv) were treated as a reference to a nonimmigrant classifiable under NATO–6 (as a member of a civilian component accompanying a force entering in accordance with the provisions of the NATO Status-of-Forces Agreement, a member of a civilian component attached to or employed by an Allied Headquarters under the "Protocol on the Status of International Military Headquarters" set up pursuant to the North Atlantic Treaty, or as a dependent); and

(iii) to the Immigration Technical Corrections Act of 1988 or to the Immigration and Nationality Technical Corrections Act of 1994 were a reference to the American Competitiveness and Workforce Improvement Act of 1998 [Pub.L. 105–277, Div. C, Title IV, Oct. 21, 1998, 112 Stat. 2681–641]

(M) subject to the numerical limitations of section 203(b)(4) [8 U.S.C.A. § 1153(b)(4)], an immigrant who seeks to enter the United States to work as a broadcaster in the United States for the International Broadcasting Bureau of the Broadcasting Board of Governors, or for a grantee of the Broadcasting Board of Governors, and the immigrant's accompanying spouse and children.

(28) The term "organization" means, but is not limited to, an organization, corporation, company, partnership, association, trust, foundation or fund; and includes a group of persons, whether or not incorporated, permanently or temporarily associated together with joint action on any subject or subjects.

(29) The term "outlying possessions of the United States" means American Samoa and Swains Island.

(30) The term "passport" means any travel document issued by competent authority showing the bearer's origin, identity, and nationality if any, which is valid for the admission of the bearer into a foreign country.

(31) The term "permanent" means a relationship of continuing or lasting nature, as distinguished from temporary, but a relationship may be permanent even though it is one that may be dissolved eventually at the instance either of the United States or of the individual, in accordance with law.

(32) The term "profession" shall include but not be limited to architects, engineers, lawyers, physicians, surgeons, and teachers in elementary or secondary schools, colleges, academies, or seminaries.

(33) The term "residence" means the place of general abode; the place of general abode of a person means his principal, actual dwelling place in fact, without regard to intent.

(34) The term "Service" means the Immigration and Naturalization Service of the Department of Justice.

(35) The term "spouse", "wife", or "husband" do not include a spouse, wife, or husband by reason of any marriage ceremony where the contracting parties thereto are not physically present in the presence of each other, unless the marriage shall have been consummated.

(36) The term "State" includes the District of Columbia, Puerto Rico, Guam, the Virgin Islands of the United States, and the Commonwealth of the Northern Mariana Islands.

(37) The term "totalitarian party" means an organization which advocates the establishment in the United States of a totalitarian dictatorship or totalitarianism. The terms "totalitarian dictatorship" and "totalitarianism" mean and refer to systems of government not representative in fact, characterized by (A) the existence of a single political party, organized on a dictatorial basis, with so close an identity between such party and its policies and the governmental policies of the country in which it exists, that the party and the government constitute an indistinguishable unit, and (B) the forcible suppression of opposition to such party.

(38) The term "United States", except as otherwise specifically herein provided, when used in a geographical sense, means the continental United States, Alaska, Hawaii, Puerto Rico, Guam, the Virgin Islands of the United States, and the Commonwealth of the Northern Mariana Islands.

(39) The term "unmarried", when used in reference to any individual as of any time, means an individual who at such time is not married, whether or not previously married.

(40) The term "world communism" means a revolutionary movement, the purpose of which is to establish eventually a Communist totalitarian dictatorship in any or all the countries of the world through the medium of an internationally coordinated Communist political movement.

(41) The term "graduates of a medical school" means aliens who have graduated from a medical school or who have qualified to practice medicine in a foreign state, other than such aliens who are of national or international renown in the field of medicine.

(42) The term "refugee" means **(A)** any person who is outside any country of such person's nationality or, in the case of a person having no nationality, is outside any country in which such person last habitually resided, and who is unable or unwilling to return to, and is unable or unwilling to avail himself or herself of the protection of, that country because of persecution or a well-founded fear of persecution on account of race, religion, nationality, membership in a particular social group, or political opinion, or **(B)** in such special circumstances as the President after appropriate consultation (as defined in section 207(e) of this Act [8 U.S.C.A. § 1157(e)]) may specify, any person who is within the country of such person's nationality or, in the case of a person having no nationality, within the country in which such person is habitually residing, and who is persecuted or who has a well-founded fear of persecution on account of race, religion, nationality, membership in a particular social group, or political opinion. The term "refugee" does not include any person who ordered, incited, assisted, or otherwise participated in the persecution of any person on account of race, religion, nationality, membership in a particular social group, or political opinion. For purposes of determinations under this Act, a person who has been forced to abort a pregnancy or to undergo involuntary sterilization, or who has been persecuted for failure or refusal to undergo such a procedure or for other resistance to a coercive population control program, shall be deemed to have been persecuted on account of political opinion, and a person who has a well founded fear that he or she will be forced to undergo such a procedure or subject to persecution for such failure, refusal, or resistance shall be deemed to have a well founded fear of persecution on account of political opinion.

(43) The term "aggravated felony" means—

(A) murder, rape, or sexual abuse of a minor;

(B) illicit trafficking in a controlled substance (as defined in section 802 of Title 21), including a drug trafficking crime (as defined in section 924(c) of Title 18);

(C) illicit trafficking in firearms or destructive devices (as defined in section 921 of Title 18) or in explosive materials (as defined in section 841(c) of that title);

(D) an offense described in section 1956 of Title 18 (relating to laundering of monetary instruments) or section 1957 of that title (relating to engaging in monetary transactions in property derived from specific unlawful activity) if the amount of the funds exceeded $10,000;

(E) an offense described in—

(i) section 842(h) or (i) of Title 18, or section 844(d), (e), (f), (g), (h), or (i) of that title (relating to explosive materials offenses);

(ii) section 922(g)(1), (2), (3), (4), or (5), (j), (n), (*o*), (p), or (r) or 924(b) or (h) of Title 18 (relating to firearms offenses); or

(iii) section 5861 of Title 26 (relating to firearms offenses);

(F) a crime of violence (as defined in section 16 of Title 18, but not including a purely political offense) for which the term of imprisonment at least one year [sic];

(G) a theft offense (including receipt of stolen property) or burglary offense for which the term of imprisonment at least one year [sic];

(H) an offense described in section 875, 876, 877, or 1202 of Title 18 (relating to the demand for or receipt of ransom);

(I) an offense described in section 2251, 2251A, or 2252 of Title 18 (relating to child pornography);

(J) an offense described in section 1962 of Title 18 (relating to racketeer influenced corrupt organizations), or an offense described in section 1084 (if it is a second or subsequent offense) or 1955 of that title (relating to gambling offenses), for which a sentence of one year imprisonment or more may be imposed;

(K) an offense that—

(i) relates to the owning, controlling, managing, or supervising of a prostitution business;

(ii) is described in section 2421, 2422, or 2423 of Title 18 (relating to transportation for the purpose of prostitution) if committed for commercial advantage; or

(iii) is described in any of sections 1581–1585 or 1588–1591 of Title 18 (relating to peonage, slavery, involuntary servitude, and trafficking in persons);

(L) an offense described in—

(i) section 793 (relating to gathering or transmitting national defense information), 798 (relating to disclosure of classified information), 2153 (relating to sabotage) or 2381 or 2382 (relating to treason) of Title 18;

(ii) section 421 of Title 50 (relating to protecting the identity of undercover intelligence agents); or

(iii) section 421 of Title 50 (relating to protecting the identity of undercover agents);

(M) an offense that—

(i) involves fraud or deceit in which the loss to the victim or victims exceeds $10,000; or

(ii) is described in section 7201 of Title 26 (relating to tax evasion) in which the revenue loss to the Government exceeds $10,000;

(N) an offense described in paragraph (1)(A) or (2) of section 274(a) [8 U.S.C.A. § 1324(a)] (relating to alien smuggling), except in the case of a first offense for which the alien has affirmatively shown that the alien committed the offense for the purpose of assisting, abetting, or aiding only the alien's spouse, child, or parent (and no other individual) to violate a provision of this Act;

(O) an offense described in section 275(a) [8 U.S.C.A. § 1325(a)] or 276 [8 U.S.C.A. § 1326] committed by an alien who was previously deported on the basis of a conviction for an offense described in another subparagraph of this paragraph;

(P) an offense **(i)** which either is falsely making, forging, counterfeiting, mutilating, or altering a passport or instrument in violation of section 1543 of Title 18, or is described in section 1546(a) of such title (relating to document fraud) and **(ii)** for which the term of imprisonment is at least 12 months, except in the case of a first offense for which the alien has affirmatively shown that the alien committed the offense for the purpose of assisting, abetting, or aiding only the alien's spouse, child, or parent (and no other individual) to violate a provision of this Act;

(Q) an offense relating to a failure to appear by a defendant for service of sentence if the underlying offense is punishable by imprisonment for a term of 5 years or more;

(R) an offense relating to commercial bribery, counterfeiting, forgery, or trafficking in vehicles the identification numbers of which have been altered for which the term of imprisonment is at least one year;

(S) an offense relating to obstruction of justice, perjury or subornation of perjury, or bribery of a witness, for which the term of imprisonment is at least one year;

(T) an offense relating to a failure to appear before a court pursuant to a court order to answer to or dispose of a charge of a felony for which a sentence of 2 years' imprisonment or more may be imposed; and

(U) an attempt or conspiracy to commit an offense described in this paragraph.

The term applies to an offense described in this paragraph whether in violation of Federal or State law and applies to such an offense in violation of the law of a foreign country for which the term of imprisonment was completed within the previous 15 years. Notwithstanding any other provision of law (including any effective date), the term applies regardless of whether the conviction was entered before, on, or after the date of enactment of this paragraph [September 30, 1996].

(44)(A) The term "managerial capacity" means an assignment within an organization in which the employee primarily—

(i) manages the organization, or a department, subdivision, function, or component of the organization;

(ii) supervises and controls the work of other supervisory, professional, or managerial employees, or manages an essential function within the organization, or a department or subdivision of the organization;

(iii) if another employee or other employees are directly supervised, has the authority to hire and fire or recommend those as well as other personnel actions (such as promotion and leave authorization) or, if no other employee is directly supervised, functions at a senior level within the organizational hierarchy or with respect to the function managed; and

(iv) exercises discretion over the day-to-day operations of the activity or function for which the employee has authority.

A first-line supervisor is not considered to be acting in a managerial capacity merely by virtue of the supervisor's supervisory duties unless the employees supervised are professional.

(B) The term "executive capacity" means an assignment within an organization in which the employee primarily—

(i) directs the management of the organization or a major component or function of the organization;

(ii) establishes the goals and policies of the organization, component, or function;

(iii) exercises wide latitude in discretionary decision-making; and

(iv) receives only general supervision or direction from higher level executives, the board of directors, or stockholders of the organization.

(C) If staffing levels are used as a factor in determining whether an individual is acting in a managerial or executive capacity, the Attorney General shall take into account the reasonable needs of the organization, component, or function in light of the overall purpose and stage of development of the organization, component, or function. An individual shall not be considered to be acting in a managerial or executive capacity (as previously defined) merely on the basis of the number of employees that the individual supervises or has supervised or directs or has directed.

(45) The term "substantial" means, for purposes of paragraph (15)(E) with reference to trade or capital, such an amount of trade or capital as is established by the Secretary of State, after consultation with appropriate agencies of Government.

(46) The term "extraordinary ability" means, for purposes of § 101(a)(15)(O)(i), in the case of the arts, distinction.

(47)(A) The term "order of deportation" means the order of the special inquiry officer, or other such administrative officer to whom the Attorney General has delegated the responsibility for determining whether an alien is deportable, concluding that the alien is deportable or ordering deportation.

(B) The order described under subparagraph (A) shall become final upon the earlier of—

(i) a determination by the Board of Immigration Appeals affirming such order; or

(ii) the expiration of the period in which the alien is permitted to seek review of such order by the Board of Immigration Appeals.

(48)(A) The term "conviction" means, with respect to an alien, a formal judgment of guilt of the alien entered by a court or, if adjudication of guilt has been withheld, where—

(i) a judge or jury has found the alien guilty or the alien has entered a plea of guilty or nolo contendere or has admitted sufficient facts to warrant a finding of guilt, and

(ii) the judge has ordered some form of punishment, penalty, or restraint on the alien's liberty to be imposed.

(B) Any reference to a term of imprisonment or a sentence with respect to an offense is deemed to include the period of incarceration or confinement ordered by a court of law regardless of any suspension of the imposition or execution of that imprisonment or sentence in whole or in part.

(49) The term "stowaway" means any alien who obtains transportation without the consent of the owner, charterer, master or person in command of any vessel or aircraft through concealment aboard such vessel or aircraft. A passenger who boards with a valid ticket is not to be considered a stowaway.

(50) The term "intended spouse" means any alien who meets the criteria set forth in section 204(a)(1)(A)(iii)(II)(aa)(BB) [8 U.S.C.A. § 1154(a)(1)(A)(iii)(II)(aa)(BB)], 204(a)(1)(B)(ii)(II)(aa)(BB) [8 U.S.C.A. § 1154(a)(1)(B)(ii)(II)(aa)(BB)], or 240A(b)(2)(A)(i)(III) [8 U.S.C.A. § 1229b(b)(2)(A)(i)(III)].

(51) The term "VAWA self-petitioner" means an alien, or a child of the alien, who qualifies for relief under—

(A) clause (iii), (iv), or (vii) of section 204(a)(1)(A) [8 U.S.C.A § 1154(a)(1)(A)];

(B) clause (ii) or (iii) of section 204(a)(1)(B) [8 U.S.C.A § 1154(a)(1)(B)];

(C) section 216(c)(4)(C) [8 U.S.C.A § 1186a(c)(4)(C)];

(D) the first section of Public Law 89–732 [8 U.S.C.A. § 1255 note] (commonly known as the Cuban Adjustment Act) as a child or spouse who has been battered or subjected to extreme cruelty;

(E) section 902(d)(1)(B) of the Haitian Refugee Immigration Fairness Act of 1998 [8 U.S.C.A. § 1255 note];

(F) section 202(d)(1) of the Nicaraguan Adjustment and Central American Relief Act; or

(G) section 309 of the Illegal Immigration Reform and Immigrant Responsibility Act of 1996 (division C of Public Law 104–208).

(52) The term "accredited language training program" means a language training program that is accredited by an accrediting agency recognized by the Secretary of Education.

(b) As used in titles I and II—

(1) The term "child" means an unmarried person under twenty-one years of age who is—

(A) a child born in wedlock;

(B) a stepchild, whether or not born out of wedlock, provided the child had not reached the age of eighteen years at the time the marriage creating the status of stepchild occurred;

(C) a child legitimated under the law of the child's residence or domicile, or under the law of the father's residence or domicile, whether in or outside the United States, if such legitimation takes place before the child reaches the age of eighteen years and the child is in the legal custody of the legitimating parent or parents at the time of such legitimation;

(D) a child born out of wedlock, by, through whom, or on whose behalf a status, privilege, or benefit is sought by virtue of the relationship of the child to its natural mother or to its natural father if the father has or had a bona fide parent-child relationship with the person;

(E)(i) a child adopted while under the age of sixteen years if the child has been in the legal custody of, and has resided with, the adopting parent or parents for at least two years or if the child has been battered or subject to extreme cruelty by the adopting parent or by a family member of the adopting parent residing in the same household: *Provided*, That no natural parent of any such adopted child shall thereafter, by virtue of such parentage, be accorded any right, privilege, or status under this Act; or

(ii) subject to the same proviso as in clause (i), a child who: **(I)** is a natural sibling of a child described in clause (i) or subparagraph (F)(i); **(II)** was adopted by the adoptive parent or parents of the sibling described in such clause or subparagraph; and **(III)** is otherwise described in clause (i), except that the child was adopted while under the age of 18 years; or

(F)(i) a child, under the age of sixteen at the time a petition is filed in his behalf to accord a classification as an immediate relative under section 201(b) [8 U.S.C.A. § 1151(b)], who is an orphan because of the death or disappearance of, abandonment or desertion by, or separation or loss from, both parents, or for whom the sole or surviving parent is incapable of providing the proper care and has in writing irrevocably released the child for emigration and adoption; who has been adopted abroad by a United States citizen and spouse jointly, or by an unmarried United States citizen at least twenty-five years of age, who personally saw and observed the child prior to or during the adoption proceedings; or who is coming to the United States for adoption by a United States citizen and spouse jointly, or by an unmarried United States citizen at least twenty-five years of age, who have or has complied with the preadoption requirements, if any, of the child's proposed residence: Provided, That the Attorney General is satisfied that proper care will be furnished the child if admitted to the United States: Provided further, That no natural parent or prior adoptive parent of any such child shall thereafter, by virtue of such parentage, be accorded any right, privilege, or status under this Act; or

(ii) subject to the same provisos as in clause (i), a child who: (I) is a natural sibling of a child described in clause (i) or subparagraph (E)(i); (II) has been adopted abroad, or is coming to the United States for adoption, by the adoptive parent (or prospective adoptive parent) or parents of the sibling described in such clause or subparagraph; and (III) is otherwise described in clause (i), except that the child is under the age of 18 at the time a petition is filed in his or her behalf to accord a classification as an immediate relative under section 201(b) [8 U.S.C.A. § 1151(b)]; or

(G)(i) a child, younger than 16 years of age at the time a petition is filed on the child's behalf to accord a classification as an immediate relative under section 201(b) [8 U.S.C.A. § 1151(b)], who has been adopted in a foreign state that is a party to the Convention on Protection of Children and Co-operation in Respect of Intercountry Adoption, done at The Hague on May 29, 1993, or who is emigrating from such a foreign state to be adopted in the United States by a United States citizen and spouse jointly or by an unmarried United States citizen who is at least 25 years of age, Provided, That—

(I) the Secretary of Homeland Security is satisfied that proper care will be furnished the child if admitted to the United States;

(II) the child's natural parents (or parent, in the case of a child who has one sole or surviving parent because of the death or disappearance of, abandonment or desertion by, the other parent), or other persons or institutions that retain legal custody of the child, have freely given their written irrevocable consent to the termination of their legal relationship with the child, and to the child's emigration and adoption;

(III) in the case of a child having two living natural parents, the natural parents are incapable of providing proper care for the child;

(IV) the Secretary of Homeland Security is satisfied that the purpose of the adoption is to form a bona fide parent-child relationship, and the parent-child relationship of the child and the natural parents has been terminated (and in carrying out both obligations under this subclause the Secretary of Homeland Security may consider whether there is a petition pending to confer immigrant status on one or both of such natural parents); and

(V) in the case of a child who has not been adopted—

(aa) the competent authority of the foreign state has approved the child's emigration to the United States for the purpose of adoption by the prospective adoptive parent or parents; and

(bb) the prospective adoptive parent or parents has or have complied with any pre-adoption requirements of the child's proposed residence; and

(ii) except that no natural parent or prior adoptive parent of any such child shall thereafter, by virtue of such parentage, be accorded any right, privilege, or status under this chapter; or

(iii) subject to the same provisos as in clauses (i) and (ii), a child who—

(I) is a natural sibling of a child described in clause (i), subparagraph (E)(i), or subparagraph (F)(i);

(II) was adopted abroad, or is coming to the United States for adoption, by the adoptive parent (or prospective adoptive parent) or parents of the sibling described in clause (i), subparagraph (E)(i), or subparagraph (F)(i); and

(III) is otherwise described in clause (i), except that the child is younger than 18 years of age at the time a petition is filed on his or her behalf for classification as an immediate relative under section 201(b) [8 U.S.C.A. § 1151(b)].

(2) The terms "parent", "father", or "mother" mean a parent, father, or mother only where the relationship exists by reason of any of the circumstances set forth in subdivision (1) of this subsection, except that, for purposes of paragraph (1)(F) (other than the second proviso therein) and paragraph (1)(G)(i) in the case of a child born out of wedlock described in paragraph (1)(D) (and not described in paragraph (1)(C)), the term "parent" does not include the natural father of the child if the father has disappeared or abandoned or deserted the child or if the father has in writing irrevocably released the child for emigration and adoption.

(3) The term "person" means an individual or an organization.

(4) The term "immigration judge" means an attorney whom the Attorney General appoints as an administrative judge within the Executive Office for Immigration Review, qualified to conduct specified classes of proceedings, including a hearing under section 240 [8 U.S.C.A. § 1229a]. An immigration judge shall be subject to such supervision and shall perform such duties as the Attorney General shall prescribe, but shall not be employed by the Immigration and Naturalization Service.

(5) The term "adjacent islands" includes Saint Pierre, Miquelon, Cuba, the Dominican Republic, Haiti, Bermuda, the Bahamas, Barbados, Jamaica, the Windward and Leeward Islands, Trinidad, Martinique, and other British, French, and Netherlands territory or possessions in or bordering on the Caribbean Sea.

(c) As used in title III—

(1) The term "child" means an unmarried person under twenty-one years of age and includes a child legitimated under the law of the child's residence or domicile, or under the law of the father's residence or domicile, whether in the United States or elsewhere, and, except as otherwise provided in sections 320 [8 U.S.C.A. § 1431] and 321 [8 U.S.C.A. § 1432], a child adopted in the United States, if such legitimation or adoption takes place before the child reaches the age of 16 years (except to the extent that the child is described in subparagraph (E)(ii) or (F)(ii) of subsection (b)(1)), and the child is in the legal custody of the legitimating or adopting parent or parents at the time of such legitimation or adoption.

(2) The terms "parent", "father", and "mother" include in the case of a posthumous child a deceased parent, father, and mother.

(d) Repealed. Pub.L. 100–525, § 9(a)(3), Oct. 24, 1988, 102 Stat. 2619.

(e) For the purposes of this Act—

(1) The giving, loaning, or promising of support or of money or any other thing of value to be used for advocating any doctrine shall constitute the advocating of such doctrine; but nothing in this paragraph shall be construed as an exclusive definition of advocating.

(2) The giving, loaning, or promising of support or of money or any other thing of value for any purpose to any organization shall be presumed to constitute affiliation therewith; but nothing in this paragraph shall be construed as an exclusive definition of affiliation.

(3) Advocating the economic, international, and governmental doctrines of world communism means advocating the establishment of a totalitarian Communist dictatorship in any or all of the countries of the world through the medium of an internationally coordinated Communist movement.

(f) For the purposes of this Act—

No person shall be regarded as, or found to be, a person of good moral character who, during the period for which good moral character is required to be established, is, or was—

(1) a habitual drunkard;

(2) Repealed. Pub.L. 97–116, § 2(c)(1), Dec. 29, 1981, 95 Stat. 1611

(3) a member of one or more of the classes of persons, whether inadmissible or not, described in paragraphs (2)(D), (6)(E), and (10)(A) of section 212(a) [8 U.S.C.A § 1182(a)]; or subparagraphs (A) and (B) of section 212(a)(2) [8 U.S.C.A § 1182(a)(2)] and subparagraph (C) thereof of such section* (except as such paragraph relates to a single offense of simple possession of 30 grams or less of marihuana), if the offense described therein, for which such person was convicted or of which he admits the commission, was committed during such period;

(4) one whose income is derived principally from illegal gambling activities;

(5) one who has been convicted of two or more gambling offenses committed during such period;

(6) one who has given false testimony for the purpose of obtaining any benefits under this Act;

(7) one who during such period has been confined, as a result of conviction, to a penal institution for an aggregate period of one hundred and eighty days or more, regardless of whether the offense, or offenses, for which he has been confined were committed within or without such period;

(8) one who at any time has been convicted of an aggravated felony (as defined in subsection (a)(43));

(9) one who at any time has engaged in conduct described in section 212(a)(3)(E) [8 U.S.C.A. § 1182(a)(3)(E)] (relating to assistance in Nazi persecution, participation in genocide, or commission of acts of torture or extrajudicial killings) or 212(a)(2)(G) [8 U.S.C.A § 1182(a)(2)(G)] (relating to severe violations of religious freedom).

The fact that any person is not within any of the foregoing classes shall not preclude a finding that for other reasons such person is or was not of good moral character.

In the case of an alien who makes a false statement or claim of citizenship, or who registers to vote or votes in a Federal, State, or local election (including an initiative, recall, or referendum) in violation of a lawful restriction of such registration or voting to citizens, if each natural parent of the alien (or, in the case of an adopted alien, each adoptive parent of the alien) is or was a citizen (whether by birth or

* So in original. The phrase "of such section" probably should not appear.

naturalization), the alien permanently resided in the United States prior to attaining the age of 16, and the alien reasonably believed at the time of such statement, claim, or violation that he or she was a citizen, no finding that the alien is, or was, not of good moral character may be made based on it.

(g) For the purposes of this Act any alien ordered deported or removed (whether before or after the enactment of this Act) who has left the United States, shall be considered to have been deported or removed in pursuance of law, irrespective of the source from which the expenses of his transportation were defrayed or of the place to which he departed.

(h) For purposes of section 212(a)(2)(E) [8 U.S.C.A. § 1182(a)(2)(E)], the term "serious criminal offense" means—

(1) any felony;

(2) any crime of violence, as defined in section 16 of Title 18; or

(3) any crime of reckless driving or of driving while intoxicated or under the influence of alcohol or of prohibited substances if such crime involves personal injury to another.

(i) With respect to each nonimmigrant alien described in subsection (a)(15)(T)(i) of this section—

(1) the Secretary of Homeland Security, the Attorney General, and other Government officials, where appropriate, shall provide the alien with a referral to a nongovernmental organization that would advise the alien regarding the alien's options while in the United States and the resources available to the alien; and

(2) the Secretary of Homeland Security shall, during the period the alien is in lawful temporary resident status under that subsection, grant the alien authorization to engage in employment in the United States and provide the alien with an "employment authorized" endorsement or other appropriate work permit.

(June 27, 1952, c. 477, Title I, § 101, 66 Stat. 166; Sept. 11, 1957, Pub.L. 85–316, §§ 1, 2, 71 Stat. 639; July 7, 1958, Pub.L. 85–508, § 22, 72 Stat. 351; Mar. 18, 1959, Pub.L. 86–3, § 20(a), 73 Stat. 13; Sept. 21, 1961, Pub.L. 87–256, § 109(a), (b), 75 Stat. 534; Sept. 26, 1961, Pub.L. 87–301, §§ 1, 2, 7, 75 Stat. 650, 653; Oct. 3, 1965, Pub.L. 89–236, §§ 8, 24, 79 Stat. 916, 922; Nov. 2, 1966, Pub.L. 89–710, 80 Stat. 1104; Apr. 7, 1970, Pub.L. 91–225, § 1, 84 Stat. 116; Dec. 16, 1975, Pub.L. 94–155, 89 Stat. 824; Oct. 12, 1976, Pub.L. 94–484, Title VI, § 601(b), (e), 90 Stat. 2301, 2302; Oct. 20, 1976, Pub.L. 94–571, § 7(a), 90 Stat. 2706; Oct. 12, 1976, Pub.L. 94–484, Title VI, § 602(c), as added Aug. 1, 1977, Pub.L. 95–83, Title III, § 307(q)(3), 91 Stat. 395; Aug. 17, 1977, Pub.L. 95–105, Title I, § 109(b)(3), 91 Stat. 847; 1977 Reorg. Plan No. 2, § 7(a)(8), 42 F.R. 62461, 91 Stat. 1637; Sept. 27, 1979, Pub.L. 96–70, Title III, § 3201(a), 93 Stat. 496; Mar. 17, 1980, Pub.L. 96–212, Title II, § 201(a), 94 Stat. 102; Dec. 29, 1981, Pub.L. 97–116, §§ 2, 5(d)(1), 18(a), 95 Stat. 1611, 1614, 1619; Oct. 30, 1984, Priv.Law 98–47, § 3, 98 Stat. 3435; Oct. 21,1986, Pub.L. 99–505, § 1, 100 Stat. 1806; Nov. 6, 1986, Pub.L. 99–603, Title III, §§ 301(a), 312, 315(a), 100 Stat. 3411, 3434, 3439; Nov. 14, 1986, Pub.L. 99–653, §§ 2, 3, 100 Stat. 3655; Oct. 1, 1988, Pub.L. 100–459, Title II, § 210(a), 102 Stat. 2203; Oct. 24, 1988, Pub.L. 100–525, §§ 2(O)(1), 8(b), 9(a), 102 Stat. 2613, 2617, 2619; Nov. 18, 1988, Pub.L. 100–690, Title VII, § 7342, 102 Stat. 4469; Nov. 21, 1989, Pub.L. 101–162, Title VI, § 611(a), 103 Stat. 1038; Dec. 18, 1989, Pub.L. 101–238, § 3(a), 103 Stat. 2100; Feb. 16, 1990, Pub.L. 101–246, Title 1, § 131(b), 104 Stat. 31; Nov. 29, 1990, Pub.L. 101–649, Title I, §§ 123, 151(a), 153(a),

162(f)(2)(A), Title II, §§ 203(c), 204(a), (c), 205(c)(1), (d), (e), 206(c), 207(a), 208, 209(a), Title IV, § 407(a)(2), Title V, §§ 501(a), 509(a), Title VI, § 603(a)(1), 104 Stat. 4995, 5004, 5005, 5012, 5018, 5019, 5020, 5022, 5023, 5024, 5026, 5027, 5040, 5048, 5051, 5082; Oct. 1, 1991, Pub.L. 102–110, § 2(a), 105 Stat. 555; Dec. 12, 1991, Pub.L. 102–232, Title II, §§ 203(a), 205(a) to (c), 206(b), (c)(1), (d), 207(b), Title III, §§ 302(e)(8)(A), 303(a)(5)(A), (7)(A), (14), 305(m)(1), 306(a)(1), 309(b)(1), (4), 105 Stat. 1737, 1740, 1741, 1746 to 1748, 1750, 1751, 1758; Apr. 30, 1994, Pub.L. 103–236, Title I, § 162(h)(1), 108 Stat. 407; Sept. 13, 1994, Pub.L. 103–322, Title XIII, § 130003(a), 108 Stat. 2024; Oct. 5, 1994, Pub.L. 103–337, Div. C, Title XXXVI, § 3605, 108 Stat. 3113; Oct. 25, 1994, Pub.L. 103–416, Title II, §§ 201, 202, 214, 219(a), 222(a), 108 Stat. 4310, 4311, 4314, 4316, 4320; Nov. 15, 1995, Pub.L. 104–51, § 1, 109 Stat. 467; Apr. 24, 1996, Pub.L. 104–132, Title IV, § 440(b), (e), 110 Stat. 1277; Sept. 30, 1996, Pub.L. 104–208, Div. C, Title I, § 104(a), Title III, §§ 301(a), 308(d)(3)(A), (4)(A), (e)(3), (f)(1)(A), (B), 321(a), (b), 322(a)(1), (2)(A), 361(a), 371(a), Title VI, §§ 601(a)(1), 625(a)(2), 671(a)(3)(B), (b)(5), (e)(2), 110 Stat. 3009–555, 3009–575, 3009–617, 3009–620, 3009–621, 3009–627, 3009–628, 3009–629, 3009–644, 3009–645, 3009–689, 3009–700, 3009–721 to 3009–723; Oct. 6, 1997, Pub.L. 105–54, § 1(a), 111 Stat. 1175; Nov. 26, 1997, Pub.L. 105–119, Title I, § 113, 111 Stat. 2460; Oct. 21, 1998, Pub.L. 105–277, Div. C, Title IV, § 421, Div. G, Title XXII, § 2222(e), 112 Stat. 2681–657, 2681–819; Oct. 30, 1998, Pub.L. 105–319, § 2(b)(1), (e)(2), 112 Stat. 3014, 3015; Nov. 12, 1999, Pub.L. 106–95, § 2(a), (c), 113 Stat. 1312; Dec. 7, 1999, Pub.L. 106–139, § (1)(a), (b)(1), 113 Stat. 1696; Oct. 6, 2000, Pub.L. 106–279, Title III, § 302(a), (c), 114 Stat. 838, 839; Oct. 28, 2000, Pub.L. 106–386, Div. A, § 107(e)(1), (4), Div. B, Title V, §§ 1503(a), 1513(b), 114 Stat. 1477, 1479, 1518, 1534; Oct. 30, 2000, Pub.L. 106–395, Title II, § 201(a)(1), 114 Stat. 1633; Nov. 1, 2000, Pub.L. 106–409, § 2(a), 114 Stat. 1787; Nov. 22, 2000, Pub.L. 106–536, § 1(a), 114 Stat. 2560; Dec. 21, 2000, Pub.L. 106–553, § 1(a)(2) [Title XI, § 1102(a), 1103(a)], 114 Stat. 2762; Jan. 16, 2002, Pub.L. 107–125, § 2(b), 115 Stat. 2403; Oct. 4, 2002, Pub.L. 107–234, § 1(4), 116 Stat. 1481; Nov. 2, 2002, Pub.L. 107–274, § 2(a), (b), 116 Stat. 1923; Sept. 3, 2003, Pub.L. 108–77, Title IV, § 402(a)(1), 117 Stat. 939; Oct. 15, 2003, Pub.L. 108–99, § 1, 117 Stat. 1176; Dec. 19, 2003, Pub.L. 108–193, §§ 4(b)(1), (5), 8(a)(1), 117 Stat. 2878, 2879, 2886; Dec. 10, 2004, Pub.L. 108–449, § 1(a)(2)(B), (b)(1), 118 Stat. 3469, 3470; Dec. 17, 2004, Pub.L. 108–458, Title V, § 5504, 118 Stat. 3741; May 11, 2005, Pub.L. 109–13, Div. B, § 501, 119 Stat. 231, 321; Oct. 18, 2005, Pub.L. 109–90, § 536, 119 Stat. 2087; Jan. 5, 2006, Pub.L. 109–162, Title VIII, §§ 801, 805(d), 811, 822(c)(1), 119 Stat. 3053, 3056, 3057, 3063; July 27, 2006, Pub.L. 109–248, Title IV, § 402(b), 120 Stat. 623; May 8, 2008, Pub.L. 110–229, Title VII, Subtitle A, § 702(j)(1)–(3), 122 Stat. 866; October 10, 2008, Pub. L. 110–391, § 2(a), 122 Stat. 4193; Dec. 23, 2008, Pub.L. 110–457, Title II, §§ 201(a), 235(d)(1), 122 Stat. 5052, 5079; Mar. 20, 2009, Pub.L. 111–9, § 1, 123 Stat. 989; Oct. 28, 2009, Pub.L. 111–83, Title V, § 568(a)(1), 123 Stat. 2186; Nov. 30, 2010, Pub.L. 111–287, § 3, 124 Stat. 3058; Pub.L. 111–306, § 1(a), (b), Dec. 14, 2010, 124 Stat. 3280; Pub.L. 112–176, § 3, Sept. 28, 2012, 126 Stat. 1325; Pub.L. 113–4, Title VIII, § 801, Title XII, §§ 1221, 1222, Mar. 7, 2013, 127 Stat. 110, 144.)

§ 102. Diplomatic and semidiplomatic immunities [8 U.S.C.A. § 1102]

Except as otherwise provided in this Act, for so long as they continue in the nonimmigrant classes enumerated in this section, the provisions of this Act relating to ineligibility to receive visas and the removal of aliens shall not be construed to apply to nonimmigrants—

(1) within the class described in paragraph (15)(A)(i) of section 101(a) [8 U.S.C.A. § 1101(a)], except those provisions relating to reasonable requirements of passports and visas as a means of identification and documentation necessary to establish their qualifications under such paragraph (15)(A)(i), and, under such rules and regulations as the President may deem to be necessary, the provisions of subparagraphs (A) through (C) of section 212(a)(3) [8 U.S.C.A. § 1182(a)(3)];

(2) within the class described in paragraph (15)(G)(i) of section 101(a) [8 U.S.C.A. § 1101(a)], except those provisions relating to reasonable requirements of passports and visas as a means of identification and documentation necessary to establish their qualifications under such paragraph (15)(G)(i), and the provisions of subparagraphs (A) through (C) of section 212(a)(3) [8 U.S.C.A. § 1182(a)(3)]; and

(3) within the classes described in paragraphs (15)(A)(ii), (15)(G)(ii), (15)(G)(iii), or (15)(G)(iv) of section 101(a) [8 U.S.C.A. § 1101(a)], except those provisions relating to reasonable requirements of passports and visas as a means of identification and documentation necessary to establish their qualifications under such paragraphs, and the provisions of subparagraphs (A) through (C) of section 212(a)(3) [8 U.S.C.A. § 1182(a)(3)].

(June 27, 1952, c. 477, Title I, § 102, 66 Stat. 173; Oct. 24, 1988, Pub.L. 100–525, § 9(b), 102 Stat. 2619; Nov. 29, 1990, Pub.L. 101–649, Title VI, § 603(a)(2), 104 Stat. 5082; Dec. 12, 1991, Pub.L. 102–232, Title III, § 307(i), 105 Stat. 1756; Sept. 30, 1996, Pub.L. 104–208, Div. C, Title III, § 308(d)(4)(B), 110 Stat. 3009–617.)

§ 103. Powers and duties of the Secretary, the Under Secretary, and the Attorney General [8 U.S.C.A. § 1103]

(a) Secretary of Homeland Security

(1) The Secretary of Homeland Security shall be charged with the administration and enforcement of this chapter and all other laws relating to the immigration and naturalization of aliens, except insofar as this chapter or such laws relate to the powers, functions, and duties conferred upon the President, Attorney General, the Secretary of State, the officers of the Department of State, or diplomatic or consular officers: *Provided, however,* That determination and ruling by the Attorney General with respect to all questions of law shall be controlling.

(2) He shall have control, direction, and supervision of all employees and of all the files and records of the Service.

(3) He shall establish such regulations; prescribe such forms of bond, reports, entries, and other papers; issue such instructions; and perform such other acts as he deems necessary for carrying out his authority under the provisions of this Act.

(4) He may require or authorize any employee of the Service or the Department of Justice to perform or exercise any of the powers, privileges, or duties conferred or imposed by this Act or regulations issued thereunder upon any other employee of the Service.

(5) He shall have the power and duty to control and guard the boundaries and borders of the United States against the illegal entry of aliens and shall, in his discretion, appoint for that purpose such number of employees of the Service as to him shall appear necessary and proper.

(6) He is authorized to confer or impose upon any employee of the United States, with the consent of the head of the Department or other independent establishment under whose jurisdiction the employee is serving, any of the powers, privileges, or duties conferred or imposed by this Act or regulations issued thereunder upon officers or employees of the Service.

(7) He may, with the concurrence of the Secretary of State, establish offices of the Service in foreign countries; and, after consultation with the Secretary of State, he may, whenever in his judgment such action may be necessary to accomplish the purposes of this chapter, detail employees of the Service for duty in foreign countries.

(8) After consultation with the Secretary of State, the Attorney General may authorize officers of a foreign country to be stationed at preclearance facilities in the United States for the purpose of ensuring that persons traveling from or through the United States to that foreign country comply with that country's immigration and related laws.

(9) Those officers may exercise such authority and perform such duties as United States immigration officers are authorized to exercise and perform in that foreign country under reciprocal agreement, and they shall enjoy such reasonable privileges and immunities necessary for the performance of their duties as the government of their country extends to United States immigration officers.

(10) In the event the Attorney General determines that an actual or imminent mass influx of aliens arriving off the coast of the United States, or near a land border, presents urgent circumstances requiring an immediate Federal response, the Attorney General may authorize any State or local law enforcement officer, with the consent of the head of the department, agency, or establishment under whose jurisdiction the individual is serving, to perform or exercise any of the powers, privileges, or duties conferred or imposed by this chapter or regulations issued thereunder upon officers or employees of the Service.

(11) The Attorney General, in support of persons in administrative detention in non–Federal institutions, is authorized—

(A) to make payments from funds appropriated for the administration and enforcement of the laws relating to immigration, naturalization, and alien registration for necessary clothing, medical care, necessary guard hire, and the housing, care, and security of persons detained by the Service pursuant to Federal law under an agreement with a State or political subdivision of a State; and

(B) to enter into a cooperative agreement with any State, territory, or political subdivision thereof, for the necessary construction, physical renovation, acquisition of equipment, supplies or materials required to establish acceptable conditions of confinement and detention services in any State or unit of local government which agrees to provide guaranteed bed space for persons detained by the Service.

(b) Land acquisition authority

(1) The Attorney General may contract for or buy any interest in land, including temporary use rights, adjacent to or in the vicinity of an international land border when the Attorney General deems the land essential to control and guard the boundaries and borders of the United States against any violation of this Act.

(2) The Attorney General may contract for or buy any interest in land identified pursuant to paragraph (1) as soon as the lawful owner of that interest fixes a price for it and the Attorney General considers that price to be reasonable.

(3) When the Attorney General and the lawful owner of an interest identified pursuant to paragraph (1) are unable to agree upon a reasonable price, the Attorney General may commence condemnation proceedings pursuant to the Act of August 1, 1888 (Chapter 728; 25 Stat. 357).

(4) The Attorney General may accept for the United States a gift of any interest in land identified pursuant to paragraph (1).

(c) Commissioner; appointment

The Commissioner shall be a citizen of the United States and shall be appointed by the President, by and with the advice and consent of the Senate. He shall be charged with any and all responsibilities and authority in the administration of the Service and of this Act which are conferred upon the Attorney General as may be delegated to him by the Attorney General or which may be prescribed by the Attorney General. The Commissioner may enter into cooperative agreements with State and local law enforcement agencies for the purpose of assisting in the enforcement of the immigration laws.

(d) Statistical information system

(1) The Commissioner, in consultation with interested academicians, government agencies, and other parties, shall provide for a system for collection and dissemination, to Congress and the public, of information (not in individually identifiable form) useful in evaluating the social, economic, environmental, and demographic impact of immigration laws.

(2) Such information shall include information on the alien population in the United States, on the rates of naturalization and emigration of resident aliens, on aliens who have been admitted, paroled, or granted asylum, on nonimmigrants in the United States (by occupation, basis for admission, and duration of stay), on aliens who have not been admitted or have been removed from the United States, on the number of applications filed and granted for cancellation of removal, and on the number of aliens estimated to be present unlawfully in the United States in each fiscal year.

(3) Such system shall provide for the collection and dissemination of such information not less often than annually.

(e) Annual report

(1) The Commissioner shall submit to Congress annually a report which contains a summary of the information collected under subsection (d) and an analysis of trends in immigration and naturalization.

(2) Each annual report shall include information on the number, and rate of denial administratively, of applications for naturalization, for each district office of the Service and by national origin group.

(f) Minimum number of agents in States

The Attorney General shall allocate to each State not fewer than 10 full-time active duty agents of the Immigration and Naturalization Service to carry out the functions of the Service, in order to ensure the effective enforcement of this Act.

(g) Attorney General

(1) In general

The Attorney General shall have such authorities and functions under this chapter and all other laws relating to the immigration and naturalization of aliens as were exercised by the Executive Office for Immigration Review, or by the Attorney General with respect to the Executive Office for Immigration Review, on the day before the effective date of the Immigration Reform, Accountability and Security Enhancement Act of 2002.

(2) Powers

The Attorney General shall establish such regulations, prescribe such forms of bond, reports, entries, and other papers, issue such instructions, review such administrative determinations in immigration proceedings, delegate such authority, and perform such other acts as the Attorney General determines to be necessary for carrying out this section.

(h) Repealed. Pub.L. 111–122, § 2(a), Dec. 22, 2009, 123 Stat. 3480.

(June 27, 1952, c. 477, Title I, § 103, 66 Stat. 173; Oct. 24, 1988, Pub.L. 100–525, § 9(c), 102 Stat. 2619, 2620; Nov. 29, 1990, Pub.L. 101–649, Title I, § 142, 104 Stat. 5004; Sept. 30, 1996, Pub.L 104–208, Div. C, Title I, §§ 102(d), 125, 134(a), Title III, §§ 308(d)(4)(C), (e)(4), 372, 373, 110 Stat. 3009–555, 3009–562, 3009–564, 3009–618, 3009–620, 3009–646, 3009–647; Nov. 25, 2002, Pub.L. 107–296, Title XI, § 1102, 116 Stat. 2273; Feb. 20, 2003, Pub.L. 108–7, Div. L, § 105(a)(1), (2), 117 Stat. 531; Dec. 17, 2004, Pub.L. 108–458, Title V, § 5505(a), 118 Stat. 3741; Dec. 22, 2009, Pub.L. 111–122, § 2(a), 123 Stat. 3480.)

§ 104. Powers and duties of Secretary of State; Bureau of Consular Affairs [8 U.S.C.A. § 1104]

(a) Powers and duties

The Secretary of State shall be charged with the administration and the enforcement of the provisions of this Act and all other immigration and nationality laws relating to **(1)** the powers, duties, and functions of diplomatic and consular officers of the United States, except those powers, duties, and functions conferred upon the consular officers relating to the granting or refusal of visas; **(2)** the powers, duties, and functions of the Administrator; and **(3)** the determination of nationality of a person not in the United States. He shall establish such regulations; prescribe such forms of reports, entries and other papers; issue such instructions; and perform such other acts as he deems necessary for carrying out such provisions. He is authorized to confer or impose upon any employee of the United States, with the consent of the head of the department or independent establishment under whose jurisdiction the employee is serving, any of the powers, functions, or duties conferred or imposed by this Act or regulations issued thereunder upon officers or employees of the Department of State or of the American Foreign Service.

(b) Designation and duties of Administrator

The Secretary of State shall designate an Administrator who shall be a citizen of the United States, qualified by experience. The Administrator shall maintain close liaison with the appropriate committees of Congress in order that they may be advised regarding the administration of this Act by consular officers. The Administrator shall be charged with any and all responsibility and authority in the administration of this Act which are conferred on the Secretary of State as may be delegated to the Administrator by the Secretary of State or which may be prescribed by the Secretary of State, and shall perform such other duties as the Secretary of State may prescribe.

(c) Passport Office, Visa Office, and other offices; Directors

Within the Department of State there shall be a Passport Office, a Visa Office, and such other offices as the Secretary of State may deem to be appropriate, each office to be headed by a director. The Directors of the Passport Office and the Visa Office shall be experienced in the administration of the nationality and immigration laws.

(d) Transfer of duties

The functions heretofore performed by the Passport Division and the Visa Division of the Department of State shall hereafter be performed by the Passport Office and the Visa Office, respectively.

(e) General Counsel of Visa Office; appointment and duties

There shall be a General Counsel of the Visa Office, who shall be appointed by the Secretary of State and who shall serve under the general direction of the Legal Advisor of the Department of State. The General Counsel shall have authority to maintain liaison with the appropriate officers of the Service with a view to securing uniform interpretations of the provisions of this Act.

(June 27, 1952, c. 477, Title I, § 104, 66 Stat. 174; June 28, 1962, Pub.L. 87–510, § 4(a)(2), 76 Stat. 123; Aug. 14, 1964, Pub.L. 88–426, Title III, § 305(43), 78 Stat. 428; Aug. 17, 1977, Pub.L. 95–105, Title I, § 109(b)(1), 91 Stat. 847; Oct. 24, 1988, Pub.L. 100–525, § 9(d), 102 Stat. 2620; Apr. 30, 1994, Pub.L. 103–236, Title I, § 162(h)(2), 108 Stat. 407.)

§ 105. Liaison with internal security officers data exchange [8 U.S.C.A. § 1105]

(a) The Commissioner and the Administrator shall have authority to maintain direct and continuous liaison with the Directors of the Federal Bureau of Investigation and the Central Intelligence Agency and with other internal security officers of the Government for the purpose of obtaining and exchanging information for use in enforcing the provisions of this Act in the interest of the internal and border security of the United States. The Commissioner and the Administrator shall maintain direct and continuous liaison with each other with a view to a coordinated, uniform, and efficient administration of this Act, and all other immigration and nationality laws.

(b)(1) The Attorney General and the Director of the Federal Bureau of Investigation shall provide the Department of State and the Service access to the criminal history record information contained in the National Crime Information Center's Interstate Identification Index (NCIC–III), Wanted Persons File, and to any other files maintained by the National Crime Information Center that may be mutually agreed upon by the Attorney General and the agency receiving the access, for the purpose of determining whether or not a visa applicant or applicant for admission has a criminal history record indexed in any such file.

(2) Such access shall be provided by means of extracts of the records for placement in the automated visa lookout or other appropriate database, and shall be provided without any fee or charge.

(3) The Federal Bureau of Investigation shall provide periodic updates of the extracts at intervals mutually agreed upon with the agency receiving the access. Upon receipt of such updated extracts, the receiving agency shall make corresponding updates to its database and destroy previously provided extracts.

(4) Access to an extract does not entitle the Department of State to obtain the full content of the corresponding automated criminal history record. To obtain the full content of a criminal history record, the Department of State shall submit the applicant's fingerprints and any appropriate fingerprint processing fee authorized by law to the Criminal

Justice Information Services Division of the Federal Bureau of Investigation.

(c) The provision of the extracts described in subsection (b) may be reconsidered by the Attorney General and the receiving agency upon the development and deployment of a more cost-effective and efficient means of sharing the information.

(d) For purposes of administering this section, the Department of State shall, prior to receiving access to NCIC data but not later than 4 months after the date of enactment of this subsection, promulgate final regulations—

(1) to implement procedures for the taking of fingerprints; and

(2) to establish the conditions for the use of the information received from the Federal Bureau of Investigation, in order—

(A) to limit the redissemination of such information;

(B) to ensure that such information is used solely to determine whether or not to issue a visa to an alien or to admit an alien to the United States;

(C) to ensure the security, confidentiality, and destruction of such information; and

(D) to protect any privacy rights of individuals who are subjects of such information.

(As amended Oct. 26, 2001, Pub.L. 107–56, Title IV, § 403(a), 115 Stat. 343.)

§ 106. Employment authorization for battered spouses of certain nonimmigrants [8 U.S.C.A. § 1105a]

(a) In general

In the case of an alien spouse admitted under subparagraph (A), (E)(iii), (G), or (H) of section 101(a)(15) [8 U.S.C.A § 1101(a)(15)] who is accompanying or following to join a principal alien admitted under subparagraph (A), (E)(iii), (G), or (H) of such section, respectively, the Secretary of Homeland Security may authorize the alien spouse to engage in employment in the United States and provide the spouse with an "employment authorized" endorsement or other appropriate work permit if the alien spouse demonstrates that during the marriage the alien spouse or a child of the alien spouse has been battered or has been the subject of extreme cruelty perpetrated by the spouse of the alien spouse. Requests for relief under this section shall be handled under the procedures that apply to aliens seeking relief under section 204(a)(1)(A)(iii) [8 U.S.C.A § 1154(a)(1)(A)(iii)].

(b) Construction

The grant of employment authorization pursuant to this section shall not confer upon the alien any other form of relief.

(June 27, 1952, c. 477, Title I, § 106, as added Jan. 5, 2006, Pub.L. 109–162, Title VIII, § 814(c), 119 Stat. 3059.)

TITLE II

IMMIGRATION

CHAPTER I—SELECTION SYSTEM

§ 201. Worldwide level of immigration [8 U.S.C.A. § 1151]

(a) In general

Exclusive of aliens described in subsection (b), aliens born in a foreign state or dependent area who may be issued immigrant visas or who may otherwise acquire the status of an alien lawfully admitted to the United States for permanent residence are limited to—

(1) family-sponsored immigrants described in section 203(a) [8 U.S.C.A. § 1153(a)] (or who are admitted under section 211(a) [8 U.S.C.A. § 1181(a)] on the basis of a prior issuance of a visa to their accompanying parent under section 203(a) [8 U.S.C.A. § 1153(a)]) in a number not to exceed in any fiscal year the number specified in subsection (c) for that year, and not to exceed in any of the first 3 quarters of any fiscal year 27 percent of the worldwide level under such subsection for all of such fiscal year;

(2) employment-based immigrants described in section 203(b) [8 U.S.C.A. § 1153(b)] (or who are admitted under section 211(a) [8 U.S.C.A. § 1181(a)] on the basis of a prior issuance of a visa to their accompanying parent under section 203(b) [8 U.S.C.A. § 1153(b)]), in a number not to exceed in any fiscal year the number specified in subsection (d) for that year, and not to exceed in any of the first 3 quarters of any fiscal year 27 percent of the worldwide level under such subsection for all of such fiscal year; and

(3) for fiscal years beginning with fiscal year 1995, diversity immigrants described in section 203(c) [8 U.S.C.A. § 1153(c)] (or who are admitted under section 211(a) [8 U.S.C.A. § 1181(a)] on the basis of a prior issuance of a visa to their accompanying parent under section 203(c) [8 U.S.C.A. § 1153(c)]) in a number not to exceed in any fiscal year the number specified in subsection (e) for that year, and not to exceed in any of the first 3 quarters of any fiscal year 27 percent of the worldwide level under such subsection for all of such fiscal year.

(b) Aliens not subject to direct numerical limitations

Aliens described in this subsection, who are not subject to the worldwide levels or numerical limitations of subsection (a), are as follows:

(1)(A) Special immigrants described in subparagraph (A) or (B) of section 101(a)(27) [8 U.S.C.A. § 1101(a)(27)].

(B) Aliens who are admitted under section 207 [8 U.S.C.A. § 1157] or whose status is adjusted under section 209 [8 U.S.C.A. § 1159].

(C) Aliens whose status is adjusted to permanent residence under section 210 [8 U.S.C.A. § 1160] or 245A [8 U.S.C.A. § 1255a].

(D) Aliens whose removal is cancelled under section 240A(a) [8 U.S.C.A. § 1229b(a)].

(E) Aliens provided permanent resident status under section 249 [8 U.S.C.A. § 1259].

(2)(A)(i) Immediate relatives.

For purposes of this subsection, the term "immediate relatives" means the children, spouses, and parents of a citizen of the United States, except that, in the case of parents, such citizens shall be at least 21 years of age. In the case of an alien who was the spouse of a citizen of the United States and was not legally separated from the citizen at the time of the citizen's death, the alien (and each child of the alien) shall be considered, for purposes of this subsection, to remain an immediate relative after the date of the citizen's death but only if the spouse files a petition under section § 204(a)(1)(A)(ii) [8 U.S.C.A. § 1154(a)(1)(A)(ii)] within 2 years after such date and only until the date the spouse remarries. For purposes of this clause, an alien who has filed a petition under clause (iii) or (iv) of section § 204(a)(1)(A) [8 U.S.C.A. § 1154(a)(1)(A)] remains an immediate relative in the event that the United States citizen spouse or parent loses United States citizenship on account of the abuse.

(ii) Aliens admitted under section 211(a) [8 U.S.C.A. § 1181(a)] on the basis of a prior issuance of a visa to their accompanying parent who is such an immediate relative.

(B) Aliens born to an alien lawfully admitted for permanent residence during a temporary visit abroad.

(c) Worldwide level of family-sponsored immigrants

(1)(A) The worldwide level of family-sponsored immigrants under this subsection for a fiscal year is, subject to subparagraph (B), equal to—

(i) 480,000, minus

(ii) the sum of the number computed under paragraph (2) and the number computed under paragraph (4), plus

(iii) the number (if any) computed under paragraph (3).

(B)(i) For each of fiscal years 1992, 1993, and 1994, 465,000 shall be substituted for 480,000 in subparagraph (A)(i).

(ii) In no case shall the number computed under subparagraph (A) be less than 226,000.

(2) The number computed under this paragraph for a fiscal year is the sum of the number of aliens described in subparagraphs (A) and (B) of subsection (b)(2) who were issued immigrant visas or who otherwise acquired the status of aliens lawfully admitted to the United States for permanent residence in the previous fiscal year.

(3)(A) The number computed under this paragraph for fiscal year 1992 is zero.

(B) The number computed under this paragraph for fiscal year 1993 is the difference (if any) between the worldwide level established under paragraph (1) for the previous fiscal year and the number of visas issued under section 203(a) [8 U.S.C.A. § 1153(a)] during that fiscal year.

(C) The number computed under this paragraph for a subsequent fiscal year is the difference (if any) between the maximum number of visas which may be issued under section 203(b) [8 U.S.C.A. § 1153(b)] (relating to employment-based immigrants) during the previous fiscal year and the number of visas issued under that section during that year.

(4) The number computed under this paragraph for a fiscal year (beginning with fiscal year 1999) is the number of aliens who were paroled into the United States under section 212(d)(5) [8 U.S.C.A. § 1182(d)(5)] in the second preceding fiscal year—

(A) who did not depart from the United States (without advance parole) within 365 days; and

(B) who (i) did not acquire the status of aliens lawfully admitted to the United States for permanent residence in the two preceding fiscal years, or (ii) acquired such status in such years under a provision of law (other than § 201(b)) which exempts such adjustment from the numerical limitation on the worldwide level of immigration under this section.

(5) If any alien described in paragraph (4) (other than an alien described in paragraph (4)(B)(ii)) is subsequently admitted as an alien lawfully admitted for permanent residence, such alien shall not again be considered for purposes of paragraph (1).

(d) Worldwide level of employment-based immigrants

(1) The worldwide level of employment-based immigrants under this subsection for a fiscal year is equal to—

(A) 140,000, plus

(B) the number computed under paragraph (2).

(2)(A) The number computed under this paragraph for fiscal year 1992 is zero.

(B) The number computed under this paragraph for fiscal year 1993 is the difference (if any) between the worldwide level established under paragraph (1) for the previous fiscal year and the number of visas issued under section 203(b) [8 U.S.C.A. § 1153(b)] during that fiscal year.

(C) The number computed under this paragraph for a subsequent fiscal year is the difference (if any) between the maximum number of visas which may be issued under section 203(a) [8 U.S.C.A. § 1153(a)] (relating to family-sponsored immigrants) during the previous fiscal year and the number of visas issued under that section during that year.

(e) Worldwide level of diversity immigrants

The worldwide level of diversity immigrants is equal to 55,000 for each fiscal year.

(f) Rules for determining whether certain aliens are immediate relatives

(1) Age on petition filing date

Except as provided in paragraphs (2) and (3), for purposes of subsection (b)(2)(A)(i) of this section, a determination of whether an alien satisfies the age requirement in the matter preceding subparagraph (A) of section 101(b)(1) [8 U.S.C.A. § 1101(b)(1)] shall be made using the age of the alien on the date on which the petition is filed with the Attorney General under section 204 [8 U.S.C.A. § 1154] to classify the alien as an immediate relative under subsection (b)(2)(A)(i) of this section.

(2) Age on parent's naturalization date

In the case of a petition under section 204 [8 U.S.C.A. § 1154] initially filed for an alien child's classification as a family–sponsored immigrant under section 203(a)(2)(A) [8 U.S.C.A. § 1153(a)(2)(A)], based on the child's parent being lawfully admitted for permanent residence, if the petition is later converted, due to the naturalization of the parent, to a petition to classify the alien as an immediate relative under subsection (b)(2)(A)(i) of this section, the determination described in paragraph (1) shall be made using the age of the alien on the date of the parent's naturalization.

(3) Age on marriage termination date

In the case of a petition under section 204 [8 U.S.C.A. § 1154] initially filed for an alien's classification as a family–sponsored immigrant under section 203(a)(3), based on the alien's being a married son or daughter of a citizen, if the petition is later converted, due to the legal termination of the alien's marriage, to a petition to classify the alien as an immediate relative under subsection (b)(2)(A)(i) of this section or as an unmarried son or daughter of a citizen under section 203(a)(1), the determination described in paragraph (1) shall be made using the age of the alien on the date of the termination of the marriage.

(4) Application to self-petitions

Paragraphs (1) through (3) shall apply to self-petitioners and derivatives of self-petitioners.

(June 27, 1952, c. 477, Title II, ch. 1, § 201, 66 Stat. 175; Oct. 3, 1965, Pub.L. 89–236, § 1, 79 Stat. 911; Oct. 20, 1976, Pub.L. 94–571, § 2, 90 Stat. 2703; Oct. 5, 1978, Pub.L. 95–412, § 1, 92 Stat. 907; Mar. 17, 1980, Pub.L. 96–212, Title II, § 203(a), 94 Stat. 106; Dec. 29, 1981, Pub.L. 97–116, § 20[(a)], 95 Stat. 1621; Nov. 29, 1990, Pub.L. 101–649, Title I, § 101(a), 104 Stat. 4980; Dec. 12, 1991, Pub.L. 102–232, Title III, § 302(a)(1), 105 Stat. 1742; Sept. 13, 1994, Pub.L. 103–322, Title IV, § 40701(b)(2), 108 Stat. 1954; Oct. 25, 1994, Pub.L. 103–416, Title II, § 219(b)(1), 108 Stat. 4316; Sept. 30, 1996, Pub.L. 104–208, Div. C, Title III, § 308(e)(5), (g)(8)(A)(i), Title VI, §§ 603, 671(d)(1)(A), 110 Stat. 3009–620, 3009–624, 3009–690, 3009–723; Oct. 28, 2000, Pub.L. 106–386, Div. B, Title V, § 1507(a)(3), 114 Stat. 1530; Aug. 6, 2002, Pub.L. 107–208, § 2, 116 Stat. 927; Jan. 5, 2006, Pub.L. 109–162, Title VIII, § 805(b)(1), 119 Stat. 3056; Oct. 28, 2009, Pub.L. 111–83, Title V, § 568(c)(1), 123 Stat. 2186.)

§ 202. Numerical limitations on individual foreign states [8 U.S.C.A. § 1152]

(a) Per country level

(1) Nondiscrimination

(A) Except as specifically provided in paragraph (2) and in sections 101(a)(27) [8 U.S.C.A. § 1101(a)(27)], 201(b)(2)(A)(i) [8 U.S.C.A. § 1151(b)(2)(A)(i)], and 203 [8 U.S.C.A. § 1153], no person shall receive any preference or priority or be discriminated against in the issuance of an immigrant visa because of the person's race, sex, nationality, place of birth, or place of residence.

(B) Nothing in this paragraph shall be construed to limit the authority of the Secretary of State to determine the procedures for the processing of immigrant visa applications or the locations where such applications will be processed.

(2) Per country levels for family-sponsored and employment-based immigrants

Subject to paragraphs (3), (4), and (5), the total number of immigrant visas made available to natives of any single foreign state or dependent area under subsections (a) and (b) of section 203 [8 U.S.C.A. § 1153] in any fiscal year may not exceed 7 percent (in the case of a single foreign state) or 2 percent (in the case of a dependent area) of the total number of such visas made available under such subsections in that fiscal year.

(3) Exception if additional visas available

If because of the application of paragraph (2) with respect to one or more foreign states or dependent areas, the total number of visas available under both subsections (a) and (b) of section 203 [8 U.S.C.A. § 1153] for a calendar quarter exceeds the number of qualified immigrants who otherwise may be issued such a visa, paragraph (2) shall not apply to visas made available to such states or areas during the remainder of such calendar quarter.

(4) Special rules for spouses and children of lawful permanent resident aliens

(A) 75 percent of 2nd preference set-aside for spouses and children not subject to per country limitation

(i) In general

Of the visa numbers made available under section 203(a) [8 U.S.C.A. § 1153(a)] to immigrants described in section 203(a)(2)(A) [8 U.S.C.A. § 1153(a)(2)(A)] in any fiscal year, 75 percent of the 2–A floor (as defined in clause (ii)) shall be issued without regard to the numerical limitation under paragraph (2).

(ii) 2–A floor defined

In this paragraph, the term "2–A floor" means, for a fiscal year, 77 percent of the total number of visas made available under section 203(a) [8 U.S.C.A. § 1153(a)] to immigrants described in section 203(a)(2) [8 U.S.C.A. § 1153(a)(2)] in the fiscal year.

(B) Treatment of remaining 25 percent for countries subject to subsection (e)

(i) In general

Of the visa numbers made available under section 203(a) [8 U.S.C.A. § 1153(a)] to immigrants described in section 203(a)(2)(A) [8 U.S.C.A. § 1153(a)(2)(A)] in any fiscal year, the remaining 25 percent of the 2–A floor shall be available in the case of a state or area that is subject to subsection (e) only to the extent that the total number of visas issued in accordance with subparagraph (A) to natives of the foreign state or area is less than the subsection (e) ceiling (as defined in clause (ii)).

(ii) Subsection (e) ceiling defined

In clause (i), the term "subsection (e) ceiling" means, for a foreign state or dependent area, 77 percent of the maximum number of visas that may be made available under section 203(a) [8 U.S.C.A. § 1153(a)] to immigrants who are natives of the state or area under section 203(a)(2) [8 U.S.C.A. § 1153(a)(2)] consistent with subsection (e).

(C) Treatment of unmarried sons and daughters in countries subject to subsection (e)

In the case of a foreign state or dependent area to which subsection (e) applies, the number of immigrant visas that may be made available to natives of the state or area under section 203(a)(2)(B) [8 U.S.C.A. § 1153(a)(2)(B)] may not exceed—

(i) 23 percent of the maximum number of visas that may be made available under section 203(a) [8 U.S.C.A.

§ 1153(a)] to immigrants of the state or area described in section 203(a)(2) [8 U.S.C.A. § 1153(a)(2)] consistent with subsection (e), or

(ii) the number (if any) by which the maximum number of visas that may be made available under section 203(a) [8 U.S.C.A. § 1153(a)] to immigrants of the state or area described in section 203(a)(2) [8 U.S.C.A. § 1153(a)(2)] consistent with subsection (e) exceeds the number of visas issued under section 203(a)(2)(A) [8 U.S.C.A. § 1153(a)(2)(A)],

whichever is greater.

(D) Limiting pass down for certain countries subject to subsection (e)

In the case of a foreign state or dependent area to which subsection (e) applies, if the total number of visas issued under section 203(a)(2) [8 U.S.C.A. § 1153(a)(2)] exceeds the maximum number of visas that may be made available to immigrants of the state or area under section 203(a)(2) [8 U.S.C.A. § 1153(a)(2)] consistent with subsection (e) (determined without regard to this paragraph), in applying paragraphs (3) and (4) of section 203(a) [8 U.S.C.A. § 1153(a)] under subsection (e)(2) all visas shall be deemed to have been required for the classes specified in paragraphs (1) and (2) of such section.

(5) Rules for employment-based immigrants

(A) Employment-based immigrants not subject to per country limitation if additional visas available

If the total number of visas available under paragraph (1), (2), (3), (4), or (5) of section 203(b) [8 U.S.C.A. § 1153(b)] for a calendar quarter exceeds the number of qualified immigrants who may otherwise be issued such visas, the visas made available under that paragraph shall be issued without regard to the numerical limitation under paragraph (2) of this subsection during the remainder of the calendar quarter.

(B) Limiting fall across for certain countries subject to subsection (e)

In the case of a foreign state or dependent area to which subsection (e) applies, if the total number of visas issued under section 203(b) [8 U.S.C.A. § 1153(b)] exceeds the maximum number of visas that may be made available to immigrants of the state or area under section 203(b) [8 U.S.C.A. § 1153(b)] consistent with subsection (e) (determined without regard to this paragraph), in applying subsection (e) all visas shall be deemed to have been required for the classes of aliens specified in section 203(b) [8 U.S.C.A. § 1153(b)].

(b) Rules for chargeability

Each independent country, self-governing dominion, mandated territory, and territory under the international trusteeship system of the United Nations, other than the United States and its outlying possessions, shall be treated as a separate foreign state for the purposes of a numerical level established under subsection (a)(2) when approved by the Secretary of State. All other inhabited lands shall be attributed to a foreign state specified by the Secretary of State. For the purposes of this Act the foreign state to which an immigrant is chargeable shall be determined by birth within such foreign state except that **(1)** an alien child, when accompanied by or following to join his alien parent or parents, may be charged to the foreign state of either parent if such parent has received or would be qualified for an immigrant visa, if necessary to prevent the separation of the child from the parent or parents, and if immigration charged to the foreign state to which such parent has been or would be chargeable has not reached a numerical level established under subsection (a)(2) for that fiscal year; **(2)** if an alien is chargeable to a different foreign state from that of his spouse, the foreign state to which such alien is chargeable may, if necessary to prevent the separation of husband and wife, be determined by the foreign state of the spouse he is accompanying or following to join, if such spouse has received or would be qualified for an immigrant visa and if immigration charged to the foreign state to which such spouse has been or would be chargeable has not reached a numerical level established under subsection (a)(2) for that fiscal year; **(3)** an alien born in the United States shall be considered as having been born in the country of which he is a citizen or subject, or, if he is not a citizen or subject of any country, in the last foreign country in which he had his residence as determined by the consular officer; and **(4)** an alien born within any foreign state in which neither of his parents was born and in which neither of his parents had a residence at the time of such alien's birth may be charged to the foreign state of either parent.

(c) Chargeability for dependent areas

Any immigrant born in a colony or other component or dependent area of a foreign state overseas from the foreign state, other than an alien described in section 201(b) [8 U.S.C.A. § 1151(b)], shall be chargeable for the purpose of the limitation set forth in subsection (a), to the foreign state.

(d) Changes in territory

In the case of any change in the territorial limits of foreign states, the Secretary of State shall, upon recognition of such change, issue appropriate instructions to all diplomatic and consular offices.

(e) Special rules for countries at ceiling

If it is determined that the total number of immigrant visas made available under subsections (a) and (b) of section 203 [8 U.S.C.A. § 1153] to natives of any single foreign state or dependent area will exceed the numerical limitation specified in subsection (a)(2) in any fiscal year, in determining the allotment of immigrant visa numbers to natives under subsections (a) and (b) of section 203 [8 U.S.C.A. § 1153], visa numbers with respect to natives of that state or area shall be allocated (to the extent practicable and otherwise consistent with this section and section 203 [8 U.S.C.A. § 1153]) in a manner so that—

(1) the ratio of the visa numbers made available under section 203(a) [8 U.S.C.A. § 1153(a)] to the visa numbers made available under section 203(b) [8 U.S.C.A. § 1153(b)] is equal to the ratio of the worldwide level of immigration under section 201(c) [8 U.S.C.A. § 1151(c)] to such level under section 201(d) [8 U.S.C.A. § 1151(d)];

(2) except as provided in subsection (a)(4), the proportion of the visa numbers made available under each of paragraphs (1) through (4) of section 203(a) [8 U.S.C.A. § 1153(a)] is equal to the ratio of the total number of visas made available under the respective paragraph to the total number of visas made available under section 203(a) [8 U.S.C.A. § 1153(a)], and

(3) except as provided in subsection (a)(5), the proportion of the visa numbers made available under each of paragraphs (1) through (5) of section 203(b) [8 U.S.C.A. § 1153(b)] is equal to the ratio of the total number of visas made available under the respective paragraph to the total number of visas made available under section 203(b) [8 U.S.C.A. § 1153(b)].

Nothing in this subsection shall be construed as limiting the number of visas that may be issued to natives of a foreign state or dependent area under section 203(a) [8 U.S.C.A. § 1153(a)] or 203(b) [8 U.S.C.A. § 1153(b)] if there is insufficient demand for visas for such natives under section 203(b) [8 U.S.C.A. § 1153(b)],or 203(a) [8 U.S.C.A. § 1153(a)], respectively, or as limiting the number of visas that may be issued under section 203(a)(2)(A) [8 U.S.C.A. § 1153(a)(2)(A)] pursuant to subsection (a)(4)(A).

(June 27, 1952, c. 477, Title II, ch. 1, § 202, 66 Stat. 176; Sept. 26, 1961, Pub.L. 87–301, § 9, 75 Stat. 654; Oct. 3, 1965, Pub.L. 89–236, § 2, 79 Stat. 911; Oct. 20, 1976, Pub.L. 94–571, § 3, 90 Stat. 2703; Oct. 5, 1978, Pub.L. 95–412, § 2, 92 Stat. 907; Mar. 17, 1980, Pub.L. 96–212, Title II, § 203(b), 94 Stat. 107; Dec. 29, 1981, Pub.L. 97–116, §§ 18(c), 20(b), 95 Stat. 1620, 1622; Nov. 6, 1986, Pub.L. 99–603, Title III, § 311(a), 100 Stat. 3434; Nov. 14, 1986, Pub.L. 99–653, § 4, 100 Stat. 3655; Oct. 24, 1988, Pub. L. 100–525, §§ 8(c), 9(f), 102 Stat. 2617, 2620; Nov. 29, 1990, Pub.L. 101–649, Title I, § 102, 104 Stat. 4982; Dec. 12, 1991, Pub.L. 102–232, Title III, § 302(a)(3), 105 Stat. 1742; Sept. 30, 1996, Pub.L. 104–208, Div. C, Title VI, § 633, 110 Stat. 3009–701; Oct. 17, 2000, Pub.L. 106–313, Title I, § 104(a), (b), 114 Stat. 1252, 1253.)

§ 203. Allocation of immigrant visas [8 U.S.C.A. § 1153]

(a) Preference allocation for family-sponsored immigrants

Aliens subject to the worldwide level specified in section 201(c) [8 U.S.C.A. § 1151(c)] for family-sponsored immigrants shall be allotted visas as follows:

(1) Unmarried sons and daughters of citizens

Qualified immigrants who are the unmarried sons or daughters of citizens of the United States shall be allocated visas in a number not to exceed 23,400, plus any visas not required for the class specified in paragraph (4).

(2) Spouses and unmarried sons and unmarried daughters of permanent resident aliens

Qualified immigrants—

(A) who are the spouses or children of an alien lawfully admitted for permanent residence, or

(B) who are the unmarried sons or unmarried daughters (but are not the children) of an alien lawfully admitted for permanent residence,

shall be allocated visas in a number not to exceed 114,200, plus the number (if any) by which such worldwide level exceeds 226,000, plus any visas not required for the class specified in paragraph (1); except that not less than 77 percent of such visa numbers shall be allocated to aliens described in subparagraph (A).

(3) Married sons and married daughters of citizens

Qualified immigrants who are the married sons or married daughters of citizens of the United States shall be allocated visas in a number not to exceed 23,400, plus any visas not required for the classes specified in paragraphs (1) and (2).

(4) Brothers and sisters of citizens

Qualified immigrants who are the brothers or sisters of citizens of the United States, if such citizens are at least 21 years of age, shall be allocated visas in a number not to exceed 65,000, plus any visas not required for the classes specified in paragraphs (1) through (3).

(b) Preference allocation for employment-based immigrants

Aliens subject to the worldwide level specified in section 201(d) [8 U.S.C.A. § 1151(d)] for employment-based immigrants in a fiscal year shall be allotted visas as follows:

(1) Priority workers

Visas shall first be made available in a number not to exceed 28.6 percent of such worldwide level, plus any visas not required for the classes specified in paragraphs (4) and (5), to qualified immigrants who are aliens described in any of the following subparagraphs (A) through (C):

(A) Aliens with extraordinary ability

An alien is described in this subparagraph if—

(i) the alien has extraordinary ability in the sciences, arts, education, business, or athletics which has been demonstrated by sustained national or international acclaim and whose achievements have been recognized in the field through extensive documentation,

(ii) the alien seeks to enter the United States to continue work in the area of extraordinary ability, and

(iii) the alien's entry into the United States will substantially benefit prospectively the United States.

(B) Outstanding professors and researchers

An alien is described in this subparagraph if—

(i) the alien is recognized internationally as outstanding in a specific academic area,

(ii) the alien has at least 3 years of experience in teaching or research in the academic area, and

(iii) the alien seeks to enter the United States—

(I) for a tenured position (or tenure-track position) within a university or institution of higher education to teach in the academic area,

(II) for a comparable position with a university or institution of higher education to conduct research in the area, or

(III) for a comparable position to conduct research in the area with a department, division, or institute of a private employer, if the department, division, or institute employs at least 3 persons full-time in research activities and has achieved documented accomplishments in an academic field.

(C) Certain multinational executives and managers

An alien is described in this subparagraph if the alien, in the 3 years preceding the time of the alien's application for classification and admission into the United States under this subparagraph, has been employed for at least 1 year by a firm or corporation or other legal entity or an affiliate or subsidiary thereof and the alien seeks to enter the United States in order to continue to render services to the same employer or to a subsidiary or affiliate thereof in a capacity that is managerial or executive.

(2) Aliens who are members of the professions holding advanced degrees or aliens of exceptional ability

(A) In general

Visas shall be made available, in a number not to exceed 28.6 percent of such worldwide level, plus any visas not required for the classes specified in paragraph (1), to qualified immigrants who are members of the professions holding advanced degrees or their equivalent or who because of their exceptional ability in the sciences, arts, or business, will substantially benefit prospectively the national economy, cultural or educational interests, or welfare of the United States, and whose services in the sciences, arts, professions, or business are sought by an employer in the United States.

(B) Waiver of job offer

(i) National interest waiver

Subject to clause (ii), the Attorney General may, when the Attorney General deems it to be in the national interest, waive the requirements of subparagraph (A) that an alien's services in the sciences, arts, professions, or business be sought by an employer in the United States.

(ii) Physicians working in shortage areas or veterans facilities

(I) In general

The Attorney General shall grant a national interest waiver pursuant to clause (i) on behalf of any alien physician with respect to whom a petition for preference classification has been filed under subparagraph (A) if—

(aa) the alien physician agrees to work full time as a physician in an area or areas designated by the Secretary of Health and Human Services as having a shortage of health care professionals or at a health care facility under the jurisdiction of the Secretary of Veterans Affairs; and

(bb) a Federal agency or a department of public health in any State has previously determined that the alien physician's work in such an area or at such facility was in the public interest.

(II) Prohibition

No permanent resident visa may be issued to an alien physician described in subclause (I) by the Secretary of State under section 204(b) [8 U.S.C.A. § 1154(b)], and the Attorney General may not adjust the status of such an alien physician from that of a nonimmigrant alien to that of a permanent resident alien under section 245 [8 U.S.C.A. § 1255], until such time as the alien has worked full time as a physician for an aggregate of 5 years (not including the time served in the status of an alien described in section 101(a)(15)(J) [8 U.S.C.A. § 1101(a)(15)(J)]), in an area or areas designated by the Secretary of Health and Human Services as having a shortage of health care professionals or at a health care facility under the jurisdiction of the Secretary of Veterans Affairs.

(III) Statutory construction

Nothing in this subparagraph may be construed to prevent the filing of a petition with the Attorney General for classification under section 204(a) [8 U.S.C.A. § 1154(a)], or the filing of an application for adjustment of status under section 245 [8 U.S.C.A. § 1255], by an alien physician described in subclause (I) prior to the date by which such alien physician has completed the service described in subclause (II).

(IV) Effective date

The requirements of this subsection do not affect waivers on behalf of alien physicians approved under subsection (b)(2)(B) of this section before the enactment date of this subsection. In the case of a physician for whom an application for a waiver was filed under subsection (b)(2)(B) of this section prior to November 1, 1998, the Attorney General shall grant a national interest waiver pursuant to subsection (b)(2)(B) of this section except that the alien is required to have worked full time as a physician for an aggregate of 3 years (not including time served in the status of an alien described in section 101(a)(15)(J) [8 U.S.C.A. § 1101(a)(15)(J)]) before a visa can be issued to the alien under section 204(b) [8 U.S.C.A. § 1154(b)] or the status of the alien is adjusted to permanent resident under section 245 [8 U.S.C.A. § 1255].

(C) Determination of exceptional ability

In determining under subparagraph (A) whether an immigrant has exceptional ability, the possession of a degree, diploma, certificate, or similar award from a college, university, school, or other institution of learning or a license to practice or certification for a particular profession or occupation shall not by itself be considered sufficient evidence of such exceptional ability.

(3) Skilled workers, professionals, and other workers

(A) In general

Visas shall be made available, in a number not to exceed 28.6 percent of such worldwide level, plus any visas not required for the classes specified in paragraphs (1) and (2), to the following classes of aliens who are not described in paragraph (2):

(i) Skilled workers

Qualified immigrants who are capable, at the time of petitioning for classification under this paragraph, of performing skilled labor (requiring at least 2 years training or experience), not of a temporary or seasonal nature, for which qualified workers are not available in the United States.

(ii) Professionals

Qualified immigrants who hold baccalaureate degrees and who are members of the professions.

(iii) Other workers

Other qualified immigrants who are capable, at the time of petitioning for classification under this paragraph, of performing unskilled labor, not of a temporary or seasonal nature, for which qualified workers are not available in the United States.

(B) Limitation on other workers

Not more than 10,000 of the visas made available under this paragraph in any fiscal year may be available for qualified immigrants described in subparagraph (A)(iii).

(C) Labor certification required

An immigrant visa may not be issued to an immigrant under subparagraph (A) until the consular officer is in receipt of a determination made by the Secretary of Labor pursuant to the provisions of section 212(a)(5)(A) [8 U.S.C.A. § 1182(a)(5)(A)].

(4) Certain special immigrants

Visas shall be made available, in a number not to exceed 7.1 percent of such worldwide level, to qualified special immigrants described in section 101(a)(27) [8 U.S.C.A. § 1101(a)(27)] (other than those described in subparagraph (A) or (B) thereof), of which not more than 5,000 may be made available in any fiscal year to special immigrants described in subclause (II) or (III) of section 101(a)(27)(C)(ii) [8 U.S.C.A. § 1101(a)(27)(C)(ii)], and not more than 100 may be made available in any fiscal year to special immigrants, excluding spouses and children, who are described in section 101(a)(27)(M) [8 U.S.C.A. § 1101(a)(27)(M)].

(5) Employment creation

(A) In general

Visas shall be made available, in a number not to exceed 7.1 percent of such worldwide level, to qualified immigrants seeking to enter the United States for the purpose of engaging in a new commercial enterprise (including a limited partnership)—

(i) in which such alien has invested (after November 29, 1990) or, is actively in the process of investing, capital in an amount not less than the amount specified in subparagraph (C), and

(ii) which will benefit the United States economy and create full–time employment for not fewer than 10 United States citizens or aliens lawfully admitted for permanent residence or other immigrants lawfully authorized to be employed in the United States (other than the immigrant and the immigrant's spouse, sons, or daughters).

(iii) Redesignated (ii)

(B) Set-aside for targeted employment areas

(i) In general

Not less than 3,000 of the visas made available under this paragraph in each fiscal year shall be reserved for qualified immigrants who invest in a new commercial enterprise described in subparagraph (A) which will create employment in a targeted employment area.

(ii) Targeted employment area defined

In this paragraph, the term "targeted employment area" means, at the time of the investment, a rural area or an area which has experienced high unemployment (of at least 150 percent of the national average rate).

(iii) Rural area defined

In this paragraph, the term "rural area" means any area other than an area within a metropolitan statistical area or within the outer boundary of any city or town having a population of 20,000 or more (based on the most recent decennial census of the United States).

(C) Amount of capital required

(i) In general

Except as otherwise provided in this subparagraph, the amount of capital required under subparagraph (A) shall be $1,000,000. The Attorney General, in consultation with the Secretary of Labor and the Secretary of State, may from time to time prescribe regulations increasing the dollar amount specified under the previous sentence.

(ii) Adjustment for targeted employment areas

The Attorney General may, in the case of investment made in a targeted employment area, specify an amount of capital required under subparagraph (A) that is less than (but not less than ½ of) the amount specified in clause (i).

(iii) Adjustment for high employment areas

In the case of an investment made in a part of a metropolitan statistical area that at the time of the investment—

(I) is not a targeted employment area, and

(II) is an area with an unemployment rate significantly below the national average unemployment rate,

the Attorney General may specify an amount of capital required under subparagraph (A) that is greater than (but not greater than 3 times) the amount specified in clause (i).

(D) Full–time employment defined

In this paragraph, the term "full–time employment" means employment in a position that requires at least 35 hours of service per week at any time, regardless of who fills the position.

(6) Special rules for "K" special immigrants

(A) Not counted against numerical limitation in year involved

Subject to subparagraph (B), the number of immigrant visas made available to special immigrants under section 101(a)(27)(K) [8 U.S.C.A. § 1101(a)(27)(K)] in a fiscal year shall not be subject to the numerical limitations of this subsection or of section 202(a) [8 U.S.C.A. § 1152(a)].

(B) Counted against numerical limitations in following year

(i) Reduction in employment-based immigrant classifications

The number of visas made available in any fiscal year under paragraphs (1), (2), and (3) shall each be reduced by ⅓ of the number of visas made available in the previous fiscal year to special immigrants described in section 101(a)(27)(K) [8 U.S.C.A. § 1101(a)(27)(K)].

(ii) Reduction in per country level

The number of visas made available in each fiscal year to natives of a foreign state under section 202(a) [8 U.S.C.A. § 1152(a)] shall be reduced by the number of visas made available in the previous fiscal year to special immigrants described in section 101(a)(27)(K) [8 U.S.C.A. § 1101(a)(27)(K)] who are natives of the foreign state.

(iii) Reduction in employment-based immigrant classifications within per country ceiling

In the case of a foreign state subject to section 202(e) [8 U.S.C.A. § 1152(e)] in a fiscal year (and in the previous fiscal year), the number of visas made available and allocated to each of paragraphs (1) through (3) of this subsection in the fiscal year shall be reduced by ⅓ of the number of visas made available in the previous fiscal year to special immigrants described in section 101(a)(27)(K) [8 U.S.C.A. § 1101(a)(27)(K)] who are natives of the foreign state.

(c) Diversity immigrants

(1) In general

Except as provided in paragraph (2), aliens subject to the worldwide level specified in section 201(e) [8 U.S.C.A. § 1151(e)] for diversity immigrants shall be allotted visas each fiscal year as follows:

(A) Determination of preference immigration

The Attorney General shall determine for the most recent previous 5–fiscal-year period for which data are available, the total number of aliens who are natives of each foreign state and who (i) were admitted or otherwise provided lawful permanent resident status (other than under this subsection) and (ii) were subject to the numerical limitations of section 201(a) [8 U.S.C.A. § 1151(a)] (other than paragraph (3) thereof) or who were admitted or otherwise provided lawful permanent resident status as an immediate relative or other alien described in section 201(b)(2) [8 U.S.C.A. § 1151(b)(2)].

(B) Identification of high-admission and low-admission regions and high-admission and low-admission states

The Attorney General—

(i) shall identify—

(I) each region (each in this paragraph referred to as a "high-admission region") for which the total of the numbers determined under subparagraph (A) for states in the region is greater than ⅙ of the total of all such numbers, and

(II) each other region (each in this paragraph referred to as a "low-admission region"); and

(ii) shall identify—

(I) each foreign state for which the number determined under subparagraph (A) is greater than 50,000 (each such state in this paragraph referred to as a "high-admission state"), and

(II) each other foreign state (each such state in this paragraph referred to as a "low-admission state").

(C) Determination of percentage of worldwide immigration attributable to high-admission regions

The Attorney General shall determine the percentage of the total of the numbers determined under subparagraph (A) that are numbers for foreign states in high-admission regions.

(D) Determination of regional populations excluding high-admission states and ratios of populations of regions within low-admission regions and high-admission regions

The Attorney General shall determine—

(i) based on available estimates for each region, the total population of each region not including the population of any high-admission state;

(ii) for each low-admission region, the ratio of the population of the region determined under clause (i) to the total of the populations determined under such clause for all the low-admission regions; and

(iii) for each high-admission region, the ratio of the population of the region determined under clause (i) to the total of the populations determined under such clause for all the high-admission regions.

(E) Distribution of visas

(i) No visas for natives of high-admission states

The percentage of visas made available under this paragraph to natives of a high-admission state is 0.

(ii) For low-admission states in low-admission regions

Subject to clauses (iv) and (v), the percentage of visas made available under this paragraph to natives (other than natives of a high-admission state) in a low-admission region is the product of—

(I) the percentage determined under subparagraph (C), and

(II) the population ratio for that region determined under subparagraph (D)(ii).

(iii) For low-admission states in high-admission regions

Subject to clauses (iv) and (v), the percentage of visas made available under this paragraph to natives (other than natives of a high-admission state) in a high-admission region is the product of—

(I) 100 percent minus the percentage determined under subparagraph (C), and

(II) the population ratio for that region determined under subparagraph (D)(iii).

(iv) Redistribution of unused visa numbers

If the Secretary of State estimates that the number of immigrant visas to be issued to natives in any region for a fiscal year under this paragraph is less than the number of immigrant visas made available to such natives under this paragraph for the fiscal year, subject to clause (v), the excess visa numbers shall be made available to natives (other than natives of a high-admission state) of the other regions in proportion to the percentages otherwise specified in clauses (ii) and (iii).

(v) Limitation on visas for natives of a single foreign state

The percentage of visas made available under this paragraph to natives of any single foreign state for any fiscal year shall not exceed 7 percent.

(F) Region defined

Only for purposes of administering the diversity program under this subsection, Northern Ireland shall be treated as a separate foreign state, each colony or other component or dependent area of a foreign state overseas from the foreign state shall be treated as part of the foreign state, and the areas described in each of the following clauses shall be considered to be a separate region:

(i) Africa.

(ii) Asia.

(iii) Europe.

(iv) North America (other than Mexico).

(v) Oceania.

(vi) South America, Mexico, Central America, and the Caribbean.

(2) Requirement of education or work experience

An alien is not eligible for a visa under this subsection unless the alien—

(A) has at least a high school education or its equivalent, or

(B) has, within 5 years of the date of application for a visa under this subsection, at least 2 years of work experience in an occupation which requires at least 2 years of training or experience.

(3) Maintenance of information

The Secretary of State shall maintain information on the age, occupation, education level, and other relevant characteristics of immigrants issued visas under this subsection.

(d) Treatment of family members

A spouse or child as defined in subparagraph (A), (B), (C), (D), or (E) of section 101(b)(1) [8 U.S.C.A. § 1101(b)(1)] shall, if not otherwise entitled to an immigrant status and the immediate issuance of a visa under subsection (a), (b), or (c), be entitled to the same status, and the same order of consideration provided in the respective subsection, if accompanying or following to join, the spouse or parent.

(e) Order of consideration

(1) Immigrant visas made available under subsection (a) or (b) shall be issued to eligible immigrants in the order in which a petition in behalf of each such immigrant is filed with the Attorney General (or in the case of special immigrants under section 101(a)(27)(D) [8 U.S.C.A. § 1101(a)(27)(D)], with the Secretary of State) as provided in section 204(a) [8 U.S.C.A. § 1154(a)].

(2) Immigrant visa numbers made available under subsection (c) (relating to diversity immigrants) shall be issued to eligible qualified immigrants strictly in a random order established by the Secretary of State for the fiscal year involved.

(3) Waiting lists of applicants for visas under this section shall be maintained in accordance with regulations prescribed by the Secretary of State.

(f) Authorization for issuance

In the case of any alien claiming in his application for an immigrant visa to be described in section 201(b)(2) [8 U.S.C.A. § 1151(b)(2)] or in subsection (a), (b), or (c) of this section, the consular officer shall not grant such status until he has been authorized to do so as provided by section 204 [8 U.S.C.A. § 1154].

(g) Lists

For purposes of carrying out the Secretary's responsibilities in the orderly administration of this section, the Secretary of State may make reasonable estimates of the anticipated numbers of visas to be issued during any quarter of any fiscal year within each of the categories under subsections (a), (b), and (c) and to rely upon such estimates in authorizing the issuance of visas. The Secretary of State shall terminate the registration of any alien who fails to apply for an immigrant visa within one year following notification to the alien of the availability of such visa, but the Secretary shall reinstate the registration of any such alien who establishes within 2 years following the date of notification of the availability of such visa that such failure to apply was due to circumstances beyond the alien's control.

(h) Rules for determining whether certain aliens are children

(1) In general

For purposes of subsections (a)(2)(A) and (d) of this section, a determination of whether an alien satisfies the age requirement in the matter preceding subparagraph (A) of section 101(b)(1) [8 U.S.C.A. § 1101(b)(1)] shall be made using—

(A) the age of the alien on the date on which an immigrant visa number becomes available for such alien (or, in the case of subsection (d) of this section, the date on which an immigrant visa number became available for the alien's parent), but only if the alien has sought to acquire the status of an alien lawfully admitted for permanent residence within one year of such availability; reduced by

(B) the number of days in the period during which the applicable petition described in paragraph (2) was pending.

(2) Petitions described

The petition described in this paragraph is—

(A) with respect to a relationship described in subsection (a)(2)(A) of this section, a petition filed under section 204 [8 U.S.C.A. § 1154] for classification of an alien child under subsection (a)(2)(A) of this section; or

(B) with respect to an alien child who is a derivative beneficiary under subsection (d) of this section, a petition filed under section 204 [8 U.S.C.A. § 1154] for classification of the alien's parent under subsection (a), (b), or (c) of this section.

(3) Retention of priority date

If the age of an alien is determined under paragraph (1) to be 21 years of age or older for the purposes of subsections (a)(2)(A) and (d) of this section, the alien's petition shall automatically be converted to the appropriate category and the alien shall retain the original priority date issued upon receipt of the original petition.

(4) Application to self-petitions

Paragraphs (1) through (3) shall apply to self-petitioners and derivatives of self-petitioners.

(June 27, 1952, c. 477, Title II, ch. 1, § 203, 66 Stat. 178; Sept. 11, 1957, Pub.L. 85–316, § 3, 71 Stat. 639; Sept. 22, 1959, Pub.L. 86–363, §§ 1–3, 73 Stat. 644; Oct. 3, 1965, Pub.L. 89–236, § 3, 79 Stat. 912; Oct. 20, 1976, Pub.L. 94–571, § 4, 90 Stat. 2705; Oct. 5, 1978, Pub.L. 95–412, § 3, 92 Stat. 907; Oct. 5, 1978, Pub.L. 95–417, § 1, 92 Stat. 917; Mar. 17, 1980, Pub.L. 96–212, Title II, § 203(c), (i), 94 Stat. 107, 108; Nov. 29, 1990, Pub.L. 101–649, Title I, §§ 111, 121(a), 131, 162(a)(1), Title VI, § 603(a)(3), 104 Stat. 4986, 4987, 4997, 5009, 5082; Oct. 1, 1991, Pub.L. 102–110, § 2(b), 105 Stat. 555; Dec. 12, 1991, Pub.L. 102–232, Title III, § 302(b)(2), (e)(3), 105 Stat. 1743, 1745; Oct. 25, 1994, Pub.L. 103–416, Title II, §§ 212(b), 219(c), 108 Stat. 4314, 4316; Nov. 12, 1999, Pub.L. 106–95, § 5, 113 Stat. 1318; Nov. 29, 1999, Pub.L. 106–113, Div. B, § 1000(a)(1) [H.R. 3421, Title I, § 117], 113 Stat. 1535, 1537; Nov. 22, 2000, Pub.L. 106–536, § 1(b)(1), 114 Stat. 2560; Aug. 6, 2002, Pub.L. 107–208, § 3, 116 Stat. 928; Nov. 2, 2002, Pub.L. 107–273, Div. C, Title I, §§ 11035, 11036(a), 116 Stat. 1846; Jan. 5, 2006, Pub.L. 109–162, Title VIII, § 805(b)(2), 119 Stat. 3056.)

§ 204. Procedure for granting immigrant status [8 U.S.C.A. § 1154]

(a) Petitioning procedure

(1)(A)(i) Except as provided in clause (viii), any citizen of the United States claiming that an alien is entitled to classification by reason of a relationship described in paragraph (1), (3), or (4) of section 203(a) [8 U.S.C.A. § 1153(a)] or to an immediate relative status under section 201(b)(2)(A)(i) [8 U.S.C.A. § 1151(b)(2)(A)(i)] may file a petition with the Attorney General for such classification.

(ii) An alien spouse described in the second sentence of section 201(b)(2)(A)(i) [8 U.S.C.A. § 1151(b)(2)(A)(i)] also may file a petition with the Attorney General under this subparagraph for classification of the alien (and the alien's children) under such section.

(iii)(I) An alien who is described in subclause (II) may file a petition with the Attorney General under this clause for classification of the alien (and any child of the alien) if the alien demonstrates to the attorney general that

(aa) the marriage or the intent to marry the United States citizen was entered into in good faith by the alien; and

(bb) during the marriage or relationship intended by the alien to be legally a marriage, the alien or a child of the alien has been battered or has been the subject of extreme cruelty perpetrated by the alien's spouse or intended spouse.

(II) For purposes of subclause (I), an alien described in this subclause is an alien

(aa)(AA) who is the spouse of a citizen of the United States;

(BB) who believed that he or she had married a citizen of the United States and with whom a marriage ceremony was actually performed and who otherwise meets any applicable requirements under this Act to establish the existence of and bona fides of a marriage, but whose marriage is not legitimate solely because of the bigamy of such citizen of the United States; or

(CC) who was a bona fide spouse of a United States citizen within the past 2 years and—

(aaa) whose spouse died within the past 2 years;

(bbb) whose spouse lost or renounced citizenship status within the past 2 years related to an incident of domestic violence; or

(ccc) who demonstrates a connection between the legal termination of the marriage within the past 2 years and battering or extreme cruelty by the United States citizen spouse;

(bb) who is a person of good moral character;

(cc) who is eligible to be classified as an immediate relative under section 201(b)(2)(A)(i) [8 U.S.C.A. § 1151(b)(2)(A)(i)] or who would have been so classified but for the bigamy of the citizen of the United States that the alien intended to marry; and

(dd) who has resided with the alien's spouse or intended spouse.

(iv) An alien who is the child of a citizen of the United States, or who was a child of a United States citizen parent who within the past 2 years lost or renounced citizenship status related to an incident of domestic violence, and who is a person of good moral character, who is eligible to be classified as an immediate relative under section 201(b)(2)(A)(i) [8 U.S.C.A. § 1151(b)(2)(A)(i)], and who resides, or has resided in the past, with the citizen parent may file a petition with the Attorney General under this subparagraph for classification of the alien (and any child of the alien) under such section if the alien demonstrates to the Attorney General that the alien has been battered by or has been the subject of extreme cruelty perpetrated by the alien's citizen parent. For purposes of this clause, residence includes any period of visitation.

(v) An alien who—

(I) is the spouse, intended spouse, or child living abroad of a citizen who—

(aa) is an employee of the United States Government;

(bb) is a member of the uniformed services (as defined in section 101(a) of Title 10); or

(cc) has subjected the alien or the alien's child to battery or extreme cruelty in the United States; and

(II) is eligible to file a petition under clause (iii) or (iv), shall file such petition with the Attorney General under the procedures that apply to self-petitioners under clause (iii) or (iv), as applicable.

(vi) For the purposes of any petition filed under clause (iii) or (iv), the denaturalization, loss or renunciation of citizenship, death of the abuser, divorce, or changes to the abuser's citizenship status after filing of the petition shall not adversely affect the approval of the petition, and for approved petitions shall not preclude the classification of the eligible self-petitioning spouse or child as an immediate relative or affect the alien's ability to adjust status under subsections (a) and (c) of section 245 [8 U.S.C.A. § 1255] or obtain status as a lawful permanent resident based on the approved self-petition under such clauses.

(vii) An alien may file a petition with the Secretary of Homeland Security under this subparagraph for classification of the alien under section 201(b)(2)(a)(i) [8 U.S.C.A § 1151(b)(2)(a)(i)] if the alien—

(I) is the parent of a citizen of the United States or was a parent of a citizen of the United States who, within the past 2 years, lost or renounced citizenship status related to an incident of domestic violence or died;

(II) is a person of good moral character;

(III) is eligible to be classified as an immediate relative under section 201(b)(2)(A)(i) [8 U.S.C.A § 1151(b)(2)(A)(i)];

(IV) resides, or has resided, with the citizen daughter or son; and

(V) demonstrates that the alien has been battered or subject to extreme cruelty by the citizen daughter or son.

(viii)(I) Clause (i) shall not apply to a citizen of the United States who has been convicted of a specified offense against a minor, unless the Secretary of Homeland Security, in the Secretary's sole and unreviewable discretion, determines that the citizen poses no risk to the alien with respect to whom a petition described in clause (i) is filed.

(II) For purposes of subclause (I), the term "specified offense against a minor" is defined as in section 111 of the Adam Walsh Child Protection and Safety Act of 2006 [Pub. L. 109–248, 120 Stat. 587].

(B)(i)(I) Except as provided in subclause (II), any alien lawfully admitted for permanent residence claiming that an alien is entitled to a classification by reason of the relationship described in section 203(a)(2) [8 U.S.C.A. § 1153(a)(2)] may file a petition with the Attorney General for such classification.

(II) Subclause (I) shall not apply in the case of an alien lawfully admitted for permanent residence who has been convicted of a specified offense against a minor (as defined in subparagraph (A)(viii)(II)), unless the Secretary of Homeland Security, in the Secretary's sole and unreviewable discretion, determines that such person poses no risk to the alien with respect to whom a petition described in subclause (I) is filed.

(ii)(I) An alien who is described in subclause (II) may file a petition with the Attorney General under this clause for classification of the alien (and any child of the alien) if such a child has not been classified under clause (iii) of section 203(a)(2)(A) [8 U.S.C.A. § 1153(a)(2)(A)] and if the alien demonstrates to the attorney general that

(aa) the marriage or the intent to marry the lawful permanent resident was entered into in good faith by the alien; and

(bb) during the marriage or relationship intended by the alien to be legally a marriage, the alien or a child of the alien has been battered or has been the subject of extreme cruelty perpetrated by the alien's spouse or intended spouse.

(II) For purposes of subclause (I), an alien described in this paragraph is an alien

(aa)(AA) who is the spouse of a lawful permanent resident of the United States; or

(BB) who believed that he or she had married a lawful permanent resident of the United States and with whom a marriage ceremony was actually performed and who otherwise meets any applicable requirements under this Act to establish the existence of and bona fides of a marriage, but whose marriage is not legitimate solely because of the bigamy of such lawful permanent resident of the United States; or

(CC) who was a bona fide spouse of a lawful permanent resident within the past 2 years and—

(aaa) whose spouse lost status within the past 2 years due to an incident of domestic violence; or

(bbb) who demonstrates a connection between the legal termination of the marriage within the past 2 years and battering or extreme cruelty by the lawful permanent resident spouse;

(bb) who is a person of good moral character;

(cc) who is eligible to be classified as a spouse of an alien lawfully admitted for permanent residence under section 203(a)(2)(A) [8 U.S.C.A. § 1153(a)(2)(A)] or who would have been so classified but for the bigamy of the lawful permanent resident of the United States that the alien intended to marry; and

(dd) who has resided with the alien's spouse or intended spouse.

(iii) An alien who is the child of an alien lawfully admitted for permanent residence, or who was the child of a lawful permanent resident who within the past 2 years lost lawful permanent resident status due to an incident of domestic violence, and who is a person of good moral character, who is eligible for classification under section 203(a)(2)(A) [8 U.S.C.A. § 1153(a)(2)(A)], and who resides, or has resided in the past, with the alien's permanent resident alien parent may file a petition with the Attorney General under this subparagraph for classification of the alien (and any child of the alien) under such section if the alien demonstrates to the Attorney General that the alien has been battered by or has been the subject of extreme cruelty perpetrated by the alien's permanent resident parent.

(iv) An alien who

(I) is the spouse, intended spouse, or child living abroad of a lawful permanent resident who—

(aa) is an employee of the United States Government;

(bb) is a member of the uniformed services (as defined in section 101(a) of Title 10); or

(cc) has subjected the alien or the alien's child to battery or extreme cruelty in the United States; and

(II) is eligible to file a petition under clause (ii) or (iii), shall file such petition with the Attorney General under the procedures that apply to self-petitioners under clause (ii) or (iii), as applicable.

(v)(I) For the purposes of any petition filed or approved under clause (ii) or (iii), divorce, or the loss of lawful permanent resident status by a spouse or parent after the filing of a petition under that clause shall not adversely affect approval of the petition, and, for an approved petition, shall not affect the alien's ability to adjust status under subsections (a) and (c) of section 245 [8 U.S.C.A. § 1255] or obtain status as a lawful permanent resident based on an approved self-petition under clause (ii) or (iii).

(II) Upon the lawful permanent resident spouse or parent becoming or establishing the existence of United States citizenship through naturalization, acquisition of citizenship, or other means, any petition filed with the Immigration and Naturalization Service and pending or approved under clause (ii) or (iii) on behalf of an alien who has been battered or subjected to extreme cruelty shall be deemed reclassified as a petition filed under subparagraph (A) even if the acquisition of citizenship occurs after divorce or termination of parental rights.

(C) Notwithstanding section 101(f) [8 U.S.C.A. § 1101(f)], an act or conviction that is waivable with respect to the petitioner for purposes of a determination of the petitioner's admissibility under section 212(a) [8 U.S.C.A. § 1182(a)] or deportability under section 237(a) [8 U.S.C.A. § 1227(a)] shall not bar the Attorney General from finding the petitioner to be of good moral character under subparagraph (A)(iii), (A)(iv), (B)(ii), or (B)(iii) if the Attorney General finds that the act or conviction was connected to the alien's having been battered or subjected to extreme cruelty.

(D)(i)(I) Any child who attains 21 years of age who has filed a petition under clause (iv) of section 204(a)(1)(A) [8 U.S.C.A § 1154(a)(1)(A)] or section 204(a)(1)(B)(iii) [8 U.S.C.A. § 1154(a)(1)(B)(iii)] that was filed or approved before the date on which the child attained 21 years of age shall be considered (if the child has not been admitted or approved for lawful permanent residence by the date the child attained 21 years of age) a petitioner for preference status under paragraph (1), (2), or (3) of section 203(a) [8 U.S.C.A § 1153(a)], whichever paragraph is applicable, with the same priority date assigned to the self-petition filed under clause (iv) of section 204(a)(1)(A) [8 U.S.C.A § 1154(a)(1)(A)] or section 204(a)(1)(B)(iii) [8 U.S.C.A. § 1154(a)(1)(B)(iii)]. No new petition shall be required to be filed.

(II) Any individual described in subclause (I) is eligible for deferred action and work authorization.

(III) Any derivative child who attains 21 years of age who is included in a petition described in clause (ii) that was filed or approved before the date on which the child attained 21 years of age shall be considered (if the child has not been admitted or approved for lawful permanent residence by the date the child attained 21 years of age) a VAWA self-petitioner with the same priority date as that assigned to the petitioner in any petition described in clause (ii). No new petition shall be required to be filed.

(IV) Any individual described in subclause (III) and any derivative child of a petition described in clause (ii) is eligible for deferred action and work authorization.

(ii) The petition referred to in clause (i)(III) is a petition filed by an alien under subparagraph (A)(iii), (A)(iv), (B)(ii) or (B)(iii) in which the child is included as a derivative beneficiary.

(iii) Nothing in the amendments made by the Child Status Protection Act shall be construed to limit or deny any right or benefit provided under this subparagraph.

(iv) Any alien who benefits from this subparagraph may adjust status in accordance with subsections (a) and (c) of section 245 [8 U.S.C.A § 1255] as an alien having an approved petition for classification under subparagraph (A)(iii), (A)(iv), (B)(ii), or (B)(iii).

(v) For purposes of this paragraph, an individual who is not less than 21 years of age, who qualified to file a petition under subparagraph (A)(iv) or (B)(iii) as of the day before the date on which the individual attained 21 years of age, and who did not file such a petition before such day, shall be treated as having filed a petition under such subparagraph as of such day if a petition is filed for the status described in such subparagraph before the individual attains 25 years of age and the individual shows that the abuse was at least one central reason for the filing delay. Clauses (i) through (iv) of this subparagraph shall apply to an individual described in this clause in the same manner as an individual filing a petition under subparagraph (A)(iv) or (B)(iii).

(E) Any alien desiring to be classified under section 203(b)(1)(A) [8 U.S.C.A. § 1153(b)(1)(A)], or any person on behalf of such an alien, may file a petition with the Attorney General for such classification.

(F) Any employer desiring and intending to employ within the United States an alien entitled to classification under section 203(b)(1)(B) [8 U.S.C.A. § 1153(b)(1)(B)], 203(b)(1)(C) [8 U.S.C.A. § 1153(b)(1)(C)], 203(b)(2) [8 U.S.C.A. § 1153(b)(2)], or 203(b)(3) [8 U.S.C.A. § 1153(b)(3)] may file a petition with the Attorney General for such classification.

(G)(i) Any alien (other than a special immigrant under section 101(a)(27)(D) [8 U.S.C.A. § 1101(a)(27)(D)]) desiring to be classified under section 203(b)(4) [8 U.S.C.A. § 1153(b)(4)], or any person on behalf of such an alien, may file a petition with the Attorney General for such classification.

(ii) Aliens claiming status as a special immigrant under section 101(a)(27)(D) [8 U.S.C.A. § 1101(a)(27)(D)] may file a petition only with the Secretary of State and only after notification by the Secretary that such status has been recommended and approved pursuant to such section.

(H) Any alien desiring to be classified under section 203(b)(5) [8 U.S.C.A. § 1153(b)(5)] may file a petition with the Attorney General for such classification.

(I)(i) Any alien desiring to be provided an immigrant visa under section 203(c) [8 U.S.C.A. § 1153(c)] may file a petition at the place and time determined by the Secretary of State by regulation. Only one such petition may be filed by an alien with respect to any petitioning period established. If more than one petition is submitted all such petitions submitted for such period by the alien shall be voided.

(ii)(I) The Secretary of State shall designate a period for the filing of petitions with respect to visas which may be issued under section 203(c) [8 U.S.C.A. § 1153(c)] for the fiscal year beginning after the end of the period.

(II) Aliens who qualify, through random selection, for a visa under section 203(c) [8 U.S.C.A. § 1153(c)] shall remain eligible to receive such visa only through the end of the specific fiscal year for which they were selected.

(III) The Secretary of State shall prescribe such regulations as may be necessary to carry out this clause.

(iii) A petition under this subparagraph shall be in such form as the Secretary of State may by regulation prescribe and shall contain such information and be supported by such documentary evidence as the Secretary of State may require.

[subsection (iv) is effective October 1, 2013 through September 30, 2014; see Pub.L. 113–6, Div. D, Title V, § 563, Mar. 26, 2013, 127 Stat. 380]

(iv) Each petition to compete for consideration for a visa under section 203(c) [8 U.S.C.A. § 1153(c)] shall be accompanied by a fee equal to $30. All amounts collected under this clause shall be deposited into the Treasury as miscellaneous receipts.

(J) In acting on petitions filed under clause (iii) or (iv) of subparagraph (A) or clause (ii) or (iii) of subparagraph (B), or in making determinations under subparagraphs (C) and (D), the Attorney General shall consider any credible evidence relevant to the petition. The determination of what evidence is credible and the weight to be given that evidence shall be within the sole discretion of the Attorney General.

(K) Upon the approval of a petition as a VAWA self-petitioner, the alien—

(i) is eligible for work authorization; and

(ii) may be provided an "employment authorized" endorsement or appropriate work permit incidental to such approval.

(L) Notwithstanding the previous provisions of this paragraph, an individual who was a VAWA petitioner or who had the status of a nonimmigrant under subparagraph (T) or (U) of section 101(a)(15) [8 U.S.C.A § 1101(a)(15)] may not file a petition for classification under this section or section 214 [8 U.S.C.A § 1184] to classify any person who committed the battery or extreme cruelty or trafficking against the individual (or the individual's child) which established the individual's (or individual's child) eligibility as a VAWA petitioner or for such nonimmigrant status.

(2)(A) The Attorney General may not approve a spousal second preference petition for the classification of the spouse of an alien if the alien, by virtue of a prior marriage, has been accorded the status of an alien lawfully admitted for permanent residence as the spouse of a citizen of the United States or as the spouse of an alien lawfully admitted for permanent residence, unless—

(i) a period of 5 years has elapsed after the date the alien acquired the status of an alien lawfully admitted for permanent residence, or

(ii) the alien establishes to the satisfaction of the Attorney General by clear and convincing evidence that the prior marriage (on the basis of which the alien obtained the status of an alien lawfully admitted for permanent residence) was not entered into for the purpose of evading any provision of the immigration laws.

In this subparagraph, the term "spousal second preference petition" refers to a petition, seeking preference status under section 203(a)(2) [8 U.S.C.A. § 1153(a)(2)], for an alien as a spouse of an alien lawfully admitted for permanent residence.

(B) Subparagraph (A) shall not apply to a petition filed for the classification of the spouse of an alien if the prior marriage of the alien was terminated by the death of his or her spouse.

(b) Investigation; consultation; approval; authorization to grant preference status

After an investigation of the facts in each case, and after consultation with the Secretary of Labor with respect to petitions to accord a status under section 203(b)(2) [8 U.S.C.A. § 1153(b)(2)] or 203(b)(3) [8 U.S.C.A. § 1153(b)(3)], the Attorney General shall, if he determines that the facts stated in the petition are true and that the alien in behalf of whom the petition is made is an immediate relative specified in section 201(b) [8 U.S.C.A. § 1151(b)] or is eligible for preference under subsection (a) or (b) of section 203 [8 U.S.C.A. § 1153], approve the petition and forward one copy thereof to the Department of State. The Secretary of State shall then authorize the consular officer concerned to grant the preference status.

(c) Prohibition against approval in cases of marriages entered into in order to evade immigration laws

Notwithstanding the provisions of subsection (b) no petition shall be approved if **(1)** the alien has previously been accorded, or has sought to be accorded, an immediate relative or preference status as the spouse of a citizen of the United States or the spouse of an alien lawfully admitted for permanent residence, by reason of a marriage determined by the Attorney General to have been entered into for the purpose of evading the immigration laws, or **(2)** the Attorney General has determined that the alien has attempted or conspired to enter into a marriage for the purpose of evading the immigration laws.

(d) Recommendation of valid home-study

(1) Notwithstanding the provisions of subsections (a) and (b) no petition may be approved on behalf of a child defined in subparagraph (F) or (G) of section 101(b)(1) [8 U.S.C.A. § 1101(b)(1)] unless a valid home-study has been favorably recommended by an agency of the State of the child's proposed residence, or by an agency authorized by that State to conduct such a study, or, in the case of a child adopted abroad, by an appropriate public or private adoption agency which is licensed in the United States.

(2) Notwithstanding the provisions of subsections (a) and (b), no petition may be approved on behalf of a child defined in section 101(b)(1)(G) [8 U.S.C.A. § 1101(b)(1)(G)] unless the Secretary of State has certified that the central authority of the child's country of origin has notified the United States central authority under the convention referred to in such section 101(b)(1)(G) [8 U.S.C.A. § 1101(b)(1)(G)] that a United States citizen habitually resident in the United States has effected final adoption of the child, or has been granted custody of the child for the purpose of emigration and adoption, in accordance with such convention and the Intercountry Adoption Act of 2000.

(e) Subsequent finding of non-entitlement to preference classification

Nothing in this section shall be construed to entitle an immigrant, in behalf of whom a petition under this section is approved, to be admitted [sic] the United States as an immigrant under subsection (a), (b), or (c) of section 203 [8 U.S.C.A. § 1153] or as an immediate relative under section 201(b) [8 U.S.C.A. § 1151(b)] if upon his arrival at a port of entry in the United States he is found not to be entitled to such classification.

(f) Preferential treatment for children fathered by United States citizens and born in Korea, Vietnam, Laos, Kampuchea, or Thailand after 1950 and before October 22, 1982

(1) Any alien claiming to be an alien described in paragraph (2)(A) of this subsection (or any person on behalf of such an alien) may file a petition with the Attorney General for classification under section 201(b) [8 U.S.C.A. § 1151(b)], 203(a)(1) [8 U.S.C.A. § 1153(a)(1)], or 203(a)(3) [8 U.S.C.A. § 1153(a)(3)], as appropriate. After an investigation of the facts of each case the Attorney General shall, if the conditions described in paragraph (2) are met, approve the petition and forward one copy to the Secretary of State.

(2) The Attorney General may approve a petition for an alien under paragraph (1) if—

(A) he has reason to believe that the alien (i) was born in Korea, Vietnam, Laos, Kampuchea, or Thailand after 1950 and before October 22, 1982, and (ii) was fathered by a United States citizen;

(B) he has received an acceptable guarantee of legal custody and financial responsibility described in paragraph (4); and

(C) in the case of an alien under eighteen years of age, (i) the alien's placement with a sponsor in the United States has been arranged by an appropriate public, private, or State child welfare agency licensed in the United States and actively involved in the intercountry placement of children and (ii) the alien's mother or guardian has in writing irrevocably released the alien for emigration.

(3) In considering petitions filed under paragraph (1), the Attorney General shall—

(A) consult with appropriate governmental officials and officials of private voluntary organizations in the country of the alien's birth in order to make the determinations described in subparagraphs (A) and (C)(ii) of paragraph 2; and

(B) consider the physical appearance of the alien and any evidence provided by the petitioner, including birth and baptismal certificates, local civil records, photographs of, and letters or proof of financial support from, a putative father who is a citizen of the United States, and the testimony of witnesses, to the extent it is relevant or probative.

(4)(A) A guarantee of legal custody and financial responsibility for an alien described in paragraph (2) must—

(i) be signed in the presence of an immigration officer or consular officer by an individual (hereinafter in this paragraph referred to as the "sponsor") who is twenty-one years of age or older, is of good moral character, and is a citizen of the United States or alien lawfully admitted for permanent residence, and

(ii) provide that the sponsor agrees **(I)** in the case of an alien under eighteen years of age, to assume legal custody for the alien after the alien's departure to the United States and until the alien becomes eighteen years of age, in accordance with the laws of the State where the alien and the sponsor will reside, and **(II)** to furnish, during the five-year period beginning on the date of the alien's acquiring the status of an alien lawfully admitted for permanent residence, or during the period beginning on the date of the alien's acquiring the status of an alien lawfully admitted for permanent residence and ending on the date on which the alien becomes twenty-one years of age, whichever period is longer, such financial support as is necessary to maintain the family in the United States of which the alien is a member at a level equal to at least 125 per centum of the current official poverty line (as established by the Director of the Office of Management and Budget, under section 9902(2) of Title 42 and as revised by the Secretary of Health and Human Services under the second and third sentences of such section) for a family of the same size as the size of the alien's family.

(B) A guarantee of legal custody and financial responsibility described in subparagraph (A) may be enforced with respect to an alien against his sponsor in a civil suit brought by the Attorney General in the United States district court for the district in which the sponsor resides, except that a sponsor or his estate shall not be liable under such a guarantee if the sponsor dies or is adjudicated a bankrupt under Title 11.

(g) Restrictions on petitions based on marriages entered while in exclusion or deportation proceedings

Notwithstanding subsection (a), except as provided in section 245(e)(3) [8 U.S.C.A. § 1255(e)(3)], a petition may not be approved to grant an alien immediate relative status or preference status by reason of a marriage which was entered into during the period described in section 245(e)(2) [8 U.S.C.A. § 1255(e)(2)], until the alien has resided outside the United States for a 2–year period beginning after the date of the marriage.

(h) Survival of rights to petition

The legal termination of a marriage may not be the sole basis for revocation under section 205 [8 U.S.C.A. § 1155] of a petition filed under subsection (a)(1)(A)(iii) or a petition filed under subsection (a)(1)(B)(ii) pursuant to conditions described in subsection (a)(1)(A)(iii)(I). Remarriage of an alien whose petition was approved under section 204(a)(1)(B)(ii) [8 U.S.C.A. § 1154(a)(1)(B)(ii)] or section 204(a)(1)(A)(iii) [8 U.S.C.A. § 1154(a)(1)(A)(iii)] or marriage of an alien described in clause (iv) or (vi) of section 204(a)(1)(A) [8 U.S.C.A. § 1154(a)(1)(A)] or in section 204(a)(1)(B)(iii) [8 U.S.C.A. § 1154(a)(1)(B)(iii)] shall not be the basis for revocation of a petition approval under section 205 [8 U.S.C.A. § 1155].

(i) Professional athletes

(1) In general

A petition under subsection (a)(4)(D) for classification of a professional athlete shall remain valid for the athlete after the athlete changes employers, if the new employer is a team in the same sport as the team which was the employer who filed the petition.

(2) Definition

For purposes of paragraph (1), the term "professional athlete" means an individual who is employed as an athlete by—

(A) a team that is a member of an association of 6 or more professional sports teams whose total combined revenues exceed $10,000,000 per year, if the association governs the conduct of its members and regulates the contests and exhibitions in which its member teams regularly engage; or

(B) any minor league team that is affiliated with such an association.

(j) Job flexibility for long delayed applicants for adjustment of status to permanent residence

A petition under subsection (a)(1)(D)* of this section for an individual whose application for adjustment of status pursuant to section 245 [8 U.S.C.A. § 1255] has been filed and remained unadjudicated for 180 days or more shall remain valid with respect to a new job if the individual changes jobs or employers if the new job is in the same or a similar occupational classification as the job for which the petition was filed.

(k) Procedures for unmarried sons and daughters of citizens

(1) In general

Except as provided in paragraph (2), in the case of a petition under this section initially filed for an alien unmarried son or daughter's classification as a family–sponsored immigrant under section 203(a)(2)(B) [8 U.S.C.A. § 1153(a)(2)(B)], based on a parent of the son or daughter being an alien lawfully admitted for permanent residence, if such parent subsequently becomes a naturalized citizen of the United States, such petition shall be converted to a

* Probably should refer to subsection (a)(1)(F)—eds.

petition to classify the unmarried son or daughter as a family–sponsored immigrant under section 203(a)(1) [8 U.S.C.A. § 1153(a)(1)].

(2) Exception

Paragraph (1) does not apply if the son or daughter files with the Attorney General a written statement that he or she elects not to have such conversion occur (or if it has occurred, to have such conversion revoked). Where such an election has been made, any determination with respect to the son or daughter's eligibility for admission as a family–sponsored immigrant shall be made as if such naturalization had not taken place.

(3) Priority date

Regardless of whether a petition is converted under this subsection or not, if an unmarried son or daughter described in this subsection was assigned a priority date with respect to such petition before such naturalization, he or she may maintain that priority date.

(4) Clarification

This subsection shall apply to a petition if it is properly filed, regardless of whether it was approved or not before such naturalization.

(*l*) Surviving relative consideration for certain petitions and applications

(1) In general

An alien described in paragraph (2) who resided in the United States at the time of the death of the qualifying relative and who continues to reside in the United States shall have such petition described in paragraph (2), or an application for adjustment of status to that of a person admitted for lawful permanent residence based upon the family relationship described in paragraph (2), and any related applications, adjudicated notwithstanding the death of the qualifying relative, unless the Secretary of Homeland Security determines, in the unreviewable discretion of the Secretary, that approval would not be in the public interest.

(2) Alien described

An alien described in this paragraph is an alien who, immediately prior to the death of his or her qualifying relative, was—

(A) the beneficiary of a pending or approved petition for classification as an immediate relative (as described in section 201(b)(2)(A)(i) [8 U.S.C.A. § 1151(b)(2)(A)(i)]);

(B) the beneficiary of a pending or approved petition for classification under section 203(a) or (d) [8 U.S.C.A. § 1153(a) or (d)];

(C) a derivative beneficiary of a pending or approved petition for classification under section 203(b) [8 U.S.C.A. § 1153(b)] (as described in section 203(d) [8 U.S.C.A. § 1153(d)]);

(D) the beneficiary of a pending or approved refugee/asylee relative petition under section 207 or 208 [8 U.S.C.A. § 1157 or 1158];

(E) an alien admitted in "T" nonimmigrant status as described in section 101(a)(15)(T)(ii) [8 U.S.C.A. § 1101(a)(15)(T)(ii)] or in "U" nonimmigrant status as described in section 101(a)(15)(U)(ii) [8 U.S.C.A. § 1101(a)(15)(U)(ii)];

(F) a child of an alien who filed a pending or approved petition for classification or application for adjustment of status or other benefit specified in section 101(a)(51) [8 U.S.C.A. § 1101(a)(51)] as a VAWA self-petitioner; or

(G) an asylee (as described in section 208(b)(3) [8 U.S.C.A. § 1158(b)(3)]).

(June 27, 1952, c. 477, Title II, ch. 1, § 204, 66 Stat. 179; Oct. 24, 1962, Pub.L. 87–885, § 3, 76 Stat. 1247; Oct. 3, 1965, Pub.L. 89–236, § 4, 79 Stat. 915; Oct. 20, 1976, Pub.L. 94–571, § 7(b), 90 Stat. 2706; Oct. 5, 1978, Pub.L. 95–417, §§ 2, 3, 92 Stat. 917; Oct. 19, 1980, Pub.L. 96–470, Title II, § 207, 94 Stat. 2245; Dec. 29, 1981, Pub.L. 97–116, §§ 3, 18(d), 95 Stat. 1611, 1620; Oct. 22, 1982, Pub.L. 97–359, 96 Stat. 1716; Nov. 10, 1986, Pub.L. 99–639, §§ 2(c), 4(a), 5(b), 100 Stat. 3541, 3543; Oct. 24, 1988, Pub. L. 100–525, § 9(g), 102 Stat. 2620; Nov. 29, 1990, Pub.L. 101–649, Title I, § 162(b), Title VII, § 702(b), 104 Stat. 5010, 5086; Dec. 12, 1991, Pub.L. 102–232, Title III, §§ 302(e)(4),(5), 308(b), 309(b)(5), 105 Stat. 1745, 1746, 1757, 1758; Sept. 13, 1994, Pub.L. 103–322, Title IV, § 40701(a), (b)(1), (c), 108 Stat. 1953, 1954; Oct. 25, 1994, Pub.L. 103–416, Title II, § 219(b)(2), 108 Stat. 4316; Sept. 30, 1996, Pub.L. 104–208, Div. C, Title III, § 308(e)(1)(A), (f)(2)(A), Title VI, § 624(b), 110 Stat. 3009–619, 3009–621, 3009–699; Oct. 6, 2000, Pub.L. 106–279, Title III, § 302(b), 114 Stat. 839; Oct. 17, 2000, Pub.L. 106–313, Title I, § 106(c)(1), 114 Stat. 1254; Oct. 28, 2000, Pub.L. 106–386, Div. B, Title V, §§ 1503(b), (c), (d), 1507(a)(1), (2), (b), 114 Stat. 1518, 1520, 1521, 1529, 1530; Aug. 6, 2002, Pub.L. 107–208, §§ 6, 7, 116 Stat. 929; Jan. 5, 2006, Pub.L. 109–162, Title VIII, §§ 805(a), (c), 814(b), (e), 816, 119 Stat. 3056, 3059, 3060; July 27, 2006, Pub.L. 109–248, Title IV, § 402(a), 120 Stat. 622; Aug. 12, 2006, Pub.L. 109–271, § 6(a), 120 Stat. 762; Oct. 28, 2009, Pub.L. 111–83, Title V, § 568(d)(1), 123 Stat. 2187; Pub.L. 113–4, Title VIII, § 803, Mar. 7, 2013, 127 Stat. 111; Pub.L. 113–6, Div. D, Title V, § 563, Mar. 26, 2013, 127 Stat. 380.)

§ 205. Revocation of approval of petitions; notice of revocation; effective date [8 U.S.C.A. § 1155]

The Secretary of Homeland Security may, at any time, for what he deems to be good and sufficient cause, revoke the approval of any petition approved by him under section 204 [8 U.S.C.A. § 1154]. Such revocation shall be effective as of the date of approval of any such petition.

(June 27, 1952, c. 477, Title II, ch. 1, § 205, 66 Stat. 180; Sept. 22, 1959, Pub.L. 86–363, § 5(a), (b), 73 Stat. 644; Sept. 26, 1961, Pub.L. 87–301, §§ 3, 10, 75 Stat. 650, 654;

Oct. 3, 1965, Pub.L. 89–236, § 5, 79 Stat. 916; Sept. 30, 1996, Pub.L. 104–208, Div. C, Title III, § 308(g)(3)(A), 110 Stat. 3009–622; Dec. 17, 2004, Pub.L. 108–458, Title V, § 5304(c), 118 Stat. 3736.)

§ 206. Unused immigrant visas [8 U.S.C.A. § 1156]

If an immigrant having an immigrant visa is denied admission to the United States and removed, or does not apply for admission before the expiration of the validity of his visa, or if an alien having an immigrant visa issued to him as a preference immigrant is found not to be a preference immigrant, an immigrant visa or a preference immigrant visa, as the case may be, may be issued in lieu thereof to another qualified alien.

(June 27, 1952, c. 477, Title II, ch. 1, § 206, 66 Stat. 181; Oct. 3, 1965, Pub.L. 89–236, § 6, 79 Stat. 916; Sept. 30, 1996, Pub.L. 104–208, Div. C, Title III, § 308(d)(4)(D), 110 Stat. 3009–618.)

§ 207. Annual admission of refugees and admission of emergency situation refugees [8 U.S.C.A. § 1157]

(a) Maximum number of admissions; increases for humanitarian concerns; allocations

(1) Except as provided in subsection (b), the number of refugees who may be admitted under this section in fiscal year 1980, 1981, or 1982, may not exceed fifty thousand unless the President determines, before the beginning of the fiscal year and after appropriate consultation (as defined in subsection (e)), that admission of a specific number of refugees in excess of such number is justified by humanitarian concerns or is otherwise in the national interest.

(2) Except as provided in subsection (b), the number of refugees who may be admitted under this section in any fiscal year after fiscal year 1982 shall be such number as the President determines, before the beginning of the fiscal year and after appropriate consultation, is justified by humanitarian concerns or is otherwise in the national interest.

(3) Admissions under this subsection shall be allocated among refugees of special humanitarian concern to the United States in accordance with a determination made by the President after appropriate consultation.

(4) In the determination made under this subsection for each fiscal year (beginning with fiscal year 1992), the President shall enumerate, with the respective number of refugees so determined, the number of aliens who were granted asylum in the previous year.

(b) Determinations by President respecting number of admissions for humanitarian concerns

If the President determines, after appropriate consultation, that (1) an unforeseen emergency refugee situation exists, (2) the admission of certain refugees in response to the emergency refugee situation is justified by grave humanitarian concerns or is otherwise in the national interest, and (3) the admission to the United States of these refugees cannot be accomplished under subsection (a), the President may fix a number of refugees to be admitted to the United States during the succeeding period (not to exceed twelve months) in response to the emergency refugee situation and such admissions shall be allocated among refugees of special humanitarian concern to the United States in accordance with a determination made by the President after the appropriate consultation provided under this subsection.

(c) Admission by Attorney General of refugees; criteria; admission status of spouse or child; applicability of other statutory requirements; termination of refugee status of alien, spouse or child

(1) Subject to the numerical limitations established pursuant to subsections (a) and (b), the Attorney General may, in the Attorney General's discretion and pursuant to such regulations as the Attorney General may prescribe, admit any refugee who is not firmly resettled in any foreign country, is determined to be of special humanitarian concern to the United States, and is admissible except as otherwise provided under paragraph (3) as an immigrant under this Act.

(2)(A) A spouse or child (as defined in section 101(b)(1)(A), (B), (C), (D), or (E) [8 U.S.C.A. § 1101(b)(1)(A), (B), (C), (D), or (E)]) of any refugee who qualifies for admission under paragraph (1) shall, if not otherwise entitled to admission under paragraph (1) and if not a person described in the second sentence of section 101(a)(42) [8 U.S.C.A. § 1101(a)(42)], be entitled to the same admission status as such refugee if accompanying, or following to join, such refugee and if the spouse or child is admissible (except as otherwise provided under paragraph (3)) as an immigrant under this chapter. Upon the spouse's or child's admission to the United States, such admission shall be charged against the numerical limitation established in accordance with the appropriate subsection under which the refugee's admission is charged.

(B) An unmarried alien who seeks to accompany, or follow to join, a parent granted admission as a refugee under this subsection, and who was under 21 years of age on the date on which such parent applied for refugee status under this section, shall continue to be classified as a child for purposes of this paragraph, if the alien attained 21 years of age after such application was filed but while it was pending.

(3) The provisions of paragraphs (4), (5), and (7)(A) of section 212(a) [8 U.S.C.A. § 1182(a)] shall not be applicable to any alien seeking admission to the United States under this subsection, and the Attorney General may waive any other provision of such section (other than paragraph (2)(C) or subparagraph (A), (B), (C), or (E) of paragraph (3)) with respect to such an alien for humanitarian purposes, to assure family unity, or when it is otherwise in the public interest. Any such waiver by the Attorney General shall be in writing and shall be granted only on an individual basis following an investigation. The Attorney General shall provide for the annual reporting to Congress of the number of waivers granted under this paragraph in the previous fiscal year and a summary of the reasons for granting such waivers.

(4) The refugee status of any alien (and of the spouse or child of the alien) may be terminated by the Attorney General pursuant to such regulations as the Attorney General may prescribe if the Attorney General determines that the alien was not in fact a refugee within the meaning of section 101(a)(42) [8 U.S.C.A. § 1101(a)(42)] at the time of the alien's admission.

(d) Oversight reporting and consultation requirements

(1) Before the start of each fiscal year the President shall report to the Committees on the Judiciary of the House of Representatives and of the Senate regarding the foreseeable number of refugees who will be in need of resettlement during the fiscal year and the anticipated allocation of refugee admissions during the fiscal year. The President shall provide for periodic discussions between designated representatives of the President and members of such committees regarding changes in the worldwide refugee situation, the progress of refugee admissions, and the possible need for adjustments in the allocation of admissions among refugees.

(2) As soon as possible after representatives of the President initiate appropriate consultation with respect to the number of refugee admissions under subsection (a) or with respect to the admission of refugees in response to an emergency refugee situation under subsection (b), the Committees on the Judiciary of the House of Representatives and of the Senate shall cause to have printed in the Congressional Record the substance of such consultation.

(3)(A) After the President initiates appropriate consultation prior to making a determination under subsection (a), a hearing to review the proposed determination shall be held unless public disclosure of the details of the proposal would jeopardize the lives or safety of individuals.

(B) After the President initiates appropriate consultation prior to making a determination, under subsection (b), that the number of refugee admissions should be increased because of an unforeseen emergency refugee situation, to the extent that time and the nature of the emergency refugee situation permit, a hearing to review the proposal to increase refugee admissions shall be held unless public disclosure of the details of the proposal would jeopardize the lives or safety of individuals.

(e) "Appropriate consultation" defined

For purposes of this section, the term "appropriate consultation" means, with respect to the admission of refugees and allocation of refugee admissions, discussions in person by designated Cabinet-level representatives of the President with members of the Committees on the Judiciary of the Senate and of the House of Representatives to review the refugee situation or emergency refugee situation, to project the extent of possible participation of the United States therein, to discuss the reasons for believing that the proposed admission of refugees is justified by humanitarian concerns or grave humanitarian concerns or is otherwise in the national interest, and to provide such members with the following information:

(1) A description of the nature of the refugee situation.

(2) A description of the number and allocation of the refugees to be admitted and an analysis of conditions within the countries from which they came.

(3) A description of the proposed plans for their movement and resettlement and the estimated cost of their movement and resettlement.

(4) An analysis of the anticipated social, economic, and demographic impact of their admission to the United States.

(5) A description of the extent to which other countries will admit and assist in the resettlement of such refugees.

(6) An analysis of the impact of the participation of the United States in the resettlement of such refugees on the foreign policy interests of the United States.

(7) Such additional information as may be appropriate or requested by such members.

To the extent possible, information described in this subsection shall be provided at least two weeks in advance of discussions in person by designated representatives of the President with such members.

(f) Training United States officials adjudicating refugee cases

(1) The Attorney General, in consultation with the Secretary of State, shall provide all United States officials adjudicating refugee cases under this section with the same training as that provided to officers adjudicating asylum cases under section 208 [8 U.S.C.A. § 1158].

(2) Such training shall include country-specific conditions, instruction on the internationally recognized right to freedom of religion, instruction on methods of religious persecution practiced in foreign countries, and applicable distinctions within a country between the nature of and treatment of various religious practices and believers.

(June 27, 1952, c. 477, Title II, ch. 1, § 207, as added Mar. 17, 1980, Pub.L. 96–212, Title II, § 201(b), 94 Stat. 103, and amended Oct. 24, 1988, Pub.L. 100–525, § 9(h), 102

Stat. 2620; Nov. 29, 1990, Pub.L. 101–649, Title I, § 104(b), Title VI, § 603(a)(4), 104 Stat. 4985, 5082; Dec. 12, 1991, Pub.L. 102–232, Title III, § 307(*l*)(1), 105 Stat. 1756; Sept. 30, 1996, Pub.L. 104–208, Div. C, Title VI, § 601(b), 110 Stat. 3009–689; Oct. 27, 1998, Pub.L. 105–292, Title VI, § 602(a), 112 Stat. 2812; Aug. 6, 2002, Pub.L. 107–208, § 5, 116 Stat. 929; May 11, 2005, Pub.L. 109–13, Div. B, § 101(g), 119 Stat. 231, 305.)

§ 208. Asylum procedure [8 U.S.C.A. § 1158]

(a) Authority to apply for asylum

(1) In general

Any alien who is physically present in the United States or who arrives in the United States (whether or not at a designated port of arrival and including an alien who is brought to the United States after having been interdicted in international or United States waters), irrespective of such alien's status, may apply for asylum in accordance with this section or, where applicable, section 235(b) [8 U.S.C.A. § 1225(b)].

(2) Exceptions

(A) Safe third country

Paragraph (1) shall not apply to an alien if the Attorney General determines that the alien may be removed, pursuant to a bilateral or multilateral agreement, to a country (other than the country of the alien's nationality or, in the case of an alien having no nationality, the country of the alien's last habitual residence) in which the alien's life or freedom would not be threatened on account of race, religion, nationality, membership in a particular social group, or political opinion, and where the alien would have access to a full and fair procedure for determining a claim to asylum or equivalent temporary protection, unless the Attorney General finds that it is in the public interest for the alien to receive asylum in the United States.

(B) Time limit

Subject to subparagraph (D), paragraph (1) shall not apply to an alien unless the alien demonstrates by clear and convincing evidence that the application has been filed within 1 year after the date of the alien's arrival in the United States.

(C) Previous asylum applications

Subject to subparagraph (D), paragraph (1) shall not apply to an alien if the alien has previously applied for asylum and had such application denied.

(D) Changed circumstances

An application for asylum of an alien may be considered, notwithstanding subparagraphs (B) and (C), if the alien demonstrates to the satisfaction of the Attorney General either the existence of changed circumstances which materially affect the applicant's eligibility for asylum or extraordinary circumstances relating to the delay in filing an application within the period specified in subparagraph (B).

(E) Applicability

Subparagraphs (A) and (B) shall not apply to an unaccompanied alien child (as defined in section 462(g) of the Homeland Security Act of 2002 [6 U.S.C.A. § 279(g)]).

(3) Limitation on judicial review

No court shall have jurisdiction to review any determination of the Attorney General under paragraph (2).

(b) Conditions for granting asylum

(1) In general

(A) Eligibility

The Secretary of Homeland Security or the Attorney General may grant asylum to an alien who has applied for asylum in accordance with the requirements and procedures established by the Secretary of Homeland Security or the Attorney General under this section if the Secretary of Homeland Security or the Attorney General determines that such alien is a refugee within the meaning of section 101(a)(42)(A) [8 U.S.C.A. § 1101(a)(42)(A)].

(B) Burden of proof

(i) In general

The burden of proof is on the applicant to establish that the applicant is a refugee, within the meaning of section 101(a)(42)(A) [8 U.S.C.A. § 1101(a)(42)(A)]. To establish that the applicant is a refugee within the meaning of such section, the applicant must establish that race, religion, nationality, membership in a particular social group, or political opinion was or will be at least one central reason for persecuting the applicant.

(ii) Sustaining burden

The testimony of the applicant may be sufficient to sustain the applicant's burden without corroboration, but only if the applicant satisfies the trier of fact that the applicant's testimony is credible, is persuasive, and refers to specific facts sufficient to demonstrate that the applicant is a refugee. In determining whether the applicant has met the applicant's burden, the trier of fact may weigh the credible testimony along with other evidence of record. Where the trier of fact determines that the applicant should provide evidence that corroborates otherwise credible testimony, such evidence must be provided unless the applicant does not have the evidence and cannot reasonably obtain the evidence.

(iii) Credibility determination

Considering the totality of the circumstances, and all relevant factors, a trier of fact may base a credibility determination on the demeanor, candor, or responsiveness of the applicant or witness, the inherent plausibility of the applicant's or witness's account, the consistency between the applicant's or witness's written and oral statements (whenever made and whether or not under oath, and considering the circumstances under which the statements were made), the internal consistency of each such statement, the consistency of such statements with other evidence of record (including the reports of the Department of State on country conditions), and any inaccuracies or falsehoods in such statements, without regard to whether an inconsistency, inaccuracy, or falsehood goes to the heart of the applicant's claim, or any other relevant factor. There is no presumption of credibility, however, if no adverse credibility determination is explicitly made, the applicant or witness shall have a rebuttable presumption of credibility on appeal.

(2) Exceptions

(A) In general

Paragraph (1) shall not apply to an alien if the Attorney General determines that—

(i) the alien ordered, incited, assisted, or otherwise participated in the persecution of any person on account of race, religion, nationality, membership in a particular social group, or political opinion;

(ii) the alien, having been convicted by a final judgment of a particularly serious crime, constitutes a danger to the community of the United States;

(iii) there are serious reasons for believing that the alien has committed a serious nonpolitical crime outside the United States prior to the arrival of the alien in the United States;

(iv) there are reasonable grounds for regarding the alien as a danger to the security of the United States;

(v) the alien is described in subclause (I), (II), (III), (IV), or (VI) of section 212(a)(3)(B)(i) [8 U.S.C.A. § 1182(a)(3)(B)(i)] or section 237(a)(4)(B) [8 U.S.C.A. § 1227(a)(4)(B)] (relating to terrorist activity), unless, in the case only of an alien described in subclause (IV) of section 212(a)(3)(B)(i) [8 U.S.C.A. § 1182(a)(3)(B)(i)], the Attorney General determines, in the Attorney General's discretion, that there are not reasonable grounds for regarding the alien as a danger to the security of the United States; or

(vi) the alien was firmly resettled in another country prior to arriving in the United States.

(B) Special rules

(i) Conviction of aggravated felony

For purposes of clause (ii) of subparagraph (A), an alien who has been convicted of an aggravated felony shall be considered to have been convicted of a particularly serious crime.

(ii) Offenses

The Attorney General may designate by regulation offenses that will be considered to be a crime described in clause (ii) or (iii) of subparagraph (A).

(C) Additional limitations

The Attorney General may by regulation establish additional limitations and conditions, consistent with this section, under which an alien shall be ineligible for asylum under paragraph (1).

(D) No judicial review

There shall be no judicial review of a determination of the Attorney General under subparagraph (A)(v).

(3) Treatment of spouse and children

(A) In general

A spouse or child (as defined in section 101(b)(1)(A), (B), (C), (D), or (E)) [8 U.S.C.A. § 1101(b)(1)(A), (B), (C), (D), or (E)] of an alien who is granted asylum under this subsection may, if not otherwise eligible for asylum under this section, be granted the same status as the alien if accompanying, or following to join, such alien.

(B) Continued classification of certain aliens as children

An unmarried alien who seeks to accompany, or follow to join, a parent granted asylum under this subsection, and who was under 21 years of age on the date on which such parent applied for asylum under this section, shall continue to be classified as a child for purposes of this paragraph and section 209(b)(3) [8 U.S.C.A. § 1159(b)(3)], if the alien attained 21 years of age after such application was filed but while it was pending.

(C) Initial jurisdiction

An asylum officer (as defined in section 235(b)(1)(E) [8 U.S.C.A. § 1225(b)(1)(E)]) shall have initial jurisdiction over any asylum application filed by an unaccompanied alien child (as defined in section 462(g) of the Homeland Security Act of 2002 [6 U.S.C.A. § 279(g)]), regardless of whether filed in accordance with this section or section 235(b) [8 U.S.C.A. § 1225(b)].

(c) Asylum status

(1) In general

In the case of an alien granted asylum under subsection (b), the Attorney General—

(A) shall not remove or return the alien to the alien's country of nationality or, in the case of a person having no nationality, the country of the alien's last habitual residence;

(B) shall authorize the alien to engage in employment in the United States and provide the alien with appropriate endorsement of that authorization; and

(C) may allow the alien to travel abroad with the prior consent of the Attorney General.

(2) Termination of asylum

Asylum granted under subsection (b) does not convey a right to remain permanently in the United States, and may be terminated if the Attorney General determines that—

(A) the alien no longer meets the conditions described in subsection (b)(1) owing to a fundamental change in circumstances;

(B) the alien meets a condition described in subsection (b)(2);

(C) the alien may be removed, pursuant to a bilateral or multilateral agreement, to a country (other than the country of the alien's nationality or, in the case of an alien having no nationality, the country of the alien's last habitual residence) in which the alien's life or freedom would not be threatened on account of race, religion, nationality, membership in a particular social group, or political opinion, and where the alien is eligible to receive asylum or equivalent temporary protection;

(D) the alien has voluntarily availed himself or herself of the protection of the alien's country of nationality or, in the case of an alien having no nationality, the alien's country of last habitual residence, by returning to such country with permanent resident status or the reasonable possibility of obtaining such status with the same rights and obligations pertaining to other permanent residents of that country; or

(E) the alien has acquired a new nationality and enjoys the protection of the country of his or her new nationality.

(3) Removal when asylum is terminated

An alien described in paragraph (2) is subject to any applicable grounds of inadmissibility or deportability under section [sic] 212(a) [8 U.S.C.A. § 1182(a)] and 237(a) [8 U.S.C.A. § 1227(a)], and the alien's removal or return shall be directed by the Attorney General in accordance with sections 240 [8 U.S.C.A. § 1229a] and 241 [8 U.S.C.A. § 1231].

(d) Asylum procedure

(1) Applications

The Attorney General shall establish a procedure for the consideration of asylum applications filed under subsection (a). The Attorney General may require applicants to submit fingerprints and a photograph at such time and in such manner to be determined by regulation by the Attorney General.

(2) Employment

An applicant for asylum is not entitled to employment authorization, but such authorization may be provided under regulation by the Attorney General. An applicant who is not otherwise eligible for employment authorization shall not be granted such authorization prior to 180 days after the date of filing of the application for asylum.

(3) Fees

The Attorney General may impose fees for the consideration of an application for asylum, for employment authorization under this section, and for adjustment of status under section 209(b) [8 U.S.C.A. § 1159(b)]. Such fees shall not exceed the Attorney General's costs in adjudicating the applications. The Attorney General may provide for the assessment and payment of such fees over a period of time or by installments. Nothing in this paragraph shall be construed to require the Attorney General to charge fees for adjudication services provided to asylum applicants, or to limit the authority of the Attorney General to set adjudication and naturalization fees in accordance with section 286(m) [8 U.S.C.A. § 1356(m)].

(4) Notice of privilege of counsel and consequences of frivolous application

At the time of filing an application for asylum, the Attorney General shall—

(A) advise the alien of the privilege of being represented by counsel and of the consequences, under paragraph (6), of knowingly filing a frivolous application for asylum; and

(B) provide the alien a list of persons (updated not less often than quarterly) who have indicated their availability to represent aliens in asylum proceedings on a pro bono basis.

(5) Consideration of asylum applications

(A) Procedures

The procedure established under paragraph (1) shall provide that—

(i) asylum cannot be granted until the identity of the applicant has been checked against all appropriate records or databases maintained by the Attorney General and by the Secretary of State, including the Automated Visa Lookout System, to determine any grounds on which the alien may be inadmissible to or deportable from the United States, or ineligible to apply for or be granted asylum;

(ii) in the absence of exceptional circumstances, the initial interview or hearing on the asylum application shall commence not later than 45 days after the date an application is filed;

(iii) in the absence of exceptional circumstances, final administrative adjudication of the asylum application, not including administrative appeal, shall be completed within 180 days after the date an application is filed;

(iv) any administrative appeal shall be filed within 30 days of a decision granting or denying asylum, or within 30 days of the completion of removal proceedings before an immigration judge under section 240 [8 U.S.C.A. § 1229a], whichever is later; and

(v) in the case of an applicant for asylum who fails without prior authorization or in the absence of exceptional circumstances to appear for an interview or hearing, including a hearing under section 240 [8 U.S.C.A. § 1229a], the application may be dismissed or the applicant may be otherwise sanctioned for such failure.

(B) Additional regulatory conditions

The Attorney General may provide by regulation for any other conditions or limitations on the consideration of an application for asylum not inconsistent with this Act.

(6) Frivolous applications

If the Attorney General determines that an alien has knowingly made a frivolous application for asylum and the alien has received the notice under paragraph (4)(A), the alien shall be permanently ineligible for any benefits under this Act, effective as of the date of a final determination on such application.

(7) No private right of action

Nothing in this subsection shall be construed to create any substantive or procedural right or benefit that is legally enforceable by any party against the United States or its agencies or officers or any other person.

(e) Commonwealth of the Northern Mariana Islands

The provisions of this section and section 209(b) [8 U.S.C.A. § 1159(b)] shall apply to persons physically present in the Commonwealth of the Northern Mariana Islands or arriving in the Commonwealth (whether or not at a designated port of arrival and including persons who are brought to the Commonwealth after having been interdicted in international or United States waters) only on or after January 1, 2014.

(June 27, 1952, c. 477, Title II, ch. 1, § 208, as added Mar. 17, 1980, Pub.L. 96–212, Title II, § 201(b), 94 Stat. 105, and amended Nov. 29, 1990, Pub.L. 101–649, Title V, § 515(a)(1), 104 Stat. 5053; Sept. 13, 1994, Pub.L. 103–322, Title XIII, § 130005(b), 108 Stat. 2028; Apr. 24, 1996, Pub.L. 104–132, Title IV, § 421(a), 110 Stat. 1270; Sept. 30, 1996, Pub.L. 104–208, Div. C, Title VI, § 604(a), 110 Stat. 3009–690; Oct. 26, 2001, Pub.L. 107–56, Title IV, § 411(b)(2), 115 Stat. 348; Aug. 6, 2002, Pub.L. 107–208, § 4, 116 Stat. 928; May 11, 2005, Pub.L. 109–13, Div. B, §§ 101(a), (b), 119 Stat. 231, 302–03; May 8, 2008, Pub.L. 110–229, Title VII, § 702(j)(4), 122 Stat. 866; Dec. 23, 2008, Pub.L. 110–457, Title II, § 235(d)(7), 122 Stat. 5071, 5080.)

§ 209. Adjustment of status of refugees [8 U.S.C.A. § 1159]

(a) Criteria and procedures applicable for admission as immigrant; effect of adjustment

(1) Any alien who has been admitted to the United States under section 207 [8 U.S.C.A. § 1157]—

(A) whose admission has not been terminated by the Secretary of Homeland Security or the Attorney General pursuant to such regulations as the Secretary of Homeland Security or the Attorney General may prescribe,

(B) who has been physically present in the United States for at least one year, and

(C) who has not acquired permanent resident status,

shall, at the end of such year period, return or be returned to the custody of the Department of Homeland Security for inspection and examination for admission to the United States as an immigrant in accordance with the provisions of sections 235 [8 U.S.C.A. § 1225], 240 [8 U.S.C.A. § 1229a], and 241 [8 U.S.C.A. § 1231].

(2) Any alien who is found upon inspection and examination by an immigration officer pursuant to paragraph (1) or after a hearing before an immigration judge to be admissible (except as otherwise provided under subsection (c)) as an immigrant under this Act at the time of the alien's inspection and examination shall, notwithstanding any numerical limitation specified in this Act, be regarded as lawfully admitted to the United States for permanent residence as of the date of such alien's arrival into the United States.

(b) Maximum number of adjustments; recordkeeping

The Secretary of Homeland Security or the Attorney General, in the Secretary's or the Attorney General's discretion and under such regulations as the Secretary or the Attorney General may prescribe, may adjust to the status of an alien lawfully admitted for permanent residence the status of any alien granted asylum who—

(1) applies for such adjustment,

(2) has been physically present in the United States for at least one year after being granted asylum,

(3) continues to be a refugee within the meaning of section 101(a)(42)(A) [8 U.S.C.A. § 1101(a)(42)(A)] or a spouse or child of such a refugee,

(4) is not firmly resettled in any foreign country, and

(5) is admissible (except as otherwise provided under subsection (c)) as an immigrant under this Act at the time of examination for adjustment of such alien.

Upon approval of an application under this subsection, the Secretary of Homeland Security or the Attorney General shall establish a record of the alien's admission for lawful permanent residence as of the date one year before the date of the approval of the application.

(c) Applicability of other Federal statutory requirements

The provisions of paragraphs (4), (5), and (7)(A) of section 212(a) [8 U.S.C.A. § 1182(a)] shall not be applicable to any alien seeking adjustment of status under this section, and the Secretary of Homeland Security or the Attorney General may waive any other provision of such section (other than paragraph (2)(C) or subparagraph (A), (B), (C), or (E) of paragraph (3)) with respect to such an alien for humanitarian purposes, to assure family unity, or when it is otherwise in the public interest.

(June 27, 1952, c. 477, Title II, ch. 1, § 209, as added Mar. 17, 1980, Pub.L. 96–212, Title II, § 201(b), 94 Stat. 105, and amended Nov. 29, 1990, Pub.L. 101–649, Title I, § 104(a)(1), Title VI, § 603(a)(4), 104 Stat. 4985, 5082; Dec. 12, 1991, Pub.L. 102–232, Title III, § 307(*l*)(1), 105 Stat. 1756; Sept. 30, 1996, Pub.L. 104–208, Div. C, Title III, §§ 308(g)(3)(A), (4)(A), 371(b)(2), 110 Stat. 3009–622, 3009–645; May 11, 2005, Pub.L. 109–13, Div. B, § 101(g), 119 Stat. 231, 305.)

§ 210. Special agricultural workers [8 U.S.C.A. § 1160]

(a) Lawful residence

(1) In general

The Attorney General shall adjust the status of an alien to that of an alien lawfully admitted for temporary residence if the Attorney General determines that the alien meets the following requirements:

(A) Application period

The alien must apply for such adjustment during the 18–month period beginning on the first day of the seventh month that begins after November 6, 1986.

(B) Performance of Seasonal Agricultural Services and residence in the United States

The alien must establish that he has—

(i) resided in the United States, and

(ii) performed seasonal agricultural services in the United States for at least 90 man-days,

during the 12–month period ending on May 1, 1986. For purposes of the previous sentence, performance of seasonal agricultural services in the United States for more than one employer on any one day shall be counted as performance of services for only 1 man-day.

(C) Admissible as immigrant

The alien must establish that he is admissible to the United States as an immigrant, except as otherwise provided under subsection (c)(2).

(2) Adjustment to permanent residence

The Attorney General shall adjust the status of any alien provided lawful temporary resident status under paragraph (1) to that of an alien lawfully admitted for permanent residence on the following date:

(A) Group 1

Subject to the numerical limitation established under subparagraph (C), in the case of an alien who has established, at the time of application for temporary residence under paragraph (1), that the alien performed seasonal agricultural services in the United States for at least 90 man-days during each of the 12–month periods ending on May 1, 1984, 1985, and 1986, the adjustment shall occur on the first day after the end of the one-year period that begins on the later of **(I)** the date the alien was granted such temporary resident status, or **(II)** the day after the last day of the application period described in paragraph (1)(A).

(B) Group 2

In the case of aliens to which subparagraph (A) does not apply, the adjustment shall occur on the day after the last day of the two-year period that begins on the later of **(I)** the date the alien was granted such temporary resident status, or **(II)** the day after the last day of the application period described in paragraph (1)(A).

(C) Numerical limitation

Subparagraph (A) shall not apply to more than 350,000 aliens. If more than 350,000 aliens meet the requirements of such subparagraph, such subparagraph shall apply to the 350,-000 aliens whose applications for adjustment were first filed under paragraph (1) and subparagraph (B) shall apply to the remaining aliens.

(3) Termination of temporary residence

(A) During the period of temporary resident status granted an alien under paragraph (1), the Attorney General may terminate such status only upon a determination under this Act that the alien is deportable.

(B) Before any alien becomes eligible for adjustment of status under paragraph (2), the Attorney General may deny adjustment to permanent status and provide for termination of the temporary resident status granted such alien under paragraph (1) if—

(i) the Attorney General finds by a preponderance of the evidence that the adjustment to temporary resident status was the result of fraud or willful misrepresentation as set out in section 212(a)(6)(C)(i) [8 U.S.C.A. § 1182(a)(6)(C)(i)], or

(ii) the alien commits an act that (I) makes the alien inadmissible to the United States as an immigrant, except as provided under subsection (c)(2), or (II) is convicted of a felony or 3 or more misdemeanors committed in the United States.

(4) Authorized travel and employment during temporary residence

During the period an alien is in lawful temporary resident status granted under this subsection, the alien has the right to travel abroad (including commutation from a residence abroad) and shall be granted authorization to engage in employment in the United States and shall be provided an "employment authorized" endorsement or other appropriate work permit, in the same manner as for aliens lawfully admitted for permanent residence.

(5) In general

Except as otherwise provided in this subsection, an alien who acquires the status of an alien lawfully admitted for temporary residence under paragraph (1), such status not having changed, is considered to be an alien lawfully admitted for permanent residence (as described in section 101(a)(20) [8 U.S.C.A. § 1101(a)(20)]), other than under any provision of the immigration laws.

(b) Applications for adjustment of status

(1) To whom may be made

(A) Within the United States

The Attorney General shall provide that applications for adjustment of status under subsection (a) may be filed—

(i) with the Attorney General, or

(ii) with a designated entity (designated under paragraph (2)), but only if the applicant consents to the forwarding of the application to the Attorney General.

(B) Outside the United States

The Attorney General, in cooperation with the Secretary of State, shall provide a procedure whereby an alien may apply for adjustment of status under subsection (a)(1) at an appropriate consular office outside the United States. If the alien otherwise qualifies for such adjustment, the Attorney General shall provide such documentation of authorization to enter the United States and to have the alien's status adjusted upon entry as may be necessary to carry out the provisions of this section.

(2) Designation of entities to receive applications

For purposes of receiving applications under this section, the Attorney General—

(A) shall designate qualified voluntary organizations and other qualified State, local community, farm labor organizations, and associations of agricultural employers, and

(B) may designate such other persons as the Attorney General determines are qualified and have substantial experience, demonstrated competence, and traditional long-term involvement in the preparation and submittal of applications for adjustment of status under section 209 [8 U.S.C.A. § 1159] or 245 [8 U.S.C.A. § 1255], Public Law 89–732 [8 U.S.C.A. § 1255 note], or Public Law 95–145.

(3) Proof of eligibility

(A) In general

An alien may establish that he meets the requirement of subsection (a)(1)(B)(ii) through government employment records, records supplied by employers or collective bargaining organizations, and such other reliable documentation as the alien may provide. The Attorney General shall establish special procedures to credit properly work in cases in which an alien was employed under an assumed name.

(B) Documentation of work history

(i) An alien applying for adjustment of status under subsection (a)(1) has the burden of proving by a preponderance of the evidence that the alien has worked the requisite number of man-days (as required under subsection (a)(1)(B)(ii)).

(ii) If an employer or farm labor contractor employing such an alien has kept proper and adequate records respecting such employment, the alien's burden of proof under clause (i) may be met by securing timely production of those records under regulations to be promulgated by the Attorney General.

(iii) An alien can meet such burden of proof if the alien establishes that the alien has in fact performed the work described in subsection (a)(1)(B)(ii) by producing sufficient evidence to show the extent of that employment as a matter of just and reasonable inference. In such a case, the burden then shifts to the Attorney General to disprove the alien's evidence with a showing which negates the reasonableness of the inference to be drawn from the evidence.

(4) Treatment of applications by designated entities

Each designated entity must agree to forward to the Attorney General applications filed with it in accordance with paragraph (1)(A)(ii) but not to forward to the Attorney General applications filed with it unless the applicant has consented to such forwarding. No such entity may make a determination required by this section to be made by the Attorney General.

(5) Limitation on access to information

Files and records prepared for purposes of this section by designated entities operating under this section are confidential and the Attorney General and the Service shall not have access to such files or records relating to an alien without the consent of the alien, except as allowed by a court order issued pursuant to paragraph (6) of this subsection.

(6) Confidentiality of information

(A) In general

Except as provided in this paragraph, neither the Attorney General, nor any other official or employee of the Department of Justice, or bureau or agency thereof, may—

(i) use the information furnished by the applicant pursuant to an application filed under this section for any purpose other than to make a determination on the application, including a determination under subsection (a)(3)(B), or for enforcement of paragraph (7);

(ii) make any publication whereby the information furnished by any particular individual can be identified; or

(iii) permit anyone other than the sworn officers and employees of the Department or bureau or agency or, with respect to applications filed with a designated entity, that designated entity, to examine individual applications.

(B) Required disclosures

The Attorney General shall provide information furnished under this section, and any other information derived from such furnished information, to a duly recognized law enforcement entity in connection with a criminal investigation or prosecution, when such information is requested in writing by such entity, or to an official coroner for purposes of affirmatively identifying a deceased individual (whether or not such individual is deceased as a result of a crime).

(C) Construction

(i) In general

Nothing in this paragraph shall be construed to limit the use, or release, for immigration enforcement purposes or law enforcement purposes of information contained in files or records of the Service pertaining to an application filed under this section, other than information furnished by an applicant pursuant to the application, or any other information derived from the application, that is not available from any other source.

(ii) Criminal convictions

Information concerning whether the applicant has at any time been convicted of a crime may be used or released for immigration enforcement or law enforcement purposes.

(D) Crime

Whoever knowingly uses, publishes, or permits information to be examined in violation of this paragraph shall be fined not more than $10,000.

(7) Penalties for false statements in applications

(A) Criminal penalty

Whoever—

(i) files an application for adjustment of status under this section and knowingly and willfully falsifies, conceals, or covers up a material fact or makes any false, fictitious, or fraudulent statements or representations, or makes or uses any false writing or document knowing the same to contain any false, fictitious, or fraudulent statement or entry, or

(ii) creates or supplies a false writing or document for use in making such an application,

shall be fined in accordance with Title 18, or imprisoned not more than five years, or both.

(B) Exclusion

An alien who is convicted of a crime under subparagraph (A) shall be considered to be inadmissible to the United States on the ground described in section 212(a)(6)(C)(i) [8 U.S.C.A. § 1182(a)(6)(C)(i)].

(c) Waiver of numerical limitations and certain grounds for exclusion

(1) Numerical limitations do not apply

The numerical limitations of sections 201 [8 U.S.C.A. § 1151] and 202 [8 U.S.C.A. § 1152] shall not apply to the adjustment of aliens to lawful permanent resident status under this section.

(2) Waiver of grounds for exclusion

In the determination of an alien's admissibility under subsection (a)(1)(C)—

(A) Grounds of exclusion not applicable

The provisions of paragraphs (5) and (7)(A) of section 212(a) [8 U.S.C.A. § 1182(a)] shall not apply.

(B) Waiver of other grounds

(i) In general

Except as provided in clause (ii), the Attorney General may waive any other provision of section 212(a) [8 U.S.C.A. § 1182(a)] in the case of individual aliens for humanitarian purposes, to assure family unity, or when it is otherwise in the public interest.

(ii) Grounds that may not be waived

The following provisions of section 212(a) [8 U.S.C.A. § 1182(a)] may not be waived by the Attorney General under clause (i):

(I) Paragraphs (2)(A) and (2)(B) (relating to criminals).

(II) Paragraph (4) (relating to aliens likely to become public charges).

(III) Paragraph (2)(C) (relating to drug offenses), except for so much of such paragraph as relates to a single offense of simple possession of 30 grams or less of marihuana.

(IV) Paragraph (3) (relating to security and related grounds), other than subparagraph (E) thereof.

(V) Omitted

(C) Special rule for determination of public charge

An alien is not ineligible for adjustment of status under this section due to being inadmissible under section 212(a)(4) [8 U.S.C.A. § 1182(a)(4)] if the alien demonstrates a history of employment in the United States evidencing self-support without reliance on public cash assistance.

(d) Temporary stay of exclusion or deportation and work authorization for certain applicants

(1) Before application period

The Attorney General shall provide that in the case of an alien who is apprehended before the beginning of the application period described in subsection (a)(1) and who can establish a nonfrivolous case of eligibility to have his status adjusted under subsection (a) (but for the fact that he may not apply for such adjustment until the beginning of such period), until the alien has had the opportunity during the first 30 days of the application period to complete the filing of an application for adjustment, the alien—

(A) may not be excluded or deported, and

(B) shall be granted authorization to engage in employment in the United States and be provided an "employment authorized" endorsement or other appropriate work permit.

(2) During application period

The Attorney General shall provide that in the case of an alien who presents a nonfrivolous application for adjustment of status under subsection (a) during the application period, and until a final determination on the application has been made in accordance with this section, the alien—

(A) may not be excluded or deported, and

(B) shall be granted authorization to engage in employment in the United States and be provided an "employment authorized" endorsement or other appropriate work permit.

(3) Use of application fees to offset program costs

No application fees collected by the Service pursuant to this subsection may be used by the Service to offset the costs of the special agricultural worker legalization program until the Service implements the program consistent with the statutory mandate as follows:

(A) During the application period described in subsection (a)(1)(A) the Service may grant temporary admission to the United States, work authorization, and provide an "employment authorized" endorsement or other appropriate work permit to any alien who presents a preliminary application for adjustment of status under subsection (a) at a designated port of entry on the southern land border. An alien who does not enter through a port of entry is subject to deportation and removal as otherwise provided in this Act.

(B) During the application period described in subsection (a)(1)(A) any alien who has filed an application for adjustment of status within the United States as provided in subsection (b)(1)(A) pursuant to the provision of 8 CFR section 210.1(j) is subject to paragraph (2) of this subsection.

(C) A preliminary application is defined as a fully completed and signed application with fee and photographs which contains specific information concerning the performance of qualifying employment in the United States and the documentary evidence which the applicant intends to submit as proof of such employment. The applicant must be otherwise admissible to the United States and must establish to the satisfaction of the examining officer during an interview that his or her claim to eligibility for special agriculture worker status is credible.

(e) Administrative and judicial review

(1) Administrative and judicial review

There shall be no administrative or judicial review of a determination respecting an application for adjustment of status under this section except in accordance with this subsection.

(2) Administrative review

(A) Single level of administrative appellate review

The Attorney General shall establish an appellate authority to provide for a single level of administrative appellate review of such a determination.

(B) Standard for review

Such administrative appellate review shall be based solely upon the administrative record established at the time of the determination on the application and upon such additional or newly discovered evidence as may not have been available at the time of the determination.

(3) Judicial review

(A) Limitation to review of exclusion or deportation

There shall be judicial review of such a denial only in the judicial review of an order of exclusion or deportation under section 106 [8 U.S.C.A. § 1105a] (as in effect before October 1, 1996).

(B) Standard for judicial review

Such judicial review shall be based solely upon the administrative record established at the time of the review by the appellate authority and the findings of fact and determinations contained in such record shall be conclusive unless the applicant can establish abuse of discretion or that the findings are directly contrary to clear and convincing facts contained in the record considered as a whole.

(f) Temporary disqualification of newly legalized aliens from receiving aid to families with dependent children

During the five-year period beginning on the date an alien was granted lawful temporary resident status under subsection (a), and notwithstanding any other provision of law, the alien is not eligible for aid under a State plan approved under part A of title IV of the Social Security Act [42 U.S.C.A. § 601 et seq.]. Notwithstanding the previous sentence, in the case of an alien who would be eligible for aid under a State plan approved under part A of title IV of the Social Security Act but for the previous sentence, the provisions of paragraph (3) of section 245A(h) [8 U.S.C.A. § 1255a(h)] shall apply in the same manner as they apply with respect to paragraph (1) of such section and, for this purpose, any reference in section 245A(h) [8 U.S.C.A. § 1255a(h)] to paragraph (1) is deemed a reference to the previous sentence.

(g) Treatment of special agricultural workers

For all purposes (subject to subsections (a)(5) and (f)) an alien whose status is adjusted under this section to that of an alien lawfully admitted for permanent residence, such status not having changed, shall be considered to be an alien lawfully admitted for permanent residence (within the meaning of section 101(a)(20) [8 U.S.C.A. § 1101(a)(20)]).

(h) "Seasonal agricultural services" defined

In this section, the term "seasonal agricultural services" means the performance of field work related to planting, cultural practices, cultivating, growing and harvesting of fruits and vegetables of every kind and other perishable commodities, as defined in regulations by the Secretary of Agriculture.

(June 27, 1952, c. 477, Title II, ch. 1, § 210, as added Nov. 6, 1986, Pub.L. 99–603, Title III, § 302(a)(1), 100 Stat. 3417, and amended Dec. 22, 1987, Pub.L. 100–202, § 101(a) [Title II, § 211], 101 Stat. 1329–18; Oct. 24, 1988, Pub. L. 100–525, § 2(m), 102 Stat. 2613; Dec. 18, 1989, Pub.L. 101–238, § 4, 103 Stat. 2103; Nov. 29, 1990, Pub.L. 101–649, Title VI, § 603(a)(5), 104 Stat. 5082; Dec. 12, 1991, Pub.L. 102–232, Title III, §§ 307(j), 309(b)(6), 105 Stat. 1756, 1758; Oct. 25, 1994, Pub.L. 103–416, Title II, § 219(d), (z)(7), 108 Stat. 4316, 4318; Apr. 24, 1996, Pub.L. 104–132, Title IV, § 431(b), 110 Stat. 1273; Aug. 22, 1996, Pub.L. 104–193, Title I, § 110(s)(1), 110 Stat. 2175; Sept. 30, 1996, Pub.L. 104–208, Div. C, Title III, §§ 308(g)(2)(B), 384(d)(1), Title VI, § 623(b), 110 Stat. 3009–622, 3009–653, 3009–697.)

CHAPTER II—ADMISSION QUALIFICATIONS FOR ALIENS; TRAVEL CONTROL OF CITIZENS AND ALIENS

§ 211. Admission of immigrants into the United States [8 U.S.C.A. § 1181]

(a) Documents required; admission under quotas before June 30, 1968

Except as provided in subsection (b) and subsection (c) no immigrant shall be admitted into the United States unless at the time of application for admission he **(1)** has a valid unexpired immigrant visa or was born subsequent to the issuance of such visa of the accompanying parent, and **(2)** presents a valid unexpired passport or other suitable travel document, or document of identity and nationality, if such document is required under the regulations issued by the Attorney General. With respect to immigrants to be admitted under quotas of quota areas prior to June 30, 1968, no immigrant visa shall be deemed valid unless the immigrant is properly chargeable to the quota area under the quota of which the visa is issued.

(b) Readmission without required documents; Attorney General's discretion

Notwithstanding the provisions of section 212(a)(7)(A) [8 U.S.C.A. § 1182(a)(7)(A)] in such cases or in such classes of cases and under such conditions as may be by regulations prescribed, returning resident immigrants, defined in section 101(a)(27)(A) [8 U.S.C.A. § 1101(a)(27)(A)], who are otherwise admissible may be readmitted to the United States by the Attorney General in his discretion without being required to obtain a passport, immigrant visa, reentry permit or other documentation.

(c) Nonapplicability to aliens admitted as refugees

The provisions of subsection (a) shall not apply to an alien whom the Attorney General admits to the United States under section 207 [8 U.S.C.A. § 1157].

(June 27, 1952, c. 477, Title II, ch. 2, § 211, 66 Stat. 181; Pub. L. 89–236, § 9, Oct. 3, 1965, 79 Stat. 917; Pub. L. 94–571, § 7(c), Oct. 20, 1976, 90 Stat. 2706; Pub. L. 96–212, Title II, § 202, Mar. 17, 1980, 94 Stat. 106; Pub.L. 101–649, Title VI, § 603(a)(7), Nov. 29, 1990, 104 Stat. 5083.)

§ 212. Excludable aliens [8 U.S.C.A. § 1182]

(a) Classes of aliens ineligible for visas or admission

Except as otherwise provided in this Act, aliens who are inadmissible under the following paragraphs are ineligible to receive visas and ineligible to be admitted to the United States:

(1) Health-related grounds

(A) In general

Any alien—

(i) who is determined (in accordance with regulations prescribed by the Secretary of Health and Human Services) to have a communicable disease of public health significance;

(ii) except as provided in subparagraph (C), who seeks admission as an immigrant, or who seeks adjustment of status to the status of an alien lawfully admitted for permanent residence, and who has failed to present documentation of having received vaccination against vaccine-preventable diseases, which shall include at least the following diseases: mumps, measles, rubella, polio, tetanus and diphtheria toxoids, pertussis, influenza type B and hepatitis B, and any other vaccinations against vaccine-preventable diseases recommended by the Advisory Committee for Immunization Practices,

(iii) who is determined (in accordance with regulations prescribed by the Secretary of Health and Human Services in consultation with the Attorney General)—

(I) to have a physical or mental disorder and behavior associated with the disorder that may pose, or has posed, a threat to the property, safety, or welfare of the alien or others, or

(II) to have had a physical or mental disorder and a history of behavior associated with the disorder, which behavior has posed a threat to the property, safety, or welfare of the alien or others and which behavior is likely to recur or to lead to other harmful behavior, or

(iv) who is determined (in accordance with regulations prescribed by the Secretary of Health and Human Services) to be a drug abuser or addict,

is inadmissible.

(B) Waiver authorized

For provision authorizing waiver of certain clauses of subparagraph (A), see subsection (g).

(C) Exception from immunization requirement for adopted children 10 years of age or younger

Clause (ii) of subparagraph (A) shall not apply to a child who—

(i) is 10 years of age or younger,

(ii) is described in subparagraph (F) or (G) of section 101(b)(1) [8 U.S.C.A. § 1101(b)(1)]; and

(iii) is seeking an immigrant visa as an immediate relative under section 201(b) [8 U.S.C.A. § 1151(b)],

if, prior to the admission of the child, an adoptive parent or prospective adoptive parent of the child, who has sponsored the child for admission as an immediate relative, has executed an affidavit stating that the parent is aware of the provisions of subparagraph (A)(ii) and will ensure that, within 30 days of the child's admission, or at the earliest time that is medically appropriate, the child will receive the vaccinations identified in such subparagraph.

(2) Criminal and related grounds

(A) Conviction of certain crimes

(i) In general

Except as provided in clause (ii), any alien convicted of, or who admits having committed, or who admits committing acts which constitute the essential elements of—

(I) a crime involving moral turpitude (other than a purely political offense) or an attempt or conspiracy to commit such a crime, or

(II) a violation of (or a conspiracy or attempt to violate) any law or regulation of a State, the United States, or a foreign country relating to a controlled substance (as defined in section 802 of Title 21),

is inadmissible.

(ii) Exception

Clause (i)(I) shall not apply to an alien who committed only one crime if—

(I) the crime was committed when the alien was under 18 years of age, and the crime was committed (and the alien released from any confinement to a prison or correctional institution imposed for the crime) more than 5 years before the date of application for a visa or other documentation and the date of application for admission to the United States, or

(II) the maximum penalty possible for the crime of which the alien was convicted (or which the alien admits having committed or of which the acts that the alien admits having committed constituted the essential elements) did not exceed imprisonment for one year and, if the alien was convicted of such crime, the alien was not sentenced to a term of imprisonment in excess of 6 months (regardless of the extent to which the sentence was ultimately executed).

(B) Multiple criminal convictions

Any alien convicted of 2 or more offenses (other than purely political offenses), regardless of whether the conviction was in a single trial or whether the offenses arose from a single scheme of misconduct and regardless of whether the offenses involved moral turpitude, for which the aggregate sentences to confinement were 5 years or more is inadmissible.

(C) Controlled substance traffickers

Any alien who the consular officer or the Attorney General knows or has reason to believe—

(i) is or has been an illicit trafficker in any controlled substance or in any listed chemical (as defined in section 102 of the Controlled Substances Act (21 U.S.C. 802)), or is or has been a knowing aider, abettor, assister, conspirator, or colluder with others in the illicit trafficking in any such controlled or listed substance or chemical, or endeavored to do so; or

(ii) is the spouse, son, or daughter of an alien inadmissible under clause (i), has, within the previous 5 years, obtained any financial or other benefit from the illicit activity of that alien, and knew or reasonably should have known that the financial or other benefit was the product of such illicit activity,

is inadmissible.

(D) Prostitution and commercialized vice

Any alien who—

(i) is coming to the United States solely, principally, or incidentally to engage in prostitution, or has engaged in prostitution within 10 years of the date of application for a visa, admission, or adjustment of status,

(ii) directly or indirectly procures or attempts to procure, or (within 10 years of the date of application for a visa, admission, or adjustment of status) procured or attempted to procure or to import, prostitutes or persons for the purpose of prostitution, or receives or (within such 10–year period) received, in whole or in part, the proceeds of prostitution, or

(iii) is coming to the United States to engage in any other unlawful commercialized vice, whether or not related to prostitution,

is inadmissible.

(E) Certain aliens involved in serious criminal activity who have asserted immunity from prosecution

Any alien—

(i) who has committed in the United States at any time a serious criminal offense (as defined in section 101(h) [8 U.S.C.A. § 1101(h)]),

(ii) for whom immunity from criminal jurisdiction was exercised with respect to that offense,

(iii) who as a consequence of the offense and exercise of immunity has departed from the United States, and

(iv) who has not subsequently submitted fully to the jurisdiction of the court in the United States having jurisdiction with respect to that offense,

is inadmissible.

(F) Waiver authorized

For provision authorizing waiver of certain subparagraphs of this paragraph, see subsection (h).

(G) Foreign government officials who have committed particularly severe violations of religious freedom

Any alien who, while serving as a foreign government official, was responsible for or directly carried out, at any time, particularly severe violations of religious freedom, as defined in section 3 of the International Religious Freedom Act of 1998 (22 U.S.C. 6402), is inadmissible.

(H) Significant traffickers in persons

(i) In general

Any alien who commits or conspires to commit human trafficking offenses in the United States or outside the United States, or who the consular officer, the Secretary of Homeland Security, the Secretary of State, or the Attorney General knows or has reason to believe is or has been a knowing aider, abettor, assister, conspirator, or colluder with such a trafficker in severe forms of trafficking in persons, as defined in the [sic] section 7102 of Title 22, is inadmissible.

(ii) Beneficiaries of trafficking

Except as provided in clause (iii), any alien who the consular officer or the Attorney General knows or has reason to believe is the spouse, son, or daughter of an alien inadmissible under clause (i), has, within the previous 5 years, obtained any financial or other benefit from the illicit activity of that alien, and knew or reasonably should have known that the financial or other benefit was the product of such illicit activity, is inadmissible.

(iii) Exception for certain sons and daughters

Clause (ii) shall not apply to a son or daughter who was a child at the time he or she received the benefit described in such clause.

(I) Money laundering

Any alien—

(i) who a consular officer or the Attorney General knows, or has reason to believe, has engaged, is engaging, or seeks to enter the United States to engage, in an offense which is described in section 1956 or 1957 of Title 18 (relating to laundering of monetary instruments); or

(ii) who a consular officer or the Attorney General knows is, or has been, a knowing aider, abettor, assister, conspirator, or colluder with others in an offense which is described in such section;

is inadmissible.

(3) Security and related grounds

(A) In general

Any alien who a consular officer or the Attorney General knows, or has reasonable ground to believe, seeks to enter the United States to engage solely, principally, or incidentally in—

(i) any activity (I) to violate any law of the United States relating to espionage or sabotage or (II) to violate or evade any law prohibiting the export from the United States of goods, technology, or sensitive information,

(ii) any other unlawful activity, or

(iii) any activity a purpose of which is the opposition to, or the control or overthrow of, the Government of the United States by force, violence, or other unlawful means,

is inadmissible.

(B) Terrorist activities

(i) In general

Any alien who—

(I) has engaged in a terrorist activity;

(II) a consular officer, the Attorney General, or the Secretary of Homeland Security knows, or has reasonable ground to believe, is engaged in or is likely to engage after entry in any terrorist activity (as defined in clause (iv));

(III) has, under circumstances indicating an intention to cause death or serious bodily harm, incited terrorist activity;

(IV) is a representative (as defined in clause (v)) of—

(aa) a terrorist organization (as defined in clause (vi)); or

(bb) a political, social, or other group that endorses or espouses terrorist activity;

(V) is a member of a terrorist organization described in subclause (I) or (II) of clause (vi);

(VI) is a member of a terrorist organization described in clause (vi)(III), unless the alien can demonstrate by clear and convincing evidence that the alien did not know, and should not reasonably have known, that the organization was a terrorist organization;

(VII) endorses or espouses terrorist activity or persuades others to endorse or espouse terrorist activity or support a terrorist organization;

(VIII) has received military-type training (as defined in section 2339D(c)(1) of title 18, United States Code) from or on behalf of any organization that, at the time the training was received, was a terrorist organization (as defined in clause (vi)); or

(IX) is the spouse or child of an alien who is inadmissible under this subparagraph, if the activity causing the alien to be found inadmissible occurred within the last 5 years,

is inadmissible. An alien who is an officer, official, representative, or spokesman of the Palestine Liberation Organization is considered, for purposes of this Act, to be engaged in a terrorist activity.

(ii) Exception

Subclause (IX) of clause (i) does not apply to a spouse or child—

(I) who did not know or should not reasonably have known of the activity causing the alien to be found inadmissible under this section; or

(II) whom the consular officer or Attorney General has reasonable grounds to believe has renounced the activity causing the alien to be found inadmissible under this section.

(iii) "Terrorist activity" defined

As used in this Act, the term "terrorist activity" means any activity which is unlawful under the laws of the place where it is committed (or which, if it had been committed in the United States, would be unlawful under the laws of the United States or any State) and which involves any of the following:

(I) The highjacking [sic] or sabotage of any conveyance (including an aircraft, vessel, or vehicle).

(II) The seizing or detaining, and threatening to kill, injure, or continue to detain, another individual in order to compel a third person (including a governmental organization) to do or abstain from doing any act as an explicit or implicit condition for the release of the individual seized or detained.

(III) A violent attack upon an internationally protected person (as defined in section 1116(b)(4) of Title 18) or upon the liberty of such a person.

(IV) An assassination.

(V) The use of any—

(a) biological agent, chemical agent, or nuclear weapon or device, or

(b) explosive, firearm, or other weapon or dangerous device (other than for mere personal monetary gain),

with intent to endanger, directly or indirectly, the safety of one or more individuals or to cause substantial damage to property.

(VI) A threat, attempt, or conspiracy to do any of the foregoing.

(iv) Engage in terrorist activity defined

As used in this Act, the term "engage in terrorist activity" means, in an individual capacity or as a member of an organization—

(I) to commit or to incite to commit, under circumstances indicating an intention to cause death or serious bodily injury, a terrorist activity;

(II) to prepare or plan a terrorist activity;

(III) to gather information on potential targets for terrorist activity;

(IV) to solicit funds or other things of value for—

(aa) a terrorist activity;

(bb) a terrorist organization described in clause (vi)(I) or (vi)(II); or

(cc) a terrorist organization described in clause (vi)(III), unless the solicitor can demonstrate by clear and convincing evidence that he did not know, and should not reasonably have known, that the organization was a terrorist organization;

(V) to solicit any individual—

(aa) to engage in conduct otherwise described in this subsection;

(bb) for membership in a terrorist organization described in clause (vi)(I) or (vi)(II); or

(cc) for membership in a terrorist organization described in clause (vi)(III) unless the solicitor can demonstrate by clear and convincing evidence that he did not know, and should not reasonably have known, that the organization was a terrorist organization; or

(VI) to commit an act that the actor knows, or reasonably should know, affords material support, including a safe house, transportation, communications, funds, transfer of funds or other material financial benefit, false documentation or identification, weapons (including chemical, biological, or radiological weapons), explosives, or training—

(aa) for the commission of a terrorist activity;

(bb) to any individual who the actor knows, or reasonably should know, has committed or plans to commit a terrorist activity;

(cc) to a terrorist organization described in subclause (I) or (II) of clause (vi) or to any member of such an organization; or

(dd) to a terrorist organization described in clause (vi)(III), or to any member of such an organization, unless the actor can demonstrate by clear and convincing evidence that the actor did not know, and should not reasonably have known, that the organization was a terrorist organization.

(v) "Representative" defined

As used in this paragraph, the term "representative" includes an officer, official, or spokesman of an organization, and any person who directs, counsels, commands, or induces an organization or its members to engage in terrorist activity.

(vi) Terrorist organization defined

As used in this section, the term "terrorist organization" means an organization—

(I) designated under section 219 [8 U.S.C.A. § 1189];

(II) otherwise designated, upon publication in the Federal Register, by the Secretary of State in consultation with or upon the request of the Attorney General or the Secretary of Homeland Security, as a terrorist organization, after finding that the organization engages in the activities described in subclauses (I) through (VI) of clause (iv); or

(III) that is a group of two or more individuals, whether organized or not, which engages in, or has a subgroup which engages in, the activities described in subclauses (I) through (VI) of clause (iv).

(C) Foreign policy

(i) In general

An alien whose entry or proposed activities in the United States the Secretary of State has reasonable ground to believe would have potentially serious adverse foreign policy consequences for the United States is inadmissible.

(ii) Exception for officials

An alien who is an official of a foreign government or a purported government, or who is a candidate for election to a foreign government office during the period immediately preceding the election for that office, shall not be excludable or subject to restrictions or conditions on entry into the United States under clause (i) solely because of the alien's past, current, or expected beliefs, statements, or associations, if such beliefs, statements, or associations would be lawful within the United States.

(iii) Exception for other aliens

An alien, not described in clause (ii), shall not be excludable or subject to restrictions or conditions on entry into the United States under clause (i) because of the alien's past, current, or expected beliefs, statements, or associations, if such beliefs, statements, or associations would be lawful within the United States, unless the Secretary of State personally determines that the alien's admission would compromise a compelling United States foreign policy interest.

(iv) Notification of determinations

If a determination is made under clause (iii) with respect to an alien, the Secretary of State must notify on a timely basis the chairmen of the Committees on the Judiciary and Foreign Affairs of the House of Representatives and of the Committees on the Judiciary and Foreign Relations of the Senate of the identity of the alien and the reasons for the determination.

(D) Immigrant membership in totalitarian party

(i) In general

Any immigrant who is or has been a member of or affiliated with the Communist or any other totalitarian party (or subdivision or affiliate thereof), domestic or foreign, is inadmissible.

(ii) Exception for involuntary membership

Clause (i) shall not apply to an alien because of membership or affiliation if the alien establishes to the satisfaction of the consular officer when applying for a visa (or to the satisfaction of the Attorney General when applying for admission) that the membership or affiliation is or was involuntary, or is or was solely when under 16 years of age, by operation of law, or for purposes of obtaining employment, food rations, or other essentials of living and whether necessary for such purposes.

(iii) Exception for past membership

Clause (i) shall not apply to an alien because of membership or affiliation if the alien establishes to the satisfaction of the consular officer when applying for a visa (or to the satisfaction of the Attorney General when applying for admission) that—

(I) the membership or affiliation terminated at least—

(a) 2 years before the date of such application, or

(b) 5 years before the date of such application, in the case of an alien whose membership or affiliation was with the party controlling the government of a foreign state that is a totalitarian dictatorship as of such date, and

(II) the alien is not a threat to the security of the United States.

(iv) Exception for close family members

The Attorney General may, in the Attorney General's discretion, waive the application of clause (i) in the case of an immigrant who is the parent, spouse, son, daughter, brother, or sister of a citizen of the United States or a spouse, son, or daughter of an alien lawfully admitted for permanent residence for humanitarian purposes, to assure family unity, or when it is otherwise in the public interest if the immigrant is not a threat to the security of the United States.

(E) Participants in Nazi persecution, genocide, or the commission of any act of torture or extrajudicial killing

(i) Participation in Nazi persecutions

Any alien who, during the period beginning on March 23, 1933, and ending on May 8, 1945, under the direction of, or in association with—

(I) the Nazi government of Germany,

(II) any government in any area occupied by the military forces of the Nazi government of Germany,

(III) any government established with the assistance or cooperation of the Nazi government of Germany, or

(IV) any government which was an ally of the Nazi government of Germany,

ordered, incited, assisted, or otherwise participated in the persecution of any person because of race, religion, national origin, or political opinion is inadmissible.

(ii) Participation in genocide

Any alien who ordered, incited, assisted, or otherwise participated in genocide, as defined in section 1091(a) of Title 18, is inadmissible.

(iii) Commission of acts of torture or extrajudicial killings

Any alien who, outside the United States, has committed, ordered, incited, assisted, or otherwise participated in the commission of—

(I) any act of torture, as defined in section 2340 of Title 18; or

(II) under color of law of any foreign nation, any extrajudicial killing, as defined in section 3(a) of the Torture Victim Protection Act of 1991 (28 U.S.C. 1350 note),

is inadmissible.

(F) Association with terrorist organizations

Any alien who the Secretary of State, after consultation with the Attorney General, or the Attorney General, after consultation with the Secretary of State, determines has been associated with a terrorist organization and intends while in the United States to engage solely, principally, or incidentally in activities that could endanger the welfare, safety, or security of the United States is inadmissible.

(G) Recruitment or use of child soldiers

Any alien who has engaged in the recruitment or use of child soldiers in violation of section 2442 of Title 18, United States Code, is inadmissible.

(4) Public charge

(A) In general

Any alien who, in the opinion of the consular officer at the time of application for a visa, or in the opinion of the Attorney General at the time of application for admission or adjustment of status, is likely at any time to become a public charge is inadmissible.

(B) Factors to be taken into account

(i) In determining whether an alien is inadmissible under this paragraph, the consular officer or the Attorney General shall at a minimum consider the alien's—

(I) age;

(II) health;

(III) family status;

(IV) assets, resources, and financial status; and

(V) education and skills.

(ii) In addition to the factors under clause (i), the consular officer or the Attorney General may also consider any affidavit of support under section 213A [8 U.S.C.A. § 1183a] for purposes of exclusion under this paragraph.

(C) Family-sponsored immigrants

Any alien who seeks admission or adjustment of status under a visa number issued under section 201(b)(2) [8 U.S.C.A. § 1151(b)(2)] or 203(a) [8 U.S.C.A. § 1153(a)] is inadmissible under this paragraph unless—

(i) the alien has obtained—

(I) status as a spouse or a child of a United States citizen pursuant to clause (ii), (iii), or (iv) of section 204(a)(1)(A) [8 U.S.C.A. § 1154(a)(1)(A)] or

(II) classification pursuant to clause (ii) or (iii) of section 204(a)(1)(B) [8 U.S.C.A. § 1154(a)(1)(B)];

(III) classification or status as a VAWA self-petitioner; or

(ii) the person petitioning for the alien's admission (and any additional sponsor required under section 213A(f) [8 U.S.C.A. § 1183a(f)] or any alternative sponsor permitted under paragraph (5)(B) of such section) has executed an affidavit of support described in section 213A [8 U.S.C.A. § 1183a] with respect to such alien.

(D) Certain employment-based immigrants

Any alien who seeks admission or adjustment of status under a visa number issued under section 203(b) [8 U.S.C.A. § 1153(b)] by virtue of a classification petition filed by a relative of the alien (or by an entity in which such relative has a significant ownership interest) is inadmissible under this paragraph unless such relative has executed an affidavit of support described in section 213A [8 U.S.C.A. § 1183a] with respect to such alien.

(E) Special rule for qualified alien victims

Subparagraphs (A), (B), and (C) shall not apply to an alien who—

(i) is a VAWA self-petitioner;

(ii) is an applicant for, or is granted, nonimmigrant status under section 101(a)(15)(U) [8 U.S.C.A. § 1101(a)(15)(U)]; or

(iii) is a qualified alien described in section 431(c) of the Personal Responsibility and Work Opportunity Reconciliation Act of 1996 [8 U.S.C.A. § 1641(c)].

(5) Labor certification and qualifications for certain immigrants

(A) Labor certification

(i) In general

Any alien who seeks to enter the United States for the purpose of performing skilled or unskilled labor is inadmissible, unless the Secretary of Labor has determined and certified to the Secretary of State and the Attorney General that—

(I) there are not sufficient workers who are able, willing, qualified (or equally qualified in the case of an alien described in clause (ii)) and available at the time of application for a visa and admission to the United States and at the place where the alien is to perform such skilled or unskilled labor, and

(II) the employment of such alien will not adversely affect the wages and working conditions of workers in the United States similarly employed.

(ii) Certain aliens subject to special rule

For purposes of clause (i)(I), an alien described in this clause is an alien who—

(I) is a member of the teaching profession, or

(II) has exceptional ability in the sciences or the arts.

(iii) Professional athletes

(I) In general

A certification made under clause (i) with respect to a professional athlete shall remain valid with respect to the athlete after the athlete changes employer, if the new employer is a team in the same sport as the team which employed the athlete when the athlete first applied for the certification.

(II) Definition

For purposes of subclause (I), the term "professional athlete" means an individual who is employed as an athlete by—

(aa) a team that is a member of an association of 6 or more professional sports teams whose total combined revenues exceed $10,000,000 per year, if the association governs the conduct of its members and regulates the contests and exhibitions in which its member teams regularly engage; or

(bb) any minor league team that is affiliated with such an association.

(iv) Long delayed adjustment applicants

A certification made under clause (i) with respect to an individual whose petition is covered by section 204(j) [8 U.S.C.A. § 1154(j)] shall remain valid with respect to a new job accepted by the individual after the individual changes jobs or employers if the new job is in the same or a similar occupational classification as the job for which the certification was issued.

(B) Unqualified physicians

An alien who is a graduate of a medical school not accredited by a body or bodies approved for the purpose by the Secretary of Education (regardless of whether such school of medicine is in the United States) and who is coming to the United States principally to perform services as a member of the medical profession is inadmissible, unless the alien (i) has passed parts I and II of the National Board of Medical Examiners Examination (or an equivalent examination as determined by the Secretary of Health and Human Services) and (ii) is competent in oral and written English. For purposes of the previous sentence, an alien who is a graduate of a medical school shall be considered to have passed parts I and II of the National Board of Medical Examiners if the alien was fully and permanently licensed to practice medicine in a State on January 9, 1978, and was practicing medicine in a State on that date.

(C) Uncertified foreign health-care workers

Subject to subsection (r), any alien who seeks to enter the United States for the purpose of performing labor as a health-care worker, other than a physician, is inadmissible unless the alien presents to the consular officer, or, in the case of an adjustment of status, the Attorney General, a certificate from the Commission on Graduates of Foreign Nursing Schools, or a certificate from an equivalent independent credentialing organization approved by the Attorney General in consultation with the Secretary of Health and Human Services, verifying that—

(i) the alien's education, training, license, and experience—

(I) meet all applicable statutory and regulatory requirements for entry into the United States under the classification specified in the application;

(II) are comparable with that required for an American health-care worker of the same type; and

(III) are authentic and, in the case of a license, unencumbered;

(ii) the alien has the level of competence in oral and written English considered by the Secretary of Health and Human Services, in consultation with the Secretary of Education, to be appropriate for health care work of the kind in which the alien will be engaged, as shown by an appropriate score on one or more nationally recognized, commercially available, standardized assessments of the applicant's ability to speak and write; and

(iii) if a majority of States licensing the profession in which the alien intends to work recognize a test predicting the success on the profession's licensing or certification examination, the alien has passed such a test or has passed such an examination.

For purposes of clause (ii), determination of the standardized tests required and of the minimum scores that are appropriate are within the sole discretion of the Secretary of Health and Human Services and are not subject to further administrative or judicial review.

(D) Application of grounds

The grounds for inadmissibility of aliens under subparagraphs (A) and (B) shall apply to immigrants seeking admission or adjustment of status under paragraph (2) or (3) of section 203(b) [8 U.S.C.A. § 1153(b)].

(6) Illegal entrants and immigration violators

(A) Aliens present without admission or parole

(i) In general

An alien present in the United States without being admitted or paroled, or who arrives in the United States at any time or place other than as designated by the Attorney General, is inadmissible.

(ii) Exception for certain battered women and children

Clause (i) shall not apply to an alien who demonstrates that—

(I) the alien is a VAWA self-petitioner;

(II) **(a)** the alien has been battered or subjected to extreme cruelty by a spouse or parent, or by a member of the spouse's or parent's family residing in the same household as the alien and the spouse or parent consented or acquiesced to such battery or cruelty, or **(b)**

the alien's child has been battered or subjected to extreme cruelty by a spouse or parent of the alien (without the active participation of the alien in the battery or cruelty) or by a member of the spouse's or parent's family residing in the same household as the alien when the spouse or parent consented to or acquiesced in such battery or cruelty and the alien did not actively participate in such battery or cruelty, and

(III) there was a substantial connection between the battery or cruelty described in subclause (I) or (II) and the alien's unlawful entry into the United States.

(B) Failure to attend removal proceeding

Any alien who without reasonable cause fails or refuses to attend or remain in attendance at a proceeding to determine the alien's inadmissibility or deportability and who seeks admission to the United States within 5 years of such alien's subsequent departure or removal is inadmissible.

(C) Misrepresentation

(i) In general

Any alien who, by fraud or willfully misrepresenting a material fact, seeks to procure (or has sought to procure or has procured) a visa, other documentation, or admission into the United States or other benefit provided under this Act is inadmissible.

(ii) Falsely claiming citizenship

(I) In general

Any alien who falsely represents, or has falsely represented, himself or herself to be a citizen of the United States for any purpose or benefit under this Act (including section 274A [8 U.S.C.A. § 1324a]) or any other Federal or State law is inadmissible.

(II) Exception

In the case of an alien making a representation described in subclause (I), if each natural parent of the alien (or, in the case of an adopted alien, each adoptive parent of the alien) is or was a citizen (whether by birth or naturalization), the alien permanently resided in the United States prior to attaining the age of 16, and the alien reasonably believed at the time of making such representation that he or she was a citizen, the alien shall not be considered to be inadmissible under any provision of this subsection based on such representation.

(iii) Waiver authorized

For provision authorizing waiver of clause (i), see subsection (i).

(D) Stowaways

Any alien who is a stowaway is inadmissible.

(E) Smugglers

(i) In general

Any alien who at any time knowingly has encouraged, induced, assisted, abetted, or aided any other alien to enter or to try to enter the United States in violation of law is inadmissible.

(ii) Special rule in the case of family reunification

Clause (i) shall not apply in the case of alien who is an eligible immigrant (as defined in section 301(b)(1) of the Immigration Act of 1990), was physically present in the United States on May 5, 1988, and is seeking admission as an immediate relative or under section 203(a)(2) [8 U.S.C.A. § 1153(a)(2)] (including under section 112 of the Immigration Act of 1990) or benefits under section 301(a) of the Immigration Act of 1990 if the alien, before May 5, 1988, has encouraged, induced, assisted, abetted, or aided only the alien's spouse, parent, son, or daughter (and no other individual) to enter the United States in violation of law.

(iii) Waiver authorized

For provision authorizing waiver of clause (i), see subsection (d)(11).

(F) Subject of civil penalty

(i) In general

An alien who is the subject of a final order for violation of section 274C [8 U.S.C.A. § 1324c] is inadmissible.

(ii) Waiver authorized

For provision authorizing waiver of clause (i), see subsection (d)(12).

(G) Student visa abusers

An alien who obtains the status of a nonimmigrant under section 101(a)(15)(F)(i) [8 U.S.C.A. § 1101(a)(15)(F)(i)] and who violates a term or condition of such status under section 214(*l*) [8 U.S.C.A. § 1184(*l*)]* is inadmissible until the alien has been outside the United States for a continuous period of 5 years after the date of the violation.

* So in original; probably should refer to section 214(m).

(7) Documentation requirements

(A) Immigrants

(i) In general

Except as otherwise specifically provided in this Act, any immigrant at the time of application for admission—

(I) who is not in possession of a valid unexpired immigrant visa, reentry permit, border crossing identification card, or other valid entry document required by this Act, and a valid unexpired passport, or other suitable travel document, or document of identity and nationality if such document is required under the regulations issued by the Attorney General under section 211(a) [8 U.S.C.A. § 1181(a)], or

(II) whose visa has been issued without compliance with the provisions of section 203 [8 U.S.C.A. § 1153],

is inadmissible.

(ii) Waiver authorized

For provision authorizing waiver of clause (i), see subsection (k).

(B) Nonimmigrants

(i) In general

Any nonimmigrant who—

(I) is not in possession of a passport valid for a minimum of six months from the date of the expiration of the initial period of the alien's admission or contemplated initial period of stay authorizing the alien to return to the country from which the alien came or to proceed to and enter some other country during such period, or

(II) is not in possession of a valid nonimmigrant visa or border crossing identification card at the time of application for admission,

is inadmissible.

(ii) General waiver authorized

For provision authorizing waiver of clause (i), see subsection (d)(4).

(iii) Guam and Northern Mariana Islands visa waiver

For provision authorizing waiver of clause (i) in the case of visitors to Guam or the Commonwealth of the Northern Mariana Islands, see subsection (*l*).

(iv) Visa waiver program

For authority to waive the requirement of clause (i) under a program, see section 217 [8 U.S.C.A. § 1187].

(8) Ineligible for citizenship

(A) In general

Any immigrant who is permanently ineligible to citizenship is inadmissible.

(B) Draft evaders

Any person who has departed from or who has remained outside the United States to avoid or evade training or service in the armed forces in time of war or a period declared by the President to be a national emergency is inadmissible, except that this subparagraph shall not apply to an alien who at the time of such departure was a nonimmigrant and who is seeking to reenter the United States as a nonimmigrant.

(9) Aliens previously removed

(A) Certain aliens previously removed

(i) Arriving aliens

Any alien who has been ordered removed under section 235(b)(1) [8 U.S.C.A. § 1225(b)(1)] or at the end of proceedings under section 240 [8 U.S.C.A. § 1229a] initiated upon the alien's arrival in the United States and who again seeks admission within 5 years of the date of such removal (or within 20 years in the case of a second or subsequent removal or at any time in the case of an alien convicted of an aggravated felony) is inadmissible.

(ii) Other aliens

Any alien not described in clause (i) who—

(I) has been ordered removed under section 240 or any other provision of law, or

(II) departed the United States while an order of removal was outstanding,

and who seeks admission within 10 years of the date of such alien's departure or removal (or within 20 years of such date in the case of a second or subsequent removal or at any time in the case of an alien convicted of an aggravated felony) is inadmissible.

(iii) Exception

Clauses (i) and (ii) shall not apply to an alien seeking admission within a period if, prior to the date of the alien's reembarkation at a place outside the United States or attempt to be admitted from foreign contiguous territory, the Attorney General has consented to the alien's reapplying for admission.

(B) Aliens unlawfully present

(i) In general

Any alien (other than an alien lawfully admitted for permanent residence) who—

(I) was unlawfully present in the United States for a period of more than 180 days but less than 1 year, voluntarily departed the United States (whether or not pursuant to section 244(e) [8 U.S.C.A. § 1254(e)])* prior to the commencement of proceedings under section 235(b)(1) [8 U.S.C.A. § 1225(b)(1)]or section 239(a) [8 U.S.C.A. § 1229(a)], and again seeks admission within 3 years of the date of such alien's departure or removal, or

(II) has been unlawfully present in the United States for one year or more, and who again seeks admission within 10 years of the date of such alien's departure or removal from the United States,

is inadmissible.

(ii) Construction of unlawful presence

For purposes of this paragraph, an alien is deemed to be unlawfully present in the United States if the alien is present in the United States after the expiration of the period of stay authorized by the Attorney General or is present in the United States without being admitted or paroled.

(iii) Exceptions

(I) Minors

No period of time in which an alien is under 18 years of age shall be taken into account in determining the period of unlawful presence in the United States under clause (i).

(II) Asylees

No period of time in which an alien has a bona fide application for asylum pending under section 208 [8 U.S.C.A. § 1158] shall be taken into account in determining the period of unlawful presence in the United States under clause (i) unless the alien during such period was employed without authorization in the United States.

* So in original. Probably should refer to the voluntary departure provisions, now in § 240B.

(III) Family unity

No period of time in which the alien is a beneficiary of family unity protection pursuant to section 301 of the Immigration Act of 1990 shall be taken into account in determining the period of unlawful presence in the United States under clause (i).

(IV) Battered women and children

Clause (i) shall not apply to an alien who would be described in paragraph (6)(A)(ii) if "violation of the terms of the alien's nonimmigrant visa" were substituted for "unlawful entry into the United States" in subclause (III) of that paragraph.

(V) Victims of a severe form of trafficking in persons

Clause (i) shall not apply to an alien who demonstrates that the severe form of trafficking (as that term is defined in section 103 of the Trafficking Victims Protection Act of 2000 (22 U.S.C. 7102)) was at least one central reason for the alien's unlawful presence in the United States.

(iv) Tolling for good cause

In the case of an alien who—

(I) has been lawfully admitted or paroled into the United States,

(II) has filed a nonfrivolous application for a change or extension of status before the date of expiration of the period of stay authorized by the Attorney General, and

(III) has not been employed without authorization in the United States before or during the pendency of such application,

the calculation of the period of time specified in clause (i)(I) shall be tolled during the pendency of such application, but not to exceed 120 days.

(v) Waiver

The Attorney General has sole discretion to waive clause (i) in the case of an immigrant who is the spouse or son or daughter of a United States citizen or of an alien lawfully admitted for permanent residence, if it is established to the satisfaction of the Attorney General that the refusal of admission to such immigrant alien would result in extreme hardship to the citizen or lawfully resident spouse or parent of such alien. No court shall have jurisdiction to review a decision or action by the Attorney General regarding a waiver under this clause.

(C) Aliens unlawfully present after previous immigration violations

(i) In general

Any alien who—

(I) has been unlawfully present in the United States for an aggregate period of more than 1 year, or

(II) has been ordered removed under section 235(b)(1) [8 U.S.C.A. § 1225(b)(1)], section 240 [8 U.S.C.A. § 1229a], or any other provision of law,

and who enters or attempts to reenter the United States without being admitted is inadmissible.

(ii) Exception

Clause (i) shall not apply to an alien seeking admission more than 10 years after the date of the alien's last departure from the United States if, prior to the alien's reembarkation at a place outside the United States or attempt to be readmitted from a foreign contiguous territory, the Secretary of Homeland Security has consented to the alien's reapplying for admission.

(iii) Waiver

The Secretary of Homeland Security may waive the application of clause (i) in the case of an alien who is a VAWA self-petitioner if there is a connection between—

(I) the alien's battering or subjection to extreme cruelty; and

(II) the alien's removal, departure from the United States, reentry or reentries into the United States; or attempted reentry into the United States.

(10) Miscellaneous

(A) Practicing polygamists

Any immigrant who is coming to the United States to practice polygamy is inadmissible.

(B) Guardian required to accompany helpless alien

Any alien—

(i) who is accompanying another alien who is inadmissible and who is certified to be helpless from sickness, mental or physical disability, or infancy pursuant to section 232(c) [8 U.S.C.A. § 1222(c)], and

(ii) whose protection or guardianship is determined to be required by the alien described in clause (i),

is inadmissible.

(C) International child abduction

(i) In general

Except as provided in clause (ii), any alien who, after entry of an order by a court in the United States granting custody to a person of a United States citizen child who detains or retains the child, or withholds custody of the child, outside the United States from the person granted custody by that order, is inadmissible until the child is surrendered to the person granted custody by that order.

(ii) Aliens supporting abductors and relatives of abductors

Any alien who—

(I) is known by the Secretary of State to have intentionally assisted an alien in the conduct described in clause (i),

(II) is known by the Secretary of State to be intentionally providing material support or safe haven to an alien described in clause (i), or

(III) is a spouse (other than the spouse who is the parent of the abducted child), child (other than the abducted child), parent, sibling, or agent of an alien described in clause (i), if such person has been designated by the Secretary of State at the Secretary's sole and unreviewable discretion, is inadmissible until the child described in clause (i) is surrendered to the person granted custody by the order described in that clause, and such person and child are permitted to return to the United States or such person's place of residence.

(iii) Exceptions

Clauses (i) and (ii) shall not apply—

(I) to a government official of the United States who is acting within the scope of his or her official duties;

(II) to a government official of any foreign government if the official has been designated by the Secretary of State at the Secretary's sole and unreviewable discretion; or

(III) so long as the child is located in a foreign state that is a party to the Convention on the Civil Aspects of International Child Abduction, done at The Hague on October 25, 1980.

(D) Unlawful voters

(i) In general

Any alien who has voted in violation of any Federal, State, or local constitutional provision, statute, ordinance, or regulation is inadmissible.

(ii) Exception

In the case of an alien who voted in a Federal, State, or local election (including an initiative, recall, or referendum) in violation of a lawful restriction of voting to citizens, if each natural parent of the alien (or, in the case of an adopted alien, each adoptive parent of the alien) is or was a citizen (whether by birth or naturalization), the alien permanently resided in the United States prior to attaining the age of 16, and the alien reasonably believed at the time of such violation that he or she was a citizen, the alien shall not be considered to be inadmissible under any provision of this subsection based on such violation.

(E) Former citizens who renounced citizenship to avoid taxation

Any alien who is a former citizen of the United States who officially renounces United States citizenship and who is determined by the Attorney General to have renounced United States citizenship for the purpose of avoiding taxation by the United States is inadmissible.

(b) Notices of denials

(1) Subject to paragraphs (2) and (3), if an alien's application for a visa, for admission to the United States, or for adjustment of status is denied by an immigration or consular officer because the officer determines the alien to be inadmissible under subsection (a), the officer shall provide the alien with a timely written notice that—

(A) states the determination, and

(B) lists the specific provision or provisions of law under which the alien is inadmissible or ineligible for entry or adjustment of status.

(2) The Secretary of State may waive the requirements of paragraph (1) with respect to a particular alien or any class or classes of inadmissible aliens.

(3) Paragraph (1) does not apply to any alien inadmissible under paragraph (2) or (3) of subsection (a).

(c) Repealed. Pub.L. 104–208, Div. C, Title III, § 304(b), Sept. 30, 1996, 110 Stat. 3009–597.

(d) Temporary admission of nonimmigrants

(1) The Attorney General shall determine whether a ground for inadmissibility exists with respect to a nonimmigrant described in section 101(a)(15)(S) [8 U.S.C.A. § 1101(a)(15)(S)]. The Attorney General, in the Attorney General's discretion, may waive the application of subsection (a) (other than paragraph (3)(E)) in the case of a nonimmigrant described in section 101(a)(15)(S) [8 U.S.C.A. § 1101(a)(15)(S)], if the Attorney General considers it to be in the national interest to do so. Nothing in this section shall be regarded as prohibiting the Immigration and Naturalization Service from instituting removal proceedings against an alien admitted as a nonimmigrant under section 101(a)(15)(S) [8 U.S.C.A. § 1101(a)(15)(S)] for conduct committed after the alien's admission into the United States, or for conduct or a condition that was not disclosed to the Attorney General prior to the alien's admission as a nonimmigrant under section 101(a)(15)(S) [8 U.S.C.A. § 1101(a)(15)(S)].

(2) Repealed. Pub.L. 101–649, Title VI, § 601(d)(2)(A), Nov. 29, 1990, 104 Stat. 5076.

(3)(A) Except as provided in this subsection, an alien **(i)** who is applying for a nonimmigrant visa and is known or believed by the consular officer to be ineligible for such visa under subsection (a) of this section (other than paragraphs (3)(A)(i)(I), (3)(A)(ii), (3)(A)(iii), (3)(C), and clauses (i) and (ii) of paragraph (3)(E) of such subsection), may, after approval by the Attorney General of a recommendation by the Secretary of State or by the consular officer that the alien be admitted temporarily despite his inadmissibility, be granted such a visa and may be admitted into the United States temporarily as a nonimmigrant in the discretion of the Attorney General, or **(ii)** who is inadmissible under subsection (a) of this section (other than paragraphs (3)(A)(i)(I), (3)(A)(ii), (3)(A)(iii), (3)(C), and clauses (i) and (ii) of paragraph (3)(E) of such subsection), but who is in possession of appropriate documents or is granted a waiver thereof and is seeking admission, may be admitted into the United States temporarily as a nonimmigrant in the discretion of the Attorney General. The Attorney General shall prescribe conditions, including exaction of such bonds as may be necessary, to control and regulate the admission and return of inadmissible aliens applying for temporary admission under this paragraph.

(B)(i) The Secretary of State, after consultation with the Attorney General and the Secretary of Homeland Security, or the Secretary of Homeland Security, after consultation with the Secretary of State and the Attorney General, may determine in such Secretary's sole unreviewable discretion that subsection (a)(3)(B) shall not apply with respect to an alien within the scope of that subsection or that subsection (a)(3)(B)(vi)(III) shall not apply to a group within the scope of that subsection, except that no such waiver may be extended to an alien who is within the scope of subsection (a)(3)(B)(i)(II), no such waiver may be extended to an alien who is a member or representative of, has voluntarily and knowingly engaged in or endorsed or espoused or persuaded others to endorse or espouse or support terrorist activity on behalf of, or has voluntarily and knowingly received military-type training from a terrorist organization that is described in subclause (I) or (II) of subsection (a)(3)(B)(vi), and no such waiver may be extended to a group that has engaged terrorist activity against the United States or another democratic country or that has purposefully engaged in a pattern or practice of terrorist activity that is directed at civilians. Such a determination shall neither prejudice the ability of the United States Government to commence criminal or civil proceedings involving a beneficiary of such a determination or any other person, nor create any substantive or procedural right or benefit for a beneficiary of such a determination or any other person. Notwithstanding any other provision of law (statutory or nonstatutory), including section 2241 of title 28, or any other habeas corpus provision, and sections 1361 and 1651 of such title, no court shall have jurisdiction to review such a determination or revocation except in a proceeding for review of a final order of removal pursuant to section 242 [8 U.S.C.A. § 1252], and review shall be limited to the extent provided in section 242(a)(2)(D) [8 U.S.C.A. § 1252(a)(2)(D)]. The Secretary of State may not exercise the discretion provided in this clause with respect to an alien at any time during which the alien is the subject of pending removal proceedings under section 240 [8 U.S.C.A. § 1229a].

(ii) Not later than 90 days after the end of each fiscal year, the Secretary of State and the Secretary of Homeland Security shall each provide to the Committees on the Judiciary of the House of Representatives and of the Senate, the Committee on International Relations of the House of Representatives, the Committee on Foreign Relations of the Senate, and the Committee on Homeland Security of the House of Representatives a report on the aliens to whom such Secretary has applied clause (i). Within one week of applying clause (i) to a group, the Secretary of State or the Secretary of Homeland Security shall provide a report to such Committees.

(4) Either or both of the requirements of paragraph (7)(B)(i) of subsection (a) may be waived by the Attorney General and the Secretary of State acting jointly **(A)** on the basis of unforeseen emergency in individual cases, or **(B)** on the basis of reciprocity with respect to nationals of foreign contiguous territory or of adjacent islands and residents thereof having a common nationality with such nationals, or **(C)** in the case of aliens proceeding in immediate and continuous transit through the United States under contracts authorized in section 233(c) [8 U.S.C.A. § 1223(c)].

(5)(A) The Attorney General may, except as provided in subparagraph (B) or in section 214(f) [8 U.S.C.A. § 1184(f)], in his discretion parole into the United States temporarily under such conditions as he may prescribe only on a case-by-case basis for urgent humanitarian reasons or significant public benefit any alien applying for admission to the United States, but such parole of such alien shall not be regarded as an admission of the alien and when the purposes of such parole shall, in the opinion of the Attorney General, have been served the alien shall forthwith return or be returned to the custody from which he was paroled and thereafter his case shall continue to be dealt with in the same manner as that of any other applicant for admission to the United States.

(B) The Attorney General may not parole into the United States an alien who is a refugee unless the Attorney General determines that compelling reasons in the public interest with respect to that particular alien require that the alien be paroled into the United States rather than be admitted as a refugee under section 207 [8 U.S.C.A. § 1157].

(6) Repealed. Pub.L. 101–649, Title VI, § 601(d)(2)(A), Nov. 29, 1990, 104 Stat. 5076.

(7) The provisions of subsection (a) (other than paragraph (7)) shall be applicable to any alien who shall leave Guam, the Commonwealth of the Northern Mariana Islands, Puerto Rico, or the Virgin Islands of the United States, and who seeks to enter the continental United States or any other place under the jurisdiction of the United States. The Attorney General shall by regulations provide a method and procedure for the temporary admission to the United States of the aliens described in this proviso. Any alien described in this paragraph, who is denied admission to the United States, shall be immediately removed in the manner provided by section 241(c) [8 U.S.C.A. § 1231(c)].

(8) Upon a basis of reciprocity accredited officials of foreign governments, their immediate families, attendants, servants, and personal employees may be admitted in immediate and continuous transit through the United States without regard to the provisions of this section except paragraphs (3)(A), (3)(B), (3)(C), and (7)(B) of subsection (a) of this section.

(9), (10) Repealed. Pub.L. 101–649, Title VI, § 601(d)(2)(A), Nov. 29, 1990, 104 Stat. 5076.

(11) The Attorney General may, in his discretion for humanitarian purposes, to assure family unity, or when it is otherwise in the public interest, waive application of clause (i) of subsection (a)(6)(E) in the case of any alien lawfully admitted for permanent residence who temporarily proceeded abroad voluntarily and not under an order of removal, and who is otherwise admissible to the United States as a returning resident under section 211(b) [8 U.S.C.A. § 1181(b)] and in the case of an alien seeking admission or adjustment of status as an immediate relative or immigrant under section 203(a) [8 U.S.C.A. § 1153(a)] (other than paragraph (4) thereof), if the alien has encouraged, induced, assisted, abetted, or aided only an individual who at the time of such action was the alien's spouse, parent, son, or daughter (and no other individual) to enter the United States in violation of law.

(12) The Attorney General may, in the discretion of the Attorney General for humanitarian purposes or to assure family unity, waive application of clause (i) of subsection (a)(6)(F)—

(A) in the case of an alien lawfully admitted for permanent residence who temporarily proceeded abroad voluntarily and not under an order of deportation or removal and who is otherwise admissible to the United States as a returning resident under section 211(b) [8 U.S.C.A. § 1181(b)], and

(B) in the case of an alien seeking admission or adjustment of status under section 201(b)(2)(A) [8 U.S.C.A. § 1151(b)(2)(A)] or under section 203(a) [8 U.S.C.A. § 1153(a)],

if no previous civil money penalty was imposed against the alien under section 274C [8 U.S.C.A. § 1324c] and the offense was committed solely to assist, aid, or support the alien's spouse or child (and not another individual). No court shall have jurisdiction to review a decision of the Attorney General to grant or deny a waiver under this paragraph.

(13)(A) The Secretary of Homeland Security shall determine whether a ground for inadmissibility exists with respect to a nonimmigrant described in section 101(a)(15)(T) [8 U.S.C.A § 1101(a)(15)(T)], except that the ground for inadmissibility described in subsection (a)(4) of this section shall not apply with respect to such a nonimmigrant.

(B) In addition to any other waiver that may be available under this section, in the case of a nonimmigrant described in section 101(a)(15)(T) [8 U.S.C.A § 1101(a)(15)(T)], if the Secretary of Homeland Security considers it to be in the National interest to do so, the Secretary of Homeland Security, in the Secretary of Homeland Security's discretion, may waive the application of

(i) subsection (a)(1) of this section; and

(ii) any other provision of subsection (a) of this section (excluding paragraphs (3), (4), (10)(C), and (10)(E)) if the activities rendering the alien inadmissible under the provision were caused by, or were incident to, the victimization described in section 101(a)(15)(T)(i)(I) [8 U.S.C.A § 1101(a)(15)(T)(i)(I)].

(14) The Secretary of Homeland Security shall determine whether a ground of inadmissibility exists with respect to a nonimmigrant described in section 101(a)(15)(U) [8 U.S.C.A § 1101(a)(15)(U)]. The Secretary of Homeland Security, in the Secretary of Homeland Security's discretion, may waive the application of subsection (a) (other than paragraph (3)(E)) in the case of a nonimmigrant described in section 101(a)(15)(U) [8 U.S.C.A

§ 1101(a)(15)(U)], if the Secretary of Homeland Security considers it to be in the public or national interest to do so.

(e) Educational visitor status; foreign residence requirement; waiver

No person admitted under section 101(a)(15)(J) [8 U.S.C.A. § 1101(a)(15)(J)] or acquiring such status after admission (i) whose participation in the program for which he came to the United States was financed in whole or in part, directly or indirectly, by an agency of the Government of the United States or by the government of the country of his nationality or his last residence, (ii) who at the time of admission or acquisition of status under section 101(a)(15)(J) [8 U.S.C.A. § 1101(a)(15)(J)] was a national or resident of a country which the Director of the United States Information Agency, pursuant to regulations prescribed by him, had designated as clearly requiring the services of persons engaged in the field of specialized knowledge or skill in which the alien was engaged, or (iii) who came to the United States or acquired such status in order to receive graduate medical education or training, shall be eligible to apply for an immigrant visa, or for permanent residence, or for a nonimmigrant visa under section 101(a)(15)(H) [8 U.S.C.A. § 1101(a)(15)(H)] or section 101(a)(15)(L) [8 U.S.C.A. § 1101(a)(15)(L)] until it is established that such person has resided and been physically present in the country of his nationality or his last residence for an aggregate of at least two years following departure from the United States: *Provided*, That upon the favorable recommendation of the Director, pursuant to the request of an interested United States Government agency (or, in the case of an alien described in clause (iii), pursuant to the request of a State Department of Public Health, or its equivalent), or of the Commissioner of Immigration and Naturalization after he has determined that departure from the United States would impose exceptional hardship upon the alien's spouse or child (if such spouse or child is a citizen of the United States or a lawfully resident alien), or that the alien cannot return to the country of his nationality or last residence because he would be subject to persecution on account of race, religion, or political opinion, the Attorney General may waive the requirement of such two-year foreign residence abroad in the case of any alien whose admission to the United States is found by the Attorney General to be in the public interest except that in the case of a waiver requested by a State Department of Public Health, or its equivalent, or in the case of a waiver requested by an interested United States Government agency on behalf of an alien described in clause (iii), the waiver shall be subject to the requirements of section 214(*l*) [8 U.S.C.A. § 1184(*l*)]: And *provided further*, That, except in the case of an alien described in clause (iii), the Attorney General may, upon the favorable recommendation of the Director, waive such two-year foreign residence requirement in any case in which the foreign country of the alien's nationality or last residence has furnished the Director a statement in writing that it has no objection to such waiver in the case of such alien.

(f) Suspension of entry or imposition of restrictions by President

Whenever the President finds that the entry of any aliens or of any class of aliens into the United States would be detrimental to the interests of the United States, he may by proclamation, and for such period as he shall deem necessary, suspend the entry of all aliens or any class of aliens as immigrants or nonimmigrants, or impose on the entry of aliens any restrictions he may deem to be appropriate. Whenever the Attorney General finds that a commercial airline has failed to comply with regulations of the Attorney General relating to requirements of airlines for the detection of fraudulent documents used by passengers traveling to the United States (including the training of personnel in such detection), the Attorney General may suspend the entry of some or all aliens transported to the United States by such airline.

(g) Bond and conditions for admission of alien excludable on health-related grounds

The Attorney General may waive the application of—

(1) subsection (a)(1)(A)(i) in the case of any alien who—

(A) is the spouse or the unmarried son or daughter, or the minor unmarried lawfully adopted child, of a United States citizen, or of an alien lawfully admitted for permanent residence, or of an alien who has been issued an immigrant visa,

(B) has a son or daughter who is a United States citizen, or an alien lawfully admitted for permanent residence, or an alien who has been issued an immigrant visa; or

(C) is a VAWA self-petitioner,

in accordance with such terms, conditions, and controls, if any, including the giving of bond, as the Attorney General, in the discretion of the Attorney General after consultation with the Secretary of Health and Human Services, may by regulation prescribe;

(2) subsection (a)(1)(A)(ii) in the case of any alien—

(A) who receives vaccination against the vaccine-preventable disease or diseases for which the alien has failed to present documentation of previous vaccination,

(B) for whom a civil surgeon, medical officer, or panel physician (as those terms are defined by section 34.2 of title 42 of the Code of Federal Regulations) certifies, according to such regulations as the Secretary of Health and Human Services may prescribe, that such vaccination would not be medically appropriate, or

(C) under such circumstances as the Attorney General provides by regulation, with respect to whom the requirement of such a vaccination would be contrary to the alien's religious beliefs or moral convictions; or

(3) subsection (a)(1)(A)(iii) in the case of any alien, in accordance with such terms, conditions, and controls, if any, including the giving of bond, as the Attorney General, in the discretion of the Attorney General after consultation with the Secretary of Health and Human Services, may by regulation prescribe.

(h) Waiver of subsection (a)(2)(A)(i)(I), (II), (B), (D), and (E)

The Attorney General may, in his discretion, waive the application of subparagraphs (A)(i)(I), (B), (D), and (E) of subsection (a)(2) and subparagraph (A)(i)(II) of such subsection insofar as it relates to a single offense of simple possession of 30 grams or less of marijuana if—

(1)(A) in the case of any immigrant it is established to the satisfaction of the Attorney General that—

(i) the alien is inadmissible only under subparagraph (D)(i) or (D)(ii) of such subsection or the activities for which the alien is inadmissible occurred more than 15 years before the date of the alien's application for a visa, admission, or adjustment of status,

(ii) the admission to the United States of such alien would not be contrary to the national welfare, safety, or security of the United States, and

(iii) the alien has been rehabilitated; or

(B) in the case of an immigrant who is the spouse, parent, son, or daughter of a citizen of the United States or an alien lawfully admitted for permanent residence if it is established to the satisfaction of the Attorney General that the alien's denial of admission would result in extreme hardship to the United States citizen or lawfully resident spouse, parent, son, or daughter of such alien; or

(C) the alien is a VAWA self-petitioner; and

(2) the Attorney General, in his discretion, and pursuant to such terms, conditions and procedures as he may by regulations prescribe, has consented to the alien's applying or reapplying for a visa, for admission to the United States, or adjustment of status.

No waiver shall be provided under this subsection in the case of an alien who has been convicted of (or who has admitted committing acts that constitute) murder or criminal acts involving torture, or an attempt or conspiracy to commit murder or a criminal act involving torture. No waiver shall be granted under this subsection in the case of an alien who has previously been admitted to the United States as an alien lawfully admitted for permanent residence if either since the date of such admission the alien has been convicted of an aggravated felony or the alien has not lawfully resided continuously in the United States for a period of not less than 7 years immediately preceding the date of initiation of proceedings to remove the alien from the United States. No court shall have jurisdiction to review a decision of the Attorney General to grant or deny a waiver under this subsection.

(i) Admission of immigrant excludable for fraud or willful misrepresentation of material fact

(1) The Attorney General may, in the discretion of the Attorney General, waive the application of clause (i) of subsection (a)(6)(C) of this section in the case of an immigrant who is the spouse, son, or daughter of a United States citizen or of an alien lawfully admitted for permanent residence if it is established to the satisfaction of the Attorney General that the refusal of admission to the United States of such immigrant alien would result in extreme hardship to the citizen or lawfully resident spouse or parent of such an alien or, in the case of a VAWA self-petitioner, the alien demonstrates extreme hardship to the alien or the alien's United States citizen, lawful permanent resident, or qualified alien parent or child.

(2) No court shall have jurisdiction to review a decision or action of the Attorney General regarding a waiver under paragraph (1).

(j) Limitation on immigration of foreign medical graduates

(1) The additional requirements referred to in section 101(a)(15)(J) [8 U.S.C.A. § 1101(a)(15)(J)] for an alien who is coming to the United States under a program under which he will receive graduate medical education or training are as follows:

(A) A school of medicine or of one of the other health professions, which is accredited by a body or bodies approved for the purpose by the Secretary of Education, has agreed in writing to provide the graduate medical education or training under the program for which the alien is coming to the United States or to assume responsibility for arranging for the provision thereof by an appropriate public or nonprofit private institution or agency, except that, in the case of such an agreement by a school of medicine, any one or more of its affiliated hospitals which are to participate in the provision of the graduate medical education or training must join in the agreement.

(B) Before making such agreement, the accredited school has been satisfied that the alien **(i)** is a graduate of a school of medicine which is accredited by a body or bodies approved for the purpose by the Secretary of Education (regardless of whether such school of medicine is in the United States); or **(ii)(I)** has passed parts I and II of the National Board of Medical Examiners Examination (or an equivalent examination as determined by the Secretary of Health and Human Services), **(II)** has competency in oral and written English, **(III)** will be able to adapt to the educational and cultural environment in which he will be receiving his education or training, and **(IV)** has adequate prior education and training to participate satisfactorily in the program for which he is coming to the United States. For the purposes of this subparagraph, an alien who is a graduate of a medical school shall be considered to have passed parts I and II of the National Board of Medical Examiners Examination if the alien was fully and permanently licensed to practice medicine in a State on January 9, 1978, and was practicing medicine in a State on that date.

(C) The alien has made a commitment to return to the country of his nationality or last residence upon completion of the education or training for which he is coming to the United States, and the government of the country of his nationality or last residence has provided a written assurance, satisfactory to the Secretary of Health and Human Services, that there is a need in that country for persons with the skills the alien will acquire in such education or training.

(D) The duration of the alien's participation in the program of graduate medical education or training for which the alien is coming to the United States is limited to the time typically required to complete such program, as determined by the Director of the United States Information Agency at the time of the alien's admission into the United States, based on criteria which are established in coordination with the Secretary of Health and Human Services and which take into consideration the published requirements of the medical specialty board which administers such education or training program; except that—

(i) such duration is further limited to seven years unless the alien has demonstrated to the satisfaction of the Director that the country to which the alien will return at the end of such specialty education or training has an exceptional need for an individual trained in such specialty, and

(ii) the alien may, once and not later than two years after the date the alien is admitted to the United States as an exchange visitor or acquires exchange visitor status, change the alien's designated program of graduate medical education or training if the Director approves the change and if a commitment and written assurance with respect to the alien's new program have been provided in accordance with subparagraph (C).

(E) The alien furnishes the Attorney General each year with an affidavit (in such form as the Attorney General shall prescribe) that attests that the alien **(i)** is in good standing in the program of graduate medical education or training in which the alien is participating, and **(ii)** will return to the country of his nationality or last residence upon completion of the education or training for which he came to the United States.

(2) An alien who is a graduate of a medical school and who is coming to the United States to perform services as a member of the medical profession may not be admitted as a nonimmigrant under section 101(a)(15)(H)(i)(b) [8 U.S.C.A. § 1101(a)(15)(H)(i)(b)] unless—

(A) the alien is coming pursuant to an invitation from a public or nonprofit private educational or research institution or agency in the United States to teach or conduct research, or both, at or for such institution or agency, or

(B)(i) the alien has passed the Federation licensing examination (administered by the Federation of State Medical Boards of the United States) or an equivalent examination as determined by the Secretary of Health and Human Services, and

(ii) (I) has competency in oral and written English or **(II)** is a graduate of a school of medicine which is accredited by a body or bodies approved for the purpose by the Secretary of Education (regardless of whether such school of medicine is in the United States).

(3) The Director of the United States Information Agency annually shall transmit to the Congress a report on aliens who have submitted affidavits described in paragraph (1)(E), and shall include in such report the name and address of each such alien, the medical education or training program in which such alien is participating, and the status of such alien in that program.

(k) Attorney General's discretion to admit otherwise inadmissible aliens who possess immigrant visas

Any alien, inadmissible from the United States under paragraph (5)(A) or (7)(A)(i) of subsection (a), who is in possession of an immigrant visa may, if otherwise admissible, be admitted in the discretion of the Attorney General if the Attorney General is satisfied that inadmissibility was not known to, and could not have been ascertained by the exercise of reasonable diligence by, the immigrant before the time of departure of the vessel or aircraft from the last port outside the United States and outside foreign contiguous territory or, in the case of an immigrant coming from foreign contiguous territory, before the time of the immigrant's application for admission.

(*l*) Guam and Northern Mariana Islands Visa Waiver Program

(1) In general

The requirement of subsection (a)(7)(B)(i) may be waived by the Secretary of Homeland Security, in the case of an alien applying for admission as a nonimmigrant visitor for business or pleasure and solely for entry into and stay in Guam or the Commonwealth of the Northern Mariana Islands for a period not to exceed 45 days, if the Secretary of Homeland Security, after consultation with the Secretary of the Interior, the Secretary of State, the Governor of Guam and the Governor of the Commonwealth of the Northern Mariana Islands, determines that—

(A) an adequate arrival and departure control system has been developed in Guam and the Commonwealth of the Northern Mariana Islands; and

(B) such a waiver does not represent a threat to the welfare, safety, or security of the United States or its territories and commonwealths.

(2) Alien waiver of rights

An alien may not be provided a waiver under this subsection unless the alien has waived any right—

(A) to review or appeal under this Act an immigration officer's determination as to the admissibility of the alien at the port of entry into Guam or the Commonwealth of the Northern Mariana Islands; or

(B) to contest, other than on the basis of an application for withholding of removal under section 241(b)(3) [8 U.S.C.A. § 1231(b)(3)] or under the Convention Against Torture, or an application for asylum if permitted under section 208 [8 U.S.C.A. § 1158], any action for removal of the alien.

(3) Regulations

All necessary regulations to implement this subsection shall be promulgated by the Secretary of Homeland Security, in consultation with the Secretary of the Interior and the Secretary of State, on or before the 180th day after the date of enactment of the Consolidated Natural Resources Act of 2008 [May 8, 2008]. The promulgation of such regulations shall be considered a foreign affairs function for purposes of section 553(a) of title 5, United States Code. At a minimum, such regulations should include, but not necessarily be limited to—

(A) a listing of all countries whose nationals may obtain the waiver also provided by this subsection, except that such regulations shall provide for a listing of any country from which the Commonwealth has received a significant economic benefit from the number of visitors for pleasure within the one-year period preceding the date of enactment of the Consolidated Natural Resources Act of 2008, [May 8, 2008] unless the Secretary of Homeland Security determines that such country's inclusion on such list would represent a threat to the welfare, safety, or security of the United States or its territories; and

(B) any bonding requirements for nationals of some or all of those countries who may present an increased risk of overstays or other potential problems, if different from such requirements otherwise provided by law for nonimmigrant visitors.

(4) Factors

In determining whether to grant or continue providing the waiver under this subsection to nationals of any country, the Secretary of Homeland Security, in consultation with the Secretary of the Interior and the Secretary of State, shall consider all factors that the Secretary deems relevant, including electronic travel authorizations, procedures for reporting lost and stolen passports, repatriation of aliens, rates of refusal for nonimmigrant visitor visas, overstays, exit systems, and information exchange.

(5) Suspension

The Secretary of Homeland Security shall monitor the admission of nonimmigrant visitors to Guam and the Commonwealth of the Northern Mariana Islands under this subsection. If the Secretary determines that such admissions have resulted in an unacceptable number of visitors from a country remaining unlawfully in Guam or the Commonwealth of the Northern Mariana Islands, unlawfully obtaining entry to other parts of the United States, or seeking withholding of removal or asylum, or that visitors from a country pose a risk to law enforcement or security interests of Guam or the Commonwealth of the Northern Mariana Islands or of the United States (including the interest in the enforcement of the immigration laws of the United States), the Secretary shall suspend the admission of nationals of such country under this subsection. The Secretary of Homeland Security may in the Secretary's discretion suspend the Guam and Northern Mariana Islands visa waiver program at any time, on a country-by-country basis, for other good cause.

(6) Addition of countries

The Governor of Guam and the Governor of the Commonwealth of the Northern Mariana Islands may request the Secretary of the Interior and the Secretary of Homeland Security to add a particular country to the list of countries whose nationals may obtain the waiver provided by this subsection, and the Secretary of Homeland Security may grant such request after consultation with the Secretary of the Interior and the Secretary of State, and may promulgate regulations with respect to the inclusion of that country and any special requirements the Secretary of Homeland Security, in the Secretary's sole discretion, may impose prior to allowing nationals of that country to obtain the waiver provided by this subsection.

(m) Requirements for admission of nonimmigrant nurses during five-year period

(1) The qualifications referred to in section 101(a)(15)(H)(i)(c) [8 U.S.C.A. § 1101(a)(15)(H)(i)(c)], with respect to an alien who is coming to the United States to perform nursing services for a facility, are that the alien—

(A) has obtained a full and unrestricted license to practice professional nursing in the country where the alien obtained nursing education or has received nursing education in the United States;

(B) has passed an appropriate examination (recognized in regulations promulgated in consultation with the Secretary of Health and Human Services) or has a full and unrestricted license under State law to practice professional nursing in the State of intended employment; and

(C) is fully qualified and eligible under the laws (including such temporary or interim licensing requirements which authorize the nurse to be employed) governing the place of intended employment to engage in the practice of professional nursing as a registered nurse immediately upon admission to the United States and is authorized under such laws to be employed by the facility.

(2)(A) The attestation referred to in section 101(a)(15)(H)(i)(c) [8 U.S.C.A. § 1101(a)(15)(H)(i)(c)], with respect to a facility for which an alien will perform services, is an attestation as to the following:

(i) The facility meets all the requirements of paragraph (6).

(ii) The employment of the alien will not adversely affect the wages and working conditions of registered nurses similarly employed.

(iii) The alien employed by the facility will be paid the wage rate for registered nurses similarly employed by the facility.

(iv) The facility has taken and is taking timely and significant steps designed to recruit and retain sufficient registered nurses who are United States citizens or immigrants who are authorized to perform nursing services, in order to remove as quickly as reasonably possible the dependence of the facility on nonimmigrant registered nurses.

(v) There is not a strike or lockout in the course of a labor dispute, the facility did not lay off and will not lay off a registered nurse employed by the facility within the period beginning 90 days before and ending 90 days after the date of filing of any visa petition, and the employment of such an alien is not intended or designed to influence an election for a bargaining representative for registered nurses of the facility.

(vi) At the time of the filing of the petition for registered nurses under section 101(a)(15)(H)(i)(c) [8 U.S.C.A. § 1101(a)(15)(H)(i)(c)], notice of the filing has been provided by the facility to the bargaining representative of the registered nurses at the facility or, where there is no such bargaining representative, notice of the filing has been provided to the registered nurses employed at the facility through posting in conspicuous locations.

(vii) The facility will not, at any time, employ a number of aliens issued visas or otherwise provided nonimmigrant status under section 101(a)(15)(H)(i)(c) [8 U.S.C.A. § 1101(a)(15)(H)(i)(c)] that exceeds 33 percent of the total number of registered nurses employed by the facility.

(viii) The facility will not, with respect to any alien issued a visa or otherwise provided nonimmigrant status under section 101(a)(15)(H)(i)(c) [8 U.S.C.A. § 1101(a)(15)(H)(i)(c)]—

(I) authorize the alien to perform nursing services at any worksite other than a worksite controlled by the facility; or

(II) transfer the place of employment of the alien from one worksite to another.

Nothing in clause (iv) shall be construed as requiring a facility to have taken significant steps described in such clause before the date of the enactment of the Nursing Relief for Disadvantaged Areas Act of 1999. A copy of the attestation shall be provided, within 30 days of the date of filing, to registered nurses employed at the facility on the date of filing.

(B) For purposes of subparagraph (A)(iv), each of the following shall be considered a significant step reasonably designed to recruit and retain registered nurses:

(i) Operating a training program for registered nurses at the facility or financing (or providing participation in) a training program for registered nurses elsewhere.

(ii) Providing career development programs and other methods of facilitating health care workers to become registered nurses.

(iii) Paying registered nurses wages at a rate higher than currently being paid to registered nurses similarly employed in the geographic area.

(iv) Providing reasonable opportunities for meaningful salary advancement by registered nurses.

The steps described in this subparagraph shall not be considered to be an exclusive list of the significant steps that may be taken to meet the conditions of subparagraph (A)(iv). Nothing in this subparagraph shall require a facility to take more than one step if the facility can demonstrate that taking a second step is not reasonable.

(C) Subject to subparagraph (E), an attestation under subparagraph (A)—

(i) shall expire on the date that is the later of—

(I) the end of the one-year period beginning on the date of its filing with the Secretary of Labor; or

(II) the end of the period of admission under section 101(a)(15)(H)(i)(c) [8 U.S.C.A. § 1101(a)(15)(H)(i)(c)] of the last alien with respect to whose admission it was applied (in accordance with clause (ii)); and

(ii) shall apply to petitions filed during the one-year period beginning on the date of its filing with the Secretary of Labor if the facility states in each such petition that it continues to comply with the conditions in the attestation.

(D) A facility may meet the requirements under this paragraph with respect to more than one registered nurse in a single petition.

(E)(i) The Secretary of Labor shall compile and make available for public examination in a timely manner in Washington, D.C., a list identifying facilities which have filed petitions for nonimmigrants under section 101(a)(15)(H)(i)(c) [8 U.S.C.A. § 1101(a)(15)(H)(i)(c)] and, for each such facility, a copy of the facility's attestation under subparagraph (A) (and accompanying documentation) and each such petition filed by the facility.

(ii) The Secretary of Labor shall establish a process, including reasonable time limits, for the receipt, investigation, and disposition of complaints respecting a facility's failure to meet conditions attested to or a facility's misrepresentation of a material fact in an attestation. Complaints may be filed by any aggrieved person or organization (including bargaining representatives, associations deemed appropriate by the Secretary, and other aggrieved parties as determined under regulations of the Secretary). The Secretary shall conduct an investigation under this clause if there is reasonable cause to believe that a facility fails to meet conditions attested to. Subject to the time limits established under this clause, this subparagraph shall apply regardless of whether an attestation is expired or unexpired at the time a complaint is filed.

(iii) Under such process, the Secretary shall provide, within 180 days after the date such a complaint is filed, for a determination as to whether or not a basis exists to make a finding described in clause (iv). If the Secretary determines that such a basis exists, the Secretary shall provide for notice of such determination to the interested parties and an opportunity for a hearing on the complaint within 60 days of the date of the determination.

(iv) If the Secretary of Labor finds, after notice and opportunity for a hearing, that a facility (for which an attestation is made) has failed to meet a condition attested to or that there was a misrepresentation of material fact in the attestation, the Secretary shall notify the Attorney General of such finding and may, in addition, impose such other administrative remedies (including civil monetary penalties in an amount not to exceed $1,000 per nurse per violation, with the total penalty not to exceed $10,000 per violation) as the Secretary determines to be appropriate. Upon receipt of such notice, the Attorney General shall not approve petitions filed with respect to a facility during a period of at least one year for nurses to be employed by the facility.

(v) In addition to the sanctions provided for under clause (iv), if the Secretary of Labor finds, after notice and an opportunity for a hearing, that a facility has violated the condition attested to under subparagraph (A)(iii) (relating to payment of registered nurses at the prevailing wage rate), the Secretary shall order the facility to provide for payment of such amounts of back pay as may be required to comply with such condition.

(F)(i) The Secretary of Labor shall impose on a facility filing an attestation under subparagraph (A) a filing fee, in an amount prescribed by the Secretary based on the costs of carrying out the Secretary's duties under this subsection, but not exceeding $250.

(ii) Fees collected under this subparagraph shall be deposited in a fund established for this purpose in the Treasury of the United States.

(iii) The collected fees in the fund shall be available to the Secretary of Labor, to the extent and in such amounts as may be provided in appropriations Acts, to cover the costs described in clause (i), in addition to any other funds that are available to the Secretary to cover such costs.

(3) The period of admission of an alien under section 101(a)(15)(H)(i)(c) [8 U.S.C.A. § 1101(a)(15)(H)(i)(c)] shall be 3 years.

(4) The total number of nonimmigrant visas issued pursuant to petitions granted under section 101(a)(15)(H)(i)(c) [8 U.S.C.A. § 1101(a)(15)(H)(i)(c)] in each fiscal year shall not exceed 500. The number of such visas issued for employment in each State in each fiscal year shall not exceed the following:

(A) For States with populations of less than 9,000,000, based upon the 1990 decennial census of population, 25 visas.

(B) For States with populations of 9,000,000 or more, based upon the 1990 decennial census of population, 50 visas.

(C) If the total number of visas available under this paragraph for a fiscal year quarter exceeds the number of qualified nonimmigrants who may be issued such visas during those quarters, the visas made available under this paragraph shall be issued without regard to the numerical limitation under subparagraph (A) or (B) of this paragraph during the last fiscal year quarter.

(5) A facility that has filed a petition under section 101(a)(15)(H)(i)(c) [8 U.S.C.A. § 1101(a)(15)(H)(i)(c)] to employ a nonimmigrant to perform nursing services for the facility—

(A) shall provide the nonimmigrant a wage rate and working conditions commensurate with those of nurses similarly employed by the facility;

(B) shall require the nonimmigrant to work hours commensurate with those of nurses similarly employed by the facility; and

(C) shall not interfere with the right of the nonimmigrant to join or organize a union.

(6) For purposes of this subsection and section 101(a)(15)(H)(i)(c) [8 U.S.C.A. § 1101(a)(15)(H)(i)(c)], the term "facility" means a subsection (d) hospital (as defined in section 1886(d)(1)(B) of the Social Security Act (42 U.S.C. 1395ww (d)(1)(B))) that meets the following requirements:

(A) As of March 31, 1997, the hospital was located in a health professional shortage area (as defined in section 332 of the Public Health Service Act (42 U.S.C. 254e)).

(B) Based on its settled cost report filed under title XVIII of the Social Security Act for its cost reporting period beginning during fiscal year 1994—

(i) the hospital has not less than 190 licensed acute care beds;

(ii) the number of the hospital's inpatient days for such period which were made up of patients who (for such days) were entitled to benefits under part A of such title is not less than 35 percent of the total number of such hospital's acute care inpatient days for such period; and

(iii) the number of the hospital's inpatient days for such period which were made up of patients who (for such days) were eligible for medical assistance under a State plan approved under title XIX of the Social Security Act, is not less than 28 percent of the total number of such hospital's acute care inpatient days for such period.

(7) For purposes of paragraph (2)(A)(v), the term "lay off", with respect to a worker—

(A) means to cause the worker's loss of employment, other than through a discharge for inadequate performance, violation of workplace rules, cause, voluntary departure, voluntary retirement, or the expiration of a grant or contract; but

(B) does not include any situation in which the worker is offered, as an alternative to such loss of employment, a similar employment opportunity with the same employer at equivalent or higher compensation and benefits than the position from which the employee was discharged, regardless of whether or not the employee accepts the offer.

Nothing in this paragraph is intended to limit an employee's or an employer's rights under a collective bargaining agreement or other employment contract.

(n) Labor condition application

(1) No alien may be admitted or provided status as an H–1B nonimmigrant in an occupational classification unless the employer has filed with the Secretary of Labor an application stating the following:

(A) The employer—

(i) is offering and will offer during the period of authorized employment to aliens admitted or provided status as a nonimmigrant described in section 101(a)(15)(H)(i)(b) [8 U.S.C.A. § 1101(a)(15)(H)(i)(b)] wages that are at least—

(I) the actual wage level paid by the employer to all other individuals with similar experience and qualifications for the specific employment in question, or

(II) the prevailing wage level for the occupational classification in the area of employment,

whichever is greater, based on the best information available as of the time of filing the application, and

(ii) will provide working conditions for such a nonimmigrant that will not adversely affect the working conditions of workers similarly employed.

(B) There is not a strike or lockout in the course of a labor dispute in the occupational classification at the place of employment.

(C) The employer, at the time of filing the application—

(i) has provided notice of the filing under this paragraph to the bargaining representative (if any) of the employer's employees in the occupational classification and area for which aliens are sought, or

(ii) if there is no such bargaining representative, has provided notice of filing in the occupational classification through such methods as physical posting in conspicuous locations at the place of employment or electronic notification to employees in the occupational classification for which H–1B nonimmigrants are sought.

(D) The application shall contain a specification of the number of workers sought, the occupational classification in which the workers will be employed, and wage rate and conditions under which they will be employed.

(E)(i) In the case of an application described in clause (ii), the employer did not displace and will not displace a United States worker (as defined in paragraph (4)) employed by the employer within the period beginning 90 days before and ending 90 days after the date of filing of any visa petition supported by the application.

(ii) An application described in this clause is an application filed on or after the date final regulations are first promulgated to carry out this subparagraph, and before, by an H–1B-dependent employer (as defined in paragraph (3)) or by an employer that has been found, on or after October 21, 1998, under paragraph (2)(C) or (5) to have committed a willful failure or misrepresentation during the 5–year period preceding the filing of the application. An application is not described in this clause if the only H–1B nonimmigrants sought in the application are exempt H–1B nonimmigrants.

(F) In the case of an application described in subparagraph (E)(ii), the employer will not place the nonimmigrant with another employer (regardless of whether or not such other employer is an H–1B-dependent employer) where—

(i) the nonimmigrant performs duties in whole or in part at one or more worksites owned, operated, or controlled by such other employer; and

(ii) there are indicia of an employment relationship between the nonimmigrant and such other employer;

unless the employer has inquired of the other employer as to whether, and has no knowledge that, within the period beginning 90 days before and ending 90 days after the date of the placement of the nonimmigrant with the other employer, the other employer has displaced or intends to displace a United States worker employed by the other employer.

(G)(i) In the case of an application described in subparagraph (E)(ii), subject to clause (ii), the employer, prior to filing the application—

(I) has taken good faith steps to recruit, in the United States using procedures that meet industry wide standards and offering compensation that is at least as great as that required to be offered to H–1B nonimmigrants under subparagraph (A), United States workers for the job for which the nonimmigrant or nonimmigrants is or are sought; and

(II) has offered the job to any United States worker who applies and is equally or better qualified for the job for which the nonimmigrant or nonimmigrants is or are sought.

(ii) The conditions described in clause (i) shall not apply to an application filed with respect to the employment of an H–1B nonimmigrant who is described in subparagraph (A), (B), or (C) of section 203(b)(1).

The employer shall make available for public examination, within one working day after the date on which an application under this paragraph is filed, at the employer's principal place of business or worksite, a copy of each such application (and such accompanying documents as are necessary). The Secretary shall compile, on a current basis, a list (by employer and by occupational classification) of the applications filed under this subsection. Such list shall include the wage rate, number of aliens sought, period of intended employment, and date of need. The Secretary shall make such list available for public examination in Washington, D.C. The Secretary of Labor shall review such an application only for completeness and obvious inaccuracies. Unless the Secretary finds that the application is incomplete or obviously inaccurate, the Secretary shall provide the certification described in section 101(a)(15)(H)(i)(b) [8 U.S.C.A. § 1101(a)(15)(H)(i)(b)] within 7 days of the date of the filing of the application. The application form shall include a clear statement explaining the liability under subparagraph (F) of a place employer if the other employer described in such subparagraph displaces a United States worker as described in such subparagraph. Nothing in subparagraph (G) shall be construed to prohibit an employer from using legitimate selection criteria relevant to the job that are normal or customary to the type of job involved, so long as such criteria are not applied in a discriminatory manner.

(2)(A) Subject to paragraph (5)(A), the Secretary shall establish a process for the receipt, investigation, and disposition of complaints respecting a petitioner's failure to meet a condition specified in an application submitted under paragraph (1) or a petitioner's misrepresentation of material facts in such an application. Complaints may be filed by any aggrieved person or organization (including bargaining representatives). No investigation or hearing shall be conducted on a complaint concerning such a failure or misrepresentation unless the complaint was filed not later than 12 months after the date of the failure or misrepresentation, respectively. The Secretary shall conduct an investigation under this paragraph if there is reasonable cause to believe that such a failure or misrepresentation has occurred.

(B) Under such process, the Secretary shall provide, within 30 days after the date such a complaint is filed, for a determination as to whether or not a reasonable basis exists to make a finding described in subparagraph (C). If the Secretary determines that such a reasonable basis exists, the Secretary shall provide for notice of such determination to the interested parties and an opportunity for a hearing on the complaint, in accordance with section 556 of Title 5, within 60 days after the date of the determination. If such a hearing is requested, the Secretary shall make a finding concerning the matter by not later than 60 days after the date of the hearing. In the case of similar complaints respecting the same applicant, the Secretary may consolidate the hearings under this subparagraph on such complaints.

(C)(i) If the Secretary finds, after notice and opportunity for a hearing, a failure to meet a condition of paragraph (1)(b), (1)(e), or (1)(f), a substantial failure to meet a condition of paragraph (1)(c), (1)(d), or (1)(g)(i)(i), or a misrepresentation of material fact in an application—

(I) the Secretary shall notify the Attorney General of such finding and may, in addition, impose such other administrative remedies (including civil monetary penalties in an amount not to exceed $1,000 per violation) as the Secretary determines to be appropriate; and

(II) the Attorney General shall not approve petitions filed with respect to that employer under section 204 [8 U.S.C.A. § 1154] or 214(c) [8 U.S.C.A. § 1184(c)] during a period of at least 1 year for aliens to be employed by the employer.

(ii) If the Secretary finds, after notice and opportunity for a hearing, a willful failure to meet a condition of paragraph (1), a willful misrepresentation of material fact in an application, or a violation of clause (iv)—

(I) the Secretary shall notify the Attorney General of such finding and may, in addition, impose such other administrative remedies (including civil monetary penalties in an amount not to exceed $5,000 per violation) as the Secretary determines to be appropriate; and

(II) the Attorney General shall not approve petitions filed with respect to that employer under section 204 [8 U.S.C.A. § 1154] or 214(c) [8 U.S.C.A. § 1184(c)] during a period of at least 2 years for aliens to be employed by the employer.

(iii) If the Secretary finds, after notice and opportunity for a hearing, a willful failure to meet a condition of paragraph (1) or a willful misrepresentation of material fact in an application, in the course of which failure or misrepresentation the employer displaced a United States worker employed by the employer within the period beginning 90 days before and ending 90 days after the date of filing of any visa petition supported by the application—

(I) the Secretary shall notify the Attorney General of such finding and may, in addition, impose such other administrative remedies (including civil monetary penalties in an amount not to exceed $35,000 per violation) as the Secretary determines to be appropriate; and

(II) the Attorney General shall not approve petitions filed with respect to that employer under section 204 [8 U.S.C.A. § 1154] or 214(c) [8 U.S.C.A. § 1184(c)] during a period of at least 3 years for aliens to be employed by the employer.

(iv) It is a violation of this clause for an employer who has filed an application under this subsection to intimidate, threaten, restrain, coerce, blacklist, discharge, or in any other manner discriminate against an employee (which term, for purposes of this clause, includes a former employee and an applicant for employment) because the employee has disclosed information to the employer, or to any other person, that the employee reasonably believes evidences a violation of this subsection, or any rule or regulation pertaining to this subsection, or because the employee cooperates or seeks to cooperate in an investigation or other proceeding concerning the employer's compliance with the requirements of this subsection or any rule or regulation pertaining to this subsection.

(v) The Secretary of Labor and the Attorney General shall devise a process under which an H–1B nonimmigrant who files a complaint regarding a violation of clause (iv) and is otherwise eligible to remain and work in the United States may be allowed to seek other appropriate employment in the United States for a period not to exceed the maximum period of stay authorized for such nonimmigrant classification.

(vi)(I) It is a violation of this clause for an employer who has filed an application under this subsection to require an H–1B nonimmigrant to pay a penalty for ceasing employment with the employer prior to a date agreed to by the nonimmigrant and the employer. The Secretary shall determine whether a required payment is a penalty (and not liquidated damages) pursuant to relevant State law.

(II) It is a violation of this clause for an employer who has filed an application under this subsection to require an alien who is the subject of a petition filed under section 214(c)(1) [8 U.S.C.A. § 1184(c)(1)], for which a fee is imposed under section 214(c)(9) [8 U.S.C.A. § 1184(c)(9)], to reimburse, or otherwise compensate, the employer for part or all of the cost of such fee. It is a violation of this clause for such an employer otherwise to accept such reimbursement or compensation from such an alien.

(III) If the Secretary finds, after notice and opportunity for a hearing, that an employer has committed a violation of this clause, the Secretary may impose a civil monetary penalty of $1,000 for each such violation and issue an administrative order requiring the return to the nonimmigrant of any amount paid in violation of this clause, or, if the nonimmigrant cannot be located, requiring payment of any such amount to the general fund of the Treasury.

(vii)(I) It is a failure to meet a condition of paragraph (1)(A) for an employer, who has filed an application under this subsection and who places an H–1B nonimmigrant designated as a full-time employee on the petition filed under section 214(c)(1) [8 U.S.C.A. § 1184(c)(1)] by the employer with respect to the nonimmigrant, after the nonimmigrant has entered into employment with the employer, in nonproductive status due to a decision by the employer (based on factors such as lack of work), or due to the nonimmigrant's lack of a permit or license, to fail to pay the nonimmigrant full-time wages in accordance with paragraph (1)(A) for all such nonproductive time.

(II) It is a failure to meet a condition of paragraph (1)(A) for an employer, who has filed an application under this subsection and who places an H–1B nonimmigrant designated as a part-time employee on the petition filed under section 214(c)(1) [8 U.S.C.A. § 1184(c)(1)] by the employer with respect to the nonimmigrant, after the nonimmigrant has entered into employment with the employer, in nonproductive status under circumstances described in subclause (I), to fail to pay such a nonimmigrant for such hours as are designated on such petition consistent with the rate of pay identified on such petition.

(III) In the case of an H–1B nonimmigrant who has not yet entered into employment with an employer who has had approved an application under this subsection, and a petition under section 214(c)(1) [8 U.S.C.A. § 1184(c)(1)], with respect to the nonimmigrant, the provisions of subclauses (I) and (II) shall apply to the employer beginning 30 days after the date the nonimmigrant first is admitted into the United States pursuant to the petition, or 60 days after the date the nonimmigrant becomes eligible to work for the employer (in the case of a nonimmigrant who is present in the United States on the date of the approval of the petition).

(IV) This clause does not apply to a failure to pay wages to an H–1B nonimmigrant for nonproductive time due to non-work-related factors, such as the voluntary request of the nonimmigrant for an absence or circumstances rendering the nonimmigrant unable to work.

(V) This clause shall not be construed as prohibiting an employer that is a school or other educational institution from applying to an H–1B nonimmigrant an established salary practice of the employer, under which the employer pays to H–1B nonimmigrants and United States workers in the same occupational classification an annual salary in disbursements over fewer than 12 months, if—

(aa) the nonimmigrant agrees to the compressed annual salary payments prior to the commencement of the employment; and

(bb) the application of the salary practice to the nonimmigrant does not otherwise cause the nonimmigrant to violate any condition of the nonimmigrant's authorization under this Act to remain in the United States.

(VI) This clause shall not be construed as superseding clause (viii).

(viii) It is a failure to meet a condition of paragraph (1)(A) for an employer who has filed an application under this subsection to fail to offer to an H–1B nonimmigrant, during the nonimmigrant's period of authorized employment, benefits and eligibility for benefits (including the opportunity to participate in health, life, disability, and other insurance plans; the opportunity to participate in retirement and savings plans; and cash bonuses and non-cash compensation, such as stock options (whether or not based on performance)) on the same basis, and in accordance with the same criteria, as the employer offers to United States workers.

(D) If the Secretary finds, after notice and opportunity for a hearing, that an employer has not paid wages at the wage level specified under the application and required under paragraph (1), the Secretary shall order the employer to provide for payment of such amounts of back pay as may be required to comply with the requirements of paragraph (1), whether or not a penalty under subparagraph (C) has been imposed.

(E) If an H–1B-dependent employer places a nonexempt H–1B nonimmigrant with another employer as provided under paragraph (1)(f) and the other employer has displaced or displaces a United States worker employed by such other employer during the period described in such paragraph, such displacement shall be considered for purposes of this paragraph a failure, by the placing employer, to meet a condition specified in an application submitted under paragraph (1); except that the attorney general may impose a sanction described in subclause (ii) of subparagraph (C)(i), (C)(ii), or (C)(iii) only if the Secretary of labor found that such placing employer

(i) knew or had reason to know of such displacement at the time of the placement of the nonimmigrant with the other employer; or

(ii) has been subject to a sanction under this subparagraph based upon a previous placement of an H–1B nonimmigrant with the same other employer.

(F) The Secretary may, on a case-by-case basis, subject an employer to random investigations for a period of up to 5 years, beginning on the date (on or after October 21, 1998) on which the employer is found by the Secretary to have committed a willful failure to meet a condition of paragraph (1) (or has been found under paragraph (5) to have committed a willful failure to meet the condition of paragraph (1)(G)(i)(II)) or to have made a willful misrepresentation of material fact in an application. The preceding sentence shall apply to an employer regardless of whether or not the employer is an H–1B-dependent employer. The authority of the Secretary under this subparagraph shall not be construed to be subject to, or limited by, the requirements of subparagraph (A).

(G)(i)* If the Secretary receives specific credible information from a source, who is likely to have knowledge of an employer's practices or employment conditions, or an employer's compliance with the employer's labor condition application under paragraph (1), and whose identity is known to the Secretary, and such information provides reasonable cause to believe that the employer has committed a willful failure to meet a condition of paragraph (1)(A), (1)(B), (1)(E), (1)(F), or (1)(G)(i)(I), has engaged in a pattern or practice of failures to meet such a condition, or has committed a substantial failure to meet such a condition that affects multiple employees, the Secretary may conduct a 30–day investigation into the alleged failure or failures. The Secretary (or the Acting Secretary in the case of the Secretary's absence or disability) shall personally certify that the requirements for conducting such an investigation have been met and shall approve commencement of the investigation. The Secretary may withhold the identity of the source from the employer, and the source's identity shall not be subject to disclosure under section 552 of Title 5.

(ii) The Secretary shall establish a procedure for any person, desiring to provide to the Secretary information described in clause (i) that may be used, in whole or in part, as the basis for commencement of an investigation described in such clause, to provide the information in writing on a form developed and provided by the Secretary and completed by or on behalf of the person. The person may not be an officer or employee of the Department of Labor, unless the information satisfies the requirement of clause (iii)(II) (although an officer or employee of the Department of Labor may complete the form on behalf of the person).

(iii) Any investigation initiated or approved by the Secretary under clause (i) shall be based on information that satisfies the requirements of such clause and that (I) originates from a source other than an officer or employee of the Department of Labor, or (II) was lawfully obtained by the Secretary of Labor in the course of lawfully conducting another Department of Labor investigation under this chapter or any other Act.

(iv) The receipt by the Secretary of information submitted by an employer to the Attorney General or the Secretary for purposes of securing the employment of an H–1B nonimmigrant shall not be considered a receipt of information for purposes of clause (i).

* So in original. Two subpars. (G) have been enacted.

(v) No investigation described in clause (i) (or hearing described in clause (vii)) may be conducted with respect to information about a failure to meet a condition described in clause (i), unless the Secretary receives the information not later than 12 months after the date of the alleged failure.

(vi) The Secretary shall provide notice to an employer with respect to whom the Secretary has received information described in clause (i), prior to the commencement of an investigation under such clause, of the receipt of the information and of the potential for an investigation. The notice shall be provided in such a manner, and shall contain sufficient detail, to permit the employer to respond to the allegations before an investigation is commenced. The Secretary is not required to comply with this clause if the Secretary determines that to do so would interfere with an effort by the Secretary to secure compliance by the employer with the requirements of this subsection. There shall be no judicial review of a determination by the Secretary under this clause.

(vii) If the Secretary determines under this subparagraph that a reasonable basis exists to make a finding that a failure described in clause (i) has occurred, the Secretary shall provide for notice of such determination to the interested parties and an opportunity for a hearing, in accordance with section 556 of Title 5, within 60 days after the date of the determination. If such a hearing is requested, the Secretary shall make a finding concerning the matter by not later than 60 days after the date of the hearing.

(G)(i)* The Secretary of Labor may initiate an investigation of any employer that employs nonimmigrants described in section 101(a)(15)(H)(i)(b) [8 U.S.C.A. § 1101(a)(15)(H)(i)(b)] if the Secretary of Labor has reasonable cause to believe that the employer is not in compliance with this subsection. In the case of an investigation under this clause, the Secretary of Labor (or the acting Secretary in the case of the absence of disability of the Secretary of Labor) shall personally certify that reasonable cause exists and shall approve commencement of the investigation. The investigation may be initiated for reasons other than completeness and obvious inaccuracies by the employer in complying with this subsection.

(ii) If the Secretary of Labor receives specific credible information from a source who is likely to have knowledge of an employer's practices or employment conditions, or an employer's compliance with the employer's labor condition application under paragraph (1), and whose identity is known to the Secretary of Labor, and such information provides reasonable cause to believe that the employer has committed a willful failure to meet a condition of paragraph (1)(A), (1)(B), (1)(C), (1)(E), (1)(F), or (1)(G)(i)(I), has engaged in a pattern or practice of failures to meet such a condition, or has

* So in original. Two subpars. (G) have been enacted.

committed a substantial failure to meet such a condition that affects multiple employees, the Secretary of Labor may conduct an investigation into the alleged failure or failures. The Secretary of Labor may withhold the identity of the source from the employer, and the source's identity shall not be subject to disclosure under section 552 of Title 5.

(iii) The Secretary of Labor shall establish a procedure for any person desiring to provide to the Secretary of Labor information described in clause (ii) that may be used, in whole or in part, as the basis for the commencement of an investigation described in such clause, to provide the information in writing on a form developed and provided by the Secretary of Labor and completed by or on behalf of the person. The person may not be an officer or employee of the Department of Labor, unless the information satisfies the requirement of clause (iv)(II) (although an officer or employee of the Department of Labor may complete the form on behalf of the person).

(iv) Any investigation initiated or approved by the Secretary of labor under clause (ii) shall be based on information that satisfies the requirements of such clause and that

(I) originates from a source other than an officer or employee of the Department of Labor; or

(II) was lawfully obtained by the Secretary of Labor in the course of lawfully conducting another Department of Labor investigation under this Act of* any other Act.

(v) The receipt by the Secretary of Labor of information submitted by an employer to the Attorney General or the Secretary of Labor for purposes of securing the employment of a nonimmigrant described in section 101(a)(15)(H)(i)(b) [8 U.S.C.A. § 1101(a)(15)(H)(i)(b)] shall not be considered a receipt of information for purposes of clause (ii).

(vi) No investigation described in clause (ii) (or hearing described in clause (viii) based on such investigation) may be conducted with respect to information about a failure to meet a condition described in clause (ii), unless the Secretary of Labor receives the information not later than 12 months after the date of the alleged failure.

(vii) The Secretary of Labor shall provide notice to an employer with respect to whom there is reasonable cause to initiate an investigation described in clauses (i) or (ii), prior to the commencement of an investigation under such clauses, of the intent to conduct an investigation. The notice shall be provided in such a manner, and shall contain sufficient detail, to permit the employer to respond to the allegations before an investigation is commenced. The Secretary

* So in original; probably should be "or".

of Labor is not required to comply with this clause if the Secretary of Labor determines that to do so would interfere with an effort by the Secretary of Labor to secure compliance by the employer with the requirements of this subsection. There shall be no judicial review of a determination by the Secretary of Labor under this clause.

(viii) An investigation under clauses (i) or (ii) may be conducted for a period of up to 60 days. If the Secretary of Labor determines after such an investigation that a reasonable basis exists to make a finding that the employer has committed a willful failure to meet a condition of paragraph (1)(A), (1)(B), (1)(C), (1)(E), (1)(F), or (1)(G)(i)(I), has engaged in a pattern or practice of failures to meet such a condition, or has committed a substantial failure to meet such a condition that affects multiple employees, the Secretary of Labor shall provide for notice of such determination to the interested parties and an opportunity for a hearing in accordance with section 556 of Title 5, within 120 days after the date of the determination. If such a hearing is requested, the Secretary of Labor shall make a finding concerning the matter by not later than 120 days after the date of the hearing.

(H)(i) Except as provided in clauses (ii) and (iii), a person or entity is considered to have complied with the requirements of this subsection, notwithstanding a technical or procedural failure to meet such requirements, if there was a good faith attempt to comply with the requirements.

(ii) Clause (i) shall not apply if—

(I) the Department of Labor (or another enforcement agency) has explained to the person or entity the basis for the failure;

(II) the person or entity has been provided a period of not less than 10 business days (beginning after the date of the explanation) within which to correct the failure; and

(III) the person or entity has not corrected the failure voluntarily within such period.

(iii) A person or entity that, in the course of an investigation, is found to have violated the prevailing wage requirements set forth in paragraph (1)(A), shall not be assessed fines or other penalties for such violation if the person or entity can establish that the manner in which the prevailing wage was calculated was consistent with recognized industry standards and practices.

(iv) Clauses (i) and (iii) shall not apply to a person or entity that has engaged in or is engaging in a pattern or practice of willful violations of this subsection.

(I) Nothing in this subsection shall be construed as superseding or preempting any other enforcement-related authority under this

Act (such as the authorities under section 274B [8 U.S.C.A. § 1324b]), or any other Act.

(3)(A) For purposes of this subsection, the term "H–1B-dependent employer" means an employer that

(i)(I) has 25 or fewer full-time equivalent employees who are employed in the United States; and **(II)** employs more than 7 H–1B nonimmigrants;

(ii)(I) has at least 26 but not more than 50 full-time equivalent employees who are employed in the United States; and **(II)** employs more than 12 H–1B nonimmigrants; or

(iii)(I) has at least 51 full-time equivalent employees who are employed in the United States; and **(II)** employs H–1B nonimmigrants in a number that is equal to at least 15 percent of the number of such full-time equivalent employees.

(B) For purposes of this subsection

(i) the term "exempt H–1B nonimmigrant" means an H–1B nonimmigrant who—

(I) receives wages (including cash bonuses and similar compensation) at an annual rate equal to at least $60,000; or

(II) has attained a master's or higher degree (or its equivalent) in a specialty related to the intended employment; and

(ii) the term "nonexempt H–1B nonimmigrant" means an H–1B nonimmigrant who is not an exempt H–1B nonimmigrant.

(C) For purposes of subparagraph (A)

(i) in computing the number of full-time equivalent employees and the number of H–1B nonimmigrants, exempt H–1B nonimmigrants shall not be taken into account during the longer of—

(I) the 6–month period beginning on October 21, 1998; or

(II) the period beginning on October 21, 1998 and ending on the date final regulations are issued to carry out this paragraph; and

(ii) any group treated as a single employer under subsection (b), (c), (m), or (*o*) of section 414 of the Internal Revenue Code of 1986 shall be treated as a single employer.

(4) For purposes of this subsection:

(A) The term "area of employment" means the area within normal commuting distance of the worksite or physical location where the work of the H–1B nonimmigrant is or will be performed. If such worksite or location is within a Metropolitan

Statistical Area, any place within such area is deemed to be within the area of employment.

(B) In the case of an application with respect to one or more H–1B nonimmigrants by an employer, the employer is considered to "displace" a United States worker from a job if the employer lays off the worker from a job that is essentially the equivalent of the job for which the nonimmigrant or nonimmigrants is or are sought. A job shall not be considered to be essentially equivalent of another job unless it involves essentially the same responsibilities, was held by a United States worker with substantially equivalent qualifications and experience, and is located in the same area of employment as the other job.

(C) The term "H–1B nonimmigrant" means an alien admitted or provided status as a nonimmigrant described in section 101(a)(15)(H)(i)(b) [8 U.S.C.A. § 1101(a)(15)(H)(i)(b)].

(D)(i) The term "lays off", with respect to a worker—

(I) means to cause the worker's loss of employment, other than through a discharge for inadequate performance, violation of workplace rules, cause, voluntary departure, voluntary retirement, or the expiration of a grant or contract (other than a temporary employment contract entered into in order to evade a condition described in subparagraph (E) or (F) of paragraph (1)); but

(II) does not include any situation in which the worker is offered, as an alternative to such loss of employment, a similar employment opportunity with the same employer (or, in the case of a placement of a worker with another employer under paragraph (1)(F), with either employer described in such paragraph) at equivalent or higher compensation and benefits than the position from which the employee was discharged, regardless of whether or not the employee accepts the offer.

(ii) Nothing in this subparagraph is intended to limit an employee's rights under a collective bargaining agreement or other employment contract.

(E) The term "United States worker" means an employee who—

(i) is a citizen or national of the United States; or

(ii) is an alien who is lawfully admitted for permanent residence, is admitted as a refugee under section 207 [8 U.S.C.A. § 1157], is granted asylum under section 208 [8 U.S.C.A. § 1158], or is an immigrant otherwise authorized, by this chapter or by the Attorney General, to be employed.

(5)(A) This paragraph shall apply instead of subparagraphs (A) through (E) of paragraph (2) in the case of a violation described in subparagraph (B), but shall not be construed to limit or affect the authority of the Secretary or the Attorney General with respect to any other violation.

(B) The Attorney General shall establish a process for the receipt, initial review, and disposition in accordance with this paragraph of complaints respecting an employer's failure to meet the condition of paragraph (1)(G)(i)(II) or a petitioner's misrepresentation of material facts with respect to such condition. Complaints may be filed by an aggrieved individual who has submitted a resume or otherwise applied in a reasonable manner for the job that is the subject of the condition. No proceeding shall be conducted under this paragraph on a complaint concerning such a failure or misrepresentation unless the Attorney General determines that the complaint was filed not later than 12 months after the date of the failure or misrepresentation, respectively.

(C) If the Attorney General finds that a complaint has been filed in accordance with subparagraph (B) and there is reasonable cause to believe that such a failure or misrepresentation described in such complaint has occurred, the Attorney General shall initiate binding arbitration proceedings by requesting the Federal Mediation and Conciliation Service to appoint an arbitrator from the roster of arbitrators maintained by such Service. The procedure and rules of such Service shall be applicable to the selection of such arbitrator and to such arbitration proceedings. The Attorney General shall pay the fee and expenses of the arbitrator.

(D)(i) The arbitrator shall make findings respecting whether a failure or misrepresentation described in subparagraph (B) occurred. If the arbitrator concludes that failure or misrepresentation was willful, the arbitrator shall make a finding to that effect. The arbitrator may not find such a failure or misrepresentation (or that such a failure or misrepresentation was willful) unless the complainant demonstrates such a failure or misrepresentation (or its willful character) by clear and convincing evidence. The arbitrator shall transmit the findings in the form of a written opinion to the parties to the arbitration and the Attorney General. Such findings shall be final and conclusive, and, except as provided in this subparagraph, no official or court of the United States shall have power or jurisdiction to review any such findings.

(ii) The Attorney General may review and reverse or modify the findings of an arbitrator only on the same bases as an award of an arbitrator may be vacated or modified under section 10 or 11 of Title 9.

(iii) With respect to the findings of an arbitrator, a court may review only the actions of the Attorney General under clause (ii) and may set aside such actions only on the grounds described in subparagraph (A), (B), or (C) of section 706(a)(2) of Title 5. Notwithstanding any other provision of law, such judicial review may only be brought in an appropriate United States court of appeals.

(E) If the attorney general receives a finding of an arbitrator under this paragraph that an employer has failed to meet the condition of paragraph (1)(g)(i)(ii) or has misrepresented a material fact with respect to such condition, unless the attorney general reverses or modifies the finding under subparagraph (d)(ii)

(i) the Attorney General may impose administrative remedies (including civil monetary penalties in an amount not to exceed $1,000 per violation or $5,000 per violation in the case of a willful failure or misrepresentation) as the Attorney General determines to be appropriate; and

(ii) the Attorney General is authorized to not approve petitions filed, with respect to that employer and for aliens to be employed by the employer, under section 204 [8 U.S.C.A. § 1154] or 214(c) [8 U.S.C.A. § 1184(c)]—

(I) during a period of not more than 1 year; or

(II) in the case of a willful failure or willful misrepresentation, during a period of not more than 2 years.

(F) The Attorney General shall not delegate, to any other employee or official of the Department of Justice, any function of the Attorney General under this paragraph, until 60 days after the Attorney General has submitted a plan for such delegation to the Committees on the Judiciary of the United States House of Representatives and the Senate.

(*o*) Repealed.

(p) Computation of prevailing wage level

(1) In computing the prevailing wage level for an occupational classification in an area of employment for purposes of subsections (a)(5)(A), (n)(1)(A)(i)(II), and (t)(1)(A)(i)(II) in the case of an employee of

(A) an institution of higher education (as defined in section 1001(a) of Title 20), or a related or affiliated nonprofit entity; or

(B) a nonprofit research organization or a Governmental research organization,

the prevailing wage level shall only take into account employees at such institutions and organizations in the area of employment.

(2) With respect to a professional athlete (as defined in subsection (a)(5)(A)(iii)(II)) when the job opportunity is covered by professional sports league rules or regulations, the wage set forth in those rules or regulations shall be considered as not adversely affecting the wages of United States workers similarly employed and be considered the prevailing wage.

(3) The prevailing wage required to be paid pursuant to subsections (a)(5)(A), (n)(1)(A)(i)(II), and (t)(1)(A)(i)(II) shall be 100 percent of the wage determined pursuant to those sections.

(4) Where the Secretary of Labor uses, or makes available to employers, a governmental survey to determine the prevailing wage, such survey shall provide at least 4 levels of wages commensurate with experience, education, and the level of supervision. Where an existing government survey has only 2 levels, 2 intermediate levels may be created by dividing by 3, the difference between the 2 levels offered, adding the quotient thus obtained to the first level and subtracting that quotient from the second level.

(q) Any alien admitted under section 101(a)(15)(B) [8 U.S.C.A. § 1101(a)(15)(B)] may accept an honorarium payment and associated incidental expenses for a usual academic activity or activities (lasting not longer than 9 days at any single institution), as defined by the Attorney General in consultation with the Secretary of Education, if such payment is offered by an institution or organization described in subsection (p)(1) and is made for services conducted for the benefit of that institution or entity and if the alien has not accepted such payment or expenses from more than 5 institutions or organizations in the previous 6–month period.

(r) Certification for certain alien nurses

Subsection (a)(5)(C) shall not apply to an alien who seeks to enter the United States for the purpose of performing labor as a nurse who presents to the consular officer (or in the case of an adjustment of status, the Attorney General) a certified statement from the Commission on Graduates of Foreign Nursing Schools (or an equivalent independent credentialing organization approved for the certification of nurses under subsection (a)(5)(C) by the Attorney General in consultation with the Secretary of Health and Human Services) that—

(1) the alien has a valid and unrestricted license as a nurse in a State where the alien intends to be employed and such State verifies that the foreign licenses of alien nurses are authentic and unencumbered;

(2) the alien has passed the National Council Licensure Examination (NCLEX);

(3) the alien is a graduate of a nursing program—

(A) in which the language of instruction was English;

(B) located in a country—

(i) designated by such commission not later than 30 days after the date of the enactment of the Nursing Relief for Disadvantaged Areas Act of 1999, based on such commission's assessment that the quality of nursing education in that country, and the English language proficiency of those who complete such programs in that country, justify the country's designation; or

(ii) designated on the basis of such an assessment by unanimous agreement of such commission and any equivalent credentialing organizations which have been approved under subsection (a)(5)(C) for the certification of nurses under this subsection; and

(C)(i) which was in operation on or before the date of the enactment of the Nursing Relief for Disadvantaged Areas Act of 1999; or

(ii) has been approved by unanimous agreement of such commission and any equivalent credentialing organizations which have been approved under subsection (a)(5)(C) for the certification of nurses under this subsection.

(s) Public charges

In determining whether an alien described in subsection (a)(4)(C)(i) is inadmissible under subsection (a)(4) or ineligible to receive an immigrant visa or otherwise to adjust to the status of permanent resident by reason of subsection (a)(4), the consular officer or the Attorney General shall not consider any benefits the alien may have received that were authorized under section 501 of the Illegal Immigration Reform and Immigrant Responsibility Act of 1996 [8 U.S.C.A. § 1641(c)].

(t)(1)* No alien may be admitted or provided status as a nonimmigrant under section 101(a)(15)(H)(i)(b1) [8 U.S.C.A. § 1101(a)(15)(H)(i)(b1)] or section 101(a)(15)(E)(iii) [8 U.S.C.A. § 1101(a)(15)(E)(iii)] in an occupational classification unless the employer has filed with the Secretary of Labor an attestation stating the following:

(A) The employer—

(i) is offering and will offer during the period of authorized employment to aliens admitted or provided status under section 101(a)(15)(H)(i)(b1) [8 U.S.C.A. § 1101(a)(15)(H)(i)(b1)] or section 101(a)(15)(E)(iii) [8 U.S.C.A. § 1101(a)(15)(E)(iii)] wages that are at least—

(I) the actual wage level paid by the employer to all other individuals with similar experience and qualifications for the specific employment in question; or

(II) the prevailing wage level for the occupational classification in the area of employment,

whichever is greater, based on the best information available as of the time of filing the attestation; and

* So in original. Two subsecs. (t) have been enacted.

(ii) will provide working conditions for such a nonimmigrant that will not adversely affect the working conditions of workers similarly employed.

(B) There is not a strike or lockout in the course of a labor dispute in the occupational classification at the place of employment.

(C) The employer, at the time of filing the attestation—

(i) has provided notice of the filing under this paragraph to the bargaining representative (if any) of the employer's employees in the occupational classification and area for which aliens are sought; or

(ii) if there is no such bargaining representative, has provided notice of filing in the occupational classification through such methods as physical posting in conspicuous locations at the place of employment or electronic notification to employees in the occupational classification for which nonimmigrants under section 101(a)(15)(H)(i)(b1) [8 U.S.C.A. § 1101(a)(15)(H)(i)(b1)] or section 101(a)(15)(E)(iii) [8 U.S.C.A. § 1101(a)(15)(E)(iii)] are sought.

(D) A specification of the number of workers sought, the occupational classification in which the workers will be employed, and wage rate and conditions under which they will be employed.

(2)(A) The employer shall make available for public examination, within one working day after the date on which an attestation under this subsection is filed, at the employer's principal place of business or worksite, a copy of each such attestation (and such accompanying documents as are necessary).

(B)(i) The Secretary of Labor shall compile, on a current basis, a list (by employer and by occupational classification) of the attestations filed under this subsection. Such list shall include, with respect to each attestation, the wage rate, number of aliens sought, period of intended employment, and date of need.

(ii) The Secretary of Labor shall make such list available for public examination in Washington, D.C.

(C) The Secretary of Labor shall review an attestation filed under this subsection only for completeness and obvious inaccuracies. Unless the Secretary of Labor finds that an attestation is incomplete or obviously inaccurate, the Secretary of Labor shall provide the certification described in section 101(a)(15)(H)(i)(b1) [8 U.S.C.A. § 1101(a)(15)(H)(i)(b1)] or section 101(a)(15)(E)(iii) [8 U.S.C.A. § 1101(a)(15)(E)(iii)] within 7 days of the date of the filing of the attestation.

(3)(A) The Secretary of Labor shall establish a process for the receipt, investigation, and disposition of complaints respecting the failure of an employer to meet a condition specified in an attestation submitted under this subsection or misrepresentation by the employer of material facts in such an attestation. Complaints may be filed by any aggrieved person or organization (including bargaining representatives). No investigation or hearing shall be conducted on a complaint concerning such a failure or misrepresentation unless the complaint was filed not later than 12 months after the date of the failure or misrepresentation, respectively. The Secretary of Labor shall conduct an investigation under this paragraph if there is reasonable cause to believe that such a failure or misrepresentation has occurred.

(B) Under the process described in subparagraph (A), the Secretary of Labor shall provide, within 30 days after the date a complaint is filed, for a determination as to whether or not a reasonable basis exists to make a finding described in subparagraph (C). If the Secretary of Labor determines that such a reasonable basis exists, the Secretary of Labor shall provide for notice of such determination to the interested parties and an opportunity for a hearing on the complaint, in accordance with section 556 of Title 5 within 60 days after the date of the determination. If such a hearing is requested, the Secretary of Labor shall make a finding concerning the matter by not later than 60 days after the date of the hearing. In the case of similar complaints respecting the same applicant, the Secretary of Labor may consolidate the hearings under this subparagraph on such complaints.

(C)(i) If the Secretary of Labor finds, after notice and opportunity for a hearing, a failure to meet a condition of paragraph (1)(b), a substantial failure to meet a condition of paragraph (1)(c) or (1)(d), or a misrepresentation of material fact in an attestation—

(I) the Secretary of Labor shall notify the Secretary of State and the Secretary of Homeland Security of such finding and may, in addition, impose such other administrative remedies (including civil monetary penalties in an amount not to exceed $1,000 per violation) as the Secretary of Labor determines to be appropriate; and

(II) the Secretary of State or the Secretary of Homeland Security, as appropriate, shall not approve petitions or applications filed with respect to that employer under section 204 [8 U.S.C.A. § 1154], 214(c) [8 U.S.C.A. § 1184(c)], 101(a)(15)(H)(i)(b1) [8 U.S.C.A. § 1101(a)(15)(H)(i)(b1)], or section 101(a)(15)(E)(iii) [8 U.S.C.A. § 1101(a)(15)(E)(iii)] during a period of at least 1 year for aliens to be employed by the employer.

(ii) If the Secretary of Labor finds, after notice and opportunity for a hearing, a willful failure to meet a condition of paragraph (1), a willful misrepresentation of material fact in an attestation, or a violation of clause (iv)—

(I) the Secretary of Labor shall notify the Secretary of State and the Secretary of Homeland Security of such finding and may, in addition, impose such other administrative remedies (including civil monetary penalties in an amount not to exceed $5,000 per violation) as the Secretary of Labor determines to be appropriate; and

(II) the Secretary of State or the Secretary of Homeland Security, as appropriate, shall not approve petitions or applications filed with respect to that employer under section 204 [8 U.S.C.A. § 1154], 214(c) [8 U.S.C.A. § 1184(c)], 101(a)(15)(H)(i)(b1) [8 U.S.C.A. § 1101(a)(15)(H)(i)(b1)], or section 101(a)(15)(E)(iii) [8 U.S.C.A. § 1101(a)(15)(E)(iii)] during a period of at least 2 years for aliens to be employed by the employer.

(iii) If the Secretary of Labor finds, after notice and opportunity for a hearing, a willful failure to meet a condition of paragraph (1) or a willful misrepresentation of material fact in an attestation, in the course of which failure or misrepresentation the employer displaced a United States worker employed by the employer within the period beginning 90 days before and ending 90 days after the date of filing of any visa petition or application supported by the attestation—

(I) the Secretary of Labor shall notify the Secretary of State and the Secretary of Homeland Security of such finding and may, in addition, impose such other administrative remedies (including civil monetary penalties in an amount not to exceed $35,000 per violation) as the Secretary of Labor determines to be appropriate; and

(II) the Secretary of State or the Secretary of Homeland Security, as appropriate, shall not approve petitions or applications filed with respect to that employer under section 204 [8 U.S.C.A. § 1154], 214(c) [8 U.S.C.A. § 1184(c)], 101(a)(15)(H)(i)(b1) [8 U.S.C.A. § 1101(a)(15)(H)(i)(b1)], or section 101(a)(15)(E)(iii) [8 U.S.C.A. § 1101(a)(15)(E)(iii)] during a period of at least 3 years for aliens to be employed by the employer.

(iv) It is a violation of this clause for an employer who has filed an attestation under this subsection to intimidate, threaten, restrain, coerce, blacklist, discharge, or in any other manner discriminate against an employee (which term, for purposes of this clause, includes a former employee and an applicant for employment) because the employee has disclosed information to the employer, or to any other person, that the employee reasonably believes evidences a violation of this subsection, or any rule or regulation pertaining to this subsection, or because the employee cooperates or seeks to cooperate in an investigation or other proceeding concerning the employer's compliance with the requirements of this subsection or any rule or regulation pertaining to this subsection.

(v) The Secretary of Labor and the Secretary of Homeland Security shall devise a process under which a nonimmigrant under section 101(a)(15)(H)(i)(b1) [8 U.S.C.A. § 1101(a)(15)(H)(i)(b1)] or section 101(a)(15)(E)(iii) [8 U.S.C.A. § 1101(a)(15)(E)(iii)] who files a complaint regarding a violation of clause (iv) and is otherwise eligible to remain and work in the United States may be allowed to seek other appropriate employment in the United States for a period not to exceed the maximum period of stay authorized for such nonimmigrant classification.

(vi)(I) It is a violation of this clause for an employer who has filed an attestation under this subsection to require a nonimmigrant under section 101(a)(15)(H)(i)(b1) [8 U.S.C.A. § 1101(a)(15)(H)(i)(b1)] or section 101(a)(15)(E)(iii) [8 U.S.C.A. § 1101(a)(15)(E)(iii)] to pay a penalty for ceasing employment with the employer prior to a date agreed to by the nonimmigrant and the employer. The Secretary of Labor shall determine whether a required payment is a penalty (and not liquidated damages) pursuant to relevant State law.

(II) If the Secretary of Labor finds, after notice and opportunity for a hearing, that an employer has committed a violation of this clause, the Secretary of Labor may impose a civil monetary penalty of $1,000 for each such violation and issue an administrative order requiring the return to the nonimmigrant of any amount paid in violation of this clause, or, if the nonimmigrant cannot be located, requiring payment of any such amount to the general fund of the Treasury.

(vii)(I) It is a failure to meet a condition of paragraph (1)(A) for an employer who has filed an attestation under this subsection and who places a nonimmigrant under section 101(a)(15)(H)(i)(b1) [8 U.S.C.A. § 1101(a)(15)(H)(i)(b1)] or section 101(a)(15)(E)(iii) [8 U.S.C.A. § 101(a)(15)(E)(iii)] designated as a full-time employee in the attestation, after the nonimmigrant has entered into employment with the employer, in nonproductive status due to a decision by the employer (based on factors such as lack of work), or due to the nonimmigrant's lack of a permit or license, to fail to pay the nonimmigrant full-time wages in accordance with paragraph (1)(A) for all such nonproductive time.

(II) It is a failure to meet a condition of paragraph (1)(A) for an employer who has filed an attestation under this subsection and who places a nonimmigrant under section 101(a)(15)(H)(i)(b1) [8 U.S.C.A. § 1101(a)(15)(H)(i)(b1)] or section 101(a)(15)(E)(iii) [8 U.S.C.A. § 1101(a)(15)(E)(iii)] designated as a part-time employee in the attestation, after the nonimmigrant has entered into employment with the employer, in nonproductive status under circumstances described in subclause (I), to fail to pay such a nonimmigrant for such hours as are designated on the attestation consistent with the rate of pay identified on the attestation.

(III) In the case of a nonimmigrant under section 101(a)(15)(H)(i)(b1) [8 U.S.C.A. § 1101(a)(15)(H)(i)(b1)] or section 101(a)(15)(E)(iii) [8 U.S.C.A. § 1101(a)(15)(E)(iii)] who has not yet entered into employment with an employer who has had approved an attestation under this subsection with respect to the nonimmigrant, the provisions of subclauses (I) and (II) shall apply to the employer beginning 30 days after the date the nonimmigrant first is admitted into the United States, or 60 days after the date the nonimmigrant becomes eligible to work for the employer in the case of a nonimmigrant who is present in the United States on the date of the approval of the attestation filed with the Secretary of Labor.

(IV) This clause does not apply to a failure to pay wages to a nonimmigrant under section 101(a)(15)(H)(i)(b1) [8 U.S.C.A. § 1101(a)(15)(H)(i)(b1)] or section 101(a)(15)(E)(iii) [8 U.S.C.A. § 1101(a)(15)(E)(iii)] for nonproductive time due to non-work-related factors, such as the voluntary request of the nonimmigrant for an absence or circumstances rendering the nonimmigrant unable to work.

(V) This clause shall not be construed as prohibiting an employer that is a school or other educational institution from applying to a nonimmigrant under section 101(a)(15)(H)(i)(b1) [8 U.S.C.A. § 1101(a)(15)(H)(i)(b1)] or section 101(a)(15)(E)(iii) [8 U.S.C.A. § 1101(a)(15)(E)(iii)] an established salary practice of the employer, under which the employer pays to nonimmigrants under section 101(a)(15)(H)(i)(b1) [8 U.S.C.A. § 1101(a)(15)(H)(i)(b1)] or section 101(a)(15)(E)(iii) [8 U.S.C.A. § 1101(a)(15)(E)(iii)] and United States workers in the same occupational classification an annual salary in disbursements over fewer than 12 months, if—

(aa) the nonimmigrant agrees to the compressed annual salary payments prior to the commencement of the employment; and

(bb) the application of the salary practice to the nonimmigrant does not otherwise cause the nonimmigrant to violate any condition of the nonimmigrant's authorization under this chapter to remain in the United States.

(VI) This clause shall not be construed as superseding clause (viii).

(viii) It is a failure to meet a condition of paragraph (1)(A) for an employer who has filed an attestation under this subsection to fail to offer to a nonimmigrant under section 101(a)(15)(H)(i)(b1) [8 U.S.C.A. § 1101(a)(15)(H)(i)(b1)] or section 101(a)(15)(E)(iii) [8 U.S.C.A. § 1101(a)(15)(E)(iii)], during the nonimmigrant's period of authorized employment, benefits and eligibility for benefits (including the opportunity to participate in health, life, disability, and other insurance plans; the opportunity to participate in retirement and savings plans; and cash bonuses and non-cash compensation, such as stock options (whether or not based on performance)) on the same basis, and in accordance with the same criteria, as the employer offers to United States workers.

(D) If the Secretary of Labor finds, after notice and opportunity for a hearing, that an employer has not paid wages at the wage level specified in the attestation and required under paragraph (1), the Secretary of Labor shall order the employer to provide for payment of such amounts of back pay as may be required to comply with the requirements of paragraph (1), whether or not a penalty under subparagraph (C) has been imposed.

(E) The Secretary of Labor may, on a case-by-case basis, subject an employer to random investigations for a period of up to 5 years, beginning on the date on which the employer is found by the Secretary of Labor to have committed a willful failure to meet a condition of paragraph (1) or to have made a willful misrepresentation of material fact in an attestation. The authority of the Secretary of Labor under this subparagraph shall not be construed to be subject to, or limited by, the requirements of subparagraph (A).

(F) Nothing in this subsection shall be construed as superseding or preempting any other enforcement-related authority under this chapter (such as the authorities under section 274B [8 U.S.C.A. § 1324b]), or any other Act.

(4) For purposes of this subsection:

(A) The term "area of employment" means the area within normal commuting distance of the worksite or physical location where the work of the nonimmigrant under section 101(a)(15)(H)(i)(b1) [8 U.S.C.A. § 1101(a)(15)(H)(i)(b1)] or section 101(a)(15)(E)(iii) [8 U.S.C.A. § 1101(a)(15)(E)(iii)] is or will be performed. If such worksite or location is within a Metropolitan Statistical Area, any place within such area is deemed to be within the area of employment.

(B) In the case of an attestation with respect to one or more nonimmigrants under section 101(a)(15)(H)(i)(b1) [8 U.S.C.A. § 1101(a)(15)(H)(i)(b1)] or section 101(a)(15)(E)(iii) [8 U.S.C.A. § 1101(a)(15)(E)(iii)] by an employer, the employer is considered to "displace" a United States worker from a job if the employer lays off the worker from a job that is essentially the equivalent of the job for which the nonimmigrant or nonimmigrants is or are sought. A job shall not be considered to be essentially equivalent of another job unless it involves essentially the same responsibilities, was held by a United States worker with substantially equivalent qualifications and experience, and is located in the same area of employment as the other job.

(C)(i) The term "lays off", with respect to a worker—

(I) means to cause the worker's loss of employment, other than through a discharge for inadequate performance, violation of workplace rules, cause, voluntary departure, voluntary retirement, or the expiration of a grant or contract; but

(II) does not include any situation in which the worker is offered, as an alternative to such loss of employment, a similar employment opportunity with the same employer at equivalent or higher compensation and benefits than the position from which the employee was discharged, regardless of whether or not the employee accepts the offer.

(ii) Nothing in this subparagraph is intended to limit an employee's rights under a collective bargaining agreement or other employment contract.

(D) The term "United States worker" means an employee who—

(i) is a citizen or national of the United States; or

(ii) is an alien who is lawfully admitted for permanent residence, is admitted as a refugee under section 207 [8 U.S.C.A. § 1157], is granted asylum under section 208 [8 U.S.C.A. § 1158], or is an immigrant otherwise authorized, by this chapter or by the Secretary of Homeland Security, to be employed.

(t)(1)* Except as provided in paragraph (2), no person admitted under section 101(a)(15)(Q)(ii)(I) [8 U.S.C.A. § 1101(a)(15)(Q)(ii)(I)], or acquiring such status after admission, shall be eligible to apply for nonimmigrant status, an immigrant visa, or permanent residence under this Act until it is established that such person has resided and been physically present in the person's country of nationality or last residence for an aggregate of at least 2 years following departure from the United States.

(2) The Secretary of Homeland Security may waive the requirement of such 2-year foreign residence abroad if the Secretary determines that—

(A) departure from the United States would impose exceptional hardship upon the alien's spouse or child (if such spouse or child is a citizen of the United States or an alien lawfully admitted for permanent residence); or

(B) the admission of the alien is in the public interest or the national interest of the United States.

(June 27, 1952, c. 477, Title II, ch. 2, § 212, 66 Stat. 182; July 18, 1956, c. 629, Title III, § 301(a), 70 Stat. 575; July 7, 1958, Pub.L. 85–508, § 23, 72 Stat. 351; Mar. 18, 1959, Pub.L. 86–3, § 20(b), 73 Stat. 13; July 14, 1960, Pub.L. 86–648, § 8, 74 Stat. 505; Sept. 21, 1961, Pub.L. 87–256, § 109(c), 75 Stat. 535; Sept. 26, 1961, Pub.L. 87–301, §§ 11–15, 75 Stat. 654, 655; Oct. 3, 1965, Pub.L. 89–236, §§ 10, 15, 79 Stat. 917, 919; Apr. 7, 1970, Pub.L. 91–225, § 2, 84 Stat. 116; Oct. 12, 1976, Pub.L. 94–484, Title VI, § 601(a), (c), (d), 90 Stat. 2300, 2301; Oct. 20, 1976, Pub.L. 94–571, §§ 5, 7(d), 90 Stat. 2705, 2706; 1966 Reorg. Plan No. 3, §§ 1, 3, 31 F.R. 8855, 80 Stat. 1610; Aug. 1, 1977, Pub.L. 95–83, Title III, § 307(q)(1), (2), 91 Stat. 394; 1977 Reorg. Plan No. 2, § 7(a)(8), 42 F.R. 62461, 91 Stat. 1637; Oct. 30, 1978, Pub.L. 95–549, Title I, §§ 101, 102, 92 Stat. 2065; Sept. 27, 1979, Pub.L. 96–70, Title III, § 3201(b), 93 Stat. 497; Oct. 17, 1979, Pub.L. 96–88, Title III, § 301(a)(1), Title I, §§ 503, 509(b), 93 Stat. 677, 690, 695; Mar. 17, 1980, Pub.L. 96–212, Title II, § 203(d), (f), 94 Stat. 107; Dec. 17, 1980, Pub.L. 96–538, Title IV, § 404, 94 Stat. 3192; Dec. 29, 1981, Pub.L. 97–116, §§ 4, 5(a)(1), (2), (b), 18(e), 95 Stat. 1611, 1612, 1620; Oct. 5, 1984, Pub.L. 98–454, Title VI, § 602(a), 98 Stat. 1737; Oct. 12, 1984, Pub.L. 98–473, Title II, § 220(a), 98 Stat. 2028; Oct. 27, 1986, Pub.L. 99–396, § 14(a), 100 Stat. 842; Oct. 27, 1986, Pub.L. 99–570, Title I, § 1751(a), 100 Stat. 3207–47; Nov. 10, 1986, Pub.L. 99–639, § 6(a), 100 Stat. 3544; Oct. 24, 1988, Pub.L. 100–525, § 7(c)(1), 102 Stat. 2616; Nov. 10, 1986, Pub.L. 99–639, § 6(b), as added Oct. 24, 1988, Pub.L. 100–525, § 7(c)(3), 102 Stat. 2617; Nov. 14, 1986, Pub.L. 99–653, § 7(a), 100 Stat. 3657; Nov. 14, 1986, Pub. L. 99–653, § 7(d)(2), as added Oct. 24, 1988, Pub.L. 100–525, § 8(f), 102 Stat. 2617; Dec. 22, 1987, Pub.L. 100–204, § 806(c), 101 Stat. 1399; Oct. 24, 1988, Pub.L. 100–525, §§ 3(1)(A), 9(i), 102 Stat. 2614, 2620; Nov. 18, 1988, Pub.L. 100–690, Title VII, § 7349(a), 102 Stat. 4473; Dec. 18, 1989, Pub.L. 101–238, § 3(b), 103 Stat. 2100; Feb. 16, 1990, Pub.L. 101–246, Title I, § 131(a), (c), 104 Stat. 31; Nov. 29, 1990, Pub.L. 101–649, Title I, § 162(e)(1), (f)(2)(B), Title II, §§ 202(b), 205(c)(3), Title V, §§ 511(a), 514(a), Title VI, § 601(a), (b), (d), 104 Stat. 5011, 5012, 5014, 5020, 5052, 5053, 5067, 5075 to 5077; Dec. 12, 1991, Pub.L. 102–232, Title III, §§ 302(e)(6), (9), 303(a)(5)(B), (6), (7)(B), 306(a)(10), (12), 307(a) to (g),

* So in original. Two subsecs. (t) have been enacted.

309(b)(7), 105 Stat. 1746 to 1748, 1751, 1753 to 1755, 1759; June 10, 1993, Pub.L. 103–43, Title XX, § 2007(a), 107 Stat. 210; Aug. 26, 1994, Pub.L. 103–317, Title V, § 506(a), 108 Stat. 1765; Sept. 13, 1994, Pub.L. 103–322, Title XIII, § 130003(b)(1), 108 Stat. 2024; Oct. 25, 1994, Pub.L. 103–416, Title II, §§ 203(a), 219(e), (z)(1), (5), 220(a), 108 Stat. 4311, 4316, 4318, 4319; Apr. 24, 1996, Pub.L. 104–132, Title IV, §§ 411, 412, 440(d), 110 Stat. 1268, 1269, 1277; Sept. 30, 1996, Pub.L. 104–208, Div. C, Title I, § 124(b)(1), Title III, §§ 301(b)(1), (c)(1), 304(b), 305(c), 306(d), 308(c)(2)(B), (d)(1), (e)(1)(B), (C), (2)(A), (6), (f)(1)(C) to (F), (3)(A), (g)(1), (4)(B), (10)(A), (H), 322(a)(2)(B), 341(a), (b), 342(a), 343, 344(a), 345(a), 346(a), 347(a), 348(a), 349, 351(a), 352(a), 355, Title V, § 531(a), Title VI, §§ 602(a), 622(b), 624(a), 671(e)(3), 110 Stat. 3009–562, 3009–576, 3009–578, 3009–597, 3009–607, 3009–612, 3009–616, 3009–619, 3009–620, 3009–621, 3009–622, 3009–625, 3009–629, 3009–635 to 3009–641, 3009–644, 3009–674, 3009–689, 3009–695, 3009–698, 3009–723; Nov. 12, 1997, Pub.L. 105–73, § 1, 111 Stat. 1459; Oct. 21, 1998, Pub.L. 105–277, Div. C, Title IV, §§ 412, 413, 415(a), 431(a), Div. G, Title XXII, § 2226, 112 Stat. 2681–642, 2681–643, 2681–645, 2681–648, 2681–649, 2681–650, 2681–651, 2681–654, 2681–658, 2681–820; Oct. 27, 1998, Pub.L. 105–292, Title VI, § 604(a), 112 Stat. 2814; Nov. 12, 1999, Pub.L. 106–95, §§ 2(b), 4(a), 113 Stat. 1312, 1317; Dec. 3, 1999, Pub.L. 106–120, Title VIII, § 809, 113 Stat. 1632; Oct. 17, 2000, Pub.L. 106–313, Title I, §§ 106(c)(2), 107(a), 114 Stat. 1254, 1255; Oct. 28, 2000, Pub.L. 106–386, Div. A, §§ 107(e)(3), 111(d), Div. B, Title V, §§ 1505(a), (c)(1), (d), (e), (f), 1513(e), 114 Stat. 1478, 1485, 1525, 1526, 1536; Oct. 30, 2000, Pub.L. 106–395, Title II, § 201(b)(1), (2), 114 Stat. 1633, 1634; Oct. 30, 2000, Pub.L. 106–396, Title I, § 101(b)(1), 114 Stat. 1638; Oct. 26, 2001, Pub.L. 107–56, Title IV, § 411(a), Title X, § 1006(a), 115 Stat. 345, 394; Mar. 13, 2002, Pub.L. 107–150, § 2, 116 Stat. 74; Nov. 2, 2002, Pub.L. 107–273, Div. C, Title I, § 11018(c), 116 Stat. 1825; Sept. 3, 2003, Pub.L. 108–77, Title IV, § 402(b), (c), 117 Stat. 940, 946; Pub.L. 108–193, §§ 4(b)(4), 8(a)(2), Dec. 19, 2003, 117 Stat. 2879; Dec. 8, 2004, Pub.L. 108–447, Div. J, Title IV, §§ 422(a), 423, 424(a)(1), (b), 118 Stat. 3353, 3354, 3355; Dec. 10, 2004, Pub.L. 108–449, § 1(b)(2), 118 Stat. 3470; Dec. 17, 2004, Pub.L. 108–458, Title V, §§ 5501(a), 5502(a), 5503, 118 Stat. 3740; May 11, 2005, Pub.L. 109–13, Div. B, §§ 103, 104, 501(d), 119 Stat. 231, 306–09, 322; Jan. 5, 2006, Pub.L. 109–162, Title VIII, § 802, 119 Stat. 3054; Aug. 12, 2006, Pub.L. 109–271, § 6(b), 120 Stat. 762; Dec. 26, 2007, Pub.L. 110–161, Div. J, Title VI, § 691(a), (c), 121 Stat. 2364, 2365; May 8, 2008, Pub.L. 110–229, Title VII, Subtitle A, § 702(b)(2), (3), (d), 122 Stat. 860, 862; July 30, 2008, Pub.L. 110–293, Title III, § 305, 122 Stat. 2963; Oct. 3, 2008, Pub.L. 110–340, § 2(b), 122 Stat. 3736; Dec. 23, 2008, Pub.L. 110–457, Title II, §§ 222(f)(1), 234, 122 Stat. 5071, 5074; Dec. 22, 2009, Pub.L. 111–122, § 3(b), 123 Stat. 3481; Nov. 30, 2010, Pub.L. 111–287, § 2, 124 Stat. 3058; Pub.L. 113–4, Title VIII, § 804, Mar. 7, 2013, 127 Stat. 111.)

§ 213. Admission of aliens on giving bond or undertaking; return upon permanent departure [8 U.S.C.A. § 1183]

An alien inadmissible under paragraph (4) of section 212(a) [8 U.S.C.A. § 1182(a)] may, if otherwise admissible, be admitted in the discretion of the Attorney General (subject to the affidavit of support requirement and attribution of sponsor's income and resources under section 213A [8 U.S.C.A. § 1183a]) upon the giving of a suitable and proper bond or undertaking approved by the Attorney General, in such amount and containing such conditions as he may prescribe, to the United States, and to all States, territories, counties, towns, municipalities, and districts thereof holding the United States and all States, territories, counties, towns, municipalities, and districts thereof harmless against such alien becoming a public charge. Such bond or undertaking shall terminate upon the permanent departure from the United States, the naturalization, or the death of such alien, and any sums or other security held to secure performance thereof, except to the extent forfeited for violation of the terms thereof, shall be returned to the person by whom furnished, or to his legal representatives. Suit may be brought thereon in the name and by the proper law officers of the United States for the use of the United States, or of any State, territory, district, county, town or municipality in which such alien becomes a public charge, irrespective of whether a demand for payment of public expenses has been made.

(June 27, 1952, c. 477, Title II, ch. 2, § 213, 66 Stat. 188; July 10, 1970, Pub.L. 91–313, § 1, 84 Stat. 413; Nov. 29, 1990, Pub.L. 101–649, Title VI, § 603(a)(8), 104 Stat. 5083; Sept. 30, 1996, Pub.L. 104–208, Div. C, Title III, § 308(d)(3)(A), Title V, § 564(f), 110 Stat. 3009–617, 3009–684.)

§ 213A. Requirements for sponsor's affidavit of support [8 U.S.C.A. § 1183a]

(a) Enforceability

(1) Terms of affidavit

No affidavit of support may be accepted by the Attorney General or by any consular officer to establish that an alien is not excludable as a public charge under section 212(a)(4) [8 U.S.C.A. § 1182(a)(4)] unless such affidavit is executed by a sponsor of the alien as a contract—

(A) in which the sponsor agrees to provide support to maintain the sponsored alien at an annual income that is not less than 125 percent of the Federal poverty line during the period in which the affidavit is enforceable;

(B) that is legally enforceable against the sponsor by the sponsored alien, the Federal Government, any State (or any political subdivision of such State), or by any other entity that provides any means-tested public benefit (as defined in subsection (e)), consistent with the provisions of this section; and

(C) in which the sponsor agrees to submit to the jurisdiction of any Federal or State court for the purpose of actions brought under subsection (b)(2).

(2) Period of enforceability

An affidavit of support shall be enforceable with respect to benefits provided for an alien before the date the alien is naturalized as a citizen of the United States, or, if earlier, the termination date provided under paragraph (3).

(3) Termination of period of enforceability upon completion of required period of employment, etc.

(A) In general

An affidavit of support is not enforceable after such time as the alien (i) has worked 40 qualifying quarters of coverage as defined under title II of the Social Security Act [42 U.S.C.A

§ 401 et seq.] or can be credited with such qualifying quarters as provided under subparagraph (B), and (ii) in the case of any such qualifying quarter creditable for any period beginning after December 31, 1996, did not receive any Federal means-tested public benefit (as provided under section 403 of the Personal Responsibility and Work Opportunity Reconciliation Act of 1996 [8 U.S.C.A. § 1613]) during any such period.

(B) Qualifying quarters

For purposes of this section, in determining the number of qualifying quarters of coverage under title II of the Social Security Act [42 U.S.C.A. § 401 et seq.] an alien shall be credited with—

(i) all of the qualifying quarters of coverage as defined under title II of the Social Security Act worked by a parent of such alien while the alien was under age 18, and

(ii) all of the qualifying quarters worked by a spouse of such alien during their marriage and the alien remains married to such spouse or such spouse is deceased.

No such qualifying quarter of coverage that is creditable under title II of the Social Security Act [42 U.S.C.A. § 401 et seq.] for any period beginning after December 31, 1996, may be credited to an alien under clause (i) or (ii) if the parent or spouse (as the case may be) of such alien received any Federal means-tested public benefit (as provided under section 403 of the Personal Responsibility and Work Opportunity Reconciliation Act of 1996 [8 U.S.C.A. § 1613]) during the period for which such qualifying quarter of coverage is so credited.

(C) Provision of information to SAVE system

The Attorney General shall ensure that appropriate information regarding the application of this paragraph is provided to the system for alien verification of eligibility (SAVE) described in section 1137(d)(3) of the Social Security Act [42 U.S.C.A. § 1320b–7(d)(3)].

(b) Reimbursement of government expenses

(1) Request for reimbursement

(A) Requirement

Upon notification that a sponsored alien has received any means-tested public benefit, the appropriate nongovernmental entity which provided such benefit or the appropriate entity of the Federal Government, a State, or any political subdivision of a State shall request reimbursement by the sponsor in an amount which is equal to the unreimbursed costs of such benefit.

(B) Regulations

The Attorney General, in consultation with the heads of other appropriate Federal agencies, shall prescribe such regulations as may be necessary to carry out subparagraph (A).

(2) Actions to compel reimbursement

(A) In case of nonresponse

If within 45 days after a request for reimbursement under paragraph (1)(A), the appropriate entity has not received a response from the sponsor indicating a willingness to commence payment an action may be brought against the sponsor pursuant to the affidavit of support.

(B) In case of failure to pay

If the sponsor fails to abide by the repayment terms established by the appropriate entity, the entity may bring an action against the sponsor pursuant to the affidavit of support.

(C) Limitation on actions

No cause of action may be brought under this paragraph later than 10 years after the date on which the sponsored alien last received any means-tested public benefit to which the affidavit of support applies.

(3) Use of collection agencies

If the appropriate entity under paragraph (1)(A) requests reimbursement from the sponsor or brings an action against the sponsor pursuant to the affidavit of support, the appropriate entity may appoint or hire an individual or other person to act on behalf of such entity acting under the authority of law for purposes of collecting any amounts owed.

(c) Remedies

Remedies available to enforce an affidavit of support under this section include any or all of the remedies described in section 3201, 3203, 3204, or 3205 of Title 28, as well as an order for specific performance and payment of legal fees and other costs of collection, and include corresponding remedies available under State law. A Federal agency may seek to collect amounts owed under this section in accordance with the provisions of subchapter II of chapter 37 of Title 31.

(d) Notification of change of address

(1) General requirement

The sponsor shall notify the Attorney General and the State in which the sponsored alien is currently a resident within 30 days of any change of address of the sponsor during the period in which an affidavit of support is enforceable.

(2) Penalty

Any person subject to the requirement of paragraph (1) who fails to satisfy such requirement shall, after notice and opportunity to be heard, be subject to a civil penalty of—

(A) not less than $250 or more than $2,000, or

(B) if such failure occurs with knowledge that the sponsored alien has received any means-tested public benefits (other than benefits described in section 401(b), 403(c)(2), or 411(b) of the Personal Responsibility and Work Opportunity Reconciliation Act of 1996 [8 U.S.C.A. § 1611(b), 1613(c)(2), or 1621(b)]) not less than $2,000 or more than $5,000.

The Attorney General shall enforce this paragraph under appropriate regulations.

(e) Jurisdiction

An action to enforce an affidavit of support executed under subsection (a) may be brought against the sponsor in any appropriate court—

(1) by a sponsored alien, with respect to financial support; or

(2) by the appropriate entity of the Federal Government, a State or any political subdivision of a State, or by any other nongovernmental entity under subsection (b)(2), with respect to reimbursement.

(f) "Sponsor" defined

(1) In general

For purposes of this section the term "sponsor" in relation to a sponsored alien means an individual who executes an affidavit of support with respect to the sponsored alien and who—

(A) is a citizen or national of the United States or an alien who is lawfully admitted to the United States for permanent residence;

(B) is at least 18 years of age;

(C) is domiciled in any of the several States of the United States, the District of Columbia, or any territory or possession of the United States;

(D) is petitioning for the admission of the alien under section 204 [8 U.S.C.A. § 1154]; and

(E) demonstrates (as provided in paragraph (6)) the means to maintain an annual income equal to at least 125 percent of the Federal poverty line.

(2) Income requirement case

Such term also includes an individual who does not meet the requirement of paragraph (1)(E) but accepts joint and several liability together with an individual under paragraph (5)(A).

(3) Active duty armed services case

Such term also includes an individual who does not meet the requirement of paragraph (1)(E) but is on active duty (other than active duty for training) in the Armed Forces of the United States, is petitioning for the admission of the alien under section 204 [8 U.S.C.A. § 1154] as the spouse or child of the individual, and demonstrates (as provided in paragraph (6)) the means to maintain an annual income equal to at least 100 percent of the Federal poverty line.

(4) Certain employment-based immigrants case

Such term also includes an individual—

(A) who does not meet the requirement of paragraph (1)(D), but is the relative of the sponsored alien who filed a classification petition for the sponsored alien as an employment-based immigrant under section 203(b) [8 U.S.C.A. § 1153(b)] or who has a significant ownership interest in the entity that filed such a petition; and

(B)(i) who demonstrates (as provided under paragraph (6)) the means to maintain an annual income equal to at least 125 percent of the Federal poverty line, or

(ii) does not meet the requirement of paragraph (1)(E) but accepts joint and several liability together with an individual under paragraph (5)(A).

(5) Non-petitioning cases

Such term also includes an individual who does not meet the requirement of paragraph (1)(D) but who—

(A) accepts joint and several liability with a petitioning sponsor under paragraph (2) or relative of an employment-based immigrant under paragraph (4) and who demonstrates (as provided under paragraph (6)) the means to maintain an annual income equal to at least 125 percent of the Federal poverty line; or

(B) is a spouse, parent, mother-in-law, father-in-law, sibling, child (if at least 18 years of age), son, daughter, son-in-law, daughter-in-law, sister-in-law, brother-in-law, grandparent, or grandchild of a sponsored alien or a legal guardian of a sponsored alien, meets the requirements of paragraph (1) (other than subparagraph (D)), and executes an affidavit of support with respect to such alien in a case in which—

(i) the individual petitioning under section 204 [8 U.S.C.A. § 1154] for the classification of such alien died after the approval of such petition, and the Secretary of Homeland Security has determined for humanitarian reasons that revocation of such petition under section 205 [8 U.S.C.A. § 1155] would be inappropriate; or

(ii) the alien's petition is being adjudicated pursuant to section 204(*l*) [8 U.S.C.A. § 1154(*l*)] (surviving relative consideration).

(6) Demonstration of means to maintain income

(A) In general

(i) Method of demonstration

For purposes of this section, a demonstration of the means to maintain income shall include provision of a certified copy of the individual's Federal income tax return for the individual's 3 most recent taxable years and a written statement, executed under oath or as permitted under penalty of perjury under section 1746 of Title 28, that the copies are certified copies of such returns.

(ii) Flexibility

For purposes of this section, aliens may demonstrate the means to maintain income through demonstration of significant assets of the sponsored alien or of the sponsor, if such assets are available for the support of the sponsored alien.

(iii) Percent of poverty

For purposes of this section, a reference to an annual income equal to at least a particular percentage of the Federal poverty line means an annual income equal to at least such percentage of the Federal poverty line for a family unit of a size equal to the number of members of the sponsor's household (including family and non-family dependents) plus the total number of other dependents and aliens sponsored by that sponsor.

(B) Limitation

The Secretary of State, or the Attorney General in the case of adjustment of status, may provide that the demonstration under subparagraph (A) applies only to the most recent taxable year.

(h) [sic] Federal poverty line defined

For purposes of this section, the term "Federal poverty line" means the level of income equal to the official poverty line (as defined by the Director of the Office of Management and Budget, as revised annually by the Secretary of Health and Human Services, in accordance with section 9902(2) of Title 42) that is applicable to a family of the size involved.

(i) Sponsor's social security account number required to be provided

(1) An affidavit of support shall include the social security account number of each sponsor.

(2) The Attorney General shall develop an automated system to maintain the social security account number data provided under paragraph (1).

(3) The Attorney General shall submit an annual report to the Committees on the Judiciary of the House of Representatives and the Senate setting forth—

(A) for the most recent fiscal year for which data are available the number of sponsors under this section and the number of sponsors in compliance with the financial obligations of this section; and

(B) a comparison of such numbers with the numbers of such sponsors for the preceding fiscal year.

(June 27, 1952, c. 477, Title II, ch. 2, § 213A, as added Aug. 22, 1996, Pub.L. 104–193, Title IV, § 423(a), 110 Stat. 2271, and amended Sept. 30, 1996, Pub.L. 104–208, Div. C, Title V, § 551(a), 110 Stat. 3009–675; Mar. 13, 2002, Pub.L. 107–150, § 2(a)(1), (3), 116 Stat. 74, 75; Oct. 28, 2009, Pub.L. 111–83, Title V, § 568(e), 123 Stat. 2187.)

§ 214. Admission of nonimmigrants [8 U.S.C.A. § 1184]

(a) Regulations

(1) The admission to the United States of any alien as a nonimmigrant shall be for such time and under such conditions as the Attorney General may by regulations prescribe, including when he deems necessary the giving of a bond with sufficient surety in such sum and containing such conditions as the Attorney General shall prescribe, to insure that at the expiration of such time or upon failure to maintain the status under which he was admitted, or to maintain any status subsequently acquired under section 248 [8 U.S.C.A. § 1258], such alien will depart from the United States. No alien admitted to Guam or the Commonwealth of the Northern Mariana Islands without a visa pursuant to section 212(*l*) [8 U.S.C.A. § 1182(*l*)] may be authorized to enter or stay in the United States other than in Guam or the Commonwealth of the Northern Mariana Islands or to remain in Guam or the Commonwealth of the Northern Mariana Islands for a period exceeding 45 days from date of admission to Guam or the Commonwealth of the Northern Mariana Islands. No alien admitted to the United States without a visa pursuant to section 217 [8 U.S.C.A. § 1187] may be authorized to remain in the United States as a nonimmigrant visitor for a period exceeding 90 days from the date of admission.

(2)(A) The period of authorized status as a nonimmigrant described in section 101(a)(15)(O) [8 U.S.C.A. § 1101(a)(15)(O)] shall be for such period as the Attorney General may specify in order to provide for the event (or events) for which the nonimmigrant is admitted.

(B) The period of authorized status as a nonimmigrant described in section 101(a)(15)(P) [8 U.S.C.A. § 1101(a)(15)(P)] shall be for such period as the Attorney General may specify in order to provide for the competition, event, or performance for which the nonimmigrant is admitted. In the case of nonimmigrants admitted as individual athletes under section 101(a)(15)(P) [8 U.S.C.A. § 1101(a)(15)(P)], the period of authorized status may be for an initial period (not to exceed 5 years) during which the nonimmigrant will perform as an athlete and such period may be extended by the Attorney General for an additional period of up to 5 years.

(b) Presumption of status; written waiver

Every alien (other than a nonimmigrant described in subparagraph (L) or (V) of section 101(a)(15) [8 U.S.C.A. § 1101(a)(15)], and other than a nonimmigrant described in any provision of section 101(a)(15)(H)(i) [8 U.S.C.A. § 1101(a)(15)(H)(i)] except subclause (b1) of such section) shall be presumed to be an immigrant until he establishes to the satisfaction of the consular officer, at the time of application for a visa, and the immigration officers, at the time of application for admission, that he is entitled to a nonimmigrant status under section 101(a)(15) [8 U.S.C.A. § 1101(a)(15)]. An alien who is an officer or employee of any foreign government or of any international organization entitled to enjoy privileges, exemptions, and immunities under the International Organizations Immunities Act [22 U.S.C.A. § 288 et seq.], or an alien who is the attendant, servant, employee, or member of the immediate family of any such alien shall not be entitled to apply for or receive an immigrant visa, or to enter the United States as an immigrant unless he executes a written waiver in the same form and substance as is prescribed by section 247(b) [8 U.S.C.A. § 1257(b)].

(c) Petition of importing employer; involvement of Departments of Labor and Agriculture

(1) The question of importing any alien as a nonimmigrant under section subparagraph (H), (L), (O), or (P)(i) of section 101(a)(15) [8 U.S.C.A. § 1101(a)(15)] (excluding nonimmigrants under section 101(a)(15)(H)(i)(b1) [8 U.S.C.A. § 1101(a)(15)(H)(i)(b1)]) in any specific case or specific cases shall be determined by the Attorney General, after consultation with appropriate agencies of the Government, upon petition of the importing employer. Such petition, shall be made and approved before the visa is granted. The petition shall be in such form and contain such information as the Attorney General shall prescribe. The approval of such a petition shall not, of itself, be construed as establishing that the alien is a nonimmigrant. For purposes of this subsection with respect to nonimmigrants described in section 101(a)(15)(H)(ii)(a) [8 U.S.C.A. § 1101(a)(15)(H)(ii)(a)], the term "appropriate agencies of Government" means the Department of Labor and includes the Department of Agriculture. The provisions of section 218 [8 U.S.C.A. § 1188] shall apply to the question of importing any alien as a nonimmigrant under section 101(a)(15)(H)(ii)(a) [8 U.S.C.A. § 1101(a)(15)(H)(ii)(a)].

(2)(A) The Attorney General shall provide for a procedure under which an importing employer which meets requirements established by the Attorney General may file a blanket petition to import aliens as nonimmigrants described in section 101(a)(15)(L) [8 U.S.C.A. § 1101(a)(15)(L)] instead of filing individual petitions under paragraph (1) to import such aliens. Such procedure shall permit the expedited processing of visas for admission of aliens covered under such a petition.

(B) For purposes of section 101(a)(15)(L) [8 U.S.C.A. § 1101(a)(15)(L)], an alien is considered to be serving in a capacity involving specialized knowledge with respect to a company if the alien has a special knowledge of the company product and its application in international markets or has an advanced level of knowledge of processes and procedures of the company.

(C) The Attorney General shall provide a process for reviewing and acting upon petitions under this subsection with respect to nonimmigrants described in section 101(a)(15)(L) [8 U.S.C.A. § 1101(a)(15)(L)] within 30 days after the date a completed petition has been filed.

(D) The period of authorized admission for—

(i) a nonimmigrant admitted to render services in a managerial or executive capacity under section 101(a)(15)(L) [8 U.S.C.A. § 1101(a)(15)(L)] shall not exceed 7 years, or

(ii) a nonimmigrant admitted to render services in a capacity that involves specialized knowledge under section 101(a)(15)(L) [8 U.S.C.A. § 1101(a)(15)(L)] shall not exceed 5 years.

(E) In the case of an alien spouse admitted under section 101(a)(15)(L) [8 U.S.C.A. § 1101(a)(15)(L)], who is accompanying or following to join a principal alien admitted under such section, the Attorney General shall authorize the alien spouse to engage in employment in the United States and provide the spouse with an "employment authorized" endorsement or other appropriate work permit.

(F) An alien who will serve in a capacity involving specialized knowledge with respect to an employer for purposes of section 101(a)(15)(L) [8 U.S.C.A. § 1101(a)(15)(L)] and will be stationed primarily at the worksite of an employer other than the petitioning employer or its affiliate, subsidiary, or parent shall not be eligible for classification under section 101(a)(15)(L) [8 U.S.C.A. § 1101(a)(15)(L)] if—

(i) the alien will be controlled and supervised principally by such unaffiliated employer; or

(ii) the placement of the alien at the worksite of the unaffiliated employer is essentially an arrangement to provide labor for hire for the unaffiliated employer, rather than a placement in connection with the provision of a product or service for which specialized knowledge specific to the petitioning employer is necessary.

(3) The Attorney General shall approve a petition—

(A) with respect to a nonimmigrant described in section 101(a)(15)(O)(i) [8 U.S.C.A. § 1101(a)(15)(O)(i)] only after consultation in accordance with paragraph (6) or, with respect to aliens seeking entry for a motion picture or television production, after consultation with the appropriate union representing the alien's occupational peers and a management organization in the area of the alien's ability, or

(B) with respect to a nonimmigrant described in section 101(a)(15)(O)(ii) [8 U.S.C.A. § 1101(a)(15)(O)(ii)] after consultation in accordance with paragraph (6) or, in the case of such an alien seeking entry for a motion picture or television production, after consultation with such a labor organization and a management organization in the area of the alien's ability.

In the case of an alien seeking entry for a motion picture or television production, **(i)** any opinion under the previous sentence shall only be advisory, **(ii)** any such opinion that recommends denial must be in writing, **(iii)** in making the decision the Attorney General shall consider the exigencies and scheduling of the production, and (iv) the Attorney General shall append to the decision any such opinion. The Attorney General shall provide by regulation for the waiver of the consultation requirement under subparagraph (A) in the case of aliens who have been admitted as nonimmigrants under section 101(a)(15)(O)(i) [8 U.S.C.A. § 1101(a)(15)(O)(i)] because of extraordinary ability in the arts and who seek readmission to perform similar services within 2 years after the date of a consultation under such subparagraph. Not later than 5 days after the date such a waiver is provided, the Attorney General shall forward a copy of the petition and all supporting documentation to the national office of an appropriate labor organization.

(4)(A) For purposes of section 101(a)(15)(P)(i)(a) [8 U.S.C.A. § 1101(a)(15)(P)(i)(a)], an alien is described in this subparagraph if the alien—

(i)(I) performs as an athlete, individually or as part of a group or team, at an internationally recognized level of performance;

(II) is a professional athlete, as defined in section 204(i)(2) [8 U.S.C.A. § 1154(i)(2)];

(III) performs as an athlete, or as a coach, as part of a team or franchise that is located in the United States and a member of a foreign league or association of 15 or more amateur sports teams, if—

(aa) the foreign league or association is the highest level of amateur performance of that sport in the relevant foreign country;

(bb) participation in such league or association renders players ineligible, whether on a temporary or permanent basis, to earn a scholarship in, or participate in, that sport at a college or university in the United States under the rules of the National Collegiate Athletic Association; and

(cc) a significant number of the individuals who play in such league or association are drafted by a major sports league or a minor league affiliate of such a sports league; or

(IV) is a professional athlete or amateur athlete who performs individually or as part of a group in a theatrical ice skating production; and

(ii) seeks to enter the United States temporarily and solely for the purpose of performing—

(I) as such an athlete with respect to a specific athletic competition; or

(II) in the case of an individual described in clause (i)(IV), in a specific theatrical ice skating production or tour.

(B)(i) For purposes of section 101(a)(15)(P)(i)(b) [8 U.S.C.A. § 1101(a)(15)(P)(i)(b)], an alien is described in this subparagraph if the alien—

(I) performs with or is an integral and essential part of the performance of an entertainment group that has (except as provided in clause (ii)) been recognized internationally as being outstanding in the discipline for a sustained and substantial period of time,

(II) in the case of a performer or entertainer, except as provided in clause (iii), has had a sustained and substantial relationship with that group (ordinarily for at least one year) and provides functions integral to the performance of the group, and

(III) seeks to enter the United States temporarily and solely for the purpose of performing as such a performer or entertainer or as an integral and essential part of a performance.

(ii) In the case of an entertainment group that is recognized nationally as being outstanding in its discipline for a sustained and substantial period of time, the Attorney General may, in consideration of special circumstances, waive the international recognition requirement of clause (i)(I).

(iii)(I) The one-year relationship requirement of clause (i)(II) shall not apply to 25 percent of the performers and entertainers in a group.

(II) The Attorney General may waive such one-year relationship requirement for an alien who because of illness or unanticipated and exigent circumstances replaces an essential member of the group and for an alien who augments the group by performing a critical role.

(iv) The requirements of subclauses (I) and (II) of clause (i) shall not apply to alien circus personnel who perform as part of a circus or circus group or who constitute an integral and essential part of the performance of such circus or circus group, but only if such personnel are entering the United States to join a circus that has been recognized nationally as outstanding for a sustained and substantial period of time or as part of such a circus.

(C) A person may petition the Attorney General for classification of an alien as a nonimmigrant under section 101(a)(15)(P) [8 U.S.C.A. § 1101(a)(15)(P)].

(D) The Attorney General shall approve petitions under this subsection with respect to nonimmigrants described in clause (i) or (iii) of section 101(a)(15)(P) [8 U.S.C.A. § 1101(a)(15)(P)] only after consultation in accordance with paragraph (6).

(E) The Attorney General shall approve petitions under this subsection for nonimmigrants described in section 101(a)(15)(P)(ii) [8 U.S.C.A. § 1101(a)(15)(P)(ii)] only after consultation with labor organizations representing artists and entertainers in the United States.

(F)(i) No nonimmigrant visa under section 101(a)(15)(P)(i)(a) [8 U.S.C.A. § 1101(a)(15)(P)(i)(a)] shall be issued to any alien who is a national of a country that is a state sponsor of international terrorism unless the Secretary of State determines, in consultation with the Secretary of Homeland Security and the heads of other appropriate United States agencies, that such alien does not pose a threat to the safety, national security, or national interest of the United States. In making a determination under this subparagraph, the Secretary of State shall apply standards developed by the Secretary of State, in consultation with the Secretary of Homeland Security and the heads of other appropriate United States agencies, that are applicable to the nationals of such states.

(ii) In this subparagraph, the term "state sponsor of international terrorism" means any country the government of which has been determined by the Secretary of State under any of the laws specified in clause (iii) to have repeatedly provided support for acts of international terrorism.

(iii) The laws specified in this clause are the following:

(I) Section 2405(j)(1)(A) of the Title 50, Appendix (or successor statute).

(II) Section 2780(d) of Title 22.

(III) Section 2371(a) of Title 22.

(G) The Secretary of Homeland Security shall permit a petition under this subsection to seek classification of more than 1 alien as a nonimmigrant under section 101(a)(15)(P)(i)(a) [8 U.S.C.A. § 1101(a)(15)(P)(i)(a)].

(H) The Secretary of Homeland Security shall permit an athlete, or the employer of an athlete, to seek admission to the United States for such athlete under a provision of this Act other than section 101(a)(15)(P)(i) [8 U.S.C.A. § 1101(a)(15)(P)(i)] if the athlete is eligible under such other provision.

(5)(A) In the case of an alien who is provided nonimmigrant status under section 101(a)(15)(H)(i)(b) [8 U.S.C.A. § 1101(a)(15)(H)(i)(b)] or 101(a)(15)(H)(ii)(b) [8 U.S.C.A. § 1101(a)(15)(H)(ii)(b)] and who is dismissed from employment by the employer before the end of the period of authorized admission, the employer shall be liable for the reasonable costs of return transportation of the alien abroad.

(B) In the case of an alien who is admitted to the United States in nonimmigrant status under section 101(a)(15)(O) [8 U.S.C.A. § 1101(a)(15)(O)] or 101(a)(15)(P) [8 U.S.C.A. § 1101(a)(15)(P)] and whose employment terminates for reasons other than voluntary resignation, the employer whose offer of employment formed the basis of such nonimmigrant status and the petitioner are jointly and severally liable for the reasonable cost of return transportation of the alien abroad. The petitioner shall provide assurance satisfactory to the Attorney General that the reasonable cost of that transportation will be provided.

(6)(A)(i) To meet the consultation requirement of paragraph (3)(A) in the case of a petition for a nonimmigrant described in section 101(a)(15)(O)(i) [8 U.S.C.A. § 1101(a)(15)(O)(i)] (other than with respect to aliens seeking entry for a motion picture or television production), the petitioner shall submit with the petition an advisory opinion from a peer group (or other person or persons of its choosing, which may include a labor organization) with expertise in the specific field involved.

(ii) To meet the consultation requirement of paragraph (3)(B) in the case of a petition for a nonimmigrant described in section 101(a)(15)(O)(ii) [8 U.S.C.A. § 1101(a)(15)(O)(ii)] (other than with respect to aliens seeking entry for a motion picture or television production), the petitioner shall submit with the petition an advisory opinion from a labor organization with expertise in the skill area involved.

(iii) To meet the consultation requirement of paragraph (4)(D) in the case of a petition for a nonimmigrant described in section 101(a)(15)(P)(i) [8 U.S.C.A. § 1101(a)(15)(P)(i)] or 101(a)(15)(P)(iii) [8 U.S.C.A. § 1101(a)(15)(P)(iii)], the petitioner shall submit with the petition an advisory opinion from a labor organization with expertise in the specific field of athletics or entertainment involved.

(B) To meet the consultation requirements of subparagraph (A), unless the petitioner submits with the petition an advisory opinion from an appropriate labor organization, the Attorney General shall forward a copy of the petition and all supporting documentation to the national office of an appropriate labor organization within 5 days of the date of receipt of the petition. If there is a collective bargaining representative of an employer's employees in the occupational classification for which the alien is being sought, that representative shall be the appropriate labor organization.

(C) In those cases in which a petitioner described in subparagraph (A) establishes that an appropriate peer group (including a labor organization) does not exist, the Attorney General shall adjudicate the petition without requiring an advisory opinion.

(D) Any person or organization receiving a copy of a petition described in subparagraph (A) and supporting documents shall have no more than 15 days following the date of receipt of such documents within which to submit a written advisory opinion or comment or to provide a letter of no objection. Once the 15–day period has expired and the petitioner has had an opportunity, where appropriate, to supply rebuttal evidence, the Attorney General shall adjudicate such petition in no more than 14 days. The Attorney General may shorten any specified time period for emergency reasons if no unreasonable burden would be thus imposed on any participant in the process.

(E)(i) The Attorney General shall establish by regulation expedited consultation procedures in the case of nonimmigrant artists or entertainers described in section 101(a)(15)(O) [8 U.S.C.A. § 1101(a)(15)(O)] or 101(a)(15)(P) [8 U.S.C.A. § 1101(a)(15)(P)] to accommodate the exigencies and scheduling of a given production or event.

(ii) The Attorney General shall establish by regulation expedited consultation procedures in the case of nonimmigrant athletes described in section 101(a)(15)(O)(i) [8 U.S.C.A. § 1101(a)(15)(O)(i)] or 101(a)(15)(P)(i) [8 U.S.C.A. § 1101(a)(15)(P)(i)] in the case of emergency circumstances (including trades during a season).

(F) No consultation required under this subsection by the Attorney General with a nongovernmental entity shall be construed as permitting the Attorney General to delegate any authority under this subsection to such an entity. The Attorney General shall give such weight to advisory opinions provided under this section as the Attorney General determines, in his sole discretion, to be appropriate.

(7) If a petition is filed and denied under this subsection, the Attorney General shall notify the petitioner of the determination and the reasons for the denial and of the process by which the petitioner may appeal the determination.

(8) The Attorney General shall submit annually to the Committees on the Judiciary of the House of Representatives and of the Senate a report describing, with respect to petitions under each subcategory of subparagraphs (H), (O), (P), and (Q) of section 101(a)(15) [8 U.S.C.A. § 1101(a)(15)] the following:

(A) The number of such petitions which have been filed.

(B) The number of such petitions which have been approved and the number of workers (by occupation) included in such approved petitions.

(C) The number of such petitions which have been denied and the number of workers (by occupation) requested in such denied petitions.

(D) The number of such petitions which have been withdrawn.

(E) The number of such petitions which are awaiting final action.

(9)(A) The attorney general shall impose a fee on an employer (excluding any employer that is a primary or secondary education institution, an institution of higher education, as defined in section 1001(a) of Title 20, a nonprofit entity related to or affiliated with any such institution, a nonprofit entity which engages in established curriculum-related clinical training of students registered at any such institution, a nonprofit research organization, or a governmental research organization) filing before a petition under paragraph (1)

(i) initially to grant an alien nonimmigrant status described in section 101(a)(15)(H)(i)(b) [8 U.S.C.A. § 1101(a)(15)(H)(i)(b)];

(ii) to extend the stay of an alien having such status (unless the employer previously has obtained an extension for such alien); or

(iii) to obtain authorization for an alien having such status to change employers.

(B) The amount of the fee shall be $1,500 for each such petition except that the fee shall be half the amount for each such petition by any employer with not more than 25 full-time equivalent employees who are employed in the United States (determined by including any affiliate or subsidiary of such employer).

(C) Fees collected under this paragraph shall be deposited in the Treasury in accordance with section 286(s) [8 U.S.C.A. § 1356(s)].

(10) An amended H–1B petition shall not be required where the petitioning employer is involved in a corporate restructuring, including but not limited to a merger, acquisition, or consolidation, where a new corporate entity succeeds to the interests and obligations of the original petitioning employer and where the terms and conditions of employment remain the same but for the identity of the petitioner.

(11)(A) Subject to subparagraph (b), the Secretary of Homeland Security or the Secretary of State, as appropriate, shall impose a fee on an employer who has filed an attestation described in section 212(t) [8 U.S.C.A. § 1182(t)]—

(i) in order that an alien may be initially granted nonimmigrant status described in section 101(a)(15)(H)(i)(b1) [8 U.S.C.A. § 1101(a)(15)(H)(i)(b1)]; or

(ii) in order to satisfy the requirement of the second sentence of subsection (g)(8)(C) of this section for an alien having such status to obtain certain extensions of stay.

(B) The amount of the fee shall be the same as the amount imposed by the Secretary of Homeland Security under paragraph (9), except that if such paragraph does not authorize such Secretary to impose any fee, no fee shall be imposed under this paragraph.

(C) Fees collected under this paragraph shall be deposited in the Treasury in accordance with section 286(s) [8 U.S.C.A. § 1356(s)].

(12)(A) In addition to any other fees authorized by law, the Secretary of Homeland Security shall impose a fraud prevention and detection fee on an employer filing a petition under paragraph (1)—

(i) initially to grant an alien nonimmigrant status described in subparagraph (H)(i)(b) or (L) of section 101(a)(15) [8 U.S.C.A. § 1101(a)(15)]; or

(ii) to obtain authorization for an alien having such status to change employers.

(B) In addition to any other fees authorized by law, the Secretary of State shall impose a fraud prevention and detection fee on an alien filing an application abroad for a visa authorizing admission to the United States as a nonimmigrant described in section 101(a)(15)(L) [8 U.S.C.A. § 1101(a)(15)(L)], if the alien is covered under a blanket petition described in paragraph (2)(A).

(C) The amount of the fee imposed under subparagraph (A) or (B) shall be $500.

(D) The fee imposed under subparagraph (A) or (B) shall only apply to principal aliens and not to the spouses or children who are accompanying or following to join such principal aliens.

(E) Fees collected under this paragraph shall be deposited in the Treasury in accordance with section 286(v) [8 U.S.C.A. § 1356(v)].

(13)(A) In addition to any other fees authorized by law, the Secretary of Homeland Security shall impose a fraud prevention and detection fee on an employer filing a petition under paragraph (1) for nonimmigrant workers described in section 101(a)(15)(H)(ii)(b) [8 U.S.C.A. § 1101(a)(15)(H)(ii)(b)].

(B) The amount of the fee imposed under subparagraph (A) shall be $150.

(14)(A) If the Secretary of Homeland Security finds, after notice and an opportunity for a hearing, a substantial failure to meet any of the conditions of the petition to admit or otherwise provide status to a nonimmigrant worker under section 101(a)(15)(H)(ii)(b) [8 U.S.C.A. § 1101(a)(15)(H)(ii)(b)] or a willful misrepresentation of a material fact in such petition—

(i) the Secretary of Homeland Security may, in addition to any other remedy authorized by law, impose such administrative remedies (including civil monetary penalties in an amount not to exceed $10,000 per violation) as the Secretary of Homeland Security determines to be appropriate; and

(ii) the Secretary of Homeland Security may deny petitions filed with respect to that employer under section 204 [8 U.S.C.A. § 1154] or paragraph (1) of this subsection during a period of at least 1 year but not more than 5 years for aliens to be employed by the employer.

(B) The Secretary of Homeland Security may delegate to the Secretary of Labor, with the agreement of the Secretary of Labor, any of the authority given to the Secretary of Homeland Security under subparagraph (A)(i).

(C) In determining the level of penalties to be assessed under subparagraph (A), the highest penalties shall be reserved for willful failures to meet any of the conditions of the petition that involve harm to United States workers.

(D) In this paragraph, the term "substantial failure" means the willful failure to comply with the requirements of this section that constitutes a significant deviation from the terms and conditions of a petition.

(d) Issuance of visa to fiancée or fiancé of citizen

(1) A visa shall not be issued under the provisions of section 101(a)(15)(K)(i) [8 U.S.C.A. § 1101(a)(15)(K)(i)] until the consular officer has received a petition filed in the United States by the fiancée or fiancé of the applying alien and approved by the Secretary of Homeland Security. The petition shall be in such form and contain such information as the Secretary of Homeland Security shall, by regulation, prescribe. Such information shall include information on any criminal convictions of the petitioner for any specified crime described in paragraph (3)(B) and information on any permanent protection or restraining order issued against the petitioner related to any specified crime described in paragraph (3)(B)(i). It shall be approved only after satisfactory evidence is submitted by the petitioner to establish that the parties have previously met in person within 2 years before the date of filing the petition, have a bona fide intention to marry, and are legally able and actually willing to conclude a valid marriage in the United States within a period of ninety days after the alien's arrival, except that the Secretary of Homeland Security in his discretion may waive the requirement that the parties have previously met in person. In the event the marriage with the petitioner does not occur within three months after the admission of the said alien and minor children, they shall be required to depart from the United States and upon failure to do so shall be removed in accordance with sections 240 [8 U.S.C.A. § 1229a] and 241 [8 U.S.C.A. § 1231].

(2)(A) Subject to subparagraphs (B) and (C), the Secretary of Homeland Security may not approve a petition under paragraph (1) unless the Secretary has verified that—

(i) the petitioner has not, previous to the pending petition, petitioned under paragraph (1) with respect to two or more applying aliens; and

(ii) if the petitioner has had such a petition previously approved, 2 years have elapsed since the filing of such previously approved petition.

(B) The Secretary of Homeland Security may, in the Secretary's discretion, waive the limitations in subparagraph (A) if justification exists for such a waiver. Except i n extraordinary circumstances and subject to subparagraph (C), such a waiver shall not be granted if the petitioner has a record of violent criminal offenses against a person or persons.

(C)(i) The Secretary of Homeland Security is not limited by the criminal court record and shall grant a waiver of the condition described in the second sentence of subparagraph (B) in the case of a petitioner described in clause (ii).

(ii) A petitioner described in this clause is a petitioner who has been battered or subjected to extreme cruelty and who is or was not the primary perpetrator of violence in the relationship upon a determination that—

(I) the petitioner was acting in self-defense;

(II) the petitioner was found to have violated a protection order intended to protect the petitioner; or

(III) the petitioner committed, was arrested for, was convicted of, or pled guilty to committing a crime that did not result in serious bodily injury and where there was a connection between the crime and the petitioner's having been battered or subjected to extreme cruelty.

(iii) In acting on applications under this subparagraph, the Secretary of Homeland Security shall consider any credible evidence relevant to the application. The determination of what evidence is credible and the weight to be given that evidence shall be within the sole discretion of the Secretary.

(3) In this subsection:

(A) The terms "domestic violence", "sexual assault", "child abuse and neglect", "dating violence", "elder abuse", and "stalking" have the meaning given such terms in section 13925 of Title 42.

(B) The term "specified crime" means the following:

(i) Domestic violence, sexual assault, child abuse and neglect, dating violence, elder abuse, stalking, or an attempt to commit any such crime.

(ii) Homicide, murder, manslaughter, rape, abusive sexual contact, sexual exploitation, incest, torture, trafficking, peonage, holding hostage, involuntary servitude, slave trade, kidnapping, abduction, unlawful criminal restraint, false imprisonment, or an attempt to commit any of the crimes described in this clause.

(iii) At least three convictions for crimes relating to a controlled substance or alcohol not arising from a single act.

(e) Nonimmigrant professionals and annual numerical limit

(1) Notwithstanding any other provision of this Act, an alien who is a citizen of Canada and seeks to enter the United States under and pursuant to the provisions of Annex 1502.1 (United States of America), Part C—Professionals, of the United States–Canada Free–Trade Agreement to engage in business activities at a professional level as provided for therein may be admitted for such purpose under regulations of the Attorney General promulgated after consultation with the Secretaries of State and Labor.

(2) An alien who is a citizen of Canada or Mexico, and the spouse and children of any such alien if accompanying or following to join such alien, who seeks to enter the United States under and pursuant to the provisions of Section D of Annex 1603 of the North American Free Trade Agreement (in this subsection referred to as "NAFTA") to engage in business activities at a professional level as provided for in such Annex, may be admitted for such purpose under regulations of the Attorney General promulgated after consultation with the Secretaries of State and Labor. For purposes of this Act, including the issuance of entry documents and the application of subsection (b), such alien shall be treated as if seeking classification, or classifiable, as a nonimmigrant under section 101(a)(15) [8 U.S.C.A. § 1101(a)(15)]. The admission of an alien who is a citizen of Mexico shall be subject to paragraphs (3), (4), and (5). For purposes of this paragraph and paragraphs (3), (4), and (5), the term "citizen of Mexico" means "citizen" as defined in Annex 1608 of NAFTA.

(3) The Attorney General shall establish an annual numerical limit on admissions under paragraph (2) of aliens who are citizens of Mexico, as set forth in Appendix 1603.D.4 of Annex 1603 of the NAFTA. Subject to paragraph (4), the annual numerical limit—

(A) beginning with the second year that NAFTA is in force, may be increased in accordance with the provisions of paragraph 5(a) of Section D of such Annex, and

(B) shall cease to apply as provided for in paragraph 3 of such Appendix.

(4) The annual numerical limit referred to in paragraph (3) may be increased or shall cease to apply (other than by operation of paragraph 3 of such Appendix) only if—

(A) the President has obtained advice regarding the proposed action from the appropriate advisory committees established under section 2155 of Title 19.

(B) the President has submitted a report to the Committee on the Judiciary of the Senate and the Committee on the Judiciary of the House of Representatives that sets forth—

(i) the action proposed to be taken and the reasons therefor, and

(ii) the advice obtained under subparagraph (A);

(C) a period of at least 60 calendar days that begins on the first day on which the President has met the requirements of subparagraphs (A) and (B) with respect to such action has expired; and

(D) the President has consulted with such committees regarding the proposed action during the period referred to in subparagraph (C).

(5) During the period that the provisions of Appendix 1603.D.4 of Annex 1603 of the NAFTA apply, the entry of an alien who is a citizen of Mexico under and pursuant to the provisions of Section D of Annex 1603 of NAFTA shall be subject to the attestation requirement of section 212(m) [8 U.S.C.A. § 1182(m)], in the case of a registered nurse, or the application requirement of section 212(n) [8 U.S.C.A. § 1182(n)], in the case of all other professions set out in Appendix 1603.D.1 of Annex 1603 of NAFTA, and the petition requirement of subsection (c), to the extent and in the manner prescribed in regulations promulgated by the Secretary of Labor, with respect to sections 212(m) [8 U.S.C.A. § 1182(m)] and 212(n) [8 U.S.C.A. § 1182(n)], and the Attorney General, with respect to subsection (c).

(6) In the case of an alien spouse admitted under section 101(a)(15)(E) [8 U.S.C.A. § 1101(a)(15)(E)], who is accompanying or following to join a principal alien admitted under such section, the Attorney General shall authorize the alien spouse to engage in employment in the United States and provide the spouse with an "employment authorized" endorsement or other appropriate work permit.

(f) Denial of crewmember status in case of certain labor disputes

(1) Except as provided in paragraph (3), no alien shall be entitled to nonimmigrant status described in section 101(a)(15)(D) [8 U.S.C.A. § 1101(a)(15)(D)] if the alien intends to land for the purpose of performing service on board a vessel of the United States (as defined in section 2101(46) of Title 46) or on an aircraft of an air carrier (as defined in section 40102(a)(2) of Title 49) during a labor dispute where there is a strike or lockout in the bargaining unit of the employer in which the alien intends to perform such service.

(2) An alien described in paragraph (1)—

(A) may not be paroled into the United States pursuant to section 212(d)(5) [8 U.S.C.A. § 1182(d)(5)] unless the Attorney General determines that the parole of such alien is necessary to protect the national security of the United States; and

(B) shall be considered not to be a bona fide crewman for purposes of section 252(b) [8 U.S.C.A. § 1282(b)].

(3) Paragraph (1) shall not apply to an alien if the air carrier or owner or operator of such vessel that employs the alien provides documentation that satisfies the Attorney General that the alien—

(A) has been an employee of such employer for a period of not less than 1 year preceding the date that a strike or lawful lockout commenced;

(B) has served as a qualified crewman for such employer at least once in each of 3 months during the 12–month period preceding such date; and

(C) shall continue to provide the same services that such alien provided as such a crewman.

(g) Temporary workers and trainees; limitation on numbers

(1) The total number of aliens who may be issued visas or otherwise provided nonimmigrant status during any fiscal year (beginning with fiscal year 1992)—

(A) under section 101(a)(15)(H)(i)(b) [8 U.S.C.A. § 1101(a)(15)(H)(i)(b)], may not exceed—

(i) 65,000 in each fiscal year before fiscal year 1999;

(ii) 115,000 in fiscal year 1999;

(iii) 115,000 in fiscal year 2000;

(iv) 195,000 in fiscal year 2001;

(v) 195,000 in fiscal year 2002;

(vi) 195,000 in fiscal year 2003; and

(vii) 65,000 in each succeeding fiscal year;

(B) under section 101(a)(15)(H)(ii)(b) [8 U.S.C.A. § 1101(a)(15)(H)(ii)(b)] may not exceed 66,000.

(2) The numerical limitations of paragraph (1) shall only apply to principal aliens and not to the spouses or children of such aliens.

(3) Aliens who are subject to the numerical limitations of paragraph (1) shall be issued visas (or otherwise provided nonimmigrant status) in the order in which petitions are filed for such visas or status. If an alien who was issued a visa or otherwise provided nonimmigrant status and counted against the numerical limitations of paragraph (1) is found to have been issued such visa or otherwise provided such status by fraud or willfully misrepresenting a material fact and such visa or nonimmigrant status is revoked, then one number shall be restored to the total number of aliens who may be issued visas or otherwise provided such status under the numerical limitations of paragraph (1) in the fiscal year in which the petition is revoked, regardless of the fiscal year in which the petition was approved.

(4) In the case of a nonimmigrant described in section 101(a)(15)(H)(i)(b) [8 U.S.C.A. § 1101(a)(15)(H)(i)(b)], the period of authorized admission as such a nonimmigrant may not exceed 6 years.

(5) The numerical limitations contained in paragraph (1)(a) shall not apply to any nonimmigrant alien issued a visa or otherwise provided status under section 101(a)(15)(h)(i)(b) [8 U.S.C.A. § 1101(a)(15)(h)(i)(b)] who—

(A) is employed (or has received an offer of employment) at an institution of higher education (as defined in section 1001(a) of Title 20), or a related or affiliated nonprofit entity;

(B) is employed (or has received an offer of employment) at a nonprofit research organization or a governmental research organization; or

(C) has earned a master's or higher degree from a United States institution of higher education (as defined in section 1101(a) of Title 20), until the number of aliens who are exempted from such numerical limitation during such year exceeds 20,000.

(6) Any alien who ceases to be employed by an employer described in paragraph (5)(A) shall, if employed as a nonimmigrant alien described in section 101(a)(15)(H)(i)(b) [8 U.S.C.A. § 1101(a)(15)(H)(i)(b)], who has not previously been counted toward the numerical limitations contained in paragraph (1)(A), be counted toward those limitations the first time the alien is employed by an employer other than one described in paragraph (5).

(7) Any alien who has already been counted, within the 6 years prior to the approval of a petition described in subsection (c), toward the numerical limitations of paragraph (1)(A) shall not again be counted toward those limitations unless the alien would be eligible for a full 6 years of authorized admission at the time the petition is filed. Where multiple petitions are approved for 1 alien, that alien shall be counted only once.

(8)(A) The agreements referred to in section 101(a)(15)(H)(i)(b1) [8 U.S.C.A. § 1101(a)(15)(H)(i)(b1)] are—

(i) the United States–Chile Free Trade Agreement; and

(ii) the United States–Singapore Free Trade Agreement.

(B)(i) The Secretary of Homeland Security shall establish annual numerical limitations on approvals of initial applications by aliens for admission under section 101(a)(15)(H)(i)(b1) [8 U.S.C.A. § 1101(a)(15)(H)(i)(b1)].

(ii) The annual numerical limitations described in clause (i) shall not exceed

(I) 1,400 for nationals of Chile (as defined in article 14.9 of the United States–Chile Free Trade Agreement) for any fiscal year; and

(II) 5,400 for nationals of Singapore (as defined in Annex 1A of the United States–Singapore Free Trade Agreement) for any fiscal year.

(iii) The annual numerical limitations described in clause (i) shall only apply to principal aliens and not to the spouses or children of such aliens.

(iv) The annual numerical limitation described in paragraph (1)(A) is reduced by the amount of the annual numerical limitations established under clause (i). However, if a numerical limitation established under clause (i) has not been exhausted at the end of a given fiscal year, the Secretary of Homeland Security shall adjust upwards the numerical limitation in paragraph (1)(A) for that fiscal year by the amount remaining in the numerical limitation under clause (i). Visas under section 101(a)(15)(H)(i)(b1) [8 U.S.C.A. § 1101(a)(15)(H)(i)(b)] may be issued pursuant to such adjustment within the first 45 days of the next fiscal year to aliens who had applied for such visas during the fiscal year for which the adjustment was made.

(C) The period of authorized admission as a nonimmigrant under section 101(a)(15)(H)(i)(b1) [8 U.S.C.A. § 1101(a)(15)(H)(i)(b1)] shall be 1 year, and may be extended, but only in 1-year increments. After every second extension, the next following extension shall not be granted unless the Secretary of Labor had determined and certified to the Secretary of Homeland Security and the Secretary of State that the intending employer has filed with the Secretary of Labor an attestation under section 212(t)(1) [8 U.S.C.A. § 1182(t)(1)] for the purpose of permitting the nonimmigrant to obtain such extension.

(D) The numerical limitation described in paragraph (1)(A) for a fiscal year shall be reduced by one for each alien granted an extension under subparagraph (C) during such year who has obtained 5 or more consecutive prior extensions.

(9)(A) Subject to subparagraphs (B) and (C), an alien who has already been counted toward the numerical limitation of paragraph (1)(B) during fiscal year 2004, 2005, or 2006 shall not again be counted toward such limitation during fiscal year 2007. Such an alien shall be considered a returning worker.

(B) A petition to admit or otherwise provide status under section 101(a)(15)(H)(ii)(b) [8 U.S.C.A. § 1101(a)(15)(H)(ii)(b)] shall include, with respect to a returning worker

(i) all information and evidence that the Secretary of Homeland Security determines is required to support a petition for status under section 101(a)(15)(H)(ii)(b) [8 U.S.C.A. § 1101(a)(15)(H)(ii)(b)];

(ii) the full name of the alien; and

(iii) a certification to the Department of Homeland Security that the alien is a returning worker.

(C) An H-2B visa or grant of nonimmigrant status for a returning worker shall be approved only if the alien is confirmed to be a returning worker by—

(i) the Department of State; or

(ii) if the alien is visa exempt or seeking to change to status under section 101(a)(15)(H)(ii)(b) [8 U.S.C.A. § 1101(a)(15)(H)(ii)(b)], the Department of Homeland Security.

(10) The numerical limitations of paragraph (1)(B) shall be allocated for a fiscal year so that the total number of aliens subject to such numerical limits who enter the United States pursuant to a visa or are accorded nonimmigrant status under section 101(a)(15)(H)(ii)(b) [8 U.S.C.A. § 1101(a)(15)(H)(ii)(b)] during the first 6 months of such fiscal year is not more than 33,000.

(11)(A) The Secretary of State may not approve a number of initial applications submitted for aliens described in section 101(a)(15)(E)(iii) [8 U.S.C.A. § 1101(a)(15)(E)(iii)] that is more than the applicable numerical limitation set out in this paragraph.

(B) The applicable numerical limitation referred to in subparagraph (A) is 10,500 for each fiscal year.

(C) The applicable numerical limitation referred to in subparagraph (A) shall only apply to principal aliens and not to the spouses or children of such aliens.

(h) Intention to abandon foreign residence

The fact that an alien is the beneficiary of an application for a preference status filed under section 204 [8 U.S.C.A. § 1154] or has otherwise sought permanent residence in the United States shall not constitute evidence of an intention to abandon a foreign residence for purposes of obtaining a visa as a nonimmigrant described in subparagraph (H)(i)(b) or (c), (L), or (V) of section 101(a)(15) [8 U.S.C.A. § 1101(a)(15)] or otherwise obtaining or maintaining the status of a nonimmigrant described in such subparagraph, if the alien had obtained a change of status under section 248 [8 U.S.C.A. § 1258] to a classification as such a nonimmigrant before the alien's most recent departure from the United States.

(i) "Specialty occupation" defined

(1) Except as provided in paragraph (3), for purposes of section 101(a)(15)(H)(i)(b) [8 U.S.C.A. § 1101(a)(15)(H)(i)(b)], section 101(a)(15)(E)(iii) [8 U.S.C.A. § 1101(a)(15)(E)(iii)], and paragraph (2), the term "specialty occupation" means an occupation that requires—

(A) theoretical and practical application of a body of highly specialized knowledge, and

(B) attainment of a bachelor's or higher degree in the specific specialty (or its equivalent) as a minimum for entry into the occupation in the United States.

(2) For purposes of section 101(a)(15)(H)(i)(b) [8 U.S.C.A. § 1101(a)(15)(H)(i)(b)], the requirements of this paragraph, with respect to a specialty occupation, are—

(A) full state licensure to practice in the occupation, if such licensure is required to practice in the occupation,

(B) completion of the degree described in paragraph (1)(B) for the occupation, or

(C) **(i)** experience in the specialty equivalent to the completion of such degree, and **(ii)** recognition of expertise in the specialty through progressively responsible positions relating to the specialty.

(3) For purposes of section 101(a)(15)(H)(i)(b1) [8 U.S.C.A. § 1101(a)(15)(H)(i)(b1)], the term "specialty occupation" means an occupation that requires—

(A) theoretical and practical application of a body of specialized knowledge; and

(B) attainment of a bachelor's or higher degree in the specific specialty (or its equivalent) as a minimum for entry into the occupation in the United States.

(j) Labor disputes

(1) Notwithstanding any other provision of this chapter, an alien who is a citizen of Canada or Mexico who seeks to enter the United States under and pursuant to the provisions of Section B, Section C, or Section D of Annex 1603 of the North American Free Trade Agreement, shall not be classified as a nonimmigrant under such provisions if there is in progress a strike or lockout in the course of a labor dispute in the occupational classification at the place or intended place of employment, unless such alien establishes, pursuant to regulations promulgated by the Attorney General, that the alien's entry will not affect adversely the settlement of the strike or lockout or the employment of any person who is involved in the strike or lockout. Notice of a determination under this paragraph shall be given as may be required by paragraph 3 of article 1603 of such Agreement. For purposes of this paragraph, the term "citizen of Mexico" means "citizen" as defined in Annex 1608 of such Agreement.

(2) Notwithstanding any other provision of this chapter except section 212(t)(1) [8 U.S.C.A. § 1182(t)(1)], and subject to regulations promulgated by the Secretary of Homeland Security, an alien who seeks to enter the United States under and pursuant to the provisions of an agreement listed in subsection (g)(8)(A) of this section, and the spouse and children of such an alien if accompanying or following to join the alien, may be denied admission as a nonimmigrant under subparagraph (E), (L), or (H)(i)(b1) of section 101(a)(15) [8 U.S.C.A. § 1101(a)(15)] if there is in progress a labor dispute in the occupational classification at the place or intended place of employment, unless such alien establishes, pursuant to regulations promulgated by the Secretary of Homeland Security after consultation with the Secretary of Labor, that the alien's entry will not affect adversely the settlement of the labor dispute or the employment of any person who is involved in the labor dispute.

Notice of a determination under this paragraph shall be given as may be required by such agreement.

(k) Numerical limitations; period of admission; conditions for admission and stay; annual report

(1) The number of aliens who may be provided a visa as nonimmigrants under section 101(a)(15)(S)(i) [8 U.S.C.A. § 1101(a)(15)(S)(i)] in any fiscal year may not exceed 200. The number of aliens who may be provided a visa as nonimmigrants under section 101(a)(15)(S)(ii) [8 U.S.C.A. § 1101(a)(15)(S)(ii)] in any fiscal year may not exceed 50.

(2) The period of admission of an alien as such a nonimmigrant may not exceed 3 years. Such period may not be extended by the Attorney General.

(3) As a condition for the admission, and continued stay in lawful status, of such a nonimmigrant, the nonimmigrant—

(A) shall report not less often than quarterly to the Attorney General such information concerning the alien's whereabouts and activities as the Attorney General may require;

(B) may not be convicted of any criminal offense punishable by a term of imprisonment of 1 year or more after the date of such admission;

(C) must have executed a form that waives the nonimmigrant's right to contest, other than on the basis of an application for withholding of removal, any action for removal of the alien instituted before the alien obtains lawful permanent resident status; and

(D) shall abide by any other condition, limitation, or restriction imposed by the Attorney General.

(4) The Attorney General shall submit a report annually to the Committee on the Judiciary of the House of Representatives and the Committee on the Judiciary of the Senate concerning—

(A) the number of such nonimmigrants admitted;

(B) the number of successful criminal prosecutions or investigations resulting from cooperation of such aliens;

(C) the number of terrorist acts prevented or frustrated resulting from cooperation of such aliens;

(D) the number of such nonimmigrants whose admission or cooperation has not resulted in successful criminal prosecution or investigation or the prevention or frustration of a terrorist act; and

(E) the number of such nonimmigrants who have failed to report quarterly (as required under paragraph (3)) or who have been convicted of crimes in the United States after the date of their admission as such a nonimmigrant.

(5) Redesignated (4)

(*l*) Restrictions on waiver

(1) In the case of a request by an interested State agency, or by an interested Federal agency, for a waiver of the 2–year foreign residence requirement under section 212(e) [8 U.S.C.A. § 1182(e)] on behalf of an alien described in clause (iii) of such section, the Attorney General shall not grant such waiver unless—

(A) in the case of an alien who is otherwise contractually obligated to return to a foreign country, the government of such country furnishes the Director of the United States Information Agency with a statement in writing that it has no objection to such waiver;

(B) in the case of a request by an interested State agency, the grant of such waiver would not cause the number of waivers allotted for that State for that fiscal year to exceed 30;

(C) in the case of a request by an interested Federal agency or by an interested State agency—

(i) the alien demonstrates a bona fide offer of full-time employment at a health facility or health care organization, which employment has been determined by the Attorney General to be in the public interest; and

(ii) the alien agrees to begin employment with the health facility or health care organization within 90 days of receiving such waiver, and agrees to continue to work for a total of not less than 3 years (unless the Attorney General determines that extenuating circumstances exist, such as closure of the facility or hardship to the alien, which would justify a lesser period of employment at such health facility or health care organization, in which case the alien must demonstrate another bona fide offer of employment at a health facility or health care organization for the remainder of such 3–year period); and

(D) in the case of a request by an interested Federal agency (other than a request by an interested Federal agency to employ the alien full-time in medical research or training) or by an interested State agency, the alien agrees to practice primary care or specialty medicine in accordance with paragraph (2) for a total of not less than 3 years only in the geographic area or areas which are designated by the Secretary of Health and Human Services as having a shortage of health care professionals, except that—

(i) in the case of a request by the Department of Veterans Affairs, the alien shall not be required to practice medicine in a geographic area designated by the Secretary;

(ii) in the case of a request by an interested State agency, the head of such State agency determines that the alien is to practice medicine under such agreement in a facility that serves patients who reside in one or more geographic areas so designated by the Secretary of Health and Human Services (without regard to whether such facility is located within such a designated geographic area), and the grant of such waiver would not cause the number of the waivers granted on behalf of aliens for such State for a fiscal year (within the limitation in subparagraph (B)) in accordance with the conditions of this clause to exceed 10; and

(iii) in the case of a request by an interested Federal agency or by an interested State agency for a waiver for an alien who agrees to practice specialty medicine in a facility located in a geographic area so designated by the Secretary of Health and Human Services, the request shall demonstrate, based on criteria established by such agency, that there is a shortage of health care professionals able to provide services in the appropriate medical specialty to the patients who will be served by the alien.

(2)(A) Notwithstanding section 248(a)(2) [8 U.S.C.A § 1258(a)(2)], the Attorney General may change the status of an alien who qualifies under this subsection and section 212(e) [8 U.S.C.A § 1182(e)] to that of an alien described in section 101(a)(15)(H)(i)(b) [8 U.S.C.A § 1101(a)(15)(H)(i)(b)]. The numerical limitations contained in subsection (g)(1)(A) of this section shall not apply to any alien whose status is changed under the preceding sentence, if the alien obtained a waiver of the 2–year foreign residence requirement upon a request by an interested Federal agency or an interested State agency.

(B) No person who has obtained a change of status under subparagraph (A) and who has failed to fulfill the terms of the contract with the health facility or health care organization named in the waiver application shall be eligible to apply for an immigrant visa, for permanent residence, or for any other change of nonimmigrant status, until it is established that such person has resided and been physically present in the country of his nationality or his last residence for an aggregate of at least 2 years following departure from the United States.

(3) Notwithstanding any other provision of this subsection, the 2–year foreign residence requirement under section 212(e) [8 U.S.C.A. § 1182(e)] shall apply with respect to an alien described in clause (iii) of such section, who has not otherwise been accorded status under section 101(a)(27)(H) [8 U.S.C.A. § 1101(a)(27)(H)], if—

(A) at any time the alien ceases to comply with any agreement entered into under subparagraph (C) or (D) of paragraph (1); or

(B) the alien's employment ceases to benefit the public interest at any time during the 3–year period described in paragraph (1)(C).

(m) Nonimmigrant elementary and secondary school students

(1) An alien may not be accorded status as a nonimmigrant under clause (i) or (iii) of section 101(a)(15)(F) [8 U.S.C.A. § 1101(a)(15)(F)] in order to pursue a course of study—

(A) at a public elementary school or in a publicly funded adult education program; or

(B) at a public secondary school unless—

(i) the aggregate period of such status at such a school does not exceed 12 months with respect to any alien, and

(ii) the alien demonstrates that the alien has reimbursed the local educational agency that administers the school for the full, unsubsidized per capita cost of providing education at such school for the period of the alien's attendance.

(2) An alien who obtains the status of a nonimmigrant under clause (i) or (iii) of section 101(a)(15)(F) [8 U.S.C.A. § 1101(a)(15)(F)] in order to pursue a course of study at a private elementary or secondary school or in a language training program that is not publicly funded shall be considered to have violated such status, and the alien's visa under section 101(a)(15)(F) [8 U.S.C.A. § 1101(a)(15)(F)] shall be void, if the alien terminates or abandons such course of study at such a school and undertakes a course of study at a public elementary school, in a publicly funded adult education program, in a publicly funded adult education language training program, or at a public secondary school (unless the requirements of paragraph (1)(B) are met).

(n) Increased portability of H–1B status

(1) A nonimmigrant alien described in paragraph (2) who was previously issued a visa or otherwise provided nonimmigrant status under section 101(a)(15)(H)(i)(b) [8 U.S.C.A. § 1101(a)(15)(H)(i)(b)] is authorized to accept new employment upon the filing by the prospective employer of a new petition on behalf of such nonimmigrant as provided under subsection (a). Employment authorization shall continue for such alien until the new petition is adjudicated. If the new petition is denied, such authorization shall cease.

(2) A nonimmigrant alien described in this paragraph is a nonimmigrant alien—

(A) who has been lawfully admitted into the United States;

(B) on whose behalf an employer has filed a nonfrivolous petition for new employment before the date of expiration of the period of stay authorized by the Attorney General; and

(C) who, subsequent to such lawful admission, has not been employed without authorization in the United States before the filing of such petition.

(*o*) Trafficking in persons; conditions of nonimmigrant status

(1) No alien shall be eligible for admission to the United States under section 101(a)(15)(T) [8 U.S.C.A. § 1101(a)(15)(T)] if there is substantial reason to believe that the alien has committed an act of a severe form of trafficking in persons (as defined in section 103 of the Trafficking Victims Protection Act of 2000 [22 U.S.C.A. § 7102]).

(2) The total number of aliens who may be issued visas or otherwise provided nonimmigrant status during any fiscal year under section 101(a)(15)(T) [8 U.S.C.A. § 1101(a)(15)(T)] may not exceed 5,000.

(3) The numerical limitation of paragraph (2) shall only apply to principal aliens and not to the spouses, sons, daughters, siblings, or parents of such aliens.

(4) An unmarried alien who seeks to accompany, or follow to join, a parent granted status under section 101(a)(15)(T)(i) [8 U.S.C.A. § 1101(a)(15)(T)(i)], and who was under 21 years of age on the date on which such parent applied for such status, shall continue to be classified as a child for purposes of section 101(a)(15)(T)(ii) [8 U.S.C.A. § 1101(a)(15)(T)(ii)], if the alien attains 21 years of age after such parent's application was filed but while it was pending.

(5) An alien described in clause (i) of section 101(a)(15)(T) [8 U.S.C.A. § 1101(a)(15)(T)] shall continue to be treated as an alien described in clause (ii)(I) of such section if the alien attains 21 years of age after the alien's application for status under such clause (i) is filed but while it is pending.

(6) In making a determination under section 101(a)(15)(T)(i)(III)(aa) [8 U.S.C.A. § 1101(a)(15)(T)(i)(III)(aa)] with respect to an alien, statements from State and local law enforcement officials that the alien has complied with any reasonable request for assistance in the investigation or prosecution of crimes such as kidnapping, rape, slavery, or other forced labor offenses, where severe forms of trafficking in persons (as defined in section 7102 of Title 22) appear to have been involved, shall be considered.

(7)(A) Except as provided in subparagraph (B), an alien who is issued a visa or otherwise provided nonimmigrant status under section 101(a)(15)(T) [8 U.S.C.A § 1101(a)(15)(T)] may be granted such status for a period of not more than 4 years.

(B) An alien who is issued a visa or otherwise provided nonimmigrant status under section 101(a)(15)(T) [8 U.S.C.A. § 1101(a)(15)(T)] may extend the period of such status beyond the period described in subparagraph (A) if—

(i) a Federal, State, or local law enforcement official, prosecutor, judge, or other authority investigating or prosecuting activity relating to human trafficking or certifies that the presence of the alien in the United States is necessary to assist in the investigation or prosecution of such activity;

(ii) the alien is eligible for relief under section 245(*l*) [8 U.S.C.A. § 1255(*l*)] and is unable to obtain such relief because regulations have not been issued to implement such section; or

(iii) the Secretary of Homeland Security determines that an extension of the period of such nonimmigrant status is warranted due to exceptional circumstances.

(C) Nonimmigrant status under section 101(a)(15)(T) [8 U.S.C.A. § 1101(a)(15)(T)] shall be extended during the pendency of an application for adjustment of status under section 245(*l*) [8 U.S.C.A. § 1255(*l*)].

(p) Requirements applicable to section 101(a)(15)(U) [8 U.S.C.A. § 1101(a)(15)(U)] visas

(1) Petitioning procedures for section 101(a)(15)(U) [8 U.S.C.A. § 1101(a)(15)(U)] visas

The petition filed by an alien under section 101(a)(15)(U)(i) [8 U.S.C.A. § 1101(a)(15)(U)(i)] shall contain a certification from a Federal, State, or local law enforcement official, prosecutor, judge, or other Federal, State, or local authority investigating criminal activity described in section 101(a)(15)(U)(iii) [8 U.S.C.A. § 1101(a)(15)(U)(iii)]. This certification may also be provided by an official of the Service whose ability to provide such certification is not limited to information concerning immigration violations. This certification shall state that the alien "has been helpful, is being helpful, or is likely to be helpful" in the investigation or prosecution of criminal activity described in section 101(a)(15)(U)(iii) [8 U.S.C.A. § 1101(a)(15)(U)(iii)].

(2) Numerical limitations

(A) The number of aliens who may be issued visas or otherwise provided status as nonimmigrants under section 101(a)(15)(U) [8 U.S.C.A. § 1101(a)(15)(U)] in any fiscal year shall not exceed 10,000.

(B) The numerical limitations in subparagraph (A) shall only apply to principal aliens described in section 101(a)(15)(U)(i) [8 U.S.C.A. § 1101(a)(15)(U)(i)], and not to spouses, children, or, in the case of alien children, the alien parents of such children.

(3) Duties of the Attorney General with respect to "U" visa nonimmigrants

With respect to nonimmigrant aliens described in subsection (a)(15)(U)[sic]—

(A) the Attorney General and other government officials, where appropriate, shall provide those aliens with referrals to nongovernmental organizations to advise the aliens regarding their options while in the United States and the resources available to them; and

(B) the Attorney General shall, during the period those aliens are in lawful temporary resident status under that subsection, provide the aliens with employment authorization.

(4) Credible evidence considered

In acting on any petition filed under this subsection, the consular officer or the Attorney General, as appropriate, shall consider any credible evidence relevant to the petition.

(5) Nonexclusive relief

Nothing in this subsection limits the ability of aliens who qualify for status under section 101(a)(15)(U) [8 U.S.C.A. § 1101(a)(15)(U)] to seek any other immigration benefit or status for which the alien may be eligible.

(6) Duration of status

The authorized period of status of an alien as a nonimmigrant under section 101(a)(15)(U) [8 U.S.C.A. § 1101(a)(15)(U)] shall be for a period of not more than 4 years, but shall be extended upon certification from a Federal, State, or local law enforcement official, prosecutor, judge, or other Federal, State, or local authority investigating or prosecuting criminal activity described in section 101(a)(15)(U)(iii) [8 U.S.C.A. § 1101(a)(15)(U)(iii)] that the alien's presence in the United States is required to assist in the investigation or prosecution of such criminal activity. The Secretary of Homeland Security may extend, beyond the 4–year period authorized under this section, the authorized period of status of an alien as a nonimmigrant under section 101(a)(15)(U) [8 U.S.C.A. § 1101(a)(15)(U)] if the Secretary determines that an extension of such period is warranted due to exceptional circumstances. Such alien's nonimmigrant status shall be extended beyond the 4–year period authorized under this section if the alien is eligible for relief under section 245(m) [8 U.S.C.A. § 1255(m)] and is unable to obtain such relief because regulations have not been issued to implement such section and shall be extended during the pendency of an application for adjustment of status under section 245(m) [8 U.S.C.A. § 1255(m)]. The Secretary may grant work authorization to any alien who has a pending, bona fide application for nonimmigrant status under section 101(a)(15)(U) [8 U.S.C.A. § 1101(a)(15)(U)].

(7) Age determinations

(A) Children

An unmarried alien who seeks to accompany, or follow to join, a parent granted status under section 101(a)(15)(U)(i) [8 U.S.C.A. § 1101(a)(15)(U)(i)], and who was under 21 years of age on the date on which such parent petitioned for such status, shall continue to be classified as a child for purposes of section 101(a)(15)(U)(ii) [8 U.S.C.A. § 1101(a)(15)(U)(ii)], if the alien attains 21 years of age after such parent's petition was filed but while it was pending.

(B) Principal aliens

An alien described in clause (i) of section 101(a)(15)(U) [8 U.S.C.A. § 1101(a)(15)(U)] shall continue to be treated as an alien described in clause (ii)(I) of such section if the alien attains 21 years of age after the alien's application for status under such clause (i) is filed but while it is pending.

(q) Nonimmigrant described in section 101(a)(15)(V) [8 U.S.C.A. § 1101(a)(15)(V)]

(1) In the case of a nonimmigrant described in section 101(a)(15)(V) [8 U.S.C.A. § 1101(a)(15)(V)]

(A) the Attorney General shall authorize the alien to engage in employment in the United States during the period of authorized admission and shall provide the alien with an "employment authorized" endorsement or other appropriate document signifying authorization of employment; and

(B) the period of authorized admission as such a nonimmigrant shall terminate 30 days after the date on which any of the following is denied:

(i) The petition filed under section 204 [8 U.S.C.A. § 1154] to accord the alien a status under section 203(a)(2)(A) [8 U.S.C.A. § 1153(a)(2)(A)] (or, in the case of a child granted nonimmigrant status based on eligibility to receive a visa under section 203(d) [8 U.S.C.A. § 1153(d)], the petition filed to accord the child's parent a status under section 203(a)(2)(A) [8 U.S.C.A. § 1153(a)(2)(A)]).

(ii) The alien's application for an immigrant visa pursuant to the approval of such petition.

(iii) The alien's application for adjustment of status under section 245 [8 U.S.C.A. § 1255] pursuant to the approval of such petition.

(2) In determining whether an alien is eligible to be admitted to the United States as a nonimmigrant under section 101(a)(15)(V) [8 U.S.C.A. § 1101(a)(15)(V)], the grounds for inadmissibility specified in section 212(a)(9)(B) [8 U.S.C.A. § 1182(a)(9)(B)] shall not apply.

(3) The status of an alien physically present in the United States may be adjusted by the attorney general, in the discretion of the attorney general and under such regulations as the attorney general may prescribe, to that of a nonimmigrant under section 101(a)(15)(v) [8 U.S.C.A. § 1101(a)(15)(v)], if the alien

(A) applies for such adjustment;

(B) satisfies the requirements of such section; and

(C) is eligible to be admitted to the United States, except in determining such admissibility, the grounds for inadmissibility specified in paragraphs (6)(A), (7), and (9)(B) of section 212(a) [8 U.S.C.A. § 1182(a)] shall not apply.

(r) Visas of nonimmigrants described in section 101(a)(15)(K)(ii) [8 U.S.C.A. § 1101(a)(15)(K)(ii)]

(1) A visa shall not be issued under the provisions of section 101(a)(15)(K)(ii) [8 U.S.C.A. § 1101(a)(15)(K)(ii)] until the consular officer has received a petition filed in the United States by the spouse of the applying alien and approved by the Attorney General. The petition shall be in such form and contain such information as the Attorney General shall, by regulation, prescribe. Such information shall include information on any criminal convictions of the petitioner for any specified crime described in paragraph (5)(B) and information on any permanent protection or restraining order issued against the petitioner related to any specified crime described in subsection (5)(B)(i).

(2) In the case of an alien seeking admission under section 101(a)(15)(K)(ii) [8 U.S.C.A. § 1101(a)(15)(K)(ii)] who concluded a marriage with a citizen of the United States outside the United States, the alien shall be considered inadmissible under section 212(a)(7)(B) [8 U.S.C.A. § 1182(a)(7)(B)] if the alien is not at the time of application for admission in possession of a valid nonimmigrant visa issued by a consular officer in the foreign state in which the marriage was concluded.

(3) In the case of a nonimmigrant described in section 101(a)(15)(K)(ii) [8 U.S.C.A. § 1101(a)(15)(K)(ii)], and any child of such a nonimmigrant who was admitted as accompanying, or following to join, such a nonimmigrant, the period of authorized admission shall terminate 30 days after the date on which any of the following is denied:

(A) The petition filed under section 204 [8 U.S.C.A. § 1154] to accord the principal alien status under section 201(b)(2)(A)(i) [8 U.S.C.A. § 1151(b)(2)(A)(i)].

(B) The principal alien's application for an immigrant visa pursuant to the approval of such petition.

(C) The principal alien's application for adjustment of status under section 245 [8 U.S.C.A. § 1255] pursuant to the approval of such petition.

(4)(A) The Secretary of Homeland Security shall create a database for the purpose of tracking multiple visa petitions filed for fiancé(e)s and spouses under clauses (i) and (ii) of section 101(a)(15)(K) [8 U.S.C.A § 1101(a)(15)(K)]. Upon approval of a second visa petition under section 101(a)(15)(K) [8 U.S.C.A § 1101(a)(15)(K)] for a fiancé(e) or spouse filed by the same United States citizen petitioner, the petitioner shall be notified by the Secretary that information concerning the petitioner has been entered into the multiple visa petition tracking database. All subsequent fiance(e) or spouse nonimmigrant visa petitions filed by that petitioner under such section shall be entered in the database.

(B)(i) Once a petitioner has had two fiance(e) or spousal petitions approved under clause (i) or (ii) of section 101(a)(15)(K) [8 U.S.C.A § 1101(a)(15)(K)], if a subsequent petition is filed under such section less than 10 years after the date the first visa petition was filed under such section, the Secretary of Homeland Security shall notify both the petitioner and beneficiary of any such subsequent petition about the number of previously approved fiance(e) or spousal petitions listed in the database.

(ii) To notify the beneficiary as required by clause (i), the Secretary of Homeland Security shall provide such notice to the Secretary of State for inclusion in the mailing to the beneficiary described in section 833(a)(5)(A)(i) of the International Marriage Broker Regulation Act of 2005 [8 U.S.C.A. § 1375a(a)(5)(A)(i)].

(5) In this subsection:

(A) The terms "domestic violence", "sexual assault", "child abuse and neglect", "dating violence", "elder abuse", and "stalking" have the meaning given such terms in section 13925 of Title 42.

(B) The term "specified crime" means the following:

(i) Domestic violence, sexual assault, child abuse and neglect, dating violence, elder abuse, stalking, or an attempt to commit any such crime.

(ii) Homicide, murder, manslaughter, rape, abusive sexual contact, sexual exploitation, incest, torture, trafficking, peonage, holding hostage, involuntary servitude, slave trade, kidnapping, abduction, unlawful criminal restraint, false imprisonment, or an attempt to commit any of the crimes described in this clause.

(iii) At least three convictions for crimes relating to a controlled substance or alcohol not arising from a single act.

(June 27, 1952, c. 477, Title II, ch. 2, § 214, 66 Stat. 189; Apr. 7, 1970, Pub.L. 91–225, § 3, 84 Stat. 117; Oct. 5, 1984, Pub.L. 98–454, Title VI, § 602(b), 98 Stat. 1737; Nov. 6, 1986, Pub.L. 99–603, Title III, §§ 301(b), 313(b), 100 Stat. 3411, 3438; Nov. 10, 1986, Pub.L. 99–639, § 3(a), (c), 100 Stat. 3542; Sept. 28, 1988, Pub.L. 100–449, Title III, § 307(b), 102 Stat. 1877; Nov. 6, 1986, Pub.L. 99–603, § 301(b); Oct. 24, 1988, Pub.L. 100–525, § 2(*l*)(1), 102 Stat. 2612; Nov. 29, 1990, Pub.L. 101–649, Title II, §§ 202(a), 205(a), (b), (c)(2), 206(b), 207(b), 104 Stat. 5014, 5019, 5020, 5023, 5025; Dec. 12, 1991, Pub.L. 102–232, Title II, §§ 202(a), 203(b), 204, 205(d), (e), 206(a), (c)(2), 207(a), (c)(1), Title III, § 303(a)(10), (11), (12), 105 Stat. 1737, 1738, 1740, 1741, 1748; Dec. 8, 1993, Pub.L. 103–182, Title III, § 341(b), (c), 107 Stat. 2116, 2117; Sept. 13, 1994, Pub.L. 103–322, Title XIII, § 130003(b)(2), 108 Stat. 2025; Oct. 25, 1994, Pub.L. 103–416, Title II, § 220(b), 108 Stat. 4319; Sept. 30, 1996, Pub.L. 104–208, Div. C, Title III, § 308(e)(1)(D), (2)(B), (f)(1)(G), (H), (3)(B), (g)(5)(A)(i), (g)(7)(A), Title VI, §§ 621, 622(c), 625(a)(1), 671(a)(3)(A), (e)(4)(A), 110 Stat. 3009–619, 3009–620, 3009–621, 3009–623, 3009–695, 3009–699, 3009–721, 3009–723; Oct. 27, 1997, Pub.L. 105–65, Title I, § 108, 111 Stat. 1350; Oct. 21, 1998, Pub.L. 105–277, Div. C, Title IV, §§ 411(a), 414(a), 112 Stat. 2681–642, 2681–651; Nov. 13, 1999, Pub.L. 106–104, § 2, 113 Stat. 1483; Oct. 17, 2000, Pub.L. 106–311, § 1, 114 Stat. 1247; Oct. 17, 2000, Pub.L. 106–313, Title I, §§ 102(a), 103, 105(a), 108, 114 Stat. 1251, 1252, 1253, 1255; Oct. 28, 2000, Pub.L. 106–386, Div. A, § 107(e)(2), Div. B, Title V, § 1513(c), 114 Stat. 1478, 1535; Oct. 30, 2000, Pub.L. 106–396, Title IV, § 401, 114 Stat. 1647; Dec. 21, 2000, Pub.L. 106–553, § 1(a)(2) [Title XI, §§ 1102(b), (d)(1), 1103(b), (c)(1)], 114 Stat. 2762; Oct. 1, 2001, Pub.L. 107–45, § 1, 115 Stat. 258; Jan. 16, 2002, Pub.L. 107–124, 115 Stat. 2402; Jan. 16, 2002, Pub.L. 107–125, §§ 1, 2(a), 115 Stat. 2403; Nov. 2, 2002, Pub.L. 107–274, § 2(c), 116 Stat. 1923; Nov. 2, 2002, Pub.L. 107–273, Div. C, Title I, § 11018(a), 116 Stat. 1825; Sept. 3, 2003, Pub.L. 108–77, Title IV, §§ 402(a)(2), (d)(1), 403, 404, 117 Stat. 940, 946, 947; Sept. 3, 2003, Pub.L. 108–78, Title IV, § 402, 117 Stat. 970; Dec. 19, 2003, Pub.L. 108–193, §§ 4(b)(2), 8(a)(3), 117 Stat. 2878, 2886; Dec. 3, 2004, Pub.L. 108–441, § 1(b), (c), (d), 118 Stat. 2630; Dec. 8, 2004, Pub.L. 108–447, Div. J, Title IV, §§ 412(a), 413(a), 422(b), 425(a), 426(a), 118 Stat. 3353, 3356, 3357; May 11, 2005, Pub.L. 109–13, Div. B, § 402(a), 403(a), 404(a), 405, 501(b), (c), 119 Stat. 231, 318–22; Jan. 5, 2006, Pub.L. 109–162, Title VIII, §§ 821(a), (b), (c)(2), 832(a)(1), (2), 119 Stat. 3062, 3066, 3067; Oct. 17, 2006, Pub.L. 109–364, Div. A, Title X, § 1074(a), 120 Stat. 2403; Dec. 22, 2006, Pub.L. 109–463, § 2, 120 Stat. 3477; May 8, 2008, Pub.L. 110–229, Title VII, Subtitle A, § 702(b)(1), 122 Stat. 860; Oct. 8, 2008, Pub.L. 110–362, § 2, 122 Stat. 4013; Dec. 23, 2008, Pub.L. 110–457, Title II, § 201(b), (c), 122 Stat. 5053; Pub.L. 113–4, Title VIII, §§ 805(a), 807(a), Mar. 7, 2013, 127 Stat. 111, 112.)

§ 215. Travel control of citizens and aliens [8 U.S.C.A. § 1185]

(a) Restrictions and prohibitions

Unless otherwise ordered by the President, it shall be unlawful—

(1) for any alien to depart from or enter or attempt to depart from or enter the United States except under such reasonable rules, regulations, and orders, and subject to such limitations and exceptions as the President may prescribe;

(2) for any person to transport or attempt to transport from or into the United States another person with knowledge or reasonable cause to believe that the departure or entry of such other person is forbidden by this section;

(3) for any person knowingly to make any false statement in an application for permission to depart from or enter the United States with intent to induce or secure the granting of such permission either for himself or for another;

(4) for any person knowingly to furnish or attempt to furnish or assist in furnishing to another a permit or evidence of permission to depart or enter not issued and designed for such other person's use;

(5) for any person knowingly to use or attempt to use any permit or evidence of permission to depart or enter not issued and designed for his use;

(6) for any person to forge, counterfeit, mutilate, or alter, or cause or procure to be forged, counterfeited, mutilated, or altered, any permit or evidence of permission to depart from or enter the United States;

(7) for any person knowingly to use or attempt to use or furnish to another for use any false, forged, counterfeited, mutilated, or altered permit, or evidence of permission, or any permit or evidence of permission which, though originally valid, has become or been made void or invalid.

(b) Citizens

Except as otherwise provided by the President and subject to such limitations and exceptions as the President may authorize and prescribe, it shall be unlawful for any citizen of the United States to depart from or enter, or attempt to depart from or enter, the United States unless he bears a valid United States passport.

(c) Definitions

The term "United States" as used in this section includes the Canal Zone, and all territory and waters, continental or insular, subject to the jurisdiction of the United States. The term "person" as used in this section shall be deemed to mean any individual, partnership, association, company, or other incorporated body of individuals, or corporation, or body politic.

(d) Nonadmission of certain aliens

Nothing in this section shall be construed to entitle an alien to whom a permit to enter the United States has been issued to enter the United States, if, upon arrival in the United States, he is found to be inadmissible under any of the provisions of this Act, or any other law, relative to the entry of aliens into the United States.

(e) Revocation of proclamation as affecting penalties

The revocation of any rule, regulation, or order issued in pursuance of this section shall not prevent prosecution for any offense committed, or the imposition of any penalties or forfeitures, liability for which was incurred under this section prior to the revocation of such rule, regulation, or order.

(f) Permits to enter

Passports, visas, reentry permits, and other documents required for entry under this Act may be considered as permits to enter for the purposes of this section.

(June 27, 1952, c. 477, Title II, ch. 2, § 215, 66 Stat. 190; Oct. 7, 1978, Pub.L. 95–426, Title VII, § 707(a)–(d), 92 Stat. 992, 993; Oct. 25, 1994, Pub.L. 103–416, Title II, § 204(a), 108 Stat. 4311.)

§ 216. Conditional permanent resident status for certain alien spouses and sons and daughters [8 U.S.C.A. § 1186a]

(a) In general

(1) Conditional basis for status

Notwithstanding any other provision of this chapter, an alien spouse (as defined in subsection (h)(1) of this section) and an alien son or daughter (as defined in subsection (h)(2) of this section) shall be considered, at the time of obtaining the status of an alien lawfully admitted for permanent residence, to have obtained such status on a conditional basis subject to the provisions of this section.

(2) Notice of requirements

(A) At time of obtaining permanent residence

At the time an alien spouse or alien son or daughter obtains permanent resident status on a conditional basis under paragraph (1), the Secretary of Homeland Security shall provide for notice to such a spouse, son, or daughter respecting the provisions of this section and the requirements of subsection (c)(1) of this section to have the conditional basis of such status removed.

(B) At time of required petition

In addition, the Secretary of Homeland Security shall attempt to provide notice to such a spouse, son, or daughter, at or about the beginning of the 90-day period described in subsection (d)(2)(A) of this section, of the requirements of subsections [sic] (c)(1) of this section.

(C) Effect of failure to provide notice

The failure of the Secretary of Homeland Security to provide a notice under this paragraph shall not affect the enforcement of the provisions of this section with respect to such a spouse, son, or daughter.

(b) Termination of status if finding that qualifying marriage improper

(1) In general

In the case of an alien with permanent resident status on a conditional basis under subsection (a) of this section, if the Secretary of Homeland Security determines, before the second anniversary of the alien's obtaining the status of lawful admission for permanent residence, that—

(A) the qualifying marriage—

(i) was entered into for the purpose of procuring an alien's admission as an immigrant, or

(ii) has been judicially annulled or terminated, other than through the death of a spouse; or

(B) a fee or other consideration was given (other than a fee or other consideration to an attorney for assistance in preparation of a lawful petition) for the filing of a petition under section 204(a) [8 U.S.C.A. § 1154(a)] or subsection (d) or (p) of section 214 [8 U.S.C.A. § 1184] with respect to the alien;

the Secretary of Homeland Security shall so notify the parties involved and, subject to paragraph (2), shall terminate the permanent resident status of the alien (or aliens) involved as of the date of the determination.

(2) Hearing in removal proceeding

Any alien whose permanent resident status is terminated under paragraph (1) may request a review of such determination in a proceeding to remove the alien. In such proceeding, the burden of proof shall be on the Secretary of Homeland Security to establish, by a preponderance of the evidence, that a condition described in paragraph (1) is met.

(c) Requirements of timely petition and interview for removal of condition

(1) In general

In order for the conditional basis established under subsection (a) for an alien spouse or an alien son or daughter to be removed—

(A) the alien spouse and the petitioning spouse (if not deceased) jointly must submit to the Secretary of Homeland Security, during the period described in subsection (d)(2) of this section, a petition which requests the removal of such conditional basis and which states, under penalty of perjury, the facts and information described in subsection (d)(1) of this section, and

(B) in accordance with subsection (d)(3) of this section, the alien spouse and the petitioning spouse (if not deceased) must appear for a personal interview before an officer or employee of the Department of Homeland Security respecting the facts and information described in subsection (d)(1) of this section.

(2) Termination of permanent resident status for failure to file petition or have personal interview

(A) In general

In the case of an alien with permanent resident status on a conditional basis under subsection (a), if—

(i) no petition is filed with respect to the alien in accordance with the provisions of paragraph (1)(A), or

(ii) unless there is good cause shown, the alien spouse and petitioning spouse fail to appear at the interview described in paragraph (1)(B),

the Secretary of Homeland Security shall terminate the permanent resident status of the alien as of the second anniversary of the alien's lawful admission for permanent residence.

(B) Hearing in removal proceeding

In any removal proceeding with respect to an alien whose permanent resident status is terminated under subparagraph (A), the burden of proof shall be on the alien to establish compliance with the conditions of paragraphs (1)(A) and (1)(B).

(3) Determination after petition and interview

(A) In general

If—

(i) a petition is filed in accordance with the provisions of paragraph (1)(A), and

(ii) the alien spouse and petitioning spouse appear at the interview described in paragraph (1)(B),

the Secretary of Homeland Security shall make a determination, within 90 days of the date of the interview, as to whether the facts and information described in subsection (d)(1) of this section and alleged in the petition are true with respect to the qualifying marriage.

(B) Removal of conditional basis if favorable determination

If the Secretary of Homeland Security determines that such facts and information are true, the Secretary of Homeland Security shall so notify the parties involved and shall remove the conditional basis of the parties effective as of the second anniversary of the alien's obtaining the status of lawful admission for permanent residence.

(C) Termination if adverse determination

If the Secretary of Homeland Security determines that such facts and information are not true, the Secretary of Homeland Security shall so notify the parties involved and, subject to subparagraph (D), shall terminate the permanent resident status of an alien spouse or an alien son or daughter as of the date of the determination.

(D) Hearing in removal proceeding

Any alien whose permanent resident status is terminated under subparagraph (C) may request a review of such determination in a proceeding to remove the alien. In such proceeding, the burden of proof shall be on the Secretary of Homeland Security to establish, by a preponderance of the evidence, that the facts and information described in subsection (d)(1) of this section and alleged in the petition are not true with respect to the qualifying marriage.

(4) Hardship waiver

The Secretary of Homeland Security, in the Secretary's discretion, may remove the conditional basis of the permanent resident status for an alien who fails to meet the requirements of paragraph (1) if the alien demonstrates that—

(A) extreme hardship would result if such alien is removed;

(B) the qualifying marriage was entered into in good faith by the alien spouse, but the qualifying marriage has been terminated (other than through the death of the spouse) and the alien was not at fault in failing to meet the requirements of paragraph (1); or

(C) the qualifying marriage was entered into in good faith by the alien spouse and during the marriage the alien spouse or child was battered by or was the subject of extreme cruelty perpetrated by his or her spouse or citizen or permanent resident parent and the alien was not at fault in failing to meet the requirements of paragraph (1); or

(D) the alien meets the requirements under section 204(a)(1)(A)(iii)(II)(aa)(BB) [8 U.S.C.A. § 1154(a)(1)(A)(iii)(II)(aa)(BB)] and following the marriage ceremony was battered by or subject to extreme cruelty perpetrated by the alien's intended spouse and was not at fault in failing to meet the requirements of paragraph (1).

In determining extreme hardship, the Secretary of Homeland Security shall consider circumstances occurring only during the period that the alien was admitted for permanent residence on a conditional basis. In acting on applications under this paragraph, the Secretary of Homeland Security shall consider any credible evidence relevant to the application. The determination of what evidence is credible and the weight to be given that evidence shall be within the sole discretion of the Secretary of Homeland Security. The Secretary of Homeland Security shall, by regulation, establish measures to protect the confidentiality of information concerning any abused alien spouse or child, including information regarding the whereabouts of such spouse or child.

(d) Details of petition and interview

(1) Contents of petition

Each petition under subsection (c)(1)(A) shall contain the following facts and information:

(A) Statement of proper marriage and petitioning process

The facts are that—

(i) the qualifying marriage—

(I) was entered into in accordance with the laws of the place where the marriage took place,

(II) has not been judicially annulled or terminated, other than through the death of a spouse, and

(III) was not entered into for the purpose of procuring an alien's admission as an immigrant; and

(ii) no fee or other consideration was given (other than a fee or other consideration to an attorney for assistance in preparation of a lawful petition) for the filing of a petition under section 204(a) [8 U.S.C.A. § 1154(a)] or subsection (d) or (p) of section 214 [8 U.S.C.A. § 1184] with respect to the alien spouse or alien son or daughter.

(B) Statement of additional information

The information is a statement of—

(i) the actual residence of each party to the qualifying marriage since the date the alien spouse obtained permanent resident status on a conditional basis under subsection (a), and

(ii) the place of employment (if any) of each such party since such date, and the name of the employer of such party.

(2) Period for filing petition

(A) 90–day period before second anniversary

Except as provided in subparagraph (B), the petition under subsection (c)(1)(A) must be filed during the 90–day period before the second anniversary of the alien's obtaining the status of lawful admission for permanent residence.

(B) Date of petitions for good cause

Such a petition may be considered if filed after such date, but only if the alien establishes to the satisfaction of the Secretary of Homeland Security good cause and extenuating circumstances for failure to file the petition during the period described in subparagraph (A).

(C) Filing of petitions during removal

In the case of an alien who is the subject of removal hearings as a result of failure to file a petition on a timely basis in accordance with subparagraph (A), the Secretary of Homeland Security may stay such removal proceedings against an alien pending the filing of the petition under subparagraph (B).

(3) Personal interview

The interview under subsection (c)(1)(B) of this section shall be conducted within 90 days after the date of submitting a petition under subsection (c)(1)(A) of this section and at a local office of the Department of Homeland Security, designated by the Secretary of Homeland Security, which is convenient to the parties involved. The Secretary of Homeland Security, in the Secretary's discretion, may waive the deadline for such an interview or the requirement for such an interview in such cases as may be appropriate.

(e) Treatment of period for purposes of naturalization

For purposes of title III, in the case of an alien who is in the United States as a lawful permanent resident on a conditional basis under this section, the alien shall be considered to have been admitted as an alien lawfully admitted for permanent residence and to be in the United States as an alien lawfully admitted to the United States for permanent residence.

(f) Treatment of certain waivers

In the case of an alien who has permanent residence status on a conditional basis under this section, if, in order to obtain such status, the alien obtained a waiver under subsection (h) or (i) of section 212 [8 U.S.C.A. § 1182] of certain grounds of inadmissibility, such waiver terminates upon the termination of such permanent residence status under this section.

(g) Service in armed forces

(1) Filing petition

The 90–day period described in subsection (d)(2)(A) shall be tolled during any period of time in which the alien spouse or petitioning spouse is a member of the Armed Forces of the United States and serving abroad in an active-duty status in the Armed Forces, except that, at the option of the petitioners, the petition may be filed during such active-duty service at any time after the commencement of such 90–day period.

(2) Personal interview

The 90–day period described in the first sentence of subsection (d)(3) shall be tolled during any period of time in which the alien spouse or petitioning spouse is a member of the Armed Forces of the

United States and serving abroad in an active-duty status in the Armed Forces, except that nothing in this paragraph shall be construed to prohibit the Secretary of Homeland Security from waiving the requirement for an interview under subsection (c)(1)(B) pursuant to the Secretary's authority under the second sentence of subsection (d)(3).

(h) Definitions

In this section:

(1) The term "alien spouse" means an alien who obtains the status of an alien lawfully admitted for permanent residence (whether on a conditional basis or otherwise)—

(A) as an immediate relative (described in section 201(b) [8 U.S.C.A. § 1151(b)]) as the spouse of a citizen of the United States,

(B) under section 214(d) [8 U.S.C.A. § 1184(d)] as the fiancee or fiance of a citizen of the United States, or

(C) under section 203(a)(2) [8 U.S.C.A. § 1153(a)(2)] as the spouse of an alien lawfully admitted for permanent residence,

by virtue of a marriage which was entered into less than 24 months before the date the alien obtains such status by virtue of such marriage, but does not include such an alien who only obtains such status as a result of section 203(d) [8 U.S.C.A. § 1153(d)].

(2) The term "alien son or daughter" means an alien who obtains the status of an alien lawfully admitted for permanent residence (whether on a conditional basis or otherwise) by virtue of being the son or daughter of an individual through a qualifying marriage.

(3) The term "qualifying marriage" means the marriage described to [sic] in paragraph (1).

(4) The term "petitioning spouse" means the spouse of a qualifying marriage, other than the alien.

(June 27, 1952, c. 477, Title II, ch. 2, § 216, as added Nov. 6, 1986, Pub.L. 99–639, § 2(a), 100 Stat. 3537, and amended Oct. 24, 1988, Pub.L. 100–525, § 7(a)(1), 102 Stat. 2616; Oct. 24, 1988, Pub.L. 100–525, § 7(a)(2), 102 Stat. 2616; Nov. 29, 1990, Pub.L. 101–649, Title VII, § 701(a), 104 Stat. 5085; Dec.12, 1991, Pub.L. 102–232, Title III, § 302(e)(8)(B), 105 Stat. 1746; Sept. 13, 1994, Pub.L. 103–322, Title IV, § 40702(a), 108 Stat. 1955; Sept. 30, 1996, Pub.L. 104–208, Div. C, Title III, § 308(d)(4)(E), (e)(7), (f)(1)(I), (J), 110 Stat. 3009–618, 3009–620, 3009–621; Dec. 21, 2000, Pub.L. 106–553, § 1(a)(2) [Title XI, § 1103(c)(2)], 114 Stat. 2762; Pub.L. 112–58, § 1, Nov. 23, 2011, 125 Stat. 747; Pub.L. 113–4, Title VIII, § 806, Mar. 7, 2013, 127 Stat. 112.)

§ 216A. Conditional permanent resident status for certain alien entrepreneurs, spouses, and children [8 U.S.C.A. § 1186b]

(a) In general

(1) Conditional basis for status

Notwithstanding any other provision of this Act, an alien entrepreneur (as defined in subsection (f)(1) of this section), alien spouse, and alien child (as defined in subsection (f)(2) of this section) shall be considered, at the time of obtaining the status of an alien lawfully admitted for permanent residence, to have obtained such status on a conditional basis subject to the provisions of this section.

(2) Notice of requirements

(A) At time of obtaining permanent residence

At the time an alien entrepreneur, alien spouse, or alien child obtains permanent resident status on a conditional basis under paragraph (1), the Attorney General shall provide for notice to such an entrepreneur, spouse, or child respecting the provisions of this section and the requirements of subsection (c)(1) to have the conditional basis of such status removed.

(B) At time of required petition

In addition, the Attorney General shall attempt to provide notice to such an entrepreneur, spouse, or child, at or about the beginning of the 90–day period described in subsection (d)(2)(A), of the requirements of subsection (c)(1).

(C) Effect of failure to provide notice

The failure of the Attorney General to provide a notice under this paragraph shall not affect the enforcement of the provisions of this section with respect to such an entrepreneur, spouse, or child.

(b) Termination of status if finding that qualifying entrepreneurship improper

(1) In general

In the case of an alien entrepreneur with permanent resident status on a conditional basis under subsection (a), if the Attorney General determines, before the second anniversary of the alien's obtaining the status of lawful admission for permanent residence, that—

(A) the investment in the commercial enterprise was intended solely as a means of evading the immigration laws of the United States,

(B)(i) the alien did not invest, or was not actively in the process of investing, the requisite capital; or

(ii) the alien was not sustaining the actions described in clause (i) throughout the period of the alien's residence in the United States; or

(C) the alien was otherwise not conforming to the requirements of section 203(b)(5) [8 U.S.C.A. § 1153(b)(5)], then the Attorney General shall so notify the alien involved and, subject to paragraph (2), shall terminate the permanent resident status of the alien (and the alien spouse and alien child) involved as of the date of the determination.

(2) Hearing in removal proceeding

Any alien whose permanent resident status is terminated under paragraph (1) may request a review of such determination in a proceeding to remove the alien. In such proceeding, the burden of proof shall be on the Attorney General to establish, by a preponderance of the evidence, that a condition described in paragraph (1) is met.

(c) Requirements of timely petition and interview for removal of condition

(1) In general

In order for the conditional basis established under subsection (a) for an alien entrepreneur, alien spouse, or alien child to be removed—

(A) the alien entrepreneur must submit to the Attorney General, during the period described in subsection (d)(2), a petition which requests the removal of such conditional basis and which states, under penalty of perjury, the facts and information described in subsection (d)(1), and

(B) in accordance with subsection (d)(3) of this section, the alien entrepreneur must appear for a personal interview before an officer or employee of the Service respecting the facts and information described in subsection (d)(1) of this section.

(2) Termination of permanent resident status for failure to file petition or have personal interview

(A) In general

In the case of an alien with permanent resident status on a conditional basis under subsection (a), if—

(i) no petition is filed with respect to the alien in accordance with the provisions of paragraph (1)(A), or

(ii) unless there is good cause shown, the alien entrepreneur fails to appear at the interview described in paragraph (1)(B) (if required under subsection (d)(3)),

the Attorney General shall terminate the permanent resident status of the alien (and the alien's spouse and children if it was obtained on a conditional basis under this section or section 216 [8 U.S.C.A. § 1186a]) as of the second anniversary of the alien's lawful admission for permanent residence.

(B) Hearing in removal proceeding

In any removal proceeding with respect to an alien whose permanent resident status is terminated under subparagraph (A), the burden of proof shall be on the alien to establish compliance with the conditions of paragraphs (1)(A) and (1)(B).

(3) Determination after petition and interview

(A) In general

If—

(i) a petition is filed in accordance with the provisions of paragraph (1)(A), and

(ii) the alien entrepreneur appears at any interview described in paragraph (1)(B),

the Attorney General shall make a determination, within 90 days of the date of the such filing or interview (whichever is later), as to whether the facts and information described in subsection (d)(1) and alleged in the petition are true with respect to the qualifying commercial enterprise.

(B) Removal of conditional basis if favorable determination

If the Attorney General determines that such facts and information are true, the Attorney General shall so notify the alien involved and shall remove the conditional basis of the alien's status effective as of the second anniversary of the alien's lawful admission for permanent residence.

(C) Termination if adverse determination

If the Attorney General determines that such facts and information are not true, the Attorney General shall so notify the alien involved and, subject to subparagraph (D), shall terminate the permanent resident status of an alien entrepreneur, alien spouse, or alien child as of the date of the determination.

(D) Hearing in removal proceeding

Any alien whose permanent resident status is terminated under subparagraph (C) may request a review of such determination in a proceeding to remove the alien. In such proceeding, the burden of proof shall be on the Attorney General to establish, by a preponderance of the evidence, that the facts and information described in subsection (d)(1) and alleged in the petition are not true with respect to the qualifying commercial enterprise.

(d) Details of petition and interview

(1) Contents of petition

Each petition under subsection (c)(1)(A) of this section shall contain facts and information demonstrating that the alien—

(A)(i) invested, or is actively in the process of investing, the requisite capital; and

(ii) sustained the actions described in clause (i) throughout the period of the alien's residence in the United States; and

(B) is otherwise conforming to the requirements of section 203(b)(5) [8 U.S.C.A. § 1153(b)(5)].

(2) Period for filing petition

(A) 90–day period before second anniversary

Except as provided in subparagraph (B), the petition under subsection (c)(1)(A) must be filed during the 90–day period before the second anniversary of the alien's lawful admission for permanent residence.

(B) Date petitions for good cause

Such a petition may be considered if filed after such date, but only if the alien establishes to the satisfaction of the Attorney General good cause and extenuating circumstances for failure to file the petition during the period described in subparagraph (A).

(C) Filing of petitions during removal

In the case of an alien who is the subject of removal hearings as a result of failure to file a petition on a timely basis in accordance with subparagraph (A), the Attorney General may stay such removal proceedings against an alien pending the filing of the petition under subparagraph (B).

(3) Personal interview

The interview under subsection (c)(1)(B) of this section shall be conducted within 90 days after the date of submitting a petition under subsection (c)(1)(A) of this section and at a local office of the Service, designated by the Attorney General, which is convenient to the parties involved. The Attorney General, in the Attorney General's discretion, may waive the deadline for such an interview or the requirement for such an interview in such cases as may be appropriate.

(e) Treatment of period for purposes of naturalization

For purposes of title III, in the case of an alien who is in the United States as a lawful permanent resident on a conditional basis under this section, the alien shall be considered to have been admitted as an alien lawfully admitted for permanent residence and to be in the United States as an alien lawfully admitted to the United States for permanent residence.

(f) Definitions

In this section:

(1) The term "alien entrepreneur" means an alien who obtains the status of an alien lawfully admitted for permanent residence (whether on a conditional basis or otherwise) under section 203(b)(5) [8 U.S.C.A. § 1153(b)(5)].

(2) The term "alien spouse" and the term "alien child" mean an alien who obtains the status of an alien lawfully admitted for permanent residence (whether on a conditional basis or otherwise) by virtue of being the spouse or child, respectively, of an alien entrepreneur.

(3) The term "commercial enterprise" includes a limited partnership.

(June 27, 1952, c. 477, Title II, ch. 2, § 216A, as added Nov. 29, 1990, Pub.L. 101–649, Title I, § 121(b)(1), 104 Stat. 4990, and amended Dec. 12, 1991, Pub.L. 102–232, Title III, § 302(b)(3), 105 Stat. 1743; Sept. 30, 1996, Pub.L. 104–208, Div. C, Title III, § 308(e)(8), 110 Stat. 3009–620; Nov. 2, 2002, Pub.L. 107–273, Div. C, Title I, § 11036(b), 116 Stat. 1847.)

§ 217. Visa waiver program for certain visitors [8 U.S.C.A. § 1187]

(a) Establishment of program

The Attorney General and the Secretary of State are authorized to establish a program (hereinafter in this section referred to as the "program") under which the requirement of paragraph (7)(B)(i)(II) of section 212(a) [8 U.S.C.A. § 1182(a)] may be waived by the Attorney General, in consultation with the Secretary of State and in accordance with this section, in the case of an alien who meets the following requirements:

(1) Seeking entry as tourist for 90 days or less

The alien is applying for admission during the program as a nonimmigrant visitor (described in section 101(a)(15)(B) [8 U.S.C.A. § 1101(a)(15)(B)]) for a period not exceeding 90 days.

(2) National of program country

The alien is a national of, and presents a passport issued by, a country which—

(A) extends (or agrees to extend), either on its own or in conjunction with one or more other countries that are described in subparagraph (B) and that have established with it a common area for immigration admissions, reciprocal privileges to citizens and nationals of the United States, and

(B) is designated as a pilot [sic] program country under subsection (c) of this section.

(3) Machine readable passport

(A) In general

Except as provided in subparagraph (B), on and after October 1, 2003, the alien at the time of application for admission is in possession of a valid unexpired machine-readable passport that satisfies the internationally accepted standard for machine readability.

(B) Limited waiver authority

For the period beginning October 1, 2003, and ending September 30, 2007, the Secretary of State may waive the requirement of subparagraph (A) with respect to nationals of a program country (as designated under subsection (c)), if the Secretary of State finds that the program country—

(i) is making progress toward ensuring that passports meeting the requirement of subparagraph (A) are generally available to its nationals; and

(ii) has taken appropriate measures to protect against misuse of passports the country has issued that do not meet the requirement of subparagraph (A).

(4) Executes immigration forms

The alien before the time of such admission completes such immigration forms as the Attorney General shall establish.

(5) Entry into the United States

If arriving by sea or air, the alien arrives at the port of entry into the United States on a carrier, including any carrier conducting operations under part 135 of title 14, Code of Federal Regulations, or a noncommercial aircraft that is owned or operated by a domestic corporation conducting operations under part 91 of title 14, Code of Federal Regulations which has entered into an agreement with the Attorney General pursuant to subsection (e). The Attorney General is authorized to require a carrier conducting operations under part 135 of title 14, Code of Federal Regulations, or a domestic corporation conducting operations under part 91 of that title, to give suitable and proper bond, in such reasonable amount and containing such conditions as the Attorney General may deem sufficient to ensure compliance with the indemnification requirements of this section, as a term of such an agreement.

(6) Not a safety threat

The alien has been determined not to represent a threat to the welfare, health, safety, or security of the United States.

(7) No previous violation

If the alien previously was admitted without a visa under this section, the alien must not have failed to comply with the conditions of any previous admission as such a nonimmigrant.

(8) Round-trip ticket

The alien is in possession of a round-trip transportation ticket (unless this requirement is waived by the Attorney General under regulations or the alien is arriving at the port of entry on an aircraft operated under part 135 of title 14, Code of Federal Regulations, or a noncommercial aircraft that is owned or operated by a domestic corporation conducting operations under part 91 of title 14, Code of Federal Regulations).

(9) Automated system check

The identity of the alien has been checked using an automated electronic database containing information about the inadmissibility of aliens to uncover any grounds on which the alien may be inadmissible to the United States, and no such ground has been found.

(10) Electronic transmission of identification information

Operators of aircraft under part 135 of title 14, Code of Federal Regulations, or operators of noncommercial aircraft that are owned or operated by a domestic corporation conducting operations under part 91 of title 14, Code of Federal Regulations, carrying any alien passenger who will apply for admission under this section shall furnish such information as the Attorney General by regulation shall prescribe as necessary for the identification of any alien passenger being transported and for the enforcement of the immigration laws. Such information shall be electronically transmitted not less than one hour prior to arrival at the port of entry for purposes of checking for inadmissibility using the automated electronic database.

(11) Eligibility determination under the electronic travel authorization system

Beginning on the date on which the electronic travel authorization system developed under subsection (h)(3) of this section is fully operational, each alien traveling under the program shall, before applying for admission to the United States, electronically provide to the system biographical information and such other information as the Secretary of Homeland Security shall determine necessary to determine the eligibility of, and whether there exists a law enforcement or security risk in permitting, the alien to travel to the United States. Upon review of such biographical information, the Secretary of Homeland Security shall determine whether the alien is eligible to travel to the United States under the program.

(b) Waiver of rights

An alien may not be provided a waiver under the program unless the alien has waived any right—

(1) to review or appeal under this Act of an immigration officer's determination as to the admissibility of the alien at the port of entry into the United States, or

(2) to contest, other than on the basis of an application for asylum, any action for removal of the alien.

(c) Designation of program countries

(1) In general

The Attorney General, in consultation with the Secretary of State, may designate any country as a program country if it meets the requirements of paragraph (2).

(2) Qualifications

Except as provided in subsection (f), a country may not be designated as a program country unless the following requirements are met:

(A) Low nonimmigrant visa refusal rate—Either—

(i) the average number of refusals of nonimmigrant visitor visas for nationals of that country during—

(I) the two previous full fiscal years was less than 2.0 percent of the total number of nonimmigrant visitor visas for nationals of that country which were granted or refused during those years; and

(II) either of such two previous full fiscal years was less than 2.5 percent of the total number of nonimmigrant visitor visas for nationals of that country which were granted or refused during that year; or

(ii) such refusal rate for nationals of that country during the previous full fiscal year was less than 3.0 percent.

(B) Machine readable passport program

(i) In general

Subject to clause (ii), the government of the country certifies that it issues to its citizens machine-readable passports that satisfy the internationally accepted standard for machine readability.

(ii) Deadline for compliance for certain countries

In the case of a country designated as a program country under this subsection prior to May 1, 2000, as a condition on the continuation of that designation, the country—

(I) shall certify, not later than October 1, 2000, that it has a program to issue machine-readable passports to its citizens not later than October 1, 2003; and

(II) shall satisfy the requirement of clause (i) not later than October 1, 2003.

(C) Law enforcement and security interests

The Attorney General, in consultation with the Secretary of State—

(i) evaluates the effect that the country's designation would have on the law enforcement and security interests of the United States (including the interest in enforcement of the immigration laws of the United States and the existence and effectiveness of its agreements and procedures for extraditing to the United States individuals, including its own nationals, who commit crimes that violate United States law);

(ii) determines that such interests would not be compromised by the designation of the country; and

(iii) submits a written report to the Committee on the Judiciary and the Committee on International Relations of the House of Representatives and the Committee on the Judiciary and the Committee on Foreign Relations of the Senate regarding the country's qualification for designation that includes an explanation of such determination.

(D) Reporting lost and stolen passports

The government of the country enters into an agreement with the United States to report, or make available through Interpol or other means as designated by the Secretary of Homeland Security, to the United States Government information about the theft or loss of passports within a strict time limit and in a manner specified in the agreement.

(E) Repatriation of aliens

The government of the country accepts for repatriation any citizen, former citizen, or national of the country against whom a final executable order of removal is issued not later than three weeks after the issuance of the final order of removal. Nothing in this subparagraph creates any duty for the United States or any right for any alien with respect to removal or release. Nothing in this subparagraph gives rise to any cause of action or claim under this paragraph or any other law against any official of the United States or of any State to compel the release, removal, or consideration for release or removal of any alien.

(F) Passenger information exchange

The government of the country enters into an agreement with the United States to share information regarding whether citizens and nationals of that country traveling to the United

States represent a threat to the security or welfare of the United States or its citizens.

(3) Continuing and subsequent qualifications

For each fiscal year after the initial period—

(A) Continuing qualification

In the case of a country which was a program country in the previous fiscal year, a country may not be designated as a program country unless the sum of—

(i) the total of the number of nationals of that country who were denied admission at the time of arrival or withdrew their application for admission during such previous fiscal year as a nonimmigrant visitor, and

(ii) the total number of nationals of that country who were admitted as nonimmigrant visitors during such previous fiscal year and who violated the terms of such admission,

was less than 2 percent of the total number of nationals of that country who applied for admission as nonimmigrant visitors during such previous fiscal year.

(B) New countries

In the case of another country, the country may not be designated as a program country unless the following requirements are met:

(i) Low nonimmigrant visa refusal rate in previous 2-year period

The average number of refusals of nonimmigrant visitor visas for nationals of that country during the two previous full fiscal years was less than 2 percent of the total number of nonimmigrant visitor visas for nationals of that country which were granted or refused during those years.

(ii) Low nonimmigrant visa refusal rate in each of the 2 previous years

The average number of refusals of nonimmigrant visitor visas for nationals of that country during either of such two previous full fiscal years was less than 2.5 percent of the total number of nonimmigrant visitor visas for nationals of that country which were granted or refused during that year.

(4) Initial period

For purposes of paragraphs (2) and (3), the term "initial period" means the period beginning at the end of the 30-day period described in subsection (b)(1) [sic] of this section and ending on the last day of the first fiscal year which begins after such 30–day period.

(5) Written reports on continuing qualification; designation terminations

(A) Periodic evaluations

(i) In general

The Secretary of Homeland Security, in consultation with the Secretary of State, periodically (but not less than once every 2 years)—

(I) shall evaluate the effect of each program country's continued designation on the law enforcement and security interests of the United States (including the interest in enforcement of the immigration laws of the United States and the existence and effectiveness of its agreements and procedures for extraditing to the United States individuals, including its own nationals, who commit crimes that violate United States law);

(II) shall determine, based upon the evaluation in subclause (I), whether any such designation ought to be continued or terminated under subsection (d);

(III) shall submit a written report to the Committee on the Judiciary, the Committee on Foreign Affairs, and the Committee on Homeland Security, of the House of Representatives and the Committee on the Judiciary, the Committee on Foreign Relations, and the Committee on Homeland Security and Governmental Affairs of the Senate regarding the continuation or termination of the country's designation that includes an explanation of such determination and the effects described in subclause (I); and

(IV) shall submit to Congress a report regarding the implementation of the electronic travel authorization system under subsection (h)(3) of this section and the participation of new countries in the program through a waiver under paragraph (8).

(ii) Effective date

A termination of the designation of a country under this subparagraph shall take effect on the date determined by the Secretary of Homeland Security, in consultation with the Secretary of State.

(iii) Redesignation

In the case of a termination under this subparagraph, the Secretary of Homeland Security shall redesignate the country as a program country, without regard to subsection

(f) or paragraph (2) or (3), when the Secretary of Homeland Security, in consultation with the Secretary of State, determines that all causes of the termination have been eliminated.

(B) Emergency termination

(i) In general

In the case of a program country in which an emergency occurs that the Secretary of Homeland Security, in consultation with the Secretary of State, determines threatens the law enforcement or security interests of the United States (including the interest in enforcement of the immigration laws of the United States), the Secretary of Homeland Security shall immediately terminate the designation of the country as a program country.

(ii) Definition

For purposes of clause (i), the term "emergency" means—

(I) the overthrow of a democratically elected government;

(II) war (including undeclared war, civil war, or other military activity) on the territory of the program country;

(III) a severe breakdown in law and order affecting a significant portion of the program country's territory;

(IV) a severe economic collapse in the program country; or

(V) any other extraordinary event in the program country that threatens the law enforcement or security interests of the United States (including the interest in enforcement of the immigration laws of the United States) and where the country's participation in the program could contribute to that threat.

(iii) Redesignation

The Secretary of Homeland Security may redesignate the country as a program country, without regard to subsection (f) or paragraph (2) or (3), when the Secretary of Homeland Security, in consultation with the Secretary of State, determines that—

(I) at least 6 months have elapsed since the effective date of the termination;

(II) the emergency that caused the termination has ended; and

(III) the average number of refusals of nonimmigrant visitor visas for nationals of that country during the period of termination under this subparagraph was less than 3.0 percent of the total number of nonimmigrant visitor visas for nationals of that country which were granted or refused during such period.

(iv) Program suspension authority

The Director of National Intelligence shall immediately inform the Secretary of Homeland Security of any current and credible threat which poses an imminent danger to the United States or its citizens and originates from a country participating in the visa waiver program. Upon receiving such notification, the Secretary, in consultation with the Secretary of State—

(I) may suspend a country from the visa waiver program without prior notice;

(II) shall notify any country suspended under subclause (I) and, to the extent practicable without disclosing sensitive intelligence sources and methods, provide justification for the suspension; and

(III) shall restore the suspended country's participation in the visa waiver program upon a determination that the threat no longer poses an imminent danger to the United States or its citizens.

(C) Treatment of nationals after termination

For purposes of this paragraph—

(i) nationals of a country whose designation is terminated under subparagraph (A) or (B) shall remain eligible for a waiver under subsection (a) until the effective date of such termination; and

(ii) a waiver under this section that is provided to such a national for a period described in subsection (a)(1) shall not, by such termination, be deemed to have been rescinded or otherwise rendered invalid, if the waiver is granted prior to such termination.

(6) Computation of visa refusal rates

For purposes of determining the eligibility of a country to be designated as a program country, the calculation of visa refusal rates shall not include any visa refusals which incorporate any procedures based on, or are otherwise based on, race, sex, or disability, unless otherwise specifically authorized by law or regulation. No court shall have jurisdiction under this paragraph to review any visa refusal, the denial of admission to the United States of any alien by the Attorney General, the Secretary's computation of the visa refusal rate, or the designation or nondesignation of any country.

(7) Visa waiver information

(A) In general

In refusing the application of nationals of a program country for United States visas, or the applications of nationals of a country seeking entry into the visa waiver program, a consular officer shall not knowingly or intentionally classify the refusal of the visa under a category that is not included in the calculation of the visa refusal rate only so that the percentage of that country's visa refusals is less than the percentage limitation applicable to qualification for participation in the visa waiver program.

(B) Reporting requirement

On May 1 of each year, for each country under consideration for inclusion in the visa waiver program, the Secretary of State shall provide to the appropriate congressional committees—

(i) the total number of nationals of that country that applied for United States visas in that country during the previous calendar year;

(ii) the total number of such nationals who received United States visas during the previous calendar year;

(iii) the total number of such nationals who were refused United States visas during the previous calendar year;

(iv) the total number of such nationals who were refused United States visas during the previous calendar year under each provision of this Act under which the visas were refused; and

(v) the number of such nationals that were refused under section 214(b) [8 U.S.C.A. § 1184(b)] as a percentage of the visas that were issued to such nationals.

(C) Certification

Not later than May 1 of each year, the United States chief of mission, acting or permanent, to each country under consideration for inclusion in the visa waiver program shall certify to the appropriate congressional committees that the information described in subparagraph (B) is accurate and provide a copy of that certification to those committees.

(D) Consideration of countries in the visa waiver program

Upon notification to the Attorney General that a country is under consideration for inclusion in the visa waiver program, the Secretary of State shall provide all of the information described in subparagraph (B) to the Attorney General.

(E) Definition

In this paragraph, the term "appropriate congressional committees" means the Committee on the Judiciary and the Committee on Foreign Relations of the Senate and the Committee on the Judiciary and the Committee on International Relations of the House of Representatives.

(8) Nonimmigrant visa refusal rate flexibility

(A) Certification

(i) In general

On the date on which an air exit system is in place that can verify the departure of not less than 97 percent of foreign nationals who exit through airports of the United States and the electronic travel authorization system required under subsection (h)(3) of this section is fully operational, the Secretary of Homeland Security shall certify to Congress that such air exit system and electronic travel authorization system are in place.

(ii) Notification to Congress

The Secretary shall notify Congress in writing of the date on which the air exit system under clause (i) fully satisfies the biometric requirements specified in subsection (i) of this section.

(iii) Temporary suspension of waiver authority

Notwithstanding any certification made under clause (i), if the Secretary has not notified Congress in accordance with clause (ii) by June 30, 2009, the Secretary's waiver authority under subparagraph (B) shall be suspended beginning on July 1, 2009, until such time as the Secretary makes such notification.

(iv) Rule of construction

Nothing in this paragraph shall be construed as in any way abrogating the reporting requirements under subsection (i)(3) of this section.

(B) Waiver

After certification by the Secretary under subparagraph (A), the Secretary, in consultation with the Secretary of State, may waive the application of paragraph (2)(A) for a country if—

(i) the country meets all security requirements of this section;

(ii) the Secretary of Homeland Security determines that the totality of the country's security risk mitigation measures provide assurance that the country's participation in the program would not compromise the law enforcement, security interests, or enforcement of the immigration laws of the United States;

(iii) there has been a sustained reduction in the rate of refusals for nonimmigrant visas for nationals of the country and conditions exist to continue such reduction;

(iv) the country cooperated with the Government of the United States on counterterrorism initiatives, information sharing, and preventing terrorist travel before the date of its designation as a program country, and the Secretary of Homeland Security and the Secretary of State determine that such cooperation will continue; and

(v)(I) the rate of refusals for nonimmigrant visitor visas for nationals of the country during the previous full fiscal year was not more than ten percent; or

(II) the visa overstay rate for the country for the previous full fiscal year does not exceed the maximum visa overstay rate, once such rate is established under subparagraph (C).

(C) Maximum visa overstay rate

(i) Requirement to establish

After certification by the Secretary under subparagraph (A), the Secretary and the Secretary of State jointly shall use information from the air exit system referred to in such subparagraph to establish a maximum visa overstay rate for countries participating in the program pursuant to a waiver under subparagraph (B). The Secretary of Homeland Security shall certify to Congress that such rate would not compromise the law enforcement, security interests, or enforcement of the immigration laws of the United States.

(ii) Visa overstay rate defined

In this paragraph the term "visa overstay rate" means, with respect to a country, the ratio of—

(I) the total number of nationals of that country who were admitted to the United States on the basis of a nonimmigrant visa whose periods of authorized stays ended during a fiscal year but who remained unlawfully in the United States beyond such periods; to

(II) the total number of nationals of that country who were admitted to the United States on the basis of a nonimmigrant visa during that fiscal year.

(iii) Report and publication

The Secretary of Homeland Security shall on the same date submit to Congress and publish in the Federal Register information relating to the maximum visa overstay rate established under clause (i). Not later than 60 days after such date, the Secretary shall issue a final maximum visa overstay rate above which a country may not participate in the program.

(9) Discretionary security-related considerations

In determining whether to waive the application of paragraph (2)(A) for a country, pursuant to paragraph (8), the Secretary of Homeland Security, in consultation with the Secretary of State, shall take into consideration other factors affecting the security of the United States, including—

(A) airport security standards in the country;

(B) whether the country assists in the operation of an effective air marshal program;

(C) the standards of passports and travel documents issued by the country; and

(D) other security-related factors, including the country's cooperation with the United States' initiatives toward combating terrorism and the country's cooperation with the United States intelligence community in sharing information regarding terrorist threats.

(10) Technical assistance

The Secretary of Homeland Security, in consultation with the Secretary of State, shall provide technical assistance to program countries to assist those countries in meeting the requirements under this section. The Secretary of Homeland Security shall ensure that the program office within the Department of Homeland Security is adequately staffed and has resources to be able to provide such technical assistance, in addition to its duties to effectively monitor compliance of the countries participating in the program with all the requirements of the program.

(11) Independent review

(A) In general

Prior to the admission of a new country into the program under this section, and in conjunction with the periodic evaluations required under subsection (c)(5)(A) of this section, the Director of National Intelligence shall conduct an independent intelligence assessment of a nominated country and member of the program.

(B) Reporting requirement

The Director shall provide to the Secretary of Homeland Security, the Secretary of State, and the Attorney General the independent intelligence assessment required under subparagraph (A).

(C) Contents

The independent intelligence assessment conducted by the Director shall include—

(i) a review of all current, credible terrorist threats of the subject country;

(ii) an evaluation of the subject country's counterterrorism efforts;

(iii) an evaluation as to the extent of the country's sharing of information beneficial to suppressing terrorist movements, financing, or actions;

(iv) an assessment of the risks associated with including the subject country in the program; and

(v) recommendations to mitigate the risks identified in clause (iv).

(d) Authority

Notwithstanding any other provision of this section, the Secretary of Homeland Security, in consultation with the Secretary of State, may for any reason (including national security) refrain from waiving the visa requirement in respect to nationals of any country which may otherwise qualify for designation or may, at any time, rescind any waiver or designation previously granted under this section. The Secretary of Homeland Security may not waive any eligibility requirement under this section unless the Secretary notifies, with respect to the House of Representatives, the Committee on Homeland Security, the Committee on the Judiciary, the Committee on Foreign Affairs, and the Committee on Appropriations, and with respect to the Senate, the Committee on Homeland Security and Governmental Affairs, the Committee on the Judiciary, the Committee on Foreign Relations, and the Committee on Appropriations not later than 30 days before the effective date of such waiver.

(e) Carrier agreements

(1) In general

The agreement referred to in subsection (a)(4) is an agreement between a carrier (including any carrier conducting operations under part 135 of title 14, Code of Federal Regulations) or a domestic corporation conducting operations under part 91 of that title and the Attorney General under which the carrier agrees, in consideration of the waiver of the visa requirement with respect to a nonimmigrant visitor under the program—

(A) to indemnify the United States against any costs for the transportation of the alien from the United States if the visitor is refused admission to the United States or remains in the United States unlawfully after the 90–day period described in subsection (a)(1)(A) of this section,

(B) to submit daily to immigration officers any immigration forms received with respect to nonimmigrant visitors provided a waiver under the program,

(C) to be subject to the imposition of fines resulting from the transporting into the United States of a national of a designated country without a passport pursuant to regulations promulgated by the Attorney General, and

(D) to collect, provide, and share passenger data as required under subsection (h)(1)(B).

(2) Termination of agreements

The Attorney General may terminate an agreement under paragraph (1) with five days' notice to the carrier (including any carrier conducting operations under part 135 of title 14, Code of Federal Regulations) or a domestic corporation conducting operations under part 91 of that title for the failure by a carrier (including any carrier conducting operations under part 135 of title 14, Code of Federal Regulations) or a domestic corporation conducting operations under part 91 of that title to meet the terms of such agreement.

(3) Business aircraft requirements

(A) In general

For purposes of this section, a domestic corporation conducting operations under part 91 of title 14, Code of Federal Regulations that owns or operates a noncommercial aircraft is a corporation that is organized under the laws of any of the States of the United States or the District of Columbia and is accredited by or a member of a national organization that sets business aviation standards. The Attorney General shall prescribe by regulation the provision of such information as the Attorney General deems necessary to identify the domestic corporation, its officers, employees, shareholders, its place of business, and its business activities.

(B) Collections

In addition to any other fee authorized by law, the Attorney General is authorized to charge and collect, on a periodic basis, an amount from each domestic corporation conducting operations under part 91 of title 14, Code of Federal Regulations, for nonimmigrant visa waiver admissions on noncommercial aircraft owned or operated by such domestic corporation equal to the total amount of fees assessed for issuance of nonimmigrant visa waiver arrival/departure forms at land border ports of entry. All fees collected under this paragraph shall be deposited into the Immigration User Fee Account established under section 286(h) [8 U.S.C.A. § 1356(h)].

(f) Duration and termination of designation

(1) In general

(A) Determination and notification of disqualification rate

Upon determination by the Attorney General that a program country's disqualification rate is 2 percent or more, the Attorney General shall notify the Secretary of State.

(B) Probationary status

If the program country's disqualification rate is greater than 2 percent but less than 3.5 percent, the Attorney General shall place the program country in probationary status for a period not to exceed 2 full fiscal years following the year in which the determination under subparagraph (A) is made.

(C) Termination of designation

Subject to paragraph (3), if the program country's disqualification rate is 3.5 percent or more, the Attorney General shall terminate the country's designation as a program country effective at the beginning of the second fiscal year following the fiscal year in which the determination under subparagraph (A) is made.

(2) Termination of probationary status

(A) In general

If the Attorney General determines at the end of the probationary period described in paragraph (1)(B) that the program country placed in probationary status under such paragraph has failed to develop a machine-readable passport program as required by section [sic] (c)(2)(C), or has a disqualification rate of 2 percent or more, the Attorney General shall terminate the designation of the country as a program country. If the Attorney General determines that the program country has developed a machine-readable passport program and has a disqualification rate of less than 2 percent, the Attorney General shall redesignate the country as a program country.

(B) Effective date

A termination of the designation of a country under subparagraph (A) shall take effect on the first day of the first fiscal year following the fiscal year in which the determination under such subparagraph is made. Until such date, nationals of the country shall remain eligible for a waiver under subsection (a) of this section.

(3) Nonapplicability of certain provisions

Paragraph (1)(C) shall not apply unless the total number of nationals of a program country described in paragraph (4)(A) exceeds 100.

(4) Definition of disqualification rate

For purposes of this subsection, the term "disqualification rate" means the percentage which—

(A) the total number of nationals of the program country who were—

(i) denied admission at the time of arrival or withdrew their application for admission during the most recent fiscal year for which data are available; and

(ii) admitted as nonimmigrant visitors during such fiscal year and who violated the terms of such admission; bears to

(B) the total number of nationals of such country who applied for admission as nonimmigrant visitors during such fiscal year.

(5) Failure to report passport thefts

If the Secretary of Homeland Security and the Secretary of State jointly determine that the program country is not reporting the theft or loss of passports, as required by subsection (c)(2)(D) of this section, the Secretary of Homeland Security shall terminate the designation of the country as a program country.

(g) Visa application sole method to dispute denial of waiver based on a ground of inadmissibility

In the case of an alien denied a waiver under the program by reason of a ground of inadmissibility described in section 212(a) [8 U.S.C.A. § 1182(a)] that is discovered at the time of the alien's application for the waiver or through the use of an automated electronic database required under subsection (a)(9), the alien may apply for a visa at an appropriate consular office outside the United States. There shall be no other means of administrative or judicial review of such a denial, and no court or person otherwise shall have jurisdiction to consider any claim attacking the validity of such a denial.

(h) Use of information technology systems

(1) Automated entry-exit control system

(A) System

Not later than October 1, 2001, the Attorney General shall develop and implement a fully automated entry and exit control system that will collect a record of arrival and departure for every alien who arrives and departs by sea or air at a port of entry into the United States and is provided a waiver under the program.

(B) Requirements

The system under subparagraph (A) shall satisfy the following requirements:

(i) Data collection by carriers

Not later than October 1, 2001, the records of arrival and departure described in subparagraph (A) shall be based, to the maximum extent practicable, on passenger data collected and electronically transmitted to the automated entry and exit control system by each carrier that has an agreement under subsection (a)(4).

(ii) Data provision by carriers

Not later than October 1, 2002, no waiver may be provided under this section to an alien arriving by sea or air at a port of entry into the United States on a carrier unless the carrier is electronically transmitting to the automated entry and exit control system passenger data determined by the Attorney General to be sufficient to permit the Attorney General to carry out this paragraph.

(iii) Calculation

The system shall contain sufficient data to permit the Attorney General to calculate, for each program country and each fiscal year, the portion of nationals of that country who are described in subparagraph (A) and for whom no record of departure exists, expressed as a percentage of the total number of such nationals who are so described.

(C) Reporting

(i) Percentage of nationals lacking departure record

As part of the annual report required to be submitted under section 110(e)(1) of the Illegal Immigration Reform and Immigrant Responsibility Act of 1996, the Attorney General shall include a section containing the calculation described in subparagraph (B)(iii) for each program country for the previous fiscal year, together with an analysis of that information.

(ii) System effectiveness

Not later than December 31, 2004, the Attorney General shall submit a written report to the Committee on the Judiciary of the United States House of Representatives and of the Senate containing the following:

(I) The conclusions of the Attorney General regarding the effectiveness of the automated entry and exit control system to be developed and implemented under this paragraph.

(II) The recommendations of the Attorney General regarding the use of the calculation described in subparagraph (B)(iii) as a basis for evaluating whether to terminate or continue the designation of a country as a program country.

The report required by this clause may be combined with the annual report required to be submitted on that date under section 110(e)(1) of the Illegal Immigration Reform and Immigrant Responsibility Act of 1996.

(2) Automated data sharing system

(A) System

The Attorney General and the Secretary of State shall develop and implement an automated data sharing system that will permit them to share data in electronic form from their respective records systems regarding the admissibility of aliens who are nationals of a program country.

(B) Requirements

The system under subparagraph (A) shall satisfy the following requirements:

(i) Supplying information to immigration officers conducting inspections at ports of entry

Not later than October 1, 2002, the system shall enable immigration officers conducting inspections at ports of entry under section 235 [8 U.S.C.A. § 1225] to obtain from the system, with respect to aliens seeking a waiver under the program—

(I) any photograph of the alien that may be contained in the records of the Department of State or the Service; and

(II) information on whether the alien has ever been determined to be ineligible to receive a visa or ineligible to be admitted to the United States.

(ii) Supplying photographs of inadmissible aliens

The system shall permit the Attorney General electronically to obtain any photograph contained in the records of the Secretary of State pertaining to an alien who is a national of a program country and has been determined to be ineligible to receive a visa.

(iii) Maintaining records on applications for admission

The system shall maintain, for a minimum of 10 years, information about each application for admission made by an alien seeking a waiver under the program, including the following:

(I) The name or Service identification number of each immigration officer conducting the inspection of the alien at the port of entry.

(II) Any information described in clause (i) that is obtained from the system by any such officer.

(III) The results of the application.

(3) Electronic travel authorization system

(A) System

The Secretary of Homeland Security, in consultation with the Secretary of State, shall develop and implement a fully automated electronic travel authorization system (referred to in this paragraph as the "System") to collect such biographical and other information as the Secretary of Homeland Security determines necessary to determine, in advance of travel, the eligibility of, and whether there exists a law enforcement or security risk in permitting, the alien to travel to the United States.

(B) Fees

(i) In general

No later than 6 months after March 4, 2010, the Secretary of Homeland Security shall establish a fee for the use of the System and begin assessment and collection of that fee. The initial fee shall be the sum of—

(I) $10 per travel authorization; and

(II) an amount that will at least ensure recovery of the full costs of providing and administering the System, as determined by the Secretary.

(ii) Disposition of amounts collected

Amounts collected under clause (i)(I) shall be credited to the Travel Promotion Fund established by subsection (d) of section 2131 of Title 22. Amounts collected under clause (i)(II) shall be transferred to the general fund of the Treasury and made available to pay the costs incurred to administer the System.

(iii) Sunset of Travel Promotion Fund fee

The Secretary may not collect the fee authorized by clause (i)(I) for fiscal years beginning after September 30, 2015.

(C) Validity

(i) Period

The Secretary of Homeland Security, in consultation with the Secretary of State, shall prescribe regulations that provide for a period, not to exceed three years, during which a determination of eligibility to travel under the program will be valid. Notwithstanding any other provision under this section, the Secretary of Homeland Security may revoke any such determination at any time and for any reason.

(ii) Limitation

A determination by the Secretary of Homeland Security that an alien is eligible to travel to the United States under the program is not a determination that the alien is admissible to the United States.

(iii) Not a determination of visa eligibility

A determination by the Secretary of Homeland Security that an alien who applied for authorization to travel to the United States through the System is not eligible to travel under the program is not a determination of eligibility for a visa to travel to the United States and shall not preclude the alien from applying for a visa.

(iv) Judicial review

Notwithstanding any other provision of law, no court shall have jurisdiction to review an eligibility determination under the System.

(D) Report

Not later than 60 days before publishing notice regarding the implementation of the System in the Federal Register, the Secretary of Homeland Security shall submit a report regarding the implementation of the system to—

(i) the Committee on Homeland Security of the House of Representatives;

(ii) the Committee on the Judiciary of the House of Representatives;

(iii) the Committee on Foreign Affairs of the House of Representatives;

(iv) the Permanent Select Committee on Intelligence of the House of Representatives;

(v) the Committee on Appropriations of the House of Representatives;

(vi) the Committee on Homeland Security and Governmental Affairs of the Senate;

(vii) the Committee on the Judiciary of the Senate;

(viii) the Committee on Foreign Relations of the Senate;

(ix) the Select Committee on Intelligence of the Senate; and

(x) the Committee on Appropriations of the Senate.

(i) Exit system

(1) In general

Not later than one year after August 3, 2007, the Secretary of Homeland Security shall establish an exit system that records the departure on a flight leaving the United States of every alien participating in the visa waiver program established under this section.

(2) System requirements

The system established under paragraph (1) shall—

(A) match biometric information of the alien against relevant watch lists and immigration information; and

(B) compare such biometric information against manifest information collected by air carriers on passengers departing the United States to confirm such aliens have departed the United States.

(3) Report

Not later than 180 days after August 3, 2007, the Secretary shall submit to Congress a report that describes—

(A) the progress made in developing and deploying the exit system established under this subsection; and

(B) the procedures by which the Secretary shall improve the method of calculating the rates of nonimmigrants who overstay their authorized period of stay in the United States.

(June 27, 1952, c. 477, Title II, ch. 2, § 217, as added Nov. 6, 1986, Pub.L. 99–603, Title III, § 313(a), 100 Stat. 3435, and amended Oct. 24, 1988, Pub.L. 100–525, § 2(p)(1), 102 Stat. 2613; Oct. 24, 1988, Pub.L. 100–525, § 2(p)(2), 102 Stat. 2613; Nov. 29, 1990, Pub.L. 101–649, Title II, § 201(a), 104 Stat. 5012; Dec. 12, 1991, Pub.L. 102–232, Title III, §§ 303(a)(1),(2), 307(*l*)(3), 105 Stat. 1746, 1756; Oct. 25, 1994, Pub.L. 103–415, § 1(m), 108 Stat. 4301; Oct. 25, 1994, Pub.L. 103–416, Title II, §§ 210, 211, 108 Stat. 4312, 4313; Sept. 30, 1996, Pub.L. 104–208, Div. C, Title III, § 308(d)(4)(F), (e)(9), Title VI, § 635(a) to (c)(1), (3), 110 Stat. 3009–618, 3009–620, 3009–702, 3009–703; Nov. 26, 1997, Pub.L. 105–119, Title I, § 125, 111 Stat. 2471; Apr. 27, 1998, Pub.L. 105–173, §§ 1, 3, 112 Stat. 56; Oct. 30, 2000, Pub.L. 106–396, Title I, §§ 101(a), Title II, §§ 201 to 207, Title IV, § 403(a) to (d), 114 Stat. 1637 to 1644, 1647, 1648; Oct. 26, 2001, Pub.L. 107–56, Title IV, §§ 417(c), (d), 115 Stat. 355; May 14, 2002, Pub.L. 107–173, Title III, § 307; Aug. 3, 2007, Pub.L. 110–53, Title VII, § 711(c), (d)(1), 121 Stat. 339, 341; Mar. 4, 2010, Pub.L. 111–145, § 9(e), 124 Stat. 62; July 2, 2010, Pub.L. 111–198, § 5(a), 124 Stat. 1357.)

§ 218. Admission of temporary H–2A workers [8 U.S.C.A. § 1188]

(a) Conditions for approval of H–2A petitions

(1) A petition to import an alien as an H–2A worker (as defined in subsection (i)(2)) may not be approved by the Attorney General unless the petitioner has applied to the Secretary of Labor for a certification that—

(A) there are not sufficient workers who are able, willing, and qualified, and who will be available at the time and place needed, to perform the labor or services involved in the petition, and

(B) the employment of the alien in such labor or services will not adversely affect the wages and working conditions of workers in the United States similarly employed.

(2) The Secretary of Labor may require by regulation, as a condition of issuing the certification, the payment of a fee to recover the reasonable costs of processing applications for certification.

(b) Conditions for denial of labor certification

The Secretary of Labor may not issue a certification under subsection (a) with respect to an employer if the conditions described in that subsection are not met or if any of the following conditions are met:

(1) There is a strike or lockout in the course of a labor dispute which, under the regulations, precludes such certification.

(2)(A) The employer during the previous two-year period employed H–2A workers and the Secretary of Labor has determined, after notice and opportunity for a hearing, that the employer at any time during that period substantially violated a material term or condition of the labor certification with respect to the employment of domestic or nonimmigrant workers.

(B) No employer may be denied certification under subparagraph (A) for more than three years for any violation described in such subparagraph.

(3) The employer has not provided the Secretary with satisfactory assurances that if the employment for which the certification is sought is not covered by State workers' compensation law, the employer will provide, at no cost to the worker, insurance covering injury and disease arising out of and in the course of the worker's employment which will provide benefits at least equal to those provided under the State workers' compensation law for comparable employment.

(4) The Secretary determines that the employer has not made positive recruitment efforts within a multi-state region of traditional or expected labor supply where the Secretary finds that there are a significant number of qualified United States workers who, if recruited, would be willing to make themselves available for work at the time and place needed. Positive recruitment under this paragraph is in addition to, and shall be conducted within the same time period as, the circulation through the interstate employment service system of the employer's job offer. The obligation to engage in positive recruitment under this paragraph shall terminate on the date the H–2A workers depart for the employer's place of employment.

(c) Special rules for consideration of applications

The following rules shall apply in the case of the filing and consideration of an application for a labor certification under this section:

(1) Deadline for filing applications

The Secretary of Labor may not require that the application be filed more than 45 days before the first date the employer requires the labor or services of the H–2A worker.

(2) Notice within seven days of deficiencies

(A) The employer shall be notified in writing within seven days of the date of filing if the application does not meet the standards (other than that described in subsection (a)(1)(A)) for approval.

(B) If the application does not meet such standards, the notice shall include the reasons therefor and the Secretary shall provide an opportunity for the prompt resubmission of a modified application.

(3) Issuance of certification

(A) The Secretary of Labor shall make, not later than 30 days before the date such labor or services are first required to be performed, the certification described in subsection (a)(1) of this section if—

(i) the employer has complied with the criteria for certification (including criteria for the recruitment of eligible individuals as prescribed by the Secretary), and

(ii) the employer does not actually have, or has not been provided with referrals of, qualified eligible individuals who have indicated their availability to perform such labor or services on the terms and conditions of a job offer which meets the requirements of the Secretary.

In considering the question of whether a specific qualification is appropriate in a job offer, the Secretary shall apply the normal and accepted qualifications required by non-H–2A-employers in the same or comparable occupations and crops.

(B)(i) For a period of 3 years subsequent to the effective date of this section, labor certifications shall remain effective only if, from the time the foreign worker departs for the employer's place of employment, the employer will provide employment to any qualified United States worker who applies to the employer until 50 percent of the period of the work contract, under which the foreign worker who is in the job was hired, has elapsed. In addition, the employer will offer to provide benefits, wages and working conditions required pursuant to this section and regulations.

(ii) The requirement of clause (i) shall not apply to any employer who—

(I) did not, during any calendar quarter during the preceding calendar year, use more than 500 man-days of agricultural labor, as defined in section 203(u) of Title 29,

(II) is not a member of an association which has petitioned for certification under this section for its members, and

(III) has not otherwise associated with other employers who are petitioning for temporary foreign workers under this section.

(iii) Six months before the end of the 3–year period described in clause (i), the Secretary of Labor shall consider the findings of the report mandated by section 403(a)(4)(D) of the Immigration Reform and Control Act of 1986 [8 U.S.C.A. § 1188 note] as well as other relevant materials, including evidence of benefits to United States workers and costs to employers, addressing the advisability of continuing a policy which requires an employer, as a condition for certification under this section, to continue to accept qualified, eligible United States workers for employment after the date the H–2A workers depart for work with the employer. The Secretary's review of such findings and materials shall lead to the issuance of findings in furtherance of the Congressional policy that aliens not be admitted under this section unless there are not sufficient workers in the United States who are able, willing, and qualified to perform the labor or service needed and that the employment of the aliens in such labor or services will not adversely affect the wages and working conditions of workers in the United States similarly employed. In the absence of the enactment of Federal legislation prior to three months before the end of the 3–year period described in clause (i) which addresses the subject matter of this subparagraph, the Secretary shall immediately publish the findings required by this clause, and shall promulgate, on an interim or final basis, regulations based on his findings which shall be effective no later than three years from the effective date of this section.

(iv) In complying with clause (i) of this subparagraph, an association shall be allowed to refer or transfer workers among its members: Provided, That for purposes of this section an association acting as an agent for its members shall not be considered a joint employer merely because of such referral or transfer.

(v) United States workers referred or transferred pursuant to clause (iv) of this subparagraph shall not be treated disparately.

(vi) An employer shall not be liable for payments under section 655.202(b)(6) of title 20, Code of Federal Regulations (or any successor regulation) with respect to an H–2A worker who is displaced due to compliance with the requirement of this subparagraph, if the Secretary of Labor certifies that the H–2A worker was displaced because of the employer's compliance with clause (i) of this subparagraph.

(vii)(I) No person or entity shall willfully and knowingly withhold domestic workers prior to the arrival of H–2A workers in order to force the hiring of domestic workers under clause (i).

(II) Upon the receipt of a complaint by an employer that a violation of subclause (I) has occurred the Secretary shall immediately investigate. He shall within 36 hours of the receipt of the complaint issue findings concerning the alleged violation. Where the Secretary finds that a violation has occurred, he shall immediately suspend the application of clause (i) of this subparagraph with respect to that certification for that date of need.

(4) Housing

Employers shall furnish housing in accordance with regulations. The employer shall be permitted at the employer's option to provide housing meeting applicable Federal standards for temporary labor camps or to secure housing which meets the local standards for rental and/or public accommodations or other substantially similar class of habitation: Provided, That in the absence of applicable local standards, State standards for rental and/or public accommodations or other substantially similar class of habitation shall be met: Provided further, That in the absence of applicable local or State standards, Federal temporary labor camp standards shall apply: Provided further, That the Secretary of Labor shall issue regulations which address the specific requirements of housing for employees principally engaged in the range production of livestock: Provided further, That when it is the prevailing practice in the area and occupation of intended employment to provide family housing, family housing shall be provided to workers with families who request it: And provided further, That nothing in this paragraph shall require an employer to provide or secure housing for workers who are not entitled to it under the temporary labor certification regulations in effect on June 1, 1986. The determination as to whether the housing furnished by an employer for an H–2A worker meets the requirements imposed by this paragraph must be made prior to the date specified in paragraph (3)(A) by which the Secretary of Labor is required to make a certification described in subsection (a)(1) with respect to a petition for the importation of such worker.

(d) Roles of agricultural associations

(1) Permitting filing by agricultural associations

A petition to import an alien as a temporary agricultural worker, and an application for a labor certification with respect to such a worker, may be filed by an association of agricultural producers which use agricultural services.

(2) Treatment of associations acting as employers

If an association is a joint or sole employer of temporary agricultural workers, the certifications granted under this section to the association may be used for the certified job opportunities of any of its producer members and such workers may be transferred among its producer members to perform agricultural services of a temporary or seasonal nature for which the certifications were granted.

(3) Treatment of violations

(A) Member's violation does not necessarily disqualify association or other members

If an individual producer member of a joint employer association is determined to have committed an act that under subsection (b)(2) results in the denial of certification with respect to the member, the denial shall apply only to that member of the association unless the Secretary determines that the association or other member participated in, had knowledge of, or reason to know of, the violation.

(B) Association's violation does not necessarily disqualify members

(i) If an association representing agricultural producers as a joint employer is determined to have committed an act that under subsection (b)(2) results in the denial of certification with respect to the association, the denial shall apply only to the association and does not apply to any individual producer member of the association unless the Secretary determines that the member participated in, had knowledge of, or reason to know of, the violation.

(ii) If an association of agricultural producers certified as a sole employer is determined to have committed an act that under subsection (b)(2) results in the denial of certification with respect to the association, no individual producer member of such association may be the beneficiary of the services of temporary alien agricultural workers admitted under this section in the commodity and occupation in which such aliens were employed by the association which was denied certification during the period such denial is in force, unless such producer member employs such aliens in the commodity and occupation in question directly or through an association which is a joint employer of such workers with the producer member.

(e) Expedited administrative appeals of certain determinations

(1) Regulations shall provide for an expedited procedure for the review of a denial of certification under subsection (a)(1) of this section or a revocation of such a certification or, at the applicant's request, for a de novo administrative hearing respecting the denial or revocation.

(2) The Secretary of Labor shall expeditiously, but in no case later than 72 hours after the time a new determination is requested, make a new determination on the request for certification in the case of an H–2A worker if able, willing, and qualified eligible individuals are not actually available at the time such labor or services are required and a certification was denied in whole or in part because of the availability of qualified workers. If the employer asserts that any eligible individual who has been referred is not able, willing, or qualified, the burden of proof is on the employer to establish that the individual referred is not able, willing, or qualified because of employment-related reasons.

(f) Violators disqualified for 5 years

An alien may not be admitted to the United States as a temporary agricultural worker if the alien was admitted to the United States as such a worker within the previous five-year period and the alien during that period violated a term or condition of such previous admission.

(g) Authorizations of appropriations

(1) There are authorized to be appropriated for each fiscal year, beginning with fiscal year 1987, $10,000,000 for the purposes—

(A) of recruiting domestic workers for temporary labor and services which might otherwise be performed by nonimmigrants described in section 101(a)(15)(H)(ii)(a) [8 U.S.C.A. § 1101(a)(15)(H)(ii)(a)], and

(B) of monitoring terms and conditions under which such nonimmigrants (and domestic workers employed by the same employers) are employed in the United States.

(2) The Secretary of Labor is authorized to take such actions, including imposing appropriate penalties and seeking appropriate injunctive relief and specific performance of contractual obligations, as may be necessary to assure employer compliance with terms and conditions of employment under this section.

(3) There are authorized to be appropriated for each fiscal year, beginning with fiscal year 1987, such sums as may be necessary for the purpose of enabling the Secretary of Labor to make determinations and certifications under this section and under section 212(a)(5)(A)(i) [8 U.S.C.A. § 1182(a)(5)(A)(i)].

(4) There are authorized to be appropriated for each fiscal year, beginning with fiscal year 1987, such sums as may be necessary for the purposes of enabling the Secretary of Agriculture to carry out the Secretary's duties and responsibilities under this section.

(h) Miscellaneous provisions

(1) The Attorney General shall provide for such endorsement of entry and exit documents of nonimmigrants described in section 101(a)(15)(H)(ii) [8 U.S.C.A. § 1101(a)(15)(H)(ii)] as may be necessary to carry out this section and to provide notice for purposes of section 274A [8 U.S.C.A. § 1324a].

(2) The provisions of subsections (a) and (c) of section 214 [8 U.S.C.A. § 1184] and the provisions of this section preempt any State or local law regulating admissibility of nonimmigrant workers.

(i) Definitions

For purposes of this section:

(1) The term "eligible individual" means, with respect to employment, an individual who is not an unauthorized alien (as defined in section 274A(h)(3) [8 U.S.C.A. § 1324a(h)(3)]) with respect to that employment.

(2) The term "H–2A worker" means a nonimmigrant described in section 101(a)(15)(H)(ii)(a) [8 U.S.C.A. § 1101(a)(15)(H)(ii)(a)].

(June 27, 1952, c. 477, Title II, ch. 2, § 218, formerly § 216, as added Nov. 6, 1986, Pub.L. 99–603, Title III, § 301(c), 100 Stat. 3411, renumbered and amended Oct. 24, 1988, Pub.L. 100–525, § 2(*l*)(2), (3), 102 Stat. 2612; Dec. 12, 1991, Pub.L. 102–232, Title III, §§ 307(*l*)(4), 309(b)(8), 105 Stat. 1756, 1759; Oct. 25, 1994, Pub.L. 103–416, Title II, § 219(z)(8), 108 Stat. 4318; Oct. 22, 1999, Pub.L. 106–78, Title VII, § 748, 113 Stat. 1167; Dec. 21, 2000, Pub.L. 106–554, § 1(a)(1) [Title I, § 105], 114 Stat. 2763.)

§ 219. Designation of foreign terrorist organizations [8 U.S.C.A. § 1189]

(a) Designation

(1) In general

The Secretary is authorized to designate an organization as a foreign terrorist organization in accordance with this subsection if the Secretary finds that—

(A) the organization is a foreign organization;

(B) the organization engages in terrorist activity (as defined in section 212(a)(3)(B) [8 U.S.C.A. § 1182(a)(3)(B)]) or terrorism (as defined in section 2656f(d)(2) of Title 22), or retains the capability and intent to engage in terrorist activity or terrorism; and

(C) the terrorist activity or terrorism of the organization threatens the security of United States nationals or the national security of the United States.

(2) Procedure

(A) Notice

(i) To Congressional leaders

Seven days before making a designation under this subsection, the Secretary shall, by classified communication, notify the Speaker and Minority Leader of the House of Representatives, the President pro tempore, Majority Leader, and Minority Leader of the Senate, and the members of the relevant committees of the House of Representatives and the Senate, in writing, of the intent to designate an organization under this subsection, together with the findings made under paragraph (1) with respect to that organization, and the factual basis therefor.

(ii) Publication in Federal Register

The Secretary shall publish the designation in the Federal Register seven days after providing the notification under clause (i).

(B) Effect of designation

(i) For purposes of section 2339B of Title 18, a designation under this subsection shall take effect upon publication under subparagraph (A)(ii).

(ii) Any designation under this subsection shall cease to have effect upon an Act of Congress disapproving such designation.

(C) Freezing of assets

Upon notification under paragraph (2)(A)(i), the Secretary of the Treasury may require United States financial institutions possessing or controlling any assets of any foreign organization included in the notification to block all financial transactions involving those assets until further directive from either the Secretary of the Treasury, Act of Congress, or order of court.

(3) Record

(A) In general

In making a designation under this subsection, the Secretary shall create an administrative record.

(B) Classified information

The Secretary may consider classified information in making a designation under this subsection. Classified information shall not be subject to disclosure for such time as it remains classified, except that such information may be disclosed to a court ex parte and in camera for purposes of judicial review under subsection (c) of this section.

(4) Period of designation

(A) In general

A designation under this subsection shall be effective for all purposes until revoked under paragraph (5) or (6) or set aside pursuant to subsection (c).

(B) Review of designation upon petition

(i) In general

The Secretary shall review the designation of a foreign terrorist organization under the procedures set forth in clauses (iii) and (iv) if the designated organization files a petition for revocation within the petition period described in clause (ii).

(ii) Petition period

For purposes of clause (i)—

(I) if the designated organization has not previously filed a petition for revocation under this subparagraph, the petition period begins 2 years after the date on which the designation was made; or

(II) if the designated organization has previously filed a petition for revocation under this subparagraph, the petition period begins 2 years after the date of the determination made under clause (iv) on that petition.

(iii) Procedures

Any foreign terrorist organization that submits a petition for revocation under this subparagraph must provide evidence in that petition that the relevant circumstances described in paragraph (1) are sufficiently different from the circumstances that were the basis for the designation such that a revocation with respect to the organization is warranted.

(iv) Determination

(I) In general

Not later than 180 days after receiving a petition for revocation submitted under this subparagraph, the Secretary shall make a determination as to such revocation.

(II) Classified information

The Secretary may consider classified information in making a determination in response to a petition for revocation. Classified information shall not be subject to disclosure for such time as it remains classified, except that such information may be disclosed to a court ex parte and in camera for purposes of judicial review under subsection (c) of this section.

(III) Publication of determination

A determination made by the Secretary under this clause shall be published in the Federal Register.

(IV) Procedures

Any revocation by the Secretary shall be made in accordance with paragraph (6).

(C) Other review of designation

(i) In general

If in a 5–year period no review has taken place under subparagraph (B), the Secretary shall review the designation of the foreign terrorist organization in order to determine whether such designation should be revoked pursuant to paragraph (6).

(ii) Procedures

If a review does not take place pursuant to subparagraph (B) in response to a petition for revocation that is filed in accordance with that subparagraph, then the review shall be conducted pursuant to procedures established by the Secretary. The results of such review and the applicable procedures shall not be reviewable in any court.

(iii) Publication of results of review

The Secretary shall publish any determination made pursuant to this subparagraph in the Federal Register.

(5) Revocation by Act of Congress

The Congress, by an Act of Congress, may block or revoke a designation made under paragraph (1).

(6) Revocation based on change in circumstances

(A) In general

The Secretary may revoke a designation made under paragraph (1) at any time, and shall revoke a designation upon completion of a review conducted pursuant to subparagraphs (B) and (C) of paragraph (4) if the Secretary finds that—

(i) the circumstances that were the basis for the designation have changed in such a manner as to warrant revocation; or

(ii) the national security of the United States warrants a revocation.

(B) Procedure

The procedural requirements of paragraphs (2) and (3) shall apply to a revocation under this paragraph. Any revocation shall take effect on the date specified in the revocation or upon publication in the Federal Register if no effective date is specified.

(7) Effect of revocation

The revocation of a designation under paragraph (5) or (6) shall not affect any action or proceeding based on conduct committed prior to the effective date of such revocation.

(8) Use of designation in trial or hearing

If a designation under this subsection has become effective under paragraph (2)(B) a defendant in a criminal action or an alien in a removal proceeding shall not be permitted to raise any question concerning the validity of the issuance of such designation as a defense or an objection at any trial or hearing.

(b) Amendments to a designation

(1) In general

The Secretary may amend a designation under this subsection if the Secretary finds that the organization has changed its name, adopted a new alias, dissolved and then reconstituted itself under a different name or names, or merged with another organization.

(2) Procedure

Amendments made to a designation in accordance with paragraph (1) shall be effective upon publication in the Federal Register. Subparagraphs (B) and (C) of subsection (a)(2) of this section shall apply to an amended designation upon such publication. Paragraphs (2)(A)(i), (4), (5), (6), (7), and (8) of subsection (a) of this section shall also apply to an amended designation.

(3) Administrative record

The administrative record shall be corrected to include the amendments as well as any additional relevant information that supports those amendments.

(4) Classified information

The Secretary may consider classified information in amending a designation in accordance with this subsection. Classified information shall not be subject to disclosure for such time as it remains classified, except that such information may be disclosed to a court ex parte and in camera for purposes of judicial review under subsection (c).

(c) Judicial review of designation

(1) In general

Not later than 30 days after publication in the Federal Register of a designation, an amended designation, or a determination in response to a petition for revocation, the designated organization may seek judicial review in the United States Court of Appeals for the District of Columbia Circuit.

(2) Basis of review

Review under this subsection shall be based solely upon the administrative record, except that the Government may submit, for ex parte and in camera review, classified information used in making the designation, amended designation, or determination in response to a petition for revocation.

(3) Scope of review

The Court shall hold unlawful and set aside a designation, amended designation, or determination in response to a petition for revocation the court finds to be—

(A) arbitrary, capricious, an abuse of discretion, or otherwise not in accordance with law;

(B) contrary to constitutional right, power, privilege, or immunity;

(C) in excess of statutory jurisdiction, authority, or limitation, or short of statutory right;

(D) lacking substantial support in the administrative record taken as a whole or in classified information submitted to the court under paragraph (2), [sic]* or

(E) not in accord with the procedures required by law.

(4) Judicial review invoked

The pendency of an action for judicial review of a designation, amended designation, or determination in response to a petition for revocation shall not affect the application of this section, unless the court issues a final order setting aside the designation, amended designation, or determination in response to a petition for revocation.

(d) Definitions

As used in this section—

(1) the term "classified information" has the meaning given that term in section 1(a) of the Classified Information Procedures Act (18 U.S.C. App.);

(2) the term "national security" means the national defense, foreign relations, or economic interests of the United States;

(3) the term "relevant committees" means the Committees on the Judiciary, Intelligence, and Foreign Relations of the Senate and the Committees on the Judiciary, Intelligence, and International Relations of the House of Representatives; and

(4) the term "Secretary" means the Secretary of State, in consultation with the Secretary of the Treasury and the Attorney General.

(June 27, 1952, c. 477, Title II, ch. 2, § 219, as added Apr. 24, 1996, Pub.L. 104–132, Title III, § 302(a), 110 Stat. 1248, and amended Sept. 30, 1996, Pub.L. 104–208, Div. C,

* So in original. The comma probably should be a semicolon.

Title III, § 356, Title VI, § 671(c)(1), 110 Stat. 3009-644, 3009–722; Oct. 26, 2001, Pub.L. 107–56, Title IV, § 411(c), 115 Stat. 349; Dec. 17, 2004, Pub.L. 108–458, Title VII, § 7119, 118 Stat. 3801 to 3803.)

CHAPTER III—ISSUANCE OF ENTRY DOCUMENTS

§ 221. Issuance of visas [8 U.S.C.A. § 1201]

(a) Immigrants; nonimmigrants

(1) Under the conditions hereinafter prescribed and subject to the limitations prescribed in this Act or regulations issued thereunder, a consular officer may issue

(A) to an immigrant who has made proper application therefor, an immigrant visa which shall consist of the application provided for in section 222 [8 U.S.C.A. § 1202], visaed by such consular officer, and shall specify the foreign state, if any, to which the immigrant is charged, the immigrant's particular status under such foreign state, the preference, immediate relative, or special immigrant classification to which the alien is charged, the date on which the validity of the visa shall expire, and such additional information as may be required; and

(B) to a nonimmigrant who has made proper application therefor, a nonimmigrant visa, which shall specify the classification under section 101(a)(15) [8 U.S.C.A. § 1101(a)(15)] of the nonimmigrant, the period during which the nonimmigrant visa shall be valid, and such additional information as may be required.

(2) The Secretary of State shall provide to the Service an electronic version of the visa file of each alien who has been issued a visa to ensure that the data in that visa file is available to immigration inspectors at the United States ports of entry before the arrival of the alien at such a port of entry.

(b) Registration; photographs; waiver of requirement

Each alien who applies for a visa shall be registered in connection with his application, and shall furnish copies of his photograph signed by him for such use as may be by regulations required. The requirements of this subsection may be waived in the discretion of the Secretary of State in the case of any alien who is within that class of nonimmigrants enumerated in sections 101(a)(15)(A) [8 U.S.C.A. § 1101(a)(15)(A)], and 101(a)(15)(G) [8 U.S.C.A. § 1101(a)(15)(G)], or in the case of any alien who is granted a diplomatic visa on a diplomatic passport or on the equivalent thereof.

(c) Period of validity; requirement of visa

An immigrant visa shall be valid for such period, not exceeding six months, as shall be by regulations prescribed, except that any visa issued to a child lawfully adopted by a United States citizen and spouse while such citizen is serving abroad in the United States Armed Forces, or is employed abroad by the United States Government, or is temporarily abroad on business, shall be valid until such time, for a period not to exceed three years, as the adoptive citizen parent returns to the United States in due course of his service, employment, or business. A nonimmigrant visa shall be valid for such periods as shall be by regulations prescribed. In prescribing the period of validity of a nonimmigrant visa in the case of nationals of any foreign country who are eligible for such visas, the Secretary of State shall, insofar as practicable, accord to such nationals the same treatment upon a reciprocal basis as such foreign country accords to nationals of the United States who are within a similar class; except that in the case of aliens who are nationals of a foreign country and who either are granted refugee status and firmly resettled in an other foreign country, or are granted permanent residence and residing in another foreign country, the Secretary of State may prescribe the period of validity of such a visa based upon the treatment granted by that other foreign country to alien refugees and permanent residents, respectively, in the United States. An immigrant visa may be replaced under the original number during the fiscal year in which the original visa was issued for an immigrant who establishes to the satisfaction of the consular officer that he was unable to use the original immigrant visa during the period of its validity because of reasons beyond his control and for which he was not responsible: Provided, That the immigrant is found by the consular officer to be eligible for an immigrant visa and the immigrant pays again the statutory fees for an application and an immigrant visa.

(d) Physical examination

Prior to the issuance of an immigrant visa to any alien, the consular officer shall require such alien to submit to a physical and mental examination in accordance with such regulations as may be prescribed. Prior to the issuance of a nonimmigrant visa to any alien, the consular officer may require such alien to submit to a physical or mental examination, or both, if in his opinion such examination is necessary to ascertain whether such alien is eligible to receive a visa.

(e) Surrender of visa

Each immigrant shall surrender his immigrant visa to the immigration officer at the port of entry, who shall endorse on the visa the date and the port of arrival, the identity of the vessel or other means of transportation by which the immigrant arrived, and such other endorsements as may be by regulations required.

(f) Surrender of documents

Each nonimmigrant shall present or surrender to the immigration officer at the port of entry such documents as may be by regulation required. In the case of an alien crewman not in possession of any individual documents other than a passport and until such time as it becomes practicable to issue individual documents, such alien crewman may be admitted, subject to the provisions of this title, if his name appears in the crew list of the vessel or aircraft on which he arrives and the crew list is visaed by a consular officer, but the consular officer shall have the right to deny admission to any alien crewman from the crew list visa.

(g) Non-issuance of visas or other documents

No visa or other documentation shall be issued to an alien if **(1)** it appears to the consular officer, from statements in the application, or in the papers submitted therewith, that such alien is ineligible to receive a visa or such other documentation under section 212 [8 U.S.C.A. § 1182], or any other provision of law, **(2)** the application fails to comply with the provisions of this Act, or the regulations issued thereunder, or **(3)** the consular officer knows or has reason to believe that such alien is ineligible to receive a visa or such other documentation under section 212 [8 U.S.C.A. § 1182], or any other provision of law: Provided, That a visa or other documentation may be issued to an alien who is within the purview of section 212(a)(4) [8 U.S.C.A. § 1182(a)(4)], if such alien is otherwise entitled to receive a visa or other documentation, upon receipt of notice by the consular officer from the Attorney General of the giving of a bond or undertaking providing indemnity as in the case of aliens admitted under section 213 [8 U.S.C.A. § 1183]: Provided further, That a visa may be issued to an alien defined in section 101(a)(15)(B) or (F) [8 U.S.C.A. § 1101(a)(15)(B) or (F)], if such alien is otherwise entitled to receive a visa, upon receipt of a notice by the consular officer from the Attorney General of the giving of a bond with sufficient surety in such sum and containing such conditions as the consular officer shall prescribe, to insure that at the expiration of the time for which such alien has been admitted by the Attorney General, as provided in section 214(a) [8 U.S.C.A. § 1184(a)], or upon failure to maintain the status under which he was admitted, or to maintain any status subsequently acquired under section 248 [8 U.S.C.A. § 1258], such alien will depart from the United States.

(h) Nonadmission upon arrival

Nothing in this Act shall be construed to entitle any alien, to whom a visa or other documentation has been issued, to be admitted [sic] the United States, if, upon arrival at a port of entry in the United States, he is found to be inadmissible under this Act, or any other provision of law. The substance of this subsection shall appear upon every visa application.

(i) Revocation of visas or documents

After the issuance of a visa or other documentation to any alien, the consular officer or the Secretary of State may at any time, in his discretion, revoke such visa or other documentation. Notice of such revocation shall be communicated to the Attorney General, and such revocation shall invalidate the visa or other documentation from the date of issuance: Provided, That carriers or transportation companies, and masters, commanding officers, agents, owners, charterers, or consignees, shall not be penalized under section 273(b) [8 U.S.C.A. § 1323(b)] for action taken in reliance on such visas or other documentation, unless they received due notice of such revocation prior to the alien's embarkation. There shall be no means of judicial review (including review pursuant to section 2241 of Title 28 or any other habeas corpus provision, and sections 1361 and 1651 of such title) of a revocation under this subsection, except in the context of a removal proceeding if such revocation provides the sole ground for removal under section 237(a)(1)(B) [8 U.S.C.A. § 1227(a)(1)(B)].

(June 27, 1952, c. 477, Title II, ch. 3, § 221, 66 Stat. 191; Sept. 26, 1961, Pub.L. 87–301, § 4, 75 Stat. 651; Oct. 3, 1965, Pub.L. 89–236, §§ 11(a), (b), 17, 79 Stat. 918, 919; Dec. 29, 1981, Pub.L. 97–116, § 18(f), 95 Stat. 1620; Nov. 14, 1986, Pub.L. 99–653, § 5(a)(1) to (3), formerly § 5(a) to (c), 100 Stat. 3656; renumbered Oct. 24, 1988, Pub.L. 100–525, § 8 (d)(1), 102 Stat. 2617, and amended Nov. 29, 1990, Pub.L. 101–649, Title VI, § 603(a)(9), 104 Stat. 5083; Dec. 12, 1991, Pub.L. 102–232, Title III, § 302(e)(8)(C), 105 Stat. 1746; Sept. 30, 1996, Pub.L. 104–208, Div. C, Title III, § 308(d)(4)(G), (f)(2)(B), Title VI, § 631, 110 Stat. 3009–618, 3009–621, 3009–700; May 14, 2002, Pub.L. 107–173, Title III, § 301, 116 Stat. 552; Dec. 17, 2004, Pub.L. 108–458, Title V, § 5304(a), 118 Stat. 3736.)

§ 222. Application for visas [8 U.S.C.A. § 1202]

(a) Immigrant visas

Every alien applying for an immigrant visa and for alien registration shall make application therefor in such form and manner and at such place as shall be by regulations prescribed. In the application the alien shall state his full and true name, and any other name which he has used or by which he has been known; age and sex; the date and place of his birth; and such additional information necessary to the identification of the applicant and the enforcement of the immigration and nationality laws as may be by regulations prescribed.

(b) Other documentary evidence for immigrant visa

Every alien applying for an immigrant visa shall present a valid unexpired passport or other suitable travel document, or document of identity and nationality, if such document is required under the regulations issued by the Secretary of State. The immigrant shall furnish to the consular officer with his application a copy of a certification by the appropriate police authorities stating what their records show concerning the immigrant; a certified copy of any existing prison record, military record, and record of his birth; and a certified copy of all other records or documents concerning him or his case which may be required by the consular officer. The copy of each document so furnished shall be permanently attached to the application and become a part thereof. In the event that the immigrant establishes to the satisfaction of the consular officer that any document or record required by this subsection is unobtainable, the consular officer may permit the immigrant to submit in lieu of such document or record other satisfactory evidence of the fact to which such document or record would, if obtainable, pertain. All immigrant visa applications shall be reviewed and adjudicated by a consular officer.

(c) Nonimmigrant visas; nonimmigrant registration; form, manner and contents of application

Every alien applying for a nonimmigrant visa and for alien registration shall make application therefor in such form and manner as shall be by regulations prescribed. In the application the alien shall state his full and true name, the date and place of birth, his nationality, the purpose and length of his intended stay in the United States; his marital status; and such additional information necessary to the identification of the applicant, the determination of his eligibility for a nonimmigrant visa, and the enforcement of the immigration and nationality laws as may be by regulations prescribed. The alien shall provide complete and accurate information in response to any request for information contained in the application. At the discretion of the Secretary of State, application forms for the various classes of nonimmigrant admissions described in section 101(a)(15) [8 U.S.C.A. § 1101(a)(15)] may vary according to the class of visa being requested.

(d) Other documentary evidence for nonimmigrant visa

Every alien applying for a nonimmigrant visa and alien registration shall furnish to the consular officer, with his application, a certified copy of such documents pertaining to him as may be by regulations required. All nonimmigrant visa applications shall be reviewed and adjudicated by a consular officer.

(e) Signing and verification of application

Except as may be otherwise prescribed by regulations, each application for an immigrant visa shall be signed by the applicant in the presence of the consular officer, and verified by the oath of the applicant administered by the consular officer. The application for an immigrant visa, when visaed by the consular officer, shall become the immigrant visa. The application for a nonimmigrant visa or other documentation as a nonimmigrant shall be disposed of as may be by regulations prescribed. The issuance of a nonimmigrant visa shall, except as may be otherwise by regulations prescribed, be evidenced by a stamp, or other [sic] placed in the alien's passport.

(f) Confidential nature of records

The records of the Department of State and of diplomatic and consular offices of the United States pertaining to the issuance or refusal of visas or permits to enter the United States shall be considered confidential and shall be used only for the formulation, amendment, administration, or enforcement of the immigration, nationality, and other laws of the United States, except that—

(1) in the discretion of the Secretary of State certified copies of such records may be made available to a court which certifies that the information contained in such records is needed by the court in the interest of the ends of justice in a case pending before the court.

(2) the Secretary of State, in the Secretary's discretion and on the basis of reciprocity, may provide to a foreign government information in the Department of State's computerized visa lookout database and, when necessary and appropriate, other records covered by this section related to information in the database—

(A) with regard to individual aliens, at any time on a case-by-case basis for the purpose of preventing, investigating, or punishing acts that would constitute a crime in the United States, including, but not limited to, terrorism or trafficking in controlled substances, persons, or illicit weapons; or

(B) with regard to any or all aliens in the database, pursuant to such conditions as the Secretary of State shall establish in an agreement with the foreign government in which that government agrees to use such information and records for the purposes described in subparagraph (A) or to deny visas to persons who would be inadmissible to the United States.

(g) Voidness of nonimmigrant visa for stay beyond authorized period

(1) In the case of an alien who has been admitted on the basis of a nonimmigrant visa and remained in the United States beyond the period of stay authorized by the Attorney General, such visa shall be void beginning after the conclusion of such period of stay.

(2) An alien described in paragraph (1) shall be ineligible to be readmitted to the United States as a nonimmigrant, except—

(A) on the basis of a visa (other than the visa described in paragraph (1)) issued in a consular office located in the country of the alien's nationality (or, if there is no office in such country, in such other consular office as the Secretary of State shall specify); or

(B) where extraordinary circumstances are found by the Secretary of State to exist.

(h) Notwithstanding any other provision of this Act, the Secretary of State shall require every alien applying for a nonimmigrant visa—

(1) who is at least 14 years of age and not more than 79 years of age to submit to an in person interview with a consular officer unless the requirement for such interview is waived—

(A) by a consular official and such alien is—

(i) within that class of nonimmigrants enumerated in subparagraph (A) or (G) of section 101(a)(15) [8 U.S.C.A. § 1101(a)(15)];

(ii) within the NATO visa category;

(iii) within that class of nonimmigrants enumerated in section 101(a)(15)(C)(iii) [sic]* [8 U.S.C.A.

* Section 101(a)(15)(C) does not have subparts.—eds.

§ 1101(a)(15)(C)(iii)] (referred to as the "C–3 visa" category); or

(iv) granted a diplomatic or official visa on a diplomatic or official passport or on the equivalent thereof;

(B) by a consular official and such alien is applying for a visa—

(i) not more than 12 months after the date on which such alien's prior visa expired;

(ii) for the visa classification for which such prior visa was issued;

(iii) from the consular post located in the country of such alien's usual residence, unless otherwise prescribed in regulations that require an applicant to apply for a visa in the country of which such applicant is a national; and

(iv) the consular officer has no indication that such alien has not complied with the immigration laws and regulations of the United States; or

(C) by the Secretary of State if the Secretary determines that such waiver is—

(i) in the national interest of the United States; or

(ii) necessary as a result of unusual or emergent circumstances; and

(2) notwithstanding paragraph (1), to submit to an in person interview with a consular officer if such alien—

(A) is not a national or resident of the country in which such alien is applying for a visa;

(B) was previously refused a visa, unless such refusal was overcome or a waiver of ineligibility has been obtained;

(C) is listed in the Consular Lookout and Support System (or successor system at the Department of State);

(D) is a national of a country officially designated by the Secretary of State as a state sponsor of terrorism, except such nationals who possess nationalities of countries that are not designated as state sponsors of terrorism;

(E) requires a security advisory opinion or other Department of State clearance, unless such alien is—

(i) within that class of nonimmigrants enumerated in subparagraph (A) or (G) of section 101(a)(15) [8 U.S.C.A. § 1101(a)(15)];

(ii) within the NATO visa category;

(iii) within that class of nonimmigrants enumerated in section 101(a)(15)(C)(iii) [sic]* [8 U.S.C.A. § 1101(a)(15)(C)(iii)] (referred to as the "C–3 visa" category); or

(iv) an alien who qualifies for a diplomatic or official visa, or its equivalent; or

(F) is identified as a member of a group or sector that the Secretary of State determines—

(i) poses a substantial risk of submitting inaccurate information in order to obtain a visa;

(ii) has historically had visa applications denied at a rate that is higher than the average rate of such denials; or

(iii) poses a security threat to the United States.

(June 27, 1952, c. 477, Title II, ch. 3, § 222, 66 Stat. 193; Sept. 26, 1961, Pub.L. 87–301, § 6, 75 Stat. 653; Oct. 3, 1965, Pub.L. 89–236 § 11(c), 79 Stat. 918; Nov. 14, 1986, Pub.L. 99–653, § 6, 100 Stat. 3656; Oct. 24, 1988, Pub.L. 100–525, §§ 8(e), 9(j), 102 Stat. 2617, 2620; Oct. 25, 1994, Pub.L. 103–416, Title II, § 205(a), 108 Stat. 4311; Sept. 30, 1996, Pub.L. 104–208, Div. C, Title VI, §§ 632(a), 634, 110 Stat. 3009–701; Oct. 26, 2001, Pub.L. 107–56, Title IV, § 413, 115 Stat. 353; Dec. 17, 2004, Pub.L. 108–458, Title V, §§ 5301, 5302, Title VII, § 7203(b), 118 Stat. 3735, 3814.)

§ 223. Re-entry permit [8 U.S.C.A. § 1203]

(a) Application; contents

(1) Any alien lawfully admitted for permanent residence, or **(2)** any alien lawfully admitted to the United States pursuant to clause 6 of section 3 of the Immigration Act of 1924, between July 1, 1924, and July 5, 1932, both dates inclusive, who intends to depart temporarily from the United States may make application to the Attorney General for a permit to reenter the United States, stating the length of his intended absence or absences, and the reasons therefor. Such applications shall be made under oath, and shall be in such form, contain such information, and be accompanied by such photographs of the applicant as may be by regulations prescribed.

(b) Issuance of permit; nonrenewability

If the Attorney General finds **(1)** that the applicant under subsection (a)(1) has been lawfully admitted to the United States for permanent residence, or that the applicant under subsection (a)(2) has since admission maintained the status required of him at the time of his admission and such applicant desires to visit abroad and to return to the United States to resume the status existing at the time of his departure for such visit, **(2)** that the application is made in good faith, and **(3)** that the alien's proposed departure from the United States would not be contrary to the interests of the United States, the Attorney General may, in his discretion, issue the permit, which shall be valid for not more than

* Section 101(a)(15)(C) does not have subparts.—eds.

two years from the date of issuance and shall not be renewable. The permit shall be in such form as shall be by regulations prescribed for the complete identification of the alien.

(c) Multiple reentries

During the period of validity, such permit may be used by the alien in making one or more applications for reentry into the United States.

(d) Presented and surrendered

Upon the return of the alien to the United States the permit shall be presented to the immigration officer at the port of entry, and upon the expiration of its validity, the permit shall be surrendered to the Service.

(e) Permit in lieu of visa

A permit issued under this section in the possession of the person to whom issued, shall be accepted in lieu of any visa which otherwise would be required from such person under this Act. Otherwise a permit issued under this section shall have no effect under the immigration laws except to show that the alien to whom it was issued is returning from a temporary visit abroad; but nothing in this section shall be construed as making such permit the exclusive means of establishing that the alien is so returning.

(June 27, 1952, c. 477, Title II, ch. 3, § 223, 66 Stat. 194; Pub. L. 97–116, § 6, Dec. 29, 1981, 95 Stat. 1615.)

§ 224. Immediate relative and special immigrant visas [8 U.S.C.A. § 1204]

A consular officer may, subject to the limitations provided in section 221 [8 U.S.C.A. § 1201], issue an immigrant visa to a special immigrant or immediate relative as such upon satisfactory proof, under regulations prescribed under this Act, that the applicant is entitled to special immigrant or immediate relative status.

(June 27, 1952, c. 477, Title II, ch. 3, § 224, 66 Stat. 195; Pub. L. 89–236, § 11(d), Oct. 3, 1965, 79 Stat. 918.)

CHAPTER IV—INSPECTION, APPREHENSION, EXAMINATION, EXCLUSION, AND REMOVAL

§ 231. Lists of alien and citizen passengers arriving and departing [8 U.S.C.A. § 1221]

(a) Arrival manifest

For each commercial vessel or aircraft transporting any person to any seaport or airport of the United States from any place outside the United States, it shall be the duty of an appropriate official specified in subsection (d) to provide to any United States border officer (as defined in subsection (i)) at that port manifest information about each passenger, crew member, and other occupant transported on such vessel or aircraft prior to arrival at that port.

(b) Departure manifests

For each commercial vessel or aircraft taking passengers on board at any seaport or airport of the United States, who are destined to any place outside the United States, it shall be the duty of an appropriate official specified in subsection (d) to provide any United States border officer (as defined in subsection (i)) before departure from such port manifest information about each passenger, crew member, and other occupant to be transported.

(c) Contents of manifest

The information to be provided with respect to each person listed on a manifest required to be provided under subsection (a) or (b) shall include—

(1) complete name;

(2) date of birth;

(3) citizenship;

(4) sex;

(5) passport number and country of issuance;

(6) country of residence;

(7) United States visa number, date, and place of issuance, where applicable;

(8) alien registration number, where applicable;

(9) United States address while in the United States; and

(10) such other information the Attorney General, in consultation with the Secretary of State, and the Secretary of Treasury determines as being necessary for the identification of the persons transported and for the enforcement of the immigration laws and to protect safety and national security.

(d) Appropriate officials specified

An appropriate official specified in this subsection is the master or commanding officer, or authorized agent, owner, or consignee, of the commercial vessel or aircraft concerned.

(e) Deadline for requirement of electronic transmission of manifest information

Not later than January 1, 2003, manifest information required to be provided under subsection (a) or (b) shall be transmitted electronically by the appropriate official specified in subsection (d) to an immigration officer.

(f) Prohibition

No operator of any private or public carrier that is under a duty to provide manifest information under this section shall be granted clearance papers until the appropriate official specified in subsection (d) has complied with the requirements of this subsection, except that, in the case of commercial vessels or aircraft that the Attorney General determines are making regular trips to the United States, the Attorney General may, when expedient, arrange for the provision of manifest information of persons departing the United States at a later date.

(g) Penalties against noncomplying shipments, aircraft, or carriers

If it shall appear to the satisfaction of the Attorney General that an appropriate official specified in subsection (d), any public or private carrier, or the agent of any transportation line, as the case may be, has refused or failed to provide manifest information required by subsection (a) or (b), or that the manifest information provided is not accurate and full based on information provided to the carrier, such official, carrier, or agent, as the case may be, shall pay to the Commissioner the sum of $1,000 for each person with respect to whom such accurate and full manifest information is not provided, or with respect to whom the manifest information is not prepared as prescribed by this section or by regulations issued pursuant thereto. No commercial vessel or aircraft shall be granted clearance pending determination of the question of the liability to the payment of such penalty, or while it remains unpaid, and no such penalty shall be remitted or refunded, except that clearance may be granted prior to the determination of such question upon the deposit with the Commissioner of a bond or undertaking approved by the Attorney General or a sum sufficient to cover such penalty.

(h) Waiver

The Attorney General may waive the requirements of subsection (a) or (b) upon such circumstances and conditions as the Attorney General may by regulation prescribe.

(i) United States border officer defined

In this section, the term "United States border officer" means, with respect to a particular port of entry into the United States, any United States official who is performing duties at that port of entry.

(j) Record of citizens and resident aliens leaving permanently for foreign countries

The Attorney General may authorize immigration officers to record the following information regarding every resident person leaving the United States by way of the Canadian or Mexican borders for permanent residence in a foreign country: Names, age, and sex; whether married or single; calling or occupation; whether able to read or write; nationality; country of birth; country of which citizen or subject; race; last permanent residence in the United States; intended future permanent residence; and time and port of last arrival in the United States; and if a United States citizen or national, the facts on which claim to that status is based.

(June 27, 1952, c. 477, Title II, ch. 4, § 231, 66 Stat. 195; Dec. 29, 1981, Pub.L. 97–116, § 18(g), 95 Stat. 1620; Nov. 29, 1990, Pub.L. 101–649, Title V, § 543(a)(1), 104 Stat. 5057; Dec. 12, 1991, Pub.L. 102–232, Title III, § 306(c)(4)(A), 105 Stat. 1752; Pub.L. 104–208,

Div. C, Title III, § 308(g)(1), Sept. 30, 1996, 110 Stat. 3009–622; Nov. 28, 2001, Pub.L. 107–77, Title I, § 115, 115 Stat. 768; May 14, 2002, Pub.L. 107–173, Title IV, § 402.)

§ 232. Detention of aliens for physical and mental examination [8 U.S.C.A. § 1222]

(a) Detention of aliens

For the purpose of determining whether aliens (including alien crewmen) arriving at ports of the United States belong to any of the classes inadmissible under this Act, by reason of being afflicted with any of the diseases or mental or physical defects or disabilities set forth in section 212(a) [8 U.S.C.A. § 1182(a)], or whenever the Attorney General has received information showing that any aliens are coming from a country or have embarked at a place where any of such diseases are prevalent or epidemic, such aliens shall be detained by the Attorney General, for a sufficient time to enable the immigration officers and medical officers to subject such aliens to observation and an examination sufficient to determine whether or not they belong to the inadmissible classes.

(b) Physical and mental examination

The physical and mental examination of arriving aliens (including alien crewmen) shall be made by medical officers of the United States Public Health Service, who shall conduct all medical examinations and shall certify, for the information of the immigration officers and the immigration judges, any physical and mental defect or disease observed by such medical officers in any such alien. If medical officers of the United States Public Health Service are not available, civil surgeons of not less than four years' professional experience may be employed for such service upon such terms as may be prescribed by the Attorney General. Aliens (including alien crewmen) arriving at ports of the United States shall be examined by at least one such medical officer or civil surgeon under such administrative regulations as the Attorney General may prescribe, and under medical regulations prepared by the Secretary of Health and Human Services. Medical officers of the United States Public Health Service who have had special training in the diagnosis of insanity and mental defects shall be detailed for duty or employed at such ports of entry as the Attorney General may designate, and such medical officers shall be provided with suitable facilities for the detention and examination of all arriving aliens who it is suspected may be inadmissible under paragraph (1) of section 212(a) [8 U.S.C.A. § 1182(a)], and the services of interpreters shall be provided for such examination. Any alien certified under paragraph (1) of section 212(a) [8 U.S.C.A. § 1182(a)], may appeal to a board of medical officers of the United States Public Health Service, which shall be convened by the Secretary of Health and Human Services, and any such alien may introduce before such board one expert medical witness at his own cost and expense.

(c) Certification of certain helpless aliens

If an examining medical officer determines that an alien arriving in the United States is inadmissible, is helpless from sickness, mental or physical disability, or infancy, and is accompanied by another alien whose protection or guardianship may be required, the officer may certify such fact for purposes of applying section 212(a)(10)(B) [8 U.S.C.A. § 1182(a)(10)(B)] with respect to the other alien.

(June 27, 1952, c. 477, Title II, ch. 4, § 232, 66 Stat. 196; Oct. 18, 1986, Pub.L. 99–500, Title I, § 101(b) [Title II, § 206(a), formerly § 206], 100 Stat. 1783–56 as renumbered and amended Oct. 24, 1988, Pub.L. 100–525, § 4(b)(1), (2), (d), 102 Stat. 2615; Sept. 30, 1996, Pub.L. 104–208, Div. C, Title III, §§ 308(b)(2), (3), (c)(2)(A), (d)(3)(A), (4)(H), 371(b)(3), 110 Stat. 3009–615, 3009–616, 3009–617, 3009–618, 3009–645.)

§ 233. Entry through or from foreign territory and adjacent islands [8 U.S.C.A. § 1223]

(a) Necessity of transportation contract

The Attorney General shall have power to enter into contracts with transportation lines for the inspection and admission of aliens coming to the United States from foreign territory or from adjacent islands. No such transportation line shall be allowed to land any such alien in the United States until and unless it has entered into any such contracts which may be required by the Attorney General.

(b) Landing stations

Every transportation line engaged in carrying alien passengers for hire to the United States from foreign territory of from adjacent islands shall provide and maintain at its expense suitable landing stations, approved by the Attorney General, conveniently located at the point or points of entry. No such transportation line shall be allowed to land any alien passengers in the United States until such landing stations are provided, and unless such stations are thereafter maintained to the satisfaction of the Attorney General.

(c) Landing agreements

The Attorney General shall have power to enter into contracts including bonding agreements with transportation lines to guarantee the passage through the United States in immediate and continuous transit of aliens destined to foreign countries. Notwithstanding any other provision of this Act, such aliens may not have their classification changed under section 248 [8 U.S.C.A. § 1258].

(d) Definitions

As used in this section the terms "transportation line" and "transportation company" include, but are not limited to, the owner, charterer, consignee, or authorized agent operating any vessel or aircraft or railroad train bringing aliens to the United States, to foreign territory, or to adjacent islands.

(e) Redesignated (d).

(June 27, 1952, c. 477, Title II, ch. 4, § 233, formerly § 238, 66 Stat. 202, as amended Nov. 14, 1986, Pub.L. 99–653, § 7(b), 100 Stat. 3657; redesignated § 233 and amended, Sept. 30, 1996, Pub.L. 104–208, Div. C, Title III, §§ 308(b)(4), (f)(4), 362, 110 Stat. 3009–615, 3009–622, 3009–645.)

§ 234. Designation of ports of entry for aliens arriving by aircraft [8 U.S.C.A. § 1224]

The Attorney General is authorized **(1)** by regulation to designate as ports of entry for aliens arriving by aircraft any of the ports of entry for civil aircraft designated as such in accordance with law; **(2)** by regulation to provide such reasonable requirements for aircraft in civil air navigation with respect to giving notice of intention to land in advance of landing, or notice of landing, as shall be deemed necessary for purposes of administration and enforcement of this Act; and **(3)** by regulation to provide for the application to civil air navigation of the provisions of this Act where not expressly so provided in this Act to such extent and upon such conditions as he deems necessary. Any person who violates any regulation made under this section shall be subject to a civil penalty of $2,000 which may be remitted or mitigated by the Attorney General in accordance with such proceedings as the Attorney General shall by regulation prescribe. In case the violation is by the owner or person in command of the aircraft, the penalty shall be a lien upon the aircraft, and such aircraft may be libeled therefor in the appropriate United States court. The determination by the Attorney General and remission or mitigation of the civil penalty shall be final. In case the violation is by the owner or person in command of the aircraft, the penalty shall be a lien upon the aircraft and may be collected by proceedings in rem which shall conform as nearly as may be to civil suits in admiralty. The Supreme Court of the United States, and under its direction other courts of the United States, are authorized to prescribe rules regulating such proceedings against aircraft in any particular not otherwise provided by law. Any aircraft made subject to a lien by this section may be summarily seized by, and placed in the custody of such persons as the Attorney General may by regulation prescribe. The aircraft may be released from such custody upon deposit of such amount not exceeding $2000 as the Attorney General may prescribe, or of a bond in such sum and with such sureties as the Attorney General may prescribe, conditioned upon the payment of the penalty which may be finally determined by the Attorney General.

(June 27, 1952, c. 477, Title II, ch. 4, § 234, formerly § 239, 66 Stat. 203, as amended Nov. 29, 1990, Pub.L. 101–649, Title V, § 543(a)(3), 104 Stat. 5058; Dec. 12, 1991, Pub.L. 102–232, Title III, § 306(c)(2), 105 Stat. 1752; renumbered § 234, Pub.L. 104–208, Div. C, Title III, § 304(a)(1), Sept. 30, 1996, 110 Stat. 3009–587.)

§ 235. Inspection by immigration officers; expedited removal of inadmissible arriving aliens; referral for hearing [8 U.S.C.A. § 1225]

(a) Inspection

(1) Aliens treated as applicants for admission

An alien present in the United States who has not been admitted or who arrives in the United States (whether or not at a designated port of arrival and including an alien who is brought to the United States after having been interdicted in international or United States waters) shall be deemed for purposes of this Act an applicant for admission.

(2) Stowaways

An arriving alien who is a stowaway is not eligible to apply for admission or to be admitted and shall be ordered removed upon inspection by an immigration officer. Upon such inspection if the alien indicates an intention to apply for asylum under section 208 [8 U.S.C.A. § 1158] or a fear of persecution, the officer shall refer the alien for an interview under subsection (b)(1)(B). A stowaway may apply for asylum only if the stowaway is found to have a credible fear of persecution under subsection (b)(1)(B). In no case may a stowaway be considered an applicant for admission or eligible for a hearing under section 240 [8 U.S.C.A. § 1229a].

(3) Inspection

All aliens (including alien crewmen) who are applicants for admission or otherwise seeking admission or readmission to or transit through the United States shall be inspected by immigration officers.

(4) Withdrawal of application for admission

An alien applying for admission may, in the discretion of the Attorney General and at any time, be permitted to withdraw the application for admission and depart immediately from the United States.

(5) Statements

An applicant for admission may be required to state under oath any information sought by an immigration officer regarding the purposes and intentions of the applicant in seeking admission to the United States, including the applicant's intended length of stay and whether the applicant intends to remain permanently or become a United States citizen, and whether the applicant is inadmissible.

(b) Inspection of applicants for admission

(1) Inspection of aliens arriving in the United States and certain other aliens who have not been admitted or paroled

(A) Screening

(i) In general

If an immigration officer determines that an alien (other than an alien described in subparagraph (F)) who is arriving in the United States or is described in clause (iii) is inadmissible under section 212(a)(6)(C) [8 U.S.C.A.

§ 1182(a)(6)(C)] or 212(a)(7) [8 U.S.C.A. § 1182(a)(7)], the officer shall order the alien removed from the United States without further hearing or review unless the alien indicates either an intention to apply for asylum under section 208 [8 U.S.C.A. § 1158] or a fear of persecution.

(ii) Claims for asylum

If an immigration officer determines that an alien (other than an alien described in subparagraph (F)) who is arriving in the United States or is described in clause (iii) is inadmissible under section 212(a)(6)(C) [8 U.S.C.A. § 1182(a)(6)(C)] or 212(a)(7) [8 U.S.C.A. § 1182(a)(7)] and the alien indicates either an intention to apply for asylum under section 208 [8 U.S.C.A. § 1158] or a fear of persecution, the officer shall refer the alien for an interview by an asylum officer under subparagraph (B).

(iii) Application to certain other aliens

(I) In general

The Attorney General may apply clauses (i) and (ii) of this subparagraph to any or all aliens described in subclause (II) as designated by the Attorney General. Such designation shall be in the sole and unreviewable discretion of the Attorney General and may be modified at any time.

(II) Aliens described

An alien described in this clause is an alien who is not described in subparagraph (F), who has not been admitted or paroled into the United States, and who has not affirmatively shown, to the satisfaction of an immigration officer, that the alien has been physically present in the United States continuously for the 2–year period immediately prior to the date of the determination of inadmissibility under this subparagraph.

(B) Asylum interviews

(i) Conduct by asylum officers

An asylum officer shall conduct interviews of aliens referred under subparagraph (A)(ii), either at a port of entry or at such other place designated by the Attorney General.

(ii) Referral of certain aliens

If the officer determines at the time of the interview that an alien has a credible fear of persecution (within the meaning of clause (v)), the alien shall be detained for further consideration of the application for asylum.

(iii) Removal without further review if no credible fear of persecution

(I) In general

Subject to subclause (III), if the officer determines that an alien does not have a credible fear of persecution, the officer shall order the alien removed from the United States without further hearing or review.

(II) Record of determination

The officer shall prepare a written record of a determination under subclause (I). Such record shall include a summary of the material facts as stated by the applicant, such additional facts (if any) relied upon by the officer, and the officer's analysis of why, in the light of such facts, the alien has not established a credible fear of persecution. A copy of the officer's interview notes shall be attached to the written summary.

(III) Review of determination

The Attorney General shall provide by regulation and upon the alien's request for prompt review by an immigration judge of a determination under subclause (I) that the alien does not have a credible fear of persecution. Such review shall include an opportunity for the alien to be heard and questioned by the immigration judge, either in person or by telephonic or video connection. Review shall be concluded as expeditiously as possible, to the maximum extent practicable within 24 hours, but in no case later than 7 days after the date of the determination under subclause (I).

(IV) Mandatory detention

Any alien subject to the procedures under this clause shall be detained pending a final determination of credible fear of persecution and, if found not to have such a fear, until removed.

(iv) Information about interviews

The Attorney General shall provide information concerning the asylum interview described in this subparagraph to aliens who may be eligible. An alien who is eligible for such interview may consult with a person or persons of the alien's choosing prior to the interview or any review thereof, according to regulations prescribed by the Attorney General. Such consultation shall be at no expense to the Government and shall not unreasonably delay the process.

(v) Credible fear of persecution defined

For purposes of this subparagraph, the term "credible fear of persecution" means that there is a significant possibility, taking into account the credibility of the statements made by the alien in support of the alien's claim and such other facts as are known to the officer, that the alien could establish eligibility for asylum under section 208 [8 U.S.C.A. § 1158].

(C) Limitation on administrative review

Except as provided in subparagraph (B)(iii)(III), a removal order entered in accordance with subparagraph (A)(i) or (B)(iii)(I) is not subject to administrative appeal, except that the Attorney General shall provide by regulation for prompt review of such an order under subparagraph (A)(i) against an alien who claims under oath, or as permitted under penalty of perjury under section 1746 of Title 28, after having been warned of the penalties for falsely making such claim under such conditions, to have been lawfully admitted for permanent residence, to have been admitted as a refugee under section 207 [8 U.S.C.A. § 1157], or to have been granted asylum under section 208 [8 U.S.C.A. § 1158].

(D) Limit on collateral attacks

In any action brought against an alien under section 275(a) [8 U.S.C.A. § 1325(a)] or section 276 [8 U.S.C.A. § 1326], the court shall not have jurisdiction to hear any claim attacking the validity of an order of removal entered under subparagraph (A)(i) or (B)(iii).

(E) Asylum officer defined

As used in this paragraph, the term "asylum officer" means an immigration officer who—

(i) has had professional training in country conditions, asylum law, and interview techniques comparable to that provided to full-time adjudicators of applications under section 208 [8 U.S.C.A. § 1158], and

(ii) is supervised by an officer who meets the condition described in clause (i) and has had substantial experience adjudicating asylum applications.

(F) Exception

Subparagraph (A) shall not apply to an alien who is a native or citizen of a country in the Western Hemisphere with whose government the United States does not have full diplomatic relations and who arrives by aircraft at a port of entry.

(G) Commonwealth of the Northern Mariana Islands

Nothing in this subsection shall be construed to authorize or require any person described in section 208(e) [8 U.S.C.A.

§ 1158(e)] to be permitted to apply for asylum under section 208 [8 U.S.C.A. § 1158] at any time before January 1, 2014.

(2) Inspection of other aliens

(A) In general

Subject to subparagraphs (B) and (C), in the case of an alien who is an applicant for admission, if the examining immigration officer determines that an alien seeking admission is not clearly and beyond a doubt entitled to be admitted, the alien shall be detained for a proceeding under section 240 [8 U.S.C.A. § 1229a].

(B) Exception

Subparagraph (A) shall not apply to an alien—

(i) who is a crewman,

(ii) to whom paragraph (1) applies, or

(iii) who is a stowaway.

(C) Treatment of aliens arriving from contiguous territory

In the case of an alien described in subparagraph (A) who is arriving on land (whether or not at a designated port of arrival) from a foreign territory contiguous to the United States, the Attorney General may return the alien to that territory pending a proceeding under section 240 [8 U.S.C.A. § 1229a].

(3) Challenge of decision

The decision of the examining immigration officer, if favorable to the admission of any alien, shall be subject to challenge by any other immigration officer and such challenge shall operate to take the alien whose privilege to be admitted is so challenged, before an immigration judge for a proceeding under section 240 [8 U.S.C.A. § 1229a].

(c) Removal of aliens inadmissible on security and related grounds

(1) Removal without further hearing

If an immigration officer or an immigration judge suspects that an arriving alien may be inadmissible under subparagraph (A) (other than clause (ii)), (B), or (C) of section 212(a)(3) [8 U.S.C.A. § 1182(a)(3)], the officer or judge shall—

(A) order the alien removed, subject to review under paragraph (2);

(B) report the order of removal to the Attorney General; and

(C) not conduct any further inquiry or hearing until ordered by the Attorney General.

(2) Review of order

(A) The Attorney General shall review orders issued under paragraph (1).

(B) If the Attorney General—

(i) is satisfied on the basis of confidential information that the alien is inadmissible under subparagraph (A) (other than clause (ii)), (B), or (C) of section 212(a)(3) [8 U.S.C.A. § 1182(a)(3)], and

(ii) after consulting with appropriate security agencies of the United States Government, concludes that disclosure of the information would be prejudicial to the public interest, safety, or security,

the Attorney General may order the alien removed without further inquiry or hearing by an immigration judge.

(C) If the Attorney General does not order the removal of the alien under subparagraph (B), the Attorney General shall specify the further inquiry or hearing that shall be conducted in the case.

(3) Submission of statement and information

The alien or the alien's representative may submit a written statement and additional information for consideration by the Attorney General.

(d) Authority relating to inspections

(1) Authority to search conveyances

Immigration officers are authorized to board and search any vessel, aircraft, railway car, or other conveyance or vehicle in which they believe aliens are being brought into the United States.

(2) Authority to order detention and delivery of arriving aliens

Immigration officers are authorized to order an owner, agent, master, commanding officer, person in charge, purser, or consignee of a vessel or aircraft bringing an alien (except an alien crewmember) to the United States—

(A) to detain the alien on the vessel or at the airport of arrival, and

(B) to deliver the alien to an immigration officer for inspection or to a medical officer for examination.

(3) Administration of oath and consideration of evidence

The Attorney General and any immigration officer shall have power to administer oaths and to take and consider evidence of or from any person touching the privilege of any alien or person he believes or suspects to be an alien to enter, reenter, transit through, or reside in the United States or concerning any matter which is material and relevant to the enforcement of this Act and the administration of the Service.

(4) Subpoena authority

(A) The Attorney General and any immigration officer shall have power to require by subpoena the attendance and testimony of witnesses before immigration officers and the production of books, papers, and documents relating to the privilege of any person to enter, reenter, reside in, or pass through the United States or concerning any matter which is material and relevant to the enforcement of this Act and the administration of the Service, and to that end may invoke the aid of any court of the United States.

(B) Any United States district court within the jurisdiction of which investigations or inquiries are being conducted by an immigration officer may, in the event of neglect or refusal to respond to a subpoena issued under this paragraph or refusal to testify before an immigration officer, issue an order requiring such persons to appear before an immigration officer, produce books, papers, and documents if demanded, and testify, and any failure to obey such order of the court may be punished by the court as a contempt thereof.

(June 27, 1952, c. 477, Title II, ch. 4, § 235, 66 Stat. 198; Nov. 29, 1990, Pub.L. 101–649, Title VI, § 603(a)(11), 104 Stat. 5083; Apr. 24, 1996, Pub.L. 104–132, Title IV, §§ 422(a), 423(b), 110 Stat. 1270, 1272; Sept. 30, 1996, Pub.L. 104–208, Div. C, Title III, §§ 302(a), 308(d)(5), 371(b)(4), 110 Stat. 3009–579, 3009–619, 3009–645; May 8, 2008, Pub.L. 110–229, Title VII, Subtitle A, § 702(j)(5), 122 Stat. 867.)

§ 235A. Preinspection at foreign airports [8 U.S.C.A. § 1225a]

(a) Establishment of preinspection stations

(1) New stations

Subject to paragraph (5), not later than October 31, 1998, the Attorney General, in consultation with the Secretary of State, shall establish and maintain preinspection stations in at least 5 of the foreign airports that are among the 10 foreign airports which the Attorney General identifies as serving as last points of departure for the greatest numbers of inadmissible alien passengers who arrive from abroad by air at ports of entry within the United States. Such preinspection stations shall be in addition to any preinspection stations established prior to the date of the enactment of such Act.

(2) Report

Not later than October 31, 1998, the Attorney General shall report to the Committees on the Judiciary of the House of Representatives and of the Senate on the implementation of paragraph (1).

(3) Data collection

Not later than November 1, 1997, and each subsequent November 1, the Attorney General shall compile data identifying—

(A) the foreign airports which served as last points of departure for aliens who arrived by air at United States ports of entry without valid documentation during the preceding fiscal years;

(B) the number and nationality of such aliens arriving from each such foreign airport; and

(C) the primary routes such aliens followed from their country of origin to the United States.

(4) Additional stations

Subject to paragraph (5), not later than January 1, 2008, the Secretary of Homeland Security, in consultation with the Secretary of State, shall establish preinspection stations in at least 25 additional foreign airports, which the Secretary of Homeland Security, in consultation with the Secretary of State, determines, based on the data compiled under paragraph (3) and such other information as may be available, would most effectively facilitate the travel of admissible aliens and reduce the number of inadmissible aliens, especially aliens who are potential terrorists, who arrive from abroad by air at points of entry within the United States. Such preinspection stations shall be in addition to those established before September 30, 1996, or pursuant to paragraph (1).

(5) Conditions

Prior to the establishment of a preinspection station, the Attorney General, in consultation with the Secretary of State, shall ensure that—

(A) employees of the United States stationed at the preinspection station and their accompanying family members will receive appropriate protection;

(B) such employees and their families will not be subject to unreasonable risks to their welfare and safety; and

(C) the country in which the preinspection station is to be established maintains practices and procedures with respect to asylum seekers and refugees in accordance with the Convention Relating to the Status of Refugees (done at Geneva, July 28, 1951), or the Protocol Relating to the Status of Refugees (done at New York, January 31, 1967), or that an alien in the country otherwise has recourse to avenues of protection from return to persecution.

(b) Establishment of carrier consultant program and immigration security initiative

The Secretary of Homeland Security shall assign additional immigration officers to assist air carriers in the detection of fraudulent documents at foreign airports which, based on the records maintained pursuant to subsection (a)(3) of this section, served as a point of departure for a significant number of arrivals at United States ports of entry without valid documentation, but where no preinspection station exists. Beginning not later than December 31, 2006, the number of airports selected for an assignment under this subsection shall be at least 50.

(June 27, 1952, c. 477, Title II, ch. 4, § 235A, as added Sept. 30, 1996, Pub.L. 104–208, Div.C, Title I, § 123(a), 110 Stat. 3009–560; Pub.L. 108–458, Title VII, §§ 7206(a), 7210(d), Dec. 17, 2004, 118 Stat. 3817, 3824.)

§ 236. Apprehension and detention of aliens [8 U.S.C.A. § 1226]

(a) Arrest, detention, and release

On a warrant issued by the Attorney General, an alien may be arrested and detained pending a decision on whether the alien is to be removed from the United States. Except as provided in subsection (c) and pending such decision, the Attorney General—

(1) may continue to detain the arrested alien; and

(2) may release the alien on—

(A) bond of at least $1,500 with security approved by, and containing conditions prescribed by, the Attorney General; or

(B) conditional parole; but

(3) may not provide the alien with work authorization (including an "employment authorized" endorsement or other appropriate work permit), unless the alien is lawfully admitted for permanent residence or otherwise would (without regard to removal proceedings) be provided such authorization.

(b) Revocation of bond or parole

The Attorney General at any time may revoke a bond or parole authorized under subsection (a), rearrest the alien under the original warrant, and detain the alien.

(c) Detention of criminal aliens

(1) Custody

The Attorney General shall take into custody any alien who—

(A) is inadmissible by reason of having committed any offense covered in section 212(a)(2) [8 U.S.C.A. § 1182(a)(2)],

(B) is deportable by reason of having committed any offense covered in section 237(a)(2)(A)(ii), (A)(iii), (B), (C), or (D) [8 U.S.C.A. § 1227(a)(2)(A)(ii), (A)(iii), (B), (C), or (D)],

(C) is deportable under section 237(a)(2)(A)(i) [8 U.S.C.A. § 1227(a)(2)(A)(i)] on the basis of an offense for which the alien has been sentence [sic] to a term of imprisonment of at least 1 year, or

(D) is inadmissible under section 212(a)(3)(B) [8 U.S.C.A. § 1182(a)(3)(B)] or deportable under section 237(a)(4)(B) [8 U.S.C.A. § 1227(a)(4)(B)],

when the alien is released, without regard to whether the alien is released on parole, supervised release, or probation, and without regard to whether the alien may be arrested or imprisoned again for the same offense.

(2) Release

The Attorney General may release an alien described in paragraph (1) only if the Attorney General decides pursuant to section 3521 of Title 18, that release of the alien from custody is necessary to provide protection to a witness, a potential witness, a person cooperating with an investigation into major criminal activity, or an immediate family member or close associate of a witness, potential witness, or person cooperating with such an investigation, and the alien satisfies the Attorney General that the alien will not pose a danger to the safety of other persons or of property and is likely to appear for any scheduled proceeding. A decision relating to such release shall take place in accordance with a procedure that considers the severity of the offense committed by the alien.

(d) Identification of criminal aliens

(1) The Attorney General shall devise and implement a system—

(A) to make available, daily (on a 24–hour basis), to Federal, State, and local authorities the investigative resources of the Service to determine whether individuals arrested by such authorities for aggravated felonies are aliens;

(B) to designate and train officers and employees of the Service to serve as a liaison to Federal, State, and local law enforcement and correctional agencies and courts with respect to the arrest, conviction, and release of any alien charged with an aggravated felony; and

(C) which uses computer resources to maintain a current record of aliens who have been convicted of an aggravated felony, and indicates those who have been removed.

(2) The record under paragraph (1)(C) shall be made available—

(A) to inspectors at ports of entry and to border patrol agents at sector headquarters for purposes of immediate identification of any alien who was previously ordered removed and is seeking to reenter the United States, and

(B) to officials of the Department of State for use in its automated visa lookout system.

(3) Upon the request of the governor or chief executive officer of any State, the Service shall provide assistance to State courts in the identification of aliens unlawfully present in the United States pending criminal prosecution.

(e) Judicial review

The Attorney General's discretionary judgment regarding the application of this section shall not be subject to review. No court may set aside any action or decision by the Attorney General under this section regarding the detention or release of any alien or the grant, revocation, or denial of bond or parole.

(June 27, 1952, c. 477, Title II, ch. 4, § 236, 66 Stat. 200; Nov. 29, 1990, Pub.L. 101–649, Title V, § 504(b), Title VI, § 603(a)(12), 104 Stat. 5050, 5083; Dec. 12, 1991, Pub.L. 102–232, Title III, § 306(a)(5), 105 Stat. 1751; Sept. 30, 1996, Pub.L. 104–208, Div. C, Title III, §§ 303(a), 371(b)(5), 110 Stat. 3009–585, 3009–645.)

§ 236A. Mandatory detention of suspected terrorists; habeas corpus; judicial review [8 U.S.C.A. § 1226a]

(a) Detention of terrorist aliens

(1) Custody

The Attorney General shall take into custody any alien who is certified under paragraph (3).

(2) Release

Except as provided in paragraphs (5) and (6), the Attorney General shall maintain custody of such an alien until the alien is removed from the United States. Except as provided in paragraph (6), such custody shall be maintained irrespective of any relief from removal for which the alien may be eligible, or any relief from removal granted the alien, until the Attorney General determines that the alien is no longer an alien who may be certified under paragraph (3). If the alien is finally determined not to be removable, detention pursuant to this subsection shall terminate.

(3) Certification

The Attorney General may certify an alien under this paragraph if the Attorney General has reasonable grounds to believe that the alien—

(A) is described in section 212(a)(3)(A)(i), 212(a)(3)(A)(iii), 212(a)(3)(B), 237(a)(4)(A)(i), 237(a)(4)(A)(iii), or 237(a)(4)(B) [8 U.S.C.A. § 1182(a)(3)(A)(i), 1182(a)(3)(A)(iii), 1182(a)(3)(B), 1227(a)(4)(A)(i), 1227(a)(4)(A)(iii), or 1227(a)(4)(B)]; or

(B) is engaged in any other activity that endangers the national security of the United States.

(4) Nondelegation

The Attorney General may delegate the authority provided under paragraph (3) only to the Deputy Attorney General. The Deputy Attorney General may not delegate such authority.

(5) Commencement of proceedings

The Attorney General shall place an alien detained under paragraph (1) in removal proceedings, or shall charge the alien with a criminal offense, not later than 7 days after the commencement of such detention. If the requirement of the preceding sentence is not satisfied, the Attorney General shall release the alien.

(6) Limitation on indefinite detention

An alien detained solely under paragraph (1) who has not been removed under section 241(a)(1)(A) [8 U.S.C.A. § 1231(a)(1)(A)], and whose removal is unlikely in the reasonably foreseeable future, may be detained for additional periods of up to six months only if the release of the alien will threaten the national security of the United States or the safety of the community or any person.

(7) Review of certification

The Attorney General shall review the certification made under paragraph (3) every 6 months. If the Attorney General determines, in the Attorney General's discretion, that the certification should be revoked, the alien may be released on such conditions as the Attorney General deems appropriate, unless such release is otherwise prohibited by law. The alien may request each 6 months in writing that the Attorney General reconsider the certification and may submit documents or other evidence in support of that request.

(b) Habeas corpus and judicial review

(1) In general

Judicial review of any action or decision relating to this section (including judicial review of the merits of a determination made under subsection (a)(3) or (a)(6)) is available exclusively in habeas corpus proceedings consistent with this subsection. Except as provided in the preceding sentence, no court shall have jurisdiction to review, by habeas corpus petition or otherwise, any such action or decision.

(2) Application

(A) In general

Notwithstanding any other provision of law, including section 2241(a) of Title 28, habeas corpus proceedings described in paragraph (1) may be initiated only by an application filed with—

(i) the Supreme Court;

(ii) any justice of the Supreme Court;

(iii) any circuit judge of the United States Court of Appeals for the District of Columbia Circuit; or

(iv) any district court otherwise having jurisdiction to entertain it.

(B) Application transfer

Section 2241(b) of Title 28 shall apply to an application for a writ of habeas corpus described in subparagraph (A).

(3) Appeals

Notwithstanding any other provision of law, including section 2253 of Title 28, in habeas corpus proceedings described in paragraph (1) before a circuit or district judge, the final order shall be subject to review, on appeal, by the United States Court of Appeals for the District of Columbia Circuit. There shall be no right of appeal in such proceedings to any other circuit court of appeals.

(4) Rule of decision

The law applied by the Supreme Court and the United States Court of Appeals for the District of Columbia Circuit shall be regarded as the rule of decision in habeas corpus proceedings described in paragraph (1).

(c) Statutory construction

The provisions of this section shall not be applicable to any other provision of this Act.

(June 27, 1952, c. 477, Title II, ch. 4, § 236A, as added Oct. 26, 2001, Pub.L. 107–56, Title IV, § 412(a), 115 Stat. 350.)

§ 237. Deportable aliens [8 U.S.C.A. § 1227]

(a) Classes of deportable aliens

Any alien (including an alien crewman) in and admitted to the United States shall, upon the order of the Attorney General, be removed if the alien is within one or more of the following classes of deportable aliens:

(1) Inadmissible at time of entry or of adjustment of status or violates status

(A) Inadmissible aliens

Any alien who at the time of entry or adjustment of status was within one or more of the classes of aliens inadmissible by the law existing at such time is deportable.

(B) Present in violation of law

Any alien who is present in the United States in violation of this Act or any other law of the United States, or whose nonimmigrant visa (or other documentation authorizing admission into the United States as a nonimmigrant) has been revoked under section 221(i) [8 U.S.C.A. § 1201(i)], is deportable.

(C) Violated nonimmigrant status or condition of admission

(i) Nonimmigrant status violators

Any alien who was admitted as a nonimmigrant and who has failed to maintain the nonimmigrant status in which the alien was admitted or to which it was changed under section 248 [8 U.S.C.A. § 1258], or to comply with the conditions of any such status, is deportable.

(ii) Violators of conditions of admission

Any alien whom the Secretary of Health and Human Services certifies has failed to comply with terms, conditions, and controls that were imposed under section 212(g) [8 U.S.C.A. § 1182(g)] is deportable.

(D) Termination of conditional permanent residence

(i) In general

Any alien with permanent resident status on a conditional basis under section 216 [8 U.S.C.A. § 1186a] (relating to conditional permanent resident status for certain alien spouses and sons and daughters) or under section 216A [8 U.S.C.A. § 1186b] (relating to conditional permanent resident status for certain alien entrepreneurs, spouses, and children) who has had such status terminated under such respective section is deportable.

(ii) Exception

Clause (i) shall not apply in the cases described in section 216(c)(4) [8 U.S.C.A. § 1186a(c)(4)] (relating to certain hardship waivers).

(E) Smuggling

(i) In general

Any alien who (prior to the date of entry, at the time of any entry, or within 5 years of the date of any entry) knowingly has encouraged, induced, assisted, abetted, or aided any other alien to enter or to try to enter the United States in violation of law is deportable.

(ii) Special rule in the case of family reunification

Clause (i) shall not apply in the case of alien who is an eligible immigrant (as defined in section 301(b)(1) of the Immigration Act of 1990), was physically present in the United States on May 5, 1988, and is seeking admission as an immediate relative or under section 203(a)(2) [8 U.S.C.A.

§ 1153(a)(2)] (including under section 112 of the Immigration Act of 1990) or benefits under section 301(a) of the Immigration Act of 1990 if the alien, before May 5, 1988, has encouraged, induced, assisted, abetted, or aided only the alien's spouse, parent, son, or daughter (and no other individual) to enter the United States in violation of law.

(iii) Waiver authorized

The Attorney General may, in his discretion for humanitarian purposes, to assure family unity, or when it is otherwise in the public interest, waive application of clause (i) in the case of any alien lawfully admitted for permanent residence if the alien has encouraged, induced, assisted, abetted, or aided only an individual who at the time of the offense was the alien's spouse, parent, son, or daughter (and no other individual) to enter the United States in violation of law.

(F) Repealed. Pub.L. 104–208, Div. C, Title VI, § 671(d)(1)(C), Sept. 30, 1996, 110 Stat. 3009–723.

(G) Marriage fraud

An alien shall be considered to be deportable as having procured a visa or other documentation by fraud (within the meaning of section 212(a)(6)(C)(i) [8 U.S.C.A. § 1182(a)(6)(C)(i)]) and to be in the United States in violation of this Act (within the meaning of subparagraph (B)) if—

(i) the alien obtains any admission into the United States with an immigrant visa or other documentation procured on the basis of a marriage entered into less than 2 years prior to such admission of the alien and which, within 2 years subsequent to any admission of the alien in the United States, shall be judicially annulled or terminated, unless the alien establishes to the satisfaction of the Attorney General that such marriage was not contracted for the purpose of evading any provisions of the immigration laws, or

(ii) it appears to the satisfaction of the Attorney General that the alien has failed or refused to fulfill the alien's marital agreement which in the opinion of the Attorney General was made for the purpose of procuring the alien's admission as an immigrant.

(H) Waiver authorized for certain misrepresentations

The provisions of this paragraph relating to the removal of aliens within the United States on the ground that they were inadmissible at the time of admission as aliens, described in section 212(a)(6)(C)(i) [8 U.S.C.A. § 1182(a)(6)(C)(i)], whether willful or innocent, may, in the discretion of the Attorney General, be waived for any alien (other than an alien described in paragraph (4)(D)) who—

(i)(I) is the spouse, parent, son, or daughter of a citizen of the United States or of an alien lawfully admitted to the United States for permanent residence; and

(II) was in possession of an immigrant visa or equivalent document and was otherwise admissible to the United States at the time of such admission except for those grounds of inadmissibility specified under paragraphs (5)(A) and (7)(A) of section 212(a) [8 U.S.C.A. § 1182(a)] which were a direct result of that fraud or misrepresentation.

(ii) is a VAWA self-petitioner.

A waiver of removal for fraud or misrepresentation granted under this subparagraph shall also operate to waive removal based on the grounds of inadmissibility directly resulting from such fraud or misrepresentation.

(2) Criminal offenses

(A) General crimes

(i) Crimes of moral turpitude

Any alien who—

(I) is convicted of a crime involving moral turpitude committed within five years (or 10 years in the case of an alien provided lawful permanent resident status under section 245(j) [8 U.S.C.A. § 1255(j)]) after the date of admission, and

(II) is convicted of a crime for which a sentence of one year or longer may be imposed,

is deportable.

(ii) Multiple criminal convictions

Any alien who at any time after admission is convicted of two or more crimes involving moral turpitude, not arising out of a single scheme of criminal misconduct, regardless of whether confined therefor and regardless of whether the convictions were in a single trial, is deportable.

(iii) Aggravated felony

Any alien who is convicted of an aggravated felony at any time after admission is deportable.

(iv) High speed flight

Any alien who is convicted of a violation of section 758 of Title 18, (relating to high speed flight from an immigration checkpoint) is deportable.

(v) Failure to register as a sex offender

Any alien who is convicted under section 2250 of title 18, United States Code, is deportable.

(vi) Waiver authorized

Clauses (i), (ii), (iii), and (iv) shall not apply in the case of an alien with respect to a criminal conviction if the alien subsequent to the criminal conviction has been granted a full and unconditional pardon by the President of the United States or by the Governor of any of the several States.

(B) Controlled substances

(i) Conviction

Any alien who at any time after admission has been convicted of a violation of (or a conspiracy or attempt to violate) any law or regulation of a State, the United States, or a foreign country relating to a controlled substance (as defined in section 802 of Title 21), other than a single offense involving possession for one's own use of 30 grams or less of marijuana, is deportable.

(ii) Drug abusers and addicts

Any alien who is, or at any time after admission has been, a drug abuser or addict is deportable.

(C) Certain firearm offenses

Any alien who at any time after admission is convicted under any law of purchasing, selling, offering for sale, exchanging, using, owning, possessing, or carrying, or of attempting or conspiring to purchase, sell, offer for sale, exchange, use, own, possess, or carry, any weapon, part, or accessory which is a firearm or destructive device (as defined in section 921(a) of Title 18) in violation of any law is deportable.

(D) Miscellaneous crimes

Any alien who at any time has been convicted (the judgment on such conviction becoming final) of, or has been so convicted of a conspiracy or attempt to violate—

(i) any offense under chapter 37 (relating to espionage), chapter 105 (relating to sabotage), or chapter 115 (relating to treason and sedition) of Title 18, for which a term of imprisonment of five or more years may be imposed;

(ii) any offense under section 871 or 960 of Title 18;

(iii) a violation of any provision of the Military Selective Service Act (50 U.S.C. App. 451 et seq.) or the Trading With the Enemy Act (50 U.S.C. App. 1 et seq.); or

(iv) a violation of section 215 [8 U.S.C.A. § 1185] or 278 [8 U.S.C.A. § 1328],

is deportable.

(E) Crimes of domestic violence, stalking, or violation of protection order, crimes against children and*

(i) Domestic violence, stalking, and child abuse

Any alien who at any time after admission is convicted of a crime of domestic violence, a crime of stalking, or a crime of child abuse, child neglect, or child abandonment is deportable. For purposes of this clause, the term "crime of domestic violence" means any crime of violence (as defined in section 16 of Title 18) against a person committed by a current or former spouse of the person, by an individual with whom the person shares a child in common, by an individual who is cohabiting with or has cohabited with the person as a spouse, by an individual similarly situated to a spouse of the person under the domestic or family violence laws of the jurisdiction where the offense occurs, or by any other individual against a person who is protected from that individual's acts under the domestic or family violence laws of the United States or any State, Indian tribal government, or unit of local government.

(ii) Violators of protection orders

Any alien who at any time after admission is enjoined under a protection order issued by a court and whom the court determines has engaged in conduct that violates the portion of a protection order that involves protection against credible threats of violence, repeated harassment, or bodily injury to the person or persons for whom the protection order was issued is deportable. For purposes of this clause, the term "protection order" means any injunction issued for the purpose of preventing violent or threatening acts of domestic violence, including temporary or final orders issued by civil or criminal courts (other than support or child custody orders or provisions) whether obtained by filing an independent action or as a pendente lite order in another proceeding.

(F) Trafficking

Any alien described in section 212(a)(2)(H) [8 U.S.C.A. § 1182(a)(2)(H)] is deportable.

(3) Failure to register and falsification of documents

(A) Change of address

* So in original.

An alien who has failed to comply with the provisions of section 265 [8 U.S.C.A. § 1305] is deportable, unless the alien establishes to the satisfaction of the Attorney General that such failure was reasonably excusable or was not willful.

(B) Failure to register or falsification of documents

Any alien who at any time has been convicted—

(i) under section 266(c) [8 U.S.C.A. § 1306(c)] or under section 36(c) of the Alien Registration Act, 1940,

(ii) of a violation of, or an attempt or a conspiracy to violate, any provision of the Foreign Agents Registration Act of 1938 (22 U.S.C. 611 et seq.), or

(iii) of a violation of, or an attempt or a conspiracy to violate, section 1546 of Title 18 (relating to fraud and misuse of visas, permits, and other entry documents),

is deportable.

(C) Document fraud

(i) In general

An alien who is the subject of a final order for violation of section 274C [8 U.S.C.A. § 1324C] is deportable.

(ii) Waiver authorized

The Attorney General may waive clause (i) in the case of an alien lawfully admitted for permanent residence if no previous civil money penalty was imposed against the alien under section 274C [8 U.S.C.A. § 1324C] and the offense was incurred solely to assist, aid, or support the alien's spouse or child (and no other individual). No court shall have jurisdiction to review a decision of the Attorney General to grant or deny a waiver under this clause.

(D) Falsely claiming citizenship

(i) In general

Any alien who falsely represents, or has falsely represented, himself to be a citizen of the United States for any purpose or benefit under this Act (including section 274A [8 U.S.C.A. § 1324a]) or any Federal or State law is deportable.

(ii) Exception

In the case of an alien making a representation described in clause (i), if each natural parent of the alien (or, in the case of an adopted alien, each adoptive parent of the alien) is or was a citizen (whether by birth or naturalization), the alien permanently resided in the United States prior to attaining the age of 16, and the alien reasonably believed at the time of making such representation that he or she was a citizen, the alien shall not be considered to be deportable under any provision of this subsection based on such representation.

(4) Security and related grounds

(A) In general

Any alien who has engaged, is engaged, or at any time after admission engages in—

(i) any activity to violate any law of the United States relating to espionage or sabotage or to violate or evade any law prohibiting the export from the United States of goods, technology, or sensitive information,

(ii) any other criminal activity which endangers public safety or national security, or

(iii) any activity a purpose of which is the opposition to, or the control or overthrow of, the Government of the United States by force, violence, or other unlawful means,

is deportable.

(B) Terrorist activities

Any alien who is described in subparagraph (B) or (F) of section 212(a)(3) [8 U.S.C.A. § 1182(a)(3)] is deportable.

(C) Foreign policy

(i) In general

An alien whose presence or activities in the United States the Secretary of State has reasonable ground to believe would have potentially serious adverse foreign policy consequences for the United States is deportable.

(ii) Exceptions

The exceptions described in clauses (ii) and (iii) of section 212(a)(3)(C) [8 U.S.C.A. § 1182(a)(3)(C)] shall apply to deportability under clause (i) in the same manner as they apply to inadmissibility under section 212(a)(3)(C)(i) [8 U.S.C.A. § 1182(a)(3)(C)(i)].

(D) Participated in Nazi persecution, genocide, or the commission of any act of torture or extrajudicial killing

Any alien described in clause (i), (ii), or (iii) of section 212(a)(3)(E) [8 U.S.C.A. § 1182(a)(3)(E)] is deportable.

(E) Participated in the Commission of severe violations of religious freedom

Any alien described in section 212(a)(2)(G) [8 U.S.C.A. § 1182(a)(2)(G)] is deportable.

(F) Recruitment or use of child soldiers

Any alien who has engaged in the recruitment or use of child soldiers in violation of section 2442 of Title 18, United States Code, is deportable.

(5) Public charge

Any alien who, within five years after the date of entry, has become a public charge from causes not affirmatively shown to have arisen since entry is deportable.

(6) Unlawful voters

(A) In general

Any alien who has voted in violation of any Federal, State, or local constitutional provision, statute, ordinance, or regulation is deportable.

(B) Exception

In the case of an alien who voted in a Federal, State, or local election (including an initiative, recall, or referendum) in violation of a lawful restriction of voting to citizens, if each natural parent of the alien (or, in the case of an adopted alien, each adoptive parent of the alien) is or was a citizen (whether by birth or naturalization), the alien permanently resided in the United States prior to attaining the age of 16, and the alien reasonably believed at the time of such violation that he or she was a citizen, the alien shall not be considered to be deportable under any provision of this subsection based on such violation.

(7) Waiver for victims of domestic violence

(A) In general

The Attorney General is not limited by the criminal court record and may waive the application of paragraph (2)(E)(i) (with respect to crimes of domestic violence and crimes of stalking) and (ii) in the case of an alien who has been battered or subjected to extreme cruelty and who is not and was not the primary perpetrator of violence in the relationship—

(i) upon a determination that—

(I) the alien was acting is* self-defense;

(II) the alien was found to have violated a protection order intended to protect the alien; or

(III) the alien committed, was arrested for, was convicted of, or pled guilty to committing a crime—

(aa) that did not result in serious bodily injury; and

* So in original. Probably should be "in".

(bb) where there was a connection between the crime and the alien's having been battered or subjected to extreme cruelty.

(B) Credible evidence considered

In acting on applications under this paragraph, the Attorney General shall consider any credible evidence relevant to the application. The determination of what evidence is credible and the weight to be given that evidence shall be within the sole discretion of the Attorney General.

(b) Deportation of certain nonimmigrants

An alien, admitted as a nonimmigrant under the provisions of either section 101(a)(15)(A)(i) [8 U.S.C.A. § 1101(a)(15)(A)(i)] or 101(a)(15)(G)(i) [8 U.S.C.A. § 1101(a)(15)(G)(i)], and who fails to maintain a status under either of those provisions, shall not be required to depart from the United States without the approval of the Secretary of State, unless such alien is subject to deportation under paragraph (4) of subsection (a).

(c) Waiver of grounds for deportation

Paragraphs (1)(A), (1)(B), (1)(C), (1)(D), and (3)(A) of subsection (a) (other than so much of paragraph (1) as relates to a ground of inadmissibility described in paragraph (2) or (3) of section 212(a) [8 U.S.C.A. § 1182(a)]) shall not apply to a special immigrant described in section 101(a)(27)(J) [8 U.S.C.A. § 1101(a)(27)(J)] based upon circumstances that existed before the date the alien was provided such special immigrant status.

(d)(1) If the Secretary of Homeland Security determines that an application for nonimmigrant status under subparagraph (T) or (U) of section 101(a)(15) [8 U.S.C.A. § 1101(a)(15)] filed for an alien in the United States sets forth a prima facie case for approval, the Secretary may grant the alien an administrative stay of a final order of removal under section 241(c)(2) [8 U.S.C.A. § 1231(c)(2)] until

(A) the application for nonimmigrant status under such subparagraph (T) or (U) is approved; or

(B) there is a final administrative denial of the application for such nonimmigrant status after the exhaustion of administrative appeals.

(2) The denial of a request for an administrative stay of removal under this subsection shall not preclude the alien from applying for a stay of removal, deferred action, or a continuance or abeyance of removal proceedings under any other provision of the immigration laws of the United States.

(3) During any period in which the administrative stay of removal is in effect, the alien shall not be removed.

(4) Nothing in this subsection may be construed to limit the authority of the Secretary of Homeland Security or the Attorney General to grant a stay of removal or deportation in any case not described in this subsection.

(e) Redesignated (b).

(f) and (g) Repealed. Pub.L. 101–649, § 602(b)(1), Nov. 29, 1990, 104 Stat. 5081.

(h) Redesignated (c).

(June 27, 1952, c. 477, Title II, ch. 5, § 237, formerly § 241, 66 Stat. 204; July 18, 1956, c. 629, Title III, § 301(b), (c), 70 Stat. 575; July 14, 1960, Pub.L. 86–648, § 9, 74 Stat. 505; Sept. 26, 1961, Pub.L. 87–301, § 16, 75 Stat. 655; Oct. 3, 1965, Pub.L. 89–236, § 11(e), 79 Stat. 918; Oct. 20, 1976, Pub.L. 94–571, § 7(e), 90 Stat. 2706; Oct. 30, 1978; Pub.L. 95–549, Title I, § 103, 92 Stat. 2065; Dec. 29, 1981, Pub.L. 97–116, § 8, 95 Stat. 1616; Oct. 27, 1986, Pub.L. 99–570, Title I, § 1751(b), 100 Stat. 3207–47; Nov. 6, 1986, Pub.L. 99–603, Title III, § 303(b), 100 Stat. 3431; Nov. 10, 1986, Pub.L. 99–639, § 2(b), 100 Stat. 3541; Nov. 14, 1986, Pub.L. 99–653, § 7(c), 100 Stat. 3657; Oct. 24, 1988, Pub.L. 100–525, §§ 2(n)(2), 9(m), 102 Stat. 2613, 2620; Nov. 18, 1988, Pub.L. 100–690, Title VII, §§ 7344(a), 7348(a), 102 Stat. 4471, 4473; Nov. 29, 1990, Pub.L. 101–649, Title I, § 153(b), Title V, §§ 505(a), 508(a), 544(b), Title VI, § 602(a), (b), 104 Stat. 5006, 5050, 5051, 5061, 5077, 5081; Dec. 12, 1991, Pub.L. 102–232, Title III, §§ 302(d)(3), 307(h), (k), 105 Stat. 1745, 1755, 1756; Sept. 13, 1994, Pub.L. 103–322, Title XIII, § 130003(d), 108 Stat. 2026; Oct. 25, 1994, Pub.L. 103–416, Title II, §§ 203(b), 219(g), 108 Stat. 4311, 4317; Apr. 24, 1996, Pub.L. 104–132, Title IV, §§ 414(a), 435(a), 110 Stat. 1270, 1274; renumbered § 237 and amended Sept. 30, 1996, Pub.L. 104–208, Div. C, Title I, § 108(c), Title III, §§ 301(d), 305(a)(2), 308(d)(2), (3)(A), (e)(1)(E), (2)(C), (f)(1)(L) to (N), (5), 344(b), 345(b), 347(b), 350(a), 351(b), Title VI, § 671(a)(4)(B), (d)(1)(C), 110 Stat. 3009–558, 3009–579, 3009–598, 3009–617, 3009–619 to 3009–622, 3009–637 to 3009–640, 3009–721, 3009–723; Oct. 28, 2000, Pub.L. 106–386, Div. B, Title V, § 1505(b)(1), (c)(2), 114 Stat. 1525, 1526; Oct. 30, 2000, Pub.L. 106–395, Title II, § 201(c)(1), (2), 114 Stat. 1634, 1635; Oct. 26, 2001, Pub.L. 107–56, Title IV, § 411(b)(1), 115 Stat. 348; Dec. 17, 2004, Pub.L. 108–458, Title V, §§ 5304(b), 5402, 5501(b), 5502(b), 118 Stat. 3736, 3737, 3740, 3741; May 11, 2005, Pub.L. 109–13, Div. B, § 105(a), 119 Stat. 231, 309; July 27, 2006, Pub.L. 109–248, Title IV, § 401, 120 Stat. 622; Aug. 12, 2006, Pub.L. 109–271, § 6(c), 120 Stat. 763; Oct. 3, 2008, Pub.L. 110–340, § 2(c), 122 Stat. 3736; Dec. 23, 2008, Pub.L. 110–457, Title II, § 204, 122 Stat. 5060; Dec. 23, 2008, Pub.L. 110–457, Title II, § 222(f)(2), 122 Stat. 5071.)

§ 238. Expedited removal of aliens convicted of committing aggravated felonies [8 U.S.C.A. § 1228]

(a) Removal of criminal aliens

(1) In general

The Attorney General shall provide for the availability of special removal proceedings at certain Federal, State, and local correctional facilities for aliens convicted of any criminal offense covered in section 237(a)(2)(A)(iii), (B), (C), or (D) [8 U.S.C.A. § 1227(a)(2)(A)(iii), (B), (C), or (D)], or any offense covered by section 237(a)(2)(A)(ii) [8 U.S.C.A. § 1227(a)(2)(A)(ii)] for which both predicate offenses are, without regard to the date of their commission, otherwise covered by section 237(a)(2)(A)(i) [8 U.S.C.A. § 1227(a)(2)(A)(i)]. Such proceedings shall be conducted in conformity with section 240 [8 U.S.C.A. § 1229a] (except as otherwise provided in this section), and in a manner which eliminates the need for additional detention at any processing center of the Service and in a manner which assures expeditious removal following the end of the alien's incarceration for the underlying sentence. Nothing in this section shall be construed to create any substantive or procedural right or benefit that is legally enforceable by any party against the United States or its agencies or officers or any other person.

(2) Implementation

With respect to an alien convicted of an aggravated felony who is taken into custody by the Attorney General pursuant to section 236(c) [8 U.S.C.A. § 1226(c)], the Attorney General shall, to the maximum extent practicable, detain any such felon at a facility at which other such aliens are detained. In the selection of such facility, the Attorney General shall make reasonable efforts to ensure that the alien's access to counsel and right to counsel under section 292 [8 U.S.C.A. § 1362] are not impaired.

(3) Expedited proceedings

(A) Notwithstanding any other provision of law, the Attorney General shall provide for the initiation and, to the extent possible, the completion of removal proceedings, and any administrative appeals thereof, in the case of any alien convicted of an aggravated felony before the alien's release from incarceration for the underlying aggravated felony.

(B) Nothing in this section shall be construed as requiring the Attorney General to effect the removal of any alien sentenced to actual incarceration, before release from the penitentiary or correctional institution where such alien is confined.

(4) Review

(A) The Attorney General shall review and evaluate removal proceedings conducted under this section.

(B) The Comptroller General shall monitor, review, and evaluate removal proceedings conducted under this section. Within 18 months after the effective date of this section, the Comptroller General shall submit a report to such Committees concerning the extent to which removal proceedings conducted under this section may adversely affect the ability of such aliens to contest removal effectively.

(b) Removal of aliens who are not permanent residents

(1) The Attorney General may, in the case of an alien described in paragraph (2), determine the deportability of such alien under section 237(a)(2)(A)(iii) [8 U.S.C.A. § 1227(a)(2)(A)(iii)] (relating to conviction of an aggravated felony) and issue an order of removal pursuant to the procedures set forth in this subsection or section 240 [8 U.S.C.A. § 1229a].

(2) An alien is described in this paragraph if the alien—

(A) was not lawfully admitted for permanent residence at the time at which proceedings under this section commenced; or

(B) had permanent resident status on a conditional basis (as described in section 216 [8 U.S.C.A. § 1186a]) at the time that proceedings under this section commenced.

(3) The Attorney General may not execute any order described in paragraph (1) until 14 calendar days have passed from the date that such order was issued, unless waived by the alien, in order that the alien has an opportunity to apply for judicial review under section 242 [8 U.S.C.A. § 1252].

(4) Proceedings before the Attorney General under this subsection shall be in accordance with such regulations as the Attorney General shall prescribe. The Attorney General shall provide that—

(A) the alien is given reasonable notice of the charges and of the opportunity described in subparagraph (C);

(B) the alien shall have the privilege of being represented (at no expense to the government) by such counsel, authorized to practice in such proceedings, as the alien shall choose;

(C) the alien has a reasonable opportunity to inspect the evidence and rebut the charges;

(D) a determination is made for the record that the individual upon whom the notice for the proceeding under this section is served (either in person or by mail) is, in fact, the alien named in such notice;

(E) a record is maintained for judicial review; and

(F) the final order of removal is not adjudicated by the same person who issues the charges.

(G) Redesignated (F).

(5) No alien described in this section shall be eligible for any relief from removal that the Attorney General may grant in the Attorney General's discretion.

(c)* [sic] Presumption of deportability

An alien convicted of an aggravated felony shall be conclusively presumed to be deportable from the United States.

(c) [sic] Judicial removal**

(1) Authority

Notwithstanding any other provision of this Act, a United States district court shall have jurisdiction to enter a judicial order of removal at the time of sentencing against an alien who is

* So in original. Two subsecs. (c) have been enacted.

** So in original. Two subsecs. (c) have been enacted.

deportable, if such an order has been requested by the United States Attorney with the concurrence of the Commissioner and if the court chooses to exercise such jurisdiction.

(2) Procedure

(A) The United States Attorney shall file with the United States district court, and serve upon the defendant and the Service, prior to commencement of the trial or entry of a guilty plea a notice of intent to request judicial removal.

(B) Notwithstanding section 242B [8 U.S.C.A. § 1252b] [sic], the United States Attorney, with the concurrence of the Commissioner, shall file at least 30 days prior to the date set for sentencing a charge containing factual allegations regarding the alienage of the defendant and identifying the crime or crimes which make the defendant deportable under section 237(a)(2)(A) [8 U.S.C.A. § 1227(a)(2)(A)].

(C) If the court determines that the defendant has presented substantial evidence to establish prima facie eligibility for relief from removal under this Act, the Commissioner shall provide the court with a recommendation and report regarding the alien's eligibility for relief. The court shall either grant or deny the relief sought.

(D)(i) The alien shall have a reasonable opportunity to examine the evidence against him or her, to present evidence on his or her own behalf, and to cross-examine witnesses presented by the Government.

(ii) The court, for the purposes of determining whether to enter an order described in paragraph (1), shall only consider evidence that would be admissible in proceedings conducted pursuant to section 240 [8 U.S.C.A. § 1229a].

(iii) Nothing in this subsection shall limit the information a court of the United States may receive or consider for the purposes of imposing an appropriate sentence.

(iv) The court may order the alien removed if the Attorney General demonstrates that the alien is deportable under this Act.

(3) Notice, appeal, and execution of judicial order of removal

(A)(i) A judicial order of removal or denial of such order may be appealed by either party to the court of appeals for the circuit in which the district court is located.

(ii) Except as provided in clause (iii), such appeal shall be considered consistent with the requirements described in section 242 [8 U.S.C.A. § 1252].

(iii) Upon execution by the defendant of a valid waiver of the right to appeal the conviction on which the order of removal is based, the expiration of the period described in section 242(b)(1) [8 U.S.C.A. § 1252(b)(1)], or the final dismissal of an appeal from such conviction, the order of removal shall become final and shall be executed at the end of the prison term in accordance with the terms of the order. If the conviction is reversed on direct appeal, the order entered pursuant to this section shall be void.

(B) As soon as is practicable after entry of a judicial order of removal, the Commissioner shall provide the defendant with written notice of the order of removal, which shall designate the defendant's country of choice for removal and any alternate country pursuant to section 243(a) [8 U.S.C.A. § 1253(a)].

(4) Denial of judicial order

Denial of a request for a judicial order of removal shall not preclude the Attorney General from initiating removal proceedings pursuant to section 240 [8 U.S.C.A. § 1229a] upon the same ground of deportability or upon any other ground of deportability provided under section 237(a) [8 U.S.C.A. § 1227(a)].

(5) Stipulated judicial order of removal

The United States Attorney, with the concurrence of the Commissioner, may, pursuant to Federal Rule of Criminal Procedure 11, enter into a plea agreement which calls for the alien, who is deportable under this Act, to waive the right to notice and a hearing under this section, and stipulate to the entry of a judicial order of removal from the United States as a condition of the plea agreement or as a condition of probation or supervised release, or both. The United States district court, in both felony and misdemeanor cases, and a United States magistrate judge in misdemeanor cases, may accept such a stipulation and shall have jurisdiction to enter a judicial order of removal pursuant to the terms of such stipulation.

(d) Redesignated (c).

(June 27, 1952, c. 477, Title II, ch. 5, § 238, formerly § 242A, as added Nov. 18, 1988, Pub.L. 100–690, Title VII, § 7347(a), 102 Stat. 4471, and amended Nov. 29, 1990, Pub.L. 101–649, Title V, § 506(a), 104 Stat. 5050; Dec. 12, 1991, Pub.L. 102–232, Title III, § 309(b)(10), 105 Stat. 1759; Sept. 13, 1994, Pub.L. 103–322, Title XIII, § 130004(a), (c), 108 Stat. 2026, 2028; Oct. 25, 1994, Pub.L. 103–416, Title II, §§ 223(a), 224(a), 108 Stat. 4322; Apr. 24, 1996, Pub.L. 104–132, Title IV, §§ 440(g), 442(a), (c), 110 Stat. 1278, 1279, 1280; redesignated § 238 and amended Sept. 30, 1996, Pub.L. 104–208, Div. C, Title III, §§ 304(c)(1), 306(d), 308(b)(5), (c)(1), (4)(A), (e)(1)(F), (2)(D), (10), (g)(1), (2)(A), (C), (5)(A)(ii), (C), (D), (10)(H), 374(a), Title VI, § 671(b)(13), (c)(5), (6), 110 Stat. 3009–597, 3009–612, 3009–615, 3009–616, 3009–619, 3009–620, 3009–622, 3009–623, 3009–625, 3009–647, 3009–722, 3009–723.)

§ 239. Initiation of removal proceedings [8 U.S.C.A. § 1229]

(a) Notice to appear

(1) In general

In removal proceedings under section 240 [8 U.S.C.A. § 1229a], written notice (in this section referred to as a "notice to appear") shall be given in person to the alien (or, if personal service is not practicable, through service by mail to the alien or to the alien's counsel of record, if any) specifying the following:

(A) The nature of the proceedings against the alien.

(B) The legal authority under which the proceedings are conducted.

(C) The acts or conduct alleged to be in violation of law.

(D) The charges against the alien and the statutory provisions alleged to have been violated.

(E) The alien may be represented by counsel and the alien will be provided (i) a period of time to secure counsel under subsection (b)(1) and (ii) a current list of counsel prepared under subsection (b)(2).

(F)(i) The requirement that the alien must immediately provide (or have provided) the Attorney General with a written record of an address and telephone number (if any) at which the alien may be contacted respecting proceedings under section 240 [8 U.S.C.A. § 1229a].

(ii) The requirement that the alien must provide the Attorney General immediately with a written record of any change of the alien's address or telephone number.

(iii) The consequences under section 240(b)(5) [8 U.S.C.A. § 1229a(b)(5)] of failure to provide address and telephone information pursuant to this subparagraph.

(G)(i) The time and place at which the proceedings will be held.

(ii) The consequences under section 240(b)(5) [8 U.S.C.A. § 1229a(b)(5)] of the failure, except under exceptional circumstances, to appear at such proceedings.

(2) Notice of change in time or place of proceedings

(A) In general

In removal proceedings under section 240(b)(5) [8 U.S.C.A. § 1229a(b)(5)], in the case of any change or postponement in the time and place of such proceedings, subject to subparagraph (B) a written notice shall be given in person to the alien (or, if personal service is not practicable, through service by mail to the alien or to the alien's counsel of record, if any) specifying—

(i) the new time or place of the proceedings, and

(ii) the consequences under section 240(b)(5) [8 U.S.C.A. § 1229a(b)(5)] of failing, except under exceptional circumstances, to attend such proceedings.

(B) Exception

In the case of an alien not in detention, a written notice shall not be required under this paragraph if the alien has failed to provide the address required under paragraph (1)(F).

(3) Central address files

The Attorney General shall create a system to record and preserve on a timely basis notices of addresses and telephone numbers (and changes) provided under paragraph (1)(F).

(b) Securing of counsel

(1) In general

In order that an alien be permitted the opportunity to secure counsel before the first hearing date in proceedings under section 240 [8 U.S.C.A. § 1229a], the hearing date shall not be scheduled earlier than 10 days after the service of the notice to appear, unless the alien requests in writing an earlier hearing date.

(2) Current lists of counsel

The Attorney General shall provide for lists (updated not less often than quarterly) of persons who have indicated their availability to represent pro bono aliens in proceedings under section 240 [8 U.S.C.A. § 1229a]. Such lists shall be provided under subsection (a)(1)(E) and otherwise made generally available.

(3) Rule of construction

Nothing in this subsection may be construed to prevent the Attorney General from proceeding against an alien pursuant to section 240 [8 U.S.C.A. § 1229a] if the time period described in paragraph (1) has elapsed and the alien has failed to secure counsel.

(c) Service by mail

Service by mail under this section shall be sufficient if there is proof of attempted delivery to the last address provided by the alien in accordance with subsection (a)(1)(F).

(d) Prompt initiation of removal

(1) In the case of an alien who is convicted of an offense which makes the alien deportable, the Attorney General shall begin any removal proceeding as expeditiously as possible after the date of the conviction.

(2) Nothing in this subsection shall be construed to create any substantive or procedural right or benefit that is legally enforceable by any party against the United States or its agencies or officers or any other person.

(e) Certification of compliance with restrictions on disclosure

(1) In general

In cases where an enforcement action leading to a removal proceeding was taken against an alien at any of the locations specified in paragraph (2), the Notice to Appear shall include a statement that the provisions of section 384 of the Illegal Immigration Reform and Immigrant Responsibility Act of 1996 [8 U.S.C.A § 1367] have been complied with.

(2) Locations

The locations specified in this paragraph are as follows:

(A) At a domestic violence shelter, a rape crisis center, supervised visitation center, family justice center, a victim services, or victim services provider, or a community-based organization.

(B) At a courthouse (or in connection with that appearance of the alien at a courthouse) if the alien is appearing in connection with a protection order case, child custody case, or other civil or criminal case relating to domestic violence, sexual assault, trafficking, or stalking in which the alien has been battered or subject to extreme cruelty or if the alien is described in subparagraph (T) or (U) of section 101(a)(15) [8 U.S.C.A. § 1101(a)(15)].

(June 27, 1952, c. 477, Title II, § 239, as added Sept. 30, 1996, Pub.L. 104–208, Div. C, Title III, § 304(a)(3), 110 Stat. 3009–587, and amended Jan. 5, 2006, Pub.L. 109–162, Title VIII, § 825(c)(1), 119 Stat. 3065; Aug. 12, 2006, Pub.L. 109–271, § 6(d), 120 Stat. 763.)

§ 240. Removal proceedings [8 U.S.C.A. § 1229a]

(a) Proceeding

(1) In general

An immigration judge shall conduct proceedings for deciding the inadmissibility or deportability of an alien.

(2) Charges

An alien placed in proceedings under this section may be charged with any applicable ground of inadmissibility under section 212(a) [8 U.S.C.A. § 1182(a)] or any applicable ground of deportability under section 237(a) [8 U.S.C.A. § 1227(a)].

(3) Exclusive procedures

Unless otherwise specified in this Act, a proceeding under this section shall be the sole and exclusive procedure for determining whether an alien may be admitted to the United States or, if the alien has been so admitted, removed from the United States. Nothing in this section shall affect proceedings conducted pursuant to section 238 [8 U.S.C.A. § 1228].

(b) Conduct of proceeding

(1) Authority of immigration judge

The immigration judge shall administer oaths, receive evidence, and interrogate, examine, and cross-examine the alien and any witnesses. The immigration judge may issue subpoenas for the attendance of witnesses and presentation of evidence. The immigration judge shall have authority (under regulations prescribed by the Attorney General) to sanction by civil money penalty any action (or inaction) in contempt of the judge's proper exercise of authority under this Act.

(2) Form of proceeding

(A) In general

The proceeding may take place—

(i) in person,

(ii) where agreed to by the parties, in the absence of the alien,

(iii) through video conference, or

(iv) subject to subparagraph (B), through telephone conference.

(B) Consent required in certain cases

An evidentiary hearing on the merits may only be conducted through a telephone conference with the consent of the alien involved after the alien has been advised of the right to proceed in person or through video conference.

(3) Presence of alien

If it is impracticable by reason of an alien's mental incompetency for the alien to be present at the proceeding, the Attorney General shall prescribe safeguards to protect the rights and privileges of the alien.

(4) Aliens [sic] rights in proceeding

In proceedings under this section, under regulations of the Attorney General—

(A) the alien shall have the privilege of being represented, at no expense to the Government, by counsel of the alien's choosing who is authorized to practice in such proceedings,

(B) the alien shall have a reasonable opportunity to examine the evidence against the alien, to present evidence on the alien's own behalf, and to cross-examine witnesses presented by the Government but these rights shall not entitle the alien to examine such national security information as the Government may proffer in opposition to the alien's admission to the United States or to an application by the alien for discretionary relief under this Act, and

(C) a complete record shall be kept of all testimony and evidence produced at the proceeding.

(5) Consequences of failure to appear

(A) In general

Any alien who, after written notice required under paragraph (1) or (2) of section 239(a) [8 U.S.C.A. § 1229(a)] has been provided to the alien or the alien's counsel of record, does not attend a proceeding under this section, shall be ordered removed in absentia if the Service establishes by clear, unequivocal, and convincing evidence that the written notice was so provided and that the alien is removable (as defined in subsection (e)(2)). The written notice by the Attorney General shall be considered sufficient for purposes of this subparagraph if provided at the most recent address provided under section 239(a)(1)(F) [8 U.S.C.A. § 1229(a)(1)(F)].

(B) No notice if failure to provide address information

No written notice shall be required under subparagraph (A) if the alien has failed to provide the address required under section 239(a)(1)(F) [8 U.S.C.A. § 1229(a)(1)(F)].

(C) Rescission of order

Such an order may be rescinded only—

(i) upon a motion to reopen filed within 180 days after the date of the order of removal if the alien demonstrates that the failure to appear was because of exceptional circumstances (as defined in subsection (e)(1)), or

(ii) upon a motion to reopen filed at any time if the alien demonstrates that the alien did not receive notice in accordance with paragraph (1) or (2) of section 239(a) [8 U.S.C.A. § 1229(a)] or the alien demonstrates that the alien was in Federal or State custody and the failure to appear was through no fault of the alien.

The filing of the motion to reopen described in clause (i) or (ii) shall stay the removal of the alien pending disposition of the motion by the immigration judge.

(D) Effect on judicial review

Any petition for review under section 242 [8 U.S.C.A. § 1252] of an order entered in absentia under this paragraph shall (except in cases described in section 242(b)(5) [8 U.S.C.A. § 1252(b)(5)]) be confined to (i) the validity of the notice provided to the alien, (ii) the reasons for the alien's not attending the proceeding, and (iii) whether or not the alien is removable.

(E) Additional application to certain aliens in contiguous territory

The preceding provisions of this paragraph shall apply to all aliens placed in proceedings under this section, including any alien who remains in a contiguous foreign territory pursuant to section 235(b)(2)(C) [8 U.S.C.A. § 1225(b)(2)(C)].

(6) Treatment of frivolous behavior

The Attorney General shall, by regulation—

(A) define in a proceeding before an immigration judge or before an appellate administrative body under this title, frivolous behavior for which attorneys may be sanctioned,

(B) specify the circumstances under which an administrative appeal of a decision or ruling will be considered frivolous and will be summarily dismissed, and

(C) impose appropriate sanctions (which may include suspension and disbarment) in the case of frivolous behavior.

Nothing in this paragraph shall be construed as limiting the authority of the Attorney General to take actions with respect to inappropriate behavior.

(7) Limitation on discretionary relief for failure to appear

Any alien against whom a final order of removal is entered in absentia under this subsection and who, at the time of the notice described in paragraph (1) or (2) of section 239(a) [8 U.S.C.A. § 1229(a)], was provided oral notice, either in the alien's native language or in another language the alien understands, of the time and place of the proceedings and of the consequences under this paragraph of failing, other than because of exceptional circumstances (as defined in subsection (e)(1)) to attend a proceeding under this section, shall not be eligible for relief under section 240A [8 U.S.C.A. § 1229b], 240B [8 U.S.C.A. § 1229c], 245 [8 U.S.C.A. § 1255], 248 [8 U.S.C.A. § 1258], or 249 [8 U.S.C.A. § 1259] for a period of 10 years after the date of the entry of the final order of removal.

(c) Decision and burden of proof

(1) Decision

(A) In general

At the conclusion of the proceeding the immigration judge shall decide whether an alien is removable from the United States. The determination of the immigration judge shall be based only on the evidence produced at the hearing.

(B) Certain medical decisions

If a medical officer or civil surgeon or board of medical officers has certified under section 232(b) [8 U.S.C.A. § 1222(b)] that an alien has a disease, illness, or addiction which would make the alien inadmissible under paragraph (1) of section

212(a) [8 U.S.C.A. § 1182(a)], the decision of the immigration judge shall be based solely upon such certification.

(2) Burden on alien

In the proceeding the alien has the burden of establishing—

(A) if the alien is an applicant for admission, that the alien is clearly and beyond doubt entitled to be admitted and is not inadmissible under section 212 [8 U.S.C.A. § 1182]; or

(B) by clear and convincing evidence, that the alien is lawfully present in the United States pursuant to a prior admission.

In meeting the burden of proof under subparagraph (B), the alien shall have access to the alien's visa or other entry document, if any, and any other records and documents, not considered by the Attorney General to be confidential, pertaining to the alien's admission or presence in the United States.

(3) Burden on service in cases of deportable aliens

(A) In general

In the proceeding the Service has the burden of establishing by clear and convincing evidence that, in the case of an alien who has been admitted to the United States, the alien is deportable. No decision on deportability shall be valid unless it is based upon reasonable, substantial, and probative evidence.

(B) Proof of convictions

In any proceeding under this Act, any of the following documents or records (or a certified copy of such an official document or record) shall constitute proof of a criminal conviction:

(i) An official record of judgment and conviction.

(ii) An official record of plea, verdict, and sentence.

(iii) A docket entry from court records that indicates the existence of the conviction.

(iv) Official minutes of a court proceeding or a transcript of a court hearing in which the court takes notice of the existence of the conviction.

(v) An abstract of a record of conviction prepared by the court in which the conviction was entered, or by a State official associated with the State's repository of criminal justice records, that indicates the charge or section of law violated, the disposition of the case, the existence and date of conviction, and the sentence.

(vi) Any document or record prepared by, or under the direction of, the court in which the conviction was entered that indicates the existence of a conviction.

(vii) Any document or record attesting to the conviction that is maintained by an official of a State or Federal penal institution, which is the basis for that institution's authority to assume custody of the individual named in the record.

(C) Electronic records

In any proceeding under this Act, any record of conviction or abstract that has been submitted by electronic means to the Service from a State or court shall be admissible as evidence to prove a criminal conviction if it is—

(i) certified by a State official associated with the State's repository of criminal justice records as an official record from its repository or by a court official from the court in which the conviction was entered as an official record from its repository, and

(ii) certified in writing by a Service official as having been received electronically from the State's record repository or the court's record repository.

A certification under clause (i) may be by means of a computer-generated signature and statement of authenticity.

(4) Applications for relief from removal

(A) In general

An alien applying for relief or protection from removal has the burden of proof to establish that the alien—

(i) satisfies the applicable eligibility requirements; and

(ii) with respect to any form of relief that is granted in the exercise of discretion, that the alien merits a favorable exercise of discretion.

(B) Sustaining burden

The applicant must comply with the applicable requirements to submit information or documentation in support of the applicant's application for relief or protection as provided by law or by regulation or in the instructions for the application form. In evaluating the testimony of the applicant or other witness in support of the application, the immigration judge will determine whether or not the testimony is credible, is persuasive, and refers to specific facts sufficient to demonstrate that the applicant has satisfied the applicant's burden of proof. In determining whether the applicant has met such burden, the immigration judge shall weigh the credible testimony along with other evidence of record. Where the immigration judge determines that the applicant should provide evidence which corroborates otherwise credible testimony, such evidence must be provided unless the applicant demonstrates that the applicant does not have the evidence and cannot reasonably obtain the evidence.

(C) Credibility determination

Considering the totality of the circumstances, and all relevant factors, the immigration judge may base a credibility determination on the demeanor, candor, or responsiveness of the applicant or witness, the inherent plausibility of the applicant's or witness's account, the consistency between the applicant's or witness's written and oral statements (whenever made and whether or not under oath, and considering the circumstances under which the statements were made), the internal consistency of each such statement, the consistency of such statements with other evidence of record (including the reports of the Department of State on country conditions), and any inaccuracies or falsehoods in such statements, without regard to whether an inconsistency, inaccuracy, or falsehood goes to the heart of the applicant's claim, or any other relevant factor. There is no presumption of credibility, however, if no adverse credibility determination is explicitly made, the applicant or witness shall have a rebuttable presumption of credibility on appeal.

(5) Notice

If the immigration judge decides that the alien is removable and orders the alien to be removed, the judge shall inform the alien of the right to appeal that decision and of the consequences for failure to depart under the order of removal, including civil and criminal penalties.

(6) Motions to reconsider

(A) In general

The alien may file one motion to reconsider a decision that the alien is removable from the United States.

(B) Deadline

The motion must be filed within 30 days of the date of entry of a final administrative order of removal.

(C) Contents

The motion shall specify the errors of law or fact in the previous order and shall be supported by pertinent authority.

(7) Motions to reopen

(A) In general

An alien may file one motion to reopen proceedings under this section, except that this limitation shall not apply so as to prevent the filing of one motion to reopen described in subparagraph (C)(iv).

(B) Contents

The motion to reopen shall state the new facts that will be proven at a hearing to be held if the motion is granted, and shall be supported by affidavits or other evidentiary material.

(C) Deadline

(i) In general

Except as provided in this subparagraph, the motion to reopen shall be filed within 90 days of the date of entry of a final administrative order of removal.

(ii) Asylum

There is no time limit on the filing of a motion to reopen if the basis of the motion is to apply for relief under sections 208 [8 U.S.C.A. § 1158] or 241(b)(3) [8 U.S.C.A. § 1231(b)(3)] and is based on changed country conditions arising in the country of nationality or the country to which removal has been ordered, if such evidence is material and was not available and would not have been discovered or presented at the previous proceeding.

(iii) Failure to appear

The filing of a motion to reopen an order entered pursuant to subsection (b)(5) is subject to the deadline specified in subparagraph (C) of such subsection.

(iv) Special rule for battered spouses, children, and parents

Any limitation under this section on the deadlines for filing such motions shall not apply—

(I) if the basis for the motion is to apply for relief under clause (iii) or (iv) of section 204(a)(1)(A) [8 U.S.C.A § 1154(a)(1)(A)], clause (ii) or (iii) of section 204(a)(1)(B) [8 U.S.C.A § 1154(a)(1)(B)], section 240A(b) [8 U.S.C.A § 1229b(b)], or section 244(a)(3) [8 U.S.C.A § 1254(a)(3)] (as in effect on March 31, 1997);

(II) if the motion is accompanied by a cancellation of removal application to be filed with the Attorney General or by a copy of the self-petition that has been or will be filed with the Immigration and Naturalization Service upon the granting of the motion to reopen;

(III) if the motion to reopen is filed within 1 year of the entry of the final order of removal, except that the Attorney General may, in the Attorney General's discretion, waive this time limitation in the case of an alien who demonstrates extraordinary circumstances or extreme hardship to the alien's child; and

(IV) if the alien is physically present in the United States at the time of filing the motion.

The filing of a motion to reopen under this clause shall only stay the removal of a qualified alien (as defined in section 431(c)(1)(B) of the Personal Responsibility and Work Opportunity Reconciliation Act of 1996 [8 U.S.C. 1641(c)(1)(B)]) pending the final disposition of the motion, including exhaustion of all appeals if the motion establishes that the alien is a qualified alien.

(d) Stipulated removal

The Attorney General shall provide by regulation for the entry by an immigration judge of an order of removal stipulated to by the alien (or the alien's representative) and the Service. A stipulated order shall constitute a conclusive determination of the alien's removability from the United States.

(e) Definitions

In this section and section 240A [8 U.S.C.A. § 1229b]:

(1) Exceptional circumstances

The term "exceptional circumstances" refers to exceptional circumstances (such as battery or extreme cruelty to the alien or any child or parent of the alien, serious illness of the alien, or serious illness or death of the spouse, child, or parent of the alien, but not including less compelling circumstances) beyond the control of the alien.

(2) Removable

The term "removable" means—

(A) in the case of an alien not admitted to the United States, that the alien is inadmissible under section 212 [8 U.S.C.A. § 1182], or

(B) in the case of an alien admitted to the United States, that the alien is deportable under section 237 [8 U.S.C.A. § 1227].

(June 27, 1952, c. 477, Title II, Ch. 4, § 240 as added Sept. 30, 1996, Pub.L. 104–208, Div. C, Title III, § 304(a)(3), 110 Stat. 3009–589, and amended Oct. 28, 2000, Pub.L. 106–386, Title V, § 1506(c)(1)(A), 114 Stat. 1528; May 11, 2005, Pub.L. 109–13, Div. B, § 101(d), 119 Stat. 231, 304–05; Jan. 5, 2006, Pub.L. 109–162, Title VIII, §§ 813(a)(1), 825(a), 119 Stat. 3057, 3063.)

§ 240A. Cancellation of removal; adjustment of status [8 U.S.C.A. § 1229b]

(a) Cancellation of removal for certain permanent residents

The Attorney General may cancel removal in the case of an alien who is inadmissible or deportable from the United States if the alien—

(1) has been an alien lawfully admitted for permanent residence for not less than 5 years,

(2) has resided in the United States continuously for 7 years after having been admitted in any status, and

(3) has not been convicted of any aggravated felony.

(b) Cancellation of removal and adjustment of status for certain nonpermanent residents

(1) In general

The Attorney General may cancel removal of, and adjust to the status of an alien lawfully admitted for permanent residence, an alien who is inadmissible or deportable from the United States if the alien—

(A) has been physically present in the United States for a continuous period of not less than 10 years immediately preceding the date of such application;

(B) has been a person of good moral character during such period;

(C) has not been convicted of an offense under section 212(a)(2) [8 U.S.C.A § 1182(a)(2)], 237(a)(2) [8 U.S.C.A § 1227(a)(2)], or 237(a)(3) [8 U.S.C.A § 1227(a)(3)], subject to paragraph (5); and

(D) establishes that removal would result in exceptional and extremely unusual hardship to the alien's spouse, parent, or child, who is a citizen of the United States or an alien lawfully admitted for permanent residence.

(2) Special rule for battered spouse or child

(A) Authority

The Attorney General may cancel removal of, and adjust to the status of an alien lawfully admitted for permanent residence, an alien who is inadmissible or deportable from the United States if the alien demonstrates that—

(i)(I) the alien has been battered or subjected to extreme cruelty by a spouse or parent who is or was a United States citizen (or is the parent of a child of a United States citizen and the child has been battered or subjected to extreme cruelty by such citizen parent);

(II) the alien has been battered or subjected to extreme cruelty by a spouse or parent who is or was a lawful permanent resident (or is the parent of a child of an alien who is or was a lawful permanent resident and the child has been battered or subjected to extreme cruelty by such permanent resident parent); or

(III) the alien has been battered or subjected to extreme cruelty by a United States citizen or lawful permanent resident whom the alien intended to marry, but whose marriage is not legitimate because of that United States citizen's or lawful permanent resident's bigamy;

(ii) the alien has been physically present in the United States for a continuous period of not less than 3 years immediately preceding the date of such application, and the issuance of a charging document for removal proceedings shall not toll the 3–year period of continuous physical presence in the United States;

(iii) the alien has been a person of good moral character during such period, subject to the provisions of subparagraph (C);

(iv) the alien is not inadmissible under paragraph (2) or (3) of section 212(a) [8 U.S.C.A § 1182(a)], is not deportable under paragraphs (1)(G) or (2) through (4) of section 237(a) [8 U.S.C.A § 1227(a)], subject to paragraph (5), and has not been convicted of an aggravated felony; and

(v) the removal would result in extreme hardship to the alien, the alien's child, or the alien's parent.

(B) Physical presence

Notwithstanding subsection (d)(2) of this section, for purposes of subparagraph (A)(ii) or for purposes of section 244(a)(3) [8 U.S.C.A § 1254(a)(3)] (as in effect before the title III–A effective date in section 309 of the Illegal Immigration Reform and Immigrant Responsibility Act of 1996), an alien shall not be considered to have failed to maintain continuous physical presence by reason of an absence if the alien demonstrates a connection between the absence and the battering or extreme cruelty perpetrated against the alien. No absence or portion of an absence connected to the battering or extreme cruelty shall count toward the 90–day or 180–day limits established in subsection (d)(2) of this section. If any absence or aggregate absences exceed 180 days, the absences or portions of the absences will not be considered to break the period of continuous presence. Any such period of time excluded from the 180–day limit shall be excluded in computing the time during which the alien has been physically present for purposes of the 3–year requirement set forth in this subparagraph, subparagraph (A)(ii), and section 244(a)(3) [8 U.S.C.A § 1254(a)(3)] (as in effect before the title III–A effective date in section 309 of the Illegal Immigration Reform and Immigrant Responsibility Act of 1996).

(C) Good moral character

Notwithstanding section 101(f) [8 U.S.C.A § 1101(f)], an act or conviction that does not bar the Attorney General from granting relief under this paragraph by reason of subparagraph (A)(iv) shall not bar the Attorney General from finding the alien to be of good moral character under subparagraph (A)(iii) or section 244(a)(3) [8 U.S.C.A § 1254(a)(3)] (as in effect before the title III–A effective date in section 309 of the Illegal Immigration Reform and Immigrant Responsibility Act of 1996), if the Attorney General finds that the act or conviction was connected to the alien's having been battered or subjected to extreme cruelty and determines that a waiver is otherwise warranted.

(D) Credible evidence considered

In acting on applications under this paragraph, the Attorney General shall consider any credible evidence relevant to the application. The determination of what evidence is credible and the weight to be given that evidence shall be within the sole discretion of the Attorney General.

(3) Recordation of date

With respect to aliens who the Attorney General adjusts to the status of an alien lawfully admitted for permanent residence under paragraph (1) or (2), the Attorney General shall record the alien's lawful admission for permanent residence as of the date of the Attorney General's cancellation of removal under paragraph (1) or (2).

(4) Children of battered aliens and parents of battered alien children

(A) In general

The Attorney General shall grant parole under section 212(d)(5) [8 U.S.C.A. § 1182(d)(5)] to any alien who is a—

(i) child of an alien granted relief under section 240A(b)(2) [8 U.S.C.A. § 1229b(b)(2)] or section 244(a)(3) (as in effect before the title III–A effective date in section 309 of the Illegal Immigration Reform and Immigrant Responsibility Act of 1996); or

(ii) parent of a child alien granted relief under section 240A(b)(2) [8 U.S.C.A. § 1229b(b)(2)] or section 244(a)(3) (as in effect before the title III–A effective date in section 309 of the Illegal Immigration Reform and Immigrant Responsibility Act of 1996).

(B) Duration of parole

The grant of parole shall extend from the time of the grant of relief under subsection (b)(2) of this section or section 244(a)(3) [8 U.S.C.A. § 1254(a)(3)] (as in effect before the title III–A effective date in section 309 of the Illegal Immigration Reform and Immigrant Responsibility Act of 1996) to the time the application for adjustment of status filed by aliens covered under this paragraph has been finally adjudicated. Applications for adjustment of status filed by aliens covered under this paragraph shall be treated as if the applicants were VAWA self-petitioners. Failure by the alien granted relief under subsection (b)(2) of this section or section 244(a)(3) [8 U.S.C.A. § 1254(a)(3)] (as in effect before the title III–A effective date in section 309 of the Illegal Immigration Reform and Immigrant Responsibility Act of 1996) to exercise due diligence in filing a visa petition on behalf of an alien described in clause (i) or (ii) may result in revocation of parole.

(5) Application of domestic violence waiver authority

The authority provided under section 237(a)(7) [8 U.S.C.A § 1227(a)(7)] may apply under paragraphs (1)(B), (1)(C), and (2)(A)(iv) in a cancellation of removal and adjustment of status proceeding.

(6) Relatives of trafficking victims

(A) In general

Upon written request by a law enforcement official, the Secretary of Homeland Security may parole under section 212(d)(5) [8 U.S.C.A. § 1182(d)(5)] any alien who is a relative of an alien granted continued presence under section 107(c)(3)(A) of the Trafficking Victims Protection Act [22 U.S.C.A. § 7105(c)(3)(A)], if the relative—

(i) was, on the date on which law enforcement applied for such continued presence—

(I) in the case of an alien granted continued presence who is under 21 years of age, the spouse, child, parent, or unmarried sibling under 18 years of age, of the alien; or

(II) in the case of an alien granted continued presence who is 21 years of age or older, the spouse or child of the alien; or

(ii) is a parent or sibling of the alien who the requesting law enforcement official, in consultation with the Secretary of Homeland Security, as appropriate, determines to be in present danger of retaliation as a result of the alien's escape from the severe form of trafficking or cooperation with law enforcement, irrespective of age.

(B) Duration of parole

(i) In general

The Secretary may extend the parole granted under subparagraph (A) until the final adjudication of the application filed by the principal alien under section 101(a)(15)(T)(ii) [8 U.S.C.A. § 1101(a)(15)(T)(ii)].

(ii) Other limits on duration

If an application described in clause (i) is not filed, the parole granted under subparagraph (A) may extend until the later of—

(I) the date on which the principal alien's authority to remain in the United States under section 107(c)(3)(A) of the Trafficking Victims Protection Act [22 U.S.C.A. § 7105(c)(3)(A)] is is terminated; or

(II) the date on which a civil action filed by the principal alien under section 1595 of Title 18, United States Code, is concluded.

(iii) Due diligence

Failure by the principal alien to exercise due diligence in filing a visa petition on behalf of an alien described in clause (i) or (ii) of subparagraph (A), or in pursuing the civil action described in clause (ii)(II) (as determined by the Secretary of Homeland Security in consultation with the Attorney General), may result in revocation of parole.

(C) Other limitations

A relative may not be granted parole under this paragraph if—

(i) the Secretary of Homeland Security or the Attorney General has reason to believe that the relative was knowingly complicit in the trafficking of an alien permitted to remain in the United States under section 107(c)(3)(A) of the Trafficking Victims Protection Act [22 U.S.C.A. § 7105(c)(3)(A)]; or

(ii) the relative is an alien described in paragraph (2) or (3) of section 212(a) [8 U.S.C.A. § 1182(a)] or paragraph (2) or (4) of section 237(a) [8 U.S.C.A. § 1227(a)].

(c) Aliens ineligible for relief

The provisions of subsections (a) and (b)(1) shall not apply to any of the following aliens:

(1) An alien who entered the United States as a crewman subsequent to June 30, 1964.

(2) An alien who was admitted to the United States as a nonimmigrant exchange alien as defined in section 101(a)(15)(J) [8 U.S.C.A. § 1101(a)(15)(J)], or has acquired the status of such a nonimmigrant exchange alien after admission, in order to receive graduate medical education or training, regardless of whether or not the alien is subject to or has fulfilled the two-year foreign residence requirement of section 212(c) [8 U.S.C.A. § 1182(c)].

(3) An alien who—

(A) was admitted to the United States as a nonimmigrant exchange alien as defined in section 101(a)(15)(J) [8 U.S.C.A. § 1101(a)(15)(J)] or has acquired the status of such a nonimmigrant exchange alien after admission other than to receive graduate medical education or training,

(B) is subject to the two-year foreign residence requirement of section 212(e) [8 U.S.C.A. § 1182(e)], and

(C) has not fulfilled that requirement or received a waiver thereof.

(4) An alien who is inadmissible under section 212(a)(3) [8 U.S.C.A. § 1182(a)(3)] or deportable under section 237(a)(4) [8 U.S.C.A. § 1227(a)(4)].

(5) An alien who is described in section 241(b)(3)(B)(i) [8 U.S.C.A. § 1231(b)(3)(B)(i)].

(6) An alien whose removal has previously been cancelled under this section or whose deportation was suspended under section 244(a) [8 U.S.C.A. § 1254(a)] or who has been granted relief under section 212(c) [8 U.S.C.A. § 1182(c)], as such sections were in effect before the date of the enactment of the Illegal Immigration Reform and Immigrant Responsibility Act of 1996 [September 30, 1996].

(d) Special rules relating to continuous residence or physical presence

(1) Termination of continuous period

For purposes of this section, any period of continuous residence or continuous physical presence in the United States shall be deemed to end (A) except in the case of an alien who applies for cancellation of removal under subsection (b)(2), when the alien is served a notice to appear under section 239(a) [8 U.S.C.A. § 1229(a)], or (B) when the alien has committed an offense referred to in section 212(a)(2) [8 U.S.C.A. § 1182(a)(2)] that renders the alien inadmissible to the United States under section 212(a)(2) [8 U.S.C.A. § 1182(a)(2)] or removable from the United States under section 237(a)(2) [8 U.S.C.A. § 1227(a)(2)] or 237(a)(4) [8 U.S.C.A. § 1227(a)(4)], whichever is earliest.

(2) Treatment of certain breaks in presence

An alien shall be considered to have failed to maintain continuous physical presence in the United States under subsections (b)(1) and (b)(2) if the alien has departed from the United States for any period in excess of 90 days or for any periods in the aggregate exceeding 180 days.

(3) Continuity not required because of honorable service in armed forces and presence upon entry into service

The requirements of continuous residence or continuous physical presence in the United States under subsections (a) and (b) shall not apply to an alien who—

(A) has served for a minimum period of 24 months in an active-duty status in the Armed Forces of the United States and, if separated from such service, was separated under honorable conditions, and

(B) at the time of the alien's enlistment or induction was in the United States.

(e) Annual limitation

(1) Aggregate limitation

Subject to paragraphs (2) and (3), the Attorney General may not cancel the removal and adjust the status under this section, nor suspend the deportation and adjust the status under section 244(a) [8 U.S.C.A. § 1254(a)] (as in effect before the enactment of the Illegal Immigration Reform and Immigrant Responsibility Act of 1996), of a total of more than 4,000 aliens in any fiscal year. The previous sentence shall apply regardless of when an alien applied for such cancellation and adjustment, or such suspension and adjustment, and whether such an alien had previously applied for suspension of deportation under such section 244(a) [8 U.S.C.A. § 1254(a)]. The numerical limitation under this paragraph shall apply to the aggregate number of decisions in any fiscal year to cancel the removal (and adjust the status) of an alien, or suspend the deportation (and adjust the status) of an alien, under this section or such section 244(a) [8 U.S.C.A. § 1254(a)].

(2) Fiscal year 1997

For fiscal year 1997, paragraph (1) shall only apply to decisions to cancel the removal of an alien, or suspend the deportation of an alien, made after April 1, 1997. Notwithstanding any other provision of law, the Attorney General may cancel the removal or suspend the deportation, in addition to the normal allotment for fiscal year 1998, of a number of aliens equal to 4,000 less the number of such cancellations of removal and suspensions of deportation granted in fiscal year 1997 after April 1, 1997.

(3) Exception for certain aliens

Paragraph (1) shall not apply to the following:

(A) Aliens described in section 309(c)(5)(C)(i) of the Illegal Immigration Reform and Immigrant Responsibility Act of 1996 (as amended by the Nicaraguan Adjustment and Central American Relief Act).

(B) Aliens in deportation proceedings prior to April 1, 1997, who applied for suspension of deportation under section 244(a)(3) [8 U.S.C.A. § 1254(a)(3)] (as in effect before Sept. 30, 1996).

(June 27, 1952, c. 477, Title II, ch. 4, § 240A, as added Sept. 30, 1996, Pub.L. 104–208, Div. C, Title III, § 304(a)(3), 110 Stat. 3009–594; Nov. 19, 1997, Pub.L. 105–100, Title I, § 204(a) to (c), 111 Stat. 2200; Oct. 28, 2000, Pub.L. 106–386, Div. B, Title V, §§ 1504(a), (b), 1505(b)(2), 1506(b)(1), 114 Stat. 1522, 1525, 1527; Jan. 5, 2006, Pub.L. 109–162, Title VIII, §§ 813(c), 822(a), (b), 119 Stat. 3058, 3062, 3063; Aug. 12, 2006, Pub.L. 109–271, § 6(e), 120 Stat. 763; Dec. 23, 2008, Pub.L. 110–457, Title II, § 205(b), 122 Stat. 5062.)

§ 240B. Voluntary departure [8 U.S.C.A. § 1229c]

(a) Certain conditions

(1) In general

The Attorney General may permit an alien voluntarily to depart the United States at the alien's own expense under this subsection, in lieu of being subject to proceedings under section 240 [8 U.S.C.A. § 1229a] or prior to the completion of such proceedings, if the alien is not deportable under section 237(a)(2)(A)(iii) [8 U.S.C.A. § 1227(a)(2)(A)(iii)] or section 237(a)(4)(B) [8 U.S.C.A. § 1227(a)(4)(B)].

(2) Period

(A) In general

Subject to subparagraph (B), permission to depart voluntarily under this subsection shall not be valid for a period exceeding 120 days.

(B) Three-year pilot program waiver

During the period October 1, 2000, through September 30, 2003, and subject to subparagraphs (C) and (D)(ii), the Attorney General may, in the discretion of the Attorney General for humanitarian purposes, waive application of subparagraph (A) in the case of an alien—

(i) who was admitted to the United States as a nonimmigrant visitor (described in section 101(a)(15)(B) [8 U.S.C.A. § 1101(a)(15)(B)]) under the provisions of the visa waiver pilot program established pursuant to section 217 [8 U.S.C.A. § 1187], seeks the waiver for the purpose of continuing to receive medical treatment in the United States from a physician associated with a health care facility, and submits to the Attorney General

(I) a detailed diagnosis statement from the physician, which includes the treatment being sought and the expected time period the alien will be required to remain in the United States;

(II) a statement from the health care facility containing an assurance that the alien's treatment is not being paid through any Federal or State public health assistance, that the alien's account has no outstanding balance, and that such facility will notify the Service when the alien is released or treatment is terminated; and

(III) evidence of financial ability to support the alien's day-to-day expenses while in the United States (including the expenses of any family member described in clause (ii)) and evidence that any such alien or family member is not receiving any form of public assistance; or

(ii) who—

(I) is a spouse, parent, brother, sister, son, daughter, or other family member of a principal alien described in clause (i); and

(II) entered the United States accompanying, and with the same status as, such principal alien.

(C) Waiver limitations

(i) Waivers under subparagraph (B) may be granted only upon a request submitted by a Service district office to Service headquarters.

(ii) Not more than 300 waivers may be granted for any fiscal year for a principal alien under subparagraph (B)(i).

(iii)(I) Except as provided in subclause (II), in the case of each principal alien described in subparagraph (B)(i) not more than one adult may be granted a waiver under subparagraph (B)(ii).

(II) Not more than two adults may be granted a waiver under subparagraph (b)(ii) in a case in which—

(aa) the principal alien described in subparagraph (B)(i) is a dependent under the age of 18; or

(bb) one such adult is age 55 or older or is physically handicapped.

(D) Report to Congress; suspension of waiver authority

(i) Not later than March 30 of each year, the Commissioner shall submit to the Congress an annual report regarding all waivers granted under subparagraph (B) during the preceding fiscal year.

(ii) Notwithstanding any other provision of law, the authority of the Attorney General under subparagraph (B) shall be suspended during any period in which an annual report under clause (i) is past due and has not been submitted.

(3) Bond

The Attorney General may require an alien permitted to depart voluntarily under this subsection to post a voluntary departure bond, to be surrendered upon proof that the alien has departed the United States within the time specified.

(4) Treatment of aliens arriving in the United States

In the case of an alien who is arriving in the United States and with respect to whom proceedings under section 240 [8 U.S.C.A. § 1229a] are (or would otherwise be) initiated at the time of such alien's arrival, paragraph (1) shall not apply. Nothing in this paragraph shall be construed as preventing such an alien from withdrawing the application for admission in accordance with section 235(a)(4) [8 U.S.C.A. § 1225(a)(4)].

(b) At conclusion of proceedings

(1) In general

The Attorney General may permit an alien voluntarily to depart the United States at the alien's own expense if, at the conclusion of a proceeding under section 240 [8 U.S.C.A. § 1229a], the immigration judge enters an order granting voluntary departure in lieu of removal and finds that—

(A) the alien has been physically present in the United States for a period of at least one year immediately preceding the date the notice to appear was served under section 239(a) [8 U.S.C.A. § 1229(a)];

(B) the alien is, and has been, a person of good moral character for at least 5 years immediately preceding the alien's application for voluntary departure;

(C) the alien is not deportable under section 237(a)(2)(A)(iii) [8 U.S.C.A. § 1227(a)(2)(A)(iii)] or section 237(a)(4) [8 U.S.C.A. § 1227(a)(4)]; and

(D) the alien has established by clear and convincing evidence that the alien has the means to depart the United States and intends to do so.

(2) Period

Permission to depart voluntarily under this subsection shall not be valid for a period exceeding 60 days.

(3) Bond

An alien permitted to depart voluntarily under this subsection shall be required to post a voluntary departure bond, in an amount necessary to ensure that the alien will depart, to be surrendered upon proof that the alien has departed the United States within the time specified.

(c) Aliens not eligible

The Attorney General shall not permit an alien to depart voluntarily under this section if the alien was previously permitted to so depart after having been found inadmissible under section 212(a)(6)(A) [8 U.S.C.A. § 1182(a)(6)(A)].

(d) Civil penalty for failure to depart

(1) In general

Subject to paragraph (2), if an alien is permitted to depart voluntarily under this section and voluntarily fails to depart the United States within the time period specified, the alien—

(A) shall be subject to a civil penalty of not less than $1,000 and not more than $5,000; and

(B) shall be ineligible, for a period of 10 years, to receive any further relief under this section and sections 240A [8 U.S.C.A § 1229b], 245 [8 U.S.C.A § 1255], 248 [8 U.S.C.A § 1258], and 249 [8 U.S.C.A § 1259].

(2) Application of VAWA protections

The restrictions on relief under paragraph (1) shall not apply to relief under section 240A [8 U.S.C.A § 1229b] or 245 [8 U.S.C.A § 1255] on the basis of a petition filed by a VAWA self-petitioner, or a petition filed under section 240A(b)(2) [8 U.S.C.A § 1229b(b)(2)], or under section 244(a)(3) [8 U.S.C.A § 1254(a)(3)] (as in effect prior to March 31, 1997), if the extreme cruelty or battery was at least one central reason for the alien's overstaying the grant of voluntary departure.

(3) Notice of penalties

The order permitting an alien to depart voluntarily shall inform the alien of the penalties under this subsection.

(e) Additional conditions

The Attorney General may by regulation limit eligibility for voluntary departure under this section for any class or classes of aliens. No court may review any regulation issued under this subsection.

(f) Judicial review

No court shall have jurisdiction over an appeal from denial of a request for an order of voluntary departure under subsection (b), nor shall any court order a stay of an alien's removal pending consideration of any claim with respect to voluntary departure.

(June 27, 1952, c. 477, Title II, ch. 4, § 240B, as added Sept. 30, 1996, Pub.L. 104–208, Div. C, Title III, § 304(a)(3), 110 Stat. 3009–596, and amended Nov. 1, 2000, Pub.L. 106–406, § 2, 114 Stat. 1755; Jan. 5, 2006, Pub.L. 109–162, Title VIII, § 812, 119 Stat. 3057).

§ 240C. Records of admission [8 U.S.C.A. § 1230]

(a) The Attorney General shall cause to be filed, as a record of admission of each immigrant, the immigrant visa required by section

211(e) [8 U.S.C.A. § 1201(e)] to be surrendered at the port of entry by the arriving alien to an immigration officer.

(b) The Attorney General shall cause to be filed such record of the admission into the United States of each immigrant admitted under section 211(b) [8 U.S.C.A. § 1181(b)] and of each nonimmigrant as the Attorney General deems necessary for the enforcement of the immigration laws.

(June 27, 1952, c. 477, Title II, ch. 4, § 240C, formerly § 240, 66 Stat. 204, redesignated and amended Sept. 30, 1996, Pub.L. 104–208, Div. C, Title III, §§ 304(a)(2), 308(f)(1)(K), 110 Stat. 3009–587, 3009–621.)

§ 241. Detention and removal of aliens ordered removed [8 U.S.C.A. § 1231]

(a) Detention, release, and removal of aliens ordered removed

(1) Removal period

(A) In general

Except as otherwise provided in this section, when an alien is ordered removed, the Attorney General shall remove the alien from the United States within a period of 90 days (in this section referred to as the "removal period").

(B) Beginning of period

The removal period begins on the latest of the following:

(i) The date the order of removal becomes administratively final.

(ii) If the removal order is judicially reviewed and if a court orders a stay of the removal of the alien, the date of the court's final order.

(iii) If the alien is detained or confined (except under an immigration process), the date the alien is released from detention or confinement.

(C) Suspension of period

The removal period shall be extended beyond a period of 90 days and the alien may remain in detention during such extended period if the alien fails or refuses to make timely application in good faith for travel or other documents necessary to the alien's departure or conspires or acts to prevent the alien's removal subject to an order of removal.

(2) Detention

During the removal period, the Attorney General shall detain the alien. Under no circumstance during the removal period shall the Attorney General release an alien who has been found inadmissible under section 212(a)(2) [8 U.S.C.A. § 1182(a)(2)] or 212(a)(3)(B) [8 U.S.C.A. § 1182(a)(3)(B)] or deportable under section

237(a)(2) [8 U.S.C.A. § 1227(a)(2)] or 237(a)(4)(B) [8 U.S.C.A. § 1227(a)(4)(B)].

(3) Supervision after 90–day period

If the alien does not leave or is not removed within the removal period, the alien, pending removal, shall be subject to supervision under regulations prescribed by the Attorney General. The regulations shall include provisions requiring the alien—

(A) to appear before an immigration officer periodically for identification;

(B) to submit, if necessary, to a medical and psychiatric examination at the expense of the United States Government;

(C) to give information under oath about the alien's nationality, circumstances, habits, associations, and activities, and other information the Attorney General considers appropriate; and

(D) to obey reasonable written restrictions on the alien's conduct or activities that the Attorney General prescribes for the alien.

(4) Aliens imprisoned, arrested, or on parole, supervised release, or probation

(A) In general

Except as provided in section 259(a) of Title 42 and paragraph (2), the Attorney General may not remove an alien who is sentenced to imprisonment until the alien is released from imprisonment. Parole, supervised release, probation, or possibility of arrest or further imprisonment is not a reason to defer removal.

(B) Exception for removal of nonviolent offenders prior to completion of sentence of imprisonment

The Attorney General is authorized to remove an alien in accordance with applicable procedures under this Act before the alien has completed a sentence of imprisonment—

(i) in the case of an alien in the custody of the Attorney General, if the Attorney General determines that (I) the alien is confined pursuant to a final conviction for a nonviolent offense (other than an offense related to smuggling or harboring of aliens or an offense described in section 101(a)(43)(B), (C), (E), (I), or (L) [8 U.S.C.A. § 1101(a)(43)(B), (C), (E), (I), or (L)] [sic] and (II) the removal of the alien is appropriate and in the best interest of the United States); or

(ii) in the case of an alien in the custody of a State (or a political subdivision of a State), if the chief State official exercising authority with respect to the incarceration of the alien determines that (I) the alien is confined pursuant to a final conviction for a nonviolent offense (other than an offense described in section 101(a)(43)(C) or (E) [8 U.S.C.A. § 1101(a)(43)(C) or (E)]), (II) the removal is appropriate and in the best interest of the State, and (III) submits a written request to the Attorney General that such alien be so removed.

(C) Notice

Any alien removed pursuant to this paragraph shall be notified of the penalties under the laws of the United States relating to the reentry of deported aliens, particularly the expanded penalties for aliens removed under subparagraph (B).

(D) No private right

No cause or claim may be asserted under this paragraph against any official of the United States or of any State to compel the release, removal, or consideration for release or removal of any alien.

(5) Reinstatement of removal orders against aliens illegally reentering

If the Attorney General finds that an alien has reentered the United States illegally after having been removed or having departed voluntarily, under an order of removal, the prior order of removal is reinstated from its original date and is not subject to being reopened or reviewed, the alien is not eligible and may not apply for any relief under this Act, and the alien shall be removed under the prior order at any time after the reentry.

(6) Inadmissible or criminal aliens

An alien ordered removed who is inadmissible under section 212 [8 U.S.C.A. § 1182], removable under section 237(a)(1)(C) [8 U.S.C.A. § 1227(a)(1)(C)], 237(a)(2) [8 U.S.C.A. § 1227(a)(2)], or 237(a)(4) [8 U.S.C.A. § 1227(a)(4)] or who has been determined by the Attorney General to be a risk to the community or unlikely to comply with the order of removal, may be detained beyond the removal period and, if released, shall be subject to the terms of supervision in paragraph (3).

(7) Employment authorization

No alien ordered removed shall be eligible to receive authorization to be employed in the United States unless the Attorney General makes a specific finding that—

(A) the alien cannot be removed due to the refusal of all countries designated by the alien or under this section to receive the alien, or

(B) the removal of the alien is otherwise impracticable or contrary to the public interest.

(b) Countries to which aliens may be removed

(1) Aliens arriving at the United States

Subject to paragraph (3)—

(A) In general

Except as provided by subparagraphs (B) and (C), an alien who arrives at the United States and with respect to whom proceedings under section 240 [8 U.S.C.A. § 1229a] were initiated at the time of such alien's arrival shall be removed to the country in which the alien boarded the vessel or aircraft on which the alien arrived in the United States.

(B) Travel from contiguous territory

If the alien boarded the vessel or aircraft on which the alien arrived in the United States in a foreign territory contiguous to the United States, an island adjacent to the United States, or an island adjacent to a foreign territory contiguous to the United States, and the alien is not a native, citizen, subject, or national of, or does not reside in, the territory or island, removal shall be to the country in which the alien boarded the vessel that transported the alien to the territory or island.

(C) Alternative countries

If the government of the country designated in subparagraph (A) or (B) is unwilling to accept the alien into that country's territory, removal shall be to any of the following countries, as directed by the Attorney General:

(i) The country of which the alien is a citizen, subject, or national.

(ii) The country in which the alien was born.

(iii) The country in which the alien has a residence.

(iv) A country with a government that will accept the alien into the country's territory if removal to each country described in a previous clause of this subparagraph is impracticable, inadvisable, or impossible.

(2) Other aliens

Subject to paragraph (3)—

(A) Selection of country by alien

Except as otherwise provided in this paragraph—

(i) any alien not described in paragraph (1) who has been ordered removed may designate one country to which the alien wants to be removed, and

(ii) the Attorney General shall remove the alien to the country the alien so designates.

(B) Limitation on designation

An alien may designate under subparagraph (A)(i) a foreign territory contiguous to the United States, an adjacent island, or an island adjacent to a foreign territory contiguous to the United States as the place to which the alien is to be removed only if the alien is a native, citizen, subject, or national of, or has resided in, that designated territory or island.

(C) Disregarding designation

The Attorney General may disregard a designation under subparagraph (A)(i) if—

(i) the alien fails to designate a country promptly;

(ii) the government of the country does not inform the Attorney General finally, within 30 days after the date the Attorney General first inquires, whether the government will accept the alien into the country;

(iii) the government of the country is not willing to accept the alien into the country; or

(iv) the Attorney General decides that removing the alien to the country is prejudicial to the United States.

(D) Alternative country

If an alien is not removed to a country designated under subparagraph (A)(i), the Attorney General shall remove the alien to a country of which the alien is a subject, national, or citizen unless the government of the country—

(i) does not inform the Attorney General or the alien finally, within 30 days after the date the Attorney General first inquires or within another period of time the Attorney General decides is reasonable, whether the government will accept the alien into the country; or

(ii) is not willing to accept the alien into the country.

(E) Additional removal countries

If an alien is not removed to a country under the previous subparagraphs of this paragraph, the Attorney General shall remove the alien to any of the following countries:

(i) The country from which the alien was admitted to the United States.

(ii) The country in which is located the foreign port from which the alien left for the United States or for a foreign territory contiguous to the United States.

(iii) A country in which the alien resided before the alien entered the country from which the alien entered the United States.

(iv) The country in which the alien was born.

(v) The country that had sovereignty over the alien's birthplace when the alien was born.

(vi) The country in which the alien's birthplace is located when the alien is ordered removed.

(vii) If impracticable, inadvisable, or impossible to remove the alien to each country described in a previous clause of this subparagraph, another country whose government will accept the alien into that country.

(F) Removal country when United States is at war

When the United States is at war and the Attorney General decides that it is impracticable, inadvisable, inconvenient, or impossible to remove an alien under this subsection because of the war, the Attorney General may remove the alien—

(i) to the country that is host to a government in exile of the country of which the alien is a citizen or subject if the government of the host country will permit the alien's entry; or

(ii) if the recognized government of the country of which the alien is a citizen or subject is not in exile, to a country, or a political or territorial subdivision of a country, that is very near the country of which the alien is a citizen or subject, or, with the consent of the government of the country of which the alien is a citizen or subject, to another country.

(3) Restriction on removal to a country where alien's life or freedom would be threatened

(A) In general

Notwithstanding paragraphs (1) and (2), the Attorney General may not remove an alien to a country if the Attorney General decides that the alien's life or freedom would be threatened in that country because of the alien's race, religion, nationality, membership in a particular social group, or political opinion.

(B) Exception

Subparagraph (A) does not apply to an alien deportable under section 237(a)(4)(D) [8 U.S.C.A. § 1227(a)(4)(D)] or if the Attorney General decides that—

(i) the alien ordered, incited, assisted, or otherwise participated in the persecution of an individual because of the individual's race, religion, nationality, membership in a particular social group, or political opinion;

(ii) the alien, having been convicted by a final judgment of a particularly serious crime is a danger to the community of the United States;

(iii) there are serious reasons to believe that the alien committed a serious nonpolitical crime outside the United States before the alien arrived in the United States; or

(iv) there are reasonable grounds to believe that the alien is a danger to the security of the United States.

For purposes of clause (ii), an alien who has been convicted of an aggravated felony (or felonies) for which the alien has been sentenced to an aggregate term of imprisonment of at least 5 years shall be considered to have committed a particularly serious crime. The previous sentence shall not preclude the Attorney General from determining that, notwithstanding the length of sentence imposed, an alien has been convicted of a particularly serious crime. For purposes of clause (iv), an alien who is described in section 237(a)(4)(B) [8 U.S.C.A. § 1227(a)(4)(B)] shall be considered to be an alien with respect to whom there are reasonable grounds for regarding as a danger to the security of the United States.

(C) Sustaining burden of proof; credibility determinations

In determining whether an alien has demonstrated that the alien's life or freedom would be threatened for a reason described in subparagraph (A), the trier of fact shall determine whether the alien has sustained the alien's burden of proof, and shall make credibility determinations, in the manner described in clauses (ii) and (iii) of section 208(b)(1)(B) [8 U.S.C.A. § 1158(b)(1)(B)].

(c) Removal of aliens arriving at port of entry

(1) Vessels and aircraft

An alien arriving at a port of entry of the United States who is ordered removed either without a hearing under section 235(b)(1) [8 U.S.C.A. § 1225(b)(1)] or 235(c) [8 U.S.C.A. § 1225(c)] or pursuant to proceedings under section 240 [8 U.S.C.A. § 1229a] initiated at the time of such alien's arrival shall be removed immediately on a vessel or aircraft owned by the owner of the vessel or aircraft on which the alien arrived in the United States, unless—

(A) it is impracticable to remove the alien on one of those vessels or aircraft within a reasonable time, or

(B) the alien is a stowaway—

(i) who has been ordered removed in accordance with section 235(a)(1) [8 U.S.C.A. § 1225(a)(1)],

(ii) who has requested asylum, and

(iii) whose application has not been adjudicated or whose asylum application has been denied but who has not exhausted all appeal rights.

(2) Stay of removal

(A) In general

The Attorney General may stay the removal of an alien under this subsection if the Attorney General decides that—

(i) immediate removal is not practicable or proper; or

(ii) the alien is needed to testify in the prosecution of a person for a violation of a law of the United States or of any State.

(B) Payment of detention costs

During the period an alien is detained because of a stay of removal under subparagraph (A)(ii), the Attorney General may pay from the appropriation "Immigration and Naturalization Service—Salaries and Expenses"—

(i) the cost of maintenance of the alien; and

(ii) a witness fee of $1 a day.

(C) Release during stay

The Attorney General may release an alien whose removal is stayed under subparagraph (A)(ii) on—

(i) the alien's filing a bond of at least $500 with security approved by the Attorney General;

(ii) condition that the alien appear when required as a witness and for removal; and

(iii) other conditions the Attorney General may prescribe.

(3) Costs of detention and maintenance pending removal

(A) In general

Except as provided in subparagraph (B) and subsection (d), an owner of a vessel or aircraft bringing an alien to the United States shall pay the costs of detaining and maintaining the alien—

(i) while the alien is detained under subsection (d)(1), and

(ii) in the case of an alien who is a stowaway, while the alien is being detained pursuant to—

(I) subsection (d)(2)(A) or (d)(2)(B)(i),

(II) subsection (d)(2)(B)(ii) or (iii) for the period of time reasonably necessary for the owner to arrange for repatriation or removal of the stowaway, including obtaining necessary travel documents, but not to extend beyond the date on which it is ascertained that such travel documents cannot be obtained from the country to which the stowaway is to be returned, or

(III) section 235(b)(1)(B)(ii), for a period not to exceed 15 days (excluding Saturdays, Sundays, and holidays) commencing on the first such day which begins on the earlier of 72 hours after the time of the initial presentation of the stowaway for inspection or at the time the stowaway is determined to have a credible fear of persecution.

(B) Nonapplication

Subparagraph (A) shall not apply if—

(i) the alien is a crewmember;

(ii) the alien has an immigrant visa;

(iii) the alien has a nonimmigrant visa or other documentation authorizing the alien to apply for temporary admission to the United States and applies for admission not later than 120 days after the date the visa or documentation was issued;

(iv) the alien has a reentry permit and applies for admission not later than 120 days after the date of the alien's last inspection and admission;

(v)(I) the alien has a nonimmigrant visa or other documentation authorizing the alien to apply for temporary admission to the United States or a reentry permit;

(II) the alien applies for admission more than 120 days after the date the visa or documentation was issued or after the date of the last inspection and admission under the reentry permit; and

(III) the owner of the vessel or aircraft satisfies the Attorney General that the existence of the condition relating to inadmissibility could not have been discovered by exercising reasonable care before the alien boarded the vessel or aircraft; or

(vi) the individual claims to be a national of the United States and has a United States passport.

(d) Requirements of persons providing transportation

(1) Removal at time of arrival

An owner, agent, master, commanding officer, person in charge, purser, or consignee of a vessel or aircraft bringing an alien (except an alien crewmember) to the United States shall—

(A) receive an alien back on the vessel or aircraft or another vessel or aircraft owned or operated by the same interests if the alien is ordered removed under this part; and

(B) take the alien to the foreign country to which the alien is ordered removed.

(2) Alien stowaways

An owner, agent, master, commanding officer, charterer, or consignee of a vessel or aircraft arriving in the United States with an alien stowaway—

(A) shall detain the alien on board the vessel or aircraft, or at such place as the Attorney General shall designate, until completion of the inspection of the alien by an immigration officer;

(B) may not permit the stowaway to land in the United States, except pursuant to regulations of the Attorney General temporarily—

(i) for medical treatment,

(ii) for detention of the stowaway by the Attorney General, or

(iii) for departure or removal of the stowaway; and

(C) if ordered by an immigration officer, shall remove the stowaway on the vessel or aircraft or on another vessel or aircraft.

The Attorney General shall grant a timely request to remove the stowaway under subparagraph (C) on a vessel or aircraft other than that on which the stowaway arrived if the requester has obtained any travel documents necessary for departure or repatriation of the stowaway and removal of the stowaway will not be unreasonably delayed.

(3) Removal upon order

An owner, agent, master, commanding officer, person in charge, purser, or consignee of a vessel, aircraft, or other transportation line shall comply with an order of the Attorney General to take on board, guard safely, and transport to the destination specified any alien ordered to be removed under this Act.

(e) Payment of expenses of removal

(1) Costs of removal at time of arrival

In the case of an alien who is a stowaway or who is ordered removed either without a hearing under section 235(a)(1) [8 U.S.C.A. § 1225(a)(1)] or 235(c) [8 U.S.C.A. § 1225(c)] or pursuant to proceedings under section 240 [8 U.S.C.A. § 1229a] initiated at the time of such alien's arrival, the owner of the vessel or aircraft (if any) on which the alien arrived in the United States shall pay the transportation cost of removing the alien. If removal is on a vessel or aircraft not owned by the owner of the vessel or aircraft on which the alien arrived in the United States, the Attorney General may—

(A) pay the cost from the appropriation "Immigration and Naturalization Service—Salaries and Expenses"; and

(B) recover the amount of the cost in a civil action from the owner, agent, or consignee of the vessel or aircraft (if any) on which the alien arrived in the United States.

(2) Costs of removal to port of removal for aliens admitted or permitted to land

In the case of an alien who has been admitted or permitted to land and is ordered removed, the cost (if any) of removal of the alien to the port of removal shall be at the expense of the appropriation for the enforcement of this Act.

(3) Costs of removal from port of removal for aliens admitted or permitted to land

(A) Through appropriation

Except as provided in subparagraph (B), in the case of an alien who has been admitted or permitted to land and is ordered removed, the cost (if any) of removal of the alien from the port of removal shall be at the expense of the appropriation for the enforcement of this Act.

(B) Through owner

(i) In general

In the case of an alien described in clause (ii), the cost of removal of the alien from the port of removal may be charged to any owner of the vessel, aircraft, or other transportation line by which the alien came to the United States.

(ii) Aliens described

An alien described in this clause is an alien who—

(I) is admitted to the United States (other than lawfully admitted for permanent residence) and is ordered removed within 5 years of the date of admission based on a ground that existed before or at the time of admission, or

(II) is an alien crewman permitted to land temporarily under section 252 [8 U.S.C.A. § 1282] and is ordered removed within 5 years of the date of landing.

(C) Costs of removal of certain aliens granted voluntary departure

In the case of an alien who has been granted voluntary departure under section 240B [8 U.S.C.A. § 1229c] and who is financially unable to depart at the alien's own expense and whose removal the Attorney General deems to be in the best interest of the United States, the expense of such removal may be paid from the appropriation for the enforcement of this Act.

(f) Aliens requiring personal care during removal

(1) In general

If the Attorney General believes that an alien being removed requires personal care because of the alien's mental or physical condition, the Attorney General may employ a suitable person for that purpose who shall accompany and care for the alien until the alien arrives at the final destination.

(2) Costs

The costs of providing the service described in paragraph (1) shall be defrayed in the same manner as the expense of removing the accompanied alien is defrayed under this section.

(g) Places of detention

(1) In general

The Attorney General shall arrange for appropriate places of detention for aliens detained pending removal or a decision on removal. When United States Government facilities are unavailable or facilities adapted or suitably located for detention are unavailable for rental, the Attorney General may expend from the appropriation "Immigration and Naturalization Service—Salaries and Expenses", without regard to section 5 of Title 41, amounts necessary to acquire land and to acquire, build, remodel, repair, and operate facilities (including living quarters for immigration officers if not otherwise available) necessary for detention.

(2) Detention facilities of the immigration and naturalization service

Prior to initiating any project for the construction of any new detention facility for the Service, the Commissioner shall consider the availability for purchase or lease of any existing prison, jail, detention center, or other comparable facility suitable for such use.

(h) Statutory construction

Nothing in this section shall be construed to create any substantive or procedural right or benefit that is legally enforceable by any party against the United States or its agencies or officers or any other person.

(i) Incarceration

(1) If the chief executive officer of a State (or, if appropriate, a political subdivision of the State) exercising authority with respect to the incarceration of an undocumented criminal alien submits a written request to the Attorney General, the Attorney General shall, as determined by the Attorney General—

(A) enter into a contractual arrangement which provides for compensation to the State or a political subdivision of the State, as may be appropriate, with respect to the incarceration of the undocumented criminal alien; or

(B) take the undocumented criminal alien into the custody of the Federal Government and incarcerate the alien.

(2) Compensation under paragraph (1)(A) shall be the average cost of incarceration of a prisoner in the relevant State as determined by the Attorney General.

(3) For purposes of this subsection, the term "undocumented criminal alien" means an alien who—

(A) has been convicted of a felony or two or more misdemeanors; and

(B)(i) entered the United States without inspection or at any time or place other than as designated by the Attorney General;

(ii) was the subject of exclusion or deportation proceedings at the time he or she was taken into custody by the State or a political subdivision of the State; or

(iii) was admitted as a nonimmigrant and at the time he or she was taken into custody by the State or a political subdivision of the State has failed to maintain the nonimmigrant status in which the alien was admitted or to which it was changed under section 248 [8 U.S.C.A. § 1258], or to comply with the conditions of any such status.

(4)(A) In carrying out paragraph (1), the Attorney General shall give priority to the Federal incarceration of undocumented criminal aliens who have committed aggravated felonies.

(B) The Attorney General shall ensure that undocumented criminal aliens incarcerated in Federal facilities pursuant to this subsection are held in facilities which provide a level of security appropriate to the crimes for which they were convicted.

(5) There are authorized to be appropriated to carry out this subsection—

(A) $750,000,000 for fiscal year 2006;

(B) $850,000,000 for fiscal year 2007; and

(C) $950,000,000 for each of the fiscal years 2008 through 2011.

(6) Amounts appropriated pursuant to the authorization of appropriations in paragraph (5) that are distributed to a State or political subdivision of a State, including a municipality, may be used only for correctional purposes.

(June 27, 1952, c. 477, Title II, ch. 4, § 241, as added and amended Sept. 30, 1996, Pub.L. 104–208, Div. C, Title III, §§ 305(a)(3), 306(a)(1), 328(a)(1), 110 Stat. 3009–598, 3009–607, 3009–630; Nov. 2, 2002, Pub.L. 107–273, Div. C, Title I, § 11014, 116 Stat. 1824; May 11, 2005, Pub.L. 109–13, Div. B, § 101(c), 119 Stat. 231, 303–04; Jan. 5, 2006, Pub.L. 109–162, Title XI, § 1196(a), (b), 119 Stat. 3130.)

§ 242. Judicial review of orders of removal [8 U.S.C.A. § 1252]

(a) Applicable provisions

(1) General orders of removal

Judicial review of a final order of removal (other than an order of removal without a hearing pursuant to section 235(b)(1) [8

U.S.C.A. § 1225(b)(1)]) is governed only by chapter 158 of Title 28, except as provided in subsection (b) and except that the court may not order the taking of additional evidence under section 2347(c) of Title 28.

(2) Matters not subject to judicial review

(A) Review relating to section 235(b)(1) [8 U.S.C.A. § 1225(b)(1)]

Notwithstanding any other provision of law (statutory or nonstatutory), including section 2241 of title 28, United States Code, or any other habeas corpus provision, and sections 1361 and 1651 of such title, no court shall have jurisdiction to review—

(i) except as provided in subsection (e), any individual determination or to entertain any other cause or claim arising from or relating to the implementation or operation of an order of removal pursuant to section 235(b)(1) [8 U.S.C.A. § 1225(b)(1)],

(ii) except as provided in subsection (e), a decision by the Attorney General to invoke the provisions of such section,

(iii) the application of such section to individual aliens, including the determination made under section 235(b)(1)(B) [8 U.S.C.A. § 1225(b)(1)(B)], or

(iv) except as provided in subsection (e), procedures and policies adopted by the Attorney General to implement the provisions of section 235(b)(1) [8 U.S.C.A. § 1225(b)(1)].

(B) Denials of discretionary relief

Notwithstanding any other provision of law (statutory or nonstatutory), including section 2241 of title 28, United States Code, or any other habeas corpus provision, and sections 1361 and 1651 of such title, and except as provided in subparagraph (D), and regardless of whether the judgment, decision, or action is made in removal proceedings, no court shall have jurisdiction to review—

(i) any judgment regarding the granting of relief under section 212(h) [8 U.S.C.A. § 1182(h)], 212(i) [8 U.S.C.A. § 1182(i)], 240A [8 U.S.C.A. § 1229b], 240B [8 U.S.C.A. § 1229c], or 245 [8 U.S.C.A. § 1255], or

(ii) any other decision or action of the Attorney General or the Secretary of Homeland Security the authority for which is specified under this title to be in the discretion of the Attorney General or the Secretary of Homeland Security, other than the granting of relief under section 208(a) [8 U.S.C.A. § 1158(a)].

(C) Orders against criminal aliens

Notwithstanding any other provision of law (statutory or nonstatutory), including section 2241 of title 28, United States Code, or any other habeas corpus provision, and sections 1361 and 1651 of such title, and except as provided in subparagraph (D), no court shall have jurisdiction to review any final order of removal against an alien who is removable by reason of having committed a criminal offense covered in section 212(a)(2) [8 U.S.C.A. § 1182(a)(2)] or 237(a)(2)(A)(iii), (B), (C), or (D) [8 U.S.C.A. § 1227(a)(2)(A)(iii), (B), (C), or (D)], or any offense covered by section 237(a)(2)(A)(ii) [8 U.S.C.A. § 1227(a)(2)(A)(ii)] for which both predicate offenses are, without regard to their date of commission, otherwise covered by section 237(a)(2)(A)(i) [8 U.S.C.A. § 1227(a)(2)(A)(i)].

(D) Judicial review of certain legal claims

Nothing in subparagraph (B) or (C), or in any other provision of this Act (other than this section) which limits or eliminates judicial review, shall be construed as precluding review of constitutional claims or questions of law raised upon a petition for review filed with an appropriate court of appeals in accordance with this section.

(3) Treatment of certain decisions

No alien shall have a right to appeal from a decision of an immigration judge which is based solely on a certification described in section 240(c)(1)(B) [8 U.S.C.A. § 1229a(c)(1)(B)].

(4) Claims under the United Nations Convention

Notwithstanding any other provision of law (statutory or nonstatutory), including section 2241 of title 28, United States Code, or any other habeas corpus provision, and sections 1361 and 1651 of such title, a petition for review filed with an appropriate court of appeals in accordance with this section shall be the sole and exclusive means for judicial review of any cause or claim under the United Nations Convention Against Torture and Other Forms of Cruel, Inhuman, or Degrading Treatment or Punishment, except as provided in subsection (e).

(5) Exclusive means of review

Notwithstanding any other provision of law (statutory or nonstatutory), including section 2241 of title 28, United States Code, or any other habeas corpus provision, and sections 1361 and 1651 of such title, a petition for review filed with an appropriate court of appeals in accordance with this section shall be the sole and exclusive means for judicial review of an order of removal entered or issued under any provision of this Act, except as provided in subsection (e). For purposes of this Act, in every provision that limits or eliminates judicial review or jurisdiction to review, the terms "judicial review" and "jurisdiction to review" include habeas corpus review pursuant to section 2241 of title 28, United States Code, or any other habeas corpus provision, sections 1361 and 1651 of such title, and review pursuant to any other provision of law (statutory or nonstatutory).

(b) Requirements for review of orders of removal

With respect to review of an order of removal under subsection (a)(1), the following requirements apply:

(1) Deadline

The petition for review must be filed not later than 30 days after the date of the final order of removal.

(2) Venue and forms

The petition for review shall be filed with the court of appeals for the judicial circuit in which the immigration judge completed the proceedings. The record and briefs do not have to be printed. The court of appeals shall review the proceeding on a typewritten record and on typewritten briefs.

(3) Service

(A) In general

The respondent is the Attorney General. The petition shall be served on the Attorney General and on the officer or employee of the Service in charge of the Service district in which the final order of removal under section 240 [8 U.S.C.A. § 1229a] was entered.

(B) Stay of order

Service of the petition on the officer or employee does not stay the removal of an alien pending the court's decision on the petition, unless the court orders otherwise.

(C) Alien's brief

The alien shall serve and file a brief in connection with a petition for judicial review not later than 40 days after the date on which the administrative record is available, and may serve and file a reply brief not later than 14 days after service of the brief of the Attorney General, and the court may not extend these deadlines except upon motion for good cause shown. If an alien fails to file a brief within the time provided in this paragraph, the court shall dismiss the appeal unless a manifest injustice would result.

(4) Scope and standard for review

Except as provided in paragraph (5)(B)—

(A) the court of appeals shall decide the petition only on the administrative record on which the order of removal is based,

(B) the administrative findings of fact are conclusive unless any reasonable adjudicator would be compelled to conclude to the contrary,

(C) a decision that an alien is not eligible for admission to the United States is conclusive unless manifestly contrary to law, and

(D) the Attorney General's discretionary judgment whether to grant relief under section 208(a) [8 U.S.C.A. § 1158(a)] shall be conclusive unless manifestly contrary to the law and an abuse of discretion.

No court shall reverse a determination made by a trier of fact with respect to the availability of corroborating evidence, as described in section 208(b)(1)(B) [8 U.S.C.A. § 1158(b)(1)(B)], 240(c)(4)(B) [8 U.S.C.A. § 1229a(c)(4)(B)], or 241(b)(3)(C) [8 U.S.C.A. § 1231(b)(3)(C)], unless the court finds, pursuant to section 242(b)(4)(B) [8 U.S.C.A. § 1252(b)(4)(B)], that a reasonable trier of fact is compelled to conclude that such corroborating evidence is unavailable.

(5) Treatment of nationality claims

(A) Court determination if no issue of fact

If the petitioner claims to be a national of the United States and the court of appeals finds from the pleadings and affidavits that no genuine issue of material fact about the petitioner's nationality is presented, the court shall decide the nationality claim.

(B) Transfer if issue of fact

If the petitioner claims to be a national of the United States and the court of appeals finds that a genuine issue of material fact about the petitioner's nationality is presented, the court shall transfer the proceeding to the district court of the United States for the judicial district in which the petitioner resides for a new hearing on the nationality claim and a decision on that claim as if an action had been brought in the district court under section 2201 of Title 28.

(C) Limitation on determination

The petitioner may have such nationality claim decided only as provided in this paragraph.

(6) Consolidation with review of motions to reopen or reconsider

When a petitioner seeks review of an order under this section, any review sought of a motion to reopen or reconsider the order shall be consolidated with the review of the order.

(7) Challenge to validity of orders in certain criminal proceedings

(A) In general

If the validity of an order of removal has not been judicially decided, a defendant in a criminal proceeding charged with violating section 243(a) [8 U.S.C.A. § 1253(a)] may challenge the validity of the order in the criminal proceeding only by filing a separate motion before trial. The district court, without a jury, shall decide the motion before trial.

(B) Claims of United States nationality

If the defendant claims in the motion to be a national of the United States and the district court finds that—

(i) no genuine issue of material fact about the defendant's nationality is presented, the court shall decide the motion only on the administrative record on which the removal order is based and the administrative findings of fact are conclusive if supported by reasonable, substantial, and probative evidence on the record considered as a whole; or

(ii) a genuine issue of material fact about the defendant's nationality is presented, the court shall hold a new hearing on the nationality claim and decide that claim as if an action had been brought under section 2201 of Title 28, United States Code.

The defendant may have such nationality claim decided only as provided in this subparagraph.

(C) Consequence of invalidation

If the district court rules that the removal order is invalid, the court shall dismiss the indictment for violation of section 243(a) [8 U.S.C.A. § 1253(a)]. The United States Government may appeal the dismissal to the court of appeals for the appropriate circuit within 30 days after the date of the dismissal.

(D) Limitation on filing petitions for review

The defendant in a criminal proceeding under section 243(a) [8 U.S.C.A. § 1253(a)] may not file a petition for review under subsection (a) during the criminal proceeding.

(8) Construction

This subsection—

(A) does not prevent the Attorney General, after a final order of removal has been issued, from detaining the alien under section 241(a) [8 U.S.C.A. § 1231(a)];

(B) does not relieve the alien from complying with section 241(a)(4) [8 U.S.C.A. § 1231(a)(4)] and section 243(g) [8 U.S.C.A. § 1253(g)]; and

(C) does not require the Attorney General to defer removal of the alien.

(9) Consolidation of questions for judicial review

Judicial review of all questions of law and fact, including interpretation and application of constitutional and statutory provisions, arising from any action taken or proceeding brought to remove an alien from the United States under this title shall be available only in judicial review of a final order under this section. Except as otherwise provided in this section, no court shall have jurisdiction, by habeas corpus under section 2241 of title 28, United States Code, or any other habeas corpus provision, by section 1361 or 1651 of such title, or by any other provision of law (statutory or nonstatutory), to review such an order or such questions of law or fact.

(c) Requirements for petition

A petition for review or for habeas corpus of an order of removal—

(1) shall attach a copy of such order, and

(2) shall state whether a court has upheld the validity of the order, and, if so, shall state the name of the court, the date of the court's ruling, and the kind of proceeding.

(d) Review of final orders

A court may review a final order of removal only if—

(1) the alien has exhausted all administrative remedies available to the alien as of right, and

(2) another court has not decided the validity of the order, unless the reviewing court finds that the petition presents grounds that could not have been presented in the prior judicial proceeding or that the remedy provided by the prior proceeding was inadequate or ineffective to test the validity of the order.

(e) Judicial review of orders under section 235(b)(1) [8 U.S.C.A. § 1225(b)(1)]

(1) Limitations on relief

Without regard to the nature of the action or claim and without regard to the identity of the party or parties bringing the action, no court may—

(A) enter declaratory, injunctive, or other equitable relief in any action pertaining to an order to exclude an alien in accordance with section 235(b)(1) [8 U.S.C.A. § 1225(b)(1)] except as specifically authorized in a subsequent paragraph of this subsection, or

(B) certify a class under Rule 23 of the Federal Rules of Civil Procedure in any action for which judicial review is authorized under a subsequent paragraph of this subsection.

(2) Habeas corpus proceedings

Judicial review of any determination made under section 235(b)(1) [8 U.S.C.A. § 1225(b)(1)] is available in habeas corpus proceedings, but shall be limited to determinations of—

(A) whether the petitioner is an alien,

(B) whether the petitioner was ordered removed under such section, and

(C) whether the petitioner can prove by a preponderance of the evidence that the petitioner is an alien lawfully admitted for permanent residence, has been admitted as a refugee under section 207 [8 U.S.C.A. § 1157], or has been granted asylum under section 208 [8 U.S.C.A. § 1158], such status not having been terminated, and is entitled to such further inquiry as prescribed by the Attorney General pursuant to section 235(b)(1)(C) [8 U.S.C.A. § 1225(b)(1)(C)].

(3) Challenges on validity of the system

(A) In general

Judicial review of determinations under section 235(b) [8 U.S.C.A. § 1225(b)] and its implementation is available in an action instituted in the United States District Court for the District of Columbia, but shall be limited to determinations of—

(i) whether such section, or any regulation issued to implement such section, is constitutional; or

(ii) whether such a regulation, or a written policy directive, written policy guideline, or written procedure issued by or under the authority of the Attorney General to implement such section, is not consistent with applicable provisions of this title or is otherwise in violation of law.

(B) Deadlines for bringing actions

Any action instituted under this paragraph must be filed no later than 60 days after the date the challenged section, regulation, directive, guideline, or procedure described in clause (i) or (ii) of subparagraph (A) is first implemented.

(C) Notice of appeal

A notice of appeal of an order issued by the District Court under this paragraph may be filed not later than 30 days after the date of issuance of such order.

(D) Expeditious consideration of cases

It shall be the duty of the District Court, the Court of Appeals, and the Supreme Court of the United States to advance on the docket and to expedite to the greatest possible extent the disposition of any case considered under this paragraph.

(4) Decision

In any case where the court determines that the petitioner—

(A) is an alien who was not ordered removed under section 235(b)(1) [8 U.S.C.A. § 1225(b)(1)], or

(B) has demonstrated by a preponderance of the evidence that the alien is an alien lawfully admitted for permanent residence, has been admitted as a refugee under section 207 [8 U.S.C.A. § 1157], or has been granted asylum under section 208 [8 U.S.C.A. § 1158],

the court may order no remedy or relief other than to require that the petitioner be provided a hearing in accordance with section 240 [8 U.S.C.A. § 1229a]. Any alien who is provided a hearing under section 240 [8 U.S.C.A. § 1229a] pursuant to this paragraph may thereafter obtain judicial review of any resulting final order of removal pursuant to subsection (a)(1) of this section.

(5) Scope of inquiry

In determining whether an alien has been ordered removed under section 235(b)(1) [8 U.S.C.A. § 1225(b)(1)], the court's inquiry shall be limited to whether such an order in fact was issued and whether it relates to the petitioner. There shall be no review of whether the alien is actually inadmissible or entitled to any relief from removal.

(f) Limit on injunctive relief

(1) In general

Regardless of the nature of the action or claim or of the identity of the party or parties bringing the action, no court (other than the Supreme Court) shall have jurisdiction or authority to enjoin or restrain the operation of the provisions of chapter 4 of title II, as amended by the Illegal Immigration Reform and Immigrant Responsibility Act of 1996, other than with respect to the application of such provisions to an individual alien against whom proceedings under such part have been initiated.

(2) Particular cases

Notwithstanding any other provision of law, no court shall enjoin the removal of any alien pursuant to a final order under this section unless the alien shows by clear and convincing evidence that the entry or execution of such order is prohibited as a matter of law.

(g) Exclusive jurisdiction

Except as provided in this section and notwithstanding any other provision of law (statutory or nonstatutory), including section 2241 of title 28, United States Code, or any other habeas corpus provision, and sections 1361 and 1651 of such title, no court shall have jurisdiction to hear any cause or claim by or on behalf of any alien arising from the decision or action by the Attorney General to commence proceedings, adjudicate cases, or execute removal orders against any alien under this Act.

(June 27, 1952, c. 477, Title II, ch. 5, § 242, 66 Stat. 208; Sept. 3, 1954, c. 1263, § 17, 68 Stat. 1232; Dec. 29, 1981, Pub.L. 97–116, § 18(h)(1), 95 Stat. 1620; Oct. 12, 1984, Pub.L. 98–473, Title II, § 220(b), 98 Stat. 2028; Nov. 6, 1986, Pub.L. 99–603, Title VII, § 701, 100 Stat. 3445; Oct. 24, 1988, Pub.L. 100–525, § 9(n) 102 Stat. 2620; Nov. 18, 1988, Pub.L. 100–690, Title VII, § 7343(a), 102 Stat. 4470; Nov. 29, 1990, Pub.L. 101–649, Title V, §§ 504(a), 545(e), Title VI, § 603(b)(2), 104 Stat. 5049, 5066, 5085; Dec. 12, 1991, Pub.L. 102–232, Title III, §§ 306(a)(4), (c)(7), 307(m)(2), 309(b)(9), 105 Stat. 1751, 1753, 1757, 1759; Sept. 13, 1994, Pub.L. 103–322, Title II, § 20301(a), Title XIII, § 130001(a), 108 Stat. 1823, 2023; Oct. 25, 1994, Pub.L. 103–416, Title II, §§ 219(h), 224(b), 108 Stat. 4317, 4324; Apr. 24, 1996, Pub.L. 104–132, Title IV, §§ 436(a), (b)(1), 438(a), 440(c), (h), 110 Stat. 1275, 1277, 1279; Sept. 30, 1996, Pub.L. 104–208, Div. C, Title III, §§ 306(a), (d), 308(g)(10)(H), 371(b)(6), 110 Stat. 3009–607, 3009–612, 3009–625, 3009–645; May 11, 2005, Pub.L. 109–13, Div. B, § 101(e), (f), 106, 119 Stat. 231, 305, 310–11.)

§ 243. Penalties related to removal [8 U.S.C.A. § 1253]

(a) Penalty for failure to depart

(1) In general

Any alien against whom a final order of removal is outstanding by reason of being a member of any of the classes described in section 237(a) [8 U.S.C.A. § 1227(a)], who—

(A) willfully fails or refuses to depart from the United States within a period of 90 days from the date of the final order of removal under administrative processes, or if judicial review is had, then from the date of the final order of the court,

(B) willfully fails or refuses to make timely application in good faith for travel or other documents necessary to the alien's departure,

(C) connives or conspires, or takes any other action, designed to prevent or hamper or with the purpose of preventing or hampering the alien's departure pursuant to such, or

(D) willfully fails or refuses to present himself or herself for removal at the time and place required by the Attorney General pursuant to such order,

shall be fined under Title 18, or imprisoned not more than four years (or 10 years if the alien is a member of any of the classes described in paragraph (1)(E), (2), (3), or (4) of section 237(a) [8 U.S.C.A. § 1227(a)]), or both.

(2) Exception

It is not a violation of paragraph (1) to take any proper steps for the purpose of securing cancellation of or exemption from such order of removal or for the purpose of securing the alien's release from incarceration or custody.

(3) Suspension

The court may for good cause suspend the sentence of an alien under this subsection and order the alien's release under such conditions as the court may prescribe. In determining whether good cause has been shown to justify releasing the alien, the court shall take into account such factors as—

(A) the age, health, and period of detention of the alien;

(B) the effect of the alien's release upon the national security and public peace or safety;

(C) the likelihood of the alien's resuming or following a course of conduct which made or would make the alien deportable;

(D) the character of the efforts made by such alien himself and by representatives of the country or countries to which the alien's removal is directed to expedite the alien's departure from the United States;

(E) the reason for the inability of the Government of the United States to secure passports, other travel documents, or removal facilities from the country or countries to which the alien has been ordered removed; and

(F) the eligibility of the alien for discretionary relief under the immigration laws.

(b) Willful failure to comply with terms of release under supervision

An alien who shall willfully fail to comply with regulations or requirements issued pursuant to section 241(a)(3) [8 U.S.C.A. § 1231(a)(3)] or knowingly give false information in response to an inquiry under such section shall be fined not more than $1,000 or imprisoned for not more than one year, or both.

(c) Penalties relating to vessels and aircraft

(1) Civil penalties

(A) Failure to carry out certain orders

If the Attorney General is satisfied that a person has violated subsection (d) or (e) of section 241 [8 U.S.C.A. § 1231], the person shall pay to the Commissioner the sum of $2,000 for each violation.

(B) Failure to remove alien stowaways

If the Attorney General is satisfied that a person has failed to remove an alien stowaway as required under section

241(d)(2) [8 U.S.C.A. § 1231(d)(2)], the person shall pay to the Commissioner the sum of $5,000 for each alien stowaway not removed.

(C) No compromise

The Attorney General may not compromise the amount of such penalty under this paragraph.

(2) Clearing vessels and aircraft

(A) Clearance before decision on liability

A vessel or aircraft may be granted clearance before a decision on liability is made under paragraph (1) only if a bond approved by the Attorney General or an amount sufficient to pay the civil penalty is deposited with the Commissioner.

(B) Prohibition on clearance while penalty unpaid

A vessel or aircraft may not be granted clearance if a civil penalty imposed under paragraph (1) is not paid.

(d) Discontinuing granting visas to nationals of country denying or delaying accepting alien

On being notified by the Attorney General that the government of a foreign country denies or unreasonably delays accepting an alien who is a citizen, subject, national, or resident of that country after the Attorney General asks whether the government will accept the alien under this section, the Secretary of State shall order consular officers in that foreign country to discontinue granting immigrant visas or nonimmigrant visas, or both, to citizens, subjects, nationals, and residents of that country until the Attorney General notifies the Secretary that the country has accepted the alien.

(June 27, 1952, c. 477, Title II, ch. 5, § 243, 66 Stat. 212; Oct. 3, 1965, Pub.L. 89–236, § 11(f), 79 Stat. 918; Oct. 30, 1978, Pub.L. 95–549, Title I, § 104, 92 Stat. 2066; Mar. 17, 1980, Pub.L. 96–212, Title II, § 203(e), 94 Stat. 107; Dec. 29, 1981, Pub.L. 97–116, § 18(i), 95 Stat. 1620; Nov. 29, 1990, Pub.L. 101–649, Title V, § 515(a)(2), Title VI, § 603(b)(3), 104 Stat. 5053, 5085; Apr. 24, 1996, Pub.L. 104–132, Title IV, § 413(a), (f), 110 Stat. 1269; Sept. 30, 1996, Pub.L. 104–208, Div. C, Title III, § 307(a), 110 Stat. 3009–612.)

§ 244. Temporary protected status [8 U.S.C.A. § 1254a]

(a) Granting of status

(1) In general

In the case of an alien who is a national of a foreign state designated under subsection (b) (or in the case of an alien having no nationality, is a person who last habitually resided in such designated state) and who meets the requirements of subsection (c), the Attorney General, in accordance with this section—

(A) may grant the alien temporary protected status in the United States and shall not remove the alien from the United States during the period in which such status is in effect, and

(B) shall authorize the alien to engage in employment in the United States and provide the alien with an "employment authorized" endorsement or other appropriate work permit.

(2) Duration of work authorization

Work authorization provided under this section shall be effective throughout the period the alien is in temporary protected status under this section.

(3) Notice

(A) Upon the granting of temporary protected status under this section, the Attorney General shall provide the alien with information concerning such status under this section.

(B) If, at the time of initiation of a removal proceeding against an alien, the foreign state (of which the alien is a national) is designated under subsection (b), the Attorney General shall promptly notify the alien of the temporary protected status that may be available under this section.

(C) If, at the time of designation of a foreign state under subsection (b), an alien (who is a national of such state) is in a removal proceeding under this title, the Attorney General shall promptly notify the alien of the temporary protected status that may be available under this section.

(D) Notices under this paragraph shall be provided in a form and language that the alien can understand.

(4) Temporary treatment for eligible aliens

(A) In the case of an alien who can establish a prima facie case of eligibility for benefits under paragraph (1), but for the fact that the period of registration under subsection (c)(1)(A)(iv) has not begun, until the alien has had a reasonable opportunity to register during the first 30 days of such period, the Attorney General shall provide for the benefits of paragraph (1).

(B) In the case of an alien who establishes a prima facie case of eligibility for benefits under paragraph (1), until a final determination with respect to the alien's eligibility for such benefits under paragraph (1) has been made, the alien shall be provided such benefits.

(5) Clarification

Nothing in this section shall be construed as authorizing the Attorney General to deny temporary protected status to an alien based on the alien's immigration status or to require any alien, as a condition of being granted such status, either to relinquish nonimmigrant or other status the alien may have or to execute any waiver of other rights under this Act. The granting of temporary protected status under this section shall not be considered to be inconsistent with the granting of nonimmigrant status under this Act.

(b) Designations

(1) In general

The Attorney General, after consultation with appropriate agencies of the Government, may designate any foreign state (or any part of such foreign state) under this subsection only if—

(A) the Attorney General finds that there is an ongoing armed conflict within the state and, due to such conflict, requiring the return of aliens who are nationals of that state to that state (or to the part of the state) would pose a serious threat to their personal safety;

(B) the Attorney General finds that—

(i) there has been an earthquake, flood, drought, epidemic, or other environmental disaster in the state resulting in a substantial, but temporary, disruption of living conditions in the area affected,

(ii) the foreign state is unable, temporarily, to handle adequately the return to the state of aliens who are nationals of the state, and

(iii) the foreign state officially has requested designation under this subparagraph; or

(C) the Attorney General finds that there exist extraordinary and temporary conditions in the foreign state that prevent aliens who are nationals of the state from returning to the state in safety, unless the Attorney General finds that permitting the aliens to remain temporarily in the United States is contrary to the national interest of the United States.

A designation of a foreign state (or part of such foreign state) under this paragraph shall not become effective unless notice of the designation (including a statement of the findings under this paragraph and the effective date of the designation) is published in the Federal Register. In such notice, the Attorney General shall also state an estimate of the number of nationals of the foreign state designated who are (or within the effective period of the designation are likely to become) eligible for temporary protected status under this section and their immigration status in the United States.

(2) Effective period of designation for foreign states

The designation of a foreign state (or part of such foreign state) under paragraph (1) shall—

(A) take effect upon the date of publication of the designation under such paragraph, or such later date as the Attorney

General may specify in the notice published under such paragraph, and

(B) shall remain in effect until the effective date of the termination of the designation under paragraph (3)(B).

For purposes of this section, the initial period of designation of a foreign state (or part thereof) under paragraph (1) is the period, specified by the Attorney General, of not less than 6 months and not more than 18 months.

(3) Periodic review, terminations, and extensions of designations

(A) Periodic review

At least 60 days before end of the initial period of designation, and any extended period of designation, of a foreign state (or part thereof) under this section the Attorney General, after consultation with appropriate agencies of the Government, shall review the conditions in the foreign state (or part of such foreign state) for which a designation is in effect under this subsection and shall determine whether the conditions for such designation under this subsection continue to be met. The Attorney General shall provide on a timely basis for the publication of notice of each such determination (including the basis for the determination, and, in the case of an affirmative determination, the period of extension of designation under subparagraph (C)) in the Federal Register.

(B) Termination of designation

If the Attorney General determines under subparagraph (A) that a foreign state (or part of such foreign state) no longer continues to meet the conditions for designation under paragraph (1), the Attorney General shall terminate the designation by publishing notice in the Federal Register of the determination under this subparagraph (including the basis for the determination). Such termination is effective in accordance with subsection (d)(3), but shall not be effective earlier than 60 days after the date the notice is published or, if later, the expiration of the most recent previous extension under subparagraph (C).

(C) Extension of designation

If the Attorney General does not determine under subparagraph (A) that a foreign state (or part of such foreign state) no longer meets the conditions for designation under paragraph (1), the period of designation of the foreign state is extended for an additional period of 6 months (or, in the discretion of the Attorney General, a period of 12 or 18 months).

(4) Information concerning protected status at time of designations

At the time of a designation of a foreign state under this subsection, the Attorney General shall make available information respecting the temporary protected status made available to aliens who are nationals of such designated foreign state.

(5) Review

(A) Designations

There is no judicial review of any determination of the Attorney General with respect to the designation, or termination or extension of a designation, of a foreign state under this subsection.

(B) Application to individuals

The Attorney General shall establish an administrative procedure for the review of the denial of benefits to aliens under this subsection. Such procedure shall not prevent an alien from asserting protection under this section in removal proceedings if the alien demonstrates that the alien is a national of a state designated under paragraph (1).

(c) Aliens eligible for temporary protected status

(1) In general

(A) Nationals of designated foreign states

Subject to paragraph (3), an alien, who is a national of a state designated under subsection (b)(1) (or in the case of an alien having no nationality, is a person who last habitually resided in such designated state) meets the requirements of this paragraph only if—

(i) the alien has been continuously physically present in the United States since the effective date of the most recent designation of that state;

(ii) the alien has continuously resided in the United States since such date as the Attorney General may designate;

(iii) the alien is admissible as an immigrant, except as otherwise provided under paragraph (2)(A), and is not ineligible for temporary protected status under paragraph (2)(B); and

(iv) to the extent and in a manner which the Attorney General establishes, the alien registers for the temporary protected status under this section during a registration period of not less than 180 days.

(B) Registration fee

The Attorney General may require payment of a reasonable fee as a condition of registering an alien under subparagraph (A)(iv) (including providing an alien with an "employment authorized" endorsement or other appropriate work permit under this section). The amount of any such fee shall not exceed $50. In the case of aliens registered pursuant to a designation under this section made after July 17, 1991, the Attorney General may impose a separate, additional fee for providing an alien with documentation of work authorization. Notwithstanding section 3302 of Title 31, all fees collected under this subparagraph shall be credited to the appropriation to be used in carrying out this section.

(2) Eligibility standards

(A) Waiver of certain grounds for inadmissibility

In the determination of an alien's admissibility for purposes of subparagraph (A)(iii) of paragraph (1)—

(i) the provisions of paragraphs (5) and (7)(A) of section 212(a) [8 U.S.C.A. § 1182(a)] shall not apply;

(ii) except as provided in clause (iii), the Attorney General may waive any other provision of section 212(a) [8 U.S.C.A. § 1182(a)] in the case of individual aliens for humanitarian purposes, to assure family unity, or when it is otherwise in the public interest; but

(iii) the Attorney General may not waive—

(I) paragraphs (2)(A) and (2)(B) (relating to criminals) of such section,

(II) paragraph (2)(C) of such section (relating to drug offenses), except for so much of such paragraph as relates to a single offense of simple possession of 30 grams or less of marijuana, or

(III) paragraphs (3)(A), (3)(B), (3)(C), and (3)(E) of such section (relating to national security and participation in the Nazi persecutions or those who have engaged in genocide).

(B) Aliens ineligible

An alien shall not be eligible for temporary protected status under this section if the Attorney General finds that—

(i) the alien has been convicted of any felony or 2 or more misdemeanors committed in the United States, or

(ii) the alien is described in section 208(b)(2)(A) [8 U.S.C.A. § 1158(b)(2)(A)].

(3) Withdrawal of temporary protected status

The Attorney General shall withdraw temporary protected status granted to an alien under this section if—

(A) the Attorney General finds that the alien was not in fact eligible for such status under this section,

(B) except as provided in paragraph (4) and permitted in subsection (f)(3), the alien has not remained continuously physically present in the United States from the date the alien first was granted temporary protected status under this section, or

(C) the alien fails, without good cause, to register with the Attorney General annually, at the end of each 12–month period after the granting of such status, in a form and manner specified by the Attorney General.

(4) Treatment of brief, casual, and innocent departures and certain other absences

(A) For purposes of paragraphs (1)(A)(i) and (3)(B), an alien shall not be considered to have failed to maintain continuous physical presence in the United States by virtue of brief, casual, and innocent absences from the United States, without regard to whether such absences were authorized by the Attorney General.

(B) For purposes of paragraph (1)(A)(ii), an alien shall not be considered to have failed to maintain continuous residence in the United States by reason of a brief, casual, and innocent absence described in subparagraph (A) or due merely to a brief temporary trip abroad required by emergency or extenuating circumstances outside the control of the alien.

(5) Construction

Nothing in this section shall be construed as authorizing an alien to apply for admission to, or to be admitted to, the United States in order to apply for temporary protected status under this section.

(6) Confidentiality of information

The Attorney General shall establish procedures to protect the confidentiality of information provided by aliens under this section.

(d) Documentation

(1) Initial issuance

Upon the granting of temporary protected status to an alien under this section, the Attorney General shall provide for the issuance of such temporary documentation and authorization as may be necessary to carry out the purposes of this section.

(2) Period of validity

Subject to paragraph (3), such documentation shall be valid during the initial period of designation of the foreign state (or part thereof) involved and any extension of such period. The Attorney General may stagger the periods of validity of the documentation and authorization in order to provide for an orderly renewal of such documentation and authorization and for an orderly transition (under paragraph (3)) upon the termination of a designation of a foreign state (or any part of such foreign state).

(3) Effective date of terminations

If the Attorney General terminates the designation of a foreign state (or part of such foreign state) under subsection (b)(3)(B), such termination shall only apply to documentation and authorization issued or renewed after the effective date of the publication of notice of the determination under that subsection (or, at the Attorney General's option, after such period after the effective date of the determination as the Attorney General determines to be appropriate in order to provide for an orderly transition).

(4) Detention of the alien

An alien provided temporary protected status under this section shall not be detained by the Attorney General on the basis of the alien's immigration status in the United States.

(e) Relation of period of temporary protected status to cancellation of removal

With respect to an alien granted temporary protected status under this section, the period of such status shall not be counted as a period of physical presence in the United States for purposes of section 240A(a) [8 U.S.C.A. § 1229b(a)], unless the Attorney General determines that extreme hardship exists. Such period shall not cause a break in the continuity of residence of the period before and after such period for purposes of such section.

(f) Benefits and status during period of temporary protected status

During a period in which an alien is granted temporary protected status under this section—

(1) the alien shall not be considered to be permanently residing in the United States under color of law;

(2) the alien may be deemed ineligible for public assistance by a State (as defined in section 101(a)(36) [8 U.S.C.A. § 1101(a)(36)]) or any political subdivision thereof which furnishes such assistance;

(3) the alien may travel abroad with the prior consent of the Attorney General; and

(4) for purposes of adjustment of status under section 245 [8 U.S.C.A. § 1255] and change of status under section 248 [8 U.S.C.A. § 1258], the alien shall be considered as being in, and maintaining, lawful status as a nonimmigrant.

(g) Exclusive remedy

Except as otherwise specifically provided, this section shall constitute the exclusive authority of the Attorney General under law to permit aliens who are or may become otherwise deportable or have been paroled into the United States to remain in the United States temporarily because of their particular nationality or region of foreign state of nationality.

(h) Limitation on consideration in Senate of legislation adjusting status

(1) In general

Except as provided in paragraph (2), it shall not be in order in the Senate to consider any bill, resolution, or amendment that—

(A) provides for adjustment to lawful temporary or permanent resident alien status for any alien receiving temporary protected status under this section, or

(B) has the effect of amending this subsection or limiting the application of this subsection.

(2) Supermajority required

Paragraph (1) may be waived or suspended in the Senate only by the affirmative vote of three-fifths of the Members duly chosen and sworn. An affirmative vote of three-fifths of the Members of the Senate duly chosen and sworn shall be required in the Senate to sustain an appeal of the ruling of the Chair on a point of order raised under paragraph (1).

(3) Rules

Paragraphs (1) and (2) are enacted—

(A) as an exercise of the rulemaking power of the Senate and as such they are deemed a part of the rules of the Senate, but applicable only with respect to the matters described in paragraph (1) and supersede other rules of the Senate only to the extent that such paragraphs are inconsistent therewith; and

(B) with full recognition of the constitutional right of the Senate to change such rules at any time, in the same manner as in the case of any other rule of the Senate.

(i) Annual report and review

(1) Annual report

Not later than March 1 of each year (beginning with 1992), the Attorney General, after consultation with the appropriate agencies of the Government, shall submit a report to the Committees on the Judiciary of the House of Representatives and of the Senate on the operation of this section during the previous year. Each report shall include—

(A) a listing of the foreign states or parts thereof designated under this section,

(B) the number of nationals of each such state who have been granted temporary protected status under this section and their immigration status before being granted such status, and

(C) an explanation of the reasons why foreign states or parts thereof were designated under subsection (b)(1) and, with respect to foreign states or parts thereof previously designated, why the designation was terminated or extended under subsection (b)(3).

(2) Committee report

No later than 180 days after the date of receipt of such a report, the Committee on the Judiciary of each House of Congress shall report to its respective House such oversight findings and legislation as it deems appropriate.

(June 27, 1952, c. 477, Title II, ch. 5, § 244, formerly § 244A, as added and amended Nov. 29, 1990, Pub.L. 101–649, Title III, § 302(a), Title VI, § 603(a)(24), 104 Stat. 5030, 5084; Dec. 12, 1991, Pub.L. 102–232, Title III, §§ 304(b), 307(*l*)(5), 105 Stat. 1749, 1756; Oct. 25, 1994, Pub.L. 103–416, Title II, § 219(j), (z)(2), 108 Stat. 4317, 4318; renumbered § 244 and amended Sept. 30, 1996, Pub.L. 104–208, Div. C, Title III, § 308(b)(7), (e)(1)(G), (11), (g)(7)(E)(i), (g)(8)(A)(i), 110 Stat. 3009–615, 3009–619, 3009–620, 3009–624.)

CHAPTER V—ADJUSTMENT AND CHANGE OF STATUS*

§ 245. Adjustment of status of nonimmigrant to that of person admitted for permanent residence [8 U.S.C.A. § 1255]

(a) Status as person admitted for permanent residence on application and eligibility for immigrant visa

The status of an alien who was inspected and admitted or paroled into the United States or the status of any other alien having an approved petition for classification as a VAWA self-petitioner may be adjusted by the Attorney General, in his discretion and under such regulations as he may prescribe, to that of an alien lawfully admitted for permanent residence if **(1)** the alien makes an application for such adjustment, **(2)** the alien is eligible to receive an immigrant visa and is admissible to the United States for permanent residence, and **(3)** an immigrant visa is immediately available to him at the time his application is filed.

(b) Record of lawful admission for permanent residence; reduction of preference visas

Upon the approval of an application for adjustment made under subsection (a), the Attorney General shall record the alien's lawful admission for permanent residence as of the date the order of the Attorney General approving the application for the adjustment of status is made, and the Secretary of State shall reduce by one the number of

* Pub.L. 104–208, section 308(a)(2), amended the table of contents of the Immigration and Nationality Act to show that renumbered §§ 242 to 244 are part of chapter IV, with chapter V starting with § 245. This suggests Congressional intent to move §§ 242 to 244 to chapter IV, but there is no specific directory language that actually moves these sections.

the preference visas authorized to be issued under sections 202 [8 U.S.C.A. § 1152] and 203 [8 U.S.C.A. § 1153] within the class to which the alien is chargeable for the fiscal year then current.

(c) Alien crewmen, aliens continuing or accepting unauthorized employment, and aliens admitted in transit without visa

Other than an alien having an approved petition for classification as a VAWA self-petitioner, subsection (a) of this section shall not be applicable to **(1)** an alien crewman; **(2)** subject to subsection (k) of this section, an alien (other than an immediate relative as defined in section 201(b) [8 U.S.C.A. § 1151(b)] or a special immigrant described in section 101(a)(27)(H), (I), (J), or (K) [8 U.S.C.A. § 1101(a)(27)(H), (I), (J), or (K)]) who hereafter continues in or accepts unauthorized employment prior to filing an application for adjustment of status or who is in unlawful immigration status on the date of filing the application for adjustment of status or who has failed (other than through no fault of his own or for technical reasons) to maintain continuously a lawful status since entry into the United States; **(3)** any alien admitted in transit without visa under section 212(d)(4)(C) [8 U.S.C.A. § 1182(d)(4)(C)]; **(4)** an alien (other than an immediate relative as defined in section 201(b) [8 U.S.C.A. § 1151(b)]) who was admitted as a nonimmigrant visitor without a visa under section 212(*l*) [8 U.S.C.A. § 1182(*l*)] or section 217 [8 U.S.C.A. § 1187]; **(5)** an alien who was admitted as a nonimmigrant described in section 101(a)(15)(S) [8 U.S.C.A. § 1101(a)(15)(S)], [sic]* **(6)** an alien who is deportable under section 237(a)(4)(B) [8 U.S.C.A. § 1227(a)(4)(B)]; **(7)** any alien who seeks adjustment of status to that of an immigrant under section 203(b) [8 U.S.C.A. § 1153(b)] and is not in a lawful nonimmigrant status; or **(8)** any alien who was employed while the alien was an unauthorized alien, as defined in section 274A(h)(3) [8 U.S.C.A. § 1324a(h)(3)], or who has otherwise violated the terms of a nonimmigrant visa.

(d) Alien admitted for permanent residence on conditional basis; fiancée or fiancé of citizen

The Attorney General may not adjust, under subsection (a), the status of an alien lawfully admitted to the United States for permanent residence on a conditional basis under section 216 [8 U.S.C.A. § 1186a]. The Attorney General may not adjust, under subsection (a), the status of a nonimmigrant alien described in section 101(a)(15)(K) [8 U.S.C.A. § 1101(a)(15)(K)] except to that of an alien lawfully admitted to the United States on a conditional basis under section 216 [8 U.S.C.A. § 1186a] as a result of the marriage of the nonimmigrant (or, in the case of a minor child, the parent) to the citizen who filed the petition to accord that alien's nonimmigrant status under section 101(a)(15)(K) [8 U.S.C.A. § 1101(a)(15)(K)].

* Comma probably should be a semi-colon.

(e) Restrictions on adjustment of status based on marriages entered while in exclusion or deportation proceedings; bona fide marriage exception

(1) Except as provided in paragraph (3), an alien who is seeking to receive an immigrant visa on the basis of a marriage which was entered into during the period described in paragraph (2) may not have the alien's status adjusted under subsection (a).

(2) The period described in this paragraph is the period during which administrative or judicial proceedings are pending regarding the alien's right to be admitted or remain in the United States.

(3) Paragraph (1) and section 204(g) [8 U.S.C.A. § 1154(g)] shall not apply with respect to a marriage if the alien establishes by clear and convincing evidence to the satisfaction of the Attorney General that the marriage was entered into in good faith and in accordance with the laws of the place where the marriage took place and the marriage was not entered into for the purpose of procuring the alien's admission as an immigrant and no fee or other consideration was given (other than a fee or other consideration to an attorney for assistance in preparation of a lawful petition) for the filing of a petition under section 204(a) [8 U.S.C.A. § 1154(a)] or subsection (d) or (p) of section 214 [8 U.S.C.A. § 1184] with respect to the alien spouse or alien son or daughter. In accordance with regulations, there shall be only one level of administrative appellate review for each alien under the previous sentence.

(f) Limitation on adjustment of status

The Attorney General may not adjust, under subsection (a), the status of an alien lawfully admitted to the United States for permanent residence on a conditional basis under section 216A [8 U.S.C.A. § 1186b].

(g) Special immigrants

In applying this section to a special immigrant described in section 101(a)(27)(K) [8 U.S.C.A. § 1101(a)(27)(K)], such an immigrant shall be deemed, for purposes of subsection (a), to have been paroled into the United States.

(h) Application with respect to special immigrants

In applying this section to a special immigrant described in section 101(a)(27)(J) [8 U.S.C.A. § 1101(a)(27)(J)]—

(1) such an immigrant shall be deemed, for purposes of subsection (a), to have been paroled into the United States; and

(2) in determining the alien's admissibility as an immigrant—

(A) paragraphs (4), (5)(A), (6)(A), (6)(C), (6)(D), (7)(A), and (9)(B) of section 212(a) [8 U.S.C.A. § 1182(a)] shall not apply; and

(B) the Attorney General may waive other paragraphs of section 212(a) [8 U.S.C.A. § 1182(a)] (other than paragraphs (2)(A), (2)(B), (2)(C) (except for so much of such paragraph as related to a single offense of simple possession of 30 grams or less of marijuana), (3)(A), (3)(B), (3)(C), and (3)(E)) in the case of individual aliens for humanitarian purposes, family unity, or when it is otherwise in the public interest.

The relationship between an alien and the alien's natural parents or prior adoptive parents shall not be considered a factor in making a waiver under paragraph (2)(B). Nothing in this subsection or section 101(a)(27)(J) [8 U.S.C.A. § 1101(a)(27)(J)] shall be construed as authorizing an alien to apply for admission or be admitted to the United States in order to obtain special immigrant status described in such section.

(i) Adjustment of status of certain aliens physically present in United States

(1) Notwithstanding the provisions of subsections (a) and (c) of this section, an alien physically present in the United States—

(A) who—

(i) entered the United States without inspection; or

(ii) is within one of the classes enumerated in subsection (c) of this section;

(B) who is the beneficiary (including a spouse or child of the principal alien, if eligible to receive a visa under section 203(d) [8 U.S.C.A. § 1153(d)]) of—

(i) a petition for classification under section 204 [8 U.S.C.A. § 1154] that was filed with the Attorney General on or before April 30, 2001; or

(ii) an application for a labor certification under section 212(a)(5)(A) [8 U.S.C.A. § 1182(a)(5)(A)] that was filed pursuant to the regulations of the Secretary of Labor on or before such date; and

(C) who, in the case of a beneficiary of a petition for classification, or an application for labor certification, described in subparagraph (B) that was filed after January 14, 1998, is physically present in the United States on the date of the enactment of the LIFE Act Amendments of 2000 [December 21, 2000];

may apply to the Attorney General for the adjustment of his or her status to that of an alien lawfully admitted for permanent residence. The Attorney General may accept such application only if the alien remits with such application a sum equalling $1,000 as of the date of receipt of the application, but such sum shall not be required from a child under the age of seventeen, or an alien who is the spouse or unmarried child of an individual who obtained temporary or permanent resident status under section 210 [8 U.S.C.A. § 1160] or 245A [8 U.S.C.A. § 1255a] or section 202 of the Immigration Reform and Control Act of 1986 at any date, who—

(i) as of May 5, 1988, was the unmarried child or spouse of the individual who obtained temporary or permanent resident status under section 210 [8 U.S.C.A. § 1160] or 245A [8 U.S.C.A. § 1255a] or section 202 of the Immigration Reform and Control Act of 1986;

(ii) entered the United States before May 5, 1988, resided in the United States on May 5, 1988, and is not a lawful permanent resident; and

(iii) applied for benefits under section 301(a) of the Immigration Act of 1990. The sum specified herein shall be in addition to the fee normally required for the processing of an application under this section.

(2) Upon receipt of such an application and the sum hereby required, the Attorney General may adjust the status of the alien to that of an alien lawfully admitted for permanent residence if—

(A) the alien is eligible to receive an immigrant visa and is admissible to the United States for permanent residence; and

(B) an immigrant visa is immediately available to the alien at the time the application is filed.

(3)(A) The portion of each application fee (not to exceed $200) that the Attorney General determines is required to process an application under this section and is remitted to the Attorney General pursuant to paragraphs (1) and (2) of this subsection shall be disposed of by the Attorney General as provided in subsections (m), (n), and (*o*) of section 286 [8 U.S.C.A. § 1356].

(B) Any remaining portion of such fees remitted under such paragraphs shall be deposited by the Attorney General into the Breached Bond/Detention Fund established under section 286(r) [8 U.S.C.A. § 1356(r)], except that in the case of fees attributable to applications for a beneficiary with respect to whom a petition for classification, or an application for labor certification, described in paragraph (1)(B) was filed after January 14, 1998, one-half of such remaining portion shall be deposited by the Attorney General into the Immigration Examinations Fee Account established under section 286(m) [8 U.S.C.A. § 1356(m)].

(j) Adjustment to permanent resident status of "S" visa nonimmigrants

(1) If, in the opinion of the Attorney General—

(A) a nonimmigrant admitted into the United States under section 101(a)(15)(S)(i) [8 U.S.C.A. § 1101(a)(15)(S)(i)] has supplied information described in subclause (I) of such section; and

(B) the provision of such information has substantially contributed to the success of an authorized criminal investigation or the prosecution of an individual described in subclause (III) of that section,

the Attorney General may adjust the status of the alien (and the spouse, married and unmarried sons and daughters, and parents of the alien if admitted under that section) to that of an alien lawfully admitted for permanent residence if the alien is not described in section 212(a)(3)(E) [8 U.S.C.A. § 1182(a)(3)(E)].

(2) If, in the sole discretion of the Attorney General—

(A) a nonimmigrant admitted into the United States under section 101(a)(15)(S)(ii) [8 U.S.C.A. § 1101(a)(15)(S)(ii)] has supplied information described in subclause (I) of such section, and

(B) the provision of such information has substantially contributed to—

(i) the prevention or frustration of an act of terrorism against a United States person or United States property, or

(ii) the success of an authorized criminal investigation of, or the prosecution of, an individual involved in such an act of terrorism, and

(C) the nonimmigrant has received a reward under section 2708(a) of Title 22,

the Attorney General may adjust the status of the alien (and the spouse, married and unmarried sons and daughters, and parents of the alien if admitted under such section) to that of an alien lawfully admitted for permanent residence if the alien is not described in section 212(a)(3)(E) [8 U.S.C.A. § 1182(a)(3)(E)].

(3) Upon the approval of adjustment of status under paragraph (1) or (2), the Attorney General shall record the alien's lawful admission for permanent residence as of the date of such approval and the Secretary of State shall reduce by one the number of visas authorized to be issued under sections 201(d) [8 U.S.C.A. § 1151(d)] and 203(b)(4) [8 U.S.C.A. § 1153(b)(4)] for the fiscal year then current.

(k) Inapplicability of certain provisions for certain employment-based immigrants

An alien who is eligible to receive an immigrant visa under paragraph (1), (2), or (3) of section 203(b) [8 U.S.C.A. § 1153(b)] (or, in the case of an alien who is an immigrant described in section 101(a)(27)(C) [8 U.S.C.A. § 1101(a)(27)(C)], under section 203(b)(4) [8 U.S.C.A. § 1153(b)(4)]) may adjust status pursuant to subsection (a) and notwithstanding subsection (c)(2), (c)(7), and (c)(8), if—

(1) the alien, on the date of filing an application for adjustment of status, is present in the United States pursuant to a lawful admission;

(2) the alien, subsequent to such lawful admission has not, for an aggregate period exceeding 180 days—

(A) failed to maintain, continuously, a lawful status;

(B) engaged in unauthorized employment; or

(C) otherwise violated the terms and conditions of the alien's admission.

(*l*) Adjustment of status for victims of trafficking

(1) If, in the opinion of the Secretary of Homeland Security, or in the case of subparagraph (C)(i), in the opinion of the Secretary of Homeland Security, in consultation with the Attorney General, as appropriate a nonimmigrant admitted into the United States under section 101(a)(15)(T)(i) [8 U.S.C.A. § 1101(a)(15)(T)(i)]—

(A) has been physically present in the United States for a continuous period of at least 3 years since the date of admission as a nonimmigrant under section 101(a)(15)(T)(i) [8 U.S.C.A. § 1101(a)(15)(T)(i)], or has been physically present in the United States for a continuous period during the investigation or prosecution of acts of trafficking and that, in the opinion of the Attorney General, the investigation or prosecution is complete, whichever period of time is less;

(B) subject to paragraph (6), has, throughout such period, been a person of good moral character; and

(C)(i) has, during such period, complied with any reasonable request for assistance in the investigation or prosecution of acts of trafficking;

(ii) the alien would suffer extreme hardship involving unusual and severe harm upon removal from the United States, the Secretary of Homeland Security may adjust the status of the alien (and any person admitted under section 101(a)(15)(T)(ii) [8 U.S.C.A. § 1101(a)(15)(T)(ii)] as the spouse, parent, sibling, or child of the alien) to that of an alien lawfully admitted for permanent residence; or

(iii) was younger than 18 years of age at the time of the victimization qualifying the alien for relief under section 101(a)(15)(T) [8 U.S.C.A. § 1101(a)(15)(T)].*

(2) Paragraph (1) shall not apply to an alien admitted under section 101(a)(15)(T) [8 U.S.C.A § 1101(a)(15)(T)] who is inadmissible to the United States by reason of a ground that has not been waived under section 212 [8 U.S.C.A § 1182], except that, if the

* Thus in original enactment (Pub. L. 110–457, § 201(d)), but the probable intent of Congress was to insert subparagraph (iii) immediately after subparagraph (ii).

Secretary of Homeland Security considers it to be in the National interest to do so, the Secretary of Homeland Security, in the Attorney General's discretion,** may waive the application of

(A) paragraphs (1) and (4) of section 212(a) [8 U.S.C.A. § 1182(a)]; and

(B) any other provision of such section (excluding paragraphs (3), (10)(C), and (10)(E)) [sic], if the activities rendering the alien inadmissible under the provision were caused by, or were incident to, the victimization described in section 101(a)(15)(T)(i)(I) [8 U.S.C.A. § 1101(a)(15)(T)(i)(I)].

(3) An alien shall be considered to have failed to maintain continuous physical presence in the United States under paragraph (1)(A) if the alien has departed from the United States for any period in excess of 90 days or for any periods in the aggregate exceeding 180 days, unless—

(A) the absence was necessary to assist in the investigation or prosecution described in paragraph (1)(A); or

(B) an official involved in the investigation or prosecution certifies that the absence was otherwise justified.

(4)(A) The total number of aliens whose status may be adjusted under paragraph (1) during any fiscal year may not exceed 5,000.

(B) The numerical limitation of subparagraph (A) shall only apply to principal aliens and not to the spouses, sons, daughters, siblings, or parents of such aliens.

(5) Upon the approval of adjustment of status under paragraph (1), the Secretary of Homeland Security shall record the alien's lawful admission for permanent residence as of the date of such approval.

(6) For purposes of paragraph (1)(B), the Secretary of Homeland Security may waive consideration of a disqualification from good moral character with respect to an alien if the disqualification was caused by, or incident to, the trafficking described in section 101(a)(15)(T)(i)(I) [8 U.S.C.A. § 1101(a)(15)(T)(i)(I)].

(7) The Secretary of Homeland Security shall permit aliens to apply for a waiver of any fees associated with filing an application for relief through final adjudication of the adjustment of status for a VAWA self-petitioner and for relief under sections 101(a)(15)(T) [8 U.S.C.A. § 1101(a)(15)(T)], 101(a)(15)(U) [8 U.S.C.A. § 1101(a)(15)(U)], 106 [8 U.S.C.A. § 1105a], 240A(b)(2) [8 U.S.C.A. § 1229b(b)(2)], and 244(a)(3) [8 U.S.C.A. § 1254a] (as in effect on March 31, 1997).

** So in original. The term "Attorney General's" probably should be "Secretary's".

(m) Adjustment of status for victims of crimes against women

(1) The Secretary of Homeland Security may adjust the status of an alien admitted into the United States (or otherwise provided nonimmigrant status) under section 101(a)(15)(U) [8 U.S.C.A. § 1101(a)(15)(U)] to that of an alien lawfully admitted for permanent residence if the alien is not described in section 212(a)(3)(E) [8 U.S.C.A. § 1182(a)(3)(E)], unless the Secretary determines based on affirmative evidence that the alien unreasonably refused to provide assistance in a criminal investigation or prosecution, if—

(A) the alien has been physically present in the United States for a continuous period of at least 3 years since the date of admission as a nonimmigrant under clause (i) or (ii) of section 101(a)(15)(U) [8 U.S.C.A. § 1101(a)(15)(U)]; and

(B) in the opinion of the Secretary of Homeland Security, the alien's continued presence in the United States is justified on humanitarian grounds, to ensure family unity, or is otherwise in the public interest.

(2) An alien shall be considered to have failed to maintain continuous physical presence in the United States under paragraph (1)(A) if the alien has departed from the United States for any period in excess of 90 days or for any periods in the aggregate exceeding 180 days unless the absence is in order to assist in the investigation or prosecution or unless an official involved in the investigation or prosecution certifies that the absence was otherwise justified.

(3) Upon approval of adjustment of status under paragraph (1) of an alien described in section 101(a)(15)(U)(i) [8 U.S.C.A § 1101(a)(15)(U)(i)] the Secretary of Homeland Security may adjust the status of or issue an immigrant visa to a spouse, a child, or, in the case of an alien child, a parent who did not receive a nonimmigrant visa under section 101(a)(15)(U)(ii) [8 U.S.C.A § 1101(a)(15)(U)(ii)] if the Secretary considers the grant of such status or visa necessary to avoid extreme hardship.

(4) Upon the approval of adjustment of status under paragraph (1) or (3), the Secretary of Homeland Security shall record the alien's lawful admission for permanent residence as of the date of such approval.

(5)(A) The Secretary of Homeland Security shall consult with the Attorney General, as appropriate, in making a determination under paragraph (1) whether affirmative evidence demonstrates that the alien unreasonably refused to provide assistance to a Federal law enforcement official, Federal prosecutor, Federal judge, or other Federal authority investigating or prosecuting criminal activity described in section 101(a)(15)(U)(iii) [8 U.S.C.A. § 1101(a)(15)(U)(iii)].

(B) Nothing in paragraph (1)(B) may be construed to prevent the Secretary from consulting with the Attorney General in making a determination whether affirmative evidence demonstrates that the alien unreasonably refused to provide assistance to a State or local law enforcement official, State or local prosecutor, State or local judge, or other State or local authority investigating or prosecuting criminal activity described in section 101(a)(15)(U)(iii) [8 U.S.C.A. § 1101(a)(15)(U)(iii)].

(June 27, 1952, c. 477, Title II, ch. 5, § 245, 66 Stat. 217; Aug. 21, 1958, Pub.L. 85–700, § 1, 72 Stat. 699; July 14, 1960, Pub.L. 86–648, § 10, 74 Stat. 505; Oct. 3, 1965, Pub.L. 89–236, § 13, 79 Stat. 918; Oct. 20, 1976, Pub.L. 94–571, § 6, 90 Stat. 2705; Dec. 29, 1981, Pub.L. 97–116, § 5(d)(2), 95 Stat. 1614; Nov. 6, 1986, Pub.L. 99–603, Title III, §§ 117, 313(c), 100 Stat. 3384, 3438; Nov. 6, 1986, Pub.L. 99–603, Title III, § 313(c), as amended Oct. 24, 1988, Pub.L. 100–525, § 2(p)(3), 102 Stat. 2613; Nov. 10, 1986, Pub.L. 99–639, §§ 2(e), 3(b), 5(a), 100 Stat. 3542, 3543; Nov. 10, 1986, Pub.L. 99–639, § 3(b), as amended Oct. 24, 1988, Pub.L. 100–525, § 7(b), 102 Stat. 2616; Oct. 24, 1988, Pub.L. 100–525, § 2(f)(1), 102 Stat. 2611; Nov. 29, 1990, Pub.L. 101–649, Title I, §§ 121(b)(4), 162(e)(3), Title VII, § 702(a), 104 Stat. 4994, 5011, 5086; Oct. 1, 1991, Pub.L. 102–110, § 2(c), 105 Stat. 556; Dec. 12, 1991, Pub.L. 102–232, Title III, §§ 302(d)(2), (e)(7), 308(a), 105 Stat. 1744, 1746, 1757; Aug. 26, 1994, Pub.L. 103–317, Title V, § 506(b), 108 Stat. 1765; Sept. 13, 1994, Pub.L. 103–322, Title XIII, § 130003(c), 108 Stat. 2025; Oct. 25, 1994, Pub.L. 103–416, Title II, § 219(k), 108 Stat. 4317; Apr. 24, 1996, Pub.L. 104–132, Title IV, § 413(d), 110 Stat. 1269; Sept. 30, 1996, Pub.L. 104–208, Div. C, Title III, §§ 308(f)(1)(O), (2)(C), (g)(10)(B), 375, 376(a), Title VI, § 671(a)(4)(A), (5), 110 Stat. 3009–621, 3009–625, 3009–648, 3009–721; Nov. 26, 1997, Pub.L. 105–119, Title I, §§ 110(3), 111(a), (c), 111 Stat. 2458; Oct. 28, 2000, Pub.L. 106–386, Div. A, § 107(f), Div. B, Title V, §§ 1506(a), 1513(f), 114 Stat. 1479, 1527, 1536; Dec. 21, 2000, Pub.L. 106–553, § 1(a)(2) [Title XI, §§ 1102(c), (d)(2), 1103(c)(3)], 114 Stat. 2762; Dec. 21, 2000, Pub.L. 106–554, § 1(a)(4) [Div. B, Title XV, § 1502], 114 Stat. 2763, 2763A–324; Pub.L. 108–193, § 4(b)(3), 8(a)(4), Dec. 19, 2003, 117 Stat. 2879; Jan. 5, 2006, Pub.L. 109–162, Title VIII, § 803, 119 Stat. 3054; Aug. 12, 2006, Pub.L. 109–271, § 6(f), 120 Stat. 763; Dec. 23, 2008, Pub.L. 110–457, Title II, §§ 201(d), (e), 235(d)(3), 122 Stat. 5053, 5080.)

§ 245A. Adjustment of status of certain entrants before January 1, 1982, to that of person admitted for lawful residence [8 U.S.C.A. § 1255a]

(a) Temporary resident status

The Attorney General shall adjust the status of an alien to that of an alien lawfully admitted for temporary residence if the alien meets the following requirements:

(1) Timely application

(A) During application period

Except as provided in subparagraph (B), the alien must apply for such adjustment during the 12–month period beginning on a date (not later than 180 days after November 6, 1986) designated by the Attorney General.

(B) Application within 30 days of show-cause order

An alien who, at any time during the first 11 months of the 12–month period described in subparagraph (A) is the subject of an order to show cause issued under section 242 [8 U.S.C.A. § 1252] (as in effect before October 1, 1996), must make application under this section not later than the end of the 30–day period beginning either on the first day of such 12–month period or on the date of the issuance of such order, whichever day is later.

(C) Information included in application

Each application under this subsection shall contain such information as the Attorney General may require, including information on living relatives of the applicant with respect to whom a petition for preference or other status may be filed by the applicant at any later date under section 204(a) [8 U.S.C.A. § 1154(a)].

(2) Continuous unlawful residence since 1982

(A) In general

The alien must establish that he entered the United States before January 1, 1982, and that he has resided continuously in the United States in an unlawful status since such date and through the date the application is filed under this subsection.

(B) Nonimmigrants

In the case of an alien who entered the United States as a nonimmigrant before January 1, 1982, the alien must establish that the alien's period of authorized stay as a nonimmigrant expired before such date through the passage of time or the alien's unlawful status was known to the Government as of such date.

(C) Exchange visitors

If the alien was at any time a nonimmigrant exchange alien (as defined in section 101(a)(15)(J) [8 U.S.C.A. § 1101(a)(15)(J)]), the alien must establish that the alien was not subject to the two-year foreign residence requirement of section 212(e) [8 U.S.C.A. § 1182(e)] or has fulfilled that requirement or received a waiver thereof.

(3) Continuous physical presence since November 6, 1986

(A) In general

The alien must establish that the alien has been continuously physically present in the United States since November 6, 1986.

(B) Treatment of brief, casual, and innocent absences

An alien shall not be considered to have failed to maintain continuous physical presence in the United States for purposes of subparagraph (A) by virtue of brief, casual, and innocent absences from the United States.

(C) Admissions

Nothing in this section shall be construed as authorizing an alien to apply for admission to, or to be admitted to, the United States in order to apply for adjustment of status under this subsection.

(4) Admissible as immigrant

The alien must establish that he—

(A) is admissible to the United States as an immigrant, except as otherwise provided under subsection (d)(2),

(B) has not been convicted of any felony or of three or more misdemeanors committed in the United States,

(C) has not assisted in the persecution of any person or persons on account of race, religion, nationality, membership in a particular social group, or political opinion, and

(D) is registered or registering under the Military Selective Service Act [50 U.S.C.A.App. § 451 et seq.], if the alien is required to be so registered under that Act.

For purposes of this subsection, an alien in the status of a Cuban and Haitian entrant described in paragraph (1) or (2)(A) of section 501(e) of Public Law 96–422 [8 U.S.C.A. § 1522 note] shall be considered to have entered the United States and to be in an unlawful status in the United States.

(b) Subsequent adjustment to permanent residence and nature of temporary resident status

(1) Adjustment to permanent residence

The Attorney General shall adjust the status of any alien provided lawful temporary resident status under subsection (a) to that of an alien lawfully admitted for permanent residence if the alien meets the following requirements:

(A) Timely application after one year's residence

The alien must apply for such adjustment during the 2–year period beginning with the nineteenth month that begins after the date the alien was granted such temporary resident status.

(B) Continuous residence

(i) In general

The alien must establish that he has continuously resided in the United States since the date the alien was granted such temporary resident status.

(ii) Treatment of certain absences

An alien shall not be considered to have lost the continuous residence referred to in clause (i) by reason of an absence from the United States permitted under paragraph (3)(A).

(C) Admissible as immigrant

The alien must establish that he—

(i) is admissible to the United States as an immigrant, except as otherwise provided under subsection (d)(2), and

(ii) has not been convicted of any felony or three or more misdemeanors committed in the United States.

(D) Basic citizenship skills

(i) In general

The alien must demonstrate that he either—

(I) meets the requirements of section 312(a) [8 U.S.C.A. § 1423(a)] (relating to minimal understanding of ordinary English and a knowledge and understanding of the history and government of the United States), or

(II) is satisfactorily pursuing a course of study (recognized by the Attorney General) to achieve such an understanding of English and such a knowledge and understanding of the history and government of the United States.

(ii) Exception for elderly or developmentally disabled individuals

The Attorney General may, in his discretion, waive all or part of the requirements of clause (i) in the case of an alien who is 65 years of age or older or who is developmentally disabled.

(iii) Relation to naturalization examination

In accordance with regulations of the Attorney General, an alien who has demonstrated under clause (i)(I) that the alien meets the requirements of section 312(a) [8 U.S.C.A. § 1423(a)] may be considered to have satisfied the requirements of that section for purposes of becoming naturalized as a citizen of the United States under title III.

(2) Termination of temporary residence

The Attorney General shall provide for termination of temporary resident status granted an alien under subsection (a)—

(A) if it appears to the Attorney General that the alien was in fact not eligible for such status;

(B) if the alien commits an act that **(i)** makes the alien inadmissible to the United States as an immigrant, except as otherwise provided under subsection (d)(2), or **(ii)** is convicted of any felony or three or more misdemeanors committed in the United States; or

(C) at the end of the 43rd month beginning after the date the alien is granted such status, unless the alien has filed an application for adjustment of such status pursuant to paragraph (1) and such application has not been denied.

(3) Authorized travel and employment during temporary residence

During the period an alien is in lawful temporary resident status granted under subsection (a)—

(A) Authorization of travel abroad

The Attorney General shall, in accordance with regulations, permit the alien to return to the United States after such brief and casual trips abroad as reflect an intention on the part of the alien to adjust to lawful permanent resident status under paragraph (1) and after brief temporary trips abroad occasioned by a family obligation involving an occurrence such as the illness or death of a close relative or other family need.

(B) Authorization of employment

The Attorney General shall grant the alien authorization to engage in employment in the United States and provide to that alien an "employment authorized" endorsement or other appropriate work permit.

(c) Applications for adjustment of status

(1) To whom may be made

The Attorney General shall provide that applications for adjustment of status under subsection (a) may be filed—

(A) with the Attorney General, or

(B) with a qualified designated entity, but only if the applicant consents to the forwarding of the application to the Attorney General.

As used in this section, the term "qualified designated entity" means an organization or person designated under paragraph (2).

(2) Designation of qualified entities to receive applications

For purposes of assisting in the program of legalization provided under this section, the Attorney General—

(A) shall designate qualified voluntary organizations and other qualified State, local, and community organizations, and

(B) may designate such other persons as the Attorney General determines are qualified and have substantial experience, demonstrated competence, and traditional long-term involvement in the preparation and submittal of applications for adjustment of status under section 209 [8 U.S.C.A. § 1159] or 245 [8 U.S.C.A. § 1255], Public Law 89–732 [8 U.S.C.A. § 1255 note], or Public Law 95–145.

(3) Treatment of applications by designated entities

Each qualified designated entity must agree to forward to the Attorney General applications filed with it in accordance with paragraph (1)(B) but not to forward to the Attorney General applications filed with it unless the applicant has consented to such forwarding. No such entity may make a determination required by this section to be made by the Attorney General.

(4) Limitation on access to information

Files and records of qualified designated entities relating to an alien's seeking assistance or information with respect to filing an application under this section are confidential and the Attorney General and the Service shall not have access to such files or records relating to an alien without the consent of the alien.

(5) Confidentiality of information

(A) In general

Except as provided in this paragraph, neither the Attorney General, nor any other official or employee of the Department of Justice, or bureau or agency thereof, may—

(i) use the information furnished by the applicant pursuant to an application filed under this section for any purpose other than to make a determination on the application, for enforcement of paragraph (6), or for the preparation of reports to Congress under section 404 of the Immigration Reform and Control Act of 1986;

(ii) make any publication whereby the information furnished by any particular applicant can be identified; or

(iii) permit anyone other than the sworn officers and employees of the Department or bureau or agency or, with respect to applications filed with a designated entity, that designated entity, to examine individual applications.

(B) Required disclosures

The Attorney General shall provide the information furnished under this section, and any other information derived from such furnished information, to a duly recognized law enforcement entity in connection with a criminal investigation or prosecution, when such information is requested in writing by such entity, or to an official coroner for purposes of affirmatively identifying a deceased individual (whether or not such individual is deceased as a result of a crime).

(C) Authorized disclosures

The Attorney General may provide, in the Attorney General's discretion, for the furnishing of information furnished under this section in the same manner and circumstances as census information may be disclosed by the Secretary of Commerce under section 8 of Title 13.

(D) Construction

(i) In general

Nothing in this paragraph shall be construed to limit the use, or release, for immigration enforcement purposes or law enforcement purposes of information contained in files or records of the Service pertaining to an application filed under this section, other than information furnished by an applicant pursuant to the application, or any other information derived from the application, that is not available from any other source.

(ii) Criminal convictions

Information concerning whether the applicant has at any time been convicted of a crime may be used or released for immigration enforcement or law enforcement purposes.

(E) Crime

Whoever knowingly uses, publishes, or permits information to be examined in violation of this paragraph shall be fined not more than $10,000.

(6) Penalties for false statements in applications

Whoever files an application for adjustment of status under this section and knowingly and willfully falsifies, misrepresents, conceals, or covers up a material fact or makes any false, fictitious, or fraudulent statements or representations, or makes or uses any false writing or document knowing the same to contain any false, fictitious, or fraudulent statement or entry, shall be fined in accordance with Title 18, or imprisoned not more than five years, or both.

(7) Application fees

(A) Fee schedule

The Attorney General shall provide for a schedule of fees to be charged for the filing of applications for adjustment under subsection (a) or (b)(1). The Attorney General shall provide for an additional fee for filing an application for adjustment under subsection (b)(1) after the end of the first year of the 2–year period described in subsection (b)(1)(A).

(B) Use of fees

The Attorney General shall deposit payments received under this paragraph in a separate account and amounts in such account shall be available, without fiscal year limitation, to cover administrative and other expenses incurred in connection with the review of applications filed under this section.

(C) Immigration-related unfair employment practices

Not to exceed $3,000,000 of the unobligated balances remaining in the account established in subparagraph (B) shall be available in fiscal year 1992 and each fiscal year thereafter for grants, contracts, and cooperative agreements to community-based organizations for outreach programs, to be administered by the Office of Special Counsel for Immigration-Related Unfair Employment Practices: Provided, That such amounts shall be in addition to any funds appropriated to the Office of Special Counsel for such purposes: Provided further, That none of the funds made available by this section shall be used by the Office of Special Counsel to establish regional offices.

(d) Waiver of numerical limitations and certain grounds for exclusion

(1) Numerical limitations do not apply

The numerical limitations of sections 201 [8 U.S.C.A. § 1151] and 202 [8 U.S.C.A. § 1152] shall not apply to the adjustment of aliens to lawful permanent resident status under this section.

(2) Waiver of grounds for exclusion

In the determination of an alien's admissibility under subsections (a)(4)(A), (b)(1)(C)(i), and (b)(2)(B)—

(A) Grounds of exclusion not applicable

The provisions of paragraphs (5) and (7)(A) of section 212(a) [8 U.S.C.A. § 1182(a)] shall not apply.

(B) Waiver of other grounds

(i) In general

Except as provided in clause (ii), the Attorney General may waive any other provision of section 212(a) [8 U.S.C.A. § 1182(a)] in the case of individual aliens for humanitarian purposes, to assure family unity, or when it is otherwise in the public interest.

(ii) Grounds that may not be waived

The following provisions of section 212(a) [8 U.S.C.A. § 1182(a)] may not be waived by the Attorney General under clause (i):

(I) Paragraphs (2)(A) and (2)(B) (relating to criminals).

(II) Paragraph (2)(C) (relating to drug offenses), except for so much of such paragraph as relates to a single offense of simple possession of 30 grams or less of marihuana.

(III) Paragraph (3) (relating to security and related grounds).

(IV) Paragraph (4) (relating to aliens likely to become public charges) insofar as it relates to an application for adjustment to permanent residence.

Subclause (IV) (prohibiting the waiver of section 212(a)(4) [8 U.S.C.A. § 1182(a)(4)]) shall not apply to an alien who is or was an aged, blind, or disabled individual (as defined in section 1382c(a)(1) of Title 42).

(iii) Special rule for determination of public charge

An alien is not ineligible for adjustment of status under this section due to being inadmissible under section 212(a)(4) [8 U.S.C.A. § 1182(a)(4)] if the alien demonstrates a history of employment in the United States evidencing self-support without receipt of public cash assistance.

(C) Medical examination

The alien shall be required, at the alien's expense, to undergo such a medical examination (including a determination of immunization status) as is appropriate and conforms to generally accepted professional standards of medical practice.

(e) Temporary stay of deportation and work authorization for certain applicants

(1) Before application period

The Attorney General shall provide that in the case of an alien who is apprehended before the beginning of the application period described in subsection (a)(1)(A) and who can establish a prima facie case of eligibility to have his status adjusted under subsection (a) (but for the fact that he may not apply for such adjustment until the beginning of such period), until the alien has had the opportunity during the first 30 days of the application period to complete the filing of an application for adjustment, the alien—

(A) may not be deported, and

(B) shall be granted authorization to engage in employment in the United States and be provided an "employment authorized" endorsement or other appropriate work permit.

(2) During application period

The Attorney General shall provide that in the case of an alien who presents a prima facie application for adjustment of status under subsection (a) during the application period, and until a final determination on the application has been made in accordance with this section, the alien—

(A) may not be deported, and

(B) shall be granted authorization to engage in employment in the United States and be provided an "employment authorized" endorsement or other appropriate work permit.

(f) Administrative and judicial review

(1) Administrative and judicial review

There shall be no administrative or judicial review of a determination respecting an application for adjustment of status under this section except in accordance with this subsection.

(2) No review for late filings

No denial of adjustment of status under this section based on a late filing of an application for such adjustment may be reviewed by a court of the United States or of any State or reviewed in any administrative proceeding of the United States Government.

(3) Administrative review

(A) Single level of administrative appellate review

The Attorney General shall establish an appellate authority to provide for a single level of administrative appellate review of a determination described in paragraph (1).

(B) Standard for review

Such administrative appellate review shall be based solely upon the administrative record established at the time of the determination on the application and upon such additional or newly discovered evidence as may not have been available at the time of the determination.

(4) Judicial review

(A) Limitation to review of deportation

There shall be judicial review of such a denial only in the judicial review of an order of deportation under section 106 [8 U.S.C.A. § 1105a] (as in effect before October 1, 1996).

(B) Standard for judicial review

Such judicial review shall be based solely upon the administrative record established at the time of the review by the appellate authority and the findings of fact and determinations contained in such record shall be conclusive unless the applicant can establish abuse of discretion or that the findings are directly contrary to clear and convincing facts contained in the record considered as a whole.

(C) Jurisdiction of courts

Notwithstanding any other provision of law, no court shall have jurisdiction of any cause of action or claim by or on behalf of any person asserting an interest under this section unless such person in fact filed an application under this section within the period specified by subsection (a)(1), or attempted to file a complete application and application fee with an authorized legalization officer of the Service but had the application and fee refused by that officer.

(g) Implementation of section

(1) Regulations

The Attorney General, after consultation with the Committees on the Judiciary of the House of Representatives and of the Senate, shall prescribe—

(A) regulations establishing a definition of the term "resided continuously", as used in this section, and the evidence needed to establish that an alien has resided continuously in the United States for purposes of this section, and

(B) such other regulations as may be necessary to carry out this section.

(2) Considerations

In prescribing regulations described in paragraph (1)(A)—

(A) Periods of continuous residence

The Attorney General shall specify individual periods, and aggregate periods, of absence from the United States which will be considered to break a period of continuous residence in the United States and shall take into account absences due merely to brief and casual trips abroad.

(B) Absences caused by deportation or advanced parole

The Attorney General shall provide that—

(i) an alien shall not be considered to have resided continuously in the United States, if, during any period for which continuous residence is required, the alien was outside the United States as a result of a departure under an order of deportation, and

(ii) any period of time during which an alien is outside the United States pursuant to the advance parole procedures of the Service shall not be considered as part of the period of time during which an alien is outside the United States for purposes of this section.

(C) Waivers of certain absences

The Attorney General may provide for a waiver, in the discretion of the Attorney General, of the periods specified under subparagraph (A) in the case of an absence from the United States due merely to a brief temporary trip abroad required by emergency or extenuating circumstances outside the control of the alien.

(D) Use of certain documentation

The Attorney General shall require that—

(i) continuous residence and physical presence in the United States must be established through documents, together with independent corroboration of the information contained in such documents, and

(ii) the documents provided under clause (i) be employment-related if employment-related documents with respect to the alien are available to the applicant.

(3) Interim final regulations

Regulations prescribed under this section may be prescribed to take effect on an interim final basis if the Attorney General determines that this is necessary in order to implement this section in a timely manner.

(h) Temporary disqualification of newly legalized aliens from receiving certain public welfare assistance

(1) In general

During the five-year period beginning on the date an alien was granted lawful temporary resident status under subsection (a), and notwithstanding any other provision of law—

(A) except as provided in paragraphs (2) and (3), the alien is not eligible for—

(i) any program of financial assistance furnished under Federal law (whether through grant, loan, guarantee, or otherwise) on the basis of financial need, as such programs are identified by the Attorney General in consultation with other appropriate heads of the various departments and agencies of Government (but in any event including the program of aid to families with dependent children under part A of title IV of the Social Security Act [42 U.S.C.A. § 601 et seq.]),

(ii) medical assistance under a State plan approved under title XIX of the Social Security Act [42 U.S.C.A. § 1396 et seq.], and

(iii) assistance under the Food and Nutrition Act of 2008 [7 U.S.C.A. § 2011 et seq.]; and

(B) a State or political subdivision therein may, to the extent consistent with subparagraph (A) and paragraphs (2) and (3), provide that the alien is not eligible for the programs of financial assistance or for medical assistance described in subparagraph (A)(ii) furnished under the law of that State or political subdivision.

Unless otherwise specifically provided by this section or other law, an alien in temporary lawful residence status granted under subsection (a) shall not be considered (for purposes of any law of a State or political subdivision providing for a program of financial assistance) to be permanently residing in the United States under color of law.

(2) Exceptions

Paragraph (1) shall not apply—

(A) to a Cuban and Haitian entrant (as defined in paragraph (1) or (2)(A) of section 501(e) of Public Law 96–422 [8 U.S.C.A. § 1522 note], as in effect on April 1, 1983), or

(B) in the case of assistance (other than aid to families with dependent children) which is furnished to an alien who is an aged, blind, or disabled individual (as defined in section 1614(a)(1) of the Social Security Act [42 U.S.C.A. § 1382c(a)(1)]).

(3) Restricted medicaid benefits

(A) Clarification of entitlement

Subject to the restrictions under subparagraph (B), for the purpose of providing aliens with eligibility to receive medical assistance—

(i) paragraph (1) shall not apply,

(ii) aliens who would be eligible for medical assistance but for the provisions of paragraph (1) shall be deemed, for purposes of title XIX of the Social Security Act [42 U.S.C.A. § 1396 et seq.], to be so eligible, and

(iii) aliens lawfully admitted for temporary residence under this section, such status not having changed, shall be considered to be permanently residing in the United States under color of law.

(B) Restriction of benefits

(i) Limitation to emergency services and services for pregnant women

Notwithstanding any provision of title XIX of the Social Security Act (including subparagraphs (B) and (C) of section 1902(a)(10) of such Act [42 U.S.C.A. § 1396a(a)(10)]) aliens who, but for subparagraph (A), would be ineligible for medical assistance under paragraph (1), are only eligible for such assistance with respect to—

(I) emergency services (as defined for purposes of section 1916(a)(2)(D) of the Social Security Act [42 U.S.C.A. § 1396o(a)(2)(D)]), and

(II) services described in section 1916(a)(2)(B) of such Act [42 U.S.C.A. § 1396o(a)(2)(B)] (relating to service for pregnant women).

(ii) No restriction for exempt aliens and children

The restrictions of clause (i) shall not apply to aliens who are described in paragraph (2) or who are under 18 years of age.

(C) Definition of medical assistance

In this paragraph, the term "medical assistance" refers to medical assistance under a State plan approved under title XIX of the Social Security Act.

(4) Treatment of certain programs

Assistance furnished under any of the following provisions of law shall not be construed to be financial assistance described in paragraph (1)(A)(i):

(A) The Richard B. Russell National School Lunch Act [42 U.S.C.A. § 1751 et seq.].

(B) The Child Nutrition Act of 1966 [42 U.S.C.A. § 1771 et seq.].

(C) The Carl D. Perkins Career and Technical Education Act of 2006 [20 U.S.C.A. § 2301 et seq.].

(D) Title I of the Elementary and Secondary Education Act of 1965 [20U.S.C.A. § 6301 et seq.].

(E) The Headstart–Follow Through Act.

(F) The Job Training Partnership Act or title I of the Workforce Investment Act of 1998 [29 U.S.C.A. § 2801 et seq.].

(G) Title IV of the Higher Education Act of 1965 [20 U.S.C.A. § 1070 et seq.].

(H) The Public Health Service Act [42 U.S.C.A. § 1201 et seq.].

(I) Titles V, XVI, and XX, and parts B, D, and E of title IV, of the Social Security Act [42 U.S.C.A. §§ 701 et seq., 1381 et seq., 1391 et seq., 620 et seq., 651 et seq., and 670 et seq., respectively] (and titles I, X, XIV, and XVI of such Act [42 U.S.C.A. §§ 301 et seq., 1201 et seq., 1351 et seq., and 1381 et seq., respectively] as in effect without regard to the amendment made by section 301 of the Social Security Amendments of 1972).

(5) Adjustment not affecting Fascell–Stone benefits

For the purpose of section 501 of the Refugee Education Assistance Act of 1980 (Public Law 96–122) [sic] [8 U.S.C.A. § 1522 note]; assistance shall be continued under such section with respect to an alien without regard to the alien's adjustment of status under this section.

(i) Dissemination of information on legalization program

Beginning not later than the date designated by the Attorney General under subsection (a)(1)(A), the Attorney General, in cooperation with qualified designated entities, shall broadly disseminate information respecting the benefits which aliens may receive under this section and the requirements to obtain such benefits.

(June 27, 1952, c. 477, Title II, ch. 5, § 245A, as added Nov. 6, 1986, Pub.L. 99–603, Title II, § 201(a), 100 Stat. 3394, and amended Oct. 24, 1988, Pub.L. 100–525, § 2(h)(1), 102 Stat. 2611; Nov. 5, 1990, Pub.L. 101–649, Title VI, § 603(a)(13), Title VII, § 703, 104 Stat. 5083, 5086; Oct. 28, 1991, Pub.L. 102–140, Title I, 105 Stat. 785; Dec. 12, 1991, Pub.L. 102–232, Title III, § 307(*l*)(6), 105 Stat. 1756; Oct. 20, 1994, Pub.L. 103–382, Title III, § 394(g), 108 Stat. 4028; Oct. 25, 1994, Pub.L. 103–416, Title I, § 108(b), Title II, § 219(*l*)(1), 108 Stat. 4310, 4317; Apr. 24, 1996, Pub.L. 104–132, Title IV, § 431(a), 110 Stat. 1273; Aug. 22, 1996, Pub.L. 104–193, Title I, § 110(s)(2), 110 Stat. 2175; Sept. 30, 1996, Pub.L. 104–208, Div. C, Title III, §§ 308(g)(2)(B), (5)(A)(iii), 377(a), 384(d)(1), Title VI, § 623(a), 110 Stat. 3009–622, 3009–623, 3009–649, 3009–653, 3009–696; Oct. 21, 1998, 112 Stat. 2681–419, 2681–430; Oct. 31, 1998, Pub.L. 105–332, § 3(a), 112 Stat. 3125, Pub.L. 105–277, Div. A, § 101(f) [Title VIII, § 405(d)(4)]; Oct. 22, 1999, Pub.L. 106–78, Title VII, § 752(b)(5), 113 Stat. 1169; Aug. 12, 2006, Pub.L. 109–270, § 2(a), 120 Stat. 746; May 22, 2008, Pub.L. 110–234, Title IV, § 4002(b)(1)(B), (2)(J), 122 Stat. 1096, 1097; June 18, 2008, Pub.L. 110–246, Title IV, § 4002(b)(1)(B), (2)(J), 122 Stat. 1857, 1858.)

§ 246. Rescission of adjustment of status; effect upon naturalized citizen [8 U.S.C.A. § 1256]

(a) If, at any time within five years after the status of a person has been otherwise adjusted under the provisions of section 245 [8 U.S.C.A. § 1255] or 249 [8 U.S.C.A. § 1259] or any other provision of law to that of an alien lawfully admitted for permanent residence, it shall appear to the satisfaction of the Attorney General that the person was not in fact eligible for such adjustment of status, the Attorney General shall rescind the action taken granting an adjustment of status to such person and cancelling removal in the case of such person if that occurred and the person shall thereupon be subject to all provisions of this Act to the same extent as if the adjustment of status had not been made. Nothing in this subsection shall require the Attorney General to rescind the alien's status prior to commencement of procedures to remove the alien under section 240 [8 U.S.C.A. § 1229a], and an order of removal issued by an immigration judge shall be sufficient to rescind the alien's status.

(b) Any person who has become a naturalized citizen of the United States upon the basis of a record of a lawful admission for permanent residence, created as a result of an adjustment of status for which such person was not in fact eligible, and which is subsequently rescinded under subsection (a) of this section, shall be subject to the provisions of section 340 of this Act [8 U.S.C.A. § 1451] as a person whose naturalization was procured by concealment of a material fact or by willful misrepresentation.

(June 27, 1952, c. 477, Title II, ch. 5, § 246, 66 Stat. 217; Oct. 25, 1994, Pub.L. 103–416, Title II, § 219(m), 108 Stat. 4317; Sept. 30, 1996, Pub.L. 104–208, Div. C, Title III, §§ 308(e)(1)(H), 378(a), 110 Stat. 3009–619, 3009–649.)

§ 247. Adjustment of status of certain resident aliens to nonimmigrant status; exceptions [8 U.S.C.A. § 1257]

(a) The status of an alien lawfully admitted for permanent residence shall be adjusted by the Attorney General, under such regulations as he may prescribe, to that of a nonimmigrant under paragraph (15)(A), (E), or (G) of section 101(a) [8 U.S.C.A. § 1101(a)], if such alien had at the time of admission or subsequently acquires an occupational status which would, if he were seeking admission to the United States, entitle him to a nonimmigrant status under such paragraphs. As of the date of the Attorney General's order making such adjustment of status, the Attorney General shall cancel the record of the alien's admission for permanent residence, and the immigrant status of such alien shall thereby be terminated.

(b) The adjustment of status required by subsection (a) shall not be applicable in the case of any alien who requests that he be permitted to retain his status as an immigrant and who, in such form as the Attorney General may require, executes and files with the Attorney General a written waiver of all rights, privileges, exemptions, and immunities under any law or any executive order which would otherwise accrue to him because of the acquisition of an occupational status entitling him to a nonimmigrant status under paragraph (15)(A), (E), or (G) of section 101(a) [8 U.S.C.A. § 1101(a)].

(June 27, 1952, c. 477, Title II, ch. 5, § 247, 66 Stat. 218; Sept. 30, 1996, Pub.L. 104–208, Div. C, Title III, § 308(f)(1)(P), 110 Stat. 3009–621.)

§ 248. Change of nonimmigrant classification [8 U.S.C.A. § 1258]

(a) The Secretary of Homeland Security may, under such conditions as he may prescribe, authorize a change from any nonimmigrant classification to any other nonimmigrant classification in the case of any alien lawfully admitted to the United States as a nonimmigrant who is continuing to maintain that status and who is not inadmissible under section 212(a)(9)(B)(i) [8 U.S.C.A § 1182(a)(9)(B)(i)] (or whose inadmissibility under such section is waived under section 212(a)(9)(B)(v) [8 U.S.C.A § 1182(a)(9)(B)(v)]), except (subject to subsection (b)) in the case of—

(1) an alien classified as a nonimmigrant under subparagraph (C), (D), (K), or (S) of section 101(a)(15) [8 U.S.C.A. § 1101(a)(15)],

(2) an alien classified as a nonimmigrant under subparagraph (J) of section 101(a)(15) [8 U.S.C.A. § 1101(a)(15)] who came to the

United States or acquired such classification in order to receive graduate medical education or training,

(3) an alien (other than an alien described in paragraph (2)) classified as a nonimmigrant under subparagraph (J) of section 101(a)(15) [8 U.S.C.A. § 1101(a)(15)] who is subject to the two-year foreign residence requirement of section 212(e) [8 U.S.C.A. § 1182(e)] and has not received a waiver thereof, unless such alien applies to have the alien's classification changed from classification under subparagraph (J) of section 101(a)(15) [8 U.S.C.A. § 1101(a)(15)] to a classification under subparagraph (A) or (G) of such section and

(4) an alien admitted as a nonimmigrant visitor without a visa under section 212(*l*) [8 U.S.C.A. § 1182(*l*)] or section 217 [8 U.S.C.A. § 1187].

(b) The exceptions specified in paragraphs (1) through (4) of subsection (a) of this section shall not apply to a change of nonimmigrant classification to that of a nonimmigrant under subparagraph (T) or (U) of section 101(a)(15) [8 U.S.C.A § 1101(a)(15)].

(June 27, 1952, c. 477, Title II, ch. 5, § 248, 66 Stat. 218; Sept. 21, 1961, Pub.L. 87–256, § 109(d), 75 Stat. 535; Dec. 29, 1981, Pub.L. 97–116, § 10, 95 Stat. 1617; Nov. 6, 1986, Pub.L. 99–603, Title III, § 313(d), 100 Stat. 3439; Sept. 13, 1994, Pub.L. 103–322, Title XIII, § 130003(b)(3), 108 Stat. 2025; Sept. 30, 1996, Pub.L. 104–208, Div. C, Title III, § 301(b)(2), Title VI, § 671(a)(2), 110 Stat. 3009–578, 3009–721; Jan. 5, 2006, Pub.L. 109–162, Title VIII, § 821(c)(1), 119 Stat. 3062.)

§ 249. Record of admission for permanent residence in the case of certain aliens who entered the United States prior to January 1, 1972 [8 U.S.C.A. § 1259]

A record of lawful admission for permanent residence may, in the discretion of the Attorney General and under such regulations as he may prescribe, be made in the case of any alien, as of the date of the approval of his application or, if entry occurred prior to July 1, 1924, as of the date of such entry, if no such record is otherwise available and such alien shall satisfy the Attorney General that he is not inadmissible under section 212(a)(3)(E) [8 U.S.C.A. § 1182(a)(3)(E)] or under section 212(a) [8 U.S.C.A. § 1182(a)] insofar as it relates to criminals, procurers and other immoral persons, subversives, violators of the narcotic laws or smugglers of aliens, and he establishes that he—

(a) entered the United States prior to January 1, 1972;

(b) has had his residence in the United States continuously since such entry;

(c) is a person of good moral character; and

(d) is not ineligible to citizenship and is not deportable under section 237(a)(4)(B) [8 U.S.C.A. § 1227(a)(4)(B)].

(June 27, 1952, c. 477, Title II, ch. 5, § 249, 66 Stat. 219; Aug. 8, 1958, Pub.L. 85–616, 72 Stat. 546; Oct. 3, 1965, Pub.L. 89–236, § 19, 79 Stat. 920; Nov. 6, 1986, Pub.L. 99–603, Title II, § 203(a), 100 Stat. 3405; Oct. 24, 1988, Pub.L. 100–525, § 2(j), 102 Stat. 2612; Nov. 29, 1990, Pub.L. 101–649, Title VI, § 603(a)(14), 104 Stat. 5083; Apr. 24, 1996, Pub.L. 104–132, Title IV, § 413(e), 110 Stat. 1269; Sept. 30, 1996, Pub.L. 104–208, Div. C, Title III, § 308(g)(10)(C), 110 Stat. 3009–625.)

§ 250. Removal of aliens falling into distress [8 U.S.C.A. § 1260]

The Attorney General may remove from the United States any alien who falls into distress or who needs public aid from causes arising subsequent to his entry, and is desirous of being so removed, to the native country of such alien, or to the country from which he came, or to the country of which he is a citizen or subject, or to any other country to which he wishes to go and which will receive him, at the expense of the appropriation for the enforcement of this Act. Any alien so removed shall be ineligible to apply for or receive a visa or other documentation for readmission, or to apply for admission to the United States except with the prior approval of the Attorney General.

(June 27, 1952, c. 477, Title II, ch. 5, § 250, 66 Stat. 219.)

Chapter VI—Special Provisions Relating to Alien Crewmen

§ 251. Alien crewmen [8 U.S.C.A. § 1281]

(a) Arrival; submission of list; exceptions

Upon arrival of any vessel or aircraft in the United States from any place outside the United States it shall be the duty of the owner, agent, consignee, master, or commanding officer thereof to deliver to an immigration officer at the port of arrival **(1)** a complete, true, and correct list containing the names of all aliens employed on such vessel or aircraft, the positions they respectively hold in the crew of the vessel or aircraft, when and where they were respectively shipped or engaged, and those to be paid off or discharged in the port of arrival; or **(2)** in the discretion of the Attorney General, such a list containing so much of such information, or such additional or supplemental information, as the Attorney General shall by regulations prescribe. In the case of a vessel engaged solely in traffic on the Great Lakes, Saint Lawrence River, and connecting waterways, such lists shall be furnished at such times as the Attorney General may require.

(b) Reports of illegal landings

It shall be the duty of any owner, agent, consignee, master, or commanding officer of any vessel or aircraft to report to an immigration officer, in writing, as soon as discovered, all cases in which any alien crewman has illegally landed in the United States from the vessel or aircraft, together with a description of such alien and any information likely to lead to his apprehension.

(c) Departure; submission of list; exceptions

Before the departure of any vessel or aircraft from any port in the United States, it shall be the duty of the owner, agent, consignee, master, or commanding officer thereof, to deliver to an immigration officer at that port **(1)** a list containing the names of all alien employees who were not employed thereon at the time of the arrival at that port but who will leave such port thereon at the time of the departure of such vessel or aircraft and the names of those, if any, who have been paid off or discharged, and of those, if any, who have deserted or landed at that port, or **(2)** in the discretion of the Attorney General, such a list containing so much of such information, or such additional or supplemental information, as the Attorney General shall by regulations prescribe. In the case of a vessel engaged solely in traffic on the Great Lakes, Saint Lawrence River, and connecting waterways, such lists shall be furnished at such times as the Attorney General may require.

(d) Violations

In case any owner, agent, consignee, master, or commanding officer shall fail to deliver complete, true, and correct lists or reports of aliens, or to report cases of desertion or landing, as required by subsections (a), (b), and (c), such owner, agent, consignee, master, or commanding officer, shall, if required by the Attorney General, pay to the Commissioner the sum of $200 for each alien concerning whom such lists are not delivered or such reports are not made as required in the preceding subsections. In the case that any owner, agent, consignee, master, or commanding officer of a vessel shall secure services of an alien crewman described in section 101(a)(15)(D)(i) [8 U.S.C.A. § 1101(a)(15)(D)(i)] to perform longshore work not included in the normal operation and service on board the vessel under section 258 [8 U.S.C.A. § 1288], the owner, agent, consignee, master, or commanding officer shall pay to the Commissioner the sum of $5,000, and such fine shall be a lien against the vessel. No such vessel or aircraft shall be granted clearance from any port at which it arrives pending the determination of the question of the liability to the payment of such fine, and if such fine is imposed, while it remains unpaid. No such fine shall be remitted or refunded. Clearance may be granted prior to the determination of such question upon deposit of a bond or a sum sufficient to cover such fine.

(e) Regulations

The Attorney General is authorized to prescribe by regulations the circumstances under which a vessel or aircraft shall be deemed to be arriving in, or departing from the United States or any port thereof within the meaning of any provision of this chapter.

(June 27, 1952, c. 477, Title II, ch. 6, § 251, 66 Stat. 219; Nov. 29, 1990, Pub.L. 101–649, Title II, § 203(b), 104 Stat. 5018; Dec. 12, 1991, Pub.L. 102–232, Title III, § 303(a)(3), 105 Stat. 1746.)

§ 252. Conditional permits to land temporarily [8 U.S.C.A. § 1282]

(a) Period of time

No alien crewman shall be permitted to land temporarily in the United States except as provided in this section and sections 212(d)(3),

(5) [8 U.S.C.A. § 1182(d)(3), (5)] and 253 [8 U.S.C.A. § 1283]. If an immigration officer finds upon examination that an alien crewman is a nonimmigrant under paragraph (15)(D) of section 101(a) [8 U.S.C.A. § 1101(a)] and is otherwise admissible and has agreed to accept such permit, he may, in his discretion, grant the crewman a conditional permit to land temporarily pursuant to regulations prescribed by the Attorney General, subject to revocation in subsequent proceedings as provided in subsection (b), and for a period of time, in any event, not to exceed—

(1) the period of time (not exceeding twenty-nine days) during which the vessel or aircraft on which he arrived remains in port, if the immigration officer is satisfied that the crewman intends to depart on the vessel or aircraft on which he arrived; or

(2) twenty-nine days, if the immigration officer is satisfied that the crewman intends to depart, within the period for which he is permitted to land, on a vessel or aircraft other than the one on which he arrived.

(b) Revocation; expenses of detention

Pursuant to regulations prescribed by the Attorney General, any immigration officer may, in his discretion, if he determines that an alien is not a bona fide crewman, or does not intend to depart on the vessel or aircraft which brought him, revoke the conditional permit to land which was granted such crewman under the provisions of subsection (a)(1), take such crewman into custody, and require the master or commanding officer of the vessel or aircraft on which the crewman arrived to receive and detain him on board such vessel or aircraft, if practicable, and such crewman shall be removed from the United States at the expense of the transportation line which brought him to the United States. Until such alien is so removed, any expenses of his detention shall be borne by such transportation company. Nothing in this section shall be construed to require the procedure prescribed in section 240 [8 U.S.C.A. § 1229a] to cases falling within the provisions of this subsection.

(c) Penalties

Any alien crewman who willfully remains in the United States in excess of the number of days allowed in any conditional permit issued under subsection (a) shall be fined under Title 18 or imprisoned not more than 6 months, or both.

(June 27, 1952, c. 477, Title II, ch. 6, § 252, 66 Stat. 220; Nov. 29, 1990, Pub.L. 101–649, Title V, § 543(b)(1), 104 Stat. 5059; Dec. 12, 1991, Pub.L. 102–232, Title III, § 306(c)(3), 105 Stat. 1752; Sept. 30, 1996, Pub.L. 104–208, Div. C, Title III, § 308(e)(2)(E), (g)(5)(A)(i), 110 Stat. 3009–620, 3009–623.)

§ 253. Hospital treatment of alien crewmen afflicted with certain diseases [8 U.S.C.A. § 1283]

An alien crewman, including an alien crewman ineligible for a conditional permit to land under section 252(a) [8 U.S.C.A. § 1282(a)], who is found on arrival in a port of the United States to be afflicted with any of the disabilities or diseases mentioned in section 255 [8 U.S.C.A. § 1285], shall be placed in a hospital designated by the immigration officer in charge at the port of arrival and treated, all expenses connected therewith, including burial in the event of death, to be borne by the owner, agent, consignee, commanding officer, or master of the vessel or aircraft, and not to be deducted from the crewman's wages. No such vessel or aircraft shall be granted clearance until such expenses are paid, or their payment appropriately guaranteed, and the collector of customs is so notified by the immigration officer in charge. An alien crewman suspected of being afflicted with any such disability or disease may be removed from the vessel or aircraft on which he arrived to an immigration station, or other appropriate place, for such observation as will enable the examining surgeons to determine definitely whether or not he is so afflicted, all expenses connected therewith to be borne in the manner hereinbefore prescribed. In cases in which it appears to the satisfaction of the immigration officer in charge that it will not be possible within a reasonable time to effect a cure, the return of the alien crewman shall be enforced on, or at the expense of, the transportation line on which he came, upon such conditions as the Attorney General shall prescribe, to insure that the alien shall be properly cared for and protected, and that the spread of contagion shall be guarded against.

(June 27, 1952, c. 477, Title II, ch. 6, § 253, 66 Stat. 221.)

§ 254. Control of alien crewmen [8 U.S.C.A. § 1284]

(a) Penalties for failure

The owner, agent, consignee, charterer, master, or commanding officer of any vessel or aircraft arriving in the United States from any place outside thereof who fails **(1)** to detain on board the vessel, or in the case of an aircraft to detain at a place specified by an immigration officer at the expense of the airline, any alien crewman employed thereon until an immigration officer has completely inspected such alien crewman, including a physical examination by the medical examiner, or **(2)** to detain any alien crewman on board the vessel, or in the case of an aircraft at a place specified by an immigration officer at the expense of the airline, after such inspection unless a conditional permit to land temporarily has been granted such alien crewman under section 252 [8 U.S.C.A. § 1282] or unless an alien crewman has been permitted to land temporarily under section 212(d)(5) [8 U.S.C.A. § 1182(d)(5)] or 253 [8 U.S.C.A. § 1283] for medical or hospital treatment, or **(3)** to remove such alien crewman if required to do so by an immigration officer, whether such removal requirement is imposed before or after the crewman is permitted to land temporarily under section 212(d)(5) [8 U.S.C.A. § 1182(d)(5)], 252 [8 U.S.C.A. § 1282], or 253 [8 U.S.C.A. § 1283], shall pay to the Commissioner the sum of $3,000 for each alien crewman in respect to whom any such failure occurs. No such vessel or aircraft shall be granted clearance pending the determination of the liability to the payment of such fine, or while the fine remains unpaid, except that clearance may be granted prior to the determination of such question upon the deposit of a sum sufficient to cover such fine, or of a bond with sufficient surety to secure the payment thereof approved by the Commissioner. The Attorney General may, upon application in writing therefor, mitigate such penalty to not less than $500 for each alien crewman in respect of whom such failure occurs, upon such terms as he shall think proper.

(b) Prima facie evidence against transportation line

Except as may be otherwise prescribed by regulations issued by the Attorney General, proof that an alien crewman did not appear upon the outgoing manifest of the vessel or aircraft on which he arrived in the United States from any place outside thereof, or that he was reported by the master or commanding officer of such vessel or aircraft as a deserter, shall be prima facie evidence of a failure to detain or remove such alien crewman.

(c) Removal on other than arriving vessel or aircraft; expenses

If the Attorney General finds that removal of an alien crewman under this section on the vessel or aircraft on which he arrived is impracticable or impossible, or would cause undue hardship to such alien crewman, he may cause the alien crewman to be removed from the port of arrival or any other port on another vessel or aircraft of the same transportation line, unless the Attorney General finds this to be impracticable. All expenses incurred in connection with such removal, including expenses incurred in transferring an alien crewman from one place in the United States to another under such conditions and safeguards as the Attorney General shall impose, shall be paid by the owner or owners of the vessel or aircraft on which the alien arrived in the United States. The vessel or aircraft on which the alien arrived shall not be granted clearance until such expenses have been paid or their payment guaranteed to the satisfaction of the Attorney General. An alien crewman who is transferred within the United States in accordance with this subsection shall not be regarded as having been landed in the United States.

(June 27, 1952, c. 477, Title II, ch. 6, § 254, 66 Stat. 221; Nov. 29, 1990, Pub.L. 101–649, Title V, § 543(a)(4), 104 Stat. 5058; Dec. 12, 1991, Pub.L. 102–232, Title III, § 306(c)(4)(C), 105 Stat. 1752; Sept. 30, 1996, Pub.L. 104–208, Div. C, Title III, § 308(e)(1)(I), (2)(F), (12), 110 Stat. 3009–619, 3009–620.)

§ 255. Employment on passenger vessels of aliens afflicted with certain disabilities [8 U.S.C.A. § 1285]

It shall be unlawful for any vessel or aircraft carrying passengers between a port of the United States and a port outside thereof to have employed on board upon arrival in the United States any alien afflicted with feeble-mindedness, insanity, epilepsy, tuberculosis in any form, leprosy, or any dangerous contagious disease. If it appears to the satisfaction of the Attorney General, from an examination made by a medical officer of the United States Public Health Service, and is so certified by such officer, that any such alien was so afflicted at the time he was shipped or engaged and taken on board such vessel or aircraft and that the existence of such affliction might have been detected by means of a competent medical examination at such time, the owner, commanding officer, agent, consignee, or master thereof shall pay for each alien so afflicted to the Commissioner the sum of $1,000. No vessel or aircraft shall be granted clearance pending the determination of the question of the liability to the payment of such sums, or while such sums remain unpaid, except that clearance may be granted prior to the determination of such question upon the deposit of an amount sufficient to cover such sums or of a bond approved by the Commissioner with sufficient surety to secure the payment thereof. Any such fine may, in the discretion of the Attorney General, be mitigated or remitted.

(June 27, 1952, c. 477, Title II, ch. 6, § 255, 66 Stat. 222; Nov. 29, 1990, Pub.L. 101–649, Title V, § 543(a)(5), 104 Stat. 5058.)

§ 256. Discharge of alien crewmen; penalties [8 U.S.C.A. § 1286]

It shall be unlawful for any person, including the owner, agent, consignee, charterer, master, or commanding officer of any vessel or aircraft, to pay off or discharge any alien crewman, except an alien lawfully admitted for permanent residence, employed on board a vessel or aircraft arriving in the United States without first having obtained the consent of the Attorney General. If it shall appear to the satisfaction of the Attorney General that any alien crewman has been paid off or discharged in the United States in violation of the provisions of this section, such owner, agent, consignee, charterer, master, commanding officer, or other person, shall pay to the Commissioner the sum of $3,000 for each such violation. No vessel or aircraft shall be granted clearance pending the determination of the question of the liability to the payment of such sums, or while such sums remain unpaid, except that clearance may be granted prior to the determination of such question upon the deposit of an amount sufficient to cover such sums, or of a bond approved by the Commissioner with sufficient surety to secure the payment thereof. Such fine may, in the discretion of the Attorney General, be mitigated to not less than $1,500 for each violation, upon such terms as he shall think proper.

(June 27, 1952, c. 477, Title II, ch. 6, § 256, 66 Stat. 223; Nov. 29, 1990, Pub.L. 101–649, Title V, § 543(a)(6), 104 Stat. 5058.)

§ 257. Alien crewmen brought into the United States with intent to evade immigration laws; penalties [8 U.S.C.A. § 1287]

Any person, including the owner, agent, consignee, master, or commanding officer of any vessel or aircraft arriving in the United States from any place outside thereof, who shall knowingly sign on the vessel's articles, or bring to the United States as one of the crew of such vessel or aircraft, any alien, with intent to permit or assist such alien to enter or land in the United States in violation of law, or who shall falsely and knowingly represent to a consular officer at the time of application for visa, or to the immigration officer at the port of arrival in the United States, that such alien is a bona fide member of the crew employed in any capacity regularly required for normal operation and services aboard such vessel or aircraft, shall be liable to a penalty not exceeding $10,000 for each such violation, for which sum such vessel or aircraft shall be liable and may be seized and proceeded against by way of libel in any district court of the United States having jurisdiction of the offense.

(June 27, 1952, c. 477, Title II, ch. 6, § 257, 66 Stat. 223; Nov. 29, 1990, Pub.L. 101–649, Title V, § 543(a)(7), 104 Stat. 5058.)

§ 258. Limitations on performance of longshore work by alien crewmen [8 U.S.C.A. § 1288]

(a) In general

For purposes of section 101(a)(15)(D)(i) [8 U.S.C.A. § 1101(a)(15)(D)(i)], the term "normal operation and service on board a vessel" does not include any activity that is longshore work (as defined in subsection (b)), except as provided under subsection (c), (d), or (e).

(b) Longshore work defined

(1) In general

In this section, except as provided in paragraph (2), the term "longshore work" means any activity relating to the loading or unloading of cargo, the operation of cargo-related equipment (whether or not integral to the vessel), and the handling of mooring lines on the dock when the vessel is made fast or let go, in the United States or the coastal waters thereof.

(2) Exception for safety and environmental protection

The term "longshore work" does not include the loading or unloading of any cargo for which the Secretary of Transportation has, under the authority contained in chapter 37 of Title 46 (relating to Carriage of Liquid Bulk Dangerous Cargoes), section 311 of the Federal Water Pollution Control Act (33 U.S.C. 1321), section 4106 of the Oil Pollution Act of 1990, or section 5103(b), 5104, 5106, 5107, or 5110 of Title 49 prescribed regulations which govern—

(A) the handling or stowage of such cargo,

(B) the manning of vessels and the duties, qualifications, and training of the officers and crew of vessels carrying such cargo, and

(C) the reduction or elimination of discharge during ballasting, tank cleaning, handling of such cargo.

(3) Construction

Nothing in this section shall be construed as broadening, limiting, or otherwise modifying the meaning or scope of longshore work for purposes of any other law, collective bargaining agreement, or international agreement.

(c) Prevailing practice exception

(1) Subsection (a) shall not apply to a particular activity of longshore work in and about a local port if—

(A) **(i)** there is in effect in the local port one or more collective bargaining agreements each covering at least 30 percent of the number of individuals employed in performing longshore work and **(ii)** each such agreement (covering such percentage of longshore workers) permits the activity to be performed by alien crewmen under the terms of such agreement; or

(B) there is no collective bargaining agreement in effect in the local port covering at least 30 percent of the number of individuals employed in performing longshore work, and an employer of alien crewmen (or the employer's designated agent or representative) has filed with the Secretary of Labor at least 14 days before the date of performance of the activity (or later, if necessary due to an unanticipated emergency, but not later than the date of performance of the activity) an attestation setting forth facts and evidence to show that—

(i) the performance of the activity by alien crewmen is permitted under the prevailing practice of the particular port as of the date of filing of the attestation and that the use of alien crewmen for such activity—

(I) is not during a strike or lockout in the course of a labor dispute, and

(II) is not intended or designed to influence an election of a bargaining representative for workers in the local port; and

(ii) notice of the attestation has been provided by the owner, agent, consignee, master, or commanding officer to the bargaining representative of longshore workers in the local port, or, where there is no such bargaining representative, notice of the attestation has been provided to longshore workers employed at the local port.

In applying subparagraph (B) in the case of a particular activity of longshore work consisting of the use of an automated self-unloading conveyor belt or vacuum-actuated system on a vessel, the attestation shall be required to be filed only if the Secretary of Labor finds, based on a preponderance of the evidence which may be submitted by any interested party, that the performance of such particular activity is not described in clause (i) of such subparagraph.

(2) Subject to paragraph (4), an attestation under paragraph (1) shall—

(A) expire at the end of the 1–year period beginning on the date of its filing with the Secretary of Labor, and

(B) apply to aliens arriving in the United States during such 1–year period if the owner, agent, consignee, master, or commanding officer states in each list under section 251 [8 U.S.C.A. § 1281] that it continues to comply with the conditions in the attestation.

(3) An owner, agent, consignee, master, or commanding officer may meet the requirements under this subsection with respect to more than one alien crewman in a single list.

(4)(A) The Secretary of Labor shall compile and make available for public examination in a timely manner in Washington, D.C., a list identifying owners, agents, consignees, masters, or commanding officers which have filed lists for nonimmigrants described in section 101(a)(15)(D)(i) [8 U.S.C.A. § 1101(a)(15)(D)(i)] with respect to whom an attestation under paragraph (1) or subsection (d)(1) is made and, for each such entity, a copy of the entity's attestation under paragraph (1) or subsection (d)(1) (and accompanying documentation) and each such list filed by the entity.

(B)(i) The Secretary of Labor shall establish a process for the receipt, investigation, and disposition of complaints respecting an entity's failure to meet conditions attested to, an entity's misrepresentation of a material fact in an attestation, or, in the case described in the last sentence of paragraph (1), whether the performance of the particular activity is or is not described in paragraph (1)(B)(i).

(ii) Complaints may be filed by any aggrieved person or organization (including bargaining representatives, associations deemed appropriate by the Secretary, and other aggrieved parties as determined under regulations of the Secretary).

(iii) The Secretary shall promptly conduct an investigation under this subparagraph if there is reasonable cause to believe that an entity fails to meet conditions attested to, an entity has misrepresented a material fact in the attestation, or, in the case described in the last sentence of paragraph (1), the performance of the particular activity is not described in paragraph (1)(B)(i).

(C)(i) If the Secretary determines that reasonable cause exists to conduct an investigation with respect to an attestation, a complaining party may request that the activities attested to by the employer cease during the hearing process described in subparagraph (D). If such a request is made, the attesting employer shall be issued notice of such request and shall respond within 14 days to the notice. If the Secretary makes an initial determination that the complaining party's position is supported by a preponderance of the evidence submitted, the Secretary shall require immediately that the employer cease and desist from such activities until completion of the process described in subparagraph (D).

(ii) If the Secretary determines that reasonable cause exists to conduct an investigation with respect to a matter under the last sentence of paragraph (1), a complaining party may request that the activities of the employer cease during the hearing process described in subparagraph (D) unless the employer files with the Secretary of Labor an attestation under paragraph (1). If such a request is made, the employer shall be issued notice of such request and shall respond within 14 days to the notice. If the Secretary makes an initial determination that the complaining party's position is supported by a preponderance of the evidence submitted, the Secretary shall require immediately that the employer cease and desist from such activities until completion of the process described in subparagraph (D) unless the employer files with the Secretary of Labor an attestation under paragraph (1).

(D) Under the process established under subparagraph (B), the Secretary shall provide, within 180 days after the date a complaint is filed (or later for good cause shown), for a determination as to whether or not a basis exists to make a finding described in subparagraph (E). The Secretary shall provide notice of such determination to the interested parties and an opportunity for a hearing on the complaint within 60 days of the date of the determination.

(E)(i) If the Secretary of Labor finds, after notice and opportunity for a hearing, that an entity has failed to meet a condition attested to or has made a misrepresentation of material fact in the attestation, the Secretary shall notify the Attorney General of such finding and may, in addition, impose such other administrative remedies (including civil monetary penalties in an amount not to exceed $5,000 for each alien crewman performing unauthorized longshore work) as the Secretary determines to be appropriate. Upon receipt of such notice, the Attorney General shall not permit the vessels owned or chartered by such entity to enter any port of the United States during a period of up to 1 year.

(ii) If the Secretary of Labor finds, after notice and opportunity for a hearing, that, in the case described in the last sentence of paragraph (1), the performance of the particular activity is not described in subparagraph (B)(i), the Secretary shall notify the Attorney General of such finding and, thereafter, the attestation described in paragraph (1) shall be required of the employer for the performance of the particular activity.

(F) A finding by the Secretary of Labor under this paragraph that the performance of an activity by alien crewmen is not permitted under the prevailing practice of a local port shall preclude for one year the filing of a subsequent attestation concerning such activity in the port under paragraph (1).

(5) Except as provided in paragraph (5) of subsection (d), this subsection shall not apply to longshore work performed in the State of Alaska.

(d) State of Alaska exception

(1) Subsection (a) shall not apply to a particular activity of longshore work at a particular location in the State of Alaska if an employer of alien crewmen has filed an attestation with the Secretary of Labor at least 30 days before the date of the first performance of the activity (or anytime up to 24 hours before the first performance of the activity, upon a showing that the employer could not have reasonably anticipated the need to file an attestation for that location at that time) setting forth facts and evidence to show that—

(A) the employer will make a bona fide request for United States longshore workers who are qualified and available in sufficient numbers to perform the activity at the particular time and location from the parties to whom notice has been provided under clauses (ii) and (iii) of subparagraph (D), except that—

(i) wherever two or more contract stevedoring companies have signed a joint collective bargaining agreement with a single labor organization described in subparagraph (D)(i), the employer may request longshore workers from only one of such contract stevedoring companies, and

(ii) a request for longshore workers to an operator of a private dock may be made only for longshore work to be performed at that dock and only if the operator meets the requirements of section 932 of Title 33;

(B) the employer will employ all those United States longshore workers made available in response to the request made pursuant to subparagraph (A) who are qualified and available in sufficient numbers and who are needed to perform the longshore activity at the particular time and location;

(C) the use of alien crewmembers for such activity is not intended or designed to influence an election of a bargaining representative for workers in the State of Alaska; and

(D) notice of the attestation has been provided by the employer to—

(i) labor organizations which have been recognized as exclusive bargaining representatives of United States longshore workers within the meaning of the National Labor Relations Act [29 U.S.C.A. § 151 et seq.] and which make available or intend to make available workers to the particular location where the longshore work is to be performed,

(ii) contract stevedoring companies which employ or intend to employ United States longshore workers at that location, and

(iii) operators of private docks at which the employer will use longshore workers.

(2)(A) An employer filing an attestation under paragraph (1) who seeks to use alien crewmen to perform longshore work shall be responsible while the attestation is valid to make bona fide requests for United States longshore workers under paragraph (1)(A) and to employ United States longshore workers, as provided in paragraph (1)(B), before using alien crewmen to perform the activity or activities specified in the attestation, except that an employer shall not be required to request longshore workers from a party if that party has notified the employer in writing that it does not intend to make available United States longshore workers to the location at which the longshore work is to be performed.

(B) If a party that has provided such notice subsequently notifies the employer in writing that it is prepared to make available United States longshore workers who are qualified and available in sufficient numbers to perform the longshore activity to the location at which the longshore work is to be performed, then the employer's obligations to that party under subparagraphs (A) and (B) of paragraph (1) shall begin 60 days following the issuance of such notice.

(3)(A) In no case shall an employer filing an attestation be required—

(i) to hire less than a full work unit of United States longshore workers needed to perform the longshore activity;

(ii) to provide overnight accommodations for the longshore workers while employed; or

(iii) to provide transportation to the place of work, except where—

(I) surface transportation is available;

(II) such transportation may be safely accomplished;

(III) travel time to the vessel does not exceed one-half hour each way; and

(IV) travel distance to the vessel from the point of embarkation does not exceed 5 miles.

(B) In the cases of Wide Bay, Alaska, and Klawock/Craig, Alaska, the travel times and travel distances specified in subclauses (III) and (IV) of subparagraph (A)(iii) shall be extended to 45 minutes and 7.5 miles, respectively, unless the party responding to the request for longshore workers agrees to the lesser time and distance limitations specified in those subclauses.

(4) Subject to subparagraphs (A) through (D) of subsection (c)(4), attestations filed under paragraph (1) of this subsection shall—

(A) expire at the end of the 1–year period beginning on the date the employer anticipates the longshore work to begin, as specified in the attestation filed with the Secretary of Labor, and

(B) apply to aliens arriving in the United States during such 1–year period if the owner, agent, consignee, master, or commanding officer states in each list under section 251 [8 U.S.C.A. § 1281] that it continues to comply with the conditions in the attestation.

(5)(A) Except as otherwise provided by subparagraph (B), subsection (c)(3) and subparagraphs (A) through (E) of subsection (c)(4) shall apply to attestations filed under this subsection.

(B) The use of alien crewmen to perform longshore work in Alaska consisting of the use of an automated self-unloading conveyor belt or vacuum-actuated system on a vessel shall be governed by the provisions of subsection (c).

(6) For purposes of this subsection—

(A) the term "contract stevedoring companies" means those stevedoring companies licensed to do business in the State of Alaska that meet the requirements of section 932 of Title 33;

(B) the term "employer" includes any agent or representative designated by the employer; and

(C) the terms "qualified" and "available in sufficient numbers" shall be defined by reference to industry standards in the State of Alaska, including safety considerations.

(e) Reciprocity exception

(1) In general

Subject to the determination of the Secretary of State pursuant to paragraph (2), the Attorney General shall permit an alien crewman to perform an activity constituting longshore work if—

(A) the vessel is registered in a country that by law, regulation, or in practice does not prohibit such activity by crewmembers aboard United States vessels; and

(B) nationals of a country (or countries) which by law, regulation, or in practice does not prohibit such activity by crewmembers aboard United States vessels hold a majority of the ownership interest in the vessel.

(2) Establishment of list

The Secretary of State shall, in accordance with section 553 of Title 5, compile and annually maintain a list, of longshore work by particular activity, or countries where performance of such a particular activity by crewmembers aboard United States vessels is prohibited by law, regulation, or in practice in the country. By not later than 90 days after November 29, 1990, the Secretary shall publish a notice of proposed rulemaking to establish such list. The Secretary shall first establish such list by not later than 180 days after November 29, 1990.

(3) In practice defined

For purposes of this subsection, the term "in practice" refers to an activity normally performed in such country during the one-year period preceding the arrival of such vessel into the United States or coastal waters thereof.

(June 27, 1952, c. 477, Title II, ch. 6, § 258, as added Nov. 29, 1990, Pub.L. 101–649, Title II, § 203(a)(1), 104 Stat. 5015, and amended Dec. 12, 1991, Pub.L. 102–232, Title III, § 303(a)(4), 105 Stat. 1747; Dec. 17, 1993, Pub.L. 103–198, § 8(a), (b), 107 Stat. 2313, 2315; Dec. 20, 1993, Pub.L. 103–206, Title III, § 323(a), (b), 107 Stat. 2428, 2430; Oct. 25, 1994, Pub.L. 103–416, Title II, § 219(f), (gg), 108 Stat. 4317, 4319; Sept. 30, 1996, Pub.L. 104–208, Div. C, Title VI, § 671(e)(4)(B), 110 Stat. 3009–723.)

CHAPTER VII—REGISTRATION OF ALIENS

§ 261. Alien seeking entry; contents [8 U.S.C.A. § 1301]

No visa shall be issued to any alien seeking to enter the United States until such alien has been registered in accordance with section 221(b) [8 U.S.C.A. § 1201(b)].

(June 27, 1952, c. 477, Title II, ch. 7, § 261, 66 Stat. 223; Pub.L. 99–653, § 8, Nov. 14, 1986, 100 Stat. 3657, as amended Pub.L. 100–525, § 8(g), Oct. 24, 1988, 102 Stat. 2617.)

§ 262. Registration of aliens [8 U.S.C.A. § 1302]

(a) It shall be the duty of every alien now or hereafter in the United States, who **(1)** is fourteen years of age or older, **(2)** has not been registered and fingerprinted under section 221(b) [8 U.S.C.A. § 1201(b)] or section 30 or 31 of the Alien Registration Act, 1940, and **(3)** remains in the United States for thirty days or longer, to apply for registration and to be fingerprinted before the expiration of such thirty days.

(b) It shall be the duty of every parent or legal guardian of any alien now or hereafter in the United States, who **(1)** is less than fourteen years of age, **(2)** has not been registered under section 221(b) [8 U.S.C.A. § 1201(b)] or section 30 or 31 of the Alien Registration Act, 1940, and **(3)** remains in the United States for thirty days or longer, to apply for the registration of such alien before the expiration of such thirty days. Whenever any alien attains his fourteenth birthday in the United States he shall, within thirty days thereafter, apply in person for registration and to be fingerprinted.

(c) The Attorney General may, in his discretion and on the basis of reciprocity pursuant to such regulations as he may prescribe, waive the requirement of fingerprinting specified in subsections (a) and (b) in the case of any nonimmigrant.

(June 27, 1952, c. 477, Title II, ch. 7, § 262, 66 Stat. 224; Nov. 14, 1986, Pub.L. 99–653, § 9, 100 Stat. 3657; Oct. 24, 1988, Pub.L. 100–525, § 8(h), 102 Stat. 2617; Oct. 25, 1994, Pub.L. 103–416, Title II, § 219(n), 108 Stat. 4317.)

§ 263. Registration of special groups [8 U.S.C.A. § 1303]

(a) Notwithstanding the provisions of sections 261 [8 U.S.C.A. § 1301] and 262 [8 U.S.C.A. § 1302], the Attorney General is authorized to prescribe special regulations and forms for the registration and fingerprinting of **(1)** alien crewmen, **(2)** holders of border-crossing identification cards, **(3)** aliens confined in institutions within the United States, **(4)** aliens under order of removal, **(5)** aliens who are or have been on criminal probation or criminal parole within the United States, and **(6)** aliens of any other class not lawfully admitted to the United States for permanent residence.

(b) The provisions of section 262 [8 U.S.C.A. § 1302] and of this section shall not be applicable to any alien who is in the United States as a nonimmigrant under section 101(a)(15)(A) or (a)(15)(G) [8 U.S.C.A. § 1101(a)(15)(A) or (a)(15)(G)] until the alien ceases to be entitled to such a nonimmigrant status.

(June 27, 1952, c. 477, Title II, ch. 7, § 263, 66 Stat. 224; Sept. 30, 1996, Pub.L. 104–208, Div. C, Title III, §§ 308(e)(1)(J), 323, 110 Stat. 3009–619, 3009–629.)

§ 264. Forms for registration and fingerprinting [8 U.S.C.A. § 1304]

(a) Preparation; contents

The Attorney General and the Secretary of State jointly are authorized and directed to prepare forms for the registration of aliens under section 261 [8 U.S.C.A. § 1301], and the Attorney General is authorized and directed to prepare forms for the registration and fingerprinting of aliens under section 262 [8 U.S.C.A. § 1302]. Such forms shall contain inquiries with respect to **(1)** the date and place of entry of the alien into the United States; **(2)** activities in which he has been and intends to be engaged; **(3)** the length of time he expects to remain in the United States; **(4)** the police and criminal record, if any, of such alien; and **(5)** such additional matters as may be prescribed.

(b) Confidential nature

All registration and fingerprint records made under the provisions of this title shall be confidential, and shall be made available only **(1)** pursuant to section 287(f)(2) [8 U.S.C.A. § 1357(f)(2)], and **(2)** to such persons or agencies as may be designated by the Attorney General.

(c) Information under oath

Every person required to apply for the registration of himself or another under this title shall submit under oath the information required for such registration. Any person authorized under regulations issued by the Attorney General to register aliens under this title shall be authorized to administer oaths for such purpose.

(d) Certificate of alien registration or alien receipt card

Every alien in the United States who has been registered and fingerprinted under the provisions of the Alien Registration Act, 1940, or under the provisions of this Act shall be issued a certificate of alien registration or an alien registration receipt card in such form and manner and at such time as shall be prescribed under regulations issued by the Attorney General.

(e) Personal possession of registration or receipt card; penalties

Every alien, eighteen years of age and over, shall at all times carry with him and have in his personal possession any certificate of alien registration or alien registration receipt card issued to him pursuant to subsection (d). Any alien who fails to comply with the provisions of this subsection shall be guilty of a misdemeanor and shall upon conviction for each offense be fined not to exceed $100 or be imprisoned not more than thirty days, or both.

(f) Social security account number

Notwithstanding any other provision of law, the Attorney General is authorized to require any alien to provide the alien's social security account number for purposes of inclusion in any record of the alien maintained by the Attorney General or the Service.

(June 27, 1952, c. 477, Title II, ch. 7, § 264, 66 Stat. 224; Nov. 14, 1986, Pub.L. 99–653, § 10, 100 Stat. 3657; Oct. 24, 1988, Pub.L. 100–525, § 8(i), 102 Stat. 2617; Nov. 29, 1990, Pub.L. 101–649, Title V, § 503(b)(2), 104 Stat. 5049; Sept. 30, 1996, Pub.L. 104–208, Div. C, Title IV, § 415, 110 Stat. 3009–669.)

§ 265. Notices of change of address [8 U.S.C.A. § 1305]

(a) Notification of change

Each alien required to be registered under this title who is within the United States shall notify the Attorney General in writing of each change of address and new address within ten days from the date of such change and furnish with such notice such additional information as the Attorney General may require by regulation.

(b) Current address of natives of any one or more foreign states

The Attorney General may in his discretion, upon ten days notice, require the natives of any one or more foreign states, or any class or group thereof, who are within the United States and who are required to be registered under this title, to notify the Attorney General of their current addresses and furnish such additional information as the Attorney General may require.

(c) Notice to parent or legal guardian

In the case of an alien for whom a parent or legal guardian is required to apply for registration, the notice required by this section shall be given to such parent or legal guardian.

(June 27, 1952, c. 477, Title II, c. 7, § 265, 66 Stat. 225; Pub.L. 97–116, § 11, Dec. 29, 1981, 95 Stat. 1617; Pub.L. 100–525, § 9(*o*), Oct. 24, 1988, 102 Stat. 2620.)

§ 266. Penalties [8 U.S.C.A. § 1306]

(a) Willful failure to register

Any alien required to apply for registration and to be fingerprinted in the United States who willfully fails or refuses to make such application or to be fingerprinted, and any parent or legal guardian required to apply for the registration of any alien who willfully fails or refuses to file application for the registration of such alien shall be guilty of a misdemeanor and shall, upon conviction thereof, be fined not to exceed $1,000 or be imprisoned not more than six months, or both.

(b) Failure to notify change of address

Any alien or any parent or legal guardian in the United States of any alien who fails to give written notice to the Attorney General, as required by section 265 [8 U.S.C.A. § 1305], shall be guilty of a misdemeanor and shall, upon conviction thereof, be fined not to exceed $200 or be imprisoned not more than thirty days, or both. Irrespective of whether an alien is convicted and punished as herein provided, any alien who fails to give written notice to the Attorney General, as required by section 265 [8 U.S.C.A. § 1305], shall be taken into custody and removed in the manner provided by chapter 4 of the title, unless such alien establishes to the satisfaction of the Attorney General that such failure was reasonably excusable or was not willful.

(c) Fraudulent statements

Any alien or any parent or legal guardian of any alien, who files an application for registration containing statements known by him to be false, or who procures or attempts to procure registration of himself or another person through fraud, shall be guilty of a misdemeanor and shall, upon conviction thereof, be fined not to exceed $1,000, or be imprisoned not more than six months, or both; and any alien so convicted shall, upon the warrant of the Attorney General, be taken into custody and be removed in the manner provided in part IV of this title.

(d) Counterfeiting

Any person who with unlawful intent photographs, prints, or in any other manner makes, or executes, any engraving, photograph, print, or impression in the likeness of any certificate of alien registration or an alien registration receipt card or any colorable imitation thereof, except when and as authorized under such rules and regulations as may be prescribed by the Attorney General, shall upon conviction be fined not to exceed $5,000 or be imprisoned not more than five years, or both.

(June 27, 1952, c. 477, Title II, ch. 7, § 266, 66 Stat. 225; Sept. 30, 1996, Pub.L. 104–208, Div. C, Title III, § 308(e)(2)(G), (g)(9)(A), 110 Stat. 3009–620, 3009–624.)

CHAPTER VIII—GENERAL PENALTY PROVISIONS

§ 271. Prevention of unauthorized landing of aliens [8 U.S.C.A. § 1321]

(a) Failure to report; penalties

It shall be the duty of every person, including the owners, masters, officers, and agents of vessels, aircraft, transportation lines, or international bridges or toll roads, other than transportation lines which may enter into a contract as provided in section 233 [8 U.S.C.A. § 1223], bringing an alien to, or providing a means for an alien to come to, the United States (including an alien crewman whose case is not covered by section 254(a) [8 U.S.C.A. § 1284(a)]) to prevent the landing of such alien in the United States at a port of entry other than as designated by the Attorney General or at any time or place other than as designated by the immigration officers. Any such person, owner, master, officer, or agent who fails to comply with the foregoing requirements shall be liable to a penalty to be imposed by the Attorney General of $3,000 for each such violation, which may, in the discretion of the Attorney General, be remitted or mitigated by him in accordance with such proceedings as he shall by regulation prescribe. Such penalty shall be a lien upon the vessel or aircraft whose owner, master, officer, or agent violates the provisions of this section, and such vessel or aircraft may be libeled therefor in the appropriate United States court.

(b) Prima facie evidence

Proof that the alien failed to present himself at the time and place designated by the immigration officers shall be prima facie evidence that such alien has landed in the United States at a time or place other than as designated by the immigration officers.

(c) Liability of owners and operators of international bridges and toll roads

(1) Any owner or operator of a railroad line, international bridge, or toll road who establishes to the satisfaction of the Attorney General that the person has acted diligently and reasonably to fulfill the duty imposed by subsection (a) shall not be liable for the penalty described in such subsection, notwithstanding the failure of the person to prevent the unauthorized landing of any alien.

(2)(A) At the request of any person described in paragraph (1), the Attorney General shall inspect any facility established, or any method utilized, at a point of entry into the United States by such person for the purpose of complying with subsection (a). The Attorney General shall approve any such facility or method (for such period of time as the Attorney General may prescribe) which the Attorney General determines is satisfactory for such purpose.

(B) Proof that any person described in paragraph (1) has diligently maintained any facility, or utilized any method, which has been approved by the Attorney General under subparagraph (A) (within the period for which the approval is effective) shall be prima facie evidence that such person acted diligently and reasonably to fulfill the duty imposed by subsection (a) (within the meaning of paragraph (1) of this subsection).

(June 27, 1952, c. 477, Title II, ch. 8, § 271, 66 Stat. 226; Nov. 6, 1986, Pub.L. 99–603, Title I, § 114, 100 Stat. 3383; Nov. 29, 1990, Pub.L. 101–649, Title V, § 543(a)(8), 104 Stat. 5058; Sept. 30, 1996, Pub.L. 104–208, Div. C, Title III, § 308(g)(1), 110 Stat. 3009–622.)

§ 272. Bringing in aliens subject to denial of admission on a health-related ground; persons liable; clearance papers; exceptions; "person" defined [8 U.S.C.A. § 1322]

(a) Any person who shall bring to the United States an alien (other than an alien crewman) who is inadmissible under section 212(a)(1) [8 U.S.C.A. § 1182(a)(1)] shall pay to the Commissioner for each and every alien so afflicted the sum of $3,000 unless (1) the alien was in possession of a valid, unexpired immigrant visa, or **(2)** the alien was allowed to land in the United States, or **(3)** the alien was in possession of a valid unexpired non-immigrant visa or other document authorizing such alien to apply for temporary admission to the United States or an unexpired reentry permit issued to him, and **(A)** such application was made within one hundred and twenty days of the date of issuance of the visa or other document, or in the case of an alien in possession of a reentry permit, within one hundred and twenty days of the date on which the alien was last examined and admitted by the Service, or **(B)** in the event the application was made later than one hundred and twenty days of the date of issuance of the visa or other document or such examination and admission, if such person establishes to the satisfaction of the Attorney General that the existence of the condition causing inadmissibility could not have been detected by the exercise of due diligence prior to the alien's embarkation.

(b) No vessel or aircraft shall be granted clearance papers pending determination of the question of liability to the payment of any fine under this section, or while the fines remain unpaid, nor shall such fines be remitted or refunded; but clearance may be granted prior to the determination of such question upon the deposit of a sum sufficient to cover such fines or of a bond with sufficient surety to secure the payment thereof, approved by the Commissioner.

(c) Nothing contained in this section shall be construed to subject transportation companies to a fine for bringing to ports of entry in the United States aliens who are entitled by law to exemption from the provisions of section 212(a) [8 U.S.C.A. § 1182(a)].

(d) As used in this section, the term "person" means the owner, master, agent, commanding officer, charterer, or consignee of any vessel or aircraft.

(June 27, 1952, c. 477, Title II, ch. 8, § 272, 66 Stat. 226; Oct. 3, 1965, Pub.L. 89–236, § 18, 79 Stat. 920; Nov. 29, 1990, Pub.L. 101–649, Title V, § 543(a)(9), Title VI, § 603(a)(15), 104 Stat. 5058, 5084; Dec. 12, 1991, Pub.L. 102–232, Title III, § 307(*l*)(7), 105 Stat. 1757; Oct. 25, 1994, Pub.L. 103–416, Title II, § 219(*o*), 108 Stat. 4317; Sept. 30, 1996, Pub.L. 104–208, Div. C, Title III, § 308(d)(3)(A), (4)(I)(i), 110 Stat. 3009–617, 3009–618.)

§ 273. Unlawful bringing of aliens into United States [8 U.S.C.A. § 1323]

(a) Persons liable

(1) It shall be unlawful for any person, including any transportation company, or the owner, master, commanding officer, agent, charterer, or consignee of any vessel or aircraft, to bring to the United States from any place outside thereof (other than from foreign contiguous territory) any alien who does not have a valid passport and an unexpired visa, if a visa was required under this Act or regulations issued thereunder.

(2) It is unlawful for an owner, agent, master, commanding officer, person in charge, purser, or consignee of a vessel or aircraft who is bringing an alien (except an alien crewmember) to the United States to take any consideration to be kept or returned contingent on whether an alien is admitted to, or ordered removed from, the United States.

(b) Evidence

If it appears to the satisfaction of the Attorney General that any alien has been so brought, such person, or transportation company, or the master, commanding officer, agent, owner, charterer, or consignee of any such vessel or aircraft, shall pay to the Commissioner a fine of $3,000 for each alien so brought and, except in the case of any such alien who is admitted, or permitted to land temporarily, in addition, an amount equal to that paid by such alien for his transportation from the initial point of departure, indicated in his ticket, to the port of the arrival, such latter fine to be delivered by the Commissioner to the alien on whose account the assessment is made. No vessel or aircraft shall be granted clearance pending the determination of the liability to the payment of such fine or while such fine remains unpaid, except that clearance may be granted prior to the determination of such question upon the deposit of an amount sufficient to cover such fine, or of a bond with sufficient surety to secure the payment thereof approved by the Commissioner.

(c) Remission or refund

Except as provided in subsection (e), such fine shall not be remitted or refunded, unless it appears to the satisfaction of the Attorney General that such person, and the owner, master, commanding officer, agent, charterer, and consignee of the vessel or aircraft, prior to the departure of the vessel or aircraft from the last port outside the United States, did not know, and could not have ascertained by the exercise of reasonable diligence, that the individual transported was an alien and that a valid passport or visa was required.

(d) Repealed. Pub.L. 104–208, Div. C, Title III, § 308(e)(13), Sept. 30, 1996, 110 Stat. 3009–620.

(e) Reduction, refund, or waiver

A fine under this section may be reduced, refunded, or waived under such regulations as the Attorney General shall prescribe in cases in which—

(1) the carrier demonstrates that it had screened all passengers on the vessel or aircraft in accordance with procedures prescribed by the Attorney General, or

(2) circumstances exist that the Attorney General determines would justify such reduction, refund, or waiver.

(June 27, 1952, c. 477, Title II, ch. 8, § 273, 66 Stat. 227; Nov. 29, 1990, Pub.L. 101–649, Title II, § 201(b), Title V, § 543(a)(10), 104 Stat. 5014, 5058; Dec. 12, 1991, Pub.L. 102–232, Title III, § 306(c)(4)(D), 105 Stat. 1752; Oct. 25, 1994, Pub.L. 103–416, Title II, §§ 209(a), 216, 219(p), 108 Stat. 4312, 4315, 4317; Sept. 30, 1996, Pub.L. 104–208, Div. C, Title III, §§ 308(c)(3), (e)(13), 371(b)(8), Title VI, § 671(b)(6), (7), 110 Stat. 3009–616, 3009–620, 3009–645, 3009–722.)

§ 274. Bringing in and harboring certain aliens [8 U.S.C.A. § 1324]

(a) Criminal penalties

(1)(A) Any person who—

(i) knowing that a person is an alien, brings to or attempts to bring to the United States in any manner whatsoever such person at a place other than a designated port of entry or place other than as designated by the Commissioner, regardless of whether such alien has received prior official authorization to come to, enter, or reside in the United States and regardless of any future official action which may be taken with respect to such alien;

(ii) knowing or in reckless disregard of the fact that an alien has come to, entered, or remains in the United States in violation of law, transports, or moves or attempts to transport or move such alien within the United States by means of transportation or otherwise, in furtherance of such violation of law;

(iii) knowing or in reckless disregard of the fact that an alien has come to, entered, or remains in the United States in violation of law, conceals, harbors, or shields from detection, or attempts to conceal, harbor, or shield from detection, such alien in any place, including any building or any means of transportation;

(iv) encourages or induces an alien to come to, enter, or reside in the United States, knowing or in reckless disregard of the fact that such coming to, entry, or residence is or will be in violation of law; or

(v)(I) engages in any conspiracy to commit any of the preceding acts, or

(II) aids or abets the commission of any of the preceding acts,

shall be punished as provided in subparagraph (B).

(B) A person who violates subparagraph (A) shall, for each alien in respect to whom such a violation occurs—

(i) in the case of a violation of subparagraph (A)(i) or (v)(I) or in the case of a violation of subparagraph (A)(ii), (iii), or (iv) in which the offense was done for the purpose of commercial advantage or private financial gain, be fined under Title 18, imprisoned not more than 10 years, or both;

(ii) in the case of a violation of subparagraph (A)(ii), (iii), (iv), or (v)(II), be fined under Title 18, imprisoned not more than 5 years, or both;

(iii) in the case of a violation of subparagraph (A)(i), (ii), (iii), (iv), or (v) during and in relation to which the person causes serious bodily injury (as defined in section 1365 of Title 18) to, or places in jeopardy the life of, any person, be fined under Title 18, imprisoned not more than 20 years, or both; and

(iv) in the case of a violation of subparagraph (A)(i), (ii), (iii), (iv), or (v) resulting in the death of any person, be punished by death or imprisoned for any term of years or for life, fined under Title 18, or both.

(C) It is not a violation of clauses (ii) or (iii) of subparagraph (A), or of clause (iv) of subparagraph (A) except where a person encourages or induces an alien to come to or enter the United States, for a religious denomination having a bona fide nonprofit, religious organization in the United States, or the agents or officers of such denomination or organization, to encourage, invite, call, allow, or enable an alien who is present in the United States to perform the vocation of a minister or missionary for the denomination or organization in the United States as a volunteer who is not compensated as an employee, notwithstanding the provision of room, board, travel, medical assistance, and other basic living expenses, provided the minister or missionary has been a member of the denomination for at least one year.

(2) Any person who, knowing or in reckless disregard of the fact that an alien has not received prior official authorization to come to, enter, or reside in the United States, brings to or attempts to bring to the United States in any manner whatsoever, such alien, regardless of any official action which may later be taken with respect to such alien shall, for each alien in respect to whom a violation of this paragraph occurs—

(A) be fined in accordance with Title 18, or imprisoned not more than one year, or both; or

(B) in the case of—

(i) an offense committed with the intent or with reason to believe that the alien unlawfully brought into the United States will commit an offense against the United States or any State punishable by imprisonment for more than 1 year,

(ii) an offense done for the purpose of commercial advantage or private financial gain, or

(iii) an offense in which the alien is not upon arrival immediately brought and presented to an appropriate immigration officer at a designated port of entry,

be fined under Title 18, and shall be imprisoned, in the case of a first or second violation of subparagraph (B)(iii), not more than 10 years, in the case of a first or second violation of subparagraph (B)(i) or (B)(ii), not less than 3 nor more than 10 years, and for any other violation, not less than 5 nor more than 15 years.

(3)(A) Any person who, during any 12–month period, knowingly hires for employment at least 10 individuals with actual knowledge that the individuals are aliens described in subparagraph (B) shall be fined under Title 18, or imprisoned for not more than 5 years, or both.

(B) An alien described in this subparagraph is an alien who—

(i) is an unauthorized alien (as defined in section 274A(h)(3) [8 U.S.C.A. § 1324a(h)(3)]), and

(ii) has been brought into the United States in violation of this subsection.

(4) In the case of a person who has brought aliens into the United States in violation of this subsection, the sentence otherwise provided for may be increased by up to 10 years if—

(A) the offense was part of an ongoing commercial organization or enterprise;

(B) aliens were transported in groups of 10 or more; and

(C)(i) aliens were transported in a manner that endangered their lives; or

(ii) the aliens presented a life-threatening health risk to people in the United States.

(b) Seizure and forfeiture

(1) Any conveyance, including any vessel, vehicle, or aircraft, that has been or is being used in the commission of a violation of subsection (a), the gross proceeds of such violation, and any property traceable to such conveyance or proceeds, shall be seized and subject to forfeiture.

(2) Seizures and forfeitures under this subsection shall be governed by the provisions of chapter 46 of title 18, United States Code, relating to civil forfeitures, including section 981(d) of such title, except that such duties as are imposed upon the Secretary of the Treasury under the customs laws described in that section shall be performed by such officers, agents, and other persons as may be designated for that purpose by the Attorney General.

(3) In determining whether a violation of subsection (a) has occurred, any of the following shall be prima facie evidence that an alien involved in the alleged violation had not received prior official authorization to come to, enter, or reside in the United States or that such alien had come to, entered, or remained in the United States in violation of law:

(A) Records of any judicial or administrative proceeding in which that alien's status was an issue and in which it was determined that the alien had not received prior official authorization to come to, enter, or reside in the United States or that such alien had come to, entered, or remained in the United States in violation of law.

(B) Official records of the Service or of the Department of State showing that the alien had not received prior official authorization to come to, enter, or reside in the United States or that such alien had come to, entered, or remained in the United States in violation of law.

(C) Testimony, by an immigration officer having personal knowledge of the facts concerning that alien's status, that the alien had not received prior official authorization to come to, enter, or reside in the United States or that such alien had come to, entered, or remained in the United States in violation of law.

(c) Authority to arrest

No officer or person shall have authority to make any arrest for a violation of any provision of this section except officers and employees of the Service designated by the Attorney General, either individually or as a member of a class, and all other officers whose duty it is to enforce criminal laws.

(d) Admissibility of videotaped witness testimony

Notwithstanding any provision of the Federal Rules of Evidence, the videotaped (or otherwise audiovisually preserved) deposition of a witness to a violation of subsection (a) who has been deported or otherwise expelled from the United States, or is otherwise unable to testify, may be admitted into evidence in an action brought for that violation if the witness was available for cross examination and the deposition otherwise complies with the Federal Rules of Evidence.

(e) Outreach program

The Secretary of Homeland Security, in consultation with the Attorney General and the Secretary of State, as appropriate, shall develop and implement an outreach program to educate the public in the United States and abroad about the penalties for bringing in and harboring aliens in violation of this section.

(June 27, 1952, c. 477, Title II, ch. 8, § 274, 66 Stat. 228; Nov. 2, 1978, Pub.L. 95–582, § 2, 92 Stat. 2479; Dec. 29, 1981, Pub.L. 97–116, § 12, 95 Stat. 1617; Nov. 6, 1986, Pub.L. 99–603, § 112, 100 Stat. 3381; Oct. 24, 1988, Pub.L. 100–525, § 2(d), 102 Stat. 2610; Sept. 13, 1994, Pub.L. 103–322, Title VI, § 60024, 108 Stat. 1981; Sept. 30, 1996, Pub.L. 104–208, Div. C, Title II, §§ 203(a) to (d), 219, Title VI, § 671(a)(1), 110 Stat. 3009–565, 3009–566, 3009–574, 3009–721; April 25, 2000, Pub.L. 106–185, § 18, 114 Stat. 222; Dec. 17, 2004, Pub.L. 108–458, Title V, § 5401, 118 Stat. 3737; Nov. 10, 2005, Pub.L. 109–97, Title VII, § 796, 119 Stat. 2165.)

§ 274A. Unlawful employment of aliens [8 U.S.C.A. § 1324a]

(a) Making employment of unauthorized aliens unlawful

(1) In general

It is unlawful for a person or other entity—

(A) to hire, or to recruit or refer for a fee, for employment in the United States an alien knowing the alien is an unauthorized alien (as defined in subsection (h)(3)) with respect to such employment, or

(B) **(i)** to hire for employment in the United States an individual without complying with the requirements of subsection (b) or **(ii)** if the person or entity is an agricultural association, agricultural employer, or farm labor contractor (as defined in section 1802 of Title 29) to hire, or to recruit or refer for a fee, for employment in the United States an individual without complying with the requirements of subsection (b).

(2) Continuing employment

It is unlawful for a person or other entity, after hiring an alien for employment in accordance with paragraph (1), to continue to employ the alien in the United States knowing the alien is (or has become) an unauthorized alien with respect to such employment.

(3) Defense

A person or entity that establishes that it has complied in good faith with the requirements of subsection (b) with respect to the hiring, recruiting, or referral for employment of an alien in the United States has established an affirmative defense that the person or entity has not violated paragraph (1)(A) with respect to such hiring, recruiting, or referral.

(4) Use of labor through contract

For purposes of this section, a person or other entity who uses a contract, subcontract, or exchange, entered into, renegotiated, or extended after the date of the enactment of this section, to obtain the labor of an alien in the United States knowing that the alien is an unauthorized alien (as defined in subsection (h)(3)) with respect to performing such labor, shall be considered to have hired the alien for employment in the United States in violation of paragraph (1)(A).

(5) Use of State employment agency documentation

For purposes of paragraphs (1)(B) and (3), a person or entity shall be deemed to have complied with the requirements of subsection (b) with respect to the hiring of an individual who was referred for such employment by a State employment agency (as defined by the Attorney General), if the person or entity has and retains (for the period and in the manner described in subsection (b)(3)) appropriate documentation of such referral by that agency, which documentation certifies that the agency has complied with the procedures specified in subsection (b) with respect to the individual's referral.

(6) Treatment of documentation for certain employees

(A) In general

For purposes of this section, if—

(i) an individual is a member of a collective-bargaining unit and is employed, under a collective bargaining agreement entered into between one or more employee organizations and an association of two or more employers, by an employer that is a member of such association, and

(ii) within the period specified in subparagraph (B), another employer that is a member of the association (or an agent of such association on behalf of the employer) has complied with the requirements of subsection (b) with respect to the employment of the individual,

the subsequent employer shall be deemed to have complied with the requirements of subsection (b) with respect to the hiring of the employee and shall not be liable for civil penalties described in subsection (e)(5).

(B) Period

The period described in this subparagraph is 3 years, or, if less, the period of time that the individual is authorized to be employed in the United States.

(C) Liability

(i) In general

If any employer that is a member of an association hires for employment in the United States an individual and relies upon the provisions of subparagraph (A) to comply with the requirements of subsection (b) and the individual is an alien not authorized to work in the United States, then for the purposes of paragraph (1)(A), subject to clause (ii), the employer shall be presumed to have known at the time of hiring or afterward that the individual was an alien not authorized to work in the United States.

(ii) Rebuttal of presumption

The presumption established by clause (i) may be rebutted by the employer only through the presentation of clear and convincing evidence that the employer did not know (and could not reasonably have known) that the individual at the time of hiring or afterward was an alien not authorized to work in the United States.

(iii) Exception

Clause (i) shall not apply in any prosecution under subsection (f)(1).

(7) Application to Federal Government

For purposes of this section, the term "entity" includes an entity in any branch of the Federal Government.

(b) Employment verification system

The requirements referred to in paragraphs (1)(B) and (3) of subsection (a) are, in the case of a person or other entity hiring, recruiting, or referring an individual for employment in the United States, the requirements specified in the following three paragraphs:

(1) Attestation after examination of documentation

(A) In general

The person or entity must attest, under penalty of perjury and on a form designated or established by the Attorney General by regulation, that it has verified that the individual is not an unauthorized alien by examining—

(i) a document described in subparagraph (B), or

(ii) a document described in subparagraph (C) and a document described in subparagraph (D).

A person or entity has complied with the requirement of this paragraph with respect to examination of a document if the document reasonably appears on its face to be genuine. If an individual provides a document or combination of documents that reasonably appears on its face to be genuine and that is sufficient to meet the requirements of the first sentence of this paragraph, nothing in this paragraph shall be construed as requiring the person or entity to solicit the production of any other document or as requiring the individual to produce such another document.

(B) Documents establishing both employment authorization and identity

A document described in this subparagraph is an individual's—

(i) United States passport;

(ii) resident alien card, alien registration card, or other document designated by the Attorney General, if the document—

(I) contains a photograph of the individual and such other personal identifying information relating to the individual as the Attorney General finds, by regulation, sufficient for purposes of this subsection,

(II) is evidence of authorization of employment in the United States, and

(III) contains security features to make it resistant to tampering, counterfeiting, and fraudulent use.

(iii), (iv) Repealed. Pub.L. 104–208, Div. C, Title IV, § 412(a)(1)(A), Sept. 30, 1996, 110 Stat. 3009–666.

(v) Redesignated (ii).

(C) Documents evidencing employment authorization

A document described in this subparagraph is an individual's—

(i) social security account number card (other than such a card which specifies on the face that the issuance of the card does not authorize employment in the United States); or

(ii) other documentation evidencing authorization of employment in the United States which the Attorney General finds, by regulation, to be acceptable for purposes of this section.

(iii) Redesignated (ii).

(D) Documents establishing identity of individual

A document described in this subparagraph is an individual's—

(i) driver's license or similar document issued for the purpose of identification by a State, if it contains a photograph of the individual or such other personal identifying information relating to the individual as the Attorney General finds, by regulation, sufficient for purposes of this section; or

(ii) in the case of individuals under 16 years of age or in a State which does not provide for issuance of an identification document (other than a driver's license) referred to in clause (i), documentation of personal identity of such other type as the Attorney General finds, by regulation, provides a reliable means of identification.

(E) Authority to prohibit use of certain documents

If the Attorney General finds, by regulation, that any document described in subparagraph (B), (C), or (D) as establishing employment authorization or identity does not reliably establish such authorization or identity or is being used fraudulently to an unacceptable degree, the Attorney General may prohibit or place conditions on its use for purposes of this subsection.

(2) Individual attestation of employment authorization

The individual must attest, under penalty of perjury on the form designated or established for purposes of paragraph (1), that the individual is a citizen or national of the United States, an alien lawfully admitted for permanent residence, or an alien who is authorized under this Act or by the Attorney General to be hired, recruited, or referred for such employment.

(3) Retention of verification form

After completion of such form in accordance with paragraphs (1) and (2), the person or entity must retain the form and make it available for inspection by officers of the Service, the Special Counsel for Immigration–Related Unfair Employment Practices, or the Department of Labor during a period beginning on the date of the hiring, recruiting, or referral of the individual and ending—

(A) in the case of the recruiting or referral for a fee (without hiring) of an individual, three years after the date of the recruiting or referral, and

(B) in the case of the hiring of an individual—

(i) three years after the date of such hiring, or

(ii) one year after the date the individual's employment is terminated,

whichever is later.

(4) Copying of documentation permitted

Notwithstanding any other provision of law, the person or entity may copy a document presented by an individual pursuant to this subsection and may retain the copy, but only (except as otherwise permitted under law) for the purpose of complying with the requirements of this subsection.

(5) Limitation on use of attestation form

A form designated or established by the Attorney General under this subsection and any information contained in or appended to such form, may not be used for purposes other than for enforcement of this Act and sections 1001, 1028, 1546, and 1621 of Title 18.

(6) Good faith compliance

(A) In general

Except as provided in subparagraphs (B) and (C), a person or entity is considered to have complied with a requirement of this subsection notwithstanding a technical or procedural failure to meet such requirement if there was a good faith attempt to comply with the requirement.

(B) Exception if failure to correct after notice

Subparagraph (A) shall not apply if—

(i) the Service (or another enforcement agency) has explained to the person or entity the basis for the failure,

(ii) the person or entity has been provided a period of not less than 10 business days (beginning after the date of the explanation) within which to correct the failure, and

(iii) the person or entity has not corrected the failure voluntarily within such period.

(C) Exception for pattern or practice violators

Subparagraph (A) shall not apply to a person or entity that has or is engaging in a pattern or practice of violations of subsection (a)(1)(A) or (a)(2).

(c) No authorization of national identification cards

Nothing in this section shall be construed to authorize, directly or indirectly, the issuance or use of national identification cards or the establishment of a national identification card.

(d) Evaluation and changes in employment verification system

(1) Presidential monitoring and improvements in system

(A) Monitoring

The President shall provide for the monitoring and evaluation of the degree to which the employment verification system established under subsection (b) provides a secure system to determine employment eligibility in the United States and shall examine the suitability of existing Federal and State identification systems for use for this purpose.

(B) Improvements to establish secure system

To the extent that the system established under subsection (b) is found not to be a secure system to determine employment eligibility in the United States, the President shall, subject to paragraph (3) and taking into account the results of any demonstration projects conducted under paragraph (4), implement such changes in (including additions to) the requirements of subsection (b) as may be necessary to establish a secure system to determine employment eligibility in the United States. Such changes in the system may be implemented only if the changes conform to the requirements of paragraph (2).

(2) Restrictions on changes in system

Any change the President proposes to implement under paragraph (1) in the verification system must be designed in a manner so the verification system, as so changed, meets the following requirements:

(A) Reliable determination of identity

The system must be capable of reliably determining whether—

(i) a person with the identity claimed by an employee or prospective employee is eligible to work, and

(ii) the employee or prospective employee is claiming the identity of another individual.

(B) Using of counterfeit-resistant documents

If the system requires that a document be presented to or examined by an employer, the document must be in a form which is resistant to counterfeiting and tampering.

(C) Limited use of system

Any personal information utilized by the system may not be made available to Government agencies, employers, and other persons except to the extent necessary to verify that an individual is not an unauthorized alien.

(D) Privacy of information

The system must protect the privacy and security of personal information and identifiers utilized in the system.

(E) Limited denial of verification

A verification that an employee or prospective employee is eligible to be employed in the United States may not be withheld or revoked under the system for any reason other than that the employee or prospective employee is an unauthorized alien.

(F) Limited use for law enforcement purposes

The system may not be used for law enforcement purposes, other than for enforcement of this Act or sections 1001, 1028, 1546, and 1621 of Title 18.

(G) Restriction on use of new documents

If the system requires individuals to present a new card or other document (designed specifically for use for this purpose) at the time of hiring, recruitment, or referral, then such document may not be required to be presented for any purpose other than under this Act (or enforcement of sections 1001, 1028, 1546, and 1621 of Title 18) nor to be carried on one's person.

(3) Notice to Congress before implementing changes

(A) In general

The President may not implement any change under paragraph (1) unless at least—

(i) 60 days,

(ii) one year, in the case of a major change described in subparagraph (D)(iii), or

(iii) two years, in the case of a major change described in clause (i) or (ii) of subparagraph (D),

before the date of implementation of the change, the President has prepared and transmitted to the Committee on the Judiciary of the House of Representatives and to the Committee on the Judiciary of the Senate a written report setting forth the proposed change. If the President proposes to make any change regarding social security account number cards, the President shall transmit to the Committee on Ways and Means of the House of Representatives and to the Committee on Finance of the Senate a written report setting forth the proposed change. The President promptly shall cause to have printed in the Federal Register the substance of any major change (described in subparagraph (D)) proposed and reported to Congress.

(B) Contents of report

In any report under subparagraph (A) the President shall include recommendations for the establishment of civil and criminal sanctions for unauthorized use or disclosure of the information or identifiers contained in such system.

(C) Congressional review of major changes

(i) Hearings and review

The Committees on the Judiciary of the House of Representatives and of the Senate shall cause to have printed in the Congressional Record the substance of any major change described in subparagraph (D), shall hold hearings respecting the feasibility and desirability of implementing such a change, and, within the two year period before implementation, shall report to their respective Houses findings on whether or not such a change should be implemented.

(ii) Congressional action

No major change may be implemented unless the Congress specifically provides, in an appropriations or other Act, for funds for implementation of the change.

(D) Major changes defined

As used in this paragraph, the term "major change" means a change which would—

(i) require an individual to present a new card or other document (designed specifically for use for this purpose) at the time of hiring, recruitment, or referral,

(ii) provide for a telephone verification system under which an employer, recruiter, or referrer must transmit to a Federal official information concerning the immigration status of prospective employees and the official transmits to the person, and the person must record, a verification code, or

(iii) require any change in any card used for accounting purposes under the Social Security Act [42 U.S.C.A. § 301 et seq.]; including any change requiring that the only social security account number cards which may be presented in order to comply with subsection (b)(1)(C)(i) are such cards as are in a counterfeit-resistant form consistent with the second sentence of section 205(c)(2)(D) of the Social Security Act [42 U.S.C.A. § 405(c)(2)(D)].

(E) General revenue funding of social security card changes

Any costs incurred in developing and implementing any change described in subparagraph (D)(iii) for purposes of this subsection shall not be paid for out of any trust fund established under the Social Security Act.

(4) Demonstration projects

(A) Authority

The President may undertake demonstration projects (consistent with paragraph (2)) of different changes in the requirements of subsection (b). No such project may extend over a period of longer than five years.

(B) Reports on projects

The President shall report to the Congress on the results of demonstration projects conducted under this paragraph.

(e) Compliance

(1) Complaints and investigations

The Attorney General shall establish procedures—

(A) for individuals and entities to file written, signed complaints respecting potential violations of subsection (a) or (g)(1),

(B) for the investigation of those complaints which, on their face, have a substantial probability of validity,

(C) for the investigation of such other violations of subsection (a) or (g)(1) as the Attorney General determines to be appropriate, and

(D) for the designation in the Service of a unit which has, as its primary duty, the prosecution of cases of violations of subsection (a) or (g)(1) under this subsection.

(2) Authority in investigations

In conducting investigations and hearings under this subsection—

(A) immigration officers and administrative law judges shall have reasonable access to examine evidence of any person or entity being investigated,

(B) administrative law judges may, if necessary, compel by subpoena the attendance of witnesses and the production of evidence at any designated place or hearing, and

(C) immigration officers designated by the Commissioner may compel by subpoena the attendance of witnesses and the production of evidence at any designated place prior to the filing of a complaint in a case under paragraph (2).

In case of contumacy or refusal to obey a subpoena lawfully issued under this paragraph and upon application of the Attorney General, an appropriate district court of the United States may issue an order requiring compliance with such subpoena and any failure to obey such order may be punished by such court as a contempt thereof.

(3) Hearing

(A) In general

Before imposing an order described in paragraph (4), (5), or (6) against a person or entity under this subsection for a violation of subsection (a) or (g)(1), the Attorney General shall provide the person or entity with notice and, upon request made within a reasonable time (of not less than 30 days, as established by the Attorney General) of the date of the notice, a hearing respecting the violation.

(B) Conduct of hearing

Any hearing so requested shall be conducted before an administrative law judge. The hearing shall be conducted in accordance with the requirements of section 554 of Title 5. The hearing shall be held at the nearest practicable place to the place where the person or entity resides or of the place where the alleged violation occurred. If no hearing is so requested, the Attorney General's imposition of the order shall constitute a final and unappealable order.

(C) Issuance of orders

If the administrative law judge determines, upon the preponderance of the evidence received, that a person or entity named in the complaint has violated subsection (a) or (g)(1), the administrative law judge shall state his findings of fact and issue and cause to be served on such person or entity an order described in paragraph (4), (5), or (6).

(4) Cease and desist order with civil money penalty for hiring, recruiting, and referral violations

With respect to a violation of subsection (a)(1)(A) or (a)(2), the order under this subsection—

(A) shall require the person or entity to cease and desist from such violations and to pay a civil penalty in an amount of—

(i) not less than $250 and not more than $2,000 for each unauthorized alien with respect to whom a violation of either such subsection occurred.

(ii) not less than $2,000 and not more than $5,000 for each such alien in the case of a person or entity previously subject to one order under this paragraph, or

(iii) not less than $3,000 and not more than $10,000 for each such alien in the case of a person or entity previously subject to more than one order under this paragraph; and

(B) may require the person or entity—

(i) to comply with the requirements of subsection (b) (or subsection (d) if applicable) with respect to individuals hired (or recruited or referred for employment for a fee) during a period of up to three years, and

(ii) to take such other remedial action as is appropriate.

In applying this subsection in the case of a person or entity composed of distinct, physically separate subdivisions each of which provides separately for the hiring, recruiting, or referring for employment, without reference to the practices of, and not under the control of or common control with, another subdivision, each such subdivision shall be considered a separate person or entity.

(5) Order for civil money penalty for paperwork violations

With respect to a violation of subsection (a)(1)(B), the order under this subsection shall require the person or entity to pay a civil penalty in an amount of not less than $100 and not more than $1,000 for each individual with respect to whom such violation occurred. In determining the amount of the penalty, due consideration shall be given to the size of the business of the employer being charged, the good faith of the employer, the seriousness of the violation, whether or not the individual was an unauthorized alien, and the history of previous violations.

(6) Order for prohibited indemnity bonds

With respect to a violation of subsection (g)(1), the order under this subsection may provide for the remedy described in subsection (g)(2).

(7) Administrative appellate review

The decision and order of an administrative law judge shall become the final agency decision and order of the Attorney General unless either **(A)** within 30 days, an official delegated by regulation to exercise review authority over the decision and order modifies or vacates the decision and order, or **(B)** within 30 days of the date of such a modification or vacation (or within 60 days of the date of decision and order of an administrative law judge if not so modified or vacated) the decision and order is referred to the Attorney General pursuant to regulations, in which case the decision and order of the Attorney General shall become the final agency decision and order under this subsection. The Attorney General may not delegate the Attorney General's authority under this paragraph to any entity which has review authority over immigration-related matters.

(8) Judicial review

A person or entity adversely affected by a final order respecting an assessment may, within 45 days after the date the final order is issued, file a petition in the Court of Appeals for the appropriate circuit for review of the order.

(9) Enforcement of orders

If a person or entity fails to comply with a final order issued under this subsection against the person or entity, the Attorney General shall file a suit to seek compliance with the order in any appropriate district court of the United States. In any such suit, the validity and appropriateness of the final order shall not be subject to review.

(f) Criminal penalties and injunctions for pattern or practice violations

(1) Criminal penalty

Any person or entity which engages in a pattern or practice of violations of subsection (a)(1)(A) or (a)(2) shall be fined not more than $3,000 for each unauthorized alien with respect to whom such a violation occurs, imprisoned for not more than six months for the entire pattern or practice, or both, notwithstanding the provisions of any other Federal law relating to fine levels.

(2) Enjoining of pattern or practice violations

Whenever the Attorney General has reasonable cause to believe that a person or entity is engaged in a pattern or practice of employment, recruitment, or referral in violation of paragraph (1)(A) or (2) of subsection (a), the Attorney General may bring a civil action in the appropriate district court of the United States requesting such relief, including a permanent or temporary injunction, restraining order, or other order against the person or entity, as the Attorney General deems necessary.

(g) Prohibition of indemnity bonds

(1) Prohibition

It is unlawful for a person or other entity, in the hiring, recruiting, or referring for employment of any individual, to require the individual to post a bond or security, to pay or agree to pay an amount, or otherwise to provide a financial guarantee or indemnity, against any potential liability arising under this section relating to such hiring, recruiting, or referring of the individual.

(2) Civil penalty

Any person or entity which is determined, after notice and opportunity for an administrative hearing under subsection (e), to have violated paragraph (1) shall be subject to a civil penalty of $1,000 for each violation and to an administrative order requiring the return of any amounts received in violation of such paragraph to the employee or, if the employee cannot be located, to the general fund of the Treasury.

(h) Miscellaneous provisions

(1) Documentation

In providing documentation or endorsement of authorization of aliens (other than aliens lawfully admitted for permanent residence) authorized to be employed in the United States, the Attorney General shall provide that any limitations with respect to the period or type of employment or employer shall be conspicuously stated on the documentation or endorsement.

(2) Preemption

The provisions of this section preempt any State or local law imposing civil or criminal sanctions (other than through licensing and similar laws) upon those who employ, or recruit or refer for a fee for employment, unauthorized aliens.

(3) Definition of unauthorized alien

As used in this section, the term "unauthorized alien" means, with respect to the employment of an alien at a particular time, that the alien is not at that time either (A) an alien lawfully admitted for permanent residence, or (B) authorized to be so employed by this Act or by the Attorney General.

(i) to (n) Repealed. Pub.L. 104–208, Div. C, Title IV, § 412(c), Sept. 30, 1996, 110 Stat. 3009–668.

(June 27, 1952, c. 477, Title II, ch. 8, § 274A, as added Nov. 6, 1986, Pub.L. 99–603, Title I, § 101(a)(1), 100 Stat. 3360, and amended Oct. 24, 1988, Pub.L. 100–525, § 2(a)(1), 102 Stat. 2609; Nov. 29, 1990, Pub.L. 101–649, Title V, §§ 521(a), 538(a), 104 Stat. 5053, 5056; Dec. 12, 1991, Pub.L. 102–232, Title III, §§ 306(b)(2), 309(b)(11), 105 Stat. 1752, 1759; Oct. 25, 1994, Pub.L. 103–416, Title II, §§ 213, 219(z)(4), 108 Stat. 4314, 4318; Sept. 30, 1996, Pub.L. 104–208, Div. C, Title III, § 379(a), Title IV, §§ 411(a), 412(a) to (d), 416, 110 Stat. 3009–649, 3009–666 to 3009–669.)

§ 274B. Unfair immigration-related employment practices [8 U.S.C.A. § 1324b]

(a) Prohibition of discrimination based on national origin or citizenship status

(1) General rule

It is an unfair immigration-related employment practice for a person or other entity to discriminate against any individual (other than an unauthorized alien, as defined in section 274A(h)(3) [8 U.S.C.A. § 1324a(h)(3)]) with respect to the hiring, or recruitment or referral for a fee, of the individual for employment or the discharging of the individual from employment—

(A) because of such individual's national origin, or

(B) in the case of a protected individual (as defined in paragraph (3)), because of such individual's citizenship status.

(2) Exceptions

Paragraph (1) shall not apply to—

(A) a person or other entity that employs three or fewer employees,

(B) a person's or entity's discrimination because of an individual's national origin if the discrimination with respect to that person or entity and that individual is covered under section 2000e–2 of Title 42, or

(C) discrimination because of citizenship status which is otherwise required in order to comply with law, regulation, or executive order, or required by Federal, State, or local government contract, or which the Attorney General determines to be essential for an employer to do business with an agency or department of the Federal, State, or local government.

(3) Definition of protected individual

As used in paragraph (1), the term "protected individual" means an individual who—

(A) is a citizen or national of the United States, or

(B) is an alien who is lawfully admitted for permanent residence, is granted the status of an alien lawfully admitted for temporary residence under section 210(a) [8 U.S.C.A. § 1160(a)] or 245A(a)(1) [8 U.S.C.A. § 1255a(a)(1)], is admitted as a refugee under section 207 [8 U.S.C.A. § 1157], or is granted asylum under section 208 [8 U.S.C.A. § 1158]; but does not include **(i)** an alien who fails to apply for naturalization within six months of the date the alien first becomes eligible (by virtue of period of lawful permanent residence) to apply for naturalization or, if later, within six months after November 6, 1986 and **(ii)** an alien who has applied on a timely basis, but has not been naturalized as a citizen within 2 years after the date of the application, unless the alien can establish that the alien is actively pursuing naturalization, except that time consumed in the Service's processing the application shall not be counted toward the 2–year period.

(4) Additional exception providing right to prefer equally qualified citizens

Notwithstanding any other provision of this section, it is not an unfair immigration-related employment practice for a person or other entity to prefer to hire, recruit, or refer an individual who is a citizen or national of the United States over another individual who is an alien if the two individuals are equally qualified.

(5) Prohibition of intimidation or retaliation

It is also an unfair immigration-related employment practice for a person or other entity to intimidate, threaten, coerce, or retaliate against any individual for the purpose of interfering with any right or privilege secured under this section or because the individual intends to file or has filed a charge or a complaint, testified, assisted, or participated in any manner in an investigation, proceeding, or hearing under this section. An individual so intimidated, threatened, coerced, or retaliated against shall be considered, for purposes of subsections (d) and (g), to have been discriminated against.

(6) Treatment of certain documentary practices as employment practices

A person's or other entity's request, for purposes of satisfying the requirements of section 274A(b) [8 U.S.C.A. § 1324a(b)], for more or different documents than are required under such section or refusing to honor documents tendered that on their face reasonably appear to be genuine shall be treated as an unfair immigration-related employment practice if made for the purpose or with the intent of discriminating against an individual in violation of paragraph (1).

(b) Charges of violations

(1) In general

Except as provided in paragraph (2), any person alleging that the person is adversely affected directly by an unfair immigration-related employment practice (or a person on that person's behalf) or an officer of the Service alleging that an unfair immigration-related employment practice has occurred or is occurring may file a charge respecting such practice or violation with the Special Counsel (appointed under subsection (c)). Charges shall be in writing under oath or affirmation and shall contain such information as the Attorney General requires. The Special Counsel by certified mail shall serve a notice of the charge (including the date, place, and circumstances of the alleged unfair immigration-related employment practice) on the person or entity involved within 10 days.

(2) No overlap with EEOC complaints

No charge may be filed respecting an unfair immigration-related employment practice described in subsection (a)(1)(A) if a charge with respect to that practice based on the same set of facts has been filed with the Equal Employment Opportunity Commission under title VII of the Civil Rights Act of 1964 [42 U.S.C.A. § 2000e et seq.], unless the charge is dismissed as being outside the scope of such title. No charge respecting an employment practice may be filed with the Equal Employment Opportunity Commission under such title if a charge with respect to such practice based on the same set of facts has been filed under this subsection, unless the charge is dismissed under this section as being outside the scope of this section.

(c) Special Counsel

(1) Appointment

The President shall appoint, by and with the advice and consent of the Senate, a Special Counsel for Immigration–Related Unfair Employment Practices (hereinafter in this section referred to as the "Special Counsel") within the Department of Justice to serve for a term of four years. In the case of a vacancy in the office of the Special Counsel the President may designate the officer or employee who shall act as Special Counsel during such vacancy.

(2) Duties

The Special Counsel shall be responsible for investigation of charges and issuance of complaints under this section and in respect of the prosecution of all such complaints before administrative law judges and the exercise of certain functions under subsection (j)(1).

(3) Compensation

The Special Counsel is entitled to receive compensation at a rate not to exceed the rate now or hereafter provided for grade GS–17 of the General Schedule, under section 5332 of Title 5.

(4) Regional offices

The Special Counsel, in accordance with regulations of the Attorney General, shall establish such regional offices as may be necessary to carry out his duties.

(d) Investigation of charges

(1) By Special Counsel

The Special Counsel shall investigate each charge received and, within 120 days of the date of the receipt of the charge, determine whether or not there is reasonable cause to believe that the charge is true and whether nor not to bring a complaint with respect to the charge before an administrative law judge. The Special Counsel may, on his own initiative, conduct investigations respecting unfair immigration-related employment practices and, based on such an investigation and subject to paragraph (3), file a complaint before such a judge.

(2) Private actions

If the Special Counsel, after receiving such a charge respecting an unfair immigration-related employment practice which alleges knowing and intentional discriminatory activity or a pattern or practice of discriminatory activity, has not filed a complaint before an administrative law judge with respect to such charge within such 120–day period, the Special Counsel shall notify the person making the charge of the determination not to file such a complaint during such period and the person making the charge may (subject to paragraph (3)) file a complaint directly before such a judge within 90 days after the date of receipt of the notice. The Special Counsel's failure to file such a complaint within such 120–day period shall not affect the right of the Special Counsel to investigate the charge or to bring a complaint before an administrative law judge during such 90–day period.

(3) Time limitations on complaints

No complaint may be filed respecting any unfair immigration-related employment practice occurring more than 180 days prior to the date of the filing of the charge with the Special Counsel. This subparagraph shall not prevent the subsequent amending of a charge or complaint under subsection (e)(1).

(e) Hearings

(1) Notice

Whenever a complaint is made that a person or entity has engaged in or is engaging in any such unfair immigration-related employment practice, an administrative law judge shall have power to issue and cause to be served upon such person or entity a copy of the complaint and a notice of hearing before the judge at a place therein fixed, not less than five days after the serving of the complaint. Any such complaint may be amended by the judge conducting the hearing, upon the motion of the party filing the complaint, in the judge's discretion at any time prior to the issuance of an order based thereon. The person or entity so complained of shall have the right to file an answer to the original or amended complaint and to appear in person or otherwise and give testimony at the place and time fixed in the complaint.

(2) Judges hearing cases

Hearings on complaints under this subsection shall be considered before administrative law judges who are specially designated by the Attorney General as having special training respecting employment discrimination and, to the extent practicable, before such judges who only consider cases under this section.

(3) Complainant as party

Any person filing a charge with the Special Counsel respecting an unfair immigration-related employment practice shall be considered a party to any complaint before an administrative law judge respecting such practice and any subsequent appeal respecting that complaint. In the discretion of the judge conducting the hearing, any other person may be allowed to intervene in the proceeding and to present testimony.

(f) Testimony and authority of hearing officers

(1) Testimony

The testimony taken by the administrative law judge shall be reduced to writing. Thereafter, the judge, in his discretion, upon notice may provide for the taking of further testimony or hear argument.

(2) Authority of administrative law judges

In conducting investigations and hearings under this subsection and in accordance with regulations of the Attorney General, the Special Counsel and administrative law judges shall have reasonable access to examine evidence of any person or entity being investigated. The administrative law judges by subpoena may compel the attendance of witnesses and the production of evidence at any designated place or hearing. In case of contumacy or refusal to obey a subpoena lawfully issued under this paragraph and upon application of the administrative law judge, an appropriate district court of the United States may issue an order requiring compliance with such subpoena and any failure to obey such order may be punished by such court as a contempt thereof.

(g) Determinations

(1) Order

The administrative law judge shall issue and cause to be served on the parties to the proceeding an order, which shall be final unless appealed as provided under subsection (i).

(2) Orders finding violations

(A) In general

If, upon the preponderance of the evidence, an administrative law judge determines that any person or entity named in the complaint has engaged in or is engaging in any such unfair immigration-related employment practice, then the judge shall state his findings of fact and shall issue and cause to be served on such person or entity an order which requires such person or entity to cease and desist from such unfair immigration-related employment practice.

(B) Contents of order

Such an order also may require the person or entity—

(i) to comply with the requirements of section 274A(b) [8 U.S.C.A. § 1324a(b)] with respect to individuals hired (or recruited or referred for employment for a fee) during a period of up to three years;

(ii) to retain for the period referred to in clause (i) and only for purposes consistent with section 274A(b)(5) [8 U.S.C.A. § 1324a(b)(5)], the name and address of each individual who applies, in person or in writing, for hiring for an existing position, or for recruiting or referring for a fee, for employment in the United States;

(iii) to hire individuals directly and adversely affected, with or without back pay;

(iv)(I) except as provided in subclauses (III) through (IV), to pay a civil penalty of not less than $250 and not more than $2,000 for each individual discriminated against,

(II) except as provided in subclauses (III) and (IV), in the case of a person or entity previously subject to a single order under this paragraph, to pay a civil penalty of not less than $2,000 and not more than $5,000 for each individual discriminated against,

(III) except as provided in subclause (IV), in the case of a person or entity previously subject to more than one order under this paragraph, to pay a civil penalty of not less than $3,000 and not more than $10,000 for each individual discriminated against, and

(IV) in the case of an unfair immigration-related employment practice described in subsection (a)(6) of this section, to pay a civil penalty of not less than $100 and not more than $1,000 for each individual discriminated against;

(v) to post notices to employees about their rights under this section and employers' obligations under section 274A [8 U.S.C.A. § 1324a];

(vi) to educate all personnel involved in hiring and complying with this section or section 274A [8 U.S.C.A. § 1324a] about the requirements of this section or such section;

(vii) to remove (in an appropriate case) a false performance review or false warning from an employee's personnel file; and

(viii) to lift (in an appropriate case) any restrictions on an employee's assignments, work shifts, or movements.

(C) Limitation on back pay remedy

In providing a remedy under subparagraph (B)(iii), back pay liability shall not accrue from a date more than two years prior to the date of the filing of a charge with the Special Counsel. Interim earnings or amounts earnable with reasonable diligence by the individual or individuals discriminated against shall operate to reduce the back pay otherwise allowable under such subparagraph. No order shall require the hiring of an individual as an employee or the payment to an individual of any back pay, if the individual was refused employment for any reason other than discrimination on account of national origin or citizenship status.

(D) Treatment of distinct entities

In applying this subsection in the case of a person or entity composed of distinct, physically separate subdivisions each of which provides separately for the hiring, recruiting, or referring for employment, without reference to the practices of, and not under the control of or common control with, another subdivision, each such subdivision shall be considered a separate person or entity.

(3) Orders not finding violations

If upon the preponderance of the evidence an administrative law judge determines that the person or entity named in the complaint has not engaged and is not engaging in any such unfair immigration-related employment practice, then the judge shall state his findings of fact and shall issue an order dismissing the complaint.

(h) Awarding of attorney's fees

In any complaint respecting an unfair immigration-related employment practice, an administrative law judge, in the judge's discretion, may allow a prevailing party, other than the United States, a reasonable attorney's fee, if the losing party's argument is without reasonable foundation in law and fact.

(i) Review of final orders

(1) In general

Not later than 60 days after the entry of such final order, any person aggrieved by such final order may seek a review of such order in the United States court of appeals for the circuit in which the violation is alleged to have occurred or in which the employer resides or transacts business.

(2) Further review

Upon the filing of the record with the court, the jurisdiction of the court shall be exclusive and its judgment shall be final, except that the same shall be subject to review by the Supreme Court of the United States upon writ of certiorari or certification as provided in section 1254 of Title 28.

(j) Court enforcement of administrative orders

(1) In general

If an order of the agency is not appealed under subsection (i)(1), the Special Counsel (or, if the Special Counsel fails to act, the person filing the charge) may petition the United States district court for the district in which a violation of the order is alleged to have occurred, or in which the respondent resides or transacts business, for the enforcement of the order of the administrative law judge, by filing in such court a written petition praying that such order be enforced.

(2) Court enforcement order

Upon the filing of such petition, the court shall have jurisdiction to make and enter a decree enforcing the order of the administrative law judge. In such a proceeding, the order of the administrative law judge shall not be subject to review.

(3) Enforcement decree in original review

If, upon appeal of an order under subsection (i)(1), the United States court of appeals does not reverse such order, such court shall have the jurisdiction to make and enter a decree enforcing the order of the administrative law judge.

(4) Awarding of attorney's fees

In any judicial proceeding under subsection (i) or this subsection, the court, in its discretion, may allow a prevailing party, other than the United States, a reasonable attorney's fee as part of costs but only if the losing party's argument is without reasonable foundation in law and fact.

(k) Termination dates

(1) This section shall not apply to discrimination in hiring, recruiting, referring, or discharging of individuals occurring after the date of any termination of the provisions of section 274A [8 U.S.C.A. § 1324a], under subsection (*l*) of that section.

(2) The provisions of this section shall terminate 30 calendar days after receipt of the last report required to be transmitted under section 274A(i) [8 U.S.C.A. § 1324a(i)] if—

(A) the Comptroller General determines, and so reports in such report that—

(i) no significant discrimination has resulted, against citizens or nationals of the United States or against any eligible workers seeking employment, from the implementation of section 274A [8 U.S.C.A. § 1324a], or

(ii) such section has created an unreasonable burden on employers hiring such workers; and

(B) there has been enacted, within such period of 30 calendar days, a joint resolution stating in substance that the Congress approves the findings of the Comptroller General contained in such report.

The provisions of subsections (m) and (n) of section 274A [8 U.S.C.A. § 1324a] shall apply to any joint resolution under subparagraph (B) in the same manner as they apply to a joint resolution under subsection (*l*) of such section.

(*l*) Dissemination of information concerning anti-discrimination provisions

(1) Not later than 3 months after November 29, 1990, the Special Counsel, in cooperation with the chairman of the Equal Employment Opportunity Commission, the Secretary of Labor, and the Administrator of the Small Business Administration, shall conduct a campaign to disseminate information respecting the rights and remedies prescribed under this section and under title VII of the Civil Rights Act of 1964 [42 U.S.C.A. § 2000e et seq.] in connection with unfair immigration-related employment practices. Such campaign shall be aimed at increasing the knowledge of employers, employees, and the general public concerning employer and employee rights, responsibilities, and remedies under this section and such title.

(2) In order to carry out the campaign under this subsection, the Special Counsel—

(A) may, to the extent deemed appropriate and subject to the availability of appropriations, contract with public and private organizations for outreach activities under the campaign, and

(B) shall consult with the Secretary of Labor, the chairman of the Equal Employment Opportunity Commission, and the heads of such other agencies as may be appropriate.

(3) There are authorized to be appropriated to carry out this subsection $10,000,000 for each fiscal year (beginning with fiscal year 1991).

(June 27, 1952, c. 477, Title II, ch. 8, § 274B, as added Nov. 6, 1986, Pub.L. 99–603, Title I, 102(a), 100 Stat. 3374, and amended Oct. 24, 1988, Pub.L. 100–525, § 2(b), 102 Stat. 2610; Nov. 29, 1990, Pub.L. 101–649, Title V, §§ 531, 532(a), 533(a), 534(a), 535(a), 536(a), 537(a), 539(a), 104 Stat. 5054, 5055, 5056; Dec. 12, 1991, Pub.L. 102–232, Title III, § 306(b)(1),(3),(c)(1), 105 Stat. 1752; Oct. 25, 1994, Pub.L. 103–416, Title II, § 219(q), 108 Stat. 4317; Sept. 30, 1996, Pub.L. 104–208, Div. C, Title IV, § 421(a), Title VI, § 671(d)(1)(B), 110 Stat. 3009–670, 3009–723.)

§ 274C. Penalties for document fraud [8 U.S.C.A. § 1324c]

(a) Activities prohibited

It is unlawful for any person or entity knowingly—

(1) to forge, counterfeit, alter, or falsely make any document for the purpose of satisfying a requirement of this Act or to obtain a benefit under this Act,

(2) to use, attempt to use, possess, obtain, accept, or receive or to provide any forged, counterfeit, altered, or falsely made document in order to satisfy any requirement of this Act or to obtain a benefit under this Act,

(3) to use or attempt to use or to provide or attempt to provide any document lawfully issued to or with respect to a person other than the possessor (including a deceased individual) for the purpose of satisfying a requirement of this Act or obtaining a benefit under this Act,

(4) to accept or receive or to provide any document lawfully issued to or with respect to a person other than the possessor (including a deceased individual) for the purpose of complying with section 274A(b) [8 U.S.C.A. § 1324a(b)] or obtaining a benefit under this Act, or

(5) to prepare, file, or assist another in preparing or filing, any application for benefits under this Act, or any document required under this Act, or any document submitted in connection with such application or document, with knowledge or in reckless disregard of the fact that such application or document was falsely made or, in whole or in part, does not relate to the person on whose behalf it was or is being submitted, or

(6) (A) to present before boarding a common carrier for the purpose of coming to the United States a document which relates to the alien's eligibility to enter the United States, and (B) to fail to present such document to an immigration officer upon arrival at a United States port of entry.

(b) Exception

This section does not prohibit any lawfully authorized investigative, protective, or intelligence activity of a law enforcement agency of the United States, a State, or a subdivision of a State, or of an intelligence agency of the United States, or any activity authorized under chapter 224 of Title 18.

(c) Construction

Nothing in this section shall be construed to diminish or qualify any of the penalties available for activities prohibited by this section but proscribed as well in Title 18.

(d) Enforcement

(1) Authority in investigations

In conducting investigations and hearings under this subsection—

(A) immigration officers and administrative law judges shall have reasonable access to examine evidence of any person or entity being investigated,

(B) administrative law judges, may, if necessary, compel by subpoena the attendance of witnesses and the production of evidence at any designated place or hearing, and

(C) immigration officers designated by the Commissioner may compel by subpoena the attendance of witnesses and the production of evidence at any designated place prior to the filing of a complaint in a case under paragraph (2).

In case of contumacy or refusal to obey a subpoena lawfully issued under this paragraph and upon application of the Attorney General, an appropriate district court of the United States may issue an order requiring compliance with such subpoena and any failure to obey such order may be punished by such court as a contempt thereof.

(2) Hearing

(A) In general

Before imposing an order described in paragraph (3) against a person or entity under this subsection for a violation of subsection (a), the Attorney General shall provide the person or entity with notice and, upon request made within a reasonable time (of not less than 30 days, as established by the Attorney General) of the date of the notice, a hearing respecting the violation.

(B) Conduct of hearing

Any hearing so requested shall be conducted before an administrative law judge. The hearing shall be conducted in accordance with the requirements of section 554 of Title 5. The hearing shall be held at the nearest practicable place to the place where the person or entity resides or of the place where the alleged violation occurred. If no hearing is so requested, the Attorney General's imposition of the order shall constitute a final and unappealable order.

(C) Issuance of orders

If the administrative law judge determines, upon the preponderance of the evidence received, that a person or entity has violated subsection (a), the administrative law judge shall state his findings of fact and issue and cause to be served on such person or entity an order described in paragraph (3).

(3) Cease and desist order with civil money penalty

With respect to a violation of subsection (a), the order under this subsection shall require the person or entity to cease and desist from such violations and to pay a civil penalty in an amount of—

(A) not less than $250 and not more than $2,000 for each document that is the subject of a violation under subsection (a), or

(B) in the case of a person or entity previously subject to an order under this paragraph, not less than $2,000 and not more than $5,000 for each document that is the subject of a violation under subsection (a).

In applying this subsection in the case of a person or entity composed of distinct, physically separate subdivisions each of which provides separately for the hiring, recruiting, or referring for employment, without reference to the practices of, and not under the control of or common control with, another subdivision, each such subdivision shall be considered a separate person or entity.

(4) Administrative appellate review

The decision and order of an administrative law judge shall become the final agency decision and order of the Attorney General unless either **(A)** within 30 days, an official delegated by regulation to exercise review authority over the decision and order modifies or vacates the decision and order, or **(B)** within 30 days of the date of such a modification or vacation (or within 60 days of the date of decision and order of an administrative law judge if not so modified or vacated) the decision and order is referred to the Attorney General pursuant to regulations, in which case the decision and order of the Attorney General shall become the final agency decision and order under this subsection.

(5) Judicial review

A person or entity adversely affected by a final order under this section may, within 45 days after the date the final order is issued, file a petition in the Court of Appeals for the appropriate circuit for review of the order.

(6) Enforcement of orders

If a person or entity fails to comply with a final order issued under this section against the person or entity, the Attorney General shall file a suit to seek compliance with the order in any appropriate district court of the United States. In any such suit, the validity and appropriateness of the final order shall not be subject to review.

(7) Waiver by Attorney General

The Attorney General may waive the penalties imposed by this section with respect to an alien who knowingly violates subsection (a)(6) if the alien is granted asylum under section 208 [8 U.S.C.A. § 1158] or withholding of removal under section 241(b)(3) [8 U.S.C.A. § 1231(b)(3)].

(e) Criminal penalties for failure to disclose role as document preparer

(1) Whoever, in any matter within the jurisdiction of the Service, knowingly and willfully fails to disclose, conceals, or covers up the fact that they have, on behalf of any person and for a fee or other remuneration, prepared or assisted in preparing an application which was falsely made (as defined in subsection (f)) for immigration benefits, shall be fined in accordance with Title 18, imprisoned for not more than 5 years, or both, and prohibited from preparing or assisting in preparing, whether or not for a fee or other remuneration, any other such application.

(2) Whoever, having been convicted of a violation of paragraph (1), knowingly and willfully prepares or assists in preparing an application for immigration benefits pursuant to this Act, or the regulations promulgated thereunder, whether or not for a fee or other remuneration and regardless of whether in any matter within the jurisdiction of the Service, shall be fined in accordance with Title 18, imprisoned for not more than 15 years, or both, and prohibited from preparing or assisting in preparing any other such application.

(f) Falsely make

For purposes of this section, the term "falsely make" means to prepare or provide an application or document, with knowledge or in reckless disregard of the fact that the application or document contains a false, fictitious, or fraudulent statement or material representation, or has no basis in law or fact, or otherwise fails to state a fact which is material to the purpose for which it was submitted.

(June 27, 1952, c. 477, Title II, ch. 8, § 274C, as added Nov. 29, 1990, Pub.L. 101–649, Title V, § 544(a), 104 Stat. 5059, and amended Dec. 12, 1991, Pub.L. 102–232, Title III, § 306(c)(5)(A), 105 Stat. 1752; Oct. 25, 1994, Pub.L. 103–416, Title II, § 219(r), 108 Stat. 4317; Sept. 30, 1996, Pub.L. 104–208, Div. C, Title II, §§ 212(a) to (d), 213, 220, Title III, §§ 308(g)(10)(D), 379(a), 110 Stat. 3009–570, 3009–571, 3009–575, 3009–625, 3009–649.)

§ 274D. Civil penalties for failure to depart [8 U.S.C.A. § 1324d]

(a) In general

Any alien subject to a final order of removal who—

(1) willfully fails or refuses to—

(A) depart from the United States pursuant to the order,

(B) make timely application in good faith for travel or other documents necessary for departure, or

(C) present for removal at the time and place required by the Attorney General; or

(2) conspires to or takes any action designed to prevent or hamper the alien's departure pursuant to the order,

shall pay a civil penalty of not more than $500 to the Commissioner for each day the alien is in violation of this section.

(b) Construction

Nothing in this section shall be construed to diminish or qualify any penalties to which an alien may be subject for activities proscribed by section 243(a) [8 U.S.C.A. § 1253(a)] or any other section of this Act.

(June 27, 1952, c. 477, Title II, ch. 8, § 274D, as added Sept. 30, 1996, Pub.L. 104–208, Div. C, Title III, § 380(a), 110 Stat. 3009–650.)

§ 275. Improper entry by alien [8 U.S.C.A. § 1325]

(a) Improper time or place; avoidance of examination or inspection; misrepresentation and concealment of facts

Any alien who **(1)** enters or attempts to enter the United States at any time or place other than as designated by immigration officers, or **(2)** eludes examination or inspection by immigration officers, or **(3)** attempts to enter or obtains entry to the United States by a willfully false or misleading representation or the willful concealment of a material fact, shall, for the first commission of any such offense, be fined under Title 18 or imprisoned not more than 6 months, or both, and, for a subsequent commission of any such offense, be fined under Title 18, or imprisoned not more than 2 years, or both.

(b) Civil penalty for illegal entry

Any alien who is apprehended while entering (or attempting to enter) the United States at a time or place other than as designated by immigration officers shall be subject to a civil penalty of—

(1) at least $50 and not more than $250 for each such entry (or attempted entry); or

(2) twice the amount specified in paragraph (1) in the case of an alien who has been previously subject to a civil penalty under this subsection.

Civil penalties under this subsection are in addition to, and not in lieu of, any criminal or other civil penalties that may be imposed.

(c) Marriage fraud

Any individual who knowingly enters into a marriage for the purpose of evading any provision of the immigration laws shall be imprisoned for not more than 5 years, or fined not more than $250,000, or both.

(d) Immigration-related entrepreneurship fraud

Any individual who knowingly establishes a commercial enterprise for the purpose of evading any provision of the immigration laws shall be imprisoned for not more than 5 years, fined in accordance with Title 18, or both.

(June 27, 1952, c. 477, Title II, ch. 8, § 275, 66 Stat. 229; Nov. 10, 1986, Pub.L. 99–639, § 2(d), 100 Stat. 3542; Nov. 29, 1990, Pub.L. 101–649, Title I, § 121(b)(3), Title V, § 543(b)(2), 104 Stat. 4994, 5059; Dec. 12, 1991, Pub.L. 102–232, Title III, § 306(c)(3), 105 Stat. 1752; Sept. 30, 1996, Pub.L. 104–208, Div C, Title I, § 105(a), 110 Stat. 3009–556.)

§ 276. Reentry of deported alien; criminal penalties for reentry of certain deported aliens [8 U.S.C.A. § 1326]

(a) Subject to subsection (b), any alien who—

(1) has been denied admission, excluded, deported, or removed or has departed the United States while an order of exclusion, deportation, or removal is outstanding, and thereafter

(2) enters, attempts to enter, or is at any time found in, the United States, unless **(A)** prior to his reembarkation at a place outside the United States or his application for admission from foreign contiguous territory, the Attorney General has expressly consented to such alien's reapplying for admission; or **(B)** with respect to an alien previously denied admission and removed, unless such alien shall establish that he was not required to obtain such advance consent under this or any prior Act,

shall be fined under Title 18, or imprisoned not more than 2 years, or both.

(b) Notwithstanding subsection (a), in the case of any alien described in such subsection—

(1) whose removal was subsequent to a conviction for commission of three or more misdemeanors involving drugs, crimes against the person, or both, or a felony (other than an aggravated felony), such alien shall be fined under Title 18, imprisoned not more than 10 years, or both;

(2) whose removal was subsequent to a conviction for commission of an aggravated felony, such alien shall be fined under such Title, imprisoned not more than 20 years, or both;

(3) who has been excluded from the United States pursuant to section 235(c) [8 U.S.C.A. § 1225(c)] because the alien was excludable under section 212(a)(3)(B) [8 U.S.C.A. § 1182(a)(3)(B)] or who has been removed from the United States pursuant to the provisions of title V, and who thereafter, without the permission of the Attorney General, enters the United States, or attempts to do so, shall be fined under Title 18, and imprisoned for a period of 10 years, which sentence shall not run concurrently with any other sentence; or

(4) who was removed from the United States pursuant to section 241(a)(4)(B) [8 U.S.C.A. § 1231(a)(4)(B)] who thereafter, without the permission of the Attorney General, enters, attempts to enter, or is at any time found in, the United States (unless the Attorney General has expressly consented to such alien's reentry) shall be fined under Title 18, imprisoned for not more than 10 years, or both.

For the purposes of this subsection, the term "removal" includes any agreement in which an alien stipulates to removal during (or not during) a criminal trial under either Federal or State law.

(c) Any alien deported pursuant to section 242(h)(2) [8 U.S.C.A. § 1252(h)(2)]* who enters, attempts to enter, or is at any time found in, the United States (unless the Attorney General has expressly consented to such alien's reentry) shall be incarcerated for the remainder of the sentence of imprisonment which was pending at the time of deportation without any reduction for parole or supervised release. Such alien shall be subject to such other penalties relating to the reentry of deported aliens as may be available under this section or any other provision of law.

(d) In a criminal proceeding under this section, an alien may not challenge the validity of the deportation order described in subsection (a)(1) or subsection (b) unless the alien demonstrates that—

(1) the alien exhausted any administrative remedies that may have been available to seek relief against the order;

(2) the deportation proceedings at which the order was issued improperly deprived the alien of the opportunity for judicial review; and

* Section 242 does not contain a subsec. (h). For provisions similar to those contained in former section 242(h), see section 241(a)(4).

(3) the entry of the order was fundamentally unfair.

(June 27, 1952, c. 477, Title II, ch. 8, § 276, 66 Stat. 229; Nov. 18, 1988, Pub.L. 100–690, Title VII, § 7345(a), 102 Stat. 4471; Nov. 29, 1990, Pub.L. 101–649, Title V, § 543(b)(3), 104 Stat. 5059; Sept. 13, 1994, Pub.L. 103–322, Title XIII, § 130001(b), 108 Stat. 2023; Apr. 24, 1996, Pub.L. 104–132, Title IV, §§ 401(c), 438(b), 441(a), 110 Stat. 1267, 1276, 1279; Sept. 30, 1996, Pub.L. 104–208, Div. C, Title III, §§ 305(b), 308(d)(4)(J), (e)(1)(K), (14)(A), 324(a), (b), 110 Stat. 3009–606, 3009–618, 3009–619, 3009–620, 3009–629.)

§ 277. Aiding or assisting certain aliens to enter [8 U.S.C.A. § 1327]

Any person who knowingly aids or assists any alien inadmissible under section 212(a)(2) [8 U.S.C.A. § 1182(a)(2)] (insofar as an alien inadmissible under such section has been convicted of an aggravated felony) or 212(a)(3) [8 U.S.C.A. § 1182(a)(3)] (other than subparagraph (E) thereof) to enter the United States, or who connives or conspires with any person or persons to allow, procure, or permit any such alien to enter the United States, shall be fined under Title 18, or imprisoned not more than 10 years, or both.

(June 27, 1952, c. 477, Title II, ch. 8, § 277, 66 Stat. 229; Nov. 18, 1988, Pub.L. 100–690, Title VII, § 7346(a), (c)(1), 102 Stat. 4471; Nov. 29, 1990, Pub.L. 101–649, Title V, § 543(b)(4), Title VI, § 603(a)(16), 104 Stat. 5059, 5084; Sept. 30, 1996, Pub.L. 104–208, Div. C, Title III, § 308(d)(3)(A), 110 Stat. 3009–617.)

§ 278. Importation of alien for immoral purpose [8 U.S.C.A. § 1328]

The importation into the United States of any alien for the purpose of prostitution, or for any other immoral purpose, is forbidden. Whoever shall, directly or indirectly, import, or attempt to import into the United States any alien for the purpose of prostitution or for any other immoral purpose, or shall hold or attempt to hold any alien for any such purpose in pursuance of such illegal importation, or shall keep, maintain, control, support, employ, or harbor in any house or other place, for the purpose of prostitution or for any other immoral purpose, any alien, in pursuance of such illegal importation, shall be fined under Title 18, or imprisoned not more than 10 years, or both. The trial and punishment of offenses under this section may be in any district to or into which such alien is brought in pursuance of importation by the person or persons accused, or in any district in which a violation of any of the provisions of this section occurs. In all prosecutions under this section, the testimony of a husband or wife shall be admissible and competent evidence against each other.

(June 27, 1952, c. 477, Title II, ch. 8, § 278, 66 Stat. 230; Nov. 29, 1990, Pub.L. 101–649, Title V, § 543(b)(5), 104 Stat. 5059.)

§ 279. Jurisdiction of district courts [8 U.S.C.A. § 1329]

The district courts of the United States shall have jurisdiction of all causes, civil and criminal, brought by the United States that arise under the provisions of this title. It shall be the duty of the United States attorney of the proper district to prosecute every such suit when brought by the United States. Notwithstanding any other law, such prosecutions or suits may be instituted at any place in the United States at which the violation may occur or at which the person charged with a violation under section 275 [8 U.S.C.A. § 1325] or 276 [8 U.S.C.A. § 1326] may be apprehended. No suit or proceeding for a violation of any of the provisions of this title shall be settled, compromised, or discontinued without the consent of the court in which it is pending and any such settlement, compromise, or discontinuance shall be entered of record with the reasons therefor. Nothing in this section shall be construed as providing jurisdiction for suits against the United States or its agencies or officers.

(June 27, 1952, c. 477, Title II, ch. 8, § 279, 66 Stat. 230; Sept. 30, 1996, Pub.L. 104–208, Div. C, Title III, § 381(a), 110 Stat. 3009–650.)

§ 280. Collection of penalties and expenses [8 U.S.C.A. § 1330]

(a) Notwithstanding any other provisions of this title, the withholding or denial of clearance of or a lien upon any vessel or aircraft provided for in section 231 [8 U.S.C.A. § 1221], 234 [8 U.S.C.A. § 1224], 243(c)(2) [8 U.S.C.A. § 1253(c)(2)], 251 [8 U.S.C.A. § 1281], 253 [8 U.S.C.A. § 1283], 254 [8 U.S.C.A. § 1284], 255 [8 U.S.C.A. § 1285], 256 [8 U.S.C.A. § 1286], 271 [8 U.S.C.A. § 1321], 272 [8 U.S.C.A. § 1322], or 273 [8 U.S.C.A. § 1323] shall not be regarded as the sole and exclusive means or remedy for the enforcement of payments of any fine, penalty or expenses imposed or incurred under such sections, but, in the discretion of the Attorney General, the amount thereof may be recovered by civil suit, in the name of the United States, from any person made liable under any of such sections.

(b)(1) There is established in the general fund of the Treasury a separate account which shall be known as the "Immigration Enforcement Account". Notwithstanding any other section of this title, there shall be deposited as offsetting receipts into the Immigration Enforcement Account amounts described in paragraph (2) to remain available until expended.

(2) The amounts described in this paragraph are the following:

(A) The increase in penalties collected resulting from the amendments made by sections 203(b) and 543(a) of the Immigration Act of 1990.

(B) Civil penalties collected under sections 240B(d) [8 U.S.C.A. § 1229c(d)], 274C [8 U.S.C.A. § 1324c], 274D [8 U.S.C.A. § 1324d], and 275(b) [8 U.S.C.A. § 1325(b)].

(3)(A) The Secretary of the Treasury shall refund out of the Immigration Enforcement Account to any appropriation the amount paid out of such appropriation for expenses incurred by the Attorney General for activities that enhance enforcement of provisions of this title. Such activities include—

(i) the identification, investigation, apprehension, detention, and removal of criminal aliens;

(ii) the maintenance and updating of a system to identify and track criminal aliens, deportable aliens, inadmissible aliens, and aliens illegally entering the United States; and

(iii) for the repair, maintenance, or construction on the United States border, in areas experiencing high levels of apprehensions of illegal aliens, of structures to deter illegal entry into the United States.

(B) The amounts which are required to be refunded under subparagraph (A) shall be refunded at least quarterly on the basis of estimates made by the Attorney General of the expenses referred to in subparagraph (A). Proper adjustments shall be made in the amounts subsequently refunded under subparagraph (A) to the extent prior estimates were in excess of, or less than, the amount required to be refunded under subparagraph (A).

(C) The amounts required to be refunded from the Immigration Enforcement Account for fiscal year 1996 and thereafter shall be refunded in accordance with estimates made in the budget request of the Attorney General for those fiscal years. Any proposed changes in the amounts designated in such budget requests shall only be made after notification to the Committees on Appropriations of the House of Representatives and the Senate in accordance with section 605 of Public Law 104–134.

(D) The Attorney General shall prepare and submit annually to the Congress statements of financial condition of the Immigration Enforcement Account, including beginning account balance, revenues, withdrawals, and ending account balance and projection for the ensuing fiscal year.

(June 27, 1952, c. 477, Title II, ch. 8, § 280, 66 Stat. 230; Nov. 29, 1990, Pub.L. 101–649, Title V, § 542(a), 104 Stat. 5057; Oct. 25, 1994, Pub.L. 103–416, Title II, § 219(s), 108 Stat. 4317; Sept. 30, 1996, Pub.L. 104–208, Div. C, Title III, §§ 308(g)(4)(C), 382(a), 110 Stat. 3009–623, 3009–651.)

CHAPTER IX. MISCELLANEOUS

§ 281. Nonimmigrant visa fees [8 U.S.C.A. § 1351]

The fees for the furnishing and verification of applications for visas by nonimmigrants of each foreign country and for the issuance of visas to nonimmigrants of each foreign country shall be prescribed by the Secretary of State, if practicable, in amounts corresponding to the total of all visa, entry, residence, or other similar fees, taxes, or charges assessed or levied against nationals of the United States by the foreign countries of which such nonimmigrants are nationals or stateless residents: *Provided,* That nonimmigrant visas issued to aliens coming to the United States in transit to and from the headquarters district of the United Nations in accordance with the provisions of the Headquarters Agreement shall be gratis. Subject to such criteria as the Secretary of State may prescribe, including the duration of stay of the alien and the financial burden upon the charitable organization, the Secretary of State shall waive or reduce the fee for application and issuance of a nonimmigrant visa for any alien coming to the United States primarily for, or in activities related to, a charitable purpose involving health or nursing care, the provision of food or housing, job training, or any other similar direct service or assistance to poor or otherwise needy individuals in the United States.

(June 27, 1952, c. 477, Title II, ch. 9, § 281, 66 Stat. 230; Oct. 3, 1965, Pub. L. 89–236, § 14, 79 Stat. 919; Oct. 21, 1968, Pub. L. 90–609, § 1, 82 Stat. 1199; Oct. 6, 1997, Pub.L. 105–54, § 2(a), 111 Stat. 1175.)

§ 282. Printing of reentry permits and blank forms of manifest and crew lists; sale to public [8 U.S.C.A. § 1352]

(a) Reentry permits issued under section 223 [8 U.S.C.A. § 1203] shall be printed on distinctive safety paper and shall be prepared and issued under regulations prescribed by the Attorney General.

(b) The Public Printer is authorized to print for sale to the public by the Superintendent of Documents, upon prepayment, copies of blank forms of manifests and crew lists and such other forms as may be prescribed and authorized by the Attorney General to be sold pursuant to the provisions of this title.

(June 27, 1952, c. 477, Title II, ch. 9, § 282, 66 Stat. 231.)

§ 283. Travel expenses and expense of transporting remains of officers and employees dying outside of United States [8 U.S.C.A. § 1353]

When officers, inspectors, or other employees of the Service are ordered to perform duties in a foreign country, or are transferred from one station to another, in the United States or in a foreign country, or while performing duties in any foreign country become eligible for voluntary retirement and return to the United States, they shall be allowed their traveling expenses in accordance with such regulations as the Attorney General may deem advisable, and they may also be allowed, within the discretion and under written orders of the Attorney General, the expenses incurred for the transfer of their wives and dependent children, their household effects and other personal property, including the expenses for packing, crating, freight, unpacking, temporary storage, and drayage thereof in accordance with subchapter II of chapter 57 of Title 5. The expense of transporting the remains of such officers, inspectors, or other employees who die while in, or in transit to, a foreign country in the discharge of their official duties, to their former homes in this country for interment, and the ordinary and necessary expenses of such interment and of preparation for shipment, are authorized to be paid on the written order of the Attorney General.

(June 27, 1952, c. 477, Title II, ch. 9, § 283, 66 Stat. 231; Pub.L. 100–525, § 9(p), Oct. 24, 1988, 102 Stat. 2621.)

§ 284. Applicability to members of the armed forces [8 U.S.C.A. § 1354]

(a) Nothing contained in this title shall be construed so as to limit, restrict, deny, or affect the coming into or departure from the United States of an alien member of the Armed Forces of the United States who is in the uniform of, or who bears documents identifying him as a member of, such Armed Forces, and who is coming to or departing from the United States under official orders or permit of such Armed Forces: *Provided,* That nothing contained in this section shall be construed to give to or confer upon any such alien any other privileges, rights, benefits, exemptions, or immunities under this Act, which are not otherwise specifically granted by this Act.

(b) If a person lawfully admitted for permanent residence is the spouse or child of a member of the armed forces of the United States, is authorized to accompany the member and reside abroad with the member pursuant to the member's official orders, and is so accompanying and residing with the member (in marital union if a spouse), then the residence and physical presence of the person abroad shall not be treated as

(1) an abandonment or relinquishment of lawful permanent resident status for purposes of clause (i) of section 101(a)(13)(C) [8 U.S.C.A. § 1101(a)(13)(C)]; or

(2) an absence from the United States for purposes of clause (ii) of such section.

(June 27, 1952, c. 477, Title II, ch. 9, § 284, 66 Stat. 232; Jan. 28, 2008, Pub.L. 110–181, Div. A, Title VI, § 673, 122 Stat. 185.)

§ 285. Disposal of privileges at immigrant stations; rentals; retail sale; disposition of receipts [8 U.S.C.A. § 1355]

(a) Subject to such conditions and limitations as the Attorney General shall prescribe, all exclusive privileges of exchanging money, transporting passengers or baggage, keeping eating houses, or other like privileges in connection with any United States immigrant station, shall be disposed of to the lowest responsible and capable bidder (other than an alien) in accordance with the provisions of section 5 of Title 41 and for the use of Government property in connection with the exercise of such exclusive privileges a reasonable rental may be charged. The feeding of aliens, or the furnishing of any other necessary service in connection with any United States immigrant station, may be performed by the Service without regard to the foregoing provisions of this subsection if the Attorney General shall find that it would be advantageous to the Government in terms of economy and efficiency. No intoxicating liquors shall be sold at any immigrant station.

(b) Such articles determined by the Attorney General to be necessary to the health and welfare of aliens detained at any immigrant station, when not otherwise readily procurable by such aliens, may be sold at reasonable prices to such aliens through Government canteens operated by the Service, under such conditions and limitations as the Attorney General shall prescribe.

(c) All rentals or other receipts accruing from the disposal of privileges, and all moneys arising from the sale of articles through Service-operated canteens, authorized by this section, shall be covered into the Treasury to the credit of the appropriation for the enforcement of this title.

(June 27, 1952, c. 477, Title II, ch. 9, § 285, 66 Stat. 232.)

§ 286. Disposition of monies collected under the provisions of this title [8 U.S.C.A. § 1356]

(a) Detention, transportation, hospitalization, and all other expenses of detained aliens; expenses of landing stations

All moneys paid into the Treasury to reimburse the Service for detention, transportation, hospitalization, and all other expenses of detained aliens paid from the appropriation for the enforcement of this Act, and all moneys paid into the Treasury to reimburse the Service for expenses of landing stations referred to in section 233(b) [8 U.S.C.A. § 1223(b)] paid by the Service from the appropriation for the enforcement of this Act, shall be credited to the appropriation for the enforcement of this Act for the fiscal year in which the expenses were incurred.

(b) Purchase of evidence

Moneys expended from appropriations for the Service for the purchase of evidence and subsequently recovered shall be reimbursed to the current appropriation for the Service.

(c) Fees and administrative fines and penalties; exception

Except as otherwise provided in subsection (a) and subsection (b), or in any other provision of this title, all moneys received in payment of fees and administrative fines and penalties under this title shall be covered into the Treasury as miscellaneous receipts: Provided, however, That all fees received from applicants residing in the Virgin Islands of the United States, and in Guam, required to be paid under section 281 [8 U.S.C.A. § 1351], shall be paid over to the Treasury of the Virgin Islands and to the Treasury of Guam, respectively.

(d) Schedule of fees

In addition to any other fee authorized by law, the Attorney General shall charge and collect $7 per individual for the immigration inspection of each passenger arriving at a port of entry in the United States, or for the preinspection of a passenger in a place outside of the United States prior to such arrival, aboard a commercial aircraft or commercial vessel.

(e) Limitations on fees

(1) Except as provided in paragraph (3), no fee shall be charged under subsection (d) for immigration inspection or preinspection provided in connection with the arrival of any passenger, other than aircraft passengers, whose journey originated in the following:

(A) Canada,

(B) Mexico,

(C) a State, territory or possession of the United States, or

(D) any adjacent island (within the meaning of section 101(b)(5) [8 U.S.C.A. § 1101(b)(5)]).

(2) No fee may be charged under subsection (d) with respect to the arrival of any passenger—

(A) who is in transit to a destination outside the United States, and

(B) for whom immigration inspection services are not provided.

(3) The Attorney General shall charge and collect $3 per individual for the immigration inspection or pre–inspection of each commercial vessel passenger whose journey originated in the United States or in any place set forth in paragraph (1): Provided, That this requirement shall not apply to immigration inspection at designated ports of entry of passengers arriving by ferry, or by Great Lakes vessels on the Great Lakes and connecting waterways when operating on a regular schedule. For the purposes of this paragraph, the term "ferry" means a vessel, in other than ocean or coastwise service, having provisions only for deck passengers and/or vehicles, operating on a short run on a frequent schedule between two points over the most direct water route, and offering a public service of a type normally attributed to a bridge or tunnel.

(f) Collection

(1) Each person that issues a document or ticket to an individual for transportation by a commercial vessel or commercial aircraft into the United States shall—

(A) collect from that individual the fee charged under subsection (d) at the time the document or ticket is issued; and

(B) identify on that document or ticket the fee charged under subsection (d) as a Federal inspection fee.

(2) If—

(A) a document or ticket for transportation of a passenger into the United States is issued in a foreign country; and

(B) the fee charged under subsection (d) is not collected at the time such document or ticket is issued;

the person providing transportation to such passenger shall collect such fee at the time such passenger departs from the United States and shall provide such passenger a receipt for the payment of such fee.

(3) The person who collects fees under paragraph (1) or (2) shall remit those fees to the Attorney General at any time before the date that is thirty-one days after the close of the calendar quarter in which the fees are collected, except the fourth quarter payment for fees collected from airline passengers shall be made on the date that is ten days before the end of the fiscal year, and the first quarter payment shall include any collections made in the preceding quarter that were not remitted with the previous payment. Regulations issued by the Attorney General under this subsection with respect to the collection of the fees charged under subsection (d) and the remittance of such fees to the Treasury of the United States shall be consistent with the regulations issued by the Secretary of the Treasury for the collection and remittance of the taxes imposed by subchapter C of chapter 33 of Title 26, but only to the extent the regulations issued with respect to such taxes do not conflict with the provisions of this section.

(g) Provision of immigration inspection and preinspection services

Notwithstanding the Act of March 2, 1931, 46 Stat. 1467 [8 U.S.C.A. § 1353b] or any other provision of law, the immigration services required to be provided to passengers upon arrival in the United States on scheduled airline flights shall be adequately provided when needed and at no cost (other than the fees imposed under subsection (d)) to airlines and airline passengers at:

(1) immigration serviced airports, and

(2) places located outside of the United States at which an immigration officer is stationed for the purpose of providing such immigration services.

(h) Disposition of receipts

(1)(A) There is established in the general fund of the Treasury a separate account which shall be known as the "Immigration User Fee Account". Notwithstanding any other section of this title, there shall be deposited as offsetting receipts into the Immigration User Fee Account all fees collected under subsection (d) of this section, to remain available until expended. At the end of each 2–year period, beginning with the creation of this account, the Attorney General, following a public rulemaking with opportunity for notice and comment, shall submit a report to the Congress concerning the status of the account, including any balances therein, and recommend any adjustment in the prescribed fee that may be required to ensure that the receipts collected from the fee charged for the succeeding two years equal, as closely as possible, the cost of providing these services.

(B) Notwithstanding any other provisions of law, all civil fines or penalties collected pursuant to sections 243(c) [8 U.S.C.A. § 1253(c)], 271 [8 U.S.C.A. § 1321], and 273 [8 U.S.C.A. § 1323] and all liquidated damages and expenses collected pursuant to this Act shall be deposited in the Immigration User Fee Account.

(2)(A) The Secretary of the Treasury shall refund out of the Immigration User Fee Account to any appropriation the amount paid out of such appropriation for expenses incurred by the Attorney General in providing immigration inspection and preinspection services for commercial aircraft or vessels and in—

(i) providing overtime immigration inspection services for commercial aircraft or vessels;

(ii) administration of debt recovery, including the establishment and operation of a national collections office;

(iii) expansion, operation and maintenance of information systems for nonimmigrant control and debt collection;

(iv) detection of fraudulent documents used by passengers traveling to the United States, including training of, and technical assistance to, commercial airline personnel regarding such detection;

(v) providing detention and removal services for inadmissible aliens arriving on commercial aircraft and vessels and for any alien who is inadmissible under section 212(a) [8 U.S.C.A. § 1182(a)] who has attempted illegal entry into the United States through avoidance of immigration inspection at air or sea ports-of-entry; and

(vi) providing removal and asylum proceedings at air or sea ports-of-entry for inadmissible aliens arriving on commercial aircraft and vessels including immigration removal proceedings resulting from presentation of fraudulent documents and failure to present documentation and for any alien who is inadmissible under section 212(a) [8 U.S.C.A. § 1182(a)] who has attempted illegal entry into the United States through avoidance of immigration inspection at air or sea ports-of-entry.

(B) The amounts which are required to be refunded under subparagraph (A) shall be refunded at least quarterly on the basis of estimates made by the Attorney General of the expenses referred to in subparagraph (A). Proper adjustments shall be made in the amounts subsequently refunded under subparagraph (A) to the extent prior estimates were in excess of, or less than, the amount required to be refunded under subparagraph (A).

The Attorney General shall provide for expenditures for training and assistance described in clause (iv) in an amount, for any fiscal year, not less than 5 percent of the total of the expenses incurred that are described in the previous sentence.

(i) Reimbursement

Notwithstanding any other provision of law, the Attorney General is authorized to receive reimbursement from the owner, operator, or agent of a private or commercial aircraft or vessel, or from any airport or seaport authority for expenses incurred by the Attorney General in providing immigration inspection services which are rendered at the request of such person or authority (including the salary and expenses of individuals employed by the Attorney General to provide such immigration inspection services). The Attorney General's authority to receive such reimbursement shall terminate immediately upon the provision for such services by appropriation.

(j) Regulations

The Attorney General may prescribe such rules and regulations as may be necessary to carry out the provisions of this section.

(k) Advisory committee

In accordance with the provisions of the Federal Advisory Committee Act [5 U.S.C.A.App. § 1 et seq.], the Attorney General shall establish an advisory committee, whose membership shall consist of representatives from the airline and other transportation industries who may be subject to any fee or charge authorized by law or proposed by the Immigration and Naturalization Service for the purpose of covering expenses incurred by the Immigration and Naturalization Service. The advisory committee shall meet on a periodic basis and shall advise the Attorney General on issues related to the performance of the inspectional services of the Immigration and Naturalization Service. This advice shall include, but not be limited to, such issues as the time periods during which such services should be performed, the proper number and deployment of inspection officers, the level of fees, and the appropriateness of any proposed fee. The Attorney General shall give substantial consideration to the views of the advisory committee in the exercise of his duties.

(*l*) Report to Congress

In addition to the reporting requirements established pursuant to subsection (h), the Attorney General shall prepare and submit annually to the Congress, not later than March 31st of each year, a statement of the financial condition of the "Immigration User Fee Account" including beginning account balance, revenues, withdrawals and their purpose, ending balance, projections for the ensuing fiscal year and a full and complete workload analysis showing on a port by port basis the current and projected need for inspectors. The statement shall indicate the success rate of the Immigration and Naturalization Service in meeting the forty-five minute inspection standard and shall provide detailed statistics regarding the number of passengers inspected within the standard, progress that is being made to expand the utilization of United States citizen by-pass, the number of passengers for whom the standard is not met and the length of their delay, locational breakdown of these statistics and the steps being taken to correct any nonconformity.

(m) Immigration Examinations Fee Account

Notwithstanding any other provisions of law, all adjudication fees as are designated by the Attorney General in regulations shall be deposited as offsetting receipts into a separate account entitled "Immigration Examinations Fee Account" in the Treasury of the United States, whether collected directly by the Attorney General or through clerks of courts: *Provided, however,* That all fees received by the Attorney General from applicants residing in the Virgin Islands of the United States, and in Guam, under this subsection shall be paid over to the treasury of the Virgin Islands and to the treasury of Guam: *Provided further,* That fees for providing adjudication and naturalization services may be set at a level that will ensure recovery of the full costs of providing all such services, including the costs of similar services provided without charge to asylum applicants or other immigrants. Such fees may also be set at a level that will recover any additional costs associated with the administration of the fees collected.

(n) Reimbursement of administrative expenses; transfer of deposits to General Fund of United States Treasury

All deposits into the "Immigration Examinations Fee Account" shall remain available until expended to the Attorney General to reimburse any appropriation the amount paid out of such appropriation for expenses in providing immigration adjudication and naturalization services and the collection, safeguarding and accounting for fees deposited in and funds reimbursed from the "Immigration Examinations Fee Account". [sic]

(*o*) Annual financial reports to Congress

The Attorney General shall prepare and submit annually to Congress statements of financial condition of the "Immigration Examinations Fee Account", including beginning account balance, revenues, withdrawals, and ending account balance and projections for the ensuing fiscal year.

(p) Additional effective dates

The provisions set forth in subsections (m), (n), and (*o*) apply to adjudication and naturalization services performed and to related fees collected on or after October 1, 1988.

(q) Land Border Inspection Fee Account

(1)(A)(i) Notwithstanding any other provision of law, the Attorney General is authorized to establish, by regulation, not more than 96 projects under which a fee may be charged and collected for inspection services provided at one or more land border points of entry. Such projects may include the establishment of commuter lanes to be made available to qualified United States citizens and aliens, as determined by the Attorney General.

(ii) This subparagraph shall take effect, with respect to any project described in clause (1)* that was not authorized to be commenced before the date of the enactment of the Illegal Immigration Reform and Immigrant Responsibility Act of 1996 [September 30, 1996], 30 days after submission of a written plan by the Attorney General detailing the proposed implementation of such project.

(iii) The Attorney General shall prepare and submit on a quarterly basis a status report on each land border inspection project implemented under this subparagraph.

(iv) Redesignated (iii).

(B) The Attorney General, in consultation with the Secretary of the Treasury, may conduct pilot projects to demonstrate the use of designated ports of entry after working hours through the use of card reading machines or other appropriate technology.

(2) All of the fees collected under this subsection, including receipts for services performed in processing forms I–94, I–94W, and I–68, and other similar applications processed at land border ports of entry, shall be deposited as offsetting receipts in a separate account within the general fund of the Treasury of the United States, to remain available until expended. Such account shall be known as the Land Border Inspection Fee Account.

(3)(A) The Secretary of the Treasury shall refund, at least on a quarterly basis amounts to any appropriations for expenses incurred in providing inspection services at land border points of entry. Such expenses shall include—

(i) the providing of overtime inspection services;

(ii) the expansion, operation and maintenance of information systems for nonimmigrant control;

(iii) the hire of additional permanent and temporary inspectors;

(iv) the minor construction costs associated with the addition of new traffic lanes (with the concurrence of the General Services Administration);

(v) the detection of fraudulent documents used by passengers travelling to the United States;

(vi) providing for the administration of said account.

* So in original; probably should be clause "(i)".

(B) The amounts required to be refunded from the Land Border Inspection Fee Account for fiscal years 1992 and thereafter shall be refunded in accordance with estimates made in the budget request of the Attorney General for those fiscal years: Provided, That any proposed changes in the amounts designated in said budget requests shall only be made after notification to the Committees on Appropriations of the House of Representatives and the Senate in accordance with section 606 of Public Law 101–162.

(4) The Attorney General will prepare and submit annually to the Congress statements of financial condition of the Land Border Immigration Fee Account, including beginning account balance, revenues, withdrawals, and ending account balance and projection for the ensuing fiscal year.

(5) Repealed. Pub.L. 104–208, Div. C, Title I, § 122(a)(2), Sept. 30, 1996, 110 Stat. 3009–560.

(r) Breached Bond/Detention Fund

(1) Notwithstanding any other provision of law, there is established in the general fund of the Treasury a separate account which shall be known as the Breached Bond/Detention Fund (in this subsection referred to as the "Fund").

(2) There shall be deposited as offsetting receipts into the Fund all breached cash and surety bonds, in excess of $8,000,000, posted under this Act, which are recovered by the Department of Justice, and amount [sic] described in section 245(i)(3)(B) [8 U.S.C.A. § 1255(i)(3)(B)].

(3) Such amounts as are deposited into the Fund shall remain available until expended and shall be refunded out of the Fund by the Secretary of the Treasury, at least on a quarterly basis, to the Attorney General for the following purposes—

(i) for expenses incurred in the collection of breached bonds, and

(ii) for expenses associated with the detention of illegal aliens.

(4) The amounts required to be refunded from the Fund for fiscal year 1998 and thereafter shall be refunded in accordance with estimates made in the budget request of the President for those fiscal years. Any proposed changes in the amounts designated in such budget requests shall only be made after Congressional reprogramming notification in accordance with the reprogramming guidelines for the applicable fiscal year.

(5) The Attorney General shall prepare and submit annually to the Congress, statements of financial condition of the Fund, including the beginning balance, receipts, refunds to appropriations, transfers to the general fund, and the ending balance.

(6) For fiscal year 1993 only, the Attorney General may transfer up to $1,000,000 from the Immigration User Fee Account to the Fund for initial expenses necessary to enhance collection efforts: Provided, That any such transfers shall be refunded from the Fund back to the Immigration User Fee Account by December 31, 1993.

(s) H–1B nonimmigrant petitioner account

(1) In general

There is established in the general fund of the Treasury a separate account, which shall be known as the "H–1B Nonimmigrant Petitioner Account". Notwithstanding any other section of this subchapter, there shall be deposited as offsetting receipts into the account all fees collected under paragraphs (9) and (11) of section 214(c) [8 U.S.C.A. § 1184(c)].

(2) Use of fees for job training

50 percent of amounts deposited into the H–1B Nonimmigrant Petitioner Account shall remain available to the Secretary of Labor until expended for demonstration programs and projects described in section 414(c) of the American Competitiveness and Workforce Improvement Act of 1998 [29 U.S.C.A. § 2916a].

(3) Use of fees for low-income scholarship program

30 percent of the amounts deposited into the H–1B Nonimmigrant Petitioner Account shall remain available to the Director of the National Science Foundation until expended for scholarships described in section 1869c of Title 42 for low-income students enrolled in a program of study leading to a degree in mathematics, engineering, or computer science.

(4) National Science Foundation competitive grant program for K–12 math, science and technology education

(A) In general

10 percent of the amounts deposited into the H–1B Nonimmigrant Petitioner Account shall remain available to the Director of the National Science Foundation until expended to carry out a direct or matching grant program to support private-public partnerships in K–12 education.

(B) Types of programs covered

The Director shall award grants to such programs, including those which support the development and implementation of standards-based instructional materials models and related student assessments that enable K–12 students to acquire an understanding of science, mathematics, and technology, as well as to develop critical thinking skills; provide systemic improvement in training K–12 teachers and education for students in science, mathematics, and technology; support the professional development of K–12 math and science teachers in the use of technology in the classroom; stimulate system-wide K–12 reform of science, mathematics, and technology in rural, economically disadvantaged regions of the United States; provide externships and other opportunities for students to increase their appreciation and understanding of science, mathematics, engineering, and technology (including summer institutes sponsored by an institution of higher education for students in grades 7–12 that provide instruction in such fields); involve partnerships of industry, educational institutions, and community organizations to address the educational needs of disadvantaged communities; provide college preparatory support to expose and prepare students for careers in science, mathematics, engineering, and technology; and provide for carrying out systemic reform activities under section 1862(a)(1) of Title 42.

(5) Use of fees for duties relating to petitions

5 percent of the amounts deposited into the H–1B Nonimmigrant Petitioner Account shall remain available to the Secretary of Homeland Security until expended to carry out duties under paragraphs (1) and (9) of section 214(c) [8 U.S.C.A. § 1184(c)] related to petitions made for nonimmigrants described in section 101(a)(15)(H)(i)(b) [8 U.S.C.A. § 1101(a)(15)(H)(i)(b)], under paragraph (1)(C) or (D) of section 204 [8 U.S.C.A. § 1154] [sic]* related to petitions for immigrants described in section 203(b) [8 U.S.C.A. § 1153(b)].

(6) Use of fees for application processing and enforcement

For fiscal year 1999, 4 percent of the amounts deposited into the H–1B Nonimmigrant Petitioner Account shall remain available to the Secretary of Labor until expended for decreasing the processing time for applications under section 212(n)(1) [8 U.S.C.A. § 1182(n)(1)] and for carrying out section 212(n)(2) [8 U.S.C.A. § 1182(n)(2)]. Beginning with fiscal year 2000, 5 percent of the amounts deposited into the H–1B Nonimmigrant Petitioner Account shall remain available to the Secretary of Labor until expended for decreasing the processing time for applications under section 212(n)(1) [8 U.S.C.A. § 1182(n)(1)] and section 212(a)(5)(A) [8 U.S.C.A. § 1182(a)(5)(A)].

(t) Genealogy fee

(1) There is hereby established the Genealogy Fee for providing genealogy research and information services. This fee shall be deposited as offsetting collections into the Examinations Fee Account. Fees for such research and information services may be set at a level that will ensure the recovery of the full costs of providing all such services.

* So in original. Probably should be "204(a) [1154(a)]".

(2) The Attorney General will prepare and submit annually to Congress statements of the financial condition of the Genealogy Fee.

(3) Any officer or employee of the Immigration and Naturalization Service shall collect fees prescribed under regulation before disseminating any requested genealogical information.

(u) Premium fee for employment-based petitions and applications

The Attorney General is authorized to establish and collect a premium fee for employment-based petitions and applications. This fee shall be used to provide certain premium-processing services to business customers, and to make infrastructure improvements in the adjudications and customer-service processes. For approval of the benefit applied for, the petitioner/applicant must meet the legal criteria for such benefit. This fee shall be set at $1,000, shall be paid in addition to any normal petition/application fee that may be applicable, and shall be deposited as offsetting collections in the Immigration Examinations Fee Account. The Attorney General may adjust this fee according to the Consumer Price Index.

(v) Fraud Prevention and Detection Account

(1) In general

There is established in the general fund of the Treasury a separate account, which shall be known as the "Fraud Prevention and Detection Account". Notwithstanding any other provision of law, there shall be deposited as offsetting receipts into the account all fees collected under paragraph (12) or (13) of section 214(c) [8 U.S.C.A. § 1184(c)].

(2) Use of fees to combat fraud

(A) Secretary of State

One-third of the amounts deposited into Fraud Prevention and Detection Account shall remain available to the Secretary of State until expended for programs and activities at United States embassies and consulates abroad—

(i) to increase the number* diplomatic security personnel assigned exclusively or primarily to the function of preventing and detecting fraud by applicants for visas described in subparagraph (H)(i), (H)(ii), or (L) of section 101(a)(15) [8 U.S.C.A. § 1101(a)(15)];

(ii) otherwise to prevent and detect visa fraud, including primarily fraud by applicants for visas described in subparagraph (H)(i), (H)(ii), or (L) of section 101(a)(15) [8 U.S.C.A. § 1101(a)(15)], in cooperation with the Secretary of Homeland Security or pursuant to the terms of a memorandum of understanding or other agreement between the

* So in original. Probably should be followed by "of".

Secretary of State and the Secretary of Homeland Security; and

(iii) upon request by the Secretary of Homeland Security, to assist such Secretary in carrying out the fraud prevention and detection programs and activities described in subparagraph (B).

(B) Secretary of Homeland Security

One-third of the amounts deposited into the Fraud Prevention and Detection Account shall remain available to the Secretary of Homeland Security until expended for programs and activities to prevent and detect immigration benefit fraud, including fraud with respect to petitions filed under paragraph (1) or (2)(A) of section 214(c) [8 U.S.C.A. § 1184(c)] to grant an alien nonimmigrant status described in subparagraph (H) or(L) of section 101(a)(15) [8 U.S.C.A. § 1101(a)(15)].

(C) Secretary of Labor

One-third of the amounts deposited into the Fraud Prevention and Detection Account shall remain available to the Secretary of Labor until expended for wage and hour enforcement programs and activities otherwise authorized to be conducted by the Secretary of Labor that focus on industries likely to employ nonimmigrants, including enforcement programs and activities described in section 212(n) [8 U.S.C.A. § 1182(n)] and enforcement programs and activities related to section 214(c)(14)(A)(i) [8 U.S.C.A. § 1184(c)(14)(A)(i)].

(D) Consultation

The Secretary of State, the Secretary of Homeland Security, and the Secretary of Labor shall consult one another with respect to the use of the funds in the Fraud Prevention and Detection Account or for programs and activities to prevent and detect fraud with respect to petitions under paragraph (1) or (2)(A) of section 214(c) [8 U.S.C.A. § 1184(c)] to grant an alien nonimmigrant status described in section 101(a)(15)(H)(ii) [8 U.S.C.A. § 1101(a)(15)(H)(ii)].

(June 27, 1952, c. 477, Title II, ch. 9, § 286, 66 Stat. 232; Dec. 29, 1981, Pub.L. 97–116, § 13, 95 Stat. 1618; Oct. 18, 1986, Pub.L. 99–500, Title I, § 101(b) [Title II, § 205(a), formerly § 205], 100 Stat. 1783–39, 1783–53, as amended Oct. 24, 1988, Pub.L. 100–525, § 4(a)(2)(A), 102 Stat. 2615; Nov. 14, 1986, Pub.L. 99–653, § 7(d)(1), as added Oct. 24, 1988, Pub.L. 100–525, § 8(f), 102 Stat. 2617; July 11, 1987, Pub.L. 100–71, Title I, § 1, 101 Stat. 394; Oct. 1, 1988, Pub.L. 100–459, § 209(a), 102 Stat. 2203, as amended Dec. 12, 1991, Pub.L. 102–232, Title III, § 309(a)(1)(A)(i)(I), 105 Stat. 1757; Oct. 24, 1988, Pub.L. 100–525, § 4(a)(1), 102 Stat. 2614; Nov. 21, 1989, Pub. L. 101–162, Title II, 103 Stat. 1000, as amended Dec. 12, 1991, Pub.L. 102–232, Title III, § 309(a)(1)(B), 105 Stat. 1758; Nov. 5, 1990, Pub.L. 101–515, Title II, § 210(a), (d), 104 Stat. 2120, 2121; Dec. 12, 1991, Pub.L. 102–232, Title III, § 309(a)(1)(A)(i), (B), (2), (b)(12), 105 Stat. 1758, 1759; Oct. 6, 1992, Pub.L. 102–395, Title I, § 112, 106 Stat. 1843; Oct. 27, 1993, Pub.L. 103–121, Title I, 107 Stat. 1161; Oct. 25, 1994, Pub.L. 103–416, Title II, § 219(t), 108 Stat. 4317; Sept. 30, 1996, Pub.L. 104–208, Div. C, Title I, §§ 122(a), 124(a)(1), Title III, §§ 308(d)(3)(A), (4)(K), (e)(1)(L), (g)(1), 376(b), 382(b), Title VI, § 671(b)(11), (e)(5), (6), 110 Stat. 3009–560, 3009–562, 3009–617 to 3009–619, 3009–622, 3009–648, 3009–651, 3009–722, 3009–723; Nov. 26, 1997, Pub.L. 105–119, Title I, § 110(1), (2), 111 Stat. 2457; Oct. 21, 1998, Pub.L. 105–277, Div. A, § 101(b) [Title I, § 114], Div. C, Title IV, § 414(b), 112 Stat. 2681–68, 2681–652; Nov. 29, 1999, Pub.L. 106–113, Div. B, § 1000(a)(1) [H.R. 3421, Title I, § 118], 113 Stat. 1535, 1537; Oct. 17, 2000, Pub.L. 106–313, Title I, §§ 110(a), 113, 114 Stat. 1255, 1261; Dec. 21, 2000, Pub.L. 106–553, § 1(a)(2) [Title I, § 112], 114 Stat. 2762; Dec. 21, 2000, Pub.L. 106–554, § 1(a)(1) [Title I, § 106], 114 Stat. 2763; Nov. 28, 2001, Pub.L. 107–77, Title I, §§ 109, 110, 115 Stat. 765; May 14, 2002, Pub.L. 107–173, Title IV, § 403; Aug. 2, 2002, Pub.L. 107–206, Title I, § 202, 116 Stat. 832; Nov. 2, 2002, Pub.L. 107–273, Div. C, Title I, § 11016(2), 116 Stat. 1824; Nov. 25, 2002, Pub.L. 107–296, Title IV, § 457, 116 Stat. 2201; Feb. 20, 2003, Pub.L. 108–7, Div. B, Title I, § 108, Div. L, § 107, 117 Stat. 67, 532; Sept. 3, 2003, Pub.L. 108–77, Title IV, § 402(d)(2), 117 Stat. 946; Dec. 8, 2004, Pub.L. 108–447, Div. J, Title IV, §§ 426(b), 427, 118 Stat. 3357,3358, as amended by Dec. 16, 2009, Pub.L. 111–117, Div. D, Title V, § 524(a), 123 Stat. 3283; May 11, 2005, Pub.L. 109–13, Div. A, Title VI, § 6046, Div. B, Title IV, § 403(b), 119 Stat. 295, 319; Jan. 11, 2007, Pub.L. 109–472, § 2, 120 Stat. 3554.)

§ 287. Powers of immigration officers and employees [8 U.S.C.A. § 1357]

(a) Powers without warrant

Any officer or employee of the Service authorized under regulations prescribed by the Attorney General shall have power without warrant—

(1) to interrogate any alien or person believed to be an alien as to his right to be or to remain in the United States;

(2) to arrest any alien who in his presence or view is entering or attempting to enter the United States in violation of any law or regulation made in pursuance of law regulating the admission, exclusion, expulsion, or removal of aliens, or to arrest any alien in the United States, if he has reason to believe that the alien so arrested is in the United States in violation of any such law or regulation and is likely to escape before a warrant can be obtained for his arrest, but the alien arrested shall be taken without unnecessary delay for examination before an officer of the Service having authority to examine aliens as to their right to enter or remain in the United States;

(3) within a reasonable distance from any external boundary of the United States, to board and search for aliens any vessel within the territorial waters of the United States and any railway car, aircraft, conveyance, or vehicle, and within a distance of twenty-five miles from any such external boundary to have access to private lands, but not dwellings, for the purpose of patrolling the border to prevent the illegal entry of aliens into the United States;

(4) to make arrests for felonies which have been committed and which are cognizable under any law of the United States regulating the admission, exclusion, expulsion, or removal of aliens, if he has reason to believe that the person so arrested is guilty of such felony and if there is likelihood of the person escaping before a warrant can be obtained for his arrest, but the person arrested shall be taken without unnecessary delay before the nearest available officer empowered to commit persons charged with offenses against the laws of the United States; and

(5) to make arrests—

(A) for any offense against the United States, if the offense is committed in the officer's or employee's presence, or

(B) for any felony cognizable under the laws of the United States, if the officer or employee has reasonable grounds to believe that the person to be arrested has committed or is committing such a felony,

if the officer or employee is performing duties relating to the enforcement of the immigration laws at the time of the arrest and if there is a likelihood of the person escaping before a warrant can be obtained for his arrest.

Under regulations prescribed by the Attorney General, an officer or employee of the Service may carry a firearm and may execute and serve any order, warrant, subpoena, summons, or other process issued under the authority of the United States. The authority to make arrests under paragraph (5)(B) shall only be effective on and after the date on which the Attorney General publishes final regulations which **(i)** prescribe the categories of officers and employees of the Service who may use force (including deadly force) and the circumstances under which such force may be used, **(ii)** establish standards with respect to enforcement activities of the Service, **(iii)** require that any officer or employee of the Service is not authorized to make arrests under paragraph (5)(B) unless the officer or employee has received certification as having completed a training program which covers such arrests and standards described in clause (ii), and **(iv)** establish an expedited, internal review process for violations of such standards, which process is consistent with standard agency procedure regarding confidentiality of matters related to internal investigations.

(b) Administration of oath; taking of evidence

Any officer or employee of the Service designated by the Attorney General, whether individually or as one of a class, shall have power and authority to administer oaths and to take and consider evidence concerning the privilege of any person to enter, reenter, pass through, or reside in the United States, or concerning any matter which is material or relevant to the enforcement of this Act and the administration of the Service; and any person to whom such oath has been administered (or who has executed an unsworn declaration, certificate, verification, or statement under penalty of perjury as permitted under section 1746 of Title 28), under the provisions of this Act, who shall knowingly or willfully give false evidence or swear (or subscribe under penalty of perjury as permitted under section 1746 of Title 28) to any false statement concerning any matter referred to in this subsection shall be guilty of perjury and shall be punished as provided by section 1621 of Title 18.

(c) Search without warrant

Any officer or employee of the Service authorized and designated under regulations prescribed by the Attorney General, whether individually or as one of a class, shall have power to conduct a search, without warrant, of the person, and of the personal effects in the possession of any person seeking admission to the United States, concerning whom such officer or employee may have reasonable cause to suspect that grounds exist for denial of admission to the United States under this Act which would be disclosed by such search.

(d) Detainer of aliens for violation of controlled substances laws

In the case of an alien who is arrested by a Federal, State, or local law enforcement official for a violation of any law relating to controlled substances, if the official (or another official)—

(1) has reason to believe that the alien may not have been lawfully admitted to the United States or otherwise is not lawfully present in the United States,

(2) expeditiously informs an appropriate officer or employee of the Service authorized and designated by the Attorney General of the arrest and of facts concerning the status of the alien, and

(3) requests the Service to determine promptly whether or not to issue a detainer to detain the alien,

the officer or employee of the Service shall promptly determine whether or not to issue such a detainer. If such a detainer is issued and the alien is not otherwise detained by Federal, State, or local officials, the Attorney General shall effectively and expeditiously take custody of the alien.

(e) Restriction on warrantless entry in case of outdoor agricultural operations

Notwithstanding any other provision of this section other than paragraph (3) of subsection (a) an officer or employee of the Service may not enter without the consent of the owner (or agent thereof) or a properly executed warrant onto the premises of a farm or other outdoor agricultural operation for the purpose of interrogating a person believed to be an alien as to the person's right to be or to remain in the United States.

(f) Fingerprinting and photographing of certain aliens

(1) Under regulations of the Attorney General, the Commissioner shall provide for the fingerprinting and photographing of each alien 14 years of age or older against whom a proceeding is commenced under section 240 [8 U.S.C.A. § 1229a].

(2) Such fingerprints and photographs shall be made available to Federal, State, and local law enforcement agencies, upon request.

(g) Acceptance of State services to carry out immigration enforcement

(1) Notwithstanding section 1342 of Title 31, the Attorney General may enter into a written agreement with a State, or any political subdivision of a State, pursuant to which an officer or employee of the State or subdivision, who is determined by the Attorney General to be qualified to perform a function of an immigration officer in relation to the investigation, apprehension, or detention of aliens in the United States (including the transportation of such aliens across State lines to detention centers), may carry out such function at the expense of the State or political subdivision and to the extent consistent with State and local law.

(2) An agreement under this subsection shall require that an officer or employee of a State or political subdivision of a State performing a function under the agreement shall have knowledge of, and adhere to, Federal law relating to the function, and shall contain a written certification that the officers or employees performing the function under the agreement have received adequate training regarding the enforcement of relevant Federal immigration laws.

(3) In performing a function under this subsection, an officer or employee of a State or political subdivision of a State shall be subject to the direction and supervision of the Attorney General.

(4) In performing a function under this subsection, an officer or employee of a State or political subdivision of a State may use Federal property or facilities, as provided in a written agreement between the Attorney General and the State or subdivision.

(5) With respect to each officer or employee of a State or political subdivision who is authorized to perform a function under this subsection, the specific powers and duties that may be, or are required to be, exercised or performed by the individual, the duration of the authority of the individual, and the position of the agency of the Attorney General who is required to supervise and direct the individual, shall be set forth in a written agreement between the Attorney General and the State or political subdivision.

(6) The Attorney General may not accept a service under this subsection if the service will be used to displace any Federal employee.

(7) Except as provided in paragraph (8), an officer or employee of a State or political subdivision of a State performing functions under this subsection shall not be treated as a Federal employee for any purpose other than for purposes of chapter 81 of Title 5 (relating to compensation for injury) and sections 2671 through 2680 of Title 28 (relating to tort claims).

(8) An officer or employee of a State or political subdivision of a State acting under color of authority under this subsection, or any agreement entered into under this subsection, shall be considered to be acting under color of Federal authority for purposes of determining the liability, and immunity from suit, of the officer or employee in a civil action brought under Federal or State law.

(9) Nothing in this subsection shall be construed to require any State or political subdivision of a State to enter into an agreement with the Attorney General under this subsection.

(10) Nothing in this subsection shall be construed to require an agreement under this subsection in order for any officer or employee of a State or political subdivision of a State—

(A) to communicate with the Attorney General regarding the immigration status of any individual, including reporting knowledge that a particular alien is not lawfully present in the United States; or

(B) otherwise to cooperate with the Attorney General in the identification, apprehension, detention, or removal of aliens not lawfully present in the United States.

(h) An alien described in section 101(a)(27)(J) [8 U.S.C.A § 1101(a)(27)(J)] who has been battered, abused, neglected, or abandoned, shall not be compelled to contact the alleged abuser (or family member of the alleged abuser) at any stage of applying for special immigrant juvenile status, including after a request for the consent of the Secretary of Homeland Security under section 101(a)(27)(J)(iii)(I) [8 U.S.C.A § 1101(a)(27)(J)(iii)(I)] of such Act.

(June 27, 1952, c. 477, Title II, ch. 9, § 287, 66 Stat. 233; Oct. 18, 1976, Pub.L. 94–550, § 7, 90 Stat. 2535; Oct. 27, 1986, Pub.L. 99–570, Title I, § 1751(d), 100 Stat. 3207–47; Nov. 6, 1986, Pub.L. 99–603, Title I, § 116, 100 Stat. 3384; Oct. 24, 1988, Pub.L. 100–525, §§ 2(e), 5, 102 Stat. 2610, 2615; Nov. 29, 1990, Pub.L. 101–649, Title V, § 503(a), (b)(1), 104 Stat. 5048; Dec. 12, 1991, Pub.L. 102–232, Title III, § 306(a)(3), 105 Stat. 1751; Sept. 30, 1996, Pub.L. 104–208, Div. C, Title I, § 133, Title III, § 308(d)(4)(L), (e)(1)(M), (g)(5)(A)(i), 110 Stat. 3009–563, 3009–618, 3009–619, 3009–623; Jan. 5, 2006, Pub.L. 109–162, Title VIII, § 826, 119 Stat. 3065; Aug. 12, 2006, Pub.L. 109–271, § 6(g), 120 Stat. 763.)

§ 288. Local jurisdiction over immigrant stations [8 U.S.C.A. § 1358]

The officers in charge of the various immigrant stations shall admit therein the proper State and local officers charged with the enforcement of the laws of the State or Territory of the United States in which any such immigrant station is located in order that such State and local officers may preserve the peace and make arrests for crimes under the laws of the States and Territories. For the purpose of this section the jurisdiction of such State and local officers and of the State and local courts shall extend over such immigrant stations.

(June 27, 1952, c. 477, Title II, ch. 9, § 288, 66 Stat. 234.)

§ 289. Application to American Indians born in Canada [8 U.S.C.A. § 1359]

Nothing in this title shall be construed to affect the right of American Indians born in Canada to pass the borders of the United States, but such right shall extend only to persons who possess at least 50 per centum of blood of the American Indian race.

(June 27, 1952, c. 477, Title II, ch. 9, § 289, 66 Stat. 234.)

§ 290. Establishment of central file; information from other departments and agencies [8 U.S.C.A. § 1360]

(a) There shall be established in the office of the Commissioner, for the use of security and enforcement agencies of the Government of the United States, a central index, which shall contain the names of all aliens heretofore admitted or denied admission to the United States, insofar as such information is available from the existing records of the Service, and the names of all aliens hereafter admitted or denied admission to the United States, the names of their sponsors of record, if any, and such other relevant information as the Attorney General shall require as an aid to the proper enforcement of this Act.

(b) Any information in any records kept by any department or agency of the Government as to the identity and location of aliens in the United States shall be made available to the Service upon request made by the Attorney General to the head of any such department or agency.

(c)(1) Not later than 3 months after the end of each fiscal year (beginning with fiscal year 1996), the Commissioner of Social Security shall report to the Committees on the Judiciary of the House of Representatives and the Senate on the aggregate quantity of social security account numbers issued to aliens not authorized to be employed, with respect to which, in such fiscal year, earnings were reported to the Social Security Administration.

(2) If earnings are reported on or after January 1, 1997, to the Social Security Administration on a social security account number issued to an alien not authorized to work in the United States, the Commissioner of Social Security shall provide the Attorney General with information regarding the name and address of the alien, the name and address of the person reporting the earnings, and the amount of the earnings. The information shall be provided in an electronic form agreed upon by the Commissioner and the Attorney General.

(d) A written certification signed by the Attorney General or by any officer of the Service designated by the Attorney General to make such certification, that after diligent search no record or entry of a specified nature is found to exist in the records of the Service, shall be admissible as evidence in any proceeding as evidence that the records of the Service contain no such record or entry, and shall have the same effect as the testimony of a witness given in open court.

(June 27, 1952, c. 477, Title II, ch. 9, § 290, 66 Stat. 234; 1953 Reorg. Plan No. 1, §§ 5, 8, eff. Apr. 11, 1953, 18 F.R. 2053, 67 Stat. 631; Oct. 24, 1988, Pub.L. 100–525, § 9(q), 102 Stat. 2621; Sept. 30, 1996, Pub.L. 104–208, Div. C, Title III, § 308(d)(4)(M), Title IV, § 414(a), 110 Stat. 3009–618, 3009–669.)

§ 291. Burden of proof upon alien [8 U.S.C.A. § 1361]

Whenever any person makes application for a visa or any other document required for entry, or makes application for admission, or otherwise attempts to enter the United States, the burden of proof shall be upon such person to establish that he is eligible to receive such visa or such document, or is not inadmissible under any provision of this Act, and, if an alien, that he is entitled to the nonimmigrant, immigrant, special immigrant, immediate relative, or refugee status claimed, as the case may be. If such person fails to establish to the satisfaction of the consular officer that he is eligible to receive a visa or other document required for entry, no visa or other document required for entry shall be issued to such person, nor shall such person be admitted to the United States unless he establishes to the satisfaction of the Attorney General that he is not inadmissible under any provision of this Act. In any removal proceeding under chapter 4 against any person, the burden of proof shall be upon such person to show the time, place, and manner of his entry into the United States, but in presenting such proof he shall be entitled to the production of his visa or other entry document, if any, and of any other documents and records, not considered by the Attorney General to be confidential, pertaining to such entry in the custody of the Service. If such burden of proof is not sustained, such person shall be presumed to be in the United States in violation of law.

(June 27, 1952, c. 477, Title II, ch. 9, § 291, 66 Stat. 234; Dec. 29, 1981, Pub.L. 97–116, § 18(k)(1), 95 Stat. 1620; Sept. 30, 1996, Pub.L. 104–208, Div. C, Title III, § 308(d)(4)(N), (e)(1)(N), (g)(9)(A), 110 Stat. 3009–618, 3009–619, 3009–624.)

§ 292. Right to counsel [8 U.S.C.A. § 1362]

In any removal proceedings before an immigration judge and in any appeal proceedings before the Attorney General from any such removal proceedings, the person concerned shall have the privilege of being represented (at no expense to the Government) by such counsel, authorized to practice in such proceedings, as he shall choose.

(June 27, 1952, c. 477, Title II, ch. 9, § 292, 66 Stat. 235; Sept. 30, 1996, Pub.L. 104–208, Div. C, Title III, §§ 308(d)(4)(O), 371(b)(9), 110 Stat. 3009–619, 3009–645.)

§ 293. Deposit of and interest on cash received to secure immigration bonds [8 U.S.C.A. § 1363]

(a) Cash received by the Attorney General as security on an immigration bond shall be deposited in the Treasury of the United States in trust for the obligor on the bond, and shall bear interest payable at a rate determined by the Secretary of the Treasury, except that in no case shall the interest rate exceed 3 per centum per annum. Such interest shall accrue from date of deposit occurring after April 27, 1966, to and including date of withdrawal or date of breach of the immigration bond, whichever occurs first: *Provided,* That cash received by the Attorney General as security on an immigration bond, and deposited by him in the postal savings system prior to discontinuance of the system, shall accrue interest as provided in this section from the date such cash ceased to accrue interest under the system. Appropriations to the Treasury Department for interest on uninvested funds shall be available for payment of said interest.

(b) The interest accruing on cash received by the Attorney General as security on an immigration bond shall be subject to the same disposition as prescribed for the principal cash, except that interest accruing to the date of breach of the immigration bond shall be paid to the obligor on the bond.

(June 27, 1952, c. 477, Title II, ch. 9, § 293; as added Pub.L. 91–313, § 2, July 10, 1970, 84 Stat. 413.)

§ 294. Undercover investigation authority [8 U.S.C.A. § 1363a]

(a) In general

With respect to any undercover investigative operation of the Service which is necessary for the detection and prosecution of crimes against the United States—

(1) sums appropriated for the Service may be used for leasing space within the United States and the territories and possessions of the United States without regard to the following provisions of law:

(A) section 3679(a) of the Revised Statutes (31 U.S.C. 1341),

(B) section 3732(a) of the Revised Statutes (41 U.S.C. 11(a)),

(C) section 305 of the Act of June 30, 1949 (63 Stat. 396; 41 U.S.C. 255),

(D) the third undesignated paragraph under the heading "Miscellaneous" of the Act of March 3, 1877 (19 Stat. 370; 40 U.S.C. 34),

(E) section 3648 of the Revised Statutes (31 U.S.C. 3324),

(F) section 3741 of the Revised Statutes (41 U.S.C. 22), and

(G) subsections (a) and (c) of section 304 of the Federal Property and Administrative Services Act of 1949 (63 Stat. 395; 41 U.S.C. 254(a) and (c));

(2) sums appropriated for the Service may be used to establish or to acquire proprietary corporations or business entities as part of an undercover operation, and to operate such corporations or business entities on a commercial basis, without regard to the provisions of section 304 of the Government Corporation Control Act (31 U.S.C. 9102);

(3) sums appropriated for the Service, and the proceeds from the undercover operation, may be deposited in banks or other financial institutions without regard to the provisions of section 648 of Title 18, and of section 3639 of the Revised Statutes (31 U.S.C. 3302); and

(4) the proceeds from the undercover operation may be used to offset necessary and reasonable expenses incurred in such operation without regard to the provisions of section 3617 of the Revised Statutes (31 U.S.C. 3302).

The authority set forth in this subsection may be exercised only upon written certification of the Commissioner, in consultation with the Deputy Attorney General, that any action authorized by paragraph (1), (2), (3), or (4) is necessary for the conduct of the undercover operation.

(b) Disposition of proceeds no longer required

As soon as practicable after the proceeds from an undercover investigative operation, carried out under paragraphs (3) and (4) of subsection (a), are no longer necessary for the conduct of the operation, the proceeds or the balance of the proceeds remaining at the time shall be deposited into the Treasury of the United States as miscellaneous receipts.

(c) Disposition of certain corporations and business entities

If a corporation or business entity established or acquired as part of an undercover operation under paragraph (2) of subsection (a) with a net value of over $50,000 is to be liquidated, sold, or otherwise disposed of, the Service, as much in advance as the Commissioner or Commissioner's designee determines practicable, shall report the circumstances to the Attorney General, the Director of the Office of Management and Budget, and the Comptroller General. The proceeds of the liquidation, sale, or other disposition, after obligations are met, shall be deposited in the Treasury of the United States as miscellaneous receipts.

(d) Financial audits

The Service shall conduct detailed financial audits of closed undercover operations on a quarterly basis and shall report the results of the audits in writing to the Deputy Attorney General.

(June 27, 1952, c. 477, Title II, ch. 9, § 294, as added Sept. 30, 1996, Pub.L. 104–208, Div. C, Title II, § 205(a), 110 Stat. 3009–567.)

TITLE III

NATIONALITY AND NATURALIZATION

CHAPTER I—NATIONALITY AT BIRTH AND COLLECTIVE NATURALIZATION

§ 301. Nationals and citizens of United States at birth [8 U.S.C.A. § 1401]

The following shall be nationals and citizens of the United States at birth:

(a) a person born in the United States, and subject to the jurisdiction thereof;

(b) a person born in the United States to a member of an Indian, Eskimo, Aleutian, or other aboriginal tribe: Provided, That the granting of citizenship under this subsection shall not in any manner impair or otherwise affect the right of such person to tribal or other property;

(c) a person born outside of the United States and its outlying possessions of parents both of whom are citizens of the United States and one of whom has had a residence in the United States or one of its outlying possessions, prior to the birth of such person;

(d) a person born outside of the United States and its outlying possessions of parents one of whom is a citizen of the United States who has been physically present in the United States or one of its outlying possessions for a continuous period of one year prior to the birth of such person, and the other of whom is a national, but not a citizen of the United States;

(e) a person born in an outlying possession of the United States of parents one of whom is a citizen of the United States who has been physically present in the United States or one of its outlying possessions for a continuous period of one year at any time prior to the birth of such person;

(f) a person of unknown parentage found in the United States while under the age of five years, until shown, prior to his attaining the age of twenty-one years, not to have been born in the United States;

(g) a person born outside the geographical limits of the United States and its outlying possessions of parents one of whom is an alien, and the other a citizen of the United States who, prior to the birth of such person, was physically present in the United States or its outlying possessions for a period or periods totaling not less than five years, at least two of which were after attaining the age of fourteen years: Provided, That any periods of honorable service in the Armed Forces of the United States, or periods of employment with the United States Government or with an international organization as that term is defined in section 288 of Title 22 by such citizen parent, or any periods during which such citizen parent is physically present abroad as the dependent unmarried son or daughter and a member of the household of a person **(A)** honorably serving with the Armed Forces of the United States, or **(B)** employed by the United States Government or an international organization as defined in section 288 of Title 22, may be included in order to satisfy the physical-presence requirement of this paragraph. This proviso shall be applicable to persons born on or after December 24, 1952, to the same extent as if it had become effective in its present form on that date; and

(h) a person born before noon (Eastern Standard Time) May 24, 1934, outside the limits and jurisdiction of the United States of an alien father and a mother who is a citizen of the United States who, prior to the birth of such person, had resided in the United States.

(June 27, 1952, c. 477, Title III, ch. 1, § 301, 66 Stat. 235; Nov. 6, 1966, Pub.L. 89–770, 80 Stat. 1322; Oct. 27, 1972, Pub.L. 92–584, §§ 1, 3, 86 Stat. 1289; Oct. 10, 1978, Pub.L. 95–432, §§ 1, 3, 92 Stat. 1046; Nov. 14, 1986, Pub.L. 99–653, § 12, 100 Stat. 3657; Oct. 25, 1994, Pub.L. 103–416, Title I, § 101(a), 108 Stat. 4306.)

§ 302. Persons born in Puerto Rico on or after April 11, 1899 [8 U.S.C.A. § 1402]

All persons born in Puerto Rico on or after April 11, 1899, and prior to January 13, 1941, subject to the jurisdiction of the United States, residing on January 13, 1941, in Puerto Rico or other territory over which the United States exercises rights of sovereignty and not citizens of the United States under any other Act, are declared to be citizens of the United States as of January 13, 1941. All persons born in Puerto Rico on or after January 13, 1941, and subject to the jurisdiction of the United States, are citizens of the United States at birth.

(June 27, 1952, c. 477, Title III, ch. 1, § 302, 66 Stat. 236.)

§ 303. Persons born in the Canal Zone or Republic of Panama on or after February 26, 1904 [8 U.S.C.A. § 1403]

(a) Any person born in the Canal Zone on or after February 26, 1904, and whether before or after the effective date of this Act, whose father or mother or both at the time of the birth of such person was or is a citizen of the United States, is declared to be a citizen of the United States.

(b) Any person born in the Republic of Panama on or after February 26, 1904, and whether before or after the effective date of this Act, whose father or mother or both at the time of the birth of such person was or is a citizen of the United States employed by the Government of the United States or by the Panama Railroad Company, or its successor in title, is declared to be a citizen of the United States.

(June 27, 1952, c. 477, Title III, ch. 1, § 303, 66 Stat. 236.)

§ 304. Persons born in Alaska on or after March 30, 1867 [8 U.S.C.A. § 1404]

A person born in Alaska on or after March 30, 1867, except a noncitizen Indian, is a citizen of the United States at birth. A noncitizen Indian born in Alaska on or after March 30, 1867, and prior to June 2, 1924, is declared to be a citizen of the United States as of June 2, 1924. An Indian born in Alaska on or after June 2, 1924, is a citizen of the United States at birth.

(June 27, 1952, c. 477, Title III, ch. 1, § 304, 66 Stat. 237.)

§ 305. Persons born in Hawaii [8 U.S.C.A. § 1405]

A person born in Hawaii on or after August 12, 1898, and before April 30, 1900, is declared to be a citizen of the United States as of April 30, 1900. A person born in Hawaii on or after April 30, 1900, is a citizen of the United States at birth. A person who was a citizen of the Republic of Hawaii on August 12, 1898, is declared to be a citizen of the United States as of April 30, 1900.

(June 27, 1952, c. 477, Title III, ch. 1, § 305, 66 Stat. 237.)

§ 306. Persons living in and born in the Virgin Islands [8 U.S.C.A. § 1406]

(a) The following persons and their children born subsequent to January 17, 1917, and prior to February 25,1927, are declared to be citizens of the United States as of February 25, 1927:

(1) All former Danish citizens who, on January 17, 1917, resided in the Virgin Islands of the United States, and were residing in those islands or in the United States or Puerto Rico on February 25, 1927, and who did not make the declaration required to preserve their Danish citizenship by article 6 of the treaty entered into on August 4, 1916, between the United States and Denmark, or who, having made such a declaration have heretofore renounced or may hereafter renounce it by a declaration before a court of record;

(2) All natives of the Virgin Islands of the United States who, on January 17, 1917, resided in those islands, and were residing in those islands or in the United States or Puerto Rico on February 25, 1927, and who were not on February 25, 1927, citizens or subjects of any foreign country;

(3) All natives of the Virgin Islands of the United States who, on January 17, 1917, resided in the United States, and were residing in those islands on February 25, 1927, and who were not on February 25, 1927, citizens or subjects of any foreign country; and

(4) All natives of the Virgin Islands of the United States who, on June 28, 1932, were residing in continental United States, the Virgin Islands of the United States, Puerto Rico, the Canal Zone, or any other insular possession or territory of the United States, and who, on June 28, 1932, were not citizens or subjects of any foreign country, regardless of their place of residence on January 17, 1917.

(b) All persons born in the Virgin Islands of the United States on or after January 17, 1917, and prior to February 25, 1927, and subject to the jurisdiction of the United States are declared to be citizens of the United States as of February 25, 1927; and all persons born in those islands on or after February 25, 1927, and subject to the jurisdiction of the United States, are declared to be citizens of the United States at birth.

(June 27, 1952, c. 477, Title III, ch. 1, § 306, 66 Stat. 237.)

§ 307. Persons living in and born in Guam [8 U.S.C.A. § 1407]

(a) The following persons, and their children born after April 11, 1899, are declared to be citizens of the United States as of August 1, 1950, if they were residing on August 1, 1950, on the island of Guam or other territory over which the United States exercises rights of sovereignty:

(1) All inhabitants of the island of Guam on April 11, 1899, including those temporarily absent from the island on that date, who were Spanish subjects, who after that date continued to reside in Guam or other territory over which the United States exercises sovereignty, and who have taken no affirmative steps to preserve or acquire foreign nationality; and

(2) All persons born in the island of Guam who resided in Guam on April 11, 1899, including those temporarily absent from the island on that date, who after that date continued to reside in Guam or other territory over which the United States exercises sovereignty, and who have taken no affirmative steps to preserve or acquire foreign nationality.

(b) All persons born in the island of Guam on or after April 11, 1899 (whether before or after August 1, 1950) subject to the jurisdiction of the United States, are declared to be citizens of the United States: *Provided,* That in the case of any person born before August 1, 1950, he has taken no affirmative steps to preserve or acquire foreign nationality.

(c) Any person hereinbefore described who is a citizen or national of a country other than the United States and desires to retain his present political status shall have made, prior to August 1, 1952, a declaration under oath of such desire, said declaration to be in form and executed in the manner prescribed by regulations. From and after the making of such a declaration any such person shall be held not to be a national of the United States by virtue of this Act.

(June 27, 1952, c. 477, Title III, ch. 1, § 307, 66 Stat. 237.)

§ 308. Nationals but not citizens of the United States at birth [8 U.S.C.A. § 1408]

Unless otherwise provided in section 301 [8 U.S.C.A. § 1401], the following shall be nationals, but not citizens, of the United States at birth:

(1) A person born in an outlying possession of the United States on or after the date of formal acquisition of such possession;

(2) A person born outside the United States and its outlying possessions of parents both of whom are nationals, but not citizens, of the United States, and have had a residence in the United States, or one of its outlying possessions prior to the birth of such person;

(3) A person of unknown parentage found in an outlying possession of the United States while under the age of five years, until shown, prior to his attaining the age of twenty-one years, not to have been born in such outlying possession; and

(4) A person born outside the United States and its outlying possessions of parents one of whom is an alien, and the other a national, but not a citizen, of the United States who, prior to the birth of such person, was physically present in the United States or its outlying possessions for a period or periods totaling not less than seven years in any continuous period of ten years—

(A) during which the national parent was not outside the United States or its outlying possessions for a continuous period of more than one year, and

(B) at least five years of which were after attaining the age of fourteen years.

The proviso of section 301(g) [8 U.S.C.A. § 1401(g)] shall apply to the national parent under this paragraph in the same manner as it applies to the citizen parent under that section.

(June 27, 1952, c. 477, Title III, ch. 1, § 308, 66 Stat. 238; Pub. L. 99–396, § 15(a), Aug. 27, 1986, 100 Stat. 842, as amended Pub.L. 100–525, § 3(2), Oct. 24, 1988, 102 Stat. 2614.)

§ 309. Children born out of wedlock [8 U.S.C.A. § 1409]

(a) The provisions of paragraphs (c), (d), (e), and (g) of section 301 [8 U.S.C.A. § 1401(c), (d), (e), and (g)], and of paragraph (2) of section 308 [8 U.S.C.A. § 1408], shall apply as of the date of birth to a person born out of wedlock if—

(1) a blood relationship between the person and the father is established by clear and convincing evidence,

(2) the father had the nationality of the United States at the time of the person's birth,

(3) the father (unless deceased) has agreed in writing to provide financial support for the person until the person reaches the age of 18 years, and

(4) while the person is under the age of 18 years—

(A) the person is legitimated under the law of the person's residence or domicile,

(B) the father acknowledges paternity of the person in writing under oath, or

(C) the paternity of the person is established by adjudication of a competent court.

(b) Except as otherwise provided in section 405 of this Act, the provisions of section 301(g) [8 U.S.C.A. § 1401(g)] shall apply to a child born out of wedlock on or after January 13, 1941, and before December 24, 1952, as of the date of birth, if the paternity of such child is established at any time and while such child is under the age of twenty-one years by legitimation.

(c) Notwithstanding the provision of subsection (a) of this section, a person born after December 23, 1952, outside the United States and out of wedlock shall be held to have acquired at birth the nationality status of his mother, if the mother had the nationality of the United States at the time of such person's birth, and if the mother had previously been physically present in the United States or one of its outlying possessions for a continuous period of one year.

(June 27, 1952, c. 477, Title III, ch. 1, § 309, 66 Stat. 238; Pub. L. 97–116, § 18(*l*), Dec. 29, 1981, 95 Stat. 1620; Pub.L. 99–653, § 13, Nov. 14, 1986, 100 Stat. 3657, as amended Pub.L. 100–525, § 8(k), Oct. 24, 1988, 102 Stat. 2617; Pub.L. 100–525, § 9(r), Oct. 24, 1988, 102 Stat. 2621.)

CHAPTER II—NATIONALITY THROUGH NATURALIZATION

§ 310. Naturalization authority [8 U.S.C.A. § 1421]

(a) Authority in Attorney General

The sole authority to naturalize persons as citizens of the United States is conferred upon the Attorney General.

(b) Court authority to administer oaths

(1) Jurisdiction

Subject to section 337(c) [8 U.S.C.A. § 1448(c)]—

(A) General jurisdiction

Except as provided in subparagraph (B), each applicant for naturalization may choose to have the oath of allegiance under section 337(a) [8 U.S.C.A. § 1448(a)] administered by the Attorney General or by an eligible court described in paragraph (5). Each such eligible court shall have authority to administer such oath of allegiance to persons residing within the jurisdiction of the court.

(B) Exclusive authority

An eligible court described in paragraph (5) that wishes to have exclusive authority to administer the oath of allegiance under section 337(a) [8 U.S.C.A. § 1448(a)] to persons residing within the jurisdiction of the court during the period described in paragraph (3)(A)(i) shall notify the Attorney General of such wish and, subject to this subsection, shall have such exclusive authority with respect to such persons during such period.

(2) Information

(A) General information

In the case of a court exercising authority under paragraph (1), in accordance with procedures established by the Attorney General—

(i) the applicant for naturalization shall notify the Attorney General of the intent to be naturalized before the court, and

(ii) the Attorney General—

(I) shall forward to the court (not later than 10 days after the date of approval of an application for naturalization in the case of a court which has provided notice under paragraph (1)(B)) such information as may be necessary to administer the oath of allegiance under section 337(a) [8 U.S.C.A. § 1448(a)], and

(II) shall promptly forward to the court a certificate of naturalization (prepared by the Attorney General).

(B) Assignment of individuals in the case of exclusive authority

If an eligible court has provided notice under paragraph (1)(B), the Attorney General shall inform each person (residing within the jurisdiction of the court), at the time of the approval of the person's application for naturalization, of—

(i) the court's exclusive authority to administer the oath of allegiance under section 337(a) [8 U.S.C.A. § 1448(a)] to such a person during the period specified in paragraph (3)(A)(i), and

(ii) the date or dates (if any) under paragraph (3)(B) on which the court has scheduled oath administration ceremonies.

If more than one eligible court in an area has provided notice under paragraph (1)(B), the Attorney General shall permit the person, at the time of the approval, to choose the court to which the information will be forwarded for administration of the oath of allegiance under this section.

(3) Scope of exclusive authority

(A) Limited period and advance notice required

The exclusive authority of a court to administer the oath of allegiance under paragraph (1)(B) shall apply with respect to a person—

(i) only during the 45–day period beginning on the date on which the Attorney General certifies to the court that an applicant is eligible for naturalization, and

(ii) only if the court has notified the Attorney General, prior to the date of certification of eligibility, of the day or days (during such 45–day period) on which the court has scheduled oath administration ceremonies.

(B) Authority of attorney general

Subject to subparagraph (C), the Attorney General shall not administer the oath of allegiance to a person under subsection (a) during the period in which exclusive authority to administer the oath of allegiance may be exercised by an eligible court under this subsection with respect to that person.

(C) Waiver of exclusive authority

Notwithstanding the previous provisions of this paragraph, a court may waive exclusive authority to administer the oath of allegiance under section 337(a) [8 U.S.C.A. § 1448(a)] to a person under this subsection if the Attorney General has not provided the court with the certification described in subparagraph (A)(i) within a reasonable time before the date scheduled by the court for oath administration ceremonies. Upon notification of a court's waiver of jurisdiction, the Attorney General shall promptly notify the applicant.

(4) Issuance of certificates

The Attorney General shall provide for the issuance of certificates of naturalization at the time of administration of the oath of allegiance.

(5) Eligible courts

For purposes of this section, the term "eligible court" means—

(A) a district court of the United States in any State, or

(B) any court of record in any State having a seal, a clerk, and jurisdiction in actions in law or equity, or law and equity, in which the amount in controversy is unlimited.

(c) Judicial review

A person whose application for naturalization under this title is denied, after a hearing before an immigration officer under section 336(a) [8 U.S.C.A. § 1447(a)], may seek review of such denial before the United States district court for the district in which such person resides in accordance with chapter 7 of Title 5. Such review shall be de novo, and the court shall make its own findings of fact and conclusions of law and shall, at the request of the petitioner, conduct a hearing de novo on the application.

(d) Sole procedure

A person may only be naturalized as a citizen of the United States in the manner and under the conditions prescribed in this title and not otherwise.

(June 27, 1952, c. 477, Title III, ch. 2, § 310, 66 Stat. 239; July 7, 1958, Pub.L. 85–508, § 25, 72 Stat. 351; Mar. 18, 1959, Pub.L. 86–3, § 20(c), 73 Stat. 13; Sept. 26, 1961, Pub.L. 87–301, § 17, 75 Stat. 656; Oct. 24, 1988, Pub.L. 100–525, § 9(s), 102 Stat. 2621; Nov. 29, 1990, Pub.L. 101–649, Title IV, § 401(a), 104 Stat. 5038; Dec. 12, 1991, Pub.L. 102–232, Title I, § 102(a), Title III, § 305(a), 105 Stat. 1734, 1749; Oct. 25, 1994, Pub.L. 103–416, Title II, § 219(u), 108 Stat. 4318.)

§ 311. Eligibility for naturalization [8 U.S.C.A. § 1422]

The right of a person to become a naturalized citizen of the United States shall not be denied or abridged because of race or sex or because such person is married.

(June 27, 1952, c. 477, Title III, ch. 2, § 311, 66 Stat. 239; Pub.L. 100–525, § 9(t), Oct. 24, 1988, 102 Stat. 2621.)

§ 312. Requirements as to understanding the English language, history, principles and form of government of the United States [8 U.S.C.A. § 1423]

(a) No person except as otherwise provided in this title shall hereafter be naturalized as a citizen of the United States upon his own application who cannot demonstrate—

(1) an understanding of the English language, including an ability to read, write, and speak words in ordinary usage in the English language: Provided, That the requirements of this paragraph relating to ability to read and write shall be met if the applicant can read or write simple words and phrases to the end that a reasonable test of his literacy shall be made and that no extraordinary or unreasonable condition shall be imposed upon the applicant; and

(2) a knowledge and understanding of the fundamentals of the history, and of the principles and form of government, of the United States.

(b)(1) The requirements of subsection (a) shall not apply to any person who is unable because of physical or developmental disability or mental impairment to comply therewith.

(2) The requirement of subsection (a)(1) shall not apply to any person who, on the date of the filing of the person's application for naturalization as provided in section 334 [8 U.S.C.A. § 1445], either—

(A) is over fifty years of age and has been living in the United States for periods totaling at least twenty years subsequent to a lawful admission for permanent residence, or

(B) is over fifty-five years of age and has been living in the United States for periods totaling at least fifteen years subsequent to a lawful admission for permanent residence.

(3) The Attorney General, pursuant to regulations, shall provide for special consideration, as determined by the Attorney General, concerning the requirement of subsection (a)(2) with respect to any person who, on the date of the filing of the person's application for naturalization as provided in section 334 [8 U.S.C.A. § 1445], is over sixty-five years of age and has been living in the United States for periods totaling at least twenty years subsequent to a lawful admission for permanent residence.

(June 27, 1952, c. 477, Title III, ch. 2, § 312, 66 Stat. 239; Nov. 2, 1978, Pub.L. 95–579, § 3, 92 Stat. 2474; Nov. 29, 1990, Pub.L. 101–649, Title IV, § 403, 104 Stat. 5039; Dec. 12, 1991, Pub.L. 102–232, Title III, § 305(m)(2), 105 Stat. 1750; Oct. 25, 1994, Pub.L. 103–416, Title I, § 108(a), 108 Stat. 4309.)

§ 313. Prohibition upon the naturalization of persons opposed to government or law, or who favor totalitarian forms of government [8 U.S.C.A. § 1424]

(a) Notwithstanding the provisions of section 405(b) of this Act [8 U.S.C.A. § 1101 note], no person shall hereafter be naturalized as a citizen of the United States—

(1) who advocates or teaches, or who is a member of or affiliated with any organization that advocates or teaches, opposition to all organized government; or

(2) who is a member of or affiliated with **(A)** the Communist Party of the United States; **(B)** any other totalitarian party of the United States; **(C)** the Communist Political Association; **(D)** the Communist or other totalitarian party of any State of the United States, of any foreign state, or of any political or geographical subdivision of any foreign state; **(E)** any section, subsidiary, branch, affiliate, or subdivision of any such association or party; or **(F)** the direct predecessors or successors of any such association or party, regardless of what name such group or organization may have used, may now bear, or may hereafter adopt, unless such alien establishes that he did not have knowledge or reason to believe at the time he became a member of or affiliated with such an organization (and did not thereafter and prior to the date upon which such organization was so registered or so required to be registered have such knowledge or reason to believe) that such organization was a Communist-front organization; or

(3) who, although not within any of the other provisions of this section, advocates the economic, international, and governmental doctrines of world communism or the establishment in the United States of a totalitarian dictatorship, or who is a member of or affiliated with any organization that advocates the economic, international, and governmental doctrines of world communism or the establishment in the United States of a totalitarian dictatorship, either through its own utterances or through any written or printed publications issued or published by or with the permission or consent of or under authority of such organization or paid for by the funds of such organization; or

(4) who advocates or teaches or who is a member of or affiliated with any organization that advocates or teaches **(A)** the overthrow by force or violence or other unconstitutional means of the Government of the United States or of all forms of law; or **(B)** the duty, necessity, or propriety of the unlawful assaulting or killing of any officer or officers (either of specific individuals or of officers generally) of the Government of the United States or of any other organized government because of his or their official character; or **(C)** the unlawful damage, injury, or destruction of property; or **(D)** sabotage; or

(5) who writes or publishes or causes to be written or published, or who knowingly circulates, distributes, prints, or displays, or knowingly causes to be circulated, distributed, printed, published, or displayed, or who knowingly has in his possession for the purpose of circulation, publication, distribution, or display, any written or printed matter, advocating or teaching opposition to all organized government, or advocating **(A)** the overthrow by force, violence, or other unconstitutional means of the Government of the United States or of all forms of law; or **(B)** the duty, necessity, or propriety of the unlawful assaulting or killing of any officer or officers (either of specific individuals or of officers generally) of the Government of the United States or of any other organized government, because of his or their official character; or **(C)** the unlawful damage, injury, or destruction of property; or **(D)** sabotage; or **(E)** the economic, international, and governmental doctrines of world communism or the establishment in the United States of a totalitarian dictatorship; or

(6) who is a member of or affiliated with any organization that writes, circulates, distributes, prints, publishes, or displays, or causes to be written, circulated, distributed, printed, published, or displayed, or that has in its possession for the purpose of circulation, distribution, publication, issue, or display, any written or printed matter of the character described in subparagraph (5) of this subsection.

(b) The provisions of this section or of any other section of this title shall not be construed as declaring that any of the organizations referred to in this section or in any other section of this title do not advocate the overthrow of the Government of the United States by force, violence, or other unconstitutional means.

(c) The provisions of this section shall be applicable to any applicant for naturalization who at any time within a period of ten years immediately preceding the filing of the application for naturalization or after such filing and before taking the final oath of citizenship is, or has been found to be within any of the classes enumerated within this section, notwithstanding that at the time the application is filed he may not be included within such classes.

(d) Any person who is within any of the classes described in subsection (a) solely because of past membership in, or past affiliation with, a party or organization may be naturalized without regard to the provisions of subsection (c) if such person establishes that such membership or affiliation is or was involuntary, or occurred and terminated prior to the attainment by such alien of the age of sixteen years, or that such membership or affiliation is or was by operation of law, or was for purposes of obtaining employment, food rations, or other essentials of living and where necessary for such purposes.

(e) A person may be naturalized under this title without regard to the prohibitions in subsections (a)(2) and (c) of this section if the person—

(1) is otherwise eligible for naturalization;

(2) is within the class described in subsection (a)(2) solely because of past membership in, or past affiliation with, a party or organization described in that subsection;

(3) does not fall within any other of the classes described in that subsection; and

(4) is determined by the Director of Central Intelligence, in consultation with the Secretary of Defense when Department of Defense activities are relevant to the determination, and with the concurrence of the Attorney General and the Secretary of Homeland Security, to have made a contribution to the national security or to the national intelligence mission of the United States.

(June 27, 1952, c. 477, Title III, ch. 2, § 313, 66 Stat. 240; Oct. 24, 1988, Pub.L. 100–525, § 9(u), 102 Stat. 2621; Nov. 29, 1990, Pub.L. 101–649, Title IV, § 407(c), 104 Stat. 5041; Dec. 12, 1991, Pub.L. 102–232, Title III, § 309(b)(13), 105 Stat. 1759; Oct. 25, 1994, Pub.L. 103–416, Title II, § 219(v), 108 Stat. 4318; Dec. 3, 1999, Pub.L. 106–120, Title III, § 306, 113 Stat. 1612; Dec. 13, 2003, Pub.L. 108–177, Title III, § 373, 117 Stat. 2628.)

§ 314. Ineligibility to naturalization of deserters from the armed forces [8 U.S.C.A. § 1425]

A person who, at any time during which the United States has been or shall be at war, deserted or shall desert the military, air, or naval forces of the United States, or who, having been duly enrolled, departed, or shall depart from the jurisdiction of the district in which enrolled, or who, whether or not having been duly enrolled, went or shall go beyond the limits of the United States, with intent to avoid any draft into the military, air, or naval service, lawfully ordered, shall, upon conviction thereof by a court martial or a court of competent jurisdiction, be permanently ineligible to become a citizen of the United States; and such deserters and evaders shall be forever incapable of holding any office of trust or of profit under the United States, or of exercising any rights of citizens thereof.

(June 27, 1952, c. 477, Title III, ch. 2, § 314, 66 Stat. 241.)

§ 315. Citizenship denied alien relieved of service in armed forces because of alienage [8 U.S.C.A. § 1426]

(a) Permanent ineligibility

Notwithstanding the provisions of section 405(b) of this Act but subject to subsection (c), any alien who applies or has applied for exemption or discharge from training or service in the Armed Forces or in the National Security Training Corps of the United States on the ground that he is an alien, and is or was relieved or discharged from such training or service on such ground, shall be permanently ineligible to become a citizen of the United States.

(b) Conclusiveness of records

The records of the Selective Service System or of the Department of Defense shall be conclusive as to whether an alien was relieved or discharged from such liability for training or service because he was an alien.

(c) Service in armed forces of a foreign country

An alien shall not be ineligible for citizenship under this section or otherwise because of an exemption from training or service in the Armed Forces of the United States pursuant to the exercise of rights under a treaty, if before the time of the exercise of such rights the alien served in the Armed Forces of a foreign country of which the alien was a national.

(June 27, 1952, c. 477, Title III, ch. 2, § 315, 66 Stat. 242; Pub.L. 100–525, § 9(v), Oct. 24, 1988, 102 Stat. 2621; Pub.L. 101–649, Title IV, § 404, Nov. 29, 1990, 104 Stat. 5039.)

§ 316. Requirements of naturalization [8 U.S.C.A. § 1427]

(a) Residence

No person, except as otherwise provided in this title, shall be naturalized unless such applicant, **(1)** immediately preceding the date of filing his application for naturalization has resided continuously, after being lawfully admitted for permanent residence, within the United States for at least five years and during the five years immediately preceding the date of filing his application has been physically present therein for periods totaling at least half of that time, and who has resided within the State or within the district of the Service in the United States in which the applicant filed the application for at least three months, **(2)** has resided continuously within the United States from the date of the application up to the time of admission to citizenship, and **(3)** during all the period referred to in this subsection has been and still is a person of good moral character, attached to the principles of the Constitution of the United States, and well disposed to the good order and happiness of the United States.

(b) Absences

Absence from the United States of more than six months but less than one year during the period for which continuous residence is required for admission to citizenship, immediately preceding the date of filing the application for naturalization, or during the period between the date of filing the application and the date of any hearing under section 336(a) [8 U.S.C.A. § 1447(a)], shall break the continuity of such residence, unless the applicant shall establish to the satisfaction of the Attorney General that he did not in fact abandon his residence in the United States during such period.

Absence from the United States for a continuous period of one year or more during the period for which continuous residence is required for admission to citizenship (whether preceding or subsequent to the filing of the application for naturalization) shall break the continuity of such residence, except that in the case of a person who has been physically present and residing in the United States, after being lawfully admitted for permanent residence, for an uninterrupted period of at least one year, and who thereafter is employed by or under contract with the Government of the United States or an American institution of research recognized as such by the Attorney General, or is employed by an American firm or corporation engaged in whole or in part in the development of foreign trade and commerce of the United States, or a subsidiary thereof more than 50 per centum of whose stock is owned by an American firm or corporation, or is employed by a public international organization of which the United States is a member by treaty or statute and by which the alien was not employed until after being lawfully admitted for permanent residence, no period of absence from the United States shall break the continuity of residence if—

(1) prior to the beginning of such period of employment (whether such period begins before or after his departure from the United States), but prior to the expiration of one year of continuous absence from the United States, the person has established to the satisfaction of the Attorney General that his absence from the United States for such period is to be on behalf of such Government, or for the purpose of carrying on scientific research on behalf of such institution, or to be engaged in the development of such foreign trade and commerce or whose residence abroad is necessary to the protection of the property rights in such countries in such firm or corporation, or to be employed by a public international organization of which the United States is a member by treaty or statute and by which the alien was not employed until after being lawfully admitted for permanent residence; and

(2) such person proves to the satisfaction of the Attorney General that his absence from the United States for such period has been for such purpose.

The spouse and dependent unmarried sons and daughters who are members of the household of a person who qualifies for the benefits of this subsection shall also be entitled to such benefits during the period for which they were residing abroad as dependent members of the household of the person.

(c) Physical presence

The granting of the benefits of subsection (b) of this section shall not relieve the applicant from the requirement of physical presence within the United States for the period specified in subsection (a) of this section, except in the case of those persons who are employed by, or under contract with, the Government of the United States. In the case of a person employed by or under contract with Central Intelligence Agency, the requirement in subsection (b) of an uninterrupted period of at least one year of physical presence in the United States may be complied with by such person at any time prior to filing an application for naturalization.

(d) Moral character

No finding by the Attorney General that the applicant is not deportable shall be accepted as conclusive evidence of good moral character.

(e) Determination

In determining whether the applicant has sustained the burden of establishing good moral character and the other qualifications for citizenship specified in subsection (a) of this section, the Attorney General shall not be limited to the applicant's conduct during the five years preceding the filing of the application, but may take into consideration as a basis for such determination the applicant's conduct and acts at any time prior to that period.

(f) Persons making extraordinary contributions to national security

(1) Whenever the Director of Central Intelligence, the Attorney General and the Commissioner of Immigration determine that an applicant otherwise eligible for naturalization has made an extraordinary contribution to the national security of the United States or to the conduct of United States intelligence activities, the applicant may be naturalized without regard to the residence and physical presence requirements of this section, or to the prohibitions of section 313 [8 U.S.C.A. § 1424], and no residence within a particular State or district of the Service in the United States shall be required: Provided, That the applicant has continuously resided in the United States for at least one year prior to naturalization: Provided, further, That the provisions of this subsection shall not apply to any alien described in clauses (i) through (iv) of section 208(b)(2)(A) [8 U.S.C.A. § 1158(b)(2)(A)].

(2) An applicant for naturalization under this subsection may be administered the oath of allegiance under section 337(a) [8 U.S.C.A. § 1448(a)] by any district court of the United States, without regard to the residence of the applicant. Proceedings under this subsection shall be conducted in a manner consistent with the protection of intelligence sources, methods and activities.

(3) The number of aliens naturalized pursuant to this subsection in any fiscal year shall not exceed five. The Director of Central Intelligence shall inform the Select Committee on Intelligence and the Committee on the Judiciary of the Senate and the Permanent Select Committee on Intelligence and the Committee on the Judiciary of the House of Representatives within a reasonable time prior to the filing of each application under the provisions of this subsection.

(g) Repealed.

(June 27, 1952, c. 477, Title III, ch. 2, § 316, 66 Stat. 242; Dec. 29, 1981, Pub.L. 97–116, § 14, 95 Stat. 1619; Dec. 4, 1985, Pub.L. 99–169, Title VI, § 601, 99 Stat. 1007; Nov. 29, 1990, Pub.L. 101–649, Title IV, §§ 402, 407(c)(2), (d)(1), (e)(1), 104 Stat. 5038, 5041, 5046; Sept. 30, 1996, Pub.L. 104–208, Div. C, Title III, § 308(g)(7)(F), 110 Stat. 3009–624; Dec. 30, 2005, Pub.L. 109–149, Title IV, § 518, 119 Stat. 2882.)

§ 317. Temporary absence of persons performing religious duties [8 U.S.C.A. § 1428]

Any person who is authorized to perform the ministerial or priestly functions of a religious denomination having a bona fide organization within the United States, or any person who is engaged solely by a religious denomination or by an interdenominational mission organization having a bona fide organization within the United States as a missionary, brother, nun, or sister, who **(1)** has been lawfully admitted to the United States for permanent residence, **(2)** has at any time thereafter and before filing an application for naturalization been physically present and residing within the United States for an uninterrupted period of at least one year, and **(3)** has heretofore been or may hereafter be absent temporarily from the United States in connection with or for the purpose of performing the ministerial or priestly functions of such religious denomination, or serving as a missionary, brother, nun, or sister, shall be considered as being physically present and residing in the United States for the purpose of naturalization within the meaning of section 316(a) [8 U.S.C.A. § 1427(a)], notwithstanding any such absence from the United States, if he shall in all other respects comply with the requirements of the naturalization law. Such person shall prove to the satisfaction of the Attorney General that his absence from the United States has been solely for the purpose of performing the ministerial or priestly functions of such religious denomination, or of serving as a missionary, brother, nun, or sister.

(June 27, 1952, c. 477, Title III, ch. 2, § 317, 66 Stat. 243; Nov. 29, 1990, Pub.L. 101–649, Title IV, § 407(c), (d)(2), 104 Stat. 5041.)

§ 318. Prerequisite to naturalization; burden of proof [8 U.S.C.A. § 1429]

Except as otherwise provided in this title, no person shall be naturalized unless he has been lawfully admitted to the United States for permanent residence in accordance with all applicable provisions of this Act. The burden of proof shall be upon such person to show that he entered the United States lawfully, and the time, place, and manner of such entry into the United States, but in presenting such proof he shall be entitled to the production of his immigrant visa, if any, or of other entry document, if any, and of any other documents and records, not considered by the Attorney General to be confidential, pertaining to such entry, in the custody of the Service. Notwithstanding the provisions of section 405(b) of this Act, and except as provided in sections 328 [8 U.S.C.A. § 1439] and 329 [8 U.S.C.A. § 1440] no person shall be naturalized against whom there is outstanding a final finding of deportability pursuant to a warrant of arrest issued under the provisions of this or any other Act; and no application for naturalization shall be considered by the Attorney General if there is pending against the applicant a removal proceeding pursuant to a warrant of arrest issued under the provisions of this or any other Act: Provided, That the findings of the Attorney General in terminating removal proceedings or in canceling the removal of an alien pursuant to the provisions of this Act, shall not be deemed binding in any way upon the Attorney General with respect to the question of whether such person has established his eligibility for naturalization as required by this title.

(June 27, 1952, c. 477, Title III, ch. 2, § 318, 66 Stat. 244; Oct. 24, 1968, Pub.L. 90–633, § 4, 82 Stat. 1344; Nov. 29, 1990, Pub.L. 101–649, Title IV, § 407(c)(4), (d)(3), 104 Stat. 5041; Sept. 30, 1996, Pub.L. 104–208, Div. C, Title III, § 308(e)(1)(O), (15), 110 Stat. 3009–620, 3009–621.)

§ 319. Married persons and employees of certain nonprofit organizations [8 U.S.C.A. § 1430]

(a) Any person whose spouse is a citizen of the United States, or any person who obtained status as a lawful permanent resident by reason of his or her status as a spouse or child of a United States citizen who battered him or her or subjected him or her to extreme cruelty, may be naturalized upon compliance with all the requirements of this title except the provisions of paragraph (1) of section 316(a) [8 U.S.C.A. § 1427(a)] if such person immediately preceding the date of filing his application for naturalization has resided continuously, after being lawfully admitted for permanent residence, within the United States for at least three years, and during the three years immediately preceding the date of filing his application has been living in marital union with the citizen spouse (except in the case of a person who has been battered or subjected to extreme cruelty by a United States citizen spouse or parent), who has been a United States citizen during all of such period, and has been physically present in the United States for periods totaling at least half of that time and has resided within the State or the district of the Service in the United States in which the applicant filed his application for at least three months.

(b) Any person, **(1)** whose spouse is **(A)** a citizen of the United States, **(B)** in the employment of the Government of the United States, or of an American institution of research recognized as such by the Attorney General, or of an American firm or corporation engaged in whole or in part in the development of foreign trade and commerce of the United States, or a subsidiary thereof, or of a public international organization in which the United States participates by treaty or statute, or is authorized to perform the ministerial or priestly functions of a religious denomination having a bona fide organization within the United States, or is engaged solely as a missionary by a religious denomination or by an interdenominational mission organization having a bona fide organization within the United States, and **(C)** regularly stationed abroad in such employment, and **(2)** who is in the United States at the time of naturalization, and **(3)** who declares before the Attorney General in good faith an intention to take up residence within the United States immediately upon the termination of such employment abroad of the citizen spouse, may be naturalized upon compliance with all the requirements of the naturalization laws, except that no prior residence or specified period of physical presence within the United States or within a State or a district of the Service in the United States or proof thereof shall be required.

(c) Any person who **(1)** is employed by a bona fide United States incorporated nonprofit organization which is principally engaged in conducting abroad through communications media the dissemination of information which significantly promotes United States interests abroad and which is recognized as such by the Attorney General, and **(2)** has been so employed continuously for a period of not less than five years after a lawful admission for permanent residence, and **(3)** who files his application for naturalization while so employed or within six months following the termination thereof, and **(4)** who is in the United States at the time of naturalization, and **(5)** who declares before the Attorney General in good faith an intention to take up residence within the United States immediately upon termination of such employment, may be naturalized upon compliance with all the requirements of this title except that no prior residence or specified period of physical presence within the United States or any State or district of the Service in the United States, or proof thereof, shall be required.

(d) Any person who is the surviving spouse, child, or parent of a United States citizen, whose citizen spouse, parent, or child dies during a period of honorable service in an active duty status in the Armed Forces of the United States and who, in the case of a surviving spouse, was living in marital union with the citizen spouse at the time of his death, may be naturalized upon compliance with all the requirements of this subchapter except that no prior residence or specified physical presence within the United States, or within a State or a district of the Service in the United States shall be required. For purposes of this subsection, the terms "United States citizen" and "citizen spouse" include a person granted posthumous citizenship under section 329A [8 U.S.C.A. § 1440–1].

(e)(1) In the case of a person lawfully admitted for permanent residence in the United States who is the spouse of a member of the armed forces of the United States, is authorized to accompany such member and reside abroad with the member pursuant to the member's official orders, and is so accompanying and residing with the member in marital union, such residence and physical presence abroad shall be treated, for purposes of subsection (a) of this section and section 316 [8 U.S.C.A. § 1427(a)], as residence and physical presence in

(A) the United States; and

(B) any State or district of the Department of Homeland Security in the United States.

(2) Notwithstanding any other provision of law, a spouse described in paragraph (1) shall be eligible for naturalization proceedings overseas pursuant to section 1701(d) of the National Defense Authorization Act for Fiscal Year 2004 [Public Law 108–136; 8 U.S.C.A. § 1443a].

(June 27, 1952, c. 477, Title III, ch. 2, § 319, 66 Stat. 244; Pub. L. 85–697, § 2, Aug. 20, 1958, 72 Stat. 687; Pub. L. 90–215, § 1(a), Dec. 18, 1967, 81 Stat. 661; Pub. L. 90–369, June 29, 1968, 82 Stat. 279; Pub.L. 101–649, Title IV, § 407(b)(1), (c), (d)(4), 104 Stat. 5040, 5041; Oct. 28, 2000, Pub.L. 106–386, Div. B, Title V, § 1503(e), 114 Stat. 1522; Nov. 24, 2003, Pub.L. 108–136, Div. A, Title XVII, § 1703(f)(1), (h), 117 Stat. 1695, 1696; Jan. 28, 2008, Pub.L. 110–181, Div. A, Title VI, § 674(a), 122 Stat. 185.)

§ 320. Children born outside the United States and residing permanently in the United States; conditions under which citizenship automatically acquired [8 U.S.C.A. § 1431]

(a) A child born outside of the United States automatically becomes a citizen of the United States when all of the following conditions have been fulfilled:

(1) At least one parent of the child is a citizen of the United States, whether by birth or naturalization.

(2) The child is under the age of eighteen years.

(3) The child is residing in the United States in the legal and physical custody of the citizen parent pursuant to a lawful admission for permanent residence.

(b) Subsection (a) shall apply to a child adopted by a United States citizen parent if the child satisfies the requirements applicable to adopted children under section 101(b)(1) [8 U.S.C.A. § 1101(b)(1)].

(c) A Certificate of Citizenship or other Federal document issued or requested to be amended under this section shall reflect the child's name and date of birth as indicated on a State court order, birth certificate, certificate of foreign birth, certificate of birth abroad, or similar State vital records document issued by the child's State of residence in the United States after the child has been adopted or readopted in that State.

(June 27, 1952, c. 477, Title III, ch. 2, § 320, 66 Stat. 245; Pub. L. 95–417, § 4, Oct. 5, 1978, 92 Stat. 917; Pub. L. 97–116, § 18(m), Dec. 29, 1981, 95 Stat. 1620; Pub.L. 99–653, § 14, Nov. 14, 1986, 100 Stat. 3658; Pub.L. 100–525, §§ 8(*l*), 9(w), Oct. 24, 1988, 102 Stat. 2618, 2621; Oct. 30, 2000, Pub.L. 106–395, Title I, § 101(a), 114 Stat. 1631; Pub.L. 113–74, § 2, Jan. 16, 2014, 127 Stat. 1212.)

§ 321. Repealed. Pub.L. 106–395, Title I, § 103(a), Oct. 30, 2000, 114 Stat. 1632 [8 U.S.C.A. § 1432]

§ 322. Child born and residing outside United States; conditions for acquiring certificate of citizenship [8 U.S.C.A. § 1433]

(a) Application by citizen parents; requirements

A parent who is a citizen of the United States (or, if the citizen parent has died during the preceding 5 years, a citizen grandparent or citizen legal guardian) may apply for naturalization on behalf of a child born outside of the United States who has not acquired citizenship automatically under section 320 [8 U.S.C.A. § 1431]. The Attorney General shall issue a certificate of citizenship to such applicant upon proof, to the satisfaction of the Attorney General, that the following conditions have been fulfilled:

(1) At least one parent (or, at the time of his or her death, was) is a citizen of the United States, whether by birth or naturalization.

(2) The United States citizen parent—

(A) has (or, at the time of his or her death, had) been physically present in the United States or its outlying possessions for a period or periods totaling not less than five years, at least two of which were after attaining the age of fourteen years; or

(B) has (or, at the time of his or her death, had) a citizen parent who has been physically present in the United States or its outlying possessions for a period or periods totaling not less than five years, at least two of which were after attaining the age of fourteen years.

(3) The child is under the age of eighteen years.

(4) The child is residing outside of the United States in the legal and physical custody of the applicant (or, if the citizen parent is deceased, an individual who does not object to the application).

(5) The child is temporarily present in the United States pursuant to a lawful admission, and is maintaining such lawful status.

(b) Attainment of citizenship status; receipt of certificate

Upon approval of the application (which may be filed from abroad) and, except as provided in the last sentence of section 337(a) [8 U.S.C.A. § 1448(a)], upon taking and subscribing before an officer of the Service within the United States to the oath of allegiance required by this Act of an applicant for naturalization, the child shall become a citizen of the United States and shall be furnished by the Attorney General with a certificate of citizenship.

(c) Adopted children

Subsections (a) and (b) shall apply to a child adopted by a United States citizen parent if the child satisfies the requirements applicable to adopted children under section 101(b)(1) [8 U.S.C.A. § 1101(b)(1)].

(d) In the case of a child of a member of the armed forces of the United States who is authorized to accompany such member and reside abroad with the member pursuant to the member's official orders, and is so accompanying and residing with the member

(1) any period of time during which the member of the Armed Forces is residing abroad pursuant to official orders shall be treated, for purposes of subsection (a)(2)(A) of this section, as physical presence in the United States;

(2) subsection (a)(5) of this section shall not apply; and

(3) the oath of allegiance described in subsection (b) of this section may be subscribed to abroad pursuant to section 1701(d) of the National Defense Authorization Act for Fiscal Year 2004 [Public Law 108–136; 8 U.S.C.A. § 1443a].

(June 27, 1952, c. 477, Title III, ch. 2, § 322, 66 Stat. 246; Oct. 5, 1978, Pub.L. 95–417, § 6, 92 Stat. 918; Dec. 29, 1981, Pub.L. 97–116, § 18(m), (n), 95 Stat. 1620, 1621; Nov. 14, 1986, Pub.L. 99–653, § 16, 100 Stat. 3658; Oct. 24, 1988, Pub.L. 100–525, § 8(*l*), 102 Stat. 2618; Nov. 29, 1990, Pub.L. 101–649, Title IV, § 407(b)(2), (c)(6), (d)(5), 104 Stat. 5040 to 5042; Dec. 12, 1991, Pub.L. 102–232, Title III, § 305(m)(3), 105 Stat. 1750; Oct. 25, 1994, Pub.L. 103–416, Title I, § 102(a), 108 Stat. 4306; Dec. 7, 1999, Pub.L. 106–139, § 1(b)(2), 113 Stat. 1697; Oct. 30, 2000, Pub.L. 106–395, Title I, § 102(a), 114 Stat. 1632; Nov. 2, 2002, Pub.L. 107–273, Div. C, Title I, § 11030B, 116 Stat. 1837; Jan. 28, 2008, Pub.L. 110–181, Div. A, Title VI, § 674(b), 122 Stat. 186.)

§ 323. Repealed. Pub. L. 95–417, § 7, Oct. 5, 1978, 92 Stat. 918 [8 U.S.C.A. § 1434]

§ 324. Former citizens regaining citizenship [8 U.S.C.A. § 1435]

(a) Requirements

Any person formerly a citizen of the United States who **(1)** prior to September 22, 1922, lost United States citizenship by marriage to an alien, or by the loss of United States citizenship of such person's spouse, or **(2)** on or after September 22, 1922, lost United States citizenship by marriage to an alien ineligible to citizenship, may if no other nationality was acquired by an affirmative act of such person other than by marriage be naturalized upon compliance with all requirements of this title, except—

(1) no period of residence or specified period of physical presence within the United States or within the State or district of the Service in the United States where the application is filed shall be required; and

(2) the application need not set forth that it is the intention of the applicant to reside permanently within the United States.

Such person, or any person who was naturalized in accordance with the provisions of section 317(a) of the Nationality Act of 1940, shall have, from and after her naturalization, the status of a native-born or naturalized citizen of the United States, whichever status existed in the case of such person prior to the loss of citizenship: Provided, That nothing contained herein or in any other provision of law shall be construed as conferring United States citizenship retroactively upon such person, or upon any person who was naturalized in accordance with the provisions of section 317(a) of the Nationality Act of 1940, during any period in which such person was not a citizen.

(b) Additional requirements

No person who is otherwise eligible for naturalization in accordance with the provisions of subsection (a) of this section shall be naturalized unless such person shall establish to the satisfaction of the Attorney General that she has been a person of good moral character, attached to the principles of the Constitution of the United States, and well disposed to the good order and happiness of the United States for a period of not less than five years immediately preceding the date of filing an application for naturalization and up to the time of admission to citizenship, and, unless she has resided continuously in the United States since the date of her marriage, has been lawfully admitted for permanent residence prior to filing her application for naturalization.

(c) Oath of allegiance

(1) A woman who was a citizen of the United States at birth and **(A)** who has or is believed to have lost her United States citizenship solely by reason of her marriage prior to September 22, 1922, to an alien, or by her marriage on or after such date to an alien ineligible to citizenship, **(B)** whose marriage to such alien shall have terminated subsequent to January 12, 1941, and **(C)** who has not acquired by an affirmative act other than by marriage any other nationality, shall, from and after taking the oath of allegiance required by section 337 [8 U.S.C.A. § 1448], be a citizen of the

United States and have the status of a citizen of the United States by birth, without filing an application for naturalization, and notwithstanding any of the other provisions of this title except the provisions of section 313 [8 U.S.C.A. § 1424]: Provided, That nothing contained herein or in any other provision of law shall be construed as conferring United States citizenship retroactively upon such person, or upon any person who was naturalized in accordance with the provisions of section 317(b) of the Nationality Act of 1940, during any period in which such person was not a citizen.

(2) Such oath of allegiance may be taken abroad before a diplomatic or consular officer of the United States, or in the United States before the Attorney General or the judge or clerk of a court described in section 310(b) [8 U.S.C.A. § 1421(b)].

(3) Such oath of allegiance shall be entered in the records of the appropriate embassy, legation, consulate, court, or the Attorney General, and, upon demand, a certified copy of the proceedings, including a copy of the oath administered, under the seal of the embassy, legation, consulate, court, or the Attorney General, shall be delivered to such woman at a cost not exceeding $5, which certified copy shall be evidence of the facts stated therein before any court of record or judicial tribunal and in any department or agency of the Government of the United States.

(d) Persons losing citizenship for failure to meet physical presence retention requirement

(1) A person who was a citizen of the United States at birth and lost such citizenship for failure to meet the physical presence retention requirements under section 301(b) [8 U.S.C.A. § 1401(b)] (as in effect before October 10, 1978), shall, from and after taking the oath of allegiance required by section 337 [8 U.S.C.A. § 1448] be a citizen of the United States and have the status of a citizen of the United States by birth, without filing an application for naturalization, and notwithstanding any of the other provisions of this title except the provisions of section 313 [8 U.S.C.A. § 1424]. Nothing in this subsection or any other provision of law shall be construed as conferring United States citizenship retroactively upon such person during any period in which such person was not a citizen.

(2) The provisions of paragraphs (2) and (3) of subsection (c) shall apply to a person regaining citizenship under paragraph (1) in the same manner as they apply under subsection (c)(1).

(June 27, 1952, c. 477, Title III, ch. 2, § 324, 66 Stat. 246; Oct. 24, 1988, Pub.L. 100–525, § 9(x), 102 Stat. 2621; Nov. 29, 1990, Pub.L. 101–649, Title IV, § 407(b)(3), (c)(7), (d)(6), 104 Stat. 5040–5042; Oct. 25, 1994, Pub.L. 103–416, Title I, § 103(a), 108 Stat. 4307.)

§ 325. Nationals but not citizens; residence within outlying possessions [8 U.S.C.A. § 1436]

A person not a citizen who owes permanent allegiance to the United States, and who is otherwise qualified, may, if he becomes a resident of any State, be naturalized upon compliance with the applicable requirements of this title, except that in applications for naturalization filed under the provisions of this section residence and physical presence within the United States within the meaning of this title shall include residence and physical presence within any of the outlying possessions of the United States.

(June 27, 1952, c. 477, Title III, ch. 2, § 325, 66 Stat. 248; Nov. 29, 1990, Pub.L. 101–649, Title IV, § 407(c)(8), 104 Stat. 5041.)

§ 326. Resident Philippine citizens excepted from certain requirements [8 U.S.C.A. § 1437]

Any person who **(1)** was a citizen of the Commonwealth of the Philippines on July 2, 1946, **(2)** entered the United States prior to May 1, 1934, and **(3)** has, since such entry, resided continuously in the United States shall be regarded as having been lawfully admitted to the United States for permanent residence for the purpose of applying for naturalization under this title.

(June 27, 1952, c. 477, Title III, ch. 2, § 326, 66 Stat. 248; Nov. 29, 1990, Pub.L. 101–649, Title IV, § 407(c)(9), 104 Stat. 5041.)

§ 327. Former citizens losing citizenship by entering armed forces of foreign countries during World War II [8 U.S.C.A. § 1438]

(a) Requirements; oath; certified copies of oath

Any person who, **(1)** during World War II and while a citizen of the United States, served in the military, air, or naval forces of any country at war with a country with which the United States was at war after December 7, 1941, and before September 2, 1945, and **(2)** has lost United States citizenship by reason of entering or serving in such forces, or taking an oath or obligation for the purpose of entering such forces, may, upon compliance with all the provisions of title III of this Act, except section 316(a) [8 U.S.C.A. § 1427(a)], and except as otherwise provided in subsection (b), be naturalized by taking before the Attorney General or before a court described in section 310(b) [8 U.S.C.A. § 1421(b)] the oath required by section 337 [8 U.S.C.A. § 1448]. Certified copies of such oath shall be sent by such court to the Department of State and to the Department of Justice and by the Attorney General to the Secretary of State.

(b) Exceptions

No person shall be naturalized under subsection (a) of this section unless he—

(1) is, and has been for a period of at least five years immediately preceding taking the oath required in subsection (a), a person of good moral character, attached to the principles of the Constitution of the United States and well disposed to the good order and happiness of the United States; and

(2) has been lawfully admitted to the United States for permanent residence and intends to reside permanently in the United States.

(c) Status

Any person naturalized in accordance with the provisions of this section, or any person who was naturalized in accordance with the provisions of section 323 of the Nationality Act of 1940, shall have, from and after such naturalization, the status of a native-born, or naturalized, citizen of the United States, whichever status existed in the case of such person prior to the loss of citizenship: *Provided,* That nothing contained herein, or in any other provision of law, shall be construed as conferring United States citizenship retroactively upon any such person during any period in which such person was not a citizen.

(d) Span of World War II

For the purposes of this section, World War II shall be deemed to have begun on September 1, 1939, and to have terminated on September 2, 1945.

(e) Inapplicability to certain persons

This section shall not apply to any person who during World War II served in the armed forces of a country while such country was at war with the United States.

(June 27, 1952, c. 477, Title III, ch. 2, § 327, 66 Stat. 248; Nov. 29, 1990, Pub.L. 101–649, Title IV, § 407(d)(7), 104 Stat. 5042.)

§ 328. Naturalization through service in the armed forces [8 U.S.C.A. § 1439]

(a) Requirements

A person who has served honorably at any time in the armed forces of the United States for a period or periods aggregating one year, and, who, if separated from such service, was never separated except under honorable conditions, may be naturalized without having resided, continuously immediately preceding the date of filing such person's application, in the United States for at least five years, and in the State or district of the Service in the United States in which the application for naturalization is filed for at least three months, and without having been physically present in the United States for any specified period, if such application is filed while the applicant is still in the service or within six months after the termination of such service.

(b) Exceptions

A person filing an application under subsection (a) of this section shall comply in all other respects with the requirements of this subchapter, except that—

(1) no residence within a State or district of the Service in the United States shall be required;

(2) notwithstanding section 318 [8 U.S.C.A. § 1429] insofar as it relates to deportability, such applicant may be naturalized immediately if the applicant be then actually in the Armed Forces of the United States, and if prior to the filing of the application, the applicant shall have appeared before and been examined by a representative of the Service;

(3) the applicant shall furnish to the Secretary of Homeland Security, prior to any hearing upon his application, a certified statement from the proper executive department for each period of his service upon which he relies for the benefits of this section, clearly showing that such service was honorable and that no discharges from service, including periods of service not relied upon by him for the benefits of this section, were other than honorable (the certificate or certificates herein provided for shall be conclusive evidence of such service and discharge); and

(4) notwithstanding any other provision of law, no fee shall be charged or collected from the applicant for filing a petition for naturalization or for the issuance of a certificate of naturalization upon citizenship being granted to the applicant, and no clerk of any State court shall charge or collect any fee for such services unless the laws of the State require such charge to be made, in which case nothing more than the portion of the fee required to be paid to the State shall be charged or collected.

(c) Periods when not in service

In the case such applicant's service was not continuous, the applicant's residence in the United States and State or district of the Service in the United States, good moral character, attachment to the principles of the Constitution of the United States, and favorable disposition toward the good order and happiness of the United States, during any period within five years immediately preceding the date of filing such application between the periods of applicant's service in the Armed Forces, shall be alleged in the application filed under the provisions of subsection (a) of this section, and proved at any hearing thereon. Such allegation and proof shall also be made as to any period between the termination of applicant's service and the filing of the application for naturalization.

(d) Residence requirements

The applicant shall comply with the requirements of section 316(a) [8 U.S.C.A. § 1427(a)], if the termination of such service has been more than six months preceding the date of filing the application for naturalization, except that such service within five years immediately preceding the date of filing such application shall be considered as residence and physical presence within the United States.

(e) Moral character

Any such period or periods of service under honorable conditions, and good moral character, attachment to the principles of the Constitution of the United States, and favorable disposition toward the good order and happiness of the United States, during such service, shall be proved by duly authenticated copies of the records of the executive departments having custody of the records of such service, and such authenticated copies of records shall be accepted in lieu of compliance with the provisions of section 316(a) [8 U.S.C.A. § 1427(a)].

(f) Revocation

Citizenship granted pursuant to this section may be revoked in accordance with section 340 [8 U.S.C.A. § 1451] if the person is separated from the Armed Forces under other than honorable conditions before the person has served honorably for a period or periods aggregating five years. Such ground for revocation shall be in addition to any other provided by law, including the grounds described in section 340 [8 U.S.C.A. § 1451]. The fact that the naturalized person was separated from the service under other than honorable conditions shall be proved by a duly authenticated certification from the executive department under which the person was serving at the time of separation. Any period or periods of service shall be proved by duly authenticated copies of the records of the executive departments having custody of the records of such service.

(g), (h) Repealed. Oct. 9, 2008, Pub.L. 110–382, §§ 3(a), 4, 122 Stat. 4088, 4089.

(June 27, 1952, c. 477, Title III, ch. 2, § 328, 66 Stat. 249; Oct. 24, 1968, Pub.L. 90–633, § 5, 82 Stat. 1344; Dec. 29, 1981, Pub.L. 97–116, § 15(e), 95 Stat. 1619; Nov. 29, 1990, Pub.L. 101–649, Title IV, § 407(b)(4), (c)(10), (d)(8), 104 Stat. 5040 to 5042; Nov. 29, 1990, Pub.L. 101–649, Title IV, § 407(d)(8); Dec. 12, 1991, Pub.L. 102–232, Title III, § 305(c), 105 Stat. 1750; Nov. 24, 2003, Pub.L. 108–136, Div. A, Title XVII, § 1701(a), 1701(b)(1), (c)(1)(A), (f), 1705(b), 117 Stat. 1691, 1692, 1696; Oct. 9, 2008, Pub.L. 110–382, § 3(a), 122 Stat. 4088.)

§ 329. Naturalization through active-duty service in the armed forces during World War I, World War II, Korean hostilities, Vietnam hostilities, or other periods of military hostilities [8 U.S.C.A. § 1440]

(a) Requirements

Any person who, while an alien or a noncitizen national of the United States, has served honorably as a member of the Selected Reserve of the Ready Reserve or in an active-duty status in the military, air, or naval forces of the United States during either World War I or during a period beginning September 1, 1939, and ending December 31, 1946, or during a period beginning June 25, 1950, and ending July 1, 1955, or during a period beginning February 28, 1961, and ending on a date designated by the President by Executive order as of the date of termination of the Vietnam hostilities, or thereafter during any other period which the President by Executive order shall designate as a period in which Armed Forces of the United States are or were engaged in military operations involving armed conflict with a hostile foreign force, and who, if separated from such service, was separated under honorable conditions, may be naturalized as provided in this section if **(1)** at the time of enlistment, reenlistment, extension of enlistment, or induction such person shall have been in the United States, the Canal Zone, American Samoa, or Swains Island, or on board a public vessel owned or operated by the United States for noncommercial service, whether or not he has been lawfully admitted to the United States for permanent residence, or **(2)** at any time subsequent to enlistment or induction such person shall have been lawfully admitted to the United States for permanent residence. The executive department under which such person served shall determine whether persons have served honorably in an active-duty status, and whether separation from such service was under honorable conditions: *Provided, however,* That no person who is or has been separated from such service on account of alienage, or who was a conscientious objector who performed no military, air, or naval duty whatever or refused to wear the uniform, shall be regarded as having served honorably or having been separated under honorable conditions for the purposes of this section. No period of service in the Armed Forces shall be made the basis of an application for naturalization under this section if the applicant has previously been naturalized on the basis of the same period of service.

(b) Exceptions

A person filing an application under subsection (a) of this section shall comply in all other respects with the requirements of this title, except that—

(1) he may be naturalized regardless of age, and notwithstanding the provisions of section 318 [8 U.S.C.A. § 1429] as they relate to deportability and the provisions of section 331 [8 U.S.C.A. § 1442];

(2) no period of residence or specified period of physical presence within the United States or any State or district of the Service in the United States shall be required;

(3) service in the military, air or naval forces of the United States shall be proved by a duly authenticated certification from the executive department under which the applicant served or is serving, which shall state whether the applicant served honorably in an active-duty status during either World War I or during a period beginning September 1, 1939, and ending December 31, 1946, or during a period beginning June 25, 1950, and ending July 1, 1955, or during a period beginning February 28, 1961, and ending on a date designated by the President by Executive order as the date of termination of the Vietnam hostilities, or thereafter during any other period which the President by Executive order shall designate as a period in which Armed Forces of the United States are or were engaged in military operations involving armed conflict with a hostile foreign force, and was separated from such service under honorable conditions; and

(4) notwithstanding any other provision of law, no fee shall be charged or collected from the applicant for filing a petition for naturalization or for the issuance of a certificate of naturalization upon citizenship being granted to the applicant, and no clerk of any State court shall charge or collect any fee for such services unless the laws of the State require such charge to be made, in which case nothing more than the portion of the fee required to be paid to the State shall be charged or collected.

(5) Repealed.

(c) Revocation

Citizenship granted pursuant to this section may be revoked in accordance with section 340 [8 U.S.C.A. § 1451] if the person is separated from the Armed Forces under other than honorable conditions before the person has served honorably for a period or periods aggregating five years. Such ground for revocation shall be in addition to any other provided by law, including the grounds described in section 340 [8 U.S.C.A. § 1451]. The fact that the naturalized person was separated from the service under other than honorable conditions shall be proved by a duly authenticated certification from the executive department under which the person was serving at the time of separation. Any period or periods of service shall be proved by duly authenticated copies of the records of the executive departments having custody of the records of such service.

(d) Repealed.

(June 27, 1952, c. 477, Title III, ch. 2, § 329, 66 Stat. 250; Pub. L. 87–301, § 8, Sept. 26, 1961, 75 Stat. 654; Pub. L. 90–633, §§ 1, 2, 6, Oct. 24, 1968, 82 Stat. 1343, 1344; Pub. L. 97–116, § 15(a), Dec. 29, 1981, 95 Stat. 1619; Pub.L. 100–525, § 9(y), Oct. 24, 1988, 102 Stat. 2621; Pub.L. 101–649, Title IV, § 407(b)(5), (c)(11), Nov. 29, 1990, 104 Stat. 5040, 5041; Dec. 12, 1991, Pub.L. 102–232, Title III, § 305(b), 105 Stat. 1749; Nov. 18, 1997, Pub.L. 105–85, Div. A, Title X, § 1080(a), 111 Stat. 1916; Nov. 24, 2003, Pub.L. 108–136, Div. A, Title XVII, §§ 1701(b)(2), 1701(c)(1)(B), 1702, 1705(b), 117 Stat. 1691, 1692, 1693, 1696.)

§ 329A. Posthumous citizenship through death while on active–duty service in the armed forces during World War I, World War II, the Korean hostilities, the Vietnam hostilities, or in other periods of military hostilities [8 U.S.C.A. § 1440–1]

(a) Permitting granting of posthumous citizenship

Notwithstanding any other provision of this subchapter, the Secretary of Homeland Security shall provide, in accordance with this section, for the granting of posthumous citizenship at the time of death to a person described in subsection (b) of this section if the Secretary of

Homeland Security approves an application for that posthumous citizenship under subsection (c) of this section.

(b) Noncitizens eligible for posthumous citizenship

A person referred to in subsection (a) of this section is a person who, while an alien or a noncitizen national of the United States—

(1) served honorably in an active–duty status in the military, air, or naval forces of the United States during any period described in the first sentence of section 329(a) [8 U.S.C.A. § 1440(a)],

(2) died as a result of injury or disease incurred in or aggravated by that service, and

(3) satisfied the requirements of clause (1) or (2) of the first sentence of section 329(a) [8 U.S.C.A. § 1440(a)].

The executive department under which the person so served shall determine whether the person satisfied the requirements of paragraphs (1) and (2).

(c) Requests for posthumous citizenship

(1) In general

A request for the granting of posthumous citizenship to a person described in subsection (b) of this section may be filed on behalf of that person—

(A) upon locating the next-of-kin, and if so requested by the next-of-kin, by the Secretary of Defense or the Secretary's designee with the Bureau of Citizenship and Immigration Services in the Department of Homeland Security immediately upon the death of that person; or

(B) by the next-of-kin.

(2) Approval

The Director of the Bureau of Citizenship and Immigration Services shall approve a request for posthumous citizenship filed by the next-of-kin in accordance with paragraph (1)(B) if—

(A) the request is filed not later than 2 years after—

(i) November 24, 2003; or

(ii) the date of the person's death;

whichever date is later;

(B) the request is accompanied by a duly authenticated certificate from the executive department under which the person served which states that the person satisfied the requirements of paragraphs (1) and (2) of subsection (b) of this section; and

(C) the Director finds that the person satisfied the requirement of subsection (b)(3) of this section.

(d) Documentation of posthumous citizenship

If the Director of the Bureau of Citizenship and Immigration Services approves the request referred to in subsection (c) of this section, the Director shall send to the next-of-kin of the person who is granted citizenship, a suitable document which states that the United States considers the person to have been a citizen of the United States at the time of the person's death.

(e) Repealed. Pub.L. 108–136, Div. A, Title XVII, § 1703(g)(1), Nov. 24, 2003, 117 Stat. 1695.

(June 27, 1952, c. 477, Title III, ch. 2, § 329A, as added Mar. 6, 1990, Pub.L. 101–249, § 2(a), 104 Stat. 94; Nov. 2, 2002, Pub.L. 107–273, Div. C, Title I, § 11030(b), 116 Stat. 1836; Nov. 24, 2003, Pub.L. 108–136, Div. A, Title XVII, §§ 1703(g), 1704, 117 Stat. 1695, 1696.)

§ 330. Constructive residence through service on certain United States vessels [8 U.S.C.A. § 1441]

Any periods of time during all of which a person who was previously lawfully admitted for permanent residence has served honorably or with good conduct, in any capacity other than as a member of the Armed Forces of the United States, **(A)** on board a vessel operated by the United States, or an agency thereof, the full legal and equitable title to which is in the United States; or **(B)** on board a vessel whose home port is in the United States, and **(i)** which is registered under the laws of the United States, or **(ii)** the full legal and equitable title to which is in a citizen of the United States, or a corporation organized under the laws of any of the several States of the United States, shall be deemed residence and physical presence within the United States within the meaning of section 316(a) [8 U.S.C.A. § 1427(a)], if such service occurred within five years immediately preceding the date such person shall file an application for naturalization. Service on vessels described in clause (A) of this section shall be proved by duly authenticated copies of the records of the executive departments or agency having custody of the records of such service. Service on vessels described in clause (B) of this section may be proved by certificates from the masters of such vessels.

(June 27, 1952, c. 477, Title III, ch. 2, § 330, 66 Stat. 251; Pub.L. 100–525, § 9(z), Oct. 24, 1988, 102 Stat. 2621; Pub.L. 101–649, Title IV, § 407(c)(12), Nov. 29, 1990, 104 Stat. 5041; Pub.L. 102–232, Title III, § 305(m)(5), Dec. 12, 1991, 105 Stat. 1750.)

§ 331. Alien enemies [8 U.S.C.A. § 1442]

(a) Naturalization under specified conditions

An alien who is a native, citizen, subject, or denizen of any country, state, or sovereignty with which the United States is at war may, after his loyalty has been fully established upon investigation by the Attorney General, be naturalized as a citizen of the United States if such alien's application for naturalization shall be pending at the beginning of the state of war and the applicant is otherwise entitled to admission to citizenship.

(b) Procedure

An alien embraced within this section shall not have his application for naturalization considered or heard except after 90 days' notice to the Attorney General to be considered at the examination or hearing, and the Attorney General's objection to such consideration shall cause the application to be continued from time to time for so long as the Attorney General may require.

(c) Exceptions from classification

The Attorney General may, in his discretion, upon investigation fully establishing the loyalty of any alien enemy who did not have an application for naturalization pending at the beginning of the state of war, except such alien enemy from the classification of alien enemy for the purposes of this title, and thereupon such alien shall have the privilege of filing an application for naturalization.

(d) Effect of cessation of hostilities

An alien who is a native, citizen, subject, or denizen of any country, state, or sovereignty with which the United States is at war shall cease to be an alien enemy within the meaning of this section upon the determination by proclamation of the President, or by concurrent resolution of the Congress, that hostilities between the United States and such country, state, or sovereignty have ended.

(e) Apprehension and removal

Nothing contained herein shall be taken or construed to interfere with or prevent the apprehension and removal, consistent with law, of any alien enemy at any time prior to the actual naturalization of such alien.

(June 27, 1952, c. 477, Title III, ch. 2, § 331, 66 Stat. 252; Nov. 29, 1990, Pub.L. 101–649, Title IV, § 407(c)(13), (d)(9), (e)(2), 104 Stat. 5041, 5042, 5046.)

§ 332. Administration [8 U.S.C.A. § 1443]

(a) Rules and regulations governing examination of petitioners

The Attorney General shall make such rules and regulations as may be necessary to carry into effect the provisions of this part and is authorized to prescribe the scope and nature of the examination of applicants for naturalization as to their admissibility to citizenship. Such examination shall be limited to inquiry concerning the applicant's residence, physical presence in the United States, good moral character, understanding of and attachment to the fundamental principles of the Constitution of the United States, ability to read, write, and speak English, and other qualifications to become a naturalized citizen as required by law, and shall be uniform throughout the United States.

(b) Instruction in citizenship

The Attorney General is authorized to promote instruction and training in citizenship responsibilities of applicants for naturalization including the sending of names of candidates for naturalization to the public schools, preparing and distributing citizenship textbooks to such candidates as are receiving instruction in preparation for citizenship within or under the supervision of the public schools, preparing and distributing monthly an immigration and naturalization bulletin and securing the aid of and cooperating with official State and national organizations, including those concerned with vocational education.

(c) Prescription of forms

The Attorney General shall prescribe and furnish such forms as may be required to give effect to the provisions of this part, and only such forms as may be so provided shall be legal. All certificates of naturalization and of citizenship shall be printed on safety paper and shall be consecutively numbered in separate series.

(d) Administration of oaths and depositions

Employees of the Service may be designated by the Attorney General to administer oaths and to take depositions without charge in matters relating to the administration of the naturalization and citizenship laws. In cases where there is a likelihood of unusual delay or of hardship, the Attorney General may, in his discretion, authorize such depositions to be taken before a postmaster without charge, or before a notary public or other person authorized to administer oaths for general purposes.

(e) Issuance of certificate of naturalization or citizenship

A certificate of naturalization or of citizenship issued by the Attorney General under the authority of this title shall have the same effect in all courts, tribunals, and public offices of the United States, at home and abroad, of the District of Columbia, and of each State, Territory, and outlying possession of the United States, as a certificate of naturalization or of citizenship issued by a court having naturalization jurisdiction.

(f) Copies of records

Certifications and certified copies of all papers, documents, certificates, and records required or authorized to be issued, used, filed, recorded, or kept under any and all provisions of this Act shall be admitted in evidence equally with the originals in any and all cases and proceedings under this Act and in all cases and proceedings in which the originals thereof might be admissible as evidence.

(g) Furnished quarters for photographic studios

The officers in charge of property owned or leased by the Government are authorized, upon the recommendation of the Attorney General, to provide quarters, without payment of rent, in any building occupied by the Service, for a photographic studio, operated by welfare organizations without profit and solely for the benefit of persons seeking to comply with requirements under the immigration and nationality laws. Such studio shall be under the supervision of the Attorney General.

(h) Public education regarding naturalization benefits

In order to promote the opportunities and responsibilities of United States citizenship, the Attorney General shall broadly distribute information concerning the benefits which persons may receive under this title and the requirements to obtain such benefits. In carrying out this subsection, the Attorney General shall seek the assistance of appropriate community groups, private voluntary agencies, and other relevant organizations. There are authorized to be appropriated (for each fiscal year beginning with fiscal year 1991) such sums as may be necessary to carry out this subsection.

(June 27, 1952, c. 477, Title III, ch. 2, § 332, 66 Stat. 252; Nov. 29, 1990, Pub.L. 101–649, Title IV, §§ 406, 407(d)(10), 104 Stat. 5040, 5042; Dec. 12, 1991, Pub.L. 102–232, Title III, § 305(m)(6), 105 Stat. 1750.)

§ 333. Photographs; number [8 U.S.C.A. § 1444]

(a) Three identical photographs of the applicant shall be signed by and furnished by each applicant for naturalization or citizenship. One of such photographs shall be affixed by the Attorney General to the original certificate of naturalization issued to the naturalized citizen and one to the duplicate certificate of naturalization required to be forwarded to the Service.

(b) Three identical photographs of the applicant shall be furnished by each applicant for—

(1) a record of lawful admission for permanent residence to be made under section 249 [8 U.S.C.A. § 1259];

(2) a certificate of derivative citizenship;

(3) a certificate of naturalization or of citizenship;

(4) a special certificate of naturalization;

(5) a certificate of naturalization or of citizenship, in lieu of one lost, mutilated, or destroyed;

(6) a new certificate of citizenship in the new name of any naturalized citizen who, subsequent to naturalization, has had his name changed by order of a court of competent jurisdiction or by marriage; and

(7) a declaration of intention.

One such photograph shall be affixed to each such certificate issued by the Attorney General and one shall be affixed to the copy of such certificate retained by the Service.

(June 27, 1952, c. 477, Title III, ch. 2, § 333, 66 Stat. 253; Nov. 29, 1990, Pub.L. 101–649, Title IV, § 407(c)(14), (d)(11), 104 Stat. 5041, 5042; Oct. 25, 1994, Pub.L. 103–416, Title II, § 219(w), 108 Stat. 4318.)

§ 334. Application for naturalization; declaration of intention [8 U.S.C.A. § 1445]

(a) Evidence and form

An applicant for naturalization shall make and file with the Attorney General a sworn application in writing, signed by the applicant in the applicant's own handwriting if physically able to write, which application shall be on a form prescribed by the Attorney General and shall include averments of all facts which in the opinion of the Attorney General may be material to the applicant's naturalization, and required to be proved under this title. In the case of an applicant subject to a requirement of continuous residence under section 316(a) or 319(a) [8 U.S.C.A. §§ 1427(a) or 1430(a)], the application for naturalization may be filed up to 3 months before the date the applicant would first otherwise meet such continuous residence requirement.

(b) Who may file

No person shall file a valid application for naturalization unless he shall have attained the age of eighteen years. An application for naturalization by an alien shall contain an averment of lawful admission for permanent residence.

(c) Hearings

Hearings under section 336(a) [8 U.S.C.A. § 1447(a)] on applications for naturalization shall be held at regular intervals specified by the Attorney General.

(d) Filing of application

Except as provided in subsection (e), an application for naturalization shall be filed in the office of the Attorney General.

(e) Substitute filing place and administering oath other than before Attorney General

A person may file an application for naturalization other than in the office of the Attorney General, and an oath of allegiance administered other than in a public ceremony before the Attorney General or a court, if the Attorney General determines that the person has an illness or other disability which—

(1) is of a permanent nature and is sufficiently serious to prevent the person's personal appearance, or

(2) is of a nature which so incapacitates the person as to prevent him from personally appearing.

(f) Declaration of intention

An alien over 18 years of age who is residing in the United States pursuant to a lawful admission for permanent residence may file with the Attorney General a declaration of intention to become a citizen of the United States. Such a declaration shall be filed in duplicate and in a form prescribed by the Attorney General and shall be accompanied by an application prescribed and approved by the Attorney General. Nothing in this subsection shall be construed as requiring any such alien to make and file a declaration of intention as a condition precedent to filing an application for naturalization nor shall any such declaration of intention be regarded as conferring or having conferred upon any such alien United States citizenship or nationality or the right to United States citizenship or nationality, nor shall such declaration be regarded as evidence of such alien's lawful admission for permanent residence in any proceeding, action, or matter arising under this or any other Act.

(June 27, 1952, c. 477, Title III, ch. 2, § 334, 66 Stat. 254; Pub. L. 97–116, § 15(b), Dec. 29, 1981, 95 Stat. 1619; Pub.L. 101–649, Title IV, §§ 401(b), 407(c)(15), (d)(12), Nov. 29, 1990, 104 Stat. 5038, 5041, 5042; Pub.L. 102–232, Title III, § 305(d), (e), (m)(7), Dec. 12, 1991, 105 Stat. 1750.)

§ 335. Investigation of applicants; examination of applications [8 U.S.C.A. § 1446]

(a) Waiver

Before a person may be naturalized, an employee of the Service, or of the United States designated by the Attorney General, shall conduct a personal investigation of the person applying for naturalization in the vicinity or vicinities in which such person has maintained his actual place of abode and in the vicinity or vicinities in which such person has been employed or has engaged in business or work for at least five years immediately preceding the filing of his application for naturalization. The Attorney General may, in his discretion, waive a personal investigation in an individual case or in such cases or classes of cases as may be designated by him.

(b) Conduct of examinations; authority of designees; record

The Attorney General shall designate employees of the Service to conduct examinations upon petitions for naturalization. For such purposes any such employee so designated is authorized to take testimony concerning any matter touching or in any way affecting the admissibility of any applicant for naturalization, to administer oaths, including the oath of the applicant for naturalization, and to require by subpoena the attendance and testimony of witnesses, including applicant, before such employee so designated and the production of relevant books, papers, and documents, and to that end may invoke the aid of any district court of the United States; and any such court may, in the event of neglect or refusal to respond to a subpoena issued by any such employee so designated or refusal to testify before such employee so designated issue an order requiring such person to appear before such employee so designated, produce relevant books, papers, and documents if demanded, and testify; and any failure to obey such order of the court may be punished by the court as a contempt thereof. The record of the examination authorized by this subsection shall be admissible as evidence in any hearing conducted by an immigration officer under section 336(a) [8 U.S.C.A. § 1447(a)]. Any such employee shall, at the examination, inform the petitioner of the remedies available to the petitioner under section 336 [8 U.S.C.A. § 1447].

(c) Transmittal of record of examination

The record of the examination upon any application for naturalization may, in the discretion of the Attorney General be transmitted to the Attorney General and the determination with respect thereto of the employee designated to conduct such examination shall when made also be transmitted to the Attorney General.

(d) Determination to grant or deny application

The employee designated to conduct any such examination shall make a determination as to whether the application should be granted or denied, with reasons therefor.

(e) Withdrawal of application

After an application for naturalization has been filed with the Attorney General, the applicant shall not be permitted to withdraw his application, except with the consent of the Attorney General. In cases where the Attorney General does not consent to the withdrawal of the application, the application shall be determined on its merits and a final order determination made accordingly. In cases where the applicant fails to prosecute his application, the application shall be decided on the merits unless the Attorney General dismisses it for lack of prosecution.

(f) Transfer of application

An applicant for naturalization who moves from the district of the Service in the United States in which the application is pending may, at any time thereafter, request the Service to transfer the application to any district of the Service in the United States which may act on the application. The transfer shall not be made without the consent of the Attorney General. In the case of such a transfer, the proceedings on the application shall continue as though the application had originally been filed in the district of the Service to which the application is transferred.

(g), (h) Repealed. Pub. L. 97–116, § 15(c)(2), Dec. 29, 1981, 95 Stat. 1619.

(i) Redesignated (f).

(June 27, 1952, c. 477, Title III, ch. 2, § 335, 66 Stat. 255; Pub. L. 97–116, § 15(c), Dec. 29, 1981, 95 Stat. 1619; Pub.L. 100–525, § 9(aa), (bb), Oct. 24, 1988, 102 Stat. 2621; Pub.L. 101–649, Title IV, §§ 401(c), 407(c)(16), (d)(13), Nov. 29, 1990, 104 Stat. 5038, 5041, 5043; Dec. 12, 1991, Pub.L. 102–232, Title III, § 305(f), 105 Stat. 1750.)

§ 336. Hearings on denials of applications for naturalization [8 U.S.C.A. § 1447]

(a) Request for hearing before immigration officer

If, after an examination under section 335 [8 U.S.C.A. § 1446], an application for naturalization is denied, the applicant may request a hearing before an immigration officer.

(b) Request for hearing before district court

If there is a failure to make a determination under section 335 [8 U.S.C.A. § 1446] before the end of the 120–day period after the date on which the examination is conducted under such section, the applicant may apply to the United States district court for the district in which the applicant resides for a hearing on the matter. Such court has jurisdiction over the matter and may either determine the matter or remand the matter, with appropriate instructions, to the Service to determine the matter.

(c) Appearance of Attorney General

The Attorney General shall have the right to appear before any immigration officer in any naturalization proceedings for the purpose of cross-examining the applicant and the witnesses produced in support of the application concerning any matter touching or in any way affecting the applicant's right to admission to citizenship, and shall have the right to call witnesses, including the applicant, produce evidence, and be heard in opposition to, or in favor of, the granting of any application in naturalization proceedings.

(d) Subpoena of witness

The immigration officer shall, if the applicant requests it at the time of filing the request for the hearing, issue a subpoena for the witnesses named by such applicant to appear upon the day set for the hearing, but in case such witnesses cannot be produced upon the hearing other witnesses may be summoned upon notice to the Attorney General, in such manner and at such time as the Attorney General may by regulation prescribe. Such subpoenas may be enforced in the same manner as subpoenas under section 335(b) [8 U.S.C.A. § 1446(b)] may be enforced.

(e) Change of name of applicant

It shall be lawful at the time and as a part of the administration by a court of the oath of allegiance under section 337(a) [8 U.S.C.A. § 1448(a)] for the court, in its discretion, upon the bona fide prayer of the applicant included in an appropriate petition to the court, to make a decree changing the name of said person, and the certificate of naturalization shall be issued in accordance therewith.

(f) Redesignated (e).

(June 27, 1952, c. 477, Title III, ch. 2, § 336, 66 Stat. 257; Pub. L. 91–136, Dec. 5, 1969, 83 Stat. 283; Pub. L. 97–116, § 15(d), Dec. 29, 1981, 95 Stat. 1619; Pub.L. 100–525, § 9(cc), Oct. 24, 1988, 102 Stat. 2621; Pub.L. 101–649, Title IV, § 407(c)(17), (d)(14), Nov. 29, 1990, 104 Stat. 5041, 5044; Dec. 12, 1991, Pub.L. 102–232, Title III, § 305(g), (h), 105 Stat. 1750.)

§ 337. Oath of renunciation and allegiance [8 U.S.C.A. § 1448]

(a) Public ceremony

A person who has applied for naturalization shall, in order to be and before being admitted to citizenship, take in a public ceremony before the Attorney General or a court with jurisdiction under section 310(b) [8 U.S.C.A. § 1421(b)] an oath **(1)** to support the Constitution of the United States; **(2)** to renounce and abjure absolutely and entirely all allegiance and fidelity to any foreign prince, potentate, state, or sovereignty of whom or which the applicant was before a subject or citizen; **(3)** to support and defend the Constitution and the laws of the United States against all enemies, foreign and domestic; **(4)** to bear true faith and allegiance to the same; and **(5)(A)** to bear arms on behalf of the United States when required by the law, or **(B)** to perform noncombatant service in the Armed Forces of the United States when required by the law, or **(C)** to perform work of national importance under civilian direction when required by the law. Any such person shall be required to take an oath containing the substance of clauses (1) to (5) of the preceding sentence, except that a person who shows by clear and convincing evidence to the satisfaction of the Attorney General that he is opposed to the bearing of arms in the Armed Forces of the United States by reason of religious training and belief shall be required to take an oath containing the substance of clauses (1) to (4) and clauses (5)(B) and (5)(C) of this subsection, and a person who shows by clear and convincing evidence to the satisfaction of the Attorney General that he is opposed to any type of service in the Armed Forces of the United States by reason of religious training and belief shall be required to take an oath containing the substance of said clauses (1) to (4) and clause (5)(C). The term "religious training and belief" as used in this section shall mean an individual's belief in a relation to a Supreme Being involving duties superior to those arising from any human relation, but does not include essentially political, sociological, or philosophical views or a merely personal moral code. In the case of the naturalization of a child under the provisions of section 322 [8 U.S.C.A. § 1433] the Attorney General may waive the taking of the oath if in the opinion of the Attorney General the child is unable to understand its meaning. The Attorney General may waive the taking of the oath by a person if in the opinion of the Attorney General the person is unable to understand, or to communicate an understanding of, its meaning because of a physical or developmental disability or mental impairment. If the Attorney General waives the taking of the oath by a person under the preceding sentence, the person shall be considered to have met the requirements of section 316(a)(3) [8 U.S.C.A. § 1427(a)(3)] with respect to attachment to the principles of the Constitution and well disposition to the good order and happiness of the United States.

(b) Hereditary titles or orders of nobility

In case the person applying for naturalization has borne any hereditary title, or has been of any of the orders of nobility in any foreign state, the applicant shall in addition to complying with the requirements of subsection (a) of this section, make under oath in the same public ceremony in which the oath of allegiance is administered, an express renunciation of such title or order of nobility, and such renunciation shall be recorded as a part of such proceedings.

(c) Expedited administration of oath

Notwithstanding section 310(b) [8 U.S.C.A. § 1421(b)], an individual may be granted an expedited judicial oath administration ceremony or administrative naturalization by the Attorney General upon demonstrating sufficient cause. In determining whether to grant an expedited judicial oath administration ceremony, a court shall consider special circumstances (such as serious illness of the applicant or a member of the applicant's immediate family, permanent disability sufficiently incapacitating as to prevent the applicant's personal appearance at the scheduled ceremony, developmental disability or advanced age, or exigent circumstances relating to travel or employment). If an expedited judicial oath administration ceremony is impracticable, the court shall refer such individual to the Attorney General who may provide for immediate administrative naturalization.

(d) Rules and regulations

The Attorney General shall prescribe rules and procedures to ensure that the ceremonies conducted by the Attorney General for the administration of oaths of allegiance under this section are public, conducted frequently and at regular intervals, and are in keeping with the dignity of the occasion.

(June 27, 1952, c. 477, Title III, ch. 2, § 337, 66 Stat. 258; Pub. L. 97–116, § 18(*o*), Dec. 29, 1981, 95 Stat. 1621; Pub.L. 101–649, Title IV, § 407(c)(18), (d)(15), Nov. 29, 1990, 104 Stat. 5041, 5044; Pub.L. 102–232, Title I, § 102(b)(2), Title III, § 305(i), Dec. 12, 1991, 105 Stat. 1736, 1750; Nov. 6, 2000, Pub.L. 106–448, § 1, 114 Stat. 1939.)

§ 338. Certificate of naturalization; contents [8 U.S.C.A. § 1449]

A person admitted to citizenship in conformity with the provisions of this title shall be entitled upon such admission to receive from the Attorney General a certificate of naturalization, which shall contain substantially the following information: Number of application for naturalization; number of certificate of naturalization; date of naturalization; name, signature, place of residence, autographed photograph, and personal description of the naturalized person, including age, sex, marital status, and country of former nationality; location of the district office of the Service in which the application was filed and the title, authority, and location of the official or court administering the oath of allegiance; statement that the Attorney General having found that the applicant had complied in all respects with all of the applicable provisions of the naturalization laws of the United States, and was entitled to be admitted a citizen of the United States of America, thereupon ordered that the applicant be admitted as a citizen of the United States of America; attestation of an immigration officer; and the seal of the Department of Justice.

(June 27, 1952, c. 447, Title III, ch. 2, § 338, 66 Stat. 259; Nov. 29, 1990, Pub.L. 101–649, Title IV, § 407(c)(19), (d)(16), 104 Stat. 5041, 5045; Dec. 12, 1991, Pub.L. 102–232, Title III, § 305(j), 105 Stat. 1750; Oct. 25, 1994, Pub.L. 103–416, Title I, § 104(a), Title II, § 219(z)(3), 108 Stat. 4308, 4318.)

§ 339. Functions and duties of clerks and records of declarations of intention and applications for naturalization [8 U.S.C.A. § 1450]

(a) The clerk of each court that administers oaths of allegiance under section 337 [8 U.S.C.A. § 1448] shall—

(1) deliver to each person administered the oath of allegiance by the court pursuant to section 337(a) [8 U.S.C.A. § 1448(a)] the certificate of naturalization prepared by the Attorney General pursuant to section 310(b)(2)(A)(ii) [8 U.S.C.A. § 1421(b)(2)(A)(ii)],

(2) forward to the Attorney General a list of applicants actually taking the oath as each scheduled ceremony and information concerning each person to whom such an oath is administered by the court, within 30 days after the close of the month in which the oath was administered,

(3) forward to the Attorney General certified copies of such other proceedings and orders instituted in or issued out of the court affecting or relating to the naturalization of persons as may be required from time to time by the Attorney General, and

(4) be responsible for all blank certificates of naturalization received by them from time to time from the Attorney General and shall account to the Attorney General for them whenever required to do so.

No certificate of naturalization received by any clerk of court which may be defaced or injured in such manner as to prevent its use as herein provided shall in any case be destroyed, but such certificates shall be returned to the Attorney General.

(b) Each district office of the Service in the United States shall maintain, in chronological order, indexed, and consecutively numbered, as part of its permanent records, all declarations of intention and applications for naturalization filed with the office.

(June 27, 1952, c. 477, Title III, ch. 2, § 339, 66 Stat. 259; Nov. 29, 1990, Pub.L. 101–649, Title IV, § 407(d)(17), 104 Stat. 5045; Dec. 12, 1991, Pub.L. 102–232, Title I, § 102(b)(1), 105 Stat. 1735.)

§ 340. Revocation of naturalization [8 U.S.C.A. § 1451]

(a) Concealment of material evidence; refusal to testify

It shall be the duty of the United States attorneys for the respective districts, upon affidavit showing good cause therefor, to institute proceedings in any district court of the United States in the judicial district in which the naturalized citizen may reside at the time of bringing suit, for the purpose of revoking and setting aside the order admitting such person to citizenship and canceling the certificate of naturalization on the ground that such order and certificate of naturalization were illegally procured or were procured by concealment of a material fact or by willful misrepresentation, and such revocation and setting aside of the order admitting such person to citizenship and such canceling of certificate of naturalization shall be effective as of the original date of the order and certificate, respectively: Provided, That refusal on the part of a naturalized citizen within a period of ten years following his naturalization to testify as a witness in any proceeding before a congressional committee concerning his subversive activities, in a case where such person has been convicted of contempt for such refusal, shall be held to constitute a ground for revocation of such person's naturalization under this subsection as having been procured by concealment of a material fact or by willful misrepresentation. If the naturalized citizen does not reside in any judicial district in the United States at the time of bringing such suit, the proceedings may be instituted in the United States District Court for the District of Columbia or in the United States district court in the judicial district in which such person last had his residence.

(b) Notice to party

The party to whom was granted the naturalization alleged to have been illegally procured or procured by concealment of a material fact or by willful misrepresentation shall, in any such proceedings under subsection (a) of this section, have sixty days' personal notice, unless waived by such party, in which to make answers to the petition of the United States; and if such naturalized person be absent from the United States or from the judicial district in which such person last had his residence, such notice shall be given either by personal service upon him or by publication in the manner provided for the service of summons by publication or upon absentees by the laws of the State or the place where such suit is brought.

(c) Membership in certain organizations; prima facie evidence

If a person who shall have been naturalized after December 24, 1952 shall within five years next following such naturalization become a member of or affiliated with any organization, membership in or affiliation with which at the time of naturalization would have precluded such person from naturalization under the provisions of section 313 [8 U.S.C.A. § 1424], it shall be considered prima facie evidence that such person was not attached to the principles of the Constitution of the United States and was not well disposed to the good order and happiness of the United States at the time of naturalization, and, in the absence of countervailing evidence, it shall be sufficient in the proper proceeding to authorize the revocation and setting aside of the order admitting such person to citizenship and the cancellation of the certificate of naturalization as having been obtained by concealment of a material fact or by willful misrepresentation, and such revocation and setting aside of the order admitting such person to citizenship and such canceling of certificate of naturalization shall be effective as of the original date of the order and certificate, respectively.

(d) Applicability to citizenship through naturalization of parent or spouse

Any person who claims United States citizenship through the naturalization of a parent or spouse in whose case there is a revocation and setting aside of the order admitting such parent or spouse to citizenship under the provisions of subsection (a) of this section on the ground that the order and certificate of naturalization were procured by concealment of a material fact or by willful misrepresentation shall be deemed to have lost and to lose his citizenship and any right or privilege of citizenship which he may have, now has, or may hereafter acquire under and by virtue of such naturalization of such parent or spouse, regardless of whether such person is residing within or without the United States at the time of the revocation and setting aside of the order admitting such parent or spouse to citizenship. Any person who claims United States citizenship through the naturalization of a parent or spouse in whose case there is a revocation and setting aside of the order admitting such parent or spouse to citizenship and the cancellation of the certificate of naturalization under the provisions of subsection (c) of this section, or under the provisions of section 329(c) [8 U.S.C.A. § 1440 (c)] on any ground other than that the order and certificate of naturalization were procured by concealment of a material fact or by willful misrepresentation, shall be deemed to have lost and to lose his citizenship and any right or privilege of citizenship which would have been enjoyed by such person had there not been a revocation and setting aside of the order admitting such parent or spouse to citizenship and the cancellation of the certificate of naturalization, unless such person is residing in the United States at the time of the revocation and setting aside of the order admitting such parent or spouse to citizenship and the cancellation of the certificate of naturalization.

(e) Citizenship unlawfully procured

When a person shall be convicted under section 1425 of Title 18 of knowingly procuring naturalization in violation of law, the court in which such conviction is had shall thereupon revoke, set aside, and declare void the final order admitting such person to citizenship, and shall declare the certificate of naturalization of such person to be canceled. Jurisdiction is conferred on the courts having jurisdiction of the trial of such offense to make such adjudication.

(f) Cancellation of certificate of naturalization

Whenever an order admitting an alien to citizenship shall be revoked and set aside or a certificate of naturalization shall be canceled, or both, as provided in this section, the court in which such judgment or decree is rendered shall make an order canceling such certificate and shall send a certified copy of such order to the Attorney General. The clerk of court shall transmit a copy of such order and judgment to the Attorney General. A person holding a certificate of naturalization or citizenship which has been canceled as provided by this section shall upon notice by the court by which the decree of cancellation was made, or by the Attorney General, surrender the same to the Attorney General.

(g) Applicability of certificates of naturalization and citizenship

The provisions of this section shall apply not only to any naturalization granted and to certificates of naturalization and citizenship issued under the provisions of this title, but to any naturalization heretofore granted by any court, and to all certificates of naturalization and citizenship which may have been issued heretofore by any court or by the Commissioner based upon naturalization granted by any court, or by a designated representative of the Commissioner under the provisions of section 702 of the Nationality Act of 1940, as amended, or by such designated representative under any other act.

(h) Power to correct, reopen, alter, modify, or vacate order

Nothing contained in this section shall be regarded as limiting, denying, or restricting the power of the Attorney General to correct, reopen, alter, modify, or vacate an order naturalizing the person.

(June 27, 1952, c. 477, Title III, ch. 2, § 340, 66 Stat. 260; Sept. 3, 1954, c. 1263, § 18, 68 Stat. 1232; Sept. 26, 1961, Pub.L. 87–301, § 18, 75 Stat. 656; Nov. 14, 1986, Pub.L. 99–653, § 17, 100 Stat. 3658; Oct. 24, 1988, Pub.L. 100–525, § 9(dd), 102 Stat. 2621; Nov. 29, 1990, Pub.L. 101–649, Title IV, § 407(d)(18), 104 Stat. 5046; Dec. 12, 1991, Pub.L. 102–232, Title III, § 305(k), 105 Stat. 1750; Oct. 25, 1994, Pub.L. 103–416, Title I, § 104(b), (c), 108 Stat. 4308.)

§ 341. Certificates of citizenship or U.S. non-citizen national status; procedure [8 U.S.C.A. § 1452]

(a) Application to Attorney General for certificate of citizenship; proof; oath of allegiance

A person who claims to have derived United States citizenship through the naturalization of a parent or through the naturalization or citizenship of a husband, or who is a citizen of the United States by virtue of the provisions of section 1993 of the United States Revised Statutes, or of section 1993 of the United States Revised Statutes, as amended by section 1 of the Act of May 24, 1934 (48 Stat. 797), or who is a citizen of the United States by virtue of the provisions of subsection (c), (d), (e), (g), or (i) of section 201 of the Nationality Act of 1940, as amended (54 Stat. 1138), or of the Act of May 7, 1934 (48 Stat. 667), or of paragraph (c), (d), (e), or (g) of section 301 [8 U.S.C.A. § 1401], or under the provisions of the Act of August 4, 1937 (50 Stat. 558), or under the provisions of section 203 or 205 of the Nationality Act of 1940 (54 Stat. 1139), or under the provisions of section 303 [8 U.S.C.A. § 1403], may apply to the Attorney General for a certificate of citizenship. Upon proof to the satisfaction of the Attorney General that the applicant is a citizen, and that the applicant's alleged citizenship was derived as claimed, or acquired, as the case may be, and upon taking and subscribing before a member of the Service within the United States to the oath of allegiance required by this chapter of an applicant for naturalization, such individual shall be furnished by the Attorney General with a certificate of citizenship, but only if such individual is at the time within the United States.

(b) Application to Secretary of State for certificate of non-citizen national status; proof; oath of allegiance

A person who claims to be a national, but not a citizen, of the United States may apply to the Secretary of State for a certificate of non-citizen national status. Upon—

(1) proof to the satisfaction of the Secretary of State that the applicant is a national, but not a citizen, of the United States, and

(2) in the case of such a person born outside of the United States or its outlying possessions, taking and subscribing, before an immigration officer within the United States or its outlying possessions, to the oath of allegiance required by this chapter of a petitioner for naturalization, the individual shall be furnished by the Secretary of State with a certificate of non-citizen national status, but only if the individual is at the time within the United States or its outlying possessions.

(June 27, 1952, c. 477, Title III, ch. 2, § 341, 66 Stat. 263; Dec. 29, 1981, Pub.L. 97–116, § 18(p), 95 Stat. 1621; Aug. 27, 1986, Pub.L. 99–396, § 16(a), 100 Stat. 843; Nov. 14, 1986, Pub.L. 99–653, § 22, 100 Stat. 3658; Oct. 24, 1988, Pub.L. 100–525, § 8(q), 102 Stat. 2618; Dec. 12, 1991, Pub.L. 102–232, Title III, § 305(m)(8), 105 Stat. 1750; Oct. 25, 1994, Pub.L. 103–416, Title I, § 102(b), 108 Stat. 4307.)

§ 342. Cancellation of certificates issued by Attorney General, the Commissioner or a Deputy Commissioner; action not to affect citizenship status [8 U.S.C.A. § 1453]

The Attorney General is authorized to cancel any certificate of citizenship, certificate of naturalization, copy of a declaration of intention, or other certificate, document or record heretofore issued or made by the Commissioner or a Deputy Commissioner or hereafter made by the Attorney General if it shall appear to the Attorney General's satisfaction that such document or record was illegally or fraudulently obtained from, or was created through illegality or by fraud practiced upon, him or the Commissioner or a Deputy Commissioner; but the person for or to whom such document or record has been issued or made shall be given at such person's last-known place of address written notice of the intention to cancel such document or record with the reasons therefor and shall be given at least sixty days in which to show cause why such document or record should not be canceled. The cancellation under this section of any document purporting to show the citizenship status of the person to whom it was issued shall affect only the document and not the citizenship status of the person in whose name the document was issued.

(June 27, 1952, c. 477, Title III, ch. 2, § 342, 66 Stat. 263.)

§ 343. Documents and copies issued by Attorney General [8 U.S.C.A. § 1454]

(a) If any certificate of naturalization or citizenship issued to any citizen or any declaration of intention furnished to any declarant is lost, mutilated, or destroyed, the citizen or declarant may make application to the Attorney General for a new certificate or declaration. If the Attorney General finds that the certificate or declaration is lost, mutilated, or destroyed, he shall issue to the applicant a new certificate or declaration. If the certificate or declaration has been mutilated, it shall be surrendered to the Attorney General before the applicant may receive such new certificate or declaration. If the certificate or declaration has been lost, the applicant or any other person who shall have, or may come into possession of it is required to surrender it to the Attorney General.

(b) The Attorney General shall issue for any naturalized citizen, on such citizen's application therefor, a special certificate of naturalization for use by such citizen only for the purpose of obtaining recognition as a citizen of the United States by a foreign state. Such certificate when issued shall be furnished to the Secretary of State for transmission to the proper authority in such foreign state.

(c) If the name of any naturalized citizen has, subsequent to naturalization, been changed by order of any court of competent jurisdiction, or by marriage, the citizen may make application for a new certificate of naturalization in the new name of such citizen. If the Attorney General finds the name of the applicant to have been changed as claimed, the Attorney General shall issue to the applicant a new certificate and shall notify the naturalization court of such action.

(d) The Attorney General is authorized to make and issue certifications of any part of the naturalization records of any court, or of any certificate of naturalization or citizenship, for use in complying with any statute, State or Federal, or in any judicial proceeding. No such certification shall be made by any clerk of court except upon order of the court.

(June 27, 1952, c. 477, Title III, ch. 2, § 343, 66 Stat. 263; Pub.L. 100–525, § 9(ee), Oct. 24, 1988, 102 Stat. 2621.)

§ 344. Fiscal provisions [8 U.S.C.A. § 1455]

(a) The Attorney General shall charge, collect, and account for fees prescribed by the Attorney General pursuant to section 9701 of Title 31 for the following:

(1) Making, filing, and docketing an application for naturalization, including the hearing on such application, if such hearing be held, and a certificate of naturalization, if the issuance of such certificate is authorized by the Attorney General.

(2) Receiving and filing a declaration of intention, and issuing a duplicate thereof.

(b) Notwithstanding the provisions of this Act or any other law, no fee shall be charged or collected for an application for declaration of intention or a certificate of naturalization in lieu of a declaration or a certificate alleged to have been lost, mutilated, or destroyed, submitted by a person who was a member of the military or naval forces of the United States at any time after April 20, 1898, and before July 5, 1902; or at any time after April 5, 1917, and before November 12, 1918; or who served on the Mexican border as a member of the Regular Army or National Guard between June 1916 and April 1917; or who has served or hereafter serves in the military, air, or naval forces of the United States after September 16, 1940, and who was not at any time during such period or thereafter separated from such forces under other than honorable conditions, who was not a conscientious objector who performed no military duty whatever or refused to wear the uniform, or who was not at any time during such period or thereafter discharged from such military, air, or naval forces on account of alienage.

(c) Except as provided by section 286(q)(2) [8 U.S.C.A. § 1356(q)(2)] or any other law, all fees collected by the Attorney General shall be deposited by the Attorney General in the Treasury of the United States except that all such fees collected or paid over on or after October 1, 1988, shall be deposited in the Immigration Examinations Fee Account established under section 286(m) [8 U.S.C.A. § 1356(m)]: *Provided, however,* That all fees received by the Attorney General from applicants residing in the Virgin Islands of the United States, and in Guam, under this title, shall be paid over to the treasury of the Virgin Islands and to the treasury of Guam, respectively.

(d) During the time when the United States is at war the Attorney General may not charge or collect a naturalization fee from an alien in the military, air, or naval service of the United States for filing an application for naturalization or issuing a certificate of naturalization upon admission to citizenship.

(e) In addition to the other fees required by this title, the applicant for naturalization shall, upon the filing of an application for naturalization, deposit with and pay to the Attorney General a sum of money sufficient to cover the expenses of subpoenaing and paying the legal fees of any witnesses for whom such applicant may request a subpoena, and upon the final discharge of such witnesses, they shall receive, if they demand the same from the Attorney General, the customary and usual witness fees from the moneys which the applicant shall have paid to the Attorney General for such purpose, and the residue, if any, shall be returned by the Attorney General to the applicant.

(f)(1) The Attorney General shall pay over to courts administering oaths of allegiance to persons under this title a specified percentage of all fees described in subsection (a)(1) collected by the Attorney General with respect to persons administered the oath of allegiance by the respective courts. The Attorney General, annually and in consultation with the courts, shall determine the specified percentage based on the proportion, of the total costs incurred by the Service and courts for essential services directly related to the naturalization process, which are incurred by courts.

(2) The Attorney General shall provide on an annual basis to the Committees on the Judiciary of the House of Representatives and of the Senate a detailed report on the use of the fees described in paragraph (1) and shall consult with such Committees before increasing such fees.

(g) to (i) Redesignated (c) to (e).

(June 27, 1952, c. 477, Title III, ch. 2, § 344, 66 Stat. 264; Pub. L. 85–508, § 26, July 7, 1958, 72 Stat. 351; Pub. L. 90–609, § 3, Oct. 21, 1968, 82 Stat. 1200; Pub. L. 97–116, § 16, Dec. 29, 1981, 95 Stat. 1619; Pub.L. 100–459, Title II, § 209(b), Oct. 1, 1988, 102 Stat. 2203; Pub.L. 100–525, § 9(ff), Oct. 24, 1988, 102 Stat. 2621; Pub.L. 101–649, Title IV, § 407(c)(20), (d)(19), Nov. 29, 1990, 104 Stat. 5041, 5046; Pub.L. 100–459, Title II, § 209(b), amended Pub.L. 102–232, Title I, § 102(b)(3), Title III, §§ 305(*l*),309(a)(1)(A)(ii), Dec. 12, 1991, 105 Stat. 1758; Pub.L. 102–232 309(b)(14), Dec. 12, 1991, 105 Stat. 1736, 1750, 1758, 1759; Nov. 2, 2002, Pub.L. 107–273, Div. C, Title I, § 11016(1), 116 Stat. 1824.)

§ 345. Repealed. Pub. L. 86–682, § 12(c), Sept. 2, 1960, 74 Stat. 708, eff. Sept. 1, 1960 [8 U.S.C.A. § 1456]

§ 346. Publication and distribution of citizenship textbooks; use of naturalization fees [8 U.S.C.A. § 1457]

Authorization is granted for the publication and distribution of the citizenship textbook described in subsection (b) of section 332 [8 U.S.C.A. § 1443(b)] and for the reimbursement of the appropriation of the Department of Justice upon the records of the Treasury Department from the naturalization fees deposited in the Treasury through the Service for the cost of such publication and distribution, such reimbursement to be made upon statements by the Attorney General of books so published and distributed.

(June 27, 1952, c. 477, Title III, ch. 2, § 346, 66 Stat. 266.)

§ 347. Compilation of naturalization statistics and payment for equipment [8 U.S.C.A. § 1458]

The Attorney General is authorized and directed to prepare from the records in the custody of the Service a report upon those heretofore seeking citizenship to show by nationalities their relation to the numbers of aliens annually arriving and to the prevailing census populations of the foreign-born, their economic, vocational, and other classification, in statistical form, with analytical comment thereon, and to prepare such report annually hereafter. Payment for the equipment used in preparing such compilation shall be made from the appropriation for the enforcement of this Act by the Service.

(June 27, 1952, c. 477, Title III, ch. 2, § 347, 66 Stat. 266.)

§ 348. Repealed [8 U.S.C.A. § 1459].

CHAPTER III—LOSS OF NATIONALITY

§ 349. Loss of nationality by native-born or naturalized citizen; voluntary action; burden of proof; presumptions [8 U.S.C.A. § 1481]

(a) A person who is a national of the United States whether by birth or naturalization, shall lose his nationality by voluntarily performing any of the following acts with the intention of relinquishing United States nationality—

(1) obtaining naturalization in a foreign state upon his own application, or upon an application filed by a duly authorized agent, after having attained the age of eighteen years; or

(2) taking an oath or making an affirmation or other formal declaration of allegiance to a foreign state or a political subdivision thereof, after having attained the age of eighteen years; or

(3) entering, or serving in, the armed forces of a foreign state if **(A)** such armed forces are engaged in hostilities against the United States, or **(B)** such persons serve as a commissioned or noncommissioned officer; or

(4)(A) accepting, serving in, or performing the duties of any office, post, or employment under the government of a foreign state or a political subdivision thereof, after attaining the age of eighteen years, if he has or acquires the nationality of such foreign state; or

(B) accepting, serving in, or performing the duties of any office, post, or employment under the government of a foreign state or a political subdivision thereof, after attaining the age of eighteen years for which office, post, or employment an oath, affirmation, or declaration of allegiance is required; or

(5) making a formal renunciation of nationality before a diplomatic or consular officer of the United States in a foreign state, in such form as may be prescribed by the Secretary of State; or

(6) making in the United States a formal written renunciation of nationality in such form as may be prescribed by, and before such officer as may be designated by, the Attorney General, whenever the United States shall be in a state of war and the Attorney General shall approve such renunciation as not contrary to the interests of national defense; or

(7) committing any act of treason against, or attempting by force to overthrow, or bearing arms against, the United States, violating or conspiring to violate any of the provisions of section 2383 of Title 18, or willfully performing any act in violation of section 2385 of Title 18, or violating section 2384 of Title 18 by engaging in a conspiracy to overthrow, put down, or to destroy by force the Government of the United States, or to levy war against them, if and when he is convicted thereof by a court martial or by a court of competent jurisdiction.

(b) Whenever the loss of United States nationality is put in issue in any action or proceeding commenced on or after September 26, 1961 under, or by virtue of, the provisions of this Act or any other Act, the burden shall be upon the person or party claiming that such loss occurred, to establish such claim by a preponderance of the evidence. Any person who commits or performs, or who has committed or performed, any act of expatriation under the provisions of this or any other Act shall be presumed to have done so voluntarily, but such presumption may be rebutted upon a showing, by a preponderance of the evidence, that the act or acts committed or performed were not done voluntarily.

(June 27, 1952, c. 477, Title III, ch. 3, § 349, 66 Stat. 267; Sept. 3, 1954, c. 1256, § 2, 68 Stat. 1146; Pub.L. 87–301, § 19, Sept. 26, 1961, 75 Stat. 656; Pub.L. 94–412, Title V, § 501(a), Sept. 14, 1976, 90 Stat. 1258; Pub.L. 95–432, §§ 2, 4, Oct. 10, 1978, 92 Stat. 1046; Pub.L. 97–116, § 18(k)(2), (q), Dec. 29, 1981, 95 Stat. 1620, 1621; Pub.L. 99–653, §§ 18, 19, Nov. 14, 1986, 100 Stat. 3658, as amended Pub.L. 100–525, §§ 8(m), (n), 9(hh), Oct. 24, 1988, 102 Stat. 2618, 2622.)

§ 350. Repealed. Pub. L. 95–432, § 1, Oct. 10, 1978, 92 Stat. 1046 [8 U.S.C.A. § 1482]

§ 351. Restrictions on loss of nationality [8 U.S.C.A. § 1483]

(a) Except as provided in paragraphs (6) and (7) of section 349(a) of this title [8 U.S.C.A. § 1481(a)], no national of the United States can lose United States nationality under this Act while within the United States or any of its outlying possessions, but loss of nationality shall result from the performance within the United States or any of its outlying possessions of any of the acts or the fulfillment of any of the conditions specified in this part if and when the national thereafter takes up a residence outside the United States and its outlying possessions.

(b) A national who within six months after attaining the age of eighteen years asserts his claim to United States nationality, in such manner as the Secretary of State shall by regulation prescribe, shall not be deemed to have lost United States nationality by the commission, prior to his eighteenth birthday, of any of the acts specified in paragraphs (3) and (5) of section 349(a) [8 U.S.C.A. § 1481(a)].

(June 27, 1952, c. 477, Title III, ch. 3, § 351, 66 Stat. 269; Dec. 29, 1981, Pub.L. 97–116, § 18(r), 95 Stat. 1621; Nov. 14, 1986, Pub.L. 99–653, § 20, 100 Stat. 3658; Oct. 24, 1988, Pub.L. 100–525, § 8(*o*), 102 Stat. 2618; Oct. 25, 1994, Pub.L. 103–416, Title I, § 105(a), 108 Stat. 4308; Sept. 30, 1996, Pub.L. 104–208, Div. C, Title VI, § 671(b)(3), 110 Stat. 3009–721.)

§§ 352 to 355. Repealed. Pub. L. 95–432, § 2, Oct. 10, 1978, 92 Stat. 1046 [8 U.S.C.A. §§ 1484 to 1487]

§ 356. Nationality lost solely from performance of acts or fulfillment of conditions [8 U.S.C.A. § 1488]

The loss of nationality under this part shall result solely from the performance by a national of the acts or fulfillment of the conditions specified in this Part.

(June 27, 1952, c. 477, Title III, ch. 3, § 356, 66 Stat. 272.)

§ 357. Application of treaties; exceptions [8 U.S.C.A. § 1489]

Nothing in this title shall be applied in contravention of the provisions of any treaty or convention to which the United States is a party and which has been ratified by the Senate before December 25, 1952: *Provided, however,* That no woman who was a national of the United States shall be deemed to have lost her nationality solely by reason of her marriage to an alien on or after September 22, 1922, or to an alien racially ineligible to citizenship on or after March 3, 1931, or, in the case of a woman who was a United States citizen at birth, through residence abroad following such marriage, notwithstanding the provisions of any existing treaty or convention.

(June 27, 1952, c. 477, Title III, ch. 3, § 357, 66 Stat. 272; Pub.L. 100–525, § 9(ii), Oct. 24, 1988, 102 Stat. 2622.)

CHAPTER IV—MISCELLANEOUS

§ 358. Certificate of diplomatic or consular officer of United States as to loss of American nationality [8 U.S.C.A. § 1501]

Whenever a diplomatic or consular officer of the United States has reason to believe that a person while in a foreign state has lost his United States nationality under any provision of chapter 3 of this title, or under any provision of chapter IV of the Nationality Act of 1940, as amended, he shall certify the facts upon which such belief is based to the Department of State, in writing, under regulations prescribed by the Secretary of State. If the report of the diplomatic or consular officer is approved by the Secretary of State, a copy of the certificate shall be forwarded to the Attorney General, for his information, and the diplomatic or consular office in which the report was made shall be directed to forward a copy of the certificate to the person to whom it relates. Approval by the Secretary of State of a certificate under this section shall constitute a final administrative determination of loss of United States nationality under this Act, subject to such procedures for administrative appeal as the Secretary may prescribe by regulation, and also shall constitute a denial of a right or privilege of United States nationality for purposes of section 360 [8 U.S.C.A. § 1503].

(June 27, 1952, c. 477, Title III, ch. 3, § 358, 66 Stat. 272; Oct. 25, 1994, Pub.L. 103–416, Title I, § 106, 108 Stat. 4309.)

§ 359. Certificate of nationality issued by Secretary of State for person not a naturalized citizen of United States for use in proceedings of a foreign state [8 U.S.C.A. § 1502]

The Secretary of State is authorized to issue, in his discretion and in accordance with rules and regulations prescribed by him, a certificate of nationality for any person not a naturalized citizen of the United States who presents satisfactory evidence that he is an American national and that such certificate is needed for use in judicial or administrative proceedings in a foreign state. Such certificate shall be solely for use in the case for which it was issued and shall be transmitted by the Secretary of State through appropriate official channels to the judicial or administrative officers of the foreign state in which it is to be used.

(June 27, 1952, c. 477, Title III, ch. 4, § 359, 66 Stat. 273.)

§ 360. Denial of rights and privileges as national [8 U.S.C.A. § 1503]

(a) Proceedings for declaration of United States nationality

If any person who is within the United States claims a right or privilege as a national of the United States and is denied such right or privilege by any department or independent agency, or official thereof, upon the ground that he is not a national of the United States, such person may institute an action under the provisions of section 2201 of Title 28 against the head of such department or independent agency for a judgment declaring him to be a national of the United States, except that no such action may be instituted in any case if the issue of such person's status as a national of the United States **(1)** arose by reason of, or in connection with any removal proceeding under the provisions of this or any other act, or **(2)** is in issue in any such removal proceeding. An action under this subsection may be instituted only within five years after the final administrative denial of such right or privilege and shall be filed in the district court of the United States for the district in which such person resides or claims a residence, and jurisdiction over such officials in such cases is conferred upon those courts.

(b) Application for certificate of identity; appeal

If any person who is not within the United States claims a right or privilege as a national of the United States and is denied such right or privilege by any department or independent agency, or official thereof, upon the ground that he is not a national of the United States, such person may make application to a diplomatic or consular officer of the

United States in the foreign country in which he is residing for a certificate of identity for the purpose of traveling to a port of entry in the United States and applying for admission. Upon proof to the satisfaction of such diplomatic or consular officer that such application is made in good faith and has a substantial basis, he shall issue to such person a certificate of identity. From any denial of an application for such certificate the applicant shall be entitled to an appeal to the Secretary of State, who, if he approves the denial, shall state in writing his reasons for his decision. The Secretary of State shall prescribe rules and regulations for the issuance of certificates of identity as above provided. The provisions of this subsection shall be applicable only to a person who at some time prior to his application for the certificate of identity has been physically present in the United States, or to a person under sixteen years of age who was born abroad of a United States citizen parent.

(c) Application for admission to United States under certificate of identity; revision of determination

A person who has been issued a certificate of identity under the provisions of subsection (b), and while in possession thereof, may apply for admission to the United States at any port of entry, and shall be subject to all the provisions of this Act relating to the conduct of proceedings involving aliens seeking admission to the United States. A final determination by the Attorney General that any such person is not entitled to admission to the United States shall be subject to review by any court of competent jurisdiction in habeas corpus proceedings and not otherwise. Any person described in this section who is finally denied admission to the United States shall be subject to all the provisions of this Act relating to aliens seeking admission to the United States.

(June 27, 1952, c. 477, Title III, ch. 3, § 360, 66 Stat. 273; Sept. 30, 1996, Pub.L. 104–208, Div. C, Title III, § 308(d)(4)(P), 110 Stat. 3009–619.)

§ 361. Cancellation of United States passports and Consular Reports of Birth [8 U.S.C.A. § 1504]

(a) The Secretary of State is authorized to cancel any United States passport or Consular Report of Birth, or certified copy thereof, if it appears that such document was illegally, fraudulently, or erroneously obtained from, or was created through illegality or fraud practiced upon, the Secretary. The person for or to whom such document has been issued or made shall be given, at such person's last known address, written notice of the cancellation of such document, together with the procedures for seeking a prompt post-cancellation hearing. The cancellation under this section of any document purporting to show the citizenship status of the person to whom it was issued shall affect only the document and not the citizenship status of the person in whose name the document was issued.

(b) For purposes of this section, the term "Consular Report of Birth" refers to the report, designated as a "Report of Birth Abroad of a Citizen of the United States", issued by a consular officer to document a citizen born abroad.

(June 27, 1952, c. 477, Title III, ch. 3, § 361, as added Oct. 25, 1994, Pub.L. 103–416, Title I, § 107(a), 108 Stat. 4309.)

TITLE IV

MISCELLANEOUS AND REFUGEE ASSISTANCE

§ 404. Authorization of appropriations [8 U.S.C.A. § 1101, note]

(a) There are authorized to be appropriated such sums as may be necessary to carry out the provisions of this Act (other than chapter 2 of title IV).

(b)(1) There are authorized to be appropriated (for fiscal year 1991 and any subsequent fiscal year) to an immigration emergency fund, to be established in the Treasury, an amount sufficient to provide for a balance of $35,000,000 in such fund, to be used to carry out paragraph (2) and to provide for an increase in border patrol or other enforcement activities of the Service and for reimbursement of State and localities in providing assistance as requested by the Attorney General in meeting an immigration emergency, except that no amounts may be withdrawn from such fund with respect to an emergency unless the President has determined that the immigration emergency exists and has certified such fact to the Judiciary Committees of the House of Representatives and of the Senate.

(2)(A) Funds which are authorized to be appropriated by paragraph (1), subject to the dollar limitation contained in subparagraph (B), shall be available, by application for the reimbursement of States and localities providing assistance as required by the Attorney General, to States and localities whenever—

> **(i)** a district director of the Service certifies to the Commissioner that the number of asylum applications filed in the respective district during a calendar quarter exceeds by at least 1,000 the number of such applications filed in that district during the preceding calendar quarter,
>
> **(ii)** the lives, property, safety, or welfare of the residents of a State or locality are endangered, or
>
> **(iii)** in any other circumstances as determined by the Attorney General.

In applying clause (i), the providing of parole at a point of entry in a district shall be deemed to constitute an application for asylum in the district.

(B) Not more than $20,000,000 shall be made available for all localities under this paragraph.

(C) For purposes of subparagraph (A), the requirement of paragraph (1) that an immigration emergency be determined shall not apply.

(D) A decision with respect to an application for reimbursement under subparagraph (A) shall be made by the Attorney General within 15 days after the date of receipt of the application.

(June 27, 1952, c. 477, Title IV, ch. 2, § 404, as amended Pub.L. 97–116, § 18(s), Dec. 29, 1981, 95 Stat. 1621; Pub.L. 99–603, Title I, § 113, Nov. 6, 1986, 100 Stat. 3383; Pub.L. 101–649, Title VII, § 705(a), Nov. 29, 1990, 104 Stat. 5087; Pub.L. 102–232, Title III, § 308(d), Dec. 12, 1991, 105 Stat. 1757.)

§ 405. Savings clause [8 U.S.C.A. § 1101, note]

(a) Nothing contained in this Act, unless otherwise specifically provided therein, shall be construed to affect the validity of any declaration of intention, petition for naturalization, certificate of naturalization, certificate of citizenship, warrant of arrest, order or warrant of deportation, order of exclusion, or other document or proceeding which shall be valid at the time this Act shall take effect; or to affect any prosecution, suit, action, or proceedings, civil or criminal, brought, or any status, condition, right in process of acquisition, act, thing, liability, obligation, or matter, civil or criminal, done or existing, at the time this Act shall take effect; but as to all such prosecutions, suits, actions, proceedings, statutes [sic] conditions, rights, acts, things, liabilities, obligations, or matters the statutes or parts of statutes repealed by this Act are, unless otherwise specifically provided therein, hereby continued in force and effect. When an immigrant, in possession of an unexpired immigrant visa issued prior to the effective date of this Act, makes application for admission, his admissibility shall be determined under the provisions of law in effect on the date of the issuance of such visa. An application for suspension of deportation under § 19 of the Immigration Act of 1917, as amended, or for adjustment of status under § 4 of the Displaced Persons Act of 1948, as amended, which is pending on the date of enactment of this Act [June 27, 1952], shall be regarded as a proceeding within the meaning of this subsection.

(b) Except as otherwise specifically provided in title III, any petition for naturalization heretofore filed which may be pending at the time this Act shall take effect shall be heard and determined in accordance with the requirements of law in effect when such petition was filed.

(c) Except as otherwise specifically provided in this Act, the repeal of any statute by this Act shall not terminate nationality heretofore lawfully acquired nor restore nationality heretofore lost under any law of the United States or any treaty to which the United States may have been a party.

(d) Except as otherwise specifically provided in this Act, or any amendment thereto, fees, charges and prices for purposes specified in title V of the Independent Offices Appropriation Act, 1952 (Public Law 137, Eighty-second Congress, approved August 31, 1951), may be fixed and established in the manner and by the head of any Federal Agency as specified in that Act.

(e) This Act shall not be construed to repeal, alter, or amend section 231(a) of the Act of April 30, 1946 (60 Stat. 148; 22 U.S.C. 1281(a)), the Act of June 20, 1949 (Public Law 110, section 8, Eighty-first Congress, first session; 63 Stat. 208 [section 403h of Title 50]), the Act of June 5, 1950 (Public Law 535, Eighty-first Congress, second session [former section 1501 et seq. of Title 22]), nor Title V of the Agricultural Act of 1949, as amended (Public Law 78, Eighty-second Congress, first session [sections 1461 to 1468 of Title 7]).

(June 27, 1952, c. 477, Title IV, ch. 2, § 405, 66 Stat. 274.)

§ 406. Separability clause [8 U.S.C.A. § 1101, note]

If any particular provision of this Act, or the application thereof to any person or circumstance, is held invalid, the remainder of the Act and the application of such provision to other persons or circumstances shall not be affected thereby.

(June 27, 1952, c. 477, Title IV, ch. 2, § 406, 66 Stat. 275.)

§ 411. Office of Refugee Resettlement; establishment; appointment of Director; functions [8 U.S.C.A. § 1521]

(a) There is established, within the Department of Health and Human Services, an office to be known as the Office of Refugee Resettlement (hereinafter in this chapter referred to as the "Office"). The head of the Office shall be a Director (hereinafter in this chapter referred to as the "Director"), to be appointed by the Secretary of Health and Human Services (hereinafter in this chapter referred to as the "Secretary").

(b) The function of the Office and its Director is to fund and administer (directly or through arrangements with other Federal agencies), in consultation with the Secretary of State, programs of the Federal Government under this chapter.

(June 27, 1952, c. 477, Title IV, ch. 2, § 411, as added Mar. 17, 1980, Pub.L. 96–212, Title III, § 311(a)(2), 94 Stat. 110, and amended Apr. 30, 1994, Pub.L. 103–236, Title I, § 162(n)(1), 108 Stat. 409.)

§ 412. Authorization for programs for domestic resettlement of and assistance to refugees [8 U.S.C.A. § 1522]

(a) Conditions and considerations

(1)(A) In providing assistance under this section, the Director shall, to the extent of available appropriations, **(i)** make available sufficient resources for employment training and placement in order to achieve economic self-sufficiency among refugees as quickly as possible, **(ii)** provide refugees with the opportunity to acquire sufficient English language training to enable them to become effectively resettled as quickly as possible, **(iii)** insure that cash assistance is made available to refugees in such a manner as not to discourage their economic self-sufficiency, in accordance with subsection (e)(2), and **(iv)** insure that women have the same opportunities as men to participate in training and instruction.

(B) it is the intent of Congress that in providing refugee assistance under this section—

(i) employable refugees should be placed on jobs as soon as possible after their arrival in the United States;

(ii) social service funds should be focused on employment-related services, English-as-a-second-language training (in non-work hours where possible), and case-management services; and

(iii) local voluntary agency activities should be conducted in close cooperation and advance consultation with State and local governments.

(2)(A) The Director and the Federal agency administering subsection (b)(1) shall consult regularly (not less often than quarterly) with State and local governments and private nonprofit voluntary agencies concerning the sponsorship process and the intended distribution of refugees among the States and localities before their placement in those States and localities.

(B) The Director shall develop and implement, in consultation with representatives of voluntary agencies and State and local governments, policies and strategies for the placement and resettlement of refugees within the United States.

(C) Such policies and strategies, to the extent practicable and except under such unusual circumstances as the Director may recognize, shall—

(i) insure that a refugee is not initially placed or resettled in an area highly impacted (as determined under regulations prescribed by the Director after consultation with such agencies and governments) by the presence of refugees or comparable populations unless the refugee has a spouse, parent, sibling, son, or daughter residing in that area,

(ii) provide for a mechanism whereby representatives of local affiliates of voluntary agencies regularly (not less often than quarterly) meet with representatives of State and local governments to plan and coordinate in advance of their arrival the appropriate placement of refugees among the various States and localities, and

(iii) take into account—

(I) the proportion of refugees and comparable entrants in the population in the area,

(II) the availability of employment opportunities, affordable housing, and public and private resources (including educational, health care, and mental health services) for refugees in the area,

(III) the likelihood of refugees placed in the area becoming self-sufficient and free from long-term dependence on public assistance, and

(IV) the secondary migration of refugees to and from the area that is likely to occur.

(D) With respect to the location of placement of refugees within a State, the Federal agency administering subsection (b)(1) shall, consistent with such policies and strategies and to the maximum extent possible, take into account recommendations of the State.

(3) In the provision of domestic assistance under this section, the Director shall make a periodic assessment, based on refugee population and other relevant factors, of the relative needs of refugees for assistance and services under this chapter and the resources available to meet such needs. The Director shall compile and maintain data on secondary migration of refugees within the United States and, by State of residence and nationality, on the proportion of refugees receiving cash or medical assistance described in subsection (e). In allocating resources, the Director shall avoid duplication of services and provide for maximum coordination between agencies providing related services.

(4)(A) No grant or contract may be awarded under this section unless an appropriate proposal and application (including a description of the agency's ability to perform the services specified in the proposal) are submitted to, and approved by, the appropriate administering official. Grants and contracts under this section shall be made to those agencies which the appropriate administering official determines can best perform the services. Payments may be made for activities authorized under this chapter in advance or by way of reimbursement. In carrying out this section, the Director, the Secretary of State, and any such other appropriate administering official are authorized—

(i) to make loans, and

(ii) to accept and use money, funds, property, and services of any kind made available by gift, devise, bequest, grant, or otherwise for the purpose of carrying out this section.

(B) No funds may be made available under this chapter (other than under subsection (b)(1)) to States or political subdivisions in the form of block grants, per capita grants, or similar consolidated grants or contracts. Such funds shall be made available under separate grants or contracts—

(i) for medical screening and initial medical treatment under subsection (b)(5),

(ii) for services for refugees under subsection (c)(1),

(iii) for targeted assistance project grants under subsection (c)(2), and

(iv) for assistance for refugee children under subsection (d)(2).

(C) The Director may not delegate to a State or political subdivision his authority to review or approve grants or contracts under this chapter or the terms under which such grants or contracts are made.

(5) Assistance and services funded under this section shall be provided to refugees without regard to race, religion, nationality, sex, or political opinion.

(6) As a condition for receiving assistance under this section, a State must—

(A) submit to the Director a plan which provides—

(i) a description of how the State intends to encourage effective refugee resettlement and to promote economic self-sufficiency as quickly as possible,

(ii) a description of how the State will insure that language training and employment services are made available to refugees receiving cash assistance,

(iii) for the designation of an individual, employed by the State, who will be responsible for insuring coordination of public and private resources in refugee resettlement,

(iv) for the care and supervision of and legal responsibility for unaccompanied refugee children in the State, and

(v) for the identification of refugees who at the time of resettlement in the State are determined to have medical conditions requiring, or medical histories indicating a need for, treatment or observation and such monitoring of such treatment or observation as may be necessary;

(B) meet standards, goals, and priorities, developed by the Director, which assure the effective resettlement of refugees and which promote their economic self-sufficiency as quickly as possible and the efficient provision of services; and

(C) submit to the Director, within a reasonable period of time after the end of each fiscal year, a report on the uses of funds provided under this chapter which the State is responsible for administering.

(7) The Secretary, together with the Secretary of State with respect to assistance provided by the Secretary of State under subsection (b), shall develop a system of monitoring the assistance provided under this section. This system shall include—

(A) evaluations of the effectiveness of the programs funded under this section and the performance of States, grantees, and contractors;

(B) financial auditing and other appropriate monitoring to detect any fraud, abuse, or mismanagement in the operation of such programs; and

(C) data collection on the services provided and the results achieved.

(8) The Attorney General shall provide the Director with information supplied by refugees in conjunction with their applications to the Attorney General for adjustment of status, and the Director shall compile, summarize, and evaluate such information.

(9) The Secretary, the Secretary of Education, the Attorney General, and the Secretary of State may issue such regulations as each deems appropriate to carry out this chapter.

(10) For purposes of this chapter, the term "refugee" includes any alien described in section 207(c)(2) [8 U.S.C.A. § 1157(c)(2)].

(b) Program of initial resettlement

(1)(A) For—

(i) fiscal years 1980 and 1981, the Secretary of State is authorized, and

(ii) fiscal year 1982 and succeeding fiscal years, the Director (except as provided in subparagraph (B)) is authorized,

to make grants to, and contracts with, public or private nonprofit agencies for initial resettlement (including initial reception and placement with sponsors) of refugees in the United States. Grants to, or contracts with, private nonprofit voluntary agencies under this paragraph shall be made consistent with the objectives of this chapter, taking into account the different resettlement approaches and practices of such agencies. Resettlement assistance under this paragraph shall be provided in coordination with the Director's provision of other assistance under this chapter. Funds provided to agencies under such grants and contracts may only be obligated or expended during the fiscal year in which they are provided (or the subsequent fiscal year or such subsequent fiscal period as the Federal contracting agency may approve) to carry out the purposes of this subsection.

(B) If the President determines that the Director should not administer the program under this paragraph, the authority of the Director under the first sentence of subparagraph (A) shall be exercised by such officer as the President shall from time to time specify.

(2) The Director is authorized to develop programs for such orientation, instruction in English, and job training for refugees, and such other education and training of refugees, as facilitates their resettlement in the United States. The Director is authorized to implement such programs, in accordance with the provisions of this section, with respect to refugees in the United States. The Secretary of State is authorized to implement such programs with respect to refugees awaiting entry into the United States.

(3) The Secretary is authorized to make arrangements (including cooperative arrangements with other Federal agencies) for the temporary care of refugees in the United States in emergency circumstances, including the establishment of processing centers, if necessary, without regard to such provisions of law (other than the Renegotiation Act of 1951 [50 App. U.S.C.A. § 1211 et seq.] and section 414(b) [8 U.S.C.A. § 1524(b)]) regulating the making, performance amendment, or modification of contracts and the expenditure of funds of the United States Government as the Secretary may specify.

(4) The Secretary shall—

(A) assure that an adequate number of trained staff are available at the location at which the refugees enter the United States to assure that all necessary medical records are available and in proper order;

(B) provide for the identification of refugees who have been determined to have medical conditions affecting the public health and requiring treatment;

(C) assure that State or local health officials at the resettlement destination within the United States of each refugee are promptly notified of the refugee's arrival and provided with all applicable medical records; and

(D) provide for such monitoring of refugees identified under subparagraph (B) as will insure that they receive appropriate and timely treatment.

The Secretary shall develop and implement methods for monitoring and assessing the quality of medical screening and related health services provided to refugees awaiting resettlement in the United States.

(5) The Director is authorized to make grants to, and enter into contracts with, State and local health agencies for payments to meet their costs of providing medical screening and initial medical treatment to refugees.

(6) The Comptroller General shall directly conduct an annual financial audit of funds expended under each grant or contract made under paragraph (1) for fiscal year 1986 and for fiscal year 1987.

(7) Each grant or contract with an agency under paragraph (1) shall require the agency to do the following:

(A) To provide quarterly performance and financial status reports to the Federal agency administering paragraph (1).

(B)(i) To provide, directly or through its local affiliate, notice to the appropriate county or other local welfare office at the time that the agency becomes aware that a refugee is offered employment and to provide notice to the refugee that such notice has been provided, and

(ii) upon request of such a welfare office to which a refugee has applied for cash assistance, to furnish that office with documentation respecting any cash or other resources provided directly by the agency to the refugee under this subsection.

(C) To assure that refugees, known to the agency as having been identified pursuant to paragraph (4)(B) as having medical conditions affecting the public health and requiring treatment, report to the appropriate county or other health agency upon their resettlement in an area.

(D) To fulfill its responsibility to provide for the basic needs (including food, clothing, shelter, and transportation for job interviews and training) of each refugee resettled and to develop and implement a resettlement plan including the early employment of each refugee resettled and to monitor the implementation of such plan.

(E) To transmit to the Federal agency administering paragraph (1) an annual report describing the following:

(i) The number of refugees placed (by county of placement) and the expenditures made in the year under the grant or contract, including the proportion of such expenditures used for administrative purposes and for provision of services.

(ii) The proportion of refugees placed by the agency in the previous year who are receiving cash or medical assistance described in subsection (e).

(iii) The efforts made by the agency to monitor placement of the refugees and the activities of local affiliates of the agency.

(iv) The extent to which the agency has coordinated its activities with local social service providers in a manner which avoids duplication of activities and has provided notices to local welfare offices and the reporting of medical conditions of certain aliens to local health departments in accordance with subparagraphs (B)(i) and (C).

(v) Such other information as the agency administering paragraph (1) deems to be appropriate in monitoring the effectiveness of agencies in carrying out their functions under such grants and contracts.

The agency administering paragraph (1) shall promptly forward a copy of each annual report transmitted under subparagraph (E) to the Committees on the Judiciary of the House of Representatives and of the Senate.

(8) The Federal agency administering paragraph (1) shall establish criteria for the performance of agencies under grants and contracts under that paragraph, and shall include criteria relating to an agency's—

(A) efforts to reduce welfare dependency among refugees resettled by that agency,

(B) collection of travel loans made to refugees resettled by that agency for travel to the United States,

(C) arranging for effective local sponsorship and other nonpublic assistance for refugees resettled by that agency,

(D) cooperation with refugee mutual assistance associations, local social service providers, health agencies, and welfare offices,

(E) compliance with the guidelines established by the Director for the placement and resettlement of refugees within the United States, and

(F) compliance with other requirements contained in the grant or contract, including the reporting and other requirements under subsection (b)(7).

The Federal administering agency shall use the criteria in the process of awarding or renewing grants and contracts under paragraph (1).

(c) Project grants and contracts for services for refugees

(1)(A) The Director is authorized to make grants to, and enter into contracts with, public or private nonprofit agencies for projects specifically designed—

(i) to assist refugees in obtaining the skills which are necessary for economic self-sufficiency, including projects for job training, employment services, day care, professional refresher training, and other recertification services;

(ii) to provide training in English where necessary (regardless of whether the refugees are employed or receiving cash or other assistance); and

(iii) to provide where specific needs have been shown and recognized by the Director, health (including mental health) services, social services, educational and other services.

(B) The funds available for a fiscal year for grants and contracts under subparagraph (A) shall be allocated among the States based on the total number or refugees (including children and adults) who arrived in the United States not more than 36 months before the beginning of such fiscal year and who are actually residing in each State (taking into account secondary migration) as of the beginning of the fiscal year.

(C) Any limitation which the Director establishes on the proportion of funds allocated to a State under this paragraph that the State may use for services other than those described in subsection (a)(1)(B)(ii) shall not apply if the Director receives a plan (established by or in consultation with local governments) and determines that the plan provides for the maximum appropriate provision of employment-related services for, and the maximum placement of, employable refugees consistent with performance standards established under section 1516 of Title 29.

(2)(A) The Director is authorized to make grants to States for assistance to counties and similar areas in the States where, because of factors such as unusually large refugee populations (including secondary migration), high refugee concentrations, and high use of public assistance by refugees, there exists and can be demonstrated a specific need for supplementation of available resources for services to refugees.

(B) Grants shall be made available under this paragraph—

(i) primarily for the purpose of facilitating refugee employment and achievement of self-sufficiency,

(ii) in a manner that does not supplant other refugee program funds and that assures that not less than 95 percent of the amount of the grant award is made available to the county or other local entity.

(d) Assistance for refugee children

(1) The Secretary of Education is authorized to make grants, and enter into contracts, for payments for projects to provide special educational services (including English language training) to refugee children in elementary and secondary schools where a demonstrated need has been shown.

(2)(A) The Director is authorized to provide assistance, reimbursement to States, and grants to and contracts with public and private nonprofit agencies, for the provision of child welfare services, including foster care maintenance payments and services and health care, furnished to any refugee child (except as provided in subparagraph (B)) during the thirty-six month period beginning with the first month in which such refugee child is in the United States.

(B)(i) In the case of a refugee child who is unaccompanied by a parent or other close adult relative (as defined by the Director), the services described in subparagraph (A) may be furnished until the month after the child attains eighteen years of age (or such higher age as the State's child welfare services plan under part B of title IV of the Social Security Act [42 U.S.C.A. § 620 et seq.] prescribes for the availability of such services to any other child in that State).

(ii) The Director shall attempt to arrange for the placement under the laws of the States of such unaccompanied refugee children, who have been accepted for admission to the United States, before (or as soon as possible after) their arrival in the United States. During any interim period while such a child is in the United States or in transit to the United States but before the child is so placed, the Director shall assume legal responsibility (including financial responsibility) for the child, if necessary, and is authorized to make necessary decisions to provide for the child's immediate care.

(iii) In carrying out the Director's responsibilities under clause (ii), the Director is authorized to enter into contracts with appropriate public or private nonprofit agencies under such conditions as the Director determines to be appropriate.

(iv) The Director shall prepare and maintain a list of (I) all such unaccompanied children who have entered the United States after April 1, 1975, (II) the names and last known residences of their parents (if living) at the time of arrival, and (III) the children's location, status, and progress.

(e) Cash assistance and medical assistance to refugees

(1) The Director is authorized to provide assistance, reimbursement to States, and grants to, and contracts with, public or private nonprofit agencies for 100 per centum of the cash assistance and medical assistance provided to any refugee during the thirty-six month period beginning with the first month in which such refugee has entered the United States and for the identifiable and reasonable administrative costs of providing this assistance.

(2)(A) Cash assistance provided under this subsection to an employable refugee is conditioned, except for good cause shown—

(i) on the refugee's registration with an appropriate agency providing employment services described in subsection (c)(1)(A)(i), or, if there is no such agency available, with an appropriate State or local employment service;

(ii) on the refugee's participation in any available and appropriate social service or targeted assistance program (funded under subsection (c)) providing job or language training in the area in which the refugee resides; and

(iii) on the refugee's acceptance of appropriate offers of employment.

(B) Cash assistance shall not be made available to refugees who are full-time students in institutions of higher education (as defined by the Director after consultation with the Secretary of Education).

(C) In the case of a refugee who—

(i) refuses an offer of employment which has been determined to be appropriate either by the agency responsible for the initial resettlement of the refugee under subsection (b) or by the appropriate State or local employment service,

(ii) refuses to go to a job interview which has been arranged through such agency or service, or

(iii) refuses to participate in a social service or targeted assistance program referred to in subparagraph (A)(ii) which such agency or service determines to be available and appropriate,

cash assistance to the refugee shall be terminated (after opportunity for an administrative hearing) for a period of three months (for the first such refusal) or for a period of six months for any subsequent refusal.

(3) The Director shall develop plans to provide English training and other appropriate services and training to refugees receiving cash assistance.

(4) If a refugee is eligible for aid or assistance under a State plan approved under part A of title IV or under title XIX of the Social Security Act [42 U.S.C.A §§ 601 et seq., 1396 et seq.], or for supplemental security income benefits (including State supplementary payments) under the program established under title XVI of that Act [42 U.S.C.A. § 1381 et seq.], funds authorized under this subsection shall only be used for the non-Federal share of such aid or assistance, or for such supplementary payments, with respect to cash and medical assistance provided with respect to such refugee under this paragraph.

(5) The Director is authorized to allow for the provision of medical assistance under paragraph (1) to any refugee, during the one-year period after entry, who does not qualify for assistance under a State plan approved under title XIX of the Social Security Act [42 U.S.C.A. § 1396 et seq.] on account of any resources or income requirement of such plan, but only if the Director determines that—

(A) this will **(i)** encourage economic self-sufficiency, or **(ii)** avoid a significant burden on State and local governments; and

(B) the refugee meets such alternative financial resources and income requirements as the Director shall establish.

(6) As a condition for receiving assistance, reimbursement, or a contract under this subsection and notwithstanding any other provision of law, a State or agency must provide assurances that whenever a refugee applies for cash or medical assistance for which assistance or reimbursement is provided under this subsection, the State or agency must notify promptly the agency (or local affiliate) which provided for the initial resettlement of the refugee under subsection (b) of the fact that the refugee has so applied.

(7)(A) The Secretary shall develop and implement alternative projects for refugees who have been in the United States less than thirty-six months, under which refugees are provided interim support, medical services, support services, and case management, as needed, in a manner that encourages self-sufficiency, reduces welfare dependency, and fosters greater coordination among the resettlement agencies and service providers. The Secretary may permit alternative projects to cover specific groups of refugees who have been in the United States 36 months or longer if the Secretary determines that refugees in the group have been significantly and disproportionately dependent on welfare and need the services provided under the project in order to become self-sufficient and that their coverage under the projects would be cost-effective.

(B) Refugees covered under such alternative projects shall be precluded from receiving cash or medical assistance under any other paragraph of this subsection or under title XIX or part A of title IV of the Social Security Act [42 U.S.C.A. §§ 601 et seq., 1396 et seq.].

(C) The Secretary shall report to Congress not later than October 31, 1985, on the results of these projects and on any recommendations respecting changes in the refugee assistance program under this section to take into account such results.

(D) To the extent that the use of such funds is consistent with the purposes of such provisions, funds appropriated under section 414(a) [8 U.S.C.A. § 1524(a)], part A of title IV of the Social Security Act [42 U.S.C.A. § 601 et seq.], or title XIX of such Act [42 U.S.C.A. § 1396 et seq.], may be used for the purpose of implementing and evaluating alternative projects under this paragraph.

(8) In its provision of assistance to refugees, a State or political subdivision shall consider the recommendations of, and assistance provided by, agencies with grants or contracts under subsection (b)(1).

(f) Assistance to States and counties for incarceration of certain Cuban nationals; priority for removal and return to Cuba

(1) The Attorney General shall pay compensation to States and to counties for costs incurred by the States and counties to confine in prisons, during the fiscal year for which such payment is made, nationals of Cuba who—

(A) were paroled into the United States in 1980 by the Attorney General,

(B) after such parole committed any violation of State or county law for which a term of imprisonment was imposed, and

(C) at the time of such parole and such violation were not aliens lawfully admitted to the United States—

(i) for permanent residence, or

(ii) under the terms of an immigrant or a nonimmigrant visa issued,

under this Act.

(2) For a State or county to be eligible to receive compensation under this subsection, the chief executive officer of the State or county shall submit to the Attorney General, in accordance with rules to be issued by the Attorney General, an application containing—

(A) the number and names of the Cuban nationals with respect to whom the State or county is entitled to such compensation, and

(B) such other information as the Attorney General may require.

(3) For a fiscal year the Attorney General shall pay the costs described in paragraph (1) to each State and county determined by the Attorney General to be eligible under paragraph (2); except that if the amounts appropriated for the fiscal year to carry out this subsection are insufficient to cover all such payments, each of such payments shall be ratably reduced so that the total of such payments equals the amount so appropriated.

(4) The authority of the Attorney General to pay compensation under this subsection shall be effective for any fiscal year only to the extent and in such amounts as may be provided in advance in appropriation Acts.

(5) Priority for removal and return to Cuba of certain Cuban nationals.

It shall be the policy of the United States Government that the President, in consultation with the Attorney General and all other appropriate Federal officials and all appropriate State and county officials referred to in paragraph (2), shall place top priority on seeking the expeditious removal from this country and the return to Cuba of Cuban nationals described in paragraph (1) by any reasonable and responsible means, and to this end the Attorney General may use the funds authorized to carry out this subsection to conduct such policy.

(June 27, 1952, c. 477, Title IV, ch. 2, § 412, as added Mar. 17, 1980, Pub.L. 96–212, Title III, § 311(a)(2), 94 Stat. 111, and amended Oct. 25, 1982, Pub.L. 97–363, §§ 3(a), 4 to 6, 96 Stat. 1734 to 1736; Nov. 22, 1983, Pub.L. 98–164, Title X, § 1011 (b), 97 Stat. 1061; Oct. 12, 1984, Pub.L. 98–473 Title I, § 101(d), 98 Stat. 1877; Pub.L. 99–605, §§ 3, 4, 5(a), (b), (c), 6(a), (b), (d), 8, 9(a), (b), 10, 12, 13, Nov. 6, 1986, 100 Stat. 3449 to 3451, 3453 to

3455; Oct. 24, 1988, Pub.L. 100–525, § 6(b), 102 Stat. 2616; Apr. 30, 1994, Pub.L. 103–236, Title I, § 162(n)(2), 108 Stat. 409; Oct. 25, 1994, Pub.L. 103–416, Title II, § 219(x), 108 Stat. 4318; Aug. 22, 1996, Pub.L. 104–193, Title I, § 110(s)(3), 110 Stat. 2175; Sept. 30, 1996, Pub.L. 104–208, Div. C, Title VI, § 671(e)(7), 110 Stat. 3009–723.)

§ 413. Congressional reports [8 U.S.C.A. § 1523]

(a) The Secretary shall submit a report on activities under this chapter to the Committees on the Judiciary of the House of Representatives and of the Senate not later than the January 31 following the end of each fiscal year, beginning with fiscal year 1980.

(b) Each such report shall contain—

(1) an updated profile of the employment and labor force statistics for refugees who have entered the United States within the five-fiscal-year period immediately preceding the fiscal year within which the report is to be made and for refugees who entered earlier and who have shown themselves to be significantly and disproportionately dependent on welfare, as well as a description of the extent to which refugees received the forms of assistance or services under this chapter during that period;

(2) a description of the geographic location of refugees;

(3) a summary of the results of the monitoring and evaluation conducted under section 412(a)(7) [8 U.S.C.A. § 1522(a)(7)] during the period for which the report is submitted;

(4) a description of **(A)** the activities, expenditures, and policies of the Office under this chapter and of the activities of States, voluntary agencies, and sponsors, and **(B)** the Director's plans for improvement of refugee resettlement;

(5) evaluations of the extent to which **(A)** the services provided under this chapter are assisting refugees in achieving economic self-sufficiency, achieving ability in English, and achieving employment commensurate with their skills and abilities, and **(B)** any fraud, abuse, or mismanagement has been reported in the provisions of services or assistance;

(6) a description of any assistance provided by the Director pursuant to section 412(e)(5) [8 U.S.C.A. § 1522(e)(5)];

(7) a summary of the location and status of unaccompanied refugee children admitted to the United States; and

(8) a summary of the information compiled and evaluation made under section 412(a)(8) [8 U.S.C.A. § 1522(a)(8)].

(June 27, 1952, c. 477, Title IV, ch. 2, § 413, as added Mar. 17, 1980, Pub.L. 96–212, Title III, § 311(a)(2), 94 Stat. 115, and amended Oct. 25, 1982, Pub.L. 97–363, §§ 3(b), 7, 96 Stat. 1734, 1737; Pub.L. 99–605, § 11, Nov. 6, 1986, 100 Stat. 3455; Oct. 24, 1988, Pub.L. 100–525, § 9(jj), 102 Stat. 2622; Apr. 30, 1994, Pub.L. 103–236, Title I, § 162(n)(3), 108 Stat. 409.)

TITLE V

ALIEN TERRORIST REMOVAL PROCEDURES

§ 501. Definitions [8 U.S.C.A. § 1531]

As used in this title—

(1) the term "alien terrorist" means any alien described in section 237(a)(4)(B) [8 U.S.C.A. § 1227(a)(4)(B)];

(2) the term "classified information" has the same meaning as in section 1(a) of the Classified Information Procedures Act (18 U.S.C. App.);

(3) the term "national security" has the same meaning as in section 1(b) of the Classified Information Procedures Act (18 U.S.C. App.);

(4) the term "removal court" means the court described in section 502 [8 U.S.C.A. § 1532];

(5) the term "removal hearing" means the hearing described in section 504 [8 U.S.C.A. § 1534];

(6) the term "removal proceeding" means a proceeding under this title; and

(7) the term "special attorney" means an attorney who is on the panel established under section 502(e) [8 U.S.C.A. § 1532(e)].

(June 27, 1952, c. 477, Title V, § 501, as added Apr. 24, 1996, Pub.L. 104–132, Title IV, § 401(a), 110 Stat. 1259, and amended Sept. 30, 1996, Pub.L. 104–208, Title III, §§ 308(g)(1), 354(a)(5), 110 Stat. 3009–622, 3009–643.)

§ 502. Establishment of removal court [8 U.S.C.A. § 1532]

(a) Designation of judges

The Chief Justice of the United States shall publicly designate 5 district court judges from 5 of the United States judicial circuits who shall constitute a court that shall have jurisdiction to conduct all removal proceedings. The Chief Justice may, in the Chief Justice's discretion, designate the same judges under this section as are designated pursuant to section 103(a) of the Foreign Intelligence Surveillance Act of 1978 (50 U.S.C. 1803(a)).

(b) Terms

Each judge designated under subsection (a) shall serve for a term of 5 years and shall be eligible for redesignation, except that of the members first designated—

(1) 1 member shall serve for a term of 1 year;

(2) 1 member shall serve for a term of 2 years;

(3) 1 member shall serve for a term of 3 years; and

(4) 1 member shall serve for a term of 4 years.

(c) Chief judge

(1) Designation

The Chief Justice shall publicly designate one of the judges of the removal court to be the chief judge of the removal court.

(2) Responsibilities

The chief judge shall—

(A) promulgate rules to facilitate the functioning of the removal court; and

(B) assign the consideration of cases to the various judges on the removal court.

(d) Expeditious and confidential nature of proceedings

The provisions of section 103(c) of the Foreign Intelligence Surveillance Act of 1978 (50 U.S.C. 1803(c)) shall apply to removal proceedings in the same manner as they apply to proceedings under that Act.

(e) Establishment of panel of special attorneys

The removal court shall provide for the designation of a panel of attorneys each of whom—

(1) has a security clearance which affords the attorney access to classified information, and

(2) has agreed to represent permanent resident aliens with respect to classified information under section 504(e)(3) [8 U.S.C.A. § 1534(e)(3)] in accordance with (and subject to the penalties under) this title.

(June 27, 1952, c. 477, Title V, § 502, as added Apr. 24, 1996, Pub.L. 104–132, Title IV, § 401(a), 110 Stat. 1259, and amended Sept. 30, 1996, Pub.L. 104–208, Div. C, Title III, § 354(a)(4), 110 Stat. 3009–643.)

§ 503. Removal court procedure [8 U.S.C.A. § 1533]

(a) Application

(1) In general

In any case in which the Attorney General has classified information that an alien is an alien terrorist, the Attorney General may seek removal of the alien under this title by filing an application with the removal court that contains—

(A) the identity of the attorney in the Department of Justice making the application;

(B) a certification by the Attorney General or the Deputy Attorney General that the application satisfies the criteria and requirements of this section;

(C) the identity of the alien for whom authorization for the removal proceeding is sought; and

(D) a statement of the facts and circumstances relied on by the Department of Justice to establish probable cause that—

(i) the alien is an alien terrorist;

(ii) the alien is physically present in the United States; and

(iii) with respect to such alien, removal under title II would pose a risk to the national security of the United States.

(2) Filing

An application under this section shall be submitted ex parte and in camera, and shall be filed under seal with the removal court.

(b) Right to dismiss

The Attorney General may dismiss a removal action under this title at any stage of the proceeding.

(c) Consideration of application

(1) Basis for decision

In determining whether to grant an application under this section, a single judge of the removal court may consider, ex parte and in camera, in addition to the information contained in the application—

(A) other information, including classified information, presented under oath or affirmation; and

(B) testimony received in any hearing on the application, of which a verbatim record shall be kept.

(2) Approval of order

The judge shall issue an order granting the application, if the judge finds that there is probable cause to believe that—

(A) the alien who is the subject of the application has been correctly identified and is an alien terrorist present in the United States; and

(B) removal under title II would pose a risk to the national security of the United States.

(3) Denial of order

If the judge denies the order requested in the application, the judge shall prepare a written statement of the reasons for the denial, taking all necessary precautions not to disclose any classified information contained in the Government's application.

(d) Exclusive provisions

If an order is issued under this section granting an application, the rights of the alien regarding removal and expulsion shall be governed solely by this title, and except as they are specifically referenced in this title, no other provisions of this Act shall be applicable.

(June 27, 1952, c. 477, Title V, § 503, as added Apr. 24, 1996, Pub.L. 104–132, Title IV, § 401(a), 110 Stat. 1259.)

§ 504. Removal hearing [8 U.S.C.A. § 1534]

(a) In general

(1) Expeditious hearing

In any case in which an application for an order is approved under section 503(c)(2) [8 U.S.C.A. § 1533(c)(2)], a removal hearing shall be conducted under this section as expeditiously as practicable for the purpose of determining whether the alien to whom the order pertains should be removed from the United States on the grounds that the alien is an alien terrorist.

(2) Public hearing

The removal hearing shall be open to the public.

(b) Notice

An alien who is the subject of a removal hearing under this title shall be given reasonable notice of—

(1) the nature of the charges against the alien, including a general account of the basis for the charges; and

(2) the time and place at which the hearing will be held.

(c) Rights in hearing

(1) Right of counsel

The alien shall have a right to be present at such hearing and to be represented by counsel. Any alien financially unable to obtain counsel shall be entitled to have counsel assigned to represent the alien. Such counsel shall be appointed by the judge pursuant to the plan for furnishing representation for any person financially unable to obtain adequate representation for the district in which the hearing is conducted, as provided for in section 3006A of Title 18. All provisions of that section shall apply and, for purposes of determining the maximum amount of compensation, the matter shall be treated as if a felony was charged.

(2) Introduction of evidence

Subject to the limitations in subsection (e), the alien shall have a reasonable opportunity to introduce evidence on the alien's own behalf.

(3) Examination of witnesses

Subject to the limitations in subsection (e), the alien shall have a reasonable opportunity to examine the evidence against the alien and to cross-examine any witness.

(4) Record

A verbatim record of the proceedings and of all testimony and evidence offered or produced at such a hearing shall be kept.

(5) Removal decision based on evidence at hearing

The decision of the judge regarding removal shall be based only on that evidence introduced at the removal hearing.

(d) Subpoenas

(1) Request

At any time prior to the conclusion of the removal hearing, either the alien or the Department of Justice may request the judge to issue a subpoena for the presence of a named witness (which subpoena may also command the person to whom it is directed to produce books, papers, documents, or other objects designated therein) upon a satisfactory showing that the presence of the witness is necessary for the determination of any material matter. Such a request may be made ex parte except that the judge shall inform the Department of Justice of any request for a subpoena by the alien for a witness or material if compliance with such a subpoena would reveal classified evidence or the source of that evidence. The Department of Justice shall be given a reasonable opportunity to oppose the issuance of such a subpoena.

(2) Payment for attendance

If an application for a subpoena by the alien also makes a showing that the alien is financially unable to pay for the attendance of a witness so requested, the court may order the costs incurred by the process and the fees of the witness so subpoenaed to be paid from funds appropriated for the enforcement of title II.

(3) Nationwide service

A subpoena under this subsection may be served anywhere in the United States.

(4) Witness fees

A witness subpoenaed under this subsection shall receive the same fees and expenses as a witness subpoenaed in connection with a civil proceeding in a court of the United States.

(5) No access to classified information

Nothing in this subsection is intended to allow an alien to have access to classified information.

(e) Discovery

(1) In general

For purposes of this title—

(A) the Government is authorized to use in a removal proceedings [sic] the fruits of electronic surveillance and unconsented physical searches authorized under the Foreign Intelligence Surveillance Act of 1978 (50 U.S.C. 1801 et seq.) without regard to subsections (c), (e), (f), (g), and (h) of section 106 of that Act [50 U.S.C.A. § 1806(c), (e), (f), (g), (h)] and discovery of information derived pursuant to such Act, or otherwise collected for national security purposes, shall not be authorized if disclosure would present a risk to the national security of the United States;

(B) an alien subject to removal under this title shall not be entitled to suppress evidence that the alien alleges was unlawfully obtained; and

(C) section 3504 of Title 18, and section 1806(c) of Title 50, shall not apply if the Attorney General determines that public disclosure would pose a risk to the national security of the United States because it would disclose classified information or otherwise threaten the integrity of a pending investigation.

(2) Protective orders

Nothing in this title shall prevent the United States from seeking protective orders and from asserting privileges ordinarily available to the United States to protect against the disclosure of classified information, including the invocation of the military and State secrets privileges.

(3) Treatment of classified information

(A) Use

The judge shall examine, ex parte and in camera, any evidence for which the Attorney General determines that public disclosure would pose a risk to the national security of the United States or to the security of any individual because it would disclose classified information and neither the alien nor the public shall be informed of such evidence or its sources other than through reference to the summary provided pursuant to this paragraph. Notwithstanding the previous sentence, the Department of Justice may, in its discretion and, in the case of classified information, after coordination with the originating agency, elect to introduce such evidence in open session.

(B) Submission

With respect to such information, the Government shall submit to the removal court an unclassified summary of the specific evidence that does not pose that risk.

(C) Approval

Not later than 15 days after submission, the judge shall approve the summary if the judge finds that it is sufficient to enable the alien to prepare a defense. The Government shall deliver to the alien a copy of the unclassified summary approved under this subparagraph.

(D) Disapproval

(i) In general

If an unclassified summary is not approved by the removal court under subparagraph (C), the Government shall be afforded 15 days to correct the deficiencies identified by the court and submit a revised unclassified summary.

(ii) Revised summary

If the revised unclassified summary is not approved by the court within 15 days of its submission pursuant to subparagraph (C), the removal hearing shall be terminated unless the judge makes the findings under clause (iii).

(iii) Findings

The findings described in this clause are, with respect to an alien, that—

(I) the continued presence of the alien in the United States would likely cause serious and irreparable harm to the national security or death or serious bodily injury to any person, and

(II) the provision of the summary would likely cause serious and irreparable harm to the national security or death or serious bodily injury to any person.

(E) Continuation of hearing without summary

If a judge makes the findings described in subparagraph (D)(iii)—

(i) if the alien involved is an alien lawfully admitted for permanent residence, the procedures described in subparagraph (F) shall apply; and

(ii) in all cases the special removal hearing shall continue, the Department of Justice shall cause to be delivered to the alien a statement that no summary is possible, and the classified information submitted in camera and ex parte may be used pursuant to this paragraph.

(F) Special procedures for access and challenges to classified information by special attorneys in case of lawful permanent aliens

(i) In general

The procedures described in this subparagraph are that the judge (under rules of the removal court) shall designate a special attorney to assist the alien—

(I) by reviewing in camera the classified information on behalf of the alien, and

(II) by challenging through an in camera proceeding the veracity of the evidence contained in the classified information.

(ii) Restrictions on disclosure

A special attorney receiving classified information under clause (i)—

(I) shall not disclose the information to the alien or to any other attorney representing the alien, and

(II) who discloses such information in violation of subclause (I) shall be subject to a fine under Title 18, imprisoned for not less than 10 years nor more than 25 years, or both.

(f) Arguments

Following the receipt of evidence, the Government and the alien shall be given fair opportunity to present argument as to whether the evidence is sufficient to justify the removal of the alien. The Government shall open the argument. The alien shall be permitted to reply. The Government shall then be permitted to reply in rebuttal. The judge may allow any part of the argument that refers to evidence received in camera and ex parte to be heard in camera and ex parte.

(g) Burden of proof

In the hearing, it is the Government's burden to prove, by the preponderance of the evidence, that the alien is subject to removal because the alien is an alien terrorist.

(h) Rules of evidence

The Federal Rules of Evidence shall not apply in a removal hearing.

(i) Determination of deportation

If the judge, after considering the evidence on the record as a whole, finds that the Government has met its burden, the judge shall order the alien removed and detained pending removal from the United States. If the alien was released pending the removal hearing, the judge shall order the Attorney General to take the alien into custody.

(j) Written order

At the time of issuing a decision as to whether the alien shall be removed, the judge shall prepare a written order containing a statement of facts found and conclusions of law. Any portion of the order that would reveal the substance or source of information received in camera and ex parte pursuant to subsection (e) shall not be made available to the alien or the public.

(k) No right to ancillary relief

At no time shall the judge consider or provide for relief from removal based on—

(1) asylum under section 208 [8 U.S.C.A. § 1158];

(2) by [sic] withholding of removal under section 237(b)(3)* [8 U.S.C.A. § 1227(b)(3)];

(3) cancellation of removal under section 240A [8 U.S.C.A. § 1229b];

(4) voluntary departure under section 244(e)** [8 U.S.C.A. § 1254(e)];

(5) adjustment of status under section 245 [8 U.S.C.A. § 1255]; or

(6) registry under section 249 [8 U.S.C.A. § 1259].

(*l*) Report on alien terrorist removal proceedings

Not later than 3 months from the date of the enactment of this subsection, the Attorney General shall submit to Congress a report concerning the effect and efficacy of alien terrorist removal proceedings, including the reasons why proceedings pursuant to this section have not been used by the Attorney General in the past and the effect on the use of these proceedings after the enactment of the USA PATRIOT Act of 2001 (Public Law 107–56).

(June 27, 1952, c. 477, Title V, § 504, as added Apr. 24, 1996, Pub.L. 104–132, Title IV, § 401(a), 110 Stat. 1260, and amended Sept. 30, 1996, Pub.L. 104–208, Div. C, Title III, §§ 308(g)(7)(B), (8)(B), 354(a)(1), (2), (b), 357, 110 Stat. 3009–623, 3009–624, 3009–641 to 3009–644; Dec. 28, 2001, Pub.L. 107–108, Title III, § 313, 115 Stat. 1401.)

§ 505. Appeals [8 U.S.C.A. § 1535]

(a) Appeal of denial of application for removal proceedings

(1) In general

The Attorney General may seek a review of the denial of an order sought in an application filed pursuant to section 503 [8 U.S.C.A. § 1533]. The appeal shall be filed in the United States Court of Appeals for the District of Columbia Circuit by notice of appeal filed not later than 20 days after the date of such denial.

(2) Record on appeal

The entire record of the proceeding shall be transmitted to the Court of Appeals under seal, and the Court of Appeals shall hear the matter ex parte.

* So in original; probably should refer to section 241(b)(3).

** So in original; probably should refer to section 240B.

(3) Standard of review

The Court of Appeals shall—

(A) review questions of law de novo; and

(B) set aside a finding of fact only if such finding was clearly erroneous.

(b) Appeal of determination regarding summary of classified information

(1) In general

The United States may take an interlocutory appeal to the United States Court of Appeals for the District of Columbia Circuit of—

(A) any determination by the judge pursuant to section 504(e)(3) [8 U.S.C.A. § 1534(e)(3)]; or

(B) the refusal of the court to make the findings permitted by section 504(e)(3) [8 U.S.C.A. § 1534(e)(3)].

(2) Record

In any interlocutory appeal taken pursuant to this subsection, the entire record, including any proposed order of the judge, any classified information and the summary of evidence, shall be transmitted to the Court of Appeals. The classified information shall be transmitted under seal. A verbatim record of such appeal shall be kept under seal in the event of any other judicial review.

(c) Appeal of decision in hearing

(1) In general

Subject to paragraph (2), the decision of the judge after a removal hearing may be appealed by either the alien or the Attorney General to the United States Court of Appeals for the District of Columbia Circuit by notice of appeal filed not later than 20 days after the date on which the order is issued. The order shall not be enforced during the pendency of an appeal under this subsection.

(2) Automatic appeals in cases of permanent resident aliens in which no summary provided

(A) In general

Unless the alien waives the right to a review under this paragraph, in any case involving an alien lawfully admitted for permanent residence who is denied a written summary of classified information under section 504(e)(3) [8 U.S.C.A. § 1534(e)(3)] and with respect to which the procedures described in section 504(e)(3)(F) [8 U.S.C.A. § 1534(e)(3)(F)] apply, any order issued by the judge shall be reviewed by the Court of Appeals for the District of Columbia Circuit.

(B) Use of special attorney

With respect to any issue relating to classified information that arises in such review, the alien shall be represented only by the special attorney designated under section 504(e)(3)(F)(i) [8 U.S.C.A. § 1534(e)(3)(F)(i)] on behalf of the alien.

(3) Transmittal of record

In an appeal or review to the Court of Appeals pursuant to this subsection—

(A) the entire record shall be transmitted to the Court of Appeals; and

(B) information received in camera and ex parte, and any portion of the order that would reveal the substance or source of such information, shall be transmitted under seal.

(4) Expedited appellate proceeding

In an appeal or review to the Court of Appeals under this subsection—

(A) the appeal or review shall be heard as expeditiously as practicable and the court may dispense with full briefing and hear the matter solely on the record of the judge of the removal court and on such briefs or motions as the court may require to be filed by the parties;

(B) the Court of Appeals shall issue an opinion not later than 60 days after the date of the issuance of the final order of the district court;

(C) the court shall review all questions of law de novo; and

(D) a finding of fact shall be accorded deference by the reviewing court and shall not be set aside unless such finding was clearly erroneous, except that in the case of a review under paragraph (2) in which an alien lawfully admitted for permanent residence was denied a written summary of classified information under section 504(c)(3) [8 U.S.C.A. § 1534(c)(3)], the Court of Appeals shall review questions of fact de novo.

(d) Certiorari

Following a decision by the Court of Appeals pursuant to subsection (c), the alien or the Attorney General may petition the Supreme Court for a writ of certiorari. In any such case, any information transmitted to the Court of Appeals under seal shall, if such information is also submitted to the Supreme Court, be transmitted under seal. Any order of removal shall not be stayed pending disposition of a writ of certiorari, except as provided by the Court of Appeals or a Justice of the Supreme Court.

(e) Appeal of detention order

(1) In general

Sections 3145 through 3148 of Title 18, pertaining to review and appeal of a release or detention order, penalties for failure to appear, penalties for an offense committed while on release, and sanctions for violation of a release condition shall apply to an alien to whom section 507(b)(1) [8 U.S.C.A. § 1537(b)(1)] applies. In applying the previous sentence—

(A) for purposes of section 3145 of Title 18 an appeal shall be taken to the United States Court of Appeals for the District of Columbia Circuit; and

(B) for purposes of section 3146 of Title 18 the alien shall be considered released in connection with a charge of an offense punishable by life imprisonment.

(2) No review of continued detention

The determinations and actions of the Attorney General pursuant to section 507(b)(2)(C) [8 U.S.C.A. § 1537(b)(2)(C)] shall not be subject to judicial review, including application for a writ of habeas corpus, except for a claim by the alien that continued detention violates the alien's rights under the Constitution. Jurisdiction over any such challenge shall lie exclusively in the United States Court of Appeals for the District of Columbia Circuit.

(June 27, 1952, c. 477, Title V, § 505, as added Apr. 24, 1996, Pub.L. 104–132, Title IV, § 401(a), 110 Stat. 1263, and amended Sept. 30, 1996, Pub.L. 104–208, Div. C, Title III, § 354(a)(3), 110 Stat. 3009–642.)

§ 506. Custody and release pending removal hearing [8 U.S.C.A. § 1536]

(a) Upon filing application

(1) In general

Subject to paragraphs (2) and (3), the Attorney General may—

(A) take into custody any alien with respect to whom an application under section 503 [8 U.S.C.A. § 1533] has been filed; and

(B) retain such an alien in custody in accordance with the procedures authorized by this title.

(2) Special rules for permanent resident aliens

(A) Release hearing

An alien lawfully admitted for permanent residence shall be entitled to a release hearing before the judge assigned to hear the removal hearing. Such an alien shall be detained pending the removal hearing, unless the alien demonstrates to the court that the alien—

(i) is a person lawfully admitted for permanent residence in the United States;

(ii) if released upon such terms and conditions as the court may prescribe (including the posting of any monetary amount), is not likely to flee; and

(iii) will not endanger national security, or the safety of any person or the community, if released.

(B) Information considered

The judge may consider classified information submitted in camera and ex parte in making a determination whether to release an alien pending the removal hearing.

(3) Release if order denied and no review sought

(A) In general

Subject to subparagraph (B), if a judge of the removal court denies the order sought in an application filed pursuant to section 503 [8 U.S.C.A. § 1533], and the Attorney General does not seek review of such denial, the alien shall be released from custody.

(B) Application of regular procedures

Subparagraph (A) shall not prevent the arrest and detention of the alien pursuant to title II.

(b) Conditional release if order denied and review sought

(1) In general

If a judge of the removal court denies the order sought in an application filed pursuant to section 503 [8 U.S.C.A. § 1533] and the Attorney General seeks review of such denial, the judge shall release the alien from custody subject to the least restrictive condition, or combination of conditions, of release described in section 3142(b) and clauses (i) through (xiv) of section 3142(c)(1)(B) of Title 18, that—

(A) will reasonably assure the appearance of the alien at any future proceeding pursuant to this title; and

(B) will not endanger the safety of any other person or the community.

(2) No release for certain aliens

If the judge finds no such condition or combination of conditions, as described in paragraph (1), the alien shall remain in custody until the completion of any appeal authorized by this title.

(June 27, 1952, c. 477, Title V, § 506, as added Apr. 24, 1996, Pub.L. 104–132, Title IV, § 401(a), 110 Stat. 1265.)

§ 507. Custody and release after removal hearing [8 U.S.C.A. § 1537]

(a) Release

(1) In general

Subject to paragraph (2), if the judge decides that an alien should not be removed, the alien shall be released from custody.

(2) Custody pending appeal

If the Attorney General takes an appeal from such decision, the alien shall remain in custody, subject to the provisions of section 3142 of Title 18.

(b) Custody and removal

(1) Custody

If the judge decides that an alien shall be removed, the alien shall be detained pending the outcome of any appeal. After the conclusion of any judicial review thereof which affirms the removal order, the Attorney General shall retain the alien in custody and remove the alien to a country specified under paragraph (2).

(2) Removal

(A) In general

The removal of an alien shall be to any country which the alien shall designate if such designation does not, in the judgment of the Attorney General, in consultation with the Secretary of State, impair the obligation of the United States under any treaty (including a treaty pertaining to extradition) or otherwise adversely affect the foreign policy of the United States.

(B) Alternate countries

If the alien refuses to designate a country to which the alien wishes to be removed or if the Attorney General, in consultation with the Secretary of State, determines that removal of the alien to the country so designated would impair a treaty obligation or adversely affect United States foreign policy, the Attorney General shall cause the alien to be removed to any country willing to receive such alien.

(C) Continued detention

If no country is willing to receive such an alien, the Attorney General may, notwithstanding any other provision of law, retain the alien in custody. The Attorney General, in coordination with the Secretary of State, shall make periodic efforts to reach agreement with other countries to accept such an alien and at least every 6 months shall provide to the attorney representing the alien at the removal hearing a written report on the Attorney General's efforts. Any alien in custody pursuant to this subparagraph shall be released from custody solely at the discretion of the Attorney General and subject to such conditions as the Attorney General shall deem appropriate.

(D) Fingerprinting

Before an alien is removed from the United States pursuant to this subsection, or pursuant to an order of removal because such alien is inadmissible under section 212(a)(3)(B) [8 U.S.C.A.

§ 1182(a)(3)(B)], the alien shall be photographed and fingerprinted, and shall be advised of the provisions of section 276(b) [8 U.S.C.A. § 1326(b)].

(c) Continued detention pending trial

(1) Delay in removal

The Attorney General may hold in abeyance the removal of an alien who has been ordered removed, pursuant to this title, to allow the trial of such alien on any Federal or State criminal charge and the service of any sentence of confinement resulting from such a trial.

(2) Maintenance of custody

Pending the commencement of any service of a sentence of confinement by an alien described in paragraph (1), such an alien shall remain in the custody of the Attorney General, unless the Attorney General determines that temporary release of the alien to the custody of State authorities for confinement in a State facility is appropriate and would not endanger national security or public safety.

(3) Subsequent removal

Following the completion of a sentence of confinement by an alien described in paragraph (1), or following the completion of State criminal proceedings which do not result in a sentence of confinement of an alien released to the custody of State authorities pursuant to paragraph (2), such an alien shall be returned to the custody of the Attorney General who shall proceed to the removal of the alien under this title.

(d) Application of certain provisions relating to escape of prisoners

For purposes of sections 751 and 752 of Title 18, an alien in the custody of the Attorney General pursuant to this title shall be subject to the penalties provided by those sections in relation to a person committed to the custody of the Attorney General by virtue of an arrest on a charge of a felony.

(e) Rights of aliens in custody

(1) Family and attorney visits

An alien in the custody of the Attorney General pursuant to this title shall be given reasonable opportunity, as determined by the Attorney General, to communicate with and receive visits from members of the alien's family, and to contact, retain, and communicate with an attorney.

(2) Diplomatic contact

An alien in the custody of the Attorney General pursuant to this title shall have the right to contact an appropriate diplomatic or consular official of the alien's country of citizenship or nationality or of any country providing representation services therefore. The Attorney General shall notify the appropriate embassy, mission, or consular office of the alien's detention.

(June 27, 1952, c. 477, Title V, § 507, as added Apr. 24, 1996, Pub.L. 104–132, Title IV, § 401(a), 110 Stat. 1266, and amended Pub.L. 104–208, Div. C, Title III, § 308(d)(4)(Q), Sept. 30, 1996, 110 Stat. 3009–619.)

II. ADDITIONAL STATUTES

Title 8, U.S. Code, Aliens and Nationality
Selected Sections Not Codified
in the Immigration and Nationality Act

Designation and Adjustment of Status of Soviet and Indochinese Refugees (Lautenberg Amendment)

Foreign Affairs Reform and Restructuring Act

Consolidated Appropriations Act of 2008

Personal Responsibility and Work Opportunity Reconciliation Act of 1996

Administrative Procedure Act

Selected Sections

Title 18, U.S. Code, Crimes and Criminal Procedure

TITLE 8, U.S. CODE, ALIENS AND NATIONALITY SELECTED SECTIONS NOT CODIFIED IN THE IMMIGRATION AND NATIONALITY ACT

§ 1373. Communication between Government agencies and the Immigration and Naturalization Service. [Illegal Immigration Reform and Immigrant Responsibility Act of 1996 § 642]

(a) In general

Notwithstanding any other provision of Federal, State, or local law, a Federal, State, or local government entity or official may not prohibit, or in any way restrict, any government entity or official from sending to, or receiving from, the Immigration and Naturalization Service information regarding the citizenship or immigration status, lawful or unlawful, of any individual.

(b) Additional authority of Government entities

Notwithstanding any other provision of Federal, State, or local law, no person or agency may prohibit, or in any way restrict, a Federal, State, or local government entity from doing any of the following with respect to information regarding the immigration status, lawful or unlawful, of any individual:

(1) Sending such information to, or requesting or receiving such information from, the Immigration and Naturalization Service.

(2) Maintaining such information.

(3) Exchanging such information with any other Federal, State, or local government entity.

(c) Obligation to respond to inquiries

The Immigration and Naturalization Service shall respond to an inquiry by a Federal, State, or local government agency, seeking to verify or ascertain the citizenship or immigration status of any individual within the jurisdiction of the agency for any purpose authorized by law, by providing the requested verification or status information.

(Pub.L. 104–208, Div. C, Title VI, § 642, Sept. 30, 1996, 110 Stat. 3009–707.)

§ 1621. Aliens who are not qualified aliens or nonimmigrants ineligible for State and local public benefits. [Personal Responsibility and Work Opportunity Reconciliation Act of 1996, § 411]

(a) In general

Notwithstanding any other provisions of law and except as provided in subsections (b) and (d) of this section, an alien who is not—

(1) a qualified alien (as defined in section 1641 of this title [8 U.S.C.A. § 1641]),

(2) a nonimmigrant under the Immigration and Nationality Act [8 U.S.C.A. § 1101 et seq.], or

(3) an alien who is paroled into the United States under section 212(d)(5) of such Act [8 U.S.C.A. § 1182(d)(5)] for less than one year,

is not eligible for any State or local public benefit (as defined in subsection (c) of this section).

(b) Exceptions

Subsection (a) of this section shall not apply with respect to the following State or local public benefits:

(1) Assistance for health care items and services that are necessary for the treatment of an emergency medical condition (as defined in section 1396b(v)(3) of Title 42) of the alien involved and are not related to an organ transplant procedure.

(2) Short-term, non-cash, in-kind emergency disaster relief.

(3) Public health assistance for immunizations with respect to immunizable diseases and for testing and treatment of symptoms of communicable diseases whether or not such symptoms are caused by a communicable disease.

(4) Programs, services, or assistance (such as soup kitchens, crisis counseling and intervention, and short-term shelter) specified by the Attorney General, in the Attorney General's sole and unreviewable discretion after consultation with appropriate Federal agencies and departments, which **(A)** deliver in-kind services at the community level, including through public or private nonprofit agencies; **(B)** do not condition the provision of assistance, the amount of assistance provided, or the cost of assistance provided on the individual recipient's income or resources; and **(C)** are necessary for the protection of life or safety.

(c) "State or local public benefit" defined

(1) Except as provided in paragraphs (2) and (3), for purposes of this subchapter the term "State or local public benefit" means—

(A) any grant, contract, loan, professional license, or commercial license provided by an agency of a State or local government or by appropriated funds of a State or local government; and

(B) any retirement, welfare, health, disability, public or assisted housing, postsecondary education, food assistance, unemployment benefit, or any other similar benefit for which payments or assistance are provided to an individual, household, or family eligibility unit by an agency of a State or local government or by appropriated funds of a State or local government.

(2) Such term shall not apply—

(A) to any contract, professional license, or commercial license for a nonimmigrant whose visa for entry is related to such employment in the United States, or to a citizen of a freely associated state, if section 141 of the applicable compact of free association approved in Public Law 99–239 [48 U.S.C.A. § 1901 note] or 99–658 [48 U.S.C.A. § 1931 note] (or a successor provision) is in effect;

(B) with respect to benefits for an alien who as a work authorized nonimmigrant or as an alien lawfully admitted for permanent residence under the Immigration and Nationality Act [8 U.S.C.A. § 1101 et seq.] qualified for such benefits and for whom the United States under reciprocal treaty agreements is required to pay benefits, as determined by the Secretary of State, after consultation with the Attorney General; or

(C) to the issuance of a professional license to, or the renewal of a professional license by, a foreign national not physically present in the United States.

(3) Such term does not include any Federal public benefit under section 1611(c) of this title [8 U.S.C.A. § 1611(c)].

(d) State authority to provide for eligibility of illegal aliens for State and local public benefits

A State may provide that an alien who is not lawfully present in the United States is eligible for any State or local public benefit for which such alien would otherwise be ineligible under subsection (a) of this section only through the enactment of a State law after August 22, 1996, which affirmatively provides for such eligibility.

(Pub.L. 104–193, Title IV, § 411, Aug. 22, 1996, 110 Stat. 2268; Pub.L. 105–33, Title V, §§ 5565, 5581(b)(1), Aug. 5, 1997, 111 Stat. 639, 642; Pub.L. 105–306, § 5(b), Oct. 28, 1998, 112 Stat. 2927.)

§ 1623. Limitation on eligibility for preferential treatment of aliens not lawfully present on basis of residence for higher education benefits. [Illegal Immigration Reform and Immigrant Responsibility Act of 1996, § 505]

(a) In general

Notwithstanding any other provision of law, an alien who is not lawfully present in the United States shall not be eligible on the basis of residence within a State (or a political subdivision) for any postsecondary education benefit unless a citizen or national of the United States is eligible for such a benefit (in no less an amount, duration, and scope) without regard to whether the citizen or national is such a resident.

(b) Effective date

This section shall apply to benefits provided on or after July 1, 1998.

(Pub.L. 104–208, Div. C, Title V, § 505, Sept. 30, 1996, 110 Stat. 3009–672.)

§ 1624. Authority of States and political subdivisions of States to limit assistance to aliens and to distinguish among classes of aliens in providing general cash public assistance. [Illegal Immigration Reform and Immigrant Responsibility Act of 1996, § 553]

(a) In general

Subject to subsection (b) of this section and notwithstanding any other provision of law, a State or political subdivision of a State is authorized to prohibit or otherwise limit or restrict the eligibility of aliens or classes of aliens for programs of general cash public assistance furnished under the law of the State or a political subdivision of a State.

(b) Limitation

The authority provided for under subsection (a) of this section may be exercised only to the extent that any prohibitions, limitations, or restrictions imposed by a State or political subdivision of a State are not more restrictive than the prohibitions, limitations, or restrictions imposed under comparable Federal programs. For purposes of this section, attribution to an alien of a sponsor's income and resources (as described in section 1631 of this title) for purposes of determining eligibility for, and the amount of, benefits shall be considered less restrictive than a prohibition of eligibility for such benefits.

(Pub.L. 104–208, Div. C, Title V, § 553, Sept. 30, 1996, 110 Stat. 3009–681.)

§ 1644. Communication between State and local government agencies and the Immigration and Naturalization Service. [Personal Responsibility and Work Opportunity Reconciliation Act of 1996, § 434]

Notwithstanding any other provision of Federal, State, or local law, no State or local government entity may be prohibited, or in any way restricted, from sending to or receiving from the Immigration and Naturalization Service information regarding the immigration status, lawful or unlawful, of an alien in the United States.

(Pub.L. 104–193, Title IV, § 434, Aug. 22, 1996, 110 Stat. 2275.)

§ 1721. Interim measures for access to and coordination of law enforcement and other information [Enhanced Border Security and Visa Entry Reform Act of 2002, § 201]

(a) Interim directive

Until the plan required by subsection (c) of this section is implemented, Federal law enforcement agencies and the intelligence community shall, to the maximum extent practicable, share any information with the Department of State and the Immigration and Naturalization Service relevant to the admissibility and deportability of aliens, consistent with the plan described in subsection (c) of this section.

(b) Report identifying law enforcement and intelligence information

(1) In general

Not later than 120 days after May 14, 2002, the President shall submit to the appropriate committees of Congress a report identifying Federal law enforcement and the intelligence community information needed by the Department of State to screen visa applicants, or by the Immigration and Naturalization Service to screen applicants for admission to the United States, and to identify those aliens inadmissible or deportable under the Immigration and Nationality Act [8 U.S.C.A. § 1101 et seq.].

(2) Omitted

(c) Coordination plan

(1) Requirement for plan

Not later than one year after October 26, 2001, the President shall develop and implement a plan based on the findings of the report under subsection (b) of this section that requires Federal law enforcement agencies and the intelligence community to provide to the Department of State and the Immigration and Naturalization Service all information identified in that report as expeditiously as practicable.

(2) Consultation requirement

In the preparation and implementation of the plan under this subsection, the President shall consult with the appropriate committees of Congress.

(3) Protections regarding information and uses thereof

The plan under this subsection shall establish conditions for using the information described in subsection (b) of this section received by the Department of State and Immigration and Naturalization Service—

(A) to limit the redissemination of such information;

(B) to ensure that such information is used solely to determine whether to issue a visa to an alien or to determine the admissibility or deportability of an alien to the United States, except as otherwise authorized under Federal law;

(C) to ensure the accuracy, security, and confidentiality of such information;

(D) to protect any privacy rights of individuals who are subjects of such information;

(E) to provide data integrity through the timely removal and destruction of obsolete or erroneous names and information; and

(F) in a manner that protects the sources and methods used to acquire intelligence information as required by section 403–3(c)(7) of Title 50.

(4) Criminal penalties for misuse of information

Any person who obtains information under this subsection without authorization or exceeding authorized access (as defined in section 1030(e) of Title 18), and who uses such information in the manner described in any of the paragraphs (1) through (7) of section 1030(a) of such title, or attempts to use such information in such manner, shall be subject to the same penalties as are applicable under section 1030(c) of such title for violation of that paragraph.

(5) Omitted

(Pub.L. 107–173, Title II, § 201, May 14, 2002, 116 Stat. 547; Pub.L. 108–177, Title III, § 377(f), Dec. 13, 2003, 117 Stat. 2631.)

§ 1722. Interoperable law enforcement and intelligence data system with name-matching capacity and training [Enhanced Border Security and Visa Entry Reform Act of 2002, § 202]

(a) Interoperable law enforcement and intelligence electronic data system

(1) Requirement for integrated immigration and naturalization data system

The Immigration and Naturalization Service shall fully integrate all databases and data systems maintained by the Service that process or contain information on aliens. The fully integrated data system shall be an interoperable component of the electronic data system described in paragraph (2).

(2) Requirement for interoperable data system

Upon the date of commencement of implementation of the plan required by section 1721(c) of this title, the President shall develop and implement an interoperable electronic data system to provide current and immediate access to information in databases of Federal law enforcement agencies and the intelligence community that is relevant to determine whether to issue a visa or to determine the admissibility or deportability of an alien (also known as the "Chimera system").

(3) Consultation requirement

In the development and implementation of the data system under this subsection, the President shall consult with the Director of the National Institute of Standards and Technology (NIST) and any such other agency as may be deemed appropriate.

(4) Technology standard

(A) In general

The data system developed and implemented under this subsection, and the databases referred to in paragraph (2), shall utilize the technology standard established pursuant to section 1379 of this title.

(B) Omitted

(5) Access to information in data system

Subject to paragraph (6), information in the data system under this subsection shall be readily and easily accessible—

(A) to any consular officer responsible for the issuance of visas;

(B) to any Federal official responsible for determining an alien's admissibility to or deportability from the United States; and

(C) to any Federal law enforcement or intelligence officer determined by regulation to be responsible for the investigation or identification of aliens.

(6) Limitation on access

The President shall, in accordance with applicable Federal laws, establish procedures to restrict access to intelligence information in the data system under this subsection, and the databases referred to in paragraph (2), under circumstances in which such information is not to be disclosed directly to Government officials under paragraph (5).

(b) Name-search capacity and support

(1) In general

The interoperable electronic data system required by subsection (a) of this section shall—

(A) have the capacity to compensate for disparate name formats among the different databases referred to in subsection (a) of this section;

(B) be searchable on a linguistically sensitive basis;

(C) provide adequate user support;

(D) to the extent practicable, utilize commercially available technology; and

(E) be adjusted and improved, based upon experience with the databases and improvements in the underlying technologies and sciences, on a continuing basis.

(2) Linguistically sensitive searches

(A) In general

To satisfy the requirement of paragraph (1)(B), the interoperable electronic database shall be searchable based on linguistically sensitive algorithms that—

(i) account for variations in name formats and transliterations, including varied spellings and varied separation or combination of name elements, within a particular language; and

(ii) incorporate advanced linguistic, mathematical, statistical, and anthropological research and methods.

(B) Languages required

(i) Priority languages

Linguistically sensitive algorithms shall be developed and implemented for no fewer than 4 languages designated as high priorities by the Secretary of State, after consultation with the Attorney General and the Director of Central Intelligence.

(ii) Implementation schedule

Of the 4 linguistically sensitive algorithms required to be developed and implemented under clause (i)—

(I) the highest priority language algorithms shall be implemented within 18 months after May 14, 2002; and

(II) an additional language algorithm shall be implemented each succeeding year for the next three years.

(3) Adequate user support

The Secretary of State and the Attorney General shall jointly prescribe procedures to ensure that consular and immigration officers can, as required, obtain assistance in resolving identity and other questions that may arise about the names of aliens seeking visas or admission to the United States that may be subject to variations in format, transliteration, or other similar phenomenon.

(4) Interim reports

Six months after May 14, 2002, the President shall submit a report to the appropriate committees of Congress on the progress in implementing each requirement of this section.

(5) Reports by intelligence agencies

(A) Current standards

Not later than 60 days after May 14, 2002, the Director of Central Intelligence shall complete the survey and issue the report previously required by section 309(a) of the Intelligence Authorization Act for Fiscal Year 1998.

(B) Guidelines

Not later than 120 days after May 14, 2002, the Director of Central Intelligence shall issue the guidelines and submit the copy of those guidelines previously required by section 309(b) of the Intelligence Authorization Act for Fiscal Year 1998.

(6) Authorization of appropriations

There are authorized to be appropriated such sums as are necessary to carry out the provisions of this subsection.

(Pub.L. 107–173, Title II, § 202, May 14, 2002, 116 Stat. 548.)

DESIGNATION AND ADJUSTMENT OF STATUS OF SOVIET AND INDOCHINESE REFUGEES (LAUTENBERG AMENDMENT)

§ 599D. Establishing Categories of Aliens for Purposes of Refugee Determinations [8 U.S.C.A. § 1157, Note]

(a) In General.—In the case of an alien who is within a category of aliens established under subsection (b), the alien may establish, for purposes of admission as a refugee under section 207 of the Immigration and Nationality Act, that the alien has a well-founded fear of persecution on account of race, religion, nationality, membership in a particular social group, or political opinion by asserting such a fear and asserting a credible basis for concern about the possibility of such persecution.

(b) Establishment of Categories.—

(1) For purposes of subsection (a), the Attorney General, in consultation with the Secretary of State and the Coordinator for Refugee Affairs, shall establish—

(A) one or more categories of aliens who are or were nationals and residents of an independent state of the former Soviet Union or of Estonia, Latvia, or Lithuania and who share common characteristics that identify them as targets of persecution in that state on account of race, religion, nationality, membership in a particular social group, or political opinion,

(B) one or more categories of aliens who are or were nationals and residents of Vietnam, Laos, or Cambodia and who share common characteristics that identify them as targets of persecution in such respective foreign state on such an account; and

(C) one or more categories of aliens who are or were nationals and residents of the Islamic Republic or Iran who, as members of a religious minority in Iran, share common characteristics that identify them as targets of persecution in that state on account of race, religion, nationality, membership in a particular social group, or political opinion.

(2)(A) Aliens who are (or were) nationals and residents of an independent state of the former Soviet Union or of Estonia, Latvia, or Lithuania and who are Jews or Evangelical Christians shall be deemed a category of alien established under paragraph (1)(A).

(B) Aliens who are (or were) nationals of an independent state of the former Soviet Union or of Estonia, Latvia, or Lithuania and who are current members of, and demonstrate public, active, and continuous participation (or attempted participation) in the religious activities of, the Ukrainian Catholic Church or the Ukrainian Orthodox Church, shall be deemed a category of alien established under paragraph (1)(A).

(C) Aliens who are (or were) nationals and residents of Vietnam, Laos, or Cambodia and who are members of categories of individuals determined, by the Attorney General in accordance with "Immigration and Naturalization Service Worldwide Guidelines for Overseas Refugee Processing" (issued by the Immigration and Naturalization Service in August 1983) shall be deemed a category of alien established under paragraph (1)(B).

(3) Within the number of admissions of refugees allocated for for [sic] each of fiscal years 1990, 1991, and 1992 for refugees who are nationals of the Soviet Union under section 207(a)(3) of the Immigration and Nationality Act [8 U.S.C.A. § 1157(a)(3)] and within the number of such admissions allocated for each of fiscal years 1993, 1994, 1995, 1996, 1997, 1998, 1999, 2000, 2001, 2002, 2003, 2004, 2005, 2006, 2007, 2008, 2009, 2010, 2011, 2012, 2013, and 2014 for refugees who are nationals of the independent states of the former Soviet Union, Estonia, Latvia, and Lithuania under such section, notwithstanding any other provision of law, the President shall allocate one thousand of such admissions for such fiscal year to refugees who are within the category of aliens described in paragraph (2)(B).

(c) Written Reasons for Denials of Refugee Status.—Each decision to deny an application for refugee status of an alien who is within a category established under this section shall be in writing and shall state, to the maximum extent feasible, the reason for the denial.

(d) Permitting Certain Aliens Within Categories to Reapply for Refugee Status.—Each alien who is within a category established under this section and who (after August 14, 1988, and before the date of the enactment of this Act [Nov. 21, 1989]) was denied refugee status shall be permitted to reapply for such status. Such an application shall be determined taking into account the application of this section.

(e) Period of Application.—

(1) Subsections (a) and (b) shall take effect on the date of the enactment of this Act [Nov. 21, 1989] and shall only apply to applications for refugee status submitted before October 1, 2014.

(2) Subsection (c) shall apply to decisions made after the date of the enactment of this Act [Nov. 21, 1989] and before October 1, 2014.

(3) Subsection (d) shall take effect on the date of the enactment of this Act [Nov. 21, 1989] and shall only apply to reapplications for refugee status submitted before October 1, 2014.

(f) Repealed. Pub.L. 102–391, Title V, § 582(c), Oct. 6, 1992, 106 Stat. 1686; Pub.L. 102–511, Title IX, § 905(c), Oct. 24, 1992, 106 Stat. 3356.

(Pub.L. 101–167, Title V, § 599D, Nov. 21, 1989, 103 Stat. 1261, as amended Pub.L. 101–513, Title V, § 598(a), Nov. 5, 1990, 104 Stat. 2063; Pub.L. 102–391, Title V, § 582(a)(1), (b)(1), and (c), Oct. 6, 1992, 106 Stat. 1686; Pub.L. 102–511, Title IX, § 905(a), (b)(1), and (c), Oct. 24, 1992, 106 Stat. 3356; Pub.L. 103–236, Title V, § 512(1), Apr. 30, 1994, 108 Stat. 466; Pub.L. 104–208, Div. A, Title I, § 101(c) [Title V, § 575(1)], Sept. 30, 1996, 110 Stat. 3009–168; Pub.L. 104–319, Title I, § 101(1), Oct. 19, 1996, 110 Stat. 3865; Pub.L. 105–118, Title V, § 574(1), Nov. 26, 1997, 111 Stat. 2432; Pub.L. 105–277, Div. A, § 101(f) [Title VII, § 705(1)], Oct. 21, 1998, 112 Stat. 2681–389; Nov. 29, 1999, Pub.L. 106–113, Div. B, § 1000(a)(4) [H.R. 3424, Title II, § 214(1)], 113 Stat. 1535, 1537; Pub.L. 106–554, § 1(a)(1) [Title II, § 212(1)], Dec. 21, 2000, 114 Stat. 2763; Pub.L. 107–116, Title II, § 213(1), Jan. 10, 2002, 115 Stat. 2177, 2200; Pub.L. 108–7, Div. G, Title II, § 213(1), Feb. 20, 2003, 117 Stat. 324; Pub. L. 108–199, Div. E, Title II, § 213(1), Jan. 23, 2004, 118 Stat. 253; Pub.L. 108–447, Div. F, Title II, § 213(1), Dec. 8, 2004, 118 Stat. 3139; Pub.L. 109–102, Title V, § 534(m)(1), Nov. 14, 2005, 119 Stat. 2211; Pub.L. 109–289, Div. B, Title II, § 20412(b)(1), as added Pub.L. 110–5, § 2, Feb. 15, 2007, 121 Stat. 25; Pub.L. 110–161, Div. J, Title VI, § 634(k)(1), Dec. 26, 2007, 121 Stat. 2329; Pub.L. 111–8, Div. H, Title VII, § 7034(g)(1), Mar. 11, 2009, 123 Stat. 878; Pub.L. 111–117 Div. F, Title VII, § 7034(f)(1), Dec. 16, 2009, 123 Stat. 3361; Pub.L. 112–10, Div. B, Title XI, § 2121(m), Apr. 15, 2011, 125 Stat. 186; Pub.L. 112–74, Div. I, Title VII, § 7034(r)(1), Dec. 23, 2011, 125 Stat. 1218; Pub.L. 113–6, Div. F, Title VII, § 1706(h)(1), Mar. 26, 2013, 127 Stat. 430; Pub.L. 113–76, Div. K, Title VII, § 7034(m)(8)(A), Jan. 17, 2014, 128 Stat. 516.)

§ 599E. Adjustment of Status for Certain Soviet and Indochinese Parolees [8 U.S.C.A. § 1255, Note]

(a) In general.—The Attorney General shall adjust the status of an alien described in subsection (b) to that of an alien lawfully admitted for permanent residence if the alien—

(1) applies for such adjustment,

(2) has been physically present in the United States for at least 1 year and is physically present in the United States on the date the application for such adjustment is filed,

(3) is admissible to the United States as an immigrant, except as provided in subsection (c), and

(4) pays a fee (determined by the Attorney General) for the processing of such application.

(b) Aliens eligible for adjustment of status.—The benefits provided in subsection (a) shall only apply to an alien who—

(1) was a national of an independent state of the former Soviet Union, Estonia, Latvia, Lithuania, Vietnam, Laos, or Cambodia, and

(2) was inspected and granted parole into the United States during the period beginning on August 15, 1988, and ending on September 30, 2014, after being denied refugee status.

(c) Waiver of certain grounds for inadmissibility.—The provisions of paragraphs (4), (5), and (7)(A) of section 212(a) of the Immigration and Nationality Act [8 U.S.C.A. § 1182(a)] shall not apply to adjustment of status under this section and the Attorney General may waive any other provision of such section (other than paragraph (2)(C) or subparagraph (A), (B), (C), or (E) of paragraph (3)) with respect to such an adjustment for humanitarian purposes, to assure family unity, or when it is otherwise in the public interest.

(d) Date of approval.—Upon the approval of such an application for adjustment of status, the Attorney General shall create a record of the alien's admission as a lawful permanent resident as of the date of the alien's inspection and parole described in subsection (b)(2).

(e) No offset in number of visas available.—When an alien is granted the status of having been lawfully admitted for permanent residence under this section, the Secretary of State shall not be required to reduce the number of immigrant visas authorized to be issued under the Immigration and Nationality Act.

(Pub.L. 101–167, Title V, § 599E, Nov. 21, 1989, 103 Stat. 1263, as amended Pub.L. 101–513, Title V, § 598(b), Nov. 5, 1990, 104 Stat. 2063, Pub.L. 101–649, Title VI, § 603(a)(22), Nov. 29, 1990, 104 Stat. 5084; Pub.L. 102–232, Title III, 307(*l*)(9), Dec. 12, 1991, 105 Stat. 1757; Pub.L. 102–391, Title V, § 582(a)(2), (b)(2), Oct. 6, 1992, 106 Stat. 1686; Pub.L. 102–511, Title IX, § 905(b)(2), Oct. 24, 1992, 106 Stat. 3356; Pub.L. 103–236, Title V, § 512(2), Apr. 30, 1994, 108 Stat. 466; Pub.L. 103–416, Title II, § 219(bb), Oct. 25, 1994, 108 Stat. 4319; Pub.L. 104–208, Div. A, Title I, § 101(c) [Title V, § 575(2)], Sept. 30, 1996, 110 Stat. 3009–168; Pub.L. 104–319, Title I, § 101(2), Oct. 19, 1996, 110 Stat. 3865; Pub.L. 105–118, Title V, § 574(2), Nov. 26, 1997, 111 Stat. 2432; Pub.L. 105–277, Div. A, § 101(f) [Title VII, § 705(2)], Oct. 21, 1998, 112 Stat. 2681; Nov. 29, 1999, Pub.L. 106–113, Div. B, § 1000(a)(4) [H.R. 3424, Title I, § 214(2)], 113 Stat. 1535, 1537; Pub.L. 106–554, § 1(a)(1) [Title II, § 212(2)], Dec. 21, 2000, 114 Stat. 2763; Pub.L. 107–116, Title II, § 213(2), Jan. 10, 2002, 115 Stat. 2177, 2200; Pub.L. 108–7, Div. G, Title II, § 213(2), Feb. 20, 2003, 117 Stat. 324; Pub.L. 108–199, Div. E, Title II, § 213(2), Jan. 23, 2004, 118 Stat. 253; Pub.L. 108–447, Div. F, Title II, § 213(2), Dec. 8, 2004, 118 Stat. 3140; Pub.L. 109–102, Title V, § 534(m)(2), Nov. 14, 2005, 119 Stat. 2211; Pub.L. 109–289, Div. B, Title II, § 20412(b)(2), as added Pub.L. 110–5, § 2, Feb. 15, 2007, 121 Stat. 25; Pub.L. 110–161, Div. J, Title VI, § 634(k)(2), Dec. 26, 2007, 121 Stat. 2329; Pub.L. 111–8, Div. H, Title VII, § 7034(g)(2), Mar. 11, 2009, 123 Stat. 878; Pub.L. 111–117, Div. F, Title VII, § 7034(f)(2), Dec. 16, 2009, 123 Stat. 3361; Pub.L. 112–10, Div. B, Title XI, § 2121(m), Apr. 15, 2011, 125 Stat. 186; Pub.L. 112–74. Div. I, Title VII, § 7034(r)(2), Dec. 23, 2011, 125 Stat. 1218; Pub.L. 113–6, Div. F, Title VII, § 1706(h)(2), Mar. 26, 2013, 127 Stat. 430; Pub.L. 113–76, Div. K, Title VII, § 7034(m)(8)(B), Jan. 17, 2014, 128 Stat. 516.)

FOREIGN AFFAIRS REFORM AND RESTRUCTURING ACT

§ 2242. United States Policy with Respect to the Involuntary Return of Persons in Danger of Subjection to Torture [8 U.S.C.A § 1231, Note]

(a) Policy.—It shall be the policy of the United States not to expel, extradite, or otherwise effect the involuntary return of any person to a country in which there are substantial grounds for believing the person would be in danger of being subjected to torture, regardless of whether the person is physically present in the United States.

(b) Regulations.—Not later than 120 days after the date of enactment of this Act [Oct. 21, 1998], the heads of the appropriate agencies shall prescribe regulations to implement the obligations of the United States under Article 3 of the United Nations Convention Against Torture and Other Forms of Cruel, Inhuman or Degrading Treatment or Punishment, subject to any reservations, understandings, declarations, and provisos contained in the United States Senate resolution of ratification of the Convention.

(c) Exclusion of certain aliens.—To the maximum extent consistent with the obligations of the United States under the Convention, subject to any reservations, understandings, declarations, and provisos contained in the United States Senate resolution of ratification of the Convention, the regulations described in subsection (b) shall exclude from the protection of such regulations aliens described in section 241(b)(3)(B) of the Immigration and Nationality Act (8 U.S.C. 1231(b)(3)(B)).

(d) Review and construction.—Notwithstanding any other provision of law, and except as provided in the regulations described in subsection (b), no court shall have jurisdiction to review the regulations adopted to implement this section, and nothing in this section shall be construed as providing any court jurisdiction to consider or review claims raised under the Convention or this section, or any other determination made with respect to the application of the policy set forth in subsection (a), except as part of the review of a final order of removal pursuant to section 242 of the Immigration and Nationality Act (8 U.S.C. 1252).

(e) Authority to detain.—Nothing in this section shall be construed as limiting the authority of the Attorney General to detain any person under any provision of law, including, but not limited to, any provision of the Immigration and Nationality Act.

(f) Definitions.—

(1) Convention defined.—In this section, the term "Convention" means the United Nations Convention Against Torture and Other Forms of Cruel, Inhuman or Degrading Treatment or Punishment, done at New York on December 10, 1984.

(2) Same terms as in the Convention.—Except as otherwise provided, the terms used in this section have the meanings given those terms in the Convention, subject to any reservations, understandings, declarations, and provisos contained in the United States Senate resolution of ratification of the Convention.

(Pub.L. 105–277, Div. G, Title XXII, § 2242, Oct. 21, 1998, 112 Stat. 2681–822.)

CONSOLIDATED APPROPRIATIONS ACT OF 2008

§ 691. Relief for Iraqi, Montagnards, Hmong and Other Refugees Who Do Not Pose a Threat to the United States

* * *

(b) Automatic relief for the Hmong and other groups that do not pose a threat to the United States.—For purposes of section 212(a)(3)(B) of the Immigration and Nationality Act (8 U.S.C.A. § 1182(a)(3)(B)), the Karen National Union/Karen Liberation Army (KNU/KNLA), the Chin National Front/Chin National Army (CNF/CNA), the Chin National League for Democracy (CNLD), the Kayan New Land Party (KNLP), the Arakan Liberation Party (ALP), the Mustangs, the Alzados, the Karenni National Progressive Party, and appropriate groups affiliated with the Hmong and the Montagnards shall not be considered to be a terrorist organization on the basis of any act or event occurring before the date of enactment of this section. Nothing in this subsection may be construed to alter or limit the authority of the Secretary of State or the Secretary of Homeland Security to exercise his discretionary authority pursuant to section 212(d)(3)(B)(i) of the Immigration and Nationality Act (8 U.S.C.A. § 1182(d)(3)(B)(i)).

* * *

(d) Designation of the Taliban as a terrorist organization.—For purposes of section 212(a)(3)(B) of the Immigration and Nationality Act (8 U.S.C.A. § 1182(a)(3)(B)), the Taliban shall be considered to be a terrorist organization described in subclause (I) of clause (vi) of that section.

(e) Report on duress waivers.—The Secretary of Homeland Security shall provide to the Committees on the Judiciary of the United States Senate and House of Representatives a report, not less than 180 days after the enactment of this Act and every year thereafter, which may include a classified annex, if appropriate, describing—

(1) the number of individuals subject to removal from the United States for having provided material support to a terrorist group who allege that such support was provided under duress;

(2) a breakdown of the types of terrorist organizations to which the individuals described in paragraph (1) have provided material support;

(3) a description of the factors that the Department of Homeland Security considers when evaluating duress waivers; and

(4) any other information that the Secretary believes that the Congress should consider while overseeing the Department's application of duress waivers.

(f) Effective date.—The amendments made by this section shall take effect on the date of enactment of this section, and these amendments and sections 212(a)(3)(B) and 212(d)(3)(B) of the Immigration and Nationality Act (8 U.S.C.A. § 1182(a)(3)(B) and § 1182(d)(3)(B)), as amended by these sections, shall apply to—

(1) removal proceedings instituted before, on, or after the date of enactment of this section; and

(2) acts and conditions constituting a ground for inadmissibility, excludability, deportation, or removal occurring or existing before, on, or after such date.

(Pub. L. 110–161, Dec. 26, 2007, 121 Stat. 1844.)

PERSONAL RESPONSIBILITY AND WORK OPPORTUNITY RECONCILIATION ACT OF 1996

§ 400. Statements of national policy concerning welfare and immigration [8 U.S.C.A. § 1601]

The Congress makes the following statements concerning national policy with respect to welfare and immigration:

(1) Self-sufficiency has been a basic principle of United States immigration law since this country's earliest immigration statutes.

(2) It continues to be the immigration policy of the United States that—

(A) aliens within the Nation's borders not depend on public resources to meet their needs, but rather rely on their own capabilities and the resources of their families, their sponsors, and private organizations, and

(B) the availability of public benefits not constitute an incentive for immigration to the United States.

(3) Despite the principle of self-sufficiency, aliens have been applying for and receiving public benefits from Federal, State, and local governments at increasing rates.

(4) Current eligibility rules for public assistance and unenforceable financial support agreements have proved wholly incapable of assuring that individual aliens not burden the public benefits system.

(5) It is a compelling government interest to enact new rules for eligibility and sponsorship agreements in order to assure that aliens be self-reliant in accordance with national immigration policy.

(6) It is a compelling government interest to remove the incentive for illegal immigration provided by the availability of public benefits.

(7) With respect to the State authority to make determinations concerning the eligibility of qualified aliens for public benefits in this chapter, a State that chooses to follow the Federal classification in determining the eligibility of such aliens for public assistance shall be considered to have chosen the least restrictive means available for achieving the compelling governmental interest of assuring that aliens be self-reliant in accordance with national immigration policy.

(Pub.L. 104–193, Title IV, § 400, Aug. 22, 1996, 110 Stat. 2260.)

§ 401. Aliens who are not qualified aliens ineligible for Federal public benefits [8 U.S.C.A. § 1611]

(a) In general

Notwithstanding any other provision of law and except as provided in subsection (b) of this section, an alien who is not a qualified alien (as defined in section 431 [8 U.S.C.A. § 1641]) is not eligible for any Federal public benefit (as defined in subsection (c) of this section).

(b) Exceptions

(1) Subsection (a) of this section shall not apply with respect to the following Federal public benefits:

(A) Medical assistance under title XIX of the Social Security Act [42 U.S.C.A § 1396 et seq.] (or any successor program to such title) for care and services that are necessary for the treatment of an emergency medical condition (as defined in section 1903(v)(3) of such Act [42 U.S.C.A. § 1396b(v)(3)]) of the alien involved and are not related to an organ transplant procedure, if the alien involved otherwise meets the eligibility requirements for medical assistance under the State plan approved under such title (other than the requirement of the receipt of aid or assistance under title IV of such Act [42 U.S.C.A § 601 et seq.], supplemental security income benefits under title XVI of such Act [42 U.S.C.A. § 1381 et seq.], or a State supplementary payment).

(B) Short-term, non-cash, in-kind emergency disaster relief.

(C) Public health assistance (not including any assistance under title XIX of the Social Security Act [42 U.S.C.A. § 1396 et seq.]) for immunizations with respect to immunizable diseases and for testing and treatment of symptoms of communicable diseases whether or not such symptoms are caused by a communicable disease.

(D) Programs, services, or assistance (such as soup kitchens, crisis counseling and intervention, and short-term shelter) specified by the Attorney General, in the Attorney General's sole and unreviewable discretion after consultation with appropriate Federal agencies and departments, which **(i)** deliver in-kind services at the community level, including through public or private nonprofit agencies; **(ii)** do not condition the provision of assistance, the amount of assistance provided, or the cost of assistance provided on the individual recipient's income or resources; and **(iii)** are necessary for the protection of life or safety.

(E) Programs for housing or community development assistance or financial assistance administered by the Secretary of

Housing and Urban Development, any program under title V of the Housing Act of 1949 [42 U.S.C.A. § 1471 et seq.], or any assistance under section 1926C of Title 7, to the extent that the alien is receiving such a benefit on August 22, 1996.

(2) Subsection (a) of this section shall not apply to any benefit payable under title II of the Social Security Act [42 U.S.C.A. § 401 et seq.] to an alien who is lawfully present in the United States as determined by the Attorney General, to any benefit if nonpayment of such benefit would contravene an international agreement described in section 233 of the Social Security Act [42 U.S.C.A. § 433], to any benefit if nonpayment would be contrary to section 202(t) of the Social Security Act [42 U.S.C.A. § 402(t)], or to any benefit payable under title II of the Social Security Act [42 U.S.C.A. § 401 et seq.] to which entitlement is based on an application filed in or before the month in which this Act becomes law.

(3) Subsection (a) of this section shall not apply to any benefit payable under title XVIII of the Social Security Act (relating to the medicare program) [42 U.S.C.A. § 1395 et seq.] to an alien who is lawfully present in the United States as determined by the Attorney General and, with respect to benefits payable under part A of such title, who was authorized to be employed with respect to any wages attributable to employment which are counted for purposes of eligibility for such benefits.

(4) Subsection (a) of this section shall not apply to any benefit payable under the Railroad Retirement Act of 1974 [45 U.S.C.A. § 231 et seq.] or the Railroad Unemployment Insurance Act [45 U.S.C.A. § 351 et seq.] to an alien who is lawfully present in the United States as determined by the Attorney General or to an alien residing outside the United States.

(5) Subsection (a) shall not apply to eligibility for benefits for the program defined in section 1612(a)(3)(A) of this title [8 U.S.C.A. § 1612(a)(3)(A)] (relating to the supplemental security income program), or to eligibility for benefits under any other program that is based on eligibility for benefits under the program so defined, for an alien who was receiving such benefits on August 22, 1996.

(c) "Federal public benefit" defined

(1) Except as provided in paragraph (2), for purposes of this chapter the term "Federal public benefit" means—

(A) any grant, contract, loan, professional license, or commercial license provided by an agency of the United States or by appropriated funds of the United States; and

(B) any retirement, welfare, health, disability, public or assisted housing, postsecondary education, food assistance, unemployment benefit, or any other similar benefit for which payments or assistance are provided to an individual, household, or family eligibility unit by an agency of the United States or by appropriated funds of the United States.

(2) Such term shall not apply—

(A) to any contract, professional license, or commercial license for a nonimmigrant whose visa for entry is related to such employment in the United States, or to a citizen of a freely associated state, if section 141 of the applicable compact of free association approved in Public Law 99–239 [48 U.S.C.A. § 1901 note] or 99–658 [48 U.S.C.A. § 1931 note] (or a successor provision) is in effect;

(B) with respect to benefits for an alien who as a work authorized nonimmigrant or as an alien lawfully admitted for permanent residence under the Immigration and Nationality Act [8 U.S.C.A. § 1101 et seq.] qualified for such benefits and for whom the United States under reciprocal treaty agreements is required to pay benefits, as determined by the Attorney General, after consultation with the Secretary of State; or

(C) to the issuance of a professional license to, or the renewal of a professional license by, a foreign national not physically present in the United States.

(Pub.L. 104–193, Title IV, § 401, Aug. 22, 1996, 110 Stat. 2261; Pub.L. 105–33, Title V, §§ 5561, 5565, Aug. 5, 1997, 111 Stat. 638, 639; Pub.L. 105–306, §§ 2, 5(a), Oct. 28, 1998, 112 Stat. 2926, 2927.)

§ 402. Limited eligibility of qualified aliens for certain Federal programs [8 U.S.C.A. § 1612]

(a) Limited eligibility for specified Federal programs

(1) In general

Notwithstanding any other provision of law and except as provided in paragraph (2), an alien who is a qualified alien (as defined in section 1641 of this title [8 U.S.C.A. § 1641]) is not eligible for any specified Federal program (as defined in paragraph (3)).

(2) Exceptions

(A) Time-limited exception for refugees and asylees

With respect to the specified Federal programs described in paragraph (3), paragraph (1) shall not apply to an alien until 7 years after the date—

(i) an alien is admitted to the United States as a refugee under section 207 of the Immigration and Nationality Act [8 U.S.C.A. § 1157];

(ii) an alien is granted asylum under section 208 of such Act [8 U.S.C.A. § 1158];

(iii) an alien's deportation is withheld under section 243(h) of such Act [8 U.S.C.A. § 1253(h)] (as in effect immediately before the effective date [April 1, 1997] of section 307 of division C of Public Law 104–208) or section 241(b)(3) [8 U.S.C.A. § 1251(b)(3)] of such Act (as amended by section 305(a) of division C of Public Law 104–208);

(iv) an alien is granted status as a Cuban and Haitian entrant (as defined in section 501(e) of the Refugee Education Assistance Act of 1980); or

(v) an alien is admitted to the United States as an Amerasian immigrant pursuant to section 584 of the Foreign Operations, Export Financing, and Related Programs Appropriations Act, 1988 (as contained in section 101(e) of Public Law 100–202 and amended by the 9th proviso under MIGRATION AND REFUGEE ASSISTANCE in title II of the Foreign Operations, Export Financing, and Related Programs Appropriations Act, 1989, Public Law 100–461, as amended).

(B) Certain permanent resident aliens

Paragraph (1) shall not apply to an alien who—

(i) is lawfully admitted to the United States for permanent residence under the Immigration and Nationality Act [8 U.S.C.A. § 1101 et seq.]; and

(ii) (I) has worked 40 qualifying quarters of coverage as defined under title II of the Social Security Act [42 U.S.C.A. § 401 et seq.] or can be credited with such qualifying quarters as provided under section 1645 of this title, and **(II)** in the case of any such qualifying quarter creditable for any period beginning after December 31, 1996, did not receive any Federal means-tested public benefit (as provided under section 1613 of this title) during any such period.

(C) Veteran and active duty exception

Paragraph (1) shall not apply to an alien who is lawfully residing in any State and is—

(i) a veteran (as defined in section 101, 1101, or 1301, or as described in section 107 of Title 38) with a discharge characterized as an honorable discharge and not on account of alienage and who fulfills the minimum active-duty service requirements of section 5303A(d) of title 38, United States Code,

(ii) on active duty (other than active duty for training) in the Armed Forces of the United States, or

(iii) the spouse or unmarried dependent child of an individual described in clause (i) or (ii) or the unremarried surviving spouse of an individual described in clause (i) or (ii) who is deceased if the marriage fulfills the requirements of section 1304 of title 38, United States Code.

(D) Transition for aliens currently receiving benefits

(i) SSI

(I) In general

With respect to the specified Federal program described in paragraph (3)(A), during the period beginning on August 22, 1996 and ending on September 30, 1998, the Commissioner of Social Security shall redetermine the eligibility of any individual who is receiving benefits under such program as of August 22, 1996 and whose eligibility for such benefits may terminate by reason of the provisions of this subsection.

(II) Redetermination criteria

With respect to any redetermination under subclause (I), the Commissioner of Social Security shall apply the eligibility criteria for new applicants for benefits under such program.

(III) Grandfather provision

The provisions of this subsection and the redetermination under subclause (I), shall only apply with respect to the benefits of an individual described in subclause (I) for months beginning on or after September 30, 1998.

(IV) Notice

Not later than March 31, 1997, the Commissioner of Social Security shall notify an individual described in subclause (I) of the provisions of this clause.

(ii) Food stamps

(I) In general

With respect to the specified Federal program described in paragraph (3)(B), ineligibility under paragraph (1) shall not apply until April 1, 1997, to an alien who received benefits under such program on August 22, 1996, unless such alien is determined to be ineligible to receive such benefits under the Food Stamp Act of 1977 [7 U.S.C.A. § 2011 et seq.]. The State agency shall recertify the eligibility of all such aliens during the period beginning April 1, 1997, and ending August 22, 1997.

(II) Recertification criteria

With respect to any recertification under subclause (I), the State agency shall apply the eligibility criteria for applicants for benefits under such program.

(III) Grandfather provision

The provisions of this subsection and the recertification under subclause (I) shall only apply with respect to the eligibility of an alien for a program for months beginning on or after the date of recertification, if on August 22, 1996 the alien is lawfully residing in any State and is receiving benefits under such program on August 22, 1996.

(E) Aliens receiving SSI on August 22, 1996

With respect to eligibility for benefits for the program defined in paragraph (3)(A) (relating to the supplemental security income program), paragraph (1) shall not apply to an alien who is lawfully residing in the United States and who was receiving such benefits on August 22, 1996.

(F) Disabled aliens lawfully residing in the United States on August 22, 1996

With respect to eligibility for benefits for the specified Federal programs described in paragraph (3), paragraph (1) shall not apply to an alien who—

(i) in the case of the specified Federal program described in paragraph (3)(A)—

(I) was lawfully residing in the United States on August 22, 1996; and

(II) is blind or disabled (as defined in paragraph (2) or (3) of section 1614(a) of the Social Security Act (42 U.S.C. 1382c(a))); and

(ii) in the case of the specified Federal program described in paragraph (3)(B), is receiving benefits or assistance for blindness or disability (within the meaning of section 3(j) of the Food Stamp Act of 1977 (7 U.S.C.A. § 2012(j))).

(G) Exception for certain Indians

With respect to eligibility for benefits for the specified Federal programs defined in paragraph (3), section 1611(a) of this title [8 U.S.C.A. § 1611(a)] and paragraph (1) shall not apply to any individual—

(i) who is an American Indian born in Canada to whom the provisions of section 1359 of this title [INA § 289] apply; or

(ii) who is a member of an Indian tribe (as defined in section 450b(e) of Title 25).

(H) SSI exception for certain recipients on the basis of very old applications

With respect to eligibility for benefits for the program defined in paragraph (3)(A) (relating to the supplemental security income program), paragraph (1) shall not apply to any individual—

(i) who is receiving benefits under such program for months after July 1996 on the basis of an application filed before January 1, 1979; and

(ii) with respect to whom the Commissioner of Social Security lacks clear and convincing evidence that such individual is an alien ineligible for such benefits as a result of the application of this section.

(I) Food stamp exception for certain elderly individuals

With respect to eligibility for benefits for the specified Federal program described in paragraph (3)(B), paragraph (1) shall not apply to any individual who on August 22, 1996—

(i) was lawfully residing in the United States; and

(ii) was 65 years of age or older.

(J) Food stamp exception for certain children

With respect to eligibility for benefits for the specified Federal program described in paragraph (3)(B), paragraph (1) shall not apply to any individual who is under 18 years of age.

(K) Food stamp exception for certain Hmong and Highland Laotians

With respect to eligibility for benefits for the specified Federal program described in paragraph (3)(B), paragraph (1) shall not apply to—

(i) any individual who—

(I) is lawfully residing in the United States; and

(II) was a member of a Hmong or Highland Laotian tribe at the time that the tribe rendered assistance to United States personnel by taking part in a military or rescue operation during the Vietnam era (as defined in section 101 of Title 38);

(ii) the spouse, or an unmarried dependent child, of such an individual; or

(iii) the unremarried surviving spouse of such an individual who is deceased.

(L) Food stamp exception for certain qualified aliens

With respect to eligibility for benefits for the specified Federal program described in paragraph (3)(B), paragraph (1) shall not apply to any qualified alien who has resided in the United States with a status within the meaning of the term "qualified alien" for a period of 5 years or more beginning on the date of the alien's entry into the United States.

(M) SSI extensions through fiscal year 2001

(i) Two-year extension for certain aliens and victims of trafficking

(I) In general

Subject to clause (ii), with respect to eligibility for benefits under subparagraph (A) for the specified Federal program described in paragraph (3)(A) of qualified aliens (as defined in section 431(b)) and victims of trafficking in persons (as defined in section 107(b)(1)(C) of division A of the Victims of Trafficking and Violence Protection Act of 2000 (Public Law 106–386) or as granted status under section 101(a)(15)(T)(ii) of the Immigration and Nationality Act), the 7–year period described in subparagraph (A) shall be deemed to be a 9–year period during fiscal years 2009 through 2011 in the case of such a qualified alien or victim of trafficking who furnishes to the Commissioner of Social Security the declaration required under subclause (IV) (if applicable) and is described in subclause (III).

(II) Aliens and victims whose benefits ceased in prior fiscal years

Subject to clause (ii), beginning on the date of the enactment of the SSI Extension for Elderly and Disabled Refugees Act, any qualified alien (as defined in section 431(b)) or victim of trafficking in persons (as defined in section 107(b)(1)(C) of division A of the Victims of Trafficking and Violence Protection Act of 2000 (Public Law 106–386) or as granted status under section 101(a)(15)(T)(ii) of the Immigration and Nationality Act) rendered ineligible for the specified Federal program described in paragraph (3)(A) during the period beginning on August 22, 1996, and ending on September 30, 2008, solely by reason of the termination of the 7–year period described in subparagraph (A) shall be eligible for such program for an additional 2–year period in accordance with this clause, if such qualified alien or victim of trafficking meets all other eligibility factors under title XVI of the Social Security Act, furnishes to the Commissioner of Social Security the declaration required under subclause (IV) (if applicable), and is described in subclause (III).

(III) Aliens and victims described

For purposes of subclauses (I) and (II), a qualified alien or victim of trafficking described in this subclause is an alien or victim who—

(aa) has been a lawful permanent resident for less than 6 years and such status has not been abandoned, rescinded under section 246 of the Immigration and Nationality Act, or terminated through removal proceedings under section 240 of the Immigration and Nationality Act, and the Commissioner of Social Security has verified such status, through procedures established in consultation with the Secretary of Homeland Security;

(bb) has filed an application, within 4 years from the date the alien or victim began receiving supplemental security income benefits, to become a lawful permanent resident with the Secretary of Homeland Security, and the Commissioner of Social Security has verified, through procedures established in consultation with such Secretary, that such application is pending;

(cc) has been granted the status of Cuban and Haitian entrant, as defined in section 501(e) of the Refugee Education Assistance Act of 1980 (Public Law 96–422), for purposes of the specified Federal program described in paragraph (3)(A);

(dd) has had his or her deportation withheld by the Secretary of Homeland Security under section 243(h) of the Immigration and Nationality Act (as in effect immediately before the effective date of section 307 of division C of Public Law 104–208), or whose removal is withheld under section 241(b)(3) of such Act;

(ee) has not attained age 18; or

(ff) has attained age 70.

(IV) Declaration required

(aa) In general

For purposes of subclauses (I) and (II), the declaration required under this subclause of a qualified alien or victim of trafficking described in either such subclause is a declaration under penalty of perjury stating that the alien or victim has made a good faith effort to pursue United States citizenship, as determined by the Secretary of Homeland Security. The Commissioner of Social Security shall develop criteria as needed, in consultation with the Secretary of Homeland Security, for consideration of such declarations.

(bb) Exception for children

A qualified alien or victim of trafficking described in subclause (I) or (II) who has not attained age 18 shall not be required to furnish to the Commissioner of Social Security a declaration described in item (aa) as a condition of being eligible for the specified Federal program described in paragraph (3)(A) for an additional 2–year period in accordance with this clause.

(V) Payment of benefits to aliens whose benefits ceased in prior fiscal years

Benefits paid to a qualified alien or victim described in subclause (II) shall be paid prospectively over the duration of the qualified alien's or victim's renewed eligibility.

(ii) Special rule in case of pending or approved naturalization application

With respect to eligibility for benefits for the specified program described in paragraph (3)(A), paragraph (1) shall not apply during fiscal years 2009 through 2011 to an alien described in one of clauses (i) through (v) of subparagraph (A) or a victim of trafficking in persons (as defined in section 107(b)(1)(C) of division A of the Victims of Trafficking and Violence Protection Act of 2000 (Public Law 106–386) or as granted status under section 101(a)(15)(T)(ii) of the Immigration and Nationality Act), if such alien or victim (including any such alien or victim rendered ineligible for the specified Federal program described in paragraph (3)(A) during the period beginning on August 22, 1996, and ending on September 30, 2008, solely by reason of the termination of the 7–year period described in subparagraph (A)) has filed an application for naturalization that is pending before the Secretary of Homeland Security or a United States district court based on section 336(b) of the Immigration and Nationality Act, or has been approved for naturalization but not yet sworn in as a United States citizen, and the Commissioner of Social Security has verified, through procedures established in consultation with the Secretary of Homeland Security, that such application is pending or has been approved.

(3) Specified Federal program defined

For purposes of this chapter, the term "specified Federal program" means any of the following:

(A) SSI

The supplemental security income program under title XVI of the Social Security Act [42 U.S.C.A. § 1381 et seq.], including supplementary payments pursuant to an agreement for Federal administration under section 1616(a) of the Social Security Act [42 U.S.C.A. § 1382e(a)] and payments pursuant to an agreement entered into under section 212(b) of Public Law 93–66.

(B) Food stamps

The food stamp program as defined in section 3(*l*) of the Food Stamp Act of 1977 [7 U.S.C.A. § 2012(*l*)].

(b) Limited eligibility for designated Federal programs

(1) In general

Notwithstanding any other provision of law and except as provided in section 1613 of this title and paragraph (2), a State is authorized to determine the eligibility of an alien who is a qualified alien (as defined in section 1641 of this title) for any designated Federal program (as defined in paragraph (3)).

(2) Exceptions

Qualified aliens under this paragraph shall be eligible for any designated Federal program.

(A) Time-limited exception for refugees and asylees

(i) Medicaid

With respect to the designated Federal program described in paragraph (3)(C), paragraph (1) shall not apply to an alien until 7 years after the date—

(I) an alien is admitted to the United States as a refugee under section 207 of the Immigration and Nationality Act [8 U.S.C.A. § 1157];

(II) an alien is granted asylum under section 208 of such Act [8 U.S.C.A. § 1158];

(III) an alien's deportation is withheld under section 243 of such Act [8 U.S.C.A. § 1253(h)] (as in effect immediately before the effective date [April 1, 1997] of section 307 of division C of Public Law 104–208) or section 241(b)(3) of such Act [8 U.S.C.A. § 1251(b)(3)](as amended by section 305(a) of division C of Public Law 104–208);

(IV) an alien is granted status as a Cuban and Haitian entrant (as defined in section 501(e) of the Refugee Education Assistance Act of 1980); or

(V) an alien admitted to the United States as an Amerasian immigrant as described in subsection (a)(2)(A)(i)(V) until 5 years after the date of such alien's entry into the United States.

(ii) Other designated Federal programs

With respect to the designated Federal programs under paragraph (3) (other than subparagraph (C)), paragraph (1) shall not apply to an alien until 5 years after the date—

(I) an alien is admitted to the United States as a refugee under section 207 of the Immigration and Nationality Act [8 U.S.C.A. § 1157];

(II) an alien is granted asylum under section 208 of such Act [8 U.S.C.A. § 1158];

(III) an alien's deportation is withheld under section 243(h) of such Act [8 U.S.C.A. § 1253(h)] (as in effect immediately before the effective date [April 1, 1997] of section 307 of division C of Public Law 104–208) or section 241(b)(3) of such Act [8 U.S.C.A. § 1251(b)(3)] (as amended by section 305(a) of division C of Public Law 104–208);

(IV) an alien is granted status as a Cuban and Haitian entrant (as defined in section 501(e) of the Refugee Education Assistance Act of 1980); or

(V) an alien admitted to the United States as an Amerasian immigrant as described in subsection (a)(2)(A)(i)(V) until 5 years after the date of such alien's entry into the United States.

(B) Certain permanent resident aliens

An alien who—

(i) is lawfully admitted to the United States for permanent residence under the Immigration and Nationality Act [8 U.S.C.A. § 1101 et seq.]; and

(ii)(I) has worked 40 qualifying quarters of coverage as defined under title II of the Social Security Act [42 U.S.C.A. § 401 et seq.] or can be credited with such qualifying quarters as provided under section 1645 of this title, and **(II)** in the case of any such qualifying quarter creditable for any period beginning after December 31, 1996, did not receive any Federal means-tested public benefit (as provided under section 1613 of this title) during any such period.

(C) Veteran and active duty exception

An alien who is lawfully residing in any State and is—

(i) a veteran (as defined in section 101, 1101, or 1301, or as described in section 107 of Title 38) with a discharge characterized as an honorable discharge and not on account of alienage, and who fulfills the minimum active-duty service requirements of section 5303A(d) of title 38, United States Code

(ii) on active duty (other than active duty for training) in the Armed Forces of the United States, or

(iii) the spouse or unmarried dependent child of an individual described in clause (i) or (ii) or the unremarried surviving spouse of an individual described in clause (i) or (ii) who is deceased if the marriage fulfills the requirements of section 1304 of title 38, United States Code.

(D) Transition for those currently receiving benefits

An alien who on August 22, 1996 is lawfully residing in any State and is receiving benefits under such program on August 22, 1996 shall continue to be eligible to receive such benefits until January 1, 1997.

(E) Medicaid exception for certain Indians

With respect to eligibility for benefits for the program defined in paragraph (3)(C) (relating to the medicaid program), section 1611(a) of this title [8 U.S.C.A. § 1611(a)] and paragraph (1) shall not apply to any individual described in subsection (a)(2)(G) of this section.

(F) Medicaid exception for aliens receiving SSI

An alien who is receiving benefits under the program defined in subsection (a)(3)(A) of this section (relating to the supplemental security income program) shall be eligible for medical assistance under a State plan under title XIX of the Social Security Act (42 U.S.C. § 1396 et seq.) under the same terms and conditions that apply to other recipients of benefits under the program defined in such subsection.

(3) "Designated Federal program" defined

For purposes of this title, the term "designated Federal program" means any of the following:

(A) Temporary assistance for needy families

The program of block grants to States for temporary assistance for needy families under part A of title IV of the Social Security Act [42 U.S.C.A. § 601 et seq.].

(B) Social services block grant

The program of block grants to States for social services under title XX of the Social Security Act [42 U.S.C.A. § 1397 et seq.].

(C) Medicaid

A State plan approved under title XIX of the Social Security Act [42 U.S.C.A. § 1396 et seq.], other than medical assistance described in section 1611(b)(1)(A) of this title.

(Pub.L. 104–193, Title IV, § 402, Aug. 22, 1996, 110 Stat. 2262; Pub.L. 104–208, Div. C, Title V, § 510, Sept. 30, 1996, 110 Stat. 3009–673; Pub.L. 105–18, Title II, § 6005, June 12, 1997, 111 Stat. 191; Pub.L. 105–33, Title V, §§ 5301, 5302(a), (b), 5303(a), (b), 5304, 5305(b), 5306(a), (b), 5562, 5563, Aug. 5, 1997, 111 Stat. 597, 598, 600, 601, 602, 638, 639; Pub.L. 105–185, Title V, §§ 503–508, June 23, 1998, 112 Stat. 578, 579; May 13, 2002, Pub.L. 107–171, Title IV, subtitle D, § 4401; Pub.L. 110–328, § 2, Sept. 30, 2008, 122 Stat. 3567; Pub.L. 110–234, Title IV, § 4115(c)(2)(D), May 22, 2008, 122 Stat. 1110; Pub.L. 110–246, Title IV, § 4115(c)(2)(D), June 18, 2008, 122 Stat. 1871.)

§ 403. Five-year limited eligibility of qualified aliens for Federal means-tested public benefit [8 U.S.C.A. § 1613]

(a) In general

Notwithstanding any other provision of law and except as provided in subsections (b), (c), and (d) of this section, an alien who is a qualified alien (as defined in section 1641 of this title) and who enters the United States on or after August 22, 1996 is not eligible for any Federal means-tested public benefit for a period of 5 years beginning on the date of the alien's entry into the United States with a status within the meaning of the term "qualified alien".

(b) Exceptions

The limitation under subsection (a) of this section shall not apply to the following aliens:

(1) Exception for refugees and asylees

(A) An alien who is admitted to the United States as a refugee under section 207 of the Immigration and Nationality Act [8 U.S.C.A. § 1157].

(B) An alien who is granted asylum under section 208 of such Act [8 U.S.C.A. § 1158].

(C) An alien whose deportation is being withheld under section 243(h) of such Act [8 U.S.C.A. § 1253(h)] (as in effect immediately before the effective date [April 1, 1997] of section 307 of division C of Public Law 104–208) or section 241(b)(3) of such Act [8 U.S.C.A. § 1251(b)(3)] (as amended by section 305(a) of division C of Public Law 104–208).

(D) An alien who is a Cuban and Haitian entrant as defined in section 501(e) of the Refugee Education Assistance Act of 1980.

(E) An alien admitted to the United States as an Amerasian immigrant as described in section 1612(a)(2)(A)(i)(V) of this title [8 U.S.C.A. § 1612(a)(2)(A)(i)(V)].

(2) Veteran and active duty exception

An alien who is lawfully residing in any State and is—

(A) a veteran (as defined in section 101, 1101, or 1301, or as described in section 107 of Title 38) with a discharge characterized as an honorable discharge and not on account of alienage and who fulfills the minimum active-duty service requirements of section 5303A(d) of title 38, United States Code.

(B) on active duty (other than active duty for training) in the Armed Forces of the United States, or

(C) the spouse or unmarried dependent child of an individual described in subparagraph (A) or (B) or the unremarried surviving spouse of an individual described in clause (i) or (ii) who is deceased if the marriage fulfills the requirements of section 1304 of title 38, United States Code.

(c) Application of term Federal means-tested public benefit

(1) The limitation under subsection (a) of this section shall not apply to assistance or benefits under paragraph (2).

(2) Assistance and benefits under this paragraph are as follows:

(A) Medical assistance described in section 1611(b)(1)(A) of this title.

(B) Short-term, non-cash, in-kind emergency disaster relief.

(C) Assistance or benefits under the Richard B. Russell National School Lunch Act [42 U.S.C.A. § 1751 et seq.].

(D) Assistance or benefits under the Child Nutrition Act of 1966 [42 U.S.C.A. § 1771 et seq.].

(E) Public health assistance (not including any assistance under title XIX of the Social Security Act [42 U.S.C.A. § 1396 et seq.]) for immunizations with respect to immunizable diseases and for testing and treatment of symptoms of communicable diseases whether or not such symptoms are caused by a communicable disease.

(F) Payments for foster care and adoption assistance under parts B and E of title IV of the Social Security Act [42 U.S.C.A. § 620 et seq. and § 670 et seq.] for a parent or a child who would, in the absence of subsection (a) of this section, be eligible to have such payments made on the child's behalf under such part, but only if the foster or adoptive parent (or parents) of such child is a qualified alien (as defined in section 1641 of this title [8 U.S.C.A. § 1641]).

(G) Programs, services, or assistance (such as soup kitchens, crisis counseling and intervention, and short-term shelter) specified by the Attorney General, in the Attorney General's sole and unreviewable discretion after consultation with appropriate Federal agencies and departments, which (i) deliver in-kind services at the community level, including through public or private nonprofit agencies; (ii) do not condition the provision of assistance, the amount of assistance provided, or the cost of assistance provided on the individual recipient's income or resources; and (iii) are necessary for the protection of life or safety.

(H) Programs of student assistance under titles IV, V, IX, and X of the Higher Education Act of 1965 [20 U.S.C.A. § 1070 et seq., § 1101 et seq., § 1134 et seq., and § 1135 et seq.], and titles III, VII, and VIII of the Public Health Service Act [42 U.S.C.A. § 241 et seq., § 292 et seq., and § 296 et seq.].

(I) Means-tested programs under the Elementary and Secondary Education Act of 1965 [20 U.S.C.A. § 6301 et seq.].

(J) Benefits under the Head Start Act [42 U.S.C.A. § 9831 et seq.].

(K) Benefits under the Job Training Partnership Act or title I of the Workforce Investment Act of 1998 [29 U.S.C.A. § 2801 et seq.].

(L) Assistance or benefits provided to individuals under the age of 18 under the Food Stamp Act of 1977 (7 U.S.C. 2011 et seq.).

(d) Benefits for certain groups

Notwithstanding any other provision of law, the limitations under section 1611(a) of this title and subsection (a) of this section shall not apply to—

(1) an individual described in section 1612(a)(2)(G) of this title [8 U.S.C.A. § 1612(a)(2)(G)], but only with respect to the programs specified in subsections (a)(3) and (b)(3)(C) of section 1612 of this title [8 U.S.C.A. § 1612]; or

(2) an individual, spouse, or dependent described in section 1612(a)(2)(K) of this title [8 U.S.C.A. § 1612(a)(2)(K)], but only with respect to the specified Federal program described in section 1612(a)(3)(B) of this title [8 U.S.C.A. § 1612(a)(3)(B)].

(Pub.L. 104–193, Title IV, § 403, Aug. 22, 1996, 110 Stat. 2265; Pub.L. 105–33, Title V, §§ 5302(c)(1), 5303(c), 5306(c), 5562, 5563(a), (b), Aug. 5, 1997, 111 Stat. 638, 639, 599, 600, 602; Pub.L. 105–185, Title V, § 509, June 23, 1998, 112 Stat. 580; Pub.L. 105–277, Div. A, § 101(f) [Title VIII, § 405(d)(3)(A)], Oct. 21, 1998, 112 Stat. 2681–419; Oct. 22, 1999, Pub.L. 106–78, Title VII, § 752(b)(6), 113 Stat. 1169; May 13, 2002, Pub.L. 107–171, Title IV, subtitle D, § 4401.)

§ 404(a). Notification and information reporting [8 U.S.C.A. § 1614]

Each Federal agency that administers a program to which section 1611, 1612 or 1613 of this title [8 U.S.C.A. § 1611, 1612 or 1613] applies shall, directly or through the States, post information and provide general notification to the public and to program recipients of the changes regarding eligibility for any such program pursuant to this subchapter.

(Pub.L. 104–193, Title IV, § 404(a), Aug. 22, 1996, 110 Stat. 2267.)

§ 411. Aliens who are not qualified aliens or nonimmigrants ineligible for State and local public benefits [8 U.S.C.A. § 1621]

[For the text of PRWORA § 411, 8 U.S.C.A. § 1621, see Title 8, U.S. Code, Aliens and Nationality: Selected Sections Not Codified in the Immigration and Nationality Act, earlier in Part II (Additional Statutes) of this Supplement.—eds.]

§ 412. State authority to limit eligibility of qualified aliens for State public benefits [8 U.S.C.A. § 1622]

(a) In general

Notwithstanding any other provision of law and except as provided in subsection (b) of this section, a State is authorized to determine the eligibility for any State public benefits of an alien who is a qualified alien (as defined in section 1641 of this title [8 U.S.C.A. § 1641]), a nonimmigrant under the Immigration and Nationality Act [8 U.S.C.A. § 1101 et seq.] or an alien who is paroled into the United States under section 212(d)(5) of such Act [8 U.S.C.A. § 1182(d)(5)] for less than one year.

(b) Exceptions

Qualified aliens under this subsection shall be eligible for any State public benefits.

(1) Time-limited exception for refugees and asylees

(A) An alien who is admitted to the United States as a refugee under section 207 of the Immigration and Nationality Act [8 U.S.C.A. § 1157] until 5 years after the date of an alien's entry into the United States.

(B) An alien who is granted asylum under section 208 of such Act [8 U.S.C.A. § 1158] until 5 years after the date of such grant of asylum.

(C) An alien whose deportation is being withheld under section 243(h) of such Act [8 U.S.C.A. § 1253(h)] (as in effect immediately before the effective date [April 1, 1997] of section 307 of division C of Public Law 104–208) or section 241(b)(3) of such Act [8 U.S.C.A. § 1251(b)(3)] (as amended by section 305(a) of division C of Public Law 104–208) until 5 years after such withholding.

(D) An alien who is a Cuban and Haitian entrant as defined in section 501(e) of the Refugee Education Assistance Act of 1980 until 5 years after the alien is granted such status.

(E) An alien admitted to the United States as an Amerasian immigrant as described in section 1612(a)(2)(A)(i)(V) of this title [8 U.S.C.A. § 1612(a)(2)(A)(i)(V)].

(2) Certain permanent resident aliens

An alien who—

(A) is lawfully admitted to the United States for permanent residence under the Immigration and Nationality Act [8 U.S.C.A. § 1101 et seq.]; and

(B)(i) has worked 40 qualifying quarters of coverage as defined under title II of the Social Security Act [42 U.S.C.A. § 401 et seq.] or can be credited with such qualifying quarters as provided under section 1645 of this title [8 U.S.C.A. § 1645], and **(ii)** in the case of any such qualifying quarter creditable for any period beginning after December 31, 1996, did not receive any Federal means-tested public benefit (as provided under section 1613 of this title [8 U.S.C.A. § 1613]) during any such period.

(3) Veteran and active duty exception

An alien who is lawfully residing in any State and is—

(A) a veteran (as defined in section 101, 1101, or 1301, or as described in section 107 of Title 38) with a discharge characterized as an honorable discharge and not on account of alienage and who fulfills the minimum active-duty service requirements of section 5303A(d) of title 38, United States Code,

(B) on active duty (other than active duty for training) in the Armed Forces of the United States, or

(C) the spouse or unmarried dependent child of an individual described in subparagraph (A) or (B) or the unremarried surviving spouse of an individual described in clause (i) or (ii) who is deceased if the marriage fulfills the requirements of section 1304 of title 38, United States Code.

(4) Transition for those currently receiving benefits

An alien who on August 22, 1996 is lawfully residing in any State and is receiving benefits on August 22, 1996 shall continue to be eligible to receive such benefits until January 1, 1997.

(Pub.L. 104–193, Title IV, § 412, Aug. 22, 1996, 110 Stat. 2269; Pub.L. 105–33, Title V, §§ 5302(c)(2), 5306(d), 5562, 5563, 5581(b)(3), Aug. 5, 1997, 111 Stat. 599, 602, 638, 639, 643.)

§ 421. Federal attribution of sponsor's income and resources to alien [8 U.S.C.A. § 1631]

(a) In general

Notwithstanding any other provision of law, in determining the eligibility and the amount of benefits of an alien for any Federal means-tested public benefits program (as provided under section 1613 of this title [8 U.S.C.A. § 1613]), the income and resources of the alien shall be deemed to include the following:

(1) The income and resources of any person who executed an affidavit of support pursuant to section 213A of the Immigration and Nationality Act [8 U.S.C.A. § 1183a] (as added by section 423) and as amended by section 551(a) of the Illegal Immigration Reform and Immigrant Responsibility Act of 1996 on behalf of such alien.

(2) The income and resources of the spouse (if any) of the person.

(b) Duration of attribution period

Subsection (a) of this section shall apply with respect to an alien until such time as the alien—

(1) achieves United States citizenship through naturalization pursuant to chapter 2 of title III of the Immigration and Nationality Act [8 U.S.C.A. § 1421 et seq.]; or

(2)(A) has worked 40 qualifying quarters of coverage as defined under title II of the Social Security Act [42 U.S.C.A. § 401 et seq.] or can be credited with such qualifying quarters as provided under section 1645 of this title [8 U.S.C.A. § 1645], and **(B)** in the case of any such qualifying quarter creditable for any period beginning after December 31, 1996, did not receive any Federal means-tested public benefit (as provided under section 1613 of this title [8 U.S.C.A. § 1613]) during any such period.

(c) Review of income and resources of alien upon reapplication

Whenever an alien is required to reapply for benefits under any Federal means-tested public benefits program, the applicable agency shall review the income and resources attributed to the alien under subsection (a) of this section.

(d) Application

(1) If on August 22, 1996, a Federal means-tested public benefits program attributes a sponsor's income and resources to an alien in determining the alien's eligibility and the amount of benefits for an alien, this section shall apply to any such determination beginning on the day after August 22, 1996.

(2) If on August 22, 1996, a Federal means-tested public benefits program does not attribute a sponsor's income and resources to an alien in determining the alien's eligibility and the amount of benefits for an alien, this section shall apply to any such determination beginning 180 days after August 22, 1996.

(3) This section shall not apply to assistance or benefits under the Food Stamp Act of 1977 (7 U.S.C. 2011 et seq.) to the extent that a qualified alien is eligible under section 402(a)(2)(J).

(e) Indigence exception

(1) In general

For an alien for whom an affidavit of support under section 213A of the Immigration and Nationality Act [8 U.S.C.A. § 1183a] has been executed, if a determination described in paragraph (2) is made, the amount of income and resources of the sponsor or the sponsor's spouse which shall be attributed to the sponsored alien shall not exceed the amount actually provided for a period beginning on the date of such determination and ending 12 months after such date.

(2) Determination described

A determination described in this paragraph is a determination by an agency that a sponsored alien would, in the absence of the assistance provided by the agency, be unable to obtain food and shelter, taking into account the alien's own income, plus any cash, food, housing, or other assistance provided by other individuals, including the sponsor. The agency shall notify the Attorney General of each such determination, including the names of the sponsor and the sponsored alien involved.

(f) Special rule for battered spouse and child

(1) In general

Subject to paragraph (2) and notwithstanding any other provision of this section, subsection (a) of this section shall not apply to benefits—

(A) during a 12 month period if the alien demonstrates that **(i)** the alien has been battered or subjected to extreme cruelty in the United States by a spouse or a parent, or by a member of the spouse or parent's family residing in the same household as the alien and the spouse or parent consented to or acquiesced to such battery or cruelty, **(ii)** the alien's child has been battered or subjected to extreme cruelty in the United States by the spouse or parent of the alien (without the active participation of the alien in the battery or cruelty), or by a member of the spouse's or parent's family residing in the same household as the alien when the spouse or parent consented or acquiesced to and the alien did not actively participate in such battery or cruelty, or **(iii)** the alien is a child whose parent (who resides in the same household as the alien child) has been battered or subjected to extreme cruelty in the United States by that parent's spouse, or by a member of the spouse's family residing in the same household as the parent and the spouse consented to, or acquiesced in, such battery or cruelty, and the battery or cruelty described in clause (i), (ii), or (iii) (in the opinion of the agency providing such public benefits, which opinion is not subject to review by any court) has a substantial connection to the need for the public benefits applied for; and

(B) after a 12 month period (regarding the batterer's income and resources only) if the alien demonstrates that such battery or cruelty under subparagraph (A) has been recognized in an order of a judge or administrative law judge or a prior determination of the Immigration and Naturalization Service, and that such battery or cruelty (in the opinion of the agency providing such public benefits, which opinion is not subject to review by any court) has a substantial connection to the need for the benefits.

(2) Limitation

The exception under paragraph (1) shall not apply to benefits for an alien during any period in which the individual responsible for such battery or cruelty resides in the same household or family eligibility unit as the individual who was subjected to such battery or cruelty.

(Pub.L. 104–193, Title IV, § 421, Aug. 22, 1996, 110 Stat. 2270; Pub.L. 104–208, Div. C, Title V, §§ 551(b)(1), 552, Sept. 30, 1996, 110 Stat. 3009–679, 3009–680; Pub.L. 105–33, Title V, § 5571(d), Aug. 5, 1997, 111 Stat. 641; May 13, 2002, Pub.L. 107–171, Title IV, subtitle D, § 4401, 116 Stat. 333.)

§ 422. Authority for States to provide for attribution of sponsors income and resources to the alien with respect to State programs [8 U.S.C.A. § 1632]

(a) Optional application to State programs

Except as provided in subsection (b) of this section, in determining the eligibility and the amount of benefits of an alien for any State public benefits, the State or political subdivision that offers the benefits is authorized to provide that the income and resources of the alien shall be deemed to include—

(1) the income and resources of any individual who executed an affidavit of support pursuant to section 1183a of this title [INA § 213A, 8 U.S.C.A. § 1183a] and as amended by section 551(a) of the Illegal Immigration Reform and Immigrant Responsibility Act of 1996 on behalf of such alien, and

(2) the income and resources of the spouse (if any) of the individual.

(b) Exceptions

Subsection (a) of this section shall not apply with respect to the following State public benefits:

(1) Assistance described in section 1621(b)(1) of this title [8 U.S.C.A. § 1621(b)(1)].

(2) Short-term, non-cash, in-kind emergency disaster relief.

(3) Programs comparable to assistance or benefits under the Richard B. Russell National School Lunch Act [42 U.S.C.A. § 1751 et seq.].

(4) Programs comparable to assistance or benefits under the Child Nutrition Act of 1966 [42 U.S.C.A. § 1771 et seq.].

(5) Public health assistance for immunizations with respect to immunizable diseases and for testing and treatment of symptoms of communicable diseases whether or not such symptoms are caused by a communicable disease.

(6) Payments for foster care and adoption assistance.

(7) Programs, services, or assistance (such as soup kitchens, crisis counseling and intervention, and short-term shelter) specified by the Attorney General of a State, after consultation with appropriate agencies and departments, which **(A)** deliver in-kind services at the community level, including through public or private nonprofit agencies; **(B)** do not condition the provision of assistance, the amount of assistance provided, or the cost of assistance provided on the individual recipient's income or resources; and **(C)** are necessary for the protection of life or safety.

(Pub.L. 104–193, Title IV, § 422, Aug. 22, 1996, 110 Stat. 2271; Pub.L. 104–208, Div. C, Title V, § 551(b)(1), Sept. 30, 1996, 110 Stat. 3009–679; Pub.L. 105–33, Title V, § 5581(b)(2), Aug. 5, 1997, 111 Stat. 643; Oct. 22, 1999, Pub.L. 106–78, Title VII, § 752(b)(6), 113 Stat. 1169.)

§ 431. Definitions [8 U.S.C.A. § 1641]

(a) In general

Except as otherwise provided in this chapter, the terms used in this chapter have the same meaning given such terms in section 101(a) of the Immigration and Nationality Act [8 U.S.C.A. § 1101(a)].

(b) Qualified alien

For purposes of this chapter, the term "qualified alien" means an alien who, at the time the alien applies for, receives, or attempts to receive a Federal public benefit, is—

(1) an alien who is lawfully admitted for permanent residence under the Immigration and Nationality Act [8 U.S.C.A. § 1101 et seq.],

(2) an alien who is granted asylum under section 208 of such Act [8 U.S.C.A. § 1158],

(3) a refugee who is admitted to the United States under section 207 of such Act [8 U.S.C.A. § 1157],

(4) an alien who is paroled into the United States under section 212(d)(5) of such Act [8 U.S.C.A. § 1182(d)(5)] for a period of at least 1 year,

(5) an alien whose deportation is being withheld under section 243(h) of such Act [8 U.S.C.A. § 1253(h)] (as in effect immediately before the effective date [April 1, 1997] of section 307 of division C of Public Law 104–208) or section 241(b)(3) of such Act [8 U.S.C.A. § 1251(b)(3)] (as amended by section 305(a) of division C of Public Law 104–208).

(6) an alien who is granted conditional entry pursuant to section 203(a)(7) of such Act as in effect prior to April 1, 1980 [8 U.S.C.A. § 1153(a)(7)]; or

(7) an alien who is a Cuban and Haitian entrant (as defined in section 501(e) of the Refugee Education Assistance Act of 1980).

(c) Treatment of certain battered aliens as qualified aliens

For purposes of this chapter, the term "qualified alien" includes—

(1) an alien who—

(A) has been battered or subjected to extreme cruelty in the United States by a spouse or a parent, or by a member of the spouse or parent's family residing in the same household as the alien and the spouse or parent consented to, or acquiesced in, such battery or cruelty, but only if (in the opinion of the agency providing such benefits) there is a substantial connection between such battery or cruelty and the need for the benefits to be provided; and

(B) has been approved or has a petition pending which sets forth a prima facie case for—

(i) status as a spouse or a child of a United States citizen pursuant to clause (ii), (iii), or (iv) of section 204(a)(1)(A) of the Immigration and Nationality Act [8 U.S.C.A. § 1154(a)(1)(A)(ii), (iii) or (iv)],

(ii) classification pursuant to clause (ii) or (iii) of section 204(a)(1)(B) of the Act [8 U.S.C.A. § 1154(a)(1)(B)(ii) or (iii)],

(iii) suspension of deportation under section 244(a)(3) of the Immigration and Nationality Act (as in effect before the title III–A effective date in section 309 of the Illegal Immigration Reform and Immigrant Responsibility Act of 1996),

(iv) status as a spouse or child of a United States citizen pursuant to clause (i) of section 204(a)(1)(A) of such Act [8 U.S.C.A. § 1154(a)(1)(A)(i)], or classification pursuant to clause (i) of section 204(a)(1)(B) of such Act [8 U.S.C.A. § 1154(a)(1)(B)(i)];

(v) cancellation of removal pursuant to section 1229b(b)(2) of this title [INA § 240A(b)(2), 8 U.S.C.A. § 1229b(b)(2)];

(2) an alien—

(A) whose child has been battered or subjected to extreme cruelty in the United States by a spouse or a parent of the alien (without the active participation of the alien in the battery or cruelty), or by a member of the spouse or parent's family residing in the same household as the alien and the spouse or parent consented or acquiesced to such battery or cruelty, and the alien did not actively participate in such battery or cruelty, but only if (in the opinion of the agency providing such benefits) there is a substantial connection between such battery or cruelty and the need for the benefits to be provided; and

(B) who meets the requirement of subparagraph (B) of paragraph (1);

(3) an alien child who—

(A) resides in the same household as a parent who has been battered or subjected to extreme cruelty in the United States by that parent's spouse or by a member of the spouse's family residing in the same household as the parent and the spouse consented or acquiesced to such battery or cruelty, but only if (in the opinion of the agency providing such benefits) there is a substantial connection between such battery or cruelty and the need for the benefits to be provided; and

(B) who meets the requirement of subparagraph (B) of paragraph (1); or

(4) an alien who has been granted nonimmigrant status under section 101(a)(15)(T) of the Immigration and Nationality Act [8 U.S.C.A. § 1101(a)(15)(T)] or who has a pending application that sets forth a prima facie case for eligibility for such nonimmigrant status.

This subsection shall not apply to an alien during any period in which the individual responsible for such battery or cruelty resides in the same household or family eligibility unit as the individual subjected to such battery or cruelty.

After consultation with the Secretaries of Health and Human Services, Agriculture, and Housing and Urban Development, the Commissioner of Social Security, and with the heads of such Federal agencies administering benefits as the Attorney General considers appropriate, the Attorney General shall issue guidance (in the Attorney General's sole and unreviewable discretion) for purposes of this subsection and section 1631(f) of this title [8 U.S.C.A. § 1631(f)], concerning the meaning of the terms "battery" and "extreme cruelty", and the standards and methods to be used for determining whether a substantial connection exists between battery or cruelty suffered and an individual's need for benefits under a specific Federal, State, or local program.

(Pub.L. 104–193, Title IV, § 431, Aug. 22, 1996, 110 Stat. 2274; Pub.L. 104–208, Div. C, Title III, § 308(g)(8)(E), Title V, § 501, Sept. 30, 1996, 110 Stat. 3009–624, 3009–670; Pub.L. 105–33, Title V, §§ 5302(c)(3), 5562, 5571(a) to (c), 5581(b)(6), (7), Aug. 5, 1997, 111 Stat. 599, 638, 640, 643; Oct. 28, 2000, Pub.L. 106–386, Div. B, Title V, § 1508, 114 Stat. 1477, 1530; Pub.L. 110–457, Title II, § 211(a), Dec. 23, 2008, 122 Stat. 5063.)

§ 432. Verification of eligibility for Federal public benefits [8 U.S.C.A. § 1642]

(a) In general

(1) Not later than 18 months after August 22, 1996, the Attorney General of the United States, after consultation with the Secretary of Health and Human Services, shall promulgate regulations requiring verification that a person applying for a Federal public benefit (as defined in section 1611(c) of this title), to which the limitation under section 1611 of this title [8 U.S.C.A. § 1611] applies, is a qualified alien and is eligible to receive such benefit. Such regulations shall, to the extent feasible, require that information requested and exchanged be similar in form and manner to information requested and exchanged under section 1320b–7 of Title 42. Not later than 90 days after the date of the enactment of the Balanced Budget Act of 1997 [Aug. 5, 1997], the Attorney General of the United States, after consultation with the Secretary of Health and Human Services, shall issue interim verification guidance.

(2) Not later than 18 months after August 22, 1996, the Attorney General, in consultation with the Secretary of Health and Human Services, shall also establish procedures for a person applying for a Federal public benefit (as defined in section 1611(c) of this title [8 U.S.C.A. § 1611(c)]) to provide proof of citizenship in a fair and nondiscriminatory manner.

(3) Not later than 90 days after the date of the enactment of the Balanced Budget Act of 1997 [Aug. 5, 1997], the Attorney General shall promulgate regulations which set forth the procedures by which a State or local government can verify whether an alien applying for a State or local public benefit is a qualified alien, a nonimmigrant under the Immigration and Nationality Act, or an alien paroled into the United States under section 1182(d)(5) of this title [INA § 212(d)(5), 8 U.S.C.A. § 1182(d)(5)] for less than 1 year, for purposes of determining whether the alien is ineligible for benefits under section 1621 of this title [8 U.S.C.A. § 1621].

(b) State compliance

Not later than 24 months after the date the regulations described in subsection (a) of this section are adopted, a State that administers a program that provides a Federal public benefit shall have in effect a verification system that complies with the regulations.

(c) Authorization of appropriations

There are authorized to be appropriated such sums as may be necessary to carry out the purpose of this section.

(d) No verification requirement for nonprofit charitable organizations

Subject to subsection (a) of this section, a nonprofit charitable organization, in providing any Federal public benefit (as defined in section 1611(c) of this title [8 U.S.C.A. § 1611(c)]) or any State or local public benefit (as defined in section 1621(c) of this title [8 U.S.C.A. § 1621(c)]), is not required under this chapter to determine, verify, or otherwise require proof of eligibility of any applicant for such benefits.

(Pub.L. 104–193, Title IV, § 432, Aug. 22, 1996, 110 Stat. 2274; Pub.L. 104–208, Div. C, Title V, §§ 504, 508, Sept. 30, 1996, 110 Stat. 3009–672, 3009–673; Pub.L. 105–33, Title V, § 5572(a), Aug. 5, 1997, 111 Stat. 641.)

§ 433. Statutory construction [8 U.S.C.A. § 1643]

(a) Limitation

(1) Nothing in this chapter may be construed as an entitlement or a determination of an individual's eligibility or fulfillment of the requisite requirements for any Federal, State, or local governmental program, assistance, or benefits. For purposes of this chapter, eligibility relates only to the general issue of eligibility or ineligibility on the basis of alienage.

(2) Nothing in this chapter may be construed as addressing alien eligibility for a basic public education as determined by the Supreme Court of the United States under Plyler v. Doe (457 U.S. 202) (1982).

(b) Benefit eligibility limitations applicable only with respect to aliens present in the United States

Notwithstanding any other provision of this title, the limitations on eligibility for benefits under this title shall not apply to eligibility for benefits of aliens who are not residing, or present, in the United States with respect to—

(1) wages, pensions, annuities, and other earned payments to which an alien is entitled resulting from employment by, or on behalf of, a Federal, State, or local government agency which was not prohibited during the period of such employment or service under section 1324a of this title [INA § 274A, 8 U.S.C.A. § 1324a] or other applicable provision of the Immigration and Nationality Act; or

(2) benefits under laws administratered by the Secretary of Veterans Affairs.

(c) Not applicable to foreign assistance

This chapter does not apply to any Federal, State, or local governmental program, assistance, or benefits provided to an alien under any program of foreign assistance as determined by the Secretary of State in consultation with the Attorney General.

(d) Severability

If any provision of this chapter or the application of such provision to any person or circumstance is held to be unconstitutional, the remainder of this chapter and the application of the provisions of such to any person or circumstance shall not be affected thereby.

(Pub.L. 104–193, Title IV, § 433, Aug. 22, 1996, 110 Stat. 2275; Pub.L. 105–33, Title V, § 5574, Aug. 5, 1997, 111 Stat. 642.)

§ 434. Communication between State and local government agencies and the Immigration and Naturalization Service. [8 U.S.C.A. § 1644].

[For the text of PRWORA § 434, 8 U.S.C.A. § 1644, see Title 8, U.S. Code, Aliens and Nationality: Selected Sections Not Codified in the Immigration and Nationality Act, earlier in Part II (Additional Statutes) of this Supplement.—eds.]

§ 435. Qualifying quarters [8 U.S.C.A. § 1645]

For purposes of this chapter, in determining the number of qualifying quarters of coverage under Title II of the Social Security Act [42 U.S.C.A. § 401 et seq.] an alien shall be credited with—

(1) all of the qualifying quarters of coverage as defined under Title II of the Social Security Act [42 U.S.C.A. § 401 et seq.] worked by a parent of such alien before the date on which the alien attains age 18, and

(2) all of the qualifying quarters worked by a spouse of such alien during their marriage and the alien remains married to such spouse or such spouse is deceased.

No such qualifying quarter of coverage that is creditable under Title II of the Social Security Act [42 U.S.C.A. § 401 et seq.] for any period beginning after December 31, 1996, may be credited to an alien under paragraph (1) or (2) if the parent or spouse (as the case may be) of such alien received any Federal means-tested public benefit (as provided under section 1613 of this title [8 U.S.C.A. § 1613]) during the period for which such qualifying quarter of coverage is so credited. Notwithstanding section 6103 of the Internal Revenue Code of 1986, the Commissioner of Social Security is authorized to disclose quarters of coverage information concerning an alien and an alien's spouse or parents to a government agency for the purposes of this title.

(Pub.L. 104–193, Title IV, § 435, Aug. 22, 1996, 110 Stat. 2275; Pub.L. 105–33, Title V, § 5573, Aug. 5, 1997, 111 Stat. 641.)

§ 742. Requirements relating to provision of benefits based on citizenship, alienage, or immigration status under the Richard B. Russell National School Lunch Act, the Child Nutrition Act of 1966, and certain other Acts [8 U.S.C.A. § 1615]

(a) School lunch and breakfast programs

Notwithstanding any other provision of this Act, an individual who is eligible to receive free public education benefits under State or local law shall not be ineligible to receive benefits provided under the school lunch program under the Richard B. Russell National School Lunch Act (42 U.S.C. 1751 et seq.) or the school breakfast program under section 4 of the Child Nutrition Act of 1966 (42 U.S.C. 1773) on the basis of citizenship, alienage, or immigration status.

(b) Other programs

(1) In general

Nothing in this Act shall prohibit or require a State to provide to an individual who is not a citizen or a qualified alien, as defined in section 1614(b) of this title [8 U.S.C.A. § 1614(b)], benefits under programs established under the provisions of law described in paragraph (2).

(2) Provisions of law described

The provisions of law described in this paragraph are the following:

(A) Programs (other than the school lunch program and the school breakfast program) under the Richard B. Russell National School Lunch Act (42 U.S.C. 1751 et seq.) and the Child Nutrition Act of 1966 (42 U.S.C. 1771 et seq.).

(B) Section 4 of the Agriculture and Consumer Protection Act of 1973 (7 U.S.C. 612c note).

(C) The Emergency Food Assistance Act of 1983 (7 U.S.C. 612c note).

(D) The food distribution program on Indian reservations established under section 2013(b) of Title 7.

(Pub.L. 104–193, Title VII, § 742, Aug. 22, 1996, 110 Stat. 2307; Oct. 22, 1999, Pub.L. 106–78, Title VII, § 752(b)(6), 113 Stat. 1169.)

ADMINISTRATIVE PROCEDURE ACT

Selected Sections

[Title 5, U.S. Code. Government Organization and Employees]

§ 551. Definitions

For the purpose of this subchapter—

(1) "agency" means each authority of the Government of the United States, whether or not it is within or subject to review by another agency, but does not include—

(A) the Congress;

(B) the courts of the United States;

(C) the governments of the territories or possessions of the United States;

(D) the government of the District of Columbia;

or except as to the requirements of section 552 of this title—

(E) agencies composed of representatives of the parties or of representatives of organizations of the parties to the disputes determined by them;

(F) courts martial and military commissions;

(G) military authority exercised in the field in time of war or in occupied territory; or

(H) functions conferred by sections 1738, 1739, 1743, and 1744 of title 12; subchapter II of chapter 471 of title 49; or sections 1884, 1891–1902, and former section 1641(b)(2), of title 50, appendix;

(2) "person" includes an individual, partnership, corporation, association, or public or private organization other than an agency;

(3) "party" includes a person or agency named or admitted as a party, or properly seeking and entitled as of right to be admitted as a party, in an agency proceeding, and a person or agency admitted by an agency as a party for limited purposes;

(4) "rule" means the whole or a part of an agency statement of general or particular applicability and future effect designed to implement, interpret, or prescribe law or policy or describing the organization, procedure, or practice requirements of an agency and includes the approval or prescription for the future of rates, wages, corporate or financial structures or reorganizations thereof, prices, facilities, appliances, services or allowances therefor or of valuations, costs, or accounting, or practices bearing on any of the foregoing;

(5) "rule making" means agency process for formulating, amending, or repealing a rule;

(6) "order" means the whole or a part of a final disposition, whether affirmative, negative, injunctive, or declaratory in form, of an agency in a matter other than rule making but including licensing;

(7) "adjudication" means agency process for the formulation of an order;

(8) "license" includes the whole or a part of an agency permit, certificate, approval, registration, charter, membership, statutory exemption or other form of permission;

(9) "licensing" includes agency process respecting the grant, renewal, denial, revocation, suspension, annulment, withdrawal, limitation, amendment, modification, or conditioning of a license;

(10) "sanction" includes the whole or a part of an agency—

(A) prohibition, requirement, limitation, or other condition affecting the freedom of a person;

(B) withholding of relief;

(C) imposition of penalty or fine;

(D) destruction, taking, seizure, or withholding of property;

(E) assessment of damages, reimbursement, restitution, compensation, costs, charges, or fees;

(F) requirement, revocation, or suspension of a license; or

(G) taking other compulsory or restrictive action;

(11) "relief" includes the whole or a part of an agency—

(A) grant of money, assistance, license, authority, exemption, exception, privilege, or remedy;

(B) recognition of a claim, right, immunity, privilege, exemption, or exception; or

(C) taking of other action on the application or petition of, and beneficial to, a person;

(12) "agency proceeding" means an agency process as defined by paragraphs (5), (7), and (9) of this section;

(13) "agency action" includes the whole or a part of an agency rule, order, license, sanction, relief, or the equivalent or denial thereof, or failure to act; and

(14) "ex parte communication" means an oral or written communication not on the public record with respect to which reasonable prior notice to all parties is not given, but it shall not include requests for status reports on any matter or proceeding covered by this subchapter.

(Pub.L. 89–554, Sept. 6, 1966, 80 Stat. 381; Pub.L. 94–409, § 4(b), Sept. 13, 1976, 90 Stat. 1247; Pub.L. 103–272, § 5(a), July 5, 1994, 108 Stat. 1373; Pub.L. 111–350, § 5(a)(2), Jan. 4, 2011, 124 Stat. 3841.)

§ 553. Rule making

(a) This section applies, according to the provisions thereof, except to the extent that there is involved—

(1) a military or foreign affairs function of the United States; or

(2) a matter relating to agency management or personnel or to public property, loans, grants, benefits, or contracts.

(b) General notice of proposed rule making shall be published in the Federal Register, unless persons subject thereto are named and either personally served or otherwise have actual notice thereof in accordance with law. The notice shall include—

(1) a statement of the time, place, and nature of public rule making proceedings;

(2) reference to the legal authority under which the rule is proposed; and

(3) either the terms or substance of the proposed rule or a description of the subjects and issues involved.

Except when notice or hearing is required by statute, this subsection does not apply—

(A) to interpretative rules, general statements of policy, or rules of agency organization, procedure, or practice; or

(B) when the agency for good cause finds (and incorporates the finding and a brief statement of reasons therefor in the rules issued) that notice and public procedure thereon are impracticable, unnecessary, or contrary to the public interest.

(c) After notice required by this section, the agency shall give interested persons an opportunity to participate in the rule making through submission of written data, views, or arguments with or without opportunity for oral presentation. After consideration of the relevant matter presented, the agency shall incorporate in the rules adopted a concise general statement of their basis and purpose. When rules are required by statute to be made on the record after opportunity for an agency hearing, sections 556 and 557 of this title apply instead of this subsection.

(d) The required publication or service of a substantive rule shall be made not less than 30 days before its effective date, except—

(1) a substantive rule which grants or recognizes an exemption or relieves a restriction;

(2) interpretative rules and statements of policy; or

(3) as otherwise provided by the agency for good cause found and published with the rule.

(e) Each agency shall give an interested person the right to petition for the issuance, amendment, or repeal of a rule.

(Pub.L. 89–554, Sept. 6, 1966, 80 Stat. 383.)

§ 701. Application; definitions

(a) This chapter applies, according to the provisions thereof, except to the extent that—

(1) statutes preclude judicial review; or

(2) agency action is committed to agency discretion by law.

(b) For the purpose of this chapter—

(1) "agency" means each authority of the Government of the United States, whether or not it is within or subject to review by another agency, but does not include—

(A) the Congress;

(B) the courts of the United States;

(C) the governments of the territories or possessions of the United States;

(D) the government of the District of Columbia;

(E) agencies composed of representatives of the parties or of representatives of organizations of the parties to the disputes determined by them;

(F) courts martial and military commissions;

(G) military authority exercised in the field in time of war or in occupied territory; or

(H) functions conferred by sections 1738, 1739, 1743, and 1744 of title 12; subchapter II of chapter 471 of title 49; or sections 1884, 1891–1902, and former section 1641(b)(2), of title 50, appendix; and

(2) "person", "rule", "order", "license", "sanction", "relief", and "agency action" have the meanings given them by section 551 of this title.

(Pub.L. 89–554, Sept. 6, 1966, 80 Stat. 392; Pub.L. 103–272, § 5(a), July 5, 1994, 108 Stat. 1373; Pub.L. 111–350, § 5(a)(3), Jan. 4, 2011, 124 Stat. 3841.)

§ 702. Right of review

A person suffering legal wrong because of agency action, or adversely affected or aggrieved by agency action within the meaning of a relevant statute, is entitled to judicial review thereof. An action in a court of the United States seeking relief other than money damages and stating a claim that an agency or an officer or employee thereof acted or failed to act in an official capacity or under color of legal authority shall not be dismissed nor relief therein be denied on the ground that it is against the United States or that the United States is an indispensable party. The United States may be named as a defendant in any such action, and a judgment or decree may be entered against the United States: *Provided,* That any mandatory or injunctive decree shall specify the Federal officer or officers (by name or by title), and their successors in office, personally responsible for compliance. Nothing herein **(1)** affects other limitations on judicial review or the power or duty of the court to dismiss any action or deny relief on any other appropriate legal or equitable ground; or **(2)** confers authority to grant relief if any other statute that grants consent to suit expressly or impliedly forbids the relief which is sought.

(Pub.L. 89–554, Sept. 6, 1966, 80 Stat. 392; Pub.L. 94–574, § 1, Oct. 21, 1976, 90 Stat. 2721.)

§ 703. Form and venue of proceeding

The form of proceeding for judicial review is the special statutory review proceeding relevant to the subject matter in a court specified by statute or, in the absence or inadequacy thereof, any applicable form of legal action, including actions for declaratory judgments or writs of prohibitory or mandatory injunction or habeas corpus, in a court of competent jurisdiction. If no special statutory review proceeding is applicable, the action for judicial review may be brought against the United States, the agency by its official title, or the appropriate officer. Except to the extent that prior, adequate, and exclusive opportunity for judicial review is provided by law, agency action is subject to judicial review in civil or criminal proceedings for judicial enforcement.

(Pub.L. 89–554, Sept. 6, 1966, 80 Stat. 392; Pub.L. 94–574, § 1, Oct. 21, 1976, 90 Stat. 2721.)

§ 704. Actions reviewable

Agency action made reviewable by statute and final agency action for which there is no other adequate remedy in a court are subject to judicial review. A preliminary, procedural, or intermediate agency action or ruling not directly reviewable is subject to review on the review of the final agency action. Except as otherwise expressly required by statute, agency action otherwise final is final for the purposes of this section whether or not there has been presented or determined an application for a declaratory order, for any form of reconsideration, or, unless the agency otherwise requires by rule and provides that the action meanwhile is inoperative, for an appeal to superior agency authority.

(Pub.L. 89–554, Sept. 6, 1966, 80 Stat. 392.)

§ 705. Relief pending review

When an agency finds that justice so requires, it may postpone the effective date of action taken by it, pending judicial review. On such conditions as may be required and to the extent necessary to prevent irreparable injury, the reviewing court, including the court to which a case may be taken on appeal from or on application for certiorari or other writ to a reviewing court, may issue all necessary and appropriate process to postpone the effective date of an agency action or to preserve status or rights pending conclusion of the review proceedings.

(Pub.L. 89–554, Sept. 6, 1966, 80 Stat. 393.)

§ 706. Scope of review

To the extent necessary to decision and when presented, the reviewing court shall decide all relevant questions of law, interpret constitutional and statutory provisions, and determine the meaning or applicability of the terms of an agency action. The reviewing court shall—

(1) compel agency action unlawfully withheld or unreasonably delayed; and

(2) hold unlawful and set aside agency action, findings, and conclusions found to be—

(A) arbitrary, capricious, an abuse of discretion, or otherwise not in accordance with law;

(B) contrary to constitutional right, power, privilege, or immunity;

(C) in excess of statutory jurisdiction, authority, or limitations, or short of statutory right;

(D) without observance of procedure required by law;

(E) unsupported by substantial evidence in a case subject to sections 556 and 557 of this title or otherwise reviewed on the record of an agency hearing provided by statute; or

(F) unwarranted by the facts to the extent that the facts are subject to trial de novo by the reviewing court.

In making the foregoing determinations, the court shall review the whole record or those parts of it cited by a party, and due account shall be taken of the rule of prejudicial error.

(Pub.L. 89–554, Sept. 6, 1966, 80 Stat. 393.)

TITLE 18, U.S. CODE, CRIMES AND CRIMINAL PROCEDURE

§ 16. Crime of violence defined

The term "crime of violence" means—

(a) an offense that has as an element the use, attempted use, or threatened use of physical force against the person or property of another, or

(b) any other offense that is a felony and that, by its nature, involves a substantial risk that physical force against the person or property of another may be used in the course of committing the offense.

(Pub.L. 98–473, Title II, § 1001(a), Oct. 12, 1984, 98 Stat. 2136.)

§ 1546. Fraud and misuse of visas, permits, and other documents

(a) Whoever knowingly forges, counterfeits, alters, or falsely makes any immigrant or nonimmigrant visa, permit, border crossing card, alien registration receipt card, or other document prescribed by statute or regulation for entry into or as evidence of authorized stay or employment in the United States, or utters, uses, attempts to use, possesses, obtains, accepts, or receives any such visa, permit, border crossing card, alien registration receipt card, or other document prescribed by statute or regulation for entry into or as evidence of authorized stay or employment in the United States, knowing it to be forged, counterfeited, altered, or falsely made, or to have been procured by means of any false claim or statement, or to have been otherwise procured by fraud or unlawfully obtained; or

Whoever, except under direction of the Attorney General or the Commissioner of the Immigration and Naturalization Service, or other proper officer, knowingly possesses any blank permit, or engraves, sells, brings into the United States, or has in his control or possession any plate in the likeness of a plate designed for the printing of permits, or makes any print, photograph, or impression in the likeness of any immigrant or nonimmigrant visa, permit or other document required for entry into the United States, or has in his possession a distinctive paper which has been adopted by the Attorney General or the Commissioner of the Immigration and Naturalization Service for the printing of such visas, permits, or documents; or

Whoever, when applying for an immigrant or nonimmigrant visa, permit, or other document required for entry into the United States, or for admission to the United States personates another, or falsely appears in the name of a deceased individual, or evades or attempts to evade the immigration laws by appearing under an assumed or fictitious name without disclosing his true identity, or sells or otherwise disposes of, or offers to sell or otherwise dispose of, or utters, such visa, permit, or other document, to any person not authorized by law to receive such document; or

Whoever knowingly makes under oath, or as permitted under penalty of perjury under section 1746 of title 28, United States Code, knowingly subscribes as true, any false statement with respect to a material fact in any application, affidavit, or other document required by the immigration laws or regulations prescribed thereunder, or knowingly presents any such application, affidavit, or other document which contains any such false statement or which fails to contain any reasonable basis in law or fact—

Shall be fined under this title or imprisoned not more than 25 years (if the offense was committed to facilitate an act of international terrorism (as defined in section 2331 of this title)), 20 years (if the offense was committed to facilitate a drug trafficking crime (as defined in section 929(a) of this title)), 10 years (in the case of the first or second such offense, if the offense was not committed to facilitate such an act of international terrorism or a drug trafficking crime), or 15 years (in the case of any other offense), or both.

(b) Whoever uses—

(1) an identification document, knowing (or having reason to know) that the document was not issued lawfully for the use of the possessor,

(2) an identification document knowing (or having reason to know) that the document is false, or

(3) a false attestation,

for the purpose of satisfying a requirement of section 274A(b) of the Immigration and Nationality Act [8 U.S.C.A. § 1324a(b)], shall be fined under this title, imprisoned not more than 5 years, or both.

(c) This section does not prohibit any lawfully authorized investigative, protective, or intelligence activity of a law enforcement agency of the United States, a State, or a subdivision of a State, or of an intelligence agency of the United States, or any activity authorized under title V of the Organized Crime Control Act of 1970 (18 U.S.C.A. note prec. 3481). For purposes of this section, the term "State" means a State of the United States, the District of Columbia, and any commonwealth, territory, or possession of the United States.

(June 25, 1948, c. 645, 62 Stat. 771; June 27, 1952, c. 477, Title IV, § 402(a), 66 Stat. 275; Oct. 18, 1976, Pub.L. 94–550, § 5, 90 Stat. 2535; Nov. 6, 1986, Pub.L. 99–603, Title I, § 103(a), 100 Stat. 3380; Oct. 24, 1988, Pub.L. 100–525, Title I, § 2(c), 102 Stat. 2610; Nov. 29, 1990, Pub.L. 101–647, Title XXXV, § 3550, 104 Stat. 4926; Sept. 13, 1994, Pub.L. 103–322, Title XIII, § 130009(a)(4), (5), Title XXXIII, § 330011(p), 108 Stat. 2030, 2145; Sept. 30, 1996, Pub.L. 104–208, Div. C, Title II, §§ 211(a)(2), 214, 110 Stat. 3009–569, 3009–572; Oct. 11, 1996, Pub.L. 104–294, Title VI, § 607(m), 110 Stat. 3512; Nov. 2, 2002, Pub.L. 107–273, Div. B, Title IV, § 4002(a)(3), 116 Stat. 1806.)

§ 2331. Definitions

As used in this chapter—

(1) the term "international terrorism" means activities that—

(A) involve violent acts or acts dangerous to human life that are a violation of the criminal laws of the United States or of any State, or that would be a criminal violation if committed within the jurisdiction of the United States or of any State;

(B) appear to be intended—

(i) to intimidate or coerce a civilian population;

(ii) to influence the policy of a government by intimidation or coercion; or

(iii) to affect the conduct of a government by mass destruction, assassination, or kidnapping; and

(C) occur primarily outside the territorial jurisdiction of the United States, or transcend national boundaries in terms of the means by which they are accomplished, the persons they appear intended to intimidate or coerce, or the locale in which their perpetrators operate or seek asylum;

(2) the term "national of the United States" has the meaning given such term in section 101(a)(22) of the Immigration and Nationality Act;

(3) the term "person" means any individual or entity capable of holding a legal or beneficial interest in property;

(4) the term "act of war" means any act occurring in the course of—

(A) declared war;

(B) armed conflict, whether or not war has been declared, between two or more nations; or

(C) armed conflict between military forces of any origin; and

(5) the term "domestic terrorism" means activities that—

(A) involve acts dangerous to human life that are a violation of the criminal laws of the United States or of any State;

(B) appear to be intended—

(i) to intimidate or coerce a civilian population;

(ii) to influence the policy of a government by intimidation or coercion; or

(iii) to affect the conduct of a government by mass destruction, assassination, or kidnapping; and

(C) occur primarily within the territorial jurisdiction of the United States.

(Pub.L. 102–572, Title X, § 1003(a)(3), Oct. 29, 1992, 106 Stat. 4521; as amended Pub.L. 107–56, Title VIII, § 802(a), Oct. 26, 2001, 115 Stat. 376.)

§ 2339A. Providing material support to terrorists

(a) Offense.—Whoever provides material support or resources or conceals or disguises the nature, location, source, or ownership of material support or resources, knowing or intending that they are to be used in preparation for, or in carrying out, a violation of section 32, 37, 81, 175, 229, 351, 831, 842(m)or (n), 844(f) or (i), 930(c), 956, 1091, 1114, 1116, 1203, 1361, 1362, 1363, 1366, 1751, 1992, 2155,2156, 2280, 2281, 2332, 2332a, 2332b, 2332f, 2340A, or 2442 of this title, section 236 of the Atomic Energy Act of 1954 (42 U.S.C. 2284), section 46502 or 60123(b) of title 49, or any offense listed in section 2332b(g)(5)(B) (except for sections 2339A and 2339B) or in preparation for, or in carrying out, the concealment of an escape from the commission of any such violation, or attempts or conspires to do such an act, shall be fined under this title, imprisoned not more than 15 years, or both, and, if the death of any person results, shall be imprisoned for any term of years or for life. A violation of this section may be prosecuted in any Federal judicial district in which the underlying offense was committed, or in any other Federal judicial district as provided by law.

(b) Definitions.—As used in this section—

(1) the term "material support or resources" means any property, tangible or intangible, or service, including currency or monetary instruments or financial securities, financial services, lodging, training, expert advice or assistance, safehouses, false documentation or identification, communications equipment, facilities, weapons, lethal substances, explosives, personnel (1 or more individuals who may be or include oneself), and transportation, except medicine or religious materials;

(2) the term "training" means instruction or teaching designed to impart a specific skill, as opposed to general knowledge; and

(3) the term "expert advice or assistance" means advice or assistance derived from scientific, technical or other specialized knowledge.

(Pub.L. 103–322, Title XII, § 120005(a), Sept. 13, 1994, 108 Stat. 2022, and amended Pub.L. 104–132, Title III, § 323, Apr. 24, 1996, 110 Stat. 1255; Pub.L. 104–294, Title VI, §§ 601(b)(2), (s)(2), (3), 604(b)(5), Oct. 11, 1996, 110 Stat. 3498, 3502, 3506; as amended Pub.L. 107–56, Title VIII, §§ 805(a), 810(c), 811(f), Oct. 26, 2001, 115 Stat. 377, 380, 381; Pub.L. 107–197, Title III, § 301(c), June 25, 2002, 116 Stat. 728; Pub.L. 107–273, Div. B, Title IV, § 4002(a)(7), (c)(1), (e)(11), Nov. 2, 2002, 116 Stat. 1807, 1808, 1811; Pub.L. 108–458, Title VI, § 6603(a)(2), (b), Dec. 17, 2004, 118 Stat. 3762; Pub.L. 109–177, Title I, § 110(b)(3)(B), Mar. 9, 2006, 120 Stat. 208; Pub.L. 111–122, § 3(d), Dec. 22, 2009, 123 Stat. 3481.)

§ 2339B. Providing material support or resources to designated foreign terrorist organizations

(a) Prohibited activities.—

(1) Unlawful conduct.—Whoever knowingly provides material support or resources to a foreign terrorist organization, or attempts or conspires to do so, shall be fined under this title or imprisoned not more than 15 years, or both, and, if the death of any person results, shall be imprisoned for any term of years or for life. To violate this paragraph, a person must have knowledge that the organization is a designated terrorist organization (as defined in subsection (g)(6)), that the organization has engaged or engages in terrorist activity (as defined in section 212(a)(3)(B) of the Immigration and Nationality Act [8 U.S.C.A. § 1182(a)(3)(B)]), or that the organization has engaged or engages in terrorism (as defined in section 140(d)(2) of the Foreign Relations Authorization Act, Fiscal Years 1988 and 1989).

(2) Financial institutions.—Except as authorized by the Secretary, any financial institution that becomes aware that it has possession of, or control over, any funds in which a foreign terrorist organization, or its agent, has an interest, shall—

(A) retain possession of, or maintain control over, such funds; and

(B) report to the Secretary the existence of such funds in accordance with regulations issued by the Secretary.

(b) Civil penalty.—Any financial institution that knowingly fails to comply with subsection (a)(2) shall be subject to a civil penalty in an amount that is the greater of—

(A) $50,000 per violation; or

(B) twice the amount of which the financial institution was required under subsection (a)(2) to retain possession or control.

(c) Injunction.—Whenever it appears to the Secretary or the Attorney General that any person is engaged in, or is about to engage in, any act that constitutes, or would constitute, a violation of this section, the Attorney General may initiate civil action in a district court of the United States to enjoin such violation.

(d) Extraterritorial jurisdiction.—

(1) In general.—There is jurisdiction over an offense under subsection (a) if—

(A) an offender is a national of the United States (as defined in section 101(a)(22) of the Immigration and Nationality Act (8 U.S.C. 1101(a)(22))) or an alien lawfully admitted for permanent residence in the United States (as defined in section 101(a)(20) of the Immigration and Nationality Act (8 U.S.C. 1101(a)(20)));

(B) an offender is a stateless person whose habitual residence is in the United States;

(C) after the conduct required for the offense occurs an offender is brought into or found in the United States, even if the conduct required for the offense occurs outside the United States;

(D) the offense occurs in whole or in part within the United States;

(E) the offense occurs in or affects interstate or foreign commerce; or

(F) an offender aids or abets any person over whom jurisdiction exists under this paragraph in committing an offense under subsection (a) or conspires with any person over whom jurisdiction exists under this paragraph to commit an offense under subsection (a).

(2) Extraterritorial jurisdiction.—There is extraterritorial Federal jurisdiction over an offense under this section.

(e) Investigations.—

(1) In general.—The Attorney General shall conduct any investigation of a possible violation of this section, or of any license, order, or regulation issued pursuant to this section.

(2) Coordination with the Department of the Treasury.—The Attorney General shall work in coordination with the Secretary in investigations relating to—

(A) the compliance or noncompliance by a financial institution with the requirements of subsection (a)(2); and

(B) civil penalty proceedings authorized under subsection (b).

(3) Referral.—Any evidence of a criminal violation of this section arising in the course of an investigation by the Secretary or any other Federal agency shall be referred immediately to the Attorney General for further investigation. The Attorney General shall timely notify the Secretary of any action taken on referrals from the Secretary, and may refer investigations to the Secretary for remedial licensing or civil penalty action.

(f) Classified information in civil proceedings brought by the United States.—

(1) Discovery of classified information by defendants.—

(A) Request by United States.—In any civil proceeding under this section, upon request made ex parte and in writing by the United States, a court, upon a sufficient showing, may authorize the United States to—

(i) redact specified items of classified information from documents to be introduced into evidence or made available to the defendant through discovery under the Federal Rules of Civil Procedure;

(ii) substitute a summary of the information for such classified documents; or

(iii) substitute a statement admitting relevant facts that the classified information would tend to prove.

(B) Order granting request.—If the court enters an order granting a request under this paragraph, the entire text of the documents to which the request relates shall be sealed and preserved in the records of the court to be made available to the appellate court in the event of an appeal.

(C) Denial of request.—If the court enters an order denying a request of the United States under this paragraph, the United States may take an immediate, interlocutory appeal in accordance with paragraph (5). For purposes of such an appeal, the entire text of the documents to which the request relates, together with any transcripts of arguments made ex parte to the court in connection therewith, shall be maintained under seal and delivered to the appellate court.

(2) Introduction of classified information; precautions by court.—

(A) Exhibits.—To prevent unnecessary or inadvertent disclosure of classified information in a civil proceeding brought by the United States under this section, the United States may petition the court ex parte to admit, in lieu of classified writings, recordings, or photographs, one or more of the following:

(i) Copies of items from which classified information has been redacted.

(ii) Stipulations admitting relevant facts that specific classified information would tend to prove.

(iii) A declassified summary of the specific classified information.

(B) Determination by court.—The court shall grant a request under this paragraph if the court finds that the redacted item, stipulation, or summary is sufficient to allow the defendant to prepare a defense.

(3) Taking of trial testimony.—

(A) Objection.—During the examination of a witness in any civil proceeding brought by the United States under this subsection, the United States may object to any question or line of inquiry that may require the witness to disclose classified information not previously found to be admissible.

(B) Action by court.—In determining whether a response is admissible, the court shall take precautions to guard against the compromise of any classified information, including—

(i) permitting the United States to provide the court, ex parte, with a proffer of the witness's response to the question or line of inquiry; and

(ii) requiring the defendant to provide the court with a proffer of the nature of the information that the defendant seeks to elicit.

(C) Obligation of defendant.—In any civil proceeding under this section, it shall be the defendant's obligation to establish the relevance and materiality of any classified information sought to be introduced.

(4) Appeal.—If the court enters an order denying a request of the United States under this subsection, the United States may take an immediate interlocutory appeal in accordance with paragraph (5).

(5) Interlocutory appeal.—

(A) Subject of appeal.—An interlocutory appeal by the United States shall lie to a court of appeals from a decision or order of a district court—

(i) authorizing the disclosure of classified information;

(ii) imposing sanctions for nondisclosure of classified information; or

(iii) refusing a protective order sought by the United States to prevent the disclosure of classified information.

(B) Expedited consideration.—

(i) In general.—An appeal taken pursuant to this paragraph, either before or during trial, shall be expedited by the court of appeals.

(ii) Appeals prior to trial.—If an appeal is of an order made prior to trial, an appeal shall be taken not later than 14 days after the decision or order appealed from, and the trial shall not commence until the appeal is resolved.

(iii) Appeals during trial.—If an appeal is taken during trial, the trial court shall adjourn the trial until the appeal is resolved, and the court of appeals—

(I) shall hear argument on such appeal not later than 4 days after the adjournment of the trial, excluding intermediate weekends and holidays;

(II) may dispense with written briefs other than the supporting materials previously submitted to the trial court;

(III) shall render its decision not later than 4 days after argument on appeal, excluding intermediate weekends and holidays; and

(IV) may dispense with the issuance of a written opinion in rendering its decision.

(C) Effect of ruling.—An interlocutory appeal and decision shall not affect the right of the defendant, in a subsequent appeal from a final judgment, to claim as error reversal by the trial court on remand of a ruling appealed from during trial.

(6) Construction.—Nothing in this subsection shall prevent the United States from seeking protective orders or asserting privileges ordinarily available to the United States to protect against the disclosure of classified information, including the invocation of the military and State secrets privilege.

(g) Definitions.—As used in this section—

(1) the term "classified information" has the meaning given that term in section 1(a) of the Classified Information Procedures Act (18 U.S.C. App.);

(2) the term "financial institution" has the same meaning as in section 5312(a)(2) of title 31, United States Code;

(3) the term "funds" includes coin or currency of the United States or any other country, traveler's checks, personal checks, bank checks, money orders, stocks, bonds, debentures, drafts, letters of credit, any other negotiable instrument, and any electronic representation of any of the foregoing;

(4) the term "material support or resources" has the same meaning given that term in section 2339A (including the definitions of "training" and "expert advice or assistance" in that section);

(5) the term "Secretary" means the Secretary of the Treasury; and

(6) the term "terrorist organization" means an organization designated as a terrorist organization under section 219 of the Immigration and Nationality Act.

(h) Provision of personnel.—No person may be prosecuted under this section in connection with the term "personnel" unless that person has knowingly provided, attempted to provide, or conspired to provide a foreign terrorist organization with 1 or more individuals (who may be or include himself) to work under that terrorist organization's direction or control or to organize, manage, supervise, or otherwise direct the operation of that organization. Individuals who act entirely independently of the foreign terrorist organization to advance its goals or objectives shall not be considered to be working under the foreign terrorist organization's direction and control.

(i) Rule of construction.—Nothing in this section shall be construed or applied so as to abridge the exercise of rights guaranteed under the First Amendment to the Constitution of the United States.

(j) Exception.—No person may be prosecuted under this section in connection with the term "personnel", "training", or "expert advice or assistance" if the provision of that material support or resources to a foreign terrorist organization was approved by the Secretary of State with the concurrence of the Attorney General. The Secretary of State may not approve the provision of any material support that may be used to carry out terrorist activity (as defined in section 212(a)(3)(B)(iii) of the Immigration and Nationality Act [8 U.S.C.A. § 1182(a)(3)(B)(iii)]).

(Pub.L. 104–132, Title III, § 303(a), Apr. 24, 1996, 110 Stat. 1250; as amended Pub.L. 107–56, Title VIII, § 810(d), Oct. 26, 2001, 115 Stat. 380; Pub.L. 108–458, Title VI, § 6603(c) to (f), Dec. 17, 2004, 118 Stat. 3762, 3763; Pub.L. 111–16, § 3(6) to (8), May 7, 2009, 123 Stat. 1608.)

III. EXCERPTS FROM CODE OF FEDERAL REGULATIONS

TITLE 8

(ALIENS AND NATIONALITY) AND TITLE 20 (EMPLOYEES' BENEFITS)

Part 204—Immigrant Petitions

Sec.

204.5 Petitions for employment-based immigrants.

Part 208—Procedures for Asylum and Withholding of Removal

Subpart A—Asylum and Withholding of Removal

208.1 General.
208.2 Jurisdiction.
208.3 Form of application.
208.4 Filing the application.
208.5 Special duties toward aliens in custody of DHS.
208.6 Disclosure to third parties.
208.7 Employment authorization.
208.8 Limitations on travel outside the United States.
208.9 Procedure for interview before an asylum officer.
208.10 Failure to appear at an interview before an asylum officer or failure to follow requirements for fingerprint processing.
208.11 Comments from the Department of State.
208.12 Reliance on information compiled by other sources.
208.13 Establishing asylum eligibility.
208.14 Approval, denial, referral, or dismissal of application.
208.15 Definition of "firm resettlement."
208.16 Withholding of removal under section 241(b)(3)(B) of the Act and withholding of removal under the Convention Against Torture.
208.17 Deferral of removal under the Convention Against Torture.
208.18 Implementation of the Convention Against Torture.
208.19 Decisions.
208.20 Determining if an asylum application is frivolous.
208.21 Admission of the asylee's spouse and children.
208.22 Effect on exclusion, deportation, and removal proceedings.
208.23 Restoration of status.
208.24 Termination of asylum or withholding of removal or deportation.
208.25–29 [Reserved.]

Subpart B—Credible Fear of Persecution

208.30 Credible fear determinations involving stowaways and applicants for admission found inadmissible pursuant to section 212(a)(6)(C) or 212(a)(7) of the Act.

PART 204—IMMIGRANT PETITIONS

§ 204.5 Petitions for employment-based immigrants.

(a) General. A petition to classify an alien under section 203(b)(1), 203(b)(2), or 203(b)(3) of the Act must be filed on Form I–140, Petition for Immigrant Worker. A petition to classify an alien under section 203(b)(4) (as it relates to special immigrants under section 101(a)(27)(C)) must be filed on Form I–360, Petition for Amerasian, Widow, or Special Immigrant. A separate Form I–140 or I–360 must be filed for each beneficiary, accompanied by the applicable fee. A petition is considered properly filed if it is:

(1) Accepted for processing under the provisions of part 103;

(2) Accompanied by any required individual labor certification, application for Schedule A designation, or evidence that the alien's occupation qualifies as a shortage occupation within the Department of Labor's Labor Market Information Pilot Program; and

(3) Accompanied by any other required supporting documentation.

(b) Jurisdiction. Form I–140 or I–360 must be filed in accordance with the instructions on the form.

(c) Filing petition. Any United States employer desiring and intending to employ an alien may file a petition for classification of the alien under section 203(b)(1)(B), 203(b)(1)(C), 203(b)(2), or 203(b)(3) of the Act. An alien, or any person in the alien's behalf, may file a petition for classification under section 203(b)(1)(A) or 203(b)(4) of the Act (as it relates to special immigrants under section 101(a)(27)(C) of the Act).

(d) Priority date. The priority date of any petition filed for classification under section 203(b) of the Act which is accompanied by an individual labor certification from the Department of Labor shall be the date the request for certification was accepted for processing by any office within the employment service system of the Department of Labor. The priority date of any petition filed for classification under section 203(b) of the Act which is accompanied by an application for Schedule A designation or with evidence that the alien's occupation is a shortage occupation within the Department of Labor's Labor Market Information Pilot Program shall be the date the completed, signed petition (including all initial evidence and the correct fee) is properly filed with the Service. The priority date of a petition filed for classification as a special immigrant under section 203(b)(4) of the Act shall be the date the completed, signed petition (including all initial evidence and the correct fee) is properly filed with the Service. The priority date of an alien who filed for classification as a special immigrant prior to October 1, 1991, and who is the beneficiary of an approved I–360 petition after October 1, 1991, shall be the date the alien applied for an immigrant visa or adjustment of status. In the case of a special immigrant alien who applied for adjustment before October 1, 1991, Form I–360 may be accepted and adjudicated at a Service District Office or sub-office.

(e) Retention of section 203(b)(1), (2), or (3) priority date.—A petition approved on behalf of an alien under sections 203(b)(1), (2), or (3) of the Act accords the alien the priority date of the approved petition for any subsequently filed petition for any classification under sections 203(b)(1), (2), or (3) of the Act for which the alien may qualify. In the event that the alien is the beneficiary of multiple petitions under sections 203(b)(1), (2), or (3) of the Act, the alien shall be entitled to the earliest priority date. A petition revoked under sections 204(e) or 205 of the Act will not confer a priority date, nor will any priority date be established as a result of a denied petition. A priority date is not transferable to another alien.

(f) Maintaining the priority date of a third or sixth preference petition filed prior to October 1, 1991—Any petition filed before October 1, 1991, and approved on any date, to accord status under section 203(a)(3) or 203(a)(6) of the Act, as in effect before October 1, 1991, shall be deemed a petition approved to accord status under section 203(b)(2) or within the appropriate classification under section 203(b)(3), respectively, of the Act as in effect on or after October 1, 1991, provided that the alien applies for an immigrant visa or adjustment of status within the two years following notification that an immigrant visa is immediately available for his or her use.

(g) Initial evidence—

(1) General. Specific requirements for initial supporting documents for the various employment-based immigrant classifications are set forth in this section. In general, ordinary legible photocopies of such documents (except for labor certifications from the Department of Labor) will be acceptable for initial filing and approval. However, at the discretion of the director, original documents may be required in individual cases. Evidence relating to qualifying experience or training shall be in the form of letter(s) from current or former employer(s) or trainer(s) and shall include the name, address, and title of the writer, and a specific description of the duties performed by the alien or of the training received. If such evidence is unavailable, other documentation relating to the alien's experience or training will be considered.

(2) Ability of prospective employer to pay wage. Any petition filed by or for an employment-based immigrant which requires an offer of employment must be accompanied by evidence that the prospective United States employer has the ability to pay the proffered wage. The petitioner must demonstrate this ability at the time the priority date is established and continuing until the beneficiary obtains lawful permanent residence. Evidence of this ability shall be either in the form of copies of annual reports, federal tax returns, or audited financial statements. In a case where the prospective United States employer employs 100 or more workers, the director may accept a statement from a financial officer of the organization which establishes the prospective employer's ability to pay the proffered wage. In appropriate cases, additional evidence, such as profit/loss statements, bank account records, or personnel records, may be submitted by the petitioner or requested by the Service.

(h) Aliens with extraordinary ability—

(1) An alien, or any person on behalf of the alien, may file an I-140 visa petition for classification under section 203(b)(1)(A) of the Act as an alien of extraordinary ability in the sciences, arts, education, business, or athletics.

(2) Definition. As used in this section:

Extraordinary ability means a level of expertise indicating that the individual is one of that small percentage who have risen to the very top of the field of endeavor.

(3) Initial evidence. A petition for an alien of extraordinary ability must be accompanied by evidence that the alien has sustained national or international acclaim and that his or her achievements have been recognized in the field of expertise. Such evidence shall include evidence of a one-time achievement (that is, a major, international recognized award), or at least three of the following:

(i) Documentation of the alien's receipt of lesser nationally or internationally recognized prizes or awards for excellence in the field of endeavor;

(ii) Documentation of the alien's membership in associations in the field for which classification is sought, which require outstanding achievements of their members, as judged by recognized national or international experts in their disciplines or fields;

(iii) Published material about the alien in professional or major trade publications or other major media, relating to the alien's work in the field for which classification is sought. Such evidence shall include the title, date, and author of the material, and any necessary translation;

(iv) Evidence of the alien's participation, either individually or on a panel, as a judge of the work of others in the same or an allied field of specification for which classification is sought;

(v) Evidence of the alien's original scientific, scholarly, artistic, athletic, or business-related contributions of major significance in the field;

(vi) Evidence of the alien's authorship of scholarly articles in the field, in professional or major trade publications or other major media;

(vii) Evidence of the display of the alien's work in the field at artistic exhibitions or showcases;

(viii) Evidence that the alien has performed in a leading or critical role for organizations or establishments that have a distinguished reputation;

(ix) Evidence that the alien has commanded a high salary or other significantly high remuneration for services, in relation to others in the field; or

(x) Evidence of commercial successes in the performing arts, as shown by box office receipts or record, cassette, compact disk, or video sales.

(4) If the above standards do not readily apply to the beneficiary's occupation, the petitioner may submit comparable evidence to establish the beneficiary's eligibility.

(5) No offer of employment required. Neither an offer for employment in the United States nor a labor certification is required for this classification; however, the petition must be accompanied by clear evidence that the alien is coming to the United States to continue work in the area of expertise. Such evidence may include letter(s) from prospective employer(s), evidence of prearranged commitments such as contracts, or a statement from the beneficiary detailing plans on how he or she intends to continue his or her work in the United States.

(i) Outstanding professors and researchers.

(1) Any United States employer desiring and intending to employ a professor or researcher who is outstanding in an academic field under section 203(b)(1)(B) of the Act may file an I–140 visa petition for such classification.

(2) Definitions. As used in this section:

Academic field means a body of specialized knowledge offered for study at an accredited United States university or institution of higher education.

Permanent, in reference to a research position, means either tenured, tenure-track, or for a term of indefinite or unlimited duration, and in which the employee will ordinarily have an expectation of continued employment unless there is good cause for termination.

(3) Initial evidence. A petition for an outstanding professor or researcher must be accompanied by:

(i) Evidence that the professor or researcher is recognized internationally as outstanding in the academic field specified in the petition. Such evidence shall consist of at least two of the following:

(A) Documentation of the alien's receipt of major prizes or awards for outstanding achievement in the academic field;

(B) Documentation of the alien's membership in associations in the academic field which require outstanding achievements of their members;

(C) Published material in professional publications written by others about the alien's work in the academic field. Such material shall include the title, date, and author of the material, and any necessary translation;

(D) Evidence of the alien's participation, either individually or on a panel, as the judge of the work of others in the same or an allied academic field;

(E) Evidence of the alien's original scientific or scholarly research contributions to the academic field; or

(F) Evidence of the alien's authorship of scholarly books or articles (in scholarly journals with international circulation) in the academic field;

(ii) Evidence that the alien has at least three years of experience in teaching and/or research in the academic field. Experience in teaching or research while working on an advanced degree will only be acceptable if the alien has acquired the degree, and if the teaching duties were such that he or she had full responsibility for the class taught or if the research conducted toward the degree has been recognized within the academic field as outstanding. Evidence of teaching and/or research experience shall be in the form of letter(s) from current or former employer(s) and shall include the name, address, and title of the writer, and a specific description of the duties performed by the alien; and

(iii) An offer of employment from a prospective United States employer. A labor certification is not required for this classification. The offer of employment shall be in the form of a letter from:

(A) A United States university or institution of higher learning offering the alien a tenured or tenure-track teaching position in the alien's academic field;

(B) A United States university or institution of higher learning offering the alien a permanent research position in the alien's academic field; or

(C) A department, division, or institute of a private employer offering the alien a permanent research position in the alien's academic field. The department, division, or institute must demonstrate that it employs at least three persons full-time in research positions, and that it has achieved documented accomplishments in an academic field.

(j) Certain multinational executives and managers.

(1) A United States employer may file a petition on Form I–140 for classification of an alien under section 203(b)(1)(C) of the Act as a multinational executive or manager.

(2) Definitions. As used in this section:

Affiliate means:

(A) One of two subsidiaries both of which are owned and controlled by the same parent or individual;

(B) One of two legal entities owned and controlled by the same group of individuals, each individual owning and controlling approximately the same share or proportion of each entity; or

(C) In the case of a partnership that is organized in the United States to provide accounting services, along with managerial and/or consulting services, and markets its accounting services under an internationally recognized name under an agreement with a worldwide coordinating organization that is owned and controlled by the member accounting firms, a partnership (or similar organization) that is organized outside the United States to provide accounting' services shall be considered to be an affiliate of the United States partnership if it markets its accounting services under the same internationally recognized name under the agreement with the worldwide coordinating organization of which the United States partnership is also a member.

Doing business means the regular, systematic, and continuous provision of goods and/or services by a firm, corporation, or other entity and does not include the mere presence of an agent or office.

Executive capacity means an assignment within an organization in which the employee primarily:

(A) Directs the management of the organization or a major component or function of the organization;

(B) Establishes the goals and policies of the organization, component, or function;

(C) Exercises wide latitude in discretionary decisionmaking; and

(D) Receives only general supervision or direction from higher level executives, the board of directors, or stockholders of the organization.

Managerial capacity means an assignment within an organization in which the employee primarily:

(A) Manages the organization, or a department, subdivision, function, or component of the organization;

(B) Supervises and controls the work of other supervisory, professional, or managerial employees, or manages an essential function within the organization, or a department or subdivision of the organization;

(C) If another employee or other employees are directly supervised, has the authority to hire and fire or recommend those as well as other personnel actions (such as promotion and leave authorization), or, if no other employee is directly supervised, functions at a senior level within the organizational hierarchy or with respect to the function managed; and

(D) Exercises direction over the day-to-day operations of the activity or function for which the employee has authority.

Multinational means that the qualifying entity, or its affiliate, or subsidiary, conducts business in two or more countries, one of which is the United States.

Subsidiary means a firm, corporation, or other legal entity of which a parent owns, directly or indirectly, more than half of the entity and controls the entity; or owns, directly or indirectly, half of the entity and controls the entity; or owns, directly or indirectly, 50 percent of a 50–50 joint venture and has equal control and veto power over the entity; or owns, directly or indirectly, less than half of the entity, but in fact controls the entity.

(3) Initial evidence—

(i) Required evidence. A petition for a multinational executive or manager must be accompanied by a statement from an authorized official of the petitioning United States employer which demonstrates that:

(A) If the alien is outside the United States, in the three years immediately preceding the filing of the petition the alien has been employed outside the United States for at least one year in a managerial or executive capacity by a firm or corporation, or other legal entity, or by an affiliate or subsidiary of such a firm or corporation or other legal entity; or

(B) If the alien is already in the United States working for the same employer or a subsidiary or affiliate of the firm or corporation, or other legal entity by which the alien was employed overseas, in the three years preceding entry as a nonimmigrant, the alien was employed by the entity abroad for at least one year in a managerial or executive capacity;

(C) The prospective employer in the United States is the same employer or a subsidiary or affiliate of the firm or corporation or other legal entity by which the alien was employed overseas; and

(D) The prospective United States employer has been doing business for at least one year.

(ii) Appropriate additional evidence. In appropriate cases, the director may request additional evidence.

(4) Determining managerial or executive capacities.—

(i) Supervisors as managers. A first-line supervisor is not considered to be acting in a managerial capacity merely by virtue of his or her supervisory duties unless the employees supervised are professional.

(ii) Staffing levels. If staffing levels are used as a factor in determining whether an individual is acting in a managerial or executive capacity, the reasonable needs of the organization, component, or function, in light of the overall purpose and stage of development of the organization, component, or function, shall be taken into account. An individual shall not be considered to be acting in a managerial or executive capacity merely on the basis of the number of employees that the individual supervises or has supervised or directs or has directed.

(5) Offer of employment. No labor certification is required for this classification; however, the prospective employer in the United States must furnish a job offer in the form of a statement which indicates that the alien is to be employed in the United States in a managerial or executive capacity. Such letter must clearly describe the duties to be performed by the alien.

(k) Aliens who are members of the professions holding advanced degrees or aliens of exceptional ability.

(1) Any United States employer may file a petition on Form I–140 for classification of an alien under section 203(b)(2) of the Act as an alien who is a member of the professions holding an advanced degree or an alien of exceptional ability in the sciences, arts, or business. If an alien is claiming exceptional ability in the sciences, arts, or business and is seeking an exemption from the requirement of a job offer in the United States pursuant to section 203(b)(2)(B) of the Act, then the alien, or anyone in the alien's behalf, may be the petitioner.

(2) Definitions. As used in this section: Advanced degree means any United States academic or professional degree or a foreign equivalent degree above that of baccalaureate. A United States baccalaureate degree or a foreign equivalent degree followed by at least five years of progressive experience in the specialty shall be considered the equivalent of a master's degree. If a doctoral degree is customarily required by the specialty, the alien must have a United States doctorate or a foreign equivalent degree.

Exceptional ability in the sciences, arts, or business means a degree of expertise significantly above that ordinarily encountered in the sciences, arts, or business.

Profession means one of the occupations listed in section 101(a)(32) of the Act, as well as any occupation for which a United States baccalaureate degree or its foreign equivalent is the minimum requirement for entry into the occupation.

(3) Initial evidence. The petition must be accompanied by documentation showing that the alien is a professional holding an advanced degree or an alien of exceptional ability in the sciences, the arts, or business.

(i) To show that the alien is a professional holding an advanced degree, the petition must be accompanied by:

(A) An official academic record showing that the alien has a United States advanced degree or a foreign equivalent degree; or

(B) An official academic record showing that the alien has a United States baccalaureate degree or a foreign equivalent degree, and evidence in the form of letters from current or former employer(s) showing that the alien has at least five years of progressive post-baccalaureate experience in the specialty.

(ii) To show that the alien is an alien of exceptional ability in the sciences, arts, or business, the petition must be accompanied by at least three of the following:

(A) An official academic record showing that the alien has a degree, diploma, certificate, or similar award from a college, university, school, or other institution of learning relating to the area of exceptional ability;

(B) Evidence in the form of letter(s) from current or former employer(s) showing that the alien has at least ten years of full-time experience in the occupation for which he or she is being sought;

(C) A license to practice the profession or certification for a particular profession or occupation;

(D) Evidence that the alien has commanded a salary, or other remuneration for services, which demonstrates exceptional ability;

(E) Evidence of membership in professional associations; or

(F) Evidence of recognition for achievements and significant contributions to the industry or field by peers, governmental entities, or professional or business organizations.

(iii) If the above standards do not readily apply to the beneficiary's occupation, the petitioner may submit comparable evidence to establish the beneficiary's eligibility.

(4) Labor certification or evidence that alien qualifies for Labor Market Information Pilot Program—

(i) General. Every petition under this classification must be accompanied by an individual labor certification from the Department of Labor, by an application for Schedule A designation (if applicable), or by documentation to establish that the alien qualifies for one of the shortage occupations in the Department of Labor's Labor Market Information Pilot Program. To apply for Schedule A designation or to establish that the alien's occupation is within the Labor Market Information Program, a fully executed uncertified Form ETA–750 in duplicate must accompany the petition. The job offer portion of the individual labor certification, Schedule A application, or Pilot Program application must demonstrate that the job requires a professional holding an advanced degree or the equivalent or an alien of exceptional ability.

(ii) Exemption from job offer. The director may exempt the requirement of a job offer, and thus of a labor certification, for aliens of exceptional ability in the sciences, arts, or business if exemption would be in the national interest. To apply for the exemption, the petitioner must submit Form ETA–750B, Statement of Qualifications of Alien, in duplicate, as well as evidence to support the claim that such exemption would be in the national interest.

(*l*) Skilled workers, professionals, and other workers.

(1) Any United States employer may file a petition on Form I–140 for classification of an alien under section 203(b)(3) as a skilled worker, professional, or other (unskilled) worker.

(2) Definitions. As used in this part:

Other worker means a qualified alien who is capable, at the time of petitioning for this classification, of performing unskilled labor (requiring less than two years training or experience), not of a temporary or seasonal nature, for which qualified workers are not available in the United States.

Professional means a qualified alien who holds at least a United States baccalaureate degree or a foreign equivalent degree and who is a member of the professions.

Skilled worker means an alien who is capable, at the time of petitioning for this classification, of performing skilled labor (requiring at least two years training or experience), not of a temporary or seasonal nature, for which qualified workers are not available in the

United States. Relevant post-secondary education may be considered as training for the purposes of this provision.

(3) Initial evidence—

(i) Labor certification or evidence that alien qualifies for Labor Market Information Pilot Program. Every petition under this classification must be accompanied by an individual labor certification from the Department of Labor, by an application for Schedule A designation, or by documentation to establish that the alien qualifies for one of the shortage occupations in the Department of Labor's Labor Market Information Pilot Program. To apply for Schedule A designation or to establish that the alien's occupation is a shortage occupation with the Labor Market Pilot Program, a fully executed uncertified Form ETA–750 in duplicate must accompany the petition. The job offer portion of an individual labor certification, Schedule A application, or Pilot Program application for a professional must demonstrate that the job requires the minimum of a baccalaureate degree.

(ii) Other documentation—

(A) General. Any requirements of training or experience for skilled workers, professionals, or other workers must be supported by letters from trainers or employers giving the name, address, and title of the trainer or employer, and a description of the training received or the experience of the alien.

(B) Skilled workers. If the petition is for a skilled worker, the petition must be accompanied by evidence that the alien meets the educational, training or experience, and any other requirements of the individual labor certification, meets the requirements for Schedule A designation, or meets the requirements for the Labor Market Information Pilot Program occupation designation. The minimum requirements for this classification are at least two years of training or experience.

(C) Professionals. If the petition is for a professional, the petition must be accompanied by evidence that the alien holds a United States baccalaureate degree or a foreign equivalent degree and by evidence that the alien is a member of the professions. Evidence of a baccalaureate degree shall be in the form of an official college or university record showing the date the baccalaureate degree was awarded and the area of concentration of study. To show that the alien is a member of the professions, the petitioner must submit evidence showing that the minimum of a baccalaureate degree is required for entry into the occupation.

(D) Other workers. If the petition is for an unskilled (other) worker, it must be accompanied by evidence that the alien meets any educational, training and experience, and other requirements of the labor certification.

(4) Differentiating between skilled and other workers. The determination of whether a worker is a skilled or other worker will be based on the requirements of training and/or experience placed on the job by the prospective employer, as certified by the Department of Labor. In the case of a Schedule A occupation or a shortage occupation within the Labor Market Pilot Program, the petitioner will be required to establish to the director that the job is a skilled job, i.e., one which requires at least two years of training and/or experience.

(m) Religious workers. This paragraph governs classification of an alien as a special immigrant religious worker as defined in section 101(a)(27)(C) of the Act and under section 203(b)(4) of the Act. To be eligible for classification as a special immigrant religious worker, the alien (either abroad or in the United States) must:

(1) For at least the two years immediately preceding the filing of the petition have been a member of a religious denomination that has a bona fide non-profit religious organization in the United States.

(2) Be coming to the United States to work in a full time (average of at least 35 hours per week) compensated position in one of the following occupations as they are defined in paragraph (m)(5) of this section:

(i) Solely in the vocation of a minister of that religious denomination;

(ii) A religious vocation either in a professional or nonprofessional capacity; or

(iii) A religious occupation either in a professional or nonprofessional capacity.

(3) Be coming to work for a bona fide non-profit religious organization in the United States, or a bona fide organization which is affiliated with the religious denomination in the United States.

(4) Have been working in one of the positions described in paragraph (m)(2) of this section, either abroad or in lawful immigration status in the United States, and after the age of 14 years continuously for at least the two-year period immediately preceding the filing of the petition. The prior religious work need not correspond precisely to the type of work to be performed. A break in the continuity of the work during the preceding two years will not affect eligibility so long as:

(i) The alien was still employed as a religious worker;

(ii) The break did not exceed two years; and

(iii) The nature of the break was for further religious training or for sabbatical that did not involve unauthorized work in the United States. However, the alien must have been a member of the petitioner's denomination throughout the two years of qualifying employment.

(5) Definitions. As used in paragraph (m) of this section, the term:

Bona fide non-profit religious organization in the United States means a religious organization exempt from taxation as described in section 501(c)(3) of the Internal Revenue Code of 1986, subsequent amendment or equivalent sections of prior enactments of the Internal Revenue Code, and possessing a currently valid determination letter from the IRS confirming such exemption.

Bona fide organization which is affiliated with the religious denomination means an organization which is closely associated with the religious denomination and which is exempt from taxation as described in section 501(c)(3) of the Internal Revenue Code of 1986, subsequent amendment or equivalent sections of prior enactments of the Internal Revenue Code and possessing a currently valid *72292 determination letter from the IRS confirming such exemption.

Denominational membership means membership during at least the two-year period immediately preceding the filing date of the petition, in the same type of religious denomination as the United States religious organization where the alien will work.

Minister means an individual who:

(A) Is fully authorized by a religious denomination, and fully trained according to the denomination's standards, to conduct such religious worship and perform other duties usually performed by authorized members of the clergy of that denomination;

(B) Is not a lay preacher or a person not authorized to perform duties usually performed by clergy;

(C) Performs activities with a rational relationship to the religious calling of the minister; and

(D) Works solely as a minister in the United States, which may include administrative duties incidental to the duties of a minister.

Petition means USCIS Form I–360, Petition for Amerasian, Widow(er), or Special Immigrant, a successor form, or other form as may be prescribed by USCIS, along with a supplement containing attestations required by this section, the fee specified in 8 CFR 103.7(b)(1), and supporting evidence filed as provided by this part.

Religious denomination means a religious group or community of believers that is governed or administered under a common type of ecclesiastical government and includes one or more of the following:

(A) A recognized common creed or statement of faith shared among the denomination's members;

(B) A common form of worship;

(C) A common formal code of doctrine and discipline;

(D) Common religious services and ceremonies;

(E) Common established places of religious worship or religious congregations; or

(F) Comparable indicia of a bona fide religious denomination.

Religious occupation means an occupation that meets all of the following requirements:

(A) The duties must primarily relate to a traditional religious function and be recognized as a religious occupation within the denomination.

(B) The duties must be primarily related to, and must clearly involve, inculcating or carrying out the religious creed and beliefs of the denomination.

(C) The duties do not include positions that are primarily administrative or support such as janitors, maintenance workers, clerical employees, fund raisers, persons solely involved in the solicitation of donations, or similar positions, although limited administrative duties that are only incidental to religious functions are permissible.

(D) Religious study or training for religious work does not constitute a religious occupation, but a religious worker may pursue study or training incident to status.

Religious vocation means a formal lifetime commitment, through vows, investitures, ceremonies, or similar indicia, to a religious way of life. The religious denomination must have a class of individuals whose lives are dedicated to religious practices and functions, as distinguished from the secular members of the religion. Examples of individuals practicing religious vocations include nuns, monks, and religious brothers and sisters.

Religious worker means an individual engaged in and, according to the denomination's standards, qualified for a religious occupation or vocation, whether or not in a professional capacity, or as a minister.

Tax-exempt organization means an organization that has received a determination letter from the IRS establishing that it, or a group that it belongs to, is exempt from taxation in accordance with sections 501(c)(3) of the Internal Revenue Code of 1986 or subsequent amendments or equivalent sections of prior enactments of the Internal Revenue Code.

(6) Filing requirements. A petition must be filed as provided in the petition form instructions either by the alien or by his or her prospective United States employer. After the date stated in section 101(a)(27)(C) of the Act, immigration or adjustment of status on the basis of this section is limited solely to ministers.

(7) Attestation. An authorized official of the prospective employer of an alien seeking religious worker status must complete, sign and date an attestation prescribed by USCIS and submit it along with the petition. If the alien is a self-petitioner and is also an authorized official of the prospective employer, the self-petitioner may sign the attestation. The prospective employer must specifically attest to all of the following:

(i) That the prospective employer is a bona fide non-profit religious organization or a bona fide organization which is affiliated with the religious denomination and is exempt from taxation;

(ii) The number of members of the prospective employer's organization;

(iii) The number of employees who work at the same location where the beneficiary will be employed and a summary of the type of responsibilities of those employees. USCIS may request a list of all employees, their titles, and a brief description of their duties at its discretion;

(iv) The number of aliens holding special immigrant or nonimmigrant religious worker status currently employed or employed within the past five years by the prospective employer's organization;

(v) The number of special immigrant religious worker and nonimmigrant religious worker petitions and applications filed by or on behalf of any aliens for employment by the prospective employer in the past five years;

(vi) The title of the position offered to the alien, the complete package of salaried or non-salaried compensation being offered, and a detailed description of the alien's proposed daily duties;

(vii) That the alien will be employed at least 35 hours per week;

(viii) The specific location(s) of the proposed employment;

(ix) That the alien has worked as a religious worker for the two years immediately preceding the filing of the application and is otherwise qualified for the position offered;

(x) That the alien has been a member of the denomination for at least two years immediately preceding the filing of the application;

(xi) That the alien will not be engaged in secular employment, and any salaried or non-salaried compensation for the work will be paid to the alien by the attesting employer; and

(xii) That the prospective employer has the ability and intention to compensate the alien at a level at which the alien and accompanying family members will not become public charges, and that funds to pay the alien's compensation do not include any monies obtained from the alien, excluding reasonable donations or tithing to the religious organization.

(8) Evidence relating to the petitioning organization. A petition shall include the following initial evidence relating to the petitioning organization:

(i) A currently valid determination letter from the Internal Revenue Service (IRS) establishing that the organization is a tax-exempt organization; or

(ii) For a religious organization that is recognized as tax-exempt under a group tax-exemption, a currently valid determination letter from the IRS *72293 establishing that the group is tax-exempt; or

(iii) For a bona fide organization that is affiliated with the religious denomination, if the organization was granted tax-exempt status under section 501(c)(3) of the Internal Revenue Code of 1986, or subsequent amendment or equivalent sections of prior enactments of the Internal Revenue Code, as something other than a religious organization:

(A) A currently valid determination letter from the IRS establishing that the organization is a tax-exempt organization;

(B) Documentation that establishes the religious nature and purpose of the organization, such as a copy of the organizing instrument of the organization that specifies the purposes of the organization;

(C) Organizational literature, such as books, articles, brochures, calendars, flyers and other literature describing the religious purpose and nature of the activities of the organization; and

(D) A religious denomination certification. The religious organization must complete, sign and date a religious denomination certification certifying that the petitioning organization is affiliated with the religious denomination. The certification is to be submitted by the petitioner along with the petition.

(9) Evidence relating to the qualifications of a minister. If the alien is a minister, the petitioner must submit the following:

(i) A copy of the alien's certificate of ordination or similar documents reflecting acceptance of the alien's qualifications as a minister in the religious denomination; and

(ii) Documents reflecting acceptance of the alien's qualifications as a minister in the religious denomination, as well as evidence that the alien has completed any course of prescribed theological education at an accredited theological institution normally required or recognized by that religious denomination, including transcripts, curriculum, and documentation that establishes that the theological institution is accredited by the denomination, or

(iii) For denominations that do not require a prescribed theological education, evidence of:

(A) The denomination's requirements for ordination to minister;

(B) The duties allowed to be performed by virtue of ordination;

(C) The denomination's levels of ordination, if any; and

(D) The alien's completion of the denomination's requirements for ordination.

(10) Evidence relating to compensation. Initial evidence must include verifiable evidence of how the petitioner intends to compensate the alien. Such compensation may include salaried or non-salaried compensation. This evidence may include past evidence of compensation for similar positions; budgets showing monies set aside for salaries, leases, etc.; verifiable documentation that room and board will be provided; or other evidence acceptable to USCIS. If IRS documentation, such as IRS Form W–2 or certified tax returns, is available, it must be provided. If IRS documentation is not available, an explanation for its absence must be provided, along with comparable, verifiable documentation.

(11) Evidence relating to the alien's prior employment. Qualifying prior experience during the two years immediately preceding the petition or preceding any acceptable break in the continuity of the religious work, must have occurred after the age of 14, and if acquired in the United States, must have been authorized under United States immigration law. If the alien was employed in the United States during the two years immediately preceding the filing of the application and:

(i) Received salaried compensation, the petitioner must submit IRS documentation that the alien received a salary, such as an IRS Form W–2 or certified copies of income tax returns.

(ii) Received non-salaried compensation, the petitioner must submit IRS documentation of the non-salaried compensation if available.

(iii) Received no salary but provided for his or her own support, and provided support for any dependents, the petitioner must show how support was maintained by submitting with the petition additional documents such as audited financial statements, financial institution records, brokerage account statements, trust documents signed by an attorney, or other verifiable evidence acceptable to USCIS.

If the alien was employed outside the United States during such two years, the petitioner must submit comparable evidence of the religious work.

(12) Inspections, evaluations, verifications, and compliance reviews. The supporting evidence submitted may be verified by USCIS through any means determined appropriate by USCIS, up to and including an on-site inspection of the petitioning organization. The inspection may include a tour of the organization's facilities, an interview with the organization's officials, a review of selected organization records relating to compliance with immigration laws and regulations, and an interview with any other individuals or review of any other records that the USCIS considers pertinent to the integrity of the organization. An inspection may include the organization headquarters, satellite locations, or the work locations planned for the applicable employee. If USCIS decides to conduct a pre-approval inspection, satisfactory completion of such inspection will be a condition for approval of any petition.

(n) Closing action—

(1) Approval. An approved employment–based petition will be forwarded to the National Visa Center of the Department of State if the beneficiary resides outside of the United States. If the Form I–140 petition indicates that the alien has filed or will file an application for adjustment to permanent residence in the United States (Form I–485) the approved visa petition (Form I–140), will be retained by the Service for consideration with the application for permanent residence (Form I–485). If a visa is available, and Form I–485 has not been filed, the alien will be instructed on the Form I–797, Notice of Action, (mailed out upon approval of the Form I–140 petition) to file the Form I–485.

(2) Denial. The denial of a petition for classification under section 203(b)(1), 203(b)(2), 203(b)(3), or 203(b)(4) of the Act (as it relates to special immigrants under section 101(a)(27)(C) of the Act) shall be appealable to the Associate Commissioner for Examinations. The petitioner shall be informed in plain language of the reasons for denial and of his or her right to appeal.

(3) Validity of approved petitions. Unless revoked under section 203(e) or 205 of the Act, an employment-based petition is valid indefinitely.

(*o*) Denial of petitions under section 204 of the Act based on a finding by the Department of Labor. Upon debarment by the Department of Labor pursuant to 20 CFR 655.31, USCIS may deny any employment-based immigrant petition filed by that petitioner for a period of at least 1 year but not more than 5 years. The time period of such bar to petition approval shall be based on the severity of the violation or violations. The decision to deny petitions, the time period for the bar to petitions, and the reasons for the time period will be explained in a written notice to the petitioner.

[30 FR 14775, Nov. 30, 1965, as amended at 41 FR 55849, Dec. 23, 1976; 52 FR 33797, Sept. 8, 1987; 53 FR 2824, Feb. 2, 1988; 56 FR 60905, Nov. 29, 1991; 59 FR 502, Jan. 5, 1994; 59 FR 27229, May 26, 1994; 59 FR 51360, Oct. 11, 1994; 60 FR 29753, June 6, 1995; 61 FR 33305, June 27, 1996; 62 FR 4631, Jan. 31, 1997; 62 Fed. Reg. 67 FR 49563, July 31, 2002; 73 FR 72291, Nov. 26, 2008; 73 FR 78127, Dec. 19, 2008; 74 FR 26936, June 5, 2009]

PART 208—PROCEDURES FOR ASYLUM AND WITHHOLDING OF REMOVAL

SUBPART A—ASYLUM AND WITHHOLDING OF REMOVAL

§ 208.1 General. [also 8 C.F.R. § 1208.1, which has minor wording changes and cross-references to part 1208]

(a) Applicability.

(1) General. Unless otherwise provided in this chapter I, this subpart A shall apply to all applications for asylum under section 208 of the Act or for withholding of deportation or withholding of removal under section 241(b)(3) of the Act, or under the Convention Against Torture, whether before an asylum officer or an immigration judge, regardless of the date of filing. For purposes of this chapter I, withholding of removal shall also mean withholding of deportation under section 243(h) of the Act, as it appeared prior to April 1, 1997, except as provided in § 208.16(d). Such applications are referred to as "asylum applications." The provisions of this part 208 shall not affect the finality or validity of any decision made by a district director, an immigration judge, or the Board of Immigration Appeals in any such case prior to April 1, 1997. No asylum application that was filed with a district director, asylum officer, or immigration judge prior to April 1, 1997, may be reopened or otherwise reconsidered under the provisions of this part 208 except by motion granted in the exercise of discretion by the Board of Immigration Appeals, an immigration judge, or an asylum officer for proper cause shown. Motions to reopen or reconsider must meet the requirements of sections 240(c)(6) and (c)(7) of the Act, and 8 CFR parts 103 and 1003, as applicable.

(2) Commonwealth of the Northern Mariana Islands. The provisions of this subpart A shall not apply prior to January 1, 2015, to an alien physically present in or arriving in the Commonwealth of the Northern Mariana Islands seeking to apply for asylum. No application for asylum may be filed prior to January 1, 2015, pursuant to section 208 of the Act by an alien physically present in or arriving in the Commonwealth of the Northern Mariana Islands. Effective on the transition program effective date, the provisions of this subpart A shall apply to aliens physically present in or arriving in the CNMI with respect to withholding of removal under section 241(b)(3) of the Act and withholding and deferral of removal under the Convention Against Torture.

(b) Training of asylum officers. The Associate Director of USCIS Refugee, Asylum, and International Operations (RAIO) shall ensure that asylum officers receive special training in international human rights law, nonadversarial interview techniques, and other relevant national and international refugee laws and principles. The Associate Director of USCIS Refugee, Asylum, and International Operations (RAIO) shall also, in cooperation with the Department of State and other appropriate sources, compile and disseminate to asylum officers information concerning the persecution of persons in other countries on account of race, religion, nationality, membership in a particular social group, or political opinion, torture of persons in other countries, and other information relevant to asylum determinations, and shall maintain a documentation center with information on human rights conditions.

[64 FR 8487, Feb. 19, 1999; 74 FR 55736, Oct. 28, 2009; 76 FR 53784, Aug. 29, 2011]

§ 208.2 Jurisdiction. [also 8 C.F.R. § 1208.2, which has minor wording changes and cross-references to part 1208]

(a) Refugee, Asylum, and International Operations (RAIO). Except as provided in paragraph (b) or (c) of this section, RAIO shall have initial jurisdiction over an asylum application filed by an alien physically present in the United States or seeking admission at a port-of-entry. RAIO shall also have initial jurisdiction over credible fear determinations under § 208.30 and reasonable fear determinations under § 208.31.

(b) Jurisdiction of Immigration Court in general. Immigration judges shall have exclusive jurisdiction over asylum applications filed by an alien who has been served a Form I–221, Order to Show Cause; Form I–122, Notice to Applicant for Admission Detained for a Hearing before an Immigration Judge; or Form I–862, Notice to Appear, after the charging document has been filed with the Immigration Court. Immigration judges shall also have jurisdiction over any asylum applications filed prior to April 1, 1997, by alien crewmembers who have remained in the United States longer than authorized, by applicants for admission under the Visa Waiver Pilot Program, and by aliens who have been admitted to the United States under the Visa Waiver Pilot Program. Immigration judges shall also have the authority to review reasonable fear determinations referred to the Immigration Court under § 208.31, and credible fear determinations referred to the Immigration Court under § 208.30.

(c) Certain aliens not entitled to proceedings under section 240 of the Act.

(1) Asylum applications and withholding of removal applications only. After Form I–863, Notice of Referral to Immigration Judge, has been filed with the Immigration Court, an immigration judge shall have exclusive jurisdiction over any asylum application filed on or after April 1, 1997, by:

(i) An alien crewmember who:

(A) Is an applicant for a landing permit;

(B) Has been refused permission to land under section 252 of the Act; or

(C) On or after April 1, 1997, was granted permission to land under section 252 of the Act, regardless of whether the alien has remained in the United States longer than authorized;

(ii) An alien stowaway who has been found to have a credible fear of persecution or torture pursuant to the procedures set forth in subpart B of this part;

(iii) An alien who is an applicant for admission pursuant to the Visa Waiver Program under section 217 of the Act, except that if such an alien is an applicant for admission to the Commonwealth of the Northern Mariana Islands, then he or she shall not be eligible for asylum prior to January 1, 2015;

(iv) An alien who was admitted to the United States pursuant to the Visa Waiver Program under section 217 of the Act and has remained longer than authorized or has otherwise violated his or her immigration status, except that if such an alien was admitted to the Commonwealth of the Northern Mariana Islands, then he or she shall not be eligible for asylum in the Commonwealth of the Northern Mariana Islands prior to January 1, 2015;

(v) An alien who has been ordered removed under § 235(c) of the Act, as described in § 235.8(a) of this chapter (applicable only in the event that the alien is referred for proceedings under this paragraph by the Regional Director pursuant to section 235.8(b)(2)(ii) of this chapter);

(vi) An alien who is an applicant for admission, or has been admitted, as an alien classified under section 101(a)(15)(S) of the Act (applicable only in the event that the alien is referred for proceedings under this paragraph by the district director);

(vii) An alien who is an applicant for admission to Guam or the Commonwealth of the Northern Mariana Islands pursuant to the Guam–CNMI Visa Waiver Program under section 212(*l*) of the Act, except that if such an alien is an applicant for admission to the Commonwealth of the Northern Mariana Islands, then he or she shall not be eligible for asylum prior to January 1, 2015; or

(viii) An alien who was admitted to Guam or the Commonwealth of the Northern Mariana Islands pursuant to the Guam–CNMI Visa Waiver Program under section 212(*l*) of the Act and has remained longer than authorized or has otherwise violated his or her immigration status, except that if such an alien was admitted to the Commonwealth of the Northern Mariana Islands, then he or she shall not be eligible for asylum in the Commonwealth of the Northern Mariana Islands prior to January 1, 2015.

(2) Withholding of removal applications only. After Form I–863, Notice of Referral to Immigration Judge, has been filed with the Immigration Court, an immigration judge shall have exclusive jurisdiction over any application for withholding of removal filed by:

(i) An alien who is the subject of a reinstated removal order pursuant to section 241(a)(5) of the Act; or

(ii) An alien who has been issued an administrative removal order pursuant to section 238 of the Act as an alien convicted of committing an aggravated felony.

(3) Rules of procedure.

(i) General. Except as provided in this section, proceedings falling under the jurisdiction of the immigration judge pursuant to paragraph (c)(1) or (c)(2) of this section shall be conducted in accordance with the same rules of procedure as proceedings conducted under 8 CFR part 240, subpart A. The scope of review in proceedings conducted pursuant to paragraph (c)(1) of this section shall be limited to a determination of whether the alien is eligible for asylum or withholding or deferral of removal, and whether asylum shall be granted in the exercise of discretion. The scope of review in proceedings conducted pursuant to paragraph (c)(2) of this section shall be limited to a determination of whether the alien is eligible for withholding or deferral of removal. During such proceedings, all parties are prohibited from raising or considering any other issues, including but not limited to issues of admissibility, deportability, eligibility for waivers, and eligibility for any other form of relief.

(ii) Notice of hearing procedures and in-absentia decisions. The alien will be provided with notice of the time and place of the proceeding. The request for asylum and withholding of removal submitted by an alien who fails to appear for the hearing shall be denied. The denial of asylum and withholding of removal for failure to appear may be reopened only upon a motion filed with the immigration judge with jurisdiction over the case. Only one motion to reopen may be filed, and it must be filed within 90 days, unless the alien establishes that he or she did not receive notice of the hearing date or was in Federal or State custody on the date directed to appear. The motion must include documentary evidence, which demonstrates that:

(A) The alien did not receive the notice;

(B) The alien was in Federal or State custody and the failure to appear was through no fault of the alien; or

(C) ''Exceptional circumstances,'' as defined in section 240(e)(1) of the Act, caused the failure to appear.

(iii) Relief. The filing of a motion to reopen shall not stay removal of the alien unless the immigration judge issues an order granting a stay pending disposition of the motion. An alien who fails to appear for a proceeding under this section shall not be eligible for relief under section 240A, 240B, 245, 248, or 249 of the Act for a period of 10 years after the date of the denial, unless the applicant can show exceptional circumstances resulted in his or her failure to appear.

[62 FR 15362, April 1, 1997; 64 FR 8487, Feb. 19, 1999; 65 FR 76130, Dec. 6, 2000; 74 FR 55736, Oct. 28, 2009; 76 FR 53784, Aug. 29, 2011.]

§ 208.3 Form of application. [also 8 C.F.R. § 1208.3, which is identical except for cross-references to part 1208]

(a) An asylum applicant must file Form I–589, Application for Asylum and for Withholding of Removal, together with any additional supporting evidence in accordance with the instructions on the form. The applicant's spouse and children shall be listed on the application and may be included in the request for asylum if they are in the United States. One additional copy of the principal applicant's Form I–589 must be submitted for each dependent included in the principal's application.

(b) An asylum application shall be deemed to constitute at the same time an application for withholding of removal, unless adjudicated in deportation or exclusion proceedings commenced prior to April 1, 1997. In such instances, the asylum application shall be deemed to constitute an application for withholding of deportation under section 243(h) of the Act, as that section existed prior to April 1, 1997. Where a determination is made that an applicant is ineligible to apply for asylum under section 208(a)(2) of the Act, an asylum application shall be construed as an application for withholding of removal.

(c) Form I–589 shall be filed under the following conditions and shall have the following consequences:

(1) If the application was filed on or after January 4, 1995, information provided in the application may be used as a basis for the initiation of removal proceedings, or to satisfy any burden of proof in exclusion, deportation, or removal proceedings;

(2) The applicant and anyone other than a spouse, parent, son, or daughter of the applicant who assists the applicant in preparing the application must sign the application under penalty of perjury. The applicant's signature establishes a presumption that the applicant is aware of the contents of the application. A person other than a relative specified in this paragraph who assists the applicant in preparing the application also must provide his or her full mailing address;

(3) An asylum application that does not include a response to each of the questions contained in the Form I–589, is unsigned, or is unaccompanied by the required materials specified in paragraph (a) of this section is incomplete. The filing of an incomplete application shall not commence the 150–day period after which the applicant may file an application for employment authorization in accordance with § 208.7. An application that is incomplete shall be returned by mail to the applicant within 30 days of the receipt of the application by the Service. If the Service has not mailed the incomplete application back to the applicant within 30 days, it shall be deemed complete. An application returned to the applicant as incomplete shall be resubmitted by the applicant with the additional information if he or she wishes to have the application considered;

(4) Knowing placement of false information on the application may subject the person placing that information on the application to criminal penalties under title 18 of the United States Code and to civil or criminal penalties under section 274C of the Act; and

(5) Knowingly filing a frivolous application on or after April 1, 1997, so long as the applicant has received the notice required by section 208(d)(4) of the Act, shall render the applicant permanently ineligible for any benefits under the Act pursuant to § 208.20.

[62 FR 10338, March 6, 1997; 65 FR 76131, Dec. 6, 2000]

§ 208.4 Filing the application. [also 8 C.F.R. § 1208.4, which has minor wording changes and cross-references to part 1208]

Except as prohibited in paragraph (a) of this section, asylum applications shall be filed in accordance with paragraph (b) of this section.

(a) Prohibitions on filing. Section 208(a)(2) of the Act prohibits certain aliens from filing for asylum on or after April 1, 1997, unless the alien can demonstrate to the satisfaction of the Attorney General that one of the exceptions in section 208(a)(2)(D) of the Act applies. Such prohibition applies only to asylum applications under section 208 of the Act and not to applications for withholding of removal under § 208.16. If an applicant files an asylum application and it appears that one or more of the prohibitions contained in section 208(a)(2) of the Act apply, an asylum officer, in an interview, or an immigration judge, in a hearing, shall review the application and give the applicant the opportunity to present any relevant and useful information bearing on any prohibitions on filing to determine if the application should be rejected. For the purpose of making determinations under section 208(a)(2) of the Act, the following rules shall apply:

(1) Authority. Only an asylum officer, an immigration judge, or the Board of Immigration Appeals is authorized to make determinations regarding the prohibitions contained in section 208(a)(2)(B) or (C) of the Act.

(2) One-year filing deadline.

(i) For purposes of section 208(a)(2)(B) of the Act, an applicant has the burden of proving:

(A) By clear and convincing evidence that the application has been filed within 1 year of the date of the alien's arrival in the United States, or

(B) To the satisfaction of the asylum officer, the immigration judge, or the Board that he or she qualifies for an exception to the 1–year deadline.

(ii) The 1–year period shall be calculated from the date of the alien's last arrival in the United States or April 1, 1997, whichever is later. When the last day of the period so computed falls on a Saturday, Sunday, or legal holiday, the period shall run until the end of the next day that is not a Saturday, Sunday, or legal holiday. For the purpose of making determinations under section 208(a)(2)(B) of the Act only, an application is considered to have been filed on the date it is received by the Service, pursuant to § 103.2(a)(7) of this chapter. In a case in which the application has not been received by the Service within 1 year from the applicant's date of entry into the United States, but the applicant provides clear and convincing documentary evidence of mailing the application within the 1–year period, the mailing date shall be considered the filing date. For cases before the Immigration Court in accordance with § 3.13 of this chapter, the application is considered to have been filed on the date it is received by the Immigration Court. For cases before the Board of Immigration Appeals, the application is considered to have been filed on the date it is received by the

Board. In the case of an application that appears to have been filed more than a year after the applicant arrived in the United States, the asylum officer, the immigration judge, or the Board will determine whether the applicant qualifies for an exception to the deadline. For aliens present in or arriving in the Commonwealth of the Northern Mariana Islands, the 1–year period shall be calculated from either January 1, 2015, or from the date of the alien's last arrival in the United States (including the Commonwealth of the Northern Mariana Islands), whichever is later. No period of physical presence in the Commonwealth of the Northern Mariana Islands prior to January 1, 2015, shall count toward the 1–year period. After November 28, 2009, any travel to the Commonwealth of the Northern Mariana Islands from any other State shall not re-start the calculation of the 1–year period.

(3) Prior denial of application. For purposes of section 208(a)(2)(C) of the Act, an asylum application has not been denied unless denied by an immigration judge or the Board of Immigration Appeals.

(4) Changed circumstances.

(i) The term "changed circumstances" in section 208(a)(2)(D) of the Act shall refer to circumstances materially affecting the applicant's eligibility for asylum. They may include, but are not limited to:

(A) Changes in conditions in the applicant's country of nationality or, if the applicant is stateless, country of last habitual residence;

(B) Changes in the applicant's circumstances that materially affect the applicant's eligibility for asylum, including changes in applicable U.S. law and activities the applicant becomes involved in outside the country of feared persecution that place the applicant at risk; or

(C) In the case of an alien who had previously been included as a dependent in another alien's pending asylum application, the loss of the spousal or parent-child relationship to the principal applicant through marriage, divorce, death, or attainment of age 21.

(ii) The applicant shall file an asylum application within a reasonable period given those "changed circumstances." If the applicant can establish that he or she did not become aware of the changed circumstances until after they occurred, such delayed awareness shall be taken into account in determining what constitutes a "reasonable period."

(5) The term "extraordinary circumstances" in section 208(a)(2)(D) of the Act shall refer to events or factors directly related to the failure to meet the 1–year deadline. Such circumstances may excuse the failure to file within the 1–year period as long as the alien filed the application within a reasonable period given those circumstances. The burden of proof is on the applicant to establish to the satisfaction of the asylum officer, the immigration judge, or the Board of Immigration Appeals that the circumstances were not intentionally created by the alien through his or her own action or inaction, that those circumstances were directly related to the alien's failure to file the application within the 1–year period, and that the delay was reasonable under the circumstances. Those circumstances may include but are not limited to:

(i) Serious illness or mental or physical disability, including any effects of persecution or violent harm suffered in the past, during the 1–year period after arrival;

(ii) Legal disability (e.g., the applicant was an unaccompanied minor or suffered from a mental impairment) during the 1–year period after arrival;

(iii) Ineffective assistance of counsel, provided that:

(A) The alien files an affidavit setting forth in detail the agreement that was entered into with counsel with respect to the actions to be taken and what representations counsel did or did not make to the respondent in this regard;

(B) The counsel whose integrity or competence is being impugned has been informed of the allegations leveled against him or her and given an opportunity to respond; and

(C) The alien indicates whether a complaint has been filed with appropriate disciplinary authorities with respect to any violation of counsel's ethical or legal responsibilities, and if not, why not;

(iv) The applicant maintained Temporary Protected Status, lawful immigrant or nonimmigrant status, or was given parole, until a reasonable period before the filing of the asylum application;

(v) The applicant filed an asylum application prior to the expiration of the 1–year deadline, but that application was rejected by the Service as not properly filed, was returned to the applicant for corrections, and was refiled within a reasonable period thereafter; and

(vi) The death or serious illness or incapacity of the applicant's legal representative or a member of the applicant's immediate family.

(6) Safe Third Country Agreement. Asylum officers have authority to apply section 208(a)(2)(A) of the Act, relating to the determination that the alien may be removed to a safe country pursuant to a bilateral or multilateral agreement, only as provided in 8 CFR 208.30(e). For provisions relating to the authority of immigration judges with respect to section 208(a)(2)(A), see 8 CFR 1240.11(g).

(b) Filing location—Form I–589, Application for Asylum and Withholding of Removal, must be filed in accordance with the instructions on the form.

(c) Amending an application after filing. Upon request of the alien and as a matter of discretion, the asylum officer or immigration judge having jurisdiction may permit an asylum applicant to amend or supplement the application, but any delay caused by such request shall extend the period within which the applicant may not apply for employment authorization in accordance with § 208.7(a).

[64 FR 8488, Feb. 19, 1999; 64 FR 13881, March 23, 1999; 65 FR 76131, Dec. 6, 2000; 69 FR 69488, Nov. 29, 2004; 74 FR 26937, June 5, 2009; 74 FR 55737, Oct. 28, 2009]

§ 208.5 Special duties toward aliens in custody of DHS. [also 8 C.F.R. § 1208.5, which has minor wording changes and cross-references to part 1208]

(a) General. When an alien in the custody of DHS requests asylum or withholding of removal, or expresses a fear of persecution or harm upon return to his or her country of origin or to agents thereof, DHS shall make available the appropriate application forms and shall provide the applicant with the information required by section 208(d)(4) of the Act, except in the case of an alien who is in custody pending a credible fear determination under 8 CFR 208.30 or a reasonable fear determination pursuant to 8 CFR 208.31. Although DHS does not have a duty in the case of an alien who is in custody pending a credible fear or reasonable fear determination under either 8 CFR 208.30 or 8 CFR 208.31, DHS may provide the appropriate forms, upon request. Where possible, expedited consideration shall be given to applications of detained aliens. Except as provided in paragraph (c) of this section, such alien shall not be excluded, deported, or removed before a decision is rendered on his or her asylum application. Furthermore, except as provided in paragraph (c) of this section, an alien physically present in or arriving in the Commonwealth of the Northern Mariana Islands shall not be excluded, deported, or removed before a decision is rendered on his or her application for withholding of removal pursuant to section 241(b)(3) of the Act and withholding of removal under the Convention Against Torture. No application for asylum may be filed prior to January 1, 2015, under section 208 of the Act by an alien physically present in or arriving in the Commonwealth of the Northern Mariana Islands.

(b) Certain aliens aboard vessels.

(1) If an alien crewmember or alien stowaway on board a vessel or other conveyance alleges, claims, or otherwise makes known to an immigration inspector or other official making an examination on the conveyance that he or she is unable or unwilling to return to his or her country of nationality or last habitual residence (if not a national of any country) because of persecution or a fear of persecution in that country on account of race, religion, nationality, membership in a particular social group, or political opinion, or if the alien expresses a fear of torture upon return to that country, the alien shall be promptly removed from the conveyance. If the alien makes such fear known to an official while off such conveyance, the alien shall not be returned to the conveyance but shall be retained in or transferred to the custody of the Service.

(i) An alien stowaway will be referred to an asylum officer for a credible fear determination under § 208.30.

(ii) An alien crewmember shall be provided the appropriate application forms and information required by section 208(d)(4) of the Act and may then have 10 days within which to submit an asylum application in accordance with the instructions on the form. DHS may extend the 10–day filing period for good cause. Once the application has been filed, DHS shall serve Form I–863 on the alien and immediately forward any such application to the appropriate Immigration Court with a copy of the Form I–863 being filed with that court.

(iii) An alien crewmember physically present in or arriving in the Commonwealth of the Northern Mariana Islands can request withholding of removal pursuant to section 241(b)(3) of the Act and withholding of removal under the Convention Against Torture. However, such an alien crewmember is not eligible to request asylum pursuant to section 208 of the Act prior to January 1, 2015.

(2) Pending adjudication of the application, and, in the case of a stowaway the credible fear determination and any review thereof, the alien may be detained by the Service or otherwise paroled in accordance with § 212.5 of this chapter. However, pending the credible fear determination, parole of an alien stowaway may be permitted only when the Secretary determines, in the exercise of discretion, that parole is required to meet a medical emergency or is necessary for a legitimate law enforcement objective.

(c) Exception to prohibition on removal. A motion to reopen or an order to remand accompanied by an asylum application pursuant to § 208.4(b)(3)(iii) shall not stay execution of a final exclusion, deportation, or removal order unless such stay is specifically granted by the Board of Immigration Appeals or the immigration judge having jurisdiction over the motion.

[64 FR 8488, Feb. 19, 1999; 65 FR 76132, Dec. 6, 2000; 74 FR 26937, June 5, 2009; 74 FR 55737, Oct. 28, 2009; 76 FR 53784, Aug. 29, 2011.]

§ 208.6 Disclosure to third parties. [also 8 C.F.R. § 1208.6, which is identical except for cross-references to part 1208]

(a) Information contained in or pertaining to any asylum application, records pertaining to any credible fear determination conducted pursuant to § 208.30, and records pertaining to any reasonable fear determination conducted pursuant to § 208.31, shall not be disclosed without the written consent of the applicant, except as permitted by this section or at the discretion of the Attorney General.

(b) The confidentiality of other records kept by the Service and the Executive Office for Immigration Review that indicate that a specific alien has applied for asylum, received a credible fear or reasonable fear interview, or received a credible fear or reasonable fear review shall also be protected from disclosure. The Service will coordinate with the Department of State to ensure that the confidentiality of those records is maintained if they are transmitted to Department of State offices in other countries.

(c) This section shall not apply to any disclosure to:

(1) Any United States Government official or contractor having a need to examine information in connection with:

(i) The adjudication of asylum applications;

(ii) The consideration of a request for a credible fear or reasonable fear interview, or a credible fear or reasonable fear review;

(iii) The defense of any legal action arising from the adjudication of, or failure to adjudicate, the asylum application, or from a credible fear determination or reasonable fear determination under § 208.30 or § 208.31;

(iv) The defense of any legal action of which the asylum application, credible fear determination, or reasonable fear determination is a part; or

(v) Any United States Government investigation concerning any criminal or civil matter; or

(2) Any Federal, State, or local court in the United States considering any legal action:

(i) Arising from the adjudication of, or failure to adjudicate, the asylum application, or from a credible fear or reasonable fear determination under § 208.30 or § 208.31; or

(ii) Arising from the proceedings of which the asylum application, credible fear determination, or reasonable fear determination is a part.

[62 Fed.Reg. 10340, March 6, 1997; 65 FR 76133, Dec. 6, 2000]

§ 208.7 Employment authorization. [also 8 C.F.R. § 1208.7, which has minor wording changes and cross-references to part 1208]

(a) Application and approval.

(1) Subject to the restrictions contained in sections 208(d) and 236(a) of the Act, an applicant for asylum who is not an aggravated felon shall be eligible pursuant to §§ 274a.12(c)(8) and 274a.13(a) of this chapter to request employment authorization. Except in the case of an alien whose asylum application has been recommended for approval, or in the case of an alien who filed an asylum application prior to January 4, 1995, the application shall be submitted no earlier than 150 days after the date on which a complete asylum application submitted in accordance with §§ 208.3 and 208.4 has been received. In the case of an applicant whose asylum application has been recommended for approval, the applicant may apply for employment authorization when he or she receives notice of the recommended approval. If an asylum application has been returned as incomplete in accordance with § 208.3(c)(3), the 150–day period will commence upon receipt by the Service of a complete asylum application. An applicant whose asylum application has been denied by an asylum officer or by an immigration judge within the 150–day period shall not be eligible to apply for employment authorization. If an asylum application is denied prior to a decision on the application for employment authorization, the application for employment authorization shall be denied. If the asylum application is not so denied, the Service shall have 30 days from the date of filing of the employment authorization request to grant or deny that application, except that no employment authorization shall be issued to an asylum applicant prior to the expiration of the 180–day period following the filing of the asylum application filed on or after April 1, 1997.

(2) The time periods within which the alien may not apply for employment authorization and within which USCIS must respond to any such application and within which the asylum application must be adjudicated pursuant to section 208(d)(5)(A)(iii) of the Act shall begin when the alien has filed a complete asylum application in accordance with SS208.3 and 208.4. Any delay requested or caused by the applicant shall not be counted as part of these time periods, including delays caused by failure without good cause to follow the requirements for fingerprint processing. Such time periods shall also be extended by the equivalent of the time between issuance of a request for evidence pursuant to § 103.2(b)(8) of this chapter and the receipt of the applicant's response to such request.

(3) The provisions of paragraphs (a)(1) and (a)(2) of this section apply to applications for asylum filed on or after January 4, 1995.

(4) Employment authorization pursuant to § 274a.12(c)(8) of this chapter may not be granted to an alien who fails to appear for a scheduled interview before an asylum officer or a hearing before an immigration judge, unless the applicant demonstrates that the failure to appear was the result of exceptional circumstances.

(b) Renewal and termination. Employment authorization shall be renewable, in increments to be determined by USCIS, for the continuous period of time necessary for the asylum officer or immigration judge to decide the asylum application and, if necessary, for completion of any administrative or judicial review.

(1) If the asylum application is denied by the asylum officer, the employment authorization shall terminate at the expiration of the employment authorization document or 60 days after the denial of asylum, whichever is longer.

(2) If the application is denied by the immigration judge, the Board of Immigration Appeals, or a Federal court, the employment authorization terminates upon the expiration of the employment authorization document, unless the applicant has filed an appropriate request for administrative or judicial review.

(c) Supporting evidence for renewal of employment authorization. In order for employment authorization to be renewed under this section, the alien must request employment authorization in accordance with the form instructions. USCIS may require that an alien establish that he or she has continued to pursue an asylum application before an immigration judge or sought administrative or judicial review. For purposes of employment authorization, pursuit of an asylum application is established by presenting one of the following, depending on the stage of the alien's immigration proceedings:

(1) If the alien's case is pending in proceedings before the immigration judge, and the alien wishes to continue to pursue his or her asylum application, a copy of any asylum denial, referral notice, or charging document placing the alien in such proceedings;

(2) If the immigration judge has denied asylum, a copy of the document issued by the Board of Immigration Appeals to show that a timely appeal has been filed from a denial of the asylum application by the immigration judge; or

(3) If the Board of Immigration Appeals has dismissed the alien's appeal of a denial of asylum, or sustained an appeal by the Service of a grant of asylum, a copy of the petition for judicial review or for habeas corpus pursuant to section 242 of the Act, date stamped by the appropriate court.

(d) In order for employment authorization to be renewed before its expiration, the application for renewal must be received by the Service 90 days prior to expiration of the employment authorization.

[62 FR 10340, March 6, 1997; as amended at 63 FR 12986, March 17, 1998; 76 FR 53784, Aug. 29, 2011.]

§ 208.8 Limitations on travel outside the United States. [also 8 C.F.R. § 1208.8, which is identical except for cross-references to part 1208]

(a) An applicant who leaves the United States without first obtaining advance parole under § 212.5(f) of this chapter shall be presumed to have abandoned his or her application under this section.

(b) An applicant who leaves the United States pursuant to advance parole under § 212.5(f) of this chapter and returns to the country of claimed persecution shall be presumed to have abandoned his or her application, unless the applicant is able to establish compelling reasons for such return.

[62 Fed. Reg. 10341, March 6, 1997; 65 FR 82255, Dec. 28, 2000; 66 FR 7863, Jan. 26, 2001]

§ 208.9 Procedure for interview before an asylum officer. [also 8 C.F.R. § 1208.9, which has minor wording changes and cross-references to part 1208]

(a) The Service shall adjudicate the claim of each asylum applicant whose application is complete within the meaning of § 208.3(c)(3) and is within the jurisdiction of the Service.

(b) The asylum officer shall conduct the interview in a nonadversarial manner and, except at the request of the applicant, separate and apart from the general public. The purpose of the interview shall be to elicit all relevant and useful information bearing on the applicant's eligibility for asylum. At the time of the interview, the applicant must provide complete information regarding his or her identity, including name, date and place of birth, and nationality, and may be required to register this identity. The applicant may have counsel or a representative present, may present witnesses, and may submit affidavits of witnesses and other evidence.

(c) The asylum officer shall have authority to administer oaths, verify the identity of the applicant (including through the use of electronic means), verify the identity of any interpreter, present and receive evidence, and question the applicant and any witnesses.

(d) Upon completion of the interview, the applicant or the applicant's representative shall have an opportunity to make a statement or comment on the evidence presented. The asylum officer may, in his or her discretion, limit the length of such statement or comment and may require its submission in writing. Upon completion of the interview, the applicant shall be informed that he or she must appear in person to receive and to acknowledge receipt of the decision of the asylum officer and any other accompanying material at a time and place designated by the asylum officer, except as otherwise provided by the asylum officer.

An applicant's failure to appear to receive and acknowledge receipt of the decision shall be treated as delay caused by the applicant for purposes of § 208.7(a)(3) and shall extend the period within which the applicant may not apply for employment authorization by the number of days until the applicant does appear to receive and acknowledge receipt of the decision or until the applicant appears before an immigration judge in response to the issuance of a charging document under § 208.14(c).

(e) The asylum officer shall consider evidence submitted by the applicant together with his or her asylum application, as well as any evidence submitted by the applicant before or at the interview. As a matter of discretion, the asylum officer may grant the applicant a brief extension of time following an interview during which the applicant may submit additional evidence. Any such extension shall extend by an equivalent time the periods specified by § 208.7 for the filing and adjudication of any employment authorization application.

(f) The asylum application, all supporting information provided by the applicant, any comments submitted by the Department of State or by the Service, and any other information specific to the applicant's case and considered by the asylum officer shall comprise the record.

(g) An applicant unable to proceed with the interview in English must provide, at no expense to the Service, a competent interpreter fluent in both English and the applicant's native language or any other language in which the applicant is fluent. The interpreter must be at least 18 years of age. Neither the applicant's attorney or representative of record, a witness testifying on the applicant's behalf, nor a representative or employee of the applicant's country of nationality, or if stateless, country of last habitual residence, may serve as the applicant's interpreter. Failure without good cause to comply with this paragraph may be considered a failure to appear for the interview for purposes of § 208.10.

[62 FR 10341, March 6, 1997; 65 FR 76133, Dec. 6, 2000; 76 FR 53784, Aug. 29, 2011.]

§ 208.10 Failure to appear at an interview before an asylum officer or failure to follow requirements for fingerprint processing. [also 8 C.F.R. § 1208.10, which has similar details]

Failure to appear for a scheduled interview without prior authorization may result in dismissal of the application or waiver of the right to an interview. Failure to comply with fingerprint processing requirements without good cause may result in dismissal of the application or waiver of the right to an adjudication by an asylum officer. Failure to appear shall be excused if the notice of the interview or fingerprint appointment was not mailed to the applicant's current address and such address had been provided to the USCIS by the applicant prior to the date of mailing in accordance with section 265 of the Act and regulations promulgated thereunder, unless the asylum officer determines that the applicant received reasonable notice of the interview or fingerprinting appointment. Failure to appear at the interview or fingerprint appointment will be excused if the applicant demonstrates that such failure was the result of exceptional circumstances.

[62 FR 10341, March 6, 1997; as amended at 63 FR 12986, March 17, 1998; 76 FR 53784, Aug. 29, 2011.]

§ 208.11 Comments from the Department of State. [also 8 C.F.R. § 1208.11, which has minor wording changes and cross-references to part 1208]

(a) U.S. Citizenship and Immigration Services (USCIS) may request, at its discretion, specific comments from the Department of State regarding individual cases or types of claims under consideration, or such other information as USCIS deems appropriate.

(b) With respect to any asylum application, the Department of State may provide, at its discretion, to USCIS:

(1) Detailed country conditions information relevant to eligibility for asylum or withholding of removal;

(2) An assessment of the accuracy of the applicant's assertions about conditions in his or her country of nationality or habitual residence and his or her particular situation;

(3) Information about whether persons who are similarly situated to the applicant are persecuted or tortured in the applicant's country of nationality or habitual residence and the frequency of such persecution or torture; or

(4) Such other information as it deems relevant.

(c) Any comments received pursuant to paragraph (b) of this section shall be made part of the record. Unless the comments are classified under the applicable Executive Order, the applicant shall be provided an opportunity to review and respond to such comments prior to the issuance of any decision to deny the application.

[64 FR 8488, Feb. 19, 1999; 74 FR 15369, April 6, 2009]

§ 208.12 Reliance on information compiled by other sources. [also 8 C.F.R. § 1208.12, which has minor wording changes and cross-references to part 1208]

(a) In deciding an asylum application, or in deciding whether the alien has a credible fear of persecution or torture pursuant to § 208.30 of this part, or a reasonable fear of persecution or torture pursuant to § 208.31, the asylum officer may rely on material provided by the Department of State, other USCIS offices, or other credible sources, such as international organizations, private voluntary agencies, news organizations, or academic institutions.

(b) Nothing in this part shall be construed to entitle the applicant to conduct discovery directed toward the records, officers, agents, or employees of the Service, the Department of Justice, or the Department of State. Persons may continue to seek documents available through a Freedom of Information Act (FOIA) request pursuant to 8 CFR part 103.

[64 FR 8488, Feb. 19, 1999; 65 FR 76133, Dec. 6, 2000; 76 FR 53784, Aug. 29, 2011.]

§ 208.13 Establishing asylum eligibility. [also 8 C.F.R. § 1208.13, which is identical except for cross-references to part 1208]

(a) Burden of proof. The burden of proof is on the applicant for asylum to establish that he or she is a refugee as defined in section 101(a)(42) of the Act. The testimony of the applicant, if credible, may be sufficient to sustain the burden of proof without corroboration. The fact that the applicant previously established a credible fear of persecution for purposes of section 235(b)(1)(B) of the Act does not relieve the alien of the additional burden of establishing eligibility for asylum.

(b) Eligibility. The applicant may qualify as a refugee either because he or she has suffered past persecution or because he or she has a well-founded fear of future persecution.

(1) Past persecution. An applicant shall be found to be a refugee on the basis of past persecution if the applicant can establish that he or she has suffered persecution in the past in the applicant's country of nationality or, if stateless, in his or her country of last habitual residence, on account of race, religion, nationality, membership in a particular social group, or political opinion, and is unable or unwilling to return to, or avail himself or herself of the protection of, that country owing to such persecution. An applicant who has been found to have established such past persecution shall also be presumed to have a well-founded fear of persecution on the basis of the original claim. That presumption may be rebutted if an asylum officer or immigration judge makes one of the findings described in paragraph (b)(1)(i) of this section. If the applicant's fear of future persecution is unrelated to the past persecution, the applicant bears the burden of establishing that the fear is well-founded.

(i) Discretionary referral or denial. Except as provided in paragraph (b)(1)(iii) of this section, an asylum officer shall, in the exercise of his or her discretion, refer or deny, or an immigration judge, in the exercise of his or her discretion, shall deny the asylum application of an alien found to be a refugee on the basis of past persecution if any of the following is found by a preponderance of the evidence:

(A) There has been a fundamental change in circumstances such that the applicant no longer has a well-founded fear of persecution in the applicant's country of nationality or, if stateless, in the applicant's country of last habitual residence, on account of race, religion, nationality, membership in a particular social group, or political opinion; or

(B) The applicant could avoid future persecution by relocating to another part of the applicant's country of nationality or, if stateless, another part of the applicant's country of last habitual residence, and under all the circumstances, it would be reasonable to expect the applicant to do so.

(ii) Burden of proof. In cases in which an applicant has demonstrated past persecution under paragraph (b)(1) of this section, the Service shall bear the burden of establishing by a preponderance of the evidence the requirements of paragraphs (b)(1)(i)(A) or (B) of this section.

(iii) Grant in the absence of well-founded fear of persecution. An applicant described in paragraph (b)(1)(i) of this section who is not barred from a grant of asylum under paragraph (c) of this section, may be granted asylum, in the exercise of the decision-maker's discretion, if:

(A) The applicant has demonstrated compelling reasons for being unwilling or unable to return to the country arising out of the severity of the past persecution; or

(B) The applicant has established that there is a reasonable possibility that he or she may suffer other serious harm upon removal to that country.

(2) Well-founded fear of persecution.

(i) An applicant has a well-founded fear of persecution if:

(A) The applicant has a fear of persecution in his or her country of nationality or, if stateless, in his or her country of last habitual residence, on account of race, religion, nationality, membership in a particular social group, or political opinion;

(B) There is a reasonable possibility of suffering such persecution if he or she were to return to that country; and

(C) He or she is unable or unwilling to return to, or avail himself or herself of the protection of, that country because of such fear.

(ii) An applicant does not have a well-founded fear of persecution if the applicant could avoid persecution by relocating to another part of the applicant's country of nationality or, if stateless, another part of the applicant's country of last habitual residence, if under all the circumstances it would be reasonable to expect the applicant to do so.

(iii) In evaluating whether the applicant has sustained the burden of proving that he or she has a well-founded fear of persecution, the asylum officer or immigration judge shall not require the applicant to provide evidence that there is a reasonable possibility he or she would be singled out individually for persecution if:

(A) The applicant establishes that there is a pattern or practice in his or her country of nationality or, if stateless, in his or her country of last habitual residence, of persecution of a group of persons similarly situated to the applicant on account of race, religion, nationality, membership in a particular social group, or political opinion; and

(B) The applicant establishes his or her own inclusion in, and identification with, such group of persons such that his or her fear of persecution upon return is reasonable.

(3) Reasonableness of internal relocation. For purposes of determinations under paragraphs (b)(1)(i), (b)(1)(ii), and (b)(2) of this section, adjudicators should consider, but are not limited to considering, whether the applicant would face other serious harm in the place of suggested relocation; any ongoing civil strife within the country; administrative, economic, or judicial infrastructure; geographical limitations; and social and cultural constraints, such as age, gender, health, and social and familial ties. Those factors may, or may not, be relevant, depending on all the circumstances of the case, and are not necessarily determinative of whether it would be reasonable for the applicant to relocate.

(i) In cases in which the applicant has not established past persecution, the applicant shall bear the burden of establishing that it would not be reasonable for him or her to relocate, unless the persecution is by a government or is government-sponsored.

(ii) In cases in which the persecutor is a government or is government-sponsored, or the applicant has established persecution in the past, it shall be presumed that internal relocation would not be reasonable, unless the Service establishes by a preponderance of the evidence that, under all the circumstances, it would be reasonable for the applicant to relocate.

(c) Mandatory denials.

(1) Applications filed on or after April 1, 1997. For applications filed on or after April 1, 1997, an applicant shall not qualify for asylum if section 208(a)(2) or 208(b)(2) of the Act applies to the applicant. If the applicant is found to be ineligible for asylum under either section 208(a)(2) or 208(b)(2) of the Act, the applicant shall be considered for eligibility for withholding of removal under section 241(b)(3) of the Act. The applicant shall also be considered for eligibility for withholding of removal under the Convention Against

Torture if the applicant requests such consideration or if the evidence presented by the alien indicates that the alien may be tortured in the country of removal.

(2) Applications filed before April 1, 1997.

(i) An immigration judge or asylum officer shall not grant asylum to any applicant who filed his or her application before April 1, 1997, if the alien:

(A) Having been convicted by a final judgment of a particularly serious crime in the United States, constitutes a danger to the community;

(B) Has been firmly resettled within the meaning of § 208.15;

(C) Can reasonably be regarded as a danger to the security of the United States;

(D) Has been convicted of an aggravated felony, as defined in section 101(a)(43) of the Act; or

(E) Ordered, incited, assisted, or otherwise participated in the persecution of any person on account of race, religion, nationality, membership in a particular social group, or political opinion.

(F) Is described within section 212(a)(3)(B)(i)(I), (II), and (III) of the Act as it existed prior to April 1, 1997, and as amended by the Anti-terrorist and Effective Death Penalty Act of 1996 (AEDPA), unless it is determined that there are no reasonable grounds to believe that the individual is a danger to the security of the United States.

(ii) If the evidence indicates that one of the above grounds apply to the applicant, he or she shall have the burden of proving by a preponderance of the evidence that he or she did not so act.

[64 FR 8488, Feb. 19, 1999; 65 FR 76133, Dec. 6, 2000]

§ 208.14 Approval, denial, referral, or dismissal of application. [also 8 C.F.R. § 1208.14, which has minor wording changes and cross-references to part 1208]

(a) By an immigration judge. Unless otherwise prohibited in § 208.13(c), an immigration judge may grant or deny asylum in the exercise of discretion to an applicant who qualifies as a refugee under section 101(a)(42) of the Act.

(b) Approval by an asylum officer. In any case within the jurisdiction of the RAIO, unless otherwise prohibited in § 208.13(c), an asylum officer may grant, in the exercise of his or her discretion, asylum to an applicant who qualifies as a refugee under section 101(a)(42) of the

Act, and whose identity has been checked pursuant to section 208(d)(5)(A)(i) of the Act.

(c) Denial, referral, or dismissal by an asylum officer. If the asylum officer does not grant asylum to an applicant after an interview conducted in accordance with § 208.9, or if, as provided in § 208.10, the applicant is deemed to have waived his or her right to an interview or an adjudication by an asylum officer, the asylum officer shall deny, refer, or dismiss the application, as follows:

(1) Inadmissible or deportable aliens. Except as provided in paragraph (c)(4) of this section, in the case of an applicant who appears to be inadmissible or deportable under section 212(a) or 237(a) of the Act, the asylum officer shall refer the application to an immigration judge, together with the appropriate charging document, for adjudication in removal proceedings (or, where charging documents may not be issued, shall dismiss the application).

(2) Alien in valid status. In the case of an applicant who is maintaining valid immigrant, nonimmigrant, or Temporary Protected Status at the time the application is decided, the asylum officer shall deny the application for asylum.

(3) Alien with valid parole. If an applicant has been paroled into the United States and the parole has not expired or been terminated by the Service, the asylum officer shall deny the application for asylum.

(4) Alien paroled into the United States whose parole has expired or is terminated.

(i) Alien paroled prior to April 1, 1997, or with advance authorization for parole. In the case of an applicant who was paroled into the United States prior to April 1, 1997, or who, prior to departure from the United States, had received an advance authorization for parole, the asylum officer shall refer the application, together with the appropriate charging documents, to an immigration judge for adjudication in removal proceedings if the parole has expired, the Service has terminated parole, or the Service is terminating parole through issuance of the charging documents, pursuant to § 212.5(d)(2)(i) of this chapter.

(ii) Alien paroled on or after April 1, 1997, without advance authorization for parole. In the case of an applicant who is an arriving alien or is otherwise subject to removal under § 235.3(b) of this chapter, and was paroled into the United States on or after April 1, 1997, without advance authorization for parole prior to departure from the United States, the asylum officer will take the following actions, if the parole has expired or been terminated:

(A) Inadmissible under section 212(a)(6)(C) or 212(a)(7) of the Act. If the applicant appears inadmissible to the United States under section 212(a)(6)(C) or 212(a)(7) of the Act and the asylum officer does not intend to lodge any additional charges of inadmissibility, the asylum officer shall proceed in accordance with § 235.3(b) of this chapter. If such applicant is found to have a credible fear of persecution or torture based on information elicited from the asylum interview, an asylum officer may refer the applicant directly to an immigration judge in removal proceedings under section 240 of the Act, without conducting a separate credible fear interview pursuant to § 208.30. If such applicant is not found to have a credible fear based on information elicited at the asylum interview, an asylum officer will conduct a credible fear interview and the applicant will be subject to the credible fear process specified at § 208.30(b).

(B) Inadmissible on other grounds. In the case of an applicant who was paroled into the United States on or after April 1, 1997, and will be charged as inadmissible to the United States under provisions of the Act other than, or in addition to, sections 212(a)(6)(C) or 212(a)(7), the asylum officer shall refer the application to an immigration judge for adjudication in removal proceedings.

(d) Applicability of § 103.2(b) of this chapter. No application for asylum or withholding of deportation shall be subject to denial pursuant to § 103.2(b) of this chapter.

(e) Duration. If the applicant is granted asylum, the grant will be effective for an indefinite period, subject to termination as provided in § 208.24.

(f) Effect of denial of principal's application on separate applications by dependents. The denial of an asylum application filed by a principal applicant for asylum shall also result in the denial of asylum status to any dependents of that principal applicant who are included in that same application. Such denial shall not preclude a grant of asylum for an otherwise eligible dependent who has filed a separate asylum application, nor shall such denial result in an otherwise eligible dependent becoming ineligible to apply for asylum due to the provisions of section 208(a)(2)(C) of the Act.

(g) Applicants granted lawful permanent residence status. If an asylum applicant is granted adjustment of status to lawful permanent resident, the Service may provide written notice to the applicant that his or her asylum application will be presumed abandoned and dismissed without prejudice, unless the applicant submits a written request within 30 days of the notice, that the asylum application be adjudicated. If an applicant does not respond within 30 days of the date the written notice was sent or served, the Service may presume the asylum application abandoned and dismiss it without prejudice.

[62 FR 10342, March 6, 1997; as amended at 63 FR 12986, March 17, 1998; 64 FR 27875, May 21, 1999; 65 FR 76134, Dec. 6, 2000; 76 FR 53784, Aug. 29, 2011.]

§ 208.15 Definition of "firm resettlement." [also 8 C.F.R. § 1208.15]

An alien is considered to be firmly resettled if, prior to arrival in the United States, he or she entered into another country with, or while in that country received, an offer of permanent resident status, citizenship, or some other type of permanent resettlement unless he or she establishes:

(a) That his or her entry into that country was a necessary consequence of his or her flight from persecution, that he or she remained in that country only as long as was necessary to arrange onward travel, and that he or she did not establish significant ties in that country; or

(b) That the conditions of his or her residence in that country were so substantially and consciously restricted by the authority of the country of refuge that he or she was not in fact resettled. In making his or her determination, the asylum officer or immigration judge shall consider the conditions under which other residents of the country live; the type of housing, whether permanent or temporary, made available to the refugee; the types and extent of employment available to the refugee; and the extent to which the refugee received permission to hold property and to enjoy other rights and privileges, such as travel documentation that includes a right of entry or reentry, education, public relief, or naturalization, ordinarily available to others resident in the country.

[62 Fed. Reg. 10343, March 6, 1997; 65 FR 76135, Dec. 6, 2000]

§ 208.16 Withholding of removal under section 241(b)(3)(B) of the Act and withholding of removal under the Convention Against Torture. [also 8 C.F.R. § 1208.16, which is identical except for cross-references to part 1208]

(a) Consideration of application for withholding of removal. An asylum officer shall not decide whether the exclusion, deportation, or removal of an alien to a country where the alien's life or freedom would be threatened must be withheld, except in the case of an alien who is otherwise eligible for asylum but is precluded from being granted such status due solely to section 207(a)(5) of the Act*. In exclusion, deportation, or removal proceedings, an immigration judge may adjudicate both an asylum claim and a request for withholding of removal whether or not asylum is granted.

(b) Eligibility for withholding of removal under section 241(b)(3) of the Act; burden of proof. The burden of proof is on the applicant for withholding of removal under section 241(b)(3) of the Act

* Because INA § 207(a)(5) has been repealed, asylum officers no longer decide applications for withholding of removal.

to establish that his or her life or freedom would be threatened in the proposed country of removal on account of race, religion, nationality, membership in a particular social group, or political opinion. The testimony of the applicant, if credible, may be sufficient to sustain the burden of proof without corroboration. The evidence shall be evaluated as follows:

(1) Past threat to life or freedom.

(i) If the applicant is determined to have suffered past persecution in the proposed country of removal on account of race, religion, nationality, membership in a particular social group, or political opinion, it shall be presumed that the applicant's life or freedom would be threatened in the future in the country of removal on the basis of the original claim. This presumption may be rebutted if an asylum officer or immigration judge finds by a preponderance of the evidence:

(A) There has been a fundamental change in circumstances such that the applicant's life or freedom would not be threatened on account of any of the five grounds mentioned in this paragraph upon the applicant's removal to that country; or

(B) The applicant could avoid a future threat to his or her life or freedom by relocating to another part of the proposed country of removal and, under all the circumstances, it would be reasonable to expect the applicant to do so.

(ii) In cases in which the applicant has established past persecution, the Service shall bear the burden of establishing by a preponderance of the evidence the requirements of paragraphs (b)(1)(i)(A) or (b)(1)(i)(B) of this section.

(iii) If the applicant's fear of future threat to life or freedom is unrelated to the past persecution, the applicant bears the burden of establishing that it is more likely than not that he or she would suffer such harm.

(2) Future threat to life or freedom. An applicant who has not suffered past persecution may demonstrate that his or her life or freedom would be threatened in the future in a country if he or she can establish that it is more likely than not that he or she would be persecuted on account of race, religion, nationality, membership in a particular social group, or political opinion upon removal to that country. Such an applicant cannot demonstrate that his or her life or freedom would be threatened if the asylum officer or immigration judge finds that the applicant could avoid a future threat to his or her life or freedom by relocating to another part of the proposed country of removal and, under all the circumstances, it would be reasonable to expect the applicant to do so. In evaluating whether it is more likely than not that the applicant's life or freedom would be threatened in a particular country on account of race, religion, nationality, membership in a particular social group, or political opinion, the asylum officer or immigration judge shall not require the applicant to provide evidence that he or she would be singled out individually for such persecution if:

(i) The applicant establishes that in that country there is a pattern or practice of persecution of a group of persons similarly situated to the applicant on account of race, religion, nationality, membership in a particular social group, or political opinion; and

(ii) The applicant establishes his or her own inclusion in and identification with such group of persons such that it is more likely than not that his or her life or freedom would be threatened upon return to that country.

(3) Reasonableness of internal relocation. For purposes of determinations under paragraphs (b)(1) and (b)(2) of this section, adjudicators should consider, among other things, whether the applicant would face other serious harm in the place of suggested relocation; any ongoing civil strife within the country; administrative, economic, or judicial infrastructure; geographical limitations; and social and cultural constraints, such as age, gender, health, and social and familial ties. These factors may or may not be relevant, depending on all the circumstances of the case, and are not necessarily determinative of whether it would be reasonable for the applicant to relocate.

(i) In cases in which the applicant has not established past persecution, the applicant shall bear the burden of establishing that it would not be reasonable for him or her to relocate, unless the persecutor is a government or is government-sponsored.

(ii) In cases in which the persecutor is a government or is government-sponsored, or the applicant has established persecution in the past, it shall be presumed that internal relocation would not be reasonable, unless the Service establishes by a preponderance of the evidence that under all the circumstances it would be reasonable for the applicant to relocate.

(c) Eligibility for withholding of removal under the Convention Against Torture.

(1) For purposes of regulations under Title II of the Act, "Convention Against Torture" shall refer to the United Nations Convention Against Torture and Other Cruel, Inhuman or Degrading Treatment or Punishment, subject to any reservations, understandings, declarations, and provisos contained in the United States Senate resolution of ratification of the Convention, as implemented by section 2242 of the Foreign Affairs Reform and Restructuring Act of 1998 (Pub.L. 105–277, 112 Stat. 2681, 2681–821). The definition of torture contained in § 208.18(a) of this part shall govern all decisions made under regulations under Title II of the Act about the applicability of Article 3 of the Convention Against Torture.

(2) The burden of proof is on the applicant for withholding of removal under this paragraph to establish that it is more likely than not that he or she would be tortured if removed to the proposed country of removal. The testimony of the applicant, if credible, may be sufficient to sustain the burden of proof without corroboration.

(3) In assessing whether it is more likely than not that an applicant would be tortured in the proposed country of removal, all evidence relevant to the possibility of future torture shall be considered, including, but not limited to:

(i) Evidence of past torture inflicted upon the applicant;

(ii) Evidence that the applicant could relocate to a part of the country of removal where he or she is not likely to be tortured;

(iii) Evidence of gross, flagrant or mass violations of human rights within the country of removal, where applicable; and

(iv) Other relevant information regarding conditions in the country of removal.

(4) In considering an application for withholding of removal under the Convention Against Torture, the immigration judge shall first determine whether the alien is more likely than not to be tortured in the country of removal. If the immigration judge determines that the alien is more likely than not to be tortured in the country of removal, the alien is entitled to protection under the Convention Against Torture. Protection under the Convention Against Torture will be granted either in the form of withholding of removal or in the form of deferral of removal. An alien entitled to such protection shall be granted withholding of removal unless the alien is subject to mandatory denial of withholding of removal under paragraphs (d)(2) or (d)(3) of this section. If an alien entitled to such protection is subject to mandatory denial of withholding of removal under paragraphs (d)(2) or (d)(3) of this section, the alien's removal shall be deferred under § 208.17(a).

(d) Approval or denial of application.

(1) General. Subject to paragraphs (d)(2) and (d)(3) of this section, an application for withholding of deportation or removal to a country of proposed removal shall be granted if the applicant's eligibility for withholding is established pursuant to paragraphs (b) or (c) of this section.

(2) Mandatory denials. Except as provided in paragraph (d)(3) of this section, an application for withholding of removal under section 241(b)(3) of the Act or under the Convention Against Torture shall be denied if the applicant falls within section 241(b)(3)(B) of the Act or, for applications for withholding of deportation adjudicated in proceedings commenced prior to April 1, 1997, within section 243(h)(2) of the Act as it appeared prior to that date. For purposes of section 241(b)(3)(B)(ii) of the Act, or section 243(h)(2)(B) of the Act as it appeared prior to April 1, 1997, an alien who has been convicted of a particularly serious crime shall be considered to constitute a danger to the community. If the evidence indicates the applicability of one or more of the grounds for denial of withholding enumerated in the Act, the applicant shall have the burden of proving by a preponderance of the evidence that such grounds do not apply.

(3) Exception to the prohibition on withholding of deportation in certain cases. Section 243(h)(3) of the Act, as added by section 413 of Pub.L. 104–132 (110 Stat. 1214), shall apply only to applications adjudicated in proceedings commenced before April 1, 1997, and in which final action had not been taken before April 24, 1996. The discretion permitted by that section to override section 243(h)(2) of the Act shall be exercised only in the case of an applicant convicted of an aggravated felony (or felonies) where he or she was sentenced to an aggregate term of imprisonment of less than 5 years and the immigration judge determines on an individual basis that the crime (or crimes) of which the applicant was convicted does not constitute a particularly serious crime. Nevertheless, it shall be presumed that an alien convicted of an aggravated felony has been convicted of a particularly serious crime. Except in the cases specified in this paragraph, the grounds for denial of withholding of deportation in section 243(h)(2) of the Act as it appeared prior to April 1, 1997, shall be deemed to comply with the Protocol Relating to the Status of Refugees, Jan. 31, 1967, T.I.A.S. No. 6577.

(e) Reconsideration of discretionary denial of asylum. In the event that an applicant is denied asylum solely in the exercise of discretion, and the applicant is subsequently granted withholding of deportation or removal under this section, thereby effectively precluding admission of the applicant's spouse or minor children following to join him or her, the denial of asylum shall be reconsidered. Factors to be considered will include the reasons for the denial and reasonable alternatives available to the applicant such as reunification with his or her spouse or minor children in a third country.

(f) Removal to third country. Nothing in this section or § 208.17 shall prevent the Service from removing an alien to a third country other than the country to which removal has been withheld or deferred.

[64 FR 8488, Feb. 19, 1999; 65 FR 76135, Dec. 6, 2000]

§ 208.17 Deferral of removal under the Convention Against Torture. [also 8 C.F.R. § 1208.17, which is identical except for cross-references to part 1208]

(a) Grant of deferral of removal. An alien who: has been ordered removed; has been found under § 208.16(c)(3) to be entitled to protection under the Convention Against Torture; and is subject to the provisions for mandatory denial of withholding of removal under § 208.16(d)(2) or (d)(3), shall be granted deferral of removal to the country where he or she is more likely than not to be tortured.

(b) Notice to Alien.

(1) After an immigration judge orders an alien described in paragraph (a) of this section removed, the immigration judge shall inform the alien that his or her removal to the country where he or she is more likely than not to be tortured shall be deferred until such time as the deferral is terminated under this section. The immigration judge shall inform the alien that deferral of removal:

(i) Does not confer upon the alien any lawful or permanent immigration status in the United States;

(ii) Will not necessarily result in the alien being released from the custody of the Service if the alien is subject to such custody;

(iii) Is effective only until terminated; and

(iv) Is subject to review and termination if the immigration judge determines that it is not likely that the alien would be tortured in the country to which removal has been deferred, or if the alien requests that deferral be terminated.

(2) The immigration judge shall also inform the alien that removal has been deferred only to the country in which it has been determined that the alien is likely to be tortured, and that the alien may be removed at any time to another country where he or she is not likely to be tortured.

(c) Detention of an alien granted deferral of removal under this section. Nothing in this section shall alter the authority of the Service to detain an alien whose removal has been deferred under this section and who is otherwise subject to detention. In the case of such an alien, decisions about the alien's release shall be made according to part 241 of this chapter.

(d) Termination of deferral of removal.

(1) At any time while deferral of removal is in effect, the INS District Counsel for the District with jurisdiction over an alien whose removal has been deferred under paragraph (a) of this section may file a motion with the Immigration Court having administrative control pursuant to § 3.11 of this chapter to schedule a hearing to consider whether deferral of removal should be terminated. The Service motion shall be granted if it is accompanied by evidence that is relevant to the possibility that the alien would be tortured in the country to which removal has been deferred and that was not presented at the previous hearing. The Service motion shall not be subject to the requirements for reopening in §§ 3.2 and 3.23 of this chapter.

(2) The Immigration Court shall provide notice to the alien and the Service of the time, place, and date of the termination hearing. Such notice shall inform the alien that the alien may supplement the information in his or her initial application for withholding of removal under the Convention Against Torture and shall provide that the alien must submit any such supplemental information within 10 calendar days of service of such notice (or 13 calendar days if service of such notice was by mail). At the expiration of this 10 or 13 day period, the Immigration Court shall forward a copy of the original application, and any supplemental information the alien or the Service has submitted, to the Department of State, together with notice to the Department of State of the time, place and date of the termination hearing. At its option, the Department of State may provide comments on the case, according to the provisions of § 208.11 of this part.

(3) The immigration judge shall conduct a hearing and make a de novo determination, based on the record of proceeding and initial application in addition to any new evidence submitted by the Service or the alien, as to whether the alien is more likely than not to be tortured in the country to which removal has been deferred. This determination shall be made under the standards for eligibility set out in § 208.16(c). The burden is on the alien to establish that it is more likely than not that he or she would be tortured in the country to which removal has been deferred.

(4) If the immigration judge determines that the alien is more likely than not to be tortured in the country to which removal has been deferred, the order of deferral shall remain in place. If the immigration judge determines that the alien has not established that he or she is more likely than not to be tortured in the country to which removal has been deferred, the deferral of removal shall be terminated and the alien may be removed to that country. Appeal of the immigration judge's decision shall lie to the Board.

(e) Termination at the request of the alien.

(1) At any time while deferral of removal is in effect, the alien may make a written request to the Immigration Court having administrative control pursuant to § 3.11 of this chapter to terminate the deferral order. If satisfied on the basis of the written submission that the alien's request is knowing and voluntary, the immigration judge shall terminate the order of deferral and the alien may be removed.

(2) If necessary the immigration judge may calendar a hearing for the sole purpose of determining whether the alien's request is knowing and voluntary. If the immigration judge determines that the alien's request is knowing and voluntary, the order of deferral shall be terminated. If the immigration judge determines that the alien's request is not knowing and voluntary, the alien's request shall not serve as the basis for terminating the order of deferral.

(f) Termination pursuant to § 208.18(c). At any time while deferral of removal is in effect, the Attorney General may determine whether deferral should be terminated based on diplomatic assurances forwarded by the Secretary of State pursuant to the procedures in § 208.18(c).

[64 FR 8489, Feb. 19, 1999]

§ 208.18 Implementation of the Convention Against Torture. [also 8 C.F.R. § 1208.18, which is identical except for cross-references to part 1208]

(a) Definitions. The definitions in this subsection incorporate the definition of torture contained in Article 1 of the Convention Against Torture, subject to the reservations, understandings, declarations, and provisos contained in the United States Senate resolution of ratification of the Convention.

(1) Torture is defined as any act by which severe pain or suffering, whether physical or mental, is intentionally inflicted on a person for such purposes as obtaining from him or her or a third person information or a confession, punishing him or her for an act he or she or a third person has committed or is suspected of having committed, or intimidating or coercing him or her or a third person, or for any reason based on discrimination of any kind, when such pain or suffering is inflicted by or at the instigation of or with the consent or acquiescence of a public official or other person acting in an official capacity.

(2) Torture is an extreme form of cruel and inhuman treatment and does not include lesser forms of cruel, inhuman or degrading treatment or punishment that do not amount to torture.

(3) Torture does not include pain or suffering arising only from, inherent in or incidental to lawful sanctions. Lawful sanctions include judicially imposed sanctions and other enforcement actions authorized by law, including the death penalty, but do not include sanctions that defeat the object and purpose of the Convention Against Torture to prohibit torture.

(4) In order to constitute torture, mental pain or suffering must be prolonged mental harm caused by or resulting from:

(i) The intentional infliction or threatened infliction of severe physical pain or suffering;

(ii) The administration or application, or threatened administration or application, of mind altering substances or other procedures calculated to disrupt profoundly the senses or the personality;

(iii) The threat of imminent death; or

(iv) The threat that another person will imminently be subjected to death, severe physical pain or suffering, or the administration or application of mind altering substances or other procedures calculated to disrupt profoundly the sense or personality.

(5) In order to constitute torture, an act must be specifically intended to inflict severe physical or mental pain or suffering. An act that results in unanticipated or unintended severity of pain and suffering is not torture.

(6) In order to constitute torture an act must be directed against a person in the offender's custody or physical control.

(7) Acquiescence of a public official requires that the public official, prior to the activity constituting torture, have awareness of such activity and thereafter breach his or her legal responsibility to intervene to prevent such activity.

(8) Noncompliance with applicable legal procedural standards does not per se constitute torture.

(b) Applicability of §§ 208.16(c) and 208.17(a).

(1) Aliens in proceedings on or after March 22, 1999. An alien who is in exclusion, deportation, or removal proceedings on or after March 22, 1999 may apply for withholding of removal under § 208.16(c), and, if applicable, may be considered for deferral of removal under § 208.17(a).

(2) Aliens who were ordered removed, or whose removal orders became final, before March 22, 1999. An alien under a final order of deportation, exclusion, or removal that became final prior to March 22, 1999 may move to reopen proceedings for the sole purpose of seeking protection under § 208.16(c). Such motions shall be governed by §§ 3.23 and 3.2 of this chapter, except that the time and numerical limitations on motions to reopen shall not apply and the alien shall not be required to demonstrate that the evidence sought to be offered was unavailable and could not have been discovered or presented at the former hearing. The motion to reopen shall not be granted unless:

(i) The motion is filed within June 21, 1999; and

(ii) The evidence sought to be offered establishes a prima facie case that the applicant's removal must be withheld or deferred under §§ 208.16(c) or 208.17(a).

(3) Aliens who, on March 22, 1999, have requests pending with the Service for protection under Article 3 of the Convention Against Torture.

(i) Except as otherwise provided, after March 22, 1999, the Service will not:

(A) Consider, under its pre-regulatory administrative policy to ensure compliance with the Convention Against Torture, whether Article 3 of that Convention prohibits the removal of an alien to a particular country, or

(B) Stay the removal of an alien based on a request filed with the Service for protection under Article 3 of that Convention.

(ii) For each alien who, on or before March 22, 1999, filed a request with the Service for protection under Article 3 of the Convention Against Torture, and whose request has not been finally decided by the Service, the Service shall provide written notice that, after March 22, 1999, consideration for protection under Article 3 can be obtained only through the provisions of this rule.

(A) The notice shall inform an alien who is under an order of removal issued by EOIR that, in order to seek consideration of a claim under §§ 208.16(c) or 208.17(a), such an alien must file a motion to reopen with the immigration court or the Board of Immigration Appeals. This notice shall be accompanied by a stay of removal, effective until 30 days after service of the notice on the alien. A motion to reopen filed under this paragraph for the limited purpose of asserting a claim under §§ 208.16(c) or 208.17(a) shall not be subject to the requirements for reopening in §§ 3.2 and 3.23 of this chapter. Such a motion shall be granted if it is accompanied by a copy of the notice described in paragraph (b)(3)(ii) or by other convincing evidence that the alien had a request pending with the Service for protection under Article 3 of the Convention Against Torture on March 22, 1999. The filing of such a motion shall extend the stay of removal during the pendency of the adjudication of this motion.

(B) The notice shall inform an alien who is under an administrative order of removal issued by the Service under section 238(b) of the Act or an exclusion, deportation, or removal order reinstated by the Service under section 241(a)(5) of the Act that the alien's claim to withholding of removal under § 208.16(c) or deferral of removal under § 208.17(a) will be considered under § 208.31.

(C) The notice shall inform an alien who is under an administrative order of removal issued by the Service under section 235(c) of the Act that the alien's claim to protection under the Convention Against Torture will be decided by the Service as provided in § 208.18(d) and 235.8(b)(4) and will not be considered under the provisions of this part relating to consideration or review by an immigration judge, the Board of Immigration Appeals, or an asylum officer.

(4) Aliens whose claims to protection under the Convention Against Torture were finally decided by the Service prior to March 22, 1999. Sections 208.16(c) and 208.17 (a) and paragraphs (b)(1) through (b)(3) of this section do not apply to cases in which, prior to March 22, 1999, the Service has made a final administrative determination about the applicability of Article 3 of the Convention Against Torture to the case of an alien who filed a request with the Service for protection under Article 3. If, prior to March 22, 1999, the Service determined that an applicant cannot be removed consistent with the Convention Against Torture, the alien shall be considered to have been granted withholding of removal under § 208.16(c), unless the alien is subject to mandatory denial of withholding of removal under § 208.16(d)(2) or (d)(3), in which case the alien will be considered to have been granted deferral of removal under 208.17(a). If, prior to March 22, 1999, the Service determined that an alien can be removed consistent with the Convention Against Torture, the alien will be considered to have been finally denied withholding of removal under § 208.16(c) and deferral of removal under § 208.17(a).

(c) Diplomatic assurances against torture obtained by the Secretary of State.

(1) The Secretary of State may forward to the Attorney General assurances that the Secretary has obtained from the government of a specific country that an alien would not be tortured there if the alien were removed to that country.

(2) If the Secretary of State forwards assurances described in paragraph (c)(1) of this section to the Attorney General for consideration by the Attorney General or her delegates under this paragraph, the Attorney General shall determine, in consultation with the Secretary of State, whether the assurances are sufficiently reliable to allow the alien's removal to that country consistent with Article 3 of the Convention Against Torture. The Attorney General's authority under this paragraph may be exercised by the Deputy Attorney General or by the Commissioner, Immigration and Naturalization Service, but may not be further delegated.

(3) Once assurances are provided under paragraph (c)(2) of this section, the alien's claim for protection under the Convention Against Torture shall not be considered further by an immigration judge, the Board of Immigration Appeals, or an asylum officer.

(d) Cases involving aliens ordered removed under section 235(c) of the Act. With respect to an alien terrorist or other alien subject to administrative removal under section 235(c) of the Act who requests protection under Article 3 of the Convention Against Torture, the Service will assess the applicability of Article 3 through the removal process to ensure that a removal order will not be executed under circumstances that would violate the obligations of the United States under Article 3. In such cases, the provisions of Part 208 relating to consideration or review by an immigration judge, the Board of Immigration Appeals, or an asylum officer shall not apply.

(e) Judicial review of claims for protection from removal under Article 3 of the Convention Against Torture.

(1) Pursuant to the provisions of section 2242(d) of the Foreign Affairs Reform and Restructuring Act of 1998, there shall be no judicial appeal or review of any action, decision, or claim raised under the Convention or that section, except as part of the review of a final order of removal pursuant to section 242 of the Act; provided however, that any appeal or petition regarding an action, decision, or claim under the Convention or under section 2242 of the Foreign Affairs Reform and Restructuring Act of 1998 shall not be deemed to include or authorize the consideration of any administrative order or decision, or portion thereof, the appeal or review of which is restricted or prohibited by the Act.

(2) Except as otherwise expressly provided, nothing in this paragraph shall be construed to create a private right of action or to authorize the consideration or issuance of administrative or judicial relief.

[64 FR 8490, Feb. 19, 1999; 64 FR 13881, March 23, 1999]

§ 208.19 Decisions. [also 8 C.F.R. § 1208.19, which is identical except for cross-references to part 1208]

The decision of an asylum officer to grant or to deny asylum or to refer an asylum application, in accordance with § 208.14(b) or (c), shall be communicated in writing to the applicant. Pursuant to § 208.9(d), an applicant must appear in person to receive and to acknowledge receipt of the decision to grant or deny asylum, or to refer an asylum application unless, in the discretion of the asylum office director, service by mail is appropriate. A letter communicating denial of asylum or referral of the application shall state the basis for denial or referral and include an assessment of the applicant's credibility.

[65 FR 76136, Dec. 6, 2000]

§ 208.20 Determining if an asylum application is frivolous. [also 8 C.F.R. § 1208.20]

For applications filed on or after April 1, 1997, an applicant is subject to the provisions of section 208(d)(6) of the Act only if a final order by an immigration judge or the Board of Immigration Appeals specifically finds that the alien knowingly filed a frivolous asylum application. For purposes of this section, an asylum application is frivolous if any of its material elements is deliberately fabricated. Such finding shall only be made if the immigration judge or the Board is satisfied that the applicant, during the course of the proceedings, has had sufficient opportunity to account for any discrepancies or implausible aspects of the claim. For purposes of this section, a finding that an alien filed a frivolous asylum application shall not preclude the alien from seeking withholding of removal.

[64 FR 8490, 8492, Feb. 19, 1999; 65 FR 76136, Dec. 6, 2000]

§ 208.21 Admission of the asylee's spouse and children. [also 8 C.F.R. § 1208.21, which has minor wording changes and cross-references to part 1208]

(a) Eligibility. In accordance with section 208(b)(3) of the Act, a spouse, as defined in section 101(a)(35) of the Act, 8 U.S.C. 1101(a)(35), or child, as defined in section 101(b)(1) of the Act, also may be granted asylum if accompanying, or following to join, the principal alien who was granted asylum, unless it is determined that the spouse or child is ineligible for asylum under section 208(b)(2)(A)(i), (ii), (iii), (iv) or (v) of the Act for applications filed on or after April 1, 1997, or under § 208.13(c)(2)(i)(A), (C), (D), (E), or (F) for applications filed before April 1, 1997.

(b) Relationship. The relationship of spouse and child as defined in sections 101(a)(35) and 101(b)(1) of the Act must have existed at the time the principal alien's asylum application was approved and must continue to exist at the time of filing for accompanying or following-to-join benefits and at the time of the spouse or child's subsequent admission to the United States. If the asylee proves that the asylee is the parent of a child who was born after asylum was granted, but who was in utero on the date of the asylum grant, the child shall be eligible to accompany or follow-to-join the asylee. The child's mother, if not the principal asylee, shall not be eligible to accompany or follow-to-join the principal asylee unless the child's mother was the principal asylee's spouse on the date the principal asylee was granted asylum.

(c) Spouse or child in the United States. When a spouse or child of an alien granted asylum is in the United States, but was not included in the asylee's benefit request, the asylee may request accompanying or following-to-join benefits for his or her spouse or child, by filing for each qualifying family member a Request for Refugee/Asylee Relative, with supporting evidence, and in accordance with the form instructions, regardless of the status of that spouse or child in the United States. A separate Request for Refugee/Asylee Relative must be filed by the asylee for each qualifying family member within two years of the date in which he or she was granted asylum status, unless it is determined by USCIS that this period should be extended for humanitarian reasons. Upon approval of the Request for Refugee/Asylee Relative, USCIS will notify the asylee of such approval. Employment will be authorized incident to status. To demonstrate employment authorization, USCIS will issue a document reflecting the derivative's current status as an asylee, or the derivative may apply, under 8 CFR 274a.12(a), for employment authorization. The approval of the Request for Refugee/Asylee Relative will remain valid for the duration of the relationship to the asylee and, in the case of a child, while the child is under 21 years of age and unmarried, provided also that the principal's status has not been revoked. However, the approved Request for Refugee/Asylee Relative will cease to confer immigration benefits after it has been used by the beneficiary for admission to the United States as a derivative of an asylee.

(d) Spouse or child outside the United States. When a spouse or child of an alien granted asylum is outside the United States, the asylee may request accompanying or following-to-join benefits for his or her spouse or child(ren) by filing a separate Request for Refugee/Asylee Relative for each qualifying family member in accordance with the form instructions. A separate Request for Refugee/Asylee Relative for each qualifying family member must be filed within two years of the date in which the asylee was granted asylum, unless USCIS determines that the filing period should be extended for humanitarian reasons. When the Request for Refugee/Asylee Relative is approved, USCIS will notify the asylee of such approval. USCIS also will send the approved request to the Department of State for transmission to the U.S. Embassy or Consulate having jurisdiction over the area in which the asylee's spouse or child is located. The approval of the Request for Refugee/Asylee Relative will remain valid for the duration of the relationship to the asylee and, in the case of a child, while the child is under 21 years of age and unmarried, provided also that the principal's status has not been revoked. However, the approved Request for Refugee/Asylee Relative will cease to confer immigration benefits after it has been used by the beneficiary for admission to the United States as a derivative of an asylee.

(e) Denial. If the spouse or child is found to be ineligible for the status accorded under section 208(c) of the Act, a written notice stating the basis for denial shall be forwarded to the principal alien. No appeal shall lie from this decision.

(f) Burden of proof. To establish the claimed relationship of spouse or child as defined in sections 101(a)(35) and 101(b)(1) of the Act, evidence must be submitted with the request as set forth in part 204 of this chapter. Where possible this will consist of the documents specified in § 204.2 (a)(1)(i)(B), (a)(1)(iii)(B), (a)(2), (d)(2), and (d)(5) of this chapter. The burden of proof is on the principal alien to establish by a preponderance of the evidence that any person on whose behalf he or she is making a request under this section is an eligible spouse or child.

(g) Duration. The spouse or child qualifying under section 208(c) of the Act shall be granted asylum for an indefinite period unless the principal's status is revoked.

[63 FR 3796, Jan. 27, 1998; 64 FR 8490, Feb. 19, 1999; 65 FR 76136, Dec. 6, 2000; 76 FR 53784, Aug. 29, 2011; 76 FR 73476, Nov. 29, 2011.]

§ 208.22 Effect on exclusion, deportation, and removal proceedings. [also 8 C.F.R. § 1208.22, which is identical except for cross-references to part 1208]

An alien who has been granted asylum may not be deported or removed unless his or her asylum status is terminated pursuant to § 208.24. An alien in exclusion, deportation, or removal proceedings who is granted withholding of removal or deportation, or deferral of removal, may not be deported or removed to the country to which his or her deportation or removal is ordered withheld or deferred unless the withholding order is terminated pursuant to § 208.24 or deferral is terminated pursuant to § 208.17(d) or (e).

[64 FR 8490, 8492, Feb. 19, 1999; 65 FR 76136, Dec. 6, 2000]

§ 208.23 Restoration of status. [also 8 C.F.R. § 1208.23]

An alien who was maintaining his or her nonimmigrant status at the time of filing an asylum application and has such application denied may continue in or be restored to that status, if it has not expired.

[64 FR 8490, Feb. 19, 1999; 65 FR 76136, Dec. 6, 2000]

§ 208.24 Termination of asylum or withholding of removal or deportation. [also 8 C.F.R. § 1208.24, which has minor wording changes and cross-references to part 1208]

(a) Termination of asylum by USCIS. Except as provided in paragraph (e) of this section, an asylum officer may terminate a grant of asylum made under the jurisdiction of USCIS if, following an interview, the asylum officer determines that:

(1) There is a showing of fraud in the alien's application such that he or she was not eligible for asylum at the time it was granted;

(2) As to applications filed on or after April 1, 1997, one or more of the conditions described in section 208(c)(2) of the Act exist; or

(3) As to applications filed before April 1, 1997, the alien no longer has a well-founded fear of persecution upon return due to a change of country conditions in the alien's country of nationality or habitual residence or the alien has committed any act that would have been grounds for denial of asylum under § 208.13(c)(2).

(b) Termination of withholding of deportation or removal by USCIS. Except as provided in paragraph (e) of this section, an asylum officer may terminate a grant of withholding of deportation or removal made under the jurisdiction of USCIS if the asylum officer determines, following an interview, that:

(1) The alien is no longer entitled to withholding of deportation or removal because, owing to a fundamental change in circumstances relating to the original claim, the alien's life or freedom no longer would be threatened on account of race, religion, nationality, membership in a particular social group, or political opinion in the country from which deportation or removal was withheld.

(2) There is a showing of fraud in the alien's application such that the alien was not eligible for withholding of removal at the time it was granted;

(3) The alien has committed any other act that would have been grounds for denial of withholding of removal under section 241(b)(3)(B) of the Act had it occurred prior to the grant of withholding of removal; or

(4) For applications filed in proceedings commenced before April 1, 1997, the alien has committed any act that would have been grounds for denial of withholding of deportation under section 243(h)(2) of the Act.

(c) Procedure. Prior to the termination of a grant of asylum or withholding of deportation or removal, the alien shall be given notice of intent to terminate, with the reasons therefor, at least 30 days prior to the interview specified in paragraph (a) of this section before an asylum officer. The alien shall be provided the opportunity to present evidence showing that he or she is still eligible for asylum or withholding of deportation or removal. If the asylum officer determines that the alien is no longer eligible for asylum or withholding of deportation or removal, the alien shall be given written notice that asylum status or withholding of deportation or removal and any employment authorization issued pursuant thereto, are terminated.

(d) Termination of derivative status. The termination of asylum status for a person who was the principal applicant shall result in termination of the asylum status of a spouse or child whose status was based on the asylum application of the principal. Such termination shall not preclude the spouse or child of such alien from separately asserting an asylum or withholding of deportation or removal claim.

(e) Removal proceedings. When an alien's asylum status or withholding of removal or deportation is terminated under this section, the Service shall initiate removal proceedings, as appropriate, if the alien is not already in exclusion, deportation, or removal proceedings. Removal proceedings may take place in conjunction with a termination hearing scheduled under § 208.24(f).

(f) Termination of asylum, or withholding of deportation or removal, by an immigration judge or the Board of Immigration Appeals. An immigration judge or the Board of Immigration Appeals may reopen a case pursuant to 8 CFR 1003.2 and 8 CFR 1003.23 for the purpose of terminating a grant of asylum, or a withholding of deportation or removal. In such a reopened proceeding, the Service must establish, by a preponderance of evidence, one or more of the grounds set forth in paragraphs (a) or (b) of this section. In addition, an immigration judge may terminate a grant of asylum, or a withholding of deportation or removal, made under the jurisdiction of the Service at any time after the alien has been provided a notice of intent to terminate by the Service. Any termination under this paragraph may occur in conjunction with an exclusion, deportation, or removal proceeding.

(g) Termination of asylum for arriving aliens. If the Service determines that an applicant for admission who had previously been granted asylum in the United States falls within conditions set forth in § 208.24 and is inadmissible, the Service shall issue a notice of intent to terminate asylum and initiate removal proceedings under section 240 of the Act. The alien shall present his or her response to the intent to terminate during proceedings before the immigration judge.

[64 FR 8490, Feb. 19, 1999; 65 FR 76136, Dec. 6, 2000; 76 FR 53784, Aug. 29, 2011; 78 FR 22771, April 17, 2013.]

§§ 208.25–29 [Reserved.] [also 8 C.F.R. § 1208.25–29]

SUBPART B—CREDIBLE FEAR OF PERSECUTION

§ 208.30 Credible fear determinations involving stowaways and applicants for admission found inadmissible pursuant to section 212(a)(6)(C) or 212(a)(7) of the Act. [also 8 C.F.R. § 1208.30, which has similar details and cross-references to part 1208]

(a) Jurisdiction. The provisions of this subpart B apply to aliens subject to sections 235(a)(2) and 235(b)(1) of the Act. Pursuant to section 235(b)(1)(B) of the Act, DHS has exclusive jurisdiction to make credible fear determinations, and the Executive Office for Immigration Review has exclusive jurisdiction to review such determinations. Except as otherwise provided in this subpart B, paragraphs (b) through (g) of this section are the exclusive procedures applicable to credible fear interviews, determinations, and reviews under section 235(b)(1)(B) of the Act. Prior to January 1, 2015, an alien present in or arriving in the Commonwealth of the Northern Mariana Islands is ineligible to apply for asylum and may only establish eligibility for withholding of removal pursuant to section 241(b)(3) of the Act or withholding or deferral of removal under the Convention Against Torture.

(b) Treatment of dependents. A spouse or child of an alien may be included in that alien's credible fear evaluation and determination, if such spouse or child:

(1) Arrived in the United States concurrently with the principal alien; and

(2) Desires to be included in the principal alien's determination. However, any alien may have his or her credible fear evaluation and determination made separately, if he or she expresses such a desire.

(c) Authority. Asylum officers conducting credible fear interviews shall have the authorities described in § 208.9(c).

(d) Interview. The asylum officer, as defined in section 235(b)(1)(E) of the Act, will conduct the interview in a nonadversarial manner, separate and apart from the general public. The purpose of the interview shall be to elicit all relevant and useful information bearing on whether the applicant has a credible fear of persecution or torture, and shall conduct the interview as follows:

(1) If the officer conducting the credible fear interview determines that the alien is unable to participate effectively in the interview because of illness, fatigue, or other impediments, the officer may reschedule the interview.

(2) At the time of the interview, the asylum officer shall verify that the alien has received Form M–444, Information about Credible Fear Interview in Expedited Removal Cases. The officer shall also determine that the alien has an understanding of the credible fear determination process.

(3) The alien may be required to register his or her identity.

(4) The alien may consult with a person or persons of the alien's choosing prior to the interview or any review thereof, and may present other evidence, if available. Such consultation shall be at no expense to the Government and shall not unreasonably delay the process. Any person or persons with whom the alien chooses to consult may be present at the interview and may be permitted, in the discretion of the asylum officer, to present a statement at the end of the interview. The asylum officer, in his or her discretion, may place reasonable limits on the number of persons who may be present at the interview and on the length of the statement.

(5) If the alien is unable to proceed effectively in English, and if the asylum officer is unable to proceed competently in a language chosen by the alien, the asylum officer shall arrange for the assistance of an interpreter in conducting the interview. The interpreter must be at least 18 years of age and may not be the applicant's attorney or representative of record, a witness testifying on the applicant's behalf, a representative or employee of the applicant's country of nationality, or, if the applicant is stateless, the applicant's country of last habitual residence.

(6) The asylum officer shall create a summary of the material facts as stated by the applicant. At the conclusion of the interview, the officer shall review the summary with the alien and provide the alien with an opportunity to correct any errors therein.

(e) Determination.

(1) The asylum officer shall create a written record of his or her determination, including a summary of the material facts as stated by the applicant, any additional facts relied on by the officer, and the officer's determination of whether, in light of such facts, the alien has established a credible fear of persecution or torture.

(2) An alien will be found to have a credible fear of persecution if there is a significant possibility, taking into account the credibility of the statements made by the alien in support of the alien's claim and such other facts as are known to the officer, the alien can establish eligibility for asylum under section 208 of the Act or for withholding of removal under section 241(b)(3) of the Act. However, prior to January 1, 2015, in the case of an alien physically present in or arriving in the Commonwealth of the Northern Mariana Islands, the officer may only find a credible fear of persecution if there is a significant possibility that the alien can establish eligibility for withholding of removal pursuant to section 241(b)(3) of the Act.

(3) An alien will be found to have a credible fear of torture if the alien shows that there is a significant possibility that he or she is eligible for withholding of removal or deferral of removal under the Convention Against Torture, pursuant to 8 CFR 208.16 or 208.17.

(4) In determining whether the alien has a credible fear of persecution, as defined in section 235(b)(1)(B)(v) of the Act, or a credible fear of torture, the asylum officer shall consider whether the alien's case presents novel or unique issues that merit consideration in a full hearing before an immigration judge.

(5) Except as provided in paragraph (e)(6) of this section, if an alien is able to establish a credible fear of persecution or torture but appears to be subject to one or more of the mandatory bars to applying for, or being granted, asylum contained in section 208(a)(2) and 208(b)(2) of the Act, or to withholding of removal contained in section 241(b)(3)(B) of the Act, the Department of Homeland Security shall nonetheless place the alien in proceedings under section 240 of the Act for full consideration of the alien's claim, if the alien is not a stowaway. If the alien is a stowaway, the Department shall place the alien in proceedings for consideration of the alien's claim pursuant to 8 CFR 208.2(c)(3).

(6) Prior to any determination concerning whether an alien arriving in the United States at a U.S.-Canada land border port-of-entry or in transit through the U.S. during removal by Canada has a credible fear of persecution or torture, the asylum officer shall conduct a threshold screening interview to determine whether such an alien is ineligible to apply for asylum pursuant to section 208(a)(2)(A) of the Act and subject to removal to Canada by operation of the Agreement Between the Government of the United States and the Government of Canada For Cooperation in the Examination of Refugee Status Claims from Nationals of Third Countries ("Agreement"). In conducting this threshold screening interview, the asylum officer shall apply all relevant interview procedures outlined in paragraph (d) of this section, provided, however, that paragraph (d)(2) of this section shall not apply to aliens described in this paragraph. The asylum officer shall advise the alien of the Agreement's exceptions and question the alien as to applicability of any of these exceptions to the alien's case.

(i) If the asylum officer, with concurrence from a supervisory asylum officer, determines that an alien does not qualify for an exception under the Agreement during this threshold screening interview, the alien is ineligible to apply for asylum in the United States. After the asylum officer's documented finding is reviewed by a supervisory asylum officer, the alien shall be advised that he or she will be removed to Canada in order to pursue his or her claims relating to a fear of persecution or torture under Canadian law. Aliens found ineligible to apply for asylum under this paragraph shall be removed to Canada.

(ii) If the alien establishes by a preponderance of the evidence that he or she qualifies for an exception under the terms of the Agreement, the asylum officer shall make a written notation of the basis of the exception, and then proceed immediately to a determination concerning whether the alien has a credible fear of persecution or torture under paragraph (d) of this section.

(iii) An alien qualifies for an exception to the Agreement if the alien is not being removed from Canada in transit through the United States and

(A) Is a citizen of Canada or, not having a country of nationality, is a habitual resident of Canada;

(B) Has in the United States a spouse, son, daughter, parent, legal guardian, sibling, grandparent, grandchild, aunt, uncle, niece, or nephew who has been granted asylum, refugee, or other lawful status in the United States, provided, however, that this exception shall not apply to an alien whose relative maintains only nonimmigrant visitor status, as defined in section 101(a)(15)(B) of the Act, or whose relative maintains only visitor status based on admission to the United States pursuant to the Visa Waiver Program;

(C) Has in the United States a spouse, son, daughter, parent, legal guardian, sibling, grandparent, grandchild, aunt, uncle, niece, or nephew who is at least 18 years of age and has an asylum application pending before U.S. Citizenship and Immigration Services, the Executive Office for

Immigration Review, or on appeal in federal court in the United States;

(D) Is unmarried, under 18 years of age, and does not have a parent or legal guardian in either Canada or the United States;

(E) Arrived in the United States with a validly issued visa or other valid admission document, other than for transit, issued by the United States to the alien, or, being required to hold a visa to enter Canada, was not required to obtain a visa to enter the United States; or

(F) The Director of USCIS, or the Director's designee, determines, in the exercise of unreviewable discretion, that it is in the public interest to allow the alien to pursue a claim for asylum, withholding of removal, or protection under the Convention Against Torture, in the United States.

(iv) As used in 8 CFR 208.30(e)(6)(iii)(B), (C) and (D) only, "legal guardian" means a person currently vested with legal custody of such an alien or vested with legal authority to act on the alien's behalf, provided that such an alien is both unmarried and less than 18 years of age, and provided further that any dispute with respect to whether an individual is a legal guardian will be resolved on the basis of U.S. law.

(7) An asylum officer's determination shall not become final until reviewed by a supervisory asylum officer.

(f) Procedures for a positive credible fear finding. If an alien, other than an alien stowaway, is found to have a credible fear of persecution or torture, the asylum officer will so inform the alien and issue a Form I–862, Notice to Appear, for full consideration of the asylum and withholding of removal claim in proceedings under section 240 of the Act. If an alien stowaway is found to have a credible fear of persecution or torture, the asylum officer will so inform the alien and issue a Form I–863, Notice of Referral to Immigration Judge, for full consideration of the asylum claim, or the withholding of removal claim, in proceedings under § 208.2(c). Parole of the alien may be considered only in accordance with section 212(d)(5) of the Act and § 212.5 of this chapter.

(g) Procedures for a negative credible fear finding.

(1) If an alien is found not to have a credible fear of persecution or torture, the asylum officer shall provide the alien with a written notice of decision and inquire whether the alien wishes to have an immigration judge review the negative decision, using Form I–869, Record of Negative Credible Fear Finding and Request for Review by Immigration Judge. The alien shall indicate whether he or she desires such review on Form I–869. A refusal by the alien to make such indication shall be considered a request for review.

(i) If the alien requests such review, or refuses to either request or decline such review, the asylum officer shall arrange for detention of the alien and serve him or her with a Form I–863, Notice of Referral to Immigration Judge, for review of the credible fear determination in accordance with paragraph (f)(2) of this section.

(ii) If the alien is not a stowaway and does not request a review by an immigration judge, the officer shall order the alien removed and issue a Form I–860, Notice and Order of Expedited Removal, after review by a supervisory asylum officer.

(iii) If the alien is a stowaway and the alien does not request a review by an immigration judge, the asylum officer shall refer the alien to the district director for completion of removal proceedings in accordance with section 235(a)(2) of the Act.

(2) Review by immigration judge of a negative credible fear finding.

(i) Immigration judges will review negative credible fear findings as provided in 8 CFR 1208.30(g)(2).

(ii) The record of the negative credible fear determination, including copies of the Form I–863, the asylum officer's notes, the summary of the material facts, and other materials upon which the determination was based shall be provided to the immigration judge with the negative determination.

[64 FR 8492, Feb. 19, 1999; 65 FR 76136, Dec. 6, 2000; 69 FR 69488, Nov. 29, 2004; 74 FR 55737, Oct. 28, 2009; 76 FR 53784, Aug. 29, 2011.]

§ 208.31 Reasonable fear of persecution or torture determinations involving aliens ordered removed under section 238(b) of the Act and aliens whose removal is reinstated under section 241(a)(5) of the Act. [also 8 C.F.R. § 1208.31, which has minor wording changes and cross-references to part 1208]

(a) Jurisdiction. This section shall apply to any alien ordered removed under section 238(b) of the Act or whose deportation, exclusion, or removal order is reinstated under section 241(a)(5) of the Act who, in the course of the administrative removal or reinstatement process, expresses a fear of returning to the country of removal. USCIS has exclusive jurisdiction to make reasonable fear determinations, and EOIR has exclusive jurisdiction to review such determinations.

(b) Initiation of reasonable fear determination process. Upon issuance of a Final Administrative Removal Order under § 238.1 of this chapter, or notice under § 241.8(b) of this chapter that an alien is subject to removal, an alien described in paragraph (a) of this section shall be referred to an asylum officer for a reasonable fear determination. In the absence of exceptional circumstances, this determination will be conducted within 10 days of the referral.

(c) Interview and Procedure. The asylum officer shall conduct the interview in a non-adversarial manner, separate and apart from the general public. At the time of the interview, the asylum officer shall determine that the alien has an understanding of the reasonable fear determination process. The alien may be represented by counsel or an accredited representative at the interview, at no expense to the Government, and may present evidence, if available, relevant to the possibility of persecution or torture. The alien's representative may present a statement at the end of the interview. The asylum officer, in his or her discretion, may place reasonable limits on the number of persons who may be present at the interview and the length of the statement. If the alien is unable to proceed effectively in English, and if the asylum officer is unable to proceed competently in a language chosen by the alien, the asylum officer shall arrange for the assistance of an interpreter in conducting the interview. The interpreter may not be a representative or employee of the applicant's country or [sic] nationality, or if the applicant is stateless, the applicant's country of last habitual residence. The asylum officer shall create a summary of the material facts as stated by the applicant. At the conclusion of the interview, the officer shall review the summary with the alien and provide the alien with an opportunity to correct errors therein. The asylum officer shall create a written record of his or her determination, including a summary of the material facts as stated by the applicant, any additional facts relied on by the officers, and the officer's determination of whether, in light of such facts, the alien has established a reasonable fear of persecution or torture. The alien shall be determined to have a reasonable fear of persecution or torture if the alien establishes a reasonable possibility that he or she would be persecuted on account of his or her race, religion, nationality, membership in a particular social group or political opinion, or a reasonable possibility that he or she would be tortured in the country of removal. For purposes of the screening determination, the bars to eligibility for withholding of removal under section 241(b)(3)(B) of the Act shall not be considered.

(d) Authority. Asylum officers conducting screening determinations under this section shall have the authority described in § 208.9(c).

(e) Referral to Immigration Judge. If an asylum officer determines that an alien described in this section has a reasonable fear of persecution or torture, the officer shall so inform the alien and issue a Form I–863, Notice of Referral to the Immigration Judge, for full consideration of the request for withholding of removal only. Such cases shall be adjudicated by the immigration judge in accordance with the provisions of § 208.16. Appeal of the immigration judge's decision shall lie to the Board of Immigration Appeals.

(f) Removal of aliens with no reasonable fear of persecution or torture. If the asylum officer determines that the alien has not established a reasonable fear of persecution or torture, the asylum officer shall inform the alien in writing of the decision and shall inquire whether the alien wishes to have an immigration judge review the negative decision, using Form I–898, Record of Negative Reasonable Fear Finding and Request for Review by Immigration Judge, on which the alien shall indicate whether he or she desires such review.

(g) Review by immigration judge. The asylum officer's negative decision regarding reasonable fear shall be subject to review by an immigration judge upon the alien's request. If the alien requests such review, the asylum officer shall serve him or her with a Form I–863. The record of determination, including copies of the Form I–863, the asylum officer's notes, the summary of the material facts, and other materials upon which the determination was based shall be provided to the immigration judge with the negative determination. In the absence of exceptional circumstances, such review shall be conducted by the immigration judge within 10 days of the filing of the Form I–863 with the immigration court. Upon review of the asylum officer's negative reasonable fear determination:

(1) If the immigration judge concurs with the asylum officer's determination that the alien does not have a reasonable fear of persecution or torture, the case shall be returned to the Service for removal of the alien. No appeal shall lie from the immigration judge's decision.

(2) If the immigration judge finds that the alien has a reasonable fear of persecution or torture, the alien may submit Form I–589, Application for Asylum and Withholding of Removal.

(i) The immigration judge shall consider only the alien's application for withholding of removal under § 208.16 and shall determine whether the alien's removal to the country of removal must be withheld or deferred.

(ii) Appeal of the immigration judge's decision whether removal must be withheld or deferred lies to the Board of Immigration Appeals. If the alien or the Service appeals the immigration judge's decision, the Board shall review only the immigration judge's decision regarding the alien's eligibility for withholding or deferral of removal under § 208.16.

[64 FR 8493, Feb. 19, 1999; 64 FR 13881, March 23, 1999; 76 FR 53784, Aug. 29, 2011.]

PART 214—NONIMMIGRANT CLASSES

§ 214.1 Requirements for admission, extension, and maintenance of status.

(a) General.

(1) Nonimmigrant classes. For the purpose of administering the nonimmigrant provisions of the Act, the following administrative subclassifications of nonimmigrant classifications as defined in section 101(a)(15) of the Act are established:

(i) Section 101(a)(15)(B) is divided into (B)(i) for visitors for business and (B)(ii) for visitors for pleasure;

(ii) Section 101(a)(15)(C) is divided into (C)(i) for aliens who are not diplomats and are in transit through the United States; (C)(ii) for aliens in transit to and from the United Nations Headquarters District; and (C)(iii) for alien diplomats in transit through the United States;

(iii) Section 101(a)(15)(H) is divided to create an (H)(iv) subclassification for the spouse and children of a nonimmigrant classified under section 101(a)(15)(H)(i), (ii), or (iii);

(iv) Section 101(a)(15)(J) is divided into (J)(i) for principal aliens and (J)(ii) for such alien's spouse and children;

(v) Section 101(a)(15)(K) is divided into (K)(i) for the fiance(e), (K)(ii) for the spouse, and (K)(iii) for the children of either;

(vi) Section 101(a)(15)(L) is divided into (L)(i) for principal aliens and (L)(ii) for such alien's spouse and children;

(vii) Section 101(a)(15)(Q)(ii) is divided to create a (Q)(iii) for subclassification for the spouse and children of a nonimmigrant classified under section 101(a)(15)(Q)(ii) of the Act;

(viii) Section 101(a)(15)(T)(ii) is divided into (T)(ii), (T)(iii) and (T)(iv) for the spouse, child, and parent, respectively, of a nonimmigrant classified under section 101(a)(15)(T)(i); and

(ix) Section 101(a)(15)(U)(ii) is divided into (U)(ii), (U)(iii), (U)(iv), and (U)(v) for the spouse, child, parent, and siblings, respectively, of a nonimmigrant classified under section 101(a)(15)(U)(i); and

(2) Classification designations. For the purpose of this chapter the following nonimmigrant designations are established. The designation in the second column may be used to refer to the appropriate nonimmigrant classification.

Section	Designation
101(a)(15)(A)(i)	A–1.
101(a)(15)(A)(ii)	A–2.
101(a)(15)(A)(iii)	A–3.
101(a)(15)(B)(i)	B–1.
101(a)(15)(B)(ii)	B–2.
101(a)(15)(C)(i)	C–1.

101(a)(15)(C)(ii)	C–2.
101(a)(15)(C)(iii)	C–3.
101(a)(15)(D)(i)	D–1.
101(a)(15)(D)(ii)	D–2.
101(a)(15)(E)(i)	E–1.
101(a)(15)(E)(ii)	E–2.
101(a)(15)(F)(i)	F–1.
101(a)(15)(F)(ii)	F–2.
101(a)(15)(G)(i)	G–1.
101(a)(15)(G)(ii)	G–2.
101(a)(15)(G)(iii)	G–3.
101(a)(15)(G)(iv)	G–4.
101(a)(15)(G)(v)	G–5.
101(a)(15)(H)(i)(B)	H–1B.
101(a)(15)(H)(i)(C)	H–1C.
101(a)(15)(H)(ii)(A)	H–2A.
101(a)(15)(H)(ii)(B)	H–2B.
101(a)(15)(H)(iii)	H–3.
101(a)(15)(H)(iv)	H–4.
101(a)(15)(I)	I.
101(a)(15)(J)(i)	J–1.
101(a)(15)(J)(ii)	J–2.
101(a)(15)(K)(i)	K–1.
101(a)(15)(K)(ii)	K–3.
101(a)(15)(K)(iii)	K–2; K–4.
101(a)(15)(L)(i)	L–1.
101(a)(15)(L)(ii)	L–2.
101(a)(15)(M)(i)	M–1.
101(a)(15)(M)(ii)	M–2.
101(a)(15)(N)(i)	N–8.
101(a)(15)(N)(ii)	N–9.
101(a)(15)(O)(i)	O–1.
101(a)(15)(O)(ii)	O–2.
101(a)(15)(O)(iii)	O–3.
101(a)(15)(P)(i)	P–1.
101(a)(15)(P)(ii)	P–2.

101(a)(15)(P)(iii)	P–3.
101(a)(15)(P)(iv)	P–4.
101(a)(15)(Q)(i)	Q–1.
101(a)(15)(Q)(ii)	Q–2.
101(a)(15)(Q)(iii)	Q–3.
101(a)(15)(R)(i)	R–1.
101(a)(15)(R)(ii)	R–2.
101(a)(15)(S)(i)	S–5.
101(a)(15)(S)(ii)	S–6.
101(a)(15)(S) qualified family members	S–7.
101(a)(15)(T)(i)	T–1.
101(a)(15)(T)(ii)	T–2.
101(a)(15)(T)(iii)	T–3.
101(a)(15)(T)(iv)	T–4.
101(a)(15)(U)(i)	U–1.
101(a)(15)(U)(ii)	U–2, U–3, U–4, U–5.
101(a)(15)(V)	V–1, V–2, or V–3.
NAFTA, Principal	TN.
NAFTA, Dependent	TD.
Visa Waiver, Business	WB.
Visa Waiver, Tourist	WT.

Note 1: The classification designation K–2 is for the child of a K–1. The classification designation K–4 is for the child of a K–3.

Note 2: The classification designation V–1 is for the spouse of a lawful permanent resident; the classification designation V–2 is for the principal beneficiary of an I–130 who is the child of an LPR; the classification V–3 is for the derivative child of a V–1 or V–2 alien.

(3) General requirements.

(i) Every nonimmigrant alien who applies for admission to, or an extension of stay in, the United States, must establish that he or she is admissible to the United States, or that any ground of inadmissibility has been waived under section 212(d)(3) of the Act. Upon application for admission, the alien must present a valid passport and valid visa unless either or both documents have been waived. A nonimmigrant alien's admission to the United States is conditioned on compliance with any inspection requirement in § 235.1(d) or of this chapter. The passport of an alien applying for admission must be valid for a minimum of six months from the expiration date of the contemplated period of stay, unless otherwise provided in this chapter, and the alien must agree to abide by the terms and conditions of his or her admission. An alien applying for extension of stay must present a passport only if requested to do so by the Department of Homeland Security. The passport of an alien applying for extension of stay must be valid at the time of application for extension, unless otherwise provided in this chapter, and the alien must agree to maintain the validity of his or her passport and to abide by all the terms and conditions of his extension.

(ii) At the time of admission or extension of stay, every nonimmigrant alien must also agree to depart the United States at the expiration of his or her authorized period of admission or extension of stay, or upon abandonment of his or her authorized nonimmigrant status, and to comply with the departure procedures at section 215.8 of this chapter if such procedures apply to the particular alien. The nonimmigrant alien's failure to comply with those departure requirements, including any requirement that the alien provide biometric identifiers, may constitute a failure of the alien to maintain the terms of his or her nonimmigrant status.

(iii) At the time a nonimmigrant alien applies for admission or extension of stay, he or she must post a bond on Form I–352 in the sum of not less than $500, to ensure the maintenance of his or her nonimmigrant status and departure from the United States, if required to do so by the Commissioner of CBP, the Director of U.S. Citizenship and Immigration Services, an immigration judge, or the Board of Immigration Appeals.

(b) Readmission of nonimmigrants under section 101(a)(15)(F), (J), (M), or (Q)(ii) to complete unexpired periods of previous admission or extension of stay—

(1) Section 101(a)(15)(F). The inspecting immigration officer shall readmit for duration of status as defined in § 214.2(f)(5)(iii), any nonimmigrant alien whose nonimmigrant visa is considered automatically revalidated pursuant to 22 CFR 41.125(f) and who is applying for readmission under section 101(a)(15)(F) of the Act, if the alien:

(i) Is admissible;

(ii) Is applying for readmission after an absence from the United States not exceeding thirty days solely in contiguous territory or adjacent islands;

(iii) Is in possession of a valid passport unless exempt from the requirement for presentation of a passport; and

(iv) Presents, or is the accompanying spouse or child of an alien who presents, an Arrival–Departure Record, Form I–94 (see § 1.4), issued to the alien in connection with the previous admission or stay, the alien's Form I–20 ID copy, and either:

(A) A properly endorsed page 4 of Form I–20A–B if there has been no substantive change in the information on the student's most recent Form I–20A since the form was initially issued; or

(B) A new Form I–20A–B if there has been any substantive change in the information on the student's most recent Form I–20A since the form was initially issued.

(2) Section 101(a)(15)(J). The inspecting immigration officer shall readmit for the unexpired period of stay authorized prior to the alien's departure, any nonimmigrant alien whose nonimmigrant visa is considered automatically revalidated pursuant to 22 CFR 41.125(f) and who is applying for readmission under section 101(a)(15)(J) of the Act, if the alien:

(i) Is admissible;

(ii) Is applying for readmission after an absence from the United States not exceeding thirty days solely in contiguous territory or adjacent islands;

(iii) Is in possession of a valid passport unless exempt from the requirement for the presentation of a passport; and

(iv) Presents, or is the accompanying spouse or child of an alien who presents, Form I–94 issued to the alien in connection with the previous admission or stay or copy three of the last Form IAP–66 issued to the alien. Form I–94 or Form IAP–66 must show the unexpired period of the alien's stay endorsed by the Service.

(3) Section 101(a)(15)(M). The inspecting immigration officer shall readmit for the unexpired period of stay authorized prior to the alien's departure, any nonimmigrant alien whose nonimmigrant visa is considered automatically revalidated pursuant to 22 CFR 41.125(f) and who is applying for readmission under section 101(a)(15)(M) of the Act, if the alien:

(i) Is admissible;

(ii) Is applying for readmission after an absence not exceeding thirty days solely in contiguous territory;

(iii) Is in possession of a valid passport unless exempt from the requirement for the presentation of a passport; and

(iv) Presents, or is the accompanying spouse or child of an alien who presents, Form I–94 issued to the alien in connection with the previous admission or stay, the alien's Form I–20 ID copy, and a properly endorsed page 4 of Form I–20M–N.

(4) Section 101(a)(15)(Q)(ii). The inspecting immigration officer shall readmit for the unexpired period of stay authorized prior to the alien's departure, if the alien:

(i) Is admissible;

(ii) Is applying for readmission after an absence from the United States not exceeding 30 days solely in contiguous territory or adjacent islands;

(iii) Is in possession of a valid passport;

(iv) Presents, or is the accompanying spouse or child of an alien who presents, an Arrival–Departure Record, Form I–94, issued to the alien in connection with the previous admission or stay. The principal alien must also present a Certification Letter issued by the Department of State's Program Administrator.

(c) Extensions of stay—

(1) Filing on Form I–129. An employer seeking the services of an E–1, E–2, H–1B, H–2A, H–2B, H–3, L–1, O–1, O–2, P–1, P–2, P–3, Q–1, R–1, or TN nonimmigrant beyond the period previously granted, must petition for an extension of stay on Form I–129. The petition must be filed with the fee required in § 103.7 of this chapter, and the initial evidence specified in § 214.2, and on the petition form. Dependents holding derivative status may be included in the petition if it is for only one worker and the form version specifically provides for their inclusion. In all other cases dependents of the worker should file on Form I–539.

(2) Filing on Form I–539. Any other nonimmigrant alien, except an alien in F or J status who has been granted duration of status, who seeks to extend his or her stay beyond the currently authorized period of admission, must apply for an extension of stay on Form I–539 with the fee required in § 103.7 of this chapter together with any initial evidence specified in the applicable provisions of § 214.2, and on the application form. More than one person may be included in an application where the co-applicants are all members of a single family group and either all hold the same nonimmigrant status or one holds a nonimmigrant status and the other co-applicants are his or her spouse and/or children who hold derivative nonimmigrant status based on his or her status. Extensions granted to members of a family group must be for the same period of time. The shortest period granted to any member of the family shall be granted to all members of the family. In order to be eligible for an extension of stay, nonimmigrant aliens in K–3/K–4 status must do so in accordance with § 214.2(k)(10).

(3) Ineligible for extension of stay. A nonimmigrant in any of the following classes is ineligible for an extension of stay:

(i) B–1 or B–2 where admission was pursuant to the Visa Waiver Pilot Program;

(ii) C–1, C–2, C–3;

(iii) D–1, D–2;

(iv) K–1, K–2;

(v) Any nonimmigrant admitted for duration of status, other than as provided in § 214.2(f)(7);

(vi) Any nonimmigrant who is classified pursuant to section 101(a)(15)(S) of the Act beyond a total of 3 years; or

(vii) Any nonimmigrant who is classified according to section 101(a)(15)(Q)(ii) of the Act beyond a total of 3 years.

(viii) Any nonimmigrant admitted pursuant to the Guam–CNMI Visa Waiver Program, as provided in section 212(*l*) of the Act.

(4) Timely filing and maintenance of status. An extension of stay may not be approved for an applicant who failed to maintain the previously accorded status or where such status expired before the application or petition was filed, except that failure to file before the period of previously authorized status expired may be excused in the discretion of the Service and without separate application, with any extension granted from the date the previously authorized stay expired, where it is demonstrated at the time of filing that:

(i) The delay was due to extraordinary circumstances beyond the control of the applicant or petitioner, and the Service finds the delay commensurate with the circumstances;

(ii) The alien has not otherwise violated his or her nonimmigrant status;

(iii) The alien remains a bona fide nonimmigrant; and

(iv) The alien is not the subject of deportation proceedings under section 242 of the Act (prior to April 1, 1997) or removal proceedings under section 240 of the Act.

(5) Decision in Form I–129 or I–539 extension proceedings. Where an applicant or petitioner demonstrates eligibility for a requested extension, it may be granted at the discretion of the Service. There is no appeal from the denial of an application for extension of stay filed on Form I–129 or I–539.

(d) Termination of status. Within the period of initial admission or extension of stay, the nonimmigrant status of an alien shall be terminated by the revocation of a waiver authorized on his or her behalf under section 212(d)(3) or (4) of the Act; by the introduction of a private bill to confer permanent resident status on such alien; or, pursuant to notification in the Federal Register, on the basis of national security, diplomatic, or public safety reasons.

(e) Employment. A nonimmigrant in the United States in a class defined in section 101(a)(15)(B) of the Act as a temporary visitor for pleasure, or section 101(a)(15)(C) of the Act as an alien in transit through this country, may not engage in any employment. Any other nonimmigrant in the United States may not engage in any employment unless he has been accorded a nonimmigrant classification which authorizes employment or he has been granted permission to engage in employment in accordance with the provisions of this chapter. A nonimmigrant who is permitted to engage in employment may engage only in such employment as has been authorized. Any unauthorized employment by a nonimmigrant constitutes a failure to maintain status within the meaning of section 241(a)(1)(C)(i) of the Act.

(f) Registration and false information. A nonimmigrant's admission and continued stay in the United States is conditioned on compliance with any registration, photographing, and fingerprinting requirements under § 264.1(f) of this chapter that relate to the maintenance of nonimmigrant status and also on the full and truthful disclosure of all information requested by the Service. Willful failure by a nonimmigrant to register or to provide full and truthful information requested by the Service (regardless of whether or not the information requested was material) constitutes a failure to maintain nonimmigrant status under section 237(a)(1)(C)(i) of the Act.

(g) Criminal activity. A condition of a nonimmigrant's admission and continued stay in the United States is obedience to all laws of United States jurisdictions which prohibit the commission of crimes of violence and for which a sentence of more than one year imprisonment may be imposed. A nonimmigrant's conviction in a jurisdiction in the United States for a crime of violence for which a sentence of more than one year imprisonment may be imposed (regardless of whether such sentence is in fact imposed) constitutes a failure to maintain status under Section 241(a)(1)(C)(i) of the Act.

(h) Education privacy and F, J, and M nonimmigrants. As authorized by section 641(c)(2) of Division C of Pub. L. 104–208, 8 U.S.C. § 1372, and § 2.1(a) of this chapter, the Service has determined that, with respect to F and M nonimmigrant students and J nonimmigrant exchange visitors, waiving the provisions of the Family Educational Rights and Privacy Act (FERPA), 20 U.S.C. § 1232g, is necessary for the proper implementation of 8 U.S.C. § 1372. An educational agency or institution may not refuse to report information concerning an F or M nonimmigrant student or a J nonimmigrant exchange visitor that the educational agency or institution is required to report under 8 U.S.C. § 1372 and § 214.3(g) (or any corresponding Department of State regulation concerning J nonimmigrants) on the basis of FERPA and any regulation implementing FERPA. The waiver of FERPA under this paragraph authorizes and requires an educational agency or institution to report information concerning an F, J or M nonimmigrant that would ordinarily be protected by FERPA, but only to the extent that 8 U.S.C. § 1372 and § 214.3(g) (or any corresponding Department of State regulation concerning J nonimmigrants) requires the educational agency or institution to report information.

(i) Employment in a health care occupation.

(1) Except as provided in 8 CFR 212.15(n), any alien described in 8 CFR 212.15(a) who is coming to the United States to perform labor in a health care occupation described in 8 CFR 212.15(c) must obtain a certificate from a credentialing organization described in 8 CFR 212.15(e). The certificate or certified statement must be presented to the Department of Homeland Security in accordance with 8 CFR 212.15(d). In the alternative, an eligible alien seeking admission as a nurse may obtain a certified statement as provided in 8 CFR 212.15(h).

(2) A TN nonimmigrant may establish that he or she is eligible for a waiver described at 8 CFR 212.15(n) by providing evidence that his or her initial admission as a TN (or TC) nonimmigrant health care worker occurred before September 23, 2003, and he or she was licensed and employed in the United States as a health care worker before September 23, 2003. Evidence may include, but is not limited to, copies of TN or TC approval notices, copies of Form I–94 Arrival/Departure Records, employment verification letters and/or pay-stubs or other employment records, and state health care worker licenses.

(j) Extension of stay or change of status for health care worker. In the case of any alien admitted temporarily as a nonimmigrant under section 212(d)(3) of the Act and 8 CFR 212.15(n) for the primary purpose of the providing labor in a health care occupation described in 8 CFR 212.15(c), the petitioning employer may file a Form I–129 to extend the approval period for the alien's classification for the nonimmigrant status. If the alien is in the United States and is eligible for an extension of stay or change of status, the Form I–129 also serves as an application to extend the period of the alien's authorized stay or to change the alien's status. Although the Form I–129 petition may be approved, as it relates to the employer's request to classify the alien, the application for an extension of stay or change of status shall be denied if:

(1) The petitioner or applicant fails to submit the certification required by 8 CFR 212.15(a) with the petition or application to extend the alien's stay or change the alien's status; or

(2) The petition or application to extend the alien's stay or change the alien's status does include the certification required by 8 CFR 212.15(a), but the alien obtained the certification more than 1 year after the date of the alien's admission under section 212(d)(3) of the Act and 8 CFR 212.15(n). While DHS may admit, extend the period of authorized stay, or change the status of a nonimmigrant health care worker for a period of 1 year if the alien does not have certification on or before July 26, 2004 (or on or before July 26, 2005, in the case of a citizen of Canada or Mexico, who, before September 23, 2003, was employed as a TN or TC nonimmigrant health care worker and held a valid license from a U.S. jurisdiction), the alien will not be eligible for a subsequent admission, change of status, or extension of stay as a health care worker if the alien has not obtained the requisite certification 1 year after the initial date of admission, change of status, or extension of stay as a health care worker.

(k) Denial of petitions under section 214(c) of the Act based on a finding by the Department of Labor. Upon debarment by the Department of Labor pursuant to 20 CFR 655.31, USCIS may deny any petition filed by that petitioner for nonimmigrant status under section 101(a)(15)(H) (except for status under sections 101(a)(15)(H)(i)(b1), (L), (O), and (P)(i) of the Act) for a period of at least 1 year but not more than 5 years. The length of the period shall be based on the severity of the violation or violations. The decision to deny petitions, the time period for the bar to petitions, and the reasons for the time period will be explained in a written notice to the petitioner.

[26 FR 12067, Dec. 16, 1961, as amended at 36 FR 8048, April 29, 1971; 37 FR 14288, June 19, 1972; 43 FR 12674, March 27, 1978; 44 FR 65727, Nov. 14, 1979; 45 FR 48867, July 22, 1980; 46 FR 25597, May 8, 1981; 48 FR 14582, April 5, 1983; 48 FR 20685, May 9, 1983; 48 FR 30350, July 1, 1983; 52 FR 45446, Nov. 30, 1987; 56 FR 38333, Aug. 13, 1991; 59 FR 1463, Jan. 11, 1994; 59 FR 26594, May 23, 1994; 60 FR 44266, Aug. 25, 1995; 62 FR 10349, March 6, 1997; 65 FR 14777, March 17, 2000; 65 FR 43531, July 13, 2000; 65 FR 67617, Nov. 13, 2000; 66 FR 31112, June 11, 2001; 66 FR 42593, Aug. 14, 2001; 66 FR 46702, Sept. 7, 2001; 66 FR 49514, Sept. 28, 2001; 67 FR 4795, Jan. 31, 2002; 67 FR 52591, Aug. 12, 2002; 67 FR 61476, Oct. 1, 2002; 67 FR 76270, Dec. 11, 2002; 68 FR 43920, July 25, 2003; 69 FR 480, Jan. 5, 2004; 69 FR 43732, July 22, 2004; 72 FR 53036, Sept. 17, 2007; 73 FR 61334, Oct. 16, 2008; 73 FR 78127, Dec. 19, 2008; 74 FR 2835, Jan. 16, 2009; 78 FR 18472, March 27, 2013]

§ 214.2 Special requirements for admission, extension, and maintenance of status. [subsections (h), (*l*)]

(h) Temporary employees—

(1) Admission of temporary employees—

(i) General. Under section 101(a)(15)(H) of the Act, an alien may be authorized to come to the United States temporarily to perform services or labor for, or to receive training from, an employer, if petitioned for by that employer. Under this nonimmigrant category, the alien may be classified as follows: under section 101(a)(15)(H)(i)(c) of the Act as a registered nurse; under section 101(a)(15)(H)(i)(b) of the Act as an alien who is coming to perform services in a specialty occupation, services relating to a Department of Defense (DOD) cooperative research and development project or coproduction project, or services as a fashion model who is of distinguished merit and ability; under section 101(a)(15)(H)(ii)(a) of the Act as an alien who is coming to perform agricultural labor or services of a temporary or seasonal nature; under section 101(a)(15)(H)(ii)(b) of the Act as an alien coming to perform other temporary services or labor; or under section 101(a)(15)(H)(iii) of the Act as an alien who is coming as a trainee or as a participant in a special education exchange visitor program. These classifications are called H–1B, H–1C, H–2A, H–2B, and H–3, respectively. The employer must file a petition with the Service for review of the services or training and for determination of the alien's eligibility for classification as a temporary employee or trainee, before the alien may apply for a visa or seek admission to the United States. This paragraph sets forth the standards and procedures applicable to these classifications.

(ii) Description of classifications.

(A) An H–1C classification applies to an alien who is coming temporarily to the United States to perform services as a registered nurse, meets the requirements of section 212(m)(1) of the Act, and will perform services at a facility (as defined at section 212(m)(6) of the Act) for which the Secretary of Labor has determined and certified to the Attorney General that an unexpired attestation is on file and in effect under section 212(m)(2) of the Act. This classification will expire 4 years from June 11, 2001.

(B) An H–1B classification applies to an alien who is coming temporarily to the United States:

(1) To perform services in a specialty occupation (except agricultural workers, and aliens described in section 101(a)(15)(O) and (P) of the Act) described in section 214(i)(1) of the Act, that meets the requirements of section 214(i)(2) of the Act, and for whom the Secretary of Labor has determined and certified to the Attorney General that the prospective employer has filed a labor condition application under section 212(n)(1) of the Act;

(2) To perform services of an exceptional nature requiring exceptional merit and ability relating to a cooperative research and development project or a co-production project provided for under a Government-to-Government agreement administered by the Secretary of Defense;

(3) To perform services as a fashion model of distinguished merit and ability and for whom the Secretary of Labor has determined and certified to the Attorney General that the prospective employer has filed a labor condition application under section 212(n)(1) of the Act.

(C) An H–2A classification applies to an alien who is coming temporarily to the United States to perform agricultural work of a temporary or seasonal nature.

(D) An H–2B classification applies to an alien who is coming temporarily to the United States to perform nonagricultural work of a temporary or seasonal nature, if there are not sufficient workers who are able, willing, qualified, and available at the time of application for a visa and admission to the United States and at the place where the alien is to perform such services or labor. This classification does not apply to graduates of medical schools coming to the United States to perform services as members of the medical profession. The temporary or permanent nature of the services or labor described on the approved temporary labor certification are subject to review by USCIS. This classification requires a temporary labor certification issued by the Secretary of Labor or the Governor of Guam prior to the filing of a petition with USCIS.

(E) An H–3 classification applies to an alien who is coming temporarily to the United States:

(1) As a trainee, other than to receive graduate medical education or training, or training provided primarily at or by an academic or vocational institution, or

(2) As a participant in a special education exchange visitor program which provides for practical training and experience in the education of children with physical, mental, or emotional disabilities.

(2) Petitions—

(i) Filing of petitions—

(A) General.A United States employer seeking to classify an alien as an H–1B, H–2A, H–2B, or H–3 temporary employee must file a petition on Form I–129, Petition for Nonimmigrant Worker, as provided in the form instructions.

(B) Service or training in more than one location. A petition that requires services to be performed or training to be received in more than one location must include an itinerary with the dates and locations of the services or training and must be filed with USCIS as provided in the form instructions. The address that the petitioner specifies as its location on the Form I–129 shall be where the petitioner is located for purposes of this paragraph.

(C) Services or training for more than one employer. If the beneficiary will perform nonagricultural services for, or receive training from, more than one employer, each employer must file a separate petition with USCIS as provided in the form instructions.

(D) Change of employers. If the alien is in the United States and seeks to change employers, the prospective new employer must file a petition on Form I–129 requesting classification and an extension of the alien's stay in the United States. If the new petition is approved, the extension of stay may be granted for the validity of the approved petition. The validity of the petition and the alien's extension of stay must conform to the limits on the alien's temporary stay that are prescribed in paragraph (h)(13) of this section. Except as provided by 8 CFR 274a.12(b)(21) or section 214(n) of the Act, 8 U.S.C. 1184(n), the alien is not authorized to begin the employment with the new petitioner until the petition is approved. An H–1C nonimmigrant alien may not change employers.

(E) Amended or new petition. The petitioner shall file an amended or new petition, with fee, with the Service Center where the original petition was filed to reflect any material changes in the terms and conditions of employment or training or the alien's eligibility as specified in the original approved petition. An amended or new H–1B, H–1C, H–2A, or H–2B petition must be accompanied by a current or new Department of Labor determination. In the case of an H–1B petition, this requirement includes a new labor condition application.

(F) Agents as petitioners. A United States agent may file a petition in cases involving workers who are traditionally self-employed or workers who use agents to arrange short-term employment on their behalf with numerous employers, and in cases where a foreign employer authorizes the agent to act on its behalf. A United States agent may be: the actual employer of the beneficiary, the representative of both the employer and the beneficiary, or, a person or entity authorized by the employer to act for, or in place of, the employer as it agent. A petition filed by a United States agent is subject to the following conditions;

(1) An agent performing the function of an employer must guarantee the wages and other terms and conditions of employment by contractual agreement with the beneficiary or beneficiaries of the petition. The agent/employer must also provide an itinerary of definite employment and information on any other services planned for the period of time requested.

(2) A person or company in business as an agent may file the H petition involving multiple employers as the representative of both the employers and the beneficiary or beneficiaries if the supporting documentation includes a complete itinerary of services or engagements. The itinerary shall specify the dates of each service or engagement, the names and addresses of the actual employers, and the names and addresses of the establishment, venues, or locations where the services will be performed. In questionable cases, a contract between the employers and the beneficiary or beneficiaries may be required. The burden is on the agent to explain the terms and conditions of the employment and to provide any required documentation.

(3) A foreign employer who, through a United States agent, files a petition for an H nonimmigrant alien is responsible for complying with all of the employer sanctions provisions of section 274A of the Act and 8 CFR part 274a.

(G) Multiple H–1B petitions. An employer may not file, in the same fiscal year, more than one H–1B petition on behalf of the same alien if the alien is subject to the numerical limitations of section 214(g)(1)(A) of the Act or is exempt from those limitations under section 214(g)(5)(C) of the Act. If an H–1B petition is denied, on a basis other than fraud or misrepresentation, the employer may file a subsequent H–1B petition on behalf of the same alien in the same fiscal year, provided that the numerical limitation has not been reached or if the filing qualifies as exempt from the numerical limitation. Otherwise, filing more than one H–1B petition by an employer on behalf of the same alien in the same fiscal year will result in the denial or revocation of all such petitions. If USCIS believes that related entities (such as a parent company, subsidiary, or affiliate) may not have a legitimate business need to file more than one H–1B petition on behalf of the same alien subject to the numerical limitations of section 214(g)(1)(A) of the Act or otherwise eligible for an exemption under section 214(g)(5)(C) of the Act, USCIS may issue a request for additional evidence or notice of intent to deny, or notice of intent to revoke each petition. If any of the related entities fail to demonstrate a legitimate business need to file an H–1B petition on behalf of the same alien, all petitions filed on that alien's behalf by the related entities will be denied or revoked.

(ii) Multiple beneficiaries. More than one beneficiary may be included in an H–1C, H–2A, H–2B, or H–3 petition if the beneficiaries will be performing the same service, or receiving the same training, for the same period of time, and in the same location. H–2A and H–2B petitions for workers from countries not designated in accordance with paragraph (h)(6)(i)(E) of this section should be filed separately.

(iii) Naming beneficiaries. H–1B, H–1C, and H–3 petitions must include the name of each beneficiary. Except as provided in this paragraph (h), all H–2A and H–2B petitions must include the name of each beneficiary who is currently in the United States, but need not name any beneficiary who is not currently in the United States. Unnamed beneficiaries must be shown on the petition by total number. USCIS may require the petitioner to name H–2B beneficiaries where the name is needed to establish eligibility for H–2B nonimmigrant status. If all of the beneficiaries covered by an H–2A or H–2B temporary labor certification have not been identified at the time a petition is filed, multiple petitions for subsequent beneficiaries may be filed at different times but must include a copy of the same temporary labor certification. Each petition must reference all previously filed petitions associated with that temporary labor certification. All H–2A and H–2B petitions on behalf of workers who are not from a country that has been designated as a participating country in accordance with paragraphs (h)(5)(i)(F)(1) or (h)(6)(i)(E)(1) of this section must name all the workers in the petition who fall within these categories. All H–2A and H–2B petitions must state the nationality of all beneficiaries, whether or not named, even if there are beneficiaries from more than one country.

(iv) [Reserved]

(v) H–2A Petitions. Special criteria for admission, extension, and maintenance of status apply to H–2A petitions and are specified in paragraph (h)(5) of this section. The other provisions of § 214.2(h) apply to H–2A only to the extent that they do not conflict with the special agricultural provisions in paragraph (h)(5) of this section.

(3) Petition for registered nurse (H–1C)—

(i) General.

(A) For purposes of H–1C classification, the term "registered nurse" means a person who is or will be authorized by a State Board of Nursing to engage in registered nurse practice in a state or U.S. territory or possession, and who is or will be practicing at a facility which provides health care services.

(B) A United States employer which provides health care services is referred to as a facility. A facility may file an H–1C petition for an alien nurse to perform the services of a registered nurse, if the facility meets the eligibility standards of 20 CFR 655.1111 and the other requirements of the Department of Labor's regulations in 20 CFR part 655, subpart L.

(C) The position must involve nursing practice and require licensure or other authorization to practice as a registered nurse from the State Board of Nursing in the state of intended employment.

(ii) [Reserved]

(iii) Beneficiary requirements. An H–1C petition for a nurse shall be accompanied by evidence that the nurse:

(A) Has obtained a full and unrestricted license to practice nursing in the country where the alien obtained nursing education, or has received nursing education in the United States;

(B) Has passed the examination given by the Commission on Graduates of Foreign Nursing Schools (CGFNS), or has obtained a full and unrestricted (permanent) license to practice as a registered nurse in the state of intended employment, or has obtained a full and unrestricted (permanent) license in any state or territory of the United States and received temporary authorization to practice as a registered nurse in the state of intended employment; and

(C) Is fully qualified and eligible under the laws (including such temporary or interim licensing requirements which authorize the nurse to be employed) governing the place of intended employment to practice as a registered nurse immediately upon admission to the United States, and is authorized under such laws to be employed by the employer. For purposes of this paragraph, the temporary or interim licensing may be obtained immediately after the alien enters the United States.

(iv) Petitioner requirements. The petitioning facility shall submit the following with an H–1C petition:

(A) A current copy of the DOL's notice of acceptance of the filing of its attestation on Form ETA 9081;

(B) A statement describing any limitations which the laws of the state or jurisdiction of intended employment place on the alien's services; and

(C) Evidence that the alien(s) named on the petition meets the definition of a registered nurse as defined at, 8 CFR 214.2(h)(3)(i)(A) and satisfies the requirements contained in section 212(m)(1) of the Act.

(v) Licensure requirements.

(A) A nurse who is granted H–1C classification based on passage of the CGFNS examination must, upon admission to the United States, be able to obtain temporary licensure or other temporary authorization to practice as a registered nurse from the State Board of Nursing in the state of intended employment.

(B) An alien who was admitted as an H–1C nonimmigrant on the basis of a temporary license or authorization to practice as a registered nurse must comply with the licensing requirements for registered nurses in the state of intended employment. An alien admitted as an H–1C nonimmigrant is required to obtain a full and unrestricted license if required by the state of intended employment. The Service must be notified pursuant to § 214.2(h)(11) when an H–1C nurse is no longer licensed as a registered nurse in the state of intended employment.

(C) A nurse shall automatically lose his or her eligibility for H–1C classification if he or she is no longer performing the duties of a registered professional nurse. Such a nurse is not authorized to remain in employment unless he or she otherwise receives authorization from the Service.

(vi) Other requirements.

(A) If the Secretary of Labor notifies the Service that a facility which employs H–1C nonimmigrant nurses has failed to meet a condition in its attestation, or that there was a misrepresentation of a material fact in the attestation, the Service shall not approve petitions for H–1C nonimmigrant nurses to be employed by the facility for a period of at least 1 year from the date of receipt of such notice. The Secretary of Labor shall make a recommendation with respect to the length of debarment. If the Secretary of Labor recommends a longer period of debarment, the Service will give considerable weight to that recommendation.

(B) If the facility's attestation expires, or is suspended or invalidated by DOL, the Service will not suspend or revoke the facility's approved petitions for nurses, if the facility has agreed to comply with the terms of the attestation under which the nurses were admitted or subsequent attestations accepted by DOL for the duration of the nurses' authorized stay.

(4) Petition for alien to perform services in a specialty occupation, services relating to a DOD cooperative research and development project or coproduction project, or services of distinguished merit and ability in the field of fashion modeling (H–1B)—

(i)(A) Types of H–1B classification. An H–1B classification may be granted to an alien who:

(1) Will perform services in a specialty occupation which requires theoretical and practical application of a body of highly specialized knowledge and attainment of a baccalaureate or higher degree or its equivalent as a minimum requirement for entry into the occupation in the United States, and who is qualified to perform services in the specialty occupation because he or she has attained a baccalaureate or higher degree or its equivalent in the specialty occupation;

(2) Based on reciprocity, will perform services of an exceptional nature requiring exceptional merit and ability relating to a DOD cooperative research and development project or a coproduction project provided for under a Government-to-Government agreement administered by the Secretary of Defense;

(3) Will perform services in the field of fashion modeling and who is of distinguished merit and ability.

(B) General requirements for petitions involving a specialty occupation.

(1) Before filing a petition for H–1B classification in a specialty occupation, the petitioner shall obtain a certification from the Department of Labor that it has filed a labor condition application in the occupational specialty in which the alien(s) will be employed.

(2) Certification by the Department of Labor of a labor condition application in an occupational classification does not constitute a determination by that agency that the occupation in question is a specialty occupation. The director shall determine if the application involves a specialty occupation as defined in section 214(i)(1) of the Act. The director shall also determine whether the particular alien for whom H–1B classification is sought qualifies to perform services in the specialty occupation as prescribed in section 214(i)(2) of the Act.

(3) If all of the beneficiaries covered by an H–1B labor condition application have not been identified at the time a petition is filed, petitions for newly identified beneficiaries may be filed at any time during the validity of the labor condition application using photocopies of the same application. Each petition must refer by file number to all previously approved petitions for that labor condition application.

(4) When petitions have been approved for the total number of workers specified in the labor condition application, substitution of aliens against previously approved openings shall not be made. A new labor condition application shall be required.

(5) If the Secretary of Labor notifies the Service that the petitioning employer has failed to meet a condition of paragraph (B) of section 212(n)(1) of the Act, has substantially failed to meet a condition of paragraphs (C) or (D) of section 212(n)(1) of the Act, has willfully failed to meet a condition of paragraph (A) of section 212(n)(1) of the Act, or has misrepresented any material fact in the application, the Service shall not approve petitions filed with respect to that employer under section 204 or 214(c) of the Act for a period of at least one year from the date of receipt of such notice.

(6) If the employer's labor condition application is suspended or invalidated by the Department of Labor, the Service will not suspend or revoke the employer's approved petitions for aliens already employed in specialty occupations if the employer has certified to the Department of Labor that it will comply with the terms of the labor condition application for the duration of the authorized stay of aliens it employs.

(C) General requirements for petitions involving an alien of distinguished merit and ability in the field of fashion modeling. H–1B classification may be granted to an alien who is of distinguished merit and ability in the field of fashion modeling. An alien of distinguished merit and ability in the field of fashion modeling is one who is prominent in the field of fashion modeling. The alien must also be coming to the United States to perform services which require a fashion model of prominence.

(ii) Definitions.

Prominence means a high level of achievement in the field of fashion modeling evidenced by a degree of skill and recognition substantially above that ordinarily encountered to the extent that a person described as prominent is renowned, leading, or well-known in the field of fashion modeling.

Recognized authority means a person or an organization with expertise in a particular field, special skills or knowledge in that field, and the expertise to render the type of opinion requested. Such an opinion must state:

(1) The writer's qualifications as an expert;

(2) The writer's experience giving such opinions, citing specific instances where past opinions have been accepted as authoritative and by whom;

(3) How the conclusions were reached; and

(4) The basis for the conclusions supported by copies or citations of any research material used.

Specialty occupation means an occupation which requires theoretical and practical application of a body of highly specialized knowledge in fields of human endeavor including, but not limited to, architecture, engineering, mathematics, physical sciences, social sciences, medicine and health, education, business specialties, accounting, law, theology, and the arts, and which requires the attainment of a bachelor's degree or higher in a specific specialty, or its equivalent, as a minimum for entry into the occupation in the United States.

United States employer means a person, firm, corporation, contractor, or other association, or organization in the United States which:

(1) Engages a person to work within the United States;

(2) Has an employer-employee relationship with respect to employees under this part, as indicated by the fact that it may hire, pay, fire, supervise, or otherwise control the work of any such employee; and

(3) Has an Internal Revenue Service Tax identification number.

(iii) Criteria for H–1B petitions involving a specialty occupation—

(A) Standards for specialty occupation position. To qualify as a specialty occupation, the position must meet one of the following criteria:

(1) A baccalaureate or higher degree or its equivalent is normally the minimum requirement for entry into the particular position;

(2) The degree requirement is common to the industry in parallel positions among similar organizations or, in the alternative, an employer may show that its particular position is so complex or unique that it can be performed only by an individual with a degree;

(3) The employer normally requires a degree or its equivalent for the position; or

(4) The nature of the specific duties are so specialized and complex that knowledge required to perform the duties is usually associated with the attainment of a baccalaureate or higher degree.

(B) Petitioner requirements. The petitioner shall submit the following with an H–1B petition involving a specialty occupation:

(1) A certification from the Secretary of Labor that the petitioner has filed a labor condition application with the Secretary,

(2) A statement that it will comply with the terms of the labor condition application for the duration of the alien's authorized period of stay,

(3) Evidence that the alien qualifies to perform services in the specialty occupation as described in paragraph (h)(4)(iii)(A) of this section, and

(C) Beneficiary qualifications. To qualify to perform services in a specialty occupation, the alien must meet one of the following criteria:

(1) Hold a United States baccalaureate or higher degree required by the specialty occupation from an accredited college or university;

(2) Hold a foreign degree determined to be equivalent to a United States baccalaureate or higher degree required by the specialty occupation from an accredited college or university;

(3) Hold an unrestricted State license, registration or certification which authorizes him or her to fully practice the specialty occupation and be immediately engaged in that specialty in the state of intended employment; or

(4) Have education, specialized training, and/or progressively responsible experience that is equivalent to completion of a United States baccalaureate or higher degree in the specialty occupation, and have recognition of expertise in the specialty through progressively responsible positions directly related to the specialty.

(D) Equivalence to completion of a college degree. For purposes of paragraph (h)(4)(iii)(C)(4) of this section, equivalence to completion of a United States baccalaureate or higher degree shall mean achievement of a level of knowledge, competence, and practice in the specialty occupation that has been determined to be equal to that of an individual who has a baccalaureate or higher degree in the specialty and shall be determined by one or more of the following:

(1) An evaluation from an official who has authority to grant college-level credit for training and/or experience in the specialty at an accredited college or university which has a program for granting such credit based on an individual's training and/or work experience;

(2) The results of recognized college-level equivalency examinations or special credit programs, such as the College Level Examination Program (CLEP), or Program on Noncollegiate Sponsored Instruction (PONSI);

(3) An evaluation of education by a reliable credentials evaluation service which specializes in evaluating foreign educational credentials;

(4) Evidence of certification or registration from a nationally-recognized professional association or society for the specialty that is known to grant certification or registration to persons in the occupational specialty who have achieved a certain level of competence in the specialty;

(5) A determination by the Service that the equivalent of the degree required by the specialty occupation has been acquired through a combination of education, specialized training, and/or work experience in areas related to the specialty and that the alien has achieved recognition of expertise in the specialty occupation as a result of such training and experience. For purposes of determining equivalency to a baccalaureate degree in the specialty, three years of specialized training and/or work experience must be demonstrated for each year of college-level training the alien lacks. For equivalence to an advanced (or Masters) degree, the alien must have a baccalaureate degree followed by at least five years of experience in the specialty. If required by a specialty, the alien must hold a Doctorate degree or its foreign equivalent. It must be clearly demonstrated that the alien's training and/or work experience included the theoretical and practical application of specialized knowledge required by the specialty occupation; that the alien's experience was gained while working with peers, supervisors, or subordinates who have a degree or its equivalent in the specialty occupation; and that the alien has recognition of expertise in the specialty evidenced by at least one type of documentation such as:

(i) Recognition of expertise in the specialty occupation by at least two recognized authorities in the same specialty occupation;

(ii) Membership in a recognized foreign or United States association or society in the specialty occupation;

(iii) Published material by or about the alien in professional publications, trade journals, books, or major newspapers;

(iv) Licensure or registration to practice the specialty occupation in a foreign country; or

(v) Achievements which a recognized authority has determined to be significant contributions to the field of the specialty occupation.

(E) Liability for transportation costs. The employer will be liable for the reasonable costs of return transportation of the alien abroad if the alien is dismissed from employment by the employer before the end of the period of authorized admission pursuant to section 214(c)(5) of the Act. If the beneficiary voluntarily terminates his or her employment prior to the expiration of the validity of the petition, the alien has not been dismissed. If the beneficiary believes that the employer has not complied with this provision, the beneficiary shall advise the Service Center which adjudicated the petition in writing. The complaint will be retained in the file relating to the petition. Within the context of this paragraph, the term "abroad" refers to the alien's last place of foreign residence. This provision applies to any employer whose offer of employment became the basis for an alien obtaining or continuing H–1B status.

(iv) General documentary requirements for H–1B classification in a specialty occupation. An H–1B petition involving a specialty occupation shall be accompanied by:

(A) Documentation, certifications, affidavits, declarations, degrees, diplomas, writings, reviews, or any other required evidence sufficient to establish that the beneficiary is qualified to perform services in a specialty occupation as described in paragraph (h)(4)(i) of this section and that the services the beneficiary is to perform are in a specialty occupation. The evidence shall conform to the following:

(1) School records, diplomas, degrees, affidavits, declarations, contracts, and similar documentation submitted must reflect periods of attendance, courses of study, and similar pertinent data, be executed by the person in charge of the records of the educational or other institution, firm, or establishment where education or training was acquired.

(2) Affidavits or declarations made under penalty of perjury submitted by present or former employers or recognized authorities certifying as to the recognition and expertise of the beneficiary shall specifically describe the beneficiary's recognition and ability in factual terms and must set forth the expertise of the affiant and the manner in which the affiant acquired such information.

(B) Copies of any written contracts between the petitioner and beneficiary, or a summary of the terms of the oral agreement under which the beneficiary will be employed, if there is no written contract.

(v) Licensure for H classification—

(A) General. If an occupation requires a state or local license for an individual to fully perform the duties of the occupation, an alien (except an H–1C nurse) seeking H classification in that occupation must have that license prior to approval of the petition to be found qualified to enter the United States and immediately engage in employment in the occupation.

(B) Temporary licensure. If a temporary license is available and the alien is allowed to perform the duties of the occupation without a permanent license, the director shall examine the nature of the duties, the level at which the duties are performed, the degree of supervision received, and any limitations placed on the alien. If an analysis of the facts demonstrates that the alien under supervision is authorized to fully perform the duties of the occupation, H classification may be granted.

(C) Duties without licensure. In certain occupations which generally require licensure, a state may allow an individual to fully practice the occupation under the supervision of licensed senior or supervisory personnel in that occupation. In such cases, the director shall examine the nature of the duties and the level at which they are performed. If the facts demonstrate that the alien under supervision could fully perform the duties of the occupation, H classification may be granted.

(D) H–1C nurses. For purposes of licensure, H–1C nurses must provide the evidence required in paragraph (h)(3)(iii) of this section.

(E) Limitation on approval of petition. Where licensure is required in any occupation, including registered nursing, the H petition may only be approved for a period of one year or for the period that the temporary license is valid, whichever is longer, unless the alien already has a permanent license to practice the occupation. An alien who is accorded H classification in an occupation which requires licensure may not be granted an extension of stay or accorded a new H classification after the one year unless he or she has obtained a permanent license in the state of intended employment or continues to hold a temporary license valid in the same state for the period of the requested extension.

(vi) Criteria and documentary requirements for H–1B petitions involving DOD cooperative research and development projects or coproduction projects—

(A) General.

(1) For purposes of H–1B classification, services of an exceptional nature relating to DOD cooperative research and development projects or coproduction projects shall be those services which require a baccalaureate or higher degree, or its equivalent, to perform the duties. The existence of this special program does not preclude the DOD from utilizing the regular H–1B provisions provided the required guidelines are met.

(2) The requirements relating to a labor condition application from the Department of Labor shall not apply to petitions involving DOD cooperative research and development projects or coproduction projects.

(B) Petitioner requirements.

(1) The petition must be accompanied by a verification letter from the DOD project manager for the particular project stating that the alien will be working on a cooperative research and development project or a coproduction project under a reciprocal Government-to-Government agreement administered by DOD. Details about the specific project are not required.

(2) The petitioner shall provide a general description of the alien's duties on the particular project and indicate the actual dates of the alien's employment on the project.

(3) The petitioner shall submit a statement indicating the names of aliens currently employed on the project in the United States and their dates of employment. The petitioner shall also indicate the names of aliens whose employment on the project ended within the past year.

(C) Beneficiary requirement. The petition shall be accompanied by evidence that the beneficiary has a baccalaureate or higher degree or its equivalent in the occupational field in which he or she will be performing services in accordance with paragraph (h)(4)(iii)(C) and/or (h)(4)(iii)(D) of this section.

(vii) Criteria and documentary requirements for H–1B petitions for aliens of distinguished merit and ability in the field of fashion modeling—

(A) General. Prominence in the field of fashion modeling may be established in the case of an individual fashion model. The work which a prominent alien is coming to perform in the United States must require the services of a prominent alien. A petition for an H–1B alien of distinguished merit and ability in the field of fashion modeling shall be accompanied by:

(1) Documentation, certifications, affidavits, writings, reviews, or any other required evidence sufficient to establish that the beneficiary is a fashion model of distinguished merit and ability. Affidavits submitted by present or former employers or recognized experts certifying to the recognition and distinguished ability of the beneficiary shall specifically describe the beneficiary's recognition and ability in factual terms and must set forth the expertise of the affiant and the manner in which the affiant acquired such information.

(2) Copies of any written contracts between the petitioner and beneficiary, or a summary of the terms of the oral agreement under which the beneficiary will be employed, if there is no written contract.

(B) Petitioner's requirements. To establish that a position requires prominence, the petitioner must establish that the position meets one of the following criteria:

(1) The services to be performed involve events or productions which have a distinguished reputation;

(2) The services are to be performed for an organization or establishment that has a distinguished reputation for, or record of, employing prominent persons.

(C) Beneficiary's requirements. A petitioner may establish that a beneficiary is a fashion model of distinguished merit and ability by the submission of two of the following forms of documentation showing that the alien:

(1) Has achieved national or international recognition and acclaim for outstanding achievement in his or her field as evidenced by reviews in major newspapers, trade journals, magazines, or other published material;

(2) Has performed and will perform services as a fashion model for employers with a distinguished reputation;

(3) Has received recognition for significant achievements from organizations, critics, fashion houses, modeling agencies, or other recognized experts in the field; or

(4) Commands a high salary or other substantial remuneration for services evidenced by contracts or other reliable evidence.

(viii) Criteria and documentary requirements for H–1B petitions for physicians—

(A) Beneficiary's requirements. An H–1B petition for a physician shall be accompanied by evidence that the physician:

(1) Has a license or other authorization required by the state of intended employment to practice medicine, or is exempt by law therefrom, if the physician will perform direct patient care and the state requires the license or authorization, and

(2) Has a full and unrestricted license to practice medicine in a foreign state or has graduated from a medical school in the United States or in a foreign state.

(B) Petitioner's requirements. The petitioner must establish that the alien physician:

(1) Is coming to the United States primarily to teach or conduct research, or both, at or for a public or nonprofit private educational or research institution or agency, and that no patient care will be performed, except that which is incidental to the physician's teaching or research; or

(2) The alien has passed the Federation Licensing Examination (or an equivalent examination as determined by the Secretary of Health and Human Services) or is a graduate of a United States medical school; and

(i) Has competency in oral and written English which shall be demonstrated by the passage of the English language proficiency test given by the Educational Commission for Foreign Medical Graduates; or

(ii) Is a graduate of a school of medicine accredited by a body or bodies approved for that purpose by the Secretary of Education.

(C) Exception for physicians of national or international renown. A physician who is a graduate of a medical school in a foreign state and who is of national or international renown in the field of medicine is exempt from the requirements of paragraph (h)(4)(viii)(B) of this section.

(5) Petition for alien to perform agricultural labor or services of a temporary or seasonal nature (H–2A)—

(i) Filing a petition—

(A) General. An H–2A petition must be filed on Form I–129 with a single valid temporary agricultural labor certification. The petition may be filed by either the employer listed on the temporary labor certification, the employer's agent, or the association of United States agricultural producers named as a joint employer on the temporary labor certification.

(B) Multiple beneficiaries. The total number of beneficiaries of a petition or series of petitions based on the same temporary labor certification may not exceed the number of workers indicated on that document. A single petition can include more than one beneficiary if the total number does not exceed the number of positions indicated on the relating temporary labor certification.

(C) [Reserved]

(D) Evidence. An H–2A petitioner must show that the proposed employment qualifies as a basis for H–2A status, and that any named beneficiary qualifies for that employment. A petition will be automatically denied if filed without the certification evidence required in paragraph (h)(5)(i)(A) of this section and, for each named beneficiary, the initial evidence required in paragraph (h)(5)(v) of this section.

(E) Special filing requirements. Where a certification shows joint employers, a petition must be filed with an attachment showing that each employer has agreed to the conditions of H–2A eligibility. A petition filed by an agent must be filed with an attachment in which the employer has authorized the agent to act on its behalf, has assumed full responsibility for all representations made by the agent on its behalf, and has agreed to the conditions of H–2A eligibility.

(F) Eligible Countries.

(1) (i) H–2A petitions may only be approved for nationals of countries that the Secretary of Homeland Security has designated as participating countries, with the concurrence of the Secretary of State, in a notice published in the Federal Register, taking into account factors, including but not limited to:

(A) The country's cooperation with respect to issuance of travel documents for citizens, subjects, nationals and residents of that country who are subject to a final order of removal;

(B) The number of final and unexecuted orders of removal against citizens, subjects, nationals and residents of that country;

(C) The number of orders of removal executed against citizens, subjects, nationals and residents of that country; and

(D) Such other factors as may serve the U.S. interest.

(ii) A national from a country not on the list described in paragraph (h)(5)(i)(F)(1)(i) of this section may be a beneficiary of an approved H–2A petition upon the request of a petitioner or potential H–2A petitioner, if the Secretary of Homeland Security, in his sole and unreviewable discretion, determines that it is in the U.S. interest for that alien to be a beneficiary of such petition. Determination of such a U.S. interest will take into account factors, including but not limited to:

(A) Evidence from the petitioner demonstrating that a worker with the required skills is not available either from among U.S. workers or from among foreign workers from a country currently on the list described in paragraph (h)(5)(i)(F)(1)(i) of this section;

(B) Evidence that the beneficiary has been admitted to the United States previously in H–2A status;

(C) The potential for abuse, fraud, or other harm to the integrity of the H–2A visa program through the potential admission of a beneficiary from a country not currently on the list; and

(D) Such other factors as may serve the U.S. interest.

(2) Once published, any designation of participating countries pursuant to paragraph (h)(5)(i)(F)(1)(i) of this section shall be effective for one year after the date of publication in the Federal Register and shall be without effect at the end of that one-year period.

(ii) Effect of the labor certification process. The temporary agricultural labor certification process determines whether employment is as an agricultural worker, whether it is open to U.S. workers, if qualified U.S. workers are available, the adverse impact of employment of a qualified alien, and whether employment conditions, including housing, meet applicable requirements. In petition proceedings a petitioner must establish that the employment and beneficiary meet the requirements of paragraph (h)(5) of this section. In a petition filed with a certification denial, the petitioner must also overcome the Department of Labor's findings regarding the availability of qualified domestic labor.

(iii) Ability and intent to meet a job offer—

(A) Eligibility requirements. An H–2A petitioner must establish that each beneficiary will be employed in accordance with the terms and conditions of the certification, which includes that the principal duties to be performed are those on the certification, with other duties minor and incidental.

(B) Intent and prior compliance. Requisite intent cannot be established for two years after an employer or joint employer, or a parent, subsidiary or affiliate thereof, is found to have violated section 274(a) of the Act or to have employed an H–2A worker in a position other than that described in the relating petition.

(C) Initial evidence. Representations required for the purpose of labor certification are initial evidence of intent.

(iv) Temporary and seasonal employment—

(A) Eligibility requirements. An H–2A petitioner must establish that the employment proposed in the certification is of a temporary or seasonal nature. Employment is of a seasonal nature where it is tied to a certain time of year by an event or pattern, such as a short annual growing cycle or a specific aspect of a longer cycle, and requires labor levels far above those necessary for ongoing operations. Employment is of a temporary nature where the employer's need to fill the position with a temporary worker will, except in extraordinary circumstances, last no longer than one year.

(B) Effect of Department of Labor findings. In temporary agricultural labor certification proceedings the Department of Labor separately tests whether employment qualifies as temporary or seasonal. Its finding that employment qualifies is normally sufficient for the purpose of an H–2A petition, However, notwithstanding that finding, employment will be found not to be temporary or seasonal where an application for permanent labor certification has been filed for the same alien, or for another alien to be employed in the same position, by the same employer or by its parent, subsidiary or affiliate. This can only be overcome by the petitioner's demonstration that there will be at least a six month interruption of employment in the United States after H–2A status ends. Also, eligibility will not be found, notwithstanding the issuance of a temporary agricultural labor certification, where there is substantial evidence that the employment is not temporary or seasonal.

(v) The beneficiary's qualifications—

(A) Eligibility requirements. An H–2A petitioner must establish that any named beneficiary met the stated minimum requirements and was fully able to perform the stated duties when the application for certification was filed. It must be established at time of application for an H–2A visa, or for admission if a visa is not required, that any unnamed beneficiary either met these requirements when the certification was applied for or passed any certified aptitude test at any time prior to visa issuance, or prior to admission if a visa is not required.

(B) Evidence of employment/job training. For petitions with named beneficiaries, a petition must be filed with evidence that the beneficiary met the certification's minimum employment and job training requirements, if any are prescribed, as of the date of the filing of the labor certification application. For petitions with unnamed beneficiaries, such evidence must be submitted at the time of a visa application or, if a visa is not required, at the time the applicant seeks admission to the United States. Evidence must be in the form of the past employer or employers' detailed statement(s) or actual employment documents, such as company payroll or tax records. Alternately, a petitioner must show that such evidence cannot be obtained, and submit affidavits from persons who worked with the beneficiary that demonstrate the claimed employment or job training.

(C) Evidence of education and other training. For petitions with named beneficiaries, a petition must be filed with evidence that the beneficiary met all of the certification's post-secondary education and other formal training requirements, if any are prescribed in the labor certification application as of date of the filing of the labor certification application. For petitions with unnamed beneficiaries, such evidence must be submitted at the time of a visa application or, if a visa is not required, at the time the applicant seeks admission to the United States. Evidence must be in the form of documents, issued by the relevant institution(s) or organization(s), that show periods of attendance, majors and degrees or certificates accorded.

(vi) Petitioner consent and notification requirements—

(A) Consent. In filing an H–2A petition, a petitioner and each employer consents to allow access to the site by

DHS officers where the labor is being performed for the purpose of determining compliance with H–2A requirements.

(B) Agreements. The petitioner agrees to the following requirements:

(1) To notify DHS, within 2 workdays, and beginning on a date and in a manner specified in a notice published in the Federal Register if:

(i) An H–2A worker fails to report to work within 5 workdays of the employment start date on the H–2A petition or within 5 workdays of the start date established by his or her employer, whichever is later;

(ii) The agricultural labor or services for which H–2A workers were hired is completed more than 30 days earlier than the employment end date stated on the H–2A petition; or

(iii) The H–2A worker absconds from the worksite or is terminated prior to the completion of agricultural labor or services for which he or she was hired.

(2) To retain evidence of such notification and make it available for inspection by DHS officers for a 1–year period beginning on the date of the notification. To retain evidence of a different employment start date if it is changed from that on the petition by the employer and make it available for inspection by DHS officers for the 1–year period beginning on the newly-established employment start date.

(3) To pay $10 in liquidated damages for each instance where the employer cannot demonstrate that it has complied with the notification requirements, unless, in the case of an untimely notification, the employer demonstrates with such notification that good cause existed for the untimely notification, and DHS, in its discretion, waives the liquidated damages amount.

(C) Process. If DHS has determined that the petitioner has violated the notification requirements in paragraph (h)(5)(vi)(B)(1) of this section and has not received the required notification, the petitioner will be given written notice and 30 days to reply before being given written notice of the assessment of liquidated damages.

(D) Failure to pay liquidated damages. If liquidated damages are not paid within 10 days of assessment, an H–2A petition may not be processed for that petitioner or any joint employer shown on the petition until such damages are paid.

(E) Abscondment. An H–2A worker has absconded if he or she has not reported for work for a period of 5 consecutive workdays without the consent of the employer.

(vii) Validity. An approved H–2A petition is valid through the expiration of the relating certification for the purpose of allowing a beneficiary to seek issuance of an H–2A nonimmigrant visa, admission or an extension of stay for the purpose of engaging in the specific certified employment.

(viii) Admission—

(A) Effect of violations of status. An alien may not be accorded H–2A status who, at any time during the past 5 years, USCIS finds to have violated, other than through no fault of his or her own (e.g., due to an employer's illegal or inappropriate conduct), any of the terms or conditions of admission into the United States as an H–2A nonimmigrant, including remaining beyond the specific period of authorized stay or engaging in unauthorized employment.

(B) Period of admission. An alien admissible as an H–2A nonimmigrant shall be admitted for the period of the approved petition. Such alien will be admitted for an additional period of up to one week before the beginning of the approved period for the purpose of travel to the worksite, and a 30–day period following the expiration of the H–2A petition for the purpose of departure or to seek an extension based on a subsequent offer of employment. Unless authorized under 8 CFR 274a.12 or section 214(n) of the Act, the beneficiary may not work except during the validity period of the petition.

(C) Limits on an individual's stay. Except as provided in paragraph (h)(5)(viii)(B) of this section, an alien's stay as an H–2A nonimmigrant is limited by the term of an approved petition. An alien may remain longer to engage in other qualifying temporary agricultural employment by obtaining an extension of stay. However, an individual who has held H–2A status for a total of 3 years may not again be granted H–2A status until such time as he or she remains outside the United States for an uninterrupted period of 3 months. An absence from the United States can interrupt the accrual of time spent as an H–2A nonimmigrant against the 3–year limit. If the accumulated stay is 18 months or less, an absence is interruptive if it lasts for at least 45 days. If the accumulated stay is greater than 18 months, an absence is interruptive if it lasts for at least 2 months. Eligibility under paragraph (h)(5)(viii)(C) of this section will be determined in admission, change of status or extension proceedings. An alien found eligible for a shorter period of H–2A status than that indicated by the petition due to the application of this paragraph (h)(5)(viii)(C) of this section shall only be admitted for that abbreviated period.

(ix) Substitution of beneficiaries after admission. An H–2A petition may be filed to replace H–2A workers whose employment was terminated earlier than the end date stated on the H–2A petition and before the completion of work; who fail to report to work within five days of the employment start date on the H–2A petition or within five days of the start date established by his or her employer, whichever is later; or who abscond from the worksite. The petition must be filed with a copy of the certification document, a copy of the approval notice covering the workers for which replacements are sought, and other evidence required by paragraph (h)(5)(i)(D) of this section. It must also be filed with a statement giving each terminated or absconded worker's name, date and country of birth, termination date, and the reason for termination, and the date that USCIS was notified that the alien was terminated or absconded, if applicable. A petition for a replacement will not be approved where the requirements of paragraph (h)(5)(vi) of this section have not been met. A petition for replacements does not constitute the notification required by paragraph (h)(5)(vi)(B)(1) of this section.

(x) Extensions in emergent circumstances. In emergent circumstances, as determined by USCIS, a single H–2A petition may be extended for a period not to exceed 2 weeks without an additional approved labor certification if filed on behalf of one or more beneficiaries who will continue to be employed by the same employer that previously obtained an approved petition on the beneficiary's behalf, so long as the employee continues to perform the same duties and will be employed for no longer than 2 weeks after the expiration of previously-approved H–2A petition. The previously approved H–2A petition must have been based on an approved temporary labor certification, which shall be considered to be extended upon the approval of the extension of H–2A status.

(xi) Treatment of petitions and alien beneficiaries upon a determination that fees were collected from alien beneficiaries.

(A) Denial or revocation of petition. As a condition to approval of an H–2A petition, no job placement fee or other compensation (either direct or indirect) may be collected at any time, including before or after the filing or approval of the petition, from a beneficiary of an H–2A petition by a petitioner, agent, facilitator, recruiter, or similar employment service as a condition of H–2A employment (other than the lesser of the fair market value or actual costs of transportation and any government-mandated passport, visa, or inspection fees, to the extent that the payment of such costs and fees by the beneficiary is not prohibited by statute or Department of Labor regulations, unless the employer agent, facilitator, recruiter, or employment service has agreed with the alien to pay such costs and fees).

(1) If USCIS determines that the petitioner has collected, or entered into an agreement to collect, such prohibited fee or compensation, the H–2A petition will be denied or revoked on notice unless the petitioner demonstrates that, prior to the filing of the petition, the petitioner has reimbursed the alien in full for such fees or compensation, or, where such fee or compensation has not yet been paid by the alien worker, that the agreement has been terminated.

(2) If USCIS determines that the petitioner knew or should have known at the time of filing the petition that the beneficiary has paid or agreed to pay any facilitator, recruiter, or similar employment service such fees or compensation as a condition of obtaining the H–2A employment, the H–2A petition will be denied or revoked on notice unless the petitioner demonstrates that, prior to the filing of the petition, the petitioner or the facilitator, recruiter, or similar employment service has reimbursed the alien in full for such fees or compensation or, where such fee or compensation has not yet been paid by the alien worker, that the agreement has been terminated.

(3) If USCIS determines that the beneficiary paid the petitioner such fees or compensation as a condition of obtaining the H–2A employment after the filing of the H–2A petition, the petition will be denied or revoked on notice.

(4) If USCIS determines that the beneficiary paid or agreed to pay the agent, facilitator, recruiter, or similar employment service such fees or compensation as a condition of obtaining the H–2A employment after the filing of the H–2A petition and with the knowledge of the petitioner, the petition will be denied or revoked unless the petitioner demonstrates that the petitioner or facilitator, recruiter, or similar employment service has reimbursed the beneficiary in full or where such fee or compensation has not yet been paid by the alien worker, that the agreement has been terminated, or notifies DHS within 2 workdays of obtaining knowledge in a manner specified in a notice published in the Federal Register.

(B) Effect of petition revocation. Upon revocation of an employer's H–2A petition based upon paragraph (h)(5)(xi)(A) of this section, the alien beneficiary's stay will be authorized and the alien will not accrue any period of unlawful presence under section 212(a)(9) of the Act (8 U.S.C. 1182(a)(9)) for a 30–day period following the date of the revocation for the purpose of departure or extension of stay based upon a subsequent offer of employment.

(C) Reimbursement as condition to approval of future H–2A petitions.

(1) Filing subsequent H–2A petitions within 1 year of denial or revocation of previous H–2A petition. A petitioner filing an H–2A petition within 1 year after the decision denying or revoking on notice an H–2A petition filed by the same petitioner on the basis of paragraph (h)(5)(xi)(A) of this section must demonstrate to the satisfaction of USCIS, as a condition of approval of such petition, that the petitioner or agent, facilitator, recruiter, or similar employment service has reimbursed the beneficiary in full or that the petitioner has failed to locate the beneficiary. If the petitioner demonstrates to the satisfaction of USCIS that the beneficiary was reimbursed in full, such condition of approval shall be satisfied with respect to any subsequently filed H–2A petitions, except as provided in paragraph (h)(5)(xi)(C)(2). If the petitioner demonstrates to the satisfaction of USCIS that it has made reasonable efforts to locate the beneficiary with respect to each H–2A petition filed within 1 year after the decision denying or revoking the previous H–2A petition on the basis of paragraph (h)(5)(xi)(A) of this section but has failed to do so, such condition of approval shall be deemed satisfied with respect to any H–2A petition filed 1 year or more after the denial or revocation. Such reasonable efforts shall include contacting any of the beneficiary's known addresses.

(2) Effect of subsequent denied or revoked petitions. An H–2A petition filed by the same petitioner subsequent to a denial under paragraph (h)(5)(xi)(A) of this section shall be subject to the condition of approval described in paragraph (h)(5)(xi)(C)(1) of this section, regardless of prior satisfaction of such condition of approval with respect to a previously denied or revoked petition.

(xii) Treatment of alien beneficiaries upon revocation of labor certification. The approval of an employer's H–2A petition is immediately and automatically revoked if the Department of Labor revokes the labor certification upon which the petition is based. Upon revocation of an H–2A petition based upon revocation of labor certification, the alien beneficiary's stay will be authorized and the alien will not accrue any period of unlawful presence under section 212(a)(9) of the Act for a 30–day period following the date of the revocation for the purpose of departure or extension of stay based upon a subsequent offer of employment.

(6) Petition for alien to perform temporary nonagricultural services or labor (H–2B)—

(i) Petition.

(A) H–2B nonagricultural temporary worker. An H–2B nonagricultural temporary worker is an alien who is coming temporarily to the United States to perform temporary services or labor without displacing qualified United States workers available to perform such services or labor and whose employment is not adversely affecting the wages and working conditions of United States workers.

(B) Denial or revocation of petition upon a determination that fees were collected from alien beneficiaries. As a condition of approval of an H–2B petition, no job placement fee or other compensation (either direct or indirect) may be collected at any time, including before or after the filing or approval of the petition, from a beneficiary of an H–2B petition by a petitioner, agent, facilitator, recruiter, or similar employment service as a condition of an offer or condition of H–2B employment (other than the lower of the actual cost or fair market value of transportation to such employment and any government-mandated passport, visa, or inspection fees, to the extent that the passing of such costs to the beneficiary is not prohibited by statute, unless the employer, agent, facilitator, recruiter, or similar employment service has agreed with the beneficiary that it will pay such costs and fees).

(1) If USCIS determines that the petitioner has collected or entered into an agreement to collect such fee or compensation, the H–2B petition will be denied or revoked on notice, unless the petitioner demonstrates that, prior to the filing of the petition, either the petitioner reimbursed the beneficiary in full for such fees or compensation or the agreement to collect such fee or compensation was terminated before the fee or compensation was paid by the beneficiary.

(2) If USCIS determines that the petitioner knew or should have known at the time of filing the petition that the beneficiary has paid or agreed to pay any agent, facilitator, recruiter, or similar employment service as a condition of an offer of the H–2B employment, the H–2B petition will be denied or revoked on notice unless the petitioner demonstrates that, prior to filing the petition, either the petitioner or the agent, facilitator, recruiter, or similar employment service reimbursed the beneficiary in full for such fees or compensation or the agreement to collect such fee or compensation was terminated before the fee or compensation was paid by the beneficiary.

(3) If USCIS determines that the beneficiary paid the petitioner such fees or compensation as a condition of an offer of H–2B employment after the filing of the H–2B petition, the petition will be denied or revoked on notice.

(4) If USCIS determines that the beneficiary paid or agreed to pay the agent, facilitator, recruiter, or similar employment service such fees or compensation after the filing of the H–2B petition and that the petitioner knew or had reason to know of the payment or agreement to pay, the petition will be denied or revoked unless the petitioner demonstrates that the petitioner or agent, facilitator, recruiter, or similar employment service reimbursed the beneficiary in full, that the parties terminated any agreement to pay before the beneficiary paid the fees or compensation, or that the petitioner has notified DHS within 2 work days of obtaining knowledge, in a manner specified in a notice published in the Federal Register.

(C) Effect of petition revocation. Upon revocation of an employer's H–2B petition based upon paragraph (h)(6)(i)(B) of this section, the alien beneficiary's stay will be authorized and the beneficiary will not accrue any period of unlawful presence under section 212(a)(9) of the Act (8 U.S.C. 1182(a)(9)) for a 30–day period following the date of the revocation for the purpose of departure or extension of stay based upon a subsequent offer of employment. The employer shall be liable for the alien beneficiary's reasonable costs of return transportation to his or her last place of foreign residence abroad, unless such alien obtains an extension of stay based on an approved H–2B petition filed by a different employer.

(D) Reimbursement as condition to approval of future H–2B petitions.

(1) Filing subsequent H–2B petitions within 1 year of denial or revocation of previous H–2B petition. A petitioner filing an H–2B petition within 1 year after a decision denying or revoking on notice an H–2B petition filed by the same petitioner on the basis of paragraph (h)(6)(i)(B) of this section must demonstrate to the satisfaction of USCIS, as a condition of the approval of the later petition, that the petitioner or agent, facilitator, recruiter, or similar employment service reimbursed in full each beneficiary of the denied or revoked petition from whom a prohibited fee was collected or that the petitioner has failed to locate each such beneficiary despite the petitioner's reasonable efforts to locate them. If the petitioner demonstrates to the satisfaction of USCIS that each such beneficiary was reimbursed in full, such condition of approval shall be satisfied with respect to any subsequently filed H–2B petitions, except as provided in paragraph (h)(6)(i)(D)(2) of this section. If the petitioner demonstrates to the satisfaction of USCIS that it has made reasonable efforts to locate but has failed to locate each such beneficiary within 1 year after the decision denying or revoking the previous H–2B petition on the basis of paragraph (h)(6)(i)(B) of this section, such condition of approval shall be deemed satisfied with respect to any H–2B petition filed 1 year or more after the denial or revocation. Such reasonable efforts shall include contacting all of each such beneficiary's known addresses.

(2) Effect of subsequent denied or revoked petitions. An H–2B petition filed by the same petitioner subsequent to a denial under paragraph (h)(6)(i)(B) of this section shall be subject to the condition of approval described in paragraph (h)(6)(i)(D)(1) of this section, regardless of prior satisfaction of such condition of approval with respect to a previously denied or revoked petition.

(E) Eligible countries.

(1) H–2B petitions may be approved for nationals of countries that the Secretary of Homeland Security has designated as participating countries, with the concurrence of the Secretary of State, in a notice published in the Federal Register, taking into account factors, including but not limited to:

(i) The country's cooperation with respect to issuance of travel documents for citizens, subjects, nationals and residents of that country who are subject to a final order of removal;

(ii) The number of final and unexecuted orders of removal against citizens, subjects, nationals, and residents of that country;

(iii) The number of orders of removal executed against citizens, subjects, nationals and residents of that country; and

(iv) Such other factors as may serve the U.S. interest.

(2) A national from a country not on the list described in paragraph (h)(6)(i)(E)(1) of this section may be a beneficiary of an approved H–2B petition upon the request of a petitioner or potential H–2B petitioner, if the Secretary of Homeland Security, in his sole and unreviewable discretion, determines that it is in the U.S. interest for that alien to be a beneficiary of such petition. Determination of such a U.S. interest will take into account factors, including but not limited to:

(i) Evidence from the petitioner demonstrating that a worker with the required skills is not available from among foreign workers from a country currently on the list described in paragraph (h)(6)(i)(E)(1) of this section;

(ii) Evidence that the beneficiary has been admitted to the United States previously in H–2B status;

(iii) The potential for abuse, fraud, or other harm to the integrity of the H–2B visa program through the potential admission of a beneficiary from a country not currently on the list; and

(iv) Such other factors as may serve the U.S. interest.

(3) Once published, any designation of participating countries pursuant to paragraph (h)(6)(i)(E)(1) of this section shall be effective for one year after the date of publication in the Federal Register and shall be without effect at the end of that one-year period.

(F) Petitioner agreements and notification requirements.

(1) Agreements. The petitioner agrees to notify DHS, within 2 work days, and beginning on a date and in a manner specified in a notice published in the Federal Register if: An H–2B worker fails to report for work within 5 work days after the employment start date stated on the petition; the nonagricultural labor or services for which H–2B workers were hired were completed more than 30 days early; or an H–2B worker absconds from the worksite or is terminated prior to the completion of the nonagricultural labor or services for which he or she was hired. The petitioner also agrees to retain evidence of such notification and make it available for inspection by DHS officers for a one-year period beginning on the date of the notification.

(2) Abscondment. An H–2B worker has absconded if he or she has not reported for work for a period of 5 consecutive work days without the consent of the employer.

(ii) Temporary services or labor—

(A) Definition. Temporary services or labor under the H–2B classification refers to any job in which the petitioner's need for the duties to be performed by the employee(s) is temporary, whether or not the underlying job can be described as permanent or temporary.

(B) Nature of petitioner's need. Employment is of a temporary nature when the employer needs a worker for a limited period of time. The employer must establish that the need for the employee will end in the near, definable future. Generally, that period of time will be limited to one year or less, but in the case of a one-time event could last up to 3 years. The petitioner's need for the services or labor shall be a one-time occurrence, a seasonal need, a peak load need, or an intermittent need.

(1) One-time occurrence. The petitioner must establish that it has not employed workers to perform the services or labor in the past and that it will not need workers to perform the services or labor in the future, or that it has an employment situation that is otherwise permanent, but a temporary event of short duration has created the need for a temporary worker.

(2) Seasonal need. The petitioner must establish that the services or labor is traditionally tied to a season of the year by an event or pattern and is of a recurring nature. The petitioner shall specify the period(s) of time during each year in which it does not need the services or labor. The employment is not seasonal if the period during which the services or labor is not needed is unpredictable or subject to change or is considered a vacation period for the petitioner's permanent employees.

(3) Peakload need. The petitioner must establish that it regularly employs permanent workers to perform the services or labor at the place of employment and that it needs to supplement its permanent staff at the place of employment on a temporary basis due to a seasonal or short-term demand and that the temporary additions to staff will not become a part of the petitioner's regular operation.

(4) Intermittent need. The petitioner must establish that it has not employed permanent or full-time workers to perform the services or labor, but occasionally or intermittently needs temporary workers to perform services or labor for short periods.

(iii) Procedures.

(A) Prior to filing a petition with the director to classify an alien as an H–2B worker, the petitioner shall apply for a temporary labor certification with the Secretary of Labor for all areas of the United States, except the Territory of Guam. In the Territory of Guam, the petitioning employer shall apply for a temporary labor certification with the Governor of Guam. The labor certification shall be advice to the director on whether or not United States workers capable of performing the temporary services or labor are available and whether or not the alien's employment will adversely affect the wages and working conditions of similarly employed United States workers.

(B) An H–2B petitioner shall be a United States employer, a United States agent, or a foreign employer filing through a United States agent. For purposes of paragraph (h) of this section, a foreign employer is any employer who is not amenable to service of process in the United States. A foreign employer may not directly petition for an H–2B nonimmigrant but must use the services of a United States agent to file a petition for an H–2B nonimmigrant. A United States agent petitioning on behalf of a foreign employer must be authorized to file the petition, and to accept service of process in the United States in proceedings under section 274A of the Act, on behalf of the employer. The petitioning employer shall consider available United States workers for the temporary services or labor, and shall offer terms and conditions of employment which are consistent with the nature of the occupation, activity, and industry in the United States.

(C) The petitioner may not file an H–2B petition unless the United States petitioner has applied for a labor certification with the Secretary of Labor or the Governor of Guam within the time limits prescribed or accepted by each, and has obtained a favorable labor certification determination as required by paragraph (h)(6)(iv) or (h)(6)(v) of this section.

(D) The Governor of Guam shall separately establish procedures for administering the temporary labor program under his or her jurisdiction. The Secretary of Labor shall separately establish for the temporary labor program under his or her jurisdiction, by regulation at 20 CFR 655, procedures for administering that temporary labor program under his or her jurisdiction, and shall determine the prevailing wage applicable to an application for temporary labor certification for that temporary labor program in accordance with the Secretary of Labor's regulation at 20 CFR 655.10.

(E) After obtaining a favorable determination from the Secretary of Labor or the Governor of Guam, as appropriate, the petitioner shall file a petition on I–129, accompanied by the labor certification determination and supporting documents, with the director having jurisdiction in the area of intended employment.

(iv) Labor certifications, except Guam—

(A) Secretary of Labor's determination. An H–2B petition for temporary employment in the United States, except for temporary employment on Guam, shall be accompanied by an approved temporary labor certification from the Secretary of Labor stating that qualified workers in the United States are not available and that the alien's employment will not adversely affect wages and working conditions of similarly employed United States workers.

(B) Validity of the labor certification. The Secretary of Labor may issue a temporary labor certification for a period of up to one year.

(C) U.S. Virgin Islands. Temporary labor certifications filed under section 101(a)(15)(H)(ii)(b) of the Act for employment in the United States Virgin Islands may be approved only for entertainers and athletes and only for periods not to exceed 45 days.

(D) Employment start date. Beginning with petitions filed for workers for fiscal year 2010, an H–2B petition must state an employment start date that is the same as the date of need stated on the approved temporary labor certification. A petitioner filing an amended H–2B petition due to the unavailability of originally requested workers may state an employment start date later than the date of need stated on the previously approved temporary labor certification accompanying the amended H–2B petition.

(v) Labor certification for Guam—

(A) Governor of Guam's determination. An H–2B petition for temporary employment on Guam shall be accompanied by an approved temporary labor certification issued by the Governor of Guam stating that qualified workers in the United States are not available to perform the required services, and that the alien's employment will not adversely affect the wages and working conditions of United States resident workers who are similarly employed on Guam.

(B) Validity of labor certification. The Governor of Guam may issue a temporary labor certification for a period up to one year.

(C) [Reserved]

(D) [Reserved]

(E) Criteria for Guam labor certifications. The Governor of Guam shall, in consultation with the Service, establish systematic methods for determining the prevailing wage rates and working conditions for individual occupations on Guam and for making determinations as to availability of qualified United States residents.

(1) Prevailing wage and working conditions. The system to determine wages and working conditions must provide for consideration of wage rates and employment conditions for occupations in both the private and public sectors, in Guam and/or in the United States (as defined in section 101(a)(38) of the Act), and may not consider wages and working conditions outside of the United States. If the system includes utilization of advisory opinions and consultations, the opinions must be provided by officially sanctioned groups which reflect a balance of the interests of the private and public sectors, government, unions and management.

(2) Availability of United States workers. The system for determining availability of qualified United States workers must require the prospective employer to:

(i) Advertise the availability of the position for a minimum of three consecutive days in the newspaper with the largest daily circulation on Guam;

(ii) Place a job offer with an appropriate agency of the Territorial Government which operates as a job referral service at least 30 days in advance of the need for the services to commence, except that for applications from the armed forces of the United States and those in the entertainment industry, the 30–day period may be reduced by the Governor to 10 days;

(iii) Conduct appropriate recruitment in other areas of the United States and its territories if sufficient qualified United States construction workers are not available on Guam to fill a job. The Governor of Guam may require a job order to be placed more than 30 days in advance of need to accommodate such recruitment;

(iv) Report to the appropriate agency the names of all United States resident workers who applied for the position, indicating those hired and the job-related reasons for not hiring;

(v) Offer all special considerations, such as housing and transportation expenses, to all United States resident workers who applied for the position, indicating those hired and the job-related reasons for not hiring;

(vi) Meet the prevailing wage rates and working conditions determined under the wages and working conditions system by the Governor; and

(vii) Agree to meet all Federal and Territorial requirements relating to employment, such as nondiscrimination, occupational safety, and minimum wage requirements.

(F) Approval and publication of employment systems on Guam—

(1) Systems. The Commissioner of Immigration and Naturalization must approve the system to determine prevailing wages and working conditions and the system to determine availability of United States resident workers and any future modifications of the systems prior to implementation. If the Commissioner, in consultation with the Secretary of Labor, finds that the systems or modified systems meet the requirements of this section, the Commissioner shall publish them as a notice in the Federal Register and the Governor shall publish them as a public record in Guam.

(2) Approval of construction wage rates. The Commissioner must approve specific wage data and rates used for construction occupations on Guam prior to implementation of new rates. The Governor shall submit new wage survey data and proposed rates to the Commissioner for approval at least eight weeks before authority to use existing rates expires. Surveys shall be conducted at least every two years, unless the Commissioner prescribes a lesser period.

(G) Reporting. The Governor shall provide the Commissioner statistical data on temporary labor certification workload and determinations. This information shall be submitted quarterly no later than 30 days after the quarter ends.

(H) Invalidation of temporary labor certification issued by the Governor of Guam—

(1) General. A temporary labor certification issued by the Governor of Guam may be invalidated by a director if it is determined by the director or a court of law that the certification request involved fraud or willful misrepresentation. A temporary labor certification may also be invalidated if the director determines that the certification involved gross error.

(2) Notice of intent to invalidate. If the director intends to invalidate a temporary labor certification, a notice of intent shall be served upon the employer, detailing the reasons for the intended invalidation. The employer shall have 30 days in which to file a written response in rebuttal to the notice of intent. The director shall consider all evidence submitted upon rebuttal in reaching a decision.

(3) Appeal of invalidation. An employer may appeal the invalidation of a temporary labor certification in accordance with Part 103 of this chapter.

(vi) Evidence for H–2B petitions. An H–2B petition shall be accompanied by:

(A) Labor certification. An approved temporary labor certification issued by the Secretary of Labor or the Governor of Guam, as appropriate;

(B) [Reserved]

(C) Alien's qualifications. In petitions where the temporary labor certification application requires certain education, training, experience, or special requirements of the beneficiary who is present in the United States, documentation that the alien qualifies for the job offer as specified in the application for such temporary labor certification. This requirement also applies to the named beneficiary who is abroad on the basis of special provisions stated in paragraph (h)(2)(iii) of this section;

(D) Statement of need. A statement describing in detail the temporary situation or conditions which make it necessary to bring the alien to the United States and whether the need is a one-time occurrence, seasonal, peakload, or intermittent. If the need is seasonal, peakload, or intermittent, the statement shall indicate whether the situation or conditions are expected to be recurrent; or

(E) Liability for transportation costs. The employer will be liable for the reasonable costs of return transportation of the alien abroad, if the alien is dismissed from employment for any reason by the employer before the end of the period of authorized admission pursuant to section 214(c)(5) of the Act. If the beneficiary voluntarily terminates his or her employment prior to the expiration of the validity of the petition, the alien has not been dismissed. If the beneficiary believes that the employer has not complied with this provision, the beneficiary shall advise the Service Center which adjudicated the petition in writing. The complaint will be retained in the file relating to the petition. Within the context of this paragraph, the term "abroad" means the alien's last place of foreign residence. This provision applies to any employer whose offer of employment became the basis for the alien obtaining or continuing H–2B status.

(vii) Traded professional H–2B athletes. In the case of a professional H–2B athlete who is traded from one organization to another organization, employment authorization for the player will automatically continue for a period of 30 days after the player's acquisition by the new organization, within which time the new organization is expected to file a new Form I–129 for H–2B nonimmigrant classification. If a new Form I–129 is not filed within 30 days, employment authorization will cease. If a new Form I–129 is filed within 30 days, the professional athlete shall be deemed to be in valid H–2B status, and employment shall continue to be authorized, until the petition is adjudicated. If the new petition is denied, employment authorization will cease.

(viii) Substitution of beneficiaries. Beneficiaries of H–2B petitions that are approved for named or unnamed beneficiaries who have not been admitted may be substituted only if the employer can demonstrate that the total number of beneficiaries will not exceed the number of beneficiaries certified in the original temporary labor certification. Beneficiaries who were admitted to the United States may not be substituted without a new petition accompanied by a newly approved temporary labor certification.

(A) To substitute beneficiaries who were previously approved for consular processing but have not been admitted with aliens who are outside of the United States, the petitioner shall, by letter and a copy of the petition approval notice, notify the consular office at which the alien will apply for a visa or the port of entry where the alien will apply for admission. The petitioner shall also submit evidence of the qualifications of beneficiaries to the consular office or port of entry prior to issuance of a visa or admission, if applicable.

(B) To substitute beneficiaries who were previously approved for consular processing but have not been admitted with aliens who are currently in the United States, the petitioner shall file an amended petition with fees at the USCIS Service Center where the original petition was filed, with a copy of the original petition approval notice, a statement explaining why the substitution is necessary, evidence of the qualifications of beneficiaries, if applicable, evidence of the beneficiaries' current status in the United States, and evidence that the number of beneficiaries will not exceed the number allocated on the approved temporary labor certification, such as employment records or other documentary evidence to establish that the number of visas sought in the amended petition were not already issued. The amended petition must retain a period of employment within the same half of the same fiscal year as the original petition. Otherwise, a new temporary labor certification issued by DOL or the Governor of Guam and subsequent H–2B petition are required.

(ix) Enforcement. The Secretary of Labor may investigate employers to enforce compliance with the conditions of a petition and Department of Labor-approved temporary labor certification to admit or otherwise provide status to an H–2B worker.

(7) Petition for alien trainee or participant in a special education exchange visitor program (H–3)—

(i) Alien Trainee. The H–3 trainee is a nonimmigrant who seeks to enter the United States at the invitation of an organization or individual for the purpose of receiving training in any field of endeavor, such as agriculture, commerce, communications, finance, government, transportation, or the professions, as well as training in a purely industrial establishment. This category shall not apply to physicians, who are statutorily ineligible to use H–3 classification in order to receive any type of graduate medical education or training.

(A) Externs. A hospital approved by the American Medical Association or the American Osteopathic Association for either an internship or residency program may petition to classify as an H–3 trainee a medical student attending a medical school abroad, if the alien will engage in employment as an extern during his/her medical school vacation.

(B) Nurses. A petitioner may seek H–3 classification for a nurse who is not H–1 if it can be established that there is a genuine need for the nurse to receive a brief period of training that is unavailable in the alien's native country and such training is designed to benefit the nurse and the overseas employer upon the nurse's return to the country of origin, if:

(1) The beneficiary has obtained a full and unrestricted license to practice professional nursing in the country where the beneficiary obtained a nursing education, or such education was obtained in the United States or Canada; and

(2) The petitioner provides a statement certifying that the beneficiary is fully qualified under the laws governing the place where the training will be received to engage in such training, and that under those laws the petitioner is authorized to give the beneficiary the desired training.

(ii) Evidence required for petition involving alien trainee—

(A) Conditions. The petitioner is required to demonstrate that:

(1) The proposed training is not available in the alien's own country;

(2) The beneficiary will not be placed in a position which is in the normal operation of the business and in which citizens and resident workers are regularly employed;

(3) The beneficiary will not engage in productive employment unless such employment is incidental and necessary to the training; and

(4) The training will benefit the beneficiary in pursuing a career outside the United States.

(B) Description of training program. Each petition for a trainee must include a statement which:

(1) Describes the type of training and supervision to be given, and the structure of the training program;

(2) Sets forth the proportion of time that will be devoted to productive employment;

(3) Shows the number of hours that will be spent, respectively, in classroom instruction and in on-the-job training;

(4) Describes the career abroad for which the training will prepare the alien;

(5) Indicates the reasons why such training cannot be obtained in the alien's country and why it is necessary for the alien to be trained in the United States; and

(6) Indicates the source of any remuneration received by the trainee and any benefit which will accrue to the petitioner for providing the training.

(iii) Restrictions on training program for alien trainee. A training program may not be approved which:

(A) Deals in generalities with no fixed schedule, objectives, or means of evaluation;

(B) Is incompatible with the nature of the petitioner's business or enterprise;

(C) Is on behalf of a beneficiary who already possesses substantial training and expertise in the proposed field of training;

(D) Is in a field in which it is unlikely that the knowledge or skill will be used outside the United States;

(E) Will result in productive employment beyond that which is incidental and necessary to the training;

(F) Is designed to recruit and train aliens for the ultimate staffing of domestic operations in the United States;

(G) Does not establish that the petitioner has the physical plant and sufficiently trained manpower to provide the training specified; or

(H) Is designed to extend the total allowable period of practical training previously authorized a nonimmigrant student.

(iv) Petition for participant in a special education exchange visitor program—

(A) General Requirements.

(1) The H–3 participant in a special education training program must be coming to the United States to participate in a structured program which provides for practical training and experience in the education of children with physical, mental, or emotional disabilities.

(2) The petition must be filed by a facility which has professionally trained staff and a structured program for providing education to children with disabilities, and for providing training and hands-on experience to participants in the special education exchange visitor program.

(3) The requirements in this section for alien trainees shall not apply to petitions for participants in a special education exchange visitor program.

(B) Evidence. An H–3 petition for a participant in a special education exchange visitor program shall be accompanied by:

(1) A description of the training program and the facility's professional staff and details of the alien's participation in the training program (any custodial care of children must be incidental to the training), and

(2) Evidence that the alien participant is nearing completion of a baccalaureate or higher degree in special education, or already holds such a degree, or has extensive prior training and experience in teaching children with physical, mental, or emotional disabilities.

(8) Numerical limits—

(i) Limits on affected categories. During each fiscal year, the total number of aliens who can be provided nonimmigrant classification is limited as follows:

(A) Aliens classified as H–1B nonimmigrants, excluding those involved in Department of Defense research and development projects or coproduction projects, may not exceed the limits identified in section 214(g)(1)(A) of the Act.

(B) Aliens classified as H–1B nonimmigrants to work for DOD research and development projects or coproduction projects may not exceed 100 at any time.

(C) Aliens classified as H–2B nonimmigrants may not exceed 66,000.

(D) Aliens classified as H–3 nonimmigrant participants in a special education exchange visitor program may not exceed 50.

(E) Aliens classified as H–1C nonimmigrants may not exceed 500 in a fiscal year.

(ii) Procedures.

(A) Each alien issued a visa or otherwise provided nonimmigrant status under sections 101(a)(15)(H)(i)(b), 101(a)(15)(H)(i)(c), or 101(a)(15)(H)(ii) of the Act shall be counted for purposes of any applicable numerical limit, unless otherwise exempt from such numerical limit. Requests for petition extension or extension of an alien's stay shall not be counted for the purpose of the numerical limit. The spouse and children of principal H aliens are classified as H–4 nonimmigrants and shall not be counted against numerical limits applicable to principals.

(B) When calculating the numerical limitations or the number of exemptions under section 214(g)(5)(C) of the Act for a given fiscal year, USCIS will make numbers available to petitions in the order in which the petitions are filed. USCIS will make projections of the number of petitions necessary to achieve the numerical limit of approvals, taking into account historical data related to approvals, denials, revocations, and other relevant factors. USCIS will monitor the number of petitions (including the number of beneficiaries requested when necessary) received and will notify the public of the date that USCIS has received the necessary number of petitions (the "final receipt date"). The day the news is published will not control the final receipt date. When necessary to ensure the fair and orderly allocation of numbers in a particular classification subject to a numerical limitation or the exemption under section 214(g)(5)(C) of the Act, USCIS may randomly select from among the petitions received on the final receipt date the remaining number of petitions deemed necessary to generate the numerical limit of approvals. This random selection will be made via computer-generated selection as validated by the Office of Immigration Statistics. Petitions subject to a numerical limitation not randomly selected or that were received after the final receipt date will be rejected. Petitions filed on behalf of aliens otherwise eligible for the exemption under section 214(g)(5)(C) of the Act not randomly selected or that were received after the final receipt date will be rejected if the numerical limitation under 214(g)(1) of the Act has been reached for that fiscal year. Petitions indicating that they are exempt from the numerical limitation but that are determined by USCIS after the final receipt date to be subject to the numerical limit will be denied and filing fees will not be returned or refunded. If the final receipt date is any of the first five business days on which petitions subject to the applicable numerical limit may be received (i.e., if the numerical limit is reached on any one of the first five business days that filings can be made), USCIS will randomly apply all of the numbers among the petitions received on any of those five business days, conducting the random selection among the petitions subject to the exemption under section 214(g)(5)(C) of the Act first.

(C) When an approved petition is not used because the beneficiary(ies) does not apply for admission to the United States, the petitioner shall notify the Service Center Director who approved the petition that the number(s) has not been used. The petition shall be revoked pursuant to paragraph (h)(11)(ii) of this section and USCIS will take into account the unused number during the appropriate fiscal year.

(D) If the total numbers available in a fiscal year are used, new petitions and the accompanying fee shall be rejected and returned with a notice that numbers are unavailable for the particular nonimmigrant classification until the beginning of the next fiscal year. Petitions received after the total numbers available in a fiscal year are used stating that the alien beneficiaries are exempt from the numerical limitation will be denied and filing fees will not be returned or refunded if USCIS later determines that such beneficiaries are subject to the numerical limitation.

(E) The 500 H–1C nonimmigrant visas issued each fiscal year shall be allocated in the following manner:

(1) For each fiscal year, the number of visas issued to the states of California, Florida, Illinois, Michigan, New York, Ohio, Pennsylvania, and Texas shall not exceed 50 each (except as provided for in paragraph (h)(8)(ii)(F)(3) of this section).

(2) For each fiscal year, the number of visas issued to the states not listed in paragraph (h)(8)(ii)(F)(1) of this section shall not exceed 25 each (except as provided for in paragraph (h)(8)(ii)(F)(3) of this section).

(3) If the total number of visas available during the first three quarters of a fiscal year exceeds the number of approvable H–1C petitions during those quarters, visas may be issued during the last quarter of the fiscal year to nurses who will be working in a state whose cap has already been reached for that fiscal year.

(4) When an approved H–1C petition is not used because the alien(s) does not obtain H–1C classification, e.g., the alien is never admitted to the United States, or the alien never worked for the facility, the facility must notify the Service according to the instructions contained in paragraph (h)(11)(ii) of this section. The Service will subtract H–1C petitions approved in the current fiscal year that are later revoked from the total count of approved H–1C petitions, provided that the alien never commenced employment with the facility.

(5) If the number of alien nurses included in an H–1C petition exceeds the number available for the remainder of a fiscal year, the Service shall approve the petition for the beneficiaries to the allowable amount in the order that they are listed on the petition. The remaining beneficiaries will be considered for approval in the subsequent fiscal year.

(6) Once the 500 cap has been reached, the Service will reject any new petitions subsequently filed requesting a work start date prior to the first day of the next fiscal year.

(9) Approval and validity of petition—

(i) Approval. The director shall consider all the evidence submitted and such other evidence as he or she may independently require to assist his or her adjudication. The director shall notify the petitioner of the approval of the petition on Form I–797, Notice of Action. The approval shall be as follows:

(A) The approval notice shall include the beneficiary's(ies') name(s) and classification and the petition's period of validity. A petition for more than one beneficiary and/or multiple services may be approved in whole or in part. The approval notice shall cover only those beneficiaries approved for classification under section 101(a)(15)(H) of the Act.

(B) The petition may not be filed or approved earlier than 6 months before the date of actual need for the beneficiary's services or training, except that an H–2B petition for a temporary nonagricultural worker may not be filed or approved more than 120 days before the date of the actual need for the beneficiary's temporary nonagricultural services that is identified on the temporary labor certification.

(ii) Recording the validity of petitions. Procedures for recording the validity period of petitions are:

(A) If a new H petition is approved before the date the petitioner indicates that the services or training will begin, the approved petition and approval notice shall show the actual dates requested by the petitioner as the validity period, not to exceed the limits specified by paragraph (h)(9)(iii) of this section or other Service policy.

(B) If a new H petition is approved after the date the petitioner indicates that the services or training will begin, the approved petition and approval notice shall show a validity period commencing with the date of approval and ending with the date requested by the petitioner, as long as that date does not exceed either the limits specified by paragraph (h)(9)(iii) of this section or other Service policy.

(C) If the period of services or training requested by the petitioner exceeds the limit specified in paragraph (h)(9)(iii) of this section, the petition shall be approved only up to the limit specified in that paragraph.

(iii) Validity. The initial approval period of an H petition shall conform to the limits prescribed as follows:

(A)(1) H–1B petition in a specialty occupation. An approved petition classified under section 101(a)(15)(H)(i)(b) of the Act for an alien in a specialty occupation shall be valid for a period of up to three years but may not exceed the validity period of the labor condition application.

(2) H–1B petition involving a DOD research and development or coproduction project. An approved petition classified under section 101(a)(15)(H)(i)(b) of the Act for an alien involved in a DOD research and development project or a coproduction project shall be valid for a period of up to five years.

(3) H–1B petition involving an alien of distinguished merit and ability in the field of fashion modeling. An approved petition classified under section 101(a)(15)(H)(i)(b) of the Act for an alien of distinguished merit and ability in the field of fashion modeling shall be valid for a period of up to three years.

(B) H–2B petition—

(1) The approval of the petition to accord an alien a classification under section 101(a)(15)(H)(ii)(b) of the Act shall be valid for the period of the approved temporary labor certification.

(2) Notice that certification cannot be made attached—

(i) Countervailing evidence. If a petition is submitted containing a notice from the Secretary of Labor or the Governor of Guam that certification cannot be made, and is not accompanied by countervailing evidence, the petitioner shall be informed that he or she may submit the countervailing evidence in accordance with paragraphs (h)(6)(iii)(E) and (h)(6)(iv)(D) of this section.

(ii) Approval. In any case where the director decides that approval of the H–2B petition is warranted despite the issuance of a notice by the Secretary of Labor or the Governor of Guam that certification cannot be made, the approval shall be certified by the Director to the Commissioner pursuant to 8 CFR 103. In emergent situations, the certification may be presented by telephone to the Director, Administrative Appeals Office, Headquarters. If approved, the petition is valid for the period of established need not to exceed one year. There is no appeal from a decision which has been certified to the Commissioner.

(C)(1) H–3 petition for alien trainee. An approved petition for an alien trainee classified under section 101(a)(15)(H)(iii) of the Act shall be valid for a period of up to two years.

(2) H–3 petition for alien participant in a special education training program. An approved petition for an alien classified under section 101(a)(15)(H)(iii) of the Act as a participant in a special education exchange visitor program shall be valid for a period of up to 18 months.

(D) H–1C petition for a registered nurse. An approved petition for an alien classified under section 101(a)(15)(H)(i)(c) of the Act shall be valid for a period of 3 years.

(iv) Spouse and dependents. The spouse and unmarried minor children of the beneficiary are entitled to H nonimmigrant classification, subject to the same period of admission and limitations as the beneficiary, if they are accompanying or following to join the beneficiary in the United States. Neither the spouse nor a child of the beneficiary may accept employment unless he or she is the beneficiary of an approved petition filed in his or her behalf and has been granted a nonimmigrant classification authorizing his or her employment.

(10) Denial of petition—

(i) Multiple beneficiaries. A petition for multiple beneficiaries may be denied in whole or in part.

(ii) Notice of denial. The petitioner shall be notified of the reasons for the denial and of the right to appeal the denial of the petition under 8 CFR part 103. The petition will be denied if it is determined that the statements on the petition were inaccurate, fraudulent, or misrepresented a material fact. There is no appeal from a decision to deny an extension of stay to the alien.

(11) Revocation of approval of petition—

(i) General.

(A) The petitioner shall immediately notify the Service of any changes in the terms and conditions of employment of a beneficiary which may affect eligibility under section 101(a)(15)(H) of the Act and paragraph (h) of this section. An amended petition on Form I–129 should be filed when the petitioner continues to employ the beneficiary. If the petitioner no longer employs the beneficiary, the petitioner shall send a letter explaining the change(s) to the director who approved the petition. However, H–2A and H–2B petitioners must send notification to DHS pursuant to paragraphs (h)(5)(vi) and (h)(6)(i)(F) of this section respectively.

(B) The director may revoke a petition at any time, even after the expiration of the petition.

(ii) Immediate and automatic revocation. The approval of any petition is immediately and automatically revoked if the petitioner goes out of business, files a written withdrawal of the petition, or the Department of Labor revokes the labor certification upon which the petition is based.

(iii) Revocation on notice—

(A) Grounds for revocation. The director shall send to the petitioner a notice of intent to revoke the petition in relevant part if he or she finds that:

(1) The beneficiary is no longer employed by the petitioner in the capacity specified in the petition, or if the beneficiary is no longer receiving training as specified in the petition; or

(2) The statement of facts contained in the petition or on the application for a temporary labor certification was not true and correct, inaccurate, fraudulent, or misrepresented a material fact; or

(3) The petitioner violated terms and conditions of the approved petition; or

(4) The petitioner violated requirements of section 101(a)(15)(H) of the Act or paragraph (h) of this section; or

(5) The approval of the petition violated paragraph (h) of this section or involved gross error.

(B) Notice and decision. The notice of intent to revoke shall contain a detailed statement of the grounds for the revocation and the time period allowed for the petitioner's rebuttal. The petitioner may submit evidence in rebuttal within 30 days of receipt of the notice. The director shall consider all relevant evidence presented in deciding whether to revoke the petition in whole or in part. If the petition is revoked in part, the remainder of the petition shall remain approved and a revised approval notice shall be sent to the petitioner with the revocation notice.

(12) Appeal of a denial or a revocation of a petition—

(i) Denial. A petition denied in whole or in part may be appealed under Part 103 of this chapter.

(ii) Revocation. A petition that has been revoked on notice in whole or in part may be appealed under Part 103 of this chapter. Automatic revocations may not be appealed.

(13) Admission—

(i) General.

(A) A beneficiary shall be admitted to the United States for the validity period of the petition, plus a period of up to 10 days before the validity period begins and 10 days after the validity period ends. The beneficiary may not work except during the validity period of the petition.

(B) When an alien in an H classification has spent the maximum allowable period of stay in the United States, a new petition under sections 101(a)(15)(H) or (L) of the Act may not be approved unless that alien has resided and been physically present outside the United States, except for brief trips for business or pleasure, for the time limit imposed on the particular H classification. Brief trips to the United States for business or pleasure during the required time abroad are not interruptive, but do not count towards fulfillment of the required time abroad. A certain period of absence from the United States of H–2A and H–2B aliens can interrupt the accrual of time spent in such status against the 3–year limit set forth in 8 CFR 214.2(h)(13)(iv). The petitioner shall provide information about the alien's employment, place of residence, and the dates and purposes of any trips to the United States during the period that the alien was required to reside abroad.

(ii) H–1C limitation on admission. The maximum period of admission for an H–1C nonimmigrant alien is 3 years. The maximum period of admission for an H–1C alien begins on the date the H–1C alien is admitted to the United and ends on the third anniversary of the alien's admission date. Periods of time spent out of the United States for business or personal reasons during the validity period of the H–1C petition count towards the alien's maximum period of admission. When an H–1C alien has reached the 3–year maximum period of admission, the H–1C alien is no longer eligible for admission to the United States as an H–1C nonimmigrant alien.

(iii) H–1B limitation on admission.

(A) Alien in a specialty occupation or an alien of distinguished merit and ability in the field of fashion modeling. An H–1B alien in a specialty occupation or an alien of distinguished merit and ability who has spent six years in the United States under section 101(a)(15)(H) and/or (L) of the Act may not seek extension, change status, or be readmitted to the United States under section 101(a)(15)(H) or (L) of the Act unless the alien has resided and been physically present outside the United States, except for brief trips for business or pleasure, for the immediate prior year.

(B) Alien involved in a DOD research and development or coproduction project. An H–1B alien involved in a DOD research and development or coproduction project who has spent 10 years in the United States under section 101(a)(15)(H) and/or (L) of the Act may not seek extension, change status, or be readmitted to the United States under section 101(a)(15)(H) or (L) of the Act to perform services involving a DOD research and development project or coproduction project. A new petition or change of status under section 101(a)(15)(H) or (L) of the Act may not be approved for such an alien unless the alien has resided and been physically present outside the United States, except for brief trips for business or pleasure, for the immediate prior year.

(iv) H–2B and H–3 limitation on admission. An H–2B alien who has spent 3 years in the United States under section 101(a)(15)(H) and/or (L) of the Act may not seek extension, change status, or be readmitted to the United States under sections 101(a)(15)(H) and/or (L) of the Act unless the alien has resided and been physically present outside the United States for the immediately preceding 3 months. An H–3 alien participant in a special education program who has spent 18 months in the United States under sections 101(a)(15)(H) and/or (L) of the Act; and an H–3 alien trainee who has spent 24 months in the United States under sections 101(a)(15)(H) and/or (L) of the Act may not seek extension, change status, or be readmitted to the United States under sections 101(a)(15)(H) and/or (L) of the Act unless the alien has resided and been physically present outside the United States for the immediate prior 6 months.

(v) Exceptions. The limitations in paragraphs (h)(13)(iii) through (h)(13)(iv) of this section shall not apply to H–1B, H–2B, and H–3 aliens who did not reside continually in the United States and whose employment in the United States was seasonal or intermittent or was for an aggregate of 6 months or less per year. In addition, the limitations shall not apply to aliens who reside abroad and regularly commute to the United States to engage in part-time employment. An absence from the United States can interrupt the accrual of time spent as an H–2B nonimmigrant against the 3–year limit. If the accumulated stay is 18 months or less, an absence is interruptive if it lasts for at least 45 days. If the accumulated stay is greater than 18 months, an absence is interruptive if it lasts for at least two months. To qualify for this exception, the petitioner and the alien must provide clear and convincing proof that the alien qualifies for such an exception. Such proof shall consist of evidence such as arrival and departure records, copies of tax returns, and records of employment abroad.

(14) Extension of visa petition validity. The petitioner shall file a request for a petition extension on Form I–129 to extend the validity of the original petition under section 101(a)(15)(H) of the Act. Supporting evidence is not required unless requested by the director. A request for a petition extension may be filed only if the validity of the original petition has not expired.

(15) Extension of stay—

(i) General. The petitioner shall apply for extension of an alien's stay in the United States by filing a petition extension on Form I–129 accompanied by the documents described for the particular classification in paragraph (h)(15)(ii) of this section. The petitioner must also request a petition extension. The dates of extension shall be the same for the petition and the beneficiary's extension of stay. The beneficiary must be physically present in the United States at the time of the filing of the extension of stay. Even though the requests to extend the petition and the alien's stay are combined on the petition, the director shall make a separate determination on each. If the alien is required to leave the United States for business or personal reasons while the extension requests are pending, the petitioner may request the director to cable notification of approval of the petition extension to the consular office abroad where the alien will apply for a visa. When the total period of stay in an H classification has been reached, no further extensions may be granted.

(ii) Extension periods—

(A) H–1C extension of stay. The maximum period of admission for an H–1C alien is 3 years. An H–1C alien who was initially admitted to the United States for less than 3 years may receive an extension of stay up to the third anniversary date of his or her initial admission. An H–1C nonimmigrant may not receive an extension of stay beyond the third anniversary date of his or her initial admission to the United States.

(B) H–1B extension of stay—

(1) Alien in a specialty occupation or an alien of distinguished merit and ability in the field of fashion modeling. An extension of stay may be authorized for a period of up to three years for a beneficiary of an H–1B petition in a specialty occupation or an alien of distinguished merit and ability. The alien's total period of stay may not exceed six years. The request for extension must be accompanied by either a new or a photocopy of the prior certification from the Department of Labor that the petitioner continues to have on file a labor condition application valid for the period of time requested for the occupation.

(2) Alien in a DOD research and development or coproduction project. An extension of stay may be authorized for a period up to five years for the beneficiary of an H–1B petition involving a DOD research and development project or coproduction project. The total period of stay may not exceed 10 years.

(C) H–2A or H–2B extension of stay. An extension of stay for the beneficiary of an H–2A or H–2B petition may be authorized for the validity of the labor certification or for a period of up to one year, except as provided for in paragraph (h)(5)(x) of this section. The alien's total period of stay as an H–2A or H–2B worker may not exceed three years, except that in the Virgin Islands, the alien's total period of stay may not exceed 45 days.

(D) H–3 extension of stay. An extension of stay may be authorized for the length of the training program for a total period of stay as an H–3 trainee not to exceed two years, or for a total period of stay as a participant in a special education training program not to exceed 18 months.

(16) Effect of approval of a permanent labor certification or filing of a preference petition on H classification—

(i) H–1B or H–1C classification. The approval of a permanent labor certification or the filing of a preference petition for an alien shall not be a basis for denying an H–1C or H–1B petition or a request to extend such a petition, or the alien's admission, change of status, or extension of stay. The alien may legitimately come to the United States for a temporary period as an H–1C or H–1B nonimmigrant and depart voluntarily at the end of his or her authorized stay and, at the same time, lawfully seek to become a permanent resident of the United States.

(ii) H–2A, H–2B, and H–3 classification. The approval of a permanent labor certification, or the filing of a preference petition for an alien currently employed by or in a training position with the same petitioner, shall be a reason, by itself, to deny the alien's extension of stay.

(17) Effect of a strike—

(i) If the Secretary of Labor certifies to the Commissioner that a strike or other labor dispute involving a work stoppage of workers is in progress in the occupation and at the place where the beneficiary is to be employed or trained, and that the employment of training of the beneficiary would adversely affect the wages and working conditions of U.S. citizens and lawful resident workers:

(A) A petition to classify an alien as a nonimmigrant as defined in section 101(a)(15)(H) of the Act shall be denied.

(B) If a petition has already been approved, but the alien has not yet entered the United States, or has entered the United States but has not commenced the employment, the approval of the petition is automatically suspended, and the application for admission on the basis of the petition shall be denied.

(ii) If there is a strike or other labor dispute involving a work stoppage of workers in progress, but such strike or other labor dispute is not certified under paragraph (h)(17)(i), the Commissioner shall not deny a petition or suspend an approved petition.

(iii) If the alien has already commenced employment in the United States under an approved petition and is participating in a strike or other labor dispute involving a work stoppage of workers, whether or not such strike or other labor dispute has been certified by the Department of Labor, the alien shall not be deemed to be failing to maintain his or her status solely on account of past, present, or future participation in a strike or other labor dispute involving a work stoppage of workers, but is subject to the following terms and conditions:

(A) The alien shall remain subject to all applicable provisions of the Immigration and Nationality Act, and regulations promulgated in the same manner as all other H nonimmigrants;

(B) The status and authorized period of stay of such an alien is not modified or extended in any way by virtue of his or her participation in a strike or other labor dispute involving a work stoppage of workers; and

(C) Although participation by an H nonimmigrant alien in a strike or other labor dispute involving a work stoppage of workers will not constitute a ground for deportation, any alien who violates his or her status or who remains in the United States after his or her authorized period of stay has expired will be subject to deportation.

(18) Use of approval notice, Form I–797. The Service shall notify the petitioner on Form I–797 whenever a visa petition, an extension of a visa petition, or an alien's extension of stay is approved under the H classification. The beneficiary of an H petition who does not require a nonimmigrant visa may present a copy of the approval notice at a port of entry to facilitate entry into the United States. A beneficiary who is required to present a visa for admission and whose visa will have expired before the date of his or her intended return may use a copy of Form I–797 to apply for a new or revalidated visa during the validity period of the petition. The copy of Form I–797 shall be retained by the beneficiary and presented during the validity of the petition when reentering the United States to resume the same employment with the same petitioner.

(19) Additional fee for filing certain H–1B petitions—

(i) A United States employer (other than an exempt employer as defined in paragraph (h)(19)(iii) of this section) who files a Form I–129, on or after December 1, 1998, and before October 1, 2001, must include the additional fee required in § 103.7(b)(1) of this chapter, if the petition is filed for any of the following purposes:

(A) An initial grant of H–1B status under section 101(a)(15)(H)(i)(b) of the Act;

(B) An initial extension of stay, as provided in paragraph (h)(15)(i) of this section; or

(C) Authorization for a change in employers, as provided in paragraph (h)(2)(i)(D) of this section.

(ii) A petitioner must submit the $110 filing fee and additional $500 filing fee in a single remittance totaling $610. Payment of the $610 sum ($110 filing fee and additional $500 filing fee) must be made at the same time to constitute a single remittance. A petitioner may submit two checks, one in the amount of $500 and the other in the amount of $110. The Service will accept remittances of the $500 fee only from the United States employer or its representative of record, as defined under 8 CFR part 292 and 8 CFR 103.2(a).

(iii) The following exempt organizations are not required to pay the additional fee:

(A) An institution of higher education, as defined in section 101(a) of the Higher Education Act of 1965;

(B) An affiliated or related nonprofit entity. A nonprofit entity (including but not limited to hospitals and medical or research institutions) that is connected or associated with an institution of higher education, through shared ownership or control by the same board or federation operated by an institution of higher education, or attached to an institution of higher education as a member, branch, cooperative, or subsidiary; or

(C) A nonprofit research organization or governmental research organization. A nonprofit research organization is an organization that is primarily engaged in basic research and/or applied research. A governmental research organization is a United States Government entity whose primary mission is the performance or promotion of basic research and/or applied research. Basic research is general research to gain more comprehensive knowledge or understanding of the subject under study, without specific applications in mind. Basic research is also research that advances scientific knowledge, but does not have specific immediate commercial objectives although it may be in fields of present or potential commercial interest. It may include research and investigation in the sciences, social sciences, or humanities. Applied research is research to gain knowledge or understanding to determine the means by which a specific, recognized need may be met. Applied research includes investigations oriented to discovering new scientific knowledge that has specific commercial objectives with respect to products, processes, or services. It may include research and investigation in the sciences, social sciences, or humanities.

(iv) Non-profit or tax exempt organizations. For purposes of paragraphs (h)(19)(iii)(B) and (C) of this section, a nonprofit organization or entity is:

(A) Defined as a tax exempt organization under the Internal Revenue Code of 1986, section 501(c)(3), (c)(4) or (c)(6), 26 U.S.C. 501(c)(3), (c)(4) or (c)(6), and

(B) Has been approved as a tax exempt organization for research or educational purposes by the Internal Revenue Service.

(v) Filing situations where the $500 filing fee is not required. The $500 filing fee is not required:

(A) If the petition is an amended H–1B petition that does not contain any requests for an extension of stay;

(B) If the petition is an H–1B petition filed for the sole purpose of correcting a Service error; or

(C) If the petition is the second or subsequent request for an extension of stay filed by the employer regardless of when the first extension of stay was filed or whether the $500 filing fee was paid on the initial petition or the first extension of stay.

(vi) Petitioners required to file Form I–129W. All petitioners must submit Form I–129W with the appropriate supporting documentation with the petition for an H–1B nonimmigrant alien. Petitioners who do not qualify for a fee exemption are required only to fill our Part A of Form I–129W.

(vii) Evidence to be submitted in support of the Form I–129W.

(A) Employer claiming to be exempt. An employer claiming to be exempt from the $500 filing fee must complete both Parts A and B of Form I–129W along with Form I–129. The employer must also submit evidence as described on Form I–129W establishing that it meets one of the exemptions described at paragraph (h)(19)(iii) of this section. A United States employer claiming an exemption from the $500 filing fee on the basis that it is a non-profit research organization must submit evidence that it has tax exempt status under the Internal Revenue Code of 1986, section 501(c)(3), (c)(4) or (c)(6), 26 U.S.C. 501(c)(3), (c)(4) or (c)(6). All other employers claiming an exemption must submit a statement describing why the organization or entity is exempt.

(B) Exempt filing situations. Any non-exempt employer who claims that the $500 filing fee does not apply with respect to a particular filing for one of the reasons described in § 214.2(h)(19)(v), must submit a statement describing why the filing fee is not required.

* * * * *

(*l*) Intracompany transferees—

(1) Admission of intracompany transferees—

(i) General. Under section 101(a)(15)(L) of the Act, an alien who within the preceding three years has been employed abroad for one continuous year by a qualifying organization may be admitted temporarily to the United States to be employed by a parent, branch, affiliate, or subsidiary of that employer in a managerial or executive capacity, or in a position requiring specialized knowledge. An alien transferred to the United States under this nonimmigrant classification is referred to as an intracompany transferee and the organization which seeks the classification of an alien as an intracompany transferee is referred to as the petitioner. The Service has responsibility for determining whether the alien is eligible for admission and whether the petitioner is a qualifying organization. These regulations set forth the standards applicable to these classifications. They also set forth procedures for admission of intracompany transferees and appeal of adverse decisions. Certain petitioners seeking the classification of aliens as intracompany transferees may file blanket petitions with the Service. Under the blanket petition process, the Service is responsible for determining whether the petitioner and its parent, branches, affiliates, or subsidiaries specified are qualifying organizations. The Department of State or, in certain cases, the Service is responsible for determining the classification of the alien.

(ii) Definitions—

(A) Intracompany transferee means an alien who, within three years preceding the time of his or her application for admission into the United States, has been employed abroad continuously for one year by a firm or corporation or other legal entity or parent, branch, affiliate, or subsidiary thereof, and who seeks to enter the United States temporarily in order to render his or her services to a branch of the same employer or a parent, affiliate, or subsidiary thereof in a capacity that is managerial, executive, or involves specialized knowledge. Periods spent in the United States in lawful status for a branch of the same employer or a parent, affiliate, or subsidiary thereof and brief trips to the United States for business or pleasure shall not be interruptive of the one year of continuous employment abroad but such periods shall not be counted toward fulfillment of that requirement.

(B) Managerial capacity means an assignment within an organization in which the employee primarily:

(1) Manages the organization, or a department, subdivision, function, or component of the organization;

(2) Supervises and controls the work of other supervisory, professional, or managerial employees, or manages an essential function within the organization, or a department or subdivision of the organization;

(3) Has the authority to hire and fire or recommend those as well as other personnel actions (such as promotion and leave authorization) if another employee or other employees are directly supervised; if no other employee is directly supervised, functions at a senior level within the organizational hierarchy or with respect to the function managed; and

(4) Exercises discretion over the day-to-day operations of the activity or function for which the employee has authority. A first-line supervisor is not considered to be acting in a managerial capacity merely by virtue of the supervisor's supervisory duties unless the employees supervised are professional.

(C) Executive capacity means an assignment within an organization in which the employee primarily:

(1) Directs the management of the organization or a major component or function of the organization;

(2) Establishes the goals and policies of the organization, component, or function;

(3) Exercises wide latitude in discretionary decision-making; and

(4) Receives only general supervision or direction from higher level executives, the board of directors, or stockholders of the organization.

(D) Specialized knowledge means special knowledge possessed by an individual of the petitioning organization's product, service, research, equipment, techniques, management, or other interests and its application in international markets, or an advanced level of knowledge or expertise in the organization's processes and procedures.

(E) Specialized knowledge professional means an individual who has specialized knowledge as defined in paragraph (*l*)(1)(ii)(D) of this section and is a member of the professions as defined in section 101(a)(32) of the Immigration and Nationality Act.

(F) New office means an organization which has been doing business in the United States through a parent, branch, affiliate, or subsidiary for less than one year.

(G) Qualifying organization means a United States or foreign firm, corporation, or other legal entity which:

(1) Meets exactly one of the qualifying relationships specified in the definitions of a parent, branch, affiliate or subsidiary specified in paragraph (*l*)(1)(ii) of this section;

(2) Is or will be doing business (engaging in international trade is not required) as an employer in the United States and in at least one other country directly or through a parent, branch, affiliate, or subsidiary for the duration of the alien's stay in the United States as an intracompany transferee; and

(3) Otherwise meets the requirements of section 101(a)(15)(L) of the Act.

(H) Doing business means the regular, systematic, and continuous provision of goods and/or services by a qualifying organization and does not include the mere presence of an agent or office of the qualifying organization in the United States and abroad.

(I) Parent means a firm, corporation, or other legal entity which has subsidiaries.

(J) Branch means an operating division or office of the same organization housed in a different location.

(K) Subsidiary means a firm, corporation, or other legal entity of which a parent owns, directly or indirectly, more than half of the entity and controls the entity; or owns, directly or indirectly, half of the entity and controls the entity; or owns, directly or indirectly, 50 percent of a 50–50 joint venture and has equal control and veto power over the entity; or owns, directly or indirectly, less than half of the entity, but in fact controls the entity.

(L) Affiliate means

(1) One of two subsidiaries both of which are owned and controlled by the same parent or individual, or

(2) One of two legal entities owned and controlled by the same group of individuals, each individual owning and controlling approximately the same share or proportion of each entity, or

(3) In the case of a partnership that is organized in the United States to provide accounting services along with managerial and/or consulting services and that markets its accounting services under an internationally recognized name under an agreement with a worldwide coordinating organization that is owned and controlled by the member accounting firms, a partnership (or similar organization) that is organized outside the United States to provide accounting services shall be considered to be an affiliate of the United States partnership if it markets its accounting services under the same internationally recognized name under the agreement with the worldwide coordinating organization of which the United States partnership is also a member.

(M) Director means a Service Center director with delegated authority at 8 CFR 103.1.

(2) Filing of petitions—

(i) Except as provided in paragraph (*l*)(2)(ii) and (*l*)(17) of this section, a petitioner seeking to classify an alien as an intracompany transferee must file a petition on Form I–129, Petition for Nonimmigrant Worker. The petitioner shall advise USCIS whether a previous petition for the same beneficiary has been filed, and certify that another petition for the same beneficiary will not be filed unless the circumstances and conditions in the initial petition have changed. Failure to make a full disclosure of previous petitions filed may result in a denial of the petition.

(ii) A United States petitioner which meets the requirements of paragraph (*l*)(4) of this section and seeks continuing approval of itself and its parent, branches, specified subsidiaries and affiliates as qualifying organizations and, later, classification under section 101(a)(15)(L) of the Act [sic]* multiple numbers of aliens employed by itself, its parent, or those branches, subsidiaries, or affiliates may file a blanket petition on Form I–129. The blanket petition shall be maintained at the adjudicating office. The petitioner shall be the single representative for the qualifying organizations with which USCIS will deal regarding the blanket petition.

(3) Evidence for individual petitions. An individual petition filed on Form I–129 shall be accompanied by:

(i) Evidence that the petitioner and the organization which employed or will employ the alien are qualifying organizations as defined in paragraph (*l*)(1)(ii)(G) of this section.

(ii) Evidence that the alien will be employed in an executive, managerial, or specialized knowledge capacity, including a detailed description of the services to be performed.

(iii) Evidence that the alien has at least one continuous year of full-time employment abroad with a qualifying organization within the three years preceding the filing of the petition.

(iv) Evidence that the alien's prior year of employment abroad was in a position that was managerial, executive, or involved specialized knowledge and that the alien's prior education, training, and employment qualifies him/her to perform the intended services in the United States; however, the work in the United States need not be the same work which the alien performed abroad.

(v) If the petition indicates that the beneficiary is coming to the United States as a manager or executive to open or to be employed in a new office in the United States, the petitioner shall submit evidence that:

(A) Sufficient physical premises to house the new office have been secured;

(B) The beneficiary has been employed for one continuous year in the three year period preceding the filing of the petition in an executive or managerial capacity and that the proposed employment involved executive or managerial authority over the new operation; and

* The word "of" probably was omitted.

(C) The intended United States operation, within one year of the approval of the petition, will support an executive or managerial position as defined in paragraphs (*l*)(1)(ii)(B) or (C) of this section, supported by information regarding:

(1) The proposed nature of the office describing the scope of the entity, its organizational structure, and its financial goals;

(2) The size of the United States investment and the financial ability of the foreign entity to remunerate the beneficiary and to commence doing business in the United States; and

(3) The organizational structure of the foreign entity.

(vi) If the petition indicates that the beneficiary is coming to the United States in a specialized knowledge capacity to open or to be employed in a new office, the petitioner shall submit evidence that:

(A) Sufficient physical premises to house the new office have been secured;

(B) The business entity in the United States is or will be a qualifying organization as defined in paragraph (*l*)(1)(ii)(G) of this section; and

(C) The petitioner has the financial ability to remunerate the beneficiary and to commence doing business in the United States.

(vii) If the beneficiary is an owner or major stockholder of the company, the petition must be accompanied by evidence that the beneficiary's services are to be used for a temporary period and evidence that the beneficiary will be transferred to an assignment abroad upon the completion of the temporary services in the United States.

(viii) Such other evidence as the director, in his or her discretion, may deem necessary.

(4) Blanket petitions—

(i) A petitioner which meets the following requirements may file a blanket petition seeking continuing approval of itself and some or all of its parent, branches, subsidiaries, and affiliates as qualifying organizations if:

(A) The petitioner and each of those entities are engaged in commercial trade or services;

(B) The petitioner has an office in the United States that has been doing business for one year or more;

(C) The petitioner has three or more domestic and foreign branches, subsidiaries, or affiliates; and

(D) The petitioner and the other qualifying organizations have obtained approval of petitions for at least ten "L" managers, executives, or specialized knowledge professionals during the previous 12 months; or have U.S. subsidiaries or affiliates with combined annual sales of at least $25 million; or have a United States work force of at least 1,000 employees.

(ii) Managers, executives, and specialized knowledge professionals employed by firms, corporations, or other entities which have been found to be qualifying organizations pursuant to an approved blanket petition may be classified as intracompany transferees and admitted to the United States as provided in paragraphs (*l*)(5) and (11) of this section.

(iii) When applying for a blanket petition, the petitioner shall include in the blanket petition all of its branches, subsidiaries, and affiliates which plan to seek to transfer aliens to the United States under the blanket petition. An individual petition may be filed by the petitioner or organizations in lieu of using the blanket petition procedure. However, the petitioner and other qualifying organizations may not seek L classification for the same alien under both procedures, unless a consular officer first denies eligibility. Whenever a petitioner which has blanket L approval files an individual petition to seek L classification for a manager, executive, or specialized knowledge professional, the petitioner shall advise the Service that it has blanket L approval and certify that the beneficiary has not and will not apply to a consular officer for L classification under the approved blanket petition.

(iv) Evidence. A blanket petition filed on Form I–129 shall be accompanied by:

(A) Evidence that the petitioner meets the requirements of paragraph (*l*)(4)(i) of this section.

(B) Evidence that all entities for which approval is sought are qualifying organizations as defined in subparagraph (*l*)(1)(ii)(G) of this section.

(C) Such other evidence as the director, in his or her discretion, deems necessary in a particular case.

(5) Certification and admission procedures for beneficiaries under blanket petition.

(i) Jurisdiction. United States consular officers shall have authority to determine eligibility of individual beneficiaries outside the United States seeking L classification under blanket petitions, except for visa-exempt nonimmigrants. An application for a visa-exempt nonimmigrant seeking L classification under a blanket petition or by an alien in the United States applying for change of status to L classification under a blanket petition shall be filed with the Service office at which the blanket petition was filed.

(ii) Procedures.

(A) When one qualifying organization listed in an approved blanket petition wishes to transfer an alien outside the United States to a qualifying organization in the United States and the alien requires a visa to enter the United States, that organization shall complete Form I–129S, Certificate of Eligibility for Intracompany Transferee under a Blanket Petition, in an original and three copies. The qualifying organization shall retain one copy for its records and send the original and two copies to the alien. A copy of the approved Form I–797 must be attached to the original and each copy of Form I–129S.

(B) After receipt of Form I–797 and Form I–129S, a qualified employee who is being transferred to the United States may use these documents to apply for visa issuance with the consular officer within six months of the date on Form I–129S.

(C) When the alien is a visa-exempt nonimmigrant seeking L classification under a blanket petition, or when the alien is in the United States and is seeking a change of status from another nonimmigrant classification to L classification under a blanket petition, the petitioner shall submit Form I–129S, Certificate of Eligibility, and a copy of the approval notice, Form I–797, to the USCIS office with which the blanket petition was filed.

(D) The consular or Service officer shall determine whether the position in which the alien will be employed in the United States is with an organization named in the approved petition and whether the specific job is for a manager, executive, or specialized knowledge professional. The consular or Service officer shall determine further whether the alien's immediate prior year of continuous employment abroad was with an organization named in the petition and was in a position as manager, executive, or specialized knowledge professional.

(E) Consular officers may grant "L" classification only in clearly approvable applications. If the consular officer determines that the alien is eligible for L classification, the consular officer may issue a nonimmigrant visa, noting the visa classification "Blanket L–1" for the principal alien and "Blanket L–2" for any accompanying or following to join spouse and children. The consular officer shall also endorse all copies of the alien's Form I–129S with the blanket L–1 visa classification and return the original and one copy to the alien. When the alien is inspected for entry into the United States, both copies of the Form I–129S shall be stamped to show a validity period not to exceed three years and the second copy collected and sent to the appropriate Regional Service Center for control purposes. Service officers who determine eligibility of aliens for L–1 classification under blanket petitions shall endorse both copies of Form I–129S with the blanket L–1 classification and the validity period not to exceed three years and retain the second copy for Service records.

(F) If the consular officer determines that the alien is ineligible for L classification under a blanket petition, the consular officer's decision shall be final. The consular officer shall record the reasons for the denial on Form I–129S, retain one copy, return the original of I–129S to the USCIS office which approved the blanket petition, and provide a copy to the alien. In such a case, an individual petition may be filed for the alien on Form I–129, Petition for Nonimmigrant Worker. The petition shall state the reason the alien was denied L classification and specify the consular office which made the determination and the date of the determination.

(G) An alien admitted under an approved blanket petition may be reassigned to any organization listed in the approved petition without referral to the Service during his/her authorized stay if the alien will be performing virtually the same job duties. If the alien will be performing different job duties, the petitioner shall complete a new Certificate of Eligibility and send it for approval to the director who approved the blanket petition.

(6) Copies of supporting documents. The petitioner may submit a legible photocopy of a document in support of the visa petition, in lieu of the original document. However, the original document shall be submitted if requested by the Service.

(7) Approval of petition—

(i) General. The director shall notify the petitioner of the approval of an individual or a blanket petition within 30 days after the date a completed petition has been filed. If additional information is required from the petitioner, the 30 day processing period shall begin again upon receipt of the information. The original Form I–797 received from the USCIS with respect to an approved individual or blanket petition may be duplicated by the petitioner for the beneficiary's use as described in paragraph (*l*)(13) of this section.

(A) Individual petition—

(1) Form I–797 shall include the beneficiary's name and classification and the petition's period of validity.

(2) An individual petition approved under this paragraph shall be valid for the period of established need for the beneficiary's services, not to exceed three years, except where the beneficiary is coming to the United States to open or to be employed in a new office.

(3) If the beneficiary is coming to the United States to open or be employed in a new office, the petition may be approved for a period not to exceed one year, after which the petitioner shall demonstrate as required by paragraph (*l*)(14)(ii) of this section that it is doing business as defined in paragraph (*l*)(1)(ii)(H) of this section to extend the validity of the petition.

(B) Blanket petition—

(1) Form I–797 shall identify the approved organizations included in the petition and the petition's period of validity.

(2) A blanket petition approved under this paragraph shall be valid initially for a period of three years and may be extended indefinitely thereafter if the qualifying organizations have complied with these regulations.

(3) A blanket petition may be approved in whole or in part and shall cover only qualifying organizations.

(C) Amendments. The petitioner must file an amended petition, with fee, at the USCIS office where the original petition was filed to reflect changes in approved relationships, additional qualifying organizations under a blanket petition, change in capacity of employment (i.e., from a specialized knowledge position to a managerial position), or any information which would affect the beneficiary's eligibility under section 101(a)(15)(L) of the Act.

(ii) Spouse and dependents. The spouse and unmarried minor children of the beneficiary are entitled to L nonimmigrant classification, subject to the same period of admission and limits as the beneficiary, if the spouse and unmarried minor children are accompanying or following to join the beneficiary in the United States. Neither the spouse nor any child may accept employment unless he or she has been granted employment authorization.

(8) Denial of petition—

(i) Individual petition. If an individual is denied, the petitioner shall be notified within 30 days after the date a completed petition has been filed of the denial, the reasons for the denial, and the right to appeal the denial.

(ii) Blanket petition. If a blanket petition is denied in whole or in part, the petitioner shall be notified within 30 days after the date a completed petition has been filed of the denial, the reasons for the denial, and the right to appeal the denial. If the petition is denied in part, the USCIS office issuing the denial shall forward to the petitioner, along with the denial, a Form I–797 listing those organizations which were found to quality. If the decision to deny is reversed on appeal, a new Form I–797 shall be sent to the petitioner to reflect the changes made as a result of the appeal.

(9) Revocation of approval of individual and blanket petitions—

(i) General. The director may revoke a petition at any time, even after the expiration of the petition.

(ii) Automatic revocation. The approval of any individual or blanket petition is automatically revoked if the petitioner withdraws the petition or the petitioner fails to request indefinite validity of a blanket petition.

(iii) Revocation on notice.

(A) The director shall send to the petitioner a notice of intent to revoke the petition in relevant part if he/she finds that:

(1) One or more entities are no longer qualifying organizations;

(2) The alien is no longer eligible under section 101(a)(15)(L) of the Act;

(3) A qualifying organization(s) violated requirements of section 101(a)(15)(L) and these regulations;

(4) The statement of facts contained in the petition was not true and correct; or

(5) Approval of the petition involved gross error; or

(6) None of the qualifying organizations in a blanket petition have used the blanket petition procedure for three consecutive years.

(B) The notice of intent to revoke shall contain a detailed statement of the grounds for the revocation and the time period allowed for the petitioner's rebuttal. Upon receipt of this notice, the petitioner may submit evidence in rebuttal within 30 days of the notice. The director shall consider all relevant evidence presented in deciding whether to revoke the petition in whole or in part. If a blanket petition is revoked in part, the remainder of the petition shall remain approved, and a revised Form I–797 shall be sent to the petitioner with the revocation notice.

(iv) Status of beneficiaries. If an individual petition is revoked, the beneficiary shall be required to leave the United States, unless the beneficiary has obtained other work authorization from the Service. If a blanket petition is revoked and the petitioner and beneficiaries already in the United States are otherwise eligible for L classification, the director shall extend the blanket petition for a period necessary to support the stay of those blanket L beneficiaries. The approval notice, Form I–171C, shall include only the names of qualifying organizations and covered beneficiaries. No new beneficiaries may be classified or admitted under this limited extension.

(10) Appeal of denial or revocation of individual or blanket petition—

(i) A petition denied in whole or in part may be appealed under 8 CFR part 103. Since the determination on the Certificate of Eligibility, Form I–129S, is part of the petition process, a denial or revocation of approval of an I–129S is appealable in the same manner as the petition.

(ii) A petition that has been revoked on notice in whole or in part may be appealed under Part 103 of this chapter. Automatic revocations may not be appealed.

(11) Admission. A beneficiary may apply for admission to the United States only while the individual or blanket petition is valid. The beneficiary of an individual petition shall not be admitted for a date past the validity period of the petition. The beneficiary of a blanket petition may be admitted for three years even though the initial validity period of the blanket petition may expire before the end of the three-year period. If the blanket petition will expire while the alien is in the United States, the burden is on the petitioner to file for indefinite validity of the blanket petition or to file an individual petition in the alien's behalf to support the alien's status in the United States. The admission period for any alien under section 101(a)(15)(L) shall not exceed three years unless an extension of stay is granted pursuant to paragraph (*l*)(15) of this section.

(12) L–1 limitation on period of stay—

(i) Limits. An alien who has spent five years in the United States in a specialized knowledge capacity or seven years in the United States in a managerial or executive capacity under section 101(a)(15)(L) and/or (H) of the Act may not be readmitted to the United States under section 101(a)(15)(L) or (H) of the Act unless the alien has resided and been physically present outside the United States, except for brief visits for business or pleasure, for the immediate prior year. Such visits do not interrupt the one year abroad, but do not count towards fulfillment of that requirement. In view of this restriction, a new individual petition may not be approved for an alien who has spent the maximum time period in the United States under section 101(a)(15)(L) and/or (H) of the Act, unless the alien has resided and been physically present outside the United States, except for brief visits for business or pleasure, for the immediate prior year. The petitioner shall provide information about the alien's employment, place of residence, and the dates and purpose of any trips to the United States for the previous year. A consular or Service officer may not grant L classification under a blanket petition to an alien who has spent five years in the United States as a professional with specialized knowledge or seven years in the United States as a manager or executive, unless the alien has met the requirements contained in this paragraph.

(ii) Exceptions. The limitations of paragraph (*l*)(12)(i) of this section shall not apply to aliens who do not reside continually in the United States and whose employment in the United States is seasonal, intermittent, or consists of an aggregate of six months or less per year. In addition, the limitations will not apply to aliens who reside abroad and regularly commute to the United States to engage in part-time employment. The petitioner and the alien must provide clear and convincing proof that the alien qualifies for an exception. Clear and convincing proof shall consist of evidence such as arrival and departure records, copies of tax returns, and records of employment abroad.

(13) Beneficiary's use of Form I–797 and Form I–129S—

(i) Beneficiary of an individual petition. The beneficiary of an individual petition who does not require a nonimmigrant visa may present a copy of Form I–797 at a port of entry to facilitate entry into the United States. The copy of Form I–797 shall be retained by the beneficiary and presented during the validity of the petition (provided that the beneficiary is entering or reentering the United States) for entry and reentry to resume the same employment with the same petitioner (within the validity period of the petition) and to apply for an extension of stay. A beneficiary who is required to present a visa for admission and whose visa will have expired before the date of his or her intended return may use an original Form I–797 to apply for a new or revalidated visa during the validity period of the petition and to apply for an extension of stay.

(ii) Beneficiary of a blanket petition. Each alien seeking L classification and admission under a blanket petition shall present a copy of Form I–797 and a Form I–129S from the petitioner which identifies the position and organization from which the employee is transferring, the new organization and position to which the employee is destined, a description of the employee's actual duties for both the new and former positions, and the positions, dates, and locations of previous L stays in the United States. A current copy of Form I–797 and Form I–129S should be retained by the beneficiary and used for leaving and reentering the United States to resume employment with a qualifying organization during his/her authorized period of stay, for applying for a new or revalidated visa, and for applying for readmission at a port of entry. The alien may be readmitted even though reassigned to a different organization named on the Form I–797 than the one shown on Form I–129S if the job duties are virtually the same.

(14) Extension of visa petition validity—

(i) Individual petition. The petitioner shall file a petition extension on Form I–129 to extend an individual petition under section 101(a)(15)(L) of the Act. Except in those petitions involving new offices, supporting documentation is not required, unless requested by the director. A petition extension may be filed only if the validity of the original petition has not expired.

(ii) New offices. A visa petition under section 101(a)(15)(L) which involved the opening of a new office may be extended by filing a new Form I–129, accompanied by the following:

(A) Evidence that the United States and foreign entities are still qualifying organizations as defined in paragraph (*l*)(1)(ii)(G) of this section;

(B) Evidence that the United States entity has been doing business as defined in paragraph (*l*)(1)(ii)(H) of this section for the previous year;

(C) A statement of the duties performed by the beneficiary for the previous year and the duties the beneficiary will perform under the extended petition;

(D) A statement describing the staffing of the new operation, including the number of employees and types of positions held accompanied by evidence of wages paid to employees when the beneficiary will be employed in a managerial or executive capacity; and

(E) Evidence of the financial status of the United States operation.

(iii) Blanket petitions—

(A) Extension procedure. A blanket petition may only be extended indefinitely by filing a new Form I–129 with a copy of the previous approval notice and a report of admissions during the preceding three years. The report of admissions shall include a list of the aliens admitted under the blanket petition during the preceding three years, including positions held during that period, the employing entity, and the dates of initial admission and final departure of each alien. The petitioner shall state whether it still meets the criteria for filing a blanket petition and shall document any changes in approved relationships and additional qualifying organizations.

(B) Other conditions. If the petitioner in an approved blanket petition fails to request indefinite validity or if indefinite validity is denied, the petitioner and its other qualifying organizations shall seek L classification by filing individual petitions until another three years have expired; after which the petitioner may seek approval of a new blanket petition.

(15) Extension of stay.

(i) In individual petitions, the petitioner must apply for the petition extension and the alien's extension of stay concurrently on Form I–129. When the alien is a beneficiary under a blanket petition, a new certificate of eligibility, accompanied by a copy of the previous approved certificate of eligibility, shall be filed by the petitioner to request an extension of the alien's stay. The petitioner must also request a petition extension. The dates of extension shall be the same for the petition and the beneficiary's extension of stay. The beneficiary must be physically present in the United States at the time the extension of stay is filed. Even though the requests to extend the visa petition and the alien's stay are combined on the petition, the director shall make a separate determination on each. If the alien is required to leave the United States for business or personal reasons while the extension requests are pending, the petitioner may request the director to cable notification of approval of the petition extension to the consular office abroad where the alien will apply for a visa.

(ii) An extension of stay may be authorized in increments of up to two years for beneficiaries of individual and blanket petitions. The total period of stay may not exceed five years for aliens employed in a specialized knowledge capacity. The total period of stay for an alien employed in a managerial or executive capacity may not exceed seven years. No further extensions may be granted. When an alien was initially admitted to the United States in a specialized knowledge capacity and is later promoted to a managerial or executive position, he or she must have been employed in the managerial or executive position for at least six months to be eligible for the total period of stay of seven years. The change to managerial or executive capacity must have been approved by the Service in an amended, new, or extended petition at the time that the change occurred.

(16) Effect of filing an application for or approval of a permanent labor certification, preference petition, or filing of an application for adjustment of status on L–1 classification. An alien may legitimately come to the United States for a temporary period as an L–1 nonimmigrant and, at the same time, lawfully seek to become a permanent resident of the United States provided he or she intends to depart voluntarily at the end of his or her authorized stay. The filing of an application for or approval of a permanent labor certification, an immigrant visa preference petition, or the filing of an application of readjustment of status for an L–1 nonimmigrant shall not be the basis for denying:

(i) An L–1 petition filed on behalf of the alien,

(ii) A request to extend an L–1 petition which had previously been filed on behalf of the alien;

(iii) An application for admission as an L–1 nonimmigrant by the alien, or as an L–2 nonimmigrant by the spouse or child of such alien;

(iv) An application for change of status to H–1 or L–2 nonimmigrant filed by the alien, or to H–1, H–4, or L–1 status filed by the L–2 spouse or child of such alien;

(v) An application for change of status to H–4 nonimmigrant filed by the L–1 nonimmigrant, if his or her spouse has been approved for classification as an H–1; or

(vi) An application for extension of stay filed by the alien, or by the L–2 spouse or child of such alien.

(17) Filing of individual petitions and certifications under blanket petitions for citizens of Canada under the North American Free Trade Agreement (NAFTA).

(i) Individual petitions. Except as provided in paragraph (1)(2)(ii) of this section (filing of blanket petitions), a United States or foreign employer seeking to classify a citizen of Canada as an intracompany transferee may file an individual petition in duplicate on Form I–129 in conjunction with an application for admission of the citizen of Canada. Such filing may be made with an immigration officer at a Class A port of entry located on the United States–Canada land border or at a United States pre-clearance/pre-flight station in Canada. The petitioning employer need not appear, but Form I–129 must bear the authorized signature of the petitioner.

(ii) Certification of eligibility for intracompany transferree under the blanket petition. An immigration officer at a location identified in paragraph (1)(17)(i) of this section may determine eligibility of individual citizens of Canada seeking L classification under approved blanket petitions. At these locations, such citizens of Canada shall present the original and two copies of Form I–129S, Intracompany Transferee Certificate of Eligibility, prepared by the approved organization, as well as three copies of Form I–797, Notice of Approval of Nonimmigrant Visa Petition.

(iii) Nothing in this section shall preclude or discourage the advance filing of petitions and certificates of eligibility in accordance with paragraph (*l*)(2) of this section.

(iv) Deficient or deniable petitions or certificates of eligibility. If a petition or certificate of eligibility submitted concurrently with an application for admission is lacking necessary supporting documentation or is otherwise deficient, the inspecting immigration officer shall return it to the applicant for admission in order to obtain the necessary documentation from the petitioner or for the deficiency to be overcome. The fee to file the petition will be remitted at such time as the documentary or other deficiency is overcome. If the petition or certificate of eligibility is clearly deniable, the immigration officer will accept the petition (with fee) and the petitioner shall be notified of the denial, the reasons for denial, and the right of appeal. If a formal denial order cannot be issued by the port of entry, the petition with a recommendation for denial shall be forwarded to the appropriate Service Center for final action. For the purposes of this provision, the appropriate Service Center will be the one within the same Service region as the location where the application for admission is made.

(v) Spouse and dependent minor children accompanying or following to join.

(A) The Canadian citizen spouse and Canadian citizen unmarried minor children of a Canadian citizen admitted under this paragraph shall be entitled to the same nonimmigrant classification and same length of stay subject to the same limits as the principal alien. They shall not be required to present visas, and they shall be admitted under the classification symbol L–2.

(B) A non-Canadian citizen spouse or non-Canadian citizen unmarried minor child shall be entitled to the same nonimmigrant classification and the same length of stay subject to the same limits as the principal, but shall be required to present a visa upon application for admission as an L–2 unless otherwise exempt under § 212.1 of this chapter.

(C) The spouse and dependent minor children shall not accept employment in the United States unless otherwise authorized under the Act.

(18) Denial of intracompany transferee status to citizens of Canada or Mexico in the case of certain labor disputes.

(i) If the Secretary of Labor certifies to or otherwise informs the Commissioner that a strike or other labor dispute involving a work stoppage of workers is in progress where the beneficiary is to be employed, and the temporary entry of the beneficiary may affect adversely the settlement of such labor dispute or the employment of any person who is involved in such dispute, a petition to classify a citizen of Mexico or Canada as an L–1 intracompany transferee may be denied. If a petition has already been approved, but the alien has not yet entered the United States, or has entered the United States but not yet commenced employment, the approval of the petition may be suspended, and an application for admission on the basis of the petition may be denied.

(ii) If there is a strike or other labor dispute involving a work stoppage of workers in progress, but such strike or other labor dispute is not certified under paragraph (*l*)(18)(i) of this section, or the Service has not otherwise been informed by the Secretary that such a strike or labor dispute is in progress, the Commissioner shall not deny a petition or suspend an approved petition.

(iii) If the alien has already commended employment in the United States under an approved petition and is participating in a strike or other labor dispute involving a work stoppage of workers, whether or not such strike or other labor dispute has been certified by the Department of Labor, the alien shall not be deemed to be failing to maintain his or her status solely on account of past, present, or future participation in a strike or other labor dispute involving a work stoppage of workers, but is subject to the following terms and conditions.

(A) The alien shall remain subject to all applicable provisions of the Immigration and Nationality Act, and regulations promulgated in the same manner as all other L nonimmigrants;

(B) The status and authorized period of stay of such an alien is not modified or extended in any way by virtue of his or her participation in a strike or other labor dispute involving work stoppage of workers; and

(C) Although participation by an L nonimmigrant alien in a strike or other labor dispute involving a work stoppage of workers will not constitute a ground for deportation, any alien who violates his or her status or who remains in the United States after his or her authorized period of stay has expired will be subject to deportation.

[38 FR 35425, Dec. 28, 1973; 48 FR 4769, Feb. 3, 1983; 48 FR 14583, April 5, 1983; 48 FR 19157, April 28, 1983; 48 FR 23159, May 24, 1983; 48 FR 30350, July 1, 1983; 48 FR 41144, Sept. 14, 1983; 49 FR 15183, April 18, 1984; 49 FR 39663, Oct. 10, 1984; 50 FR 42007, Oct. 17, 1985; 51 FR 44267, Dec. 9, 1986; 52 FR 5750, Feb. 26, 1987; 52 FR 7063, March 6, 1987; 52 FR 13226, April 22, 1987; 52 FR 20555, June 1, 1987; 52 FR 48084, Dec. 18, 1987; 53 FR 3331, Feb. 5, 1988; 53 FR 24900, June 30, 1988; 53 FR 26231, July 12, 1988; 53 FR 30017, Aug. 10, 1988; 53 FR 46852, Nov. 21, 1988; 54 FR 14, Jan. 3, 1989; 54 FR 10979, March 16, 1989; 54 FR 48577, Nov. 24, 1989; 54 FR 51816, Dec. 18, 1989; 55 FR 2621, Jan. 26, 1990; 55 FR 5573, Feb. 16, 1990; 55 FR 7881, March 6, 1990; 55 FR 34897, 34900, 34901, Aug. 27, 1990; 56 FR 480, 482, Jan. 7, 1991; 56 FR 2841, Jan. 25, 1991; 56 FR 11916, 11917, March 21, 1991; 56 FR 26017, June 6, 1991; 56 FR 33371, July 22, 1991; 56 FR 38333, Aug. 13, 1991; 56 FR 41624, Aug. 22, 1991; 56 FR 55613, Oct. 29, 1991; 56 FR 61119, 61127, 61130, Dec. 2, 1991; 56 FR 66967, Dec. 27, 1991; 57 FR 749, Jan. 8, 1992; 57 FR 6184, Feb. 21, 1992; 57 FR 10978, April 1, 1992; 57 FR 12178, 12181, 12182, 12186, 12190, April 9, 1992; 57 FR 29193, July 1, 1992; 57 FR 31955, 31956, July 20, 1992; 57 FR 33426, July 29, 1992; 57 FR 40832, Sept. 8, 1992; 57 FR 42884, Sept. 17, 1992; 57 FR 55060, Nov. 24, 1992; 58 FR 58097, Oct. 29, 1993; 58 FR 69210, Dec. 30, 1993; 59 FR 1470, Jan. 11, 1994; 59 FR 26594, May 23, 1994; 59 FR 41830, Aug. 15, 1994; 59 FR 42487, Aug. 18, 1994; 59 FR 51102, Oct. 7, 1994; 59 FR 55910, Nov. 9, 1994; 60 FR 21975, May 4, 1995; 60 FR 44266, Aug. 25, 1995; 60 FR 49195, Sept. 22, 1995; 60 FR 52248, Oct. 5, 1995; 60 FR 62022, Dec. 4, 1995; 61 FR 35935, July 9, 1996; 62 FR 10424, 10425, March 7, 1997; 62 FR 18511, 18512, April 16, 1997; 62 FR 48146, Sept. 12, 1997; 62 FR 50435, Sept. 25, 1997; 62 FR 60122, Nov. 6, 1997; 63 FR 1334, Jan. 9, 1998; 63 FR 31873, June 10, 1998; 63 FR 32115, June 12, 1998; 63 FR 65659, Nov. 30, 1998; 63 FR 71342, Dec. 24, 1998; 64 FR 29211, June 1, 1999; 64 FR 30103, June 4, 1999; 64 FR 32147, June 15, 1999; 64 FR 33346, June 22, 1999; 64 FR 36423, July 6, 1999; 65 FR 7715, Feb. 16, 2000; 65 FR 10684, Feb. 29, 2000; 65 FR 14778, 14779, March 17, 2000; 65 FR 18432, April 7, 2000; 65 FR 43531, July 13, 2000; 65 FR 67617, Nov. 13, 2000; 66 FR 31112, June 11, 2001; 66 FR 42593, Aug. 14, 2001; 66 FR 46702, Sept. 7, 2001; 66 FR 49514, Sept. 28, 2001; 67 FR 18063, April 12, 2002; 67 FR 54945, Aug. 27, 2002; 67 FR 61476, Oct. 1, 2002; 67 FR 71449, Dec. 2, 2002; 67 FR 76270, 76276, Dec. 11, 2002; 68 FR 46929, Aug. 7, 2003; 69 FR 39825, July 1, 2004; 70 FR 23783, May 5, 2005; 72 FR 18860, April 16, 2007; 72 FR 19107, April 17, 2007; 73 FR 15394, Mar. 24, 2008; 73 FR 18954, Apr. 8, 2008; 73 FR 72293, Nov. 26, 2008; 73 FR 76911, Dec. 18, 2008; 73 FR 78127, Dec. 19, 2008; 74 FR 2837, Jan. 16, 2009; 74 FR 26515, June 3, 2009; 74 FR 26938, June 5, 2009; 74 FR 55109, Oct. 27, 2009; 75 FR 47701, Aug. 9, 2010; 75 FR 79277, Dec. 20, 2010; 78 FR 24061, April 24, 2013]

PART 216—CONDITIONAL BASIS OF LAWFUL PERMANENT RESIDENCE STATUS

§ 216.1 Definition of conditional permanent resident. [also 8 C.F.R. § 1216.1]

A conditional permanent resident is an alien who has been lawfully admitted for permanent residence within the meaning of section 101(a)(20) of the Act, except that a conditional permanent resident is also subject to the conditions and responsibilities set forth in section 216 or 216A of the Act, whichever is applicable, and Part 216 of this chapter. Unless otherwise specified, the rights, privileges, responsibilities and duties which apply to all other lawful permanent residents apply equally to conditional permanent residents, including but not limited to the right to apply for naturalization (if otherwise eligible), the right to file petitions on behalf of qualifying relatives, the privilege of residing permanently in the United States as an immigrant in accordance with the immigration laws, such status not having changed; the duty to register with the Selective Service System, when required; and the responsibility for complying with all laws and regulations of the United States. All references within this chapter to lawful permanent residents apply equally to conditional permanent residents, unless otherwise specified. The conditions of section 216 of the Act shall not apply to lawful permanent resident status based on a self-petitioning relationship under section 204(a)(1)(A)(iii), 204(a)(1)(A)(iv), 204(a)(1)(b)(ii), or 204(a)(1)(B)(iii) of the Act or based on eligibility as the derivative child of a self-petitioning spouse under section 204(a)(1)(A)(iii) or 204(a)(1)(B)(ii) of the Act, regardless of the date on which the marriage to the abusive citizen or lawful permanent resident occurred.

[59 FR 26590, May 23, 1994; 61 FR 13079, March 26, 1996]

§ 216.2 Notification requirements. [also 8 C.F.R. § 1216.2]

(a) When alien acquires status of conditional permanent resident. At the time an alien acquires conditional permanent residence through admission to the United States with an immigrant visa or adjustment of status under section 245 of the Act, the Service shall notify the alien of the conditional basis of the alien's status, of the requirement that the alien apply for removal of the conditions within the ninety days immediately preceding the second anniversary of the alien's having been granted such status, and that failure to apply for removal of the conditions will result in automatic termination of the alien's lawful status in the United States.

(b) When alien is required to apply for removal of the conditional basis of lawful permanent resident status. Approximately 90 days before the second anniversary of the date on which the alien obtained conditional permanent residence, the Service should notify the alien a second time of the requirement that the alien and the petitioning spouse or the alien entrepreneur must file a petition to remove the conditional basis of the alien's lawful permanent residence. Such notification shall be mailed to the alien's last known address.

(c) Effect of failure to provide notification. Failure of the Service to provide notification as required by either paragraph (a) or (b) of this section does not relieve the alien and the petitioning spouse, or the alien entrepreneur of the requirement to file a petition to remove conditions within the 90 days immediately preceding the second anniversary of the date on which the alien obtained permanent residence.

[53 FR 30018, Aug. 10, 1988, as amended at 59 FR 26590, May 23, 1994]

§ 216.3 Termination of conditional resident status. [also 8 C.F.R. § 1216.3]

(a) During the two-year conditional period. The director shall send a formal written notice to the conditional permanent resident of the termination of the alien's conditional permanent resident status if the director determines that any of the conditions set forth in section 216(b)(1) or 216A(b)(1) of the Act, whichever is applicable, are true, or it becomes known to the government that an alien entrepreneur who was admitted pursuant to section 203(b)(5) of the Act obtained his or her investment capital through other than legal means (such as through the sale of illegal drugs). If the Service issues a notice of intent to terminate an alien's conditional resident status, the director shall not adjudicate Form I–751 or Form I–829 until it has been determined that the alien's status will not be terminated. During this time, the alien shall continue to be a lawful conditional permanent resident with all the rights, privileges, and responsibilities provided to persons possessing such status. Prior to issuing the notice of termination, the director shall provide the alien with an opportunity to review and rebut the evidence upon which the decision is to be based, in accordance with § 103.2(b)(2) of this chapter. The termination of status, and all of the rights and privileges concomitant thereto (including authorization to accept or continue in employment in this country), shall take effect as of the date of such determination by the director, although the alien may request a review of such determination in removal proceedings. In addition to the notice of termination, the director shall issue a notice to appear in accordance with 8 CFR part 239. During the ensuing removal proceedings, the alien may submit evidence to rebut the determination of the director. The burden of proof shall be on the Service to establish, by a preponderance of the evidence, that one or more of the conditions in section 216(b)(1) or 216A(b)(1) of the Act, whichever is applicable, are true, or that an alien entrepreneur who was admitted pursuant to section 203(b)(5) of the Act obtained his or her investment capital through other than legal means (such as through the sale of illegal drugs).

(b) Determination of fraud after two years. If, subsequent to the removal of the conditional basis of an alien's permanent resident status, the director determines that an alien spouse obtained permanent resident status through a marriage which was entered into for the purpose of evading the immigration laws or an alien entrepreneur obtained permanent resident status through a commercial enterprise which was improper under section 216A(b)(1) of the Act, the director may institute rescission proceedings pursuant to section 246 of the Act (if otherwise appropriate) or removal proceedings under section 240 of the Act.

[53 FR 30019, Aug. 10, 1988; as amended at 59 FR 26590, May 23, 1994; 62 FR 10349, March 6, 1997]

§ 216.4 Joint petition to remove conditional basis of lawful permanent resident status or alien spouse. [also 8 C.F.R. § 1216.4]

(a) Filing the petition—

(1) General procedures. Within the 90–day period immediately preceding the second anniversary of the date on which the alien obtained permanent residence, the alien and the alien's spouse who filed the original immigrant visa petition or fiance/fiancee petition through which the alien obtained permanent residence must file a Petition to Remove the Conditions on Residence (Form I–751) with the Service. The petition shall be filed within this time period regardless of the amount of physical presence which the alien has accumulated in the United States. Before Form I–751 may be considered as properly filed, it must be accompanied by the fee required under § 103.7(b) of this chapter and by documentation as described in paragraph (a)(5) of this section, and it must be properly signed by the alien and the alien's spouse. If the joint petition cannot be filed due to the termination of the marriage through annulment, divorce, or the death of the petitioning spouse, or if the petitioning spouse refuses to join in the filing of the petition, the conditional permanent resident may apply for a waiver of the requirement to file the joint petition in accordance with the provisions of § 216.5 of this part. Upon receipt of a properly filed Form I–751, the alien's conditional permanent resident status shall be extended automatically, if necessary, until such time as the director has adjudicated the petition.

(2) Dependent children. Dependent children of a conditional permanent resident who acquired conditional permanent resident status concurrently with the parent may be included in the joint petition filed by the parent and the parent's petitioning spouse. A child shall be deemed to have acquired conditional residence status concurrently with the parent if the child's residence was acquired on the same date or within 90 days thereafter. Children who cannot be included in a joint petition filed by the parent and parent's petitioning spouse due to the child's not having acquired conditional resident status concurrently with the parent, the death of the parent, or other reasons may file a separate Petition to Remove the Conditions on Residence (Form I–751).

(3) [Reserved.]

(4) Physical presence at time of filing. A petition may be filed regardless of whether the alien is physically present in the United States. However, if the alien is outside the United States at the time of filing, he or she must return to the United States, with his or her spouse and dependent children, to comply with the interview requirements contained in the Act. Furthermore, if the documentation submitted in support of the petition includes affidavits of third parties having knowledge of the bona fides of the marital relationship, the petitioner must arrange for the affiants to be present at the interview, at no expense to the government. Once the petition has been properly filed, the alien may travel outside the United States and return if in possession of documentation as set forth in § 211.1(b)(1) of this chapter, provided the alien and the petitioning spouse comply with the interview requirements described in § 216.4(b). An alien who is not physically present in the United States during the filing period but subsequently applies for admission to the United States shall be processed in accordance with § 235.11 of this chapter.

(5) Documentation. Form I–751 shall be accompanied by evidence that the marriage was not entered into for the purpose of evading the immigration laws of the United States. Such evidence may include:

(i) Documentation showing joint ownership of property;

(ii) Lease showing joint tenancy of a common residence;

(iii) Documentation showing commingling of financial resources;

(iv) Birth certificates of children born to the marriage;

(v) Affidavits of third parties having knowledge of the bona fides of the marital relationship, or

(vi) Other documentation establishing that the marriage was not entered into in order to evade the immigration laws of the United States.

(6) Termination of status for failure to file petition. Failure to properly file Form I–751 within the 90–day period immediately preceding the second anniversary of the date on which the alien obtained lawful permanent residence on a conditional basis shall result in the automatic termination of the alien's permanent residence status and the initiation of proceedings to remove the alien from the United States. In such proceedings the burden shall be on the alien to establish that he or she complied with the requirement to file the joint petition within the designated period. Form I–751 may be filed after the expiration of the 90–day period only if the alien establishes to the satisfaction of the director, in writing, that there was good cause for the failure to file Form I–751 within the required time period. If the joint petition is filed prior to the jurisdiction vesting with the immigration judge in removal proceedings and the director excuses the late filing and approves the petition, he or she shall restore the alien's permanent residence status, remove the conditional basis of such status and cancel any outstanding notice to appear in accordance with § 239.2 of this chapter. If the joint petition is not filed until after jurisdiction vests with the immigration judge, the immigration judge may terminate the matter upon joint motion by the alien and the Service.

(b) Interview—

(1) Authority to waive interview. The director of the regional service center shall review the Form I–751 filed by the alien and the alien's spouse to determine whether to waive the interview required by the Act. If satisfied that the marriage was not for the purpose of evading the immigration laws, the regional service center director may waive the interview and approve the petition. If not so satisfied, then the regional service center director shall forward the petition to the district director having jurisdiction over the place of the alien's residence so that an interview of both the alien and the alien's spouse may be conducted. The director must either waive the requirement for an interview and adjudicate the petition or arrange for an interview within 90 days of the date on which the petition was properly filed.

(2) Location of interview. Unless waived, an interview on the Form I–751 shall be conducted by an immigration examiner or other officer so designated by the district director at the district office, files control office or suboffice having jurisdiction over the residence of the joint petitioners.

(3) Termination of status for failure to appear for interview. If the conditional resident alien and/or the petitioning spouse fail to appear for an interview in connection with the joint petition required by section 216(c) of the Act, the alien's permanent residence status will be automatically terminated as of the second anniversary of the date on which the alien obtained permanent residence. The alien shall be provided with written notification of the termination and the reasons therefor, and a notice to appear shall be issued placing the alien under removal proceedings. The alien may seek review of the decision to terminate his or her status in such proceedings, but the burden shall be on the alien to establish compliance with the interview requirements. If the alien submits a written request that the interview be rescheduled or that the interview be waived, and the director determines that there is good cause for granting the request, the interview may be rescheduled or waived, as appropriate. If the interview is rescheduled at the request of the petitioners, the Service shall not be required to conduct the interview within the 90–day period following the filing of the petition.

(c) Adjudication of petition. The director shall adjudicate the petition within 90 days of the date of the interview, unless the interview is waived in accordance with paragraph (b)(1) of this section. In adjudicating the petition the director shall determine whether—

(1) The qualifying marriage was entered into in accordance with the laws of the place where the marriage took place;

(2) The qualifying marriage has been judicially annulled or terminated, other than through the death of a spouse;

(3) The qualifying marriage was entered into for the purpose of procuring permanent residence status for the alien; or

(4) A fee or other consideration was given (other than a fee or other consideration to an attorney for assistance in preparation of a lawful petition) in connection with the filing of the petition through which the alien obtained conditional permanent residence. If derogatory information is determined regarding any of these issues, the director shall offer the petitioners the opportunity to rebut such information. If the petitioners fail to overcome such derogatory information the director may deny the joint petition, terminate the alien's permanent residence, and issue a notice to appear to initiate removal proceedings. If derogatory information not relating to any of these issues is determined during the course of the interview, such information shall be forwarded to the investigations unit for appropriate action. If no unresolved derogatory information is determined relating to these issues, the petition shall be approved and the conditional basis of the alien's permanent residence status removed, regardless of any action taken or contemplated regarding other possible grounds for removal.

(d) Decision—

(1) Approval. If the director approves the joint petition he or she shall provide written notice of the decision to the alien and shall require the alien to report to the appropriate office of the Service for processing for a new Permanent Resident Card (if necessary), at which time the alien shall surrender any Permanent Resident Card previously issued.

(2) Denial. If the director denies the joint petition, he or she shall provide written notice to the alien of the decision and the reason(s) therefor and shall issue a notice to appear under section 239 of the Act and 8 CFR part 239. The alien's lawful permanent resident status shall be terminated as of the date of the director's written decision. The alien shall also be instructed to surrender any Permanent Resident Card previously issued by the Service. No appeal shall lie from the decision of the director; however, the alien may seek review of the decision in removal proceedings. In such proceedings the burden of proof shall be on the Service to establish, by a preponderance of the evidence, that the facts and information set forth by the petitioners are not true or that the petition was properly denied.

[54 FR 30369, July 20, 1989; 59 FR 26590, 26591, May 23, 1994; 62 FR 10349, March 6, 1997; 63 FR 70315, Dec. 21, 1998; 74 FR 26939, June 5, 2009]

§ 216.5 Waiver of requirement to file joint petition to remove conditions by alien spouse. [also 8 C.F.R. § 1216.5]

(a) General.

(1) A conditional resident alien who is unable to meet the requirements under section 216 of the Act for a joint petition for removal of the conditional basis of his or her permanent resident status may file Form I–751, Petition to Remove the Conditions on

Residence, if the alien requests a waiver, was not at fault in failing to meet the filing requirement, and the conditional resident alien is able to establish that:

(i) Deportation or removal from the United States would result in extreme hardship;

(ii) The marriage upon which his or her status was based was entered into in good faith by the conditional resident alien, but the marriage was terminated other than by death, and the conditional resident was not at fault in failing to file a timely petition; or

(iii) The qualifying marriage was entered into in good faith by the conditional resident but during the marriage the alien spouse or child was battered by or subjected to extreme cruelty committed by the citizen or permanent resident spouse or parent.

(2) A conditional resident who is in exclusion, deportation, or removal proceedings may apply for the waiver only until such time as there is a final order of exclusion, deportation or removal.

(b) Fee. Form I–751 shall be accompanied by the appropriate fee required under § 103.7(b) of this Chapter.

(c) [Reserved.]

(d) Interview. The service center director may refer the application to the appropriate local office and require that the alien appear for an interview in connection with the application for a waiver. The director shall deny the application and initiate removal proceedings if the alien fails to appear for the interview as required, unless the alien establishes good cause for such failure and the interview is rescheduled.

(e) Adjudication of waiver application.

(1) Application based on claim of hardship. In considering an application for a waiver based upon an alien's claim that extreme hardship would result from the alien's removal from the United States, the director shall take into account only those factors that arose subsequent to the alien's entry as a conditional permanent resident. The director shall bear in mind that any removal from the United States is likely to result in a certain degree of hardship, and that only in those cases where the hardship is extreme should the application for a waiver be granted. The burden of establishing that extreme hardship exists rests solely with the applicant.

(2) Application for waiver based upon the alien's claim that the marriage was entered into in good faith. In considering whether an alien entered into a qualifying marriage in good faith, the director shall consider evidence relating to the amount of commitment by both parties to the marital relationship. Such evidence may include—

(i) Documentation relating to the degree to which the financial assets and liabilities of the parties were combined;

(ii) Documentation concerning the length of time during which the parties cohabited after the marriage and after the alien obtained permanent residence;

(iii) Birth certificates of children born to the marriage; and

(iv) Other evidence deemed pertinent by the director.

(3) Application for waiver based on alien's claim of having been battered or subjected to extreme mental cruelty. A conditional resident who entered into the qualifying marriage in good faith, and who was battered or was the subject of extreme cruelty or whose child was battered by or was the subject of extreme cruelty perpetrated by the United States citizen or permanent resident spouse during the marriage, may request a waiver of the joint filing requirement. The conditional resident parent of a battered or abused child may apply for the waiver regardless of the child's citizenship or immigration status.

(i) For the purpose of this chapter the phrase "was battered by or was the subject of extreme cruelty" includes, but is not limited to, being the victim of any act or threatened act of violence, including any forceful detention, which results or threatens to result in physical or mental injury. Psychological or sexual abuse or exploitation, including rape, molestation, incest (if the victim is a minor) or forced prostitution shall be considered acts of violence.

(ii) A conditional resident or former conditional resident who has not departed the United States after termination of resident status may apply for the waiver. The conditional resident may apply for the waiver regardless of his or her present marital status. The conditional resident may still be residing with the citizen or permanent resident spouse, or may be divorced or separated.

(iii) Evidence of physical abuse may include, but is not limited to, expert testimony in the form of reports and affidavits from police, judges, medical personnel, school officials and social service agency personnel. The Service must be satisfied with the credibility of the sources of documentation submitted in support of the application.

(iv) The Service is not in a position to evaluate testimony regarding a claim of extreme mental cruelty provided by unlicensed or untrained individuals. Therefore, all waiver applications based upon claims of extreme mental cruelty must be supported by the evaluation of a professional recognized by the Service as an expert in the field. An evaluation which was obtained in the course of the divorce proceedings may be submitted if it was provided by a professional recognized by the Service as an expert in the field.

(v) The evaluation must contain the professional's full name, professional address and license number. It must also identify the licensing, certifying, or registering authority. The Service retains the right to verify the professional's license.

(vi) The Service's decision on extreme mental cruelty waivers will be based upon the evaluation of the recognized professional. The Service reserves the right to request additional evaluations from expert witnesses chosen by the Service. Requests for additional evaluations must be authorized by the Assistant Regional Commissioner for Adjudications.

(vii) Licensed clinical social workers, psychologists, and psychiatrists are professionals recognized by the Service for the purpose of this section. A clinical social worker who is not licensed only because the state in which he or she practices does not provide for licensing will be considered a licensed professional recognized by the Service if he or she is included in the Register of Clinical Social Workers published by the National Association of Social Workers or is certified by the American Board of Examiners in Clinical Social Work.

(viii) As directed by the statute, the information contained in the application and supporting documents shall not be released without a court order or the written consent of the applicant; or, in the case of a child, the written consent of the parent or legal guardian who filed the waiver application on the child's behalf. Information may be released only to the applicant, his or her authorized representative, an officer of the Department of Justice, or any federal or State law enforcement agency. Any information provided under this part may be used for the purposes of enforcement of the Act or in any criminal proceeding.

(f) Decision. The director shall provide the alien with written notice of the decision on the application for waiver. If the decision is adverse, the director shall advise the alien of the reasons therefor, notify the alien of the termination of his or her permanent residence status, instruct the alien to surrender any Permanent Resident Card issued by the Service and issue a notice to appear placing the alien in removal proceedings. No appeal shall lie from the decision of the director; however, the alien may seek review of such decision in removal proceedings.

[56 FR 22637, May 16, 1991; 59 FR 26591, May 23, 1994; 62 FR 10350, March 6, 1997; 63 FR 70315, Dec. 21, 1998; 74 FR 26939, June 5, 2009]

PART 223—REENTRY PERMITS, REFUGEE TRAVEL DOCUMENTS, AND ADVANCE PAROLE DOCUMENTS

§ 223.1 Purpose of documents.

(a) Reentry permit. A reentry permit allows a permanent resident to apply for admission to the United States upon return from abroad during the period of the permit's validity without the necessity of obtaining a returning resident visa.

(b) Refugee travel document. A refugee travel document is issued pursuant to this part and article 28 of the United Nations Convention of July 29, 1951, for the purpose of travel. Except as provided in § 223.3(d)(2)(i), a person who holds refugee status pursuant to section 207 of the Act, or asylum status pursuant to section 208 of the Act, must have a refugee travel document to return to the United States after temporary travel abroad unless he or she is in possession of a valid advance parole document.

[59 FR 47063, Sept. 14, 1994; 62 FR 10352, March 6, 1997]

§ 223.2 Application and processing.

(a) Application. An applicant must submit an application for a reentry permit, refugee travel document, or advance parole on the form designated by USCIS with the fee prescribed in 8 CFR 103.7(b)(1) and in accordance with the form instructions.

(b) Filing eligibility—

(1) Reentry permit. An applicant for a reentry permit must file such application while in the United States and in status as a lawful permanent resident or conditional permanent resident.

(2) Refugee travel document—

(i) Except as provided in paragraph (b)(2)(ii) of this section, an applicant for a refugee travel document must submit the application while in the United States and in valid refugee status under section 207 of the Act, valid asylum status under section 208 of the Act or is a permanent resident who received such status as a direct result of his or her asylum or refugee status.

(ii) Discretionary authority to accept a refugee travel document application from an alien not within the United States. As a matter of discretion, the Service office with jurisdiction over a port-of-entry or pre-flight inspection location where the alien is seeking admission, or the overseas Service office where the alien is physically present, may accept and adjudicate an application for a refugee travel document from an alien who previously had been admitted to the United

States as a refugee, or who previously had been granted asylum status in the United States, and who departed from the United States without having applied for such refugee travel document, provided the officer:

(A) Is satisfied that the alien did not intend to abandon his or her refugee or asylum status at the time of departure from the United States;

(B) The alien did not engage in any activities while outside the United States that would be inconsistent with continued refugee or asylum status; and

(C) The alien has been outside the United States for less than 1 year since his or her last departure.

(c) Ineligibility—

(1) Prior document still valid. An application for a reentry permit or refugee travel document will be denied if the applicant was previously issued a reentry permit or refugee travel document which is still valid, unless it was returned to USCIS or it is demonstrated that it was lost.

(2) Extended absences. A reentry permit issued to a person who, since becoming a permanent resident, or during the last five years, whichever is less, has been outside the United States for more than four years in the aggregate, shall be limited to a validity of one year, except that a permit with a validity of two years may be issued to:

(i) A permanent resident described in 8 CFR 211.1(a)(6) or (a)(7);

(ii) A permanent resident employed by a public international organization of which the United States is a member by treaty or statute, and his or her permanent resident spouse and children; or

(iii) A permanent resident who is a professional athlete who regularly competes in the United States and worldwide.

(3) Permanent resident entitled to nonimmigrant diplomatic or treaty status. A permanent resident entitled to nonimmigrant status under section 101(a)(15)(A), (E), or (G) of the Act because of occupational status may only be issued a reentry permit if the applicant executes and submits with the application, or has previously executed and submitted, a written waiver as required by 8 CFR part 247.

(d) Effect of travel before a decision is made. Departure from the United States before a decision is made on an application for a reentry permit or refugee travel document will not affect the application.

(e) Processing. USCIS may approve or deny a request for a reentry permit or refugee travel document as an exercise of discretion. If it approves the application, USCIS will issue an appropriate document.

(f) Effect on proceedings. Issuance of a reentry permit or refugee travel document to a person in exclusion, deportation, or removal proceedings shall not affect those proceedings.

(g) Appeal. Denial of an application for a reentry permit or refugee travel document may be appealed in accordance with 8 CFR 103.3.

[62 FR 10352, March 6, 1997; 76 FR 53784, Aug. 29, 2011.]

§ 223.3 Validity and effect on admissibility.

(a) Validity—

(1) Reentry permit. Except as provided in § 223.2(c)(2), a reentry permit issued to a permanent resident shall be valid for 2 years from the date of issuance. A reentry permit issued to a conditional permanent resident shall be valid for 2 years from the date of issuance, or to the date the conditional permanent resident must apply for removal of the conditions on his or her status, whichever comes first.

(2) Refugee travel document. A refugee travel document shall be valid for 1 year, or to the date the refugee or asylee status expires, whichever comes first.

(b) Invalidation. A document issued under this part is invalid if obtained through material false representation or concealment, or if the person is ordered excluded or deported. A refugee travel document is also invalid if the United Nations Convention of July 28, 1951, ceases to apply or does not apply to the person as provided in Article 1C, D, E, or F of the convention.

(c) Extension. A reentry permit or refugee travel document may not be extended.

(d) Effect on admissibility—

(1) Reentry permit. A permanent resident or conditional permanent resident in possession of a valid reentry permit who is otherwise admissible shall not be deemed to have abandoned status based solely on the duration of an absence or absences while the permit is valid.

(2) Refugee travel document—

(i) Inspection and immigration status. Upon arrival in the United States, an alien who presents a valid unexpired refugee travel document, or who has been allowed to file an application for a refugee travel document and this application has been approved under the procedure set forth in § 223.2(b)(2)(ii), shall be examined as to his or her admissibility under the Act. An alien shall be accorded the immigration status endorsed in his or her refugee travel document, or (in the case of an alien discussed in § 223.2(b)(2)(ii)) which will be endorsed in such document, unless he or she is no longer eligible for that status, or he or she applies for and is found eligible for some other immigration status.

(ii) Inadmissibility. If an alien who presents a valid unexpired refugee travel document appears to the examining immigration officer to be inadmissible, he or she shall be referred for proceedings under section 240 of the Act. Section 235(c) of the Act shall not be applicable.

[62 FR 10353, March 6, 1997]

PART 235—INSPECTION OF PERSONS APPLYING FOR ADMISSION

§ 235.1 Scope of examination.

(a) General. Application to lawfully enter the United States shall be made in person to an immigration officer at a U.S. port-of-entry when the port is open for inspection, or as otherwise designated in this section.

(b) U.S. Citizens. A person claiming U.S. citizenship must establish that fact to the examining officer's satisfaction and must present a U.S. passport or alternative documentation as required by 22 CFR part 53. If such applicant for admission fails to satisfy the examining immigration officer that he or she is a U.S. citizen, he or she shall thereafter be inspected as an alien. A U.S. citizen must present a valid unexpired U.S. passport book upon entering the United States, unless he or she presents one of the following documents:

(1) Passport Card. A U.S. citizen who possesses a valid unexpired United States passport card, as defined in 22 CFR 53.1, may present the passport card when entering the United States from contiguous territory or adjacent islands at land or sea ports-of-entry.

(2) Merchant Mariner Document. A U.S. citizen who holds a valid Merchant Mariner Document (MMD) issued by the U.S. Coast Guard may present an unexpired MMD used in conjunction with official maritime business when entering the United States.

(3) Military Identification. Any U.S. citizen member of the U.S. Armed Forces who is in the uniform of, or bears documents identifying him or her as a member of, such Armed Forces, and who is coming to or departing from the United States under official orders or permit of such Armed Forces, may present a military identification card and the official orders when entering the United States.

(4) Trusted Traveler Programs. A U.S. citizen who travels as a participant in the NEXUS, FAST, or SENTRI programs may present a valid NEXUS program card when using a NEXUS Air kiosk or a valid NEXUS, FAST, or SENTRI card at a land or sea port-of-entry prior to entering the United States from contiguous territory or adjacent islands. A U.S. citizen who enters the United States by pleasure vessel from Canada using the remote inspection system may present a NEXUS program card.

(5) Certain Cruise Ship Passengers. A U.S. citizen traveling entirely within the Western Hemisphere is permitted to present a government-issued photo identification document in combination with either an original or a copy of his or her birth certificate, a Consular Report of Birth Abroad issued by the Department of State, or a Certificate of Naturalization issued by U.S. Citizenship and Immigration Services for entering the United States when the United States citizen:

(i) Boards a cruise ship at a port or place within the United States; and,

(ii) Returns on the return voyage of the same cruise ship to the same United States port or place from where he or she originally departed.

On such cruises, U.S. Citizens under the age of 16 may present an original or a copy of a birth certificate, a Consular Report of Birth Abroad, or a Certificate of Naturalization issued by U.S. Citizenship and Immigration Services.

(6) Native American Holders of an American Indian Card. A Native American holder of a Form I–872 American Indian Card arriving from contiguous territory or adjacent islands may present the Form I–872 card prior to entering the United States at a land or sea port-of-entry.

(7) Native American Holders of Tribal Documents. A U.S. citizen holder of a tribal document issued by a United States qualifying tribal entity or group of United States qualifying tribal entities, as provided in paragraph (e) of this section, who is arriving from contiguous territory or adjacent islands may present the tribal document prior to entering the United States at a land or sea port-of-entry.

(8) Children. A child who is a United States citizen entering the United States from contiguous territory at a sea or land ports-of-entry may present certain other documents, if the arrival falls under subsection (i) or (ii).

(i) Children Under Age 16. A U.S. citizen who is under the age of 16 is permitted to present either an original or a copy of his or her birth certificate, a Consular Report of Birth Abroad issued by the Department of State, or a Certificate of Naturalization issued by U.S. Citizenship and Immigration Services when entering the United States from contiguous territory at land or sea ports-of-entry.

(ii) Groups of Children Under Age 19. A U.S. citizen, who is under age 19 and is traveling with a public or private school group, religious group, social or cultural organization, or team associated with a youth sport organization is permitted to present either an original or a copy of his or her birth certificate, a Consular Report of Birth Abroad issued by the Department of State, or a Certificate of Naturalization issued by U.S. Citizenship and Immigration Services when arriving from contiguous territory at land or sea ports-of-entry, when the group, organization, or team is under the supervision of an adult affiliated with the group, organization, or team and when the child has parental or legal guardian consent to travel. For purposes of this paragraph, an adult is considered to be a person age 19 or older. The following requirements will apply:

(A) The group or organization must provide to CBP upon crossing the border, on organizational letterhead:

(1) The name of the group, organization or team, and the name of the supervising adult;

(2) A list of the children on the trip;

(3) For each child, the primary address, primary phone number, date of birth, place of birth, and name of a parent or legal guardian.

(B) The adult leading the group, organization, or team must demonstrate parental or legal guardian consent by certifying in the writing submitted in paragraph (b)(8)(ii)(A) of this section that he or she has obtained for each child the consent of at least one parent or legal guardian.

(C) The inspection procedure described in this paragraph is limited to members of the group, organization, or team who are under age 19. Other members of the group, organization, or team must comply with other applicable document and/or inspection requirements found in this part.

(c) Alien members of United States Armed Forces and members of a force of a NATO country. Any alien member of the United States Armed Forces who is in the uniform of, or bears documents identifying him or her as a member of, such Armed Forces, and who is coming to or departing from the United States under official orders or permit of such Armed Forces is not subject to the removal provisions of the Act. A member of the force of a NATO country signatory to Article III of the Status of Forces Agreement seeking to enter the United States under official orders is exempt from the control provision of the Act. Any alien who is a member of either of the foregoing classes may, upon request, be inspected and his or her entry as an alien may be recorded. If the alien does not appear to the examining immigration officer to be clearly and beyond a doubt entitled to enter the United States under the provisions of the Act, the alien shall be so informed and his or her entry shall not be recorded.

(d) Enhanced Driver's License Projects; alternative requirements. Upon the designation by the Secretary of Homeland Security of an enhanced driver's license as an acceptable document to denote identity and citizenship for purposes of entering the United States, U.S. and Canadian citizens may be permitted to present these documents in lieu of a passport upon entering or seeking admission to the United States according to the terms of the agreements entered between the Secretary of Homeland Security and the entity. The Secretary of Homeland Security will announce, by publication of a notice in the Federal Register, documents designated under this paragraph. A list of the documents designated under this paragraph will also be made available to the public.

(e) Native American Tribal Cards; alternative requirements. Upon the designation by the Secretary of Homeland Security of a United States qualifying tribal entity document as an acceptable document to denote identity and citizenship for purposes of entering the United States, Native Americans may be permitted to present tribal cards upon entering or seeking admission to the United States according to the terms of the voluntary agreement entered between the Secretary of Homeland Security and the tribe. The Secretary of Homeland Security will announce, by publication of a notice in the Federal Register, documents designated under this paragraph. A list of the documents designated under this paragraph will also be made available to the public.

(f) Alien applicants for admission.

(1) Each alien seeking admission at a United States port-of-entry must present whatever documents are required and must establish to the satisfaction of the inspecting officer that the alien is not subject to removal under the immigration laws, Executive Orders, or Presidential Proclamations, and is entitled, under all of the applicable provisions of the immigration laws and this chapter, to enter the United States.

(i) A person claiming to have been lawfully admitted for permanent residence must establish that fact to the satisfaction of the inspecting officer and must present proper documents in accordance with § 211.1 of this chapter.

(ii) The Secretary of Homeland Security or his designee may require any alien, other than aliens exempted under paragraph (iv) of this section or Canadian citizens under section 101(a)(15)(B) of the Act who are not otherwise required to present a visa or be issued Form I–94 (see § 1.4) or Form I–95 for admission or parole into the United States, to provide fingerprints, photograph(s) or other specified biometric identifiers, documentation of his or her immigration status in the

United States, and such other evidence as may be requested to determine the alien's identity and whether he or she has properly maintained his or her status while in the United States and/or whether he or she is admissible. The failure of an alien at the time of inspection to comply with any requirement to provide biometric identifiers may result in a determination that the alien is inadmissible under section 212(a) of the Immigration and Nationality Act or any other law.

(iii) Aliens who are required under paragraph (d)(1)(ii) to provide biometric identifier(s) at inspection may also be subject to the departure requirements for biometrics contained in § 215.8 of this chapter, unless otherwise exempted.

(iv) The requirements of paragraph (d)(1)(ii) shall not apply to:

(A) Aliens younger than 14 or older than 79 on date of admission;

(B) Aliens admitted on A–1, A–2, C–3 (except for attendants, servants, or personal employees of accredited officials), G–1, G–2, G–3, G–4, NATO–1, NATO–2, NATO–3, NATO–4, NATO–5, or NATO–6 visas, and certain Taiwan officials who hold E–1 visas and members of their immediate families who hold E–1 visas unless the Secretary of State and the Secretary of Homeland Security jointly determine that a class of such aliens should be subject to the requirements of paragraph (d)(1)(ii);

(C) Classes of aliens to whom the Secretary of Homeland Security and the Secretary of State jointly determine it shall not apply; or

(D) An individual alien to whom the Secretary of Homeland Security, the Secretary of State, or the Director of Central Intelligence determines it shall not apply.

(2) An alien present in the United States who has not been admitted or paroled or an alien who seeks entry at other than an open, designated port-of-entry, except as otherwise permitted in this section, is subject to the provisions of section 212(a) of the Act and to removal under section 235(b) or 240 of the Act.

(3) An alien who is brought to the United States, whether or not to a designated port-of-entry and regardless of the means of transportation, after having been interdicted in international or United States waters, is considered an applicant for admission and shall be examined under section 235(b) of the Act.

(4) An alien stowaway is not an applicant for admission and may not be admitted to the United States. A stowaway shall be removed from the United States under section 235(a)(2) of the Act. The provisions of section 240 of the Act are not applicable to stowaways, nor is the stowaway entitled to further hearing or review of the removal, except that an alien stowaway who indicates an intention to apply for asylum, or expresses a fear of persecution, a fear of torture, or a fear of return to the country of proposed removal shall be referred to an asylum officer for a determination of credible fear of persecution or torture in accordance with section 235(b)(1)(B) of the Act and § 208.30 of this chapter. An alien stowaway who is determined to have a credible fear of persecution or torture shall have his or her asylum application adjudicated in accordance with § 208.2(b)(2) of this chapter.

(g) U.S. citizens, lawful permanent residents of the United States, and other aliens, entering the United States along the northern border, other than at a port–of–entry. A citizen of Canada or a permanent resident of Canada who is a national of a country listed in § 217.2(a) of this chapter may, if in possession of a valid, unexpired, Canadian Border Boat Landing Permit (Form I–68) or evidence of enrollment in any other Service Alternative Inspections program (e.g., the Immigration and Naturalization Service Passenger Accelerated Service System (INSPASS) or the Port Passenger Accelerated Service System (PORTPASS)), enter the United States by means of a pleasure craft along the northern border of the United States from time–to–time without further inspection. No persons other than those described in this paragraph may participate in this program. Permanent residents of Canada who are nationals of a designated Visa Waiver Program country listed in § 217.2(a) of this chapter must be in possession of a valid, unexpired passport issued by his or her country of nationality, and an unexpired multiple entry Form I–94W, Nonimmigrant Visa Waiver Arrival/Departure Form, or an unexpired passport, valid unexpired United States visa and I–94 Arrival/Departure Form. When an entry to the United States is made by a person who is a Canadian citizen or a permanent resident of *5194 Canada who is a national of a designated Visa Waiver Program country listed in § 217.2(a) of this chapter, entry may be made under this program only for a purpose as described in section 101(a)(15)(B)(ii) of the Act as a visitor for pleasure. Persons seeking to enter the United States for any other purpose must do so at a port–of–entry staffed by immigration inspectors. Persons aboard a vessel which has crossed the international boundary between the United States and Canada and who do not intend to land in the United States, other than at a staffed port–of–entry, are not required to be in possession of Form I–68, Canadian Border Boat Landing Permit, or evidence of enrollment in an Alternative Inspections program merely because they have crossed the international boundary. However, the Service retains the right to conduct inspections or examinations of all persons applying for admission or readmission to or seeking transit through the United States in accordance with the Act.

(1) Application. An eligible applicant may apply for a Canadian Border Boat Landing Permit by completing the Form I–68 in triplicate. Application forms will be made readily available through the Internet, from a Service office, or by mail. A family may apply on a single application. For the purposes of this paragraph, a family is defined as a husband, wife, unmarried children under the age of 21, and the parents of either husband or wife, who reside at the same address. In order for the I–68 application to be considered complete, it must be accompanied by the following:

(i) For each person included on the application, evidence of citizenship, and, if not a citizen of the United States or Canada, evidence of legal permanent resident status in either the United States or Canada. Evidence of residency must be submitted by all applicants. It is not required that all persons on the application be of the same nationality; however, they must all be individually eligible to participate in this program.

(ii) If multiple members of a family, as defined in paragraph (e)(1) of this section, are included on a single application, evidence of the familial relationship.

(iii) A fee as prescribed in § 103.7(b)(1) of this chapter.

(iv) A copy of any previously approved Form I–68.

(v) A permanent resident of Canada who is a national of a Visa Waiver Program may apply for admission simultaneously with the Form I–68 application and thereby obtain a Form I–94 or I–94W.

(2) Submission of Form I–68. Except as indicated in this paragraph, Form I–68 shall be properly completed and submitted in person, along with the documentary evidence and the required fee as specified in § 103.7(b)(1) of this chapter, to a United States immigration officer at a Canadian border Port-of-Entry located within the district having jurisdiction over the applicant's residence or intended place of landing. Persons previously granted Form I–68 approval may apply by mail to the issuing Service office for renewal if a copy of the previous Form I–68 is included in the application. At the discretion of the district director concerned, any applicant for renewal of Form I–68 may be required to appear for an interview in person if the applicant does not appear to be clearly eligible for renewal.

(3) Denial of Form I–68. If the applicant has committed a violation of any immigration or customs regulation or, in the case of an alien, is inadmissible to the United States, approval of the Form I–68 shall be denied. However, if, in the exercise of discretion, the district director waives under section 212(d)(3) of the Act all applicable grounds of inadmissibility, the I–68 application may be approved for such non-citizens. If the Form I–68 application is denied, the applicant shall be given written notice of and the reasons for the denial by letter from the district director. There is no appeal from the denial of the Form I–68 application, but the denial is without prejudice to a subsequent application for this program or any other

Service benefit, except that the applicant may not submit a subsequent Form I–68 application for 90 days after the date of the last denial.

(4) Validity. Form I–68 shall be valid for 1 year from the date of issuance, or until revoked or violated [sic] by the Service.

(5) Conditions for participation in the I–68 program. Upon being inspected and positively identified by an immigration officer and found admissible and eligible for participation in the I–68 program, a participant must agree to abide by the following conditions:

(i) Form I–68 may be used only when entering the United States by means of a vessel exclusively used for pleasure, including chartered vessels when such vessel has been chartered by an approved Form I–68 holder. When used by a person who is a not a citizen or a lawful permanent resident of the United States, admission shall be for a period not to exceed 72 hours to visit within 25 miles of the shore line along the northern border of the United States, including the shore line of Lake Michigan and Puget Sound.

(ii) Participants must be in possession of any authorization documents issued for participation in this program or another Service Alternative Inspections program (INSPASS or PORTPASS). Participants over the age of 15 years and who are not in possession of an INSPASS or PORTPASS enrollment card must also be in possession of a photographic identification document issued by a governmental agency. Participants who are permanent residents of Canada who are nationals of a Visa Waiver Program country listed in § 217.2(a) of this chapter must also be in possession of proper documentation as described in paragraph (e) of this section.

(iii) Participants may not import merchandise or transport controlled or restricted items while entering the United States under this program. The entry of any merchandise or goods must be in accordance with the laws and regulations of all Federal Inspection Services.

(iv) Participants must agree to random checks or inspections that may be conducted by the Service, at any time and at any location, to ensure compliance.

(v) Participants must abide by all Federal, state, and local laws regarding the importation of alcohol or agricultural products or the importation or possession of controlled substances as defined in section 101 of the Controlled Substance Act (21 U.S.C. 802).

(vi) Participants acknowledge that all devices, decals, cards, or other Federal Government supplied identification or technology used to identify or inspect persons or vessels seeking entry via this program remain the property of the United States Government at all times, and must be surrendered upon request by a Border Patrol Agent or any other officer of a Federal Inspection Service.

(vii) The captain, charterer, master, or owner (if aboard) of each vessel bringing persons into the United States is responsible for determining that all persons aboard the vessel are in possession of a valid, unexpired Form I–68 or other evidence of participation in a Service Alternative Inspections program (INSPASS or PORTPASS) prior to entry into the territorial waters of the United States. If any person on board is not in possession of such evidence, the captain, charterer, master, or owner must transport such person to a staffed United States Port-of-Entry for an in-person immigration inspection.

(6) Revocation. The district director, the chief patrol agent, or their designated representatives may revoke the designation of any participant who violates any condition of this program, as contained in paragraph (e)(5) of this section, or who has violated any immigration law or regulation, or a law or regulation of the United States Customs Service or other Federal Inspection Service, has abandoned his or her residence in the United States or Canada, is inadmissible to the United States, or who is otherwise determined by an immigration officer to be ineligible for continued participation in this program. Such persons may be subject to other applicable sanctions, such as criminal and/or administrative prosecution or deportation, as well as possible seizure of goods and/or vessels. If permission to participate is revoked, a written request to the district director for restoration of permission to participate may be made. The district director will notify the person of his or her decision and the reasons therefore in writing.

(7) Compliance checking. Participation in this program does not relieve the holder from responsibility to comply with all other aspects of United States Immigration, Customs, or other Federal inspection service laws or regulations. To prevent abuse, the United States Immigration and Naturalization Service retains the right to conduct inspections or examinations of all persons applying for admission or readmission to or seeking transit through the United States in accordance with the Immigration and Nationality Act.

(h) Form I–94, Arrival Departure Record.

(1) Unless otherwise exempted, each arriving nonimmigrant who is admitted to the United States will be issued a Form I–94 as evidence of the terms of admission. For land border admission, a Form I–94 will be issued only upon payment of a fee, and will be considered issued for multiple entries unless specifically annotated for a limited number of entries. A Form I–94 issued at other than a land border port-of-entry, unless issued for multiple entries, must be surrendered upon departure from the United States in accordance with the instructions on the form. Form I–94 is not required by:

(i) Any nonimmigrant alien described in § 212.1(a) of this chapter and 22 CFR 41.33 who is admitted as a visitor for business or pleasure or admitted to proceed in direct transit through the United States;

(ii) Any nonimmigrant alien residing in the British Virgin Islands who was admitted only to the U.S. Virgin Islands as a visitor for business or pleasure under § 212.1(b) of this chapter;

(iii) Except as provided in paragraph (h)(1)(v) of this section, any Mexican national admitted as a nonimmigrant visitor who is:

(A) Exempt from a visa and passport pursuant to § 212.1(c)(1) of this chapter and is admitted for a period not to exceed 30 days to visit within 25 miles of the border; or

(B) In possession of a valid visa and passport and is admitted for a period not to exceed 72 hours to visit within 25 miles of the border;

(iv) Bearers of Mexican diplomatic or official passports described in § 212.1(c) of this chapter; or

(v) Any Mexican national admitted as a nonimmigrant visitor who is:

(A) Exempt from a visa and passport pursuant to § 212.1(c)(1) of this chapter and is admitted at the Mexican border POEs in the State of Arizona at Sasabe, Nogales, Mariposa, Naco or Douglas to visit within the State of Arizona within 75 miles of the border for a period not to exceed 30 days; or

(B) In possession of a valid visa and passport and is admitted at the Mexican border POEs in the State of Arizona at Sasabe, Nogales, Mariposa, Naco or Douglas to visit within the State of Arizona within 75 miles of the border for a period not to exceed 72 hours; or

(C) Exempt from visa and passport pursuant to § 212.1(c)(1) of this chapter and is admitted for a period not to exceed 30 days to visit within the State of New Mexico within 55 miles of the border or the area south of and including Interstate Highway I–10, whichever is further north; or

(D) In possession of a valid visa and passport and is admitted for a period not to exceed 72 hours to visit within the State of New Mexico within 55 miles of the border or the area south of and including Interstate Highway I–10, whichever is further north.

(2) Paroled aliens. Any alien paroled into the United States under section 212(d)(5) of the Act, including any alien crewmember, shall be issued a completely executed Form I–94, endorsed with the parole stamp.

[32 FR 9627, July 4, 1967; 32 FR 11628, Aug. 11, 1967; 42 FR 41848, Aug. 19, 1977; 45 FR 19545, March 26, 1980; 45 FR 63483, Sept. 25, 1980; 45 FR 70428, Oct. 24, 1980; 46 FR 43826, Sept. 1, 1981; 47 FR 49953, Nov. 4, 1982; 49 FR 33434, Aug. 23, 1984; 58 FR 69217, Dec. 30, 1993; 60 FR 40068, Aug. 7, 1995; 60 FR 50389, Sept. 29, 1995; 61 FR 53831, Oct. 16, 1996; 62 FR 10353, March 6, 1997; 62 FR 47751, Sept. 11, 1997; 63 FR 1334, Jan. 9, 1998; 64 FR 8494, Feb. 19, 1999; 64 FR 36561, July 7, 1999; 64 FR 68617, Dec. 8, 1999; 67 FR 71449, Dec. 2, 2002; 68 FR 5193, Jan. 31, 2003; 69 FR 480, Jan. 5, 2004; 69 FR 50053, Aug. 13, 2004; 69 FR 53333, Aug. 31, 2004; 69 FR 58037, Sept. 29, 2004; 71 FR 68429, Nov. 24, 2006; 73 FR 18416, Apr. 3, 2008; 73 FR 77491, Dec. 19, 2008; 74 FR 2837, Jan. 16, 2009; 78 FR 18472, March 27, 2013; 78 FR 35107, June 12, 2013]

§ 235.2 Parole for deferred inspection. [also 8 C.F.R. § 1235.2]

(a) A district director may, in his or her discretion, defer the inspection of any vessel or aircraft, or of any alien, to another Service office or port-of-entry. Any alien coming to a United States port from a foreign port, from an outlying possession of the United States, from Guam, Puerto Rico, or the Virgin Islands of the United States, or from another port of the United States at which examination under this part was deferred, shall be regarded as an applicant for admission at that onward port.

(b) An examining immigration officer may defer further examination and refer the alien's case to the district director having jurisdiction over the place where the alien is seeking admission, or over the place of the alien's residence or destination in the United States, if the examining immigration officer has reason to believe that the alien can overcome a finding of inadmissibility by:

(1) Posting a bond under section 213 of the Act;

(2) Seeking and obtaining a waiver under section211 or 212(d)(3) or (4) of the Act; or

(3) Presenting additional evidence of admissibility not available at the time and place of the initial examination.

(c) Such deferral shall be accomplished pursuant to the provisions of section 212(d)(5) of the Act for the period of time necessary to complete the deferred inspection.

(d) Refusal of a district director to authorize admission under section 213 of the Act, or to grant an application for the benefits of section 211 or section 212(d)(3) or (4) of the Act, shall be without prejudice to the renewal of such application or the authorizing of such admission by the immigration judge without additional fee.

(e) Whenever an alien on arrival is found or believed to be suffering from a disability that renders it impractical to proceed with the examination under the Act, the examination of such alien, members of his or her family concerning whose admissibility it is necessary to have such alien testify, and any accompanying aliens whose protection or guardianship will be required should such alien be found inadmissible shall be deferred for such time and under such conditions as the district director in whose district the port is located imposes.

[22 FR 9791, Dec. 6, 1957; 62 FR 10355, March 6, 1997]

§ 235.3 Inadmissible aliens and expedited removal. [also 8 C.F.R. § 1235.3]

(a) Detention prior to inspection. All persons arriving at a port-of-entry in the United States by vessel or aircraft shall be detained aboard the vessel or at the airport of arrival by the owner, agent, master, commanding officer, person in charge, purser, or consignee of such vessel or aircraft until admitted or otherwise permitted to land by an officer of the Service. Notice or order to detain shall not be required. The owner, agent, master, commanding officer, person in charge, purser, or consignee of such vessel or aircraft shall deliver every alien requiring examination to an immigration officer for inspection or to a medical officer for examination. The Service will not be liable for any expenses related to such detention or presentation or for any expenses of a passenger who has not been presented for inspection and for whom a determination has not been made concerning admissibility by a Service officer.

(b) Expedited removal.

(1) Applicability. The expedited removal provisions shall apply to the following classes of aliens who are determined to be inadmissible under section 212(a)(6)(C) or (7) of the Act:

(i) Arriving aliens, as defined 8 CFR 1.2, except for citizens of Cuba arriving at a United States port-of-entry by aircraft;

(ii) As specifically designated by the Commissioner, aliens who arrive in, attempt to enter, or have entered the United States without having been admitted or paroled following inspection by an immigration officer at a designated port-of-entry, and who have not established to the satisfaction of the immigration officer that they have been physically present in the United States continuously for the 2–year period immediately prior to the date of determination of inadmissibility. The Commissioner shall have the sole discretion to apply the provisions of section 235(b)(1) of the Act, at any time, to any class of aliens described in this section. The Commissioner's designation shall become effective upon publication of a notice in the Federal Register. However, if the Commissioner determines, in the exercise of discretion, that the delay caused by publication would adversely affect the interests of the United States or the effective enforcement of the immigration laws, the Commissioner's designation shall become effective immediately upon issuance, and shall be published in the Federal Register as soon as practicable thereafter. When these provisions are in effect for aliens who enter without inspection, the burden of proof rests with the alien to affirmatively show that he or she has the required continuous physical presence in the United States. Any absence from the United States shall serve to break the period of continuous physical presence. An alien who was not inspected and admitted or paroled into the United States but who establishes that he or she has been continuously physically present in the United States for the 2–year period immediately prior to the date of determination of inadmissibility shall be detained in accordance with section 235(b)(2) of the Act for a proceeding under section 240 of the Act.

(2) Determination of inadmissibility.

(i) Record of proceeding. An alien who is arriving in the United States, or other alien as designated pursuant to paragraph (b)(1)(ii) of this section, who is determined to be inadmissible under section 212(a)(6)(C) or 212(a)(7) of the Act (except an alien for whom documentary requirements are waived under § 211.1(b)(3) or § 212.1 of this chapter), shall be ordered removed from the United States in accordance with section 235(b)(1) of the Act. In every case in which the expedited removal provisions will be applied and before removing an alien from the United States pursuant to this section, the examining immigration officer shall create a record of the facts of the case and statements made by the alien. This shall be accomplished by means of a sworn statement using Form I–867AB, Record of Sworn Statement in Proceedings under Section 235(b)(1) of the Act. The examining immigration officer shall read (or have read) to the alien all information contained on Form I–867A. Following questioning and recording of the alien's statement regarding identity, alienage, and inadmissibility, the examining immigration officer shall record the alien's response to the questions contained on Form I–867B, and have the alien read (or have read to him or her) the statement, and the alien shall sign and initial each page of the statement and each correction. The examining immigration officer shall advise the alien of the charges against him or her on Form I–860, Notice and Order of Expedited Removal, and the alien shall be given an opportunity to respond to those charges in the sworn statement. After obtaining supervisory concurrence in accordance with paragraph (b)(7) of this section, the examining immigration official shall serve the alien with Form I–860 and the alien shall sign the reverse of the form acknowledging receipt. Interpretative assistance shall be used if necessary to communicate with the alien.

(ii) No entitlement to hearings and appeals. Except as otherwise provided in this section, such alien is not entitled to a hearing before an immigration judge in proceedings conducted pursuant to section 240 of the Act, or to an appeal of the expedited removal order to the Board of Immigration Appeals.

(iii) Detention and parole of alien in expedited removal. An alien whose inadmissibility is being considered under this section or who has been ordered removed pursuant to this section shall be detained pending determination and removal, except that parole of such alien, in accordance with section 212(d)(5) of the Act, may be permitted only when the Attorney General determines, in the exercise of discretion, that parole is required to meet a medical emergency or is necessary for a legitimate law enforcement objective.

(3) Additional charges of inadmissibility. In the expedited removal process, the Service may not charge an alien with any additional grounds of inadmissibility other than section 212(a)(6)(C) or 212(a)(7) of the Act. If an alien appears to be inadmissible under other grounds contained in section 212(a) of the Act, and if the Service wishes to pursue such additional grounds of inadmissibility, the alien shall be detained and referred for a removal hearing before an immigration judge pursuant to sections 235(b)(2) and 240 of the Act for inquiry into all charges. Once the alien is in removal proceedings under section 240 of the Act, the Service is not precluded from lodging additional charges against the alien. Nothing in this paragraph shall preclude the Service from pursuing such additional grounds of inadmissibility against the alien in any subsequent attempt to reenter the United States, provided the additional grounds of inadmissibility still exist.

(4) Claim of asylum or fear of persecution or torture. If an alien subject to the expedited removal provisions indicates an intention to apply for asylum, or expresses a fear of persecution or torture, or a fear of return to his or her country, the inspecting officer shall not proceed further with removal of the alien until the alien has been referred for an interview by an asylum officer in accordance with 8 CFR 208.30. The examining immigration officer shall record sufficient information in the sworn statement to establish and record that the alien has indicated such intention, fear, or concern, and to establish the alien's inadmissibility.

(i) Referral. The referring officer shall provide the alien with a written disclosure on Form M–444, Information About Credible Fear Interview, describing:

(A) The purpose of the referral and description of the credible fear interview process;

(B) The right to consult with other persons prior to the interview and any review thereof at no expense to the United States Government;

(C) The right to request a review by an immigration judge of the asylum officer's credible fear determination; and

(D) The consequences of failure to establish a credible fear of persecution or torture.

(ii) Detention pending credible fear interview. Pending the credible fear determination by an asylum officer and any review of that determination by an immigration judge, the alien shall be detained. Parole of such alien in accordance with section 212(d)(5) of the Act may be permitted only when the Attorney General determines, in the exercise of discretion, that parole is required to meet a medical emergency or is necessary for a legitimate law enforcement objective. Prior to the interview, the alien shall be given time to contact and consult with any person or persons of his or her choosing. Such consultation shall be made available in accordance with the policies and procedures of the detention facility where the alien is detained, shall be at no expense to the government, and shall not unreasonably delay the process.

(5) Claim to lawful permanent resident, refugee, or asylee status or U.S. citizenship.—

(i) Verification of status. If an applicant for admission who is subject to expedited removal pursuant to section 235(b)(1) of the Act claims to have been lawfully admitted for permanent residence, admitted as a refugee under section 207 of the Act, granted asylum under section 208 of the Act, or claims to be a U.S. citizen, the immigration officer shall attempt to verify the alien's claim. Such verification shall include a check of all available Service data systems and any other means available to the officer. An alien whose claim to lawful permanent resident, refugee, asylee status, or U.S. citizen status cannot be verified will be advised of the penalties for perjury, and will be placed under oath or allowed to make a declaration as permitted under 28 U.S.C. 1746, concerning his or her lawful admission for permanent residence, admission as a refugee under section 207 of the Act, grant of asylum status under section 208 of the Act, or claim to U.S. citizenship. A written statement shall be taken from the alien in the alien's own language and handwriting, stating that he or she declares, certifies, verifies, or states that the claim is true and correct. The immigration officer shall issue an expedited order of removal under section 235(b)(1)(A)(i) of the Act and refer the alien to the immigration judge for review of the order in accordance with paragraph (b)(5)(iv) of this section and § 235.6(a)(2)(ii). The person shall be detained pending review of the expedited removal order under this section. Parole of such person, in accordance with section 212(d)(5) of the Act, may be permitted only when the Attorney General determines, in the exercise of discretion, that parole is required to meet a medical emergency or is necessary for a legitimate law enforcement objective.

(ii) Verified lawful permanent residents. If the claim to lawful permanent resident status is verified, and such status has not been terminated in exclusion, deportation, or removal proceedings, the examining immigration officer shall not order the alien removed pursuant to section 235(b)(1) of the Act. The examining immigration officer will determine in accordance with section 101(a)(13)(C) of the Act whether the alien is considered to be making an application for admission. If the alien is determined to be seeking admission and the alien is otherwise admissible, except that he or she is not in possession of the required documentation, a discretionary waiver of documentary requirements may be considered in accordance with section 211(b) of the Act and § 211.1(b)(3) of this chapter or the alien's inspection may be deferred to an onward office for presentation of the required documents. If the alien appears to be inadmissible, the immigration officer may initiate removal proceedings against the alien under section 240 of the Act.

(iii) Verified refugees and asylees. If a check of Service records or other means indicates that the alien has been granted refugee status or asylee status, and such status has not been terminated in deportation, exclusion, or removal proceedings, the immigration officer shall not order the alien removed pursuant to section 235(b)(1) of the Act. If the alien is not in possession of a valid, unexpired refugee travel document, the examining immigration officer may accept an application for a refugee travel document in accordance with § 223.2(b)(2)(ii) of this chapter. If accepted, the immigration officer shall readmit the refugee or asylee in accordance with § 223.3(d)(2)(i) of this chapter. If the alien is determined not to be eligible to file an application for a refugee travel document the immigration officer may initiate removal proceedings against the alien under section 240 of the Act.

(iv) Review of order for claimed lawful permanent residents, refugees, asylees, or U.S. citizens. A person whose claim to U.S. citizenship has been verified may not be ordered removed. When an alien whose status has not been verified but who is claiming under oath or under penalty of perjury to be a lawful permanent resident, refugee, asylee, or U.S. citizen is ordered removed pursuant to section 235(b)(1) of the Act, the case will be referred to an immigration judge for review of the expedited removal order under section 235(b)(1)(C) of the Act and § 235.6(a)(2)(ii). If the immigration judge determines that the alien has never been admitted as a lawful permanent resident or as a refugee, granted asylum status, or is not a U.S. citizen, the order issued by the immigration officer will be affirmed and the Service will remove the alien. There is no appeal from the decision of the immigration judge. If the immigration judge determines that the alien was once so admitted as a lawful permanent resident or as a refugee, or was granted asylum status, or is a U.S. citizen, and such status has not been terminated by final administrative action, the immigration judge will terminate proceedings and vacate the expedited removal order. The Service may initiate removal proceedings against such an alien, but not against a person determined to be a U.S. citizen, in proceedings under section 240 of the Act. During removal proceedings, the immigration judge may consider any waivers, exceptions, or requests for relief for which the alien is eligible.

(6) Opportunity for alien to establish that he or she was admitted or paroled into the United States. If the Commissioner determines that the expedited removal provisions of section 235(b)(1) of the Act shall apply to any or all aliens described in paragraph (b)(2)(ii) of this section, such alien will be given a reasonable opportunity to establish to the satisfaction of the examining immigration officer that he or she was admitted or paroled into the United States following inspection at a port-of-entry. The alien will be allowed to present evidence or provide sufficient information to support the claim. Such evidence may consist of documentation in the possession of the alien, the Service, or a third party. The examining immigration officer will consider all such evidence and information, make further inquiry if necessary, and will attempt to verify the alien's status through a check of all available Service data systems. The burden rests with the alien to satisfy the examining immigration officer of the claim of lawful admission or parole. If the alien establishes that he or she was lawfully admitted or paroled, the case will be examined to determine if grounds of deportability under section 237(a) of the Act are applicable, or if paroled, whether such parole has been, or should be, terminated, and whether the alien is inadmissible under section 212(a) of the Act. An alien who cannot satisfy the examining officer that he or she was lawfully admitted or paroled will be ordered removed pursuant to section 235(b)(1) of the Act.

(7) Review of expedited removal orders. Any removal order entered by an examining immigration officer pursuant to section 235(b)(1) of the Act must be reviewed and approved by the appropriate supervisor before the order is considered final. Such supervisory review shall not be delegated below the level of the second line supervisor, or a person acting in that capacity. The supervisory review shall include a review of the sworn statement and any answers and statements made by the alien regarding a fear of removal or return. The supervisory review and approval of an expedited removal order for an alien described in section

235(b)(1)(A)(iii) of the Act must include a review of any claim of lawful admission or parole and any evidence or information presented to support such a claim, prior to approval of the order. In such cases, the supervisor may request additional information from any source and may require further interview of the alien.

(8) Removal procedures relating to expedited removal. An alien ordered removed pursuant to section 235(b)(1) of the Act shall be removed from the United States in accordance with section 241(c) of the Act and 8 CFR part 241.

(9) Waivers of documentary requirements. Nothing in this section limits the discretionary authority of the Attorney General, including authority under sections 211(b) or 212(d) of the Act, to waive the documentary requirements for arriving aliens.

(10) Applicant for admission under section 217 of the Act. The provisions of § 235.3(b) do not apply to an applicant for admission under section 217 of the Act.

(c) Arriving aliens placed in proceedings under section 240 of the Act. Except as otherwise provided in this chapter, any arriving alien who appears to the inspecting officer to be inadmissible, and who is placed in removal proceedings pursuant to section 240 of the Act shall be detained in accordance with section 235(b) of the Act. Parole of such alien shall only be considered in accordance with § 212.5(b) of this chapter. This paragraph shall also apply to any alien who arrived before April 1, 1997, and who was placed in exclusion proceedings.

(d) Service custody. The Service will assume custody of any alien subject to detention under paragraph (b) or (c) of this section. In its discretion, the Service may require any alien who appears inadmissible and who arrives at a land border port-of-entry from Canada or Mexico, to remain in that country while awaiting a removal hearing. Such alien shall be considered detained for a proceeding within the meaning of section 235(b) of the Act and may be ordered removed in absentia by an immigration judge if the alien fails to appear for the hearing.

(e) Detention in non-Service facility. Whenever an alien is taken into Service custody and detained at a facility other than at a Service Processing Center, the public or private entities contracted to perform such service shall have been approved for such use by the Service's Jail Inspection Program or shall be performing such service under contract in compliance with the Standard Statement of Work for Contract Detention Facilities. Both programs are administered by the Detention and Deportation section having jurisdiction over the alien's place of detention. Under no circumstances shall an alien be detained in facilities not meeting the four mandatory criteria for usage. These are:

(1) 24–Hour supervision,

(2) Conformance with safety and emergency codes,

(3) Food service, and

(4) Availability of emergency medical care.

(f) Privilege of communication. The mandatory notification requirements of consular and diplomatic officers pursuant to § 236.1(e) of this chapter apply when an inadmissible alien is detained for removal proceedings, including for purpose of conducting the credible fear determination.

[32 FR 9628, July 4, 1967, as amended at 34 FR 14727, Sept. 24, 1969; 47 FR 30046, July 9, 1982; 47 FR 46494, Oct. 19, 1982; 54 FR 101, Jan. 4, 1989; 54 FR 6365, Feb. 9, 1989; 60 FR 16043, March 29, 1995; 62 FR 10355, March 6, 1997; 64 FR 8494, Feb. 19, 1999; 65 FR 82256, Dec. 28, 2000; 66 FR 7863, Jan. 26, 2001; 69 FR 69490, Nov. 29, 2004; 76 FR 53784, Aug. 29, 2011.]

§ 235.4 Withdrawal of application for admission. [also 8 C.F.R. § 1235.4]

The Attorney General may, in his or her discretion, permit any alien applicant for admission to withdraw his or her application for admission in lieu of removal proceedings under section 240 of the Act or expedited removal under section 235(b)(1) of the Act. The alien's decision to withdraw his or her application for admission must be made voluntarily, but nothing in this section shall be construed as to give an alien the right to withdraw his or her application for admission. Permission to withdraw an application for admission should not normally be granted unless the alien intends and is able to depart the United States immediately. An alien permitted to withdraw his or her application for admission shall normally remain in carrier or Service custody pending departure, unless the district director determines that parole of the alien is warranted in accordance with § 212.5(b) of this chapter.

[22 FR 9791, Dec. 6, 1957, as amended at 33 FR 4562, March 15, 1968; 48 FR 35349, Aug. 4, 1983; 62 FR 10358, March 6, 1997; 62 FR 15363, April 1, 1997; 65 FR 82256, Dec. 28, 2000; 66 FR 7863, Jan. 26, 2001]

§ 235.5 Preinspection. [also 8 C.F.R. § 1235.5]

(a) In United States territories and possessions. In the case of any aircraft proceeding from Guam, the Commonwealth of the Northern Mariana Islands (beginning November 28, 2009), Puerto Rico, or the United States Virgin Islands destined directly and without touching at a foreign port or place, to any other of such places, or to one of the States of the United States or the District of Columbia, the examination of the passengers and crew required by the Act may be made prior to the departure of the aircraft, and in such event, final determination of admissibility will be made immediately prior to such departure. The examination will be conducted in accordance with sections 232, 235, and 240 of the Act and 8 CFR parts 235 and 240. If it appears to the immigration officer that any person in the United States being examined under this section is prima facie removable from the United States, further action with respect to his or her examination will be deferred and further proceedings regarding removability conducted as provided in section 240 of the Act and 8 CFR part 240. When the foregoing inspection procedure is applied to any aircraft, persons examined and found admissible will be placed aboard the aircraft, or kept at the airport separate and apart from the general public until they are permitted to board the aircraft. No other person will be permitted to depart on such aircraft until and unless he or she is found to be admissible as provided in this section.

(b) In foreign territory. In the case of any aircraft, vessel, or train proceeding directly, without stopping, from a port or place in foreign territory to a port-of-entry in the United States, the examination and inspection of passengers and crew required by the Act and final determination of admissibility may be made immediately prior to such departure at the port or place in the foreign territory and shall have the same effect under the Act as though made at the destined port-of-entry in the United States.

[23 FR 3997, June 7, 1958, as amended at 24 FR 2583, Apr. 3, 1959; 50 FR 11842, March 26, 1985; 54 FR 101, Jan. 4, 1989; 62 FR 10358, March 6, 1997; 74 FR 2836, Jan. 16, 2009; 74 FR 25388, May 28, 2009]

§ 235.6 Referral to immigration judge. [also 8 C.F.R. § 1235.6]

(a) Notice.

(1) Referral by Form I–862, Notice to Appear. An immigration officer or asylum officer will sign and deliver a Form I–862 to an alien in the following cases:

(i) If, in accordance with the provisions of section 235(b)(2)(A) of the Act, the examining immigration officer detains an alien for a proceeding before an immigration judge under section 240 of the Act; or

(ii) If an asylum officer determines that an alien in expedited removal proceedings has a credible fear of persecution or torture and refers the case to the immigration judge for consideration of the application for asylum, except that, prior to January 1, 2015, an alien arriving in the Commonwealth of the Northern Mariana Islands is not eligible to apply for asylum but the immigration judge may consider eligibility for withholding of removal pursuant to section 241(b)(3) of the Act or withholding or deferral of removal under the Convention Against Torture.

(iii) If the immigration judge determines that an alien in expedited removal proceedings has a credible fear of persecution or torture and vacates the expedited removal order issued by the asylum officer, except that, prior to January 1, 2015, an alien physically present in or arriving in the Commonwealth of the Northern Mariana Islands is not eligible to apply for asylum but an immigration judge may consider eligibility for withholding of removal pursuant to section 241(b)(3) of the Act or withholding or deferral of removal under the Convention Against Torture.

(iv) If an immigration officer verifies that an alien subject to expedited removal under section 235(b)(1) of the Act has been admitted as a lawful permanent resident refugee, or asylee, or upon review pursuant to § 235.3(b)(5)(iv) an immigration judge determines that the alien was once so admitted, provided that such status has not been terminated by final administrative action, and the Service initiates removal proceedings against the alien under section 240 of the Act.

(2) Referral by Form I–863, Notice of Referral to Immigration Judge. An immigration officer will sign and deliver a Form I–863 to an alien in the following cases:

(i) If an asylum officer determines that an alien does not have a credible fear of persecution or torture, and the alien requests a review of that determination by an immigration judge; or

(ii) If, in accordance with section 235(b)(1)(C) of the Act, an immigration officer refers an expedited removal order entered on an alien claiming to be a lawful permanent resident, refugee, asylee, or U.S. citizen for whom the officer could not verify such status to an immigration judge for review of the order.

(iii) If an immigration officer refers an applicant described in § 208.2(b)(1) of this chapter to an immigration judge for an asylum hearing under § 208.2(b)(2) of this chapter.

(b) Certification for mental condition; medical appeal. An alien certified under sections 212(a)(1) and 232(b) of the Act shall be advised by the examining immigration officer that he or she may appeal to a board of medical examiners of the United States Public Health Service pursuant to section 232 of the Act. If such appeal is taken, the district director shall arrange for the convening of the medical board.

[24 FR 6477, Aug. 12, 1959, as amended at 44 FR 4653, Jan. 23, 1979; 56 FR 50812, Oct. 9, 1991; 62 FR 9074, Feb. 28, 1997; 62 FR 10358, March 6, 1997; 64 FR 8494, Feb. 19, 1999; 74 FR 55739, Oct. 28, 2009]

PART 274a—CONTROL OF EMPLOYMENT OF ALIENS

Subpart A—Employer Requirements

§ 274a.1 Definitions. [also 8 C.F.R. § 1274a.1]

For the purpose of this part—

(a) The term "unauthorized alien" means, with respect to employment of an alien at a particular time, that the alien is not at that time either: (1) Lawfully admitted for permanent residence, or (2) authorized to be so employed by this Act or by the Attorney General;

(b) The term "entity" means any legal entity, including but not limited to, a corporation, partnership, joint venture, governmental body, agency, proprietorship, or association;

(c) The term "hire" means the actual commencement of employment of an employee for wages or other remuneration. For purposes of section 274A(a)(4) of the Act and 8 CFR 274a.5, a hire occurs when a person or entity uses a contract, subcontract, or exchange entered into, renegotiated, or extended after November 6, 1986 (or, with respect to the Commonwealth of the Northern Mariana Islands, after the transition program effective date as defined in 8 CFR 1.1), to obtain the labor of an alien in the United States, knowing that the alien is an unauthorized alien;

(d) The term "refer for a fee" means the act of sending or directing a person or transmitting documentation or information to another, directly or indirectly, with the intent of obtaining employment in the United States for such person, for remuneration whether on a retainer or contingency basis; however, this term does not include union hiring halls that refer union members or non-union individuals who pay union membership dues;

(e) The term "recruit for a fee" means the act of soliciting a person, directly or indirectly, and referring that person to another with the intent of obtaining employment for that person, for remuneration whether on a retainer or contingency basis; however, this term does not include union hiring halls that refer union members or non-union individuals who pay union membership dues;

(f) The term "employee" means an individual who provides services or labor for an employer for wages or other remuneration but does not mean independent contractors as defined in paragraph (j) of this section or those engaged in casual domestic employment as stated in paragraph (h) of this section;

(g) The term "employer" means a person or entity, including an agent or anyone acting directly or indirectly in the interest thereof, who engages the services or labor of an employee to be performed in the United States for wages or other remuneration. In the case of an independent contractor or contract labor or services, the term "employer" shall mean the independent contractor or contractor and not the person or entity using the contract labor;

(h) The term "employment" means any service or labor performed by an employee for an employer within the United States, including service or labor performed on a vessel or aircraft that has arrived in the United States and has been inspected, or otherwise included within the provisions of the Anti–Reflagging Act codified at 46 U.S.C. 8704, but not including duties performed by nonimmigrant crewmen defined in sections 101(a)(10) and (a)(15)(D) of the Act. However, employment does not include casual employment by individuals who provide domestic service in a private home that is sporadic, irregular or intermittent;

(i) The term "State employment agency" means any State government unit designated to cooperate with the United States Employment Service in the operation of the public employment service system;

(j) The term "independent contractor" includes individuals or entities who carry on independent business, contract to do a piece of work according to their own means and methods, and are subject to control only as to results. Whether an individual or entity is an independent contractor, regardless of what the individual or entity calls itself, will be determined on a case-by-case basis. Factors to be considered in that determination include, but are not limited to, whether the individual or entity: supplies the tools or materials; makes services available to the general public; works for a number of clients at the same time; has an opportunity for profit or loss as a result of labor or services provided; invests in the facilities for work; directs the order or sequence in which the work is to be done and determines the hours during which the work is to be done. The use of labor or services of an independent contractor are subject to the restrictions in section 274A(a)(4) of the Act and § 274a.5 of this part;

(k) The term "pattern or practice" means regular, repeated, and intentional activities, but does not include isolated, sporadic, or accidental acts;

(*l*)(1) The term "knowing" includes not only actual knowledge but also knowledge which may fairly be inferred through notice of certain facts and circumstances which would lead a person, through the exercise of reasonable care, to know about a certain condition. Constructive knowledge may include, but is not limited to, situations where an employer:

(i) Fails to complete or improperly completes the Employment Eligibility Verification, Form I–9;

(ii) Has information available to it that would indicate that the alien is not authorized to work, such as Labor Certification and/or an Application for Prospective Employer; or

(iii) Acts with reckless and wanton disregard for the legal consequences of permitting another individual to introduce an unauthorized alien into its work force or to act on its behalf.

(2) Knowledge that an employee is unauthorized may not be inferred from an employee's foreign appearance or accent. Nothing in this definition should be interpreted as permitting an employer to request more or different documents than are required under section 274(b) of the Act or to refuse to honor documents tendered that on their face reasonably appear to be genuine and to relate to the individual.

[52 FR 16221, May 1, 1987, as amended at 53 FR 8612, Mar. 16, 1988; 55 FR 25931, June 25, 1990; 56 FR 41783, Aug. 23, 1991; 72 FR 45623, Aug. 15, 2007; 73 FR 63867, Oct. 28, 2008; 74 FR 51452, Oct. 7, 2009; 74 FR 55739, Oct. 28, 2009]

§ 274a.2 Verification of identity and employment authorization.

(a) General. This section establishes requirements and procedures for compliance by persons or entities when hiring, or when recruiting or referring for a fee, or when continuing to employ individuals in the United States.

(1) Recruiters and referrers for a fee. For purposes of complying with section 274A(b) of the Act and this section, all references to recruiters and referrers for a fee are limited to a person or entity who is either an agricultural association, agricultural employer, or farm labor contractor (as defined in section 3 of the Migrant and Seasonal Agricultural Worker Protection Act, Pub.L. 97–470 (29 U.S.C. 1802)).

(2) Verification form. Form I–9, Employment Eligibility Verification Form, is used in complying with the requirements of this 8 CFR 274a.1—274a.11. Form I–9 can be in paper or electronic format. In paper format, the Form I–9 may be obtained in limited quantities at USCIS district offices, or ordered from the Superintendent of Documents, Washington, DC 20402. In electronic format, a fillable electronic Form I–9 may be downloaded from http://www.uscis.gov. Alternatively, Form I–9 can be electronically generated or retained, provided that the resulting form is legible; there is no change to the name, content, or sequence of the data elements and instructions; no additional data elements or language are inserted; and the standards specified under 8 CFR 274a.2(e), (f), (g), (h), and (i), as applicable, are met. When copying or printing the paper Form I–9, the text of the two-sided form may be reproduced by making either double-sided or single-sided copies.

(3) Attestation Under Penalty and Perjury. In conjunction with completing the Form I–9, an employer or recruiter or referrer for a fee must examine documents that evidence the identity and employment authorization of the individual. The employer or recruiter or referrer for a fee and the individual must each complete an attestation on the Form I–9 under penalty of perjury.

(b) Employment verification requirements—

(1) Examination of documents and completion of Form I–9.

(i) A person or entity that hires or recruits or refers for a fee an individual for employment must ensure that the individual properly:

(A) Completes section 1—"Employee Information and Verification"—on the Form I–9 at the time of hire and signs the attestation with a handwritten or electronic signature in accordance with paragraph (h) of this section; or if an individual is unable to complete the Form I–9 or needs it translated, someone may assist him or her. The preparer or translator must read the Form I–9 to the individual, assist him or her in completing Section 1—"Employee Information and Verification," and have the individual sign or mark the Form I–9 by a handwritten signature, or an electronic signature in accordance with paragraph (h) of this section, in the appropriate place; and

(B) Present to the employer or the recruiter or referrer for a fee documentation as set forth in paragraph (b)(1)(v) of this section establishing his or her identity and employment authorization within the time limits set forth in paragraphs (b)(1)(ii) through (b)(1)(v) of this section.

(ii) Except as provided in paragraph (b)(1)(viii) of this section, an employer, his or her agent, or anyone acting directly or indirectly in the interest thereof, must within three business days of the hire:

(A) Physically examine the documentation presented by the individual establishing identity and employment authorization as set forth in paragraph (b)(1)(v) of this section and ensure that the documents presented appear to be genuine and to relate to the individual; and

(B) Complete section 2—"Employer Review and Verification"—on the Form I–9 within three business days of the hire and sign the attestation with a handwritten signature or electronic signature in accordance with paragraph (i) of this section.

(iii) An employer who hires an individual for employment for a duration of less than three business days must comply with paragraphs (b)(1)(ii)(A) and (b)(1)(ii)(B) of this section at the time of the hire. An employer may not accept a receipt, as described in paragraph (b)(1)(vi) of this section, in lieu of the required document if the employment is for less than three business days.

(iv) A recruiter or referrer for a fee for employment must comply with paragraphs (b)(1)(ii)(A) and (b)(1)(ii)(B) of this section within three business days of the date the referred individual is hired by the employer. Recruiters and referrers may designate agents to complete the employment verification procedures on their behalf including but not limited to notaries, national associations, or employers. If a recruiter or referrer designates an employer to complete the employment verification procedures, the employer need only provide the recruiter or referrer with a photocopy or printed electronic image of the Form I–9, electronic Form I–9, or a Form I–9 on microfilm or microfiche.

(v) The individual may present either an original document which establishes both employment authorization and identity, or an original document which establishes employment authorization and a separate original document which establishes identity. Only unexpired documents are acceptable. The identification number and expiration date (if any) of all documents must be noted in the appropriate space provided on the Form I–9.

(A) The following documents, so long as they appear to relate to the individual presenting the document, are acceptable to evidence both identity and employment authorization:

(1) A United States passport;

(2) An Alien Registration Receipt Card or Permanent Resident Card (Form I–551);

(3) A foreign passport that contains a temporary I–551 stamp, or temporary I–551 printed notation on a machine-readable immigrant visa;

(4) An Employment Authorization Document which contains a photograph (Form I–766);

(5) In the case of a nonimmigrant alien authorized to work for a specific employer incident to status, a foreign passport with a Form I–94 (see § 1.4) or Form I–94A bearing the same name as the passport and containing an endorsement of the alien's nonimmigrant status, as long as the period of endorsement has not yet expired and the proposed employment is not in conflict with any restrictions or limitations identified on the Form;

(6) A passport from the Federated States of Micronesia (FSM) or the Republic of the Marshall Islands (RMI) with Form I–94 or Form I–94A indicating nonimmigrant admission under the Compact of Free Association Between the United States and the FSM or RMI;

(7) In the case of an individual lawfully enlisted for military service in the Armed Forces under 10 U.S.C. 504, a military identification card issued to such individual may be accepted only by the Armed Forces.

(B) The following documents are acceptable to establish identity only:

(1) For individuals 16 years of age or older:

(i) A driver's license or identification card containing a photograph, issued by a state (as defined in section 101(a)(36) of the Act) or an outlying possession of the United States (as defined by section 101(a)(29) of the Act). If the driver's license or identification card does not contain a photograph, identifying information shall be included such as: name, date of birth, sex, height, color of eyes, and address;

(ii) School identification card with a photograph;

(iii) Voter's registration card;

(iv) U.S. military card or draft record;

(v) Identification card issued by federal, state, or local government agencies or entities. If the identification card does not contain a photograph, identifying information shall be included such as: name, date of birth, sex, height, color of eyes, and address;

(vi) Military dependent's identification card;

(vii) Native American tribal documents;

(viii) United States Coast Guard Merchant Mariner Card;

(ix) Driver's license issued by a Canadian government authority;

(2) For individuals under age 18 who are unable to produce a document listed in paragraph (b)(1)(v)(B)(1) of this section, the following documents are acceptable to establish identity only:

(i) School record or report card;

(ii) Clinic doctor or hospital record;

(iii) Daycare or nursery school record.

(3) Minors under the age of 18 who are unable to produce one of the identity documents listed in paragraph (b)(1)(v)(B)(1) or (2) of this section are exempt from producing one of the enumerated identity document if:

(i) The minor's parent or legal guardian completes on the Form I–9 Section 1—"Employee Information and Verification" and in the space for the minor's signature, the parent or legal guardian writes the words, "minor under age 18."

(ii) The minor's parent or legal guardian completes on the Form I–9 the "Preparer/Translator certification."

(iii) The employer or the recruiter or referrer for a fee writes in Section 2—"Employer Review and Verification" under List B in the space after the words "Document Identification #" the words, "minor under age 18."

(4) Individuals with handicaps, who are unable to produce one of the identity documents listed in paragraph (b)(1)(v)(B)(1) or (2) of this section, who are being placed into employment by a nonprofit organization, association or as part of a rehabilitation program, may follow the procedures for establishing identity provided in this section for minors under the age of 18, substituting where appropriate, the term "special placement" for "minor under age 18", and permitting, in addition to a parent or legal guardian, a representative from the nonprofit organization, association or rehabilitation program placing the individual into a position of employment, to fill out and sign in the appropriate section, the Form I–9. For purposes of this section the term "individual with handicaps" means any person who

(i) Has a physical or mental impairment which substantially limits one or more of such person's major life activities,

(ii) Has a record of such impairment, or

(iii) Is regarded as having such impairment.

(C) The following are acceptable documents to establish employment authorization only:

(1) A Social Security account number card other than one that specifies on the face that the issuance of the card does not authorize employment in the United States;

(2) Certification of Birth issued by the Department of State, Form FS–545;

(3) Certification of Report of Birth issued by the Department of State, Form DS–1350;

(4) An original or certified copy of a birth certificate issued by a State, county, municipal authority or outlying possession of the United States bearing an official seal;

(5) Native American tribal document;

(6) United States Citizen Identification Card, Form I–197;

(7) Identification card for use of resident citizen in the United States, Form I–179;

(8) An employment authorization document issued by the Department of Homeland Security.

(D) The following are acceptable documents to establish both identity and employment authorization in the Commonwealth of the Northern Mariana Islands only, for a two-year period starting from the transition program effective date (as defined in 8 CFR 1.1), in addition to those documents listed in paragraph (b)(1)(v)(A) of this section:

(1) In the case of an alien with employment authorization in the Commonwealth of the Northern Mariana Islands incident to status for a period of up to two years following the transition program effective date that is unrestricted or otherwise authorizes a change of employer:

(i) The unexpired foreign passport and an Alien Entry Permit with red band issued to the alien by the Office of the Attorney General, Division of Immigration of the Commonwealth of the Northern Mariana Islands before the transition program effective date, as long as the period of employment authorization has not yet expired, or

(ii) An unexpired foreign passport and temporary work authorization letter issued by the Department of Labor of the Commonwealth of the Northern Mariana Islands before the transition program effective date, and containing the name and photograph of the individual, as long as the period of employment authorization has not yet expired and the proposed employment is not in conflict with any restrictions or limitations identified on the Temporary Work Authorization letter;

(iii) An unexpired foreign passport and a permanent resident card issued by the Commonwealth of the Northern Mariana Islands.

(2) [Reserved.]

(vi) Special rules for receipts. Except as provided in paragraph (b)(1)(iii) of this section, unless the individual indicates or the employer or recruiter or referrer for a fee has actual or constructive knowledge that the individual is not authorized to work, an employer or recruiter or referrer for a fee must accept a receipt for the application for a replacement document or a document described in paragraphs (b)(1)(vi)(B)(1) and (b)(1)(vi)(C)(1) of this section in lieu of the required document in order to comply with any requirement to examine documentation imposed by this section, in the following circumstances:

(A) Application for a replacement document. The individual:

(1) Is unable to provide the required document within the time specified in this section because the document was lost, stolen, or damaged;

(2) Presents a receipt for the application for the replacement document within the time specified in this section; and

(3) Presents the replacement document within 90 days of the hire or, in the case of reverification, the date employment authorization expires; or

(B) Form I–94 or I–94A indicating temporary evidence of permanent resident status. The individual indicates in section 1 of the Form I–9 that he or she is a lawful permanent resident and the individual:

(1) Presents the arrival portion of Form I–94 or Form I–94A containing an unexpired "Temporary I–551" stamp and a photograph of the individual, which is designated for purposes of this section as a receipt for Form I–551; and

(2) Presents the Form I–551 by the expiration date of the "Temporary I–551" stamp or, if the stamp has no expiration date, within one year from the issuance date of the arrival portion of the Form I–94 or Form I–94A; or

(C) Form I–94 or I–94A indicating refugee status. The individual indicates in section 1 of the Form I–9 that he or she is an alien authorized to work and the individual:

(1) Presents the departure portion of Form I–94 or I–94A containing an unexpired refugee admission stamp, which is designated for purposes of this section as a receipt for the Form I–766, or a social security account number card that contains no employment restrictions; and

(2) Presents, within 90 days of the hire or, in the case of reverification, the date employment authorization expires, either an unexpired Form I–766, or a social security account number card that contains no employment restrictions and a document described under paragraph (b)(1)(v)(B) of this section.

(vii) If an individual's employment authorization expires, the employer, recruiter or referrer for a fee must reverify on the Form I–9 to reflect that the individual is still authorized to work in the United States; otherwise the individual may no longer be employed, recruited, or referred. Reverification on the

Form I–9 must occur not later than the date work authorization expires. In order to reverify on the Form I–9, the employee or referred individual must present a document that either shows continuing employment eligibility or is a new grant of work authorization. The employer or the recruiter or referrer for a fee must review this document, and if it appears to be genuine and relate to the individual, re-verify by noting the document's identification number and expiration date, if any, on the Form I–9 and signing the attestation by a handwritten signature or electronic signature in accordance with paragraph (i) of this section.

(viii) An employer will not be deemed to have hired an individual for employment if the individual is continuing in his or her employment and has a reasonable expectation of employment at all times.

(A) An individual is continuing in his or her employment in one of the following situations:

(1) An individual takes approved paid or unpaid leave on account of study, illness or disability of a family member, illness or pregnancy, maternity or paternity leave, vacation, union business, or other temporary leave approved by the employer;

(2) An individual is promoted, demoted, or gets a pay raise;

(3) An individual is temporarily laid off for lack of work;

(4) An individual is on strike or in a labor dispute;

(5) An individual is reinstated after disciplinary suspension for wrongful termination, found unjustified by any court, arbitrator, or administrative body, or otherwise resolved through reinstatement or settlement;

(6) An individual transfers from one distinct unit of an employer to another distinct unit of the same employer; the employer may transfer the individual's Form I–9 to the receiving unit;

(7) An individual continues his or her employment with a related, successor, or reorganized employer, provided that the employer obtains and maintains from the previous employer records and Forms I–9 where applicable. For this purpose, a related, successor, or reorganized employer includes:

(i) The same employer at another location;

(ii) An employer who continues to employ some or all of a previous employer's workforce in cases involving a corporate reorganization, merger, or sale of stock or assets;

(iii) An employer who continues to employ any employee of another employer's workforce where both employers belong to the same multi-employer association and the employee continues to work in the same bargaining unit under the same collective bargaining agreement. For purposes of this subsection, any agent designated to complete and maintain the Form I–9 must record the employee's date of hire and/or termination each time the employee is hired and/or terminated by an employer of the multi-employer association; or

(8) An individual is engaged in seasonal employment.

(B) The employer who is claiming that an individual is continuing in his or her employment must also establish that the individual expected to resume employment at all times and that the individual's expectation is reasonable. Whether an individual's expectation is reasonable will be determined on a case-by-case basis taking into consideration several factors. Factors which would indicate that an individual has a reasonable expectation of employment include, but are not limited to, the following:

(1) The individual in question was employed by the employer on a regular and substantial basis. A determination of a regular and substantial basis is established by a comparison of other workers who are similarly employed by the employer;

(2) The individual in question complied with the employer's established and published policy regarding his or her absence;

(3) The employer's past history of recalling absent employees for employment indicates a likelihood that the individual in question will resume employment with the employer within a reasonable time in the future;

(4) The former position held by the individual in question has not been taken permanently by another worker;

(5) The individual in question has not sought or obtained benefits during his or her absence from employment with the employer that are inconsistent with an expectation of resuming employment with the employer within a reasonable time in the future. Such benefits include, but are not limited to, severance and retirement benefits;

(6) The financial condition of the employer indicates the ability of the employer to permit the individual in question to resume employment within a reasonable time in the future; or

(7) The oral and/or written communication between employer, the employer's supervisory employees and the individual in question indicates that it is reasonably likely that the individual in question will resume employment with the employer within a reasonable time in the future.

(2) Retention and Inspection of Form I–9.

(i) A paper (with original handwritten signatures), electronic (with acceptable electronic signatures that meet the requirements of paragraphs (h) and (i) of this section or original paper scanned into an electronic format, or a combination of paper and electronic formats that meet the requirements of paragraphs (e), (f), and (g) of this section), or microfilm or microfiche copy of the original signed version of Form I–9 must be retained by an employer or a recruiter or referrer for a fee for the following time periods:

(A) In the case of an employer, three years after the date of the hire or one year after the date the individual's employment is terminated, whichever is later; or

(B) In the case of a recruiter or referrer for a fee, three years after the date of the hire.

(ii) Any person or entity required to retain Forms I–9 in accordance with this section shall be provided with at least three business days notice prior to an inspection of Forms I–9 by officers of an authorized agency of the United States. At the time of inspection, Forms I–9 must be made available in their original paper, electronic form, a paper copy of the electronic form, or on microfilm or microfiche at the location where the request for production was made. If Forms I–9 are kept at another location, the person or entity must inform the officer of the authorized agency of the United States of the location where the forms are kept and make arrangements for the inspection. Inspections may be performed at an office of an authorized agency of the United States. A recruiter or referrer for a fee who has designated an employer to complete the employment verification procedures may present a photocopy or printed electronic image of the Form I–9 in lieu of presenting the Form I–9 in its original paper or electronic form or on microfilm or microfiche, as set forth in paragraph (b)(1)(iv) of this section. Any refusal or delay in presentation of the Forms I–9 for inspection is a violation of the retention requirements as set forth in section 274A(b)(3) of the Act. No Subpoena or warrant shall be required for such inspection, but the use of such enforcement tools is not precluded. In addition, if the person or entity has not complied with a request to present the Forms I–9, any officer listed in 8 CFR 287.4 may compel production of the Forms I–9 and any other relevant documents by issuing a subpoena. Nothing in this section is intended to limit the subpoena power under section 235(d)(4) of the Act.

(iii) The following standards shall apply to Forms I–9 presented on microfilm or microfiche submitted to an officer of the Service, the Special Counsel for Immigration–Related Unfair Employment Practices, or the Department of Labor: Microfilm, when displayed on a microfilm reader (viewer) or reproduced on paper must exhibit a high degree of legibility and readability. For this purpose, legibility is defined as the quality of a letter or numeral which enables the observer to positively and quickly identify it to the exclusion of all other letters or numerals. Readability is defined as the quality of a group of letters or numerals being recognizable as words or whole numbers. A detailed index of all microfilmed data shall be maintained and arranged in such a manner as to permit the immediate location of any particular record. It is the responsibility of the employer, recruiter or referrer for a fee:

(A) To provide for the processing, storage and maintenance of all microfilm, and

(B) To be able to make the contents thereof available as required by law. The person or entity presenting the microfilm will make available a reader-printer at the examination site for the ready reading, location and reproduction of any record or records being maintained on microfilm. Reader-printers made available to an officer of the Service, the Special Counsel for Immigration–Related Unfair Employment Practices, or the Department of Labor shall provide safety features and be in clean condition, properly maintained and in good working order. The reader-printers must have the capacity to display and print a complete page of information. A person or entity who is determined to have failed to comply with the criteria established by this regulation for the presentation of microfilm or microfiche to the Service, the Special Counsel for Immigration–Related Unfair Employment Practices, or the Department of Labor, and at the time of the inspection does not present a properly completed Form I–9 for the employee, is in violation of section 274A(a)(1)(B) of the Act and § 274a.2(b)(2).

(iv) Paragraphs (e), (f), (g), (h), and (i) of this section specify the standards for electronic Forms I–9.

(3) Copying of documentation. An employer, or a recruiter or referrer for a fee may, but is not required to, copy or make an electronic image of a document presented by an individual solely for the purpose of complying with the verification requirements of this section. If such a copy or electronic image is made, it must either be retained with the Form I–9 or stored with the employee's records and be retrievable consistent with paragraphs (e), (f), (g), (h), and (i) of this section. The copying or electronic imaging of any such document and retention of the copy or electronic image does not relieve the employer from the requirement to fully complete section 2 of the Form I–9. An employer, recruiter or referrer for a fee should not, however, copy or electronically image only the documents of individuals of certain national origins or citizenship statuses. To do so may violate section 274B of the Act.

(4) Limitation on use of Form I–9. Any information contained in or appended to the Form I–9, including copies or electronic images of documents listed in paragraph (c) of this section used to verify an individual's identity or employment eligibility, may be used only for enforcement of the Act and 18 U.S.C. 1001, 1028, 1546, or 1621.

(c) Employment verification requirements in the case of hiring an individual who was previously employed.

(1) When an employer hires an individual whom that person or entity has previously employed, if the employer has previously completed the Form I–9 and complied with the verification requirements set forth in paragraph (b) of this section with regard to the individual, the employer may (in lieu of completing a new Form I–9) inspect the previously completed Form I–9 and:

(i) If upon inspection of the Form I–9, the employer determines that the Form I–9 relates to the individual and that the individual is still eligible to work, that previously executed Form I–9 is sufficient for purposes of section 274A(b) of the Act if the individual is hired within three years of the date of the initial execution of the Form I–9 and the employer updates the Form I–9 to reflect the date of rehire; or

(ii) If upon inspection of the Form I–9, the employer determines that the individual's employment authorization has expired, the employer must reverify on the Form I–9 in accordance with paragraph (b)(1)(vii); otherwise the individual may no longer be employed.

(2) For purposes of retention of the Form I–9 by an employer for a previously employed individual hired pursuant to paragraph (c)(1) of this section, the employer shall retain the Form I–9 for a period of three years commencing from the date of the initial execution of the Form I–9 or one year after the individual's employment is terminated, whichever is later.

(d) Employment verification requirements in the case of recruiting or referring for a fee an individual who was previously recruited or referred.

(1) When a recruiter or referrer for a fee refers an individual for whom that recruiter or referrer for a fee has previously completed a Form I–9 and complied with the verification requirements set forth in paragraph (b) of this section with regard to the individual, the recruiter or referrer may (in lieu of completing a new Form I–9) inspect the previously completed Form I–9 and:

(i) If upon inspection of the Form I–9, the recruiter or referrer for a fee determines that the Form I–9 relates to the individual and that the individual is still eligible to work, that previously executed Form I–9 is sufficient for purposes of section 274A(b) of the Act if the individual is referred within three years of the date of the initial execution of the Form I–9 and the recruiter or referrer for a fee updates the Form I–9 to reflect the date of rehire; or

(ii) If upon inspection of the Form I–9, the recruiter or referrer determines that the individual's employment authorization has expired, the recruiter or referrer for a fee must reverify on the Form I–9 in accordance with paragraph (b)(1)(vii) of this section; otherwise the individual may no longer be recruited or referred.

(2) For purposes of retention of the Form I–9 by a recruiter or referrer for a previously recruited or referred individual pursuant to paragraph (d)(1) of this section, the recruiter or referrer shall retain the Form I–9 for a period of three years from the date of the rehire.

(e) Standards for electronic retention of Form I–9.

(1) Any person or entity who is required by this section to complete and retain Forms I–9 may complete or retain electronically only those pages of the Form I–9 on which employers and employees enter data in an electronic generation or storage system that includes:

(i) Reasonable controls to ensure the integrity, accuracy and reliability of the electronic generation or storage system;

(ii) Reasonable controls designed to prevent and detect the unauthorized or accidental creation of, addition to, alteration of, deletion of, or deterioration of an electronically completed or stored Form I–9, including the electronic signature if used;

(iii) An inspection and quality assurance program evidenced by regular evaluations of the electronic generation or storage system, including periodic checks of the electronically stored Form I–9, including the electronic signature if used;

(iv) In the case of electronically retained Forms I–9, a retrieval system that includes an indexing system that permits searches consistent with the requirements of paragraph (e)(6) of this section; and

(v) The ability to reproduce legible and readable hardcopies.

(2) All documents reproduced by the electronic retention system must exhibit a high degree of legibility and readability when displayed on a video display terminal or when printed on paper, microfilm, or microfiche. The term "legibility" means the observer must be able to identify all letters and numerals positively and quickly, to the exclusion of all other letters or numerals. The term "readability" means that the observer must be able to recognize any group of letters or numerals that form words or numbers as those words or complete numbers. The employer, or recruiter or referrer for a fee, must ensure that the reproduction process maintains the legibility and readability of the electronically stored document.

(3) An electronic generation or storage system must not be subject, in whole or in part, to any agreement (such as a contract or license) that would limit or restrict access to and use of the electronic generation or storage system by an agency of the United States, on the premises of the employer, recruiter or referrer for a fee (or at any other place where the electronic generation or storage system is maintained), including personnel, hardware, software, files, indexes, and software documentation.

(4) A person or entity who chooses to complete or retain Forms I–9 electronically may use one or more electronic generation or storage systems. Each electronic generation or storage system must meet the requirements of this paragraph, and remain available as long as required by the Act and these regulations. Employers may implement new electronic storage systems provided:

(i) All systems meet the requirements of paragraphs (e), (f), (g), (h) and (i) of this section; and

(ii) Existing Forms I–9 are retained in a system that remains fully accessible.

(5) For each electronic generation or storage system used, the person or entity retaining the Form I–9 must maintain, and make available upon request, complete descriptions of:

(i) The electronic generation and storage system, including all procedures relating to its use; and

(ii) The indexing system.

(6) An "indexing system" for the purposes of paragraphs (e)(1)(iv) and (e)(5) of this section is a system that permits the identification and retrieval for viewing or reproducing of relevant documents and records maintained in an electronic storage system. For example, an indexing system might consist of assigning each electronically stored document a unique identification number and maintaining a separate database that contains descriptions of all electronically stored books and records along with their identification numbers. In addition, any system used to maintain, organize, or coordinate multiple electronic storage systems is treated as an indexing system. The requirement to maintain an indexing system will be satisfied if the indexing system is functionally comparable to a reasonable hardcopy filing system. The requirement to maintain an indexing system does not require that a separate electronically stored documents and records description database be maintained if comparable results can be achieved without a separate description database.

(7) Any person or entity choosing to retain completed Forms I–9 electronically may use reasonable data compression or formatting technologies as part of the electronic storage system as long as the requirements of 8 CFR 274a.2 are satisfied.

(8) At the time of an inspection, the person or entity required to retain completed Forms I–9 must:

(i) Retrieve and reproduce (including printing copies on paper, if requested) only the Forms I–9 electronically retained in the electronic storage system and supporting documentation specifically requested by an agency of the United States, along with associated audit trails. Generally, an audit trail is a record showing who has accessed a computer system and the actions performed within or on the computer system during a given period of time;

(ii) Provide a requesting agency of the United States with the resources (e.g., appropriate hardware and software, personnel and documentation) necessary to locate, retrieve, read, and reproduce (including paper copies) any electronically stored Forms I–9, any supporting documents, and their associated audit trails, reports, and other data used to maintain the authenticity, integrity, and reliability of the records; and

(iii) Provide, if requested, any reasonably available or obtainable electronic summary file(s), such as a spreadsheet, containing all of the information fields on all of the electronically stored Forms I–9 requested by a requesting agency of the United States.

(f) Documentation.

(1) A person or entity who chooses to complete and/or retain Forms I–9 electronically must maintain and make available to an agency of the United States upon request documentation of the business processes that:

(i) Create the retained Forms I–9;

(ii) Modify and maintain the retained Forms I–9; and

(iii) Establish the authenticity and integrity of the Forms I–9, such as audit trails.

(2) Insufficient or incomplete documentation is a violation of section 274A(a)(1)(B) of the Act.

(3) Any officer listed in 8 CFR 287.4 may issue a subpoena to compel production of any documentation required by 8 CFR 274a.2. Nothing in this section is intended to limit the subpoena power of an agency of the United States under section 235(d)(4) of the Act.

(g) Security.

(1) Any person or entity who elects to complete or retain Forms I–9 electronically must implement an effective records security program that:

(i) Ensures that only authorized personnel have access to electronic records;

(ii) Provides for backup and recovery of records to protect against information loss, such as power interruptions;

(iii) Ensures that employees are trained to minimize the risk of unauthorized or accidental alteration or erasure of electronic records; and

(iv) Ensure that whenever the electronic record is created, completed, updated, modified, altered, or corrected, a secure and permanent record is created that establishes the date of access, the identity of the individual who accessed the electronic record, and the particular action taken.

(2) An action or inaction resulting in the unauthorized alteration, loss, or erasure of electronic records, if it is known, or reasonably should be known, to be likely to have that effect, is a violation of section 274A(b)(3) of the Act.

(h) Electronic signatures for employee.

(1) If a Form I–9 is completed electronically, the attestations in Form I–9 must be completed using a system for capturing an electronic signature that meets the standards set forth in this paragraph. The system used to capture the electronic signature must include a method to acknowledge that the attestation to be signed has been read by the signatory. The electronic signature must be attached to, or logically associated with, an electronically completed Form I–9. In addition, the system must:

(i) Affix the electronic signature at the time of the transaction;

(ii) Create and preserve a record verifying the identity of the person producing the signature; and

(iii) Upon request of the employee, provide a printed confirmation of the transaction to the person providing the signature.

(2) Any person or entity who is required to ensure proper completion of a Form I–9 and who chooses electronic signature for a required attestation, but who has failed to comply with the standards set forth in this paragraph, is deemed to have not properly completed the Form I–9, in violation of section 274A(a)(1)(B) of the Act and 8 CFR 274a.2(b)(2).

(i) Electronic signatures for employer, recruiter or referrer, or representative. If a Form I–9 is completed electronically, the employer, the recruiter or referrer for a fee, or the representative of the employer or the recruiter or referrer, must attest to the required information in Form I–9. The system used to capture the electronic signature should include a method to acknowledge that the attestation to be signed has been read by the signatory. Any person or entity who has failed to comply with the criteria established by this regulation for electronic signatures, if used, and at the time of inspection does not present a properly completed Form I–9 for the employee, is in violation of section 274A(a)(1)(B) of the Act and 8 CFR 274a.2(b)(2).

[53 FR 8612, March 16, 1988; 55 FR 25932 to 25934, June 25, 1990; 56 FR 41782, 41784–41786, Aug. 23, 1991; 58 FR 48780, Sept. 20, 1993; 59 FR 47063, Sept. 14, 1994; 60 FR 14353, March 17, 1995; 61 FR 46537, Sept. 4, 1996; 61 FR 52236, Oct. 7, 1996; 62 FR 51005, Sept. 30, 1997; 64 FR 6189, Feb. 9, 1999; 64 FR 11533, March 9, 1999; 71 FR 34514, June 15, 2006; 73 FR 76511, Dec. 17, 2008; 74 FR 2838, Jan. 16, 2009; 74 FR 5899, Feb. 3, 2009; 74 FR 7995, Feb. 23, 2009; 74 FR 10455, March 11, 2009; 74 FR 55739, Oct. 28, 2009; 74 FR 62207, 62208, Nov. 27, 2009; 75 FR 42578, July 22, 2010; 76 FR 21232, April 15, 2011; 78 FR 18472, March 27, 2013]

Subpart B—Employment Authorization

§ 274a.12 Classes of aliens authorized to accept employment. [also 8 C.F.R. § 1274a.12]

(a) Aliens authorized employment incident to status. Pursuant to the statutory or regulatory reference cited, the following classes of aliens are authorized to be employed in the United States without restrictions as to location or type of employment as a condition of their admission or subsequent change to one of the indicated classes. Any alien who is within a class of aliens described in paragraphs (a)(3), (a)(4), (a)(6)–(a)(8), (a)(10)–(a)(15), or (a)(20) of this section, and who seeks to be employed in the United States, must apply to U.S. Citizenship and Immigration Services (USCIS) for a document evidencing such employment authorization. USCIS may, in its discretion, determine the validity period assigned to any document issued evidencing an alien's authorization to work in the United States.

(1) An alien who is a lawful permanent resident (with or without conditions pursuant to section 216 of the Act), as evidenced by Form I–551 issued by the Service. An expiration date on the

Form I–551 reflects only that the card must be renewed, not that the bearer's work authorization has expired;

(2) An alien admitted to the United States as a lawful temporary resident pursuant to section 245A or 210 of the Act, as evidenced by an employment authorization document issued by the Service;

(3) An alien admitted to the United States as a refugee pursuant to section 207 of the Act for the period of time in that status, as evidenced by an employment authorization document issued by the Service;

(4) An alien paroled into the United States as a refugee for the period of time in that status, as evidenced by an employment authorization document issued by the Service;

(5) An alien granted asylum under section 208 of the Act for the period of time in that status, as evidenced by an employment authorization document, issued by USCIS to the alien. An expiration date on the employment authorization document issued by USCIS reflects only that the document must be renewed, and not that the bearer's work authorization has expired. Evidence of employment authorization shall be granted in increments not exceeding 5 years for the period of time the alien remains in that status;

(6) An alien admitted to the United States as a nonimmigrant fiance or fiancee pursuant to section 101(a)(15)(K)(i) of the Act, or an alien admitted as a child of such alien, for the period of admission in that status, as evidenced by an employment authorization document issued by the Service;

(7) An alien admitted as a parent (N–8) or dependent child (N–9) of an alien granted permanent residence under section 101(a)(27)(I) of the Act, as evidenced by an employment authorization document issued by the Service;

(8) An alien admitted to the United States as a nonimmigrant pursuant to the Compact of Free Association between the United States and of the Federated States of Micronesia, the Republic of the Marshall Islands, or the Republic of Palau;

(9) Any alien admitted as a nonimmigrant spouse pursuant to section 101(a)(15)(K)(ii) of the Act, or an alien admitted as a child of such alien, for the period of admission in that status, as evidenced by an employment authorization document, with an expiration date issued by the Service;

(10) An alien granted withholding of deportation or removal for the period of time in that status, as evidenced by an employment authorization document issued by the Service;

(11) An alien whose enforced departure from the United States has been deferred in accordance with a directive from the President of the United States to the Secretary. Employment is authorized for the period of time and under the conditions established by the Secretary pursuant to the Presidential directive;

(12) An alien granted Temporary Protected Status under section 244 of the Act for the period of time in that status, as evidenced by an employment authorization document issued by the Service;

(13) An alien granted voluntary departure by the Attorney General under the Family Unity Program established by section 301 of the Immigration Act of 1990, as evidenced by an employment authorization document issued by the Service;

(14) An alien granted Family Unity benefits under section 1504 of the Legal Immigrant Family Equity (LIFE) Act Amendments, Public Law 106–554, and the provisions of 8 CFR part 245a, Subpart C of this chapter, as evidenced by an employment authorization document issued by the Service; or

(15) Any alien in V nonimmigrant status as defined in section 101(a)(15)(V) of the Act and 8 CFR 214.15;

(16) An alien authorized to be admitted to or remain in the United States as a nonimmigrant alien victim of a severe form of trafficking in persons under section 101(a)(15)(T)(i) of the Act. Employment authorization granted under this paragraph shall expire upon the expiration of the underlying T–1 nonimmigrant status granted by the Service.

(17) [Reserved]

(18) [Reserved]

(19) Any alien in U–1 nonimmigrant status, pursuant to 8 CFR 214.14, for the period of time in that status, as evidenced by an employment authorization document issued by USCIS to the alien.

(20) Any alien in U–2, U–3, U–4, or U–5 nonimmigrant status, pursuant to 8 CFR 214.14, for the period of time in that status, as evidenced by an employment authorization document issued by USCIS to the alien.

(b) Aliens authorized for employment with a specific employer incident to status. The following classes of nonimmigrant aliens are authorized to be employed in the United States by the specific employer and subject to the restrictions described in the section(s) of this chapter indicated as a condition of their admission in, or subsequent change to, such classification. An alien in one of these classes is not issued an employment authorization document by the Service:

(1) A foreign government official (A–1 or A–2), pursuant to § 214.2(a) of this chapter. An alien in this status may be employed only by the foreign government entity;

(2) An employee of a foreign government official (A–3), pursuant to § 214.2(a) of this chapter. An alien in this status may be employed only by the foreign government official;

(3) A foreign government official in transit (C–2 or C–3), pursuant to § 214.2(c) of this chapter. An alien in this status may be employed only by the foreign government entity;

(4) [Reserved]

(5) A nonimmigrant treaty trader (E–1) or treaty investor (E–2), pursuant to § 214.2(e) of this chapter. An alien in this status may be employed only by the treaty-qualifying company through which the alien attained the status. Employment authorization does not extend to the dependents of the principal treaty trader or treaty investor (also designated "E–1" or "E–2"), other than those specified in paragraph (c)(2) of this section;

(6) A nonimmigrant (F–1) student who is in valid nonimmigrant student status and pursuant to 8 CFR 214.2(f) is seeking:

(i) On-campus employment for not more than twenty hours per week when school is in session or full-time employment when school is not in session if the student intends and is eligible to register for the next term or session. Part-time on-campus employment is authorized by the school and no specific endorsement by a school official or Service officer is necessary;

(ii) [Reserved].

(iii) Curricular practical training (internships, cooperative training programs, or work–study programs which are part of an established curriculum) after having been enrolled full–time in a Service approved institution for one full academic year. Curricular practical training (part–time or full–time) is authorized by the Designated School Official on the student's Form I–20. No Service endorsement is necessary.

(iv) An employment authorization document under paragraph (c)(3)(i)(C) of this section based on a 17-month STEM Optional Practical Training extension, and whose timely filed employment authorization request is pending and employment authorization issued under paragraph (c)(3)(i)(B) of this section has expired. Employment is authorized beginning on the expiration date of the authorization issued under paragraph (c)(3)(i)(B) of this section and ending on the date of USCIS' written decision on the current employment authorization request, but not to exceed 180 days; or

(v) Pursuant to 8 CFR 214.2(h) is seeking H–1B nonimmigrant status and whose duration of status and employment authorization have been extended pursuant to 8 CFR 214.2(f)(5)(vi).

(7) A representative of an international organization (G–1, G–2, G–3, or G–4), pursuant to § 214.2(g) of this chapter. An alien in this status may be employed only by the foreign government entity or the international organization;

(8) A personal employee of an official or representative of an international organization (G–5), pursuant to § 214.2(g) of this chapter. An alien in this status may be employed only by the official or representative of the international organization;

(9) A temporary worker or trainee (H–1, H–2A, H–2B, or H–3), pursuant to § 214.2(h) of this chapter. An alien in this status may be employed only by the petitioner through whom the status was obtained. In the case of a professional H–2B athlete who is traded from one organization to another organization, employment authorization for the player will automatically continue for a period of 30 days after acquisition by the new organization, within which time the new organization is expected to file a new Form I–129 to petition for H–2B classification. If a new Form I–129 is not filed within 30 days, employment authorization will cease. If a new Form I–129 is filed within 30 days, the professional athlete's employment authorization will continue until the petition is adjudicated. If the new petition is denied, employment authorization will cease;

(10) An information media representative (I), pursuant to § 214.2(i) of this chapter. An alien in this status may be employed only for the sponsoring foreign news agency or bureau. Employment authorization does not extend to the dependents of an information media representative (also designated "I");

(11) An exchange visitor (J–1), pursuant to § 214.2(j) of this chapter and 22 CFR part 62. An alien in this status may be employed only by the exchange visitor program sponsor or appropriate designee and within the guidelines of the program approved by the Department of State as set forth in the Form DS–2019, Certificate of Eligibility, issued by the program sponsor;

(12) An intra-company transferee (L–1), pursuant to § 214.2(1) of this chapter. An alien in this status may be employed only by the petitioner through whom the status was obtained;

(13) An alien having extraordinary ability in the sciences, arts, education, business, or athletics (O–1), and an accompanying alien (O–2), pursuant to § 214.2(*o*) of this chapter. An alien in this status may be employed only by the petitioner through whom the status was obtained. In the case of a professional O–1 athlete who is traded from one organization to another organization, employment authorization for the player will automatically continue for a period of 30 days after the acquisition by the new organization, within which time the new organization is expected to file a new Form I–129 petition for O nonimmigrant classification. If a new Form I–129 is not filed within 30 days, employment authorization will cease. If a new Form I–129 is filed within 30 days, the professional athlete's employment authorization will continue until the petition is adjudicated. If the new petition is denied, employment authorization will cease.

(14) An athlete, artist, or entertainer (P–1, P–2, or P–3), pursuant to § 214.2(p) of this chapter. An alien in this status may be employed only by the petitioner through whom the status was obtained. In the case of a professional P–1 athlete who is traded from one organization to another organization, employment authorization for the player will automatically continue for a period of 30 days after the acquisition by the new organization, within which time the new organization is expected to file a new Form I–129 for P–1 nonimmigrant classification. If a new Form I–129 is not filed within 30 days, employment authorization will cease. If a new Form I–129 is filed within 30 days, the professional athlete's employment authorization will continue until the petition is adjudicated. If the new petition is denied, employment authorization will cease;

(15) An international cultural exchange visitor (Q–1), according to § 214.2(q)(1) of this chapter. An alien may only be employed by the petitioner through whom the status was obtained;

(16) An alien having a religious occupation, pursuant to § 214.2(r) of this chapter. An alien in this status may be employed only by the religious organization through whom the status was obtained;

(17) Officers and personnel of the armed services of nations of the North Atlantic Treaty Organization, and representatives, officials, and staff employees of NATO (NATO–1, NATO–2, NATO–3, NATO–4, NATO–5 and NATO–6), pursuant to § 214.2(*o*) of this chapter. An alien in this status may be employed only by NATO;

(18) An attendant, servant or personal employee (NATO–7) of an alien admitted as a NATO–1, NATO–2, NATO–3, NATO–4, NATO–5, or NATO–6, pursuant to § 214.2(*o*) of this chapter. An alien admitted under this classification may be employed only by the NATO alien through whom the status was obtained;

(19) A nonimmigrant pursuant to section 214(e) of the Act. An alien in this status must be engaged in business activities at a professional level in accordance with the provisions of Chapter 16 of the North American Free Trade Agreement (NAFTA);

(20) A nonimmigrant alien within the class of aliens described in paragraphs (b)(2), (b)(5), (b)(8), (b)(9), (b)(10), (b)(11), (b)(12), (b)(13), (b)(14), (b)(16), and (b)(19) of this section whose status has expired but who has filed a timely application for an extension of such stay pursuant to §§ 214.2 or 214.6 of this chapter. These aliens are authorized to continue employment with the same employer for a period not to exceed 240 days beginning on the date of the expiration of the authorized period of stay. Such authorization shall be subject to any conditions and limitations noted on the initial authorization. However, if the district director or service center director adjudicates the application prior to the expiration of this 240 day period and denies the application for extension of stay, the employment authorization under this paragraph shall automatically terminate upon notification of the denial decision;

(21) A nonimmigrant alien within the class of aliens described in 8 CFR 14.2(h)(1)(ii)(C) who filed an application for an extension of stay pursuant to 8 CFR 214.2 during his or her period of admission. Such alien is authorized to be employed by a new employer that has filed an H–2A petition naming the alien as a beneficiary and requesting an extension of stay for the alien for a period not to exceed 120 days beginning from the "Received Date" on Form I–797 (Notice of Action) acknowledging receipt of the petition requesting an extension of stay, provided that the employer has enrolled in and is a participant in good standing in the E–Verify program, as determined by USCIS in its discretion. Such authorization will be subject to any conditions and limitations noted on the initial authorization, except as to the employer and place of employment. However, if the District Director or Service Center director adjudicates the application prior to the expiration of this 120–day period and denies the application for extension of stay, the employment authorization under this paragraph (b)(21) shall automatically terminate upon 15 days after the date of the denial decision. The employment authorization shall also terminate automatically if the employer fails to remain a participant in good standing in the E–Verify program, as determined by USCIS in its discretion;

(22) An alien in E–2 CNMI Investor nonimmigrant status pursuant to 8 CFR 214.2(e)(23). An alien in this status may be employed only by the qualifying company through which the alien attained the status. An alien in E–2 CNMI Investor nonimmigrant status may be employed only in the Commonwealth of the Northern Mariana Islands for a qualifying entity. An alien who attained E–2 CNMI Investor nonimmigrant status based upon a Foreign Retiree Investment Certificate or Certification is not employment-authorized. Employment authorization does not extend to the dependents of the principal investor (also designated E–2 CNMI Investor nonimmigrants) other than those specified in paragraph (c)(12) of this section;

(23) A Commonwealth of the Northern Mariana Islands transitional worker (CW–1) pursuant to 8 CFR 214.2(w). An alien in this status may be employed only in the CNMI during the transition period, and only by the petitioner through whom the status was obtained, or as otherwise authorized by 8 CFR 214.2(w). An alien who is lawfully present in the CNMI (as defined by 8 CFR 214.2(w)(1)(v)) on or before November 27, 2011, is authorized to be employed in the CNMI, and is so employed in the CNMI by an employer properly filing an application under 8 CFR 214.2(w)(14)(ii) on or before such date for a grant of CW–1 status to its employee in the CNMI for the purpose of the alien continuing the employment, is authorized to continue such employment on or after November 27, 2011, until a decision is made on the application; or

(24) An alien who is authorized to be employed in the Commonwealth of the Northern Mariana Islands for a period of up to 2 years following the transition program effective date, under section 6(e)(2) of Public Law 94–241, as added by section 702(a) of Public Law 110–229. Such alien is only authorized to continue in the same employment that he or she had on the transition program effective date as defined in 8 CFR 1.1 until the earlier of the date that is 2 years after the transition program effective date or the date of expiration of the alien's employment authorization, unless the alien had unrestricted employment authorization or was otherwise authorized as of the transition program effective date to change employers, in which case the alien may have such employment privileges as were authorized as of the transition program effective date for up to 2 years.

(c) Aliens who must apply for employment authorization. An alien within a class of aliens described in this section must apply for work authorization. If authorized, such an alien may accept employment subject to any restrictions stated in the regulations or cited on the employment authorization document. USCIS, in its discretion, may establish a specific validity period for an employment authorization document, which may include any period when an administrative appeal or judicial review of an application or petition is pending.

(1) An alien spouse or unmarried dependent child; son or daughter of a foreign government official (A–1 or A–2) pursuant to 8 CFR 214.2(a)(2) and who presents an endorsement from an authorized representative of the Department of State;

(2) An alien spouse or unmarried dependent son or daughter of an alien employee of the Coordination Council for North American Affairs (E–1) pursuant to § 214.2(e) of this chapter;

(3) A nonimmigrant (F–1) student who:

(i)(A) Is seeking pre-completion practical training pursuant to 8 CFR 214.2(f)(10)(ii)(A)(1)–(2);

(B) Is seeking authorization to engage in post-completion Optional Practical Training (OPT) pursuant to 8 CFR 214.2(f)(10)(ii)(A)(3); or

(C) Is seeking a 17–month STEM OPT extension pursuant to 8 CFR 214.2(f)(10)(ii)(C);

(ii) Has been offered employment under the sponsorship of an international organization within the meaning of the International Organization Immunities Act (59 Stat. 669) and who presents a written certification from the international organization that the proposed employment is within the scope of the organization's sponsorship. The F–1 student must also present a

Form I–20 ID or SEVIS Form I–20 with employment page completed by DSO certifying eligibility for employment; or

(iii) Is seeking employment because of severe economic hardship pursuant to 8 CFR 214.2(f)(9)(ii)(C) and has filed the Form I–20 ID and Form I–538 (for non–SEVIS schools), or SEVIS Form I–20 with employment page completed by the DSO certifying eligibility, and any other supporting materials such as affidavits which further detail the unforeseen economic circumstances that require the student to seek employment authorization.

(4) An alien spouse or unmarried dependent child; son or daughter of a foreign government official (G–1, G–3 or G–4) pursuant to 8 CFR 214.2(g) and who presents an endorsement from an authorized representative of the Department of State;

(5) An alien spouse or minor child of an exchange visitor (J–2) pursuant to § 214.2(j) of this chapter;

(6) A nonimmigrant (M–1) student seeking employment for practical training pursuant to 8 CFR 214.2(m) following completion of studies. The alien may be employed only in an occupation or vocation directly related to his or her course of study as recommended by the endorsement of the designated school official on the I–20 ID;

(7) A dependent of an alien classified as NATO–1 through NATO–7 pursuant to § 214.2(n) of this chapter;

(8) An alien who has filed a complete application for asylum or withholding of deportation or removal pursuant to 8 CFR part 208, whose application:

(i) Has not been decided, and who is eligible to apply for employment authorization under § 208.7 of this chapter because the 150–day period set forth in that section has expired. Employment authorization may be granted according to the provisions of § 208.7 of this chapter in increments to be determined by the Commissioner and shall expire on a specified date; or

(ii) Has been recommended for approval, but who has not yet received a grant of asylum or withholding or deportation or removal;

(9) An alien who has filed an application for adjustment of status to lawful permanent resident pursuant to part 245 of this chapter. For purposes of section 245(c)(8) of the Act, an alien will not be deemed to be an "unauthorized alien" as defined in section 274A(h)(3) of the Act while his or her properly filed Form I–485 application is pending final adjudication, if the alien has otherwise obtained permission from the Service pursuant to 8 CFR 274a.12 to engage in employment, or if the alien had been granted employment authorization prior to the filing of the adjustment application and such authorization does not expire during the pendency of the adjustment application. Upon meeting these conditions, the adjustment applicant need not file an application for employment authorization to continue employment during the period described in the preceding sentence;

(10) An alien who has filed an application for suspension of deportation under section 244 of the Act (as it existed prior to April 1, 1997), cancellation of removal pursuant to section 240A of the Act, or special rule cancellation of removal under section 309(f)(1) of the Illegal Immigration Reform and Immigrant Responsibility Act of 1996, enacted as Pub.L. 104–208 (110 Stat. 3009–625) (as amended by the Nicaraguan Adjustment and Central American Relief Act (NACARA)), title II of Pub.L. 105–100 (111 Stat. 2160, 2193) and whose properly filed application has been accepted by the Service or EOIR;

(11) An alien paroled into the United States temporarily for emergency reasons or reasons deemed strictly in the public interest pursuant to § 212.5 of this chapter;

(12) An alien spouse of a long-term investor in the Commonwealth of the Northern Mariana Islands (E–2 CNMI Investor) other than an E–2 CNMI investor who obtained such status based upon a Foreign Retiree Investment Certificate, pursuant to 8 CFR 214.2(e)(23). An alien spouse of an E–2 CNMI Investor is eligible for employment in the CNMI only;

(13) [Reserved]

(14) An alien who has been granted deferred action, an act of administrative convenience to the government which gives some cases lower priority, if the alien establishes an economic necessity for employment;

(15) [Reserved]

(16) Any alien who has filed an application for creation of record of lawful admission for permanent residence pursuant to part 249 of this chapter;

(17) A nonimmigrant visitor for business (B–1) who:

(i) Is a personal or domestic servant who is accompanying or following to join an employer who seeks admission into, or is already in, the United States as a nonimmigrant defined under sections 101(a)(15)(B), (E), (F), (H), (I), (J), (L) or section 214(e) of the Act. The personal or domestic servant shall have a residence abroad which he or she has no intention of abandoning and shall demonstrate at least one year's experience as a personal or domestic servant. The nonimmigrant's employer shall demonstrate that the employer/employee relationship has existed for at least one year prior to the employer's admission to the United States; or, if the employer/employee relationship existed for less than one year, that the employer has regularly employed (either year-round or seasonally) personal or domestic servants over a period of several years preceding the employer's admission to the United States;

(ii) Is a domestic servant of a United States citizen accompanying or following to join his or her United States citizen employer who has a permanent home or is stationed in a foreign country, and who is visiting temporarily in the United States. The employer/employee relationship shall have existed prior to the commencement of the employer's visit to the United States; or

(iii) Is an employee of a foreign airline engaged in international transportation of passengers freight, whose position with the foreign airline would otherwise entitle the employee to classification under section 101(a)(15)(E)(i) of the Immigration and Nationality Act, and who is precluded from such classification solely because the employee is not a national of the country of the airline's nationality or because there is no treaty of commerce and navigation in effect between the United States and the country of the airline's nationality.

(18) An alien against whom a final order of deportation or removal exists and who is released on an order of supervision under the authority contained in section 241(a)(3) of the Act may be granted employment authorization in the discretion of the district director only if the alien cannot be removed due to the refusal of all countries designated by the alien or under section 241 of the Act to receive the alien, or because the removal of the alien is otherwise impracticable or contrary to the public interest. Additional factors which may be considered by the district director in adjudicating the application for employment authorization include, but are not limited to, the following:

(i) The existence of economic necessity to be employed;

(ii) The existence of a dependent spouse and/or children in the United States who rely on the alien for support; and

(iii) The anticipated length of time before the alien can be removed from the United States.

(19) An alien applying for Temporary Protected Status pursuant to section 244 of the Act shall apply for employment authorization only in accordance with the procedures set forth in part 244 of this chapter.

(20) Any alien who has filed a completed legalization application pursuant to section 210 of the Act (and part 210 of this chapter).

(21) A principal nonimmigrant witness or informant in S classification, and qualified dependent family members.

(22) Any alien who has filed a completed legalization application pursuant to section 245A of the Act (and part 245a of this chapter). Employment authorization shall be granted in increments not exceeding 1 year during the period the application is pending (including any period when an administrative appeal is pending) and shall expire on a specified date.

(23) Reserved.

(24) An alien who has filed an application for adjustment pursuant to section 1104 of the LIFE Act, Public Law 106–553, and the provisions of 8 CFR part 245a, Subpart B of this chapter.

(25) An immediate family member of a T–1 victim of a severe form of trafficking in persons designated as a T–2, T–3 or T–4 nonimmigrant pursuant to § 214.11 of this chapter. Aliens in this status shall only be authorized to work for the duration of their T nonimmigrant status.

(d) An alien lawfully enlisted in one of the Armed Forces, or whose enlistment the Secretary with jurisdiction over such Armed Force has determined would be vital to the national interest under 10 U.S.C. 504(b)(2), is authorized to be employed by that Armed Force in military service, if such employment is not otherwise authorized under this section and the immigration laws. An alien described in this section is not issued an employment authorization document.

(e) Basic criteria to establish economic necessity. Title 45—Public Welfare, Poverty Guidelines, 45 CFR 1060.2 should be used as the basic criteria to establish eligibility for employment authorization when the alien's economic necessity is identified as a factor. The alien shall submit an application for employee authorization listing his or her assets, income, and expenses as evidence of his or her economic need to work. Permission to work granted on the basis of the alien's application for employment authorization may be revoked under § 274a.14 of this chapter upon a showing that the information contained in the statement was not true and correct.

[53 FR 8614, March 16, 1988; 53 FR 46855, Nov. 21, 1988; 54 FR 16, Jan. 3, 1989; 54 FR 48577, Nov. 24, 1989; 55 FR 5576, Feb. 16, 1990; 55 FR 25935, 25936, June 25, 1990; 56 FR 624, Jan. 7, 1991; 56 FR 23496, 23499, May 22, 1991; 56 FR 41782, 41786, 41787, Aug. 23, 1991; 56 FR 55616, Oct. 29, 1991; 57 FR 6462, Feb. 25, 1992; 57 FR 31956, July 20, 1992; 57 FR 42884, Sept. 17, 1992; 58 FR 48780, Sept. 20, 1993; 58 FR 69217, Dec. 30, 1993; 59 FR 42487, Aug. 15, 1994; 59 FR 47063, Sept. 14, 1994; 59 FR 52894, Oct. 20, 1994; 59 FR 62302, Dec. 5, 1994; 60 FR 14353, March 17, 1995; 60 FR 21976, May 4, 1995; 60 FR 44271, Aug. 25, 1995; 60 FR 66067, 66069, Dec. 21, 1995; 61 FR 46537, Sept. 4, 1996; 62 FR 10389, March 6, 1997; 62 FR 18514, April 16, 1997; 62 FR 39425, July 23, 1997; 62 FR 46553, Sept. 3, 1997; 63 FR 1334, Jan. 9, 1998; 63 FR 27833, May 21, 1998; 63 FR 63597, Nov. 16, 1998; 64 FR 25773, May 12, 1999; 64 FR 27881, May 21, 1999; 65 FR 14780, March 17, 2000; 65 FR 14774, March 24, 2000; 65 FR 43680, July 14, 2000; 66 FR 29681, June 1, 2001; 66 FR 42595, Aug. 14, 2001; 66 FR 46704, Sept. 7, 2001; 67 FR 4803, Jan. 31, 2002; 67 FR 38350, June 4, 2002; 67 FR 76280, Dec. 11, 2002; 69 FR 45557, July

30, 2004; 69 FR 47763, Aug. 6, 2004; 72 FR 53041, Sept. 17, 2007; 73 FR 18956, Apr. 8, 2008; 73 FR 76914, Dec. 18, 2008; 74 FR 7995, Feb. 23, 2009; 74 FR 26515, June 3, 2009; 74 FR 55111, Oct. 27, 2009; 74 FR 55740, Oct. 28, 2009; 75 FR 47701, Aug. 9, 2010; 75 FR 58990, Sept. 24, 2010; 75 FR 79277, Dec. 20, 2010; 76 FR 53784, Aug. 29, 2011; 76 FR 55538, Sept. 7, 2011.]

§ 274a.13 Application for employment authorization. [also 8 C.F.R. § 1274a.13]

(a) Application. Aliens authorized to be employed under sections 274a.12(a)(3), (4), (6) through (8), (a)(10) through (15), and (a)(20) must file an application in order to obtain documentation evidencing this fact.

(1) Aliens who may apply for employment authorization under 8 CFR 274a.12(c), except for those who may apply under 8 CFR 274a.12(c)(8), must apply on the form designated by USCIS with the fee prescribed in 8 CFR 103.7(b)(1) and in accordance with the form instructions. The approval of applications filed under 8 CFR 274a.12(c), except for 8 CFR 274a.12(c)(8), are within the discretion of USCIS. Where economic necessity has been identified as a factor, the alien must provide information regarding his or her assets, income, and expenses.

(2) An initial employment authorization request for asylum applicants under 8 CFR 274a.12(c)(8) must be filed on the form designated by USCIS in accordance with the form instructions. The applicant also must submit a copy of the underlying application for asylum or withholding of deportation, together with evidence that the application has been filed in accordance with 8 CFR 208.3 and 208.4. An application for an initial employment authorization or for a renewal of employment authorization filed in relation to a pending claim for asylum shall be adjudicated in accordance with 8 CFR 208.7. An application for renewal or replacement of employment authorization submitted in relation to a pending claim for asylum, as provided in 8 CFR 208.7, must be filed, with fee or application for waiver of such fee.

(b) Approval of application. If the application is granted, the alien shall be notified of the decision and issued an employment authorization document valid for a specific period and subject to any terms and conditions as noted.

(c) Denial of application. If the application is denied, the applicant shall be notified in writing of the decision and the reasons for the denial. There shall be no appeal from the denial of the application.

(d) Interim employment authorization. USCIS will adjudicate the application within 90 days from the date of receipt of the application, except in the case of an initial application for employment authorization under 8 CFR 274a.12(c)(8), which is governed by paragraph (a)(2) of this section, and 8 CFR 274a.12(c)(9) in so far as it is governed by 8 CFR 245.13(j) and 245.15(n). Failure to complete the adjudication within 90 days will result in the grant of an employment authorization document for a period not to exceed 240 days. Such authorization will be subject to any conditions noted on the employment authorization document. However, if USCIS adjudicates the application prior to the expiration date of the interim employment authorization and denies the individual's employment authorization application, the interim employment authorization granted under this section will automatically terminate as of the date of the adjudication and denial.

[53 FR 8614, March 16, 1988; 55 FR 25937, June 25, 1990; 56 FR 41782, 41787, Aug. 23, 1991; 57 FR 6462, Feb. 25, 1992; 57 FR 14627, April 21, 1992; 58 FR 12149, March 3, 1993; 58 FR 14145, March 16, 1993; 59 FR 33905, July 1, 1994; 59 FR 62303, Dec. 5, 1994; 60 FR 21976, May 4, 1995; 60 FR 66067, Dec. 21, 1995; 63 FR 27833, May 21, 1998; 63 FR 39121, July 21, 1998; 64 FR 25773, May 12, 1999; 65 FR 14774, March 24, 2000; 72 FR 53042, Sept. 17, 2007; 74 FR 26940, June 5, 2009; 76 FR 53784, Aug. 29, 2011.]

§ 274a.14 Termination of employment authorization. [also 8 C.F.R. § 1274a.14]

(a) Automatic termination of employment authorization—

(1) Employment authorization granted under § 274a.12(c) of this chapter shall automatically terminate upon the occurrence of one of the following events:

(i) The expiration date specified by the Service on the employment authorization document is reached;

(ii) Exclusion or deportation proceedings are instituted (however, this shall not preclude the authorization of employment pursuant to § 274a.12(c) of this part where appropriate); or

(iii) The alien is granted voluntary departure.

(2) Termination of employment authorization pursuant to this paragraph does not require the service of a notice of intent to revoke; employment authorization terminates upon the occurrence of any event enumerated in paragraph (a)(1) of this section.

However, automatic revocation under this section does not preclude reapplication for employment authorization under § 274.12(c) of this part.

(b) Revocation of employment authorization—

(1) Basis for revocation of employment authorization. Employment authorization granted under § 274a.12(c) of this chapter may be revoked by the district director:

(i) Prior to the expiration date, when it appears that any condition upon which it was granted has not been met or no longer exists, or for good cause shown; or

(ii) Upon a showing that the information contained in the application is not true and correct.

(2) Notice of intent to revoke employment authorization. When a district director determines that employment authorization should be revoked prior to the expiration date specified by the Service, he or she shall serve written notice of intent to revoke the employment authorization. The notice will cite the reasons indicating that revocation is warranted. The alien will be granted a period of fifteen days from the date of service of the notice within which to submit countervailing evidence. The decision by the district director shall be final and no appeal shall lie from the decision to revoke the authorization.

(c) Automatic termination of temporary employment authorization granted prior to June 1, 1987—

(1) Temporary employment authorization granted prior to June 1, 1987, pursuant to 8 CFR 274a.12(c) (s 109.1(b) contained in the 8 CFR edition revised as of January 1, 1987), shall automatically terminate on the date specified by the Service on the document issued to the alien, or on December 31, 1996, whichever is earlier. Automatic termination of temporary employment authorization does not preclude a subsequent application for temporary employment authorization.

(2) A document issued by the Service prior to June 1, 1987, that authorized temporary employment authorization for any period beyond December 31, 1996, is null and void pursuant to paragraph (c)(1) of this section. The alien shall be issued a new employment authorization document upon application to the Service if the alien is eligible for temporary employment authorization pursuant to 274A.12(c).

(3) No notice of intent to revoke is necessary for the automatic termination of temporary employment authorization pursuant to this part.

[53 FR 8614, March 16, 1988; 53 FR 20087, June 1, 1988; 61 FR 46537, Sept. 4, 1996]

PART 292—REPRESENTATION AND APPEARANCES

§ 292.1 Representation of others. [also 8 C.F.R. § 1292.1]

(a) A person entitled to representation may be represented by any of the following, subject to the limitations in 8 CFR 103.2(a)(3):

(1) Attorneys in the United States. Any attorney as defined 8 CFR 1.2.

(2) Law students and law graduates not yet admitted to the bar. A law student who is enrolled in an accredited U.S. law school, or a graduate of an accredited U.S. law school who is not yet admitted to the bar, provided that:

(i) He or she is appearing at the request of the person entitled to representation;

(ii) In the case of a law student, he or she has filed a statement that he or she is participating, under the direct supervision of a faculty member, licensed attorney, or accredited representative, in a legal aid program or clinic conducted by a law school or non-profit organization, and that he or she is appearing without direct or indirect remuneration from the alien he or she represents;

(iii) In the case of a law graduate, he or she has filed a statement that he or she is appearing under the supervision of a licensed attorney or accredited representative and that he or she is appearing without direct or indirect remuneration from the alien he or she represents; and

(iv) The law student's or law graduate's appearance is permitted by the DHS official before whom he or she wishes to appear. The DHS official may require that a law student be accompanied by the supervising faculty member, attorney, or accredited representative.

(3) Reputable individuals. Any reputable individual of good moral character, provided that:

(i) He is appearing on an individual case basis, at the request of the person entitled to representation;

(ii) He is appearing without direct or indirect remuneration and files a written declaration to that effect;

(iii) He has a pre-existing relationship or connection with the person entitled to representation (e.g., as a relative, neighbor, clergyman, business associate or personal friend), provided that such requirement may be waived, as a matter of administrative discretion, in cases where adequate representation would not otherwise be available; and

(iv) His or her appearance is permitted by the DHS official before whom he or she seeks to appear, provided that such permission will not be granted with respect to any individual who regularly engages in immigration and naturalization practice or preparation, or holds himself or herself out to the public as qualified to do so.

(4) Accredited representatives. A person representing an organization described in § 292.2 of this chapter who has been accredited by the Board.

(5) Accredited officials. An accredited official, in the United States, of the government to which an alien owes allegiance, if the official appears solely in his official capacity and with the alien's consent.

(6) Attorneys outside the United States. An attorney, other than one described in 8 CFR 1.2, who is licensed to practice law and is in good standing in a court of general jurisdiction of the country in which he or she resides and who is engaged in such practice, may represent parties in matters before DHS, provided that he or she represents persons only in matters outside the geographical confines of the United States as defined in section 101(a)(38) of the Act, and that the DHS official before whom he or she wishes to appear allows such representation as a matter of discretion.

(b) Persons formerly authorized to practice. A person, other than a representative of an organization described in § 292.2 of this chapter, who on December 23, 1952, was authorized to practice before the Board and the Service may continue to act as a representative, subject to the provisions of § 292.3 of this chapter.

(c) Former employees. No person previously employed by the Department of Justice shall be permitted to act as a representative in any case in violation of the provisions of 28 CFR 45.735–7.

(d) Amicus curiae. The Board may grant permission to appear, on a case-by-case basis, as amicus curiae, to an attorney or to an organization represented by an attorney, if the public interest will be served thereby.

(e) Except as set forth in this section, no other person or persons shall represent others in any case.

[40 FR 23271, May 29. 1975; 53 FR 7728, March 10, 1988; 55 FR 49251, Nov. 27, 1990; 61 FR 53610, Oct. 15, 1996; 62 FR 23634, May 1, 1997; 75 FR 5227, Feb. 2, 2010; 76 FR 53784, Aug. 29, 2011.]

§ 292.2 Organizations qualified for recognition; requests for recognition; withdrawal of recognition; accreditation of representatives; roster. [also 8 C.F.R. § 1292.2]

(a) Qualifications of organizations. A non-profit religious, charitable, social service, or similar organization established in the United States and recognized as such by the Board may designate a representative or representatives to practice before the Service alone or the Service and the Board (including practice before the Immigration Court). Such organization must establish to the satisfaction of the Board that:

(1) It makes only nominal charges and assesses no excessive membership dues for persons given assistance; and

(2) It has at its disposal adequate knowledge, information and experience.

(b) Requests for recognition. An organization having the qualifications prescribed in paragraph (a) of this section may file an application for recognition on a Form G–27 directly with the Board, along with proof of service of a copy of the application on the district director having jurisdiction over the area in which the organization is located. The district director, within 30 days from the date of service, shall forward to the Board a recommendation for approval or disapproval of the application and the reasons therefor, or request a specified period of time in which to conduct an investigation or otherwise obtain relevant information regarding the applicant. The district director shall include proof of service of a copy of such recommendation or request on the organization. The organization shall have 30 days in which to file a response with the Board to a recommendation by a district director that is other than favorable, along with proof of service of a copy of such response on the district director. If the Board approves a request for time to conduct an investigation, or in its discretion remands the application to the district director for further information, the organization shall be advised of the time granted for such purpose. The Service shall promptly forward the results of any investigation or inquiry to the Board, along with its recommendations for approval or disapproval and the reasons therefor, and proof of service of a copy of the submission on the organization. The organization shall have 30 days from the date of such service to file a response with the Board to any matters raised therein, with proof of service of a copy of the response on the district director. Requests for extensions of filing times must be submitted in writing with the reasons therefor and may be granted by the Board in its discretion. Oral argument may be heard before the Board in its discretion at such date and time as the Board may direct. The organization and Service shall be informed by the Board of the action taken regarding an application. Any recognized organization shall promptly notify the Board of any changes in its name, address, or public telephone number.

(c) Withdrawal of recognition. The Board may withdraw the recognition of any organization which has failed to maintain the qualifications required by § 292.2(a). Withdrawal of recognition may be accomplished in accordance with the following procedure:

(1) The Service, by the district director within whose jurisdiction the organization is located, may conduct an investigation into any organization it believes no longer meets the standards for recognition.

(2) If the investigation establishes to the satisfaction of the district director that withdrawal proceedings should be instituted, he shall cause a written statement of the grounds upon which withdrawal is sought to be served upon the organization, with notice to show cause why its recognition should not be withdrawn. The notice will call upon the organization to appear before a special inquiry officer for a hearing at a time and place stated, not less than 30 days after service of the notice.

(3) The special inquiry officer shall hold a hearing, receive evidence, make findings of fact, state his recommendations, and forward the complete record to the Board.

(4) The organization and the Service shall have the opportunity of appearing at oral argument before the Board at a time specified by the Board.

(5) The Board shall consider the entire record and render its decision. The order of the Board shall constitute the final disposition of the proceedings.

(d) Accreditation of representatives. An organization recognized by the Board under paragraph (b) of this section may apply for accreditation of persons of good moral character as its representatives. An organization may apply to have a representative accredited to practice before the Service alone or the Service and the Board (including practice before immigration judges). An application for accreditation shall fully set forth the nature and extent of the proposed representative's experience and knowledge of immigration and naturalization law and procedure and the category of accreditation sought. No individual may submit an application on his or her own behalf. An application shall be filed directly with the Board, along with proof of service of a copy of the application on the district director having jurisdiction over the area in which the requesting organization is located. The district director, within 30 days from the date of service, shall forward to the Board a recommendation for approval or disapproval of the application and the reasons therefor, or request a specified period of time in which to conduct an investigation or otherwise obtain relevant information regarding the applicant. The district director shall include proof of service of a copy of such recommendation or request on the organization. The organization shall have 30 days in which to file a response with the Board to a recommendation by a district director that is other than favorable, with proof of service of a copy of such response on the district director. If the Board approves a request for time to conduct an investigation, or in its discretion remands the application to the district director for further information, the organization shall be advised of the time granted for such purpose. The district director shall promptly forward the results of any investigation or inquiry to the Board, along with a recommendation for approval or disapproval and the reasons therefor, and proof of service of a copy of the submission on the organization. The organization shall have 30 days from the date of service to file a response with the Board to any matters raised therein, with proof or service of a copy of the response on the district director. Requests for extensions of filing times must be submitted in writing with the reasons therefor and may be granted by the Board in its discretion. Oral argument may be heard before the Board in its discretion at such date and time as the Board may direct. The Board may approve or disapprove an application in whole or in part and shall inform the organization and the district director of the action taken with regard to an application. The accreditation of a representative shall be valid for a period of three years only; however, the accreditation shall remain valid pending Board consideration of an application for renewal of accreditation if the application is filed at least 60 days before the third anniversary of the date of the Board's prior accreditation of the representative. Accreditation terminates when the Board's recognition of the organization ceases for any reason or when the representative's employment or other connection with the organization ceases. The organization shall promptly notify the Board of such changes.

(e) Roster. The Board shall maintain an alphabetical roster of recognized organizations and their accredited representatives. A copy of the roster shall be furnished to the Commissioner and he shall be advised from time to time of changes therein.

[40 FR 23272, May 29, 1975; 49 FR 44086, Nov. 2, 1984; 62 FR 9075, Feb. 28, 1997]

TITLE 20—EMPLOYEES' BENEFITS

Part 656—Labor Certification Process for Permanent Employment of Aliens in the United States

Sec.

PART 656—LABOR CERTIFICATION PROCESS FOR PERMANENT EMPLOYMENT OF ALIENS IN THE UNITED STATES

§ 656.3 Definitions, for purposes of this part, of terms used in this part.

Act means the Immigration and Nationality Act, as amended, 8 U.S.C. 1101 et seq.

Agent means a person who is not an employee of an employer, and who has been designated in writing to act on behalf of an alien or employer in connection with an application for labor certification.

Applicant means a U.S. worker (see definition of U.S. worker below) who is applying for a job opportunity for which an employer has filed an Application for Permanent Employment Certification (ETA Form 9089).

Application means an Application for Permanent Employment Certification submitted by an employer (or its agent or attorney) in applying for a labor certification under this part.

Area of intended employment means the area within normal commuting distance of the place (address) of intended employment. There is no rigid measure of distance which constitutes a normal commuting distance or normal commuting area, because there may be widely varying factual circumstances among different areas (e.g., normal commuting distances might be 20, 30, or 50 miles). If the place of intended employment is within a Metropolitan Statistical Area (MSA) or a Primary Metropolitan Statistical Area (PMSA), any place within the MSA or PMSA is deemed to be within normal commuting distance of the place of intended employment; however, not all locations within a Consolidated Metropolitan Statistical Area (CMSA) will be deemed automatically to be within normal commuting distance. The borders of MSA's and PMSA's are not controlling in the identification of the normal commuting area; a location outside of an MSA or PMSA (or a CMSA) may be within normal commuting distance of a location that is inside (e.g., near the border of) the MSA or PMSA (or CMSA). The terminology CMSAs and PMSAs are being replaced by the Office of Management and Budget (OMB). However, ETA will continue to recognize the use of these area concepts as well as their replacements.

Attorney means any person who is a member in good standing of the bar of the highest court of any state, possession, territory, or commonwealth of the United States, or the District of Columbia, and who is not under suspension or disbarment from practice before any court or before DHS or the United States Department of Justice's Executive Office for Immigration Review. Such a person is permitted to act as an agent, representative, or attorney for an employer and/or alien under this part.

Barter, for purposes of an Application for Permanent Employment Certification (Form ETA 9089) or an Application for Alien Labor Certification (Form ETA 750), means the transfer of ownership of a labor certification application or certification from one person to another by voluntary act or agreement in exchange for a commodity, service, property or other valuable consideration.

Board of Alien Labor Certification Appeals (BALCA or Board) means the permanent Board established by this part, chaired by the Chief Administrative Law Judge, and consisting of Administrative Law Judges assigned to the Department of Labor and designated by the Chief Administrative Law Judge to be members of the Board of Alien Labor Certification Appeals. The Board of Alien Labor Certification Appeals is located in Washington, DC, and reviews and decides appeals in Washington, DC.

Certifying Officer (CO) means a Department of Labor official who makes determinations about whether or not to grant applications for labor certifications.

Closely-held Corporation means a corporation that typically has relatively few shareholders and whose shares are not generally traded in the securities market.

Employer means:

(1) A person, association, firm, or a corporation that currently has a location within the United States to which U.S. workers may be referred for employment and that proposes to employ a full-time employee at a place within the United States, or the authorized representative of such a person, association, firm, or corporation. An employer must possess a valid Federal Employer Identification Number (FEIN). For purposes of this definition, an "authorized representative" means an employee of the employer whose position or legal status authorizes the employee to act for the employer in labor certification matters. A labor certification can not be granted for an Application for Permanent Employment Certification filed on behalf of an independent contractor.

(2) Persons who are temporarily in the United States, including but not limited to, foreign diplomats, intra-company transferees, students, and exchange visitors, visitors for business or pleasure, and representatives of foreign information media can not be employers for the purpose of obtaining a labor certification for permanent employment.

Employment means:

(1) Permanent, full-time work by an employee for an employer other than oneself. For purposes of this definition, an investor is not an employee. In the event of an audit, the employer must be prepared to document the permanent and full-time nature of the position by furnishing position descriptions and payroll records for the job opportunity involved in the Application for Permanent Employment Certification.

(2) Job opportunities consisting solely of job duties that will be performed totally outside the United States, its territories, possessions, or commonwealths can not be the subject of an Application for Permanent Employment Certification.

Employment and Training Administration (ETA) means the agency within the Department of Labor (DOL) that includes the Office of Foreign Labor Certification (OFLC).

Immigration Officer means an official of the Department of Homeland Security, United States Citizenship and Immigration Services (USCIS) who handles applications for labor certifications under this part.

Job opportunity means a job opening for employment at a place in the United States to which U.S. workers can be referred.

Nonprofessional occupation means any occupation for which the attainment of a bachelor's or higher degree is not a usual requirement for the occupation.

Non-profit or tax-exempt organization for the purposes of § 656.40 means an organization that:

(1) Is defined as a tax exempt organization under the Internal Revenue Code of 1986, section 501(c)(3), (c)(4), or (c)(6) (26 U.S.C. 501(c)(3), (c)(4) or (c)(6)); and

(2) Has been approved as a tax-exempt organization for research or educational purposes by the Internal Revenue Service.

O*NET means the system developed by the Department of Labor, Employment and Training Administration, to provide to the general public information on skills, abilities, knowledge, work activities, interests and specific vocational preparation levels associated with occupations. O*NET is based on the Standard Occupational Classification system. Further information about O*NET can be found at http://www.onetcenter.org.

Office of Foreign Labor Certification means the organizational component within the Employment and Training Administration that provides national leadership and policy guidance and develops regulations and procedures to carry out the responsibilities of the Secretary of Labor under the Immigration and Nationality Act, as amended, concerning alien workers seeking admission to the United States in order to work under section 212(a)(5)(A) of the Immigration and Nationality Act, as amended.

Prevailing wage determination (PWD) means the prevailing wage provided or approved by an OFLC National Processing Center (NPC), in accordance with OFLC guidance governing foreign labor certification programs. This includes PWD requests processed for purposes of employer petitions filed with DHS under Schedule A or for sheepherders.

Professional occupation means an occupation for which the attainment of a bachelor's or higher degree is a usual education requirement. A beneficiary of an application for permanent alien employment certification involving a professional occupation need not have a bachelor's or higher degree to qualify for the professional occupation. However, if the employer is willing to accept work experience in lieu of a baccalaureate or higher degree, such work experience must be attainable in the U.S. labor market and must be stated on the application form. If the employer is willing to accept an equivalent foreign degree, it must be clearly stated on the Application for Permanent Employment Certification form.

"Purchase" for purposes of an Application for Permanent Employment Certification (Form ETA 9089) or an Application for Alien Labor Certification (Form ETA 750), means the transfer of ownership of a labor certification application or certification from one person to another by voluntary act and agreement, based on a valuable consideration.

"Sale" for purposes of an Application for Permanent Employment Certification (Form ETA 9089) or an Application for Alien Labor Certification (Form ETA 750), means an agreement between two parties, called, respectively, the seller (or vendor) and the buyer (or purchaser)

by which the seller, in consideration of the payment or promise of payment of a certain price in money terms, transfers ownership of a labor certification application or certification to the buyer.

Secretary means the Secretary of Labor, the chief official of the U.S. Department of Labor, or the Secretary's designee.

Secretary of Homeland Security means the chief official of the U.S. Department of Homeland Security or the Secretary of Homeland Security's designee.

Secretary of State means the chief official of the U.S. Department of State or the Secretary of State's designee.

Specific vocational preparation (SVP) means the amount of lapsed time required by a typical worker to learn the techniques, acquire the information, and develop the facility needed for average performance in a specific job-worker situation. Lapsed time is not the same as work time. For example, 30 days is approximately 1 month of lapsed time and not six 5–day work weeks, and 3 months refers to 3 calendar months and not 90 work days. The various levels of specific vocational preparation are provided below.

Level	Time
1	Short demonstration.
2	Anything beyond short demonstration up to and including 30 days.
3	Over 30 days up to and including 3 months.
4	Over 3 months up to and including 6 months.
5	Over 6 months up to and including 1 year.
6	Over 1 year up to and including 2 years.
7	Over 2 years up to and including 4 years.
8	Over 4 years up to and including 10 years.
9	Over 10 years.

"State Workforce Agency (SWA)", formerly known as State Employment Security Agency (SESA), means the state agency that receives funds under the Wagner–Peyser Act to provide employment-related services to U.S. workers and employers and/or administers the public labor exchange delivered through the state's one-stop delivery system in accordance with the Wagner–Peyser Act.

United States, when used in a geographic sense, means the 50 states, the District of Columbia, Puerto Rico, the U.S. Virgin Islands, and Guam.

United States worker means any worker who is:

(1) A U.S. citizen;

(2) A U.S. national;

(3) Lawfully admitted for permanent residence;

(4) Granted the status of an alien lawfully admitted for temporary residence under 8 U.S.C. 1160(a), 1161(a), or 1255a(a)(1);

(5) Admitted as a refugee under 8 U.S.C. 1157; or

(6) Granted asylum under 8 U.S.C. 1158.

[71 FR 35522, June 21, 2006; 72 FR 27944, May 17, 2007; 73 FR 78068, Dec. 19, 2008]

§ 656.5 Schedule A.

We have determined there are not sufficient United States workers who are able, willing, qualified, and available for the occupations listed below on Schedule A and the wages and working conditions of United States workers similarly employed will not be adversely affected by the employment of aliens in Schedule A occupations. An employer seeking a labor certification for an occupation listed on Schedule A may apply for that labor certification under § 656.15.

Schedule A

(a) Group I:

(1) Persons who will be employed as physical therapists, and who possess all the qualifications necessary to take the physical therapist licensing examination in the state in which they propose to practice physical therapy.

(2) Aliens who will be employed as professional nurses; and

(i) Who have received a Certificate from the Commission on Graduates of Foreign Nursing Schools (CGFNS);

(ii) Who hold a permanent, full and unrestricted license to practice professional nursing in the state of intended employment; or

(iii) Who have passed the National Council Licensure Examination for Registered Nurses (NCLEX–RN), administered by the National Council of State Boards of Nursing.

(3) Definitions of Group I occupations:

(i) Physical therapist means a person who applies the art and science of physical therapy to the treatment of patients with disabilities, disorders and injuries to relieve pain, develop or restore function, and maintain performance, using physical means, such as exercise, massage, heat, water, light, and electricity, as prescribed by a physician (or a surgeon).

(ii) Professional nurse means a person who applies the art and science of nursing which reflects comprehension of principles derived from the physical, biological and behavioral sciences. Professional nursing generally includes making clinical judgments involving the observation, care and counsel of persons requiring nursing care; administering of medicines and treatments prescribed by the physician or dentist; and participation in the activities for the promotion of health and prevention of illness in others. A program of study for professional nurses generally includes theory and practice in clinical areas such as obstetrics, surgery, pediatrics, psychiatry, and medicine.

(b) Group II:

(1) Sciences or arts (except performing arts). Aliens (except for aliens in the performing arts) of exceptional ability in the sciences or arts including college and university teachers of exceptional ability who have been practicing their science or art during the year prior to application and who intend to practice the same science or art in the United States. For purposes of this group, the term "science or art" means any field of knowledge and/or skill with respect to which colleges and universities commonly offer specialized courses leading to a degree in the knowledge and/or skill. An alien, however, need not have studied at a college or university in order to qualify for the Group II occupation.

(2) Performing arts. Aliens of exceptional ability in the performing arts whose work during the past 12 months did require, and whose intended work in the United States will require, exceptional ability.

[69 FR 77326, 77389, Dec. 27, 2004]

§ 656.10 General instructions.

(a) Filing of applications. A request for a labor certification on behalf of any alien who is required by the Act to be a beneficiary of a labor certification in order to obtain permanent resident status in the United States may be filed as follows:

(1) Except as provided in paragraphs (a)(2), (3), and (4) of this section, an employer seeking a labor certification must file under this section and § 656.17.

(2) An employer seeking a labor certification for a college or university teacher must apply for a labor certification under this section and must also file under either § 656.17 or § 656.18.

(3) An employer seeking labor certification for an occupation listed on Schedule A must apply for a labor certification under this section and § 656.15.

(4) An employer seeking labor certification for a sheepherder must apply for a labor certification under this section and must also choose to file under either § 656.16 or § 656.17.

(b) Representation.

(1) Employers may have agents or attorneys represent them throughout the labor certification process. If an employer intends to be represented by an agent or attorney, the employer must sign the statement set forth on the Application for Permanent Employment Certification form: That the attorney or agent is representing the employer and the employer takes full responsibility for the accuracy of any representations made by the attorney or agent. Whenever, under this part, any notice or other document is required to be sent to the employer, the document will be sent to the attorney or agent who has been authorized to represent the employer on the Application for Permanent Employment Certification form.

(2)(i) It is contrary to the best interests of U.S. workers to have the alien and/or agents or attorneys for either the employer or the alien participate in interviewing or considering U.S. workers for the job offered the alien. As the beneficiary of a labor certification application, the alien can not represent the best interests of U.S. workers in the job opportunity. The alien's agent and/or attorney can not represent the alien effectively and at the same time truly be seeking U.S. workers for the job opportunity. Therefore, the alien and/or the alien's agent and/or attorney may not interview or consider U.S. workers for the job offered to the alien, unless the agent and/or attorney is the employer's representative, as described in paragraph (b)(2)(ii) of this section.

(ii) The employer's representative who interviews or considers U.S. workers for the job offered to the alien must be the person who normally interviews or considers, on behalf of the employer, applicants for job opportunities such as that offered the alien, but which do not involve labor certifications.

(3) No person under suspension or disbarment from practice before any court or before the DHS or the United States Department of Justice's Executive Office for Immigration Review is permitted to act as an agent, representative, or attorney for an employer and/or alien under this part.

(c) Attestations. The employer must certify to the conditions of employment listed below on the Application for Permanent Employment Certification under penalty of perjury under 18 U.S.C. 1621(2). Failure to attest to any of the conditions listed below results in a denial of the application.

(1) The offered wage equals or exceeds the prevailing wage determined pursuant to § 656.40 and § 656.41, and the wage the employer will pay to the alien to begin work will equal or exceed the prevailing wage that is applicable at the time the alien begins work or from the time the alien is admitted to take up the certified employment;

(2) The wage offered is not based on commissions, bonuses or other incentives, unless the employer guarantees a prevailing wage paid on a weekly, bi-weekly, or monthly basis that equals or exceeds the prevailing wage;

(3) The employer has enough funds available to pay the wage or salary offered the alien;

(4) The employer will be able to place the alien on the payroll on or before the date of the alien's proposed entrance into the United States;

(5) The job opportunity does not involve unlawful discrimination by race, creed, color, national origin, age, sex, religion, handicap, or citizenship;

(6) The employer's job opportunity is not:

(i) Vacant because the former occupant is on strike or locked out in the course of a labor dispute involving a work stoppage;

(ii) At issue in a labor dispute involving a work stoppage.

(7) The job opportunity's terms, conditions and occupational environment are not contrary to Federal, state or local law;

(8) The job opportunity has been and is clearly open to any U.S. worker;

(9) The U.S. workers who applied for the job opportunity were rejected for lawful job-related reasons;

(10) The job opportunity is for full-time, permanent employment for an employer other than the alien.

(d) Notice.

(1) In applications filed under §§ 656.15 (Schedule A), 656.16 (Sheepherders), 656.17 (Basic Process), 656.18 (College and University Teachers), and 656.21 (Supervised Recruitment), the employer must give notice of the filing of the Application for Permanent Employment Certification and be able to document that notice was provided, if requested by the Certifying Officer, as follows:

(i) To the bargaining representative(s) (if any) of the employer's employees in the occupational classification for which certification of the job opportunity is sought in the employer's location(s) in the area of intended employment. Documentation may consist of a copy of the letter and a copy of the Application for Permanent Employment Certification form that was sent to the bargaining representative.

(ii) If there is no such bargaining representative, by posted notice to the employer's employees at the facility or location of the employment. The notice must be posted for at least 10 consecutive business days. The notice must be clearly visible and unobstructed while posted and must be posted in conspicuous places where the employer's U.S. workers can readily read the posted notice on their way to or from their place of employment. Appropriate locations for posting notices of the job opportunity include locations in the immediate vicinity of the wage and hour notices required by 29 CFR 516.4 or occupational safety and health notices required by 29 CFR 1903.2(a). In addition, the employer must publish the notice in any and all in-house media, whether electronic or printed, in accordance with the normal procedures used for the recruitment of similar positions in the employer's organization. The documentation requirement may be satisfied by providing a copy of the posted notice and stating where it was posted, and by providing copies of all the in-house media, whether electronic or print, that were used to distribute notice of the application in accordance with the procedures used for similar positions within the employer's organization.

(2) In the case of a private household, notice is required under this paragraph (d) only if the household employs one or more U.S. workers at the time the application for labor certification is filed. The documentation requirement may be satisfied by providing a copy of the posted notice to the Certifying Officer.

(3) The notice of the filing of an Application for Permanent Employment Certification must:

(i) State the notice is being provided as a result of the filing of an application for permanent alien labor certification for the relevant job opportunity;

(ii) State any person may provide documentary evidence bearing on the application to the Certifying Officer of the Department of Labor;

(iii) Provide the address of the appropriate Certifying Officer; and

(iv) Be provided between 30 and 180 days before filing the application.

(4) If an application is filed under § 656.17, the notice must contain the information required for advertisements by § 656.17(f), must state the rate of pay (which must equal or exceed the prevailing wage entered by the SWA on the prevailing wage request form), and must contain the information required by paragraph (d)(3) of this section.

(5) If an application is filed on behalf of a college and university teacher selected in a competitive selection and recruitment process, as provided by § 656.18, the notice must include the information required for advertisements by § 656.18(b)(3), and must include the information required by paragraph (d)(3) of this section.

(6) If an application is filed under the Schedule A procedures at § 656.15, or the procedures for sheepherders at § 656.16, the notice must contain a description of the job and rate of pay, and must meet the requirements of this section.

(e)(1)(i) Submission of evidence. Any person may submit to the Certifying Officer documentary evidence bearing on an application for permanent alien labor certification filed under the basic labor certification process at § 656.17 or an application involving a college and university teacher selected in a competitive recruitment and selection process under § 656.18.

(ii) Documentary evidence submitted under paragraph (e)(1)(i) of this section may include information on available workers, information on wages and working conditions, and information on the employer's failure to meet the terms and conditions for the employment of alien workers and co-workers. The Certifying Officer must consider this information in making his or her determination.

(2)(i) Any person may submit to the appropriate DHS office documentary evidence of fraud or willful misrepresentation in a Schedule A application filed under § 656.15 or a sheepherder application filed under § 656.16.

(ii) Documentary evidence submitted under paragraph (e)(2) of this section is limited to information relating to possible fraud or willful misrepresentation. The DHS may consider this information under § 656.31.

(f) Retention of Documents. Copies of applications for permanent employment certification filed with the Department of Labor and all supporting documentation must be retained by the employer for 5 years from the date of filing the Application for Permanent Employment Certification.

[71 FR 35523, June 21, 2006]

§ 656.15 Applications for labor certification for Schedule A occupations.

(a) Filing application. An employer must apply for a labor certification for a Schedule A occupation by filing an application with the appropriate DHS office, and not with an ETA application processing center.

(b) General documentation requirements. A Schedule A application must include:

(1) An Application for Permanent Employment Certification form, which includes a prevailing wage determination in accordance with § 656.40 and § 656.41.

(2) Evidence that notice of filing the Application for Permanent Employment Certification was provided to the bargaining representative or the employer's employees as prescribed in § 656.10(d).

(c) Group I documentation. An employer seeking labor certification under Group I of Schedule A must file with DHS, as part of its labor certification application, documentary evidence of the following:

(1) An employer seeking Schedule A labor certification for an alien to be employed as a physical therapist (§ 656.5(a)(1)) must file as part of its labor certification application a letter or statement, signed by an authorized state physical therapy licensing official in the state of intended employment, stating the alien is qualified to take that state's written licensing examination for physical therapists. Application for certification of permanent employment as a physical therapist may be made only under this § 656.15 and not under § 656.17.

(2) An employer seeking a Schedule A labor certification for an alien to be employed as a professional nurse (§ 656.5(a)(2)) must file as part of its labor certification application documentation that the alien has received a Certificate from the Commission on Graduates of Foreign Nursing Schools (CGFNS); that the alien holds a full and unrestricted (permanent) license to practice nursing in the state of intended employment; or that the alien has passed the National Council Licensure Examination for Registered Nurses (NCLEX–RN). Application for certification of employment as a professional nurse may be made only under this § 656.15(c) and not under § 656.17.

(d) Group II documentation. An employer seeking a Schedule A labor certification under Group II of Schedule A must file with DHS, as part of its labor certification application, documentary evidence of the following:

(1) An employer seeking labor certification on behalf of an alien to be employed as an alien of exceptional ability in the sciences or arts (excluding those in the performing arts) must file documentary evidence showing the widespread acclaim and international recognition accorded the alien by recognized experts in the alien's field; and documentation showing the alien's work in that field during the past year did, and the alien's intended work in the United States will, require exceptional ability. In addition, the employer must file documentation about the alien from at least two of the following seven groups:

(i) Documentation of the alien's receipt of internationally recognized prizes or awards for excellence in the field for which certification is sought;

(ii) Documentation of the alien's membership in international associations, in the field for which certification is sought, which require outstanding achievement of their members, as judged by recognized international experts in their disciplines or fields;

(iii) Published material in professional publications about the alien, about the alien's work in the field for which certification is sought, which shall include the title, date, and author of such published material;

(iv) Evidence of the alien's participation on a panel, or individually, as a judge of the work of others in the same or in an allied field of specialization to that for which certification is sought;

(v) Evidence of the alien's original scientific or scholarly research contributions of major significance in the field for which certification is sought;

(vi) Evidence of the alien's authorship of published scientific or scholarly articles in the field for which certification is sought, in international professional journals or professional journals with an international circulation;

(vii) Evidence of the display of the alien's work, in the field for which certification is sought, at artistic exhibitions in more than one country.

(2) An employer seeking labor certification on behalf of an alien of exceptional ability in the performing arts must file documentary evidence that the alien's work experience during the past twelve months did require, and the alien's intended work in the United States will require, exceptional ability; and must submit documentation to show this exceptional ability, such as:

(i) Documentation attesting to the current widespread acclaim and international recognition accorded to the alien, and receipt of internationally recognized prizes or awards for excellence;

(ii) Published material by or about the alien, such as critical reviews or articles in major newspapers, periodicals, and/or trade journals (the title, date, and author of such material shall be indicated);

(iii) Documentary evidence of earnings commensurate with the claimed level of ability;

(iv) Playbills and star billings;

(v) Documents attesting to the outstanding reputation of theaters, concert halls, night clubs, and other establishments in which the alien has appeared or is scheduled to appear; and/or

(vi) Documents attesting to the outstanding reputation of theaters or repertory companies, ballet troupes, orchestras, or other organizations in which or with which the alien has performed during the past year in a leading or starring capacity.

(e) Determination. An Immigration Officer determines whether the employer and alien have met the applicable requirements of § 656.10 and of Schedule A (§ 656.5); reviews the application; and determines whether or not the alien is qualified for and intends to pursue the Schedule A occupation. The Schedule A determination of DHS is conclusive and final. The employer, therefore, may not appeal from any such determination under the review procedures at § 656.26.

(f) Refiling after denial. If an application for a Schedule A occupation is denied, the employer, except where the occupation is as a physical therapist or a professional nurse, may at any time file for a labor certification on the alien beneficiary's behalf under § 656.17. Labor certifications for professional nurses and for physical therapists shall not be considered under § 656.17.

[69 FR 77326, 77390, Dec. 27, 2004; 72 FR 27944, May 17, 2007; 73 FR 78068, Dec. 19, 2008]

§ 656.17 Basic labor certification process.

(a) Filing applications.

(1) Except as otherwise provided by §§ 656.15, 656.16, and 656.18, an employer who desires to apply for a labor certification on behalf of an alien must file a completed Department of Labor Application for Permanent Employment Certification form (ETA Form 9089). The application must be filed with an ETA application processing center. Incomplete applications will be denied. Applications filed and certified electronically must, upon receipt of the labor certification, be signed immediately by the employer in order to be valid. Applications submitted by mail must contain the original signature of the employer, alien, attorney, and/or agent when they are received by the application processing center. DHS will not process petitions unless they are supported by an original certified ETA Form 9089 that has been signed by the employer, alien, attorney and/or agent.

(2) The Department of Labor may issue or require the use of certain identifying information, including user identifiers, passwords, or personal identification numbers (PINS). The purpose of these personal identifiers is to allow the Department of Labor to associate a given electronic submission with a single, specific individual. Personal identifiers can not be issued to a company or business. Rather, a personal identifier can only be issued to specific individual. Any personal identifiers must be used solely by the individual to whom they are assigned and can not be used or transferred to any other individual. An individual assigned a personal identifier must take all reasonable steps to ensure that his or her personal identifier can not be compromised. If an individual assigned a personal identifier suspects, or becomes aware, that his or her personal identifier has been compromised or is being used by someone else, then the individual must notify the Department of Labor immediately of the incident and cease the electronic transmission of any further submissions under that personal identifier until such time as a new personal identifier is provided. Any electronic transmissions submitted with a personal identifier will be presumed to be a submission by the individual assigned that personal identifier. The Department of Labor's system will notify those making submissions of these requirements at the time of each submission.

(3) Documentation supporting the application for labor certification should not be filed with the application, however in the event the Certifying Officer notifies the employer that its application is to be audited, the employer must furnish required supporting documentation prior to a final determination.

(b) Processing.

(1) Applications are screened and are certified, are denied, or are selected for audit.

(2) Employers will be notified if their applications have been selected for audit by the issuance of an audit letter under § 656.20.

(3) Applications may be selected for audit in accordance with selection criteria or may be randomly selected.

(c) Filing date. Non-electronically filed applications accepted for processing shall be date stamped. Electronically filed applications will be considered filed when submitted.

(d) Refiling Procedures.

(1) Employers that filed applications under the regulations in effect prior to March 28, 2005, may, if a job order has not been placed pursuant to those regulations, refile such applications under this part without loss of the original filing date by:

(i) Submitting an application for an identical job opportunity after complying with all of the filing and recruiting requirements of this part 656; and

(ii) Withdrawing the original application in accordance with ETA procedures. Filing an application under this part stating the employer's desire to use the original filing date will be deemed to be a withdrawal of the original application. The original application will be deemed withdrawn regardless of whether the employer's request to use the original filing date is approved.

(2) Refilings under this paragraph must be made within 210 days of the withdrawal of the prior application.

(3) A copy of the original application, including amendments, must be sent to the appropriate ETA application processing center when requested by the CO under § 656.20.

(4) For purposes of paragraph (d)(1)(i) of this section, a job opportunity shall be considered identical if the employer, alien, job title, job location, job requirements, and job description are the same as those stated in the original application filed under the regulations in effect prior to March 28, 2005. For purposes of determining identical job opportunity, the original application includes all accepted amendments up to the time the application was withdrawn, including amendments in response to an assessment notice from a

SWA pursuant to § 656.21(h) of the regulations in effect prior to March 28, 2005.

(e) Required pre-filing recruitment. Except for labor certification applications involving college or university teachers selected pursuant to a competitive recruitment and selection process (§ 656.18), Schedule A occupations (§§ 656.5 and 656.15), and sheepherders (§ 656.16), an employer must attest to having conducted the following recruitment prior to filing the application:

(1) Professional occupations. If the application is for a professional occupation, the employer must conduct the recruitment steps within 6 months of filing the application for alien employment certification. The employer must maintain documentation of the recruitment and be prepared to submit this documentation in the event of an audit or in response to a request from the Certifying Officer prior to rendering a final determination.

(i) Mandatory steps. Two of the steps, a job order and two print advertisements, are mandatory for all applications involving professional occupations, except applications for college or university teachers selected in a competitive selection and recruitment process as provided in § 656.18. The mandatory recruitment steps must be conducted at least 30 days, but no more than 180 days, before the filing of the application.

(A) Job order. Placement of a job order with the SWA serving the area of intended employment for a period of 30 days. The start and end dates of the job order entered on the application shall serve as documentation of this step.

(B) Advertisements in newspaper or professional journals.

(1) Placing an advertisement on two different Sundays in the newspaper of general circulation in the area of intended employment most appropriate to the occupation and the workers likely to apply for the job opportunity and most likely to bring responses from able, willing, qualified, and available U.S. workers.

(2) If the job opportunity is located in a rural area of intended employment that does not have a newspaper with a Sunday edition, the employer may use the edition with the widest circulation in the area of intended employment.

(3) The advertisements must satisfy the requirements of paragraph (f) of this section. Documentation of this step can be satisfied by furnishing copies of the newspaper pages in which the advertisements appeared or proof of publication furnished by the newspaper.

(4) If the job involved in the application requires experience and an advanced degree, and a professional journal normally would be used to advertise the job opportunity, the employer may, in lieu of one of the Sunday advertisements, place an advertisement in the professional journal most likely to bring responses from able, willing, qualified, and available U.S. workers. Documentation of this step can be satisfied by providing a copy of the page in which the advertisement appeared.

(ii) Additional recruitment steps. The employer must select three additional recruitment steps from the alternatives listed in paragraphs (e)(1)(ii)(A)–(J) of this section. Only one of the additional steps may consist solely of activity that took place within 30 days of the filing of the application. None of the steps may have taken place more than 180 days prior to filing the application.

(A) Job fairs. Recruitment at job fairs for the occupation involved in the application, which can be documented by brochures advertising the fair and newspaper advertisements in which the employer is named as a participant in the job fair.

(B) Employer's Web site. The use of the employer's Web site as a recruitment medium can be documented by providing dated copies of pages from the site that advertise the occupation involved in the application.

(C) Job search Web site other than the employer's. The use of a job search Web site other than the employer's can be documented by providing dated copies of pages from one or more website(s) that advertise the occupation involved in the application. Copies of web pages generated in conjunction with the newspaper advertisements required by paragraph (e)(1)(i)(B) of this section can serve as documentation of the use of a Web site other than the employer's.

(D) On-campus recruiting. The employer's on-campus recruiting can be documented by providing copies of the notification issued or posted by the college's or university's placement office naming the employer and the date it conducted interviews for employment in the occupation.

(E) Trade or professional organizations. The use of professional or trade organizations as a recruitment source can be documented by providing copies of pages of newsletters or trade journals containing advertisements for the occupation involved in the application for alien employment certification.

(F) Private employment firms. The use of private employment firms or placement agencies can be documented by providing documentation sufficient to demonstrate that recruitment has been conducted by a private firm for the occupation for which certification is sought. For example, documentation might consist of copies of contracts between the employer and the private employment firm and copies of advertisements placed by the private employment firm for the occupation involved in the application.

(G) Employee referral program with incentives. The use of an employee referral program with incentives can be documented by providing dated copies of employer notices or memoranda advertising the program and specifying the incentives offered.

(H) Campus placement offices. The use of a campus placement office can be documented by providing a copy of the employer's notice of the job opportunity provided to the campus placement office.

(I) Local and ethnic newspapers. The use of local and ethnic newspapers can be documented by providing a copy of the page in the newspaper that contains the employer's advertisement.

(J) Radio and television advertisements. The use of radio and television advertisements can be documented by providing a copy of the employer's text of the employer's advertisement along with a written confirmation from the radio or television station stating when the advertisement was aired.

(2) Nonprofessional occupations. If the application is for a nonprofessional occupation, the employer must at a minimum, place a job order and two newspaper advertisements within 6 months of filing the application. The steps must be conducted at least 30 days but no more that 180 days before the filing of the application.

(i) Job order. Placing a job order with the SWA serving the area of intended employment for a period of 30 days. The start and end dates of the job order entered on the application serve as documentation of this step.

(ii) Newspaper advertisements.

(A) Placing an advertisement on two different Sundays in the newspaper of general circulation in the area of intended employment most appropriate to the occupation and the workers likely to apply for the job opportunity.

(B) If the job opportunity is located in a rural area of intended employment that does not have a newspaper that publishes a Sunday edition, the employer may use the newspaper edition with the widest circulation in the area of intended employment.

(C) Placement of the newspaper advertisements can be documented in the same way as provided in paragraph (e)(1)(i)(B)(3) of this section for professional occupations.

(D) The advertisements must satisfy the requirements of paragraph (f) of this section.

(f) Advertising requirements. Advertisements placed in newspapers of general circulation or in professional journals before filing the Application for Permanent Employment Certification must:

(1) Name the employer;

(2) Direct applicants to report or send resumes, as appropriate for the occupation, to the employer;

(3) Provide a description of the vacancy specific enough to apprise the U.S. workers of the job opportunity for which certification is sought;

(4) Indicate the geographic area of employment with enough specificity to apprise applicants of any travel requirements and where applicants will likely have to reside to perform the job opportunity;

(5) Not contain a wage rate lower than the prevailing wage rate;

(6) Not contain any job requirements or duties which exceed the job requirements or duties listed on the ETA Form 9089; and

(7) Not contain wages or terms and conditions of employment that are less favorable than those offered to the alien.

(g) Recruitment report.

(1) The employer must prepare a recruitment report signed by the employer or the employer's representative noted in § 656.10(b)(2)(ii) describing the recruitment steps undertaken and the results achieved, the number of hires, and, if applicable, the number of U.S. workers rejected, categorized by the lawful job related reasons for such rejections. The Certifying Officer, after reviewing the employer's recruitment report, may request the U.S. workers' resumes or applications, sorted by the reasons the workers were rejected.

(2) A U.S. worker is able and qualified for the job opportunity if the worker can acquire the skills necessary to perform the duties involved in the occupation during a reasonable period of on-the-job training. Rejecting U.S. workers for lacking skills necessary to perform the duties involved in the occupation, where the U.S. workers are capable of acquiring the skills during a reasonable period of on-the-job training is not a lawful job-related reason for rejection of the U.S. workers.

(h) Job duties and requirements.

(1) The job opportunity's requirements, unless adequately documented as arising from business necessity, must be those normally required for the occupation and must not exceed the Specific Vocational Preparation level assigned to the occupation as shown in the O*NET Job Zones. To establish a business necessity, an employer must demonstrate the job duties and requirements bear a reasonable relationship to the occupation in the context of the employer's business and are essential to perform the job in a reasonable manner.

(2) A foreign language requirement can not be included, unless it is justified by business necessity. Demonstrating business necessity for a foreign language requirement may be based upon the following:

(i) The nature of the occupation, e.g., translator; or

(ii) The need to communicate with a large majority of the employer's customers, contractors, or employees who can not communicate effectively in English, as documented by:

(A) The employer furnishing the number and proportion of its clients, contractors, or employees who can not communicate in English, and/or a detailed plan to market products or services in a foreign country; and

(B) A detailed explanation of why the duties of the position for which certification is sought requires frequent contact and communication with customers, employees or contractors who can not communicate in English and why it is reasonable to believe the allegedly foreign-language-speaking customers, employees, and contractors can not communicate in English.

(3) If the job opportunity involves a combination of occupations, the employer must document that it has normally employed persons for that combination of occupations, and/or workers customarily perform the combination of occupations in the area of intended employment, and/or the combination job opportunity is based on a business necessity. Combination occupations can be documented by position descriptions and relevant payroll records, and/or letters from other employers stating their workers normally perform the combination of occupations in the area of intended employment, and/or documentation that the combination occupation arises from a business necessity.

(4)(i) Alternative experience requirements must be substantially equivalent to the primary requirements of the job opportunity for which certification is sought; and

(ii) If the alien beneficiary already is employed by the employer, and the alien does not meet the primary job requirements and only potentially qualifies for the job by virtue of the employer's alternative requirements, certification will be denied unless the application states that any suitable combination of education, training, or experience is acceptable.

(i) Actual minimum requirements. DOL will evaluate the employer's actual minimum requirements in accordance with this paragraph (i).

(1) The job requirements, as described, must represent the employer's actual minimum requirements for the job opportunity.

(2) The employer must not have hired workers with less training or experience for jobs substantially comparable to that involved in the job opportunity.

(3) If the alien beneficiary already is employed by the employer, in considering whether the job requirements represent the employer's actual minimums, DOL will review the training and experience possessed by the alien beneficiary at the time of hiring by the employer, including as a contract employee. The employer can not require domestic worker applicants to possess training and/or experience beyond what the alien possessed at the time of hire unless:

(i) The alien gained the experience while working for the employer, including as a contract employee, in a position not substantially comparable to the position for which certification is being sought, or

(ii) The employer can demonstrate that it is no longer feasible to train a worker to qualify for the position.

(4) In evaluating whether the alien beneficiary satisfies the employer's actual minimum requirements, DOL will not consider any education or training obtained by the alien beneficiary at the employer's expense unless the employer offers similar training to domestic worker applicants.

(5) For purposes of this paragraph (i):

(i) The term "employer" means an entity with the same Federal Employer Identification Number (FEIN), provided it meets the definition of an employer at § 656.3.

(ii) A "substantially comparable" job or position means a job or position requiring performance of the same job duties more than 50 percent of the time. This requirement can be documented by furnishing position descriptions, the percentage of time spent on the various duties, organization charts, and payroll records.

(j) Conditions of employment.

(1) Working conditions must be normal to the occupation in the area and industry.

(2) Live-in requirements are acceptable for household domestic service workers only if the employer can demonstrate the requirement is essential to perform, in a reasonable manner, the job duties as described by the employer and there are not cost-effective alternatives to a live-in household requirement. Mere employer assertions do not constitute acceptable documentation. For example, a live-in requirement could be supported by documenting two working parents and young children in the household, and/or the existence of erratic work schedules requiring frequent travel and a need to entertain business associates and clients on short notice. Depending upon the situation, acceptable documentation could consist of travel vouchers, written estimates of costs of alternatives such as babysitters, or a detailed listing of the frequency and length of absences of the employer from the home.

(k) Layoffs.

(1) If there has been a layoff by the employer applicant in the area of intended employment within 6 months of filing an application involving the occupation for which certification is sought or in a related occupation, the employer must document it has notified and considered all potentially qualified laid off (employer applicant) U.S. workers of the job opportunity involved in the application and the results of the notification and consideration. A layoff shall be considered any involuntary separation of one or more employees without cause or prejudice.

(2) For the purposes of paragraph (k)(1) of this section, a related occupation is any occupation that requires workers to perform a majority of the essential duties involved in the occupation for which certification is sought.

(*l*) Alien influence and control over job opportunity. If the employer is a closely held corporation or partnership in which the alien has an ownership interest, or if there is a familial relationship between the stockholders, corporate officers, incorporators, or partners, and the alien, or if the alien is one of a small number of employees, the employer in the event of an audit must be able to demonstrate the existence of a bona fide job opportunity, i.e. the job is available to all U.S. workers, and must provide to the Certifying Officer, the following supporting documentation:

(1) A copy of the articles of incorporation, partnership agreement, business license or similar documents that establish the business entity;

(2) A list of all corporate/company officers and shareholders/partners of the corporation/firm/business, their titles and positions in the business' structure, and a description of the relationships to each other and to the alien beneficiary;

(3) The financial history of the corporation/company/partnership, including the total investment in the business entity and the amount of investment of each officer, incorporator/partner and the alien beneficiary; and

(4) The name of the business' official with primary responsibility for interviewing and hiring applicants for positions within the organization and the name(s) of the business' official(s) having control or influence over hiring decisions involving the position for which labor certification is sought.

(5) If the alien is one of 10 or fewer employees, the employer must document any family relationship between the employees and the alien.

[69 FR 77326, 77392, Dec. 27, 2004]

§ 656.18 Optional special recruitment and documentation procedures for college and university teachers.

(a) Filing requirements. Applications for certification of employment of college and university teachers must be filed by submitting a completed Application for Permanent Employment Certification form to the appropriate ETA application processing center.

(b) Recruitment. The employer may recruit for college and university teachers under § 656.17 or must be able to document the alien was selected for the job opportunity in a competitive recruitment and selection process through which the alien was found to be more qualified than any of the United States workers who applied for the job. For purposes of this paragraph (b), documentation of the "competitive recruitment and selection process" must include:

(1) A statement, signed by an official who has actual hiring authority from the employer outlining in detail the complete recruitment procedures undertaken; and which must set forth:

(i) The total number of applicants for the job opportunity;

(ii) The specific lawful job-related reasons why the alien is more qualified than each U.S. worker who applied for the job; and

(2) A final report of the faculty, student, and/or administrative body making the recommendation or selection of the alien, at the completion of the competitive recruitment and selection process;

(3) A copy of at least one advertisement for the job opportunity placed in a national professional journal, giving the name and the date(s) of publication; and which states the job title, duties, and requirements;

(4) Evidence of all other recruitment sources utilized; and

(5) A written statement attesting to the degree of the alien's educational or professional qualifications and academic achievements.

(c) Time limit for filing. Applications for permanent alien labor certification for job opportunities as college and university teachers must be filed within 18 months after a selection is made pursuant to a competitive recruitment and selection process.

(d) Alternative procedure. An employer that can not or does not choose to satisfy the special recruitment procedures for a college or university teacher under this section may avail itself of the basic process at § 656.17. An employer that files for certification of employment of college and university teachers under § 656.17 or this section must be able to document, if requested by the Certifying Officer, in accordance with § 656.24(a)(2)(ii), the alien was found to be more qualified than each U.S. worker who applied for the job opportunity.

[69 FR 77326, 77395, Dec. 27, 2004]

§ 656.21 Supervised recruitment.

(a) Supervised recruitment. Where the Certifying Officer determines it appropriate, post-filing supervised recruitment may be required of the employer for the pending application or future applications pursuant to § 656.20(b).

(b) Requirements. Supervised recruitment shall consist of advertising for the job opportunity by placing an advertisement in a newspaper of general circulation or in a professional, trade, or ethnic publication, and any other measures required by the CO. If placed in a newspaper of general circulation, the advertisement must be published for 3 consecutive days, one of which must be a Sunday; or, if placed in a professional, trade, or ethnic publication, the advertisement must be published in the next available published edition. The advertisement must be approved by the Certifying Officer before publication, and the CO will direct where the advertisement is to be placed.

(1) The employer must supply a draft advertisement to the CO for review and approval within 30 days of being notified that supervised recruitment is required.

(2) The advertisement must:

(i) Direct applicants to send resumes or applications for the job opportunity to the CO for referral to the employer;

(ii) Include an identification number and an address designated by the Certifying Officer;

(iii) Describe the job opportunity;

(iv) Not contain a wage rate lower than the prevailing wage rate;

(v) Summarize the employer's minimum job requirements, which can not exceed any of the requirements entered on the application form by the employer;

(vi) Offer training if the job opportunity is the type for which employers normally provide training; and

(vii) Offer wages, terms and conditions of employment no less favorable than those offered to the alien.

(c) Timing of advertisement.

(1) The advertisement shall be placed in accordance with the guidance provided by the CO.

(2) The employer will notify the CO when the advertisement will be placed.

(d) Additional or substitute recruitment. The Certifying Officer may designate other appropriate sources of workers from which the employer must recruit for U.S. workers in addition to the advertising described in paragraph (b) of this section.

(e) Recruitment report. The employer must provide to the Certifying Officer a signed, detailed written report of the employer's supervised recruitment, signed by the employer or the employer's representative described in § 656.10(b)(2)(ii), within 30 days of the Certifying Officer's request for such a report. The recruitment report must:

(1) Identify each recruitment source by name and document that each recruitment source named was contacted. This can include, for example, copies of letters to recruitment sources such as unions, trade associations, colleges and universities and any responses received to the employer's inquiries. Advertisements placed in newspapers, professional, trade, or ethnic publications can be documented by furnishing copies of the tear sheets of the pages of the publication in which the advertisements appeared, proof of publication furnished by the publication, or dated copies of the web pages if the advertisement appeared on the web as well as in the publication in which the advertisement appeared.

(2) State the number of U.S. workers who responded to the employer's recruitment.

(3) State the names, addresses, and provide resumes (other than those sent to the employer by the CO) of the U.S. workers who applied for the job opportunity, the number of workers interviewed, and the job title of the person who interviewed the workers.

(4) Explain, with specificity, the lawful job-related reason(s) for not hiring each U.S. worker who applied. Rejection of one or more U.S. workers for lacking skills necessary to perform the duties involved in the occupation, where the U.S. workers are capable of acquiring the skills during a reasonable period of on-the-job training, is not a lawful job-related reason for rejecting the U.S. workers. For the purpose of this paragraph (e)(4), a U.S. worker is able and qualified for the job opportunity if the worker can acquire the skills necessary to perform the duties involved in the occupation during a reasonable period of on-the-job training.

(f) The employer shall supply the CO with the required documentation or information within 30 days of the date of the request. If the employer does not do so, the CO shall deny the application.

(g) The Certifying Officer in his or her discretion, for good cause shown, may provide one extension to any request for documentation or information.

[69 FR 77326, 77396, Dec. 27, 2004]

§ 656.24 Labor certification determinations.

(a)(1) The Office of Foreign Labor Certification Administrator (OFLC Administrator) is the National Certifying Officer. The OFLC Administrator and the certifying officers in the ETA application processing centers have the authority to certify or deny labor certification applications.

(2) If the labor certification presents a special or unique problem, the Director of an ETA application processing center may refer the matter to the Office of Foreign Labor Certification Administrator (OFLC Administrator). If the OFLC Administrator has directed that certain types of applications or specific applications be handled in the ETA national office, the Directors of the ETA application processing centers shall refer such applications to the OFLC Administrator.

(b) The Certifying Officer makes a determination either to grant or deny the labor certification on the basis of whether or not:

(1) The employer has met the requirements of this part.

(2) There is in the United States a worker who is able, willing, qualified, and available for and at the place of the job opportunity.

(i) The Certifying Officer must consider a U.S. worker able and qualified for the job opportunity if the worker, by education, training, experience, or a combination thereof, is able to perform in the normally accepted manner the duties involved in the occupation as customarily performed by other U.S. workers similarly employed. For the purposes of this paragraph (b)(2)(i), a U.S. worker is able and qualified for the job opportunity if the worker can acquire the skills necessary to perform the duties involved in the occupation during a reasonable period of on-the-job training.

(ii) If the job involves a job opportunity as a college or university teacher, the U.S. worker must be at least as qualified as the alien.

(3) The employment of the alien will not have an adverse effect upon the wages and working conditions of U.S. workers similarly employed. In making this determination, the Certifying Officer considers such things as: labor market information, the special circumstances of the industry, organization, and/or occupation, the prevailing wage in the area of intended employment, and prevailing working conditions, such as hours, in the occupation.

(c) The Certifying Officer shall notify the employer in writing (either electronically or by mail) of the labor certification determination.

(d) If a labor certification is granted, except for a labor certification for an occupation on Schedule A (§ 656.5) or for employment as a sheepherder under § 656.16, the Certifying Officer must send the certified application and complete Final Determination form to the employer, or, if appropriate, to the employer's agent or attorney, indicating the employer may file all the documents with the appropriate DHS office.

(e) If the labor certification is denied, the Final Determination form will:

(1) State the reasons for the determination;

(2) Quote the request for review procedures at § 656.26(a) and (b);

(3) Advise that failure to request review within 30 days of the date of the determination, as specified in § 656.26(a), constitutes a failure to exhaust administrative remedies;

(4) Advise that, if a request for review is not made within 30 days of the date of the determination, the denial shall become the final determination of the Secretary;

(5) Advise that if an application for a labor certification is denied, and a request for review is not made in accordance with the procedures at § 656.26(a) and (b), a new application may be filed at any time; and

(6) Advise that a new application in the same occupation for the same alien can not be filed while a request for review is pending with the Board of Alien Labor Certification Appeals.

(f) If the Certifying Officer determines the employer substantially failed to produce required documentation, or the documentation was inadequate, or determines a material misrepresentation was made with respect to the application, or if the Certifying Officer determines it is appropriate for other reasons, the employer may be required to conduct supervised recruitment pursuant to § 656.21 in future filings of labor certification applications for up to two years from the date of the Final Determination.

(g)(1) The employer may request reconsideration within 30 days from the date of issuance of the denial.

(2) For applications submitted after July 16, 2007, a request for reconsideration may include only:

(i) Documentation that the Department actually received from the employer in response to a request from the Certifying Officer to the employer; or

(ii) Documentation that the employer did not have an opportunity to present previously to the Certifying Officer, but that existed at the time the Application for Permanent Labor Certification was filed, and was maintained by the employer to support the application for permanent labor certification in compliance with the requirements of § 656.10(f).

(3) Paragraphs (g)(1) and (2) of this section notwithstanding, the Certifying Officer will not grant any request for reconsideration where the deficiency that caused denial resulted from the applicant's disregard of a system prompt or other direct instruction.

(4) The Certifying Officer may, in his or her discretion, reconsider the determination or treat it as a request for review under § 656.26(a).

[71 FR 35523, June 21, 2006; 72 FR 27945, May 17, 2007]

§ 656.26 Board of Alien Labor Certification Appeals review of denials of labor certification.

(a) Request for review.

(1) If a labor certification is denied, if a labor certification is revoked pursuant to § 656.32, or if a debarment is issued under § 656.31(f), a request for review of the denial, revocation, or debarment may be made to the Board of Alien Labor Certification Appeals by the employer or debarred person or entity by making a request for such an administrative review in accordance with the procedures provided in paragraph (a) of this section. In the case of a finding of debarment, receipt by the Department of a request for review, if made in accordance with this section, shall stay the debarment until such time as the review has been completed and a decision rendered thereon.

(2) A request for review of a denial or revocation:

(i) Must be sent within 30 days of the date of the determination to the Certifying Officer who denied the application or revoked the certification;

(ii) Must clearly identify the particular labor certification determination for which review is sought;

(iii) Must set forth the particular grounds for the request; and

(iv) Must include a copy of the Final Determination.

(3) A request for review of debarment:

(i) Must be sent to the Administrator, Office of Foreign Labor Certification, within 30 days of the date of the debarment determination;

(ii) Must clearly identify the particular debarment determination for which review is sought;

(iii) Must set forth the particular grounds for the request; and

(iv) Must include a copy of the Notice of Debarment.

(4) **(i)** With respect to a denial of the request for review, statements, briefs, and other submissions of the parties and amicus curiae must contain only legal argument and only such evidence that was within the record upon which the denial of labor certification was based.

(ii) With respect to a revocation or a debarment determination, the BALCA proceeding may be de novo.

(b) Upon the receipt of a request for review, the Certifying Officer immediately must assemble an indexed Appeal File:

(1) The Appeal File must be in chronological order, must have the index on top followed by the most recent document, and must have consecutively numbered pages. The Appeal File must contain the request for review, the complete application file, and copies of all the written material, such as pertinent parts and pages of surveys and/or reports upon which the denial was based.

(2) The Certifying Officer must send the Appeal File to the Board of Alien Labor Certification Appeals, Office of Administrative Law Judges, 800 K Street, NW., Suite 400–N, Washington, DC 20001–8002.

(3) The Certifying Officer must send a copy of the Appeal File to the employer. The employer may furnish or suggest directly to the Board of Alien Labor Certification Appeals the addition of any documentation that is not in the Appeal File, but that was submitted to DOL before the issuance of the Final Determination. The employer must submit such documentation in writing, and must send a copy to the Associate Solicitor for Employment and Training Legal Services, Office of the Solicitor, U.S. Department of Labor, Washington, DC 20210.

(c) **Debarment Appeal File**. Upon the receipt of a request for review of debarment, the Administrator, Office of Foreign Labor Certification, immediately must assemble an indexed Appeal File:

(1) The Appeal File must be in chronological order, must have the index on top followed by the most recent document, and must have consecutively numbered pages. The Appeal File must contain the request for review, the complete application file(s), and copies of all written materials, such as pertinent parts and pages of surveys and/or reports or documents received from any court, DHS, or the Department of State, upon which the debarment was based.

(2) The Administrator, Office of Foreign Labor Certification, must send the Appeal File to the Board of Alien Labor Certification Appeals, Office of Administrative Law Judges, 800 K St., NW., Suite 400–N, Washington, DC 20001–8002.

(3) The Administrator, Office of Foreign Labor Certification, must send a copy of the Appeal File to the debarred person or entity. The debarred person or entity may furnish or suggest directly to the Board of Alien Labor Certification Appeals the addition of any documentation that is not in the Appeal File. The debarred person or entity must submit such documentation in writing, and must send a copy to the Associate Solicitor for Employment and Training Legal Services, Office of the Solicitor, U.S. Department of Labor, 200 Constitution Ave., NW., Washington, DC 20210.

[69 FR 77326, 77397, Dec. 27, 2004; 72 FR 27944, May 17, 2007]

§ 656.27 Consideration by and decisions of the Board of Alien Labor Certification Appeals.

(a) Panel designations. In considering requests for review before it, the Board of Alien Labor Certification Appeals may sit in panels of three members. The Chief Administrative Law Judge may designate any Board of Alien Labor Certification Appeals member to submit proposed findings and recommendations to the Board of Alien Labor Certification Appeals or to any duly designated panel thereof to consider a particular case.

(b) Briefs and Statements of Position. In considering the requests for review before it, the Board of Alien Labor Certification Appeals must afford all parties 30 days to submit or decline to submit any appropriate Statement of Position or legal brief. The Certifying Officer is to be represented solely by the Solicitor of Labor or the Solicitor's designated representative.

(c) Review on the record. The Board of Alien Labor Certification Appeals must review a denial of labor certification under § 656.24, a revocation of a certification under § 656.32, or an affirmation of a prevailing wage determination under § 656.41 on the basis of the record upon which the decision was made, the request for review, and any Statements of Position or legal briefs submitted and must:

(1) Affirm the denial of the labor certification, the revocation of certification, or the affirmation of the PWD; or

(2) Direct the Certifying Officer to grant the certification, overrule the revocation of certification, or overrule the affirmation of the PWD; or

(3) Direct that a hearing on the case be held under paragraph (e) of this section.

(d) Notifications of decisions. The Board of Alien Labor Certification Appeals must notify the employer, the Certifying Officer, and the Solicitor of Labor of its decision, and must return the record to the Certifying Officer unless the case has been set for hearing under paragraph (e) of this section.

(e) Hearings.

(1) Notification of hearing. If the case has been set for a hearing, the Board of Alien Labor Certification Appeals must notify the employer, the alien, the Certifying Officer, and the Solicitor of Labor of the date, time, and place of the hearing, and that the hearing may be rescheduled upon written request and for good cause shown.

(2) Hearing procedure.

(i) The "Rules of Practice and Procedure For Administrative Hearings Before the Office of Administrative Law Judges," at 29 CFR part 18, apply to hearings under this paragraph (e).

(ii) For the purposes of this paragraph (e)(2), references in 29 CFR part 18 to: "administrative law judge" mean the Board of Alien Labor Certification Appeals member or the Board of Alien Labor Certification Appeals panel duly designated under § 656.27(a); "Office of Administrative Law Judges" means the Board of Alien Labor Certification Appeals; and "Chief Administrative Law Judge" means the Chief Administrative Law Judge in that official's function of chairing the Board of Alien Labor Certification Appeals.

[69 FR 77326, 77397, Dec. 27, 2004]

§ 656.30 Validity of and invalidation of labor certifications.

(a) Priority Date.

(1) The filing date for a Schedule A occupation or sheepherders is the date the application was dated by the Immigration Officer.

(2) The filing date, established under § 656.17(c), of an approved labor certification may be used as a priority date by the Department of Homeland Security and the Department of State, as appropriate.

(b) Expiration of labor certifications. For certifications resulting from applications filed under this part and 20 CFR part 656 in effect prior to March 28, 2005, the following applies:

(1) An approved permanent labor certification granted on or after July 16, 2007 expires if not filed in support of a Form I–140 petition with the Department of Homeland Security within 180 calendar days of the date the Department of Labor granted the certification.

(2) An approved permanent labor certification granted before July 16, 2007 expires if not filed in support of a Form I–140 petition with the Department of Homeland Security within 180 calendar days of July 16, 2007.

(c) Scope of validity. For certifications resulting from applications filed under this part or 20 CFR part 656 in effect prior to March 28, 2005, the following applies:

(1) A permanent labor certification for a Schedule A occupation or sheepherders is valid only for the occupation set forth on the Application for Alien Employment Certification (Form ETA 750) or the Application for Permanent Employment Certification (Form ETA 9089) and only for the alien named on the original application, unless a substitution was approved prior to July 16, 2007. The certification is valid throughout the United States unless the certification contains a geographic limitation.

(2) A permanent labor certification involving a specific job offer is valid only for the particular job opportunity, the alien named on the original application (unless a substitution was approved prior to July 16, 2007), and the area of intended employment stated on the Application for Alien Employment Certification (Form ETA 750) or the Application for Permanent Employment Certification (Form ETA 9089).

(d) Invalidation of labor certifications. After issuance, a labor certification may be revoked by ETA using the procedures described in § 656.32. Additionally, after issuance, a labor certification is subject to invalidation by the DHS or by a Consul of the Department of State upon a determination, made in accordance with those agencies' procedures or by a court, of fraud or willful misrepresentation of a material fact involving the labor certification application. If evidence of such fraud or willful misrepresentation becomes known to the CO or to the Chief, Division of Foreign Labor Certification, the CO, or the Chief of the Division of Foreign Labor Certification, as appropriate, shall notify in writing the DHS or Department of State, as appropriate. A copy of the notification must be sent to the regional or national office, as appropriate, of the Department of Labor's Office of Inspector General.

(e) Duplicate labor certifications.

(1) The Certifying Officer shall issue a duplicate labor certification at the written request of a Consular or Immigration Officer. The Certifying Officer shall issue such duplicate labor certifications only to the Consular or Immigration Officer who initiated the request.

(2) The Certifying Officer shall issue a duplicate labor certification to a Consular or Immigration Officer at the written request of an alien, employer, or an alien's or employer's attorney/agent. Such request for a duplicate labor certification must be addressed to the Certifying Officer who issued the labor certification; must include documentary evidence from a Consular or Immigration Officer that a visa application or visa petition, as appropriate, has been filed; and must include a Consular Office or DHS tracking number.

(3) A duplicate labor certification shall be issued by the Certifying Officer with the same filing and expiration dates, as described in paragraphs (a) and (b) of this section, as the original approved labor certification.

[69 FR 77326, 77398, Dec. 27, 2004; 72 FR 27944, May 17, 2007]

§ 656.31 Labor certification applications involving fraud, willful misrepresentation, or violations of this part.

The following provisions apply to applications filed under both this part and 20 CFR part 656 in effect prior to March 28, 2005, and to any certifications resulting from those applications.

(a) Denial. A Certifying Officer may deny any application for permanent labor certification if the officer finds the application contains false statements, is fraudulent, or was otherwise submitted in violation of the Department's permanent labor certification regulations.

(b) Possible fraud or willful misrepresentation.

(1) If the Department learns an employer, attorney, or agent is involved in possible fraud or willful misrepresentation in connection with the permanent labor certification program, the Department will refer the matter to the Department of Justice, Department of Homeland Security, or other government entity, as appropriate, for investigation, and send a copy of the referral to the Department of Labor's Office of Inspector General (OIG). In these cases, or if the Department learns an employer, attorney, or agent is under investigation by the Department of Justice, Department of Homeland Security, or other government entity for possible fraud or willful misrepresentation in connection with the permanent labor certification program, the Department may suspend processing of any permanent labor certification application involving such employer, attorney, or agent until completion of any investigation and/or judicial proceedings. Unless the investigatory agency, in writing, requests the Department to do otherwise, the Department shall provide written notification to the employer of the suspension in processing.

(2) A suspension pursuant to paragraph (b)(1) of this section may last initially for up to 180 days. No later than 180 days after the suspension began, if no criminal indictment or information has been issued, or judicial proceedings have not been concluded, the National Certifying Officer may resume processing some or all of the applications, or may extend the suspension in processing until completion of any investigation and/or judicial proceedings.

(c) Criminal indictment or information. If the Department learns that an employer, attorney, or agent is named in a criminal indictment or information in connection with the permanent labor certification program, the processing of applications related to that employer, attorney, or agent may be suspended until the judicial process is completed. Unless the investigatory or prosecutorial agency, in writing, requests the Department to do otherwise, the Department shall provide written notification to the employer of the suspension in processing.

(d) No finding of fraud or willful misrepresentation. If an employer, attorney, or agent is acquitted of fraud or willful misrepresentation charges, or if such criminal charges are withdrawn or otherwise fail to result in a finding of fraud or willful misrepresentation, the Certifying Officer shall decide each pending permanent labor certification application related to that employer, attorney, or agent on the merits of the application.

(e) Finding of fraud or willful misrepresentation. If an employer, attorney, or agent is found to have committed fraud or willful misrepresentation involving the permanent labor certification program, whether by a court, the Department of State or DHS, as referenced in § 656.30(d), or through other proceedings:

(1) Any suspension of processing of pending applications related to that employer, attorney, or agent will terminate.

(2) The Certifying Officer will decide each such application on its merits, and may deny any such application as provided in § 656.24 and in paragraph (a) of this section.

(3) In the case of a pending application involving an attorney or agent found to have committed fraud or willful misrepresentation, DOL will notify the employer associated with that application of the finding and require the employer to notify DOL in writing, within 30 days of the notification, whether the employer will withdraw the application, designate a new attorney or agent, or continue the application without representation. Failure of the employer to respond within 30 days of the notification will result in a denial. If the employer elects to continue representation by the attorney or agent, DOL will suspend processing of affected applications while debarment proceedings are conducted under paragraph (f) of this section.

(f) Debarment.

(1) No later than six years after the date of filing of the labor certification application that is the basis for the finding, or, if such basis requires a pattern or practice as provided in paragraphs (f)(1)(iii), (iv), and (v) of this section, no later than six years after the date of filing of the last labor certification application which constitutes a part of the pattern or practice, the Administrator, Office of Foreign Labor Certification, may issue to an employer, attorney, agent, or any combination thereof a Notice of Debarment from the permanent labor certification program for a reasonable period of no more than three years, based upon any action that was prohibited at the time the action occurred, upon determining the employer, attorney, or agent has participated in or facilitated one or more of the following:

(i) The sale, barter, or purchase of permanent labor applications or certifications, or any other action prohibited under § 656.12;

(ii) The willful provision or willful assistance in the provision of false or inaccurate information in applying for permanent labor certification;

(iii) A pattern or practice of a failure to comply with the terms of the Form ETA 9089 or Form ETA 750;

(iv) A pattern or practice of failure to comply in the audit process pursuant to § 656.20;

(v) A pattern or practice of failure to comply in the supervised recruitment process pursuant to § 656.21; or

(vi) Conduct resulting in a determination by a court, DHS or the Department of State of fraud or willful misrepresentation involving a permanent labor certification application, as referenced in § 656.31(e).

(2) The Notice of Debarment shall be in writing; shall state the reason for the debarment finding, including a detailed explanation of how the employer, attorney or agent has participated in or facilitated one or more of the actions listed in paragraphs (f)(1)(i) through (v) of this section; shall state the start date and term of the debarment; and shall identify appeal opportunities under § 656.26. The debarment shall take effect on the start date identified in the Notice of Debarment unless a request for review is filed within the time permitted by § 656.26. DOL will notify DHS and the Department of State regarding any Notice of Debarment.

(g) False Statements. To knowingly and willfully furnish any false information in the preparation of the Application for Permanent Employment Certification (Form ETA 9089) or the Application for Alien Employment Certification (Form ETA 750) and any supporting documentation, or to aid, abet, or counsel another to do so is a Federal offense, punishable by fine or imprisonment up to five years, or both under 18 U.S.C. 2 and 1001. Other penalties apply as well to fraud or misuse of ETA immigration documents and to perjury with respect to such documents under 18 U.S.C. 1546 and 1621.

[69 FR 77326, 77398, Dec. 27, 2004; 72 FR 27944, May 17, 2007]

§ 656.32 Revocation of approved labor certifications.

(a) Basis for DOL revocation. The Certifying Officer in consultation with the Chief, Division of Foreign Labor Certification may take steps to revoke an approved labor certification, if he/she finds the certification was not justified. A labor certification may also be invalidated by DHS or the Department of State as set forth in § 656.30(d).

(b) Department of Labor procedures for revocation.

(1) The Certifying Officer sends to the employer a Notice of Intent to Revoke an approved labor certification which contains a detailed statement of the grounds for the revocation and the time period allowed for the employer's rebuttal. The employer may submit evidence in rebuttal within 30 days of receipt of the notice. The Certifying Officer must consider all relevant evidence presented in deciding whether to revoke the labor certification.

(2) If rebuttal evidence is not filed by the employer, the Notice of Intent to Revoke becomes the final decision of the Secretary.

(3) If the employer files rebuttal evidence and the Certifying Officer determines the certification should be revoked, the employer may file an appeal under § 656.26.

(4) The Certifying Officer will inform the employer within 30 days of receiving any rebuttal evidence whether or not the labor certification will be revoked.

(5) If the labor certification is revoked, the Certifying Officer will also send a copy of the notification to the DHS and the Department of State.

[69 FR 77326, 77399, Dec. 27, 2004]

§ 656.40 Determination of prevailing wage for labor certification purposes.

(a) Application process. The employer must request a PWD from the NPC, on a form or in a manner prescribed by OFLC. Prior to January 1, 2010, the SWA having jurisdiction over the area of intended employment shall continue to receive and process prevailing wage determination requests in accordance with the regulatory provisions and Department guidance in effect prior to January 1, 2009. On or after January 1, 2010, the NPC shall receive and process prevailing wage determination requests in accordance with these regulations and with Department guidance. The NPC will provide the employer with an appropriate prevailing wage rate. The NPC shall determine the wage in accordance with sec. 212(t) of the INA. Unless the employer chooses to appeal the center's PWD under § 656.41(a) of this part, it files the Application for Permanent Employment Certification either electronically or by mail with the processing center of jurisdiction and maintains the PWD in its files. The determination shall be submitted to the CO, if requested.

(b) Determinations. The National Processing Center will determine the appropriate prevailing wage as follows:

(1) Except as provided in paragraphs (e) and (f) of this section, if the job opportunity is covered by a collective bargaining agreement (CBA) that was negotiated at arms-length between the union and the employer, the wage rate set forth in the CBA agreement is considered as not adversely affecting the wages of U.S. workers similarly employed, that is, it is considered the "prevailing wage" for labor certification purposes.

(2) If the job opportunity is not covered by a CBA, the prevailing wage for labor certification purposes shall be the arithmetic mean, except as provided in paragraph (b)(3) of this section, of the wages of workers similarly employed in the area of intended employment. The wage component of the DOL Occupational Employment Statistics Survey shall be used to determine the arithmetic mean, unless the employer provides an acceptable survey under paragraph (g) of this section.

(3) If the employer provides a survey acceptable under paragraph (g) of this section that provides a median and does not provide an arithmetic mean, the prevailing wage applicable to the employer's job opportunity shall be the median of the wages of workers similarly employed in the area of intended employment.

(4) The employer may utilize a current wage determination in the area under the Davis–Bacon Act, 40 U.S.C. 276a et seq., 29 CFR part 1, or the McNamara–O'Hara Service Contract Act, 41 U.S.C. 351 et seq.

(c) Validity Period. The National Processing Center must specify the validity period of the prevailing wage, which in no event may be less than 90 days or more than 1 year from the determination date. To use a prevailing wage rate provided by the NPC, employers must file their applications or begin the recruitment period required by §§ 656.17(e) or 656.21 of this part within the validity period specified by the NPC.

(d) Similarly employed. For purposes of this section, similarly employed means having substantially comparable jobs in the occupational category in the area of intended employment, except that, if a representative sample of workers in the occupational category can not be obtained in the area of intended employment, similarly employed means:

(1) Having jobs requiring a substantially similar level of skills within the area of intended employment; or

(2) If there are no substantially comparable jobs in the area of intended employment, having substantially comparable jobs with employers outside of the area of intended employment.

(e) Institutions of higher education and research entities. In computing the prevailing wage for a job opportunity in an occupational classification in an area of intended employment for an employee of an institution of higher education, or an affiliated or related nonprofit entity, a nonprofit research organization, or a Governmental research organization, the prevailing wage level takes into account the wage levels of employees only at such institutions and organizations in the area of intended employment.

(1) The organizations listed in this paragraph (e) are defined as follows:

(i) Institution of higher education means an institution of higher education as defined in section 101(a) of the Higher Education Act of 1965. Section 101(a) of that Act, 20 U.S.C. 1001(a)(2000), provides an institution of higher education is an educational institution in any state that:

(A) Admits as regular students only persons having a certificate of graduation from a school providing secondary education, or the recognized equivalent of such a certificate;

(B) Is legally authorized within such state to provide a program of education beyond secondary education;

(C) Provides an educational program for which the institution awards a bachelor's degree or provides not less than a two-year program that is acceptable for full credit toward such a degree;

(D) Is a public or other nonprofit institution; and

(E) Is accredited by a nationally recognized accrediting agency or association or, if not so accredited, is an institution that has been granted preaccreditation status by such an agency or association that has been recognized by the Secretary of Education for the granting of preaccreditation status, and the Secretary of Education has determined there is satisfactory assurance the institution will meet the accreditation standards of such an agency or association within a reasonable time.

(ii) Affiliated or related nonprofit entity means a nonprofit entity (including but not limited to a hospital and a medical or research institution) connected or associated with an institution of higher education, through shared ownership or control by the same board or federation, operated by an institution of higher education, or attached to an institution of higher education as a member, branch, cooperative, or subsidiary.

(iii) Nonprofit research organization or Governmental research organization means a research organization that is either a nonprofit organization or entity primarily engaged in basic research and/or applied research, or a United States Government entity whose primary mission is the performance or promotion of basic research and/or applied research. Basic research is general research to gain more comprehensive knowledge or understanding of the subject under study, without specific applications in mind. Basic research is also research that advances scientific knowledge, but does not have specific immediate commercial objectives although it may be in fields of present or commercial interest. It may include research and investigation in the sciences, social sciences, or humanities. Applied research is research to gain knowledge or understanding to determine the means by which a specific, recognized need may be met.

Applied research includes investigations oriented to discovering new scientific knowledge that has specific commercial objectives with respect to products, processes, or services. It may include research and investigation in the sciences, social sciences, or humanities.

(2) Nonprofit organization or entity, for the purpose of this paragraph (e), means an organization qualified as a tax exempt organization under the Internal Revenue Code of 1986, section 501(c)(3), (c)(4), or (c)(6) (26 U.S.C. 501(c)(3), (c)(4) or (c)(6)), and which has received approval as a tax exempt organization from the Internal Revenue Service, as it relates to research or educational purposes.

(f) Professional athletes. In computing the prevailing wage for a professional athlete (defined in Section 212(a)(5)(A)(iii)(II) of the Act) when the job opportunity is covered by professional sports league rules or regulations, the wage set forth in those rules or regulations is considered the prevailing wage (see Section 212(p)(2) of the Act). INA Section 212(a)(5)(A)(iii)(II), 8 U.S.C. 1182(a)(5)(A)(iii)(II) (1999), defines "professional athlete" as an individual who is employed as an athlete by—

(1) A team that is a member of an association of six or more professional sports teams whose total combined revenues exceed $10,000,000 per year, if the association governs the conduct of its members and regulates the contests and exhibitions in which its member teams regularly engage; or

(2) Any minor league team that is affiliated with such an association.

(g) Employer-provided wage information.

(1) If the job opportunity is not covered by a CBA, or by a professional sports league's rules or regulations, the NPC will consider wage information provided by the employer in making a PWD. An employer survey can be submitted either initially or after NPC issuance of a PWD derived from the OES survey. In the latter situation, the new employer survey submission will be deemed a new PWD request.

(2) In each case where the employer submits a survey or other wage data for which it seeks acceptance, the employer must provide the NPC with enough information about the survey methodology, including such items as sample size and source, sample selection procedures, and survey job descriptions, to allow the NPC to make a determination about the adequacy of the data provided and validity of the statistical methodology used in conducting the survey in accordance with guidance issued by the OFLC national office.

(3) The survey submitted to the NPC must be based upon recently collected data.

(i) A published survey must have been published within 24 months of the date of submission to the NPC, must be the most current edition of the survey, and the data upon which the survey is based must have been collected within 24 months of the publication date of the survey.

(ii) A survey conducted by the employer must be based on data collected within 24 months of the date it is submitted to the NPC.

(4) If the employer-provided survey is found not to be acceptable, the NPC will inform the employer in writing of the reasons the survey was not accepted.

(5) The employer, after receiving notification that the survey it provided for NPC consideration is not acceptable, may file supplemental information as provided by paragraph (h) of this section, file a new request for a PWD, or appeal under § 656.41.

(h) Submittal of supplemental information by employer.

(1) If the employer disagrees with the skill level assigned to its job opportunity, or if the NPC informs the employer its survey is not acceptable, or if there are other legitimate bases for such a review, the employer may submit supplemental information to the NPC.

(2) The NPC will consider one supplemental submission about the employer's survey or the skill level the NPC assigned to the job opportunity or any other legitimate basis for the employer to request such a review. If the NPC does not accept the employer's survey after considering the supplemental information, or affirms its determination concerning the skill level, it will inform the employer of the reasons for its decision.

(3) The employer may then apply for a new wage determination or appeal under § 656.41 of this part.

(i) Frequent users. The Secretary will issue guidance regarding the process by which employers may obtain a wage determination to apply to a subsequent application, when the wage is for the same occupation, skill level, and area of intended employment. In no case may the wage rate the employer provides the NPC be lower than the highest wage required by any applicable Federal, State, or local law.

(j) Fees prohibited. No SWA or SWA employee may charge a fee in connection with the filing of a request for a PWD, responding to such a request, or responding to a request for a review of a SWA prevailing wage determination under § 656.41.

[69 FR 77326, 77399, Dec. 27, 2004; 73 FR 78068, Dec. 19, 2008]

IV. OTHER FEDERAL MATERIALS

Fiscal Year 2014 Refugee Admissions Numbers

Presidential Determination No. 2014–01
78 Fed. Reg. 62415
October 2, 2013

Memorandum for the Secretary of State

In accordance with section 207 of the Immigration and Nationality Act (the "Act") (8 U.S.C. 1157), as amended, and after appropriate consultations with the Congress, I hereby make the following determinations and authorize the following actions:

The admission of up to 70,000 refugees to the United States during Fiscal Year (FY) 2014 is justified by humanitarian concerns or is otherwise in the national interest; provided that this number shall be understood as including persons admitted to the United States during FY 2014 with Federal refugee resettlement assistance under the Amerasian immigrant admissions program, as provided below.

The 70,000 admissions numbers shall be allocated among refugees of special humanitarian concern to the United States in accordance with the following regional allocations; provided that the number of admissions allocated to the East Asia region shall include persons admitted to the United States during FY 2014 with Federal refugee resettlement assistance under section 584 of the Foreign Operations, Export Financing, and Related Programs Appropriations Act of 1988, as contained in section 101(e) of Public Law 100–202 (Amerasian immigrants and their family members):

Africa	15,000
East Asia	14,000
Europe and Central Asia	1,000
Latin America/Caribbean	5,000
Near East/South Asia	33,000
Unallocated Reserve	2,000

The 2,000 unallocated refugee numbers shall be allocated to regional ceilings, as needed. Upon providing notification to the Judiciary Committees of the Congress, you are hereby authorized to use unallocated admissions in regions where the need for additional admissions arises.

Additionally, upon notification to the Judiciary Committees of the Congress, you are further authorized to transfer unused admissions allocated to a particular region to one or more other regions, if there is a need for greater admissions for the region or regions to which the admissions are being transferred. Consistent with section 2(b)(2) of the Migration and Refugee Assistance Act of 1962, as amended, I hereby determine that assistance to or on behalf of persons applying for admission to the United States as part of the overseas refugee admissions program will contribute to the foreign policy interests of the United States and designate such persons for this purpose.

Consistent with section 101(a)(42) of the Act (8 U.S.C. 1101(a)(42)), and after appropriate consultation with the Congress, I also specify that, for FY 2014, the following persons may, if otherwise qualified, be considered refugees for the purpose of admission to the United States within their countries of nationality or habitual residence:

a. Persons in Cuba

b. Persons in Eurasia and the Baltics

c. Persons in Iraq

d. In exceptional circumstances, persons identified by a United States Embassy in any location.

You are authorized and directed to report this determination to the Congress immediately and to publish it in the *Federal Register*.

BARACK OBAMA
THE WHITE HOUSE,
Washington, October 2, 2013

V. STATE AND LOCAL PROVISIONS

PROPOSITION 187 (CALIFORNIA)

November 8, 1994

Section 1. Findings and Declaration.

The People of California find and declare as follows:

That they have suffered and are suffering economic hardship caused by the presence of illegal aliens in this state.

That they have suffered and are suffering personal injury and damage by the criminal conduct of illegal aliens in this state.

That they have a right to the protection of their government from any person or persons entering this country unlawfully.

Therefore, the People of California declare their intention to provide for cooperation between their agencies of state and local government with the federal government, and to establish a system of required notification by and between such agencies to prevent illegal aliens in the United States from receiving benefits or public services in the State of California.

Section 2. Manufacture, Distribution or Sale of False Citizenship or Resident Alien Documents: Crime and Punishment.

Section 113 is added to the Penal Code, to read:

Section 113. Any person who manufactures, distributes or sells false documents to conceal the true citizenship or resident alien status of another person is guilty of a felony, and shall be punished by imprisonment in the state prison for five years or by a fine of seventy–five thousand dollars ($75,000).

Section 3. Use of False Citizenship or Resident Alien Documents: Crime and Punishment.

Section 114 is added to the Penal Code, to read:

Section 114. Any person who uses false documents to conceal his or her true citizenship or resident alien status is guilty of a felony, and shall be punished by imprisonment in the state prison for five years or by a fine of twenty–five thousand dollars ($25,000).

Section 4. Law Enforcement Cooperation with INS.

Section 834b is added to the Penal Code, to read:

Section 834b. (a) Every law enforcement agency in California shall fully cooperate with the United States Immigration and Naturalization Service regarding any person who is arrested if he or she is suspected of being present in the United States in violation of federal immigration laws.

(b) With respect to any such person who is arrested, and suspected of being present in the United States in violation of federal immigration laws, every law enforcement agency shall do the following:

(1) Attempt to verify the legal status of such person as a citizen of the United States, an alien lawfully admitted as a permanent resident, an alien lawfully admitted for a temporary period of time or as an alien who is present in the United States in violation of immigration laws. The verification process may include, but shall not be limited to, questioning the person regarding his or her date and place of birth and entry into the United States, and demanding documentation to indicate his or her legal status.

(2) Notify the person of his or her apparent status as an alien who is present in the United States in violation of federal immigration laws and inform him or her that, apart from any criminal justice precedings [sic], he or she must either obtain legal status or leave the United States.

(3) Notify the Attorney General of California and the United States Immigration and Naturalization Service of the apparent illegal status and provide any additional information that may be requested by any other public entity.

(c) Any legislative, administrative, or other action by a city, county, or other legally authorized local governmental entity with jurisdictional boundaries, or by a law enforcement agency, to prevent or limit the cooperation required by subdivision (a) is expressly prohibited.

Section 5. Exclusion of Illegal Aliens from Public Social Services.

Section 10001.5 is added to the Welfare and Institutions Code, to read:

Section 10001.5. (a) In order to carry out the intention of the People of California that only citizens of the United States and aliens lawfully admitted to the United States may receive the benefits of public social services and to ensure that all persons employed in the providing of those services shall diligently protect public funds from misuse, the provisions of this section are adopted.

(b) A person shall not receive any public social services to which he or she may be otherwise entitled until the legal status of that person has been verified as one of the following:

(1) A citizen of the United States.

(2) An alien lawfully admitted as a permanent resident.

(3) An alien lawfully admitted for a temporary period of time.

(c) If any public entity in this state to whom a person has applied for public social services determines or reasonably suspects, based upon the information provided to it, that the person is an alien in the United States in violation of federal law, the following procedures shall be followed by the public entity:

(1) The entity shall not provide the person with benefits or services.

(2) The entity shall, in writing, notify the person of his or her apparent illegal immigration status, and that the person must either obtain legal status or leave the United States.

(3) The entity shall also notify the State Director of Social Services, the Attorney General of California and the United States Immigration and Naturalization Service of the apparent illegal status, and shall provide any additional information that may be requested by any other public entity.

Section 6. Exclusion of Illegal Aliens from Publicly Funded Health Care.

Chapter 1.3 (commencing with Section 130) is added to Part 1 of Division 1 of the Health and Safety Code, to read:

Chapter 1.3. Publicly-funded Health-care Services

Section 130. (a) In order to carry out the intention of the People of California that, excepting emergency medical care as required by federal law, only citizens of the United States and aliens lawfully admitted to the United States may receive the benefits of publicly–funded health care, and to ensure that all persons employed in the providing of those services shall diligently protect public funds from misuse, the provisions of this section are adopted.

(b) A person shall not receive any health care services from a publicly–funded health care facility, to which he or she is otherwise entitled until the legal status of that person has been verified as one of the following:

(1) A citizen of the United States.

(2) An alien lawfully admitted as a permanent resident.

(3) An alien lawfully admitted for a temporary period of time.

(c) If any publicly–funded health care facility in this state from whom a person seeks health care services, other than emergency medical care as required by federal law, determines or reasonably suspects, based upon the information provided to it, that the person is an alien in the United States in violation of federal law, the following procedures shall be followed by the facility:

(1) The facility shall not provide the person with services.

(2) The facility shall, in writing, notify the person of his or her apparent illegal immigration status, and that the person must either obtain legal status or leave the United States.

(3) The facility shall also notify the State Director of Social Services, the Attorney General of California and the United States Immigration and Naturalization Service of the apparent illegal status, and shall provide any additional information that may be requested by any other public entity.

(d) For purposes of this section "publicly–funded health care facility" shall be defined as specified in Section 1200 and 1250 of the Health and Safety Code as of January 1, 1993.

Section 7. Exclusion of Illegal Aliens From Public Elementary and Secondary Schools.

Section 48215 is added to the Education Code to read:

Section 48215. (a) No public elementary or secondary school shall admit, or permit the attendance of, any child who is not a citizen of the United States, an alien lawfully admitted as a permanent resident, or a person who is otherwise authorized under federal law to be present in the United States.

(b) Commencing January 1, 1995, each school district shall verify the legal status of each child enrolling in the school district for the first time in order to ensure the enrollment or attendance only of citizens, aliens lawfully admitted as permanent residents, or persons who are otherwise authorized to be present in the United States.

(c) By January 1, 1996, each school district shall have verified the legal status of each child already enrolled and in attendance in the school district in order to ensure the enrollment or attendance only of citizens, aliens lawfully admitted as permanent residents, or persons who are otherwise authorized under federal law to be present in the United States.

(d) By January 1, 1996, each school district shall also have verified the legal status of each parent or guardian of each child referred to in subdivision (b) and (c) above, to determine whether such parent or guardian is one of the following:

(1) A citizen of the United States.

(2) An alien lawfully admitted as a permanent resident.

(3) An alien admitted lawfully for a temporary period of time.

(e) Each school district shall provide information to the State Superintendent of Public Instruction, the Attorney General of California and the United States Immigration and Naturalization Service regarding any enrollee or pupil, or parent or guardian, attending a public elementary or secondary school in the school district determined or reasonably suspected to be in violation of federal immigration laws within forty five days after becoming aware of an apparent violation. The notice shall also be provided to the parent or legal guardian of the enrollee or pupil, and shall state that an existing pupil may not continue to attend the school after ninety calendar days from the date of the notice, unless legal status is established.

(f) For each child who cannot establish legal status in the United States, each school district shall continue to provide education for a period of ninety days from the date of the notice. Such ninety day period shall be utilized to accomplish an orderly transition to a school in the child's country of origin. Each school district shall fully cooperate in this transition effort to ensure that the educational needs of the child are best served for that period of time.

Section 8. Exclusion of Illegal Aliens from Public Postsecondary Educational Institutions.

Section 66010.8. is added to the Education Code, to read:

Section 66010.8. (a) No public institution of postsecondary education shall admit, enroll, or permit the attendance of any person who is not a citizen of the United States, an alien lawfully admitted as a permanent resident, in the United States, or a person who is otherwise authorized under federal law to be present in the United States.

(b) Commencing with the first term or semester that begins after January 1, 1995, and at the commencement of each term or semester thereafter, each public postsecondary educational institution shall verify the status of each person enrolled or in attendance at that institution in order to ensure the enrollment or attendance only of United States citizens, aliens lawfully admitted as permanent residents in the United States, and persons who are otherwise authorized under federal law to be present in the United States.

(c) No later than 45 days after the admissions officer of a public postsecondary educational institution becomes aware of the application, enrollment, or attendance of a person determined to be, or who is under reasonable suspicion of being, in the United States in violation of federal immigration laws, that officer shall provide that information to the State Superintendent of Public Instruction, the Attorney General of California and the United States Immigration and Naturalization Service. The information shall also be provided to the applicant, enrollee, or person admitted.

Section 9. Attorney General cooperation with the INS.

Section 53069.65 is added to the Government Code, to read:

53069.65. Whenever the state or a city, or a county, or any other legally authorized local governmental entity with jurisdictional boundaries reports the presence of a person who is suspected of being present in the United States in violation of federal immigration laws to the Attorney General of California, that report shall be transmitted to the United States Immigration and Naturalization Service. The Attorney General shall be responsible for maintaining on-going and accurate records of such reports, and shall provide any additional information that may be requested by any other government entity.

Section 10. Amendment and Severability.

The statutory provisions contained in this measure may not be amended by the Legislature except to further its purposes by statute passed in each house by roll call vote entered in the journal, two–thirds of the membership concurring, or by a statute that becomes effective only when approved by the voters.

In the event that any portion of this act or the application thereof to any person or circumstance is held invalid, that invalidity shall not affect any other provision or application of the act, which can be given effect without the invalid provision or application, and to that end the provisions of this act are severable.

CITY OF HAZLETON ILLEGAL IMMIGRATION RELIEF ACT ORDINANCE 2006–18 (AS AMENDED BY ORDINANCE 2006–40, ORDINANCE 2007–6)

ORDINANCE 2006–18 ILLEGAL IMMIGRATION RELIEF ACT ORDINANCE

BE IT ORDAINED BY THE COUNCIL OF THE CITY OF HAZLETON AS FOLLOWS:

Section 1. Title

This chapter shall be known and may be cited as the "City of Hazleton Illegal Immigration Relief Act Ordinance."

Section 2. Findings and Declaration of Purpose

The People of the City of Hazleton find and declare:

A. That state and federal law require that certain conditions be met before a person may be authorized to work or reside in this country.

B. That unlawful workers and illegal aliens, as defined by this ordinance and state and federal law, do not normally meet such conditions as a matter of law when present in the City of Hazleton.

C. That unlawful employment, the harboring of illegal aliens in dwelling units in the City of Hazleton, and crime committed by illegal aliens harm the health, safety and welfare of authorized US workers and legal residents in the City of Hazleton. Illegal immigration leads to higher crime rates, subjects our hospitals to fiscal hardship and legal residents to substandard quality of care, contributes to other burdens on public services, increasing their cost and diminishing their availability to legal residents, and diminishes our overall quality of life.

D. That the City of Hazleton is authorized to abate public nuisances and empowered and mandated by the people of Hazleton to abate the nuisance of illegal immigration by diligently prohibiting the acts and policies that facilitate illegal immigration in a manner consistent with federal law and the objectives of Congress.

E. That United States Code Title 8, subsection 1324(a)(1)(A) prohibits the harboring of illegal aliens. The provision of housing to illegal aliens is a fundamental component of harboring.

F. This ordinance seeks to secure to those lawfully present in the United States and this City, whether or not they are citizens of the United States, the right to live in peace free of the threat crime, to enjoy the public services provided by this city without being burdened by the cost of providing goods, support and services to aliens unlawfully present in the United States, and to be free of the debilitating effects on their economic and social well being imposed by the influx of illegal aliens to the fullest extent that these goals can be achieved consistent with the Constitution and Laws of the United States and the Commonwealth of Pennsylvania.

G. The City shall not construe this ordinance to prohibit the rendering of emergency medical care, emergency assistance, or legal assistance to any person.

Section 3. Definitions

When used in this chapter, the following words, terms and phrases shall have the meanings ascribed to them herein, and shall be construed so as to be consistent with state and federal law, including federal immigration law:

A. "Business entity" means any person or group of persons performing or engaging in any activity, enterprise, profession, or occupation for gain, benefit, advantage, or livelihood, whether for profit or not for profit.

B. "City" means the City of Hazleton.

C. "Contractor" means a person, employer, subcontractor or business entity that enters into an agreement to perform any service or work or to provide a certain product in exchange for valuable consideration. This definition shall include but not be limited to a subcontractor, contract employee, or a recruiting or staffing entity.

D. "Illegal Alien" means an alien who is not lawfully present in the United States, according to the terms of United States Code Title 8, section 1101 et seq. The City shall not conclude that a person is an illegal alien unless and until an authorized representative of the City has verified with the federal government, pursuant to United States Code Title 8, subsection 1373(c), that the person is an alien who is not lawfully present in the United States.

E. "Unlawful worker" means a person who does not have the legal right or authorization to work due to an impediment in any provision of federal, state or local law, including but not limited to a minor disqualified by nonage, or an unauthorized alien as defined by United States Code Title 8, subsection 1324a(h)(3).

F. "Work" means any job, task, employment, labor, personal services, or any other activity for which compensation is provided, expected, or due, including but not limited to all activities conducted by business entities.

G. "Basic Pilot Program" means the electronic verification of work authorization program of the Illegal Immigration Reform and Immigration Responsibility Act of 1996, P.L. 104–208, Division C, Section 403(a); United States Code Title 8, subsection 1324a, and operated by the United States Department of Homeland Security (or a successor program established by the federal government.)

***Section 4.* Business Permits, Contracts, or Grants**

A. It is unlawful for any business entity to recruit, hire for employment, or continue to employ, or to permit, dispatch, or instruct any person who is an unlawful worker to perform work in whole or part within the City. Every business entity that applies for a business permit to engage in any type of work in the City shall sign an affidavit, prepared by the City Solicitor, affirming that they do not knowingly utilize the services or hire any person who is an unlawful worker.

B. Enforcement: The Hazleton Code Enforcement Office shall enforce the requirements of this section.

    (1) An enforcement action shall be initiated by means of a written signed complaint to the Hazleton Code Enforcement Office submitted by any City official, business entity, or City resident. A valid complaint shall include an allegation which describes the alleged violator(s) as well as the actions constituting the violation, and the date and location where such actions occurred.

    (2) A complaint which alleges a violation solely or primarily on the basis of national origin, ethnicity, or race shall be deemed invalid and shall not be enforced.

    (3) Upon receipt of a valid complaint, the Hazleton Code Enforcement Office shall, within three business days, request identity information from the business entity regarding any persons alleged to be unlawful workers. The Hazleton Code Enforcement Office shall suspend the business permit of any business entity which fails, within three business days after receipt of the request, to provide such information. In instances where an unlawful worker is alleged to be an unauthorized alien, as defined in United States Code Title 8, subsection 1324a(h)(3), the Hazleton Code Enforcement Office shall submit identity data required by the federal government to verify, pursuant to United States Code Title 8, section 1373, the immigration status of such person(s), and shall provide the business entity with written confirmation of that verification.

    (4) The Hazleton Code Enforcement Office shall suspend the business permit of any business entity which fails correct a violation

of this section within three business days after notification of the violation by the Hazleton Code Enforcement Office.

(5) The Hazleton Code Enforcement Office shall not suspend the business permit of a business entity if, prior to the date of the violation, the business entity had verified the work authorization of the alleged unlawful worker(s) using the Basic Pilot Program.

(6) The suspension shall terminate one business day after a legal representative of the business entity submits, at a City office designated by the City Solicitor, a sworn affidavit stating that the violation has ended.

(a) The affidavit shall include a description of the specific measures and actions taken by the business entity to end the violation, and shall include the name, address and other adequate identifying information of the unlawful workers related to the complaint.

(b) Where two or more of the unlawful workers were verified by the federal government to be unauthorized aliens, the legal representative of the business entity shall submit to the Hazleton Code Enforcement Office, in addition to the prescribed affidavit, documentation acceptable to the City Solicitor which confirms that the business entity has enrolled in and will participate in the Basic Pilot Program for the duration of the validity of the business permit granted to the business entity.

(7) For a second or subsequent violation, the Hazleton Code Enforcement Office shall suspend the business permit of a business entity for a period of twenty days. After the end of the suspension period, and upon receipt of the prescribed affidavit, the Hazleton Code Enforcement Office shall reinstate the business permit. The Hazleton Code Enforcement Office shall forward the affidavit, complaint, and associated documents to the appropriate federal enforcement agency, pursuant to United States Code Title 8, section 1373. In the case of an unlawful worker disqualified by state law not related to immigration, the Hazleton Code Enforcement Office shall forward the affidavit, complaint, and associated documents to the appropriate state enforcement agency.

C. All agencies of the City shall enroll and participate in the Basic Pilot Program.

D. As a condition for the award of any City contract or grant to a business entity for which the value of employment, labor or, personal services shall exceed $10,000, the business entity shall provide documentation confirming its enrollment and participation in the Basic Pilot Program.

E. Private Cause of Action for Unfairly Discharged Employees

(1) The discharge of any employee who is not an unlawful worker by a business entity in the City is an unfair business practice if, on the date of the discharge, the business entity was not participating in the Basic Pilot program and the business entity was employing an unlawful worker.

(2) The discharged worker shall have a private cause of action in the Municipal Court of Hazleton against the business entity for the unfair business practice. The business entity found to have violated this subsection shall be liable to the aggrieved employee for:

(a) three times the actual damages sustained by the employee, including but not limited to lost wages or compensation from the date of the discharge until the date the employee has procured new employment at an equivalent rate of compensation, up to a period of one hundred and twenty days; and

(b) reasonable attorney's fees and costs.

Section 5. Harboring Illegal Aliens

A. It is unlawful for any person or business entity that owns a dwelling unit in the City to harbor an illegal alien in the dwelling unit, knowing or in reckless disregard of the fact that an alien has come to, entered, or remains in the United States in violation of law, unless such harboring is otherwise expressly permitted by federal law.

(1) For the purposes of this section, to let, lease, or rent a dwelling unit to an illegal alien, knowing or in reckless disregard of the fact that an alien has come to, entered, or remains in the United States in violation of law, shall be deemed to constitute harboring. To suffer or permit the occupancy of the dwelling unit by an illegal alien, knowing or in reckless disregard of the fact that an alien has come to, entered, or remains in the United States in violation of law, shall also be deemed to constitute harboring.

(2) A separate violation shall be deemed to have been committed on each day that such harboring occurs, and for each adult illegal alien harbored in the dwelling unit, beginning one business day after receipt of a notice of violation from the Hazleton Code Enforcement Office.

(3) A separate violation of this section shall be deemed to have been committed for each business day on which the owner fails to provide the Hazleton Code Enforcement Office with identity data needed to obtain a federal verification of immigration status, beginning three days after the owner receives written notice from the Hazleton Code Enforcement Office.

B. Enforcement: The Hazleton Code Enforcement Office shall enforce the requirements of this section.

(1) An enforcement action shall be initiated by means of a written signed complaint to the Hazleton Code Enforcement Office submitted by any official, business entity, or resident of the City. A valid complaint shall include an allegation which describes the alleged violator(s) as well as the actions constituting the violation, and the date and location where such actions occurred.

(2) A complaint which alleges a violation solely or primarily on the basis of national origin, ethnicity, or race shall be deemed invalid and shall not be enforced.

(3) Upon receipt of a valid written complaint, the Hazleton Code Enforcement Office shall, pursuant to United States Code Title 8, section 1373(c), verify with the federal government the immigration status of a person seeking to use, occupy, lease, or rent a dwelling unit in the City. The Hazleton Code Enforcement Office shall submit identity data required by the federal government to verify immigration status. The City shall forward identity data provided by the owner to the federal government, and shall provide the property owner with written confirmation of that verification.

(4) If after five business days following receipt of written notice from the City that a violation has occurred and that the immigration status of any alleged illegal alien has been verified, pursuant to United States Code Title 8, section 1373(c), the owner of the dwelling unit fails to correct a violation of this section, the Hazleton Code Enforcement Office shall deny or suspend the rental license of the dwelling unit.

(5) For the period of suspension, the owner of the dwelling unit shall not be permitted to collect any rent, payment, fee, or any other form of compensation from, or on behalf of, any tenant or occupant in the dwelling unit.

(6) The denial or suspension shall terminate one business day after a legal representative of the dwelling unit owner submits to the Hazleton Code Enforcement Office a sworn affidavit stating that each and every violation has ended. The affidavit shall include a description of the specific measures and actions taken by the business entity to end the violation, and shall include the name, address and other adequate identifying information for the illegal aliens who were the subject of the complaint.

(7) The Hazleton Code Enforcement Office shall forward the affidavit, complaint, and associated documents to the appropriate federal enforcement agency, pursuant to United States Code Title 8, section 1373.

(8) Any dwelling unit owner who commits a second or subsequent violation of this section shall be subject to a fine of two hundred and fifty dollars ($250) for each separate violation. The suspen-

sion provisions of this section applicable to a first violation shall also apply.

(9) Upon the request of a dwelling unit owner, the Hazleton Code Enforcement Office shall, pursuant to United States Code Title 8, section 1373(c), verify with the federal government the lawful immigration status of a person seeking to use, occupy, lease, or rent a dwelling unit in the City. The penalties in this section shall not apply in the case of dwelling unit occupants whose status as an alien lawfully present in the United States has been verified.

***Section 6.* Construction and Severability**

A. The requirements and obligations of this section shall be implemented in a manner fully consistent with federal law regulating immigration and protecting the civil rights of all citizens and aliens.

B. If any part of provision of this Chapter is in conflict or inconsistent with applicable provisions of federal or state statutes, or is otherwise held to be invalid or unenforceable by any court of competent jurisdiction, such part of provision shall be suspended and superseded by such applicable laws or regulations, and the remainder of this Chapter shall not be affected thereby.

ORDAINED by Council this 21st day of September, 2006.

ORDINANCE 2006–40

Illegal Immigration Relief Act Implementation Amendment

BE IT ORDAINED BY THE COUNCIL OF THE CITY OF HAZLETON AS FOLLOWS:

To clarify the intent of the City of Hazleton with respect to the implementation of Ordinance 2006–18 (the City of Hazleton Illegal Immigration Relief Act Ordinance), Ordinance 2006–18 is hereby amended by adding the following:

***Section 7.* Implementation and Process**

A. Prospective Application Only. The default presumption with respect to Ordinances of the City of Hazleton—that such Ordinances shall apply only prospectively—shall pertain to the Illegal Immigration Relief Act Ordinance. The Illegal Immigration Relief Act Ordinance shall be applied only to employment contracts, agreements to perform service or work, and agreements to provide a certain product in exchange for valuable consideration that are entered into or are renewed after the date that the Illegal Immigration Relief Act Ordinance becomes effective and any judicial injunction prohibiting its implementation is removed. The Illegal Immigration Relief Act Ordinance shall be applied only to contracts to let, lease, or rent dwelling units that are entered into or are renewed after the date that the Illegal Immigration Relief Act Ordinance becomes effective and any judicial injunction prohibiting its implementation is removed. The renewal of a month-to-month lease or other type of tenancy which automatically renews absent notice by either party will not be considered as entering into a new contract to let, lease or rent a dwelling unit.

B. Condition of Lease. Consistent with the obligations of a rental unit owner described in Section 5.A., a tenant may not enter into a contract for the rental or leasing of a dwelling unit unless the tenant is either a U.S. citizen or an alien lawfully present in the United States according to the terms of United States Code Title 8, Section 1101 et seq. A tenant who is neither a U.S. citizen nor an alien lawfully present in the United States who enters into such a contract shall be deemed to have breached a condition of the lease under 68 P.S. Section 250.501. A tenant who is not a U.S. citizen who subsequent to the beginning of his tenancy becomes unlawfully present in the United States shall be deemed to have breached a condition of the lease under 68 P.S. Section 250.501.

C. Corrections of Violations—Employment of Unlawful Workers. The correction of a violation with respect to the employment of an unlawful worker shall include any of the following actions:

(1) The business entity terminates the unlawful worker's employment.

(2) The business entity, after acquiring additional information from the worker, requests a secondary or additional verification by the federal government of the worker's authorization, pursuant to the procedures of the Basic Pilot Program. While this verification is pending, the three business day period described in Section 4.B.(4) shall be tolled.

(3) The business entity attempts to terminate the unlawful worker's employment and such termination is challenged in a court of the Commonwealth of Pennsylvania. While the business entity pursues the termination of the unlawful worker's employment in such forum, the three business day period described in Section 4.B.(4) shall be tolled.

D. Corrections of Violations—Harboring Illegal Aliens. The correction of a violation with respect to the harboring of an illegal alien in a dwelling unit shall include any of the following actions:

(1) A notice to quit, in writing, issued and served by the dwelling unit owner, as landlord, to the tenant declaring a forfeiture of the lease for breach of the lease condition describe in Section 7.B.

(2) The dwelling unit owner, after acquiring additional information from the alien, requests the City of Hazleton to obtain a secondary or additional verification by the federal government that the alien is lawfully present in the United States, under the procedures designated by the federal government, pursuant to United

States Code Title 8, Subsection 1373(c). While this second verification is pending, the five business day period described in Section 5.B.(4) shall be tolled.

(3) The commencement of an action for the recovery of possession of real property in accordance with Pennsylvania law by the landlord against the illegal alien. If such action is contested by the tenant in court, the dwelling unit owner shall be deemed to have complied with this Ordinance while the dwelling unit owner is pursuing the action in court. While this process is pending, the five business day period described in Section 5.B.(4) shall be tolled.

E. Procedure if Verification is Delayed. If the federal government notifies the City of Hazleton that it is unable to verify whether a tenant is lawfully present in the United States or whether an employee is authorized to work in the United States, the City of Hazleton shall take no further action on the complaint until a verification from the federal government concerning the status of the individual is received. At no point shall any City official attempt to make an independent determination of any alien's legal status, without verification from the federal government, pursuant to United States Code Title 8, Subsection 1373(c).

F. Venue for Judicial Process. Any business entity or rental unit owner subject to a complaint and subsequent enforcement under this ordinance, or any employee of such a business entity or tenant of such a rental unit owner, may challenge the enforcement of this Ordinance with respect to such entity or individual in the Magisterial District Court for the City of Hazleton, subject to the right of appeal to the Luzerne County Court of Common Pleas. Such an entity or individual may alternatively challenge the enforcement of this Ordinance with respect to such entity or individual in any other court of competent jurisdiction in accordance with applicable law, subject to all rights of appeal.

G. Deference to Federal Determinations of Status. The determination of whether a tenant of a dwelling is lawfully present in the United States, and the determination of whether a worker is an unauthorized alien shall be made by the federal government, pursuant to United States Code Title 8, Subsection 1373(c). A determination of such status of an individual by the federal government shall create a rebuttable presumption as to that individual's status in any judicial proceedings brought pursuant to this ordinance. The Court may take judicial notice of any verification of the individual previously provided by the federal government and may request the federal government to provide automated or testimonial verification pursuant to United States Code Title 8, Subsection 1373(c).

ORDAINED AND ENACTED by Council this 28th day of December, 2006.

ORDINANCE 2007–6

An Ordinance Amending Ordinance 2006–18 (Illegal Immigration Relief Act)

WHEREAS, the City of Hazleton (hereinafter "City") is desirous of amending Ordinance 2006–18;

BE IT ORDAINED AND ENACTED and is **HEREBY ORDAINED AND ENACTED** by the Council of the City of Hazleton, Pennsylvania, Section 4B(2) and Section 5B(2) of the Illegal Immigration Relief Act Ordinance shall be amended to remove the words "solely and primarily" from said Sections as follows:

> *Section 4B(2)*—A complaint which alleges a violation on the basis of national origin, ethnicity or race shall be deemed invalid and shall not be enforced.
>
> *Section 5B(2)*—A complaint which alleges a violation on the basis of national origin, ethnicity or race shall be deemed invalid and shall not be enforced.
>
> *Section 4A* shall be amended to read as follows:
>
> It is unlawful for any business entity to knowingly recruit, hire for employment, or continue to employ, or to permit, dispatch, or instruct any person who is an unlawful worker to perform work in whole or part within the City. Every business entity that applies for a business permit to engage in any type of work in the City shall sign an affidavit, prepared by the City Solicitor, affirming that they do not knowingly utilize the services or hire any person who is an unlawful worker.

Sections 4A, 4B(2) and 5B(2) of Ordinance 2006–18 are hereby amended and replaced as provided in this Ordinance. The remainder of Ordinance 2006–18 shall remain unchanged.

ORDAINED AND ENACTED into law by the Council of the City of Hazleton this 21st day of March, 2007.

CITY OF HAZLETON
TENANT REGISTRATION ORDINANCE
ORDINANCE 2006–13

ORDINANCE 2006–13

ESTABLISHING A REGISTRATION PROGRAM FOR RESIDENTIAL RENTAL PROPERTIES; REQUIRING ALL OWNERS OF RESIDENTIAL RENTAL PROPERTIES TO DESIGNATE AN AGENT FOR SERVICE OF PROCESS; AND PRESCRIBING DUTIES OF OWNERS, AGENTS AND OCCUPANTS; DIRECTING THE DESIGNATION OF AGENTS; ESTABLISHING FEES FOR THE COSTS ASSOCIATED WITH THE REGISTRATION OF RENTAL PROPERTY; AND PRESCRIBING PENALTIES FOR VIOLATIONS

BE IT ORDAINED BY THE GOVERNING BODY OF THE CITY OF HAZLETON and it is hereby ordained and with the authority of the same as follows:

Section 1. **Definitions and Interpretation.**

The following words, when used in this ordinance, shall have the meanings ascribed to them in this section, except in those instances where the context clearly indicates otherwise. When not inconsistent with the context, words used in the present tense include the future; words in the plural number include the singular number; words in the singular shall include the plural, and words in the masculine shall include the feminine and the neuter.

a. **AGENT**—Individual of legal majority who has been designated by the Owner as the agent of the Owner or manager of the Property under the provisions of this ordinance.

b. **CITY**—City of Hazleton

c. **CITY CODE**—the building code (property Maintenance Code 1996 as amended or superceded) officially adopted by the governing body of the City, or other such codes officially designated by the governing body of the City for the regulation of construction, alteration, addition, repair, removal, demolition, location, occupancy and maintenance of buildings and structures.

d. **ZONING ORDINANCE**—Zoning ordinance as officially adopted by the City of Hazleton, File of Council #95–26 (as amended).

e. **OFFICE**—The Office of Code Enforcement for the City of Hazleton.

f. **DWELLING UNIT**—a single habitable unit, providing living facilities for one or more persons, including permanent space for living, sleeping, eating, cooking and bathing and sanitation, whether furnished or unfurnished. There may be more than one Dwelling Unit on a Premises.

g. **DORMITORY**—a residence hall offered as student or faculty housing to accommodate a college or university, providing living or sleeping rooms for individuals or groups of individuals, with or without cooking facilities and with or without private baths

h. **INSPECTOR**—any person authorized by Law or Ordinance to inspect buildings or systems, e.g. zoning, housing, plumbing, electrical systems, heat systems, mechanical systems and health necessary to operate or use buildings within the City of Hazleton. An Inspector would include those identified in Section 8—Enforcement.

i. **FIRE DEPARTMENT**—the Fire Department of the City of Hazleton or any member thereof, and includes the Chief of Fire or his designee.

j. **HOTEL**—a building or part of a building in which living and sleeping accommodations are used primarily for transient occupancy, may be rented on a daily basis, and desk service is provided, in addition to one or more of the following services: maid, telephone, bellhop service, or the furnishing or laundering of linens.

k. **LET FOR OCCUPANCY**—to permit, provide or offer, for consideration, possession or occupancy of a building, dwelling unit, rooming unit, premise or structure by a person who is not the legal owner of record thereof, pursuant to a written or unwritten lease, agreement or license, or pursuant to a recorded or unrecorded agreement or contract for the sale of land.

l. **MOTEL**—a building or group of buildings which contain living and sleeping accommodations used primarily for transient occupancy, may be rented on a daily basis, and desk service is provided, and has individual entrances from outside the building to serve each such living or sleeping unit.

m. **OCCUPANT**—a person age 18 or older who resides at a Premises.

n. **OPERATOR**—any person who has charge, care or control of a Premises which is offered or let for occupancy.

o. **OWNER**—any Person, Agent, or Operator having a legal or equitable interest in the property; or recorded in the official records of the state, county, or municipality as holding title to the property; or otherwise having control of the property, including the guardian of the estate of any such person, and the executor or administrator of the estate of such person if ordered to take possession of real property by a Court of competent jurisdiction.

p. **OWNER—OCCUPANT**—an owner who resides in a Dwelling Unit on a regular permanent basis, or who otherwise occupies a non-residential portion of the Premises on a regular permanent basis.

q. **PERSON**—any person, partnership, firm, association, corporation, or municipal authority or any other group acting as a single unit.

r. **POLICE DEPARTMENT**—the Police Department of the City of Hazleton or any member thereof sworn to enforce laws and ordinances in the City, and includes the Chief of Police or his designee.

s. **PREMISES**— any parcel of real property in the City, including the land and all buildings and structures in which one or more Rental Units are located.

t. **RENTAL UNIT**—means a Dwelling Unit or Rooming Unit which is Let for Occupancy and is occupied by one or more Tenants.

u. **ROOMING UNIT**—any room or groups of rooms forming a single habitable unit occupied or intended to be occupied for sleeping or living, but not for cooking purposes.

v. **TENANT**—any Person authorized by the Owner or Agent who occupies a Rental Unit within a Premises regardless of whether such Person has executed a lease for said Premises.

Section 2. Appointment of an Agent and/or Manager

Each Owner who is not an Owner-occupant, or who does not reside in the City of Hazleton or within a ten (10) mile air radius of the City limits, shall appoint an Agent who shall reside in the City or within a ten (10) mile air radius of the City limits.

Section 3. Duties of the Owner and/or Agent

a. The Owner has the duty to maintain the Premises in good repair, clean and sanitary condition, and to maintain the Premises in compliance with the current Codes, Building Codes and Zoning Ordinance of the City of Hazleton. The Owner may delegate implementation of these responsibilities to an Agent.

b. The duties of the Owner and/or Agent shall be to receive notices and correspondence, including service of process, from the City of Hazleton; to arrange for the inspection of the Rental Units; do or arrange for the performance of maintenance, cleaning, repair, pest control, snow and ice removal, and ensure continued compliance of the Premises with the current Codes, Building Codes and Zoning Ordinance in effect in the City of Hazleton, as well as arrange for garbage removal.

c. The name, address and telephone number of the Owner and Agent, if applicable, shall be reported to the Code Enforcement Office in writing upon registering the Rental Units.

d. No Dwelling Unit shall be occupied, knowingly by the Owner or Agent, by a number of persons that is in excess of the requirements outlined in 2003 International Property Maintenance Code, Chapter 4, Light, Ventilation, and Occupancy Limits, Section PM–404.5, Overcrowding, or any update thereof, a copy of which is appended hereto and made a part hereof.

Section 4. **Notices**

a. Whenever an Inspector or Code Enforcement Officer determines that any Rental Unit or Premises fails to meet the requirements set forth in the applicable Codes, the Inspector or Code Enforcement Officer shall issue a correction notice setting forth the violations and ordering the Occupant, Owner or Agent, as appropriate, to correct such violations. The notice shall:

1) Be in writing;

2) Describe the location and nature of the violation;

3) Establish a reasonable time for the correction of the violation.

b. All notices shall be served upon the Occupant, Owner or Agent, as applicable, personally or by certified mail, return receipt requested. A copy of any notices served solely on an Occupant shall also be provided to the Owner or Agent. In the event service is first attempted by mail and the notice is returned by the postal authorities marked "unclaimed" or "refused", then the Code Enforcement Office or Police Department shall attempt delivery by personal service on the Occupant, Owner or Agent, as applicable. The Code Enforcement Office shall also post the notice at a conspicuous place on the Premises. If personal service directed to the Owner or Agent cannot be accomplished after a reasonable attempt to do so, then the notice may be sent to the Owner or Agent, as applicable, at the address stated on the most current registration application for the Premises in question, by regular first class mail, postage prepaid. If such notice is not returned by the postal authorities within five (5) days of its deposit in the U.S. Mail, then it shall be deemed to have been delivered to and received by the addressee on the fifth day following its deposit in the United States Mail.

c. For purposes of this Ordinance, any notice hereunder that is given to the Agent shall be deemed as notice given to the Owner.

d. There shall be a rebuttable presumption that any notice that is given to the Occupant, Owner or Agent under this ordinance shall have been received by such Occupant, Owner or Agent if the notice was served in the manner provided by this ordinance.

e. Subject to paragraph 4.d above, a claimed lack of knowledge by the Owner or Agent, if applicable, of any violation hereunder cited shall be no defense to closure of rental units pursuant to Section 9, as long as all notices prerequisite to such proceedings have been given and deemed received in accordance with the provisions of this ordinance.

f. All notices shall contain a reasonable time to correct, or take steps to correct, violations of the above. The Occupant, Owner or Agent to whom the notice was addressed may request additional time to correct violations. Requests for additional time must be in writing and either deposited in the U.S. Mail (post-marked) or hand-delivered to the Code Enforcement Office within five (5) days of receipt of the notice by the Occupant, Owner or Agent. The City retains the right to deny or modify time extension requests. If the Occupant, Owner or Agent is attempting in good faith to correct violations but is unable to do so within the time specified in the notice, the Occupant, Owner or Agent shall have the right to request such additional time as may be needed to complete the correction work, which request shall not be unreasonably withheld.

g. Failure to correct violations within the time period stated in the notice of violation shall result in such actions or penalties as are set forth in Section 10 of this ordinance. If the notice of violation relates to actions or omissions of the Occupant, and the Occupant fails to make the necessary correction, the Owner or Agent may be required to remedy the condition. No adverse action shall be taken against an Owner or Agent for failure to remedy a condition so long as the Owner or Agent is acting with due diligence and taking bona fide steps to correct the violation, including but not limited to pursuing remedies under a lease agreement with an Occupant or Tenant. The City shall not be precluded from pursuing an enforcement action against any Occupant or Tenant who is deemed to be in violation.

Section 5. **Insurance**

In order to protect the health, safety and welfare of the residents of the City, it is hereby declared that the city shall require hazard and general liability insurance for all property owners letting property for occupancy in the City.

a. *Minimum coverage; use of insurance proceeds.* All Owners shall be required to obtain a minimum of fifty thousand ($50,000.00) dollars in general liability insurance, and hazard and casualty insurance in an amount sufficient to either restore or remove the building in the event of a fire or other casualty. Further, in the event of any fire or loss covered by such insurance, it shall be the obligation of the Owner to use such insurance proceeds to cause the restoration or demolition or other repair of the property in adherence to the City Code and all applicable ordinances.

b. *Property owners to provide City with insurance information.* Owners shall be required to place their insurance company name, policy number and policy expiration date on their Rental Property Registration form, or in the alternative, to provide the Code Enforcement Office with a copy of a certificate of insurance. A registration Certificate (see Section 6 below) shall not be issued to any Owner or Agent unless the aforementioned information has been provided to the Code Enforcement Office. The Code Enforcement Office shall be informed of any change in policies for a particular rental property or cancellation of a policy for said property within thirty (30) days of said change or cancellation.

Section 6. Rental Registration and License Requirements

a. No Person shall hereafter occupy, allow to be occupied, advertise for occupancy, solicit occupants for, or let to another person for occupancy any Rental Unit within the City for which an application for license has not been made and filed with the Code Enforcement Office and for which there is not an effective license. Initial application and renewal shall be made upon forms furnished by the Code Enforcement Office for such purpose and shall specifically require the following minimum information:

1) Name, mailing address, street address and phone number of the Owner, and if the Owner is not a natural person, the name, address and phone number of a designated representative of the Owner.
2) Name, mailing address, street address and phone number of the Agent of the Owner, if applicable.
3) The street address of the Premises being registered.
4) The number and types of units within the Premises (Dwelling Units or Rooming Units)

The Owner or Agent shall notify the Code Enforcement Office of any changes of the above information within thirty (30) days of such change.

b. The initial application for registration and licensing shall be made by personally filing an application with the Code Enforcement Office by October 1, 2006. Thereafter, any new applicant shall file an application before the Premises is let for occupancy, or within thirty (30) days of becoming an Owner of a currently registered Premises. One application per property is required, as each property will receive its own license.

c. Upon receipt of the initial application or any renewal thereof and the payment of applicable fees as set forth in Section 7 below, the Code Enforcement Office shall issue a Rental Registration License to the Owner within thirty (30) days of receipt of payment.

d. Each new license issued hereunder, and each renewal license, shall expire on October 31 of each year. The Code Enforcement Office shall mail license renewal applications to the Owner or designated Agent on or before September 1 of each year. Renewal applications and fees may be returned by mail or in person to the Code Enforcement Office. A renewal license will not be issued unless the application and appropriate fee has been remitted.

Section 7. **Fees.**

a. *Annual License Fee.* There shall be a license fee for the initial license and an annual renewal fee thereafter. Fees shall be assessed against and payable by the Owner in the amount of $5.00 per Rental Unit, payable at the time of initial registration and annual renewal, as more specifically set forth in Section 6 above.

b. *Occupancy Permit Fee.* There shall be a one-time occupancy permit fee of $10.00 for every new Occupant, which is payable by the Occupant. For purposes of initial registration under this ordinance, this fee shall be paid for all current Occupants by October 1, 2006. Thereafter, prior to occupying any Rental Unit, all Occupants shall obtain an occupancy permit. It shall be the Occupant's responsibility to submit an occupancy permit application to the Code Enforcement Office, pay the fee and obtain the occupancy permit. If there are multiple Occupants in a single Rental Unit, each Occupant shall obtain his or her own permit. Owner or Agent shall notify all prospective Occupants of this requirement and shall not permit occupancy of a Rental Unit unless the Occupant first obtains an occupancy permit. Each occupancy permit issued is valid only for the Occupant for as long as the Occupant continues to occupy the Rental Unit for which such permit was applied. Any relocation to a different Rental Unit requires a new occupancy permit. All Occupants age 65 and older, with adequate proof of age, shall be exempt from paying the permit fee, but shall be otherwise required to comply with this section and the rest of the Ordinance.

1. Application for occupancy permits shall be made upon forms furnished by the Code Enforcement Office for such purpose and shall specifically require the following minimum information:
   a) Name of Occupant
   b) Mailing address of Occupant
   c) Street address of Rental Unit for which Occupant is applying, if different from mailing address
   d) Name of Landlord
   e) Date of lease commencement
   f) Proof of age if claiming exemption from the permit fee
   g) Proper identification showing proof of legal citizenship and/or residency
2. Upon receipt of the application and the payment of applicable fees as set forth above, the Code Enforcement Office shall issue an Occupancy Permit to the Occupant immediately.

Section 8. **Enforcement**

a. The following persons are hereby authorized to enforce this Ordinance:

1. The Chief of Police
2. Any Police Officer

3. Code Enforcement Officer
4. The Fire Chief
5. Deputy Fire Chief of the City of Hazleton.
6. Health Officer

b. The designation of any person to enforce this Ordinance or authorization of an Inspector, when in writing, and signed by a person authorized by Section 8.a to designate or authorize an Inspector to enforce this Ordinance, shall be prima facie evidence of such authority before the Magisterial District Judge, Court of Common Pleas, or any other Court, administrative body of the City, or of this Commonwealth, and the designating Director or Supervisor need not be called as a witness thereto.

Section 9. Failure to Correct Violations.

If any Person shall fail, refuse or neglect to comply with a notice of violation as set forth in Section 4 above, the City shall have the right to file an enforcement action with the Magisterial District Judge against any Person the City deems to be in violation. If, after hearing, the Magisterial District Judge determines that such Person or Persons are in violation, the Magisterial District Judge may, at the City's request, order the closure of the Rental Unit(s), or assess fines in accordance with Section 10 below, until such violations are corrected. Such order shall be stayed pending any appeal to the Court of Common Pleas of Luzerne County.

Section 10. Failure to Comply With This Ordinance; Penalties

a. Except as provided in subsections 10.b and 10.c below, any Person who shall violate any provision of the Ordinance shall, upon conviction thereof after notice and a hearing before the Magisterial District Judge, be sentenced to pay a fine of not less than $100.00 and not more than $300.00 plus costs, or imprisonment for a term not to exceed ninety (90) days in default of payment. Every day that a violation of this Ordinance continues shall constitute a separate offense, provided, however, that failure to register or renew or pay appropriate fees in a timely manner shall not constitute a continuing offense but shall be a single offense not subject to daily fines.

b. Any Owner or Agent who shall allow any Occupant to occupy a Rental Unit without first obtaining an occupancy permit is in violation of Section 7.b and shall, upon conviction thereof after notice and a hearing before the Magisterial District Judge, be sentenced to pay a fine of $1,000 for each Occupant that does not have an occupancy permit and $100 per Occupant per day for each day that Owner or Agent continues to allow each such Occupant to occupy the Rental Unit without an occupancy permit after Owner or Agent is given notice of such violation pursuant to Section 4 above. Owner or Agent shall not be held liable for the actions of Occupants who allow additional occupancy in any Rental

Unit without the Owner or Agent's written permission, provided that Owner or Agent takes reasonable steps to remove or register such unauthorized Occupant(s) within ten (10) days of learning of their unauthorized occupancy in the Rental Unit. c. Any Occupant having an occupancy permit but who allows additional occupancy in a Rental Unit without first obtaining the written permission of the Owner or Agent and without requiring each such additional Occupant to obtain his or her own occupancy permit is in violation of Section 7.b of this ordinance and shall, upon conviction thereof after notice and a hearing before the Magisterial District Judge, be sentenced to pay a fine of $1,000 for each additional Occupant permitted by Occupant that does not have an occupancy permit and $100 per additional Occupant per day for each day that Occupant continues to allow each such additional Occupant to occupy the Rental Unit without an occupancy permit after Occupant is given written notice of such violation by Owner or Agent or pursuant to Section 4 above.

Section 11. Applicability and Exemptions to the Ordinance

The provisions of the ordinance shall not apply to the following properties, which are exempt from registration and license requirements:

a. Hotels, Motels and Dormitories.

b. Rental Units owned by Public Authorities as defined under the Pennsylvania Municipal Authorities Act, and Dwelling Units that are part of an elderly housing multi-unit building which is 75% occupied by individuals over the age of sixty-five.

c. Multi-dwelling units that operate under Internal Revenue Service Code Section 42 concerning entities that operate with an elderly component.

d. Properties which consist of a double home, half of which is let for occupancy and half of which is Owner-occupied as the Owner's residence.

Section 12. Confidentiality of Information

All registration information collected by the City under this Ordinance shall be maintained as confidential and shall not be disseminated or released to any individual, group or organization for any purpose except as provided herein or required by law. Information may be released only to authorized individuals when required during the course of an official City, state or federal investigation or inquiry.

Section 13. Saving Clause

This ordinance shall not affect violations of any other ordinance, code or regulation existing prior to the effective date thereof and any such violations shall be governed and shall continue to be punishable to the full extent of the law under the provisions of those ordinances, codes or regulations in effect at the time the violation was committed.

Section 14. **Severability**

If any section, clause, provision or portion of this Ordinance shall be held invalid or unconstitutional by any Court of competent jurisdiction, such decision shall not affect any other section, clause, provision or portion of this Ordinance so long as it remains legally enforceable without the invalid portion. The City reserves the right to amend this Ordinance or any portion thereof from time to time as it shall deem advisable in the best interest of the promotion of the purposes and intent of this Ordinance, and the effective administration thereof.

Section 15. **Effective Date**

This Ordinance shall become effective immediately upon approval. **This Ordinance repeals Ordinance number 2004–11 and replaces same in its entirety**.

Section 16.

This Ordinance is enacted by the Council of the City of Hazleton under the authority of the Act of Legislature, April 13, 1972, Act No. 62, known as the "Home Rule Charter and Optional Plans Law", and all other laws enforceable the State of Pennsylvania.

ORDAINED AND ENACTED by Council this 15th day of August 2006.

ARIZONA SENATE BILL 1070

April 23, 2010

Editors' note: Arizona Senate Bill 1070, Ariz. Sess. Laws 113, which became law on April 23, 2010, added several new sections to the Arizona statutes and amended several preexisting sections. On April 30, 2010, Arizona House Bill 2162, 2010 Ariz. Sess. Laws 211, became law and amended several of the new provisions that SB 1070 had added.

Below is SB 1070, as amended by HB 2162. As indicated for each section in footnotes *infra*, new provisions in each enactment are in ALL CAPS; deleted text is in ~~strikethrough~~.

ARIZONA 49TH LEGISLATURE—SECOND REGULAR SESSION

CHAPTER 113

SENATE BILL 1070

as amended by House Bill 2162, 2010 Ariz. Sess. Laws 211

2010 Ariz. ALS 113; 2010 Ariz. Sess. Laws 113; 2010 Ariz. Ch. 113; 2010 Ariz. SB 1070

Be it enacted by the Legislature of the State of Arizona:

Section 1. Intent

The legislature finds that there is a compelling interest in the cooperative enforcement of federal immigration laws throughout all of Arizona. The legislature declares that the intent of this act is to make attrition through enforcement the public policy of all state and local government agencies in Arizona. The provisions of this act are intended to work together to discourage and deter the unlawful entry and presence of aliens and economic activity by persons unlawfully present in the United States.

Sec. 2. Title 11, chapter 7, Arizona Revised Statutes, is amended by adding article 8, to read:

ARTICLE 8. ENFORCEMENT OF IMMIGRATION LAWS

11–1051. Cooperation and assistance in enforcement of immigration laws; indemnification[1]

A. No official or agency of this state or a county, city, town or other political subdivision of this state may limit or restrict the enforce-

1. This new § 11–1051, added by SB 1070, was later amended by HB 2162, § 3. In this section, text in ALL CAPS was added by HB 2162, and text in ~~strikethrough~~ was deleted by HB 2162.—eds.

ment of federal immigration laws to less than the full extent permitted by federal law.

B. For any lawful ~~contact~~ STOP, DETENTION OR ARREST made by a law enforcement official or a law enforcement agency of this state or a law enforcement official or a law enforcement agency of a county, city, town or other political subdivision of this state IN THE ENFORCEMENT OF ANY OTHER LAW OR ORDINANCE OF A COUNTY, CITY OR TOWN OR THIS STATE where reasonable suspicion exists that the person is an alien ~~who~~ AND is unlawfully present in the United States, a reasonable attempt shall be made, when practicable, to determine the immigration status of the person, except if the determination may hinder or obstruct an investigation. Any person who is arrested shall have the person's immigration status determined before the person is released. The person's immigration status shall be verified with the federal government pursuant to 8 United States code section 1373(c). A law enforcement official or agency of this state or a county, city, town or other political subdivision of this state may not ~~solely~~ consider race, color or national origin in implementing the requirements of this subsection except to the extent permitted by the United States or Arizona Constitution. A person is presumed to not be an alien who is unlawfully present in the United States if the person provides to the law enforcement officer or agency any of the following:

1. A valid Arizona driver license.

2. A valid Arizona nonoperating identification license.

3. A valid tribal enrollment card or other form of tribal identification.

4. If the entity requires proof of legal presence in the United States before issuance, any valid United States federal, state or local government issued identification.

C. If an alien who is unlawfully present in the United States is convicted of a violation of state or local law, on discharge from imprisonment or on the assessment of any monetary obligation that is imposed, the United States immigration and customs enforcement or the United States customs and border protection shall be immediately notified.

D. Notwithstanding any other law, a law enforcement agency may securely transport an alien who the agency has received verification is unlawfully present in the united states and who is in the agency's custody to a federal facility in this state or to any other point of transfer into federal custody that is outside the jurisdiction of the law enforcement agency. A law enforcement agency shall obtain judicial authorization before securely transporting an alien who is unlawfully present in the United States to a point of transfer that is outside of this state.

E. IN THE IMPLEMENTATION OF THIS SECTION, AN ALIEN'S IMMIGRATION STATUS MAY BE DETERMINED BY:

1. A LAW ENFORCEMENT OFFICER WHO IS AUTHORIZED BY THE FEDERAL GOVERNMENT TO VERIFY OR ASCERTAIN AN ALIEN'S IMMIGRATION STATUS.

2. THE UNITED STATES IMMIGRATION AND CUSTOMS ENFORCEMENT OR THE UNITED STATES CUSTOMS AND BORDER PROTECTION PURSUANT TO 8 UNITED STATES CODE SECTION 1373(C).

~~E.~~ **F.** Except as provided in federal law, officials or agencies of this state and counties, cities, towns and other political subdivisions of this state may not be prohibited or in any way be restricted from sending, receiving or maintaining information relating to the immigration status, lawful or unlawful, of any individual or exchanging that information with any other federal, state or local governmental entity for the following official purposes:

1. Determining eligibility for any public benefit, service or license provided by any federal, state, local or other political subdivision of this state.

2. Verifying any claim of residence or domicile if determination of residence or domicile is required under the laws of this state or a judicial order issued pursuant to a civil or criminal proceeding in this state.

3. If the person is an alien, determining whether the person is in compliance with the federal registration laws prescribed by title II, chapter 7 of the federal immigration and Nationality act.

4. Pursuant to 8 United States Code section 1373 and 8 United States Code section 1644.

~~F.~~ **G.** This section does not implement, authorize or establish and shall not be construed to implement, authorize or establish the REAL ID act of 2005 (P.L. 109–13, division B; 119 Stat. 302), including the use of a radio frequency identification chip.

~~G.~~ **H.** A person who is a legal resident of this state may bring an action in superior court to challenge any official or agency of this state or a county, city, town or other political subdivision of this state that adopts or implements a policy ~~or practice~~ that limits or restricts the enforcement of federal immigration laws, INCLUDING 8 UNITED STATES CODE SECTIONS 1373 AND 1644, to less than the full extent permitted by federal law. If there is a judicial finding that an entity has violated this section, the court shall order that the entity pay a civil penalty of not less than ~~one thousand~~ FIVE HUNDRED dollars and not more than five thousand dollars for each day that the policy has remained in effect after the filing of an action pursuant to this subsection.

~~H.~~ **I.** A court shall collect the civil penalty prescribed in subsection ~~G~~ **H** of this section and remit the civil penalty to the state treasurer for deposit in the gang and immigration intelligence team enforcement mission fund established by section 41–1724.

~~I.~~ **J.** The court may award court costs and reasonable attorney fees to any person or any official or agency of this state or a county, city, town or other political subdivision of this state that prevails by an adjudication on the merits in a proceeding brought pursuant to this section.

~~J.~~ **K.** Except in relation to matters in which the officer is adjudged to have acted in bad faith, a law enforcement officer is indemnified by the law enforcement officer's agency against reasonable costs and expenses, including attorney fees, incurred by the officer in connection with any action, suit or proceeding brought pursuant to this section in which the officer may be a defendant by reason of the officer being or having been a member of the law enforcement agency.

~~K.~~ **L.** This section shall be implemented in a manner consistent with federal laws regulating immigration, protecting the civil rights of all persons and respecting the privileges and immunities of United States citizens.

Sec. 3. Title 13, chapter 15, Arizona Revised Statutes, is amended by adding section 13–1509, to read:

13–1509. Willful failure to complete or carry an alien registration document; assessment; exception; authenticated records; classification[2]

A. In addition to any violation of federal law, a person is guilty of willful failure to complete or carry an alien registration document if the person is in violation of 8 United States Code section 1304(e) or 1306(a).

B. In the enforcement of this section, an alien's immigration status may be determined by:

1. A law enforcement officer who is authorized by the federal government to verify or ascertain an alien's immigration status.

2. The United States immigration and customs enforcement or the United States customs and border protection pursuant to 8 United States Code section 1373(c).

C. A LAW ENFORCEMENT OFFICIAL OR AGENCY OF THIS STATE OR A COUNTY, CITY, TOWN OR OTHER POLITICAL SUBDIVISION OF THIS STATE MAY NOT CONSIDER RACE, COLOR OR NATIONAL ORIGIN IN THE ENFORCEMENT OF THIS SECTION EXCEPT TO THE EXTENT PERMITTED BY THE UNITED STATES OR ARIZONA CONSTITUTION.

~~C.~~ **D.** A person who is sentenced pursuant to this section is not eligible for suspension of sentence, probation, pardon, commutation of sentence, or release from confinement on any basis except as authorized by section 31–233, subsection A or B until the sentence imposed by the

2. This new § 13–1509, added by SB 1070, was later amended by HB 2162, § 4. In this section, text in ALL CAPS was added by HB 2162, and text in ~~strikethrough~~ was deleted by HB 2162.—eds.

court has been served or the person is eligible for release pursuant to section 41–1604.07.

~~D.~~ **E.** In addition to any other penalty prescribed by law, the court shall order the person to pay jail costs**.** ~~and an additional assessment in the following amounts:~~

~~1. At least five hundred dollars for a first violation.~~

~~2. Twice the amount specified in paragraph 1 of this subsection if the person was previously subject to an assessment pursuant to this subsection.~~

~~E. A court shall collect the assessments prescribed in subsection D of this section and remit the assessments to the department of public safety, which shall establish a special subaccount for the monies in the account established for the gang and immigration intelligence team enforcement mission appropriation. Monies in the special subaccount are subject to legislative appropriation for distribution for gang and immigration enforcement and for county jail reimbursement costs relating to illegal immigration.~~

F. This section does not apply to a person who maintains authorization from the federal government to remain in the United States.

G. Any record that relates to the immigration status of a person is admissible in any court without further foundation or testimony from a custodian of records if the record is certified as authentic by the government agency that is responsible for maintaining the record.

H. A violation of this section is a class 1 misdemeanor, except that THE MAXIMUM FINE IS ONE HUNDRED DOLLARS AND FOR a FIRST violation of this section ~~is:~~ THE COURT SHALL NOT SENTENCE THE PERSON TO MORE THAN TWENTY DAYS IN JAIL AND FOR A SECOND OR SUBSEQUENT VIOLATION THE COURT SHALL NOT SENTENCE THE PERSON TO MORE THAN THIRTY DAYS IN JAIL.

~~1. A class 3 felony if the person violates this section while in possession of any of the following:~~

~~(a) A dangerous drug as defined in section 13–3401.~~

~~(b) Precursor chemicals that are used in the manufacturing of methamphetamine in violation of section 13–3404.01.~~

~~(c) A deadly weapon or a dangerous instrument, as defined in section 13–105.~~

~~(d) Property that is used for the purpose of committing an act of terrorism as prescribed in section 13–2308.01.~~

~~2. A class 4 felony if the person either:~~

~~(a) Is convicted of a second or subsequent violation of this section.~~

~~(b) Within sixty months before the violation, has been removed from the United States pursuant to 8 United States Code section 1229a or has accepted a voluntary removal from the United States pursuant to 8 United States Code section 1229c.~~

Sec. 4. Section 13–2319, Arizona Revised Statutes, is amended to read:

13–2319. Smuggling; classification; definitions[3]

A. It is unlawful for a person to intentionally engage in the smuggling of human beings for profit or commercial purpose.

B. A violation of this section is a class 4 felony.

C. Notwithstanding subsection B of this section, a violation of this section:

1. Is a class 2 felony if the human being who is smuggled is under eighteen years of age and is not accompanied by a family member over eighteen years of age or the offense involved the use of a deadly weapon or dangerous instrument.

2. Is a class 3 felony if the offense involves the use or threatened use of deadly physical force and the person is not eligible for suspension of sentence, probation, pardon or release from confinement on any other basis except pursuant to section 31–233, subsection A or B until the sentence imposed by the court is served, the person is eligible for release pursuant to section 41–1604.07 or the sentence is commuted.

D. Chapter 10 of this title does not apply to a violation of subsection C, paragraph 1 of this section.

E. NOTWITHSTANDING ANY OTHER LAW, IN THE ENFORCEMENT OF THIS SECTION A PEACE OFFICER MAY LAWFULLY STOP ANY PERSON WHO IS OPERATING A MOTOR VEHICLE IF THE OFFICER HAS REASONABLE SUSPICION TO BELIEVE THE PERSON IS IN VIOLATION OF ANY CIVIL TRAFFIC LAW.

~~E.~~ **F.** For the purposes of this section:

1. "Family member" means the person's parent, grandparent, sibling or any other person who is related to the person by consanguinity or affinity to the second degree.

2. "Procurement of transportation" means any participation in or facilitation of transportation and includes:

(a) Providing services that facilitate transportation including travel arrangement services or money transmission services.

3. This § 13–2319 was amended by SB 1070 and not affected by HB 2162. In this section, text in ALL CAPS was added by SB 1070, and text in ~~strikethrough~~ was deleted by SB 1070.—eds.

(b) Providing property that facilitates transportation, including a weapon, a vehicle or other means of transportation or false identification, or selling, leasing, renting or otherwise making available a drop house as defined in section 13–2322.

3. "Smuggling of human beings" means the transportation, procurement of transportation or use of property or real property by a person or an entity that knows or has reason to know that the person or persons transported or to be transported are not United States citizens, permanent resident aliens or persons otherwise lawfully in this state or have attempted to enter, entered or remained in the United States in violation of law.

Sec. 5. Title 13, chapter 29, Arizona Revised Statutes, is amended by adding sections 13–2928 and 13–2929, to read:

13–2928. Unlawful stopping to hire and pick up passengers for work; unlawful application, solicitation or employment; classification; definitions[4]

A. It is unlawful for an occupant of a motor vehicle that is stopped on a street, roadway or highway to attempt to hire or hire and pick up passengers for work at a different location if the motor vehicle blocks or impedes the normal movement of traffic.

B. It is unlawful for a person to enter a motor vehicle that is stopped on a street, roadway or highway in order to be hired by an occupant of the motor vehicle and to be transported to work at a different location if the motor vehicle blocks or impedes the normal movement of traffic.

C. It is unlawful for a person who is unlawfully present in the United States and who is an unauthorized alien to knowingly apply for work, solicit work in a public place or perform work as an employee or independent contractor in this state.

D. A LAW ENFORCEMENT OFFICIAL OR AGENCY OF THIS STATE OR A COUNTY, CITY, TOWN OR OTHER POLITICAL SUBDIVISION OF THIS STATE MAY NOT CONSIDER RACE, COLOR OR NATIONAL ORIGIN IN THE ENFORCEMENT OF THIS SECTION EXCEPT TO THE EXTENT PERMITTED BY THE UNITED STATES OR ARIZONA CONSTITUTION.

E. IN THE ENFORCEMENT OF THIS SECTION, AN ALIEN'S IMMIGRATION STATUS MAY BE DETERMINED BY:

1. A LAW ENFORCEMENT OFFICER WHO IS AUTHORIZED BY THE FEDERAL GOVERNMENT TO VERIFY OR ASCERTAIN AN ALIEN'S IMMIGRATION STATUS.

4. This new § 13–2928, added by SB 1070, was later amended by HB 2162, § 5. In this section, text in ALL CAPS was added by HB 2162, and text in ~~strikethrough~~ was deleted by HB 2162.—eds.

2. THE UNITED STATES IMMIGRATION AND CUSTOMS ENFORCEMENT OR THE UNITED STATES CUSTOMS AND BORDER PROTECTION PURSUANT TO 8 UNITED STATES CODE SECTION 1373(C).

~~D.~~ **F.** A violation of this section is a class 1 misdemeanor.

~~E.~~ **G.** For the purposes of this section:

1. "Solicit" means verbal or nonverbal communication by a gesture or a nod that would indicate to a reasonable person that a person is willing to be employed.

2. "Unauthorized alien" means an alien who does not have the legal right or authorization under federal law to work in the United States as described in 8 United States Code section 1324a(h)(3).

13–2929. Unlawful transporting, moving, concealing, harboring or shielding of unlawful aliens; vehicle impoundment; exception; classification[5]

A. It is unlawful for a person who is in violation of a criminal offense to:

1. Transport or move or attempt to transport or move an alien in this state, in furtherance of the illegal presence of the alien in the United States, in a means of transportation if the person knows or recklessly disregards the fact that the alien has come to, has entered or remains in the United States in violation of law.

2. Conceal, harbor or shield or attempt to conceal, harbor or shield an alien from detection in any place in this state, including any building or any means of transportation, if the person knows or recklessly disregards the fact that the alien has come to, has entered or remains in the United States in violation of law.

3. Encourage or induce an alien to come to or reside in this state if the person knows or recklessly disregards the fact that such coming to, entering or residing in this state is or will be in violation of law.

B. A means of transportation that is used in the commission of a violation of this section is subject to mandatory vehicle immobilization or impoundment pursuant to section 28–3511.

C. A LAW ENFORCEMENT OFFICIAL OR AGENCY OF THIS STATE OR A COUNTY, CITY, TOWN OR OTHER POLITICAL SUBDIVISION OF THIS STATE MAY NOT CONSIDER RACE, COLOR OR NATIONAL ORIGIN IN THE ENFORCEMENT OF THIS SECTION EXCEPT TO THE EXTENT PERMITTED BY THE UNITED STATES OR ARIZONA CONSTITUTION.

5. This new § 13–2929, added by SB 1070, was later amended by HB 2162, § 6. In this section, text in ALL CAPS was added by HB 2162, and text in ~~strikethrough~~ was deleted by HB 2162.—eds.

D. IN THE ENFORCEMENT OF THIS SECTION, AN ALIEN'S IMMIGRATION STATUS MAY BE DETERMINED BY:

1. A LAW ENFORCEMENT OFFICER WHO IS AUTHORIZED BY THE FEDERAL GOVERNMENT TO VERIFY OR ASCERTAIN AN ALIEN'S IMMIGRATION STATUS.

2. THE UNITED STATES IMMIGRATION AND CUSTOMS ENFORCEMENT OR THE UNITED STATES CUSTOMS AND BORDER PROTECTION PURSUANT TO 8 UNITED STATES CODE SECTION 1373(C).

~~C.~~ **E.** This section does not apply to a child protective services worker acting in the worker's official capacity or a person who is acting in the capacity of a first responder, an ambulance attendant or an emergency medical technician and who is transporting or moving an alien in this state pursuant to title 36, chapter 21.1.

~~D.~~ **F.** A person who violates this section is guilty of a class 1 misdemeanor and is subject to a fine of at least one thousand dollars, except that a violation of this section that involves ten or more illegal aliens is a class 6 felony and the person is subject to a fine of at least one thousand dollars for each alien who is involved.

Sec. 6. Section 13–3883, Arizona Revised Statutes, is amended to read:

13–3883. Arrest by officer without warrant[6]

A. A peace officer ~~may~~, without a warrant, MAY arrest a person if ~~he~~ THE OFFICER has probable cause to believe:

1. A felony has been committed and probable cause to believe the person to be arrested has committed the felony.

2. A misdemeanor has been committed in ~~his~~ THE OFFICER'S presence and probable cause to believe the person to be arrested has committed the offense.

3. The person to be arrested has been involved in a traffic accident and violated any criminal section of title 28, and that such violation occurred prior to or immediately following such traffic accident.

4. A misdemeanor or a petty offense has been committed and probable cause to believe the person to be arrested has committed the offense. A person arrested under this paragraph is eligible for release under section 13–3903.

5. THE PERSON TO BE ARRESTED HAS COMMITTED ANY PUBLIC OFFENSE THAT MAKES THE PERSON REMOVABLE FROM THE UNITED STATES.

6. This § 13–3883 was amended by SB 1070 and not affected by HB 2162. In this section, text in ALL CAPS was added by SB 1070, and text in ~~strikethrough~~ was deleted by SB 1070.—eds.

B. A peace officer may stop and detain a person as is reasonably necessary to investigate an actual or suspected violation of any traffic law committed in the officer's presence and may serve a copy of the traffic complaint for any alleged civil or criminal traffic violation. A peace officer who serves a copy of the traffic complaint shall do so within a reasonable time of the alleged criminal or civil traffic violation.

Sec. 7. Section 23–212, Arizona Revised Statutes, is amended to read:

23–212. Knowingly employing unauthorized aliens; prohibition; false and frivolous complaints; violation; classification; license suspension and revocation; affirmative defense[7]

A. An employer shall not knowingly employ an unauthorized alien. If, in the case when an employer uses a contract, subcontract or other independent contractor agreement to obtain the labor of an alien in this state, the employer knowingly contracts with an unauthorized alien or with a person who employs or contracts with an unauthorized alien to perform the labor, the employer violates this subsection.

B. The attorney general shall prescribe a complaint form for a person to allege a violation of subsection A of this section. The complainant shall not be required to list the complainant's social security number on the complaint form or to have the complaint form notarized. On receipt of a complaint on a prescribed complaint form that an employer allegedly knowingly employs an unauthorized alien, the attorney general or county attorney shall investigate whether the employer has violated subsection A of this section. If a complaint is received but is not submitted on a prescribed complaint form, the attorney general or county attorney may investigate whether the employer has violated subsection A of this section. This subsection shall not be construed to prohibit the filing of anonymous complaints that are not submitted on a prescribed complaint form. The attorney general or county attorney shall not investigate complaints that are based solely on race, color or national origin. A complaint that is submitted to a county attorney shall be submitted to the county attorney in the county in which the alleged unauthorized alien is or was employed by the employer. The county sheriff or any other local law enforcement agency may assist in investigating a complaint. When investigating a complaint, the attorney general or county attorney shall verify the work authorization of the alleged unauthorized alien with the federal government pursuant to 8 United States Code section 1373(c). A state, county or local official shall not attempt to independently make a final determination on whether an alien is authorized to work in the United States. An alien's immigration status or work authorization status shall be verified with the federal

7. This § 23–212 was amended by SB 1070 and not affected by HB 2162. In this section, text in ALL CAPS was added by SB 1070, and text in ~~strikethrough~~ was deleted by SB 1070.—eds.

government pursuant to 8 United States Code section 1373(c). A person who knowingly files a false and frivolous complaint under this subsection is guilty of a class 3 misdemeanor.

C. If, after an investigation, the attorney general or county attorney determines that the complaint is not false and frivolous:

1. The attorney general or county attorney shall notify the United States immigration and customs enforcement of the unauthorized alien.

2. The attorney general or county attorney shall notify the local law enforcement agency of the unauthorized alien.

3. The attorney general shall notify the appropriate county attorney to bring an action pursuant to subsection D of this section if the complaint was originally filed with the attorney general.

D. An action for a violation of subsection A of this section shall be brought against the employer by the county attorney in the county where the unauthorized alien employee is or was employed by the employer. The county attorney shall not bring an action against any employer for any violation of subsection A of this section that occurs before January 1, 2008. A second violation of this section shall be based only on an unauthorized alien who is or was employed by the employer after an action has been brought for a violation of subsection A of this section or section 23–212.01, subsection A.

E. For any action in superior court under this section, the court shall expedite the action, including assigning the hearing at the earliest practicable date.

F. On a finding of a violation of subsection A of this section:

1. For a first violation, as described in paragraph 3 of this subsection, the court:

(a) Shall order the employer to terminate the employment of all unauthorized aliens.

(b) Shall order the employer to be subject to a three year probationary period for the business location where the unauthorized alien performed work. During the probationary period the employer shall file quarterly reports in the form provided in section 23–722.01 with the county attorney of each new employee who is hired by the employer at the business location where the unauthorized alien performed work.

(c) Shall order the employer to file a signed sworn affidavit with the county attorney within three business days after the order is issued. The affidavit shall state that the employer has terminated the employment of all unauthorized aliens in this state and that the employer will not intentionally or knowingly employ an unauthorized alien in this state. The court shall order the appropriate agencies to suspend all licenses subject to this subdivision that are held by the employer if the employer fails to file a signed sworn affidavit with the county attorney within three business days after the order is issued. All licenses that are suspended under this subdivision shall remain suspended until the employer files a signed sworn affidavit with the county attorney. Notwithstanding any other law, on filing of the affidavit the suspended licenses shall be reinstated immediately by the appropriate agencies. For the purposes of this subdivision, the licenses that are subject to suspension under this subdivision are all licenses that are held by the employer specific to the business location where the unauthorized alien performed work. If the employer does not hold a license specific to the business location where the unauthorized alien performed work, but a license is necessary to operate the employer's business in general, the licenses that are subject to suspension under this subdivision are all licenses that are held by the employer at the employer's primary place of business. On receipt of the court's order and notwithstanding any other law, the appropriate agencies shall suspend the licenses according to the court's order. The court shall send a copy of the court's order to the attorney general and the attorney general shall maintain the copy pursuant to subsection G of this section.

(d) May order the appropriate agencies to suspend all licenses described in subdivision (c) of this paragraph that are held by the employer for not to exceed ten business days. The court shall base its decision to suspend under this subdivision on any evidence or information submitted to it during the action for a violation of this subsection and shall consider the following factors, if relevant:

(i) The number of unauthorized aliens employed by the employer.

(ii) Any prior misconduct by the employer.

(iii) The degree of harm resulting from the violation.

(iv) Whether the employer made good faith efforts to comply with any applicable requirements.

(v) The duration of the violation.

(vi) The role of the directors, officers or principals of the employer in the violation.

(vii) Any other factors the court deems appropriate.

2. For a second violation, as described in paragraph 3 of this subsection, the court shall order the appropriate agencies to permanently revoke all licenses that are held by the employer specific to the business location where the unauthorized alien performed work. If the employer does not hold a license specific to the business location where the unauthorized alien performed work, but a license is necessary to operate the employer's business in general, the court

shall order the appropriate agencies to permanently revoke all licenses that are held by the employer at the employer's primary place of business. On receipt of the order and notwithstanding any other law, the appropriate agencies shall immediately revoke the licenses.

3. The violation shall be considered:

(a) A first violation by an employer at a business location if the violation did not occur during a probationary period ordered by the court under this subsection or section 23–212.01, subsection F for that employer's business location.

(b) A second violation by an employer at a business location if the violation occurred during a probationary period ordered by the court under this subsection or section 23–212.01, subsection F for that employer's business location.

G. The attorney general shall maintain copies of court orders that are received pursuant to subsection F of this section and shall maintain a database of the employers and business locations that have a first violation of subsection A of this section and make the court orders available on the attorney general's website.

H. On determining whether an employee is an unauthorized alien, the court shall consider only the federal government's determination pursuant to 8 United States Code section 1373(c). The federal government's determination creates a rebuttable presumption of the employee's lawful status. The court may take judicial notice of the federal government's determination and may request the federal government to provide automated or testimonial verification pursuant to 8 United States Code section 1373(c).

I. For the purposes of this section, proof of verifying the employment authorization of an employee through the e-verify program creates a rebuttable presumption that an employer did not knowingly employ an unauthorized alien.

J. For the purposes of this section, an employer that establishes that it has complied in good faith with the requirements of 8 United States Code section 1324a(b) establishes an affirmative defense that the employer did not knowingly employ an unauthorized alien. An employer is considered to have complied with the requirements of 8 United States Code section 1324a(b), notwithstanding an isolated, sporadic or accidental technical or procedural failure to meet the requirements, if there is a good faith attempt to comply with the requirements.

K. IT IS AN AFFIRMATIVE DEFENSE TO A VIOLATION OF SUBSECTION A OF THIS SECTION THAT THE EMPLOYER WAS ENTRAPPED. TO CLAIM ENTRAPMENT, THE EMPLOYER MUST ADMIT BY THE EMPLOYER'S TESTIMONY OR OTHER EVIDENCE THE SUBSTANTIAL ELEMENTS OF THE VIOLATION. AN EMPLOYER WHO ASSERTS AN ENTRAPMENT DEFENSE HAS THE

BURDEN OF PROVING THE FOLLOWING BY A PREPONDERANCE OF THE EVIDENCE:

1. THE IDEA OF COMMITTING THE VIOLATION STARTED WITH LAW ENFORCEMENT OFFICERS OR THEIR AGENTS RATHER THAN WITH THE EMPLOYER.

2. THE LAW ENFORCEMENT OFFICERS OR THEIR AGENTS URGED AND INDUCED THE EMPLOYER TO COMMIT THE VIOLATION.

3. THE EMPLOYER WAS NOT PREDISPOSED TO COMMIT THE VIOLATION BEFORE THE LAW ENFORCEMENT OFFICERS OR THEIR AGENTS URGED AND INDUCED THE EMPLOYER TO COMMIT THE VIOLATION.

L. AN EMPLOYER DOES NOT ESTABLISH ENTRAPMENT IF THE EMPLOYER WAS PREDISPOSED TO VIOLATE SUBSECTION A OF THIS SECTION AND THE LAW ENFORCEMENT OFFICERS OR THEIR AGENTS MERELY PROVIDED THE EMPLOYER WITH AN OPPORTUNITY TO COMMIT THE VIOLATION. IT IS NOT ENTRAPMENT FOR LAW ENFORCEMENT OFFICERS OR THEIR AGENTS MERELY TO USE A RUSE OR TO CONCEAL THEIR IDENTITY. THE CONDUCT OF LAW ENFORCEMENT OFFICERS AND THEIR AGENTS MAY BE CONSIDERED IN DETERMINING IF AN EMPLOYER HAS PROVEN ENTRAPMENT.

Sec. 8. Section 23–212.01, Arizona Revised Statutes, is amended to read:

23–212.01. Intentionally employing unauthorized aliens; prohibition; false and frivolous complaints; violation; classification; license suspension and revocation; affirmative defense[8]

A. An employer shall not intentionally employ an unauthorized alien. If, in the case when an employer uses a contract, subcontract or other independent contractor agreement to obtain the labor of an alien in this state, the employer intentionally contracts with an unauthorized alien or with a person who employs or contracts with an unauthorized alien to perform the labor, the employer violates this subsection.

B. The attorney general shall prescribe a complaint form for a person to allege a violation of subsection A of this section. The complainant shall not be required to list the complainant's social security number on the complaint form or to have the complaint form notarized. On receipt of a complaint on a prescribed complaint form that an employer allegedly intentionally employs an unauthorized alien, the attorney general or county attorney shall investigate whether the employer has violated subsection A of this section. If a complaint is received but is not

8. This § 23–212.01 was amended by SB 1070 and not affected by HB 2162. In this section, text in ALL CAPS was added by SB 1070, and text in ~~strikethrough~~ was deleted by SB 1070.—eds.

submitted on a prescribed complaint form, the attorney general or county attorney may investigate whether the employer has violated subsection A of this section. This subsection shall not be construed to prohibit the filing of anonymous complaints that are not submitted on a prescribed complaint form. The attorney general or county attorney shall not investigate complaints that are based solely on race, color or national origin. A complaint that is submitted to a county attorney shall be submitted to the county attorney in the county in which the alleged unauthorized alien is or was employed by the employer. The county sheriff or any other local law enforcement agency may assist in investigating a complaint. When investigating a complaint, the attorney general or county attorney shall verify the work authorization of the alleged unauthorized alien with the federal government pursuant to 8 United States Code section 1373(c). A state, county or local official shall not attempt to independently make a final determination on whether an alien is authorized to work in the United States. An alien's immigration status or work authorization status shall be verified with the federal government pursuant to 8 United States Code section 1373(c). A person who knowingly files a false and frivolous complaint under this subsection is guilty of a class 3 misdemeanor.

C. If, after an investigation, the attorney general or county attorney determines that the complaint is not false and frivolous:

1. The attorney general or county attorney shall notify the United States immigration and customs enforcement of the unauthorized alien.

2. The attorney general or county attorney shall notify the local law enforcement agency of the unauthorized alien.

3. The attorney general shall notify the appropriate county attorney to bring an action pursuant to subsection D of this section if the complaint was originally filed with the attorney general.

D. An action for a violation of subsection A of this section shall be brought against the employer by the county attorney in the county where the unauthorized alien employee is or was employed by the employer. The county attorney shall not bring an action against any employer for any violation of subsection A of this section that occurs before January 1, 2008. A second violation of this section shall be based only on an unauthorized alien who is or was employed by the employer after an action has been brought for a violation of subsection A of this section or section 23–212, subsection A.

E. For any action in superior court under this section, the court shall expedite the action, including assigning the hearing at the earliest practicable date.

F. On a finding of a violation of subsection A of this section:

1. For a first violation, as described in paragraph 3 of this subsection, the court shall:

(a) Order the employer to terminate the employment of all unauthorized aliens.

(b) Order the employer to be subject to a five year probationary period for the business location where the unauthorized alien performed work. During the probationary period the employer shall file quarterly reports in the form provided in section 23–722.01 with the county attorney of each new employee who is hired by the employer at the business location where the unauthorized alien performed work.

(c) Order the appropriate agencies to suspend all licenses described in subdivision (d) of this paragraph that are held by the employer for a minimum of ten days. The court shall base its decision on the length of the suspension under this subdivision on any evidence or information submitted to it during the action for a violation of this subsection and shall consider the following factors, if relevant:

(i) The number of unauthorized aliens employed by the employer.

(ii) Any prior misconduct by the employer.

(iii) The degree of harm resulting from the violation.

(iv) Whether the employer made good faith efforts to comply with any applicable requirements.

(v) The duration of the violation.

(vi) The role of the directors, officers or principals of the employer in the violation.

(vii) Any other factors the court deems appropriate.

(d) Order the employer to file a signed sworn affidavit with the county attorney. The affidavit shall state that the employer has terminated the employment of all unauthorized aliens in this state and that the employer will not intentionally or knowingly employ an unauthorized alien in this state. The court shall order the appropriate agencies to suspend all licenses subject to this subdivision that are held by the employer if the employer fails to file a signed sworn affidavit with the county attorney within three business days after the order is issued. All licenses that are suspended under this subdivision for failing to file a signed sworn affidavit shall remain suspended until the employer files a signed sworn affidavit with the county attorney. For the purposes of this subdivision, the licenses that are subject to suspension under this subdivision are all licenses that are held by the employer specific to the business location where the unauthorized alien performed work. If the employer does not hold a license specific to the business location where the unauthorized alien performed work, but a license is necessary to operate the employer's business in general, the licenses that are subject to suspension under this subdivision are all licenses that are held by the employer at the employer's primary place of business. On receipt of the court's order and notwithstanding any other law, the appropriate agencies shall suspend the licenses according to the court's order. The court shall send a copy of the court's order to the attorney general and the attorney general shall maintain the copy pursuant to subsection G of this section.

2. For a second violation, as described in paragraph 3 of this subsection, the court shall order the appropriate agencies to permanently revoke all licenses that are held by the employer specific to the business location where the unauthorized alien performed work. If the employer does not hold a license specific to the business location where the unauthorized alien performed work, but a license is necessary to operate the employer's business in general, the court shall order the appropriate agencies to permanently revoke all licenses that are held by the employer at the employer's primary place of business. On receipt of the order and notwithstanding any other law, the appropriate agencies shall immediately revoke the licenses.

3. The violation shall be considered:

(a) A first violation by an employer at a business location if the violation did not occur during a probationary period ordered by the court under this subsection or section 23–212, subsection F for that employer's business location.

(b) A second violation by an employer at a business location if the violation occurred during a probationary period ordered by the court under this subsection or section 23–212, subsection F for that employer's business location.

G. The attorney general shall maintain copies of court orders that are received pursuant to subsection F of this section and shall maintain a database of the employers and business locations that have a first violation of subsection A of this section and make the court orders available on the attorney general's website.

H. On determining whether an employee is an unauthorized alien, the court shall consider only the federal government's determination pursuant to 8 United States Code section 1373(c). The federal government's determination creates a rebuttable presumption of the employee's lawful status. The court may take judicial notice of the federal government's determination and may request the federal government to provide automated or testimonial verification pursuant to 8 United States Code section 1373(c).

I. For the purposes of this section, proof of verifying the employment authorization of an employee through the e-verify program creates a rebuttable presumption that an employer did not intentionally employ an unauthorized alien.

J. For the purposes of this section, an employer that establishes that it has complied in good faith with the requirements of 8 United States Code section 1324a(b) establishes an affirmative defense that the employer did not intentionally employ an unauthorized alien. An employer is considered to have complied with the requirements of 8 United States Code section 1324a(b), notwithstanding an isolated, sporadic or accidental technical or procedural failure to meet the requirements, if there is a good faith attempt to comply with the requirements.

K. IT IS AN AFFIRMATIVE DEFENSE TO A VIOLATION OF SUBSECTION A OF THIS SECTION THAT THE EMPLOYER WAS ENTRAPPED. TO CLAIM ENTRAPMENT, THE EMPLOYER MUST ADMIT BY THE EMPLOYER'S TESTIMONY OR OTHER EVIDENCE THE SUBSTANTIAL ELEMENTS OF THE VIOLATION. AN EMPLOYER WHO ASSERTS AN ENTRAPMENT DEFENSE HAS THE BURDEN OF PROVING THE FOLLOWING BY A PREPONDERANCE OF THE EVIDENCE:

1. THE IDEA OF COMMITTING THE VIOLATION STARTED WITH LAW ENFORCEMENT OFFICERS OR THEIR AGENTS RATHER THAN WITH THE EMPLOYER.

2. THE LAW ENFORCEMENT OFFICERS OR THEIR AGENTS URGED AND INDUCED THE EMPLOYER TO COMMIT THE VIOLATION.

3. THE EMPLOYER WAS NOT PREDISPOSED TO COMMIT THE VIOLATION BEFORE THE LAW ENFORCEMENT OFFICERS OR THEIR AGENTS URGED AND INDUCED THE EMPLOYER TO COMMIT THE VIOLATION.

L. AN EMPLOYER DOES NOT ESTABLISH ENTRAPMENT IF THE EMPLOYER WAS PREDISPOSED TO VIOLATE SUBSECTION A OF THIS SECTION AND THE LAW ENFORCEMENT OFFICERS OR THEIR AGENTS MERELY PROVIDED THE EMPLOYER WITH AN OPPORTUNITY TO COMMIT THE VIOLATION. IT IS NOT ENTRAPMENT FOR LAW ENFORCEMENT OFFICERS OR THEIR AGENTS MERELY TO USE A RUSE OR TO CONCEAL THEIR IDENTITY. THE CONDUCT OF LAW ENFORCEMENT OFFICERS AND THEIR AGENTS MAY BE CONSIDERED IN DETERMINING IF AN EMPLOYER HAS PROVEN ENTRAPMENT.

Sec. 9. Section 23–214, Arizona Revised Statutes, is amended to read:

23–214. Verification of employment eligibility; e-verify program; economic development incentives; list of registered employers[9]

A. After December 31, 2007, every employer, after hiring an employee, shall verify the employment eligibility of the employee through

9. This § 23–214 was amended by SB 1070 and not affected by HB 2162. In this section, text in ALL CAPS was added by SB 1070, and text in ~~strikethrough~~ was deleted by SB 1070.—eds.

the e-verify program AND SHALL KEEP A RECORD OF THE VERIFICATION FOR THE DURATION OF THE EMPLOYEE'S EMPLOYMENT OR AT LEAST THREE YEARS, WHICHEVER IS LONGER.

B. In addition to any other requirement for an employer to receive an economic development incentive from a government entity, the employer shall register with and participate in the e-verify program. Before receiving the economic development incentive, the employer shall provide proof to the government entity that the employer is registered with and is participating in the e-verify program. If the government entity determines that the employer is not complying with this subsection, the government entity shall notify the employer by certified mail of the government entity's determination of noncompliance and the employer's right to appeal the determination. On a final determination of noncompliance, the employer shall repay all monies received as an economic development incentive to the government entity within thirty days of the final determination. For the purposes of this subsection:

1. "Economic development incentive" means any grant, loan or performance-based incentive from any government entity that is awarded after September 30, 2008. Economic development incentive does not include any tax provision under title 42 or 43.

2. "Government entity" means this state and any political subdivision of this state that receives and uses tax revenues.

C. Every three months the attorney general shall request from the United States department of homeland security a list of employers from this state that are registered with the e-verify program. On receipt of the list of employers, the attorney general shall make the list available on the attorney general's website.

Sec. 10. Section 28–3511, Arizona Revised Statutes, is amended to read:

28–3511. Removal and immobilization or impoundment of vehicle[10]

A. A peace officer shall cause the removal and either immobilization or impoundment of a vehicle if the peace officer determines that a person is driving the vehicle while any of the following applies:

1. The person's driving privilege is suspended or revoked for any reason.

2. The person has not ever been issued a valid driver license or permit by this state and the person does not produce evidence of ever having a valid driver license or permit issued by another

10. This § 28–3511 was amended by SB 1070 and not affected by HB 2162. In this section, text in ALL CAPS was added by SB 1070, and text in ~~strikethrough~~ was deleted by SB 1070.—eds.

jurisdiction. This paragraph does not apply to the operation of an implement of husbandry.

3. The person is subject to an ignition interlock device requirement pursuant to chapter 4 of this title and the person is operating a vehicle without a functioning certified ignition interlock device. This paragraph does not apply to a person operating an employer's vehicle or the operation of a vehicle due to a substantial emergency as defined in section 28–1464.

4. IN FURTHERANCE OF THE ILLEGAL PRESENCE OF AN ALIEN IN THE UNITED STATES AND IN VIOLATION OF A CRIMINAL OFFENSE, THE PERSON IS TRANSPORTING OR MOVING OR ATTEMPTING TO TRANSPORT OR MOVE AN ALIEN IN THIS STATE IN A VEHICLE IF THE PERSON KNOWS OR RECKLESSLY DISREGARDS THE FACT THAT THE ALIEN HAS COME TO, HAS ENTERED OR REMAINS IN THE UNITED STATES IN VIOLATION OF LAW.

5. THE PERSON IS CONCEALING, HARBORING OR SHIELDING OR ATTEMPTING TO CONCEAL, HARBOR OR SHIELD FROM DETECTION AN ALIEN IN THIS STATE IN A VEHICLE IF THE PERSON KNOWS OR RECKLESSLY DISREGARDS THE FACT THAT THE ALIEN HAS COME TO, ENTERED OR REMAINS IN THE UNITED STATES IN VIOLATION OF LAW.

B. A peace officer shall cause the removal and impoundment of a vehicle if the peace officer determines that a person is driving the vehicle and if all of the following apply:

1. The person's driving privilege is canceled, suspended or revoked for any reason or the person has not ever been issued a driver license or permit by this state and the person does not produce evidence of ever having a driver license or permit issued by another jurisdiction.

2. The person is not in compliance with the financial responsibility requirements of chapter 9, article 4 of this title.

3. The person is driving a vehicle that is involved in an accident that results in either property damage or injury to or death of another person.

C. Except as provided in subsection D of this section, while a peace officer has control of the vehicle the peace officer shall cause the removal and either immobilization or impoundment of the vehicle if the peace officer has probable cause to arrest the driver of the vehicle for a violation of section 4–244, paragraph 34 or section 28–1382 or 28–1383.

D. A peace officer shall not cause the removal and either the immobilization or impoundment of a vehicle pursuant to subsection C of this section if all of the following apply:

1. The peace officer determines that the vehicle is currently registered and that the driver or the vehicle is in compliance with the financial responsibility requirements of chapter 9, article 4 of this title.

2. The spouse of the driver is with the driver at the time of the arrest.

3. The peace officer has reasonable grounds to believe that the spouse of the driver:

(a) Has a valid driver license.

(b) Is not impaired by intoxicating liquor, any drug, a vapor releasing substance containing a toxic substance or any combination of liquor, drugs or vapor releasing substances.

(c) Does not have any spirituous liquor in the spouse's body if the spouse is under twenty-one years of age.

4. The spouse notifies the peace officer that the spouse will drive the vehicle from the place of arrest to the driver's home or other place of safety.

5. The spouse drives the vehicle as prescribed by paragraph 4 of this subsection.

E. Except as otherwise provided in this article, a vehicle that is removed and either immobilized or impounded pursuant to subsection A, B or C of this section shall be immobilized or impounded for thirty days. An insurance company does not have a duty to pay any benefits for charges or fees for immobilization or impoundment.

F. The owner of a vehicle that is removed and either immobilized or impounded pursuant to subsection A, B or C of this section, the spouse of the owner and each person identified on the department's record with an interest in the vehicle shall be provided with an opportunity for an immobilization or poststorage hearing pursuant to section 28–3514.

Sec. 11. Title 41, chapter 12, article 2, Arizona Revised Statutes, is amended by adding section 41–1724, to read:

41–1724. GANG AND IMMIGRATION INTELLIGENCE TEAM ENFORCEMENT MISSION FUND[11]

THE GANG AND IMMIGRATION INTELLIGENCE TEAM ENFORCEMENT MISSION FUND IS ESTABLISHED CONSISTING OF MONIES DEPOSITED PURSUANT TO SECTION 11–1051 AND MONIES APPROPRIATED BY THE LEGISLATURE. THE DEPARTMENT SHALL ADMINISTER THE FUND. MONIES IN THE FUND ARE SUBJECT TO LEGISLATIVE APPROPRIATION AND SHALL BE USED FOR GANG AND IMMIGRATION ENFORCEMENT AND FOR

11. This new § 41–1724 was added by SB 1070 and not affected by HB 2162. In this section, text in ALL CAPS was added by SB 1070.—eds.

COUNTY JAIL REIMBURSEMENT COSTS RELATING TO ILLEGAL IMMIGRATION.

Sec. 12. Severability, implementation and construction

A. If a provision of this act or its application to any person or circumstance is held invalid, the invalidity does not affect other provisions or applications of the act that can be given effect without the invalid provision or application, and to this end the provisions of this act are severable.

B. The terms of this act regarding immigration shall be construed to have the meanings given to them under federal immigration law.

C. This act shall be implemented in a manner consistent with federal laws regulating immigration, protecting the civil rights of all persons and respecting the privileges and immunities of United States citizens.

D. Nothing in this act shall implement or shall be construed or interpreted to implement or establish the REAL ID act of 2005 (P.L. 109–13, division B; 119 Stat. 302) including the use of a radio frequency identification chip.

Sec. 13. Short title

This act may be cited as the "Support Our Law Enforcement and Safe Neighborhoods Act".

Approved by the Governor April 23, 2010

CALIFORNIA LEGISLATURE
2013–14 REGULAR SESSION

CHAPTER 570

ASSEMBLY BILL 4

[Transparency and Responsibility Using State Tools (TRUST) Act]

AN ACT to add Chapter 17.1 (commencing with Section 7282) to Division 7 of Title 1 of the Government Code, relating to state government.

[Filed with Secretary of State October 5, 2013.]

LEGISLATIVE COUNSEL'S DIGEST

AB 4, Ammiano. State government: federal immigration policy enforcement.

Existing federal law authorizes any authorized immigration officer to issue an immigration detainer that serves to advise another law enforcement agency that the federal department seeks custody of an alien presently in the custody of that agency, for the purpose of arresting and removing the alien. Existing federal law provides that the detainer is a request that the agency advise the department, prior to release of the alien, in order for the department to arrange to assume custody in situations when gaining immediate physical custody is either impracticable or impossible.

This bill would prohibit a law enforcement official, as defined, from detaining an individual on the basis of a United States Immigration and Customs Enforcement hold after that individual becomes eligible for release from custody, unless, at the time that the individual becomes eligible for release from custody, certain conditions are met, including, among other things, that the individual has been convicted of specified crimes.

The people of the State of California do enact as follows:

Section 1. The Legislature finds and declares all of the following:

(a) The United States Immigration and Customs Enforcement's (ICE) Secure Communities program shifts the burden of federal civil immigration enforcement onto local law enforcement. To operate the Secure Communities program, ICE relies on voluntary requests, known as ICE holds or detainers, to local law enforcement to hold individuals in local jails for additional time beyond when they would be eligible for release in a criminal matter.

(b) State and local law enforcement agencies are not reimbursed by the federal government for the full cost of responding to a detainer, which can include, but is not limited to, extended detention time and the administrative costs of tracking and responding to detainers.

(c) Unlike criminal detainers, which are supported by a warrant and require probable cause, there is no requirement for a warrant and no established standard of proof, such as reasonable suspicion or probable cause, for issuing an ICE detainer request. Immigration detainers have erroneously been placed on United States citizens, as well as immigrants who are not deportable.

(d) The Secure Communities program and immigration detainers harm community policing efforts because immigrant residents who are victims of or witnesses to crime, including domestic violence, are less likely to report crime or cooperate with law enforcement when any contact with law enforcement could result in deportation. The program can result in a person being held and transferred into immigration detention without regard to whether the arrest is the result of a mistake, or merely a routine practice of questioning individuals involved in a dispute without pressing charges. Victims or witnesses to crimes may otherwise have recourse to lawful status (such as U-visas or T-visas) that detention resulting from the Secure Communities program obstructs.

(e) It is the intent of the Legislature that this act shall not be construed as providing, expanding, or ratifying the legal authority for any state or local law enforcement agency to detain an individual on an immigration hold.

Section 2. Chapter 17.1 (commencing with Section 7282) is added to Division 7 of Title 1 of the Government Code, to read:

Chapter 17.1. Standards for Responding to United States Immigration and Customs Enforcement Holds

7282. For purposes of this chapter, the following terms have the following meanings:

(a) "Conviction" shall have the same meaning as subdivision (d) of Section 667 of the Penal Code.

(b) "Eligible for release from custody" means that the individual may be released from custody because one of the following conditions has occurred:

(1) All criminal charges against the individual have been dropped or dismissed.

(2) The individual has been acquitted of all criminal charges filed against him or her.

(3) The individual has served all the time required for his or her sentence.

(4) The individual has posted a bond.

(5) The individual is otherwise eligible for release under state or local law, or local policy.

(c) "Immigration hold" means an immigration detainer issued by an authorized immigration officer, pursuant to Section 287.7 of Title 8 of the Code of Federal Regulations, that requests that the law enforcement official to maintain custody of the individual for a period not to exceed 48 hours, excluding Saturdays, Sundays, and holidays, and to advise the authorized immigration officer prior to the release of that individual.

(d) "Law enforcement official" means any local agency or officer of a local agency authorized to enforce criminal statutes, regulations, or local ordinances or to operate jails or to maintain custody of individuals in jails, and any person or local agency authorized to operate juvenile detention facilities or to maintain custody of individuals in juvenile detention facilities.

(e) "Local agency" means any city, county, city and county, special district, or other political subdivision of the state.

(f) "Serious felony" means any of the offenses listed in subdivision (c) of Section 1192.7 of the Penal Code and any offense committed in another state which, if committed in California, would be punishable as a serious felony as defined by subdivision (c) of Section 1192.7 of the Penal Code.

(g) "Violent felony" means any of the offenses listed in subdivision (c) of Section 667.5 of the Penal Code and any offense committed in another state which, if committed in California, would be punishable as a violent felony as defined by subdivision (c) of Section 667.5 of the Penal Code.

7282.5. (a) A law enforcement official shall have discretion to cooperate with federal immigration officials by detaining an individual on the basis of an immigration hold after that individual becomes eligible for release from custody only if the continued detention of the individual on the basis of the immigration hold would not violate any federal, state, or local law, or any local policy, and only under any of the following circumstances:

(1) The individual has been convicted of a serious or violent felony identified in subdivision (c) of Section 1192.7 of, or subdivision (c) of Section 667.5 of, the Penal Code.

(2) The individual has been convicted of a felony punishable by imprisonment in the state prison.

(3) The individual has been convicted within the past five years of a misdemeanor for a crime that is punishable as either a misdemeanor or a felony for, or has been convicted at any time of a felony for, any of the following offenses:

(A) Assault, as specified in, but not limited to, Sections 217.1, 220, 240, 241.1, 241.4, 241.7, 244, 244.5, 245, 245.2, 245.3, 245.5, 4500, and 4501 of the Penal Code.

(B) Battery, as specified in, but not limited to, Sections 242, 243.1, 243.3, 243.4, 243.6, 243.7, 243.9, 273.5, 347, 4501.1, and 4501.5 of the Penal Code.

(C) Use of threats, as specified in, but not limited to, Sections 71, 76, 139, 140, 422, 601, and 11418.5 of the Penal Code.

(D) Sexual abuse, sexual exploitation, or crimes endangering children, as specified in, but not limited to, Sections 266, 266a, 266b, 266c, 266d, 266f, 266g, 266h, 266i, 266j, 267, 269, 288, 288.5, 311.1, 311.3, 311.4, 311.10, 311.11, and 647.6 of the Penal Code.

(E) Child abuse or endangerment, as specified in, but not limited to, Sections 270, 271, 271a, 273a, 273ab, 273d, 273.4, and 278 of the Penal Code.

(F) Burglary, robbery, theft, fraud, forgery, or embezzlement, as specified in, but not limited to, Sections 211, 215, 459, 463, 470, 476, 487, 496, 503, 518, 530.5, 532, and 550 of the Penal Code.

(G) Driving under the influence of alcohol or drugs, but only for a conviction that is a felony.

(H) Obstruction of justice, as specified in, but not limited to, Sections 69, 95, 95.1, 136.1, and 148.10 of the Penal Code.

(I) Bribery, as specified in, but not limited to, Sections 67, 67.5, 68, 74, 85, 86, 92, 93, 137, 138, and 165 of the Penal Code.

(J) Escape, as specified in, but not limited to, Sections 107, 109, 110, 4530, 4530.5, 4532, 4533, 4534, 4535, and 4536 of the Penal Code.

(K) Unlawful possession or use of a weapon, firearm, explosive device, or weapon of mass destruction, as specified in, but not limited to, Sections 171b, 171c, 171d, 246, 246.3, 247, 417, 417.3, 417.6, 417.8, 4574, 11418, 11418.1, 12021.5, 12022, 12022.2, 12022.3, 12022.4, 12022.5, 12022.53, 12022.55, 18745, 18750, and 18755 of, and subdivisions (c) and (d) of Section 26100 of, the Penal Code.

(L) Possession of an unlawful deadly weapon, under the Deadly Weapons Recodification Act of 2010 (Part 6 (commencing with Section 16000) of the Penal Code).

(M) An offense involving the felony possession, sale, distribution, manufacture, or trafficking of controlled substances.

(N) Vandalism with prior convictions, as specified in, but not limited to, Section 594.7 of the Penal Code.

(O) Gang-related offenses, as specified in, but not limited to, Sections 186.22, 186.26, and 186.28 of the Penal Code.

(P) An attempt, as defined in Section 664 of, or a conspiracy, as defined in Section 182 of, the Penal Code, to commit an offense specified in this section.

(Q) A crime resulting in death, or involving the personal infliction of great bodily injury, as specified in, but not limited to, subdivision (d) of Section 245.6 of, and Sections 187, 191.5, 192, 192.5, 12022.7, 12022.8, and 12022.9 of, the Penal Code.

(R) Possession or use of a firearm in the commission of an offense.

(S) An offense that would require the individual to register as a sex offender pursuant to Section 290, 290.002, or 290.006 of the Penal Code.

(T) False imprisonment, slavery, and human trafficking, as specified in, but not limited to, Sections 181, 210.5, 236, 236.1, and 4503 of the Penal Code.

(U) Criminal profiteering and money laundering, as specified in, but not limited to, Sections 186.2, 186.9, and 186.10 of the Penal Code.

(V) Torture and mayhem, as specified in, but not limited to, Section 203 of the Penal Code.

(W) A crime threatening the public safety, as specified in, but not limited to, Sections 219, 219.1, 219.2, 247.5, 404, 404.6, 405a, 451, and 11413 of the Penal Code.

(X) Elder and dependent adult abuse, as specified in, but not limited to, Section 368 of the Penal Code.

(Y) A hate crime, as specified in, but not limited to, Section 422.55 of the Penal Code.

(Z) Stalking, as specified in, but not limited to, Section 646.9 of the Penal Code.

(AA) Soliciting the commission of a crime, as specified in, but not limited to, subdivision (c) of Section 286 of, and Sections 653j and 653.23 of, the Penal Code.

(AB) An offense committed while on bail or released on his or her own recognizance, as specified in, but not limited to, Section 12022.1 of the Penal Code.

(AC) Rape, sodomy, oral copulation, or sexual penetration, as specified in, but not limited to, paragraphs (2) and (6) of subdivision (a) of Section 261 of, paragraphs (1) and (4) of subdivision (a) of Section 262 of, Section 264.1 of, subdivisions (c) and (d) of Section 286 of, subdivisions (c) and (d) of Section 288a of, and subdivisions (a) and (j) of Section 289 of, the Penal Code.

(AD) Kidnapping, as specified in, but not limited to, Sections 207, 209, and 209.5 of the Penal Code.

(AE) A violation of subdivision (c) of Section 20001 of the Vehicle Code.

(4) The individual is a current registrant on the California Sex and Arson Registry.

(5) The individual is arrested and taken before a magistrate on a charge involving a serious or violent felony, as identified in subdivision (c) of Section 1192.7 or subdivision (c) of Section 667.5 of the Penal Code, a felony punishable by imprisonment in state prison, or any felony listed in paragraph (2) or (3) other than domestic violence, and the magistrate makes a finding of probable cause as to that charge pursuant to Section 872 of the Penal Code.

(6) The individual has been convicted of a federal crime that meets the definition of an aggravated felony as set forth in subparagraphs (A) to (P), inclusive, of paragraph (43) of subsection (a) of Section 101 of the federal Immigration and Nationality Act [8 U.S.C.A § 1101 et seq.], or is identified by the United States Department of Homeland Security's Immigration and Customs Enforcement as the subject of an outstanding federal felony arrest warrant.

(b) If none of the conditions listed in subdivision (a) is satisfied, an individual shall not be detained on the basis of an immigration hold after the individual becomes eligible for release from custody.

Section 3. The provisions of this act are severable. If any provision of this act or its application is held invalid, that invalidity shall not affect other provisions or applications that can be given effect without the invalid provision or application.

VI. TREATIES AND RELATED MATERIALS

CONVENTION RELATING TO THE STATUS OF REFUGEES

Done at Geneva, July 28, 1951

Entry into force, April 22, 1954

189 U.N.T.S. 137

PREAMBLE

THE HIGH CONTRACTING PARTIES

Considering that the Charter of the United Nations and the Universal Declaration of Human Rights approved on 10 December 1948 by the General Assembly have affirmed the principle that human beings shall enjoy fundamental rights and freedoms without discrimination,

Considering that the United Nations has, on various occasions, manifested its profound concern for refugees and endeavoured to assure refugees the widest possible exercise of these fundamental rights and freedoms,

Considering that it is desirable to revise and consolidate previous international agreements relating to the status of refugees and to extend the scope of and the protection accorded by such instruments by means of a new agreement,

Considering that the grant of asylum may place unduly heavy burdens on certain countries, and that a satisfactory solution of a problem of which the United Nations has recognized the international scope and nature cannot therefore be achieved without international co-operation,

Expressing the wish that all States, recognizing the social and humanitarian nature of the problem of refugees, will do everything within their power to prevent this problem from becoming a cause of tension between States,

Noting that the United Nations High Commissioner for Refugees is charged with the task of supervising international conventions providing for the protection of Refugees, and recognizing that the effective co-ordination of measures taken to deal with this problem will depend upon the co-operation of States with the High Commissioner,

Have agreed as follows:

CHAPTER I. GENERAL PROVISIONS

Article 1. Definition of the term "Refugee"

A. For the purposes of the present Convention, the term "refugee" shall apply to any person who:

(1) Has been considered a refugee under the Arrangements of 12 May 1926 and 30 June 1928 or under the Conventions of 28 October 1933 and 10 February 1938, the Protocol of 14 September 1939 or the Constitution of the International Refugee Organization;

Decisions of non-eligibility taken by the International Refugee Organization during the period of its activities shall not prevent the status of refugee being accorded to persons who fulfil the conditions of paragraph 2 of this section;

(2) As a result of events occurring before 1 January 1951 and owing to well-founded fear of being persecuted for reasons of race, religion, nationality, membership of a particular social group or political opinion, is outside the country of his nationality and is unable or, owing to such fear, is unwilling to avail himself of the protection of that country; or who, not having a nationality and being outside the country of his former habitual residence as a result of such events, is unable or, owing to such fear, is unwilling to return to it.

In the case of a person who has more than one nationality, the term "the country of his nationality" shall mean each of the countries of which he is a national, and a person shall not be deemed to be lacking the protection of the country of his nationality if, without any valid reason based on well-founded fear, he has not availed himself of the protection of one of the countries of which he is a national.

B. **(1)** For the purposes of this Convention, the words "events occurring before 1 January 1951" in Article 1, Section A, shall be understood to mean either:

(a) "events occurring in Europe before 1 January 1951" or

(b) "events occurring in Europe or elsewhere before 1 January 1951"

and each Contracting State shall make a declaration at the time of signature, ratification or accession, specifying which of these meanings it applies for the purpose of its obligations under this Convention.

(2) Any Contracting State which has adopted alternative *(a)* may at any time extend its obligations by adopting alternative *(b)* by means of a notification addressed to the Secretary–General of the United Nations.

C. This Convention shall cease to apply to any person falling under the terms of Section A if:

(1) He has voluntarily re-availed himself of the protection of the country of his nationality; or

(2) Having lost his nationality, he has voluntarily re-acquired it; or

(3) He has acquired a new nationality, and enjoys the protection of the country of his new nationality; or

(4) He has voluntarily re-established himself in the country which he left or outside which he remained owing to fear of persecution; or

(5) He can no longer, because the circumstances in connexion with which he has been recognized as a refugee have ceased to exist, continue to refuse to avail himself of the protection of the country of his nationality;

Provided that this paragraph shall not apply to a refugee falling under section A(1) of this Article who is able to invoke compelling reasons arising out of previous persecution for refusing to avail himself of the protection of the country of nationality;

(6) Being a person who has no nationality he is, because the circumstances in connexion with which he has been recognized as a refugee have ceased to exist, able to return to the country of his former habitual residence;

Provided that this paragraph shall not apply to a refugee falling under section A(1) of this Article who is able to invoke compelling reasons arising out of previous persecution for refusing to return to the country of his former habitual residence.

D. This Convention shall not apply to persons who are at present receiving from organs or agencies of the United Nations other than the United Nations High Commissioner for Refugees protection or assistance.

When such protection or assistance has ceased for any reason, without the position of such persons being definitively settled in accordance with the relevant resolutions adopted by the General Assembly of the United Nations, these persons shall *ipso facto* be entitled to the benefits of this Convention.

E. This Convention shall not apply to a person who is recognized by the competent authorities of the country in which he has taken residence as having the rights and obligations which are attached to the possession of the nationality of that country.

F. The provisions of this Convention shall not apply to any person with respect to whom there are serious reasons for considering that:

(a) he has committed a crime against peace, a war crime, or a crime against humanity, as defined in the international instruments drawn up to make provision in respect of such crimes;

(b) he has committed a serious non-political crime outside the country of refuge prior to his admission to that country as a refugee;

(c) he has been guilty of acts contrary to the purposes and principles of the United Nations.

Article 2. General obligations

Every refugee has duties to the country in which he finds himself, which require in particular that he conform to its laws and regulations as well as to measures taken for the maintenance of public order.

Article 3. Non-discrimination

The Contracting States shall apply the provisions of this Convention to refugees without discrimination as to race, religion or country of origin.

Article 4. Religion

The Contracting States shall accord to refugees within their territories treatment at least as favourable as that accorded to their nationals with respect to freedom to practise their religion and freedom as regards the religious education of their children.

Article 5. Rights granted apart from this Convention

Nothing in this Convention shall be deemed to impair any rights and benefits granted by a Contracting State to refugees apart from this Convention.

Article 6. The term "in the same circumstances"

For the purpose of this Convention, the term "in the same circumstances" implies that any requirements (including requirements as to length and conditions of sojourn or residence) which the particular individual would have to fulfil for the enjoyment of the right in question, if he were not a refugee, must be fulfilled by him, with the exception of requirements which by their nature a refugee is incapable of fulfilling.

Article 7. Exemption from reciprocity

1. Except where this Convention contains more favourable provisions, a Contracting State shall accord to refugees the same treatment as is accorded to aliens generally.

2. After a period of three years' residence, all refugees shall enjoy exemption from legislative reciprocity in the territory of the Contracting States.

3. Each Contracting State shall continue to accord to refugees the rights and benefits to which they were already entitled, in the absence of reciprocity, at the date of entry into force of this Convention for that State.

4. The Contracting States shall consider favourably the possibility of according to refugees, in the absence of reciprocity, rights and benefits beyond those to which they are entitled according to paragraphs 2 and 3, and to extending exemption from reciprocity to refugees who do not fulfil the conditions provided for in paragraphs 2 and 3.

5. The provisions of paragraphs 2 and 3 apply both to the rights and benefits referred to in articles 13, 18, 19, 21 and 22 of this Convention and to rights and benefits for which this Convention does not provide.

Article 8. Exemption from exceptional measures

With regard to exceptional measures which may be taken against the person, property or interests of nationals of a foreign State, the Contracting States shall not apply such measures to a refugee who is formally a national of the said State solely on account of such nationality. Contracting States which, under their legislation, are prevented from applying the general principle expressed in this article, shall, in appropriate cases, grant exemptions in favour of such refugees.

Article 9. Provisional measures

Nothing in this Convention shall prevent a Contracting State, in time of war or other grave and exceptional circumstances, from taking provisionally measures which it considers to be essential to the national security in the case of a particular person, pending a determination by the Contracting State that that person is in fact a refugee and that the continuance of such measures is necessary in his case in the interests of national security.

Article 10. Continuity of residence

1. Where a refugee has been forcibly displaced during the Second World War and removed to the territory of a Contracting State, and is resident there, the period of such enforced sojourn shall be considered to have been lawful residence within that territory.

2. Where a refugee has been forcibly displaced during the Second World War from the territory of a Contracting State and has, prior to the date of entry into force of this Convention, returned there for the purpose of taking up residence, the period of residence before and after such enforced displacement shall be regarded as one uninterrupted period for any purposes for which uninterrupted residence is required.

Article 11. Refugee seamen

In the case of refugees regularly serving as crew members on board a ship flying the flag of a Contracting State, that State shall give sympathetic consideration to their establishment on its territory and the issue of travel documents to them on their temporary admission to its territory particularly with a view to facilitating their establishment in another country.

CHAPTER II. JURIDICAL STATUS

Article 12. Personal status

1. The personal status of a refugee shall be governed by the law of the country of his domicile or, if he has no domicile, by the law of the country of his residence.

2. Rights previously acquired by a refugee and dependent on personal status, more particularly rights attaching to marriage, shall be respected by a Contracting State, subject to compliance, if this be necessary, with the formalities required by the law of that State, provided that the right in question is one which would have been recognized by the law of that State had he not become a refugee.

Article 13. Movable and immovable property

The Contracting States shall accord to a refugee treatment as favourable as possible and, in any event, not less favourable than that accorded to aliens generally in the same circumstances as regards the acquisition of movable and immovable property and other rights pertaining thereto, and to leases and other contracts relating to movable and immovable property.

Article 14. Artistic rights and industrial property

In respect of the protection of industrial property, such as inventions, designs or models, trade marks, trade names, and of rights in literary, artistic and scientific works, a refugee shall be accorded in the country in which he has his habitual residence the same protection as is accorded to nationals of that country. In the territory of any other Contracting State, he shall be accorded the same protection as is accorded in that territory to nationals of the country in which he has habitual residence.

Article 15. Right of association

As regards non-political and non-profit-making associations and trade unions the Contracting States shall accord to refugees lawfully staying in their territory the most favourable treatment accorded to nationals of a foreign country, in the same circumstances.

Article 16. Access to courts

1. A refugee shall have free access to the courts of law on the territory of all Contracting States.

2. A refugee shall enjoy in the Contracting State in which he has his habitual residence the same treatment as a national in matters pertaining to access to the Courts, including legal assistance and exemption from *cautio judicatum solvi.*

3. A refugee shall be accorded in the matters referred to in paragraph 2 in countries other than that in which he has his habitual residence the treatment granted to a national of the country of his habitual residence.

CHAPTER III. GAINFUL EMPLOYMENT

Article 17. Wage-earning employment

1. The Contracting State shall accord to refugees lawfully staying in their territory the most favourable treatment accorded to nationals of a foreign country in the same circumstances, as regards the right to engage in wage-earning employment.

2. In any case, restrictive measures imposed on aliens or the employment of aliens for the protection of the national labour market shall not be applied to a refugee who was already exempt from them at the date of entry into force of this Convention for the Contracting States concerned, or who fulfils one of the following conditions:

(a) He has completed three years' residence in the country;

(b) He has a spouse possessing the nationality of the country of residence. A refugee may not invoke the benefits of this provision if he has abandoned his spouse;

(c) He has one or more children possessing the nationality of the country of residence.

3. The Contracting States shall give sympathetic consideration to assimilating the rights of all refugees with regard to wage-earning employment to those of nationals, and in particular of those refugees who have entered their territory pursuant to programmes of labour recruitment or under immigration schemes.

Article 18. Self-employment

The Contracting States shall accord to a refugee lawfully in their territory treatment as favourable as possible and, in any event, not less favourable than that accorded to aliens generally in the same circumstances, as regards the right to engage on his own account in agriculture, industry, handicrafts and commerce and to establish commercial and industrial companies.

Article 19. Liberal professions

1. Each Contracting State shall accord to refugees lawfully staying in their territory who hold diplomas recognized by the competent authorities of that State, and who are desirous of practising a liberal profession, treatment as favourable as possible and, in any event, not less favourable than that accorded to aliens generally in the same circumstances.

2. The Contracting States shall use their best endeavours consistently with their laws and constitutions to secure the settlement of such refugees in the territories, other than the metropolitan territory, for whose international relations they are responsible.

CHAPTER IV. WELFARE

Article 20. Rationing

Where a rationing system exists, which applies to the population at large and regulates the general distribution of products in short supply, refugees shall be accorded the same treatment as nationals.

Article 21. Housing

As regards housing, the Contracting States, in so far as the matter is regulated by laws or regulations or is subject to the control of public authorities, shall accord to refugees lawfully staying in their territory treatment as favourable as possible and, in any event, not less favourable than that accorded to aliens generally in the same circumstances.

Article 22. Public education

1. The Contracting States shall accord to refugees the same treatment as is accorded to nationals with respect to elementary education.

2. The Contracting States shall accord to refugees treatment as favourable as possible, and, in any event, not less favourable than that accorded to aliens generally in the same circumstances, with respect to education other than elementary education and, in particular, as regards access to studies, the recognition of foreign school certificates, diplomas and degrees, the remission of fees and charges and the award of scholarships.

Article 23. Public relief

The Contracting States shall accord to refugees lawfully staying in their territory the same treatment with respect to public relief and assistance as is accorded to their nationals.

Article 24. Labour legislation and social security

1. The Contracting States shall accord to refugees lawfully staying in their territory the same treatment as is accorded to nationals in respect of the following matters:

(a) In so far as such matters are governed by laws or regulations or are subject to the control of administrative authorities: remuneration, including family allowances where these form part of remuneration, hours of work, overtime arrangements, holidays with pay, restrictions on home work, minimum age of employment, apprenticeship and training, women's work and the work of young persons, and the enjoyment of the benefits of collective bargaining;

(b) Social security (legal provisions in respect of employment injury, occupational diseases, maternity, sickness, disability, old age, death, unemployment, family responsibilities and any other contingency which, according to national laws or regulations, is covered by a social security scheme), subject to the following limitations:

(i) There may be appropriate arrangements for the maintenance of acquired rights and rights in course of acquisition;

(ii) National laws or regulations of the country of residence may prescribe special arrangements concerning benefits or portions of benefits which are payable wholly out of public funds, and concerning allowances paid to persons who do not fulfil the contribution conditions prescribed for the award of a normal pension.

2. The right to compensation for the death of a refugee resulting from employment injury or from occupational disease shall not be affected by the fact that the residence of the beneficiary is outside the territory of the Contracting State.

3. The Contracting States shall extend to refugees the benefits of agreements concluded between them, or which may be concluded between them in the future, concerning the maintenance of acquired rights and rights in the process of acquisition in regard to social security, subject only to the conditions which apply to nationals of the States signatory to the agreements in question.

4. The Contracting States will give sympathetic consideration to extending to refugees so far as possible the benefits of similar agreements which may at any time be in force between such Contracting States and non-contracting States.

CHAPTER V. ADMINISTRATIVE MEASURES

Article 25. Administrative assistance

1. When the exercise of a right by a refugee would normally require the assistance of authorities of a foreign country to whom he cannot have recourse, the Contracting States in whose territory he is residing shall arrange that such assistance be afforded to him by their own authorities or by an international authority.

2. The authority or authorities mentioned in paragraph 1 shall deliver or cause to be delivered under their supervision to refugees such documents or certifications as would normally be delivered to aliens by or through their national authorities.

3. Documents or certifications so delivered shall stand in the stead of the official instruments delivered to aliens by or through their national authorities, and shall be given credence in the absence of proof to the contrary.

4. Subject to such exceptional treatment as may be granted to indigent persons, fees may be charged for the services mentioned herein, but such fees shall be moderate and commensurate with those charged to nationals for similar services.

5. The provisions of this article shall be without prejudice to articles 27 and 28.

Article 26. Freedom of movement

Each Contracting State shall accord to refugees lawfully in its territory the right to choose their place of residence and to move freely within its territory, subject to any regulations applicable to aliens generally in the same circumstances.

Article 27. Identity papers

The Contracting States shall issue identity papers to any refugee in their territory who does not possess a valid travel document.

Article 28. Travel documents

1. The Contracting States shall issue to refugees lawfully staying in their territory travel documents for the purpose of travel outside their territory unless compelling reasons of national security or public order otherwise require, and the provisions of the Schedule to this Convention shall apply with respect to such documents. The Contracting States may issue such a travel document to any other refugee in their territory; they shall in particular give sympathetic consideration to the issue of such a travel document to refugees in their territory who are unable to obtain a travel document from the country of their lawful residence.

2. Travel documents issued to refugees under previous international agreements by parties thereto shall be recognized and treated by the Contracting States in the same way as if they had been issued pursuant to this article.

Article 29. Fiscal charges

1. The Contracting States shall not impose upon refugees duties, charges or taxes, of any description whatsoever, other or higher than those which are or may be levied on their nationals in similar situations.

2. Nothing in the above paragraph shall prevent the application to refugees of the laws and regulations concerning charges in respect of the issue to aliens of administrative documents including identity papers.

Article 30. Transfer of assets

1. A Contracting State shall, in conformity with its laws and regulations permit refugees to transfer assets which they have brought into its territory, to another country where they have been admitted for the purposes of resettlement.

2. A Contracting State shall give sympathetic consideration to the application of refugees for permission to transfer assets wherever they may be and which are necessary for their resettlement in another country to which they have been admitted.

Article 31. Refugees unlawfully in the country of refuge

1. The Contracting States shall not impose penalties, on account of their illegal entry or presence, on refugees who, coming directly from a territory where their life or freedom was threatened in the sense of Article 1, enter or are present in their territory without authorization, provided they present themselves without delay to the authorities and show good cause for their illegal entry or presence.

2. The Contracting States shall not apply to the movements of such refugees restrictions other than those which are necessary and such restrictions shall only be applied until their status in the country is regularized or they obtain admission into another country. The Contracting States shall allow such refugees a reasonable period and all the necessary facilities to obtain admission into another country.

Article 32. Expulsion

1. The Contracting States shall not expel a refugee lawfully in their territory save on grounds of national security or public order.

2. The expulsion of such a refugee shall be only in pursuance of a decision reached in accordance with due process of law. Except where compelling reasons of national security otherwise require, the refugee shall be allowed to submit evidence to clear himself, and to appeal to and be represented for the purpose before competent authority or a person or persons specially designated by the competent authority.

3. The Contracting States shall allow such a refugee a reasonable period within which to seek legal admission into another country. The Contracting States reserve the right to apply during that period such internal measures as they may deem necessary.

Article 33. Prohibition of expulsion or return ("refoulement")

1. No Contracting State shall expel or return ("*refouler*") a refugee in any manner whatsoever to the frontiers of territories where his life or freedom would be threatened on account of his race, religion, nationality, membership of a particular social group or political opinion.

2. The benefit of the present provision may not, however, be claimed by a refugee whom there are reasonable grounds for regarding as a danger to the security of the country in which he is, or who, having been convicted by a final judgement of a particularly serious crime, constitutes a danger to the community of that country.

Article 34. Naturalization

The Contracting States shall as far as possible facilitate the assimilation and naturalization of refugees. They shall in particular make every effort to expedite naturalization proceedings and to reduce as far as possible the charges and costs of such proceedings.

CHAPTER VI. EXECUTORY AND TRANSITORY PROVISIONS

Article 35. Co-operation of the national authorities with the United Nations

1. The Contracting States undertake to co-operate with the Office of the United Nations High Commissioner for Refugees, or any other agency of the United Nations which may succeed it, in the exercise of its functions, and shall in particular facilitate its duty of supervising the application of the provisions of this Convention.

2. In order to enable the Office of the High Commissioner or any other agency of the United Nations which may succeed it, to make reports to the competent organs of the United Nations, the Contracting States undertake to provide them in the appropriate form with information and and statistical data requested concerning:

(a) the condition of refugees,

(b) the implementation of this Convention, and

(c) laws, regulations and decrees which are, or may hereafter be, in force relating to refugees.

Article 36. Information on national legislation

The Contracting States shall communicate to the Secretary–General of the United Nations the laws and regulations which they may adopt to ensure the application of this Convention.

Article 37. Relation to previous conventions

Without prejudice to article 28, paragraph 2, of this Convention, this Convention replaces, as between parties to it, the Arrangements of 5 July 1922, 31 May 1924, 12 May 1926, 30 June 1928 and 30 July 1935, the Conventions of 28 October 1933 and 10 February 1938, the Protocol of 14 September 1939 and the Agreement of 15 October 1946.

CHAPTER VII. FINAL CLAUSES

Article 38. Settlement of disputes

Any dispute between parties to this Convention relating to its interpretation or application, which cannot be settled by other means, shall be referred to the International Court of Justice at the request of any one of the parties to the dispute.

Article 39. Signature, ratification and accession

1. This Convention shall be opened for signature at Geneva on 28 July 1951 and shall thereafter be deposited with the Secretary–General of the United Nations. It shall be open for signature at the European Office of the United Nations from 28 July to 31 August 1951 and shall be reopened for signature at the Headquarters of the United Nations from 17 September 1951 to 31 December 1952.

2. This Convention shall be open for signature on behalf of all States Members of the United Nations, and also on behalf of any other State invited to attend the Conference of Plenipotentiaries on the Status of Refugees and Stateless Persons or to which an invitation to sign will have been addressed by the General Assembly. It shall be ratified and the instruments of ratification shall be deposited with the Secretary–General of the United Nations.

3. This Convention shall be open from 28 July 1951 for accession by the States referred to in paragraph 2 of this Article. Accession shall be effected by the deposit of an instrument of accession with the Secretary–General of the United Nations.

Article 40. Territorial application clause

1. Any State may, at the time of signature, ratification or accession, declare that this Convention shall extend to all or any of the territories for the international relations of which it is responsible. Such a declaration shall take effect when the Convention enters into force for the States concerned.

2. At any time thereafter any such extension shall be made by notification addressed to the Secretary–General of the United Nations and shall take effect as from the ninetieth day after the day of receipt by the Secretary–General of the United Nations of this notification, or as from the date of entry into force of the Convention for the State concerned, whichever is the later.

3. With respect to those territories to which this Convention is not extended at the time of signature, ratification or accession, each State concerned shall consider the possibility of taking the necessary steps in order to extend the application of this Convention to such territories, subject where necessary for constitutional reasons, to the consent of the governments of such territories.

Article 41. Federal clause

In the case of a Federal or non-unitary State, the following provisions shall apply:

(a) With respect to those articles of this Convention that come within the legislative jurisdiction of the federal legislative authority, the obligations of the Federal Government shall to this extent be the same as those of Parties which are not Federal States,

(b) With respect to those articles of this Convention that come within the legislative jurisdiction of constituent States, provinces or cantons which are not, under the constitutional system of the federation, bound to take legislative action, the Federal Government shall bring such articles with a favourable recommendation, to the notice of the appropriate authorities of States, provinces or cantons at the earliest possible moment.

(c) A Federal State Party to this Convention shall, at the request of any other Contracting State transmitted through the Secretary–General of the United Nations, supply a statement of the law and practice of the Federation and its constituent units in regard to any particular provision of the Convention showing the extent to which effect has been given to that provision by legislative or other action.

Article 42. Reservations

1. At the time of signature, ratification or accession, any State may make reservations to articles of the Convention other than to articles 1, 3, 4, 16(1), 33, 36 to 46 inclusive.

2. Any State making a reservation in accordance with paragraph 1 of this article may at any time withdraw the reservation by a communication to that effect addressed to the Secretary–General of the United Nations.

Article 43. Entry into force

1. This Convention shall come into force on the ninetieth day following the day of deposit of the sixth instrument of ratification or accession.

2. For each State ratifying or acceding to the Convention after the deposit of the sixth instrument of ratification or accession, the Convention shall enter into force on the ninetieth day following the day of deposit by such State of its instrument of ratification or accession.

Article 44. Denunciation

1. Any Contracting State may denounce this Convention at any time by a notification addressed to the Secretary–General of the United Nations.

2. Such denunciation shall take effect for the Contracting State concerned one year from the date upon which it is received by the Secretary–General of the United Nations.

3. Any State which has made a declaration or notification under article 40 may, at any time thereafter, by a notification to the Secretary–General of the United Nations, declare that the Convention shall cease to extend to such territory one year after the date of receipt of the notification by the Secretary–General.

Article 45. Revision

1. Any Contracting State may request revision of this Convention at any time by a notification addressed to the Secretary–General of the United Nations.

2. The General Assembly of the United Nations shall recommend the steps, if any, to be taken in respect of such request.

Article 46. Notifications by the Secretary–General of the United Nations

The Secretary–General of the United Nations shall inform all Members of the United Nations and non-member States referred to in article 39:

(a) of declarations and notifications in accordance with Section B of Article 1;

(b) of signatures, ratifications and accessions in accordance with article 39;

(c) of declarations and notifications in accordance with article 40;

(d) of reservations and withdrawals in accordance with article 42;

(e) of the date on which this Convention will come into force in accordance with article 43;

(f) of denunciations and notifications in accordance with article 44;

(g) of requests for revision in accordance with article 45.

In faith whereof the undersigned, duly authorized, have signed this Convention on behalf of their respective Governments,

Done at Geneva, this twenty-eighth day of July, one thousand nine hundred and fifty-one, in a single copy, of which the English and French texts are equally authentic and which shall remain deposited in the archives of the United Nations, and certified true copies of which shall be delivered to all Members of the United Nations and to the non-member States referred to in article 39.

Schedule

Paragraph 1

1. The travel document referred to in Article 28 of this Convention shall be similar to the specimen annexed hereto.

2. The document shall be made out in at least two languages, one of which shall be English or French.

Paragraph 2

Subject to the regulations obtaining in the country of issue, children may be included in the travel document of a parent or, in exceptional circumstances, of another adult refugee.

Paragraph 3

The fees charged for issue of the document shall not exceed the lowest scale of charges for national passports.

Paragraph 4

Save in special or exceptional cases, the document shall be made valid for the largest possible number of countries.

Paragraph 5

The document shall have a validity of either one or two years, at the discretion of the issuing authority.

Paragraph 6

1. The renewal or extension of the validity of the document is a matter for the authority which issued it, so long as the holder has not established lawful residence in another territory and resides lawfully in the territory of the said authority. The issue of a new document is, under the same conditions, a matter for the authority which issued the former document.

2. Diplomatic or consular authorities, specially authorized for the purpose, shall be empowered to extend, for a period not exceeding six months, the validity of travel documents issued by their Governments.

3. The Contracting States shall give sympathetic consideration to renewing or extending the validity of travel documents or issuing new documents to refugees no longer lawfully resident in their territory who are unable to obtain a travel document from the country of their lawful residence.

Paragraph 7

The Contracting States shall recognize the validity of the documents issued in accordance with the provisions of Article 28 of this Convention.

Paragraph 8

The competent authorities of the country to which the refugee desires to proceed shall, if they are prepared to admit him and if a visa is required, affix a visa on the document of which he is the holder.

Paragraph 9

1. The Contracting States undertake to issue transit visas to refugees who have obtained visas for a territory of Final destination.

2. The issue of such visas may be refused on grounds which would justify refusal of a visa to any alien.

Paragraph 10

The fees for the issue of exit, entry or transit visas shall not exceed the lowest scale of charges for visas on foreign passports.

Paragraph 11

When a refugee has lawfully taken up residence in the territory of another Contracting State, the responsibility for the issue of a new document, under the terms and conditions of Article 28, shall be that of the competent authority of that territory, to which the refugee shall be entitled to apply.

Paragraph 12

The authority issuing a new document shall withdraw the old document and shall return it to the country of issue, if it is stated in the document that it should be so returned; otherwise it shall withdraw and cancel the document.

Paragraph 13

1. Each Contracting State undertakes that the holder of a travel document issued by it in accordance with Article 28 of this Convention shall be re-admitted to its territory at any time during the period of its validity,

2. Subject to the provisions of the preceding sub-paragraph, a Contracting State may require the holder of the document to comply with such formalities as may be prescribed in regard to exit from or return to its territory.

3. The Contracting States reserve the right, in exceptional cases, or in cases where the refugee's stay is authorized for a specific period, when issuing the document, to limit the period during which the refugee may return to a period of not less than three months.

Paragraph 14

Subject only to the terms of paragraph 13, the provisions of this Schedule in no way affect the laws and regulations governing the conditions of admission to, transit through, residence and establishment in, and departure from, the territories of the Contracting States.

Paragraph 15

Neither the issue of the document nor the entries made thereon determine or affect the status of the holder, particularly as regards nationality.

Paragraph 16

The issue of the document does not in any way entitle the holder to the protection of the diplomatic or consular authorities of the country of issue, and does not confer on these authorities a right of protection.

ANNEX

Specimen Travel Document

The document will be in booklet form (approximately 15 x 10 centimetres).

It is recommended that it be so printed that any erasure or alteration by chemical or other means can be readily detected, and that the words "Convention of 28 July 1951" be printed in continuous repetition on each page, in the language of the issuing country.

(Cover of booklet)

TRAVEL DOCUMENT

(Convention of 28 July 1951)

No. ________

(1)

TRAVEL DOCUMENT

(Convention of 28 July 1951)

This document expires on ....
unless its validity is extended or renewed.

Name ....

Forename(s) ....

Accompanied by ....child (children)

1. This document is issued solely with a view to providing the holder with a travel document which can serve in lieu of a national passport. It is without prejudice to and in no way affects the holder's nationality.

2. The holder is authorized to return to ....
....[state here the country whose authorities are issuing the document] on or before ....unless some later date is hereafter specified.
[The period during which the holder is allowed to return must not be less than three months]

3. Should the holder take up residence in a country other than that which issued the present document, he must, if he wishes to travel again, apply to the competent authorities of his country of residence for a new document. [The old travel document shall be withdrawn by the authority issuing the new document and returned to the authority which issued it.][1]

(This document contains .... pages, exclusive of cover.)

[1]The sentence in brackets to be inserted by Governments which so desire.

---

(2)

Place and date of birth ....
Occupation ....
Present residence..
*Maiden name and forename(s) of wife ....
....
*Name and forename(s) of husband..
....

Description

Height____________________
Hair____________________
Colour of eyes____________________
Nose ____________________
Shape of face ____________________
Complexion ____________________
Special peculiarities ____________________

Children accompanying holder

Name	Forename(s)	Place and date of birth	Sex
________	________	________	________
________	________	________	________
________	________	________	________
________	________	________	________

*Strike out whichever does not apply.

(This document contains _____ pages, exclusive of cover.)

---

(3)

Photograph of holder and stamp of issuing authority
Finger-prints of holder (if required)

Signature of holder ____________________

(This document contains _____ pages, exclusive of cover.)

---

(4)

1. This document is valid for the following countries:

____
____
____
____

2. Document or documents on the basis of which the present document is issued:

____
____
____

Issued at ____________________
Date ____________________

Signature and stamp of authority issuing the document:

Fee paid: ____________________

(This document contains _____ pages, exclusive of cover.)

(5)

Extension or renewal of validity

Fee paid: From ______________________
To ______________________
Done at ______________________ Date ______________________

Signature and stamp of authority extending or renewing the validity of the document:

____

Extension or renewal of validity

Fee paid: From ______________________
To ______________________
Done at ______________________ Date ______________________

Signature and stamp of authority extending or renewing the validity of the document:

(This document contains _____ pages, exclusive of cover.)

---

(6)

Extension or renewal of validity

Fee paid: From ______________________
To ______________________
Done at ______________________ Date ______________________

Signature and stamp of authority extending or renewing the validity of the document:

____

Extension or renewal of validity

Fee paid: From ______________________
To ______________________
Done at ______________________ Date ______________________

Signature and stamp of authority extending or renewing the validity of the document:

(This document contains _____ pages, exclusive of cover.)

(7-32)

Visas

The name of the holder of the document must be repeated in each visa.
(This document contains _____ pages, exclusive of cover.

PROTOCOL RELATING TO THE STATUS OF REFUGEES

Done January 31, 1967

Entry into force, October 4, 1967

606 U.N.T.S. 267, 19 U.S.T. 6223, T.I.A.S. No. 6577

The States Parties to the present Protocol,

Considering that the Convention relating to the Status of Refugees done at Geneva on 28 July 1951 (hereinafter referred to as the Convention) covers only those persons who have become refugees as a result of events occurring before 1 January 1951,

Considering that new refugee situations have arisen since the Convention was adopted and that the refugees concerned may therefore not fall within the scope of the Convention,

Considering that it is desirable that equal status should be enjoyed by all refugees covered by the definition in the Convention irrespective of the dateline 1 January 1951,

Have agreed as follows:

Article I. General provision

1. The States Parties to the present Protocol undertake to apply articles 2 to 34 inclusive of the Convention to refugees as hereinafter defined.

2. For the purpose of the present Protocol, the term "refugee" shall, except as regards the application of paragraph 3 of this article, mean any person within the definition of article 1 of the Convention as if the words "As a result of events occurring before 1 January 1951 and . . ." and the words ". . . as a result of such events", in article 1A(2) were omitted.

3. The present Protocol shall be applied by the States Parties hereto without any geographic limitation, save that existing declarations made by States already Parties to the Convention in accordance with article 1B(1)*(a)* of the Convention, shall, unless extended under article 1B(2) thereof, apply also under the present Protocol.

Article II. Co-operation of the national authorities with the United Nations

1. The States Parties to the present Protocol undertake to co-operate with the Office of the United Nations High Commissioner for Refugees, or any other agency of the United Nations which may succeed it, in the exercise of its functions, and shall in particular facilitate its duty of supervising the application of the provisions of the present Protocol.

2. In order to enable the Office of the High Commissioner, or any other agency of the United Nations which may succeed it, to make reports to the competent organs of the United Nations, the States Parties to the present Protocol undertake to provide them with the information and statistical data requested, in the appropriate form, concerning:

(a) The condition of refugees;

(b) The implementation of the present Protocol;

(c) Laws, regulations and decrees which are, or may hereafter be, in force relating to refugees.

Article III. Information on national legislation

The States Parties to the present Protocol shall communicate to the Secretary–General of the United Nations the laws and regulations which they may adopt to ensure the application of the present Protocol.

Article IV. Settlement of disputes

Any dispute between States Parties to the present Protocol which relates to its interpretation or application and which cannot be settled by other means shall be referred to the International Court of Justice at the request of any one of the parties to the dispute.

Article V. Accession

The present Protocol shall be open for accession on behalf of all States Parties to the Convention and of any other State Member of the United Nations or member of any of the specialized agencies or to which an invitation to accede may have been addressed by the General Assembly of the United Nations. Accession shall be effected by the deposit of an instrument of accession with the Secretary–General of the United Nations.

Article VI. Federal clause

In the case of a Federal or non-unitary State, the following provisions shall apply:

(a) With respect to those articles of the Convention to be applied in accordance with article I, paragraph 1, of the present Protocol that come within the legislative jurisdiction of the federal legislative authority, the obligations of the Federal Government shall to this extent be the same as those of States Parties which are not Federal States;

(b) With respect to those articles of the Convention to be applied in accordance with article I, paragraph 1, of the present Protocol that come within the legislative jurisdiction of constituent States, provinces or cantons which are not, under the constitutional system of the federation, bound to take legislative action, the Federal Government shall bring such articles with a favourable recommendation to

the notice of the appropriate authorities of States, provinces or cantons at the earliest possible moment;

(c) A Federal State Party to the present Protocol shall, at the request of any other State Party hereto transmitted through the Secretary–General of the United Nations, supply a statement of the law and practice of the Federation and its constituent units in regard to any particular provision of the Convention to be applied in accordance with article I, paragraph 1, of the present Protocol, showing the extent to which effect has been given to that provision by legislative or other action.

Article VII. Reservations and Declarations

1. At the time of accession, any State may make reservations in respect of article IV of the present Protocol and in respect of the application in accordance with article I of the present Protocol of any provisions of the Convention other than those contained in articles 1, 3, 4, 16(1) and 33 thereof, provided that in the case of a State Party to the Convention reservations made under this article shall not extend to refugees in respect of whom the Convention applies.

2. Reservations made by States Parties to the Convention in accordance with article 42 thereof shall, unless withdrawn, be applicable in relation to their obligations under the present Protocol.

3. Any State making a reservation in accordance with paragraph 1 of this article may at any time withdraw such reservation by a communication to that effect addressed to the Secretary–General of the United Nations.

4. Declarations made under article 40, paragraphs 1 and 2, of the Convention by a State Party thereto which accedes to the present Protocol shall be deemed to apply in respect of the present Protocol, unless upon accession a notification to the contrary is addressed by the State Party concerned to the Secretary–General of the United Nations. The provisions of article 40, paragraphs 2 and 3, and of article 44, paragraph 3, of the Convention shall be deemed to apply *mutatis mutandis* to the present Protocol.

Article VIII. Entry into force

1. The present Protocol shall come into force on the day of deposit of the sixth instrument of accession.

2. For each State acceding to the Protocol after the deposit of the sixth instrument of accession, the Protocol shall come into force on the date of deposit by such State of its instrument of accession.

Article IX. Denunciation

1. Any State Party hereto may denounce this Protocol at any time by a notification addressed to the Secretary–General of the United Nations.

2. Such denunciation shall take effect for the State Party concerned one year from the date on which it is received by the Secretary–General of the United Nations.

Article X. Notifications by the Secretary–General of the United Nations

The Secretary–General of the United Nations shall inform the States referred to in article V above of the date of entry into force, accessions, reservations and withdrawals of reservations to and denunciations of the present Protocol, and of declarations and notifications relating hereto.

Article XI. Deposit in the Archives of the Secretariat of the United Nations

A copy of the present Protocol, of which the Chinese, English, French, Russian and Spanish texts are equally authentic, signed by the President of the General Assembly and by the Secretary–General of the United Nations, shall be deposited in the archives of the Secretariat of the United Nations. The Secretary–General will transmit certified copies thereof to all States Members of the United Nations and to the other States referred to in article V above.

CONVENTION AGAINST TORTURE AND OTHER CRUEL, INHUMAN, OR DEGRADING TREATMENT OR PUNISHMENT

Done Dec. 10, 1984

Entered into force, June 26, 1987

1468 U.N.T.S. 85

The States Parties to this Convention,

Considering that, in accordance with the principles proclaimed in the Charter of the United Nations, recognition of the equal and inalienable rights of all members of the human family is the foundation of freedom, justice and peace in the world,

Recognizing that those rights derive from the inherent dignity of the human person,

Considering the obligation of States under the Charter, in particular Article 55, to promote universal respect for, and observance of, human rights and fundamental freedoms,

Having regard to article 5 of the Universal Declaration of Human Rights and article 7 of the International Covenant on Civil and Political Rights, both of which provide that no one may be subjected to torture or to cruel, inhuman or degrading treatment or punishment,

Having regard also to the Declaration on the Protection of All Persons from Being Subjected to Torture and Other Cruel, Inhuman or Degrading Treatment or Punishment, adopted by the General Assembly on 9 December 1975 (resolution 3452 (XXX)),

Desiring to make more effective the struggle against torture and other cruel, inhuman or degrading treatment or punishment throughout the world,

Have agreed as follows:

Part I

Article 1

1. For the purposes of this Convention, torture means any act by which severe pain or suffering, whether physical or mental, is intentionally inflicted on a person for such purposes as obtaining from him or a third person information or a confession, punishing him for an act he or a third person has committed or is suspected of having committed, or intimidating or coercing him or a third person, or for any reason based on discrimination of any kind, when such pain or suffering is inflicted by or at the instigation of or with the consent or acquiescence of a public official or other person acting in an official capacity. It does not include pain or suffering arising only from, inherent in or incidental to lawful sanctions.

2. This article is without prejudice to any international instrument or national legislation which does or may contain provisions of wider application.

Article 2

1. Each State Party shall take effective legislative, administrative, judicial or other measures to prevent acts of torture in any territory under its jurisdiction.

2. No exceptional circumstances whatsoever, whether a state of war or a threat or war, internal political instability or any other public emergency, may be invoked as a justification of torture.

3. An order from a superior officer or a public authority may not be invoked as a justification of torture.

Article 3

1. No State Party shall expel, return ("refouler") or extradite a person to another State where there are substantial grounds for believing that he would be in danger of being subjected to torture.

2. For the purpose of determining whether there are such grounds, the competent authorities shall take into account all relevant considerations including, where applicable, the existence in the State concerned of a consistent pattern of gross, flagrant or mass violations of human rights.

Article 4

1. Each State Party shall ensure that all acts of torture are offences under its criminal law. The same shall apply to an attempt to commit torture and to an act by any person which constitutes complicity or participation in torture.

2. Each State Party shall make these offences punishable by appropriate penalties which take into account their grave nature.

Article 5

1. Each State Party shall take such measures as may be necessary to establish its jurisdiction over the offences referred to in article 4 in the following cases:

(a) When the offences are committed in any territory under its jurisdiction or on board a ship or aircraft registered in that State;

(b) When the alleged offender is a national of that State;

(c) When the victim is a national of that State if that State considers it appropriate.

2. Each State Party shall likewise take such measures as may be necessary to establish its jurisdiction over such offences in cases where the alleged offender is present in any territory under its jurisdiction and it does not extradite him pursuant to article 8 to any of the States mentioned in paragraph I of this article.

3. This Convention does not exclude any criminal jurisdiction exercised in accordance with internal law.

Article 6

1. Upon being satisfied, after an examination of information available to it, that the circumstances so warrant, any State Party in whose territory a person alleged to have committed any offence referred to in article 4 is present shall take him into custody or take other legal measures to ensure his presence. The custody and other legal measures shall be as provided in the law of that State but may be continued only for such time as is necessary to enable any criminal or extradition proceedings to be instituted.

2. Such State shall immediately make a preliminary inquiry into the facts.

3. Any person in custody pursuant to paragraph I of this article shall be assisted in communicating immediately with the nearest appropriate representative of the State of which he is a national, or, if he is a stateless person, with the representative of the State where he usually resides.

4. When a State, pursuant to this article, has taken a person into custody, it shall immediately notify the States referred to in article 5, paragraph 1, of the fact that such person is in custody and of the circumstances which warrant his detention. The State which makes the preliminary inquiry contemplated in paragraph 2 of this article shall promptly report its findings to the said States and shall indicate whether it intends to exercise jurisdiction.

Article 7

1. The State Party in the territory under whose jurisdiction a person alleged to have committed any offence referred to in article 4 is found shall in the cases contemplated in article 5, if it does not extradite him, submit the case to its competent authorities for the purpose of prosecution.

2. These authorities shall take their decision in the same manner as in the case of any ordinary offence of a serious nature under the law of that State. In the cases referred to in article 5, paragraph 2, the standards of evidence required for prosecution and conviction shall in no way be less stringent than those which apply in the cases referred to in article 5, paragraph 1.

3. Any person regarding whom proceedings are brought in connection with any of the offences referred to in article 4 shall be guaranteed fair treatment at all stages of the proceedings.

Article 8

1. The offences referred to in article 4 shall be deemed to be included as extraditable offences in any extradition treaty existing between States Parties. States Parties undertake to include such offences as extraditable offences in every extradition treaty to be concluded between them.

2. If a State Party which makes extradition conditional on the existence of a treaty receives a request for extradition from another State Party with which it has no extradition treaty, it may consider this Convention as the legal basis for extradition in respect of such offences. Extradition shall be subject to the other conditions provided by the law of the requested State.

3. States Parties which do not make extradition conditional on the existence of a treaty shall recognize such offences as extraditable offences between themselves subject to the conditions provided by the law of the requested State.

4. Such offences shall be treated, for the purpose of extradition between States Parties, as if they had been committed not only in the place in which they occurred but also in the territories of the States required to establish their jurisdiction in accordance with article 5, paragraph 1.

Article 9

1. States Parties shall afford one another the greatest measure of assistance in connection with criminal proceedings brought in respect of any of the offences referred to in article 4, including the supply of all evidence at their disposal necessary for the proceedings.

2. States Parties shall carry out their obligations under paragraph I of this article in conformity with any treaties on mutual judicial assistance that may exist between them.

Article 10

1. Each State Party shall ensure that education and information regarding the prohibition against torture are fully included in the training of law enforcement personnel, civil or military, medical personnel, public officials and other persons who may be involved in the custody, interrogation or treatment of any individual subjected to any form of arrest, detention or imprisonment.

2. Each State Party shall include this prohibition in the rules or instructions issued in regard to the duties and functions of any such person.

Article 11

Each State Party shall keep under systematic review interrogation rules, instructions, methods and practices as well as arrangements for the custody and treatment of persons subjected to any form of arrest, detention or imprisonment in any territory under its jurisdiction, with a view to preventing any cases of torture.

Article 12

Each State Party shall ensure that its competent authorities proceed to a prompt and impartial investigation, wherever there is reasonable ground to believe that an act of torture has been committed in any territory under its jurisdiction.

Article 13

Each State Party shall ensure that any individual who alleges he has been subjected to torture in any territory under its jurisdiction has the right to complain to, and to have his case promptly and impartially examined by, its competent authorities. Steps shall be taken to ensure that the complainant and witnesses are protected against all ill–treatment or intimidation as a consequence of his complaint or any evidence given.

Article 14

1. Each State Party shall ensure in its legal system that the victim of an act of torture obtains redress and has an enforceable right to fair and adequate compensation, including the means for as full rehabilitation as possible. In the event of the death of the victim as a result of an act of torture, his dependants shall be entitled to compensation.

2. Nothing in this article shall affect any right of the victim or other persons to compensation which may exist under national law.

Article 15

Each State Party shall ensure that any statement which is established to have been made as a result of torture shall not be invoked as evidence in any proceedings, except against a person accused of torture as evidence that the statement was made.

Article 16

1. Each State Party shall undertake to prevent in any territory under its jurisdiction other acts of cruel, inhuman or degrading treatment or punishment which do not amount to torture as defined in article I, when such acts are committed by or at the instigation of or with the consent or acquiescence of a public official or other person acting in an official capacity. In particular, the obligations contained in articles 10, 11, 12 and 13 shall apply with the substitution for references to torture of references to other forms of cruel, inhuman or degrading treatment or punishment.

2. The provisions of this Convention are without prejudice to the provisions of any other international instrument or national law which prohibits cruel, inhuman or degrading treatment or punishment or which relates to extradition or expulsion.

* * *

CONVENTION AGAINST TORTURE— U.S. RESOLUTION OF ADVICE AND CONSENT (WITH RESERVATIONS, UNDERSTANDINGS AND DECLARATIONS)

136 Cong. Rec. 36198–99 (1990).

Resolved (two–thirds of the Senators present concurring therein), That the Senate advise and consent to the ratification of the Convention Against Torture and Other Cruel, Inhuman or Degrading Treatment or Punishment, adopted by unanimous agreement of the United Nations General Assembly on December 10, 1984, and signed by the United States on April 18, 1988: Provided, That:

I. The Senate's advice and consent is subject to the following reservations:

(1) That the United States considers itself bound by the obligation under Article 16 to prevent "cruel, inhuman or degrading treatment or punishment," only insofar as the term "cruel, inhuman or degrading treatment or punishment" means the cruel, unusual and inhumane treatment or punishment prohibited by the Fifth, Eighth, and/or Fourteenth Amendments to the Constitution of the United States.

(2) That pursuant to Article 30(2) the United States declares that it does not consider itself bound by Article 30(1), but reserves the right specifically to agree to follow this or any other procedure for arbitration in a particular case.

II. The Senate's advice and consent is subject to the following understandings, which shall apply to the obligations of the United States under this Convention:

(1)(a) That with reference to Article 1, the United States understands that, in order to constitute torture, an act must be specifically intended to inflict severe physical or mental pain or suffering and that mental pain or suffering refers to prolonged mental harm caused by or resulting from: **(1)** the intentional infliction or threatened infliction of severe physical pain or suffering; **(2)** the administration or application, or threatened administration or application, of mind altering substances or other procedures calculated to disrupt profoundly the senses or the personality; **(3)** the threat of imminent death; or (4) the threat that another person will imminently be subjected to death, severe physical pain or suffering, or the administration or application of mind altering substances or other procedures calculated to disrupt profoundly the senses or personality.

(b) That the United States understands that the definition of torture in Article 1 is intended to apply only to acts directed against persons in the offender's custody or physical control.

(c) That with reference to Article 1 of the Convention, the United States understands that "sanctions" includes judicially imposed sanctions and other enforcement actions authorized by United States law or by judicial interpretation of such law. Nonetheless, the United States understands that a State Party could not through its domestic sanctions defeat the object and purpose of the Convention to prohibit torture.

(d) That with reference to Article 1 of the Convention, the United States understands that the term "acquiescence" requires that the public official, prior to the activity constituting torture, have awareness of such activity and thereafter breach his legal responsibility to intervene to prevent such activity.

(e) That with reference to Article 1 of the Convention, the United States understands that noncompliance with applicable legal procedural standards does not per se constitute torture.

(2) That the United States understands the phrase, "where there are substantial grounds for believing that he would be in danger of being subjected to torture," as used in Article 3 of the Convention, to mean "if it is more likely than not that he would be tortured."

(3) That it is the understanding of the United States that Article 14 requires a State Party to provide a private right of action for damages only for acts of torture committed in territory under the jurisdiction of that State Party.

(4) That the United States understands that international law does not prohibit the death penalty, and does not consider this Convention to restrict or prohibit the United States from applying the death penalty consistent with the Fifth, Eighth and/or Fourteenth Amendments to the Constitution of the United States, including any constitutional period of confinement prior to the imposition of the death penalty.

(5) That the United States understands that this Convention shall be implemented by the United States Government to the extent that it exercises legislative and judicial jurisdiction over the matters covered by the Convention and otherwise by the state and local governments. Accordingly, in implementing Articles 10–14 and 16, the United States Government shall take measures appropriate to the Federal system to the end that the competent authorities of the constituent units of the United States of America may take appropriate measures for the fulfillment of the Convention.

III. The Senate's advice and consent is subject to the following declarations:

(1) That the United States declares that the provisions of Articles 1 through 16 of the Convention are not self-executing.

(2) That the United States declares, pursuant to Article 21, paragraph 1, of the Convention, that it recognizes the competence of the Committee against Torture to receive and consider communications to the effect that a State Party claims that another State Party is not fulfilling its obligations under the Convention. It is the understanding of the United States that, pursuant to the above mentioned article, such communications shall be accepted and processed only if they come from a State Party which has made a similar declaration.

IV. The Senate's advice and consent is subject to the following proviso, which shall not be included in the instrument of ratification to be deposited by the President:

The President of the United States shall not deposit the instrument of ratification until such time as he has notified all present and prospective ratifying parties to this Convention that nothing in this Convention requires or authorizes legislation, or other action, by the United States of America prohibited by the Constitution of the United States as interpreted by the United States.

VII. THE CONSTITUTION OF THE UNITED STATES

Preamble

We the People of the United States, in Order to form a more perfect Union, establish Justice, insure domestic Tranquility, provide for the common defence, promote the general Welfare, and secure the Blessings of Liberty to ourselves and our Posterity, do ordain and establish this Constitution for the United States of America.

Article I

Section 1. All legislative Powers herein granted shall be vested in a Congress of the United States, which shall consist of a Senate and House of Representatives.

Section 2. [1] The House of Representatives shall be composed of Members chosen every second Year by the People of the several States, and the Electors in each State shall have the Qualifications requisite for Electors of the most numerous Branch of the State Legislature.

[2] No Person shall be a Representative who shall not have attained to the Age of twenty five Years, and been seven Years a Citizen of the United States, and who shall not, when elected, be an Inhabitant of that State in which he shall be chosen.

[3] Representatives and direct Taxes shall be apportioned among the several States which may be included within this Union, according to their respective Numbers, which shall be determined by adding to the whole Number of free Persons, including those bound to Service for a Term of Years, and excluding Indians not taxed, three fifths of all other Persons. The actual Enumeration shall be made within three Years after the first Meeting of the Congress of the United States, and within every subsequent Term of ten Years, in such Manner as they shall by Law direct. The Number of Representatives shall not exceed one for every thirty Thousand, but each State shall have at Least one Representative; and until such enumeration shall be made, the State of New Hampshire shall be entitled to chuse three, Massachusetts eight, Rhode Island and Providence Plantations one, Connecticut five, New York six, New Jersey four, Pennsylvania eight, Delaware one, Maryland six, Virginia ten, North Carolina five, South Carolina five, and Georgia three.

[4] When vacancies happen in the Representation from any State, the Executive Authority thereof shall issue Writs of Election to fill such Vacancies.

[5] The House of Representatives shall chuse their Speaker and other Officers; and shall have the sole Power of Impeachment.

Section 3. [1] The Senate of the United States shall be composed of two Senators from each State, chosen by the Legislature thereof, for six Years; and each Senator shall have one Vote.

[2] Immediately after they shall be assembled in Consequence of the first Election, they shall be divided as equally as may be into three Classes. The Seats of the Senators of the first Class shall be vacated at the Expiration of the Second Year, of the second Class at the Expiration of the fourth Year, and of the third Class at the Expiration of the sixth Year, so that one third may be chosen every second Year; and if Vacancies happen by Resignation, or otherwise, during the Recess of the Legislature of any State, the Executive thereof may make temporary Appointments until the next Meeting of the Legislature, which shall then fill such Vacancies.

[3] No Person shall be a Senator who shall not have attained to the Age of thirty Years, and been nine Years a Citizen of the United States, and who shall not, when elected, by an Inhabitant of that State for which he shall be chosen.

[4] The Vice President of the United States shall be President of the Senate, but shall have no Vote, unless they be equally divided.

[5] The Senate shall chuse their other Officers, and also a President pro tempore, in the Absence of the Vice President, or when he shall exercise the Office of President of the United States.

[6] The Senate shall have the sole Power to try all Impeachments. When sitting for that Purpose, they shall be on Oath or Affirmation. When the President of the United States is tried, the Chief Justice shall preside: And no Person shall be convicted without the Concurrence of two thirds of the Members present.

[7] Judgment in Cases of Impeachment shall not extend further than to removal from Office, and disqualification to hold and enjoy any Office of honor, Trust, or Profit under the United States: but the Party convicted shall nevertheless be liable and subject to Indictment, Trial, Judgment, and Punishment, according to Law.

Section 4. [1] The Times, Places and Manner of holding Elections for Senators and Representatives, shall be prescribed in each State by the Legislature thereof; but the Congress may at any time by Law make or alter such Regulations, except as to the Places of chusing Senators.

[2] The Congress shall assemble at least once in every Year, and such Meeting shall be on the first Monday in December, unless they shall by Law appoint a different Day.

Section 5. [1] Each House shall be the Judge of the Elections, Returns, and Qualifications of its own Members, and a Majority of each shall constitute a Quorum to do Business; but a smaller Number may adjourn from day to day, and may be authorized to compel the Attendance of absent Members, in such Manner, and under such Penalties as each House may provide.

[2] Each House may determine the Rules of its Proceedings, punish its Members for disorderly Behavior, and, with the Concurrence of two thirds, expel a Member.

[3] Each House shall keep a Journal of its Proceedings, and from time to time publish the same, excepting such Parts as may in their Judgment require Secrecy; and the Yeas and Nays of the Members of either House on any question shall, at the Desire of one fifth of those Present, be entered on the Journal.

[4] Neither House, during the Session of Congress, shall without the Consent of the other, adjourn for more than three days, nor to any other Place than that in which the two Houses shall be sitting.

Section 6. [1] The Senators and Representatives shall receive a Compensation for their Services, to be ascertained by Law, and paid out of the Treasury of the United States. They shall in all Cases, except Treason, Felony and Breach of the Peace, be privileged from Arrest during their Attendance at the Session of their respective Houses, and in going to and returning from the same; and for any Speech or Debate in either House, they shall not be questioned in any other Place.

[2] No Senator or Representative shall, during the Time for which he was elected, be appointed to any civil Office under the Authority of the United States, which shall have been created, or the Emoluments whereof shall have been increased during such time; and no Person holding any Office under the United States, shall be a Member of either House during his Continuance in Office.

Section 7. [1] All Bills for raising Revenue shall originate in the House of Representatives; but the Senate may propose or concur with Amendments as on other Bills.

[2] Every Bill which shall have passed the House of Representatives and the Senate, shall, before it become a Law, be presented to the President of the United States; If he approve he shall sign it, but if not he shall return it, with his Objections at large on their Journal, and proceed to reconsider it. If after such Reconsideration two thirds of that House shall agree to pass the Bill, it shall be sent together with the Objections, to the other House, by which it shall likewise be reconsidered, and if approved by two thirds of that House, it shall become a Law. But in all such Cases the Votes of both Houses shall be determined by yeas and Nays, and the Names of the Persons voting for and against the Bill shall be entered on the Journal of each House respectively. If any Bill shall not be returned by the President within ten Days (Sundays excepted) after it shall have been presented to him, the Same shall be a Law, in like Manner as if he had signed it, unless the Congress by their Adjournment prevent its Return in which Case it shall not be a Law.

[3] Every Order, Resolution, or Vote, to Which the Concurrence of the Senate and House of Representatives may be necessary (except on a question of Adjournment) shall be presented to the President of the United States; and before the Same shall take Effect, shall be approved

by him, or being disapproved by him, shall be repassed by two thirds of the Senate and House of Representatives, according to the Rules and Limitations prescribed in the Case of a Bill.

Section 8. [1] The Congress shall have Power To lay and collect Taxes, Duties, Imposts and Excises, to pay the Debts and provide for the common Defence and general Welfare of the United States; but all Duties, Imposts and Excises shall be uniform throughout the United States;

[2] To borrow money on the credit of the United States;

[3] To regulate Commerce with foreign Nations, and among the several States, and with the Indian Tribes;

[4] To establish an uniform Rule of Naturalization, and uniform Laws on the subject of Bankruptcies throughout the United States;

[5] To coin Money, regulate the Value thereof, and of foreign Coin, and fix the Standard of Weights and Measures;

[6] To provide for the Punishment of counterfeiting the Securities and current Coin of the United States;

[7] To Establish Post Offices and Post Roads;

[8] To promote the Progress of Science and useful Arts, by securing for limited Times to Authors and Inventors the exclusive Right to their respective Writings and Discoveries;

[9] To constitute Tribunals inferior to the supreme Court;

[10] To define and punish Piracies and Felonies committed on the high Seas, and Offenses against the Law of Nations;

[11] To declare War, grant Letters of Marque and Reprisal, and make Rules concerning Captures on Land and Water;

[12] To raise and support Armies, but no Appropriation of Money to that Use shall be for a longer Term than two Years;

[13] To provide and maintain a Navy;

[14] To make Rules for the Government and Regulation of the land and naval Forces;

[15] To provide for calling forth the Militia to execute the Laws of the Union, suppress Insurrections and repel Invasions;

[16] To provide for organizing, arming, and disciplining, the Militia, and for governing such Part of them as may be employed in the Service of the United States, reserving to the States respectively, the Appointment of the Officers, and the Authority of training the Militia according to the discipline prescribed by Congress;

[17] To exercise exclusive Legislation in all Cases whatsoever, over such District (not exceeding ten Miles square) as may, by Cession of particular States, and the Acceptance of Congress, become the Seat of the Government of the United States, and to exercise like Authority over all Places purchased by the Consent of the Legislature of the State in

which the Same shall be, for the Erection of Forts, Magazines, Arsenals, dock-Yards, and other needful Buildings;—And

[18] To make all Laws which shall be necessary and proper for carrying into Execution the foregoing Powers, and all other Powers vested by this Constitution in the Government of the United States, or in any Department or Officer thereof.

Section 9. [1] The Migration or Importation of Such Persons as any of the States now existing shall think proper to admit, shall not be prohibited by the Congress prior to the Year one thousand eight hundred and eight, but a Tax or duty may be imposed on such Importation, not exceeding ten dollars for each Person.

[2] The privilege of the Writ of Habeas Corpus shall not be suspended, unless when in Cases of Rebellion or Invasion the public Safety may require it.

[3] No Bill of Attainder or ex post facto Law shall be passed.

[4] No Capitation, or other direct, Tax shall be laid, unless in Proportion to the Census or Enumeration herein before directed to be taken.

[5] No Tax or Duty shall be laid on Articles exported from any State.

[6] No Preference shall be given by any Regulation of Commerce or Revenue to the Ports of one State over those of another: nor shall Vessels bound to, or from, one State be obliged to enter, clear, or pay Duties in another.

[7] No money shall be drawn from the Treasury, but in Consequence of Appropriations made by Law; and a regular Statement and Account of the Receipts and Expenditures of all public Money shall be published from time to time.

[8] No Title of Nobility shall be granted by the United States: And no Person holding any Office of Profit or Trust under them, shall, without the Consent of the Congress, accept of any present, Emolument, Office, or Title, of any kind whatever, from any King, Prince, or foreign State.

Section 10. [1] No State shall enter into any Treaty, Alliance, or Confederation; grant Letters of Marque and Reprisal; coin Money; emit Bills of Credit; make any Thing but gold and silver Coin a Tender in Payment of Debts; pass any Bill of Attainder, ex post facto Law, or Law impairing the Obligation of Contracts, or grant any Title of Nobility.

[2] No State shall, without the Consent of the Congress, lay any Imposts or Duties on Imports or Exports, except what may be absolutely necessary for executing it's inspection Laws: and the net Produce of all Duties and Imposts, laid by any State on Imports or Exports, shall be for the Use of the Treasury of the United States; and all such Laws shall be subject to the Revision and Controul of the Congress.

[3] No State shall, without the Consent of Congress, lay any Duty of Tonnage, keep Troops, or Ships of War in time of Peace, enter into any Agreement or Compact with another State, or with a foreign Power, or engage in War, unless actually invaded, or in such imminent Danger as will not admit of delay.

Article II

Section 1. [1] The executive Power shall be vested in a President of the United States of America. He shall hold his Office during the Term of four Years, and, together with the Vice President, chosen for the same Term, be elected, as follows:

[2] Each State shall appoint, in such Manner as the Legislature thereof may direct, a Number of Electors, equal to the whole Number of Senators and Representatives to which the State may be entitled in the Congress; but no Senator or Representative, or Person holding an Office of Trust or Profit under the United States, shall be appointed an Elector.

[3] The Electors shall meet in their respective States, and vote by Ballot for two Persons, of whom one at least shall not be an Inhabitant of the same State with themselves. And they shall make a List of all the Persons voted for, and of the Number of Votes for each; which List they shall sign and certify, and transmit sealed to the Seat of the Government of the United States, directed to the President of the Senate. The President of the Senate shall, in the Presence of the Senate and House of Representatives, open all the Certificates, and the Votes shall then be counted. The Person having the greatest Number of Votes shall be the President, if such Number be a Majority of the whole Number of Electors appointed; and if there be more than one who have such Majority, and have an equal Number of Votes, then the House of Representatives shall immediately chuse by Ballot one of them for President; and if no Person have a Majority, then from the five highest on the List the said House shall in like Manner chuse the President. But in chusing the President, the Votes shall be taken by States the Representation from each State having one Vote; A quorum for this Purpose shall consist of a Member or Members from two thirds of the States, and a Majority of all the States shall be necessary to a Choice. In every Case, after the Choice of the President, the Person having the greater Number of Votes of the Electors shall be the Vice President. But if there should remain two or more who have equal Votes, the Senate shall chuse from them by Ballot the Vice President.

[4] The Congress may determine the Time of chusing the Electors, and the Day on which they shall give their Votes; which Day shall be the same throughout the United States.

[5] No person except a natural born Citizen, or a Citizen of the United States, at the time of the Adoption of this Constitution, shall be eligible to the Office of President; neither shall any Person be eligible to that Office who shall not have attained to the Age of thirty five Years, and been fourteen Years a Resident within the United States.

[6] In case of the removal of the President from Office, or of his Death, Resignation or Inability to discharge the Powers and Duties of the said Office, the Same shall devolve on the Vice President, and the Congress may by Law provide for the Case of Removal, Death, Resignation or Inability, both of the President and Vice President, declaring what Officer shall then act as President, and such Officer shall act accordingly, until the Disability be removed, or a President shall be elected.

[7] The President shall, at stated Times, receive for his Services, a Compensation, which shall neither be increased nor diminished during the Period for which he shall have been elected, and he shall not receive within that Period any other Emolument from the United States, or any of them.

[8] Before he enter on the Execution of his Office, he shall take the following Oath or Affirmation: "I do solemnly swear (or affirm) that I will faithfully execute the Office of President of the United States, and will to the best of my Ability, preserve, protect and defend the Constitution of the United States."

Section 2. [1] The President shall be Commander in Chief of the Army and Navy of the United States, and of the militia of the several States, when called into the actual Service of the United States; he may require the Opinion, in writing, of the principal Officer in each of the Executive Departments, upon any Subject relating to the Duties of their respective Offices, and he shall have Power to grant Reprieves and Pardons for Offenses against the United States, except in Cases of Impeachment.

[2] He shall have Power, by and with the Advice and Consent of the Senate to make Treaties, provided two thirds of the Senators present concur; and he shall nominate, and by and with the Advice and Consent of the Senate, shall appoint Ambassadors, other public Ministers and Consuls, Judges of the supreme Court, and all other Officers of the United States, whose Appointments are not herein otherwise provided for, and which shall be established by Law; but the Congress may by Law vest the Appointment of such inferior Officers, as they think proper, in the President alone, in the Courts of Law, or in the Heads of Departments.

[3] The President shall have Power to fill up all Vacancies that may happen during the Recess of the Senate, by granting Commissions which shall expire at the End of their next Session.

Section 3. He shall from time to time give to the Congress Information of the State of the Union, and recommend to their Consideration such Measures as he shall judge necessary and expedient; he may, on extraordinary Occasions, convene both Houses, or either of them, and in Case of Disagreement between them, with Respect to the Time of Adjournment, he may adjourn them to such Time as he shall think proper; he shall receive Ambassadors and other public Ministers; he shall take Care that the Laws be faithfully executed, and shall Commission all the Officers of the United States.

Section 4. The President, Vice President and all civil Officers of the United States, shall be removed from Office on Impeachment for, and Conviction of, Treason, Bribery, or other high Crimes and Misdemeanors.

Article III

Section 1. The judicial Power of the United States, shall be vested in one supreme Court, and in such inferior Courts as the Congress may from time to time ordain and establish. The Judges, both of the supreme and inferior Courts, shall hold their Offices during good Behaviour, and shall, at stated Times, receive for their Services a Compensation, which shall not be diminished during their Continuance in Office.

Section 2. [1] The Judicial Power shall extend to all Cases, in Law and Equity, arising under this Constitution, the Laws of the United States, and Treaties made, or which shall be made, under their Authority;—to all Cases affecting Ambassadors, other public Ministers and Consuls;—to all Cases of admiralty and maritime Jurisdiction;—to Controversies to which the United States shall be a Party;—to Controversies between two or more States;—between a State and Citizens of another State;—between Citizens of different States;—between Citizens of the same State claiming Lands under the Grants of different States, and between a State, or the Citizens thereof, and foreign States, Citizens or Subjects.

[2] In all Cases affecting Ambassadors, other public Ministers and Consuls, and those in which a State shall be a Party, the supreme Court shall have original Jurisdiction. In all the other Cases before mentioned, the supreme Court shall have appellate Jurisdiction, both as to Law and Fact, with such Exceptions, and under such Regulations as the Congress shall make.

[3] The trial of all Crimes, except in Cases of Impeachment, shall be by Jury; and such Trial shall be held in the State where the said Crimes shall have been committed; but when not committed within any State, the Trial shall be at such Place or Places as the Congress may by Law have directed.

Section 3. [1] Treason against the United States, shall consist only in levying War against them, or, in adhering to their Enemies, giving them Aid and Comfort. No Person shall be convicted of Treason unless on the Testimony of two Witnesses to the same overt Act, or on Confession in open Court.

[2] The Congress shall have Power to declare the Punishment of Treason, but no Attainder of Treason shall work Corruption of Blood, or Forfeiture except during the Life of the Person attainted.

ARTICLE IV

Section 1. Full Faith and Credit shall be given in each State to the public Acts, Records, and judicial Proceedings of every other State. And the Congress may by general Laws prescribe the Manner in which such Acts, Records and Proceedings shall be proved, and the Effect thereof.

Section 2. [1] The Citizens of each State shall be entitled to all Privileges and Immunities of Citizens in the several States.

[2] A Person charged in any State with Treason, Felony, or other Crime, who shall flee from Justice, and be found in another State, shall on demand of the executive Authority of the State from which he fled, be delivered up, to be removed to the State having Jurisdiction of the Crime.

[3] No Person held to Service or Labour in one State, under the Laws thereof, escaping into another, shall, in Consequence of any Law or Regulation therein, be discharged from such Service or Labour, but shall be delivered up on Claim of the Party to whom such Service or Labour may be due.

Section 3. [1] New States may be admitted by the Congress into this Union; but no new State shall be formed or erected within the Jurisdiction of any other State; nor any State be formed by the Junction of two or more States, or Parts of States, without the Consent of the Legislatures of the States concerned as well as of the Congress.

[2] The Congress shall have Power to dispose of and make all needful Rules and Regulations respecting the Territory or other Property belonging to the United States; and nothing in this Constitution shall be so construed as to Prejudice any Claims of the United States, or of any particular State.

Section 4. The United States shall guarantee to every State in this Union a Republican Form of Government, and shall protect each of them against Invasion; and on Application of the Legislature, or of the Executive (when the Legislature cannot be convened) against domestic Violence.

ARTICLE V

The Congress, whenever two thirds of both Houses shall deem it necessary, shall propose Amendments to this Constitution, or, on the Application of the Legislatures of two thirds of the several States, shall call a Convention for proposing Amendments, which, in either Case, shall be valid to all Intents and Purposes, as part of this Constitution, when ratified by the Legislatures of three fourths of the several States, or by Conventions in three fourths thereof, as the one or the other Mode of Ratification may be proposed by the Congress; Provided that no Amendment which may be made prior to the Year One thousand eight hundred and eight shall in any Manner affect the first and fourth Clauses in the Ninth Section of the first Article; and that no State, without its Consent, shall be deprived of its equal Suffrage in the Senate.

Article VI

[1] All Debts contracted and Engagements entered into, before the Adoption of this Constitution shall be as valid against the United States under this Constitution, as under the Confederation.

[2] This Constitution, and the Laws of the United States which shall be made in Pursuance thereof; and all Treaties made, or which shall be made, under the Authority of the United States, shall be the supreme Law of the Land; and the Judges in every State shall be bound thereby, any Thing in the Constitution or Laws of any State to the Contrary notwithstanding.

[3] The Senators and Representatives before mentioned, and the Members of the several State Legislatures, and all executive and judicial Officers, both of the United States and of the several States, shall be bound by Oath or Affirmation, to support this Constitution; but no religious Test shall ever be required as a Qualification to any Office or public Trust under the United States.

Article VII

The Ratification of the Conventions of nine States shall be sufficient for the Establishment of this Constitution between the States so ratifying the Same.

ARTICLES IN ADDITION TO, AND AMENDMENT OF, THE CONSTITUTION OF THE UNITED STATES OF AMERICA, PROPOSED BY CONGRESS, AND RATIFIED BY THE LEGISLATURES OF THE SEVERAL STATES PURSUANT TO THE FIFTH ARTICLE OF THE ORIGINAL CONSTITUTION.

Amendment I [1791]

Congress shall make no law respecting an establishment of religion, or prohibiting the free exercise thereof; or abridging the freedom of speech, or of the press; or the right of the people peaceably to assemble, and to petition the Government for a redress of grievances.

Amendment II [1791]

A well regulated Militia, being necessary to the security of a free State, the right of the people to keep and bear Arms, shall not be infringed.

Amendment III [1791]

No Soldier shall, in time of peace be quartered in any house, without the consent of the Owner, nor in time of war, but in a manner to be prescribed by law.

Amendment IV [1791]

The right of the people to be secure in their persons, houses, papers, and effects, against unreasonable searches and seizures, shall not be violated, and no Warrants shall issue, but upon probable cause, supported by Oath or affirmation and particularly describing the place to be searched, and the persons or things to be seized.

Amendment V [1791]

No person shall be held to answer for a capital, or otherwise infamous crime, unless on a presentment or indictment of a Grand Jury, except in cases arising in the land or naval forces, or in the Militia, when in actual service in time of War or public danger; nor shall any person be subject for the same offence to be twice put in jeopardy of life or limb; nor shall be compelled in any criminal case to be a witness against himself, nor be deprived of life, liberty, or property, without due process of law; nor shall private property be taken for public use, without just compensation.

Amendment VI [1791]

In all criminal prosecutions, the accused shall enjoy the right to a speedy and public trial, by an impartial jury of the State and district wherein the crime shall have been committed, which district shall have been previously ascertained by law, and to be informed of the nature and cause of the accusation; to be confronted with the witnesses against him; to have compulsory process for obtaining witnesses in his favor, and to have the Assistance of Counsel for his defence.

Amendment VII [1791]

In Suits at common law, where the value in controversy shall exceed twenty dollars, the right of trial by jury shall be preserved, and no fact tried by jury, shall be otherwise re-examined in any Court of the United States, than according to the rules of the common law.

Amendment VIII [1791]

Excessive bail shall not be required, nor excessive fines imposed, nor cruel and unusual punishments inflicted.

Amendment IX [1791]

The enumeration in the Constitution, of certain rights, shall not be construed to deny or disparage others retained by the people.

Amendment X [1791]

The powers not delegated to the United States by the Constitution, nor prohibited by it to the States, are reserved to the States respectively, or to the people.

* * *

Amendment XIV [1868]

Section 1. All persons born or naturalized in the United States, and subject to the jurisdiction thereof, are citizens of the United States and of the State wherein they reside. No State shall make or enforce any law which shall abridge the privileges or immunities of citizens of the United States; nor shall any State deprive any person of life, liberty, or property, without due process of law; nor deny to any person within its jurisdiction the equal protection of the laws.

Section 2. Representatives shall be apportioned among the several States according to their respective numbers, counting the whole number of persons in each State, excluding Indians not taxed. But when the right to vote at any election for the choice of electors for President and Vice President of the United States, Representatives in Congress, the Executive and Judicial officers of a State, or the members of the Legislature thereof, is denied to any of the male inhabitants of such State, being twenty-one years of age, and citizens of the United States, or in any way abridged, except for participation in rebellion, or other crime, the basis of representation therein shall be reduced in the proportion which the number of such male citizens shall bear to the whole number of male citizens twenty-one years of age in such State.

Section 3. No person shall be a Senator or Representative in Congress, or elector of President and Vice President, or hold any office, civil or military, under the United States, or under any State, who having previously taken an oath, as a member of Congress, or as an officer of the United States, or as a member of any State legislature, or as an executive or judicial officer of any State, to support the Constitution of the United States, shall have engaged in insurrection or rebellion against the same, or given aid or comfort to the enemies thereof. But Congress may by a vote of two-thirds of each House, remove such disability.

Section 4. The validity of the public debt of the United States, authorized by law, including debts incurred for payment of pensions and bounties for services in suppressing insurrection or rebellion, shall not be questioned. But neither the United States nor any State shall assume or pay any debt or obligation incurred in aid of insurrection or rebellion against the United States, or any claim for the loss or emancipation of any slave; but all such debts, obligations and claims shall be held illegal and void.

Section 5. The Congress shall have power to enforce, by appropriate legislation, the provisions of this article.

AMENDMENT XV [1870]

Section 1. The right of citizens of the United States to vote shall not be denied or abridged by the United States or by any State on account of race, color, or previous condition of servitude.

Section 2. The Congress shall have power to enforce this article by appropriate legislation.

* * *

AMENDMENT XIX [1920]

[1] The right of citizens of the United States to vote shall not be denied or abridged by the United States or by any State on account of sex.

[2] Congress shall have power to enforce this article by appropriate legislation.

* * *

AMENDMENT XXIV [1964]

Section 1. The right of citizens of the United States to vote in any primary or other election for President or Vice President, for electors for President or Vice President, or for Senator or Representative in Congress, shall not be denied or abridged by the United States or any State by reason of failure to pay any poll tax or other tax.

Section 2. The Congress shall have power to enforce this article by appropriate legislation.

* * *

AMENDMENT XXVI [1971]

Section 1. The right of citizens of the United States, who are eighteen years of age or older, to vote shall not be denied or abridged by the United States or by any State on account of age.

Section 2. The Congress shall have power to enforce this article by appropriate legislation.

VIII. SELECTED IMMIGRATION FORMS

List of Principal Forms Arranged by Subject Matter (includes guide to forms available online)

Form **Page***

* Documents designated “online” are available at http://www.uscis.gov/forms.

** Note: In 2013 CBP ceased using this paper form for most purposes, instead capturing relevant information digitally from other records. See http://www.cbp.gov/sites/default/files/documents/i94_factsheet_2.pdf. For samples of a completed I–94 card showing class of admission and relevant dates, see the M–274 Handbook for Employers below.

SELECTED IMMIGRATION FORMS

Set forth here are the forms in current use as of May 15, 2014. Online forms are regularly updated by USCIS at its website. Forms reprinted here sometimes contain earlier expiration dates in an upper corner of the first page, but may nonetheless remain in use while updated forms are under review at the Office of Management and Budget.

BASIC DOCUMENTS

Form I–94 Arrival-departure record

DEPARTMENT OF HOMELAND SECURITY
U.S. Customs and Border Protection

OMB No. 1651-0111

Welcome to the United States
I-94 Arrival/Departure Record
Instructions

This form must be completed by all persons except U.S. Citizens, returning resident aliens, aliens with immigrant visas, and Canadian Citizens visiting or in transit.

Type or print legibly with pen in ALL CAPITAL LETTERS. Use English. Do not write on the back of this form.

This form is in two parts. Please complete both the Arrival Record (Items 1 through 17) and the Departure Record (Items 18 through 21).

When all items are completed, present this form to the CBP Officer.

Item 9 - If you are entering the United States by land, enter LAND in this space. If you are entering the United States by ship, enter SEA in this space.

5 U.S.C. § 552a(e)(3) Privacy Act Notice: Information collected on this form is required by Title 8 of the U.S. Code, including the INA (8 U.S.C. 1103, 1187), and 8 CFR 235.1, 264, and 1235.1. The purposes for this collection are to give the terms of admission and document the arrival and departure of nonimmigrant aliens to the U.S. The information solicited on this form may be made available to other government agencies for law enforcement purposes or to assist DHS in determining your admissibility. All nonimmigrant aliens seeking admission to the U.S., unless otherwise exempted, must provide this information. Failure to provide this information may deny you entry to the United States and result in your removal.

CBP Form I-94 (05/08)

OMB No. 1651-0111

Arrival Record

Admission Number

OOOOOOOOO OO

1. Family Name

2. First (Given) Name

3. Birth Date (DD/MM/YY)

4. Country of Citizenship

5. Sex (Male or Female)

6. Passport Issue Date (DD/MM/YY)

7. Passport Expiration Date (DD/MM/YY)

8. Passport Number

9. Airline and Flight Number

10. Country Where You Live

11. Country Where You Boarded

12. City Where Visa Was Issued

13. Date Issued (DD/MM/YY)

14. Address While in the United States (Number and Street)

15. City and State

16. Telephone Number in the U.S. Where You Can be Reached

17. Email Address

CBP Form I-94 (05/08)

OMB No. 1651-0111

DEPARTMENT OF HOMELAND SECURITY
U.S. Customs and Border Protection

Departure Record

Admission Number

OOOOOOOOO OO

18. Family Name

19. First (Given) Name

20. Birth Date (DD/MM/YY)

21. Country of Citizenship

CBP Form I-94 (05/08)

See Other Side STAPLE HERE

This Side For Government Use Only

Primary Inspection

Applicant's Name ____________

Date Referred ________ Time ________ Insp. # ________

Reason Referred

☐ 212A ☐ ☐ ☐ PP ☐ Visa ☐ Parole ☐ LO ☐ TWOV

Other ____________

Secondary Inspection

End Secondary Time ________ Insp. # ________

Disposition ____________

22. Occupation	23. Waivers
24. CIS A Number A-	25. CIS FCO
26. Petition Number	27. Program Number
28. ☐ Bond	29. ☐ Prospective Student

30. Itinerary/Comments

31. TWOV Ticket Number

Paperwork Reduction Act Statement: An agency may not conduct or sponsor an information collection and a person is not required to respond to this information unless it displays a current valid OMB control number. The control number for this collection is 1651-0111. The estimated average time to complete this application is 8 minutes per respondent. If you have any comments regarding the burden estimate you can write to U.S. Customs and Border Protection, Asset Management, 1300 Pennsylvania Avenue, NW, Washington DC 20229

Warning A nonimmigrant who accepts unauthorized employment is subject to deportation.
Important Retain this permit in your possession; ***you must surrender it when you leave the U.S.*** Failure to do so may delay your entry into the U.S. in the future.
You are authorized to stay in the U.S. only until the date written on this form. To remain past this date, without permission from Department of Homeland Security authorities, is a violation of the law.
Surrender this permit when you leave the U.S.:
- By sea or air, to the transportation line;
- Across the Canadian border, to a Canadian Official;
- Across the Mexican border, to a U.S. Official

Students planning to reenter the U.S. within 30 days to return to the same school, see "Arrival-Departure" on page 2 of Form I-20 **prior to surrendering this permit.**

Record of Changes

Departure Record

Port:

Date:

Carrier:

Flight No./ Ship Name:

Sample nonimmigrant visa

Reading a US Nonimmigrant Visa

This is a simple guide to reading the data contained in a US Nonimmigrant Visa. Data and format are identical for each version of the visa. Earlier versions have slight variations.

MRV 2000
(First issued at certain posts beginning May 2000)

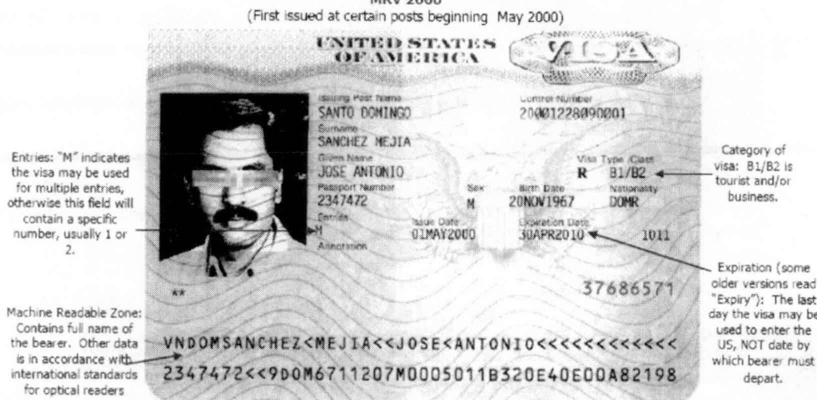

Lincoln Visa
(First issued at certain posts beginning February 2002)

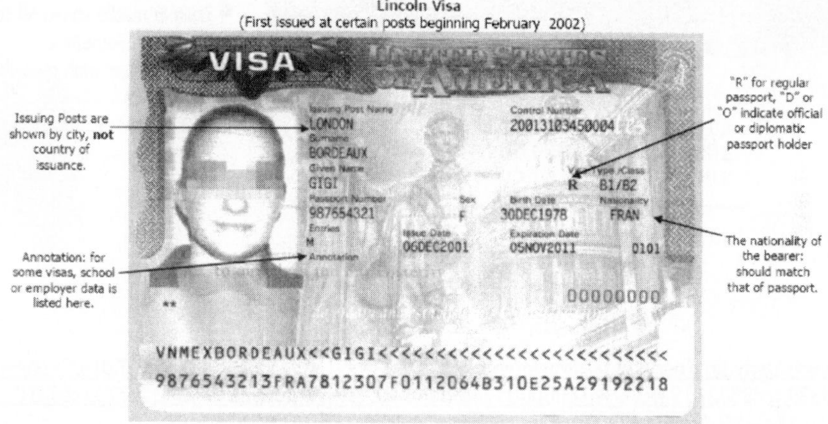

Form I–551 Permanent resident card

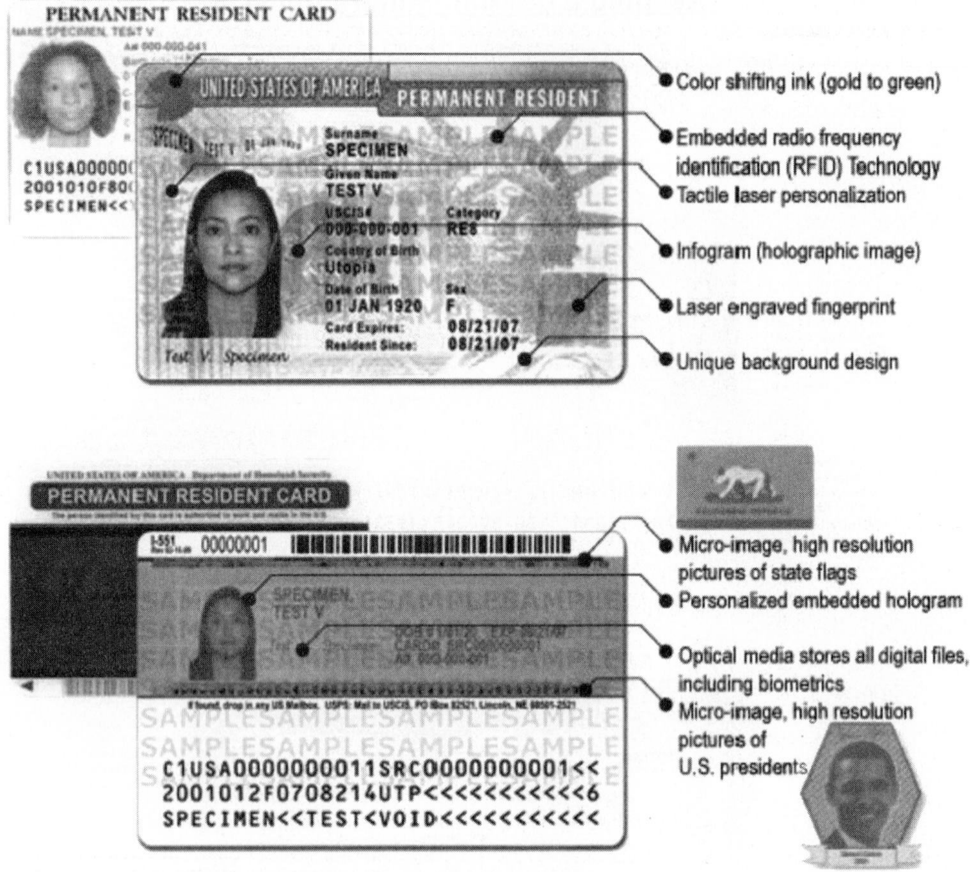

Source:
http://www.uscis.gov/portal/site/uscis/menuitem.5af9bb95919f35e66f614176543f6d1a/?vgnextoid=34233893c4888210VgnVCM100000082ca60aRCRD&vgnextchannel=68439c7755cb9010VgnVCM10000045f3d6a1RCRD

(Newer version of the card appears in the foreground.)

Form I–797A Notice of action (sample)

Department of Homeland Security
U.S. Citizenship and Immigration Services

I-797A, Notice of Action

THE UNITED STATES OF AMERICA

RECEIPT NUMBER WAC-[redacted]		CASE TYPE I129 PETITION FOR A NONIMMIGRANT WORKER
RECEIPT DATE September 8, 2008	PRIORITY DATE	PETITIONER [redacted]
NOTICE DATE September 19, 2008	PAGE 1 of 1	BENEFICIARY [redacted]

CHARLES MEDINA ESQ
[redacted]

Notice Type: Approval Notice
Class: E2
Valid from 10/01/2008 to 09/30/2010

The above petition and change of status have been approved. The status of the named foreign worker(s) in this classification is valid as indicated above. The foreign worker(s) can work for the petitioner, but only as detailed in the petition and for the period authorized. Any change in employment requires a new petition. Since this employment authorization stems from the filing of this petition, separate employment authorization documentation is not required. Please contact the IRS with any questions about tax withholding.

The petitioner should keep the upper portion of this notice. The lower portion should be given to the worker. He or she should keep the right part with his or her form I-94, *Arrival-Departure Record*. This should be turned in with the I-94 when departing the U.S. The left part is for his or her records. A person granted a change of status who leaves the U.S. must normally obtain a visa in the new classification before returning. The left part can be used in applying for the new visa. The petitioner may also file Form I-824, *Application for Action on an Approved Application or Petition*, with this office to request that we notify a consulate, port of entry, or pre-flight inspection office of this approval.

The approval of this visa petition does not in itself grant any immigration status and does not guarantee that the alien beneficiary will subsequently be found to be eligible for a visa, for admission to the United States, or for an extension, change, or adjustment of status.

THIS FORM IS NOT A VISA NOR MAY IT BE USED IN PLACE OF A VISA.

Please see the additional information on the back. You will be notified separately about any other cases you filed.
U.S. CITIZENSHIP & IMMIGRATION SVC
CALIFORNIA SERVICE CENTER
P. O. BOX 30111
LAGUNA NIGUEL CA 92607-0111
Customer Service Telephone: (800) 375-5283

Form I797A (Rev. 09/07/93)N

PLEASE TEAR OFF FORM I-94 PRINTED BELOW, AND STAPLE TO ORIGINAL I-94 IF AVAILABLE

Detach This Half for Personal Records

Receipt # WAC-[redacted]
I-94# [redacted]
NAME [redacted]
CLASS E2
VALID FROM 10/01/2008 UNTIL 09/30/2010

PETITIONER:

Receipt Number WAC-[redacted]
Immigration and Naturalization Service
I-94
Departure Record Petitioner: [redacted]

14. Family Name [redacted]
15. First (Given) Name [redacted]
16. Date of Birth [redacted]
17. Country of Citizenship KOREA, SOUTH

Form I-797A (Rev. 10/31/05) N

Form DSP–150 Border crossing card ("laser visa," as issued from 10/1/2008)

The new border crossing card being issued by the U.S. Department of State in cooperation with the Department of Homeland Security is a credit card-sized plastic card that conveys the same purpose and effect as a B1/B2 Visa foil. However, the Border Crossing Card will be issued only to Mexican nationals. The purpose of the BCC is to facilitate travel and inspection at land border crossings for Mexican nationals in general, and especially to facilitate frequent crossings for those persons living in Mexican border communities along the southwestern tier of the United States. The BCC permits the bearer to travel to the U.S. for tourism and/or business but does not authorize employment in the United States.

Like the U.S. Passport Card, the new BCC will contain a radio frequency identification chip (RFID chip) and an integrated contactless circuit (ICC) antenna, which will be recognized by DHS' PASS System and will respond with a unique 'read-only' electronic number. No BCC card recipient's personal information is written to the RFID chip itself.

For further information about visas and the regulations coming into force to facilitate and govern travel and inspection under the terms of the Western Hemisphere Travel Initiative (WHTI), please visit the Department of State's website located at www.travel.state.gov.

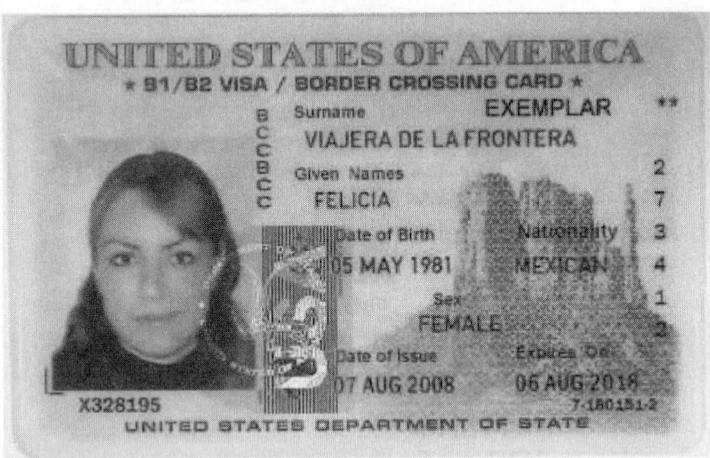

Source: http://monterrey.usconsulate.gov/press_bol100108.html

Form EOIR–28 Notice of entry of appearance as attorney or representative before the immigration court

U.S. Department of Justice
Executive Office for Immigration Review
Immigration Court

OMB#1125-0006

Notice of Entry of Appearance as Attorney or Representative Before the Immigration Court

(Type or print)
NAME AND ADDRESS OF REPRESENTED PARTY

(First) (Middle Initial) (Last)

(Number and Street) (Apt. No.)

(City) (State) (Zip Code)

ALIEN (A) NUMBER (S)
(List number(s) of all parties represented in this case.)

For disciplinary case, enter docket number.

NAME OF ATTORNEY OR REPRESENTATIVE, ADDRESS, FAX & PHONE NUMBERS, & E-MAIL ADDRESS

☐ Check here if new address

Please check one of the following:

☐ I am an attorney eligible to practice law in, and a member in good standing of, the bar of the highest court(s) of the following state(s), possession(s), territory(ies), commonwealth(s), or the District of Columbia (use additional space on reverse side if necessary) and I am not subject to any order disbarring, suspending, or otherwise restricting me in the practice of law (if subject to such an order, explain on reverse).

Full Name of Court **Bar Number (if applicable)**

☐ I am an accredited representative as defined in 8 C.F.R. § 1292.1(a)(4) with the following recognized organization:

☐ I am a law student or law graduate of an accredited U.S. law school as defined in 8 C.F.R. § 1292.1(a)(2).

☐ I am a reputable individual as defined in 8 C.F.R. § 1292.1(a)(3).

☐ I am an accredited foreign government official as defined in 8 C.F.R. § 1292.1(a)(5).

☐ I am a person who was authorized to practice on December 23, 1952, under 8 C.F.R. § 1292.1(b).

I hereby enter my appearance as attorney or representative for, and at the request of, the party named above. I have read and understand the statements provided on the reverse side of this form that set forth the regulations and conditions governing appearances and representation before the Immigration Court. I declare under penalty of perjury under the laws of the United States of America that the foregoing is true and correct.

SIGNATURE OF ATTORNEY OR REPRESENTATIVE **EOIR ID NUMBER** **DATE**

X

Form EOIR - 28
Rev. Oct. 2013

Indicate type of appearance

☐ Primary Attorney/Representative ☐ Non-primary Attorney/Representative

☐ **On behalf of Attorney** ______________________________ .

I am providing pro bono representation. Check one: yes ☐ **no** ☐

Proof of Service

I (Name) ______________________ mailed or delivered a copy of the foregoing Form EOIR-28 on (Date)______________

to the ☐ DHS (U.S. Immigration and Customs Enforcement - ICE) at ______________________________

X ______________________________

Signature of Attorney or Representative

APPEARANCES - An appearance shall be filed on a Form EOIR-28 by the attorney or representative appearing in each case before an Immigration Judge (see 8 C.F.R. § 1003.17). When an appearance is made by a person acting in a representative capacity, his/her personal appearance or signature constitutes a representation that, under the provisions of 8 C.F.R. part 1003, he/she is authorized and qualified to represent individuals and will comply with the EOIR Rules of Professional Conduct in 8 C.F.R. § 1003.102. Thereafter, substitution or withdrawal may be permitted upon the approval of the Immigration Judge of a request by the attorney or representative of record in accordance with 8 C.F.R. § 1003.17(b). Please note that appearances for limited purposes are not permitted. *See Matter of Velasquez*, 19 I&N Dec. 377, 384 (BIA 1986). A separate appearance form (Form EOIR-27) must be filed with an appeal to the Board of Immigration Appeals (see 8 C.F.R. § 1003.38(g)).

AVAILABILITY OF RECORDS - During the time a case is pending, a party to a proceeding or his/her attorney or representative will be permitted to examine the Record of Proceeding in the Immigration Court having administrative control over the Record of Proceeding, in accordance with the standard procedures of the Court.

FREEDOM OF INFORMATION ACT - This form may not be used to request records under the Freedom of Information Act or the Privacy Act. The manner of requesting such records is in 28 C.F.R. §§ 16.1-16.11 and appendices. For further information about requesting records from EOIR under the Freedom of Information Act, see How to File a Freedom of Information Act (FOIA) Request With the Executive Office for Immigration Review, available on EOIRs website at http://www.justice.gov/eoir.

PRIVACY ACT NOTICE - The information requested on this form is authorized by 8 U.S.C. §§ 1229a, 1362 and 8 C.F.R. § 1003.17 in order to enter an appearance to represent a party before the Immigration Court. The information you provide is mandatory and required to enter an appearance. Failure to provide the requested information will result in an inability to represent a party or receive notice of actions in a proceeding. EOIR may share this information with others in accordance with approved routine uses described in EOIRs system of records notice, EOIR-001, Records and Management Information System, and Practitioner Complaint-Disciplinary Files.

CASES BEFORE EOIR - Automated information about cases before EOIR is available by calling 1-800-898-7180 or (240) 314-1500.

ADDITIONAL INFORMATION:

Under the Paperwork Reduction Act, a person is not required to respond to a collection of information unless it displays a valid OMB control number. We try to create forms and instructions that are accurate, can be easily understood, and which impose the least possible burden on you to provide us with information. The estimated average time to complete this form is six (6) minutes. If you have comments regarding the accuracy of this estimate, or suggestions for making this form simpler, you can write to the Executive Office for Immigration Review, Office of the General Counsel, 5107 Leesburg Pike, Suite 2600, Falls Church, Virginia 20530.

Form EOIR - 28
Rev. Oct. 2013

PETITIONS AND APLICATIONS

Form ETA 9089 Application for permanent employment certification

OMB Approval: 1205-0451
Expiration Date: 08/31/2014

Application for Permanent Employment Certification

ETA Form 9089

U.S. Department of Labor

Please read and review the filing instructions before completing this form. A copy of the instructions can be found at http://www.foreignlaborcert.doleta.gov/pdf/9089inst.pdf

Employing or continuing to employ an alien unauthorized to work in the United States is illegal and may subject the employer to criminal prosecution, civil money penalties, or both.

A. Refiling Instructions

1. Are you seeking to utilize the filing date from a previously submitted Application for Alien Employment Certification (ETA 750)?	☐ Yes ☐ No
1-A. If Yes, enter the previous filing date	
1-B. Indicate the previous SWA or local office case number OR if not available, specify state where case was originally filed:	

B. Schedule A or Sheepherder Information

1. Is this application in support of a Schedule A or Sheepherder Occupation?	☐ Yes ☐ No
If Yes, do NOT send this application to the Department of Labor. All applications in support of Schedule A or Sheepherder Occupations must be sent directly to the appropriate Department of Homeland Security office.	

C. Employer Information (Headquarters or Main Office)

1. Employer's name			
2. Address 1			
Address 2			
3. City	State/Province	Country	Postal code
4. Phone number		Extension	
5. Number of employees		6. Year commenced business	
7. FEIN(Federal Employer Identification Number)		8. NAICS Code	
9. Is the employer a closely held corporation, partnership, or sole proprietorship in which the alien has an ownership interest, or is there a familial relationship between the owners, stockholders, partners, corporate officers, incorporators, and the alien?			☐ Yes ☐ No

D. Employer Contact Information (This section must be filled out. This information must be different from the agent or attorney information listed in Section E).

1. Contact's last name		First name	Middle initial
2. Address 1			
Address 2			
3. City	State/Province	Country	Postal code
4. Phone number		Extension	
5. E-mail address			

ETA Form 9089 This Certification is valid from ____________ to ____________ Page 1 of

ETA Case Number:

OMB Approval: 1205-0451
Expiration Date: 08/31/2014

Application for Permanent Employment Certification

ETA Form 9089

U.S. Department of Labor

E. Agent or Attorney Information (If applicable)

1. Agent or attorney's last name	First name		Middle initial
2. Firm name			
3. Firm EIN	4. Phone number	Extension	
5. Address 1			
Address 2			
6. City	State/Province	Country	Postal code
7. E-mail address			

F. Prevailing Wage Information (as provided by the State Workforce Agency)

1. Prevailing wage tracking number (if applicable)	2. SOC/O*NET(OES) code
3. Occupation Title	4. Skill Level
5. Prevailing wage $	Per: (Choose only one) ☐ Hour ☐ Week ☐ Bi-Weekly ☐ Month ☐ Year
6. Prevailing wage source (Choose only one) ☐ OES ☐ CBA ☐ Employer Conducted Survey ☐ DBA ☐ SCA ☐ Other	
6-A. If Other is indicated in question 6, specify:	
7. Determination date	8. Expiration date

G. Wage Offer Information

1. Offered wage From: $	To: (Optional) $	Per: (Choose only one) ☐ Hour ☐ Week ☐ Bi-Weekly ☐ Month ☐ Year

H. Job Opportunity Information (Where work will be performed)

1. Primary worksite (where work is to be performed) address 1		
Address 2		
2. City	State	Postal code
3. Job title		
4. Education: minimum level required: ☐ None ☐ High School ☐ Associate's ☐ Bachelor's ☐ Master's ☐ Doctorate ☐ Other		
4-A. If Other is indicated in question 4, specify the education required:		
4-B. Major field of study		
5. Is training required in the job opportunity? ☐ Yes ☐ No	5-A. If Yes, number of months of training required:	

ETA Form 9089 This Certification is valid from ______________ to ______________ Page 2 of

ETA Case Number:

OMB Approval: 1205-0451
Expiration Date: 08/31/2014

Application for Permanent Employment Certification

ETA Form 9089

U.S. Department of Labor

H. Job Opportunity Information Continued

5-B. Indicate the field of training:

6. Is experience in the job offered required for the job? ☐ Yes ☐ No

6-A. If Yes, number of months experience required:

7. Is there an alternate field of study that is acceptable? ☐ Yes ☐ No

7-A. If Yes, specify the major field of study:

8. Is there an alternate combination of education and experience that is acceptable? ☐ Yes ☐ No

8-A. If Yes, specify the alternate level of education required:

☐ None ☐ High School ☐ Associate's ☐ Bachelor's ☐ Master's ☐ Doctorate ☐ Other

8-B. If Other is indicated in question 8-A, indicate the alternate level of education required:

8-C. If applicable, indicate the number of years experience acceptable in question 8:

9. Is a foreign educational equivalent acceptable? ☐ Yes ☐ No

10. Is experience in an alternate occupation acceptable? ☐ Yes ☐ No

10-A. If Yes, number of months experience in alternate occupation required:

10-B. Identify the job title of the acceptable alternate occupation:

11. Job duties – If submitting by mail, add attachment if necessary. Job duties description must begin in this space.

12. Are the job opportunity's requirements normal for the occupation? ☐ Yes ☐ No

If the answer to this question is No, the employer must be prepared to provide documentation demonstrating that the job requirements are supported by business necessity.

13. Is knowledge of a foreign language required to perform the job duties? ☐ Yes ☐ No

If the answer to this question is Yes, the employer must be prepared to provide documentation demonstrating that the language requirements are supported by business necessity.

14. Specific skills or other requirements – If submitting by mail, add attachment if necessary. Skills description must begin in this space.

ETA Case Number:

OMB Approval: 1205-0451
Expiration Date: 08/31/2014

Application for Permanent Employment Certification
ETA Form 9089
U.S. Department of Labor

H. Job Opportunity Information Continued

15. Does this application involve a job opportunity that includes a combination of occupations?	☐ Yes ☐ No
16. Is the position identified in this application being offered to the alien identified in Section J?	☐ Yes ☐ No
17. Does the job require the alien to live on the employer's premises?	☐ Yes ☐ No
18. Is the application for a live-in household domestic service worker?	☐ Yes ☐ No
18-A. If Yes, have the employer and the alien executed the required employment contract and has the employer provided a copy of the contract to the alien?	☐ Yes ☐ No ☐ NA

I. Recruitment Information

a. Occupation Type – All must complete this section.

1. Is this application for a **professional occupation**, other than a college or university teacher? Professional occupations are those for which a bachelor's degree (or equivalent) is normally required.	☐ Yes ☐ No
2. Is this application for a college or university teacher? **If Yes, complete questions 2-A and 2-B below.**	☐ Yes ☐ No
2-A. Did you select the candidate using a competitive recruitment and selection process?	☐ Yes ☐ No
2-B. Did you use the basic recruitment process for professional occupations?	☐ Yes ☐ No

b. Special Recruitment and Documentation Procedures for College and University Teachers – Complete only if the answer to question I.a.2-A is Yes.

3. Date alien selected:
4. Name and date of national professional journal in which advertisement was placed:
5. Specify additional recruitment information in this space. Add an attachment if necessary.

c. Professional/Non-Professional Information – Complete this section unless your answer to question B.1 or I.a.2-A is YES.

6. Start date for the SWA job order	7. End date for the SWA job order
8. Is there a Sunday edition of the newspaper in the area of intended employment?	☐ Yes ☐ No
9. Name of newspaper (of general circulation) in which the first advertisement was placed:	
10. Date of first advertisement identified in question 9:	
11. Name of newspaper or professional journal (if applicable) in which second advertisement was placed:	☐ Newspaper ☐ Journal

ETA Form 9089 This Certification is valid from ____________ ___to______ ________ Page 4 of

ETA Case Number:

OMB Approval: 1205-0451
Expiration Date: 08/31/2014

Application for Permanent Employment Certification

ETA Form 9089

U.S. Department of Labor

I. Recruitment Information Continued

12. Date of second newspaper advertisement or date of publication of journal identified in question 11:

d. Professional Recruitment Information – Complete if the answer to question I.a.1 is YES or if the answer to I.a.2-B is YES. Complete at least 3 of the items.

13. Dates advertised at job fair From: To:	14. Dates of on-campus recruiting From: To:
15. Dates posted on employer web site From: To:	16. Dates advertised with trade or professional organization From: To:
17. Dates listed with job search web site From: To:	18. Dates listed with private employment firm From: To:
19. Dates advertised with employee referral program From: To:	20. Dates advertised with campus placement office From: To:
21. Dates advertised with local or ethnic newspaper From: To:	22. Dates advertised with radio or TV ads From: To:

e. General Information – All must complete this section.

23. Has the employer received payment of any kind for the submission of this application?	☐ Yes ☐ No
23-A. If Yes, describe details of the payment including the amount, date and purpose of the payment :	
24. Has the bargaining representative for workers in the occupation in which the alien will be employed been provided with notice of this filing at least 30 days but not more than 180 days before the date the application is filed?	☐ Yes ☐ No ☐ NA
25. If there is no bargaining representative, has a notice of this filing been posted for 10 business days in a conspicuous location at the place of employment, ending at least 30 days before but not more than 180 days before the date the application is filed?	☐ Yes ☐ No ☐ NA
26. Has the employer had a layoff in the area of intended employment in the occupation involved in this application or in a related occupation within the six months immediately preceding the filing of this application?	☐ Yes ☐ No
26-A. If Yes, were the laid off U.S. workers notified and considered for the job opportunity for which certification is sought?	☐ Yes ☐ No ☐ NA

J. Alien Information (This section must be filled out. This information must be different from the agent or attorney information listed in Section E).

1. Alien's last name		First name	Full middle name
2. Current address 1			
Address 2			
3. City	State/Province	Country	Postal code
4. Phone number of current residence			
5. Country of citizenship		6. Country of birth	
7. Alien's date of birth		8. Class of admission	
9. Alien registration number (A#)		10. Alien admission number (I-94)	
11. Education: highest level achieved relevant to the requested occupation: ☐ None ☐ High School ☐ Associate's ☐ Bachelor's ☐ Master's ☐ Doctorate ☐ Other			

ETA Form 9089 This Certification is valid from ___________ to ___________ Page 5 of

ETA Case Number:

OMB Approval: 1205-0451
Expiration Date: 08/31/2014

Application for Permanent Employment Certification
ETA Form 9089
U.S. Department of Labor

J. Alien Information Continued

11-A. If Other indicated in question 11, specify	
12. Specify major field(s) of study	
13. Year relevant education completed	
14. Institution where relevant education specified in question 11 was received	
15. Address 1 of conferring institution	
Address 2	
16. City State/Province Country Postal code	
17. Did the alien complete the training required for the requested job opportunity, as indicated in question H.5?	☐ Yes ☐ No ☐ NA
18. Does the alien have the experience as required for the requested job opportunity indicated in question H.6?	☐ Yes ☐ No ☐ NA
19. Does the alien possess the alternate combination of education and experience as indicated in question H.8?	☐ Yes ☐ No ☐ NA
20. Does the alien have the experience in an alternate occupation specified in question H.10?	☐ Yes ☐ No ☐ NA
21. Did the alien gain any of the qualifying experience with the employer in a position substantially comparable to the job opportunity requested?	☐ Yes ☐ No ☐ NA
22. Did the employer pay for any of the alien's education or training necessary to satisfy any of the employer's job requirements for this position?	☐ Yes ☐ No
23. Is the alien currently employed by the petitioning employer?	☐ Yes ☐ No

K. Alien Work Experience

List all jobs the alien has held during the past 3 years. Also list any other experience that qualifies the alien for the job opportunity for which the employer is seeking certification.

a. Job 1

1. Employer name			
2. Address 1			
Address 2			
3. City	State/Province	Country	Postal code
4. Type of business		5. Job title	
6. Start date	7. End date	8. Number of hours worked per week	

Job 1 continued on next page

OMB Approval: 1205-0451
Expiration Date: 08/31/2014

Application for Permanent Employment Certification

ETA Form 9089

U.S. Department of Labor

K. Alien Work Experience Continued

9. Job details (duties performed, use of tools, machines, equipment, skills, qualifications, certifications, licenses, etc. Include the phone number of the employer and the name of the alien's supervisor.)

b. Job 2

1. Employer name			
2. Address 1			
Address 2			
3. City	State/Province	Country	Postal code
4. Type of business		5. Job title	
6. Start date	7. End date	8. Number of hours worked per week	
9. Job details (duties performed, use of tools, machines, equipment, skills, qualifications, certifications, licenses, etc. Include the phone number of the employer and the name of the alien's supervisor.)			

c. Job 3

1. Employer name			
2. Address 1			
Address 2			
3. City	State/Province	Country	Postal code
4. Type of business		5. Job title	
6. Start date	7. End date	8. Number of hours worked per week	

Job 3 continued on next page

ETA Case Number:

OMB Approval: 1205-0451
Expiration Date: 08/31/2014

Application for Permanent Employment Certification

ETA Form 9089

U.S. Department of Labor

K. Alien Work Experience Continued

9. Job details (duties performed, use of tools, machines, equipment, skills, qualifications, certifications, licenses, etc. Include the phone number of the employer and the name of the alien's supervisor.)

L. Alien Declaration

I declare under penalty of perjury that Sections J and K are true and correct. *I understand that to knowingly furnish false information in the preparation of this form and any supplement thereto or to aid, abet, or counsel another to do so is a federal offense punishable by a fine or imprisonment up to five years or both under 18 U.S.C. §§ 2 and 1001. Other penalties apply as well to fraud or misuse of ETA immigration documents and to perjury with respect to such documents under 18 U.S.C. §§ 1546 and 1621.*

In addition, I ***further declare*** *under penalty of perjury that I intend to accept the position offered in Section H of this application if a labor certification is approved and I am granted a visa or an adjustment of status based on this application.*

1. Alien's last name	First name	Full middle name
2. Signature	Date signed	

Note – The signature and date signed do not have to be filled out when electronically submitting to the Department of Labor for processing, but must be complete when submitting by mail. If the application is submitted electronically, any resulting certification MUST be signed *immediately upon receipt* from DOL before it can be submitted to USCIS for final processing.

M. Declaration of Preparer

1. **Was the application completed by the employer?** If No, you must complete this section.	☐ Yes ☐ No

I hereby certify that I have prepared this application at the direct request of the employer listed in Section C and that to the best of my knowledge the information contained herein is true and correct. *I understand that to knowingly furnish false information in the preparation of this form and any supplement thereto or to aid, abet, or counsel another to do so is a federal offense punishable by a fine, imprisonment up to five years or both under 18 U.S.C. §§ 2 and 1001. Other penalties apply as well to fraud or misuse of ETA immigration documents and to perjury with respect to such documents under 18 U.S.C. §§ 1546 and 1621.*

2. Preparer's last name	First name	Middle initial
3. Title		
4. E-mail address		
5. Signature	Date signed	

Note – The signature and date signed do not have to be filled out when electronically submitting to the Department of Labor for processing, but must be complete when submitting by mail. If the application is submitted electronically, any resulting certification MUST be signed *immediately upon receipt* from DOL before it can be submitted to USCIS for final processing.

ETA Form 9089 This Certification is valid from ____________ to ____________ Page 8 of

ETA Case Number:

OMB Approval: 1205-0451
Expiration Date: 08/31/2014

Application for Permanent Employment Certification
ETA Form 9089
U.S. Department of Labor

N. Employer Declaration

By virtue of my signature below, ***I HEREBY CERTIFY*** *the following conditions of employment:*

1. The offered wage equals or exceeds the prevailing wage and I will pay at least the prevailing wage.
2. The wage is not based on commissions, bonuses or other incentives, unless I guarantees a wage paid on a weekly, bi-weekly, or monthly basis that equals or exceeds the prevailing wage.
3. I have enough funds available to pay the wage or salary offered the alien.
4. I will be able to place the alien on the payroll on or before the date of the alien's proposed entrance into the United States.
5. The job opportunity does not involve unlawful discrimination by race, creed, color, national origin, age, sex, religion, handicap, or citizenship.
6. The job opportunity is not:
   a. Vacant because the former occupant is on strike or is being locked out in the course of a labor dispute involving a work stoppage; or
   b. At issue in a labor dispute involving a work stoppage.
7. The job opportunity's terms, conditions, and occupational environment are not contrary to Federal, state or local law.
8. The job opportunity has been and is clearly open to any U.S. worker.
9. The U.S. workers who applied for the job opportunity were rejected for lawful job-related reasons.
10. The job opportunity is for full-time, permanent employment for an employer other than the alien.

I hereby designate the agent or attorney identified in section E (if any) to represent me for the purpose of labor certification and, by virtue of my signature in Block 3 below, **I take full responsibility** for the accuracy of any representations made by my agent or attorney.

I declare under penalty of perjury that I have read and reviewed this application and that to the best of my knowledge the information contained herein is true and accurate. *I understand that to knowingly furnish false information in the preparation of this form and any supplement thereto or to aid, abet, or counsel another to do so is a federal offense punishable by a fine or imprisonment up to five years or both under 18 U.S.C. §§ 2 and 1001. Other penalties apply as well to fraud or misuse of ETA immigration documents and to perjury with respect to such documents under 18 U.S.C. §§ 1546 and 1621.*

1. Last name	First name	Middle initial
2. Title		
3. Signature	Date signed	

Note – The signature and date signed do not have to be filled out when electronically submitting to the Department of Labor for processing, but must be complete when submitting by mail. If the application is submitted electronically, any resulting certification MUST be signed *immediately upon receipt* from DOL before it can be submitted to USCIS for final processing.

O. U.S. Government Agency Use Only

Pursuant to the provisions of Section 212 (a)(5)(A) of the Immigration and Nationality Act, as amended, I hereby certify that there are not sufficient U.S. workers available and the employment of the above will not adversely affect the wages and working conditions of workers in the U.S. similarly employed.

This Certification is valid from ____________ to ____________

Signature of Certifying Officer

Date Signed

Case Number

Filing Date

OMB Approval: 1205-0451
Expiration Date: 08/31/2014

Application for Permanent Employment Certification

ETA Form 9089

U.S. Department of Labor

P. OMB Information *Paperwork Reduction Act Information Control Number 1205-0451*

Persons are not required to respond to this collection of information unless it displays a currently valid OMB control number.

Respondent's reply to these reporting requirements is required to obtain the benefits of permanent employment certification (Immigration and Nationality Act, Section 212(a)(5)). Public reporting burden for this collection of information is estimated to average 1¼ hours per response, including the time for reviewing instructions, searching existing data sources, gathering and maintaining the data needed, and completing and reviewing the collection of information. Send comments regarding this burden estimate to the Division of Foreign Labor Certification * U.S. Department of Labor * Room C4312 * 200 Constitution Ave., NW * Washington, DC * 20210.

Do NOT send the completed application to this address.

Q. Privacy Statement Information

In accordance with the Privacy Act of 1974, as amended (5 U.S.C. 552a), you are hereby notified that the information provided herein is protected under the Privacy Act. The Department of Labor (Department or DOL) maintains a System of Records titled Employer Application and Attestation File for Permanent and Temporary Alien Workers (DOL/ETA-7) that includes this record.

Under routine uses for this system of records, case files developed in processing labor certification applications, labor condition applications, or labor attestations may be released as follows: in connection with appeals of denials before the DOL Office of Administrative Law Judges and Federal courts, records may be released to the employers that filed such applications, their representatives, to named alien beneficiaries or their representatives, and to the DOL Office of Administrative Law Judges and Federal courts; and in connection with administering and enforcing immigration laws and regulations, records may be released to such agencies as the DOL Office of Inspector General, Employment Standards Administration, the Department of Homeland Security, and the Department of State.

Further relevant disclosures may be made in accordance with the Privacy Act and under the following circumstances: in connection with federal litigation; for law enforcement purposes; to authorized parent locator persons under Pub. L. 93-647; to an information source or public authority in connection with personnel, security clearance, procurement, or benefit-related matters; to a contractor or their employees, grantees or their employees, consultants, or volunteers who have been engaged to assist the agency in the performance of Federal activities; for Federal debt collection purposes; to the Office of Management and Budget in connection with its legislative review, coordination, and clearance activities; to a Member of Congress or their staff in response to an inquiry of the Congressional office made at the written request of the subject of the record; in connection with records management; and to the news media and the public when a matter under investigation becomes public knowledge, the Solicitor of Labor determines the disclosure is necessary to preserve confidence in the integrity of the Department, or the Solicitor of Labor determines that a legitimate public interest exists in the disclosure of information, unless the Solicitor of Labor determines that disclosure would constitute an unwarranted invasion of personal privacy.

ETA Form 9089 This Certification is valid from ____________ to ____________ Page 10 of

ETA Case Number:

Addendum

H. 11. Job duties

ETA Form 9089 This Certification is valid from ____________ to ____________ Page of

ETA Case Number:

Addendum

H. 14. Specific skills or other requirements

ETA Form 9089 This Certification is valid from ______________ to ______________ Page of

ETA Case Number:

Addendum

I. 5. Specify additional recruitement information in this space

ETA Form 9089 This Certification is valid from to Page of

ETA Case Number:

Addendum

K. 9. Job - Job Details

ETA Form 9089 This Certification is valid from ______________ to ______________ Page of

ETA Case Number:

Addendum

K. Alien Work Experience Continued

1. Employer name			
2. Address 1			
Address 2			
3. City	State/Province	Country	Postal code
4. Type of business		5. Job title	
6. Start date	7. End date	8. Number of hours worked per week	
9. Job details (duties performed, use of tools, machines, equipment, skills, qualifications, certifications, licenses, etc. Include the phone number of the employer and the name of the alien's supervisor.)			

1. Employer name			
2. Address 1			
Address 2			
3. City	State/Province	Country	Postal code
4. Type of business		5. Job title	
6. Start date	7. End date	8. Number of hours worked per week	
9. Job details (duties performed, use of tools, machines, equipment, skills, qualifications, certifications, licenses, etc. Include the phone number of the employer and the name of the alien's supervisor.)			

ETA Form 9089 This Certification is valid from __________ to __________ Page of

ETA Case Number:

VISA APPLICATIONS

Form DS–156 Nonimmigrant visa application

[The DS–156 is now used only for K, N, S, T, or U visas. Other nonimmigrant visa applicants use the online DS–160 Nonimmigrant Visa Application Form (an interactive form not reproducible here), which can be found at https://ceac.state.gov/genniv/.]

U.S. Department of State
NONIMMIGRANT VISA APPLICATION

Approved OMB 1405-0018
Expires 06/30/2014
Estimated Burden 1 hour
See Page 2

PLEASE TYPE OR PRINT YOUR ANSWERS IN THE SPACE PROVIDED BELOW EACH ITEM

1. Passport Number
2. Place of Issuance: City | Country | State/Province
3. Issuing Country
4. Issuance Date *(dd-mmm-yyyy)*
5. Expiration Date *(dd-mmm-yyyy)*
6. Surnames *(As in Passport)*
7. First and Middle Names *(As in Passport)*
8. Other Surnames Used *(Maiden, Religious, Professional, Aliases)*
9. Other First and Middle Names Used
10. Date of Birth *(dd-mmm-yyyy)*
11. Place of Birth: City | Country | State/Province
12. Nationality

DO NOT WRITE IN THIS SPACE
B-1/B-2 MAX B-1 MAX B-2 MAX
Other ____________ MAX
Visa Classification
Mult or ____________
Number of Applications
Months ____________
Validity
Issued/Refused
On ____________ By ____________
Under SEC. 214(b) 221(g)
Other ____________ INA
Reviewed By ____________

13. Sex ☐ Male ☐ Female
14. National Identification Number *(If Applicable)*
15. Home Address *(Include Apartment Number, Street, City, State or Province, Postal Zone and Country)*
16. Home Telephone Number | Business Phone Number | Mobile/Cell Number
Fax Number | Business Fax Number | Pager Number
17. Marital Status ☐ Married ☐ Single *(Never Married)* ☐ Widowed ☐ Divorced ☐ Separated
18. Spouse's Full Name *(Even if divorced or separated, include maiden name.)*
19. Spouse's DOB *(dd-mmm-yyyy)*
20. Name and Address of Present Employer or School
Name Address
21. Present Occupation *(If retired, write "retired". If student, write "student".)*
22. When do you intend to arrive in the U.S.? *(Provide specific date if known) (dd-mmm-yyyy)*
23. E-Mail Address
24. At what address will you stay in the U.S.?
25. Name and telephone numbers of person in U.S. who you will be staying with or visiting for tourism or business:
Name Home Phone
Business Phone Cell Phone
26. How long do you intend to stay in the U.S.?
27. What is the purpose of your trip?
28. Who will pay for your trip?
29. Have you ever been in the U.S.? ☐ Yes ☐ No
When? ____________
For how long? ____________

BARCODE

DO NOT WRITE IN THIS SPACE

50 mm x 50 mm
PHOTO
staple or glue photo here

DS-156
06-2011
PREVIOUS EDITIONS OBSOLETE
Page 1 of 2

30. Have you ever issued a U.S. visa? ☐ Yes ☐ No
When? ______
Where? ______
What type of visa? ______

31. Have you ever been refused a U.S. visa? ☐ Yes ☐ No
When? ______
Where? ______
What type of visa? ______

32. Do you intend to work in the U.S.? ☐ Yes ☐ No
(If YES, give the name and complete address of U.S. employer.)

33. Do you intend to study in the U.S.? ☐ Yes ☐ No
(If YES, give the name and complete address of the school.)

34. Names and relationships of persons traveling with you

35. Has your U.S. visa ever been cancelled or revoked?
☐ Yes ☐ No

36. Has anyone ever filed an immigrant visa petition on your behalf?
☐ Yes ☐ No If Yes, who?

37. Are any of the following persons in the U.S., or do they have U.S. legal permanent residence or U.S. citizenship?
Mark YES or NO and indicate that person's status in the U.S. (i.e., U.S. legal permanent resident, U.S. citizen, visiting, studying, working, etc.).

☐ Yes ☐ No Husband/Wife ______ ☐ Yes ☐ No Fiance/Fiancee ______ ☐ Yes ☐ No
☐ Yes ☐ No Father/Mother ______ ☐ Yes ☐ No Son/Daughter ______ Brother/Sister ______

38. **IMPORTANT: ALL APPLICANTS MUST READ AND CHECK THE APPROPRIATE BOX FOR EACH ITEM.**
A visa may not be issued to persons who are within specific categories defined by law as inadmissible to the United States (except when a waiver is obtained in advance). Is any of the following applicable to you?

- Have you ever been arrested or convicted for any offense or crime, even though subject of a pardon, amnesty or other similar legal action? Have you ever unlawfully distributed or sold a controlled substance (drug), or been a prostitute or procurer for prostitutes? ☐ Yes ☐ No
- Have you ever been refused admission to the U.S., or been the subject of a deportation hearing, or sought to obtain or assist others to obtain a visa, entry into the U.S., or any other U.S. immigration benefit by fraud or willful misrepresentation or other unlawful means? Have you attended a U.S. public elementary school on student (F) status or a public secondary school after November 30, 1996 without reimbursing the school? ☐ Yes ☐ No
- Do you seek to enter the United States to engage in export control violations, subversive or terrorist activities, or any other unlawful purpose? Are you a member or representative of a terrorist organization as currently designated by the U.S. Secretary of State? Have you ever participated in persecutions directed by the Nazi government of Germany; or have you ever participated in genocide? Have you ever participated in, ordered, or engaged in genocide, torture, or extrajudicial killings? Have you ever engaged in the recruitment of or the use of child soldiers? ☐ Yes ☐ No
- Have you ever violated the terms of a U.S. visa, or been unlawfully present in, or deported from, the United States? ☐ Yes ☐ No
- Have you ever withheld custody of a U.S. citizen child outside the United States from a person granted legal custody by a U.S. court, voted in the United States in violation of any law or regulation, or renounced U.S. citizenship for the purpose of avoiding taxation? ☐ Yes ☐ No
- Have you ever been afflicted with a communicable disease of public health significance or a dangerous physical or mental disorder, or ever been a drug abuser or addict? ☐ Yes ☐ No

While a YES answer does not automatically signify ineligibility for a visa, if you answered YES you may be required to personally appear before a consular officer.

39. Was this application prepared by another person on your behalf?
(If answer is YES, then have that person complete item 40.) ☐ Yes ☐ No

40. Application Prepared By
Name ______ Relationship to Applicant ______
Address ______
Signature of Person Preparing Form ______ Date *(dd-mmm-yyyy)* ______

41. I certify that I have read and understood all the questions set forth in this application and the answers I have furnished on this form are true and correct to the best of my knowledge and belief. I understand that any false or misleading statement may result in the permanent refusal of a visa or denial of entry into the United States. I understand that possession of a visa does not automatically entitle the bearer to enter the United States of America upon arrival at a port of entry if he or she is found inadmissible.

Applicant's Signature ______ Date *(dd-mmm-yyyy)* ______

Privacy Act and Paperwork Reduction Act Statements

INA Section 222(f) provides that visa issuance and refusal records shall be considered confidential and shall be used only for the formulation, amendment, administration, or enforcement of the immigration, nationality, and other laws of the United States. Certified copies of visa records may be made available to a court which certifies that the information contained in such records is needed in a case pending before the court.
Public reporting burden for this collection of information is estimated to average 1 hour per response, including time required for searching existing data sources, gathering the necessary data, providing the information required, and reviewing the final collection. You do not have to provide the information unless this collection displays a currently valid OMB number. Send comments on the accuracy of this estimate of the burden and recommendations for reducing it to: U.S. Department of State, A/GIS/DIR, Washington, DC 20520.

DS-156 Page 2 of 2

Form DS–230 Application for immigrant visa and alien registration

U.S. Department of State

APPLICATION FOR IMMIGRANT VISA AND ALIEN REGISTRATION

OMB APPROVAL NO. 1405-0015
EXPIRES: 06/30/2015
ESTIMATED BURDEN: 1 HOUR*
(See Page 2)

PART I - BIOGRAPHIC DATA

Instructions: Complete one copy of this form for yourself and each member of your family, regardless of age, who will immigrate with you. Please print or type your answers to all questions. Mark questions that are **Not Applicable** with **"N/A"**. If there is insufficient room on the form, answer on a separate sheet using the same numbers that appear on the form. **Attach any additional sheets to this form.**

Warning: Any false statement or concealment of a material fact may result in your permanent exclusion from the United States.
This form *(DS-230 Part I)* is the first of two parts. This part, together with Form DS-230 Part II, constitutes the complete Application for Immigrant Visa and Alien Registration.

1. Family Name | First Name | Middle Name

2. Other Names Used or Aliases *(If married woman, give maiden name)*

3. Full Name in Native Alphabet *(If Roman letters not used)*

4. Date of Birth *(mm-dd-yyyy)* | 5. Age | 6. Place of Birth *(City or Town)* *(Province)* *(Country)*

7. Nationality *(If dual national, give both.)* | 8. Gender ☐ Female ☐ Male | 9. Marital Status ☐ Single *(Never Married)* ☐ Married ☐ Widowed ☐ Divorced ☐ Separated
Including my present marriage, I have been married ______ times.

10. Permanent address in the United States where you intend to live, if known *(street address including ZIP code)*. Include the name of a person who currently lives there.
Telephone number

11. Address in the United States where you want your Permanent Resident Card *(Green Card)* mailed, if different from address in item #10 *(include the name of a person who currently lives there)*.
Telephone number

12. Present Occupation

13. Present Address *(Street Address) (City or Town) (Province) (Country)*
Telephone Number *(Home)* | Telephone Number *(Office)* | E-mail Address

14. Spouse's Maiden or Family Name | First Name | Middle Name

15. Date *(mm-dd-yyyy)* and Place of Birth of Spouse

16. Address of Spouse *(If different from your own)*

17. Spouse's Occupation

18. Date of Marriage *(mm-dd-yyyy)*

19. Father's Family Name | First Name | Middle Name

20. Father's Date of Birth *(mm-dd-yyyy)* | 21. Place of Birth | 22. Current Address | 23. If Deceased, Give Year of Death

24. Mother's Family Name at Birth | First Name | Middle Name

25. Mother's Date of Birth *(mm-dd-yyyy)* | 26. Place of Birth | 27. Current Address | 28. If Deceased, Give Year of Death

DS-230 Part I
07-2012

This Form May be Obtained Free at Consular Offices of the United States of America
Previous Editions Obsolete

Page 1 of 4

29. List Names, Dates and Places of Birth, and Addresses of **ALL** Children.

Name	Date *(mm-dd-yyyy)*	Place of Birth	Address *(If different from your own)*

30. List below all places you have lived for at least six months since reaching the age of 16, including places in your country of nationality. Begin with your present residence.

City or Town	Province	Country	From/To *(mm-yyyy)* or "Present"

31a. Person(s) named in 14 and 29 who will accompany you to the United States now.

31b. Person(s) named in 14 and 29 who will follow you to the United States at a later date.

32. List below all employment for the last ten years.

Employer	Location	Job Title	From/To *(mm-yyyy)* or "Present"

In what occupation do you intend to work in the United States? ______

33. List below all educational institutions attended.

School and Location	From/To *(mm-yyyy)*	Course of Study	Degree or Diploma

Languages spoken or read ______

Professional associations to which you belong ______

34. Previous Military Service ☐ Yes ☐ No

Branch ______ Dates of Service *(mm-dd-yyyy)* ______

Rank/Position ______ Military Speciality/Occupation ______

35. List dates of all previous visits to or residence in the United States. *(If never, write "never")* Give type of visa status, if known. Give DHS "A" number if any.

From/To *(mm-yyyy)*	Location	Type of Visa	"A" Number *(If known)*

Signature of Applicant ______ Date *(mm-dd-yyyy)* ______

Privacy Act and Paperwork Reduction Act Statements

The information asked for on this form is requested pursuant to Section 222 of the Immigration and Nationality Act. The U.S. Department of State uses the facts you provide on this form primarily to determine your classification and eligibility for a U.S. immigrant visa. Individuals who fail to submit this form or who do not provide all the requested information may be denied a U.S. immigrant visa. If you are issued an immigrant visa and are subsequently admitted to the United States as an immigrant, the Department of Homeland Security will use the information on this form to issue you a Permanent Resident Card, and, if you so indicate, the Social Security Administration will use the information to issue you a social security number and card.

*Public reporting burden for this collection of information is estimated to average 1 hour per response, including time required for searching existing data sources, gathering the necessary documentation, providing the information and/or documents required, and reviewing the final collection. You do not have to supply this information unless this collection displays a currently valid OMB control number. If you have comments on the accuracy of this burden estimate and/or recommendations for reducing it, please send them to: A/GIS/DIR, Room 2400 SA-22, U.S. Department of State, Washington, DC 20522-2202. Please do not send Visa Applications to this address. Send Visa Applications to your nearest U.S Embassy or Consulate for processing.

DS-230 Part I **Page 2 of 4**

U.S. Department of State

APPLICATION FOR IMMIGRANT VISA AND ALIEN REGISTRATION

OMB APPROVAL NO. 1405-0015
EXPIRES: 06/30/2015
ESTIMATED BURDEN: 1 HOUR*

PART II - SWORN STATEMENT

Instructions: Complete one copy of this form for yourself and each member of your family, regardless of age, who will immigrate with you. Please print or type your answers to all questions. Mark questions that are **Not Applicable** with **"N/A"**. If there is insufficient room on the form, answer on a separate sheet using the same numbers that appear on the form. Attach any additional sheets to this form. The fee should be paid in United States dollars or local currency equivalent, or by bank draft.

Warning: Any false statement or concealment of a material fact may result in your permanent exclusion from the United States. Even if you are issued an immigrant visa and are subsequently admitted to the United States, providing false information on this form could be grounds for your prosecution and/or deportation.

This form *(DS-230 Part II)*, together with Form DS-230 Part I, constitutes the complete Application for Immigrant Visa and Alien Registration.

36. Family Name | First Name | Middle Name

37. Other Names Used or Aliases *(If married woman, give maiden name)*

38. Full Name in Native Alphabet *(If Roman letters not used)*

39. Name and Address of Petitioner | Telephone number | E-mail Address

40. United States laws governing the issuance of visas require each applicant to state whether or not he or she is a member of any class of individuals excluded from admission into the United States. The excludable classes are described below in general terms. You should read carefully the following list and answer **Yes** or **No** to each category. The answers you give will assist the consular officer to reach a decision on your eligibility to receive a visa.

Except as Otherwise Provided by Law, Aliens Within the Following Classifications are Ineligible to Receive a Visa. Do Any of the Following Classes Apply to You?

a. An alien who has a communicable disease of public health significance; who has failed to present documentation of having received vaccinations in accordance with U.S. law; who has or has had a physical or mental disorder that poses or is likely to pose a threat to the safety or welfare of the alien or others; or who is a drug abuser or addict. ☐ Yes ☐ No

b. An alien convicted of, or who admits having committed, a crime involving moral turpitude or violation of any law relating to a controlled substance or who is the spouse, son or daughter of such a trafficker who knowingly has benefited from the trafficking activities in the past five years; who has been convicted of 2 or more offenses for which the aggregate sentences were 5 years or more; who is coming to the United States to engage in prostitution or commercialized vice or who has engaged in prostitution or procuring within the past 10 years; who is or has been an illicit trafficker in any controlled substance; who has committed a serious criminal offense in the United States and who has asserted immunity from prosecution; who, while serving as a foreign government official, was responsible for or directly carried out particularly severe violations of religious freedom; or whom the President has identified as a person who plays a significant role in a severe form of trafficking in persons, who otherwise has knowingly aided, abetted, assisted or colluded with such a trafficker in severe forms of trafficking in persons, or who is the spouse, son or daughter of such a trafficker who knowingly has benefited from the trafficking activities within the past five years. ☐ Yes ☐ No

c. An alien who seeks to enter the United States to engage in espionage, sabotage, export control violations, terrorist activities, the overthrow of the Government of the United States or other unlawful activity; who is a member of or affiliated with the Communist or other totalitarian party; who participated, engaged or ordered genocide, torture, or extrajudicial killings; or who is a member or representative of a terrorist organization as currently designated by the U.S. Secretary of State. ☐ Yes ☐ No

d. An alien who is likely to become a public charge. ☐ Yes ☐ No

e. An alien who seeks to enter for the purpose of performing skilled or unskilled labor who has not been certified by the Secretary of Labor; who is a graduate of a foreign medical school seeking to perform medical services who has not passed the NBME exam or its equivalent; or who is a health care worker seeking to perform such work without a certificate from the CGFNS or from an equivalent approved independent credentialing organization. ☐ Yes ☐ No

f. An alien who failed to attend a hearing on deportation or inadmissibility within the last 5 years; who seeks or has sought a visa, entry into the United States, or any immigration benefit by fraud or misrepresentation; who knowingly assisted any other alien to enter or try to enter the United States in violation of law; who, after November 30, 1996, attended in student (F) visa status a U.S. public elementary school or who attended a U.S. public secondary school without reimbursing the school; or who is subject to a civil penalty under INA 274C. ☐ Yes ☐ No

Privacy Act and Paperwork Reduction Act Statements

The information asked for on this form is requested pursuant to Section 222 of the Immigration and Nationality Act. The U.S. Department of State uses the facts you provide on this form primarily to determine your classification and eligibility for a U.S. immigrant visa. Individuals who fail to submit this form or who do not provide all the requested information may be denied a U.S. immigrant visa. If you are issued an immigrant visa and are subsequently admitted to the United States as an immigrant, the Department of Homeland Security will use the information on this form to issue you a Permanent Resident Card, and, if you so indicate, the Social Security Administration will use the information to issue you a social security number and card.

*Public reporting burden for this collection of information is estimated to average 1 hour per response, including time required for searching existing data sources, gathering the necessary documentation, providing the information and/or documents required, and reviewing the final collection. You do not have to supply this information unless this collection displays a currently valid OMB control number. If you have comments on the accuracy of this burden estimate and/or recommendations for reducing it, please send them to: A/GIS/DIR, Room 2400 SA-22, U.S. Department of State, Washington, DC 20522-2202. Please do not send Visa Applications to this address. Send Visa Applications to your nearest U.S Embassy or Consulate for processing.

DS-230 Part II **Previous Editions Obsolete** **Page 3 of 4**

g. An alien who is permanently ineligible for U.S. citizenship; or who departed the United States to evade military service in time of war. ☐ Yes ☐ No

h. An alien who was previously ordered removed within the last 5 years or ordered removed a second time within the last 20 years; who was previously unlawfully present and ordered removed within the last 10 years or ordered removed a second time within the last 20 years; who was convicted of an aggravated felony and ordered removed; who was previously unlawfully present in the United States for more than 180 days but less than one year who voluntarily departed within the last 3 years; or who was unlawfully present for more than one year or an aggregate of one year within the last 10 years. ☐ Yes ☐ No

i. An alien who is coming to the United States to practice polygamy; who withholds custody of a U.S. citizen child outside the United States from a person granted legal custody by a U.S. court or intentionally assists another person to do so; who has voted in the United States in violation of any law or regulation; or who renounced U.S. citizenship to avoid taxation. ☐ Yes ☐ No

j. An alien who is a former exchange visitor who has not fulfilled the 2-year foreign residence requirement. ☐ Yes ☐ No

k. An alien determined by the Attorney General to have knowingly made a frivolous application for asylum. ☐ Yes ☐ No

l. An alien who has ordered, carried out or materially assisted in extrajudicial and political killings and other acts of violence against the Haitian people; who has directly or indirectly assisted or supported any of the groups in Colombia known as FARC, ELN, or AUC; who through abuse of a governmental or political position has converted for personal gain, confiscated or expropriated property in Cuba, a claim to which is owned by a national of the United States, has trafficked in such property or has been complicit in such conversion, has committed similar acts in another country, or is the spouse, minor child or agent of an alien who has committed such acts; who has been directly involved in the establishment or enforcement of population controls forcing a woman to undergo an abortion against her free choice or a man or a woman to undergo sterilization against his or her free choice; or who has disclosed or trafficked in confidential U.S. business information obtained in connection with U.S. participation in the Chemical Weapons Convention or is the spouse, minor child or agent of such a person; or who has ever engaged in the recruitment of or the use of child solders. ☐ Yes ☐ No

41. Have you ever been charged, arrested or convicted of any offense or crime? *(If answer is Yes, please explain)* ☐ Yes ☐ No

42. Have you ever been refused admission to the United States at a port-of-entry? *(If answer is Yes, please explain)* ☐ Yes ☐ No

43a. Have you ever applied for a Social Security Number *(SSN)*?

☐ Yes

Give the number ____________
Would you like to receive a replacement card? (You must answer YES to question 43b. to receive a card.)

☐ Yes ☐ No

☐ No

Do you want the Social Security Administration to assign you a SSN and issue a card? (You must answer YES to question 43b. to receive a number and a card.)

☐ Yes ☐ No

43b. **Consent to Disclosure:** I authorize disclosure of information from this form to the Department of Homeland Security *(DHS)*, the Social Security Administration *(SSA)*, such other U.S. Government agencies as may be required for the purpose of assigning me an SSN and issuing me a Social Security card, and I authorize the SSA to share my SSN with the INS. ☐ Yes ☐ No

The applicant's response does not limit or restrict the Government's ability to obtain his or her SSN, or other information on this form, for enforcement or other purposes as authorized by law.

44. Were you assisted in completing this application? ☐ Yes ☐ No
(If answer is Yes, give name and address of person assisting you, indicating whether relative, friend, travel agent, attorney, or other)

DO NOT WRITE BELOW THE FOLLOWING LINE
The consular officer will assist you in answering item 45.
DO NOT SIGN this form until instructed to do so by the consular officer

45. I claim to be:

☐ A Family-Sponsored Immigrant
☐ An Employment-Based Immigrant
☐ A Diversity Immigrant
☐ A Special Category *(Specify)* ____________
(Returning resident, Hong Kong, Tibetan, Private Legislation, etc.)

☐ I derive foreign state chargeability under Sec. 202(b) through my ____________

☐ Preference ____________

☐ Numerical limitation *(foreign state)* ____________

I understand that I am required to surrender my visa to the United States Immigration Officer at the place where I apply to enter the United States, and that the possession of a visa does not entitle me to enter the United States if at that time I am found to be inadmissible under the immigration laws.

I understand that any willfully false or misleading statement or willful concealment of a material fact made by me herein may subject me to permanent exclusion from the United States and, if I am admitted to the United States, may subject me to criminal prosecution and/or deportation.

I, the undersigned applicant for a United States immigrant visa, do solemnly swear *(or affirm)* that all statements which appear in this application, consisting of Form DS-230 Part I and Part II combined, have been made by me, including the answers to items 1 through 45 inclusive, and that they are true and complete to the best of my knowledge and belief. I do further swear *(or affirm)* that, if admitted into the United States, I will not engage in activities which would be prejudicial to the public interest, or endanger the welfare, safety, or security of the United States; in activities which would be prohibited by the laws of the United States relating to espionage, sabotage, public disorder, or in other activities subversive to the national security; in any activity a purpose of which is the opposition to or the control, or overthrow of, the Government of the United States, by force, violence, or other unconstitutional means.

I understand that completion of this form by persons required by law to register with the Selective Service System *(males 18 through 25 years of age)* constitutes such registration in accordance with the Military Selective Service Act.

I understand all the foregoing statements, having asked for and obtained an explanation on every point which was not clear to me.

____
Signature of Applicant

Subscribed and sworn to before me this ______ day of ____________ ______ at: ____________

____
Consular Officer

DS-230 Part II **This Form May be Obtained Free at Consular Offices of The United States of America** **Page 4 of 4**

EMPLOYMENT

Form M–274 Handbook for employers (excerpts)

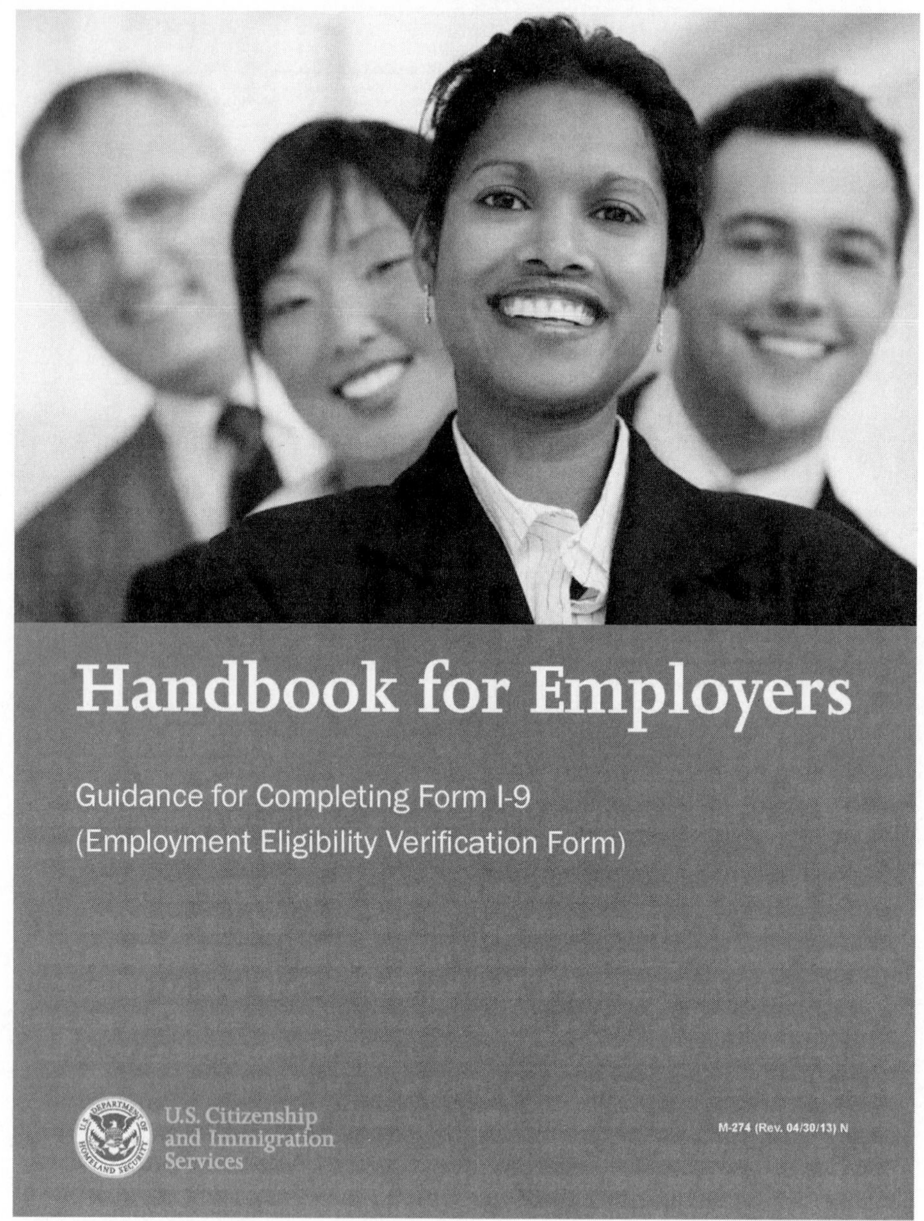

Handbook for Employers

Guidance for Completing Form I-9
(Employment Eligibility Verification Form)

U.S. Citizenship and Immigration Services

M-274 (Rev. 04/30/13) N

Part Eight
Acceptable Documents for Verifying Employment Authorization and Identity

The following documents have been designated as acceptable for Form I-9 to establish an employee's employment authorization and identity. The comprehensive Lists of Acceptable Documents can be found on the next pages of this Handbook and on the last page of Form I-9. Samples of many of the acceptable documents appear on the following pages.

To establish both identity and employment authorization, a person must present to his or her employer a document or combination of documents, if applicable, from List A, which shows both identity and employment authorization; or one document from List B, which shows only identity, and one document from List C, which shows only employment authorization.

If a person is unable to present the required document(s) within three business days of the date work for pay begins, he or she must present an acceptable receipt within that time. The person then must present the actual document when the receipt period ends. The person must have indicated on or before the time employment began, by having checked an appropriate box in Section 1, that he or she is already authorized to be employed in the United States. Receipts showing that a person has applied for an initial grant of employment authorization, or for renewal of employment authorization, are not acceptable. Receipts are also not acceptable if employment is for fewer than three business days.

The following pages show the most recent versions and representative images of some of the various acceptable documents on the list. These images can assist you in your review of the document presented to you. These pages are not, however, comprehensive. In some cases, many variations of a particular document exist and new versions may be published subsequent to the publication date of this Handbook. Keep in mind that USCIS does not expect you to be a document expert. You are expected to accept documents that reasonably appear to be genuine and to relate to the person presenting them. For a list of acceptable receipts for Form I-9, see Table 1 in Part Two.

LIST A: Documents That Establish Both Identity and Employment Authorization
All documents must be unexpired.

1. U.S. Passport or Passport Card
2. Permanent Resident Card or Alien Registration Receipt Card (Form I-551)
3. Foreign passport that contains a temporary I-551 stamp or temporary I-551 printed notation on a machine-readable immigrant visa (MRIV)
4. Employment Authorization Document (Card) that contains a photograph (Form I-766)
5. In the case of a nonimmigrant alien authorized to work for a specific employer incident to status, a foreign passport with Form I-94 or Form I-94A bearing the same name as the passport and containing an endorsement of the alien's nonimmigrant status, as long as the period of endorsement has not yet expired and the proposed employment is not in conflict with any restrictions or limitations identified on the form
6. Passport from the Federated States of Micronesia (FSM) or the Republic of the Marshall Islands (RMI) with Form I-94 or Form I-94A indicating nonimmigrant admission under the Compact of Free Association Between the United States and the FSM or RMI

LIST B: Documents That Establish Identity
All documents must be unexpired.

For individuals 18 years of age or older:

1. Driver's license or ID card issued by a state or outlying possession of the United States, provided it contains a photograph or information such as name, date of birth, gender, height, eye color, and address
2. ID card issued by federal, state, or local government agencies or entities, provided it contains a photograph or information such as name, date of birth, gender, height, eye color, and address
3. School ID card with a photograph
4. Voter's registration card
5. U.S. military card or draft record
6. Military dependent's ID card
7. U.S. Coast Guard Merchant Mariner Card
8. Native American tribal document
9. Driver's license issued by a Canadian government authority

For persons under age 18 who are unable to present a document listed above:

10. School record or report card
11. Clinic, doctor, or hospital record
12. Day-care or nursery school record

LIST C: Documents That Establish Employment Authorization
All documents must be unexpired.

1. A Social Security Account Number card unless the card includes one of the following restrictions:

   (1) NOT VALID FOR EMPLOYMENT

   (2) VALID FOR WORK ONLY WITH INS AUTHORIZATION

   (3) VALID FOR WORK ONLY WITH DHS AUTHORIZATION

   NOTE: A copy (such as a metal or plastic reproduction) is not acceptable.
2. Certification of Birth Abroad issued by the U.S. Department of State (Form FS-545)
3. Certification of Report of Birth issued by the U.S. Department of State (Form DS-1350)
4. Original or certified copy of a birth certificate issued by a state, county, municipal authority, or outlying possession of the United States bearing an official seal
5. Native American tribal document
6. U.S. Citizen Identification Card (Form I-197)
7. Identification Card for Use of Resident Citizen in the United States (Form I-179)
8. Employment authorization document issued by DHS

54

List A—Documents That Establish Both Identity and Employment Authorization

U.S. Passport

The U.S. Department of State issues the U.S. passport to U.S. citizens and noncitizen nationals. There are a small number of versions still in circulation that may differ from the main versions shown here.

The illustrations in this Handbook do not necessarily reflect the actual size of the documents.

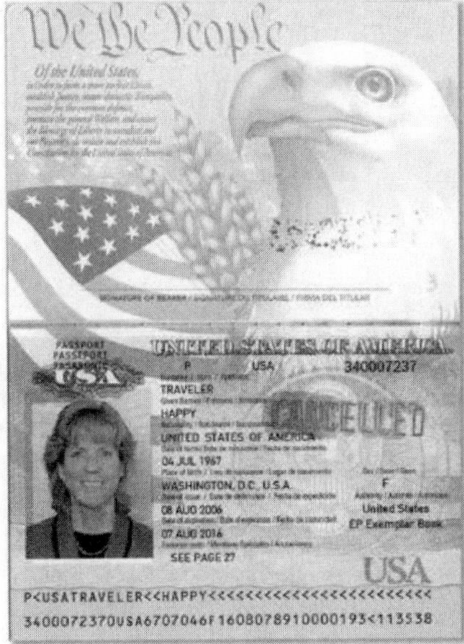

Current U.S. Passport cover and open

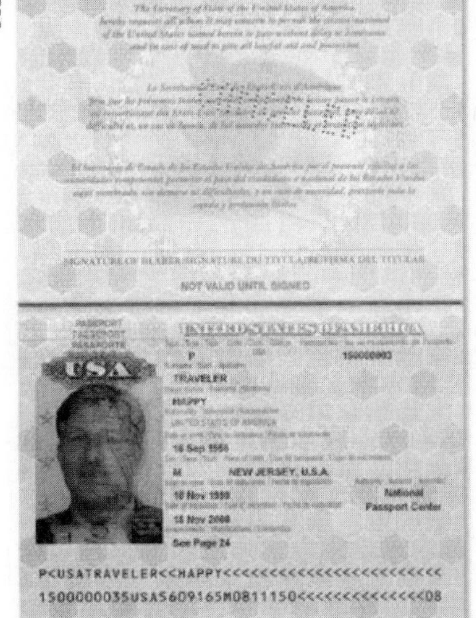

Older U.S. Passport cover and open

U.S. Passport Card

The U.S. Department of State began producing the passport card in July 2008. The passport card is a wallet-size card that can only be used for land and sea travel between the United States and Canada, Mexico, the Caribbean, and Bermuda.

Passport Card front and back

Permanent Resident Card (Form I-551)

On May 11, 2010, USCIS began issuing the newly re-designed Permanent Resident Card, also known as the Green Card, which is now green in keeping with its long-standing nickname. The card is personalized with the bearer's photo, name, USCIS number, alien registration number, date of birth, and laser-engraved fingerprint, as well as the card expiration date.

Note that on the new card, shown below, the lawful permanent resident's alien registration number, commonly known as the A number, is found under the USCIS # heading. The A number is also located on the back of the card.

Current Permanent Resident Card (Form I-551) front and back

56

This most recent older version of the Permanent Resident Card shows the DHS seal and contains a detailed hologram on the front of the card. Each card is personalized with an etching showing the bearer's photo, name, fingerprint, date of birth, alien registration number, card expiration date, and card number.

Also in circulation are older Resident Alien cards, issued by the U.S. Department of Justice, Immigration and Naturalization Service, which do not have expiration dates and are valid indefinitely. These cards are peach in color and contain the bearer's fingerprint and photograph.

PERMANENT RESIDENT CARD
NAME VOID, VOID V
A# 000-000-000
Country of Birth
El Salvador
Resident Since 01/01/80
C1USA0000000392SRC0000000000<<
2001010F8001022SLV<<<<<<<<<<<0
VOID<<VOID<<<<<<<<<<<<<<<<<<<<

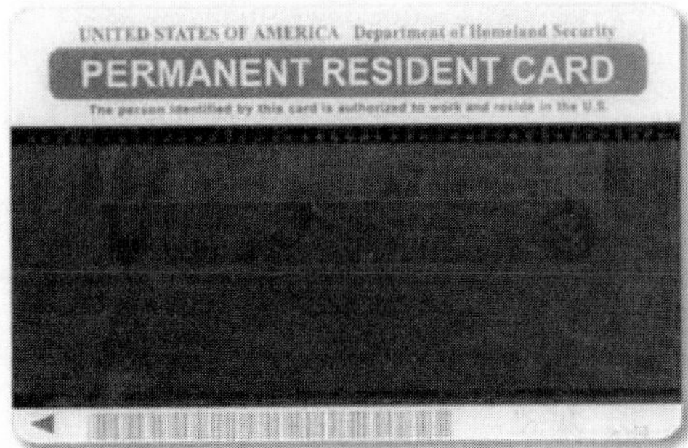

Older version Permanent Resident Card (Form I-551) front and back

---

Foreign Passport with I-551 Stamp or MRIV

Unexpired Foreign Passport with I-551 Stamp

USCIS uses either an I-551 stamp or a temporary I-551 printed notation on a machine-readable immigrant visa (MRIV) to denote temporary evidence of lawful permanent residence. Sometimes, if no foreign passport is available, USCIS will place the I-551 stamp on a Form I-94 and affix a photograph of the bearer to the form. This document is considered a receipt.

Reverify the employee in Section 3 of Form I-9 when the stamp in the passport expires, or one year after the issuance date if the stamp does not include an expiration date. For temporary I-551 receipts, at the end of the receipt validity period, the individual must present the Permanent Resident Card (Form I-551) for Section 2 of Form I-9.

The MRIV demonstrates permanent resident status for one year from the date of admission found in the foreign passport that contains the MRIV.

PROCESSED FOR I-551.
TEMPORARY EVIDENCE OF
LAWFUL ADMISSION FOR
PERMANENT RESIDENCE
VALID UNTIL___________.
EMPLOYMENT AUTHORIZED

I-551 Stamp

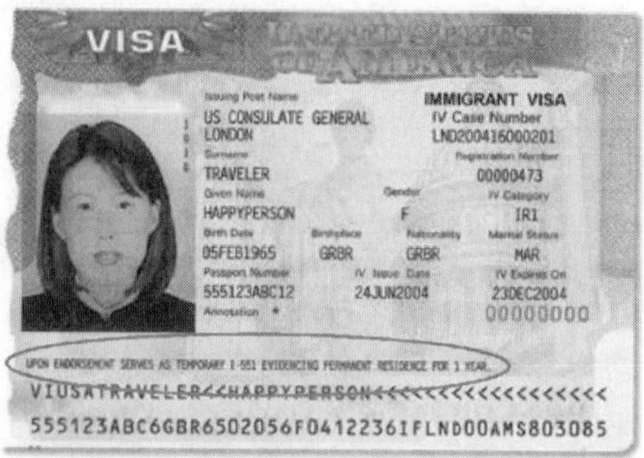

The temporary Form I-551 MRIV is evidence of permanent resident status for one year from the date of admission.

Temporary I-551 printed notation on a machine-readable immigrant visa (MRIV)

Employment Authorization Document (Form I-766)

USCIS issues the Employment Authorization Document (Form I-766) to individuals granted temporary employment authorization in the United States. The card contains the bearer's photograph, fingerprint, card number, Alien number, birth date, and signature, along with a holographic film and the DHS seal. The expiration date is located at the bottom of the card. Cards may contain one of the following notations above the expiration date: "Not Valid for Reentry to U.S.", "Valid for Reentry to U.S." or "Serves as I-512 Advance Parole."

Employment Authorization Document (Form I-766) with notation "NOT VALID FOR REENTRY TO U.S."

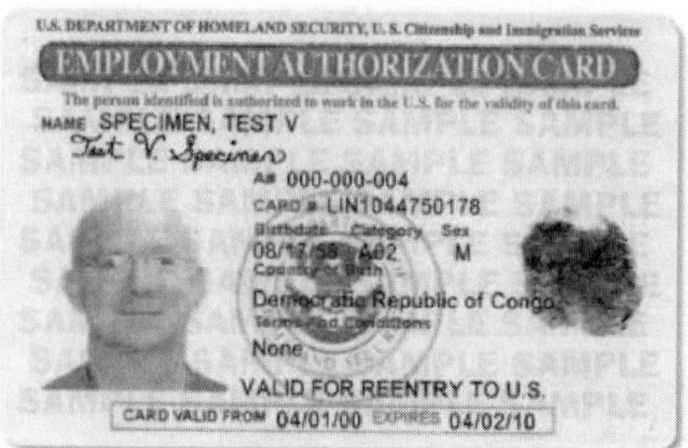

Employment Authorization Document (Form I-766) with notation "VALID FOR REENTRY TO U.S."

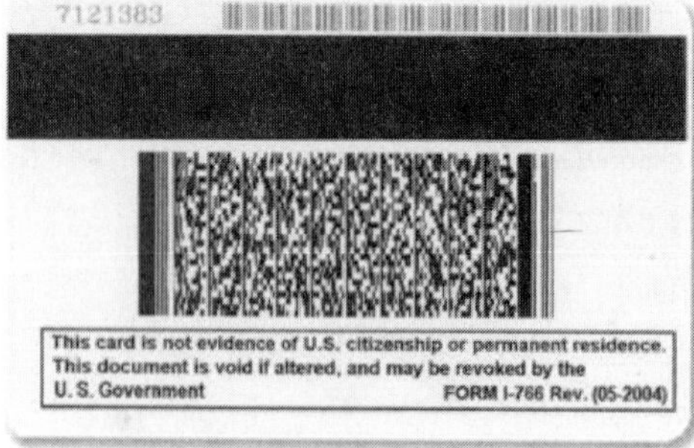

Previous back of EAD card

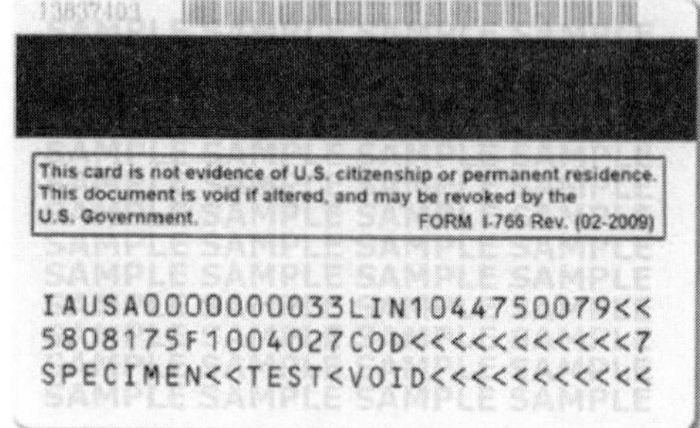

Newly redesigned back of EAD card

58

Form I-20 Accompanied by Form I-94 or Form I-94A

Form I-94 or Form I-94A for F-1 nonimmigrant students must be accompanied by a Form I-20, *Certificate of Eligibility for Nonimmigrant Students*, endorsed with employment authorization by the designated school official for off-campus employment or curricular practical training. USCIS will issue an Employment Authorization Document (Form I-766) to all students (F-1 and M-1) authorized for a post-completion OPT period.

(See Form I-94 on next page.)

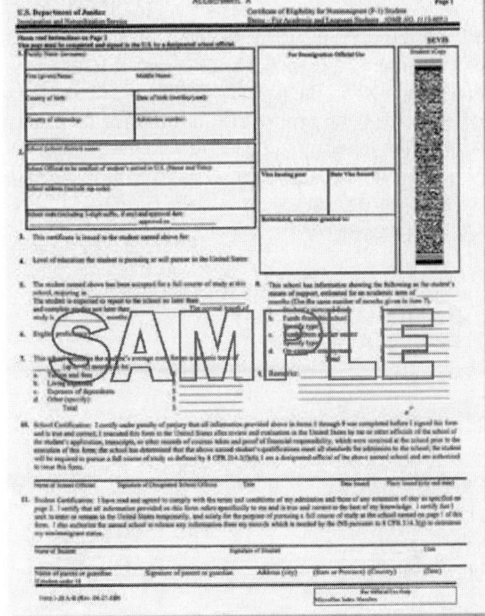

Attachment A

SAMPLE

Form I-20 Accompanied by Form I-94 or Form I-94A

Form DS-2019 Accompanied by Form I-94 or Form I-94A

Nonimmigrant exchange visitors (J-1) must have a Form I-94 or Form I-94A accompanied by an unexpired Form DS-2019, *Certificate of Eligibility for ExchangeVisitor (J-1) Status*, issued by the U.S. Department of State, that specifies the sponsor. J-1 exchange visitors working outside the program indicated on the Form DS-2019 also need a letter from their responsible officer.

(See Form I-94 on next page.)

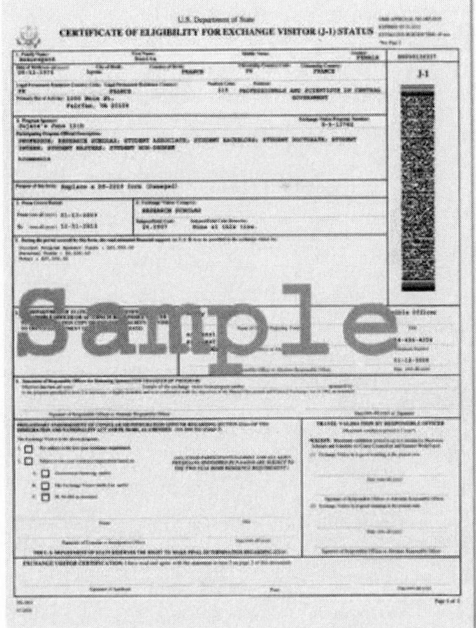

U.S. Department of State

CERTIFICATE OF ELIGIBILITY FOR EXCHANGE VISITOR (J-1) STATUS

Sample

Form DS-2019 Accompanied by Form I-94 or Form I-94A

Form I-94 or Form I-94A Arrival/Departure Record

CBP and sometimes USCIS issue arrival-departure records to nonimmigrants. This document indicates the bearer's immigration status, the date that the status was granted, and when the status expires. The immigration status notation within the stamp on the card varies according to the status granted, e.g., L-1, F-1, J-1. The Form I-94 has a handwritten date and status, and the Form I-94A has a computer-generated date and status. Both may be presented with documents that Form I-9 specifies are valid only when Form I-94 or Form I-94A also is presented, such as the foreign passport, Form DS-2019, or Form I-20.

Form I-9 provides space for you to record the document number and expiration date for both the passport and Form I-94 or Form I-94A.

Departure Number OMB No. 1651-0111

000000000 00

Sample APR 2 0 2011 F-1 D/S

I-94
Departure Record

14. Family Name
STUDENT
15. First (Given) Name
IMA
16. Birth Date (Day/Mo/Yr)
010170
17. Country of Citizenship
ANY COUNTRY

CBP Form I-94 (10/04)
See Other Side STAPLE HERE

Form I-94 Arrival/Departure Record

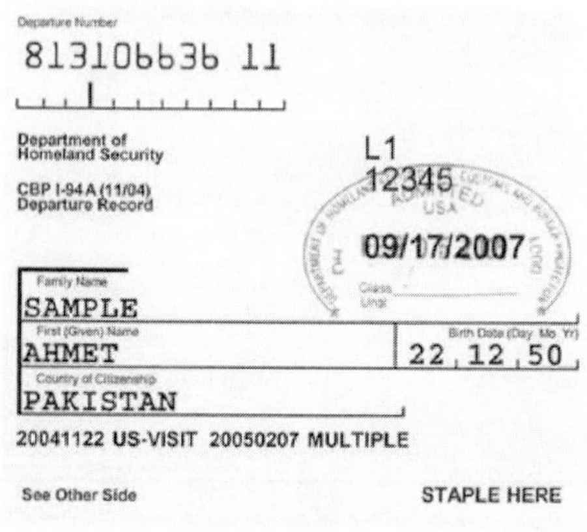

Departure Number
81310663b 11

Department of Homeland Security
CBP I-94A (11/04)
Departure Record

L1
12345
09/17/2007

Family Name
SAMPLE
First (Given) Name
AHMET
Birth Date (Day Mo Yr)
22 12 50
Country of Citizenship
PAKISTAN

20041122 US-VISIT 20050207 MULTIPLE

See Other Side STAPLE HERE

Form I-94A Arrival/Departure Record

Passports of the Federated States of Micronesia and the Republic of the Marshall Islands

In 2003, Compacts of Free Association (CFA) between the United States and the Federated States of Micronesia (FSM) and Republic of the Marshall Islands (RMI) were amended to allow citizens of these countries to work in the United States without obtaining an Employment Authorization Document (Form I-766).

For Form I-9 purposes, citizens of these countries may present FSM or RMI passports accompanied by a Form I-94 or Form I-94A indicating nonimmigrant admission under the CFA, which are acceptable documents under List A. The exact notation on Form I-94 or Form I-94A may vary and is subject to change. The notation on Form I-94 or Form I-94A typically states "CFA/FSM" for an FSM citizen and "CFA/MIS" for an RMI citizen.

Passports from the Federated States of Micronesia and the Republic of the Marshall Islands

60

List B—Documents That Establish Identity Only

State-Issued Driver's License

A driver's license can be issued by any state or territory of the United States (including the District of Columbia, Puerto Rico, the U.S. Virgin Islands, Guam, American Samoa, and the Commonwealth of the Northern Mariana Islands) or by a Canadian government authority, and is acceptable if it contains a photograph or other identifying information such as name, date of birth, gender, height,eye color, and address.

Some states may place notations on their drivers' licenses that state the card does not confirm employment authorization. For Form I-9 purposes, these drivers' licenses, along with every other state's, establish the identity of an employee. When presenting any driver's license, the employee must also present a List C document that establishes employment authorization.

State-issued drivers' licenses vary from state to state.

The illustrations below do not necessarily reflect the actual size of the documents.

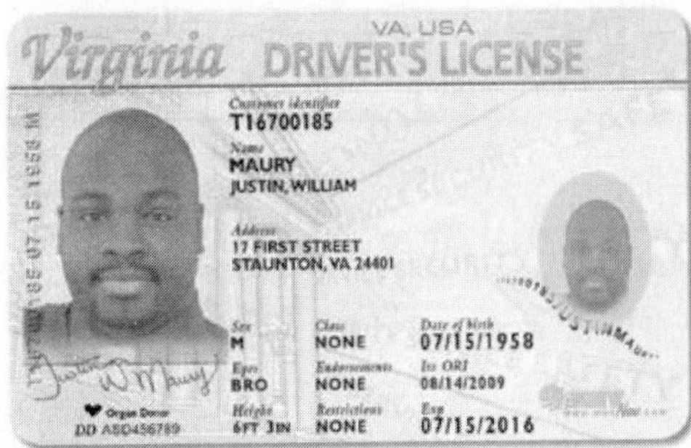

Driver's License from the Commonwealth ofVirginia

State-issued ID Card

An ID card can be issued by any state (including the District of Columbia, Puerto Rico, the U.S. Virgin Islands, Guam, American Samoa, and the Commonwealth of the Northern Mariana Islands) or by a local government, and is acceptable if it contains a photograph or other identifying information such as name, date of birth, gender, height,eye color, and address.

Some states may place notations on their ID cards that state the card does not confirm employment authorization. For Form I-9 purposes, these cards, along with every other state's, establish the identity of an employee. When presenting any state-issued ID card, the employee must also present a List C document that establishes employment authorization.

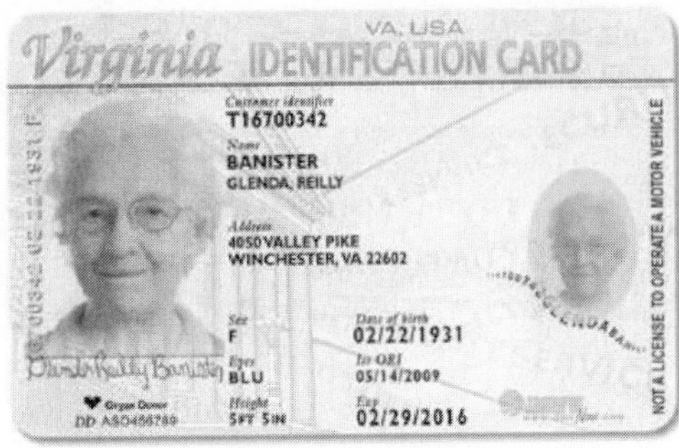

Identification card from the Commonwealth ofVirginia

List C — Documents That Establish Employment Authorization Only

The following illustrations in this Handbook do not necessarily reflect the actual size of the documents.

U.S. Social Security Account Number Card

The U.S. Social Security account number card is issued by the Social Security Administration (older versions were issued by the U.S. Department of Health and Human Services), and can be presented as a List C document unless the card specifies that it does not authorize employment in the United States. Metal or plastic reproductions are not acceptable.

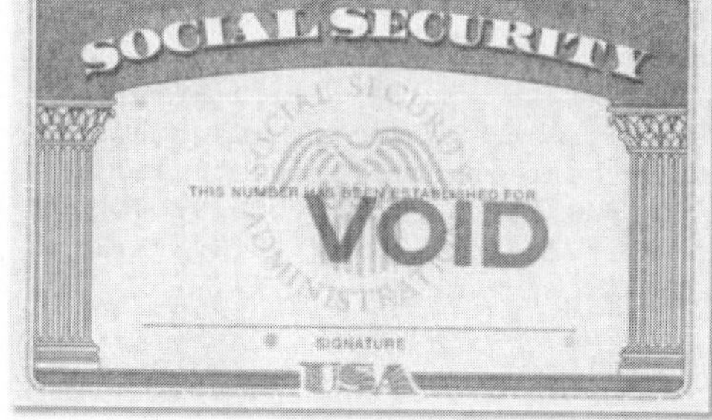

U.S. Social Security Card

Certifications of Birth Issued by the U.S. Department of State

These documents may vary in color and paper used. All will include a raised seal of the office that issued the document, and may contain a watermark and raised printing.

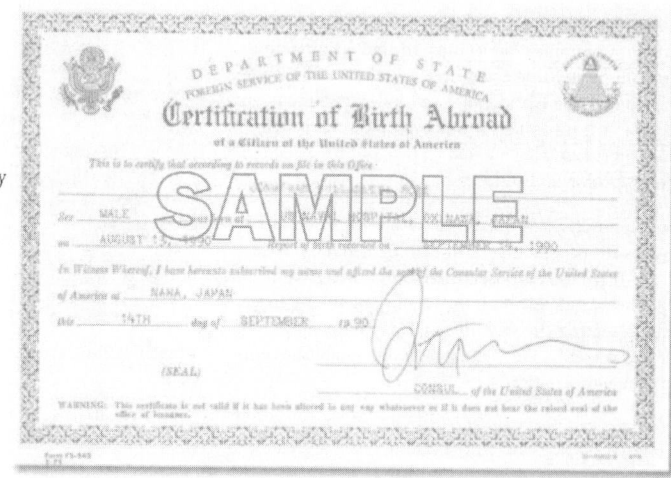

DEPARTMENT OF STATE
FOREIGN SERVICE OF THE UNITED STATES OF AMERICA

Certification of Birth Abroad
of a Citizen of the United States of America

This is to certify that according to records on file in this Office:

SAMPLE

Sex MALE ... on AUGUST 13, 1990 Report of Birth recorded on SEPTEMBER 14, 1990

In Witness Whereof, I have hereunto subscribed my name and affixed the seal of the Consular Service of the United States of America at NAHA, JAPAN this 14TH day of SEPTEMBER 19 90

(SEAL)

CONSUL of the United States of America

Certification of Birth Abroad Issued by the U.S. Department of State (FS-545)

62

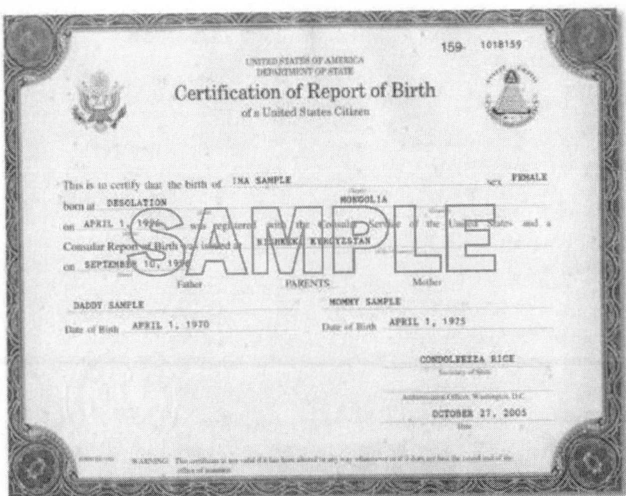

159- 1018159

UNITED STATES OF AMERICA
DEPARTMENT OF STATE

Certification of Report of Birth
of a United States Citizen

This is to certify that the birth of INA SAMPLE sex FEMALE
born at DESOLATION MONGOLIA
on APRIL 1, 199_ was registered with the Consular Service of the United States and a Consular Report of Birth was issued at BISHKEK KYRGYZSTAN
on SEPTEMBER 10, 199_

PARENTS

Father	Mother
DADDY SAMPLE	MOMMY SAMPLE
Date of Birth APRIL 1, 1970	Date of Birth APRIL 1, 1975

CONDOLEEZZA RICE
Secretary of State

Authentication Office, Washington, D.C.

OCTOBER 27, 2005
Date

SAMPLE

Certification of Report of Birth Issued by the U.S. Department of State (DS-1350)

Birth Certificate

Only an original or certified copy of a birth certificate issued by a state, county, municipal authority, or outlying possession of the United States that bears an official seal is acceptable. Versions will vary by state and year of birth.

Beginning October 31, 2010, only Puerto Rico birth certificates issued on or after July 1, 2010 are valid. Please check www.uscis.gov for guidance on the validity of Puerto Rico birth certificates for Form I-9 purposes.

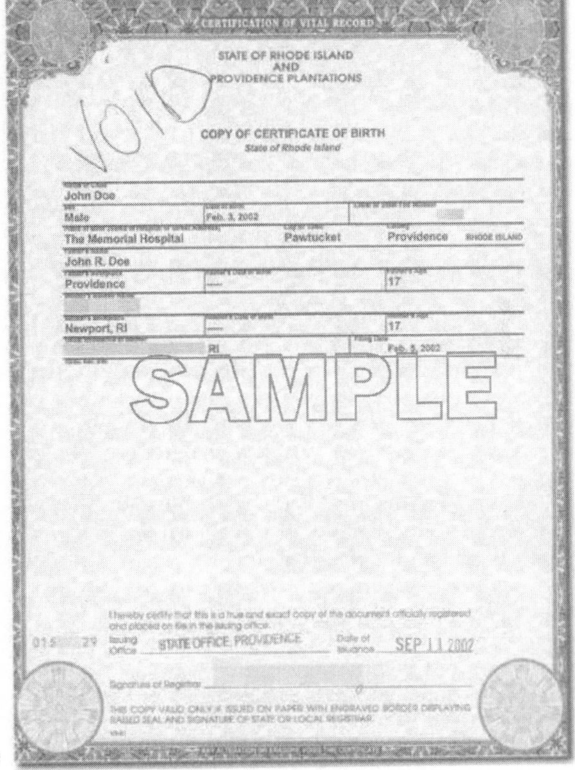

CERTIFICATION OF VITAL RECORD

STATE OF RHODE ISLAND
AND
PROVIDENCE PLANTATIONS

VOID

COPY OF CERTIFICATE OF BIRTH
State of Rhode Island

John Doe
Male | Feb. 3, 2002
The Memorial Hospital | Pawtucket | Providence | RHODE ISLAND
John R. Doe
Providence | — | 17
Newport, RI | — | 17
RI | Feb. 5, 2002

SAMPLE

I hereby certify that this is a true and exact copy of the document officially registered and placed on file in the issuing office.

015___29 Issuing Office STATE OFFICE, PROVIDENCE Date of Issuance SEP 11 2002

Signature of Registrar

THIS COPY VALID ONLY IF ISSUED ON PAPER WITH ENGRAVED BORDER DISPLAYING RAISED SEAL AND SIGNATURE OF STATE OR LOCAL REGISTRAR.

Birth Certificate

U.S. Citizen Identification Card (Form I-197)

Form I-197 was issued by the former Immigration and Naturalization Service (INS) to naturalized U.S. citizens. Although this card is no longer issued, it is valid indefinitely.

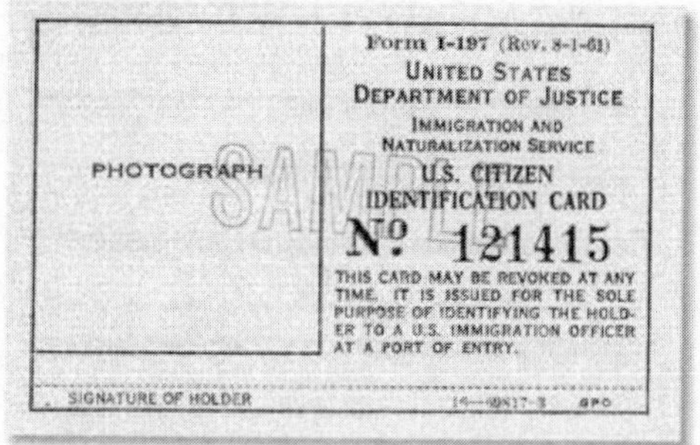

Form I-197 (Rev. 8-1-61)
UNITED STATES
DEPARTMENT OF JUSTICE
IMMIGRATION AND
NATURALIZATION SERVICE
U.S. CITIZEN
IDENTIFICATION CARD
No 121415
THIS CARD MAY BE REVOKED AT ANY TIME. IT IS ISSUED FOR THE SOLE PURPOSE OF IDENTIFYING THE HOLDER TO A U.S. IMMIGRATION OFFICER AT A PORT OF ENTRY.
PHOTOGRAPH
SIGNATURE OF HOLDER
SAMPLE

U.S. Citizen Identification Card (Form I-197)

Identification Card for Use of Resident Citizen in the United States (Form I-179)

Form I-179 was issued by INS to U.S. citizens who are residents of the United States. Although this card is no longer issued, it is valid indefinitely.

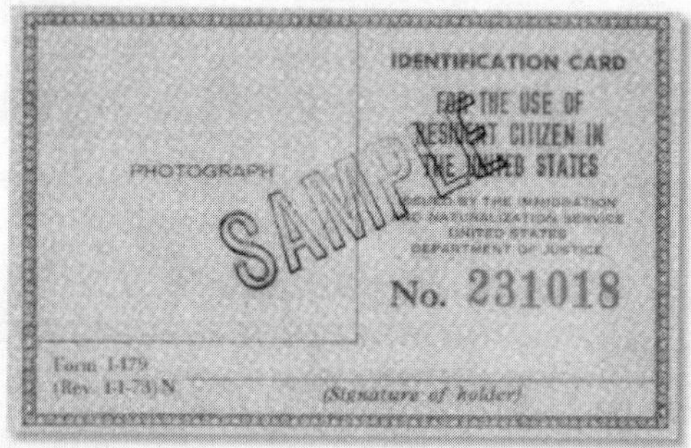

IDENTIFICATION CARD
FOR THE USE OF
RESIDENT CITIZEN IN
THE UNITED STATES
UNITED STATES
DEPARTMENT OF JUSTICE
No. 231018
PHOTOGRAPH
SAMPLE
Form I-179
(Rev. 1-1-73) N
(Signature of holder)

Identification Card for Use of Resident Citizen in the United States (Form I-179)

Form I–766 Employment authorization document (EAD) (as issued from 5/26/2010)

FRONT

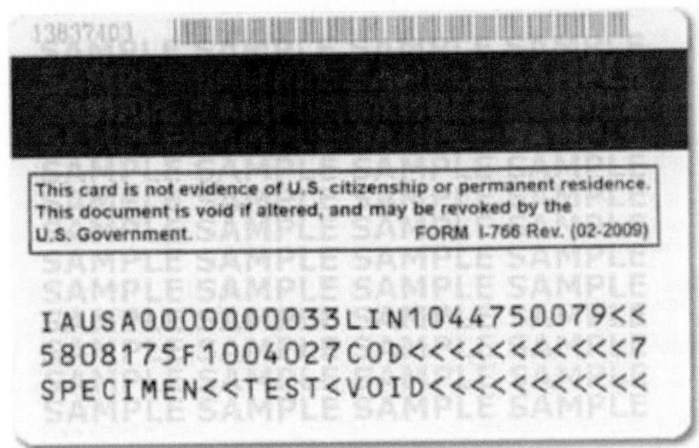

BACK

ADMINISTRATIVE REMOVAL AND REINSTATEMENT OF PRIOR ORDER

Form I-851 Notice of intent to issue a final administrative removal order

Notice of Intent to Issue a Final Administrative Removal Order

In removal proceedings under section 238(b) of the Immigration and Nationality Act

FIN #

Event No:

File Number ______________________

To: Sample Form ______________________

Address: ______________________
(Number, Street, City, State and ZIP Code)

Telephone: ______________________
(Area Code and Phone Number)

Pursuant to section 238(b) of the Immigration and Nationality Act (Act) as amended, 8 U.S.C. 1228(b), the Department of Homeland Security (Department) has determined that you are amenable to administrative removal proceedings. The determination is based on the following allegations:

1. You are not a citizen or national of the United States.
2. You are a native of ______________ and a citizen of ______________
3. You entered the United States (at)(near) ______________ on or about ______________
4. At that time you entered ______________
5. You are not lawfully admitted for permanent residence.
6. You were, on ______________, convicted in the ______________ Court ______________ for the offense of ______________ in violation of ______________ for which the term of imprisonment imposed was ______________.

Charge:
You are deportable under section 237(a)(2)(A)(iii) of the Act, 8 U.S.C. 1227(a)(2)(A)(iii), as amended, because you have been convicted of an aggravated felony as defined in section 101(a)(43)(   ) of the Act, 8 U.S.C. 1101(a)(43)(   ).

Based upon section 238(b) of the Act, 8 U.S.C. 1228(b), the Department is serving upon you this NOTICE OF INTENT TO ISSUE A FINAL ADMINISTRATIVE REMOVAL ORDER ("Notice of Intent") without a hearing before an Immigration Judge.

Your Rights and Responsibilities:
You may be represented (at no expense to the United States government) by counsel, authorized to practice in this proceeding. If you wish legal advice and cannot afford it, you may contact legal counsel from the list of available free legal services provided to you.

You must respond to the above charges in writing to the Department address provided on the other side of this form within 10 calendar days of service of this notice (or 13 calendar days if service is by mail). **The Department must RECEIVE your response within that time period.**

In your response you may: request, for good cause, an extension of time; rebut the charges stated above (with supporting evidence); request an opportunity to review the government's evidence; admit deportability; designate the country to which you choose to be removed in the event that a final order of removal is issued (which designation the Department will honor only to the extent permitted under section 241of the Act, 8 U.S.C. 1231); and/or, if you fear persecution in any specific country or countries on account of race, religion, nationality, membership in a particular social group, or political opinion or, if you fear torture in any specific country or countries, you may request withholding of removal under section 241(b)(3) of the Act, 8 U.S.C. 1231(b)(3), or withholding/deferral of removal under the Convention Against Torture and Other Cruel, Inhuman, or Degrading Treatment or Punishment (Convention Against Torture). A grant of withholding or deferral of removal would prohibit your return to a country or countries where you would be persecuted or tortured, but would not prevent your removal to a safe third country.

You have the right to remain in the United States for 14 calendar days so that you may file a petition for review of this order to the appropriate U.S. Circuit Court of Appeals as provided for in section 242 of the Act, 8 U.S.C. 1252. You may waive your right to remain in the United States for this 14-day period. If you do not file a petition for review within this 14-day period, you will still be allowed to file a petition from outside of the United States so long as that petition is filed with the appropriate U.S. Circuit Court of Appeals within 30 calendar days of the date of your final order of removal.

(Signature and Title of Issuing Officer) (City and State of Issuance) (Date and Time)

Form I-851 (Rev. 08/01/07)

Certificate of Service

I served this Notice of Intent. I have determined that the person served with this document is the individual named on the other side of the form.

(Signature and Title of Officer) (Date and Manner of Service)

☐ I explained and/or served this Notice of Intent to the alien in the ______________________ language.

(Name of interpreter) (Signature of interpreter)

Location/Employer:

I Acknowledge that I Have Received this Notice of Intent to Issue a Final Administrative Removal Order.

(Signature of Respondent) (Date and Time)

☐ The alien refused to acknowledge receipt of this document.

(Signature and Title of Officer) (Date and Time)

☐ **I Wish to Contest and/or to Request Withholding of Removal**

☐ I contest my deportability because: *(Attach any supporting documentation)*

- ☐ I am a citizen or national of the United States.
- ☐ I am a lawful permanent resident of the United States.
- ☐ I was not convicted of the criminal offense described in allegation number 6 above.
- ☐ I am attaching documents in support of my rebuttal and request for further review.

☐ I request withholding or deferral of removal to ______________________ [Name of Country or Countries]:

- ☐ Under section 241(b)(3) of the Act, 8 U.S.C. 1231(b)(3), because I fear persecution on account of my race, religion, nationality, membership in a particular social group, or political opinion in that country or those countries.
- ☐ Under the Convention Against Torture, because I fear torture in that country or those countries.

(Signature of Respondent) (Printed Name of Respondent) (Date and Time)

☐ **I Do Not Wish to Contest and/or to Request Withholding of Removal**

☐ I admit the allegations and charge in this Notice of Intent. I admit that I am deportable and acknowledge that I am not eligible for any form of relief from removal. I waive my right to rebut and contest the above charges. I do not wish to request withholding or deferral of removal. I wish to be removed to

____

☐ I understand that I have the right to remain in the United States for 14 calendar days in order to apply for judicial review. I do not wish this opportunity. I waive this right.

(Signature of Respondent) (Printed Name of Respondent) (Date and Time)

(Signature of Witness) (Printed Name of Witness) (Date and Time)

RETURN THIS FORM TO:
Department Of Homeland Security

____

____

____

ATTENTION: **The Department office at the above address must <u>RECEIVE</u> your response within 10 calendar days from the date of service of this Notice of Intent (13 calendar days if service is by mail).**

Form I-851 (Rev. 08/01/07)

Form I–851A Final administrative removal order

Final Administrative Removal Order

In removal proceedings under section 238(b) of the Immigration and Nationality Act

Event No:
FIN #
File Number ______________________
Date ______________________

To: Sample Form

Address: ______________________
(Number, Street, City, State and ZIP Code)

Telephone: ______________________
(Area Code and Phone Number)

ORDER

Based upon the allegations set forth in the Notice of Intent to Issue a Final Administrative Removal Order and evidence contained in the administrative record, I, the undersigned Deciding Officer of the Department of Homeland Security, make the following findings of fact and conclusions of law. I find that you are not a citizen or national of the United States and that you are not lawfully admitted for permanent residence. I further find that you have a final conviction for an aggravated felony as defined in section 101(a)(43)(   ) of the Immigration and Nationality Act (Act) as amended, 8 U.S.C. 1101(a)(43)(   ), and are ineligible for any relief from removal that the Secretary of Homeland Security, may grant in an exercise of discretion. I further find that the administrative record established by clear, convincing, and unequivocal evidence that you are deportable as an alien convicted of an aggravated felony pursuant to section 237(a)(2)(A)(iii) of the Act, 8 U.S.C. 1227(a)(2)(A)(iii). By the power and authority vested in the Secretary of Homeland Security, and in me as the Secretary's delegate under the laws of the United States, I find you deportable as charged and order that you be removed from the United States to:

____

or to any alternate country prescribed in section 241 of the Act.

____
(Signature of Authorized Official)

____
(Title of Official)

____
(Date and Office Location)

Certificate of Service

I served this FINAL ADMINISTRATIVE REMOVAL ORDER upon the above named individual.

____
(Date, Time, Place and Manner of Service)

____
(Signature and Title of Officer)

Form I-851A (Rev. 08/01/07)

Form I–871 Notice of intent/decision to reinstate prior order

U.S. Department of Homeland Security

Notice of Intent/Decision to Reinstate Prior Order

File No. ______________

Date: ______________

Name: ____

In accordance with section 241(a)(5) of the Immigration and Nationality Act (Act) and 8 CFR 241.8, you are hereby notified that the Secretary of Homeland Security intends to reinstate the order of ______________ (Deportation / exclusion / removal) entered against you. This intent is based on the following determinations:

1. You are an alien subject to a prior order of deportation / exclusion / removal entered on ______________ (Date) at ______________ (Location).

2. You have been identified as an alien who:

   ☐ was removed on ______________ (Date) pursuant to an order of deportation / exclusion / removal.

   ☐ departed voluntarily on ______________ (Date) pursuant to an order of deportation / exclusion / removal on or after the date on which such order took effect (i.e., who self-deported).

3. You illegally reentered the United States on or about ______________ (Date) at or near ______________ (Location)

In accordance with Section 241(a)(5) of the Act, you are removable as an alien who has illegally reentered the United States after having been previously removed or departed voluntarily while under an order of exclusion, deportation or removal and are therefore subject to removal by reinstatement of the prior order. You may contest this determination by making a written or oral statement to an immigration officer. You **do not** have a right to a hearing before an immigration judge.

The facts that formed the basis of this determination, and the existence of a right to make a written or oral statement contesting this determination, were communicated to the alien in the ______________ language.

______________ (Printed or typed name of official)

______________ (Signature of officer)

______________ (Title of officer)

Acknowledgment and Response

I ☐ do ☐ do not wish to make a statement contesting this determination.

______________ (Date)

______________ (Signature of Alien)

Decision, Order, and Officer's Certification

Having reviewed all available evidence, the administrative file and any statements made or submitted in rebuttal, I have determined that the above-named alien is subject to removal through reinstatement of the prior order, in accordance with section 241(a)(5) of the Act.

______________ (Date)

______________ (Location)

______________ (Signature of authorized deciding official)

______________ (Printed or typed name of official)

______________ (Title)

Form I-871 (Rev. 08/01/07)

EXPEDITED REMOVAL

Form I–867AB Record of sworn statement in proceedings under section 235(b)(1) of the Act

U.S. Department of Homeland Security

Record of Sworn Statement in Proceedings under Section 235(b)(1) of the Act

Office:____________________ File No:________________

Statement by:____________________________________

In the case of:____________________________________

Date of Birth:____________________ Gender (circle one): Male Female

At:____________________ Date:________________

Before:____________________________________
(Name and Title)

In the__________ language. Interpreter________________ Employed by________________

I am an officer of the United States Department of Homeland Security. I am authorized to administer the immigration laws and to take sworn statements. I want to take your sworn statement regarding your application for admission to the United States. Before I take your statement, I also want to explain your rights, and the purpose and consequences of this interview.

You do not appear to be admissible or to have the required legal papers authorizing your admission to the United States. This may result in your being denied admission and immediately returned to your home country without a hearing. If a decision is made to refuse your admission into the United States, you may be immediately removed from this country, and if so, you may be barred from reentry for a period of 5 years or longer.

This may be your only opportunity to present information to me and the Department of Homeland Security to make a decision. It is very important that you tell me the truth. If you lie or give misinformation, you may be subject to criminal or civil penalties, or barred from receiving immigration benefits or relief now or in the future.

Except as I will explain to you, you are not entitled to a hearing or review.

> U.S. law provides protection to certain persons who face persecution, harm or torture upon return to their home country. If you fear or have a concern about being removed from the United States or about being sent home, you should tell me so during this interview because you may not have another chance. You will have the opportunity to speak privately and confidentially to another officer about your fear or concern. That officer will determine if you should remain in the United States and not be removed because of that fear.

Until a decision is reached in your case, you will remain in the custody of the Department of Homeland Security.

Any statement you make may be used against you in this or any subsequent administrative proceeding.

Page 1 of 1 I-867A (08/01/07)

U.S. Department of Homeland Security

Jurat for Record of Sworn Statement in Proceedings under Section 235(b)(1) of the Act

Q: Why did you leave your home country or country of last residence?

A.

Q. Do you have any fear or concern about being returned to your home country or being removed from the United States?

A.

Q. Would you be harmed if you are returned to your home country or country of last residence?

A.

Q. Do you have any question or is there anything else you would like to add?

A.

I have read (or have had read to me) this statement, consisting of __1__ pages (including this page). I state that my answers are true and correct to the best of my knowledge and that this statement is a full, true and correct record of my interrogation on the date indicated by the above named officer of the Department of Homeland Security. I have initialed each page of this statement (and the corrections noted on page(s)__________).

Signature: ______________________________

Sworn and subscribed to before me at ____
on __________________.

____
Signature of Immigration Officer

Witnessed by:____

Page __1__ of __1__

I-867B (08/01/07)

Form M–444 Information about credible fear interview

U.S. Department of Homeland Security **Information about Credible Fear Interview**

Purpose of this notice

The purpose of this notice is to explain what will happen while you are in detention, what rights you have, and what may happen to you as a result of statements you make. It is important that you understand your rights and what will happen. **PLEASE READ THIS NOTICE CAREFULLY.**

You have been detained because the U.S. Department of Homeland Security (DHS) believes that you may not have the right to stay in the United States. You have indicated an intention to apply for asylum or a fear of persecution or return to your country. You will be interviewed by a specially-trained asylum officer to determine if you have a "credible fear of persecution." You will be detained until that interview takes place. If the DHS finds that you have a credible fear of persecution, you may or may not be released.

Right to consult with other persons

Normally, the interview will not take place sooner than 48 hours after you arrive at the detention facility. You may use this time to rest and consult with family members, friends, or other representatives. In unusual circumstances, you may be given additional time to contact someone. If you need this additional time, you should inform a DHS officer. You may request that the interview take place sooner if you are prepared to discuss your fears or claim immediately.

You may consult with a person or persons of your choosing, provided that such consultation is at no expense to the government and does not delay the process. A person of your choice can be present with you at your interview. A list of representatives who may be able to speak to you free of charge is attached to this notice. You may use the telephone while you are in detention to call a representative, friend or family member in the United States, collect or at your own expense. If you wish to call someone, you should inform an DHS officer for assistance. You also may contact the United States Office of the United Nations High Commissioner for Refugees, at (202) 296-5191 from 9:00 a.m - 5:00 p.m. (eastern standard time), Monday thru Friday.

Description of credible fear interview

The purpose of the credible fear interview is to determine whether you might be eligible to apply for asylum before an immigration judge. This interview is not your formal asylum hearing. It is only to help us determine whether there is a significant possibility that you may qualify as a refugee.

At your interview, you will have the opportunity to explain to the asylum officer why you think you should not be returned to your home country. If you want to apply for asylum in the United States, or think you will be harmed, persecuted or tortured if you return to your home country, you must show an asylum officer that you have a credible fear of being harmed or persecuted because of your race, religion, nationality, membership in a particular social group or political opinion, or that it is likely that you will be tortured.

If the officer determines that you have a credible fear or persecution or that you might face torture if you are returned to your home country, you may be eligible to remain in the United States.

It is very important that you tell the officer all the reasons why you have concerns about returning to your home country or are afraid to return to your home country. There are regulations protecting the confidentiality of asylum claims.

It is also very important that you tell the truth during your interview. Although the purpose of this interview is not to gather evidence against you, failure to tell the truth could be used against you in this or any future immigration proceeding.

Form M-444 (Rev. 08/01/07)

Need for interpreter or special consideration

If you do not speak English well or if you prefer to be interviewed in your own language, DHS will provide an interpreter for the interview. The interpreter has been told to keep the information you discuss confidential. If the interpreter is not translating correctly or you don't feel comfortable with the interpreter, you may request another interpreter. The officer will take written notes.

If you will need to tell the asylum officer information that is very personal and very difficult to talk about, you may request a female officer and female interpreter, or a male officer and male interpreter. The DHS will provide them if they are available. You will also have the opportunity to speak with the asylum officer separately from your family if you so desire.

Consequences of failure to establish credible fear and review of determination

If the asylum officer determines that you do not have a credible fear of persecution, you may request to have that decision reviewed by an immigration judge. The immigration judge's review will be in person or by telephone or video connection. The review will happen as soon as possible, to the maximum extent practicable within 24 hours, but in no case later than 7 days from the date of the asylum officer's decision. You may consult with a person or person of your choosing before the review by the immigration judge, provided it does not cause unreasonable delay. You will be given a copy of the asylum officer's record of determination to examine prior to the review by the immigration judge. If any of the information is incorrect, you should notify the immigration judge. The immigration judge may decide that you do have a credible fear and that you are eligible for a full asylum hearing before an immigration judge. If you are ordered removed, you may be barred from reentry to the United States for a period of 5 years or longer.

Interpreter Certification

I ____________________________ (name of interpreter) certify that I am fluent in both the ________________ and English languages, that I interpreted the above information from English to ______________________ completely and accurately, and that the recipient understood my interpretation.

____
Signature of interpreter

____
Date

Alien Acknowledgment of Receipt

I acknowledge that I have been given notice concerning my credible fear interview. I understand that I may consult with a person or persons of my choosing prior to the interview as long as it does not unreasonably delay the process and is at no expense to the Government.

____
Alien's signature

____
Date

Form M-444 (Rev. 08/01/07)

Form I–869 Record of negative credible fear finding and request for review by immigration judge

U. S. Department of Justice
Immigration and Naturalization Service

Record of Negative Credible Fear Finding and Request for Review by Immigration Judge

Alien File Number _ _ _ _ _ _ _ _

1. To be explained to the alien by the asylum officer:

The INS has determined that you do not have a credible fear of persecution or torture pursuant to 8 CFR 208.30 for the following reason(s):

A. You have not established a credible fear of return to your country of nationality or country of last residence because:

☐ You have not indicated that you were harmed in the past and you have not expressed fear of future harm.

☐ There is no significant possibility that you could establish in an asylum hearing that the harm you experienced and/or the harm you fear is on account of one or more of the five grounds for asylum (race, religion, nationality, political opinion, or social group).

☐ You have not indicated that you were harmed in the past, and there is no significant possibility that you could establish in an asylum hearing that the harm you fear is well founded.

AND

☐ You have not expressed a fear that you would be intentionally subjected to serious physical or mental harm in a country to which you may be removed.

☐ There is no significant possibility you could establish that the harm you fear would be inflicted by, or at the instigation of, or with the consent or acquiescence of, a government official or other person acting in an official capacity.

B. There is no significant possibility that your claim is credible because your testimony was inconsistent or lacked detail on material issues. When you were given an opportunity to explain you were unable to give a reasonable explanation about the following issues:

☐ Your testimony was internally inconsistent on material issues.

☐ Your testimony was not consistent with country conditions on material issues.

☐ Your testimony lacked reasonably sufficient detail on material issues.

Therefore, you are ordered removed from the United States. You may request that an Immigration Judge review this decision.

If you request that an Immigration Judge review this decision, you will remain in detention until an Immigration Judge reviews your case. That review could occur as long as 7 days after you receive this decision.

If you do not request that an Immigration Judge review the decision, you may be removed from the United States immediately.

2. To be completed by the alien:

☐ **Yes, I request Immigration Judge review** of the decision that I do not have a credible fear of persecution or torture.

☐ **No, I do not request Immigration Judge review** of the decision that I do not have a credible fear of persecution or torture.

____________________ Applicant's Last Name/ Family Name (Print) ____________________ Applicant's First Name (Print) ____________________ Applicant's Signature

____________________ Asylum Officer's Last Name (Print) ____________________ Asylum Officer's First Name, (Print) _ _/_ _/_ _ Date

The contents of this form were read and explained to the applicant in the ____________________ language

Interpreter used:

By telephone (list interpreter service /ID number used ____________________).

In person (I, ____________________, certify that I am fluent in both the ________________ and English languages. I interpreted the above information completely and accurately to the alien.)

____________________ Interpreter's Signature _ _/_ _/_ _ Date

Form I-869 (Rev. 3/22/99)N

Form I–863 Notice of referral to immigration judge

U.S. Department of Homeland Security | **Notice of Referral to Immigration Judge**

	Date
	A-File
Name	Country of Citizenship
Place and Manner of Arrival null	Date of Arrival

To immigration judge:

☐ 1. The above-named alien has been found inadmissible to the United States and ordered removed pursuant to section 235(b)(1) of the Immigration and Nationality Act (Act). A copy of the removal order is attached. The alien has requested asylum and/or protection under the Convention against Torture and the matter has been reviewed by an asylum officer who has concluded the alien does not have a credible fear of persecution or torture. The alien has requested a review of that determination in accordance with section 235(b)(1)(B)(iii)(III) of the Act and 8 CFR § 208.30(g).

☐ 2. The above-named alien arrived in the United States as a stowaway and has been ordered removed pursuant to section 235(a)(2) of the Act. The alien has requested asylum and/or withholding of removal under the Convention against Torture and the matter has been reviewed by an asylum officer who has concluded the alien does not have a credible fear of persecution or torture. The alien has requested a review of that determination in accordance with section 235(b)(1)(B)(iii)(III) of the Act.

☐ 3. The above-named alien arrived in the United States in the manner described below and has requested asylum and/or withholding of removal under the Convention against Torture. The matter is referred for a determination in accordance with 8 CFR § 208.2(c). Arrival category (check one):

☐ Crewmember/applicant	☐ Crewmember/refused	☐ Crewmember/landed
☐ Crewmember/violator	☐ VWP/applicant	☐ VWP/violator
☐ 235(c) order	☐ S-visa nonimmigrant	☐ Stowaway: credible fear determination attached

☐ 4. The above-named alien has been ordered removed by an immigration officer pursuant to section 235(b)(1) of the Act. A copy of the removal order is attached. In accordance with section 235(b)(1)(C) of the Act, the matter is referred for review of that order. The above-named alien claims to be (check one):

☐ a United States citizen	☐ a lawful permanent resident alien
☐ an alien granted refugee status under section 207 of the Act	☐ an alien granted asylum under section 208 of the Act.

☐ 5. The above-named alien has been ordered removed pursuant to section 238(b) of the Act, or the Department of Homeland Security (DHS) has reinstated a prior exclusion, deportation, or removal order of the above-named alien pursuant to section 241(a)(5) of the Act. A copy of the removal order and, if applicable, the notice of reinstatement, are attached. The alien has expressed fear of persecution or torture and the claim has been reviewed by an asylum officer who has concluded the alien **does not** have a reasonable fear of persecution or torture. The alien has requested a review of that determination in accordance with 8 CFR §§ 208.31(f) and (g).

☐ 6. The above-named alien has been ordered removed pursuant to section 238(b) of the Act, or the DHS has reinstated a prior exclusion, deportation, or removal order of the above-named alien pursuant to section 241(a)(5) of the Act. A copy of the removal order and, if applicable, the notice of reinstatement, are attached. The alien has expressed fear of persecution or torture and the claim has been reviewed by an asylum officer who has concluded the alien **has** a reasonable fear of persecution or torture. The matter is referred for a determination in accordance with 8 CFR § 208.31(e).

☐ 7. The Secretary of Homeland Security has determined that the release from custody of the above-named alien who is under a final order of removal would pose a special danger to the public according to the standards set in 8 CFR § 241.14(f)(1). The DHS has therefore invoked procedures to continue the alien's detention even though there is no significant likelihood that the alien will be removed from the United States in the reasonably foreseeable future. The matter is referred to the immigration judge for a review of this determination in accordance with 8 CFR § 241.14(g).

Page 1 of 2 Form I-863 (Rev. 08/01/07)

U.S. Department of Homeland Security

Notice of Referral to Immigration Judge

NOTICE TO APPLICANT

You are ordered to report for a hearing before an immigration judge for the reasons stated above. Your hearing is scheduled on

____________________ at ____________________ . You are to appear at ____________________
(Date) (Time)

____
(Complete office address)

☐ You may be represented in this proceeding, at no expense to the government, by an attorney or other individual authorized and qualified to represent persons before an Immigration Court. If you wish to be so represented, your attorney or representative should appear with you at this hearing. In the event of your release from custody, you must immediately report any change of your address to the Immigration Court on Form EOIR-33, which is provided with this notice. If you fail to appear for a scheduled hearing, a decision may be rendered in your absence.

☐ You may consult with a person or persons of your own choosing prior to your appearance in Immigration Court. Such consultation is at no expense to the government and may not unreasonably delay the process.

☐ Attached is a list of recognized organizations and attorneys that provide free legal service.

____
(Signature and title of immigration officer)

CERTIFICATE OF SERVICE

☐ The contents of this notice were read and explained to the applicant in the ____________________ language.

☐ The original of this notice was delivered to the above-named applicant by the undersigned on ________________ and the alien has been advised of communication privileges pursuant to 8 CFR 236.1(e). Delivery was made:

☐ in person ☐ by certified mail, return receipt requested ☐ by regular mail

____
(Signature and title of immigration officer)

Attachments to copy presented to immigration judge:

☐ Passport
☐ Visa
☐ Form I-94
☐ Forensic document analysis
☐ Fingerprints and photographs
☐ EOIR-33
☐ Form I-860
☐ Form I-869
☐ Form I-898
☐ Asylum officer's reasonable fear determination worksheet (I-899)
☐ Asylum officer's credible fear determination worksheet (I-870)

☐ **FOR 8 CFR 241.14(f) CASES ONLY:** Written statement including summary of the basis for the Secretary's determination to continue the alien in detention, and description of the evidence relied on in finding the alien specially dangerous (with supporting documents attached).

☐ **FOR 8 CFR 241.14(f) CASES ONLY:** Written notice advising the alien of initiation of proceedings and informing alien of procedures governing the Reasonable Cause Hearing at 8 CFR 241.14(h).

☐ Other (specify): ____

Page 2 of 2 Form I-863 (Rev. 08/01/07)

Form I–860 Notice and order of expedited removal

U.S. Department of Homeland Security

Notice and Order of Expedited Removal

DETERMINATION OF INADMISSIBILITY

File No: ______________

Date: ______________

In the Matter of: ____

Pursuant to section 235(b)(1) of the Immigration and Nationality Act (Act), (8 U.S.C. 1225(b)(1)), the Department of Homeland Security has determined that you are inadmissible to the United States under section(s) 212(a) ☐ (6)(C)(i); ☐ (6)(C)(ii); ☐ (7)(A)(i)(I); ☐ (7)(A)(i)(II); ☐ (7)(B)(i)(I); and/or ☐ (7)(B)(i)(II) of the Act, as amended, and therefore are subject to removal, in that:

______________________________ Name and title of immigration officer (Print)

______________________________ Signature of immigration officer

ORDER OF REMOVAL UNDER SECTION 235(b)(1) OF THE ACT

Based upon the determination set forth above and evidence presented during inspection or examination pursuant to section 235 of the Act, and by the authority contained in section 235(b)(1) of the Act, you are found to be inadmissible as charged and ordered removed from the United States.

______________________________ Name and title of immigration officer (Print)

______________________________ Signature of immigration officer

______________________________ Name and title of supervisor (Print)

______________________________ Signature of supervisor, if available

☐ Check here if supervisory concurrence was obtained by telephone or other means (no supervisor on duty).

CERTIFICATE OF SERVICE

I personally served the original of this notice upon the above-named person on ______________ (Date)

______________________________ Signature of immigration officer

Form I-860 (Rev. 08/01/07)

IMMIGRATION COURT

Form I–862 Notice to appear

U.S. Department of Homeland Security

Notice to Appear

In removal proceedings under section 240 of the Immigration and Nationality Act:

File No:________________

In the Matter of:

Respondent: ____ currently residing at:

____

(Number, street, city and ZIP code) (Area code and phone number)

☐ 1. You are an arriving alien.

☐ 2. You are an alien present in the United States who has not been admitted or paroled.

☐ 3. You have been admitted to the United States, but are removable for the reasons stated below.

The Department of Homeland Security alleges that you:

On the basis of the foregoing, it is charged that you are subject to removal from the United States pursuant to the following provision(s) of law:

☐ This notice is being issued after an asylum officer has found that the respondent has demonstrated a credible fear of persecution or torture.

☐ Section 235(b)(1) order was vacated pursuant to: ☐8CFR 208.30(f)(2) ☐8CFR 235.3(b)(5)(iv)

YOU ARE ORDERED to appear before an immigration judge of the United States Department of Justice at:

____

(Complete Address of Immigration Court, including Room Number, if any)

on ______________ at ____________ to show why you should not be removed from the United States based on the

(Date) *(Time)*

charge(s) set forth above. ____________________________________

(Signature and Title of Issuing Officer)

Date: ______________ ____________________________________

(City and State)

See reverse for Important Information

Form I-862 (Rev. 08/01/07)

Notice to Respondent

Warning: Any statement you make may be used against you in removal proceedings.

Alien Registration: This copy of the Notice to Appear served upon you is evidence of your alien registration while you are under removal proceedings. You are required to carry it with you at all times.

Representation: If you so choose, you may be represented in this proceeding, at no expense to the Government, by an attorney or other individual authorized and qualified to represent persons before the Executive Office for Immigration Review, pursuant to 8 CFR 3.16. Unless you so request, no hearing will be scheduled earlier than ten days from the date of this notice, to allow you sufficient time to secure counsel. A list of qualified attorneys and organizations who may be available to represent you at no cost will be provided with this notice.

Conduct of the hearing: At the time of your hearing, you should bring with you any affidavits or other documents, which you desire to have considered in connection with your case. If you wish to have the testimony of any witnesses considered, you should arrange to have such witnesses present at the hearing.

At your hearing you will be given the opportunity to admit or deny any or all of the allegations in the Notice to Appear and that you are inadmissible or removable on the charges contained in the Notice to Appear. You will have an opportunity to present evidence on your own behalf, to examine any evidence presented by the Government, to object, on proper legal grounds, to the receipt of evidence and to cross examine any witnesses presented by the Government. At the conclusion of your hearing, you have a right to appeal an adverse decision by the immigration judge.

You will be advised by the immigration judge before whom you appear of any relief from removal for which you may appear eligible including the privilege of departure voluntarily. You will be given a reasonable opportunity to make any such application to the immigration judge.

Failure to appear: You are required to provide the DHS, in writing, with your full mailing address and telephone number. You must notify the Immigration Court immediately by using Form EOIR-33 whenever you change your address or telephone number during the course of this preceeding. You will be provided with a copy of this form. Notices of hearing will be mailed to this address. If you do not submit Form EOIR-33 and do not otherwise provide an address at which you may be reached during proceedings, then the Government shall not be required to provide you with written notice of your hearing. If you fail to attend the hearing at the time and place designated on this notice, or any date and time later directed by the Immigration Court, a removal order may be made by the immigration judge in your absence, and you may be arrested and detained by the DHS.

Mandatory Duty to Surrender for Removal: If you become subject to a final order of removal, you must surrender for removal to one of the offices listed in 8 CFR 241.16(a). Specific addresses on locations for surrender can be obtained from your local DHS office or over the internet at http://www.ice.gov/about/dro/contact.htm. You must surrender within 30 days from the date the order becomes administratively final, unless you obtain an order from a Federal court, immigration court, or the Board of Immigration Appeals staying execution of the removal order. Immigration regulations at 8 CFR 241.1 define when the removal order becomes administratively final. If you are granted voluntary departure and fail to depart the United States as required, fail to post a bond in connection with voluntary departure, or fail to comply with any other condition or term in connection with voluntary departure, you must surrender for removal on the next business day thereafter. If you do not surrender for removal as required, you will be ineligible for all forms of discretionary relief for as long as you remain in the United States and for ten years after departure or removal. This means you will be ineligible for asylum, cancellation of removal, voluntary departure, adjustment of status, change of nonimmigrant status, registry, and related waivers for this period. If you do not surrender for removal as required, you may also be criminally prosecuted under section 243 of the Act.

Request for Prompt Hearing

To expedite a determination in my case, I request an immediate hearing. I waive my right to a 10-day period prior to appearing before an immigration judge.

Before: ______________________
(Signature of Respondent)

Date: ______________

____
(Signature and Title of Immigration Officer)

Certificate of Service

This Notice To Appear was served on the respondent by me on ______________, in the following manner and in compliance with section 239(a)(1)(F) of the Act.

☐ in person ☐ by certified mail, returned receipt requested ☐ by regular mail

☐ Attached is a credible fear worksheet.

☐ Attached is a list of organization and attorneys which provide free legal services.

The alien was provided oral notice in the ______________ language of the time and place of his or her hearing and of the consequences of failure to appear as provided in section 240(b)(7) of the Act.

______________________ (Signature of Respondent if Personally Served)

______________________ (Signature and Title of officer)

Form I-862 Page 2 (Rev. 08/01/07)

Form EOIR–42A Application for cancellation of removal for certain permanent residents

OMB#1125-0001

U.S. Department of Justice
Executive Office for Immigration Review

Application for Cancellation of Removal for Certain Permanent Residents

ADVICE TO APPLICANT

PLEASE READ CAREFULLY. FEES WILL NOT BE RETURNED.

I. **Permanent Resident Aliens Eligible for Cancellation of Removal:** You may be eligible to have your removal cancelled under section 240A(a) of the Immigration and Nationality Act (INA). To qualify for this benefit, you must establish in a hearing before an Immigration Judge that:

A. You have been a permanent resident for at least five (5) years;

B. Prior to service of the Notice to Appear, or prior to committing a criminal or related offense referred to in sections 212(a)(2) and 237(a)(2) of the INA, or prior to committing a security or related offense referred to in section 237(a)(4) of the INA;

-- you have at least seven (7)years continuous residence in the United States after having been lawfully admitted in any status; and

C. You have not been convicted of an aggravated felony.

NOTE: If you have served on active duty in the Armed Forces of the United States for at least 24 months, you do not have to meet the requirements of continuous residence in the United States. You must, however, have been in the United States when you entered the Armed Forces. If you are no longer in the Armed Forces, you must have been separated under honorable conditions.

II. **Permanent Resident Aliens NOT Eligible for Cancellation of Removal:** You are not eligible to have your removal cancelled under section 240A(a) of the INA if you:

A. Entered the United States as a crewman after June 30, 1964;

B. Were admitted to the United States as, or later became, a nonimmigrant exchange alien as defined in section 101(a)(15)(J) of the INA in order to receive a graduate medical education or training, regardless of whether you are subject to or have fulfilled the 2-year foreign residence requirement of section 212(e) of the INA;

C. Were admitted to the United States as, or later became, a nonimmigrant exchange alien as defined in section 101(a)(15)(J) of the INA, other than to receive graduate medical education or training, and are subject to the 2-year foreign residence requirement of section 212(e) of the INA but have neither fulfilled nor obtained a waiver of that requirement;

D. Are an alien who is either inadmissible under section 212(a)(3) of the INA or deportable under section 237(a)(4) of the INA;

E. Are an alien who ordered, incited, assisted, or otherwise participated in the persecution of an individual because of the individual's race, religion, nationality, membership in a particular social group, or political opinion; or

F. Are an alien who was previously granted relief under section 212(c) of the INA, or section 244(a) of the INA as such sections were in effect prior to the enactment of the Illegal Immigration Reform and Immigrant Responsibility Act of 1996, or whose removal has previously been cancelled under section 240A of the INA.

Form EOIR-42A
Revised October 2013

OMB#1125-0001

U.S. Department of Justice
Executive Office for Immigration Review

Application for Cancellation of Removal for Certain Permanent Residents

III. How Permanent Resident Aliens Can Apply for Cancellation of Removal

If you believe that you have met all the requirements for cancellation of removal, you must answer all the questions on the attached Form EOIR-42A fully and accurately. You must pay the filing and biometrics fees and comply with the Department of Homeland Security (DHS) instructions for providing biometric and biographic information to USCIS [available at http://uscis.gov]. You must also serve a copy of your application on the Assistant Chief Counsel for the DHS, U.S. Immigration and Customs Enforcement (ICE) as required in the proof of service on page 7 of this application, and you must file your application with the appropriate Immigration Court. Please read the following instructions carefully before completing your application.

Form EOIR-42A
Revised October 2013

OMB#1125-0001

U.S. Department of Justice
Executive Office for Immigration Review

Application for Cancellation of Removal for Certain Permanent Residents

INSTRUCTIONS

1. PREPARATION OF APPLICATION.

To apply for cancellation of removal as a permanent resident alien under section 240A(a) of the Immigration and Nationality Act (INA), you must fully and accurately answer all questions on the attached Form EOIR-42A. You must also comply with all of the instructions on this form. These instructions have the force of law. A separate application must be prepared and executed for each person applying for cancellation of removal. An application on behalf of an alien who is mentally incompetent or is a child under 14 years of age shall be executed by a parent or guardian.

Your responses must be typed or printed legibly in ink. Do not leave any questions unanswered or blank. If any questions do not apply to you, write "none" or "not applicable" in the appropriate space.

To the extent possible, answer all questions directly on the form. If there is insufficient room to respond fully to a question, please continue your response on an additional sheet of paper. Please indicate the number of the question being answered next to your response on the additional sheet, write your alien registration number, print your name, and sign, date, and securely attach each additional sheet to the Form EOIR-42A.

2. BURDEN OF PROOF.

The burden of proof is on you to prove that you meet all of the statutory requirements for cancellation of removal for certain permanent resident aliens under section 240A(a) of the INA and that you are entitled to such relief as a matter of discretion. To meet this burden, your responses to the questions on the application should be as detailed and complete as possible. You should also attach to your application any documents that demonstrate your eligibility for relief (see "SUPPORTING DOCUMENTS" below).

3. SUPPORTING DOCUMENTS.

You should submit documentary evidence to show both that you have been a permanent resident alien for at least five (5) years, and that you have seven (7) years of continuous residence in the United States after having been lawfully admitted in any status. This evidence may include, but is not limited to, immigration stamps in passports, DHS Form I-94, leases, deeds, receipts, letters, church records, school records, employment records, and tax payment records.

The original of all supporting documents must be available for inspection at the hearing. If you wish to have the original documents returned to you, you should also present reproductions.

4. REQUIRED BIOMETRIC AND BIOGRAPHIC INFORMATION.

Each applicant 14 years of age or older must also comply with the requirement to supply biometric and biographic information. You will be given instructions on how to complete this requirement. You will be notified in writing of the location of the Application Support Center (ASC) or the designated Law Enforcement Agency where you must go to provide biometric and biographic information. You will also be given a date and time for the appointment. It is important to furnish all the required information. Failure to comply with this requirement may result in a delay in your appointment or in your application being deemed abandoned and dismissed by the Immigration Court.

5. TRANSLATIONS.

Any document in a foreign language must be accompanied by an English language translation and a certificate signed by the translator stating that he/she is competent to translate the document and that the translation is true and accurate to the best of the translator's abilities. Such certification must be printed legibly or typed.

Form EOIR-42A
Revised October 2013

OMB#1125-0001

U.S. Department of Justice
Executive Office for Immigration Review

Application for Cancellation of Removal for Certain Permanent Residents

6. FEES.

Before you file your Form EOIR-42A with the Immigration Court, you must pay the required $100 filing fee and the biometrics fee to the Department of Homeland Security (DHS). Evidence of payment of these fees in the form of a copy of the DHS, U.S. Citizenship and Immigration Services (USCIS) ASC notice of fee receipt and biometrics appointment instructions must accompany your Form EOIR-42A. These fees will not be refunded, regardless of the action taken on your application. Therefore, it is important that you read the advice, instructions, and application carefully before responding. **If you are unable to pay the filing fee, you may ask the Immigration Judge to permit you to file your Form EOIR-42A without fee (fee waiver).**

DO NOT SEND CASH. All fees must be submitted in the exact amount. Remittance may be made by personal check, cashier's check, certified bank check, bank international money order, or foreign draft drawn on a financial institution in the United States and payable to the "Department of Homeland Security" in United States currency. If the applicant resides in the Virgin Islands, the check or money order must be payable to the "Commissioner of Finance of the Virgin Islands." If the applicant resides in Guam, the check or money order must be made payable to the "Treasurer, Guam." Personal checks are accepted subject to collectibility. An uncollectible check will render the application and any documents issued pursuant thereto invalid. A charge of $30.00 will be imposed if a check in payment of a fee is not honored by the bank on which it is drawn. When the check is drawn on an account of a person other than the applicant, the name and alien registration number of the applicant must be entered on the face of the check. All checks must be drawn on a bank located in the United States.

7. SERVING & FILING YOUR APPLICATION.

A. You must first comply with the DHS instructions for providing biometric and biographic information to USCIS, which involves sending a copy of the application to the appropriate USCIS Service Center. The DHS instructions also address payment of the application fees.

B. You must then serve the following documents on the Assistant Chief Counsel for DHS, U.S. Immigration and Customs Enforcement (ICE):

- a copy of your Form EOIR-42A, Application for Cancellation of Removal, with all supporting documents and additional sheets;
- a copy of the USCIS ASC notice of fee receipt and biometrics appointment instructions; and
- the original Biographical Information Form G-325A.

You must file the following documents with the appropriate Immigration Court:

- the original Form EOIR-42A with all supporting documents and additional sheets;
- a copy of the USCIS ASC notice of fee receipt and biometrics appointment instructions;
- a copy of the Biographical Information Form G-325A; and
- a completed certificate showing service of these documents (See Part 10 of the Application on page 7) on the ICE Assistant Chief Counsel, unless service is made on the record at the hearing.

Retain your USCIS ASC biometrics confirmation document or a copy of your Fingerprint Card, FD-258, if applicable, as proof that your biometrics were taken, and bring it to your future Immigration Court hearings.

8. PENALTIES.

You must answer all questions on Form EOIR-42A truthfully and submit only genuine documents in support of your application. **You will be required to swear or affirm that the contents of your application and the supporting documents are true to the best of your knowledge.** Your answer to the questions on this form and the supporting documents you present will be used to determine whether your removal should be cancelled and whether you should be permitted to retain your permanent resident status. Any answer you give and any supporting document you present may also be used as evidence in any proceeding to determine your right to be admitted or readmitted, re-enter, pass through, or reside in the United States. Your application may be denied if any of your answers or supporting documents are found to be false.

Form EOIR-42A
Revised October 2013

OMB#1125-0001

U.S. Department of Justice
Executive Office for Immigration Review

Application for Cancellation of Removal for Certain Permanent Residents

Presenting false answers or false documents may also subject you to criminal prosecution under 18 U.S.C. section 1546 and/or subject you to civil penalties under 8 U.S.C. section 1324c if you submit your application knowing that the application, or any supporting document, contains any false statement with respect to a material fact, or if you swear or affirm that the contents of your application and the supporting documents are true, knowing that the application or any supporting documents contain any false statement with respect to a material fact. If convicted, you could be fined up to $250,000, imprisoned for up to ten (10) years, or both. 18 U.S.C. sections 1546(a), 3559(a)(4), 3571(b)(3). If it is determined you have violated the prohibition against document fraud and a final order is entered against you, you could be subject to a civil penalty up to $2,000 for each document used or created for the first offense, and up to $5,000 for any second, or subsequent offense. In addition, if you are the subject of a final order for violating 8 U.S.C. section 1324c, relating to civil penalties for document fraud, you will be removable from the United States.

9. PAPERWORK REDUCTION ACT NOTICE.

Under the Paperwork Reduction Act, a person is not required to respond to a collection of information unless it displays a currently valid OMB control number. We try to create forms and instructions that are accurate, can easily be understood, and which impose the least possible burden on you to provide us with information. Often, this process is difficult because some immigration laws are very complex. The reporting burden for this collection of information is computed as follows: (1) learning about the form, 50 minutes, (2) completing the form, 2 hours, and (3) assembling and filing the form, 3 hours, for an average of 5 hours, 50 minutes per application. If you have comments regarding the accuracy of this burden estimate, or any other aspect of this collection of information, including suggestions for reducing this burden, you may write to the U.S. Department of Justice, Executive Office for Immigration Review, Office of the General Counsel, 5107 Leesburg Pike, Suite 2600, Falls Church, Virginia 20530.

Form EOIR-42A
Revised October 2013

U.S. Department of Justice
Executive Office for Immigration Review

OMB#1125-0001

Application for Cancellation of Removal for Certain Permanent Residents

PLEASE READ ADVICE AND INSTRUCTIONS BEFORE FILLING IN FORM

PLEASE TYPE OR PRINT

Fee Stamp (Official Use Only)

PART 1 - INFORMATION ABOUT YOURSELF

1) My present true name is: *(Last, First, Middle)*

2) Alien Registration (or "A") Number(s):

3) My name given at birth was: *(Last, First, Middle)*

4) Birth Place: *(City and Country)*

5) Date of Birth: *(Month, Day, Year)*

6) Gender: ❑ Male ❑ Female

7) Height:

8) Hair Color:

9) Eye Color:

10) Current Nationality and Citizenship:

11) Social Security Number:

12) Home Phone Number: (   )

13) Work Phone Number: (   )

14) I currently reside at:

Apt. number and/or in care of

Number and Street

City or Town *State* *Zip Code*

15) I have been known by these additional name(s):

16) I have resided in the following locations in the United States: (List PRESENT ADDRESS FIRST, and work back in time for at least 7 years.)

Street and Number - Apt. or Room # - City or Town - State - Zip Code	Resided From: *(Month, Day, Year)*	Resided To: *(Month, Day, Year)*
		PRESENT

PART 2 - INFORMATION ABOUT THIS APPLICATION

17) I, the undersigned, hereby request that my removal be cancelled under the provisions of section 240A(a) of the Immigration and Nationality Act (INA). I believe that I am eligible for this relief because I have been a lawful permanent resident alien for 5 or more years, have 7 years of continuous residence in the United States, and have not been convicted of an aggravated felony. I was admitted as or adjusted to the status of an alien lawfully admitted for permanent residence on ____________ *(Date)*

at ____________________________________ . *(Place)*

Please continue answers on a separate sheet as needed.

(1)

Form EOIR-42A
Revised October 2013

PART 3 - INFORMATION ABOUT YOUR PRESENCE IN THE UNITED STATES

18) My first arrival into the United States was under the name of: *(Last, First, Middle)*	19) My first arrival to the United States was on: *(Month, Day, Year)*

20) Place or port of first arrival: *(Place or Port, City, and State)*

21) I: ❑ was inspected and admitted.
☐ I entered using my Lawful Permanent Resident card which is valid until ____________ *(Month, Day, Year)*.
☐ I entered using a ____________ *(Specify Type of Visa)* visa which is valid until ____________ *(Month, Day, Year)*.
❑ was not inspected and admitted.
☐ I entered without documents. Explain: ____________.
☐ I entered without inspection. Explain: ____________.
❑ Other. Explain: ____________.

22) I applied on ____________ *(Month, Day, Year)* for additional time to stay and it was ❑ granted on ____________ *(Month, Day, Year)* and valid until ____________ *(Month, Day, Year)*, or ❑ denied on ____________ *(Month, Day, Year)*.

23) Since the date of my first entry, I departed from and returned to the United States at the following places and on the following dates:
(Please list all departures regardless of how briefly you were absent from the United States.)
If you have never departed from the United States since your original date of entry, please mark an X in this box: ☐

1	Port of Departure *(Place or Port, City and State)*	Departure Date *(Month, Day, Year)*	Purpose of Travel	Destination
	Port of Return *(Place or Port, City and State)*	Return Date *(Month, Day, Year)*	Manner of Return	Inspected and Admitted? ❑ Yes ❑ No
2	Port of Departure *(Place or Port, City and State)*	Departure Date *(Month, Day, Year)*	Purpose of Travel	Destination
	Port of Return *(Place or Port, City and State)*	Return Date *(Month, Day, Year)*	Manner of Return	Inspected and Admitted? ❑ Yes ❑ No

24) Have you ever departed the United States: a) under an order of deportation, exclusion, or removal?................................ ❑ Yes ❑ No
b) pursuant to a grant of voluntary departure?.. ❑ Yes ❑ No

PART 4 - INFORMATION ABOUT YOUR MARITAL STATUS AND SPOUSE *(Continued on page 3)*

25) I am not married: ❑ I am married: ❑	26) If married, the name of my spouse is: *(Last, First, Middle)*	27) My spouse's name before marriage was:

28) The marriage took place in: *(City and Country)*	29) Date of marriage: *(Month, Day, Year)*
30) My spouse currently resides at: *Apt. number and/or in care of* / *Number and Street* / *City or Town* *State/Country* *Zip Code*	31) Place and date of birth of my spouse: *(City & Country; Month, Day, Year)* 32) My spouse is a citizen of: *(Country)*

33) If your spouse is other than a native born United States citizen, answer the following:
He/she arrived in the United States at: *(Place or Port, City and State)* ____________.
He/she arrived in the United States on: *(Month, Day, Year)* ____________.
His/her alien registration number(s) is: A# ____________.
He/she was naturalized on: *(Month, Day, Year)* ____________ at ____________ *(City and State)*.

34) My spouse ❑ - is ❑ - is not employed. If employed, please give salary and the name and address of the place(s) of employment.

Full Name and Address of Employer	Earnings Per Week *(Approximate)*
	$
	$
	$

Please continue answers on a separate sheet as needed.

(2)

Form EOIR-42A
Revised October 2013

PART 4 - INFORMATION ABOUT YOUR MARITAL STATUS AND SPOUSE *(Continued)*

35) I ❑ - have ❑ - have not been previously married: *(If previously married, list the name of each prior spouse, the dates on which each marriage began and ended, the place where the marriage terminated, and describe how each marriage ended.)*

Name of prior spouse: *(Last, First, Middle)*	Date marriage began: Date marriage ended:	Place marriage ended: *(City and Country)*	Description or manner of how marriage was terminated or ended:

Name of prior spouse: *(Last, First, Middle)*	Date marriage began: Date marriage ended:	Place marriage ended: *(City and Country)*	Description or manner of how marriage was terminated or ended:

36) Have you been ordered by any court, or are otherwise under any legal obligation, to provide child support and/or spousal maintenance as a result of a separation and/or divorce? ❑ - Yes ❑ - No

PART 5 - INFORMATION ABOUT YOUR EMPLOYMENT AND FINANCIAL STATUS

37) Since my arrival into the United States, I have been employed by the following named persons or firms: *(Please begin with present employment and work back in time. Any periods of unemployment or school attendance should be specified. Attach a separate sheet for additional entries if necessary.)*

Full Name and Address of Employer	Earnings Per Week *(Approximate)*	Type of Work Performed	Employed From: *(Month, Day, Year)*	Employed To: *(Month, Day, Year)*
	$			PRESENT
	$			
	$			

38) If self-employed, describe the nature of the business, the name of the business, its address, and net income derived therefrom:

39) My assets (and if married, my spouse's assets) in the United States and other countries, not including clothing and household necessities, are:

Self		**Jointly Owned With Spouse**	
Cash, Stocks, and Bonds................................	$	Cash, Stocks, and Bonds................................	$
Real Estate..	$	Real Estate..	$
Auto (dollar value minus amount owed).......	$	Auto (dollar value minus amount owed).......	$
Other (describe on line below).......................	$	Other (describe on line below).......................	$
TOTAL	**$**	**TOTAL**	**$**

40) I ❑ - have ❑ - have not received public or private relief or assistance (e.g. Welfare, Unemployment Benefits, Medicaid, TANF, AFDC, etc.). If you have, please give full details including the type of relief or assistance received, date for which relief or assistance was received, place, and total amount received during this time:

41) Please list each of the years in which you have filed an income tax return with the Internal Revenue Service:

Please continue answers on a separate sheet as needed.

(3)

Form EOIR-42A
Revised October 2013

PART 6 - INFORMATION ABOUT YOUR FAMILY *(Continued on page 5)*

42) I have ____________ *(Number of)* children. Please list information for each child below, include assets and earnings information for children over the age of 16 who have separate incomes:

Name of Child: *(Last, First, Middle)* Child's Alien Registration Number:	Citizen of What Country: Birth Date: *(Month, Day, Year)*	Now Residing At: *(City and Country)* Birth Date: *(City and Country)*	Immigration Status of Child
A#:			
Estimated Total of Assets: $ ____________		Estimated Average Weekly Earnings: $____________	
A#:			
Estimated Total of Assets: $ ____________		Estimated Average Weekly Earnings: $____________	
A#:			
Estimated Total of Assets: $ ____________		Estimated Average Weekly Earnings: $ ____________	

43) If your application is denied, would your spouse and all of your children accompany you to your:

Country of Birth - ☐ Yes ☐ No

Country of Nationality - ☐ Yes ☐ No

Country of Last Residence - ☐ Yes ☐ No

If you answered "No" to any of the responses, please explain: ____________

44) Members of my family, including my spouse and/or child(ren) ☐ - have ☐ - have not received public or private relief or assistance (e.g., Welfare, Unemployment Benefits, Medicaid, TANF, AFDC, etc.). If any member of your immediate family has received such relief or assistance, please give full details including identity of person(s) receiving relief or assistance, dates for which relief or assistance was received, place, and total amount received during this time: ____________

45) Please give the requested information about your parents, brothers, sisters, aunts, uncles, and grandparents, living or deceased. As to residence, show street address, city, and state, if in the United States; otherwise show only country:

Name: *(Last, First, Middle)* Alien Registration Number:	Citizen of What Country: Birth Date: *(Month, Day, Year)*	Relationship to Me: Birth Date: *(City and Country)*	Immigration Status of Listed Relative
A#:			
Complete Address of Current Residence, if Living: ____________			
A#:			
Complete Address of Current Residence, if Living: ____________			

Please continue answers on a separate sheet as needed.

(4)

Form EOIR-42A
Revised October 2013

PART 7 - MISCELLANEOUS INFORMATION *(Continued on page 6)*

46) I ❑ - have ❑ - have not entered the United States as a crewman after June 30, 1964.

47) I ❑ - have ❑ - have not been admitted as, or after arrival in the United States acquired the status of, an exchange alien.

48) I ❑ - have ❑ - have not submitted address reports as required by section 265 of the Immigration and Nationality Act.

49) I ❑ - have ❑ - have never (either in the United States or in any foreign country) been arrested, summoned into court as a defendant, convicted, fined, imprisoned, placed on probation, or forfeited collateral for an act involving a felony, misdemeanor, or breach of any public law or ordinance (including, but not limited to, traffic violations or driving incidents involving alcohol). *(If answer is in the affirmative, please give a brief description of each offense including the name and location of the offense, date of conviction, any penalty imposed, any sentence imposed, and the time actually served.)*

____

____

____

____

50) Have you ever served in the Armed Forces of the United States? ❑ - Yes ❑ - No. If "Yes" please state branch *(Army, Navy, etc.)* and service number: ______________________________

Place of entry on duty: *(City and State)* ______________________________

Date of entry on duty: *(Month, Day, Year)* ______________ Date of discharge: *(Month, Day, Year)* ______________

Type of discharge: *(Honorable, Dishonorable, etc.)* ______________________________

I served in active duty status from: *(Month, Day, Year)* ______________ to *(Month, Day, Year)* ______________

51) Have you ever left the United States or the jurisdiction of the district where you registered for the draft to avoid being drafted into the military or naval forces of the United States? ❑ Yes ❑ No

52) Have you ever deserted from the military or naval forces of the United States while the United States was at war? ❑ Yes ❑ No

53) If male, did you register under the Military Selective Service Act or any applicable previous Selective Service (Draft) Laws? ❑ Yes ❑ No
If "Yes," please give date, Selective Service number, local draft board number, and your last draft classification: ______________________________

____

54) Were you ever exempted from service because of conscientious objection, alienage, or any other reason? ❑ Yes ❑ No

55) Please list your present or past membership in or affiliation with every political organization, association, fund, foundation, party, club, society, or similar group in the United States or any other place since your 16th birthday. Include any foreign military service in this part. If none, write "None." Include the name of the organization, location, nature of the organization, and the dates of membership.

Name of Organization	Location of Organization	Nature of Organization	Member From: *(Month, Day, Year)*	Member To: *(Month, Day, Year)*

Please continue answers on a separate sheet as needed.

(5)

Form EOIR-42A
Revised October 2013

PART 7 - MISCELLANEOUS INFORMATION *(Continued)*

56) Have you ever:

- ❑ Yes ❑ No been ordered deported, excluded, or removed?
- ❑ Yes ❑ No overstayed a grant of voluntary departure from an Immigration Judge or the Department of Homeland Security (DHS), formerly the Immigration and Naturalization Service (INS)?
- ❑ Yes ❑ No failed to appear for deportation or removal?

57) Have you ever been:

- ❑ Yes ❑ No a habitual drunkard?
- ❑ Yes ❑ No one whose income is derived principally from illegal gambling?
- ❑ Yes ❑ No one who has given false testimony for the purpose of obtaining immigration benefits?
- ❑ Yes ❑ No one who has engaged in prostitution or unlawful commercialized vice?
- ❑ Yes ❑ No involved in a serious criminal offense and asserted immunity from prosecution?
- ❑ Yes ❑ No a polygamist?
- ❑ Yes ❑ No one who brought in or attempted to bring in another to the United States illegally?
- ❑ Yes ❑ No a trafficker of a controlled substance, or a knowing assister, abettor, conspirator, or colluder with others in any such controlled substance offense (not including a single offense of simple possession of 30 grams or less of marijuana)?
- ❑ Yes ❑ No inadmissible or deportable on security-related grounds under sections 212(a)(3) or 237(a)(4) of the INA?
- ❑ Yes ❑ No one who has ordered, incited, assisted, or otherwise participated in the persecution of an individual on account of his or her race, religion, nationality, membership in a particular social group, or political opinion?
- ❑ Yes ❑ No a person previously granted relief under sections 212(c) or 244(a) of the INA or whose removal has previously been cancelled under section 240A of the INA?

If you answered "Yes" to any of the above questions, explain:

____

____

____

58) The following certificates or other supporting documents are attached hereto as a part of this application: *(Refer to the Instructions for documents which **should be attached.**)*

______________	______________
______________	______________
______________	______________
______________	______________
______________	______________
______________	______________
______________	______________
______________	______________
______________	______________
______________	______________
______________	______________
______________	______________

Please continue answers on a separate sheet as needed.

(6)

Form EOIR-42A
Revised October 2013

PART 8 - SIGNATURE OF PERSON PREPARING FORM, IF OTHER THAN APPLICANT

(Read the following information and sign below)

I declare that I have prepared this application at the request of the person named in Part 1, that the responses provided are based on all information of which I have knowledge, or which was provided to me by the applicant, and that the completed application was read to the applicant in a language the applicant speaks fluently for verification before he or she signed the application in my presence. I am aware that the knowing placement of false information on the Form EOIR-42A may subject me to civil penalties under 8 U.S.C. 1324c.

Signature of Preparer:	Print Name:	Date:

Daytime Telephone #: ( )	Address of Preparer: *(Number and Street, City, State, Zip Code)*

PART 9 - SIGNATURE

APPLICATION NOT TO BE SIGNED BELOW UNTIL APPLICANT APPEARS BEFORE AN IMMIGRATION JUDGE

I swear or affirm that I know the contents of this application that I am signing, including the attached documents and supplements, and that they are all true to the best of my knowledge, taking into account the correction(s) numbered ______ to ______, if any, that were made by me or at my request.

____
(Signature of Applicant or Parent or Guardian)

Subscribed and sworn to before me by the above-named applicant at ______________________________

____
Immigration Judge

____
Date: (Month, Day, Year)

PART 10 - PROOF OF SERVICE

I hereby certify that a copy of the foregoing Form EOIR-42A was: ☐ - delivered in person ☐ - mailed first class, postage prepaid

on ____________________ to the Assistant Chief Counsel for the DHS (U.S. Immigration and Customs Enforcement-ICE)
(Month, Day, Year)

at ______________________________
(Number and Street, City, State, Zip Code)

____
Signature of Applicant (or Attorney or Representative)

Please continue answers on a separate sheet as needed.
(7)

Form EOIR-42A
Revised October 2013

Form EOIR–42B Application for cancellation of removal and adjustment of status for certain nonpermanent residents

OMB#1125-0001

U.S. Department of Justice
Executive Office for Immigration Review

Application for Cancellation of Removal and Adjustment of Status for Certain Nonpermanent Residents

ADVICE TO APPLICANT

PLEASE READ CAREFULLY. FEES WILL NOT BE RETURNED.

I. **Aliens Eligible for Cancellation of Removal**: You may be eligible to have your removal cancelled under section 240A(b) of the Immigration and Nationality Act (INA). To qualify for this benefit, you must establish in a hearing before an Immigration Judge that:

A. 1. Prior to the service of the Notice to Appear, you have maintained continuous physical presence in the United States for ten (10) years or more, and you have been a person of good moral character as defined in section 101(f) of the INA during such period;

2. You have not been convicted of an offense covered under sections 212(a)(2), 237(a)(2), or 237(a)(3) of the INA; and

3. Your removal would result in exceptional and extremely unusual hardship to your United States citizen or lawful permanent resident spouse, parent, or child, and you are deserving of a favorable exercise of discretion on your application.

OR

B. 1. You have been battered or subjected to extreme cruelty in the United States by your United States citizen or lawful permanent resident spouse or parent, or you are the parent of a child of a United States citizen or lawful permanent resident and the child has been battered or subjected to extreme cruelty in the United States by such citizen or lawful permanent resident parent;

2. Prior to the service of the Notice to Appear, you have maintained continuous physical presence in the United States for three (3) years or more and you have been a person of good moral character as defined in section 101(f) of the INA during such period;

3. You are not inadmissible under sections 212(a)(2) or 212(a)(3) of the INA, you are not deportable under section 237(a)(1)(G) or sections 237(a)(2)-(4) of the INA, and you have not been convicted of an aggravated felony as defined under the INA;

4. a. Your removal would result in extreme hardship to you or your child who is the child of a United States citizen or lawful permanent resident; or

b. You are a child whose removal would result in extreme hardship to you or your parent; and

5. You are deserving of a favorable exercise of discretion on your application.

Note: If you have served on active duty in the Armed Forces of the United States for at least 24 months, you do not have to meet the requirements of continuous physical presence in the United States. You must, however, have been in the United States when you entered the Armed Forces. If you are no longer in the Armed Forces, you must have been separated under honorable conditions.

II. **Aliens NOT Eligible for Cancellation of Removal**: You are not eligible for cancellation of removal under section 240A(b)(1) of the INA if you:

A. Entered the United States as a crewman after June 30, 1964;

Form EOIR-42B
Revised October 2013

OMB#1125-0001

U.S. Department of Justice
Executive Office for Immigration Review

Application for Cancellation of Removal and Adjustment of Status for Certain Nonpermanent Residents

B. Were admitted to the United States as, or later became, a nonimmigrant exchange alien as defined in section 101(a)(15)(J) of the INA in order to receive graduate medical education or training, regardless of whether you are subject to or have fulfilled the 2-year foreign residence requirement of section 212(e) of the INA;

C. Were admitted to the United States as, or later became, a nonimmigrant exchange alien as defined in section 101(a)(15)(J) of the INA, other than to receive graduate medical education or training, and are subject to the 2-year foreign residence requirement of section 212(e) of the INA, but have neither fulfilled nor obtained a waiver of that requirement;

D. Are an alien who is either inadmissible under section 212(a)(3) of the INA or deportable under section 237(a)(4) of the INA;

E. Are an alien who ordered, incited, assisted, or otherwise participated in the persecution of an individual because of the individual's race, religion, nationality, membership in a particular social group, or political opinion; or

F. Are an alien who was previously granted relief under section 212(c) of the INA, or section 244(a) of the INA as such sections were in effect prior to the enactment of the Illegal Immigration Reform and Immigrant Responsibility Act of 1996, whose removal has previously been cancelled under section 240A of the INA.

III. How to Apply for Cancellation of Removal

If you believe that you have met all the requirements for cancellation of removal, you must answer all the questions on the attached Form EOIR-42B fully and accurately. You must pay the filing and biometrics fees and comply with the Department of Homeland Security (DHS) instructions for providing biometric and biographic information to USCIS, [available at http://uscis.gov]. You must also serve a copy of your application on the Assistant Chief Counsel for the DHS, U.S. Immigration and Customs Enforcement (ICE) as required in the proof of service on page 8 of this application, and you must file your application with the appropriate Immigration Court. Please read the following instructions carefully before completing your application.

OMB#1125-0001

U.S. Department of Justice
Executive Office for Immigration Review

Application for Cancellation of Removal and Adjustment of Status for Certain Nonpermanent Residents

INSTRUCTIONS

1. PREPARATION OF APPLICATION.

To apply for cancellation of removal under section 240A(b) of the Immigration and Nationality Act (INA), you must fully and accurately answer all questions on the attached Form EOIR-42B. You must also comply with all of the instructions contained in this form. These instructions have the force of law. A separate application must be prepared and executed for each person applying for cancellation of removal. An application on behalf of an alien who is mentally incompetent or is a child under 14 years of age shall be executed by a parent or guardian.

Your responses must be typed or printed legibly in ink. Do not leave any questions unanswered or blank. If any questions do not apply to you, write "none" or "not applicable" in the appropriate space.

To the extent possible, answer all questions directly on the form. If there is insufficient room to respond fully to a question, please continue your response on an additional sheet of paper. Please indicate the number of the question being answered next to your response on the additional sheet, write your alien registration number, print your name, and sign, date, and securely attach each additional sheet to the Form EOIR-42B.

2. BURDEN OF PROOF.

The burden of proof is on you to prove that you meet all of the statutory requirements for cancellation of removal for certain nonpermanent resident aliens under section 240A(b) of the INA and that you are entitled to such relief as a matter of discretion. To meet this burden, your responses to the questions on the application should be as detailed and complete as possible. You should also attach to your application any documents that demonstrate your eligibility for cancellation of removal (see "SUPPORTING DOCUMENTS" below).

3. SUPPORTING DOCUMENTS.

You should submit documentary evidence to show that you have maintained continuous physical presence in the United States for the required period. Documents which may show evidence of your physical presence in the United States include, but are not limited to, bankbooks, leases, deeds, licenses, receipts, letters, birth records, church records, school records, employment records, and evidence of tax payments.

You should submit documents which help to show that you are, and have been, a person of good moral character during the entire period of continuous physical presence in the United States required for eligibility for cancellation of removal. You should submit police records from each jurisdiction in which you resided during such period. To show good moral character, it is recommended that you submit the affidavits of witnesses attesting to your good moral character, preferably citizens of the United States, and if you are employed, your employer. The affidavit from your employer should include information regarding the nature and duration of your employment and your earnings.

You should submit official certification to establish your relationship to those you claim would suffer hardship by your removal, and if such persons are citizens of the United States or lawful permanent residents, evidence of their citizenship or lawful permanent resident status. Documentary evidence of such relationships may include, but are not limited to, birth records, marriage certificates, proof of divorce or termination of marriage, and death certificates.

You should also submit with your application copies of any documents which you were issued by the Department of Homeland Security (DHS), formerly the Immigration and Naturalization Service. The Immigration Judge may require you to submit additional records relating to your request for cancellation of removal. These documents may include, but are not limited to, documents which reflect payment of taxes, court convictions, and payment of child support during your physical presence in the United States.

The original of all supporting documents must be available for inspection at the hearing. If you wish to have the original documents returned to you, you should also present reproductions.

Form EOIR-42B
Revised October 2013

OMB#1125-0001

U.S. Department of Justice
Executive Office for Immigration Review

Application for Cancellation of Removal and Adjustment of Status for Certain Nonpermanent Residents

4. REQUIRED BIOMETRIC AND BIOGRAPHIC INFORMATION.

Each applicant 14 years of age or older must also comply with the requirement to supply biometric and biographic information. You will be given instructions on how to complete this requirement. You will be notified in writing of the location of the Application Support Center (ASC) or the designated Law Enforcement Agency where you must go to provide biometric and biographic information. You will also be given a date and time for the appointment. It is important to furnish all the required information. Failure to comply with this requirement may result in a delay in your application or in your application being deemed abandoned and dismissed by the Immigration Court.

5. TRANSLATIONS.

Any document in a foreign language must be accompanied by an English language translation and a certificate signed by the translator stating that he/she is competent to translate the document and that the translation is true and accurate to the best of the translator's abilities. Such certification must be printed legibly or typed.

6. PHOTOGRAPHS.

Unless you are incarcerated or detained in a facility which prevents your compliance with this instruction, you must submit two glossy, unretouched, color photographs of yourself taken within 30 days of the date of this application. These photos must have a white background and must not be mounted. The dimension of your facial image in the photograph should be about one (1) inch from the chin to the top of your hair and you should be shown in full frontal/passport-style view with your eyes open. Using a pencil or felt pen, you should lightly print your name and alien registration number on the back of each photograph.

7. FEES.

Before you file your Form EOIR-42B with the Immigration Court, you must pay the required $100 filing fee and the biometrics fee to the Department of Homeland Security (DHS). Evidence of payment of these fees in the form of a copy of the DHS, U.S. Citizenship and Immigration Services (USCIS) ASC notice of fee receipt and biometrics appointment instructions must accompany your Form EOIR-42B. These fees will not be refunded, regardless of the action taken on your application. Therefore, it is important that you read the advice, instructions, and application carefully before responding. **If you are unable to pay the filing fee, you may ask the Immigration Judge to permit you to file your Form EOIR-42B without fee (fee waiver).**

DO NOT SEND CASH. All fees must be submitted in the exact amount. Remittance may be made by personal check, cashier's check, certified bank check, bank international money order, or foreign draft drawn on a financial institution in the United States and payable to the "Department of Homeland Security" in United States currency. If the applicant resides in the Virgin Islands, the check or money order must be payable to the "Commissioner of Finance of the Virgin Islands." If the applicant resides in Guam, the check or money order must be made payable to the "Treasurer, Guam." Personal checks are accepted subject to collectibility. An uncollectible check will render the application and any documents issued pursuant thereto invalid. A charge of $30.00 will be imposed if a check in payment of a fee is not honored by the bank on which it is drawn. When the check is drawn on an account of a person other than the applicant, the name and alien registration number of the applicant must be entered on the face of the check. All checks must be drawn on a bank located in the United States.

8. SERVING & FILING YOUR APPLICATION.

A. You must first comply with the DHS instructions for providing biometric and biographic information to USCIS, which involves sending a copy of the application to the appropriate USCIS Service Center. The DHS instructions also address payment of the application fees.

B. You must then serve the following documents on the Assistant Chief Counsel for DHS, U.S. Immigration and Customs Enforcement (ICE):

Form EOIR-42B
Revised October 2013

OMB#1125-0001

U.S. Department of Justice
Executive Office for Immigration Review

Application for Cancellation of Removal and Adjustment of Status for Certain Nonpermanent Residents

- a copy of your Form EOIR-42B, Application for Cancellation of Removal, with all supporting documents and additional sheets;
- a copy of the USCIS ASC notice of fee receipt and biometrics appointment instructions;
- the original Biographical Information Form G-325A; and
- a photograph of you which meets the requirements of instruction #6 above.

You must file the following documents with the appropriate Immigration Court:

- the original Form EOIR-42B with all supporting documents and additional sheets;
- a copy of the USCIS ASC notice of fee receipt and biometrics appointment instructions;
- a copy of Biographical Information Form G-325A;
- a photograph of you which meets the requirements of instruction #6 above; and
- a completed certificate showing service of these documents (See Part 10 of the Application on page 8) on the ICE Assistant Chief Counsel, unless service is made on the record at the hearing.

Retain your USCIS ASC biometrics confirmation document or a copy of your Fingerprint Card, FD-258, if applicable, as proof that your biometrics were taken, and bring it to your future Immigration Court hearings.

9. PENALTIES.

You must answer all questions on Form EOIR-42B truthfully and submit only genuine documents in support of your application. **You will be required to swear or affirm that the contents of your application and the supporting documents are true to the best of your knowledge.** Your answer to the questions on this form and the supporting documents you present will be used to determine whether your removal should be cancelled and whether you should be permitted to adjust your status. Any answer you give and any supporting document you present may also be used as evidence in any proceeding to determine your right to be admitted or readmitted, re-enter, pass through, or reside in the United States. Your application may be denied if any of your answers or supporting documents are found to be false.

Presenting false answers or false documents may also subject you to criminal prosecution under 18 U.S.C. section 1546 and/or subject you to civil penalties under 8 U.S.C. section 1324c if you submit your application knowing that the application, or any supporting document, contains any false statement with respect to a material fact, or if you swear or affirm that the contents of your application and the supporting documents are true, knowing that the application or any supporting documents contain any false statement with respect to a material fact. If convicted, you could be fined up to $250,000, imprisoned for up to ten (10) years, or both. 18 U.S.C. sections 1546(a), 3559(a)(4), 3571(b)(3). If it is determined you have violated the prohibition against document fraud and a final order is entered against you, you could be subject to a civil penalty up to $2,000 for each document used or created for the first offense, and up to $5,000 for any second, or subsequent offense. In addition, if you are the subject of a final order for violating 8 U.S.C. section 1324c, relating to civil penalties for document fraud, you will be removable from the United States.

10. PAPERWORK REDUCTION ACT NOTICE.

Under the Paperwork Reduction Act, a person is not required to respond to a collection of information unless it displays a currently valid OMB control number. We try to create forms and instructions that are accurate, can easily be understood, and which impose the least possible burden on you to provide us with information. Often, this process is difficult because some immigration laws are very complex. The reporting burden for this collection of information is computed as follows: (1) learning about the form, 50 minutes, (2) completing the form, 2 hours, and (3) assembling and filing the form, 3 hours, for an average of 5 hours, 50 minutes per application. If you have comments regarding the accuracy of this burden estimate, or any other aspect of this collection of information, including suggestions for reducing this burden, you may write to the U.S. Department of Justice, Executive Office for Immigration Review, Office of the General Counsel, 5107 Leesburg Pike, Suite 2600, Falls Church, Virginia 20530.

Form EOIR-42B
Revised October 2013

OMB#1125-0001

U.S. Department of Justice
Executive Office for Immigration Review

Application for Cancellation of Removal and Adjustment of Status for Certain Nonpermanent Residents

PLEASE READ ADVICE AND INSTRUCTIONS BEFORE FILLING IN FORM

PLEASE TYPE OR PRINT

Fee Stamp (Official Use Only)

PART 1 - INFORMATION ABOUT YOURSELF

1) My present true name is: *(Last, First, Middle)*		2) Alien Registration (or "A") Number(s):	
3) My name given at birth was: *(Last, First, Middle)*		4) Birth Place: *(City and Country)*	
5) Date of Birth: *(Month, Day, Year)*	6) Gender: ❑ Male ❑ Female	7) Height: 8) Hair Color:	9) Eye Color:
10) Current Nationality and Citizenship:	11) Social Security Number:	12) Home Phone Number: ( )	13) Work Phone Number: ( )

14) I currently reside at:

Apt. number and/or in care of

Number and Street

City or Town _State_ _Zip Code_

15) I have been known by these additional name(s):

16) I have resided in the following locations in the United States: (List PRESENT ADDRESS FIRST, and work back in time for at least 10 years.)

Street and Number - Apt. or Room # - City or Town - State - Zip Code	Resided From: *(Month, Day, Year)*	Resided To: *(Month, Day, Year)*
		PRESENT

PART 2 - INFORMATION ABOUT THIS APPLICATION

17) I, the undersigned, hereby request that my removal be cancelled under the provisions of section 240A(b) of the Immigration and Nationality Act (INA). I believe that I am eligible for cancellation of removal because: (Check all that apply.)

❑ My removal would result in exceptional and extremely unusual hardship to my:

	UNITED STATES CITIZEN	LEGAL PERMANENT RESIDENT	TEMPORARY STATUS	NO STATUS
❑ spouse, who is a	___	___	___	___
❑ father, who is a	___	___	___	___
❑ mother, who is a	___	___	___	___
❑ child/children, who is/are a	___	___	___	___

With the exception of absences described in question #23, I have resided in the United States since:

(Month, Day, Year) ______________________.

❑ I, or my child, have been battered or subjected to extreme cruelty by a United States citizen or lawful permanent resident spouse or parent.

With the exception of absences described in question #23, I have resided in the United States since:

(Month, Day, Year) ______________________.

Please continue answers on a separate sheet as needed.

(1)

Form EOIR-42B
Revised October 2013

PART 3 - INFORMATION ABOUT YOUR PRESENCE IN THE UNITED STATES

18) I first arrived in the United States under the name of: *(Last, First, Middle)*	19) I first arrived in the United States on: *(Month, Day, Year)*

20) Place or port of first arrival: *(Place or Port, City, and State)*

21) I: ❑ was inspected and admitted.
- ☐ I entered using my Lawful Permanent Resident card which is valid until ______________ *(Month, Day, Year)*.
- ☐ I entered using a ______________ *(Specify Type of Visa)* visa which is valid until ______________ *(Month, Day, Year)*.

❑ was not inspected and admitted.
- ☐ I entered without documents. Explain: ______________.
- ☐ I entered without inspection. Explain: ______________.

❑ Other. Explain: ______________.

22) I applied on ______________ *(Month, Day, Year)* for additional time to stay and it was ❑ granted on ______________ *(Month, Day, Year)* and valid until ______________ *(Month, Day, Year)*, or ❑ denied on ______________ *(Month, Day, Year)*.

23) Since the date of my first entry, I departed from and returned to the United States at the following places and on the following dates:
(Please list all departures regardless of how briefly you were absent from the United States.)
If you have never departed from the United States since your original date of entry, please mark an X in this box: ❑

1	Port of Departure *(Place or Port, City and State)*	Departure Date *(Month, Day, Year)*	Purpose of Travel	Destination
	Port of Return *(Place or Port, City and State)*	Return Date *(Month, Day, Year)*	Manner of Return	Inspected and Admitted? ❑ Yes ❑ No
2	Port of Departure *(Place or Port, City and State)*	Departure Date *(Month, Day, Year)*	Purpose of Travel	Destination
	Port of Return *(Place or Port, City and State)*	Return Date *(Month, Day, Year)*	Manner of Return	Inspected and Admitted? ❑ Yes ❑ No

24) Have you ever departed the United States: a) under an order of deportation, exclusion, or removal?.. ❑ Yes ❑ No
b) pursuant to a grant of voluntary departure?.. ❑ Yes ❑ No

PART 4 - INFORMATION ABOUT YOUR MARITAL STATUS AND SPOUSE *(Continued on page 3)*

25) I am not married: ❑ I am married: ❑	26) If married, the name of my spouse is: *(Last, First, Middle)*	27) My spouse's name before marriage was:

28) The marriage took place in: *(City and Country)*	29) Date of marriage: *(Month, Day, Year)*
30) My spouse currently resides at: ______________ *Apt. number and/or in care of* ______________ *Number and Street* ______________ *City or Town* *State/Country* *Zip Code*	31) Place and date of birth of my spouse: *(City & Country; Month, Day, Year)* 32) My spouse is a citizen of: *(Country)*

33) If your spouse is other than a native born United States citizen, answer the following:
He/she arrived in the United States at: *(Place or Port, City and State)* ______________.
He/she arrived in the United States on: *(Month, Day, Year)* ______________.
His/her alien registration number(s) is: A# ______________.
He/she was naturalized on: *(Month, Day, Year)* ______________ at ______________ *(City and State)*.

34) My spouse ❑ - is ❑ - is not employed. If employed, please give salary and the name and address of the place(s) of employment.

Full Name and Address of Employer	Earnings Per Week *(Approximate)*
	$
	$
	$

Please continue answers on a separate sheet as needed.
(2)
Form EOIR-42B
Revised October 2013

PART 4 - INFORMATION ABOUT YOUR MARITAL STATUS AND SPOUSE *(Continued)*

35) I ❑ - have ❑ - have not been previously married: *(If previously married, list the name of each prior spouse, the dates on which each marriage began and ended, the place where the marriage terminated, and describe how each marriage ended.)*

Name of prior spouse: *(Last, First, Middle)*	Date marriage began: Date marriage ended:	Place marriage ended: *(City and Country)*	Description or manner of how marriage was terminated or ended:

36) My present spouse ❑ - has ❑ - has not been previously married: *(If previously married, list the names of each prior spouse, the dates on which each marriage began and ended, the place where the marriage terminated, and describe how each marriage ended.)*

Name of prior spouse: *(Last, First, Middle)*	Date marriage began: Date marriage ended:	Place marriage ended: *(City and Country)*	Description or manner of how marriage was terminated or ended:

37) Have you been ordered by any court, or are otherwise under any legal obligation, to provide child support and/or spousal maintenance as a result of a separation and/or divorce? ❑ Yes ❑ No

PART 5 - INFORMATION ABOUT YOUR EMPLOYMENT AND FINANCIAL STATUS

38) Since my arrival into the United States, I have been employed by the following named persons or firms: *(Please begin with present employment and work back in time. Any periods of unemployment or school attendance should be specified. Attach a separate sheet for additional entries if necessary.)*

Full Name and Address of Employer	Earnings Per Week *(Approximate)*	Type of Work Performed	Employed From: *(Month, Day, Year)*	Employed To: *(Month, Day, Year)*
	$			PRESENT
	$			
	$			

39) If self-employed, describe the nature of the business, the name of the business, its address, and net income derived therefrom:

40) My assets (and if married, my spouse's assets) in the United States and other countries, not including clothing and household necessities, are:

Self		**Jointly Owned With Spouse**	
Cash, Stocks, and Bonds	$	Cash, Stocks, and Bonds	$
Real Estate	$	Real Estate	$
Auto (dollar value minus amount owed)	$	Auto (dollar value minus amount owed)	$
Other (describe on line below)	$	Other (describe on line below)	$
TOTAL	$	**TOTAL**	$

41) I ❑ - have ❑ - have not received public or private relief or assistance (e.g. Welfare, Unemployment Benefits, Medicaid, TANF, AFDC, etc.). If you have, please give full details including the type of relief or assistance received, date for which relief or assistance was received, place, and total amount received during this time:

42) Please list each of the years in which you have filed an income tax return with the Internal Revenue Service:

Please continue answers on a separate sheet as needed.

(3)

Form EOIR-42B
Revised October 2013

PART 6 - INFORMATION ABOUT YOUR FAMILY *(Continued on page 5)*

43) I have______________*(Number of)* children. Please list information for each child below, include assets and earnings information for children over the age of 16 who have separate incomes:

Name of Child: *(Last, First, Middle)* Child's Alien Registration Number:	Citizen of What Country: Birth Date: *(Month, Day, Year)*	Now Residing At: *(City and Country)* Birth Date: *(City and Country)*	Immigration Status of Child
A#:			
Estimated Total of Assets: $		Estimated Average Weekly Earnings: $	
A#:			
Estimated Total of Assets: $		Estimated Average Weekly Earnings: $	
A#:			
Estimated Total of Assets: $		Estimated Average Weekly Earnings: $	

44) If your application is denied, would your spouse and all of your children accompany you to your:

Country of Birth - ☐ Yes ☐ No

Country of Nationality - ☐ Yes ☐ No

Country of Last Residence - ☐ Yes ☐ No

If you answered "No" to any of the responses, please explain: ________________

45) Members of my family, including my spouse and/or child(ren) ☐ - have ☐ - have not received public or private relief or assistance (e.g., Welfare, Unemployment Benefits, Medicaid, TANF, AFDC, etc.). If any member of your immediate family has received such relief or assistance, please give full details including identity of person(s) receiving relief or assistance, dates for which relief or assistance was received, place, and total amount received during this time: ________________

46) Please give the requested information about your parents, brothers, sisters, aunts, uncles, and grandparents, living or deceased. As to residence, show street address, city, and state, if in the United States; otherwise show only country:

Name: *(Last, First, Middle)* Alien Registration Number:	Citizen of What Country: Birth Date: *(Month, Day, Year)*	Relationship to Me: Birth Date: *(City and Country)*	Immigration Status of Listed Relative
A#:			
Complete Address of Current Residence, if Living:			
A#:			
Complete Address of Current Residence, if Living:			

Please continue answers on a separate sheet as needed.

(4)

Form EOIR-42B
Revised October 2013

PART 6 - INFORMATION ABOUT YOUR FAMILY *(Continued)*

IF THIS APPLICATION IS BASED ON HARDSHIP TO A PARENT OR PARENTS, QUESTIONS 47-50 MUST BE ANSWERED.

47) If your parent is not a citizen of the United States, give the date and place of arrival in the United States including full details as to the date, manner, and terms of admission into the United States: ______

______

______

48) My father ❑ - is ❑ - is not employed. If employed, please give salary and the name and address of the place(s) of employment.

Full Name and Address of Employer	Earnings Per Week *(Approximate)*
	$

49) My mother ❑ - is ❑ - is not employed. If employed, please give salary and the name and address of place(s) of employment.

Full Name and Address of Employer	Earnings Per Week *(Approximate)*
	$

50) My parent's assets in the United States and other countries not including clothing and household necessities are:

Assets of father consist of the following:

Cash, Stocks, and Bonds.............................. $______
Real Estate.. $______
Auto (dollar value minus amount owed)....... $______
Other (describe on line below)...................... $______
______ **TOTAL $**______

Assets of mother consist of the following:

Cash, Stocks, and Bonds.............................. $______
Real Estate.. $______
Auto (dollar value minus amount owed)....... $______
Other (describe on line below)...................... $______
______ **TOTAL $**______

PART 7 - MISCELLANEOUS INFORMATION *(Continued on page 6)*

51) I ❑ - have ❑ - have not entered the United States as a crewman after June 30, 1964.

52) I ❑ - have ❑ - have not been admitted as, or after arrival in the United States acquired the status of, an exchange alien.

53) I ❑ - have ❑ - have not submitted address reports as required by section 265 of the Immigration and Nationality Act.

54) I ❑ - have ❑ - have never (either in the United States or in any foreign country) been arrested, summoned into court as a defendant, convicted, fined, imprisoned, placed on probation, or forfeited collateral for an act involving a felony, misdemeanor, or breach of any public law or ordinance (including, but not limited to, traffic violations or driving incidents involving alcohol). *(If answer is in the affirmative, please give a brief description of each offense including the name and location of the offense, date of conviction, any penalty imposed, any sentence imposed, and the time actually served.)*

______

______

______

______

55) Have you ever served in the Armed Forces of the United States? ❑ Yes ❑ No. If "Yes" please state branch *(Army, Navy, etc.)* and service number: ______

Place of entry on duty: *(City and State)* ______

Date of entry on duty: *(Month, Day, Year)* ______ Date of discharge: *(Month, Day, Year)* ______

Type of discharge: *(Honorable, Dishonorable, etc.)* ______

I served in active duty status from: *(Month, Day, Year)* ______ to *(Month, Day, Year)* ______

56) Have you ever left the United States or the jurisdiction of the district where you registered for the draft to avoid being drafted into the military or naval forces of the United States? ❑ Yes ❑ No

Please continue answers on a separate sheet as needed.

(5)

Form EOIR-42B
Revised October 2013

PART 7 - MISCELLANEOUS INFORMATION *(Continued)*

57) Have you ever deserted from the military or naval forces of the United States while the United States was at war? ❑ Yes ❑ No

58) If male, did you register under the Military Selective Service Act or any applicable previous Selective Service (Draft) Laws? ❑ Yes ❑ No
If "Yes," please give date, Selective Service number, local draft board number, and your last draft classification: ______________

____

59) Were you ever exempted from service because of conscientious objection, alienage, or any other reason? ❑ Yes ❑ No

60) Please list your present or past membership in or affiliation with every political organization, association, fund, foundation, party, club, society, or similar group in the United States or any other place since your 16th birthday. Include any foreign military service in this part. If none, write "None." Include the name of the organization, location, nature of the organization, and the dates of membership.

Name of Organization	Location of Organization	Nature of Organization	Member From: *(Month, Day, Year)*	Member To: *(Month, Day, Year)*

61) Have you ever:

❑ Yes ❑ No been ordered deported, excluded, or removed?
❑ Yes ❑ No overstayed a grant of voluntary departure from an Immigration Judge or the Department of Homeland Security (DHS), formerly the Immigration and Naturalization Service (INS)?
❑ Yes ❑ No failed to appear for removal or deportation?

62) Have you ever been:

❑ Yes ❑ No a habitual drunkard?
❑ Yes ❑ No one whose income is derived principally from illegal gambling?
❑ Yes ❑ No one who has given false testimony for the purpose of obtaining immigration benefits?
❑ Yes ❑ No one who has engaged in prostitution or unlawful commercialized vice?
❑ Yes ❑ No involved in a serious criminal offense and asserted immunity from prosecution?
❑ Yes ❑ No a polygamist?
❑ Yes ❑ No one who brought in or attempted to bring in another to the United States illegally?
❑ Yes ❑ No a trafficker of a controlled substance, or a knowing assister, abettor, conspirator, or colluder with others in any such controlled substance offense (not including a single offense of simple possession of 30 grams or less of marijuana)?
❑ Yes ❑ No inadmissible or deportable on security-related grounds under sections 212(a)(3) or 237(a)(4) of the INA?
❑ Yes ❑ No one who has ordered, incited, assisted, or otherwise participated in the persecution of an individual on account of his or her race, religion, nationality, membership in a particular social group, or political opinion?
❑ Yes ❑ No a person previously granted relief under sections 212(c) or 244(a) of the INA or whose removal has previously been cancelled under section 240A of the INA?

If you answered "Yes" to any of the above questions, explain: ______________

____

____

Please continue answers on a separate sheet as needed.

(6)

Form EOIR-42B
Revised October 2013

PART 7 - MISCELLANEOUS INFORMATION *(Continued)*

63) Are you the beneficiary of an approved visa petition? ❑ Yes ❑ No

If yes, can you arrange a trip outside the United States to obtain an immigrant visa? ❑ Yes ❑ No If no, please explain:

64) The following certificates or other supporting documents are attached hereto as a part of this application: *(Refer to the Instructions for documents which **should be attached.**)*

PART 8 - SIGNATURE OF PERSON PREPARING FORM, IF OTHER THAN APPLICANT

(Read the following information and sign below)

I declare that I have prepared this application at the request of the person named in Part 1, that the responses provided are based on all information of which I have knowledge, or which was provided to me by the applicant, and that the completed application was read to the applicant in a language the applicant speaks fluently for verification before he or she signed the application in my presence. I am aware that the knowing placement of false information on the Form EOIR-42B may subject me to civil penalties under 8 U.S.C. 1324c.

Signature of Preparer:	Print Name:	Date:

Daytime Telephone #: ( )	Address of Preparer: *(Number and Street, City, State, Zip Code)*

Please continue answers on a separate sheet as needed.

(7)

Form EOIR-42B
Revised October 2013

PART 9 - SIGNATURE

APPLICATION NOT TO BE SIGNED BELOW UNTIL APPLICANT APPEARS BEFORE AN IMMIGRATION JUDGE

I swear or affirm that I know the contents of this application that I am signing, including the attached documents and supplements, and that they are all true to the best of my knowledge, taking into account the correction(s) numbered ______ to ______, if any, that were made by me or at my request.

____
(Signature of Applicant or Parent or Guardian)

Subscribed and sworn to before me by the above-named applicant at ______________________________

____
Immigration Judge

____
Date (Month, Day, Year)

PART 10 - PROOF OF SERVICE

I hereby certify that a copy of the foregoing Form EOIR-42B was: ☐ - delivered in person ☐ - mailed first class, postage prepaid

on ____________________ to the Assistant Chief Counsel for the DHS (U.S. Immigration and Customs Enforcement - ICE)
(Month, Day, Year)

at ______________________________
(Number and Street, City, State, Zip Code)

____
Signature of Applicant (or Attorney or Representative)

Please continue answers on a separate sheet as needed.
(8)

Form EOIR-42B
Revised October 2013

TOPICAL INDEX

CITATIONS

INA §	Section number of the Immigration and Nationality Act
___ USCA § ___	Title and section number of the U.S. Code
___ CFR § ___	Title and section number of the Code of Federal Regulations

---

TOPICAL INDEX

* Available online at: http://www.uscis.gov/forms.

TOPICAL INDEX

---

* Available online at: http://www.uscis.gov/forms.

* Available online at: http://www.uscis.gov/forms.

TOPICAL INDEX

TOPICAL INDEX

* Available online at: http://www.uscis.gov/forms.

* Available online at: http://www.uscis.gov/forms.

* Available online at: http://www.uscis.gov/forms.

TOPICAL INDEX

* Available online at: http://www.uscis.gov/forms.

* Available online at: http://www.uscis.gov/forms.

* Available online at: http://www.uscis.gov/forms.

* Available online at: http://www.uscis.gov/forms.

TOPICAL INDEX

* Available online at: http://www.uscis.gov/forms.